Arthur W. Pink's Doctrine Collection

Printed in the United States of America and Australia.

Bottom of the Hill Publishing
Memphis, TN
www.BottomoftheHillPublishing.com

ISBN: 978-1-61203-542-0

Contents

The Doctrine of Election

Contents

Chapter 1
Introduction

Election is a foundational doctrine. In the past, many of the ablest teachers were accustomed to commence their systematic theology with a presentation of the attributes of God, and then a contemplation of His eternal decrees; and it is our studied conviction, after perusing the writings of many of our moderns, that the method followed by their predecessors cannot be improved upon. God existed before man, and His eternal purpose long antedated His works in time. "Known unto God are all his works from the beginning of the world" (Acts 15:18). The divine councils went before creation. As a builder draws his plans before he begins to build, so the great Architect predestinated everything before a single creature was called into existence. Nor has God kept this a secret locked in His own bosom; it has pleased Him to make known in His Word the everlasting counsels of His grace, His design in the same, and the grand end He has in view.

When a building is in course of construction onlookers are often at a loss to perceive the reason for many of the details. As yet, they discern no order or design; everything appears to be in confusion. But if they could carefully scan the builder's "plan" and visualize the finished production, much that had puzzled would become clear to them. It is the same with the outworking of God's eternal purpose. Unless we are acquainted with His eternal decrees, history remains an insoluble enigma. God is not working at random: the gospel has been sent forth on no uncertain mission: the final outcome in the conflict between good and evil has not been left indeterminate; how many are to be saved or lost depends not on the will of the creature. Everything was infallibly determined and immutably fixed by God from the beginning, and all that happens in time is but the accomplishment of what was ordained in eternity.

The grand truth of election, then, takes us back to the beginning of all things. It antedated the entrance of sin into the universe, the fall of man, the advent of Christ, and the proclamation of the gospel. A right understanding of it, especially in its relation to the everlasting covenant, is absolutely essential if we are to be preserved from fundamental error. If the foundation itself be faulty, then the building erected on it cannot be sound; and if we err in our conceptions of this basic truth, then just in proportion as we do so will our grasp of all other truth be inaccurate. God's dealings with Jew and Gentile, His object in sending His Son into this world, His design by the gospel, yea, the whole of His providential dealings, cannot be seen in their proper perspective till they are viewed in the light of His eternal election. This will become the more evident as we proceed.

It is a difficult doctrine, and this in three respects. First, in the understanding of it. Unless we are privileged to sit under the ministry of some Spirit-taught servant of God, who presents the truth to us systematically, great pains and diligence are called for in the searching of the Scriptures, so that we may collect and tabulate their scattered statements on this subject. It has not pleased the Holy Spirit to give us one complete and orderly setting forth of the doctrine of election, but instead "here a little, there a little"—in typical history, in psalm and prophecy, in the great prayer of Christ (John 17), in the epistles of the apostles. Second, in the acceptation of it. This presents a much greater difficulty, for when the mind perceives what the Scriptures reveal thereon, the heart is loath to receive such an humbling and flesh-withering truth. How earnestly we need to pray for God to subdue our enmity against Him and our prejudice against His truth. Third, in the proclamation of it. No novice is competent to present this subject in its scriptural perspective and proportions.

But notwithstanding, these difficulties should not discourage, still less deter us, from an honest and serious effort to understand and heartily receive all that God has been pleased to reveal thereon. Difficulties are designed to humble us, to exercise us, to make us feel our need of wisdom from on high. It is not easy to arrive at a clear and adequate grasp of any of the great doctrines of Holy Writ, and God never intended it should be so. Truth has to be "bought" (Prov. 23:23): alas that so few are willing to pay the price—devote to the prayerful study of the Word the time wasted on newspapers or idle recreations. These difficulties are not insurmountable, for the Spirit has been given to God's people to guide them into all truth. Equally so for the minister of the Word: an humble waiting upon God, coupled with a diligent effort to be a workman that needeth not to be ashamed, will in due time fit him to expound this truth to the glory of God and the blessing of his hearers.

It is an important doctrine, as is evident from various considerations. Perhaps we can express most impressively the momentousness of this truth by pointing out that apart from eternal election there had never been any Jesus Christ, and therefore, no divine gospel; for if God had never chosen a people unto salvation, He had never sent His Son; and if He had sent no Savior, none had ever been saved. Thus, the gospel itself originated in this vital matter of election. "But we are bound to give thanks always to God for you, brethren beloved of the Lord, because God hath from the beginning chosen you to salvation" (2 Thess. 2:13). And why are we "bound to give thanks"? Because election is the root of all blessings, the spring of every mercy that the soul receives. If election be taken away, everything is taken away, for those who have any spiritual blessing are they who have all spiritual blessings "according as he hath chosen us in him before the foundation of the world" (Eph. 1:3, 4).

It was well said by Calvin, "We shall never be clearly convinced, as we ought to be, that our salvation flows from the fountain of God's free mercy, till we are acquainted with His eternal election, which illustrates the grace of God by this comparison; that He adopts not all promiscuously to the hope of salvation, but He gives to some what He refuses to others. Ignorance of this principle evidently detracts from the divine glory, and diminishes real humility—If, then, we need to be recalled to the origin of election, to prove that we obtain salvation from no other source than the mere good pleasure of God, then they who desire to extinguish this principle, do all they can to obscure what ought to be magnificently and loudly celebrated."

It is a blessed doctrine, for election is the spring of all blessings. This is made unmistakably clear by Ephesians 1:3, 4. First, the Holy Spirit declares that the saints have been blessed with all spiritual blessings in the heavenlies in Christ. Then He proceeds to show why and how they were so blessed: it is according as God hath chosen us in Christ before the foundation of the world. Election in Christ, therefore, precedes being blessed with all spiritual blessings, for we are blessed with them only as being in Him, and we are only in Him as chosen in Him. We see, then, what a grand and glorious truth this is, for all our hopes and prospects belong to it. Election, though distinct and personal, is not, as is sometimes carelessly stated, a mere abstract choice of persons unto eternal salvation, irrespective of union with their Covenant-Head, but a choice of them in Christ. It therefore implies every other blessing, and all other blessings are given only through it and in accordance with it.

Rightly understood there is nothing so calculated to impart comfort and courage, strength and security, as a heart-apprehension of this truth. To be assured that I am one of the high favorites of Heaven imparts the confidence that God most certainly will supply my every need and make all things work together for my good. The knowledge that God has predestinated me unto eternal glory supplies an absolute guarantee that no efforts of Satan can possibly bring about my destruction, for if the great God be for me, who can be against me! It brings great peace to the preacher, for he now discovers that God has not sent him forth to draw a bow at a venture, but that His Word shall accomplish that which He pleases, and shall prosper whereto He sends it (Isa. 55:11). And what encouragement it should afford the awakened sinner. As he learns that election is solely a matter of divine grace, hope is kindled in his heart: as he discovers, that election singled out some of the vilest of the vile to be the monuments of divine mercy, why should he despair!

It is a distasteful doctrine. One had naturally thought that a truth so God-honoring, Christ-exalting, and so blessed, had been cordially espoused by all professing Christians who had had it clearly presented to them. In view of the fact that the terms "predestinated," "elect," and "chosen," occur so frequently in the Word, one would surely conclude that all who claim to accept the Scriptures as divinely inspired would receive with implicit faith this grand truth, referring the act itself—as becometh sinful and ignorant creatures so to do— unto the sovereign good pleasure of God. But such is far, very far from being the actual case. No doctrine is so detested by proud human nature as this one, which make nothing of the creature and everything of the Creator; yea, at no other point is the enmity of the carnal mind so blatantly and hotly evident.

We commenced our addresses in Australia by saying, "I am going to speak tonight on one of the most hated doctrines of the Bible, namely, that of God's sovereign election." Since then we have encircled this globe, and come into more or less close contact with thousands of people belonging to many denominations, and thousands more of professing Christians attached to none, and today the only change we would make in that statement is, that while the truth of eternal punishment is the one most objectionable to non-professors, that of God's sovereign election is the truth most loathed and reviled by the majority of those claiming to be believers. Let it be plainly announced that salvation originated not in the will of man, but in the will of God (see John 1:13; Rom. 9:16), that were it not so none would or could be saved—for as the result of the fall man has lost all desire and will unto that which is good (John 5:40; Rom. 3:11)—and that even the elect themselves have to be made willing (Ps. 110:3), and loud will be the cries of indignation raised against such teaching.

It is at this point the issue is drawn. Merit-mongers will not allow the supremacy of the divine will and the impotency unto good of the human will, consequently they who are the most bitter in denouncing election by the sovereign pleasure of God, are the warmest in crying up the freewill of fallen man. In the decrees of the council of Trent—wherein the Papacy definitely defined her position on the leading points raised by the Reformers, and which Rome has never rescinded— occurs the following: "If anyone should affirm that since the fall of Adam man's free will is lost, let him be accursed." It was for their faithful adherence to the truth of election, with all that it involves, that Bradford and hundreds of others were burned at the stake by the agents of the pope. Unspeakably sad is it to see so many professing Protestants agree with the mother of harlots in this fundamental error.

But whatever aversion men may now have to this blessed truth, they will be compelled to hear it in the last day, hear it as the voice of final, unalterable, and eternal decision. When death and Hades, the sea and dry land, shall give up the dead, then shall the Book of Life—the register in which was recorded from before the foundation of the world the whole election of grace—be opened in the presence of angels and demons, in the presence of the saved and of the lost, and that voice shall sound to the highest arches of Heaven, to the lowest depths of hell, to the uttermost bound of the universe: "And whosoever was not found written in the Book of Life was cast into the lake of fire" (Rev. 20:15). Thus, this truth which is hated by the non-elect above all others, is the one that shall ring in the ears of the lost as they enter their eternal doom! Ah, my reader, the reason why people do not receive and duly prize the truth of election, is because they do not feel their due need of it.

It is a separating doctrine. The preaching of the sovereignty of God, as exercised by Him in foreordaining the eternal destiny of each of His creatures, serves as an effectual flail to divide the chaff from the wheat. "He that is of God heareth God's words" (John 8:47): yes, no matter how contrary they may be to his ideas. It is one of the marks of the regenerate that they set to their seal that God is true. Nor do they pick and choose, as will religious hypocrites: once they perceive a truth is clearly taught in the Word, even though it be utterly opposed to their own reason and inclinations, they humbly bow to it and implicitly receive it, and would do so though not another person in whole world believed it. But it is far otherwise with the unregenerate. As the apostle declares, "They are of the world: therefore speak they of the world, and the world heareth them. We are of God: he that knoweth God heareth us; he that is not of God heareth not us. Hereby know we the spirit of truth, and the spirit of error" (1 John 4:5, 6).

We know of nothing so devisive between the sheep and the goats as a faithful exposition of this doctrine. If a servant of God accepts some new charge, and he wishes to ascertain which of his people desire the pure milk of the Word, and which prefer the Devil's substitutes, let him deliver a series of sermons on this subject, and it will quickly be the means of "taking forth the precious from the vile" (Jer. 15:19). It was thus in the experience of the Divine Preacher: when Christ announced "no man can come unto me, except it were given unto him of my Father," we are told, "from that time many of his disciples went back, and walked no more with him" (John 6:65, 66)! True it is that by no means all who intellectually receive "Calvinism" as a philosophy or theology, give evidence (in their daily lives) of regeneration; yet equally true is it that those who continue to cavil against and steadfastly refuse any part of the truth, are not entitled to be regarded as Christians.

It is a neglected doctrine. Though occupying so prominent a place in the Word of God, it is today but little preached, and still less understood. Of course, it is not to be expected that the "higher critics" and their blinded dupes should preach that which makes nothing of man; but even among those who wish to be looked up to as "orthodox" and "evangelical," there are scarcely any who give this grand truth a real place in either their pulpit ministrations or their writings. In some cases this is due to ignorance: not having been taught it in the seminary, and certainly not in the "Bible Institutes," they have never perceived its great importance and value. But in too many cases it is a desire to be popular with their hearers which muzzles their mouths. Nevertheless, neither ignorance, prejudice, nor enmity can do away with the doctrine itself, or lessen its vital momentousness.

In bringing to a close these introductory remarks, let it be pointed out that this blessed doctrine needs to be handled reverently. It is not a subject to be reasoned about and speculated upon, but approached in a spirit of holy awe and devotion. It is to be handled soberly, "When thou art in disputation, engaged upon a just quarrel to vindicate the truth of God from heresy and distortion, look into thy heart, set a watch on thy lips, beware of wild fire in thy zeal" (E. Reynolds, 1648). Nevertheless, this truth is to be dealt with uncompromisingly, and plainly, irrespective of the fear or favor of man, confidently leaving all "results" in the hand of God. May it be graciously granted us to write in a manner pleasing to God, and you to receive whatever is from Himself.

Chapter 2
Its Source

Accurately speaking, election is a branch of predestation, the latter being a more comprehensive term than the former. Predestination relates to all creatures, things, and events; but election is restricted to rational beings—angels and humans. As the word predestinate signifies, God from all eternity sovereignly ordained and immutably determined the history and destiny of each and all of His creatures. But in this study we shall confine ourselves to predestination as it relates to or concerns rational creatures. And here too a further distinction must be noticed. There cannot be an election without a rejection, a taking without a passing by, a choice without a refusal. As Psalm 78 expresses it, "He refused the tabernacle of Joseph, and chose not the tribe of Ephraim; but chose the tribe of Judah" (vv. 67, 68). Thus predestination includes both reprobation (the preterition or passing by of the non-elect, and then the foreordaining of them to condemnation—Jude 4—because of their sins) and election unto eternal life, the former of which we shall not now discuss.

The doctrine of election means, then, that God singled out certain ones in His mind both from among angels (1 Tim. 5:21) and from among men, and ordained them unto eternal life and blessedness; that before He created them, He decided their destiny, just as a builder draws his plans and determines every part of the building before any of the materials are assembled for the carrying out of his design. Election may thus be defined: it is that part of the counsel of God whereby He did from all eternity purpose in Himself to display His grace upon certain of His creatures. This was made effectual by a definite decree concerning them. Now in every decree of God three things must be considered: the beginning, the matter or substance, the end or design. Let us offer a few remarks upon each.

The beginning of the decree is the will of God. It originates solely in His own sovereign determination. Whilst determining the estate of His creatures God's own will is the alone and absolute cause thereof. As there is nothing above God to rule Him, so there is nothing outside of Himself which can be in any wise an impulsive cause unto Him; to say otherwise is to make the will of God no will at all. Herein He is infinitely exalted above us, for not only are we subject to One above us, but our wills are being constantly moved and disposed by external causes. The will of God could have no cause outside of itself, or otherwise there would be something prior to itself (for a cause ever precedes the effect) and something more excellent (for the cause is ever superior to the effect), and thus God would not be the independent Being which He is.

The matter or substance of a divine decree is God's purpose to manifest one or more of His attributes or perfections. This is true of all the divine decrees, but as there is variety in God's attributes so there is in the things He decrees to bring into existence. The two principal attributes He exercises upon His rational creatures are His grace and His justice. In the case of the elect God determined to exemplify the riches of His amazing grace, but in the case of the non-elect He saw fit to demonstrate His justice and severity—withholding His grace from them because it was His good pleasure so to do. Yet it must not be allowed for a moment that this latter was a point of cruelty in God, for His nature is not grace alone, nor justice alone, but both together; and therefore in determining to display both of them there could not be a point of injustice.

The end or design of every divine decree is God's own glory, for nothing less than this could be worthy of Himself. As God swears by Himself because He can swear by none greater, so because a greater and grander end cannot be proposed than His own glory, God has set up that as the supreme end of all His decrees and works. "The Lord hath made all things for himself" (Prov. 16:4)—for His own glory. As all things are from Him as the first cause, so all things are to Him (Rom. 11:36) as the final end. The good of His creatures is but the secondary end; His own glory is the supreme end, and everything else is subordinate thereto. In the case of the elect it is God's amazing grace which will be magnified; in the case of the reprobate His pure justice will be glorified. What follows in this chapter will largely be an amplification of these three points.

The source of election, then, is the will of God. It should be scarcely necessary to point out that by "God" we mean, Father, Son, and Holy Spirit. Though there are three persons in the Godhead, there is but one undivided nature common to Them all, and so but one will. They are one, and They agree in one: "He is in one mind, and who can turn him?" (Job 23:13). Let it also be pointed out that the will of God is not a thing apart from God, nor is it to be considered only as a part of God: the will of God is God Himself willing: it is, if we may so speak, His very nature in activity, for His will is His very essence. Nor is God's will subject to any fluctuation or change: when we affirm that God's will is immutable, we are only saying that God Himself is, "without variableness or shadow or turning" (James 1:17). Therefore the will of God is eternal, for since God Himself had no beginning, and since His will is His very nature, then His will must be from everlasting.

To proceed one step further. The will of God is absolutely free, uninfluenced and uncontrolled by anything outside of itself. This appears from the making of the world—as well as of everything in it. The world is not eternal, but was made by God, yet whether it should be or should not be created, was determined by Himself alone. The time when it was made—whether sooner or later; the size of it—whether smaller or larger; the duration of it—whether for a season or forever; the condition of it—whether it should remain "very good" or be defiled by sin; was all settled by the sovereign decree of the Most High. Had He so pleased, God could have brought this world into existence millions of ages earlier than He did. Had He so pleased, He could have made it and all things in it in a moment of time, instead of in six days and nights. Had He so pleased, He could have limited the human family to a few thousand or hundred, or have made it a thousand times larger than it is. No other reason can be assigned why God created it when and as it is than His own imperial will.

God's will was absolutely free in connection with election. In choosing a people unto eternal life and glory, there was nothing outside Himself which moved God to form such a purpose. As He expressly declares, "I will have mercy on whom I will have mercy, and I will have compassion on whom I will have compassion" (Rom. 9:15)—language could not state more definitely the absoluteness of divine sovereignty in this matter. "Having predestinated us unto the adoption of children by Jesus Christ to himself, according to the good pleasure of his will" (Eph. 1:5): here again all is resolved into the mere pleasure of God. He bestows His favors or withholds them as pleaseth Himself. Nor does He stand in any need of our vindicating His procedure. The Almighty is not to be brought down to the bar of human reason: instead of seeking to justify God's high sovereignty, we are only required to believe it, on the authority of His own Word. "I thank thee, O Father, Lord of heaven and earth, because thou hast hid these things from the wise and prudent, and hast revealed them unto babes: even so, Father; for so it seemed good in thy sight" (Matt. 11:25, 26)—the Lord Jesus was content to rest there, and so must we be.

Some of the ablest expositors of this profound truth have affirmed that the love of God is the moving cause of our election, citing "In love having predestinated us" (Eph. 1:5); yet in so doing, we think they are chargeable with a slight inaccuracy or departure from the rule of faith. While fully agreeing that the last two words of Ephesians 1:4 (as they stand in the A.V.) belong properly to the beginning of verse 5, yet it should be carefully noted that verse 5 is not speaking of our original election, but of our being predestinated unto the adoption of children: the two things are quite distinct, separate acts on the part of God, the second following upon the first. There is an order in the divine counsels, as there is in God's works of creation, and it is as important to heed what is said of the former as it is to attend unto the divine procedure in the six days work of Genesis 1.

An object must exist or subsist before it can be loved. Election was the first act in the mind of God, whereby He chose the persons of the elect to be holy and without blame (v. 4). Predestination was God's second act, whereby He ratified by decree the state of those to whom His election had given a real subsistence before Him. Having chosen them in His dear Son unto a perfection of holiness and righteousness, God's love went forth to them, and bestowed upon them the chiefest and highest blessing His love could confer: to make them His children by adoption. God is love, and all His love is exercised upon Christ and those in Him. Having made the elect His own by the sovereign choice of His will, God's heart was set upon them as His special treasure.

Others have attributed our election to the grace of God, quoting "There is a remnant according to the election of grace" (Rom. 11:5). But here again we must distinguish between things that differ, namely, between the beginning of a divine decree and its matter or substance. It is true, blessedly true, that the elect are the objects upon which the grace of God is specially exercised, but that is quite another thing from saying that their election originated in God's grace. The order we are here insisting upon is clearly expressed in Ephesians 1. First, "He [God] hath chosen us in him [Christ] before the foundation of the world: that we should be holy and without blame [righteous] before him" (v. 4): that was the initial act in the divine mind. Second, "in love having predestinated us unto the adoption of children by Jesus Christ to himself." and that "according to the good pleasure of his will" (v. 5): that was God enriching those upon whom He had set His heart. Third, "to the praise of the glory of his grace, wherein he hath made us accepted in the beloved" (v. 6): that was both the subject and design of God's decree—the manifestation and magnification of His grace.

"The election of grace" (Rom. 11:5), then, is not to be understood as the genitive of origin, but of object or character, as in "the Rose of Sharon," "the tree of life," "the children of disobedience." The election of the church, as of all His acts and works, is to be traced right back to the uncontrolled and uncontrollable will of God. Nowhere else in Scripture is the order of the divine counsels so definitely revealed as in Ephesians 1, and nowhere else is emphasis placed so strongly upon God's will. He predestinated unto the adoption of children "according to the good pleasure of his will" (v. 5). He has made known to us "the mystery of his will" (not "grace") and that "according to his good pleasure which he hath purposed in himself" (v. 9). And then, as though that was not sufficiently explicit, the passage closes with "being predestinated according to the purpose of him who worketh all things after the counsel of his own will, that we should be to the praise of his glory" (vv. 11, 12).

Let us dwell for a moment longer upon that remarkable expression "who worketh all things after the counsel of his own will"(v. 11). Note well it is not "the counsel of his own heart," nor even "the counsel of his own mind," but WILL: not "the will of his own counsel," but "the counsel of his own will." Herein God differs radically from us. Our wills are influenced by the thoughts of our minds and moved by the affections of our hearts; but not so God's. "He doeth according to his will in the army of heaven, and among the inhabitants of the earth" (Dan. 4:35). God's will is supreme, determining the exercise of all His perfections. He is infinite in wisdom, yet His will regulates the operations of it. He is full of mercy, but His will determines when and to whom He shows it. He is inflexibly just, yet His will decides whether or not justice shall be put forth: observe carefully not "Who can by no means clear the guilty" (as is so generally misquoted), but "Who will by no means clear the guilty" (Exod. 34:7). God first wills or determines that a thing shall be, and then His wisdom contrives the execution of it.

Let us now point out what has been disproved. From all that has been said above it is clear, first, that our good works are not the thing which induced God to elect us, for that act passed in the divine mind in eternity—long before we had any actual existence. See how this very point is set aside in, "For the children being not yet born, neither having done any good or evil, that the purpose of God according to election might stand, not for works, but of him that calleth" (Rom. 9:11). Again we read, "For we are his workmanship, created in Christ Jesus unto good works, which God hath before ordained that we should walk in them" (Eph. 2:10). Since, then, we were elected prior to our creation, then good works could not be the moving cause of it: no, they are the fruits and effects of it.

Second, the holiness of men, whether in principle or in practice, or both, is not the moving cause of election, for as Ephesians 1:4 so plainly declares "He hath chosen us in him before the foundation of the world, that we should be holy and without blame before him"— not because we were holy, but so that we might be. That we "should be holy" was something future, which follows upon it, and is the means to a further end, namely, our salvation, to which men are chosen. "God hath from the beginning chosen you to salvation, through sanctification of the Spirit" (2 Thess. 2:13). Since, then, the sanctification of God's people was the design of His election, it could not be the cause of it. "This is the will of God, even your sanctification" (1 Thess. 4:3): not merely the approving will of God, as being agreeable to His nature; nor merely His preceptive will, as required by the Law; but His decretive will, His determinate counsel.

Third, nor is faith the cause of our election. How could it be? Throughout their unregeneracy all men are in a state of unbelief, living in this world without God and without hope. And when we had faith, it was not of ourselves—either of our goodness, power, or will. No, it was a gift from God (Eph. 2:9), and the operation of the Spirit (Col. 2:12), flowing from His grace. "As many as were ordained to eternal life believed" (Acts 13:48), and not "as many as believed, were ordained to eternal life." Since, then, faith flows from divine grace, it cannot be the cause of our election. The reason why other men do not believe, is because they are not of Christ's sheep (John 10:26); the reason why any believe is because God gives them faith, and therefore it is called "the faith of God's elect" (Titus 1:1).

Fourth, it is not God's foreview of these things in men which moved Him to choose them. God's foreknowledge of the future is founded upon the determination of His will concerning it. The divine decree, the divine foreknowledge, and the divine predestination is the order set forth in the Scriptures. First, "Who are the called according to his purpose"; second, "for whom he did foreknow"; third, "he also did predestinate" (Rom. 8:28, 29). The decree of God as preceding His foreknowledge is also stated in, "Him, being delivered by the determinate counsel and foreknowledge of God" (Acts 2:23). God foreknows everything that will be, because He has ordained everything that shall be; then it is to put the cart before the horse when we make foreknowledge the cause of God's election.

In conclusion let it be said that the end of God in His decree of election is the manifestation of His own glory, but before entering into detail upon this point we will quote several passages which state the broad fact itself. "But know that the Lord hath set apart him that is godly for himself" (Ps. 4:3). "Set apart" here signifies chosen or severed from the rest; "him that is godly" refers to David himself (Ps. 89:19, 20); "for himself," and not merely for the throne and kingdom of Israel. "For the Lord hath chosen Jacob unto himself, and Israel for his peculiar treasure" (Ps. 135:4). "To give drink to my people, my chosen. This people have I formed for myself; they shall show forth my praise" (Isa. 43:20, 21), which is parallel with Ephesians 1:5, 6. So in the New Testament: when Christ was pleased to give to Ananias an account of the conversion of His beloved Paul, He said, "he is a chosen vessel unto me" (Acts 9:15). Again, "I have reserved to myself seven thousand men, who have not bowed the knee to Baal" (Rom. 11:4 ASV), which is explained in the next verse as "a remnant according to the election of grace."

Chapter 3
Its Grand Original

The decrees of God, His eternal purpose, the inscrutable counsels of His will, are indeed a great deep; yet this we know, that from first to last they have a definite relation to Christ, for He is the Alpha and the Omega in all covenant transactions. Beautifully did Spurgeon express it: "Search for the celestial fountain, from which the divine streams of grace flow to us, and you will find Jesus Christ the well-spring in covenant love. If your eyes shall ever see the covenant roll, if you shall ever be permitted in a future state to see the whole plan of redemption as it was mapped out in the chambers of eternity, you shall see the blood-red line of atoning sacrifice running across the margin of every page, and you shall see that from the beginning to the end one object was always in view—the glory of the Son of God." It therefore seems strange that many who see that election is the foundation of salvation, yet overlook the glorious Head of election, in whom the elect were chosen and from whom they receive all blessings.

"Blessed be the God and Father of our Lord Jesus Christ, who hath blessed us with all spiritual blessings in the heavenlies in Christ: according as he hath chosen us in him before the foundation of the world" (Eph. 1:3, 4). Since we were chosen in Christ, it is evident that we were chosen out of ourselves; and since we were chosen in Christ, it necessarily follows that He was chosen before we were. This is clearly implied in the preceding verse, wherein the Father is expressly designated "the God and Father of our Lord Jesus Christ." Now according to the analogy of Scripture (i.e., when He is said to be "the God" of any one) God was "the God" of Christ first, because He chose Him to that grace and union. Christ as man was predestinated as truly as we were, and so has God to be His God by predestination and free grace. Second, because the Father made a covenant with Him (Isa. 42:6). In view of the covenant made with them, He became known as "the God of Abraham, of Isaac and of Jacob;" so in view of the covenant He made with Christ, He became His "God." Third, because God is the author of all Christ's blessedness (Ps. 45:2, 7).

"According as He [God] hath chosen us in him" means, then, that in election Christ was made the Head of the elect. "In the womb of election He, the Head, came out first [adumbrated in every normal birth, A. W. P.], and then we, the members" (Thos. Goodwin). In all things Christ must have the "preeminence," and therefore is He "the Firstborn" in election (Rom. 8:29). In the order of nature Christ was chosen first, but in the order of time we were elected with Him. We were not chosen for ourselves apart, but in Christ, which denotes three things. First, we were chosen in Christ as the members of His body. Second, we were chosen in Him as the pattern which we should be conformed unto. Third, we were chosen in Him as the final end, i.e., it was for Christ's glory, to be His "fullness" (Eph. 1:23).

"Behold my servant, whom I uphold: mine elect, in whom my soul delighteth" (Isa. 42:1): that this passage refers to none other than the Lord Jesus Christ is unmistakably plain from the Spirit's citation of it in Matthew 12:15-21. Here, then, is the grand original of election: in its first and highest instance election is spoken of and applied to the Lord Jesus! It was the will of the eternal three to elect and predestinate the second person into creature being and existence, so that as God-man, "the firstborn of every creature" (Col. 1:15), He was the subject of the divine decrees and the immediate and principal object of the love of the co-essential three. And as the Father hath life in Himself, so hath He given to the Son—considered as God-man—to have life in Himself (John 5:26), to be a fountain of life, of grace and glory, unto His beloved Spouse, who received her being and wellbeing from Jehovah's free grace and everlasting love.

When God determined to create, among all the myriad creatures, both angelic and human, which rose up in the divine mind, to be brought into being by Him, the man Christ Jesus was singled out of them, and appointed to union with the second person in the blessed trinity, and was accordingly sanctified and set up. This original and highest act of election was one of pure sovereignty and amazing grace. The celestial hosts were passed by, and the seed of the woman was determined upon. Out of the innumerable seeds which were to be created in Adam, the line of Abraham was selected, then of Isaac, and then of Jacob. Of the twelve tribes which were to issue from Jacob, that of Judah was chosen, God elected not an angel to the high union with His Son, but "one chosen out of the people" (Ps. 89:19). What shall those say who so much dislike the truth that the heirs of heaven are elected, when they learn that Jesus Christ Himself is the subject of eternal election!

"Jehovah is the first cause and the last end of all things. His essence and existence are of and from Himself. He is Jehovah, the self-existing essence: the fountain of life, and essential blessedness—'The King eternal, immortal, invisible, the only wise God, who alone hath immortality, dwelling in that light to which no mortal eye can approach.' And throughout a vast eternity the eternal three enjoyed boundless and incomprehensible blessedness in the contemplation of those essential perfections which belong to the Father, Son, and Spirit, the everlasting Jehovah: who is His own eternity, and cannot receive any addition to His essential happiness or glory by any or all of His creatures. He is exalted above all blessing and praise. The whole creation before Him, and as viewed by Him, is less than nothing and vanity. If any should curiously inquire, what was God engaged in before He stretched out the heavens and laid the foundations of the earth? The answer is: the blessed, co-equal, and co-essential three, Father, Son, and Spirit, had a mutual in being and society together, and were essentially blessed in that divine eternal life, in the mutual interests or propriety they have in each other, in mutual love and delight—as also in the possession of one common glory.

But as it is the nature of goodness to be communicative of itself, so it pleased the eternal trinity to purpose to go forth into creature acts. The ever blessed three, to whom nothing can be added or diminished, the spring and fountain of whose essential blessedness arises from the immense perfections in the infinite nature in which they exist—in the mutual love they have to each other—and their mutual converse together—were pleased to delight in creature fellowship and society. The eternal Father predestinated His co-essential Son into creature being and existence, and from everlasting He wore the form and bore the personage of God-man. The creation of all things is attributed in Scripture to divine sovereignty: 'Thou hast created all things, and for thy pleasure they are and were created' (Rev. 4:11). Nothing out of God can move Him: or be a motive to Him; His will is His rule, His glory His ultimate end. 'For of Him (as the first cause), and through Him (as the preserving cause), and to Him (as the final cause), are all things' (Rom. 11:36).

God in His actual creation of all, is the end of all. 'The Lord hath made all things for himself' (Prov. 16:4), and the sovereignty of God naturally ariseth from the relation of all things to Himself as their Creator, and their natural and inseparable dependence upon Him, in regard of their being and well-being. He had the being of all things in His own will and power, and it was at His own pleasure whether He would impart it or not. 'Known unto God are all his works from the beginning of the world' (Acts 15:18). He comprehends and grasps all things in His infinite understanding. As He hath an incomprehensible essence, to which ours is but as the drop in a bucket, so He hath an incomprehensible knowledge, to which ours is but as a grain of dust. His primitive decree and view, in the creation of heaven and earth, angels and men, being His own glory, and that which gave foundation to it and was the basis to support it, was Jehovah's design to exalt His Son as God-man, to be the foundation and corner-stone of the whole creation of God. God had never gone forth into creature acts, had not the second person condescended by the assumption of our nature to become a creature. Though this took place after the fall, yet the decree concerning it was before the fall. Jesus Christ, the fellow of the Lord of hosts, was the first of all the ways of God" (S. E. Pierce).

Nowhere does the sovereignty of God shine forth so conspicuously as in His acts of election and reprobation, which took place in eternity past, and which nothing in the creature was the cause of. God's act of choosing His people in Christ was before the foundation of the world, without the consideration of the fall, nor was it upon the foresight and footing of works, but was wholly, of grace, and all to the praise and glory of it. In nothing else is Jehovah's sovereignty so manifest: indeed the highest instance of it was in predestinating the second person in the Trinity to be the God-man. That this came under the decree of God is clear, again, from the words of the apostle: "Who verily [says he in speaking of Christ] was foreordained before the foundation of the world" (1 Pet. 1:20) and who is said to be laid "in Sion a chief cornerstone, elect, precious" (1 Pet. 2:6). This grand original of election, so little known today, is of such transcendent importance that we dwell upon it a little longer, to point out some of the reasons why God was pleased to predestinate the man Christ Jesus unto personal union with His Son.

Christ was predestinated for higher ends than the saving of His people from the effects of their fall in Adam. First, He was chosen for God Himself to delight in, far more so and infinitely above all other creatures. Being united to the second person, the man Christ Jesus was exalted to a closer union and communion with God. The Lord of hosts speaks of Him as "the man that is my fellow" (Zech. 13:7), "mine elect, in whom my soul delighteth" (Isa. 42:1). Second, Christ was chosen that God might behold the image of Himself and all His perfections in a creature, so that His excellences are seen in Christ as in no other: "Who being the brightness of his glory and the express image of his person" (Heb. 1:3), which is spoken of the person of Christ as God-man. Third, by the union of the man Christ Jesus with the everlasting Son of God, the whole fullness of the Godhead was to dwell personally in Him, He being "the Image of the invisible God" (Col. 1:15, 19).

The Man Christ Jesus, then, was chosen unto the highest union and communion with God Himself. In Him the love and grace of Jehovah shine forth in their superlative glory. The Son of God gave subsistence and personality to His human nature, so that the Son of God and His human nature are not merely one flesh as man and wife (which is the closest union with us), nor one spirit only (as is the case between Christ and the Church: 1 Cor. 6:17), but one person, and hence this creature nature is advanced to a fellowship in the society of the blessed Trinity, and therefore to Him God communicates Himself without measure (John 3:34). Descending now to a lower plane, the Man Christ Jesus was also chosen to be an Head to an elect seed, who were chosen in Him, given a super-creation subsistence, and blessed in Him with all spiritual blessings.

If God will love, He must have an object for His love, and the object must have an existence before Him to exercise His love upon, for He cannot love a non-entity. It must therefore be that the God-man, and the elect in Him existed in the divine mind as objects of God's everlasting love, before all time. In Christ the Church was chosen from everlasting: the one the Head, the other His body; the one being the bridegroom, the other His bride: the one being chosen and appointed for the other. They were chosen together, yet Christ first in the order of the divine decrees. As, then, Christ and the Church had existed in the will, thoughts, and purpose of the Father from the beginning, He could love them and rejoice in them. As the God-man declares "Thou hast sent me, and hast loved them, as thou hast loved me...for thou lovest me before the foundation of the world" (John 17:23, 24).

The Son of God being, before all time, predestinated to be God-man, He was secretly anointed or set up as such, and His human nature had a covenant subsistence before God. In consequence of this, He was the Son of man in heaven before He became the Son of man on earth; He was the Son of man secretly before God before He became the Son of man openly and manifestly in this world. Therefore did the Psalmist exclaim, "Let thy hand be upon the man of thy right hand, upon the son of man whom thou madest strong for Thyself" (80:17); and therefore did Christ Himself declare, "What and if ye shall see the Son of man ascend up where he was before?" (John 6:62). "God, out of His eternal and infinite goodness of love, and purposing Christ to become a creature, and communicate with His creatures, ordained in His eternal counsel that person in the Godhead should be united to our nature and to one particular of His creatures, that so in the person of the Mediator the true ladder of salvation might be fixed, whereby God might descend to His creatures and His creatures ascend unto Him" (Sir Francis Bacon).

"Christ was first elected as Head and Mediator, and as the Cornerstone to bear up the whole building; for the act of the Father's election in Christ supposeth Him first chosen to this mediatory work and to be the Head of the elect part of the world. After this election of Christ, others were predestinated 'to be conformed unto His image' (Rom 8:29) i.e., to Christ as Mediator, and taking human nature; not to Christ barely considered as God. This conformity being specially intended in election, Christ was in the purpose of the Father the first exemplar and copy of it. One foot of the compass of grace stood in Christ as the center, while the other walked about the circumference, pointing one here and another there, to draw a line, as it were, between every one of those points and Christ. The Father, then, being the prime cause of the election of some out of the mass of mankind, was the prime cause of the election of Christ to bring them to the enjoyment of that to which they were elected. Is it likely that God, in founding an everlasting kingdom, should consult about the members before He did about the Head? Christ was registered at the top of the book of election, and His members after Him. It is called, therefore, 'the book of the Lamb'" (S. Charnock).

That passage of Scripture which enters most fully into what we are here contemplating is Proverbs 8, at which we will now glance. There are many passages in that book wherein the "wisdom" spoken of signifies far more than a moral excellency, and something even more blessed than the personification of one of the divine attributes. In not a few passages (1:20, 21, for example) the reference is to Christ, one of whose titles is "the wisdom of God" (1 Cor. 1:24). It is as such He is to be regarded here in chapter 8. That it is a person which is there in view is clear from verse 17, and that it is a divine person appears from verse 15; yet not a divine person considered abstractedly, but as the God-man. This is evident from what is there predicated of Him.

"The Lord possessed me in the beginning of his way, before his works of old" (v. 22). The speaker is Christ Himself, the alone Mediator between the Creator and His creatures. The words "The Lord possessed me in the beginning of his way" tend to hide what is there affirmed. There is no prefix in the original Hebrew, nothing there to warrant the interposed "in," while the word rendered "beginning" signifies the first or chief. Thus it should be translated "the Lord possessed me: the beginning (or Chief) of his way, before his works of old." Christ was the firstborn of all God's thoughts and designs, delighted in by Him long before the universe was brought into existence.

"I was set up from everlasting, from the beginning, or ever the earth was" (v. 23). "Our Redeemer came forth of the womb of a decree from eternity, before He came out of the womb of the virgin in time; He was hid in the will of God before He was made manifest in the flesh of a Redeemer; He was a lamb slain in decree before He was slain upon the cross; He was possessed by God in the beginning, or the beginning of His way, the Head of His works, and set up from everlasting to have His delights among the sons of men" (Prov. 8:22, 23, 31), (S. Charnock).

"When there were no depths, I was brought forth; when there were no fountains abounding with water. Before the mountains were settled, before the hills was I brought forth" (vv. 24, 25). Christ is here referring to His being "brought forth" in God's mind, being predestinated into creature existence before the world was made. The first of all God's intentions respected the union of the Man Christ Jesus unto His Son. The Mediator became the foundation of all the divine counsels: see Ephesians 3:11 and 1:9, 10. As such the triune Jehovah "possessed" Him as a treasury in which were laid up all His designs. He was then "set up" or "anointed" (v. 23) in His official character as Mediator and Head of the Church. As the God-man He had a virtual influence and was the Executor of all the works and will of God.

"Then I was by him, as one brought up with him: and I was daily his delight, rejoicing always before him" (v. 30). It is not the complacency of the Father in the Son considered absolutely as the second Person, but His satisfaction and joy in the Mediator as He viewed Him in the glass of His decrees. It was as incarnate that the Father said, "This is my beloved Son in whom I am well pleased" (Matt. 3:17), and it was with the foreordained God-man, who had a real subsistence before the divine mind, that He was delighted in by Jehovah before the world was. In His eternal thoughts and primitive views, the man that was His fellow became the Object of God's ineffable love and complacency. It was far more than that Jehovah simply purposed that the Son should become incarnate; His decree gave Christ a real subsistence before Him, and as such afforded infinite satisfaction to His heart.

So little understood is this blessed aspect of our subject, and so important do we deem it, that some further remarks thereon seem called for. That Christ is the firstborn or head of the election of grace was prefigured at the beginning of God's works, in fact the creation of this world and the formation of the first man were on purpose to make Christ known. As we are told in Romans 5:14 "which is the figure of Him that was to come." In his creation, formation, and constitution as the federal head of our race, Adam was a remarkable type of Christ as God's Elect. In amplifying this statement it will be necessary to go over some of the same ground that we covered in Spiritual Union and Communion, but we trust the reader will bear with us if we here repeat a number of the things.

There is a certain class of people—despising all doctrine, and particularly disliking the doctrine of God's absolute sovereignty—who often exhort us to "preach Christ," but we have long observed that they never preach Christ in His highest official character, as the Covenant-Head of God's people, that they never say one word about Him as God's "Elect, in whom my soul delighteth!" Preaching Christ is a far more comprehensive task than many suppose, nor can it be done intelligently by any man until he begins at the beginning and shows that the man Christ Jesus was eternally predestinated unto union with the second person of the Godhead. "I have exalted one chosen out of the people" (Ps. 89:19): that exaltation commenced with the elevation of Christ's humanity to personal union with the eternal Word— unique honor!

The very words "chosen in Christ" necessarily imply that He was chosen first, as the soil in which we were set. When God chose Christ it was not as a single or private person, but as a public person, as Head of His body, we being chosen in Him as the members thereof. Thus, inasmuch as we were then given a representative subsistence before God, God could make a covenant with Christ on our behalf. That He did so enter into an eternal compact with Christ in this character as Head of the election of grace is clear from, "I have made a covenant with my chosen, I have sworn unto David my servant" (Ps. 89:3)— adumbrated in the covenant He made in time with him who was typically "the man after his own heart," for David was as truly shadowing forth

Christ when God made a covenant with him as Joseph was when he supplied food to his needy brethren, or as Moses was when he led forth the Hebrews out of the house of bondage.

Let those, then, who desire to preach Christ, see to it that they give Him the preeminence in all things—election not excepted! Let them learn to give unto Jesus of Nazareth His full honor, that which the Father Himself hath given to Him It is a superlative honor that Christ is the channel through which all the grace and glory we have, or shall have, flows to us, and was set up as such from the beginning. As Romans 8:29 so plainly teaches, it was in connection with election that God appointed His own beloved Son to be "the firstborn among many brethren." Christ being appointed as the masterpiece of divine wisdom, the grand prototype, and we ordained to be so many little copies and models of Him. Christ is the first and last of all God's thoughts, counsels, and ways.

The universe is but the theatre and this world the principal stage on which the Lord God thinks fit to act out some of His deepest designs. His creating of Adam was a shadow to point to a better Adam, who was to have an universal headship over all the creatures of God, and whose glories were to shine forth visibly in and through every part of the creation. When the world was created and furnished, man was brought forth. But before his formation we read of that renowned consultation of the eternal three: "And God said, Let us make man in our image" (Gen. 1:26). This respected Christ, the God-man, who was from all eternity the object and subject of all the counsels of the Trinity. Adam, created and made after God's Image, which consisted of righteousness and true holiness, was the type, for Christ is par excellent "the image of the invisible God" (Col. 1:15).

The formation of Adam's body, by God's immediate hand, out of the dust of the ground, was a figure or shadow of the assumption of human nature by the Son of God, whose humanity was formed immediately by the Holy Spirit: as Adam's body was produced from the virgin earth, so Christ's human nature was produced from the virgin's womb. Again; that union of soul and body in Adam was a type to express that most profound and greatest of all mysteries, the hypostatical union of our nature in the person of Christ: as it is justly expressed in what is commonly called the Athanasian Creed, "As the reasonable soul and flesh is one man, so God and man is one Christ." Again; as Adam's person comprised the perfections of all creatures, and was suited to take in all the comforts and pleasures they could afford and impart, so the glory of Christ's humanity excels all creatures, even the angels themselves. The more attentively we consider the person and position of the first Adam the better may we discern how fully and fittingly he was a figure of the last Adam.

As Adam, placed in paradise, had all the creatures of the earth brought before him and was made to have dominion over them all (Gen. 1:28), thus being crowned with mundane glory and honor, so in this too he accurately foreshadowed Christ, who hath universal empire and dominion over all worlds, beings, and things, as may be seen from Psalm 8, which is applied to the Savior in Hebrews 2:9, where sovereignty over all creatures is ascribed to Him, the earth and the heavens, sun, moon and stars magnifying Him. For though He was for a little while abased beneath the angels in His humiliation, yet now in His exaltation, He is crowned King of kings and Lord of lords. Moreover, though the God-man, the "fellow of the Lord of hosts," went through a season of degradation before His exaltation, nevertheless His glorification was foreordained before the world began: "I appoint unto you a kingdom, as my Father hath appointed unto me" (Luke 22:29); "It is he which was ordained of God to be the Judge of quick and dead" (Acts 10:42).

That Christ had both a precedency and presidency in election was also shadowed forth in this primo-primitive type, for we read, "And Adam gave names to all cattle, and to the fowl of the air, and to every beast of the field; but for Adam there was not found a help meet for him" (Gen. 2:20). Yet mark the perfect accuracy of the type: when God created Adam, He created Eve in him (and in blessing Adam— Gen. 1:28—He blessed all mankind in him); so when God elected Christ, His people were chosen in Him (Eph. 1:4), and therefore they had a virtual being and subsistence in Him from all eternity, and consequently He was styled "the everlasting Father" (Isa. 9:6 and cf. Heb. 2:13); and consequently in blessing Christ, God blessed all the elect in Him and together with Him (Eph. 1:3; 2:5).

Though Adam came forth "very good" from the hands of his Maker and was given dominion over all the creatures of the earth, yet we read "but for Adam there was not found a help meet for him." Consequently, He provided a suitable partner for him, which being taken out of his side was then "built" (Gen. 2:22 margin), brought to, and welcomed by him. In like manner, though Christ was the beginning of God's way, set up from everlasting, and delighted in by the Father (Prov. 8:22, 23, 30), yet God did not think it good for him to be alone, and therefore He decreed a spouse for Him, who should share His communicable graces, honors, riches, and glories; a spouse which, in due time, was the fruit of His pierced side, and brought to Him by the gracious operations of the Holy Spirit.

When Eve was formed by the Lord God and brought to Adam so as to effect a marriage union, there was shadowed forth that highest mystery of grace, of God the Father presenting His elect and giving them to Christ: "Thine they were, and thou gayest them me" (John 17:6). Foreviewing them in the glass of the divine decrees, the Mediator loved and delighted in them (Prov. 8:31), betrothed them unto Himself, taking the Church as thus presented by God unto Him in a deed of marriage settlement and covenant contract as the gift of the Father. As Adam owned the relation between Eve and himself saying, "This is now bone of my bones, and flesh of my flesh" (Gen. 2:23), so Christ became an everlasting husband unto the Church. And as Adam and Eve were united before the fall, so Christ and the Church were one in the mind of God prior to any foreviews of sin.

If, then, we are to "preach Christ" in His highest official glory, it must be plainly shown that He was not ordained in God's eternal purpose for the Church, but the Church was ordained for Him. Notice how the Holy Spirit has emphasized this particular point in the type. "For a man indeed ought not to cover his head, forasmuch as he is the image and glory of God: but the woman is the glory of the man. For the man is not of the woman; but the woman of the man. Neither was the man created for the woman; but the woman for the man" (1 Cor. 11:7-9). Yet as Adam was not complete without Eve, so neither is Christ without the Church: she is His "fullness" or "complement" (Eph. 1:23), yea, she is His crown of glory and royal diadem (Isa. 62: 3)—the Church may be said to be necessary for Christ as an empty vessel for Him to supply with grace and glory. All His delights are in her, and He will be glorified in her and by her through all eternity, putting His glory upon her (John 17:22). "Come hither, I will show thee the Bride, the Lamb's wife. . . descending out of heaven from God, having the glory of God" (Rev. 2 1:9-11)

In His character as God's "Elect" Christ was shadowed forth by others than Adam. Indeed it is striking to see what a number of those who were prominent types of Christ were made the subjects of a real election of God, by which they were designated to some special office. Concerning Moses we read "Therefore he said that he would destroy them, had not Moses his chosen stood before him in the breach, to turn away his wrath" (Ps. 106:23). Of Aaron it is said, "No man taketh this honor unto himself, but he that is called of God, as was Aaron" (Heb. 5:4). Of the priests of Israel it is recorded, "The sons of Levi shall come near; for them the Lord thy God hath chosen to minister unto him; and to bless in the name of the Lord" (Deut. 21:5). Regarding David and the tribe from which he came, it is written, "He refused the tabernacle of Joseph, and chose not the tribe of Ephraim; but chose the tribe of Judah, the mount Zion which he loved.... He chose David also his servant, and took him from the sheepfolds" (Ps. 78:67, 68, 70). Each of these cases adumbrated the grand truth that the Man Christ Jesus was chosen by God to the highest degree of glory and blessedness of all His creatures.

"And there shall in no wise enter into it anything that defileth, neither whatsoever worketh abomination, or maketh a lie: but they which are written in the Lamb's book of life" (Rev. 21:27). This expression "The Book of Life" is doubtless a figurative one, for the Holy Spirit delights to represent spiritual, heavenly, and eternal things—as well as the blessing and benefits of them— under a variety of images and metaphors, that our minds may the more readily understand and our hearts feel the reality of them, and thus we be made more capable of receiving them. Yet this we are to know: the similitude thus made use of to represent them to our spiritual view are but shadows, yet what is shadowed forth by them has real being and substance.

The sun in the firmament is an instituted emblem in the nature of Christ—He being that to the spiritual world which the former is to the natural—yet the former is but the shadow, and Christ is the real substance, hence He is styled "the Sun of righteousness." So when Christ is compared to the light, He is the "true Light" (John 1:9), when compared to a vine, He is the "true Vine" (John 15:1), when to bread, He is "the true Bread," the Bread of life, that Bread of God which came down from heaven (John 6). Let this principle, then, be duly kept in mind by us as we come across the many metaphors which are applied to the Redeemer in the Scriptures. So here in Revelation 21:27 while allowing that "the Book of Life" is a figurative expression, we are far from granting that there is not in heaven that which is figured by it, nay, the very reality itself.

This expression "the Book of Life" has its roots in Isaiah 4:3, wherein God refers to His chosen remnant as "every one that is written among the living in Jerusalem," and it is this which explains the meaning of all the later references thereto. God's eternal act of election is spoken of as writing the names of His chosen ones in the Book of Life, and the following things are suggested by this figure. First, the exact knowledge which God has of all the elect, His particular remembrance of them, His love for and delight in them. Second, that His eternal election is one of particular persons whose names are definitely recorded by Him. Third, to show they are absolutely safe and secure, for God having written their names in the Book of Life, they shall never be blotted out (Rev. 3:5). When the seventy returned from their missionary journey, elated because the very demons were subject to them, Christ said, "But rather rejoice, because your names are written in heaven" (Luke 10:20 and cf. Phil. 4:3; Heb. 12:23), which shows that God's election to eternal life is of particular persons—by name—and therefore is sure and immutable.

Let us now particularly observe that this election-register is designated "the Lamb's Book of Life," and this for at least two reasons. First, because the Lamb's name heads it, His being the first one written therein, for He must have the preeminence; after which follows the enrollment of the particular names of all His people—note how His name is the first one recorded in the New Testament: Matthew 1:1! Second, because Christ, is the root and His elect are branches, so that they receive their life from Him as they are in Him and supported by Him. It is written "When Christ, who is our life, shall appear, then shall ye also appear with Him in glory" (Col. 3:4). Christ is our life because He is the very "Prince of life" (Acts 3:15). Thus, the divine register of election in which are enrolled all the names of Christ's members, is aptly termed "the Lamb's Book of Life," for they are entirely dependent upon Him for life.

But it is in connection with the first reason that we would offer a further remark. It is called the Lamb's Book of Life because His is the first name in it. This is no arbitrary assertion of ours, but one that is clearly warranted by the Bible, "Lo, I come (in the volume of the book it is written of Me)" (Heb. 10:7). The speaker here is the Lord Jesus and, as is so often the case (such is the fullness of His words), there is a double reference in it: first to the archives of God's eternal counsels, the scroll of His decrees; second, to the Holy Scriptures, which are a partial transcript of them.

In keeping with this twofold reference is the double meaning of the word "volume." In Psalm 40:7 "volume" is unquestionably the signification of the Hebrew word there used; but in Hebrews 10:7 the Greek word most certainly ought to be rendered "head"—kephale occurs seventy-six times in the New Testament, and it is always rendered "head" except here. Thus, properly translated, Hebrews 10:7 reads "at the head of the book it is written of me."

Here, then is the proof of our assertion. The Book of Life—the Divine register of election—is termed the Lamb's Book of Life" because His name is the first one written therein, and He who had Himself scanned that roll said, as He entered this world, "at the head of the book it is written of me." A further reference to this Book was made by Christ in "In thy book all my members were written" (Ps. 139:16). The Psalmist was referring to his natural body, first as formed in the womb (v. 15), and then as being the subject of the divine decrees (v. 16). But the deeper reference is to Christ, speaking, as the antitypical David, of the members of His mystical body. "The substance of the Church, whereof it was to be formed, was under the eyes of God, as proposed in the decree of election" (John Owen).

Should an exercised reader be asking, How may I now be assured that my name is written in the Lamb's Book of Life? We answer, very briefly. First, by God's having taught you to see and brought you to feel your inward corruption, your personal vileness, your awful guilt, your dire need of the sacrifice of the Lamb. Second, by causing you to make Christ of first importance in your thoughts and estimation, perceiving that He alone can save you. Third, by bringing you to believe in Him, rest your whole soul upon Him, desiring to be found in Him, not having your own righteousness, but His. Fourth, by making Him infinitely precious to you, so that He is all your desire. Fifth, by working in you a determination to please and glorify Him.

Chapter 4
Its Verity

Before proceeding further with an orderly opening up of this profound but precious doctrine, it may be better (especially for the benefit of those less familiar with the subject) if we now demonstrate its Scripturalness. We must not take anything for granted, and as numbers of our readers have never received any systematic instruction upon the subject—yea, some of them know next to nothing about it—and as others have heard and read only perversions and caricatures of this doctrine, it seems essential that we should pause and establish its verity. In other words, our present object is to furnish proof that what we are now writing upon is not some theological invention of Calvin's or any other man's, but is clearly revealed in Holy Writ, namely, that God, before the foundation of the world, made a difference between His creatures, singling out certain ones to be the special objects of His favor.

We shall deal with the subject in a more or less general way—occupying ourselves with the fact itself; reserving the more detailed analysis and the drawing of distinctions for later chapters. Let us begin by asking, Has God an elect people? Now this question must be propounded to God Himself, for He alone is competent to answer it. It is, therefore, to His holy Word we have to turn, if we would learn His answer thereto. But ere doing so, we need to earnestly beg God to grant us a teachable spirit, that we may humbly receive the divine testimony. The things of God can no man know, till God Himself declares them; but when He has declared them, it is not only crass folly, but wicked presumption, for anyone to contend or disbelieve. The Holy Scriptures are the rule of faith, as well as the rule of conduct. To the law and the testimony, then, we now turn.

Concerning the nation of Israel we read, "The Lord thy God hath chosen thee to be a special people unto Himself, above all people that are upon the face of the earth" (Deut. 7:6); "For the Lord hath chosen Jacob unto himself, and Israel for his peculiar treasure" (Ps. 135:4); "But thou, Israel, art my servant, Jacob whom I have chosen, the seed of Abraham my friend. Thou whom I have taken from the ends of the earth, and called thee from the chief men thereof, and said unto thee, thou art my servant; I have chosen thee, and not cast thee away" (Isa. 41:8, 9). These testimonies make it unmistakably plain that ancient Israel were the favored, elect people of God. We do not here take up the question as to why God chose them, or as to what they were chosen unto; but notice only the bare fact itself. In Old Testament times God had an elect nation.

Next, it is to be observed that even in favored Israel God made a distinction: there was an election within an election; or, in other words, God had a special people of His own from among the nation itself. "For they are not all Israel, which are of Israel: neither, because they are the seed of Abraham, are they all children: but, in Isaac shall thy seed by called" (Rom. 9:6-8). "God hath not cast away his people which he foreknew.... I have reserved to myself seven thousand men who have not bowed the knee to the image of Baal: even so that at this present time also there is a remnant according to the election of grace....Israel hath not obtained that which he seeketh for; but the election hath obtained it" (Rom. 11:2-7). Thus we see that even in visible Israel, the nation chosen to outward privileges, God had an election—a spiritual Israel, the objects of His love.

The same principle of Divine selection appears plainly and conspicuously in the teaching of the New Testament. There too it is revealed that God has a peculiar people, the subjects of His special favor, His own dear children. The Savior and His apostles describe this people in various ways, and often designate them by the term of which we here treat. "For the elect's sake those days shall be shortened . . . insomuch that, if it were possible, they shall deceive the very elect ... and they shall gather together His elect from the four winds" (Matt. 24:22, 24, 31). "Shall not God avenge His own elect, which cry day and night unto Him?" (Luke 18:7). "Who shall lay anything to the charge of God's elect?" (Rom. 8:33). "That the purpose of God according to election might stand" (Rom. 9:11). "I endure all things for the elect's sake" (2 Tim. 2:10), "The faith of God's elect" (Titus 1:1). Many other passages might be quoted, but these are sufficient to clearly demonstrate that God has an elect people. God Himself says He has, who will dare say He has not!

The word "elected" in one of its forms, or its synonym "chosen" in one of its forms, occurs upon the sacred page considerably over one hundred times. The term, then, belongs to the divine vocabulary. It must mean something; it must convey some definite idea. What, then, is its significance? The humble inquirer will not force a construction upon the word, or seek to read into it his own preconceptions, but will prayerfully endeavor to ascertain the mind of the Spirit. Nor should this be difficult, for there is no word in human language which has a more specific meaning. The concept universally expressed by it is that one is taken and another left, for if all were taken there would be no "choice." Moreover, the right of choice always belongs to him who chooses: the act is his, the motive is his. Therein "choice" differs from compulsion, the paying of a debt, discharging an obligation, or responding to the requirements of justice. Choice is a free and sovereign act.

Let there be no uncertainty about the meaning of our term. God has made a choice, for election signifies selection and appointment. God has exercised His own sovereign will and singled out from the mass of His creatures those upon whom He determined to bestow His special favors. There cannot be an election without a singling out, and there cannot be a singling out without a passing by. The doctrine of election means that from all eternity God made a choice of those who were to be His special treasure, His dear children, the coheirs of Christ. The doctrine of election means that before His Son became incarnate God marked out the ones who should be saved by Him. The doctrine of election means that God has left nothing to chance: the accomplishment of His purpose, the success of Christ's undertaking, the peopling of heaven, is not contingent upon the fickle caprice of the creature. God's will, and not man's will, fixes destiny.

Let us now call attention to a most remarkable and little known example of divine election. "I charge thee before God, and the Lord Jesus Christ, and the elect angels" (1 Tim. 5:21). If then, there are "elect angels" there must necessarily be non-elect, for there cannot be the one without the other. God, then, in the past made a selection among the hosts of heaven, choosing some to be vessels of honor and others to be vessels of dishonor. Those whom He chose unto His favor, stood steadfast, remained in subjection to His will. The rest fell when Satan revolted, for upon his apostasy he dragged down with himself one third of the angels (Rev. 12:4). Concerning them we read, "God spared not the angels that sinned, but cast them down to hell, and delivered them into chains of darkness" (2 Pet. 2:4). But those of them who belong to the election of grace are "the holy angels": holy as the consequence of their election, and not elected because they were holy, for election antedated their creation. The supreme example of election is seen in Christ; the next highest in that God made choice among the celestial hierarchies.

Let us next observe and admire the marvel and singularity of God's choice among men. He has selected a portion of Adam's race to be the high favorites of heaven. "Now this is a wonder of wonders, when we come to consider that the heaven, even the heaven of heavens, is the Lord's. If God must have a chosen race, why did He not select one from the majestic order of angels, or from the flashing cherubim and seraphim who stand around His throne? Why was not Gabriel fixed upon? Why was he not so constituted that from his loins there might spring a mighty race of angels, and why were not those chosen of God from before the foundation of the world? What could there be in man, a creature lower than the angels, that God should select him rather than the angelic spirits? Why were not the cherubim and seraphim given to Christ? Why did He not assume the nature of angels, and take them into union with Himself? An angelic body might be more in keeping with the person of Deity than a body of weak and suffering flesh and blood. There was something congruous if He had said unto the angels, 'Ye shall be My Sons.' But no! though all these were His own; He passes them by and stoops to man" (C. H. Spurgeon).

Some may suggest that the reason why God made choice of Adam's descendants in preference to the angels, was that the human race fell in Adam and thus afforded a more suitable case for God to display His rich mercy upon. But such a supposition is entirely fallacious, for, as we have seen, one third of the angels themselves fell from their high estate, yet so far from God showing them mercy, He "hath reserved in everlasting chains under darkness unto the judgment of the great day" (Jude 6). No Savior was provided for them, no gospel has ever been preached to them. How striking and how solemn is this: the fallen angels passed by; the fallen sons of Adam made the recipients of the overtures of divine mercy.

Here is a truly marvelous thing. God determined to have a people who should be His peculiar treasure, nearer and dearer to Himself than any other creatures; a people who should be conformed to the very image of His Son. And that people was chosen from the descendants of Adam. Why? Why not have reserved that supreme honor for the celestial hosts? They are a higher order of beings; they were created before us. They were heavenly creatures, yet God passed them by; we are earthly, yet the Lord set His heart upon us. Again we ask, why? Ah, let those who hate the truth of God's high sovereignty and contend against the doctrine of unconditional election, carefully ponder this striking example of it. Let those who so blatantly insist that it would be unjust for God to show partiality between man and man, tell us why did He show partiality between race and race, bestowing favors upon men which He never has upon angels? Only one answer is possible: because it so pleased Him.

Election is a divine secret, an act in the will of God in eternity past. But it does not forever remain such. No, in due time, God is pleased to make openly manifest His everlasting counsels. This He has done in varying degrees, since the beginning of human history. In Genesis 3:15 He made known the fact that there would be two distinct lines: the woman's "seed," which denoted Christ and His people, and the Serpent's "seed," which signified Satan and those who are conformed to his likeness; God placing an irreconcilable "enmity" between them. These two "seeds" comprehend the elect and the non-elect. Abel belonged to the election of grace: evidence of this being furnished in his "faith" (Heb. 11:4), for only those "ordained to eternal life" (Acts 13:48) savingly "believe." Cain belonged to the non-elect: evidence of this is found in the statement "Cain, who was of that Wicked one" (1 John 3:12). Thus at the beginning of history, in the two sons of Adam and Eve, God "took" the one into His favor, and "left" the other to suffer the due reward of his iniquities.

Next, we behold election running in the line of Seth, for it was of his descendants (and not those of Cain's) we read, "Then began men to call upon the name of the Lord" (Gen. 4:26). But in the course of time they too were corrupted, until the entire human race became so evil that God sent the flood and swept them all away. Yet even then the principle of divine election was exemplified: not only in Enoch, but that "Noah found grace in the eyes of the Lord" (Gen. 6:8). It was the same after the flood, for a marked discrimination was made between the sons of Noah: "Blessed be the Lord God of Shem" (Gen. 9:26), which imports that God had chosen and blessed him. On the other hand, "Cursed be Canaan: a servant of servants shall he be unto his brethren" (Gen. 9:25), which is expressive of preterition and all that is involved in God's rejection. Thus, even of those who emerged from the ark, God made one to differ from another.

From the sons of Noah sprang the nations which have peopled the world. "By these [i.e., Noah's three sons] were the nations divided in the earth after the flood" (Gen. 10:32). From those seventy nations God chose the one in which the great current of His election would run. In Genesis 10:25 we read that this dividing of the nations was made in the time of Eber, the grandson of Shem. Why are we told this? To intimate that God then began to separate the Jewish nation unto Himself in Eber, for Eber was their father; hence it is also that at the beginning of Shem's genealogy we are told, "Shem also (the elected and blessed of God), the father of all the children of Eber" (10:21). This is very striking, for Shem had other and older children (whose line of descendants is also recorded), as Asshur and Elim, the fathers of the Assyrians and the Persians.

The seemingly dry and uninteresting detail in Genesis 10 to which we have just alluded, marked a most important step forward in the outworking of the divine counsels, for it was then that God began to separate unto Himself the Israelites in Eber, whom He had appointed to be their father. Till then the Hebrews had lain promiscuously mingled with the other nations, but now God "divided" them from the rest, as the other nations were divided from one another. Accordingly, we find Eber's posterity, even when very few in number, were designated "Hebrews" as their national denomination ("Israel" being their religious name) in distinction from those among whom they lived: "Abraham the Hebrew" (Gen. 14:13), "Joseph the Hebrew" (Gen. 39:14). Hence, when they became a nation in numbers, and while living in the midst of the Egyptians, they are again styled "Hebrews" (Exod. 1:15), while in Numbers 24:24 they are distinctly called "Eber"!

What we have sought to explain above is definitely confirmed by "Remember the days of old, consider the years of many generations: ask thy father, and he will show thee; thy elders, and they will tell thee. When the most High divided to the nations their inheritance, when he separated the sons of Adam, he set the bounds of the people according to the number of the children of Israel. For the Lord's portion is his people; Jacob is the lot of his inheritance" (Deut. 32:7-9). Notice, first, the Lord here bade Israel cast their minds back to ancient times, the traditions of which had been handed down by their fathers. Second, the particular event alluded to was when God "divided" to the nations their inheritance, the reference being to that famous division of Genesis 10. Third, those nations are spoken of not "as the sons of Noah" (who was in the elect line), but as "the sons of Adam"—another plain hint that he headed the line of the reprobate. Fourth, that when God allotted to the non-elect nations their earthly portion, even then the eye of grace and favor was upon the children of Israel. Fifth, "according to the number of the children of Israel," which was seventy when they first settled in Egypt (Gen. 46:27)—the exact number of the nations mentioned in Genesis 10!

The chief link of connection between Eber and the nation of Israel was, of course, Abraham, and in his case the principle of divine election shines forth with sunlight clearness. The divine call which he received marked another important stage in the development of God's eternal purpose. At the tower of Babel God gave over the nations to walk in their own evil ways, afterward taking up Abraham to be the founder of the favored nation. "Thou art the Lord the God, who didst choose Abraham, and broughtest him forth out of Ur" (Neh. 9:7). It was not Abraham who chose God, but God who chose Abraham. "The God of glory appeared unto our father Abraham, when he was in Mesopotamia" (Acts 7:2): this title "the God of glory" is employed here to emphasize the signal favor which was shown to Abraham, the glory of His grace in electing him, for there was nothing in him by nature that lifted him above his fellows and entitled him to the divine notice. It was unmerited kindness, sovereign mercy, which was shown him.

This is made very evident by what is told us in Joshua 24 of his condition before Jehovah appeared to him: "Thus saith the God of Israel, your fathers dwelt on the other side of the flood in old time, even Terah, the father of Abraham, and the father of Nachor: and they served other gods" (v. 2). Abraham was living in the heathen city of Ur, and belonged to an idolatrous family! At a later date God pressed this very fact upon his descendants, reminding them of the lowly and corrupt state of their original, and giving them to know it was for no good in him that he had been chosen: "Hearken to me, ye that follow after righteousness, ye that seek the Lord: look unto the rock whence ye are hewn, and to the hole of the pit whence ye are dug. Look unto Abraham your father, and unto Sarah that bare you; for I called him alone, and blessed him" (Isa. 51:1, 2). What a flesh-withering word is that: the great Abraham is here likened (by God) to "the hole of the pit"—such was his condition when the Lord first appeared unto him.

But there is more in the above passage. Observe carefully the words "I called him alone." Remember that this was while he dwelt in Ur, and as modern excavations have shown, that was a city of vast extent: out of all its huge number of inhabitants God revealed himself to one only! The Lord here emphasized that very fact and calls upon us to mark the singularity of His election by this word "alone." See here, then, the absolute sovereignty of God, exercising His own imperial will, choosing whom He pleases. He had mercy upon Abraham simply because He was pleased to do so, and He left the remainder of his countrymen in heathen darkness simply because it so seemed good in His sight. There was nothing more in Abraham than in any of his fellows why God should have selected him: whatever goodness was found in him later was what God Himself put there, and therefore it was the consequence and not the cause of His choice.

Striking as is the case of Abraham's own election, yet God's dealings with his offspring is equally if not more noteworthy. Therein God furnished an epitome of what has largely characterized the history of all His elect, for it is a very rare thing to find a whole family which (not simply makes a profession, but) gives evidence of enjoying His special favor. The common rule is that one is taken and other is left, for those who are given to really believe this precious but solemn truth, are made to experimentally realize its force in connection with their own kin. Thus Abraham's own family furnished in his next and immediate successors, a prototype of the future experience of the elect. In his family we behold the most striking instances of both election and preterition, first in his sons, and then in his grandsons.

That Isaac was a child of pure electing grace (which was the cause and not the consequence of his faith and holiness), and that as such he was placed in Abraham's family as a precious gift, while Ishmael was excluded from that preeminent favor, is quite evident from the history of Genesis. Before he was born, yea, before he was conceived in the womb, God declared unto Abraham that Isaac was heir of the same salvation with him, and had irrevocably estated the covenant of grace upon him thereby distinguishing him from Ishmael; who, though blessed with temporal mercies, was not in the covenant of grace, but rather was under the covenant of works (see Gen. 17:19-21 and compare the Spirit's comments thereon in Gal. 4:22-26).

Later, while Isaac was yet young, and lay bound as a sacrifice upon the altar, God ratified the promises of blessing which He had made before his birth, confirming them with a solemn oath: "By myself have I sworn, saith the Lord, for because thou hast done this thing, hast not withheld thy son, thine only son: that in blessing I will bless thee, and in multiplying I will multiply thy seed as the stars of the heaven" (Gen. 22:16, 17). That oath respected the spiritual seed, the heirs of promise, such as Isaac was, the declared son of promise. To that the apostle referred when he said, "wherein God; willing more abundantly to show unto the heirs of promise the immutability of his counsel, confirmed it by an oath" (Heb. 6:17). And what was His "immutable counsel" but His eternal decree, His purpose of election? God's counsels are His decrees within Himself from everlasting (Eph. 1:4, 9,10). And what is a promise with an oath but God's immutable counsel or election put into promissory form. And who are the "heirs of promise" but the elect, such as Isaac was.

An objector would argue that the choosing of Isaac in preference to Ishmael was not an act of pure sovereignty, seeing that the former was the son of Sarah, while the latter was the child of Hagar, the Egyptian bondwoman—thus supposing that God's gifts are regulated by something in the creature. But the next instance precludes even that sophistry and entirely shuts us up to the uncaused and uninfluenced will of the Most High. Jacob and Esau were by the same father and mother, twins. Concerning them we read, "(For the children being not yet born, neither having done any good or evil, that the purpose of God according to election might stand, not of works, but of him that calleth;) It was said unto her, The elder shall serve the younger. As it is written, Jacob have I loved, but Esau have I hated" (Rom. 9:11-13). Let us bow in awed silence before such a passage.

The nation which sprang from Abraham, Isaac, and Jacob, was God's chosen and favored people, singled out and separated from all other nations, to be the recipients of the rich blessings of God. It was that very fact which added so greatly to the enormity of their sins, for increased privileges entail increased responsibility, and increased responsibility not discharged involves increased guilt. "Hear this word that the Lord hath spoken against you, 0 children of Israel.... You only have I known of all the families of the earth: therefore I will punish you for all your iniquities" (Amos 3:1, 2). From the days of Moses until the time of Christ, a period of fifteen hundred years, God suffered all the heathen nations to walk in their own ways, leaving them to the corruptions and darkness of their own evil hearts. No other nation had God's Word, no other nation had a divinely appointed priesthood. Israel alone was favored with a written revelation from heaven.

And why did the Lord choose Israel to be His special favorites? The Chaldeans were more ancient, the Egyptians were far wiser, the Canaanites were more numerous; yet they were passed by. What, then, was the reason why the Lord singled out Israel? Certainly it was not because of any excellency in them, as the whole of their history shows. From Moses till Malachi they were a stiff-necked and hardhearted people, unappreciative of divine favors, unresponsive to the divine will. It could not have been because of any goodness in them: it was a clear case of the divine sovereignty: "The Lord thy God hath chosen thee to be a special people unto himself, above all people that are upon the face of the earth. The Lord did not set his love upon you, nor choose you because ye were more in number than any people; for ye were the fewest of all people; but because the Lord loved you, and because He would keep the oath which He had sworn unto your fathers" (Deut. 7:6-8). The explanation of all God's acts and works was to be found in Himself—in the sovereignty of His will, and not anything in the creature.

The same principle of divine selection is as plainly and prominently revealed in the New Testament as in the Old. It was strikingly exemplified in connection with the birth of Christ. First, in the place where He was born. How startlingly the sovereignty of God was displayed in that momentous event. Jerusalem was not the Savior's birthplace, nor was it one of the prominent towns of Palestine; instead, it was in a small village! The Holy Spirit has called particular attention to this point in one of the leading Messianic prophecies: "But thou, Bethlehem Ephratah, though thou be little among the thousands of Judah, yet out of thee shall he come forth unto me that is to be ruler in Israel" (Mic. 5:2). How different are God's thoughts and ways from man's! How He despises what we most esteem, and honors that which we look down upon. One of the most insignificant of all places was chosen by God to be the scene of the most stupendous of all events.

Again; the high sovereignty of God and the principle of His singular election appeared in those to whom He first communicated these glad tidings. To whom was it God sent the angels to announce the blessed fact of the Savior's birth? Suppose Scripture had been silent upon the point: how differently would we have conceived of the matter. Would we not have naturally thought that the first ones to be informed of this glorious event had been the ecclesiastical and religious leaders in Israel? Surely the angels would deliver the message in the temple. But no, it was neither to the chief priests nor to the rulers they were sent, but unto the lowly shepherds keeping watch over their flocks in the fields. And again we say, how entirely different are God's thoughts and ways from man's. And what thus took place at the beginning of this Christian era was indicative of God's way throughout its entire course (see 1 Cor. 1:26-29).

Let us next observe that this same grand truth was emphasized by Christ Himself in His public ministry. Look at His first message in the Nazareth synagogue. "And there was delivered unto him the book of the prophet Esaias. And when he had opened the book, he found the place where it was written, the Spirit of the Lord is upon me, because he hath anointed me to preach the gospel to the poor [i.e., the poor in spirit, and not to wealthy Laodiceans]; he hath sent me to heal the broken-hearted [not the stout-hearted, but those sorrowing before God over their sins] , to preach deliverance to the captives [and not to those who prate about their "free will"] , and recovering of sight to the blind [not those who think they can see] , and to set at liberty them that are bruised [not those who deem themselves whole], To preach the acceptable year of the Lord" (Luke 4:17-19).

The immediate sequel is indeed solemn: "And He began to say unto them, This day is this Scripture fulfilled in your ears. And all bear him witness, and wondered at the gracious words which proceeded out of his mouth" (vv. 21, 22). So far so good: they were pleased at His "gracious words"; yes, but would they tolerate the preaching of sovereign grace? "But I tell you of a truth, many widows were in Israel in the days of Elias, when the heaven was shut up three years and six months, when great famine was throughout the land; but unto none of them was Elias sent, save unto Sarepta, a city of Sidon, unto a woman that was a widow. And many lepers were in Israel in the time of Eliseus the prophet; and none of them was cleansed, saving Naaman the Syrian" (vv. 25-27). Here Christ pressed upon them the truth of God's high sovereignty, and that they could not endure: "And all they in the synagogue, when they heard these things, were filled with wrath; and rose up, and thrust Him out of the city" (vv. 28, 29) and mark it well that it was the respectable worshippers of the synagogue who thus gave vent to their hatred of this precious truth! Then let not the servant today be surprised if he meet with the same treatment as his Master.

His sermon at Nazareth was by no means the only time when the Lord Jesus proclaimed the doctrine of election. In Matthew 11 we hear Him saying, "I thank Thee, 0 Father, Lord of heaven and earth, because thou hast hid these things from the wise and prudent, and hast revealed them unto babes. Even so, Father: for so it seemed good in thy sight" (vv. 25, 26). To the seventy He said, "Notwithstanding, in this rejoice not, that the spirits are subject unto you; but rather rejoice, because your names are written in heaven" (Luke 10:20). In John 6 it will be found that Christ, in the hearing of the multitude, hesitated not to speak openly of a company whom the Father had "given to him" (vv. 37, 39). To the apostles He said, "Ye have not chosen me, but I have chosen you, and ordained you, that ye should go and bring forth fruit" (John 15:16): how shocked would the great majority of church goers be today if they heard the Lord say such words unto His own! In John 17:9 we find Him saying, "I pray not for the world, but for them which thou hast given me."

As an interesting and instructive illustration of the emphasis which the Holy Spirit has placed upon this truth we would call attention to the fact that in the New Testament God's people are termed "believers" but twice, "Christians" only three times, whereas the designation elect, is found fourteen times and saints or separated ones sixty-two times! We would also point out that various other terms and phrases are used in the Scriptures to express election: "And the Lord said unto Moses, I will do this thing also that thou hast spoken: for thou hast found grace in my sight, and I know thee by name" (Exod. 33:17); "Before I formed thee in the belly I knew thee, and before thou camest forth out of the womb I sanctified thee" (Jer. 1:5; cf. Amos 3:2). "I speak not of you all: I know whom I have chosen" (John 13:18; cf. Matt. 20:16). "As many as were ordained to eternal life believed" (Acts 13:48). "God at the first did visit the Gentiles, to take out of them a people for his name" (Acts 15:14). "Church of the firstborn, which are written in heaven" (Heb. 12:23).

This basic truth of election undergirds the whole scheme of salvation: that is why we are told "the foundation of God standeth sure, having this seal, the Lord knoweth them that are his" (2 Tim. 2:19). Election is necessarily and clearly implied by some of the most important terms used in Scripture concerning various aspects of our salvation, yea, they are unintelligible without it. For example, every passage which makes mention of "redemption" presupposes eternal election. How so? Because "redemption" implies a previous possession: it is Christ buying back and delivering those who were God's at the beginning. Again; the words "regeneration" and "renewing" necessarily signify a previous spiritual life—lost when we fell in Adam (1 Cor. 15:22). So again the term "reconciliation:" this not only denotes a state of alienation before the reconciliation, but a condition of harmony and amity, before the alienation. But enough: the truth of election has now been abundantly demonstrated from the Scriptures. If these many and indubitable proofs are not sufficient, it would be a waste of time to further multiply them.

Let it now be pointed out that this grand truth was definitely held and owned by our forefathers. First, a brief quotation from the ancient Creed of the Waldenses (eleventh century)—those renowned confessors of the Christian Faith in the dark ages, in the midst of the most terrible persecutions from the Papacy: "That God saves from corruption and damnation those whom He has chosen from the foundation of the world, not for any disposition, faith, or holiness that He foresaw in them, but of His mere mercy in Christ Jesus His Son; passing by all the rest, according to the irreprehensible reason of His own free will and justice." Here is one of the Thirty-nine Articles of the Church of England: "Predestination to life is the everlasting purpose of God whereby, before the foundations of the world were laid, He hath constantly decreed by His secret counsel to us to deliver from curse and condemnation those whom He had chosen in Christ out of mankind, and to bring by Christ to everlasting salvation as vessels made to honor."

This is from the Westminster Confession of Faith, subscribed to by all Presbyterian ministers, "By the decree of God, for the manifestation of His glory, some men and angels are predestinated unto everlasting life, and others foreordained to everlasting death. These angels and men, thus predestinated and foreordained, are particularly and unchangeably designed; and their number is so certain and definite, that it cannot be either increased or diminished." And here is the third article from the old Baptist (English) Confession: "By the decree of God, for the manifestation of His glory, some men and angels are predestinated or foreordained to eternal life through Jesus Christ, to the praise of His glorious grace; others being left to act in their sin to their just condemnation, to the praise of His glorious justice."

Let it not be thought that we have quoted from these human standards in order to bolster up our cause. Not so: the present writer, by divine grace, would believe and teach this grand truth if none before him had ever held it, and if everyone in Christendom now repudiated it. But what has just been adduced is good evidence that we are here advancing no heretical novelty, but a doctrine proclaimed in the past in each section of the orthodox Church upon earth. We have also made the above quotations for the purpose of showing how far the present generation of professing Christians have departed from the Faith of those to whom under God, they owe their present religious liberties. Just as the modern denials of the divine inspiration and authority of the Scriptures (by the higher critics), the denial of immediate creation (by evolutionists), the denial of the deity of Christ (by Unitarians), so the present denial of God's sovereign election and of man's spiritual impotency, are equally departures from the Faith of our forefathers, which was based upon the inerrant Word of God.

The truth of divine election has been most conspicuously exemplified in the history of Christendom. If it be true that during the last two thousand years of the Old Testament dispensation the spiritual blessings of God were largely confined to a single people, it is equally true that for the last five hundred years one section of the human race has been more signally favored by heaven than all the other sections put together. God's dealings with the Anglo-Saxons have been as singular and sovereign as His dealings with the Hebrews of old. Here is a fact which cannot be gainsaid, staring us all in the face, exposing the madness of those who deny this doctrine: for centuries past the vast majority of God's saints have been gathered out of the Anglo-Saxons! Thus, the very testimony of modern history unmistakably rebukes the folly of those who repudiate the teachings of God's Word on this subject, rendering their unbelief without excuse.

Tell us, ye who murmur against the divine sovereignty, why is it that the Anglo-Saxon race has been singled out for the enjoyment of far the greater part of God's spiritual blessings? Were there no other races equally needy? The Chinese practiced a nobler system of morality and were far more numerous: why, then, were they left for so long in gospel darkness? Why was the whole African continent left for many centuries before the Sun of Righteousness shone there again with healing in His wings? Why is America today a thousand times more favored than India, which has thrice the population? To all of these questions we are compelled to fall back upon the answer of our blessed Lord: "Even so, Father: for so it seemed good in thy sight." And just as with Israel of old there was an election within an election, so in Germany, in Great Britain, and in the U.S.A., certain particular places have been favored with one faithful minister after another, while other places have been cursed with false prophets. "I caused it to rain upon one city, and caused it not to rain upon another city" (Amos 4:7)—true now in a spiritual way.

Finally, the veracity of election is clearly evidenced by the fierce opposition of Satan against it. The Devil fights truth, not error. He vented His hatred against it when Christ proclaimed it (Luke 4:28, 29); he did so when Paul preached it (as Rom. 9:14, 19 more than hints); he did so when the Waldenses, the Reformers, and the Puritans heralded it—using the Papists as his tools to torment and murder thousands of them who confessed it. He still opposes it. Today he does so in his guise as an angel of light. He pretends to be very jealous of the honor of God's character, and declares that election makes Him out to be a monster of injustice. He uses the weapon of ridicule: if election be true, why preach the gospel? He seeks to intimidate: even if the doctrine of election be Scriptural, it is not wise to preach it. Thus, the teaching of Scripture, the testimony of history, and the opposition of Satan, all witness to the veracity of this doctrine.

Chapter 5
Its Justice

Somewhat against our inclinations we have decided to depart again from the logical method of exposition, and instead of now proceeding with an orderly unfolding of this doctrine, we pause to deal with the principal objection which is made against the same. No sooner is the truth set forth of God's singling out certain of His creatures to be subjects of His special favors, than a general cry of protest is heard. No matter how much Scripture is quoted to the point nor how many plain passages be adduced in illustration and demonstration of it, the majority of those who profess to be Christians loudly object, alleging that such teaching slanders the divine character, making God guilty of gross injustice. It seems, then, that this difficulty should be met, that reply should be made to such a criticism of the doctrine, ere we proceed any further with our attempt to give a systematic setting forth of it.

In such an age as ours, when the principles of democracy, socialism and communism are so widely and warmly espoused, in a day when human authority and dominion are being more and more despised, when it is the common custom to "speak evil of dignities" (Jude 8), it is scarcely surprising that so many who make no pretension of bowing to the authority of Holy Writ should rebel against the concept of God's being partial. But it is unspeakably dreadful to find the great majority of those who profess to receive the Scriptures as divinely inspired, gnashing their teeth against its author when informed that He has sovereignly elected a people to be His peculiar treasure, and to hear them charging Him with being a hateful tyrant, a monster of cruelty. Yet such blasphemies only go to show that "the carnal mind is enmity against God."

It is not because we have any hope of converting such rebels from the error of their ways that we feel constrained to take up the present aspect of our subject—though it may please God in His infinite grace to use these feeble lines to the enlightening and convicting of a few of them. No, rather is it that some of God's dear people are disturbed by these ravings of His enemies, and know not how to answer in their own minds this objection, that if God makes a sovereign selection from among His creatures and predestinates them to blessings which He withholds from countless millions of their fellows, then such partiality makes Him guilty of treating the latter unjustly. And yet the fact stares them in the face on every hand, both in creation and providence, that God distributes His mercies most unevenly. There is no equality in His bestowments either in physical health and strength, mental capacities, social status, or the comforts of this life. Why, then, should we be staggered when we learn that His spiritual blessings are distributed unevenly?

Before proceeding further it should be pointed out that the design of every false scheme and system of religion is to depict the character of God in such a way that it is agreeable to the tastes of the carnal heart, acceptable to depraved human nature. And that can only be done by a species of misrepresentation: the ignoring of those of His prerogatives and perfections which are objectionable, and the disproportionate emphasizing of those of His attributes which appeal to their selfishness—such as His love, mercy, and long-sufferance. But let the character of God be faithfully presented as it is actually portrayed in the Scriptures—in the Old Testament as well as the New—and nine out of every ten of church-goers will frankly state that they find it impossible to love Him." The plain fact is, dear reader, that to the present generation the Most High of Holy Writ is "the unknown God."

It is just because people today are so ignorant of the divine character and so lacking in godly fear, that they are quite in the dark as to the nature and glory of divine justice, presuming to arraign it. This is an age of blatant irreverence, wherein lumps of animate clay dare to prescribe what the Almighty ought and ought not to do. Our forefathers sowed the wind, and today their children are reaping the whirlwind. The "divine rights of kings" was scoffed at and tabooed by the sires, and now their offspring repudiate the "divine rights of the King of kings." Unless the supposed "rights" of the creature are "respected," then our modems have no respect for the Creator, and if His high sovereignty and absolute dominion over all be insisted upon, they hesitate not to vomit forth their condemnation of Him. And, "evil communications corrupt good manners" (1 Cor. 15:33)! God's own people are in danger of being infected by the poisonous gas which now fills the air of the religious world.

Not only is the miasmic atmosphere obtaining in most of the "churches" a serious menace to the Christian, but there is in each of us a serious tendency to humanize God: viewing His perfections through our own intellectual lenses instead of through the glass of Scripture, interpreting His attributes by human qualities. It was of this very thing that God complained of old when He said, "Thou thoughtest that I was altogether such an one as thyself" (Ps. 50:21), which is a solemn warning for us to take to heart. What we mean is this: when we read of God's mercy or righteousness we are very apt to think of them according to the qualities of man's mercy and justice. But this is a serious mistake. The Almighty is not to be measured by any human standard: He is so infinitely above us that any comparison is utterly impossible, and therefore it is the height of madness for any finite creature to sit in judgment upon the ways of Jehovah.

Again; we need to be much on our guard against the folly of making invidious distinctions between the divine perfections. For example, it is quite wrong for us to suppose that God is more glorious in His grace and mercy than He is in His power and majesty. But this mistake is often made. How many are more thankful unto God for blessing them with health than they are for His bestowing the gospel upon them: but does it therefore follow that God's goodness in giving material things is greater than His goodness in bestowing spiritual blessings? Certainly not. Scripture often speaks of God's wisdom and power being manifested in creation, but where are we told of His grace and mercy in making the world? Inasmuch as men commonly fail to glorify God for His wisdom and power, does it thence follow that He is not to be so much adored for them? Beware of extolling one of the divine perfections above another.

What is justice? It is treating each person equitably and fairly, giving to him his due. Divine justice is simply doing that which is right. But this raises the question, What is due unto the creature? what is it that God ought to bestow upon him? Ah, my friend, every sober-minded person will at once object to the introduction of the word "ought" in such a connection. And rightly so. The Creator is under no obligation whatever unto the works of His own hands. He alone has the right to decide whether such and such a creature should exist at all. He alone has the prerogative to determine the nature, status, and destiny of that creature; whether it shall be an animal, a man, or an angel; whether it shall be endowed with a soul and subsist forever, or be without a soul and endure only for a brief time; whether it shall be a vessel unto honor and taken into communion with Himself, or a vessel unto dishonor which is rejected by Him.

As the great Creator possessed perfect freedom to create or not create, to bring into existence whatever creatures He pleased (and a visit to the zoo will show He has created some which strike the beholder as exceedingly queer ones); and therefore He has the unquestionable right to decree concerning them as He pleases. The justice of God in election and preterition, then, is grounded upon His high sovereignty. The dependence of all creatures upon Him is entire. His proprietorship of all creatures is indisputable. His dominion over all creatures is absolute. Let these facts be established from Scripture— and their complete demonstration therefrom is a very simple matter— and where is the creature who can with the slightest propriety say unto the Lord most high "What doest Thou?" Instead of the Creator being under any obligation to His creature, it is the creature who is under binding obligations to the One who gave it existence and now sustains its very life.

God has the absolute right to do as He pleases with the creatures of His own hand: "Hath not the potter power over the clay; of the same lump to make one vessel unto honor and another unto dishonor?" (Rom. 9:2 1) is His own assertion. Therefore He may give to one and withhold from another, bestow five talents on one and only a single talent on another, without any imputation of injustice. If He may give grace and glory to whom He will without such a charge, then He may also decree to do so without any such charge. Are men chargeable with injustice when they choose their own favorites, friends, companions, and confidants? Then obviously there is no injustice in God's choosing whom He will to bestow His special favors upon, to indulge with communion with Himself now and to dwell with Him for all eternity. Is a man free to make selection of the woman which he desires for his wife? and does he in anywise wrong the other women whom he passes by? Then is the great God less free to make selection of those who constitute the spouse of His Son? Shame, shame, upon those who would ascribe less freedom to the Creator than to the creature.

Upon a little reflection it should be evident to all right-minded people that there is no parity between human and divine justice: human justice requires that we should give each of our fellows his due, whereas no creature is due anything from God, not even what He is pleased to sovereignly give him. In his most reverent discussion of the nature of God's attributes W. Twisse (moderator of the Westminster Assembly) pointed out that if human justice be of the same nature with divine justice then it necessarily follows: first, that which is just in man is just with God. Second, that it must be after the same manner just: as human justice consists in subjection and obedience to God's law, so God Himself must be under obligation to His own Law. Third, as a man is under obligation to be just, so God is under obligation to be just, and therefore as Saul sinned and acted unjustly in slaying the priests, so had God been unjust in doing the like.

Unless the perversity of their hearts blinded their judgment men would readily perceive that divine justice must necessarily be of quite another order and character than human, yea, as different from and superior to it as divine love is from human. All are agreed that a man acts unjustly, that he sins, if he suffers his brother to transgress when it lies in his power to keep him from so doing. Then if divine justice were the same in kind, though superior in degree, it would necessarily follow that God sins every time He allows one of His creatures to transgress, for most certainly He has the power to prevent it; yea, and can exercise that power without destroying the liberty of the creature: "I also withheld thee from sinning against Me; therefore suffered I thee not to touch her" (Gen. 20:6). Cease, then, ye rebels from arraigning the Most High, and attempting to measure His justice by your petty tape-lines—as well seek to fathom His wisdom or define His power, as comprehend His inscrutable justice. "Clouds and darkness are round about him," and this be it noted, is expressly said in connection with: "righteousness [justice] and judgment are the habitation of His throne" (Ps. 97:2).

Lest some of our readers demur at our quoting from such a high Calvinist as Mr. Twisse, we append the following from the milder James Ussher. "What is the divine justice? It is an essential property of God, whereby He is infinitely just in himself, of himself, for, from, and by Himself, and none other: 'For the righteous Lord loveth righteousness' (Ps. 11:7). What is the rule of His justice? Answer: His own free will, and nothing else: for whatsoever He willeth is just, and because He willeth it therefore it is just; not because it is just, therefore He willeth it (Eph. 1:11; Ps. 115:3)." Such men as these were conscious of their ignorance, and therefore they cried unto Heaven for instruction, and God was pleased to grant them clear vision. But the pride-inflated pharisees of our day think they can already see, and therefore feel no need of Divine illumination: consequently they remain blind (John 9:40, 41).

So again that justly renowned teacher W. Perkins: "We must not think that God doeth a thing because it is good and right, but rather is the thing good and right because God willeth and worketh it. Examples hereof we have in the Word. God commanded Abimelech to deliver Sarah to Abraham, or else He would destroy him and all his household (Gen. 20:7). To man's reason that might seem unjust, for why should Abimelech's servants be punished for their master's fault? So again Achan sinned, and all the house of Israel were penalized for it (Josh. 7). David numbered the people, and the whole nation was smitten by a plague (2 Sam. 24). All these to man's reason may seem unequal; yet being the works of God we must with all reverence judge them most just and holy." Alas, how little of this humility and reverence is manifested in the churches today! How ready is the present generation to criticize and condemn whatever of God's ways and works suit them not!

So far from the truth are most of those who are now looked up to as "the champions of orthodoxy," that even they are often guilty of turning things upside down, or putting the cart in front of the horse. It is commonly assumed by them that God Himself is under law, that He is under a moral constraint to do what he does, so that He cannot do otherwise. Others wrap this up in more sophisticated terms, insisting that it is His own nature which regulates all His actions. But this is merely an artful subterfuge. Is it by a necessity of His nature or by the free exercise of His sovereignty that He bestows favor upon His creatures? Let Scripture answer: "Therefore hath he mercy on whom he will have mercy, and whom he will he hardeneth" (Rom. 9:18). Why, my reader, if God's nature obliged Him to show saving mercy to any, then by parity of reason it would oblige Him to show mercy to all, and thus bring every fallen creature to repentance, faith, and obedience. But enough of this nonsense.

Let us now approach this aspect of our subject from an entirely different angle. How could there possibly be any injustice in God's electing those whom He did, when had He not done so all had inevitably perished, angels and men alike? This is neither an invention nor an inference of ours, for Scripture itself expressly declares "Except the Lord of Sabbaoth had left us a seed, we had been as Sodom" (Rom. 9:29). Not one of God's rational creatures, either celestial or earthly, had ever been eternally and effectually saved apart from the grave of divine election. Though both angels and men were created in a state of perfect holiness, yet they were mutable creatures, liable to change and fall. Yea, inasmuch as their continuance in holiness was dependent upon the exercise of their own wills, unless God was pleased to supernaturally preserve them, their fall was certain.

"Behold, he put no trust in his servants; and his angels he charged with folly" (Job 4:18). The angels were perfectly holy, yet if God gave them no other assistance than that with which He had capacitated them at their creation, then no "trust" or reliance was to be placed in them, or their standing. If they were holy today, they were liable to sin tomorrow. If God but sent them on an errand to this world, they might fall before they returned to Heaven. The "folly" which God imputes to them in the above passage is their creature mutability: for them to maintain their holiness unchangeably to eternity, without the danger of losing the same, was utterly beyond their creature endowment. Therefore, for them to be immutably preserved is a grace which issues from another and higher spring than the covenant of works or creation endowment, namely, that of election grace, super-creation grace.

It was meet that God should, from the beginning, make manifest the infinite gulf which divides the creature from the Creator. God alone is immutable, without variableness or shadow of turning. Fitting was it, then, that God should withdraw His preserving hand from those whom He had created upright, so that it might appear that the highest creature of all (Satan, "the anointed cherub" Ezek. 28:14) was mutable, and would inevitably fall into sin when left to the exercise of his own free will. Of God alone can it be predicated that He "cannot be tempted with evil" (James 1:13). The creature, though holy, may be tempted to sin, fall, and be irretrievably lost. The fall of Satan, then, made way for evidencing the more plainly the absolute necessity of electing grace— the imparting to the creature the image of God's own immutable holiness.

Because of the mutability of the creature-state God foresaw that if all His creatures were left to the conduct of their own wills, they were in a continual hazard of falling. He, therefore, made an election of grace to remove all hazard from the case of His chosen ones. This we know from what is revealed of their history. Jude tells us of "the angels which kept not their first estate, but left their own habitation" (v. 6), and the remainder of them would, sooner or later, have done so too, if left to the mutability of their own wills. So also it proved with Adam and Eve: both of them evidenced the mutability of their wills by apostatizing. Accordingly, God foreseeing all of this from the beginning, made a "reserve" (Rom. 11:4—explained in v. 5 as "election), determining to have a remnant who should be blessed of Him and who would everlastingly bless Him in return. Election and preserving grace are never to be severed.

We have thus far pointed out, first that divine justice is of an entirely different order and character than human justice; second that divine justice is grounded upon God's sovereign dominion over all the works of His hands, being the exercise of His own imperial will. Third, that nothing whatever is due the creature from the Creator, not even what He is pleased to give, and that so far from God's being under any obligation to it, it is under lasting obligations to Him. Fourth, that whatever God wills and works is right and must be reverently submitted to, yea, adored by us. Fifth, that it is impossible to charge God with injustice in His electing certain ones to be the objects of His amazing grace, since that apart from it, all had eternally perished. Let us now descend to a lower and simpler level, and contemplate God's election in connection with the human race fallen in Adam.

If there was no injustice in God's making a choice of some unto special favor and eternal blessing as He viewed His creatures in the glass of His purpose to create, then certainly there could be no injustice in His determining to show them mercy as He foreviewed them among the mass of Adam's ruined race; for if a sinless creature has no claim whatever upon its maker, being entirely dependent upon His charity, then most assuredly a fallen creature is entitled to nothing good at the hands of its offended judge. And this is the angle from which we must now view our subject. Fallen man is a criminal, an outlaw and if bare justice is to be meted out to him, then he must be left to receive the due reward of his iniquities, and that can mean nothing less than eternal punishment, for his transgressions have incurred infinite guilt.

Before enlarging upon what has just been said, it also needs to be pointed out that if the only hope for a holy creature lies in God's electing grace, then doubly is this the case with one that is unholy, totally depraved. If an holy angel was in constant danger, incapable of maintaining his purity, because of the mutability of his nature and the fickleness of his will, what shall be said of an unholy creature? Why, nothing less than this: fallen man has a nature that is confirmed in evil, and therefore his will no longer has any power to turn unto that which is spiritual, yea, it is inveterately steeled against God; hence, his case is utterly and eternally hopeless, unless God, in

His sovereign grace, is pleased to save him from himself

Preachers may prate all they please about man's inherent powers, the freedom of his will, and his capacity for good, yet it is useless and madness to ignore the solemn fact of the fall. The difference and disadvantage between our case and that of unfallen Adam's can scarcely be conceived. Instead of a perfect holiness possessing and inclining our minds and wills, as it did his, there is no such vital principle left in our hearts. Instead, there is a thorough disability unto what is spiritual and holy, yea, contrary enmity and opposition thereto. "Men err, not knowing the power of original sin, nor the depth of corruption that is in their own hearts. The will of man now is the prime and proper seat of sin: the throne thereof is seated therein" (Thos. Goodwin). Outward helps and aids are of no account, for nothing short of a new creation is of any avail.

No matter what instruction fallen men receive, what inducements be offered them, the Ethiopian cannot change his skin. Neither light, conviction, nor the general operations of the Holy Spirit, are of any avail, unless God over and above them impart a new principle of holiness to the heart. This has been clearly and fully demonstrated under both Law and Gospel. Read Exodus 20 and Deuteronomy 5 and see the wondrous and awe-inspiring manifestation of Himself which God granted unto Israel at Sinai: did that change their hearts and incline their wills to obey Him? Then read through the four Gospels and behold the incarnate Son of God dwelling in the midst of men, not as a judge, but as a benefactor—going about doing good, feeding the hungry, healing the sick, proclaiming the gospel: did that melt their hearts and win them to God? No, they hated and crucified Him.

Behold, then, the case of fallen mankind: alienated from the life of God, dead in trespasses and sins, with no heart, no will for spiritual things. In themselves their case is desperate, irretrievable, hopeless. Apart from divine election none would, none could, ever be saved. Election means that God was pleased to reserve a remnant, so that the entire race of Adam should not eternally perish. And what thanks does He receive for this? None at all, save from those who have their sin-blinded eyes opened to perceive the inexpressible blessedness of such a fact. Thanks, no; instead, the vast majority even of those in professing Christendom when they hear of this truth, ignorant of their own interests and of the ways of God, quarrel at His election, revile Him for the same, charge Him with gross injustice, and accuse Him of being a merciless tyrant.

Now the great God stands in no need of any defense from us: in due time He will effectually close the mouth of every rebel. But we must address a few more remarks to those believers who are disturbed by such as insist so loudly that God is guilty of injustice when He sovereignly elects some. First, then, we ask these slanderers of Jehovah to make good their charge. The burden of proof falls upon them to do so. They affirm that an electing God is unjust, then let them demonstrate how such be the case. They cannot. In order to do so they must show that lawbreakers merit something good at the hands of the lawgiver. They must show that the King of kings is morally obliged to smile upon those who have blasphemed His name, desecrated His sabbaths, slighted His Word, reviled His servants, and above all, despised and rejected His Son.

"Is there one man in the whole world who would have the impertinence to say that he merits anything of his Maker? If so, be it known unto you that he shall have all he merits; and his reward will be the flames of hell forever, for that is the utmost that any man ever merited of God. God is in no debt to man, and at the last great day every man shall have as much love, as much pity, and as much goodness, as he deserves. Even the lost in hell shall have all they deserve; ay, and woe worth the day for them when they shall have the wrath of God, which will be the summit of their deservings. If God gives to every man as much as he merits, is He therefore to be accused of injustice because He gives to some infinitely more than they merit?" (C. H. Spurgeon). How many who now speak of him eulogistically, and refer to him as "beloved Spurgeon," would gnash their teeth and execrate him were they to hear his faithful and plain-spoken preaching.

Second, we would inform these detractors of God that His salvation is not a matter of justice, but of pure grace, and grace is something that can be claimed by none. Where is the injustice if any one does as he wills with his own? If I am free to disburse my charity as I see fit, shall God be conceded less freedom to bestow His gifts upon whom He pleases! God is indebted to none, and therefore if He grants His favors in a sovereign way who can complain. If God passes thee by, He has not injured thee; but if He enriches thee, then art thou a debtor to His grace, and then wilt thou cease prating about His justice and injustice, and wilt gladly join with those who astonishingly exclaim, "He hath not dealt with us after our sins; nor rewarded us according to our iniquities" (Ps. 103:10). Salvation is God's free gift, and therefore He bestows it on whom He pleases.

Third, we would ask these haughty creatures, to whom has God ever refused His mercy when it was sincerely and penitently sought? Does He not freely proclaim the gospel to every creature? Does not His Word bid all men to throw down the weapons of their warfare against Him and come to Christ for pardon? Does He not promise to blot out your iniquities if you will turn unto Him in the way of His appointing? If you refuse to do so, if you are so thoroughly in love with sin, so wedded to your lusts that you are determined to destroy your own soul, then who is to blame? Most certainly God is not. His gospel promises are reliable, and anyone is at liberty to prove them for himself. If he does so, if he renounces sin and puts his trust in Christ, then he will discover for himself that he is one of God's chosen ones. On the other hand, if he deliberately spurns the gospel and rejects the Savior then his blood is on his own head.

This leads us to ask, fourth, You say it is unjust that some should be lost while others are saved: but who makes them to be lost that are lost? Whom has God ever caused to sin?—rather doth He warn and exhort against it. Whom has the Holy Spirit ever prompted to a wrong action?—rather doth He uniformly incline against evil. Where do the Scriptures bolster up any in his wickedness?—rather do they constantly condemn it in all its forms. Then is God unjust if He condemns those who willfully disobey Him? Is He unrighteous if He punishes those who defiantly disregard His danger-signals and expostulations? Assuredly not. To each such one God will yet say, "Thou hast destroyed thyself" (Hos. 13:9). It is the creature who commits moral suicide. It is the creature who breaks through every restraint and hurls himself into the precipice of eternal woe. In the last great day it will appear that God is justified when He speaks, and clear when He judges (Ps. 51:4).

Election is the taking of one and leaving of another, and implies freedom on the part of the elector to choose or refuse. Hence the choosing of one does no injury to the other which is not chosen. If I select one out of a hundred men to a position of honor and profit, I do no injury to the ninety and nine not elected. If I take two from a score of ragged and hungry children, and adopt them as my son and daughter, feed and clothe, house and educate them, I do them an immense benefit; but while disbursing my bounty as I choose and making two happy, I do no injury to the eighteen who are left. True, they remain ragged, ill-fed, and uneducated, yet they are in no worse condition for my having shown favor to their late companions—they only continue precisely in the situation in which they were.

Again; if among ten convicts justly sentenced to death, the king of England was pleased to choose five to be the recipients of his sovereign mercy, pardoned and released them, they would owe their very lives to his royal favor; nevertheless, by extending kindness to them, no injury is done to the other five: they are left to suffer the righteous penalty of the law, due to them for their transgressions. They only suffer what they would have suffered if the king's mercy had not been extended toward their fellows. Who, then, can fail to see that it would be a misuse of terms, a grievous slander of the king, to charge him with injustice, because he was pleased to exercise his royal prerogative and evidence his favor in this discriminating manner.

Our Savior definitely expressed this idea of election when He said, "Then shall two be in the field; the one shall be taken, and the other left" (Matt. 24:40). If both had been "left," then both had perished: hence the "taking" of the one did no injury to his fellow. "Two women shall be grinding at the mill; the one shall be taken, and the other left" (Matt. 24:41). The taking of the one was a great favor to her, but the leaving of her companion did her no wrong. Divine election, then, is a choice to favor from among those who have no claims upon God. It therefore does no injustice to them that are passed by, for they only continue as and where they were, and as and where they would have been if none had been taken from among them. In the exercise of His electing grace God has mercy upon whom He will have mercy, and in the bestowment of His favor He does what He wills with His own.

It is not difficult to perceive the ground upon which the false reasoning of God's detractors rests: behind all the murmurings of objectors against the Divine justice lies the concept that God is under obligation to provide salvation for all His fallen creatures. But such reasoning fails to see that if such a contention were valid, then no thanks could be returned to God. How could we praise Him for redeeming those whom He was bound to redeem? If salvation be a debt which God owes man for allowing him to fall, then salvation cannot be a matter of mercy. But we must not expect that those whose eyes are blinded by pride should understand anything of the infinite demerits of sin, of their own utter unworthiness and vileness; and therefore it is impossible that they should form any true concept of Divine grace, and perceive that when grace is exercised it is necessarily exercised in a sovereign manner.

But after all that has been pointed out above some will be ready to sneeringly ask, "Does not the Bible declare that God is 'no respecter of persons': how then can He make a selection from among men?" The calumniators of Divine predestination suppose that either the Scriptures are inconsistent with themselves, or that in His election God has regard to merits. Let us first quote from Calvin: "The Scripture denies that God is a respecter of persons, in a different sense from that in which they understand it; for by the word person it signifies not a man, but those things in a man which, being conspicuous to the eyes, usually conciliate favor, honor, and dignity, or attract hatred, contempt, and disgrace. Such are riches, power, nobility, magistracy, country, elegance of form, on the one hand; and on the other hand, poverty, necessity, ignoble birth, slovenliness, contempt, and the like. Thus Peter and Paul declare that God is not a respecter of persons because He makes no difference between the Jew and Greek, to reject one and receive the other, merely on account of his nation (Acts 10:34, Rom. 2:11). So James uses the same language when he asserts that God in His judgment pays no regard to riches (2:5).

"There will, therefore, be no contradiction in our affirming, that according to the good pleasures of His will, God chooses whom He will as His children, irrespective of all merit, while He rejects and reprobates others. Yet, for the sake of further satisfaction, the matter may be explained in the following manner. They ask how it happens, that of two persons distinguished from each other by no merit, God, in His election, leaves one and takes another. I, on the other hand, ask them, whether they suppose him that is taken to possess anything that can attract the favor of God? If they confess that he has not, as indeed they must, it will follow, that God looks not at man, but derives His motive to favor him from His own goodness. God's election of one man, therefore, while He rejects another, proceeds not from any respect of man, but solely from His own mercy; which may freely display and exert itself wherever and whenever it pleases."

To have "respect of persons" is to regard and treat them differently on account of some supposed or real difference in them or their circumstances, which is no warrantable ground or reason for such preferential regard and treatment. This character of a respecter of persons belongs rather to one who examines and rewards others according to their characters and works. Thus, for a judge to justify and reward one rather than another because he is rich and the other poor, or because he has given him a bribe, or is a near relative or an intimate friend, while the character and conduct of the other is more upright and his cause more just. But such a denomination is inapplicable to a disburser of charity, who is granting his favors and bestowing freely undeserved gifts to one rather than to another, doing so without any consideration of personal merit. The benefactor has a perfect right to do what he will with his own, and those who are neglected by him have no valid ground for complaint.

Even if this expression be taken in its more popular acceptation, nothing so strikingly evidences that God is "no respecter of persons" than the character of the ones He has chosen. When the angels sinned and fell God provided no Savior for them, yet when the human race sinned and fell a Savior was provided for many of them. Let the unfriendly critic carefully weigh this fact: had God been a "respecter of persons" would He not have selected the angels and passed by men? The fact that He did the very reverse clears Him of this calumny. Take again that nation which God chose to be the recipients of earthly and temporal favors above all others during the last two thousand years of Old Testament history. What sort of characters were they? Why, an unappreciative and murmuring, stiffnecked and hardhearted, rebellious and impenitent people, from the beginning of their history until the end. Had God been a respecter of persons He surely had never singled out the Jews for such favor and blessing!

The very character, then, of those whom God chooses refutes this silly objection. The same is equally apparent in the New Testament. "Hath not God chosen the poor of this world" (James 2:5): blessed be His name, that it is so, for had He chosen the wealthy it had fared ill with many of us, had it not? God did not pick out magnates and millionaires, financiers and bankers, to be objects of His grace. Nor are those of royal blood or the peers of the realm, the wise, the gifted, the influential of this world, for few among them have their names written in the Lamb's Book of Life. No, it is the despised, the weak, the base, the non-entities of this world, whom God has chosen (1 Cor. 1:26-29), and this, in order that "no flesh should glory in his presence." Pharisees passed by and publicans and harlots brought in! "Jacob have I loved": and what was there in him to love!—and echo still asks "what?" Had God been "a respecter of persons" He certainly had never chosen worthless me!

Chapter 6
Its Nature

It has been well said that, "The reason why any one believes in election is, that he finds it in the Bible. No man could ever imagine such a doctrine—for it is, in itself, contrary to the thinking and the wishes of the human heart. Every one, at first, opposes the doctrine, and it is only after many struggles, under the working of the Spirit of God, that we are made to receive it. A perfect acquiescence in this doctrine—an absolute lying still, in adoring wonder, at the footstool of God's sovereignty, is the last attainment of the sanctified soul in this life, as it is the beginning of Heaven. The reason why any one believes in election is just this, and only this, that God has made it known. Had the Bible been a counterfeit it never could have contained the doctrine of election, for men are too averse to such a thought to give it expression, much more to give it prominence." (G. S. Bishop).

Thus far, in our exposition of this blessed truth, we have shown that the source of election is the will of God, for nothing exists or can exist apart from that. Next, we have seen, that the Grand Original of election is the man Christ Jesus, who was ordained unto union with the second person in the Godhead. Then, in order to clear the way for a more detailed examination of this truth as it bears upon us, we demonstrated the verity and then the justice of it, seeking to remove from the minds of Christian readers the defiling and disturbing effects of the principal objection which is made against divine election by its enemies. And now we shall endeavor to point out the principal elements which enter into election.

First, it is an act by God. True it is that there comes a day when each of the elect chooses God for his absolute Lord and supreme Good, but this is the effect and in no sense the cause of the former. Our choosing of Him is in time, His choosing of us was before time began; and certain it is that unless He had first chosen us, we would never choose Him at all. God, who is a sovereign being, does whatsoever He pleases both in heaven and in earth, having an absolute right to do as He will with His own creatures, and therefore did He choose a certain number of human beings to be His people, His children, His peculiar treasure. Having done this, it is called "election of God" (1 Thess. 1:4), for He is the efficient cause of it; and the persons chosen are denominated "His own elect" (Luke 18:7; cf. Rom. 8:33).

This choice of God's is an absolute one, being entirely gratuitous, depending on nothing whatever outside of Himself. God elected the ones He did simply because He chose to do so: from no good, merit, or attraction in the creature, and from no foreseen merit or attraction to be in the creature. God is absolutely self-sufficient, and therefore He never goes outside of Himself to find a reason for anything that He does. He cannot be swayed by the works of His own hand. No, He is the One who sways them, as He alone is the One who gave them existence. "In Him we live, and are moved [Greek], and have our being." It was, then, simply out of the spontaneous goodness of His own volition that God singled out from the mass of those He purposed to create a people who should show forth His praises for all eternity, to the glory of His sovereign grace forever and ever.

This choice of God's is an unchangeable one. Necessarily so, for it is not founded upon anything in the creature, or grounded upon anything outside of Himself. It is before everything, even before His "foreknowledge." God does not decree because He foreknows, but He foreknows because He has infallibly and irrevocably fixed it—otherwise He would merely guess it. But since He foreknows it, then He does not guess—it is certain; and if certain, then He must have fixed it. Election being the act of God, it is forever, for whatever He does in a way of special grace, is irreversible and unalterable. Men may choose some to be their favorites and friends for a while, and then change their minds and choose others in their room. But God does not act such a part: He is of one mind, and none can turn Him; His purpose according to election stands firm, sure, unalterable (Rom. 9:11; 2 Tim 2:19).

Second, God's act of election is made in Christ: "according as he hath chosen us in him" (Eph. 1:4). Election does not find men in Christ, but puts them there. It gives them a being in Christ and union to Him, which is the foundation of their manifestative being in Him at conversion. In the infinite mind of God, He willed to love a company of Adam's posterity with an immutable love, and out of the love wherewith He loves them, He chose them in Christ. By this act in His infinite mind, God gave them being and blessedness in Christ from everlasting. Though, while all fell in Adam, yet all did not fall alike. The non-elect fell so as to be damned, they being left to perish in their sins, because they had no relation to Christ—He was not related to them as the Mediator of union with God.

The non-elect had their all in Adam, their natural head. But the elect had all spiritual blessing bestowed upon them in Christ, their gracious and glorious Head (Eph. 1:3). They could not lose these, because they were secured for them in Christ. God had chosen them as His own: He their God, they His people; He their Father, they His children. He gave them to Christ to be His brethren, His companions, His bride, His partners in all His communicable grace and glory. On the foresight of their fall in Adam, and what would be the effects thereof, the Father proposed to raise them up from the ruins of the fall, upon the consideration of His Son's undertaking to perform all righteousness for them, and as their Surety, bear all their sins in His own body on the tree, making His soul an offering for sin. To carry all of this unto execution, the beloved Son became incarnate.

It was to this that the Lord Jesus referred in His high priestly prayer, when He said to the Father "I have manifested thy name unto the men which thou gayest me out of the world: thine they were, and thou gavest them me" (John 17:6). He was alluding to the whole election of grace. They were the objects of the Father's delight: His jewels, His portion; and in Christ's eyes they were what the Father beheld them to be. How highly, then, did the Father esteem the Mediator, or He would never have bestowed His elect on Him and committed them all to His care and management! And how highly did Christ value this love-gift of the Father's, or He would not have undertaken their salvation at such tremendous cost to Himself! Now the giving of the elect to Christ was a different act, a distinct act from that of their election. The elect were first the Father's by election, who singled out the persons; and then He bestowed them upon Christ as His love gift: "Thine they were [by election] and thou gavest them me"—in the same way that grace is said to be given us in Christ Jesus before the world began (2 Tim. 1:9).

Third, this act of God was irrespective of and anterior to any foresight of the entrance of sin. We have somewhat anticipated this branch of our subject, yet as it is one upon which very few today are clear, and one we deem of considerable importance, we propose to give it separate consideration. The particular point which we are now to ponder is, as to whether His people were viewed by God, in His act of election, as fallen or unfallen; as in the corrupt mass through their defection in Adam, or in the pure mass of creaturehood, as to be created. Those who took the former view are known as Sublapsarians; those who took the latter as Supralapsarians, and in the past this question was debated considerably between high and low Calvinists. This writer unhesitatingly (after prolonged study) takes the Supralapsarian position, though he is well aware that few indeed will be ready to follow him.

Sin having drawn a veil over the greatest of all the divine mysteries of grace—that of the divine incarnation alone excepted—renders our present task the more difficult. It is much easier for us to apprehend our misery, and our redemption from it—by the incarnation, obedience, and sacrifice of the Son of God—than it is for us to conceive of the original glory, excellency, purity, and dignity of the Church of Christ, as the eternal object of God's thoughts, counsels, and purpose. Nevertheless, if we adhere closely to the Holy Scriptures, it is evident (to the writer, at least) that God's people had a super-creation and spiritual union with Christ before ever they had a creature and natural union with Adam; that they were blessed with all spiritual blessings in the heavenlies in Christ (Eph. 1:3), before they fell in Adam and became subject to all the evils of the curse. First, we will summarize the reasons given by John Gill in support of this.

God's decree of election is to be divided into two parts or degrees, namely, His purpose concerning the end and His purpose concerning the means. The first part has to do with the purpose of God in Himself, in which He determined to have an elect people and that for His own glory. The second part has to do with the actual execution of the first, by fixing upon the means whereby the end shall be accomplished. These two parts in the divine decree are neither to be severed nor confounded, but considered distinctly. God's purpose concerning the end means that He ordained a certain people to be the recipients of His special favor, for the glorifying of His sovereign goodness and grace. His purpose concerning the means signifies that He determined to create that people, permit them to fall, and to recover them out of it by Christ's redemption and the Spirit's sanctification. These are not to be regarded as separate decrees, but as component parts and degrees of one purpose. There is an order in the divine counsels as real and definite as Genesis 1 shows there was in connection with creation.

As the purpose of the end is first in view (in the order of nature) before the determination of the means, therefore what is first in intention is last in execution. Now as the glory of God is the last in execution, it necessarily follows that it was first in intention. Wherefore men must be considered in the Divine purpose concerning the end as neither yet created nor fallen, since both their creation and the permission of sin belong to God's counsel concerning the means. Is it not obvious that if God first decreed to create men and suffer them to fall, and then out of the fallen mass chose some to grace and glory, that He purposed to create men without any end in view? And is not that charging God with what a wise man would never do, for when man determines to do a thing he proposes an end (say the building of an house) and then fixes on ways and means to bring about the end. Can it be thought for a moment that the Omniscient One should act otherwise?

The above distinction between the divine purpose concerning the end and God's appointing of means to secure that end, is clearly borne out by Scripture. For example, "For it became him, for whom are all things, and by whom are all things, in bringing many sons unto glory, to make the captain of their salvation perfect through sufferings" (Heb. 2:10). Here is first the decree concerning the end: God ordained His many sons "unto glory"; in His purpose of the means God ordained that the captain of their salvation should be made perfect "through sufferings." In like manner was it in connection with Christ Himself. "The Lord said unto my Lord, Sit thou at my right hand" (Ps. 110:1). God decreed that the Mediator should have this high honor conferred upon Him, yet in order thereto it was ordained that "He shall drink of the brook in the way" (v. 7): God, then, decreed that the Redeemer should drink of the fullness of those pleasures which are at His right hand for evermore (Ps. 16:11), but before that He must drain the bitter cup of anguish. So it is with His people: Canaan is their destined portion, but the wilderness is appointed as that through which they shall pass on their way thereto.

God's foreordination of His people unto holiness and glory anterior to His foreview of their fall in Adam, comports far better with the instances given of Jacob and Esau in Romans 9:11 than does the sublapsarian view that His decree contemplated them as sinful creatures. There we read, "(For the children being not yet born, neither having done any good or evil, that the purpose of God according to election might stand, not of works, but of Him that calleth;) It was said unto her, The elder shall serve the younger." The apostle is showing that the preference was given to Jacob independent of all ground of merit, because it was made before the children were born. If it be kept in mind that what God does in time is only a making manifest of what He secretly decreed in eternity, the point we are here pressing will be the more conclusive. God's acts both of election and preterition—choosing and passing by—were entirely irrespective of any foreseen "good or evil." Note, too, how this compound expression "the purpose of God according to election" supports the contention of there being two parts to God's decree.

It should also be pointed out that God's foreordination of His people unto everlasting bliss before He contemplated them as sinful creatures, agrees far better than does the sublapsarian idea, with the unformed clay of the Potter: "Hath not the potter power [the right] over the clay; of the same lump to make one vessel unto honor and another unto dishonor?" (Rom. 9:2 1). Upon this Beza (co-pastor with Calvin of the church at Geneva) remarked that "if the apostle had considered mankind as corrupted, he would not have said that some vessels were made unto honor and some unto dishonor, but rather that seeing all the vessels were fit for dishonor, some were left in that dishonor, and others translated from dishonor to honor"

But leaving inferences and deductions, let us turn now to something more express and definite. In Ephesians 1:11 we are told, "Being predestinated according to the purpose of Him who worketh all things after the counsel of His own will." Now a careful study of what precedes reveals a clear distinction in the "all things" which God works "according to the counsel of His own will," or, to state it in another way, the spiritual blessings which God bestows upon His people are divided into two distinct classes, according as He contemplated them first in an unfallen state and then in a fallen. The first and highest class of blessings are enumerated in verses 4-6 and have to do with God's decree concerning the end; the second and subordinate class of blessings are described in verses 7-9 and have to do with God's decree concerning the means which He has appointed for the accomplishment of that end.

These two parts in the mystery of God's will towards His people from everlasting are clearly marked by the change of tense which is used: the past tense of "he hath chosen us" (v. 4), "having predestinated us unto the adoption of children" (v. 5) and "hath made us accepted in the beloved" (v. 6), becomes the present tense in verse 7: in whom we have redemption through His blood." The benefits spoken of in verses 4-6 are such as in no way depended upon a consideration of the fall, but follow from our being chosen in Christ, being given upon grounds higher and distinct from that of His being our Redeemer. God's choice of us in Christ our Head, that we should be "holy" signifies not that imperfect holiness which we have in this life, but a perfect and immutable one such as even the unfallen angels had not by nature; and our predestination to adoption denotes an immediate communion with God Himself—blessings which had been ours had sin never entered.

As Thomas Goodwin pointed out in his unrivalled exposition of Ephesians 1, "The first source of blessings—perfect holiness, adoption, etc.—were ordained us without consideration of the Fall, though not before the consideration of the Fall; for all the things which God decrees are at once in His mind; they were all, both one another, ordained to our persons. But God in the decrees about these first sort of blessings viewed us as creatures which He could and would make so and so glorious. .. . But the second sort of blessings were ordained us merely upon consideration of the fall, and to our persons considered as sinners and unbelievers. The first sort were to the 'praise of God's grace,' taking grace for the freeness of love; whereas the latter sort are to 'the praise of the glory of his grace,' taking grace for free mercy."

The first and higher blessings are to have their full accomplishment in heaven, being suited to that state into which we shall then be installed, and as in God's primary intention they are before the other and are said to have been "before the foundation of the world" (Eph. 1:4), so they are to be realized after this world is ended—the "adoption" to which we are predestinated (Eph. 1:5) we still await (Rom. 8:23); whereas the second blessings are bestowed upon us in the lower world, for it is here and now we receive "forgiveness of sins" through the blood of Christ. Again; the first blessings are founded solely upon our relation to the person of Christ, as is evident from "chosen in Him. .. accepted in the beloved"; but the second sort are grounded upon His work, redemption issuing from Christ's sacrifice. Thus the latter blessings are but the removing of those obstacles which by reason of sin stand in our way of that intended glory.

Again; this distinction of blessings which we receive in Christ as creatures, and through Christ as sinners, is confirmed by the twofold office which He sustains toward us. This is clearly expressed in "for the husband is the head of the wife, even as Christ is the head of the church, and he is the savior of the body" (Eph. 5:23). Notice carefully the order of those titles: Christ is first as head and husband to us, which lays the foundation of that relation to God of being His adopted children—as by marriage with His Son. Second, He is our "Savior," which necessarily respects sin. With Ephesians 5:23 should be compared Colossians 1:18-20, where the same order is set forth: in verses 18 and 19 we learn of what Christ is absolutely ordained to and His church with Him, by which He is the founder of that state we shall enter after the resurrection: and then in verse 20 we see Him as redeemer and reconciler: first the "head" of His Church, and then its "Savior!" From this twofold relation of Christ to the elect arises a double glory which He is ordained unto: the one intrinsical, due to Him as the Son of God dwelling in human nature and being there in the head of a glorious Church (see John 17:5); and the other more extrinsical, as acquired by His work of redemption and purchased with the agony of His soul (see Phil. 2:8-10)!

We have called attention to the fact that the only reason why any God-fearing soul believes in the doctrine of election is because he finds it clearly and prominently revealed in God's Word, and hence it follows that our only source of information thereon is the Word itself. Yet, what has just been said is much too general to be of specific help to the earnest inquirer. In turning to the Scriptures for light upon the mystery of election, it is most essential that we should bear in mind that Christ is the key to every part of them: "In the volume of the Book it is written of me" He declares, and therefore if we attempt to study this subject apart from Him we are certain to err. In preceding chapters we have evidenced that Christ is the grand original of election, and it is from that starting point we must proceed if we are to make any right advance.

What has just been pointed out holds good not only in the general, but in the particular: for instance, in connection with that special branch of our subject which was discussed we will now follow up from this particular viewpoint. If we go right back to the beginning itself then it will appear that God was pleased, and so resolved, to go forth into creature communion, which is to say that He determined to bring into existence creatures who should enjoy fellowship with Himself. His own glory was alone the supreme end in this determination, for "the Lord hath made all things for himself" (Prov. 16:4). We repeat, that His own glory was the sole and sufficient motive which induced God to create at all: "Who hath first given to him, and it shall be recompensed unto him again? For of him, and through him and to him, are all things: to whom be glory forever. Amen" (Rom. 11:35, 36).

The principal glory which God designed to Himself in election was the manifestation of the glory of His grace. This is irrefutably established by "Having predestinated us unto the adoption of children through [Greek] Jesus Christ to himself, according to the good pleasure of his will, to the praise of the glory of his grace" (Eph. 1:5, 6). Grace is one of those illustrious perfections in the divine character, which is glorious in itself, and had ever remained so though no creature had been formed; but God has so displayed this attribute in election that His people will praise and render glory to it throughout the endless ages yet to be. God showed His holiness in the giving of the Law, His power in the making of the world, His justice in casting the wicked into hell, but His grace shines forth especially in predestination and what His elect are predestinated unto. So, too, when it is said to God "that he might make known the riches of his glory on the vessels of mercy, which he had afore prepared unto glory" (Rom. 9:23), the prime reference is to His grace as Ephesians 1:7 shows.

The second person in the Trinity was predestinated to be God-man, being first decreed, for we are "chosen in Him" (Eph. 1:4), which presupposes Him to be chosen first, as the soil in which we are set. We are predestinated unto the adoption of children, yet it is "through Jesus Christ" (Eph. 1:5). So we read "Who verily was foreordained [as "Christ"—see previous verse] before the foundation of the world" (1 Pet. 1:20); as we shall show later that expression "before the foundation of the world" is not merely a note of time, but chiefly one of eminence or preference, that God had Christ in His view before His intention to create the world for Him and His people. Now we have shown that Christ was ordained to be God-man for much higher ends than our salvation, namely, for God's own self to delight in, to behold the perfect image of Himself in a creature, and by that union to communicate Himself to that man in a manner and degree not possible to any mere creature as such.

Together with the Son's being predestinated to be God-man, there falls unto His glorious person, as His inheritance, to be the sovereign end of all things else which God should make and the end of whatever His intelligent creatures He should be pleased to choose unto glory. This is clear from "For all things are yours ... and ye are Christ's, and Christ is God's" (1 Cor. 3:21-23), which is spoken of in reference of endship. As you, the saints, are the end for which all things were ordained, so Christ is the end of you, and Christ is God's end or design m acting. We say that Christ is "the sovereign end," and not the supreme end, for God Himself is above and over all; but Christ is the sovereign end unto all creation, having joint-authority with God, under God. So it is declared that "by Him" and "for Him" were all things created (Col. 1:16), as it is said of God in Romans 11:36. Thus this sovereign end in creation fell to Him as the inheritance of the Mediator: "The Father loveth the Son, and hath given all things into His hand" (John 3:35).

In the predestination of the Son of man unto union with the Son of God, and in the constituting of Him through that union to be the sovereign end of us and of all things, there was conferred upon the man Christ Jesus thus exalted the highest possible favor, immeasurably transcending all the grace shown unto the elect any way considered, so that if the election of us be to the praise of the glory of God's grace, His much more so. More honor has been conferred upon "that holy thing" born of the virgin than upon all the members of His mystical body put together; and it was grace pure and simple, sovereign grace, which bestowed it. What was there in His humanity, simply considered, which entitled it to such an exaltation? nor could there be any desert foreseen which required it, for it must be said of the man Christ Jesus, as of every other creature, "for who maketh thee to differ from another? and what hast thou that thou didst not receive?" (1 Cor. 4:7).

Let it not be forgotten that in decreeing the Son of man into union with the second person of the Trinity, with all the honor and glory involved therein, that God was perfectly free, as in everything else, to have decreed Him or not decreed Him, as He would; yea, had He pleased, He could have appointed the arch-angel rather than the seed of the woman, to that inestimable privilege. It was therefore free grace in God which made that decree, and by how much loftier was the dignity conferred upon Christ above His fellows, so much greater was the grace. The predestination of the man Jesus, then, is the highest example of grace, and thus God's greatest end in predestination to manifest His grace (from whence election hath its title to be styled "the election of grace": Rom 11:5) was accomplished in Him above His brethren, that He should be to the praise of the glory of God's grace, far above what we are.

Since in the case of Christ we have both the pattern and example of election—the grand original—it is quite evident that grace is not to be limited or understood only of the divine favor toward creatures that are fallen and are delivered out of ruin and misery. Grace does not necessarily presuppose sin in the objects it is shown unto, for the highest instance of all, that of the grace bestowed upon the man Christ Jesus, was conferred upon One who had no sin and was incapable of it. Grace is favor shown to the undeserving, for the human nature in the God-man merited not the distinction conferred upon it. When extended to fallen creatures, it is favor shown to the ill-deserving and Hell-deserving, yet this is not implied in the term itself, as may further be seen in the case of divine grace being extended to the unfallen angels. Thus, as Christ is the pattern to whom God has predestinated His people to be conformed, His election of them to everlasting glory was under His view of them as unfallen and not as corrupt creatures.

God having thus absolutely chosen the Son of man and therewith endowed Him with such royalty as to be the sovereign end of all whom He should create or elect to glory, it therefore follows that those who were chosen of us men were intended by the very ordination of God in our choice to be for Christ's glory as the end of our election, as well as for God's own glory. We were not absolutely ordained—as Christ in His unique predestination was in the first design of it—but from the first of ours the intention of God concerning us was that we should be Christ's and have our glory from Him who is "the Lord of glory" (1 Cor. 2:8). Here, as everywhere, Christ has the preeminence, for the person of Christ, God-man, was predestinated for the dignity of Himself, but we for the glory of God and of Christ. Though God the Father, first and alone, designed who the favored ones should be, yet that there should be an election of any was for Christ's sake, as well as His own.

In our election God had His Son in view as God-man, and in His design of Him as our end, He chose us for His sake, that we might be His "fellows" or companions (Ps. 45:7), that as He was God's delight (Isa. 42:1), so we might be His delight (Prov. 8:31). Thus we were given to Christ first, not as sinners to be saved by Him, but as sinless members to a sinless Head, as a sovereign gift to His person, for His honor and pleasure, and to be partakers of a supernatural glory with Him and from Him. "And the glory which thou gayest me [as the God-man] I have given them" as concurring with Thy election of them and Thy giving of them to Me to be Mine. Thou hast loved them as Thou hast loved Me (i.e., with an everlasting love in election), yea, thou gayest them to me for my glory as their end, and for which chiefly Thou lovest them (John 17:22, 23).

And what immediately follows in John 17? This, "Father, I will that they also, whom thou hast given me, be with me where I am; that they may behold my glory, which thou hast given me: for Thou lovedst me before the foundation of the world" (v. 24). Christ was loved in His election from everlasting, and out of God's love for Him His people were given to Him—with what intent? Even to behold, admire, and adore Him in His person and glory, as being that very thing they were ordained for, more than for their own glory, for their glory arises from beholding His (2 Cor. 3:18). And what is this glory which Christ was ordained unto? The glory of His person first absolutely decreed Him which is the height of His glory in heaven, where it is we are ordained to behold it. And observe how He here (John 17:24) reveals the main motive to God in this: "for thou lovedst me"—Christ's being chosen first in the intention of God, the members were chosen and given to Him so that they should redound to His glory.

We being chosen for Christ's glory as our end, and for His sake, as well as to the glory of God's grace towards us, God did ordain a double relation of Christ unto us for His glory, additional unto that absolute glory of His person. First the relation of an "Head," wherein we were given to Him as members of His body, and as a spouse unto her husband to be her head. Second, the relation of a "Savior" and Redeemer, which is in addition to His headship; and both of these for the further glory of Christ, and also for the demonstration of God's grace towards us. These two relations are quite distinct and must not be confounded. "For the husband is the head of the wife, even as Christ is the head of the church; and he is the Savior of the body" (Eph. 5:23): each of those offices were appointed Him by the good pleasure of God's will. This same twofold relation of Christ to His people is set forth again in Colossians 1:18-20: this double official honor conferred upon Him is further and above the absolute royalties of His person as the God-man.

Now that twofold relation of Christ to His people has, answerably a double and distinct aspect and consideration upon us and of us in our election by God, which was not absolute as Christ's was, but relative unto His two principal offices. The first concerns our persons without the consideration of our fall in Adam, whereby we were contemplated in the pure lump of creatureship as to be created, and in that consideration God ordained us unto ultimate glory, under relation to Christ as an "Head": whether as members of His body or as His bride, or rather both as He is the Head of the Church; of either or both which our persons were fully capable of before or without any consideration of our fall. Second, of our persons viewed as fallen, as corrupt and sinful, and therefore as objects to be saved and redeemed from the thraldom thereof, under our relation to Him as a "Savior"

Each of these relations was for the glory of God's grace. First, in His design to advance us, considered purely as creatures, to an higher glory by His Christ than was attainable by the law of creation. To ordain us unto this glory was pure grace, no less so than to redeem us from sin and misery when fallen; for it was wholly independent of works or merit, even as Christ's election (which is the pattern of ours) was apart from the consideration of works of any kind: as He declared, "my goodness extendeth not to thee" (Ps. 16:2). "Although the life-work and death-agony of the Son did reflect unparalleled luster upon every attribute of God, yet the most blessed and infinitely happy God stood in no need of the obedience and death of His Son: it was for our sakes that the work of redemption was undertaken" (C. H. Spurgeon). It is to this original grace that 2 Timothy 1:9 refers: grace alone moving God to redeem and call us, apart from works, "according to" that mother grace whereby we were ordained to glory from the beginning.

In that original grace lay God's grand and ultimate design, for it will have its accomplishment last of all, and as the perfection of all. God might immediately, upon our first creation, have taken us up into that glory. But second, for the further magnifying of Christ and the ampler demonstration of His grace—to extend it to its utmost reach: as the word in the Hebrew is "draw out at length thy lovingkindness" (Ps. 36:10)—He was not pleased to bring us unto the full possession of our inheritance in beholding the personal glory of Christ our head; but permissively ordained that we should fall into sin, and therefore decreed to create us in mutable condition (as the law of creation required), which made way for the abounding of His grace (Rom. 5:15). This is confirmed by, "But God, who is rich in mercy [a term which denotes our ill-desert], for his great love wherewith he loved us" (Eph. 2:4): first God loved us, viewed as sinless creatures; and this became the foundation of "mercy" to us considered as sinners.

It was upon this divine determination that the elect should not immediately upon their creation enter into the glory unto which they were ordained, but should first be suffered to fall into sin and wretchedness and then be delivered out of the same, that Christ had for His great and further glory the office of Redeemer and Savior superadded to His election of Headship. It is our being sinful and miserable which occupies our present and immediate concern, as that which we are most solicitous about while left in this world, and therefore it is that the Scriptures do principally set forth Christ as Redeemer and Savior. We say "principally" for as we have seen they are by no means silent upon the higher glory of His headship; yea, sufficient is said thereon to draw out our thoughts, affections and hopes unto the beholding Him in His grandest glory.

In bringing to a close this outline of the divine order of Christ's election, and of ours, as it is represented in Scripture, let it be pointed out that we are not to suppose an interval of time between God's foreordination of Christ as Head and of Him as Savior, for all was simultaneous in the mind of God; but the distinction is in the order of nature, and for our better understanding thereof. Christ could not be the "Head" without the correlate of His mystical "body," as He could not be our "Savior" except we had fallen. "Behold my servant, whom I uphold; mine elect, in whom my soul delighteth" (Isa. 42:1): Christ was first God's elect and delight and then His servant—upheld by Him in the work of redeeming. Absolutely and primarily Christ as God-man was ordained for Himself, for His own glory; relatively and secondarily, He was chosen for us and our salvation.

The glory of the person of the God-man, absolutely considered, was the primo-primitive design of God, that upon which He set His heart; next unto this was His ordination of Christ to be an Head unto us and we a body to Him that by our union to Him as our Head, He was the sufficient and efficient author of such blessings as our becoming immutably holy, of sonship from His Sonship, and the gracious acceptance of our persons in Him as the chief Beloved, and heirs of the same glory with Him—all of which we were capable of in God's considering us as pure creatures through our union with Christ, and needed not His death to have purchased them for us, being quite distinct from the blessing of redemption as Ephesians 1: 7 (following vv. 3-6) clearly enough shows. As this was the first in God's design, so it is the last in execution, being greater than all "salvation" blessings, the crown of all, when we shall be "forever with the Lord."

Descending to a much lower level, let it be pointed out that most certainly the holy angels could not be regarded in the corrupt mass when they were chosen, since they never fell; therefore it is most reasonable to suppose we were regarded by God as in the same pure mass of creatureship, when He elected us. Thus it was with the human nature of Christ, which is the object of election, for it never fell in Adam, nor ever came into a corrupt state, yet it was "chosen out of the people" (Ps. 89:19), and consequently the people out of which it was chosen must be considered as yet unfallen. This alone agrees with the type of Eve (the Church) being given to Adam (Christ) before sin entered. So God's double ordination of the elect to glory and then to salvation (in view of the fall) agrees with the double ordination of the non-elect: preterition as creatures and condemnation as sinners.

N.B. For most of the above we are indebted to Thomas Goodwin. In some places we have purposely repeated ourselves in this chapter, as much of the ground gone over is entirely new to most of our readers.

Chapter 7
Its Design

In the last chapter we have sought to go right back to the very beginning of all things and trace out the order of God's counsels in connection with His eternal decree in election, so far as they are revealed in Holy Writ. Now we shall seek to project our thoughts forward to the future, and contemplate God's grand design, or what it was He ordained His people unto. Here we shall be on more familiar ground to many of our readers, yet we must not overlook the fact that even this phase of our subject will be entirely new to quite a few of those who will scan these lines, and for their sakes especially it will behoove us to proceed slowly, taking nothing for granted, but furnishing clear Scriptural proof for what we advance. That which is to be before us is inexpressibly blessed, O that it may please God to so quicken the hearts of both writer and reader that we may actually rejoice and adore.

1. God's design in our election was that we should be holy: "According as he hath chosen us in him before the foundation of the world, that we should be holy and without blame before him" (Eph. 1:4). There has been much difference of opinion among the commentators as to whether this refers to that imperfect holiness of grace which we have in this world, or to that perfect holiness of glory which will be ours in the world to come. Personally, we believe that both are included, but that the latter is chiefly intended; and so we shall expound it. First, of that perfect holiness is heaven. That this is the prime reference appears from the amplifying clause "and without blame before him": it is such a holiness that God Himself can find no flaw in. Now the imperfect holiness which the saints have personally in this life, though it be a holiness before God in truth and sincerity, yet it is not one "without blame": it is not one God can fully delight in.

Second, as God hath ordained us to perfect holiness in the world to come, so He hath ordained us to an evangelical holiness in this world, or else we shall never come to heaven: unless we be made pure in heart here, we shall never see God there. Holiness is the image of God upon the soul, a likeness to Him which makes us capable of communion with Him; and therefore the apostle declares that we should "follow holiness, without which no man shall see the Lord" (Heb. 12:14). As reason is the foundation of learning, no man being able to attain it unless he hath reason, so we cannot reach the glory of Heaven unless the principle of holiness be divinely communicated to us. Therefore, as God's first design in our election was that we should be holy before Him, let us now make this our paramount concern. Here too is solid comfort for those who find indwelling sin to be their heaviest burden: though thy holiness be most imperfect in this life, yet is it the earnest of a perfect holiness in the life to come.

Holiness must needs be the fruit of our being chosen in Christ, for it is essential to our having a being in Him. It would be a contradiction in terms to say that God chose a man to be in Christ and did not make him to be holy. If God ordains a man to be in Christ, then He ordains him to be a member of Christ, and there must be conformity between Head and members. The election of grace was given to Christ as His spouse, and husband and wife must be of the same kind and image. When Adam was to have a wife she must be the same specie: none of the beasts was fit to be a partner for him. God brought them all before him, but among them all "For Adam was not found a help meet for him" (Gen. 2:20), because they had not the same image and kind. So if God chooses a man in Christ—the Holy One—he must necessarily be holy, and this is the reason why our holiness is annexed to our being chosen in Him (Eph. 1:4).

God, then, has decreed that His people shall be perfectly holy before Him, that they shall be in His presence forever, there to enjoy Him everlastingly, and delight themselves in that enjoyment, for as the Psalmist tells us "in thy presence is fullness of joy." Therein is revealed to us of what consists the ineffable bliss of our eternal inheritance: it is perfect holiness, perfect love to God; this is the essence of celestial glory. If the entire apostolate had spent the whole of their remaining lifetime in an attempt to depict and describe what heaven is, they could have done no more than enlarge upon these words: perfect holiness in God's presence, perfect love to Him, perfect enjoyment of Him, even as we are beloved by Him. This is heaven, and this is what God has decreed to bring His people unto. This is His first design in our election: to bring us into an unblemished holiness before Him.

2. God's design in our election was that we should be His sons: "Having foreordained us unto adoption as sons through Jesus Christ unto Himself according to the good pleasure of His will" (Eph. 1:5 ASV.). Holiness is that which fits us for heaven, for an unholy person could not possibly enjoy heaven: were he to enter it, he would be altogether out of his native element. Holiness, then, is that which constitutes the saints meetness for their inheritance in light (Col. 1:12). But adoption is that which gives the right to the glory of heaven, being bestowed upon them as a dignity or prerogative (John 1:12). As we have pointed out on other occasions, the last two words of Ephesians 1:4 belong properly to verse 5: "In love having predestinated us unto the adoption." God's love unto His dear Son was so great that, having chosen us in Him, His heart went out toward us as one with Christ, and therefore did He ordain us unto this further honor and privilege. This agrees perfectly with "Behold, what manner of love the Father hath bestowed upon us, that we should be called the sons of God" (1 John 3:1).

God might have made us perfectly holy in Christ and added no further blessing to it. "Ye have your fruits unto holiness" says the apostle (Rom. 6:22), and precious fruit that is; but he did not stop there—"and the end everlasting life:" that is added as a further fruit and privilege. In like manner, God added adoption to holiness: as the Psalmist says "the Lord will give grace and glory" (84:11). As our God, He chose us to holiness, according to that express saying "ye shall be holy: for I the Lord your God am holy" (Lev. 19:2). But as He became our Father in Christ, He predestinated us unto the adoption of sons. Here, then, is the twofold relation which the Most High sustains to His people in and through Christ, and there is the consequent twofold blessing of our persons because of Christ. Observe how minutely this corresponds with "Blessed be the God and Father of our Lord Jesus Christ, who hath blessed us with all spiritual blessings in the heavenly places in Christ" (Eph. 1:3).

By adoption we become God's sons in law, as by regeneration we are made His children in nature. By the new birth we become (experimentally) members of God's family; by adoption we have the legal status of sons, with all the high privileges that relationship involves: "Because ye are sons, God hath sent forth the Spirit of his Son into your hearts" (Gal. 4:6). Adoption makes known the high prerogatives and blessings which are ours by virtue of union with Christ, the legal right which we have unto all the blessings we enjoy, both here and hereafter. As the apostle reminds us, if we are children then are we "heirs," co-heirs with Christ; yea, heirs of God (Rom. 8:17)—to possess and enjoy God as Christ doth. "Seemeth it to you a light thing to be a king's son-in-law?" exclaimed David (1 Sam. 18:23), when it was suggested that he marry Michal: you may haply be the king's favorite and he may make you great, but to become his son-in-law is the highest honor of all. This is why we are told immediately after I John 3:1, "Beloved, now are we the sons of God, and it doth not yet appear what we shall be: but we know that when he shall appear, we shall be like him" (v. 2)—like Him in our proportion: as He perfectly enjoys God, so shall we.

Let it be duly noted that it is "through Jesus Christ" we are sons and heirs of God. Christ is our pattern in election, the One to whose image we are predestinated to be conformed. Christ is God's natural Son, and we become (by union with Christ) God's legal sons. "That he might be the firstborn among many brethren" (Rom. 8:29) signifies that God did set up Christ as the prototype and masterpiece, and made us to be so many little copies and models of Him. Every dignity we possess, every blessing we enjoy—save our election when God chose us in Him—we owe to Christ. He is the virtual cause of our adoption. Christ, as we have said, is God's natural Son; how, then, do we become His sons? Thus: God gave us to Christ to be married to Him, and He betrothed us to Him from everlasting, and so we become sons-in-law unto God, even as a woman comes to be a man's daughter-in-law by marrying his son.

We owe our adoption to our relation unto Christ's person, and not to His atoning work. Our adoption as originally it was in predestination bestowed upon us, was not founded upon redemption or Christ's obedience, but on Christ's being God's natural Son. Our justification is indeed grounded upon Christ's obedience and sufferings: "In whom we have redemption through his blood, the forgiveness of sins" (Eph. 1:7). But our adoption and becoming sons-in-law to God is through Christ's being His natural Son, and we His brethren in relation to His person. "God is faithful by whom ye were called unto the fellowship of his Son Jesus Christ our Lord" (1 Cor. 1:9). That fellowship or communion involves our participation of His dignities and whatever else in Him we were capable of; just as a woman acquires a legal title unto all the possessions of the man she marries. As Christ being God's natural Son was the foundation of His work possessing infinite worth, so our adoption is founded on our relation to His person, and then our justification upon His meritorious work.

We must, however, add this word of caution to what has just been pointed out: when we fell in Adam we lost all our privileges, and therefore Christ was fain to purchase them anew; and hence it follows that adoption, and all other blessings, are the fruits of His merit so far as their actual bestowment is concerned. Thus the apostle tells us Christ became incarnate "to redeem them that were under the law, that we might receive the adoption of sons" (Gal. 4:5)—our sins and bondage under the law and its curse interposing an obstacle against God's actual bestowment of adoption. But mark the minute accuracy of the language used: Christ's redemption is not said to procure adoption for us, but only that we might receive it. That which procured adoption was our relation to Christ as God's sons-in-law: this being God's purpose from everlasting.

Let us duly consider now the greatness of this privilege. Adam was created holy, and Luke 3:38 tells us he was "the son of God," but nowhere is it said that he was the son of God by adoption through Christ. So too in Job 38:7 the angels are called "morning stars" and "sons of God," yet we are never told they are such by adoption through Christ. They were "sons" indeed by creation, for God made them; but not sons-in-law of God by being married unto His Son, which is a grace and dignity peculiar to believers. Thus we excel the angels by our special relation to the Son of God's love: Christ nowhere calls the angels His "brethren," as He doth us! This is borne out by Hebrews 12:22 where, in contrast from the angels mentioned previously, we read of "the Church of the firstborn," a title denoting superiority (Gen. 49:3): we being related to God's "Firstborn," have higher privilege of sonship than the angels have.

"A figure may perhaps help us here. A father chooses a bride for his son, as Abraham chose one of his own kin for Isaac, and gives her a goodly dowry, besides presenting her with bridal ornaments, such as Eliezer put upon Rebekah. But on becoming the spouse of his son, she becomes his daughter, and now his affections flow forth to her, not only as a suitable bride for his dear son; not only does he admire her beauty and grace, and is charmed with the sweetness of her disposition, but he is moved also with fatherly love towards her as adopted unto himself, and thus occupying a newer and nearer relationship. Figures are, of course, necessarily imperfect, and as such must not be pressed too far; but if the one which we have adduced at all help us to a clearer understanding of the wondrous love of God in the adoption of us unto Himself, it will not be out of place. We thus see that predestination to the adoption of children, is a higher, richer, and greater blessing than being chosen unto holiness, and may thus be said to follow upon it as an additional and special fruit of God's love.

"But the love of God, in predestinating the church unto the adoption of children by Jesus Christ to Himself, has even a deeper root than viewing her as the bride of His dear Son. It springs out of and is most closely and intimately connected with the true, real, and eternal sonship of Jesus. Being chosen in Christ, the elect become the sons of God. Why? Because He is the true, real, and essential Son of the Father; and thus, as in union with Him, who is the Son of God by nature, they become the sons of God by adoption. Were He a Son merely by office, or by incarnation, this would not be the case, for He would then only be a Son by adoption Himself. But being the Son of God by eternal subsistence, He can say, 'Behold I and the children which Thou hast given Me: I Thy Son by nature, they Thy sons by adoption.' We see, then, that so great, so special was the love of God to His only begotten Son, that, viewing the Church in union with Him, His heart embraced Her with the same love as that wherewith He loved Him" (J. C. Philpot).

3. God's design in our election was that we should be saved: saved from the fall and its effects, from sin and its attendant consequences. This particular ordination of God was upon His foreview of our defection in Adam, who was our natural head and representative; for as pointed out in previous chapters, God decreed to permit the fall of His people in order to the greater manifestation of His own grace and increased glory of the Mediator. Obviously the very term "salvation" implies sin, and that in turn presupposes the fall. But this determination of God to suffer His people to fall into sin and then deliver them from it, was entirely subservient to His prime design concerning the elect and the ultimate glory to which He ordained them. The subordination of this third design of God in our election to those we have already considered appears in "who hath saved us, and called us with a holy calling, not according to our works, but according to His own purpose and grace, which was given us in Christ Jesus before the world began" (2 Tim. 1:9).

If the above Scripture be carefully analyzed it will be seen, first, that God formed a "purpose" concerning His people and that "grace" was given them in Christ Jesus "before the world began" either historically or in the mind of God: the reference being to His sovereign act in singling them out from the pure mass of creatureship, giving them being in Christ, and bestowing upon them the grace of sonship. Second, that God "hath saved us" (the reference being to believers) and "called us with a holy calling," which refers to what takes place in time when He brings us forth from our death in sin by an effectual call unto holiness (cf. Titus 3:5). Third, that this saving and calling for us was "not according to our works" either actual or foreseen, but "according to His own purpose," i.e., was based upon His original intention that we should be His sons. Neither our merits (for we have none), nor our misery, moved God to save us, but His having given us to Christ from the beginning.

As we have previously pointed out, God assigned unto Christ a double relation to His people: "Christ is the head of the church: and he is the savior of the Body" (Eph. 5:23). In the same Epistle He is seen first as the Head in whom we were originally "blessed with all spiritual blessings in the heavenly places" (1:3); later, He is presented as Savior, as the One who "loved the church and gave himself for it; that he might sanctify and cleanse it" (5:25, 26). In speaking of

Him as "the Savior of the Body" it is intimated that He is the Savior of none else, which is clearly confirmed by "therefore I endure all things for the elect's sake, that they may also obtain the salvation which is in Christ Jesus with eternal glory" (2 Tim. 2:10): note, not merely, "Salvation" indefinitely, but "the salvation" decreed by God for His own. Nor does "we trust in the living God, who is the Savior of all men, specially of those that believe" (1 Tim. 4:10) in anywise clash with this: the "living God" has reference to the Father, and "Savior" is more correctly rendered "Preserver" in Baxter's Interlinear.

Now this "salvation" which God has decreed for His elect, viewed as fallen in Adam, may be summed up under two heads: from the guilt and penalty of sin, and from its dominion and power, these having to do, respectively, with the legal and experimental sides. They are accomplished in time by what Christ did for us, and by what the Spirit works in us. Of the former it is written, "For God hath not appointed us to wrath, but to obtain salvation by our Lord Jesus Christ" (1 Thess. 5:9); of the latter we read "God hath from the beginning chosen you to salvation through sanctification of the Spirit and belief of the truth" (1 Thess. 2:13). It is by the latter we obtain evidence and assurance of the former: "Knowing, brethren beloved, your election of God. For our gospel came not unto you in word only, but also in power and in the Holy Ghost" (1 Thess. 1:4, 5). When our salvation from sin is consummated we shall be delivered from the very presence of it.

4. God's design in our election was that we should be for Christ: "All things were created by him, and for him," (Col. 1:16). God not only chose us in Christ and predestinated us unto sonship through Him, but gave us to Him, so that Christ was likewise the end of God's purpose in choosing to perfect holiness and adoption. God having a natural Son, the second person in the Trinity, whom He designed to make visible in human nature, through an union of it to His Son, did decree for His greater glory to ordain us unto the adoption of sons to Him and as brethren unto Him, so that He should not be alone, but rather "the firstborn among many brethren." As in Zechariah 13:7 the man Christ Jesus is designated Jehovah's "fellow," so from Psalm 45:7 we learn that God predestinated others to be for his Son, to be His companions: "Hath anointed thee above thy fellows.

The subject of the divine decrees is so vast in its range (whether we look backward or forward) and so comprehensive in its scope (when we contemplate all that is involved and included in it), that it is far from being an easy task to present a summarized sketch (which is as high as this writer aspires) of the same; and when attempt is made to furnish an orderly outline and deal separately with its most essential and distinctive features, it is almost impossible to prevent a measure of overlapping; yet if such repetition renders it easier for the reader to take in the prime aspects, our object will be accomplished. Part of what we now wish to contemplate in connection with God's design in our election was somewhat anticipated—unavoidably so—in the chapter on the nature of election, when, in showing that God's original intention was anterior to His foreview of our fall, we touched upon the positive side of His design.

We have sought to point out the infinite distance between the creature and the Creator, the high and lofty One, and that because of the mutability of our first estate by nature there was a necessity of super creation grace if the condition and standing of either men or angels was to be immutably fixed, which God was pleased to appoint by an election of grace. And therefore did God by that election also ordain those whom He singled out unto a super-creation union with Himself and communication of Himself, as our highest and ultimate end, which is far above that relation we had to Him by mere creation; this being accomplished by and through Christ. "Yet to us there is one God, the Father, of whom are all things, and we unto Him and one Lord, Jesus Christ, through whom are all things, and we through Him" (1 Cor. 8:6, ASV.). Let us note first the discriminating language used in this verse: there is a pointed difference made here between the "us" and the "all things," as of a select and special company, which is repeated in the second half of the verse.

We and all other things are from the Father—"of Him" or by His will and power, as the originating cause: this is common to "us" and all of His creatures. But the "we" He speaks of as a severed remnant, set apart to some higher excellency and dignity, and this special company is also referred to as "we through Him" (the Lord Jesus) in contrast from the "through whom are all things." The A.V. gives "one God, the Father, of whom are all things, and we in (Greek eis) Him," which is quite warrantable, the reference there being to God's taking us into Himself out of a special love and by a special union with Himself: compare "the church of the Thessalonians which is in God the Father" (1 Thess. 1:1). But the Greek also imports our being singled out unto His glory, "for Him": our being in Him is the foundation of our being for Him

The distinction to which we have just adverted receives further illustration and confirmation in "One God and Father of all, who is above all, and through all, and in you all" (Eph. 4:6). Here again we find the same difference used about the phrases of the all things and the us. Of the all things God is said to be "above all," whereby we understand the sublimity and transcendence of the divine nature and essence as being infinitely superior to that being which all creatures have by participation from Him. Yet, second, the transcendent One is also imminent, near to, piercing "through" all creatures. He is present with all, yet holding a different being from all—as the air permeates all our dwellings, be they palaces or hovels. But third, when it comes to the saints, it is "in you all": this is sovereign grace making them to differ from all the rest. God is so united to them as to be made one with them, in a special manner and by a special relationship.

How amazing is that grace which has taken such creatures as we are into union with One so elevated and ineffable as God is! This is the very summit of our privilege and happiness. If we compare Isaiah 57:15 with 66:1, 2 we shall see how God Himself has there emphasized both the sublimity and the transcendence of His own person and the marvel and measure of His grace toward us. In the former God speaks of Himself as "the high and lofty One that inhabiteth eternity, whose name is holy; I dwell in the high and holy place, with him also that is of a contrite and humble spirit"; while in the other He declares "The heaven is my throne and the earth is my footstool. . .but to this man will I look even to him that is poor and of a contrite spirit." How this demonstrates the infinite condescension of His favor that picks up animated dust, indwells us, communicates Himself to us as to none others: we have a participation of Him such as the angels have not!

Before proceeding further with our exposition of 1 Corinthians 8:6 so far as it bears upon our present subject, perhaps we should digress for a moment and make a brief remark upon the words "But to us there is but one God, the Father," which has been grossly perverted by those who deny a trinity of persons in the Godhead. The term "Father" here (as in Matt. 5:16; James 3:9, etc.) is not used of the first person in contradistinction to the second and third, but refers to God as God, to the Divine nature as such. If it could be shown from this verse that Christ is not God in the most absolute sense (see Titus 2:13), then by parity of reason it necessarily follows that "one Lord" would deny the Father is Lord, giving the lie to Revelation 11:15, etc. The main thought of 1 Corinthians 8:6 becomes quite intelligible when we perceive that this verse furnishes a perfect antithesis and opposition to the false devices of the heathen religion mentioned in verse 5.

Among the pagans there were many "gods" or supreme deities and many "lords" or middle persons and mediators. But Christians have only one supreme Deity, the Triune God, and only one Mediator, the Lord Jesus Christ (cf. John 17:3). Christ has a double "Lordship." First a natural, essential, underived one, belonging to Him considered simply as the second person of the Trinity.

Second (to which 1 Cor. 8:6 refers), a derived, economical and dispensatory Lordship, received by commission from God, considered as God-man. It was to this allusion was made previously, wherein it was stated that God decreed the man Christ Jesus should be taken into union with His Son, and so appointed Him His "sovereign end." The administration of the universe has been placed under Him: all power is committed to Him (John 5:22, 27; Acts 2:36; Heb. 1:2). Christ as God-man has equal authority with God (John 5:23), yet under Him, as Corinthians 3:23, "ask of Me" (Ps. 2:8), Philippians 2:11 shows.

The next thing in I Corinthians 8:6 we would dwell upon is the clause "and we in Him" (Greek) or as the margin has it "we for Him." Such a supernatural union with God and communication of God is His ultimate design towards us in His choosing of us. Hence it is that we so often read that "for the Lord hath chosen Jacob unto Himself, and Israel for His peculiar treasure" (Ps. 135:4). "This people have I formed for myself" (Isa. 43:21). "I have reserved to myself seven thousand men" (Rom. 11:4). This choosing of us is not merely a setting apart from all others to be His peculiar treasure (Exod. 19:5), nor only that God hath separated us for His peculiar worship and service to be holy unto Himself (Jer. 2:3), nor only that we should show forth His praise (Isa. 43:21), for even the wicked shall do that (Prov. 16:4; Phil. 2:11); but we are peculiarly for Himself and His glory, wholly in a way of grace and loving kindness.

All that which grace can do for us in communicating God Himself to us, and all that He will do for us unto the magnifying of His glory, arises wholly out of the free favor He shows us. In other words, God will have no more glory in us and on us, than arises out of what He bestows in grace upon us, so that our happiness as the effect will extend as far as His own glory as the end. How wondrous, how grand, how inexpressibly blessed, that God's glory in us should not be severed in anything from our good: God has so ordered things that not only are the two things inseparable, but co-extensive. If, therefore, God has designed to have a manifestative glory unto the uttermost, He will show forth unto us grace unto the uttermost. It is not merely that God bestows gifts, showers blessings, but communicates to us Himself to the utmost that we as creatures are capacitated for.

This is so far above poor human reason that nothing but faith can apprehend it, that we are yet to be "filled with all the fullness of God" (Eph. 3:19). In communicating Himself, God communicates the whole of Himself, whether of His divine perfections so far as to bless us therewith, or of all three persons, Father, Son, and Holy Spirit, for us to enjoy and have fellowship with. All in God shall as truly serve to make the elect blessed (according to a creature capacity) as serves to make Him blessed in His own immense infinity. If we have God Himself, and the whole of Himself, then are we "heirs of God" (Rom. 8:17), for we are "joint heirs with Christ"; and that God Himself is Christ's inheritance is proved by His own declaration "the Lord is the portion of mine inheritance" (Ps. 16:5). More than this we cannot have or wish: "He that overcometh shall inherit all things; and I will be his God, and he shall be my son" (Rev. 21:7).

In consequence of having chosen us for Himself, God reserves Himself for us, and all that is in Him. If Romans 11:4 speaks of God's having "reserved to himself" the elect (see v. 5 and note the "also"), so 1 Peter 1:4 tells that God is "reserved in heaven for us" as is clear from the fact that God Himself is our "inheritance," and none shall share in this wondrous inheritance but the destined heirs. And there He waits, as it were, till such time as we are gathered to Himself. There He has waited throughout the centuries, suffering the great ones of each generation to pass by, reserving Himself (as in election He did design) for His saints—"as if a great prince in a dream or vision should see the image of a woman yet to be born, and should so fall in love with his foreview of her that he should reserve himself till she is born and grown up, and will not think of or entertain any other love" (T. Goodwin). Christian reader, if God hath such love for thee, what ought to be thy love to Him! If He hath given Himself wholly to thee, how entire should be thy dedication unto Him!

When God hath brought us safely through all the trials and troubles of this lower world to heaven, then will He make it manifest that His first and ultimate design in electing us was for Himself, and therefore our first welcome there will be a presenting of us to Himself: "Now unto him that is able to keep you from falling, and to present you faultless before the presence of His glory with exceeding joy" (Jude 24), which is here mentioned that we might praise and give Him glory beforehand. The reference here is (we believe) not to Christ (that we have in Eph. 5:27; Heb. 2:13), but to the Father Himself, as "the presence of his glory" intimates, that being what we are "presented" before. It is the same Person who presents us to Himself whose glory it is. This is further borne out by "to the only wise God our Savior [note the "Father" is distinctly called "our Savior" in Titus 3:4] be glory and majesty, dominion and power, now and ever. Amen" (v. 25), all which attributes are those of God the Father in the usual current of doxologies.

God will present us to Himself "with exceeding joy." This "presentation" takes place at the first coming of each individual saint into heaven, though it will be more formally repeated when the entire election of grace arrive there. As we on our part—and with good reason—shall rejoice, so God on His part, too. He is pleased to present us with great joy to Himself, as making our entrance into Heaven more His own concern than it is ours. This presenting us to Himself "before the presence of His glory" is a matter of great joy to Himself to have us so with Himself: as parents are overjoyed when children long absent return home to them—compare the joy of the Father in Luke 15. It is because His purpose is accomplished, His eternal design realized, His glory secured, that He rejoices. With this agrees, "He will rejoice over thee with joy; he will rest in his love: he will joy over thee with singing" (Zeph. 3:17). It was for Himself God first chose us as His ultimate end, and this is now perfected.

Another Scripture which teaches that God has chosen His people for Himself is "Having predestinated us unto the adoption of children by Christ to himself" (Eph. 1:5). The Greek word rendered "to Himself" may as indifferently (with a variation of the aspirate) be rendered "for Him," so that with equal warrant and propriety we may understand it, first, as relating to God the Father, He having predestinated us to Himself as His ultimate end of this adoption; or second, to Jesus Christ, who is also one end in God thus predestinating us unto adoption. That the preposition eis often signifies "for" as denoting the end or final cause, appears from many places: for example, in the very next verse, "to [or "for"] the praise of the glory of His grace" as His grand design; so too in Romans 11:36 "to Him" (or "for Him") are all things." We shall therefore take this expression in its most comprehensive sense and give it a twofold meaning according to its context and the analogy of faith.

God's having predestinated us "to Himself" is not to be understood as referring primarily or alone to adopting us as sons to Himself, but as denoting distinctly and immediately His having elected and predestinated us to His own great and glorious self, and for His great and blessed Son. In other words, the clause we are now considering points to another and larger end of His predestinating us than simply our adoption; although that be mentioned as a special end, yet it is but a lower and subordinate end in comparison with God's predestinating us to Himself. First, He chose us in Christ unto an impeccable holiness which would satisfy His own nature; in addition, He predestinated us unto the honor and glory of adoption; but over and above all, His grace reached to the utmost extent by predestinating us to Himself— the meaning and marvel of which we have already dwelt upon.

God's having predestinated us "to Himself" denotes a special propriety in us. The cattle upon a thousand hills are His, and they honor Him in their kind (Isa. 43:20), but the Church is His peculiar treasure and medium of glory. The elect are consecrated to Him out of the whole in a peculiar way: "Israel was holiness unto the Lord, and the first fruits of his increase" (Jer. 2:3), which denotes His consecrating them to Himself, as the type in Numbers 18 explains it. Christ made a great matter of this in God's taking us to be His: "I pray not for the world, but for them which thou hast given me; for they are thine" (John 17:9); so too the apostle Paul emphasized the same note in "The Lord knoweth them that are his" (2 Tim. 2:19). It denotes too a choosing of us to be holy before Him, as consecrating us unto His service and worship, which is specially instanced in Romans 11:4, where the "I have reserved to Myself" is in contrast from the rest which He left to the worshipping of Baal. But above all, it imports His taking us into the nearest oneness and communion with and participation of Himself.

Consider now the phrase in Ephesians 1:5 as meaning "for Him," that is, for Jesus Christ. The Greek words autos and hautos are used promiscuously, either for "him" or "himself," so that we are not straining it at all in rendering "for Him." It is in the prepositions which are used with reference to Christ in connection with the Church's relation to Him that His glory is told out: they are in Him, through Him, for Him. Each of these is employed here in Ephesians 1:4, 5 and in that order: we were chosen in Him as our Head, predestinated to adoption through Him as the means of our sonship, and appointed for Him as an end—the honor of Christ as well as the glory of His own grace was made God's aim in His predestinating of us. The same three things are attributed to Christ in connection with creation and providence: see Greek of Colossians 1:16. But it is of God the Father alone, as the fountain, we read "of Him" (the Originator) (Rom. 11:36; 1 Cor. 8:6; 2 Cor. 5:18).

First God decreed that His own dear Son should be made visibly glorious in a human nature, through an union with it to His own person; and then for His greater glory God decreed us to be adopted sons through Him, as brethren unto Him, for God would not His Son in humanity should be alone, but have "fellows" or companions to enhance His glory. First, by His comparison with them, for He is "anointed above His fellows" (Ps. 45:7), being "the firstborn among many brethren" (Rom. 8:29). Second, God gave to His Son an unique honor and matchless glory by ordaining Him to be God-man, and for the enhancing of the same He ordained that there should be those about Him who might see His glory and magnify Him for the same (John 17:24). Third, God ordained us to adoption that Christ might be the means of all the glory of our sonship, which we have through Him, for He is not only our pattern in predestination, but the virtual cause of it.

Now in God's councils of election, the consideration of Christ's assumption of man's nature was not founded upon the supposition or foresight of the Fall, as our being predestinated for Him as the end intimates. Surely, this is obvious. Why, to bring Christ into the world only on account of sin and for the work of redemption were to subject Him unto us, making our interests the end of His becoming incarnate! That is indeed to get things upside down, for Christ, as God-man is the end of us, and of all things else. Moreover, this were to subordinate the infinite value of His person to the benefits we receive from His work; whereas redemption is far inferior to the gift of Himself unto us and we unto Him. It might also be shown that redemption itself was designed by God first for Christ's own glory rather than to meet our need.

N. B. We are again indebted to the invaluable writings of Thomas Goodwin.

Chapter 8
Its Manifestation

By His electing act God took the Church into a definite and personal relation to Himself, so that He reckons and regards its members as His own dear children and people. Consequently, even while they are in a state of nature, before their regeneration, He views and owns them as such. This is very blessed and wonderful, though alas it is a truth which is almost unknown in present-day Christendom. It is now commonly assumed that we only become the children of God when we are born again, that we have no relation to Christ until we have embraced Him with the arms of faith. But with the Scriptures in our hands there is no excuse for such ignorance, and woe be unto those who deliberately repudiate their plain testimony: to their divine Author will they yet have to answer for such wickedness.

It seems strange that the very ones who are foremost in propagating (unwittingly, we would feign believe) the error alluded to above, are they who have probably said and written more upon the typical teaching of the Book of Exodus than anyone else. We would ask such, Were not the Hebrews definitely owned by God as belonging to Him before He sent Moses to deliver them from the house of bondage, before the blood of the paschal lamb was shed, yea, while they were utterly idolatrous (Ezek. 20:5-9)? Verily, for to Moses He declared, "I have surely seen the affliction of my people which are in Egypt, and have heard their cry by reason of their taskmasters; for I know their sorrows" (Exod. 3:7); and of Pharaoh He demanded, "Thus saith the Lord God of Israel, Let my people go, that they may hold a feast unto me in the wilderness" (5:1). And the Hebrews were a divinely ordained type of the Israel of God, the spiritual election of grace!

It is quite true that God's elect are "by nature the children of wrath, even as others" (Eph. 2:3), nevertheless their persons have been loved by Him with an everlasting love. Consequently, before the Spirit is sent to quicken them into newness of life, the Lord God contemplates and speaks of them as His own. As this is now so little known, we will pause and offer proof from the Word. First, God calls them His children: "All thy children shall be taught of the Lord" (Isa. 54:13)—His children before taught by Him; and again, "He should gather together in one the children of God that were scattered abroad" (John 11:52)—His children before "gathered" by Him. Second, He designates them His people. "Thy people shall be willing in the day of thy power" (Ps. 110:3)—His people before "made willing," "I am with thee, and no man shall set on thee to hurt thee, for I have much people in this city" (Acts 18:10)—before Paul preached the gospel in that heathen center.

Third, Christ denominates God's elect His sheep before they are brought into the fold: "And other sheep I have, which are not of this fold: them also I must bring" (John 10:16)—who were those "other sheep" but those of His elect among the Gentiles? Fourth, the elect are spoken of as the tabernacle of David while they are in the ruins of the fall: "God at the first did visit the Gentiles to take out of them a people for his name. And to this agree the words of the prophets; as it is written, after this I will return, and will build again the tabernacle of David, which is fallen down" (Acts 15:14-16). In the apostolic age God began to take out of the Gentiles a people for His name, and concerning this Amos had prophesied of old: "The tabernacle of David, that is, the elect of God, once stood in Adam with the non-elect, and with them they fell; but the Lord will set up His elect again, not in the first Adam, but in the second Adam, in whom they shall be for an habitation of God through the Spirit" (James Wells).

Love in the heart of God was a secret in Himself from everlasting, being wholly unknown before the world began, except to Christ, God-man, yet it has been exercised towards the whole election of grace. Though they were beloved with such a love as contained the uttermost of God's good will unto them, and to the uttermost of blessing, grace and glory, yet it was in such a way and manner that for a season they were altogether unacquainted with the same. Though the acts of God's will in Christ's Person concerning them and upon them were such as could never cease, nevertheless they were to be in a state for a season in the which none of them were to be opened and made known to them. All was in the incomprehensible mind of Jehovah from everlasting, and the same it will be to everlasting; but the revelation and manifestation of the same has been made at different times and in various degrees.

The various conditions in which God's elect find themselves not only exhibit the manifold wisdom of God, but illustrate our last remark above. The elect were to be in a creature state of purity and holiness; as such they were made naturally in Adam. From that they fell into a state of sin and misery, sharing the guilt and depravity of their federal head. They were to be brought therefrom into a redeemed state by the atoning work of Christ, and given a knowledge of this through the quickening and sanctifying operations of the Spirit. After their earthly course is finished they are brought into a sinless state, while they rest from their labors and await the consummation of their salvation. In due course they shall be brought into the resurrection state, and from thence into the state of everlasting glory and unutterable bliss.

In like manner there are different stages in the unfolding of God's eternal purpose concerning His people. The principle of divine election has operated from the beginning of human history. No sooner did the Fall take place than the Lord announced the line of distinction which was drawn between the woman's seed and the seed of the Serpent, first exemplified in the clear-cut case of Cain and Abel (1 John 3:12). In an earlier chapter we called attention to the continuous operation of this selective principle, as was seen in the families of Noah, Abraham, Isaac and Jacob, and later still more conspicuously in the separating of Israel from all other nations, as the people of Jehovah's choice and the objects of His special favor. But what we would now consider is not so much the operation of God's eternal purpose of grace, as the manifestation of it.

In all these states through which the elect are ordained to pass the love of God is exercised and displayed toward them and upon them, agreeably to the good pleasure of His will. The secret and everlasting love of God to His chosen and His open disclosure of the same, though distinct parts, are one and the same love. The first act of God's love to the persons of those whom He chose in Christ consisted in giving them being in Christ, wellbeing in Christ from everlasting: that was the fundamental act of all grace and glory for God then "blessed them with all spiritual blessings in heavenly places in Christ" (Eph. 1:3). The love of God in His own heart towards the person of Christ, the Head of the whole election of grace, cannot be expressed, and His love towards the persons of the elect in Christ is so great and infinite that the Scriptures themselves declare "it passeth knowledge." The open expression and manifestation of this love it is now our design to ponder.

First, the incarnation and mission of Christ: "In this was manifested the love of God toward us, because that God sent his only-begotten Son into the world, that we might live through him" (1 John 4:9). Take notice of the persons unto whom the love of God was thus manifested, expressed in the word "us." This is a term made use of by the sacred writers to include and express the saints of God by. It is a distinguishing excellency of the apostles that they bring home their subjects with all their energy to the minds of saints, and then apply them so that hereby the truth might be felt in all its vast importance. Let the subject be election, redemption, effectual calling or glorification, and most generally they use the term "us," as thereby including themselves and all the believers to whom they wrote. This serves fitly to evince that all of them are alike interested in all the blessings and benefits of grace, which opens the way for them to appropriate and enjoy the good of them in the Scriptures.

To illustrate what has just been pointed out: "Blessed be the God and Father of our Lord Jesus Christ, who hath blessed us with all spiritual blessings in the heavenly places in Christ: according as he hath chosen us in Him before the foundation of the world, that we should be holy and without blame before him in love: having predestinated us unto the adoption of children by Jesus Christ. . .to the praise of the glory of his grace, wherein he hath made us accepted in the beloved" (Eph. 1:3-6). In that passage the repeated "us" shows the interest which all the saints have in their eternal election in Christ. With respect to effectual calling the apostle uses the word "us" in Romans 9:24. So in connection with salvation (note the "us" in 2 Tim. 1:9) and glorification (see Eph. 2:7; Rom. 8:18). Let it be carefully observed that whereas this repeated "us" in the Epistles includes the whole election of grace, yet it excludes all other and cannot with any truth or propriety be applied to any but the called of God in Christ Jesus.

We next consider in what this open manifestation of the love of God consisted, namely, in the incarnation and mission of Christ. In the infinite mind of Jehovah all His love concerning the persons of the elect was conceived from everlasting, with the various ways and means by which the same should be displayed and made known in a time state, so that the Church might be the more sensibly taken therewith. As it pleased the Lord, notwithstanding His eternal love to His people in Christ, to will their fall from a state of creature purity into depravity, so also their redemption from the same was predetermined. An everlasting covenant transaction took place between the Father and the Son, wherein the latter engaged to assume human nature and act as their Surety and Redeemer. His incarnation, life and death were fixed upon as the means of their salvation. This became the subject of Old Testament prophecy: that Christ was to be manifested in the flesh, with what He was to do and suffer, in order to take away sin and bring in everlasting righteousness.

That which was revealed in the Scriptures of the prophets concerning Christ made it fully evident that it was of God that the whole of it was originally council-transaction in Heaven before time began, the fruit of consultation between Jehovah and the Branch, of which the eternal Spirit was witness, He communicating the same to holy men, who spoke as they were moved by Him, for He searcheth all things, even the deep things of God. In the person of Immanuel, God with us, by His open incarnation and the salvation He wrought out and most honorably completed, all the love of the blessed Trinity is reflected most gloriously. God has shone forth in all the greatness and majesty of His love upon His Church in Christ, and thus displayed His everlasting good will unto them. He has so loved them as to give His only begotten Son. This is clearly set forth in His Word, so that it is all-sufficient to keep up a lively sense thereof in our minds, as the Spirit is pleased to maintain a believing knowledge of it in our hearts.

A brief word upon the end of this manifestation of the love of God as spoken of in 1 John 4:9: it is "that we might live through him." "It is through the incarnation and mediation of the Lord Jesus Christ that we live through Him a life of justification, peace, pardon, acceptance, and access to God. The elect of God in their fallen state were all sin, corruption, misery, and death; in these circumstances God commended His love toward them, in that while they were yet sinners Christ died for them. He by His death removed their sins from them. He loved them and washed them from their sins in His own blood, and brought them nigh unto God, so that herein the Father's everlasting love of them is most distinctly evidenced" (S. E. Pierce, to whose lovely sermon on 1

John 4:9 we here gladly acknowledge our indebtedness).

A most striking parallel with the Scripture we have looked at above is the statement made by the Lord to His Father in John 17:6: "I have manifested thy name unto the men which thou gavest me out of the world: thine they were, and thou gavest them me." The manifesting of the name of God, or the secret mystery of His mind and will, could only be performed by Christ, who had been in the bosom of the Father from everlasting, who became incarnate in order to make visible Him who is invisible. It was the office and work of the Messiah to open the "hidden wisdom" (1 Cor. 2:7), to unlock the holy of holies, to declare what had been kept secret from the foundation of the world; and here in John 17 He declares that He had faithfully discharged it. But mark well how the "us" of 1 John 4:9 is here defined as "the men which thou gavest me out of the world." Yes, it was to them Christ manifested God's ineffable name.

In John 17 Christ opened the whole heart of God, making known His everlasting love as was never revealed before. Therein He expounded the good will which the Father bore to the elect in Christ Jesus, in a manner sufficient to fill the spiritual mind with knowledge and understanding, even such as was calculated to lead to an entire trust and confidence in the Lord for all the blessings of this life and that which is to come. And who could give this information but Himself? He came down from heaven with this express end and design. He was the great Prophet over the House of God. He had the key of all the treasury of grace and glory. In Him personally was "hid all the treasures of wisdom and knowledge" (Col. 2:3). By the "Name" of God is meant all that He is in a manifestative and communicative way. It is His love to the Church, His covenant relation to His people in Christ, the eternal delight of His heart to them, which Christ has been pleased to so fully reveal.

It is by the Lord's admitting us into the knowledge of Himself that we are led to know our election of God. The true apprehension of this is a ground for joy, therefore did Christ say, "Rejoice, because your names are written in heaven" (Luke 10:20). As we cannot know that we are the beloved of God but by believing on His Son, so this is the fruit of spiritual knowledge. Christ has the key of knowledge and opens the door of faith, so that we receive Him as revealed in the Word. It is He, who by His Spirit, is pleased to shed abroad the love of God in the heart. He gives the Spirit to make a revelation of the everlasting covenant to our minds, and thereby we are made to know and feel the love of God to be the fountain and spring of all grace and everlasting consolation. As Jehovah caused all His goodness to pass before Moses and showed him His glory (Exod. 33:19), so He admits us into the knowledge of Himself as "The Lord God merciful and gracious."

Second, by a supernatural call. We have somewhat anticipated this in the last two paragraphs, but must now consider it more distinctly. A saint's being called is the first immediate fruit and breaking forth of God's purpose of electing grace. "The river ran underground from eternity and rises and bubbles up therein first, and then runs above ground to everlasting. It is the initial and grand difference which God puts between man and man, the first mark which He sets upon His sheep, whereby He owns them and visibly signifies that they are His" (T. Goodwin). "Whom He did predestinate, them he also called" (Rom. 8:30). The original benefit was His predestination of us, and the next blessing is His calling of us. The same order is observed in "Who hath saved us, and called us. . . according to his own purpose and grace which was given us in Christ Jesus before the world began" (2 Tim. 1:9). The eternal purpose is made evident in time by a divine call.

Another Scripture which presents this same truth are those well-known words "give diligence to make your calling and election sure" (2 Pet. 1:10). It is not our faith nor our justification which is here specifically singled out, but our "calling," which we are bidden to "make sure," for thereby our election will be attested to us, that is, confirmed to our faith. It is not that election is not sure without it, for "the foundation of God [His eternal decree] standeth sure" (2 Tim. 2:19) before our calling; but hereby it is certified unto our faith. Thus the apostles speak one uniform language, and therefore when writing to believers show that the two terms are co-extensive. Thus, Paul "unto the church of God which is at Corinth . . . called to be saints"—saints by calling (1 Cor. 1:2). Peter unto "the church that is at Babylon, elected together with you" (1 Pet. 5:13). The terms are equivalent, the apostles acknowledging none other to be true "calling" but what was the immediate proof of election, being commensurate to the same persons.

It is indeed blessed to observe—so graciously has the Spirit condescended to stoop to and help our infirmity—how frequently this precious truth is iterated in the Word, so that there might be no room whatever for doubt on the point. "The Lord hath appeared of old unto me, saying, Yea, I have loved thee with an everlasting love: therefore with loving-kindness have I drawn thee" (Jer. 31:3). Two things are here affirmed, and the intimate and inseparable relation between them is emphatically stated. First, the everlasting love of God unto His own; second, the effect and showing forth of the same. It is by the Spirit's effectual call the elect are brought out of their natural state of alienation and drawn to God in Christ. That supernatural call or drawing is here expressly attributed to the Lord's "loving kindness," and the connection between this and His everlasting love for them is pointed by the "therefore." Thus, it is by means of God's reconciling us to Himself that we obtain proof of His everlasting good will toward us.

The everlasting love and grace of the triune God unto His chosen ones is made apparent to them in this world by means of the fruit or immediate effects of the same: that which was secret in the heart of Jehovah is gradually brought into open manifestation through His own wondrous works unto the Church. It cannot be expected that the world of the ungodly should take any interest in these transactions, but to the regenerate they must be a source of unfailing and ever increasing delight. As we pointed out earlier, the electing love of God was evidenced, first, in the incarnation and mission of His own dear Son, who was ordained to accomplish the redemption of His people that had fallen in Adam. Second, the eternal purpose of God's grace is revealed in and through a divine call which the elect receive while here on earth. We must now consider more definitely what this divine call really is.

First of all we must distinguish carefully between this call which is received by the elect and that which comes to all who are under the sound of the Word: the one is particular, the other general. Whosoever comes under the sound of the Word, yea, all who have it in their hands in its written form, are called by God to forsake their sins and seek His mercy in Christ. This general call comes to the elect and non-elect alike: but alas, it is refused by all of them. It is described in such passages as, "Unto you, 0 men, I call; and my voice is to the sons of man" (Prov. 8:4), "many [are] called, but few chosen" (Matt. 20:16). Their rejection of the same is depicted thus: "Because I have called, and ye refused; I have stretched out my hand, and no man regarded" (Prov. 1:24), "They all with one consent began to make excuse" (Luke 14:18). But it is with the special and particular call, of which the elect alone are the subjects, that we are now concerned.

Second, then, this calling of the elect is an individual and inward one, falling not upon the outward ear, but penetrating to their very hearts. It is the Word of God's power, reaching them in their natural state of spiritual death and quickening them into newness of life. It is the Good Shepherd seeking and saving His lost sheep and restoring them to His Father: as it is written, "He calleth His own sheep by name, and leadeth them out. And when He putteth forth His own sheep, He goeth before them, and the sheep follow Him; for they know His voice" (John 10:3, 4). From the legal side of things the salvation of God's elect became an accomplished fact when Christ died and rose again, but not until the Spirit of God's Son is sent into their hearts— "whereby they cry Abba, Father"—is it made good in their actual experience. It is by the Spirit alone that we are given a saving knowledge of the Truth, being led by Him into a right apprehension thereof: The

Spirit so shines upon our understanding that we are enabled to take in the spiritual knowledge of God and His Son Jesus Christ.

Third, then, it is an effectual call, being accomplished by the supernatural operations of the Spirit. It holds equally good of the new creation as of the old that, "He [God] spoke, and it was done; He commanded, and it stood fast" (Ps. 33:9). It is in such passages as "Thy people shall be willing in the day of Thy power" (Ps. 110:3), this effectual call is referred to—their natural unwillingness to surrender themselves completely to the Lord's claims is sweetly melted down by the communication of an overwhelming sense of God's grace and love to them. Again; "All Thy children shall be taught of the Lord" (Isa. 54:13), so taught that He "hath given us an understanding, that we may know Him that is true" (1 John 5:20). Once more, this effectual call is God's making good the promises of the new covenant: "I will put My laws into their mind, and write them in their hearts: and I will be to them a God, and they shall be to me a people" (Heb. 8:10).

Theologians have wisely designated this the "effectual call" so as to distinguish it from the general and outward one which comes to all who hear the gospel. This effectual call is not an invitation, but is the actual bestowment of life and light. It is the immediate fruit of God's wondrous and infinite love to our persons when we are altogether unlovely, yea, the subjects of nothing but what renders us repulsive and hateful (see Ezek. 16:4-8!). It is then that the Holy Spirit is given to the elect—given to make good in them what Christ wrought out for them. Let it be clearly recognized and thankfully owned that the gift of the Spirit to us is as great and grand a gift as the gift of Christ for us. By the Spirit's inhabiting us we are sanctified and sealed unto the day of redemption. By the Spirit's indwelling of us we become the temples of the living God, His dwelling-place on earth.

It is not sufficiently recognized that all covenant mercies are in the hand of the blessed Holy Spirit, whose office and work it is to bring home the elect (by effectual calling) to Christ, and to make known and apply to their souls the salvation which the Lord Jesus has fulfilled and wrought out for them. He comes from Heaven in consequence of Christ's atonement and ascension, and proclaims salvation from the Lord for wretched sinners. He enters their hearts of sin and woe and makes known the salvation of God. He puts them by believing on the person and work of Christ into possession of the things that accompany salvation, and then He becomes a Comforter to them. Such do not pray for the Spirit to come and regenerate them, for they have already received Him as a life-giving and sanctifying Spirit. What they must now do is pray for grace to receive Him as the Spirit of adoption, that He may witness with their spirit that they are the children of God.

Now this effectual call is a necessary and proper consequence and effect of God's eternal election, for none are the recipients of this supernatural vocation but His chosen ones. Wherever predestination unto everlasting glory goes before concerning any person, then effectual calling unto faith and holiness infallibly follows. "God hath from the beginning chosen you to salvation through sanctification of the Spirit and belief of the truth" (2 Thess. 2:13). The elect are chosen unto salvation by the free and sovereign grace of God; but how is that salvation actually obtained? How are His favored ones brought into the personal possession of it? Through sanctification of the Spirit and belief of the truth, and not otherwise. God's decree of election is an ordination unto everlasting life and glory, and it is evident by holiness being effectually wrought in its objects by the regenerating and sanctifying operations of the Spirit. It is thereby that the Spirit communicates what Christ purchased for them.

"And that He might make known the riches of His glory on the vessels of mercy, which He had afore prepared unto glory, even us, whom He hath called, not of the Jews only, but also of the Gentiles" (Rom. 9:23, 24). In the verses immediately preceding the apostle had treated of the unspeakably solemn subject of how God shows His wrath and makes known His power in connection with the non-elect, but here he takes up the blessed theme of how God discovers the riches of His glory on the vessels of mercy. This is by the effectual call which is received individually by His people. That call is what serves to make manifest God's everlasting grace toward us: as Romans 8:28 expresses it we are "the called according to His purpose"; in other words, the Spirit is given to us in order to the accomplishment of God's decree, or to put it in another way, through his effectual call the believer may look upward to the eternal love of God unto him, much as he might through a chink in his wall peer through to the shining of the sun in the heavens.

As the love of God the Father is chiefly spoken of under the act of election and expressed by Him giving His only begotten Son to be our Head and Mediator, and as the love of God the Son shines forth brightest in His incarnation, obedience, and laying down His life for us, so the love of God the Spirit is displayed in His revealing in the Word the eternal transactions between the Father and the Son and by enlightening our minds into a true, vital, and spiritual knowledge of the Father and the Son. It is at effectual calling that the Spirit is pleased to make an inward revelation and application of the salvation of Christ to the soul, which is indeed heaven dawning upon us, for by it dead sinners are quickened, hard hearts softened, stubborn wills rendered pliable, great sins manifestatively forgiven, and infinite mercy displayed and magnified. It is then that the Holy Spirit, who is the Lord and giver of all spiritual life, enables great sinners to know that God is love.

By His Spirit Christ is pleased to shed abroad the love of God in the heart, and through the gospel He manifests the knowledge of the Father's love to us. He gives the Spirit to make a revelation of this to our minds, and thus we are led to know and feel the love of God to be the foundation of all grace and of everlasting consolation. As the knowledge of our personal election (obtained through our effectual calling) makes it evident to us that we are near and dear to God, so it follows that we perceive we are dear to Christ. As the Spirit imparts to us a knowledge of the Father's love unto us in His dear Son, we are led to search into and study this wondrous subject of election, and the more we know of it, the more we are astonished at it. Hereby, under the influences of the Holy Spirit, we are led to such views of the grace of the Lord Jesus as fills the heart with holy contentment and delight.

Third, the eternal purpose of God's grace unto us is manifested by a supernatural change in us. Strictly speaking this is not a distinct branch of our subject, for the new birth is one and the same as our effectual calling; nevertheless, for the sake of clarity and to resolve those doubts which the regenerate are the subjects of, we deem it well to give the same a separate consideration. When a sincere soul learns that there is both a general and external call, and a particular and inward one, he is deeply concerned to ascertain which of these he has received, or rather, whether he has been favored with the latter, for it is only the supernatural call of the Spirit which is effectual unto salvation. It is on this point that many of God's dear people are so deeply perplexed and exercised: to ascertain and make sure that they have passed from death unto life and been brought into a vital union with Christ.

In seeking to clear this point the writer has to guard against infringing too much upon the next branch of our subject, namely, the knowledge of our election. At present we are treating of the manifestation of it, particularly as it is seen in that supernatural change which is wrought in its subjects at the moment they receive God's effectual call. We shall therefore content ourselves here with endeavoring to describe some of the principal features of this supernatural change. That supernatural change is described in general terms in, "If any man be in Christ, he is a new creature" (2 Cor. 5:17). Another passage treating of the same thing is, "According as His divine power [he] hath given unto us all things that pertain unto life and godliness, through the knowledge of him that hath called us unto glory and virtue" (2 Pet. 1:3). It will at once appear that this verse is very much to the point, for it refers specifically to our effectual call and attributes the same to God's Divine power.

This supernatural change consists, then, in our being made new creatures in Christ Jesus. That which is brought forth by the Spirit at the new birth, though but a feeble and tiny spiritual babe, is nevertheless "a new creature"; a new life has been imparted, new principles communicated from which new actions proceed. It is then that "Of His [Christ's] fullness have all we received, and grace for grace" (John 1:16), that is, every spiritual grace in the Head is transmitted to His members; every grace from Christ in the Christian is now complete for parts: "grace for grace" as a child receives limb for limb from its parents. At our effectual calling divine power gives to us "all things pertaining to life and godliness": what they comprise we must now briefly consider.

First, a spiritual understanding. The natural man can neither perceive nor receive spiritual things in a spiritual way (though he can ponder them in a natural and intellectual way), because he is devoid of spiritual discernment (1 Cor. 2:14). But when we are effectually called God gives us "an understanding that we may know him that is true." Hence 2 Peter 1:3 declares that the all things pertaining to life and godliness are given us "through the knowledge of Him that has called us." The first light which the soul receives when the Spirit enters his heart is a new view of God, and in that light we begin to see what sin is, as it is in itself against a holy God, and thus perceive what holiness is. It is this new and spiritual knowledge of God Himself which constitutes the very core and essence of the blessing and work of the new covenant of grace: "They shall not teach every man his neighbor, and every man his brother, saying, Know the Lord: for all shall know Me, from the least to the greatest" (Heb. 8:11). This spiritual knowledge of God, then, is the germ and root of the spiritual change which accompanies the effectual call.

Second, a principle of holiness is wrought in the soul. God chose His people in Christ that they should be "holy" (Eph. 1:4), and therefore does He call them "with a holy calling" (2 Tim. 1:9). Thereby we are made "meet to be partakers of the inheritance of the saints in light" (Col. 1:12). Our title to heaven rests upon what Christ did for us, but our fitness for heaven consists of the image of Christ being wrought in us. This principle of holiness is planted in the heart by the Spirit, and is termed "the new nature" by some writers. It evidences itself by the mind's pondering again and again that God is a holy God, whose pure eyes can endure no iniquity, and by the heart's cleaving to Him under this apprehension of Him. Here, then, is the test by which we are to examine and measure ourselves: do I—notwithstanding so much in my heart and life which humbles me and causes me to mourn as contrary to divine holiness—approve of all God's commands as holy and good, though opposite to my lusts? And is it my constant longing for God to make me, increasingly, a partaker of this holiness?

Third, a love for spiritual objects and things. Not only is a "new heart" communicated at our effectual calling, but there is such a divine renewing of our will that it is now enabled to choose what is spiritually good—a power which the natural man has not in his fallen condition. It is the turning of the heart unto and longing after holy objects which carries the will along with it. When the love of God is shed abroad in our hearts we cannot but love Him and all that He loves. A true and sincere love to God is the fruit and effect of His effectual call: the two things are inseparable: "to them that love God, to them who are the called according to His purpose" (Rom. 8:28). Alas, our natural lusts still crave that which is unholy, nevertheless, in the renewed heart there is a principle which delights in and seeks after that which is pure and holy: "We know that we have passed from death unto life, because we love the brethren" (1 John 3:14). Do you not find (intermingled with other workings in you) true strains of love toward God Himself?

Fourth, a spiritual principle of faith. Natural faith suffices for natural objects, but spiritual and supernatural objects require a spiritual and supernatural faith. That spiritual faith is "the gift of God" (Eph. 2:8), wrought in the regenerate by "the operation of God" (Col. 2:12). This faith is the effect and accompaniment of our effectual call: "with lovingkindness have I drawn thee" (Jer. 31:3) signifies, first, that the heart is drawn unto the Lord, so that it rests on His promises, reposes in His love, and responds to His voice. "By faith Abraham, when he was called to go out into a place which he should after receive for an inheritance, obeyed" (Heb. 11:8): the two things are inseparable—faith responds to God's call. Therefore do we read of "the faith of God's elect" (Titus 1:1), which differs radically from the "faith" of formal religionists and wild enthusiasts. First, because it is a divine gift and not the working of a natural principle. Second, because it receives with childlike simplicity whatever is stated in the Word, quibbling not at "difficulties" therein. Third, because its possessor realizes that only God can sustain and maintain that faith in his soul, for it lies not in the power of the creature to either exercise or increase it.

In conclusion, let us point out that this supernatural change wrought in the elect at their effectual call, this working in them a spiritual understanding that they may know God, the imparting to them of a principle of holiness, of love and of faith, is the foundation of all the actings of grace which do follow. Every acting of grace, to the end of the believer's life, evidences this first work of effectual calling to be sound and saving. At regeneration God endows the soul with all the principles and seeds of all graces, and the future life of the Christian and his growth in grace (through the conflict between the "flesh" and "spirit") is but a calling of them into operation and manifestation.

We will now treat God's making known in time that purpose of grace which He formed concerning the Church in eternity past. The everlasting love of God unto His chosen people is discovered in a variety of ways and means, chief among them being the inestimable gifts of His Son for them and of His Spirit to them. Thus, we have so far dwelt upon, first, the incarnation and mission of Christ as the principal opening of the Father's heart unto His own, for while the glorification of the Godhead was His chief design therein, yet inseparably connected therewith was the blessing of His saints. Second, God's gracious design is manifested by the communication of the Spirit unto the elect, whereby they are made the subjects of a supernatural call. Third, this is made still further evident by the supernatural change wrought in them by the Spirit's regeneration and sanctification.

Fourth, by Divine preservation. "But the God of all grace, who hath called us unto His eternal glory by Christ Jesus, after that ye have suffered a while, make you perfect, establish, strengthen, settle you" (1 Pet. 5:10). This verse sets forth the wondrous and mighty grace of God dispensed to His elect in effectually calling them, in preserving them from temptation and sin, in strengthening and enabling them to persevere unto the end, and—notwithstanding all the opposition of the flesh, the world, and the devil—bring them at last securely unto eternal glory; for as Romans 8:30 declares, "Whom He called, them He also justified, and whom he justified, them he also glorified." Once again we shall draw freely from the most excellent writings of the Puritan, Thomas Goodwin, first because his works are now out of print and unknown to our generation, and second because having personally received so much help therefrom, we wish to share the same with our readers.

It is to be duly noted that in the immediate context (1 Pet. 5:8) the Devil is set forth in all his terribleness: as our "adversary" for malice, likened unto "a lion" for strength, unto a "roaring lion" for dread, "walking about seeking" such is his unwearied diligence; "whom he may devour" if God prevent not. Now observe the blessed and consolatory contrast: "But God": the Almighty, the self-sufficient and all sufficient One; "the God of grace": how comforting is the singling out of this attribute when we have to do with Satan in point of temptation. If the God of grace be for us, who can be against us? When Paul was under temptation a messenger (or angel) from Satan being sent to buffet him, what was it that God did immediately set before him for relief? This: "My grace is sufficient for thee" (2 Cor. 12:9)—the grace in God's heart toward him and the grace working in his own heart, both to assist him effectually.

But there is something yet more precious here in 1 Peter 5:10: "the God of all grace," which has reference first to the exceeding riches of grace that are in His nature, then to the benevolent designs which He has toward His own, and then to His gracious dealings with them. The grace in His nature is the fountain, the grace of His purpose or counsels is the wellhead, and the grace in His dispensations or dealings with us are the streams. God is an all-gracious God in Himself, even as He is the Almighty, which is an essential attribute. There is a limitless ocean of grace in Himself to feed all streams in which His purposes and designs of grace are to issue forth. Our consolation from hence is, that all the grace which is in the nature of God is in the promise of His being "the God of all grace" to His Church, declared to be so engaged as to afford supplies unto them, yea, to the utmost expenditure of these riches as their needs shall require.

Nor is God known to be such only by His people in the New Testament era. David, who was the greatest subject as well as adorer of this grace that we find in the Old Testament, apprehended and acknowledged the same. "According to Thine own heart, hast thou done all this greatness, in making known all these great things" (1 Chron. 17:19). And mark what immediately follows, "O Lord, there is none like thee, neither is there any God beside thee": that is, Thou art the God of all grace, for it was a point of grace, high grace, David is there extolling, namely, God's covenant of grace with him in Christ, just revealed to him. "What can David say more?" (v. 18); such divine favor is beyond him; just as Paul in Romans 8:3 1, "what shall we then say to these things?" When God pardons, He does so after the manner of a great God, full of all grace: He will "abundantly pardon" (Isa. 55:7), not according to our thoughts saith He (v. 8) but according to His own.

That to which the old divines referred when they spoke of God's purposing grace was the ocean thereof in His own nature, from which flow those beneficent designs which He hath toward His people, designs which the prophet described as "thoughts of peace" (Jer. 29:11), which He took up unto them or which He "thinks toward" them. It would be impossible to speak of all these thoughts, for as David declares, "Many, O Lord my God, are thy wonderful works which thou hast done, and thy thoughts which are to us-ward: they cannot be reckoned up in order" (Ps. 40:5). We must then summarize them and dwell only on those particulars which directly serve to the point before us, namely, our preservation, or God's carrying us safely through all temptations unto everlasting glory.

First Peter 5:10 manifestly speaks of God's purposing grace, that grace which was in His heart toward His people before He calls them from which in fact that call proceeds and which moved Him thereunto, as it is expressly affirmed in 2 Timothy 1:9. The first act of His purposing grace was in His choosing of us, His singling out of those persons whom He designed to be a God of grace unto. Choice of their persons is therefore styled "the election of grace" (Rom. 11:5), that being the fundamental act of grace, upon which all others are built. To be a God of grace unto His Church is to love its members merely because He chose to love them, for grace is the freeness of love. Receive us graciously" is the prayer of the Church (Hos. 14:2); "I will love them freely (v. 4) is the Lord's response. Divine grace and human merits are as far apart as the poles: as Romans 11:6 shows, the one mutually excludes the other.

For God to be the God of all grace unto His people is for Him to resolve to love them, and that forever; to be unchanging in His love and never to have His heart taken from off them. This is clearly denoted in the language of 1 Peter 5:10, for He "called us unto His eternal glory." It is not simply that He hath called us into His grace or favor, but into glory, and that, "eternal glory": that is, by the effectual call He estates us into the whole and full right thereof forever. What can this mean but that God called us out of such grace and love as He did and doth resolve to be the God of all grace to us for everlasting, and therefore calls us beyond recall (Rom. 11:29). This is clearly borne out by what immediately follows: "after that ye have suffered awhile, make you perfect, establish, strengthen, settle you.

This grace thus fixed in the divine will is the most sovereign and predominating principle in the heart of God, overruling all other things He willeth, so as to effectually carry on and carry out His resolution of free grace. Grace, as it is the most resolute, so it is the most absolute principle in the heart of God; for unto it belongeth the dominion. What else means "the throne of grace" (Heb. 4:16)? Why else is grace said to "reign . . . unto eternal life" (Rom. 5:21)? The same thing appears in the context of 1 Peter 5:10: "Humble yourselves [or submit to] therefore under the mighty hand of God [that is, to His sovereign power] that He may exalt you in due time" (v. 6): He "careth for you" (v. 7); all of which is carried down to "the God of all grace" in verse 10; which is followed by "To Him be glory and dominion for ever and ever. Amen" (v. 11), that is, to Him as "the God of all grace."

But it is as the God of all grace by way of execution or performance that we must now contemplate Him in His gracious dispensations of all sorts, which are the effects of the ocean of grace in His nature and the purpose of grace in His heart. We may turn back for a moment to 1 Peter 5:5: "God giveth grace to the humble," which refers to His actual bestowment of grace. In like manner, James declares, "He giveth more grace" (4:6), where he quotes the same passage as Peter's. In James it is spoken of in reference to subduing His people's lusts, particularly lusting after envy. Truly this is grace indeed, that when lust is raging, the grace of God should move Him to give more grace whereby He subdueth; unto them that humble themselves for their lusts, He giveth more grace.

It will help us to a better understanding of this divine title "the God of all grace" if we compare it with "the God of all comfort" in 2 Corinthians 1:3. Now that is spoken of in relation to effects of comfort: as the Psalmist says "He is good, and doeth good"; so immediately after He is spoken of as "the God of all comfort" it follows, "who comforteth us in all our tribulations." He is "the God of all comfort" in relation unto all sorts of distresses, which the saints at any time have; in like manner, He is the God of all grace in respect of its gracious effects. Yet this may be added—for the due magnifying of free grace—that the two are not commensurate, for the dispensations of His grace are wider than the dispensations of His comfort. God often gives grace where He does not bestow comfort, so that He is the God of all grace to a larger extent than He is of all comfort.

Now since there is a fullness, an ocean, all dispensatory grace to be given forth by God, what necessarily follows? This, first, that there is no temptation that doth or can befall a saint that is under the dominion of free grace, but God hath a grace prepared to be applied when His hour arrives. It clearly implies that God hath a grace fitted and suited as every need and occasion should arise. There is no sore in the heart but He hath a plaster ready for it, to be laid thereon in due season. The very word "grace" is a relative to need and temptation, and so "all grace" must be a relative to all or any needs whatsoever. If there were any want in the large subjects of free grace of which they are capable, and God had not a special grace for it, He were not the God of all grace. But it can never be said that the misery of His people is more extensive than the scope of God's grace.

As God hath grace for all the manifold needs of His people, so He is the God of all grace in giving forth help as their occasions require, for such is the season for grace to be displayed. "Let us therefore come boldly unto the throne of grace, that we may obtain mercy, and find grace to help in time of need" (Heb. 4:16). So again, "that He maintain the cause of his servant, and the cause of his people Israel at all times, as the matter shall require" (1 Kings 8:59), which is to be viewed as a type of the intercession of the antitypical Solomon, the Prince of peace. Thus God's favor is manifested unto His people at all times of need and in all manner of ways. If God were to fail His people in any one season and help them not in any one need, then He is not the God of all grace, for it is the chiefest part of being gracious to relieve in time of greatest need.

The fact that He is the God of all grace in respect to dispensing the same, demonstrates that He takes not this title upon Himself potentially, but that He is so actually, it is merely that He has in Himself sufficient grace to meet all the varied needs of His people, but also that He really does so. By instances of all sorts, God gives full proof of the same. In the day to come, He will have the honor of being not only the God of all grace potentially, but really so in the performance of it, for it will then be seen that He fully made good that word, "There hath no temptation taken you but such as is common to man: but God is faithful, who will not suffer you to be tempted above that ye are able; but will with the temptation also make a way to escape, that ye may be able to bear it" (1 Cor. 10:13). The greatest and acutest need of the Christian springs out of his indwelling sin, yet ample provision is made here, too, for "Where sin abounded, grace did much more abound" (Rom. 5:20).

This superabounding of divine grace is gloriously displayed when God effectually calls His people. Let us mention one or two eminent details in proof. First, God then shows Himself to be the God of all grace in the pardon He bestows. Consider what an incalculable debt of sinning we had incurred! From the earliest infancy the carnal mind is enmity against God: "The wicked are estranged from the womb: they go astray as soon as they be born, speaking lies" (Ps. 58:3). Every thought from the first dawning of reason has been only evil continually. Our sins were more in number than the hairs of our head. Suppose, Christian reader, thou hadst lived for twenty or thirty years before God effectually called thee: during all that time thou hadst done no good—not a single act acceptable to the thrice holy God; instead, all thy ways were abominable to Him. Nor hadst thou any concern about God's being so grievously dishonored, nor the fearfulness of thine estate. And then, lo!—wonder of wonders—by one act, in a single moment, God blotted out all thy sins: "having forgiven you all trespasses" (Col. 2:13).

Second, God showed Himself to be the God of all grace in bestowing on thee a righteousness which met every requirement of His holy Law: a perfect righteousness, even the righteousness of Christ, which contained in it all obedience. That infinitely meritorious righteousness was imputed to thy account wholly and at once: not piecemeal, abit at a time, but in one entire gift. "For if by one man's offence death reigned by one; much more they which receive abundance of grace and of the gift of righteousness shall reign in life by one, Jesus Christ" (Rom. 5:17). Verily, that was indeed "abundance of grace." That perfect righteousness of Christ is fully commensurate with all the designs of grace in God's heart toward thee, and the whole of this thou receivest at thy calling, so that thou mayest exclaim, "I will greatly rejoice in the Lord, my soul shall be joyful in my God; for he hath clothed me with the garments of salvation, he hath covered me with the robe of righteousness, as a bridegroom decketh himself with ornaments, and as a bride adorneth herself with her jewels" (Isa. 61:10). It was the realization of this which moved Paul to extol the grace bestowed on him at his first conversion: "And the grace of our Lord was exceeding abundant" (1 Tim. 1:14).

Third, God showed Himself to be the God of all grace in sanctifying thee. This includes first and foremost the bestowment of the Holy Spirit, who takes up His residence in the heart, so that thy body is the temple of God, whereby thou art set apart and consecrated to Him. In consequence of this, mortifying grace was bestowed, so that every lust then received its death-wound: "They that are Christ's have crucified the flesh with the affections and lusts" (Gal. 5:24). Quickening grace was also imparted, whereby the spirit is enabled to resist the flesh: "According as his divine power hath given unto us all things that pertain unto life and godliness, through the knowledge of him that hath called us to glory and virtue" (2 Pet. 1:3). Justification and sanctification are inseparably conjoined: as the former provides an inalienable standing for us, so the latter secures our state; and thereby is the foundation laid for our glorification.

These inestimable blessings were the pledges and earnests of thy preservation, for "He which hath begun a good work in you will perform it until the day of Jesus Christ" (Phil 1:6). It is in no wise a question of thy worthiness, but solely a matter of divine grace: "I know that, whatsoever God doeth, it shall be forever: nothing can be put to it, nor any thing taken from it" (Eccl. 3:14). True, sin is still left within thee—to further humble thy heart—and thy lusts are ever active; nevertheless, you may be fully assured with David "The Lord will perfect that which concerneth me; Thy mercy, O Lord, endureth forever" (Ps. 138:8). True, thou hast a most inadequate appreciation of such wondrous favor being shown thee, and to thine unutterable shame thou must confess that your daily conduct is utterly unworthy thereof; nevertheless, that too serves to bring out the amazing grace which bears with so ungrateful and vile a creature.

Before looking at some of the obstacles which might be supposed to stand in the way of the believer being carried safely through all temptation into eternal glory, we must guard against a possible misconception. It is not the prerogative of divine grace to save men who continue how they will in sin, to save out of an absolute sovereignty because it will save them. No indeed: God saves none without rule, much less against rule. The very verse which speaks of Him being the "God of all grace" adds "who hath called us" and as 2 Timothy 1:9 declares, God calls us "with an holy calling . . . according to his own purpose and grace"; for "without holiness no man shall see the Lord." The monarchy of grace hath fundamental laws, as all well-regulated monarchies have. Let the foundation of God be never so sure that "the Lord knoweth [loveth] them that are his," yet it is added "Let everyone that nameth the name of Christ depart from iniquity" (2 Tim. 2:19).

On the other hand, we do unhesitatingly declare the Scriptures teach that the saving grace of God is an effectual, all-powerful, infallible principle in the hearts of the regenerate, enabling them to keep those rules that are set them as essentially requisite to salvation. The one thing which Arminians suppose stands in the way of this is man's free will—as if God had made a creature which He was unable to rule. We are not ashamed to affirm that there is such a supremacy in divine grace that it engages all in God to its triumphant issue. If on the one hand grace complies with divine wisdom, justice, and holiness in setting rules; on the other hand grace draws all other attributes of God into an engagement for the preserving of us, keeping our otherwise perverse wills within the compass of those rules, and overcoming all opposition to the contrary. Hence it is that God makes so absolute a covenant: "I will not turn away from them, to do them good, ... they shall not depart from me" (Jer. 32:40).

We now desire to point out the arguments of comfort and support which may be drawn from this grand truth that the God of all grace will safely carry His people through all temptations. Having begun as the God of all grace in justifying them after this manner, and in sanctifying them at their effectual call, what is there which should divert and hinder Him from conducting them to eternal glory? Is it the guilt of sin, incurred by transgressions after calling? or the power of sin again recovering its strength in them? If neither of these, then nothing else remains. As both of them, at times, acutely distress the consciences and minds of Christians, it is advisable for us to point out that there is nothing in either of them which can even begin to turn God's heart from off His beloved children. May the Lord graciously help us to make this quite clear.

If anything was calculated to provoke God not to continue His grace unto the Christian it would be the guilt of those sins committed after his calling. But that shall not be able to so do. If God justified them at the first from sins mountain high, and thereby became engaged to continue a God of all grace ever after to them, then surely He will not fail to pardon their after-sins. Compare matters as they stood in this respect afore calling with the state thereof after. First, at thy calling God pardoned a continued course of sinning for many years, wherein there had been laid up a multitude too great for thee to number; but a pardoning thy sins after conversion it is at worst but of backslidings, and those repaired by many sincere repentings coming between. If then, God pardoned an entire course of sinning, will He not much more easily continue to pardon backsliding intermingled with repentings, even though they are sins committed again and again?

"Turn, 0 backsliding children, saith the Lord; for I am married unto you" (Jer. 3:14). Married Israel had been to God afore, but she had gone a-whoring from Him. At his first conversion God is espoused to the believer and He did then give up Himself to be a God of all grace to him. How marvelous is such grace to His unfaithful spouse! "Return, thou backsliding Israel, saith the Lord; and I will not cause mine anger to fall upon you: for I am merciful, saith the Lord" (Jer. 3:12). So merciful is He and He pardons on the lowest terms we could desire: "Only acknowledge thine iniquity, that thou hast transgressed against the Lord thy God, and hast scattered thy ways to the strangers under every green tree, and ye have not obeyed my voice" (v. 13). The same is found again in Isaiah 57:17, 18 and Hosea 14:4, where He promises to heal their backsliding.

Now if the God of all grace picked us up out of the mire when our hearts were wholly hard and impenitent, broke them, and forgave us all our years of sinning: then shall He not continue to melt our hearts when we backslide and recover us? Then, He forgave thee all thy past sins in one immeasurable lump; now He distributes His pardon, daily as thou humblest thyself for transgressions. That fountain opened "for sin and for uncleanness" (Zech. 13:1) is constantly available for us. Dost thou not confess thy sins, plead the blood of Christ, seek for mercy at the throne of grace, and beg forgiveness through Christ's intercession? If so, thou shalt not seek in vain; for though God pardoneth not because of thy humblings and seekings (as they are thy doings), yet in this course runs His pardoning grace.

But will not those who have been effectually called, reply: Alas, my sins since conversion have been greater and grosser than any I committed before. Answer: first, thou mayest have been very young when first converted: since then, as you have developed according to the course of nature, lusts too have grown, and you are more conscious of them than in early youth. Second, thy circumstances may account for them, though not excuse them. Some do sin worse after conversion than before: Job and Jeremiah sinned more grievously in later life than during their earlier years, for their temptations grew much higher. Third, consider not only thine awful sins, but thy sincere repentings too—thy earnest cryings to God against them, which were not disregarded by Him—demonstrating again that He is "the God of all grace."

One other thing which might be supposed to obstruct the course of God's grace begun in us at effectual calling, causing His heart to be diverted from us, is the power and ragings of sin within the Christian. But if He did sanctify us at the first as the God of all grace, then surely that affords a sure ground of confirmation that, notwithstanding the hazards with which our remaining corruptions might seem to threaten us, He will assuredly preserve grace in us despite all the temptations we are subject to. At his sanctification God laid in the soul of the Christian the seeds of every grace and gracious disposition that he shall ever possess: is He not well able to nourish and preserve this garden of His own planting? Listen to His most precious promise, "I the Lord do keep it; I will water it every moment; lest any hurt it, I will keep it night and day" (Isa. 27:3).

"Do ye think that the Scripture saith in vain, The spirit that dwelleth in us lusteth to envy? But He giveth more grace. Wherefore He saith, God resisteth the proud, but giveth grace unto the humble" (James 4:5, 6). This clearly denotes that our fiercest and most perilous conflicts are with some particular lust or temptation, for so the apostle's instance here carries it—the lust of envy. But when a regenerated soul is conscious of this corruption and doth humble himself under it and for it, bewailing the same before God, this shows that a contrary grace is working within him opposing the activities of that lust, resisting that envy (and the pride from which it springs), and therefore it is that he seeks for humility (the contrary grace to pride); and the Lord as the God of all grace giveth him "more grace.

But many a poor soul will reply: alas, I greatly fear that my condition is far worse now than ever it was previously. Answer: take the very worst condition that you have ever been in since conversion, and consider the frame of your heart therein, and then compare it with the best mood you were ever in before conversion. Honestly, dare you exchange this now for that then? Before conversion you had not the least iota of holy affection in thee, no aim at the glory of God; but since conversion thou hast (take the whole course of your Christian life) had an eye unto God and sought to please Him. True, like David, you must say, "I have gone astray like [not a sow but] a lost sheep"; yet can you also add with him "seek thy servant; for I do not forget thy commandments" (Ps. 119:176).

Before thy conversion thou never callest upon God, unless a formality; but now thou often criest unto Him unfeignedly. Before, you had no real hatred of sin and no pursuit after holiness; but now thou hast though falling far short of what thou wouldest be. Thou talkest of lusts harrying thee with temptations; yes, but once thou hadst the Devil dwelling within thee, as in his own house, in peace, and taking thee captive at his will. You complain of coldness in the performance of spiritual duties; yes, but once thou wast wholly dead. It may be thy graces are not shining, and yet there are in thee longings after God, desires to fear His name. There is, then, a living spiritual creature in thee, which, like the mole underground, is working up towards the air, heaving up the earth.

A further proof (in 1 Pet. 5:10) that the God of all grace will carry safely through all suffering and temptations into heaven those whom he has called, is contained in the words "called us unto His eternal glory." Though we are not yet in actual possession and full enjoyment thereof, nevertheless God has already invested us with a full and indefeasible right thereunto. This "glory" was the firstborn of all God's thoughts and intentions concerning us, for it was the end or upshot of His gracious designs with us. Said the Lord Jesus, "Fear not, little flock: for it is your Father's good pleasure to give you the kingdom" (Luke 12:32), and He will exclaim in the day to come, "Come, ye blessed of my Father, inherit the kingdom prepared for you from the foundation of the world" (Matt. 25:34), which refers unto heaven itself, where God reigns as undisputed King.

Now God's heart is so set upon this glory as His first and last end for His people that, when His electing grace is made known at our calling, He does then give us a full right thereto. Though He suspends the giving us the full possession of it for some years, yet He does not suspend the complete title thereto, for the whole of salvation is then stated upon them. A beautiful (and designed) type of this is found in 1 Samuel 16:18. In the open view of his brethren, God sent Samuel to David while he was yet young, and anointed him king, thereby investing him unto a sure right to the kingdom of Israel—that anointing being the earnest and pledge of all the rest. But for many years David's possession of the kingdom was delayed, and during that time he suffered much at the hands of Saul; nevertheless, God miraculously preserved him and brought him safely into it.

But note well that God has not only called us unto His glory, but unto "His eternal glory," whereby is implied not simply that the glory is eternal as an adjunct of it, but that our calling and estate thereby is into the eternity of that glory, as well as unto the glory itself. This implies two things. First, he that is called of God hath a spiritual life or glory begun in his soul which is eternal—note how the image of Christ wrought in the believer in this life is termed "glory" in 2 Corinthians 3:18. This glory of spiritual life in the Christian is indestructible; "Whosoever liveth and believeth in me shall never die" (John 11:25). Second, it imports that when a man is called, he is put into possession of an eternal right of glory—not a present right to glory only, but a perpetual right; a present right that reaches to eternity. We are "made heirs according to the hope of eternal life" (Titus 3:7).

There is yet one other phrase in 1 Peter 5:10 which remains to be considered: "by Jesus Christ." There is a security which Jesus Christ gives, as well as that of the Father's, to confirm the believer's faith that he shall be strengthened and enabled to persevere. God is the God of all grace to us by Jesus Christ: all His acts of grace towards us are in and through Him: He elected us at first and then loved us only as considered in Jesus Christ. God having thus laid Christ as Mediator, or rather as the foundation of His grace, it is a sure ground of its continuance to us. All God's purposes of grace were made in Christ, and all His promises are established and performed in and through Him.

There are two persons engaged for the preservation of saints unto glory: God the Father and Jesus Christ. We have seen what confirmation to our faith the interests that God the Father hath to us doth afford; equally full and strong is that supplied by the interest which Jesus Christ hath to them. The making of our salvation sure and steadfast against all opposition is directly founded upon Him and committed to Him. Concerning Jesus Christ God says, "Behold, I lay in Zion for a foundation of stone, a tried stone, a precious cornerstone, a sure foundation: he that believeth shall not make haste" (Isa. 28:16), or as the apostle explains it "shall not be confounded" (1 Pet. 2:6). We are "the called of Jesus Christ" (Rom. 1:6). We have "eternal life through Jesus Christ our Lord" (Rom. 6:23). God "establisheth us with you in Christ" (2 Cor. 1:21).

Little space remains for us to consider the security which a due contemplation of Christ's person, His relation to us, and office for us, affords to our faith that we shall be divinely strengthened to persevere unto the end. Only a few details can therefore be mentioned. First, His redemptive work. This is of such infinite worth that it not only purchased for us our first calling unto grace (Rom. 5:2), but together therewith, our continuance in that grace. Christ meritoriously bought off all our temptations and an ability in Himself to succor and establish us to the end. "Who gave Himself for our sins, that He might deliver us from this present evil world" (Gal. 1:4). "Who gave Himself for us, that He might redeem us from all iniquity, and purify us unto Himself a peculiar people, zealous of good works" (Titus 2:14). While His precious blood retains its infinite value in the esteem of God, not one of His sheep can perish.

Second, Christ's tender pity. "For in that he himself hath suffered being tempted, he is able to succor them that are tempted" (Heb. 2:18). In the previous verse it is declared that He is a merciful High Priest" to pity us, so that He hath a heart and willingness to help His people; but in verse 18 it is added that He is able so to do. And mark, it is not affirmed that He is able in respect of His personal power, as He is God, but there is a further and acquired ability as He is man. He was made a frail man, subject to temptations, and the painful experiences through which He passed in the days of His humiliation engages His heart to pity us when in distress, and because of this acquired tenderness, He is able to succor us in temptation.

Third, His intercession. "For if, when we were enemies, we were reconciled to God by the death of His Son, much more, being reconciled, we shall be saved by His life" (Rom. 5:10), that is, by His life for us in heaven. "Wherefore He is able also to save them to the uttermost that come unto God by him, seeing he ever liveth to make intercession for them" (Heb. 7:25). If, then, thou hast come unto God by Him, Christ's intercession effectually secures thine uttermost salvation. Because He hath taken thee into His heart, He has taken thee into His prayers. Once Christ takes us into

His prayers, He will never leave us out, but prevail for us, whatever be our case or whatever we fall into (1 John 2:1)—clear proof of this was furnished by the case of Peter. A man may be cast out of the prayers of a saint, as Saul was out of Samuel's; but none was ever cast out of Christ's prayers whom He once took in. His prayers will prevail to prevent thee from falling into such sins as God will not forgive.

Fourth, Christ's interest in that glory we are called unto and our interest in Christ's glory, for they are one. "God is faithful, by whom ye were called unto the fellowship of his Son, Jesus Christ our Lord" (1 Cor. 1:9); that is, to be partakers of the same things (in our measure) that He is partaker of. "For if we have been planted together in the likeness of his death, we shall be also in the likeness of his resurrection" (Rom. 6:5). The apostle declares that God "calls you by our gospel to the obtaining of the glory of our Lord Jesus Christ" (2 Thess. 2:14). It is Christ's own glory—the reward of that wondrous work by which He so illustriously magnified the Father—which His people are brought into, for nothing short of this would satisfy the heart of Christ: "Father, I will that they also, whom thou hast given me, be with me where I am; that they may behold my glory" (John 17:24).

Here, then, is how the secret election of God in eternity past is openly manifested unto His people in this time state: by a supernatural call, and by miraculously bringing them through a world which is as hostile to their souls as Babylon's furnace was to the bodies of the three Hebrews.

Chapter 9
Its Perception

Thus far we have dwelt mainly upon the doctrinal side of election; now we turn more directly to its experimental and practical aspect. The entire doctrine of Scripture is a perfect and harmonious unit, yet for our clearer apprehension thereof it may be considered distinctively in its component parts. Strictly speaking it is inadmissible to talk of "the doctrines of grace," for there is but one grand and divine doctrine of grace, though that precious diamond has many facets in it. We are not warranted by the Language of Holy Writ to employ the expression the doctrines of election, regeneration, justification, and sanctification, for in reality they are but parts of one doctrine; yet it is not easy to find an alternative term. When the plural "doctrines" is used in the Word of God, it alludes to what is false and erroneous:" doctrines of men" (Col. 2:22), "doctrines of devils" (1 Tim. 4:1), "divers and strange doctrines" (Heb. 13:9)—"divers" because there is not agreement among them.

In contrast from the false and conflicting doctrines of men, the truth of God is one grand and consistent whole, and it is uniformly spoken of as "the doctrine" (1 Tim. 4:16), "sound doctrine" (Titus 2:1). Its distinctive mark is described as "the doctrine which is according to godliness" (1 Tim. 6:3)—the doctrine which produces and promotes godliness. Every part of that doctrine is intensely practical and experimental in all its bearings. It is no mere abstraction addressed to the intellect, but, when duly apprehended, exerts a spiritual influence upon the heart and life. Thus it is with that particular phase of God's doctrine which is now before us. The blessed truth of election is revealed not for carnal speculation and controversy, but to yield the lovely fruits of holiness. The choice is God's, but the salutary effects are in us. True that doctrine must be applied by the power of the Holy Spirit to the soul before those effects are produced; for here, as everywhere, we are entirely dependent upon His gracious operations.

The first effect produced in the soul by the Spirit's application of the truth of divine election is the promotion of true humility. Pride and presumption now receive their death wound: self-complacency is shattered, and the subject of this experience is shaken to his very foundations. He may for years past have made a Christian profession, and entertained no serious doubts of the sincerity and genuineness thereof. He may have had a strong and unshaken assurance that he was journeying to heaven; and during that time he was utterly ignorant of the truth of election. But what a change has come over him! Now that he learns God has made an eternal choice from among the children of men, he is deeply concerned to ascertain whether or not he is one of heaven's favorites. Realizing something of the tremendous issues involved, and painfully conscious of his own utter depravity, he is filled with fear and trembling. This is most painful and unsettling, for as yet he knows not that such exercises of soul are a healthy sign.

It is just because the preaching of election, when accompanied by the power of the Holy Spirit (and what preaching is more calculated to have His blessing than that which most magnifies God and abases man!) produces such an harrowing of heart, that is so distasteful to those who wish to be "at ease in Zion." Nothing is more calculated to expose an empty profession, to arouse the slumbering victims of Satan. But alas, those who have nothing better than a fleshly assurance do not wish to have their false peace disturbed, and consequently they are the very ones who are the loudest in their outcries against the proclamation of discriminating grace. But the howling and snapping of dogs is no reason why the children of God should be deprived of their necessary bread. And no matter how unpleasant be the first effects produced in him by the heart's reception of this truth, it will not be long before the humbled one will be truly thankful for that which causes him to dig more deeply and make sure that his hope is founded on the Rock of ages.

Divine chastisement is a painful thing; nevertheless, to them that are exercised thereby, it afterwards yieldeth the peaceable fruits of righteousness (Heb. 12:11). So it is a grievous thing for our complacency to be rudely shattered, but if the sequel be that we exchange a false confidence for a Scripturally grounded assurance, we have indeed cause for fervent praise. To discover that God's purpose of grace is restricted to an elect people, is alarming to one who has imagined that He loves all mankind alike. To be made to seriously wonder if I am one of those whom God chose in Christ before the foundation of the world, raises a question which it is not easy to answer satisfactorily; and to be made to diligently inquire into my actual state, to solemnly examine myself before God, is a task which no hypocrite will prosecute; yet is it one which the regenerate will not shrink from, but on the contrary will pursue it with earnest zeal and fervent prayers to God for help therein.

It is not (as some foolishly suppose) that the one who is now so seriously concerned about his spiritual condition and eternal destiny is in such alarm because he doubts God's Word. Far from it: it is just because he believes God's Word that he doubts himself, doubts the validity of his Christian profession. It is because he believes the Scriptures when they declare the Lord's flock is a "very little one" (Greek, Luke 12:32), he is fearful that he belongs not to it. It is because he believes God when He says, "There is a generation that are pure in their own eyes, and yet is not washed from their filthiness" (Prov. 30:12), and that finding so much filth in his own soul, he trembles lest that be true of him. It is because he believes God when He says "the heart is deceitful above all things, and desperately wicked" (Jer. 17:9), that he is deeply exercised lest he be fatally deluded. Ah, my reader, the more firmly we believe God's Word, the more cause have we to doubt ourselves.

To obtain assurance that they have received a supernatural call from God, which has brought them from death unto life, is a matter of paramount concern to those who really value their souls. Those to whom God has imparted an honest heart abhor hypocrisy, refuse to take anything for granted, and greatly fear lest they impose upon themselves by passing a more favorable verdict than is warranted. Others may laugh at their concern and mock at their fears, but this moves them not. Too much is at stake for such a matter to be lightly and hurriedly dismissed. They know full well that it is one which must be settled in the presence of God, and if they are deceived, they beg Him to make them aware of it. It is God who has wounded them, and He alone can heal; it is God who has disturbed their carnal complacency, and none but He can bestow real spiritual rest.

Is it possible for a person, in this life, to really ascertain his eternal election of God? Papists reply dogmatically that no man can certainly know his own election unless he is certified thereof by some special, immediate, and personal revelation from God. But this is manifestly false and erroneous. When the disciples of Christ returned from their preaching tour and reported to Him the wonders they had wrought and being elated that even the demons were subject to them, He bade them "notwithstanding in this rejoice not, that the spirits are subject unto you; but rather rejoice, because your names are written in heaven" (Luke 10:20). Is it not perfectly plain in these words of our Savior that men may attain unto a sure knowledge of their eternal election? Surely we cannot, nor do we, rejoice in things which are unknown or even in things uncertain.

Did not Paul bid the Corinthians "Examine yourselves, whether ye be in the faith, prove your own selves" (2 Cor. 13:5). Here it is certainly taken for granted that he who hath faith may know that he hath it, and therefore may also know his election, for saving faith is an infallible mark of election: "As many as were ordained to eternal life believed" (Acts 13:48). Would that more ministers took a page out of the apostle's book and urged their hearers to real self-examination: true, it would not increase their present popularity, but it would probably result in thanksgiving from some of their hearers in a future day. Did not another of the apostles exhort his readers, "Give diligence to make your calling and election sure" (2 Pet. 1:10)? But what force would such an injunction possess if assurance be unattainable in this life? It would be utterly vain to use diligence if knowledge of our election is impossible without an extraordinary revelation from God.

But how may a man come to know his election? Certainly it is not by ascending up as it were into heaven, there to search into the counsels of God, and afterwards come down to himself. None of us can obtain access to the Lamb's book of life: God's decrees are secret. Nevertheless it is possible for the saints to know they are among that company whom God has predestinated to be conformed to the image of His Son. But how? Not by some extraordinary revelation from God, for Scripture nowhere promises any such thing to exercised souls. Spurgeon put it bluntly when he said, "We know of some who imagine themselves to be elect because of the vision they have seen when they were asleep, or when they were awake—for men have waking dreams; but these are as much value as cobwebs would be for a garment, they will be of as much service to them at the day of judgment as a thief's convictions would be to him if he were in need of a character to commend him to mercy" (from Sermon on 1 Thess. 1:4-6).

In order to ascertain our election we have to descend into our own hearts, and then go up from ourselves as it were by Jacob's ladder to God's eternal purpose. It is by the signs and testimonies described in the Scriptures, which we are to search for within ourselves, and from them discover the counsel of God concerning our salvation. In making this assertion we are not unmindful of the satirical comment which it is likely to meet with in certain quarters. There is a class of professing Christians who entertain no doubts whatever about their salvation, who are fond of saying, as well look to an iceberg for heat or into a grave to find the tokens of life, as search within ourselves for proofs of the new birth. But is it not akin to blasphemy to suggest that God the Spirit can take up His residence in a person and yet for there to be no definite evidences of His presence.

There are two testifiers to the believer from which he may assuredly learn the eternal counsels of God respecting his salvation: the witness of God's Spirit and the witness of his own spirit (Rom. 8:16). By what means does God's Spirit furnish testimony to a Christian conscience from the Word, but rather by His application of the promises of the Gospel in the form of a syllogism: whosoever believeth in Christ is chosen to everlasting life. That proposition is clearly set forth in God's Word, and is expressly propounded by His ministers of the gospel. The Spirit of God accompanies their preaching with effectual power, so that the hearts of God's elect are opened to receive the truth, their eyes enlightened to perceive its blessedness, and their wills moved to renounce all other dependencies and give up themselves to the mercy of God in Christ.

But the question arises, how may I distinguish between the witness of the Spirit and Satan's delusive imitation thereof? for as there is a sure persuasion of God's favor from His Spirit, so there are frauds of the Devil whereby he flatters and soothes men in their sins. Moreover, there is in all men natural presumption which is often mistaken for faith, in fact there is far more of this mock-faith in the world than there if of true faith. It is really tragic to find what multitudes there are in the religious world today who are carried away by the "strange fire" of wild enthusiasm, supposing that the exciting of their animal spirits and emotions is sure proof that they have received the Spirit's "baptism" and thus are certain of heaven. At the other extreme is a large company who disdain and discredit all religious feelings and pin their faith to an "I am resting on John 5:24," and boast that they have not had a doubt of their salvation for many years past.

Now the true witness of the Spirit may be discerned from natural presumption and Satanic deception by its effects and fruits. First, the Spirit bestows upon God's elect praying hearts. "Shall not God avenge his own elect, which cry day and night unto him" (Luke 18:7). Notice how right after making that statement the Lord Jesus went on to give an illustration of the nature of their praying. It is true that formalists and hypocrites pray, but vastly different is that from the crying of the sin-conscious, guilt-burdened, distressed people of God, as appears from the vivid contrast between the Pharisee and publican. Ah, it is not until we are brought to feel our utter unworthiness and Hell deservingness, our ruin and wretchedness, our abject poverty and absolute dependency on God's sovereign bounty, that we begin to "cry" unto Him and that, "day and night"—to pray experimentally, to pray perseveringly, to pray with "groanings which cannot be uttered," and thus, to pray effectually.

Let us look for a moment at a prayer of one of God's people, "Remember me, O Lord, with the favor that thou bearest unto thy people: O visit me with thy salvation" (Ps. 106:4). Now my reader, you are either earnestly seeking that favor by which the Lord remembers His people, or you are not. It is only when we are brought to the place where we are pressed down with a sense of our sinfulness and vileness that we can say in our souls before God, "O visit me with thy salvation." But the Psalmist did not stop there, no more must we: he went on to say, "That I may see the good of thy chosen, that I may rejoice in the gladness of thy nation, that I may glory with thine inheritance" (v. 5). God's elect pray for and seek after that which no other men pray for and seek after: they long to see the good of God's chosen, they seek to be saved with His salvation, and to dwell in the order of His everlasting covenant and eternal establishment.

A second effect of the Spirit's witness is a bringing of us to submit to God's sovereignty. Not only do God's elect pray for something which no other men pray for, but they do so in a different manner from all others. They approach the Almighty not as equals, but as beggars; they make "requests" of Him, and not demands; and they present their requests in strict subserviency to His own imperial will. How utterly different are their humble petitions from the arrogance and dictatorialness of empty professors. They know they have no claims upon the Lord, that they deserve no mercy at His hands, and therefore they raise no outcry against His express assertion, "I will have mercy on whom I will have mercy, and I will have compassion on whom I will have compassion" (Rom. 9:15). That person whose heart is indwelt by the Spirit of God takes his place in the dust, and says with pious Eli, "It is the Lord: let him do what seemeth him good" (1 Sam. 3:18).

We read in Matthew 20:3 of a number of men "standing idle in the marketplace," which we understand to signify that they were not actively engaged in the Devil's service, but that they had not yet entered God's service. Their attitude was indicative of a desire to be religious. Very well, said the Lord, go and work in My vineyard. But a little later the Lord of the vineyard displayed His sovereignty, and they were highly displeased. The Lord gave unto the last even as unto the first, and they murmured. The Lord answered "I do thee no wrong. . . .Is it not lawful for me to do what I will with mine own?" (v. 15). That was what offended them; they would not submit to His sovereignty, yet He exercised it notwithstanding. "Is thine eye evil, because I am good?" He asked and still asks to everyone who in the pride and unbelief of his heart rises up against God's discriminating grace. But not so with God's elect: they bow before His throne and leave themselves entirely in His hands.

Third, God's elect have imparted to them a filial spirit so that they have the affections of dutiful children to their heavenly Father. It inspires them with an awe of His majesty, so that they are conscious of every evil way. It draws out their hearts in love to God, so that they crave for the conscious enjoyment of His smiling countenance, esteeming fellowship with Him high above all other privileges. That filial spirit produces confidence toward God so that they plead His promises, count on His mercy, and rely on His goodness. His high authority is respected and they tremble at His Word. That filial spirit produces subjection to God, so that they desire to obey Him in all things, and sincerely endeavor to walk according to His commandments and precepts. True, they are yet very far from being that they should be, and what they would be could their earnest longings be realized; nevertheless, it is their fervent desire to please Him in all their ways.

"The Spirit himself beareth witness with our spirit, that we are the children of God" (Rom 8:16). The office of a "witness" is to give testimony or supply evidence for the purpose of adducing proof, either of innocence or guilt. This may be seen from "which show the work of the law written in their hearts, their conscience also bearing witness, and their thoughts the mean while accusing or else excusing one another" (Rom. 2:15). Though the heathen had not received a written revelation from God (as was the case with the Jews), nevertheless they were His creatures, accountable to Him, subject to His authority, and will yet be judged by Him. The grounds on which their responsibility rest are: the revelation which God has made of Himself in nature which renders them "without excuse" (Rom. 1:19, 20) and the work of the law written on their hearts, which is rationality or "the light of nature." Their moral instincts instruct them in the difference between right and wrong and warn of a future day of reckoning. While their conscience also "bears witness," supplies evidence that God is their governor and judge.

Now the Christian has a renewed conscience, and it supplies the proof that he is a renewed person, and consequently, one of God's elect. "We trust we have a good conscience, in all things willing to live honestly" (Heb. 13:18): the bent of his heart was for God and obedience to Him. Not only does the Christian sincerely desire to honor God and be honest with his fellows, but he makes a genuine endeavor thereunto: "Herein do I exercise myself, to have always a conscience void of offence toward God and toward men" (Acts 24:16). And it is the office of a good conscience to witness favorably for us and unto us. To it the Christian may appeal. Paul did so again and again, for example, in Romans 9:1 we find him declaring, "I say the truth in Christ, I lie not, my conscience also bearing me witness in the Holy Ghost," which means that his conscience testified to his sincerity in the matter. Thus we see again how Scripture interprets Scripture: Romans 2:15 and 9:1 define the meaning of "our spirit bearing witness"—adducing evidence, establishing the verity of a case.

Romans 8:16 declares that our spirit (supported by the Holy Spirit) furnishes proof that we are "the children of God," and, as the apostle goes on to show, if children, "then heirs" (v. 17) and "God's elect" (v. 33). Now this witness of our spirit is the testimony of our heart and conscience, purged and sanctified by the blood of Christ. It testifies in two ways, by inward tokens in itself, and by outward proofs. As this is so little understood to-day, we must enlarge thereon. Those inward tokens are certain special graces implanted in our spirit at the new birth, whereby a person may be certainly assured of His divine adoption, and therefore of his election to salvation. Those tokens regard first our sins, and second the mercy of God in Christ. And for the sake of clarity we will consider the former in connection with our sins past, present, and to come.

The token or sign in our "spirit" or heart which concerns sins past is "godly sorrow" (2 Cor. 7:10), which is really a mother grace of many other gifts and graces of God. The nature of it may the better be conceived if we compare it with its opposite. Worldly sorrow issues from sin, and is nothing else but terror of conscience and an apprehension of the wrath of God for the same; whereas godly sorrow though it be indeed occasioned by our sins, springs from a grief of conscience caused by a sense of the goodness and grace of God. Worldly sorrow is horror only in respect of the punishment, whereas godly sorrow is grief for sin as sin, which is increased by the realization that there will be no personal punishment for it, since that was inflicted upon Christ in my stead. In order that no one may deceive himself in discerning this "godly sorrow," the Holy Spirit in 2 Corinthians 7:11 has given seven marks by which it may be identified.

The, first is "For behold this selfsame thing ["godly sorrow"] that ye sorrowed after a godly sort, what carefulness it wrought in you." The word for "carefulness" signifies first "haste" and then diligence—the opposite of negligence and indifference. There is not only mourning over, but going to work with a will so as to rectify the misconduct. Second, "yea, what clearing of yourselves": the Greek word signifies "to apologize," seeking forgiveness: it is the reverse of self-extenuation. Third, yea, "what indignation," instead of unconcern: the penitent one is exceedingly angry with himself for committing such offenses. Fourth, "yea, what fear," lest there be any repetition of the same: it is an anxiety of mind against a further lapse. Fifth, "yea what vehement desire": for divine assistance and strength against any recurrence of it. Sixth, "yea, what zeal," in performing the holy duties which are the opposite of those sins. Seventh, "yea what revenge," upon himself, by daily mortifying his members. When a man finds these fruits in himself, he need not doubt the "godliness" of his repentance.

The token in our spirit with respect of sins present is the resistance made by the new nature against the old, or the principle of holiness against that of evil (see Gal. 5:17). This is proper to the regenerate as they are dual creatures—children of men and children of God. It is far more than the checks of conscience which all men, both good and bad, find in themselves as often as they offend God. No; it is that striving and fighting of the mind, affections, and will with themselves, whereby as far as they are renewed and sanctified they carry the man one way, and as they are still corrupt they carry him the flat contrary. It is this painful and protracted warfare which the Christian discovers to be going on within himself, which evidences him to be a new creature in Christ. If he reviews and recalls the past, he will find in his experience nothing like this before his regeneration.

Everything in the natural adumbrates spiritual realities, did we but have eyes to see and understandings to properly interpret them. There is a disease called ephialtes which causes its victims when they are half asleep to feel as though some heavy weight was lying across their chest, bearing them down; and they strive with hands and feet, with all their might, to remove that weight, but cannot. Such is the case of the genuine Christian: he is conscious of something within that drags him down, which clips the wings of faith and hope, which hinders his affections being set upon things above. It oppresses him and he wrestles with it, but in vain. It is the "flesh," his inborn corruptions, indwelling sin, against which all the graces of the new nature strive and struggle. It is an intolerable burden which disturbs his rest, and prevents him doing the things which he would.

The token in our spirit which respects sins to come is an earnest care to prevent them. That this is a mark of God's children appears from "We know that whosoever is born of God sinneth not: but he that is begotten of God keepeth himself, and that wicked one toucheth him not" (1 John 5:18). Note carefully the tense of the verb, it is not, "he doth not sin," but "sinneth not" as a regular practice and constant course. From that he "keepeth himself." This carefulness consists not only in the ordering of our outward conduct, but extends to the very thoughts of the heart. It was to this the apostle referred when he said "I keep under my body, and bring it into subjection" (1 Cor. 9:27)—not his physical body, but the body of sin within him. The more we are conscious of evil thoughts and unlawful imaginations, the more we sit in judgment upon our motives, the less likely is our external behavior to be displeasing unto God.

We turn now to consider the tokens or signs in the Christian's spirit with respect to God's mercy, tokens which evidence him to be one of God's elect. The first one is when a man feels himself to be heavily burdened and deeply disturbed with the guilt and pollution of his iniquities, and when he apprehends the heavy displeasure of God in his conscience for them. This far outweighs any physical ills or temporal calamities which he may be subject to. Sin is now his greatest burden of all, making him quite unable to enjoy worldly pleasures or relish the society of worldly companions. Now it is that he feels his urgent need of Christ, and pants after Him as the parched hart does for the refreshing stream. Carnal ambitions and worldly hopes fade into utter insignificance before this overwhelming yearning for reconciliation with God through the merits of the Redeemer. "Give me Christ or else I die is now his agonizing cry.

Now to all such sin-sick, conscience-tormented, Spirit-convicted souls, Christ has made some exceedingly great and precious promises, promises which pertain unto none but the quickened elect of God. "If any man thirst, let him come unto me, and drink. He that believeth on me, as the scripture hath said, out of his belly shall flow rivers of living water" (John 7:37, 38). Is not that exactly suited to the deep needs of one who feels the flames of hell upon his conscience? He hungers and thirsts after righteousness, for he knows that he has none of his own. He thirsts for peace, for he has none night or day. He thirsts for pardon and cleansing for he sees himself to be a leprous felon. Then come to Me, says Christ, and I will meet your every need. "I will give unto him that is athirst of the fountain of the water of life freely" (Rev. 2 1:6). And mark what follows his thus coming to Christ: "Whosoever drinketh of this water that I shall give him shall never thirst" (John 4:14).

The second token is a new affection which is implanted in the heart by the Holy Spirit, whereby a man doth so esteem and value and set such a high price upon the blood and righteousness of Christ that he accounts the most precious things of this world as but dross and dung in comparison. This affection was evidenced by Paul (see Phil. 3:7, 8). Now it is true that almost every professor will say that he values the person and work of Christ high above all the things of this world, when the fact is that the vast majority of them are of Esau's mind, preferring a mess of pottage to Jacob's portion. With very, very few exceptions those who bear the name of Christians much prefer the flesh pots of Egypt to the blessings of God in the land of promise. Their actions, their lives demonstrate it, for where a man's treasure is there is his heart also.

That no man may deceive himself in connection with this particular sign of regeneration and election, God has given us two identifying and corroboratory marks. First, when there is a genuine prizing of and delighting in Christ above all other objects, there is an unfeigned love for His members. "We know that we have passed from death unto life, because we love the brethren" (2 John 3:14): that is, such as are members of the mystical body of Christ, and because they are so. Those who are dear to God must be dear to His people. No matter what differences there may be between them in nationality, social position, personal temperament, there is a spiritual bond which unites them. If Christ be dwelling in my heart, then my affections will necessarily be drawn forth unto all in whom I perceive, however faintly, the lineaments of His holy image. And just so far as I allow the spirit of animosity to alienate me from them, will my evidence of election be overclouded.

The second corroboratory mark of a genuine valuing of Christ is a love and longing for His coming: whether it be by death, or by His second advent. Though nature shrinks from physical dissolution, and though the sin which indwells the Christian renders him uneasy at the thought of being ushered into the immediate presence of the Holy One of God, nevertheless, the actings of the new nature carries the soul above these obstacles. A renewed heart cannot rest satisfied with its present, fitful, and imperfect communion with his beloved. He yearns for full and complete fellowship with Him. This was clearly the case with Paul: "Having a desire to depart, and to be with Christ; which is far better" (Phil. 1:23). That this was not peculiar to himself, but something which is common to the entire election of grace, appears from his word "Henceforth there is laid up for me a crown of righteousness, which the Lord, the righteous judge, shall give me at that day: and not to me only, but unto all them that love His appearing" (2 Tim. 4:8).

Next we turn to the external token of our adoption. This is evangelical obedience, whereby the believer sincerely endeavors to obey God's commands in his daily life. "Hereby we do know that we know Him, if we keep His commandments" (1 John 2:3). God does not judge disobedience by the rigor of the Law for then it would be no token of grace but a means of damnation. Rather does God esteem and consider that obedience according to the tenor of the new covenant. Concerning those who fear Him the Lord declares, "I will spare them, as a man spareth his own son that serveth him" (Mal. 3:17). God regards the things done not by their effects or absolute doing of them, but by the affection of the doer. It is at the heart God chiefly looks. And yet, lest any be deceived on this point, let the following qualifications be prayerfully pondered.

That external obedience which God requires of His children and which for Christ's sake He accepts from them is not one which has respect to only a few of the divine commands, but unto all without exception. Herod heard the Baptist gladly, and did many things (Mark 6:20), but he drew the line at complying with the seventh commandment to leave his brother Philip's wife. Judas forsook the world for Christ, and became a preacher of the gospel, yet he failed to mortify the lust of covetousness, and perished. On the contrary David exclaimed, "Then shall I not be ashamed, when I have respect unto all thy commandments" (Ps. 119:6). He that repents of one sin truly repents of all sins, and he that lives in any one known sin without repentance, actually repents of no sin at all.

Again, for our external obedience to be acceptable to God, it must extend itself to the whole course of a Christian's life after conversion. We are not to judge ourselves (or anyone else) by a few odd actions, but by the general tenor of our lives. As the course of a man's life is, such is the man himself; though he, because of the sin which still indwells him, fails in this or that particular action, yet doth it not prejudice his estate before God, so long as he renews his repentance for his offenses—not lying down in any one sin. Finally, it is required that this external obedience proceed from the whole man: all that is within him is to show forth God praises. At the new birth all the faculties of the soul are renewed, and henceforth are to be employed in the service of God, as formerly they had been in the service of sin.

Let it be said once more that it is most important that the Christian should be quite clear as to exactly what it is his spirit bears witness unto. It is not to any improvement in his carnal nature, nor to sin being less active within him; rather is it to the fact that he is a child of God, as is evident from his heart going out after Him, yearning for fellowship with Him, and his sincere endeavor to please Him. Just as an affectionate and dutiful child has within his own bosom proof of the peculiar relationship which he stands in to his father, so the filial inclinations and aspirations of the believer prove that God is his heavenly Father. True, there is still much in him which is constantly rising up in opposition to God, nevertheless there is something else which was not in him by nature.

Let us here anticipate an objection: some say that it is a sin for the Christian to question his acceptance with God because he is still so depraved, or to doubt his salvation because he can perceive little or no holiness within. They say that such doubting is to call God's truth and faithfulness into question, for He has assured us of His love and His readiness to save all who believe in His Son. They deny that it is our duty to examine our hearts and say that we shall never obtain any assurance by so doing; that we must look to Christ alone, and rest on His naked Word. But this is a serious mistake. We do rest on His Word when we search for those evidences which that

Word itself describes as the marks of a child of God. Said the apostle, "For our rejoicing is this, the testimony of our conscience. . ." (2 Cor. 1:12). "Let us not love in word, neither in tongue; but in deed and in truth. And hereby we know that we are of the truth, and shall assure our hearts before him" (1 John 3:18, 19).

But notwithstanding the evidences which a Christian has of his divine sonship, he finds it no easy matter to be assured of his sincerity or to establish solid comfort in his soul. His moods are fitful, his frames variable. It is at this very point the blessed Spirit of God helpeth our infirmities. He adds His witness to the testimony of our renewed conscience, so that at times the Christian is assured of his salvation, and can say "my conscience is also bearing me witness in the Holy Spirit" (Rom. 9:1).

"The sole way of God's appointment whereby we may come to an apprehension of an interest in election is by the fruits of it in our own souls. Nor is it lawful for us to inquire into it or after it in any other way." With those words of the judicious Owen we are in full accord. For our part, we would not dare to place any reliance of an everlasting hope upon any dream or vision we had received, or any voice we had heard. Even if a celestial being appeared before us and declared that he had seen our name written in the Lamb's book of life, we should place no credence in it, for we would have no means of knowing that it might not be the Devil himself "transformed into an angel of light" (2 Cor. 11:14) come to deceive us. Our election must be certified to us by the unerring Word of God, and there we have a sure foundation on which to rest our faith.

The obligation which the gospel puts upon us to believe anything respects the order of the things themselves and the order of our obedience. When it is declared by the gospel that Christ died for sinners, I am not immediately required to believe that Christ died for me in particular—that were to invert the divine order of the gospel. The grand and simple message of the evangel of God's grace is, that Christ Jesus came into the world to procure a way of salvation for them who are lost, that He died for the ungodly, that He so perfectly satisfied the claims of the divine justice that God can righteously justify every sinner who truly believes in His Son, Jesus Christ (Rom. 3:26). Consequently since I find myself a member of that class, since I know myself to be a sinner, an ungodly person, lost, then I have full warrant to believe the good news of the gospel. Thus the gospel requires from me faith and obedience and I am under an obligation to render them withal.

Until I believe and obey the gospel I am under no obligation to believe that Christ died for me in particular; but having done so, I am warranted to enjoy that assurance. In like manner, I am required to believe the doctrine of election upon my first hearing of the gospel, because it is therein clearly declared. But as for my own personal election I cannot Scripturally believe it, nor am I obligated to believe it any otherwise, but as God reveals it by its effects. No man may justly disbelieve in or deny his election until he be in a condition where it is impossible for the effects of election to be wrought in him. While he is unholy a man can have no evidence that he is elected; so he can have none that he is not elected while it is possible for him to be made holy. Thus, whether men are elected or no, is not that which God calls any immediately to be conversant about: faith, obedience, holiness are what are first required from us.

Before proceeding further let it be pointed out that the elect are usually to be found where the ministers of Christ labor much. Said Paul, "Therefore I endure all things for the elect's sake, that they may also obtain the salvation which is in Christ Jesus with eternal glory" (2 Tim. 2:10). That illustrates the principle: the apostle knew that in his evangelical labors he was being employed in executing God's purpose in carrying the message of salvation to His people. To that very end was the apostle sustained by divine providence and directed by the Spirit of the Lord. Take a brief specimen of the method in which he was divinely guided. In his second journey publishing the glad tidings in heathen lands, Paul had been led through Phrygia and the region of Galatia, and would have preached the Word in Asia, but was "forbidden of the Holy Spirit" (Acts 16:6)—for what possible reason? but that God had none of His elect there, or if any, that the time had not yet arrived for their spiritual deliverance.

The apostle then essayed to go into Bithynia, but again we are told, "the Spirit suffered him not" (Acts 16:7). Very striking indeed is that, though it seems to make little or no impression upon people today. Next we read, "And they passing by Mysia [how solemn!] came down to Troas." There the Lord appeared unto him in a vision directing him to go to Macedonia, and from this he assuredly gathered that He had called him to preach the gospel there. He thereupon entered that country and proclaimed the good news, and in consequence, God's elect in Thessalonica obtained salvation. Later, he came to Corinth, where he met with much opposition, and with little success. He seems to have been on the point of departing, when the Lord appeared to him, strengthened his heart, and assured him "I have much people in this city" (Acts 18:10). As the result, he remained there eighteen months and the Corinthian Church was formed.

This grand principle of the Lord's so directing His servants that His elect are caused to hear His gospel from their lips, receives many striking illustrations in the Scriptures. The remarkable way in which Philip was conducted with the word of salvation to the Ethiopian eunuch, and Peter with the same word to Cornelius and his company, are cases in point. Another example, perhaps more striking still, is the way in which the apostles obtained access to the Philippian jailer with the word of life, who, because of his calling, probably found it impossible to hear their public preaching. Most blessedly do these instances exemplify the words of the Savior who, when referring to that company which the Father had given Him in Gentile lands, declared "And other sheep I have which are not of this fold; them also I must bring, and they shall hear my voice" (John 10:16)—hear His voice through His servants and be quickened by the power of His Spirit.

The Lord Jesus never yet sent His servants to labor where He had not a people, which being given to Him by the Father, were by Him to be brought into the fold. And He never will so send them. But where He has a people, He will there direct His own servants to call that people to Himself, and they like Paul of old will "endure all things for the elect's sake, that they may also obtain the salvation which is in Christ Jesus." Only the day to come will fully reveal how much— by His upholding grace—they did endure so that the elect might be saved. The elect, then, are to be found where the faithful ministers of Christ labor much. Now, my reader, if you are privileged to live in such a place, then in your own midst you may look for the favored people of God. The day of golden opportunity is now yours, and it is your bounden duty to respond and yield to the call made by Christ's servants.

Let us now pass on to something yet more specific. God not only sends His servants to those places where His providence has situated some of His elect, but He clothes His word with power and makes their labors effective. "Knowing, brethren beloved, your election of God. For our gospel came not unto you, in word only, but also in power, and in the Holy Spirit, and in much assurance" (1 Thess. 1:4, 5). That passage is very much to the point, and each clause in it calls for our closest attention. It tells us how the apostle became assured that the Thessalonian saints were among God's chosen people, and how by parity of reason, they too might know and rejoice in their election. Those details have been placed on record for our instruction, and if the Lord is pleased to grant us a spiritual understanding of them, we shall be on safe and sure ground. But in order for this, we must prayerfully ponder these verses word by word.

"Knowing brethren, beloved, your election of God." How did the apostle know their election of God? Let it be most particularly observed that this assurance of his was obtained not by any immediate revelation from Heaven, not by a supernatural vision or angelic message, nor by the

Lord Himself, directly informing him to that effect. No; rather was it by what he had witnessed in and from them. It was by the visible fruits of their election that he perceived them to be "brethren beloved." In other words, he traced back those effects of grace which had been wrought in them at their conversion, to the source thereof in God's eternal purpose of mercy. Those tiny rivulets of grace in their hearts the apostle traced back to the ocean of God's everlasting love from which they proceeded. Therein, he indicated to us the course which we must follow, the method we are to pursue in order to ascertain our predestination to glory.

"For our gospel came not unto you in word only, but also in power." All who pretend to preach the gospel do not actually do so. To allow that they did, would be to grant that there are as many different gospels as there are sects and sentiments in Christendom, all claiming theirs to be the true gospel, to the exclusion of every other. It is therefore a matter of the very highest importance that each of us should know what the gospel of Christ really is, and this must be learned from the Holy Scriptures, under the guidance of God the Spirit. There are numerous counterfeits of it in the world today, and their fraudulency can only be discovered by weighing them in "the balances of the Sanctuary." Equally necessary and important is it that we ascertain how the gospel should be received by us if the soul is to be permanently benefited by it, for according to the apostle there is a twofold reception thereof.

"For our gospel came not unto you in word only." For the gospel to come to us in word only" is for God to leave it to its natural efficacy, or the force of its arguments and persuasion on the human mind. Multitudes, in many places have heard the gospel, yet continue in idolatry and in iniquity, notwithstanding the profession which many of them make. When the gospel comes to us "in word only" it reaches the intellect and understanding, but makes no real impression on the conscience and heart. Consequently, it produces only a feigned and presumptuous faith, a faith which is inferior even to that which the demons have, for they "believe and tremble" (James 2:19). It is only when the gospel comes to us "in power and in the Holy Spirit" that it is received with a true and saving faith. How necessary it is then, to test ourselves at this point.

There are two extremes into which men fall through lack of the right receiving of God's Word. The one supposes he is possessed of both will and power to perform works of righteousness sufficient to commend him to the favor of God, and so he becomes "zealously affected, but not well" (Gal. 4:17). He fasts, prays, gives alms, attends church, etc.; and wherein he thinks he fails or comes short, he calls in the merits of Christ as a make weight for his deficiency. This is but taking a piece of new cloth (Christ's Atonement) and patching into his garment a legal righteousness, hoping thereby to appease a guilty conscience. He continues his religious performances the year round, but never attains to a vital and experimental knowledge of the gospel. All his service is but dead works.

The other extreme is the very reverse of this, but equally dangerous. Instead of toiling to the point of weariness, these work not at all. Being conscious more or less, as all natural men are, that they are sinners, and hearing of free salvation by Jesus Christ, they readily fall m with it, receiving it in their minds but not in their consciences. A superficial and presumptuous faith is begotten, and by a single leap they arrive at a supposed assurance of heaven. But, says Solomon, "An inheritance may be gotten hastily at the beginning; but the end thereof shall not be blessed" (Prov. 20:21). These people are great talkers, boast much of their freedom from the law, but are themselves the slaves of sin. They are ever learning, yet never able to come to a knowledge of the truth. They laugh at those who have doubts and fears, yet they themselves have the most cause of all to fear.

Now in marked contrast from both of these classes, are they who receive the gospel not in word only "but in power and in the Holy Spirit." This is a middle way between these two extremes, and one that is hidden from all unregenerate, for "the natural man receiveth not the things of the Spirit of God, for they are foolishness unto him, neither can he know them, because they are spiritually discerned" (1 Cor. 2:14). When God begins "the work of faith with power" (2 Thess. 1:11), and leads that soul in this middle way, he can at first neither see nor understand it. As it was with the father of all who believe, so it is with all his children: when Abraham was effectually called, he "went out, not knowing whither he went" (Heb. 11:8). Those born of the Spirit are led forth by "a way that they know not" (Isa. 42:16), and until darkness is made light before them and crooked things straight, they cannot understand the way of the Spirit; but when that is done, then the highway is "cast up" for them (Isa. 62:10).

The all-important question, then, is, Has the gospel come to me in word only, or in saving power? If the former, then it has been received without anguish, trouble, or distress of conscience, for those are the common marks of divine power working in the sinner's soul. When God's Word comes to us "in power," it comes as a "two-edged sword" (Heb. 4:12), having the same effect on the heart as a sword does when it is thrust into the body. If the wound be deep, the pain and smart will be very acute. So when the Word of God pierces "even to the dividing asunder of soul and spirit, and of the joints and marrow and is a discerner of the thoughts and intents of the heart" it produces real anguish and deep distress. Said Job, "The arrows of the Almighty are within me, the poison whereof drinketh up my spirit [explained in the next words] ; the terrors of God do set themselves in array against me" (6:4). And thus, too, David exclaimed, "Thine arrows stick fast in me, and thy hand presseth me sore" (Ps. 38:2).

It was thus in the experience of Paul. Before the Spirit applied the law to his heart, he was alive in his own eyes, though dead in God's; but when the commandment came home to him in divine power, sin revived and he died—in his own esteem (Rom. 7:9). The fact is that he, like every other Pharisee, supposed that the law reached no further than the external letter, touching which he considered himself blameless. But when its high demands and searching spirituality was made known to him he found it reached the very thoughts and intents of the heart, and discovered to him the awful depths of depravity in him which was hid before. He found the law was spiritual, but himself carnal, sold under sin. He found—as very, very few do—that his heart was in the very state described by Christ in Mark 7:21, 22. He was compelled to believe what Christ there declared, because he now saw and felt the same within himself.

The first act of faith brings a man to believe that he is in the very state Scripture declares him to be; at enmity against God (Rom. 8:7), a child of wrath (Eph. 2:3), under the curse of a broken law (Gal. 3:10), led captive by the Devil (2 Tim. 2:26). A heavy burden of sin lies on his conscience (Ps. 38:4), an active fountain of iniquity like the troubled sea casts up its mire and dirt (Isa. 57:20), which baffles all the efforts of an arm of flesh, bringing him into terrible bondage: "our iniquities, like the wind, have taken us away" (Isa. 64:6). He finds himself bound hand and foot with the cords of his sins, and he cries earnestly to God to take pity upon him, and out of his great mercy loose him. He now needs no set forms of prayer, but night and day he cries "God be merciful to me a sinner."

And how does the Lord set him at liberty? By the gospel coming to him "in power and in the Holy Spirit." God exhibits to him in a new light, the sufferings and death of His Son, by whom His justice was satisfied, His law magnified, His wrath appeased, and a way of reconciliation opened between God and sinners. It is the Spirit's office to work faith in the heart and to apply the atoning blood and righteousness of Christ to the conscience, by whom the burden of sin and death is removed, the love of God is made known, peace is imparted to the soul, and joy to the heart. Thus, the same instrument which wounded, brings healing. Therefore did the apostle here add, "For our gospel came not unto you in word only, but also in power, and in the Holy Spirit, and in much assurance"—assurance of its divine verity and authority, of its perfect adaptability and suitability to our case, of its ineffable blessedness.

"I remember, too, when the truth came home to my heart, and made me leap for very joy, for it took all my load away; it showed me Christ's power to save. I had known the truth before, but now I felt it. I went to Jesus just as I was, I touched the hem of His garment; I was made whole. I found now that the Word was not a fiction—that it was the one reality. I had listened scores of times, and he that spoke was as one that played a tune upon an instrument; but now he seemed to be dealing with me, putting his hand right into my heart. He brought me first to God's judgment seat, and there I stood and heard the thunders roll; then he brought me to the mercy seat, and I saw the blood sprinkled on it, and I went home triumphing because sin was washed away" (C. H. Spurgeon).

"Knowing, brethren beloved, your election of God" (1 Thess. 1:4). How did the apostle know that those Thessalonians were among God's elect? The next verses tell us: by the visible fruits thereof which he perceived in them. Discerning in their lives those effects of grace which had been wrought in them at their conversion, he traced back the same unto God's eternal purpose of mercy concerning them. And, my reader, the way in which Paul knew the Thessalonian believers were "from the beginning chosen . . . to salvation" (2 Thess. 2:13) must be the method by which every Christian today is to ascertain his or her election of God.

"For our gospel came not unto you in word only, but also in power, and in the Holy Spirit" (1 Thess. 1:5). Everything turns upon how the (true) Gospel is received by us: whether it is merely apprehended by the intellect, or whether it really reaches the conscience and heart for only then is it received with a saving faith. When God's Word comes to us "in power," it comes as "a two-edged sword"— cutting, wounding, causing pain and deep distress. When the Word comes to us in power it is not due to any learning or eloquence of the preacher, nor to any pathos which he may employ. The fact that his hearers' emotions are deeply stirred so that they are moved to tears, is no proof whatever that the gospel is come to them in divine efficacy: creature passions are often stirred by the actings of the stage and thousands are moved to weep in the theater. Such superficial emotionalism is but evanescent, having no lasting and spiritual effects. The test is whether we are broken and bowed before God.

The same thought is expressed again in the next verse, as though this is the particular detail by which we most need to test ourselves: "having received the Word in much affliction, with joy of the Holy Ghost" (v. 6). How that exposes the worthlessness of the light and frothy "evangelism" of the day! How solemn it is to remember that Christ described the stony-ground hearer as "he that heareth the Word and anon with joy receiveth it; yet hath he not root in himself" (Matt. 13:20, 21). Very different was it with those who were converted on the day of Pentecost, for the first thing recorded of them is, that they were "pricked in their heart" (Acts 2:37). Travail precedes birth, and then comes the rejoicing (see John 16:2 1). These are the questions to be considered—and answered before God: Has the Word rebuked and condemned me? Has it stripped me of my self-complacency and self-righteousness? Has it cut down my hopes, and brought me to lie as a self-condemned felon before the mercy seat?

"People come and hear sermons in this place, and then they go out and say, 'How did you like it?'—as if that signified to anybody. 'How did you like it?' and one says, 'Oh, very well,' and another says 'Oh, not at all.' Do you think we live on the breath of your nostrils? Do you believe that God's servants, if they are really His, care for what you think of them? Nay, verily; but if you should reply 'I enjoyed the sermon,' they are inclined to say, 'Then we must have been unfaithful, or else you would have been angry; we must surely have slurred over something, or else the Word would have cut your conscience as with the jagged edges of a knife. You would have said,

'I did not think how I liked it; I was thinking how I liked myself, and about my own state before God; that was the matter that exercised me, not whether he preached well, but whether I stood accepted in Christ, or whether I was a castaway.' My dear hearers, Are you learning to hear like that? If you are not, if going to church and to chapel be to you like going to an oratorio, or like listening to some orator who speaks upon temporal matters, then you lack the evidence of election; the Word had not come to your souls with power" (C. H. Spurgeon).

In between the portions quoted above from I Thessalonians 1:5, 6 are two other details: first, "and in much assurance." When the Word comes home in converting power to a man's soul, all his doubts concerning its authenticity and authority are removed, and he needs no human arguments to convince him that its author is God. All the skepticism of the rationalists and higher critics would be dispelled like mist before the rising sun, if the Spirit was pleased to effectually apply the Word to their hearts. Those who have been made to feel their dire need of Christ and have perceived His perfect suitability to their desperate condition, have "much assurance" of what the gospel affirms of His person and work. Whatever may have been the case with them formerly, they have no doubt now about His absolute Deity, His virgin birth, His vicarious death, His pre-eminent dignity, as prophet, priest, and king. These all-important things are settled for him, settled forever, and he will declare himself with a positiveness and dogmatism which will shock the sensibilities of the supercilious.

Again it is said, "ye become followers of us and of the Lord." Here is another mark of election: those who are chosen by the Lord desire to be like Him. "Ye became followers of us" does not mean that they said, 'I am of Paul, I am of Silas, I am of Timothy,' but that they imitated those eminent evangelists so far as they followed the example which Christ has left us. Ah, that is the test my readers. Are we Christlike? or do we honestly wish to be so? Then that is a sure evidence of our election. Do we live by every word of God (Matt. 4:4)?—Christ did. Do we take everything to God in prayer?—Christ did. Do we pray God to bless those who curse us? It is not that we are sinless, perfect; but are we, though often "afar off," really following Christ? If we are, it is not proud boastfulness to acknowledge it, nor is it self-righteousness to derive comfort therefrom, providing we also grieve over our many shortcomings and mourn over our sins.

"With joy of the Holy Spirit." Mark the qualifying language: it is not carnal mirth, but spiritual gladness. And observe too, that this concludes the list, for it is ever the Lord's way to reserve the best wine for the last. Alas, how few professors know anything, experimentally, about this deep, spiritual joy. The religion of the vast majority consists of a slavish attendance upon forms that they delight not in. How many go to some place of worship simply because it is not respectable to stay away, though they often wish it were. Not so with the Christian—when he is in his right mind: he goes to worship the Lord, to hear the voice of his beloved, seeking a fresh love-token from Him, desiring to bask in the sunshine of His presence. And when he is favored with a visit from Christ he exclaims with Jacob, "This is the house of God," a foretaste of heaven.

And now in drawing to a conclusion our remarks upon this fascinating aspect of the subject, there remains one other verse we must ponder: "Wherefore the rather, brethren, give diligence to make your calling and election sure" (2 Pet. 1:10). Those words have been fearfully wrested by errorists. Enemies of the truth have perverted them to signify that, the divine decree concerning salvation is but provisional, conditional on the sinner's own efforts. They deny that any man's predestination to eternal life is absolute and irrevocable, insisting that it is contingent upon our own personal diligence. In other words, man himself must decide and determine whether God's desire for him is to be realized. Not only is such a concept entirely foreign to the teaching of Holy Writ, but to say that the ratification and realization of God's eternal purpose is left dependent on something from the creature, is sheer blasphemy; and were it true, would not only render our election uncertain, but utterly hopeless.

"Wherefore the rather, brethren, give diligence to make your calling and election sure." These words have also presented a real problem to not a few of God's people. They have been sorely perplexed to understand how any diligence on their part could possibly make God's calling and election sure; and even when that difficulty is cleared up, they are quite at a loss to know what form their diligence is to take. Ah, my friends, God has often expressed Himself in the Scriptures in such a way as to test our faith, humble our hearts, and drive us to our knees. Perhaps it may afford most help if we concentrate on the following points. First, the particular people here addressed. Second, the unusual order of "calling and election. Third, what is the "diligence" here required. Fourth, in what sense can we make our calling and election "sure"?

First, the people addressed. If this simple but essential principle were duly heeded what a mass of erroneous expositions would be avoided. It is the mis-application of Scripture which is responsible for so much faulty interpretation. When the children's bread be cast unto the dogs, the former are robbed and the latter given that which they cannot digest. To take an exhortation which is addressed to believers and appropriate it, or rather misappropriate it, to unbelievers, is an excuseless offense: yet such has often been done with the verse before us. There is no difficulty whatever in ascertaining the addressees of this divine injunction. The opening verse of the epistle tells us that the apostle is here writing to those who had "obtained like precious faith," so that they were believers; while in the verse itself they are styled "brethren" and exhorted as such.

This exhortation, then, is addressed to living saints and not to dead sinners. To teach that the unregenerate can do anything at all toward securing their calling and election, is not only colossal ignorance, but it gives the lie of God's Word. When they are delivering a divine message, the first duty of God's ministers is to draw very definitely the line of demarcation between the Church and the world: it is failure at this point which causes so many children of the Devil to claim relationship with the people of God. Attention to the context will almost always make it clear to whom a passage pertains: whether to the children of men in general or to the children of God in particular. The simplest and most effectual way of making this plain to their hearers, is for them to carefully delineate the characters (the identifying marks) of the one and of the other—note how the apostle followed this very course in the first four verses of the epistle.

Second, the unusual order that is found here: "your calling and election." Though at first sight this presents a difficulty, yet further study will show it really supplies an important key to the opening of this exhortation. That which puzzles the thoughtful reader is, why "calling" comes before "election," for as we have sought so show at length in previous chapters, effectual calling is the consequence of election, as it is also the manifestation thereof. As Romans 8:28 declares believers are "the called according to His purpose": that is, the calling is in pursuance of God's purpose. So too in Romans 8:30 it is said, "Whom He did predestinate, them He also called." Likewise "Who hath saved us and called us with a holy calling, not according to our works, but according to His own purpose" (2 Tim. 1:9). Why, then, are these two things inverted in the passage we are now considering?

It is to be carefully noted that Romans 8:28, 30 and 2 Timothy 1:9 are treating of God's acts, whereas 2 Peter 1:10 mentions calling and election in connection with our diligence. It is only by duly noting such distinctions that we can hope to arrive at a right understanding of many of the details of Holy Writ. In Romans 8 the apostle is propounding doctrine, whereas in 2 Peter 1:10 he is pressing an exhortation, and there is a marked difference between those things. When the ways of God are being expounded, they are presented in their natural or logical order (as in Rom. 8:30), but when Christian experience is being dealt with, the order in which we apprehend the truth is the one followed. Thus it is here: we are first to make sure that we have been the recipients of an effectual call, for that in turn will furnish proof of our election. The order of God's thoughts toward us was, election and then calling; but in our experience we apprehend calling before election.

Third, what is the "diligence" here required? There are multitudes who fancy they have received an effectual call from God, but it is merely fancy: instead of prayerfully and diligently devoting themselves to the duty here enjoined, they give themselves the benefit of the doubt. Probably many are quite sincere in their supposition, but they are sincerely mistaken, being led astray by their deceitful hearts. It is far from being sufficient to adopt the doctrine of election as an article of our creed. As one tersely put it:

> Though God's election is a truth,
> Small comfort there I see,
> Till I am told by God's own mouth,
> That He hath chosen me.

And I have no right or warrant to expect that He will ever do any such thing, till I have complied with His requirements in the verse now before us.

That to which I am here exhorted is to first make sure my "calling" of God. This is to be done by accumulating and strengthening my evidence that I am His born-again child; and that, in turn, is accomplished by cultivating the character and conduct of a saint. And how is that to be achieved? By using the means of grace which God has provided: such as the daily reading of the Scriptures with spiritual meditation thereon; by secret and fervent prayer for divine succor and grace; by cultivating fellowship with God's people, so far as His providence permits this; by keeping faithful watch over our hearts, disallowing all that is unholy; by the strict denial of self and mortification of our members. But we shall receive most help at this point if we attend unto something yet more specific in the context.

In verses 5-7 we are exhorted, "giving all diligence, add to your faith virtue; and to virtue knowledge; and to knowledge temperance; and to temperance patience; and to patience godliness; and to godliness brotherly kindness; and to brotherly kindness love." Now verse 10 expresses the same duty, but in different words. There is a striking parallelism in this chapter, and it is by noting the repetition (in variation of thought) that we find the chief key to our verse. In verses 5-7 we have an exhortation, and in verse 8 we are shown the result of heeding it. In verse 10 we also have a similar exhortation, and then in verse 11 the result of compliance therewith is shown. Thus our text is to be interpreted in the light of its context. What is the "diligence" here required? Of what does it consist? Verses 5 to 7 tell us. It is by carefully cultivating the spiritual graces therein mentioned that I may ascertain my calling and election.

Fourth, in what sense do we make our calling and election "sure"? First, observe it is not "make secure": they are already secured to every saint by the immutability of the divine purpose, for "the gifts and calling of God are without repentance" (Rom. 11:29). It is not the making of our calling and election sure Godwards, but manwards. Nor is it something future which is here in view: it is the present enjoyment to ourselves of our calling and election, and of evidencing the same to our brethren. By heeding the exhortation of verses 5-7 I am to prove my calling and election, and demonstrate the same to the Church. A man may tell me he believes in election and is sure that he has been called of God, but unless I can see in his character and conduct the spiritual graces of verses 5-7 then I have to say of him (as Paul did of the Galatians) "I stand in doubt of you." Here, then, is the meaning: make steadfast in your own conscience your calling and election, and make good to others your profession, by walking as a child of God.

Finally, two consequences of complying with those exhortations are pointed out. First, "For if ye do these things, ye shall never fall" (v. 10.) Those who give all diligence to cultivate the spiritual graces mentioned in verses 5-7 (thereby making their calling and election sure, both to themselves and to their brethren), shall never fall from the place of communion with God; shall never fall from the truth into false doctrine and error; shall never fall into grievous sins, and so disgrace their Christian profession; shall never fall into a state of backsliding, so that they lose their relish for spiritual things; shall never fall under sore discipline from God; shall never fall into a despondency so as to lose all assurance; shall never fall into a condition of spiritual uselessness. But, second, "For so an entrance shall be ministered unto you abundantly into the everlasting kingdom of our Lord and Savior Jesus Christ" (v. 11): experimentally so here; fully and honorably so in the future. This is the result and reward of "diligence": the Greek word for "ministered" in verse 11 is the same as "added" in verse 5!

And now to summarize. How may a real believer ascertain that he is one of God's elect? Why, the very fact he is a genuine Christian evidences it, for a believing into Christ is the sure consequence of God's having ordained him to eternal life (Acts. 13:48). But to be more specific. How may I know my election? First, by the Word of God, having come in Divine power to the soul, so that my self-complacency is shattered and my self-righteousness renounced. Second, by the Spirit's having convicted me to my woeful, guilty, and lost condition. Third, by having had revealed to me the suitability and sufficiency of Christ to meet my desperate case, and by a divinely given faith causing me to lay hold of and rest upon Him as my only hope. Fourth, by the marks of the new nature within me: a love for God, an appetite for spiritual things, a longing for holiness, a seeking after conformity to Christ. Fifth, by the resistance which the new nature makes to the old, causing me to hate sin and loathe myself for it. Sixth, by sedulously avoiding everything which is condemned by God's Word, and by sincerely repenting of and humbly confessing every transgression thereof. Failure at this point will most surely and quickly bring a dark cloud over our assurance, causing the Spirit to withhold His witness. Seventh, by giving all diligence to cultivate the Christian graces, and using all legitimate means to this end. Thus, knowledge of election is cumulative.

Chapter 10
Its Blessedness

First, the doctrine of election magnifies the character of God. It exemplifies His grace. Election makes known the fact that salvation is God's free gift, gratuitously bestowed upon whom He pleases. This must be so, for those who receive it are themselves no different from and no better than those who receive it not. Election allows some to go to hell, to show that all deserved to perish. But grace comes in like a dragnet and draws out from a ruined humanity a little flock, to be throughout eternity the monument of God's sovereign mercy. It exhibits His omnipotency. Election makes known the fact that God is all powerful, ruling and reigning over the earth, and declares that none can successfully resist His will or thwart His secret purposes. Election reveals God breaking down the opposition of the human heart, subduing the enmity of the carnal mind, and with irresistible power drawing His chosen ones to Christ. Election confesses that "we love him because he first loved us," and that we believe because He made us willing in the day of His power (Ps. 110:3).

The doctrine of election ascribes all the glory to God. It disallows any credit to the creature. It denies that the unregenerate are capable of predicting a right thought, generating a right affection, or originating a right volition. It insists that God must work in us both to will and to do. It declares that repentance and faith are themselves God's gifts, and not something which the sinner contributes towards the price of his salvation. His language is, "Not unto us, not unto us," but "Unto him that loved us and washed us from our sins in his own blood." These paragraphs were written by us almost a quarter of a century since, and today we neither rescind nor modify them.

"The Lord makes distinctions among guilty men according to the sovereignty of His grace. 'I will no more have mercy upon the house of Israel: but I will have mercy upon the house of Judah.' Had not Judah sinned too? Might not the Lord have given up Judah also? Indeed He might justly have done so, but He delighteth in mercy. Many sin, and righteously bring upon themselves the punishment due to sin: they believe not in Christ, and die in their sins. But God has mercy, according to the greatness of His heart upon many, who could not be saved upon any other footing but that of undeserved mercy. Claiming His royal right He says, 'I will have mercy on whom I will have mercy.' The prerogative of mercy is vested in the sovereignty of God: that prerogative He exercises. He gives where He pleases, and He has a right to do so, since none have any claim upon Him" (C. H. Spurgeon: "The Lord's Own Salvation"—Hos. 1:7).

The above makes it sufficiently plain that it is no light thing to reject this blessed part of eternal truth: nay, it is a most solemn and serious matter so to do. God's Word is not given us to pick and choose from—to single out those portions which appeal to us, and to disdain whatever commends itself not to our reason and sentiments. It is given to us as a whole, and by it each of us must yet be judged. To reject the grand truth we are here treating of is the height of impiety, for to repudiate the election of God is to repudiate the God of election. It is a refusal to bow before His high sovereignty. It is the corrupt preacher opposing himself against the holy Creator. It is presumptuous pride which insists upon being the determiner of its own destiny. It is the spirit of

Lucifer, who said, "I will exalt my throne above the stars of God . . . I will be like the Most High" (Isa. 14:13, 14).

Second, the blessedness of this doctrine appears in that it is all important in the plan of salvation. Consider this first from the divine side. A Scriptural presentation of this grand truth is indispensable if the distinctive acts of the triune God in salvation matters are to be recognized, honored, and owned. Salvation proceeds not from one divine person only, but equally from the everlasting three. Jehovah has so ordered things that each one in the Godhead should be magnified and glorified alike. The Father is as really and truly the Christian's Savior as is the Lord Jesus, and so too is the Holy Spirit—note how the Father is expressly designated "God our Savior" in Titus 3:4, as distinct from "Jesus Christ our Savior" in verse 5. But this is ignored and lost sight of if this precious doctrine be omitted. Predestination pertains to the Father, propitiation to the Son, regeneration to the Spirit. The Father originated, the Son effectuated our salvation, and by the Spirit it is consummated. To repudiate the former is to take away the very foundation.

Consider it now from the human side: election lies at the very base of a sinner's hope. By nature all are the children of wrath. In practice, all have gone astray. The whole world has become guilty before God, all are exposed to wrath, and if left to themselves would be involved in one common ruin. They are "clay of the same lump," and continuing under nature's forming hand would be all "vessels to dishonor" (Rom. 9:21). That any are saved is of the grace of God (Rom. 11:4-7). Jesus Christ, the redeemer of sinners, is Himself the elect one, as described by the prophet (Isa. 42:1). And all who shall ever be saved are elected in Him, given to Him of the Father, chosen in Him before the foundation of the world. It was to accomplish their salvation that God gave His only begotten Son, and that Jesus Christ assumed our nature and gave His life a ransom.

It is to call the elect that the Scriptures are given, that ministers are sent, that the gospel is preached, and the Holy Spirit is here. It is to accomplish election that men are taught of God, drawn of the Father, regenerated by the Holy Spirit, made partakers of precious faith, endued with the spirit of adoption, the spirit of prayer, and the spirit of holiness. It is in consequence of their election that men are made obedient to the gospel, are sanctified by the Spirit, and become holy and without blame before God. Had there been no divine election, there had been no divine salvation. Nor is this a mere arbitrary assertion of ours: "Except the Lord of Sabbaoth had left us a seed, we had been as Sodom, and been made like unto Gomorrah" (Rom. 9:29). Lost sinners cannot save themselves. God was under no obligation to save them. If He be pleased to save, He saves whom He will.

Election not only lies at the foundation of a sinner's hope, but also accompanies every step of the Christian's progress to heaven. It carries to him the glad tidings of salvation. It opens his heart to receive the Savior. It is seen in every act of faith, in every holy duty, and in every effectual prayer. It calls him. It quickens him in Christ. It beautifies his soul. It crowns him with righteousness and life and glory. It contains within it the precious assurance that "He which hath begun a good work in you will perform it until the day of Jesus Christ" (Phil. 1:6). There was nothing in them which moved God to choose. His people, and He so deals with them as not to permit anything in or from them as to cause Him to reverse that choice. As Romans 8:30 so definitely intimates, predestination involves glorification, and therefore guarantees the supply of the elect's every need in between the two.

Third, the blessedness of this doctrine appears in its essential elements. We will single out three or four of the principal of these. First, the superlative honor of being chosen by God. In all choices the person choosing puts a value on the chosen. To be selected by a king unto an office, or to be called to some employment by the state, how it will dignify a man. Thus it is in spiritual affairs. It was a special commendation of Titus that he had been "chosen of the churches" (2 Cor. 8:19). But that the great God, the blessed and only potentate, should choose such poor, contemptible, worthless, and vile creatures as we are, passeth knowledge. Ponder 1 Corinthians 1:26-29, and see how this is there dwelt upon. How it should amaze us. How it should humble us. Note how this honorable emphasis is put upon the Lord Jesus: "Behold my servant, whom I have chosen" (Matt. 12:18); so upon His members too: "The elect's sake, whom he hath chosen" (Mark 13:20).

Again; the consequent excellency of this. They are the elect: the ones which God hath chosen, and doth not high worth, honor, excellency, necessarily follow from this? The chosen of God must needs be choice: the act of God makes them so. Observe the order in 1 Peter 2:6, "chief cornerstone, elect, precious"—precious because elect. Take the most eminent of God's saints, and what is their highest title and honor? This: "For David My servant's sake, whom I chose" (1 Kings 11:34). "Aaron whom He had chosen" (Ps. 105:26). Paul, "he is a chosen vessel unto Me" (Acts 9:15). "Ye are a chosen generation, a peculiar people" (1 Pet. 2:9), that is, elect. That expression is taken from "Ye shall be a peculiar treasure unto me above all people" (Ex. 19:5). It imports that which is dear to God: "since thou wast precious in my sight, thou hast been honorable" (Isa. 43:4).

Again, mark the fullness of such high privilege. "Blessed is the man whom thou choosest, and causest to approach unto thee, that he may dwell in thy courts" (Ps. 65:4); yea, he is "most blessed forever" (Ps. 21:6), or as the Hebrew has it (see mar.) "set for blessings," that is, set apart or appointed for naught but blessings. As the New Testament expresses it, "Blessed be the God and Father of our Lord Jesus Christ, who hath blessed us with all spiritual blessings in the heavenly places in Christ: according as he hath chosen us in him" (Eph. 1:3, 4). Election, then, is the treasury-fountain of all blessedness. The elect are chosen unto the nearest approach and union unto God that is possible for creatures, to the highest communion with Himself. Consider too the time when He chose us. Paul dates it from "the beginning" (2 Thess. 2:13). God hath loved us ever since He was God, and while He is God He will continue to do so. God is from everlasting and He continues to be God to everlasting (Ps. 90:2), and His love to us is as old: "I have loved thee with an everlasting love." And His love is like Himself: causeless, changeless, endless.

The blessedness of election appears again in the comparative fewness of the elect. The paucity of men enjoying any privilege magnifies it the more, as in the case of the preservation of Noah and his family: "The ark . . . wherein few, that is, eight souls were saved" (1 Pet. 3:20). What a contrast was that from the whole world "of the ungodly," which all perished! The same fact and contrast was emphasized by Christ in Luke 12. "For all these things do the nations of the world seek after" (v. 30): that is, the things of time and sense, and God gives such to them. But in opposition thereto, the Lord says, "Fear not, little flock; for it is your Father's good pleasure to give you the kingdom" (v. 32). His design was to show the greater mercy of God that so few are reserved unto spiritual and eternal favors, while all others have only material and temporal things as their portion.

How this solemn fact should affect our hearts. Turn your eyes, dear reader, upon the world today, and look where you will, what do you behold? Are you not compelled to say of the present generation, in all nations alike, that God has left them to walk "in their own ways?" Must we not mournfully conclude of the men and women of this age that "the whole world lieth in wickedness" (1 John 5:19)? The sparse number that are of God, are indeed thinly sown, a small handful of gleaning in comparison with the whole great crop of mankind. And let it not be forgotten that what appears now before our eyes is but the actualization of that which was foreordained in eternity. There is no disappointed and defeated God on the throne of the universe. He has His way "in the whirlwind and in the storm" (Nab. 1:3).

And again we say how deeply should this startling contrast affect our hearts. "For a few to be singled forth and saved, when a multitude, yea, a generality of others are suffered to perish, how doth it heighten the mercy and grace of salvation to us; for God in His providence to order many outward means to deliver a few which He denies to others, who perish: how doth this affect the persons that are preserved? How much more when it is 'so great a salvation'" (T. Goodwin). This appears from what were types and mere shadows of it in Old Testament times, as in the case of the one small family of Noah alone being spared from the universal deluge. So, too, by the example of Lot, pulled out of Sodom by the hand of angels. And why? "The Lord being merciful unto him" says Genesis 19:16. Mark what a deep sense of and valuation upon Lot had of the same: "Behold now thy servant hath found grace in thy sight, and thou hast magnified thy mercy, which thou hast showed unto me in saving my life" (Gen. 19:19).

But there is this further to be considered: our being delivered from a condition of like wretchedness and wrath as pertains to the non-elect, which held not in the cases mentioned above. Noah was "A just man, and perfect in his generations" (Gen. 6:9), and Lot was "righteous" and "vexed with the filthy conversation of the wicked" (2 Pet. 2:7, 8). They were not guilty of those awful sins because of which God sent the flood and fire upon their fellows. But when we were ordained to salvation, we lay before God in a like condition of corruption and guilt as all mankind are in. It was only the sovereign decree of a sovereign God which purposed our being brought out of a state of sin and wrath into a state of grace and righteousness. How stupendous, then, was the mercy of God unto us, in making this difference (1 Cor. 4:7) between those in whom there was "no difference" (Rom. 3:22)! 0 what love, what wholehearted obedience, what praise are due unto Him.

Fourth, the blessedness of this doctrine appears in that a true apprehension thereof is a great promoter of holiness. According to the divine purpose the elect are destined to a holy calling (2 Tim. 1:9). In the accomplishment of that purpose, they are actually and effectually brought to holiness. God separates them from an ungodly world. He writes upon their hearts His Law and affixes to them His seal. They are made partakers of the divine nature, being renewed in the image of Him who created them. They are an habitation of God, their bodies becoming the temple of the Holy Spirit, and they are led by Him. A glorious change is thus wrought in them, transforming their character and conduct. They wash their robes and make them white in the blood of the Lamb. To them, old things are passed away and all things are become new: forgetting the things which are behind, they press forward to the things which are before. They are kings and priests unto God, and shall yet be adorned with crowns of glory.

There are those who, in their ignorance, say that the doctrine of election is a licentious one, that a belief of it is calculated to produce carelessness and a sense of security in sin. Such a charge is a blasphemous reflection upon the divine author of it. This truth, as we have shown at length, occupies a prominent place in the Word of God, and that Word is holy, and the whole of it profitable for instruction in righteousness (2 Tim. 3:16). The apostles one and all believed and taught this doctrine, and they were promoters of piety and not encouragers of loose living. It is true that this doctrine, like every other Scripture, may be perverted by wicked men and put to an evil use, but so far as militating against the truth, it only serves to demonstrate the fearful extent of human depravity. We also grant that unregenerate men may intellectually espouse this doctrine and then settle down into a fatalistic inertia. But we emphatically deny that a heart reception thereof will produce any such effect.

That faith, obedience, holiness are the inseparable consequences and fruits of election is unmistakably clear from the Scriptures (Acts 13:48; Eph. 1:4; 1 Thess. 1:4-7; Titus 1:1), and has been fully set forth by us in previous chapters. How can it be otherwise? Election always involves regeneration and sanctification, and when a regenerated and sanctified soul discovers that he owes his spiritual renewal solely to the sovereign predestination of God, how can he but be truly grateful and deeply thankful? And in what other way can he express his gratitude than in a holy course of fruitful obedience? An apprehension of the everlasting love of God for him will of necessity awaken in him a responsive love to God, and wherever that exists there will be a sincere effort to please Him in all things. The fact is that a spiritual sense of the distinguishing grace of God is the most powerful constraining motive unto genuine godliness.

Were we to enter into detail upon the principal elements of holiness this chapter would be extended indefinitely. A due consideration of the fact that there was nothing in us which moved God to fix His heart upon us, and that He foresaw us as ruined and hell-deserving creatures, will humble our souls as nothing else will. A spiritual realization that all our concerns are entirely at the disposal of God, will work in us a submission to His sovereign will as nothing else can. A believing perception that God set His heart upon us from everlasting, choosing us to be His peculiar treasure, will work in us a contempt of the world. The knowledge that fellow-Christians are the elect and beloved of God will evoke love and kindness unto them. The assurance that God's eternal purpose is immutable and guarantees the supply of our every need will impart solid comfort in every trial.

Chapter 11
Its Opposition

Wherever the doctrine of election is Scripturally presented it meets with fierce opposition and bitter declamation. It has been so throughout the entire course of this Christian era, and that, among all races and classes of people. Let the high prerogatives of God be set forth, let the sovereignty of His grace be proclaimed, let men be told they are but clay in the hands of the divine potter to be shaped into vessels of wrath or vessels of mercy as seemeth good in His sight, and at once there is an uproar and outcries of protest. Let the preacher insist that the fallen creature has no claim whatever upon his maker, that he stands before Him as a convicted felon, and is entitled to naught but everlasting judgment, and let him declare that all of Adam's progeny are so utterly depraved that their minds are "enmity against God" and therefore in a state of inveterate insubordination, that their hearts are so corrupt they have no desire for spiritual things, their wills so completely under the domination of evil they cannot turn unto the Lord, and he will he denounced as a heretic.

But this should neither surprise nor stagger the child of God. As he becomes more familiar with the Scriptures, he will find that in every generation the faithful servants of God have been hated and persecuted, some for proclaiming one part of the truth, some for another. When the sun shines on a dunghill, an odious stench is the consequence; when its rays fall upon the stagnant waters of a swamp, disease germs are multiplied. But is the sun to be blamed? Certainly not. So when the sword of the Spirit cuts to the root of human pride, reveals man to be a fallen and foul being, reduces him to an impotent creature, laying him in the dust as a bankrupt pauper, and declares him to be entirely dependent upon the discriminating pleasure of a sovereign God, there is a storm of opposition evoked, and a determined effort is made to silence such flesh-withering teaching.

The method which is usually followed by those who reject this truth is one of misrepresentation. The doctrine of election is so grand and glorious that to bear any opposition at all it must be perverted. Those who hate it can neither look upon nor speak of it as it really deserves. Election is treated by them as though it did not include a designation to faith and holiness, as though it was not a conforming of them unto the image of Christ; yea, as though the elect of God might continue to commit all manner of wickedness and yet go to heaven; and that the non-elect, no matter how virtuous they be, or how ardently they long for and strive after righteousness, must assuredly perish. False inferences are drawn, grotesque parodies exhibited, and unscrupulous tactics are employed to create prejudice.

By such devilish efforts do the enemies of God seek to distort and destroy this blessed doctrine. They besmirch it with mire, seek to overwhelm it with things odious, and present it to the indignant gaze of men as something to be repudiated and abominated. A monster of iniquity is thus created and christened "Election," and then presented to the world as something to be cast out as evil. Thereby multitudes have been cheated out of one of the most precious portions of divine truth, and thereby some of God's own people have been sorely perplexed and harassed. That the avowed opponents of Christ should revile a doctrine taught by Him and His apostles is only to be expected; but when those who profess to be His friends and followers join in denouncing this truth, it only serves to demonstrate the cunning of that old serpent the devil, who is never more pleased than when he can persuade nominal Christians to do his vile work for him. Then let not the reader be moved by such opposition.

The vast majority of these opposers have little or no real understanding of that which they set themselves against. They are largely ignorant of what the Scriptures teach thereon, and are too indolent to make any serious study of the subject. Whatever attention they do pay to it is mostly neutralized by the veil of prejudice which obstructs their vision. But when such persons examine the doctrine with sufficient diligence to discover that it leads only to holiness—holiness in heart and life—then they redouble their efforts to do away with it. When professing Christians unite with its detractors, charity obliges us to conclude that it is because of failure to properly understand the doctrine. They take a one-sided view of this truth: they view it through distorted lenses: they contemplate it from the wrong angle. They fail to see that election originated in everlasting love, that it is the choosing of a company to eternal salvation, who otherwise would have inevitably perished, and that it makes that company a willing, obedient, and holy people.

We shall not now attempt to cover the whole range of objections which have been brought against the doctrine of election, yet our discussion would be incomplete if we totally ignored them. The workings of unbelief are always endless in number. The child of God needs to be occupied with something more profitable. Yet we feel that we should at least consider briefly the ones which the enemy suppose are the most forceful and formidable. Not that our object is to try and convince them of their errors, but rather with the design of seeking to help fellow-believers who may have been shaken if not stumbled thereby. Our business is not to refute error, but (under God) to establish our readers in the truth. Yet in order to do this, it is sometimes needful to expose the wiles of Satan, show how baseless are the most insidious of his lies, and seek to remove from the Christian's mind any injurious effect they may have had upon him.

Before starting on this unwelcome task let it be pointed out that any lack of ability on our part to refute the calumnies of opponents, is no proof that their position is impregnable. As the renowned Butler pointed out long ago in his masterly "Analogy," "If a truth is established, objections are nothing. The one (i.e., Truth) is founded upon our knowledge, and the other on our ignorance." Once it is established that two and two make four, no quibbling or juggling with figures can disprove it. "We should never suffer what we know to be disturbed by what we know not" said that master of logic, Paley. Once we see anything to be clearly taught in Holy Writ, we must not allow either our own prejudices or the antagonism of others to shake our confidence in or adherence to it. If we are satisfied that we have a "thus saith the Lord" to rest upon, it matters nothing if we be unable to show the sophistry in the arguments brought to bear against it. Be assured that God is true, even if that involves our accounting every man a liar.

The bitterest enemies against the doctrine of election are the Papists: This is exactly what might be expected, for the truth of election can never be made to square with the dogma of human merits—the one is diametrically opposed to the other. Every man who loves himself and seeks salvation by his own works, will loathe sovereign grace, and seek to load it with contempt. On the other hand, those who have been effectually humbled by the Holy Spirit and brought to realize that they are utterly dependent upon the discriminating mercy of God, will have no hankerings after nor patience with a system which sets the crown of honor upon the creature. History bears ample testimony that Rome detests the very name of Calvinism. "From all sects there may be some hope of obtaining converts to Rome except Calvinism" said the late "Cardinal" Manning. And he was right, as our own degenerate age bears full witness, for while no regenerated Calvinist will ever be fatally deceived by the wiles of the mother of harlots, yet thousands of

"Protestant" Arminians are annually rushing to her arms.

It is an irrefutable fact that as Calvinism has met with less and less favor in the leading Protestant bodies, as the sovereignty of God and His electing love have been more and more crowded out of their pulpits, that Rome has made increasing progress, until today she must have, both in England and in the U.S.A., a greater number of followers than any single evangelical denomination. But what is saddest of all is that, the vast majority of those now occupying so-called Protestant pulpits are preaching the very things which further Rome's interests. Their insistence upon the freedom of fallen man's will-to-good must fill the Papist leaders with delight—in the Council of Trent she anathematized all who affirmed the contrary. To what extent the leaven of Popery has spread may be seen in that "Evangelical Protestants" who oppose the doctrine of election are now employing the self-same objections as were used by the Italian doctors four hundred years ago.

But to come now to some of the objections. First, such a doctrine is utterly unreasonable. When it suits her purpose Rome makes a big pretense of appealing to human reason, but at other times she demands that her children close their mental eyes and accept blindly whatever their unholy "mother" is pleased to palm upon them. Yet Rome is by no means the only offender at this point: multitudes of those who regard themselves as Protestants are guilty of the same thing. So too almost the first response of those who make no religious profession, when they have this truth presented to their notice, is to exclaim, "Such a concept does not appeal to me at all. If there is a God, and if He has anything at all to do with our present lives, I believe He will give us all an equal chance, balance our good deeds against our bad, and be merciful unto us. To say that He has favorites among His creatures, and that He fixed the destiny of every one before his birth, strikes me as outrageous."

Our first reply to such an objection is that, it is quite beside the point. The only matter which needs deciding at the outset is, What saith the Scriptures? If election be clearly taught therein, that settles the matter for the child of God, settles it once and for all. Whether he understands it or no, he knows that God cannot lie, and that His Word is "true from the beginning" (Ps. 119:160). If his opponent will not allow this, then there is no common ground on which they can meet, and it is utterly futile to discuss the matter with him. Under no circumstances must the Christian allow himself to be drawn away from his stand on the impregnable rock of Holy Writ, and descend to the treacherous ground of human reason. Only on that high plane can he successfully withstand the onslaughts of Satan. Reread Matthew 4 and observe how Christ vanquished the tempter.

The holy Word of God does not come to us craving acceptance at the bar of human reason. Instead, it demands that human reason surrender itself to its divine authority and receive unmurmuringly its inerrant contents. It emphatically and repeatedly warns men that if they despise its authority and reject its teachings, it is to their certain eternal undoing. It is by that Word each of us shall be weighed, measured, judged in the day to come; and therefore it is the part of human wisdom to bow to and thankfully receive its inspired declarations. The supreme act of right reason, my reader, is to submit unreservedly unto divine wisdom, and accept with childlike simplicity the revelation which God has graciously given us. Any other, any different attitude thereto, is utterly unreasonable—the derangement of pride. How thankful we should be that the ancient of days condescends to instruct us.

Our second reply to the above objection is that, in a written revelation from heaven we should fully expect to find much that transcends the grasp of our poor earth-bound minds. What was the use of God communicating to us only that which we already knew? Nor are the Scriptures given to us as a field on which reason may be exercised: what they require are faith and obedience. And faith is not a blind, unintelligible thing, but confidence in its Author, an assurance that He is too wise to err, too righteous to be unjust; and therefore that He is infinitely worthy of our trust and subjection to His holy will. But just because God's Word is addressed to faith, there is much in it which is contrary to nature, much that is most mysterious, much that leaves us wondering. Faith must be tested—to prove its genuineness. And God delights to honor faith: though His Word be not written to satisfy curiosity, and though many questions are not there fully answered, yet the more faith be exercised, the fuller is the light granted.

God Himself is profoundly mysterious. "Lo, these are parts of His ways: but how little a portion is heard of Him!" (Job 26:14); "How unsearchable are his judgments, and his ways past finding out" (Rom. 11:33). We must therefore expect to find in the Bible much that strikes us as strange: things "hard to be understood" (2 Peter 3:16). The creation of the universe out of nothing, at the mere fiat of the Almighty, is beyond the grasp of the finite mind. The divine incarnation transcends human reason: "Great is the mystery of godliness: God was manifest in the flesh" (2 Tim. 3:16): that Christ should be conceived and born of a woman who had known no contact with man, cannot be accounted for by human reason. The resurrection of our bodies, thousands of years after they had gone to dust, is inexplicable. Is it not, then, most unreasonable to reject the truth of election because human reason cannot fathom it!

Second, it is highly unjust. Rebels against the supreme sovereign hesitate not to charge Him with unrighteousness because He is pleased to exercise His own rights, and determine the destiny of His creatures. They argue that all men should be dealt with on the same footing, that all should be given an equal opportunity of salvation. They say that if God shows mercy unto one and withholds it from another, such partiality is grossly unfair. To such an objector we reply in the language of Holy Writ: "Nay but, O man, who art thou that repliest against God? Shall the thing formed say to him that formed it, Why hast thou made me thus? Hath not the potter power over the clay of the same lump, to make one vessel unto honor, and another unto dishonor?" (Rom. 9:20, 21). And there we leave him.

But some of the Lord's own people are disturbed by this difficulty. First, then, we would remind them that God is "light" (1 John 1:5), as well as "love." God is ineffably holy, as well as infinitely gracious. As the Holy One He abhors all evil, and as the moral governor of His creatures it becomes Him to eternally manifest His hatred of sin. As the gracious one He is pleased to bestow favors upon the undeserving, and to give an everlasting demonstration that He is "the Father of mercies." Now in election both of these designs are unmistakably accomplished. In the preterition and condemnation of the non-elect, God gives full proof of His holiness and justice, by visiting upon them the due reward of their iniquities. In the foreordination and salvation of His chosen people, God makes a clear display of the exceeding riches of His grace.

Suppose that God had willed the destruction of the entire human race: then what? Had that been unjust? Certainly not. There could be no injustice whatever in visiting upon criminals the penalty of that law which they had defiantly broken. But what had then become of God's mercy? Had naught but inexorable justice been exercised by an offended God, then every descendant of fallen Adam had inevitably been consigned to hell. Now on the other hand. Suppose God had decided to open wide the floodgates of mercy, and carry the whole human race to heaven: then what? The wages of sin is death—eternal death. But if every man sinned, and none died, what evidence would there be that divine justice was anything more than an empty name? If God had saved all sinners, would not that necessarily inculcate light views of sin? If all were taken to heaven, should we not conclude that this was due us as a right?

Because all are guilty, are the hands of divine mercy to be tied? If not, if mercy may be exercised, then is God obliged to wholly renounce His justice? If God be pleased to exercise mercy upon some, who have no claim thereto, cannot He also show Himself to be a just judge by inflicting upon others the punishment to which they are entitled? What wrong does a creditor do if he releases one and enforces his demands on another? Am I unjust because I bestow charity on a beggar, and decline doing so to his fellow? Then is the great God less free to impart His gifts where He pleases? Before the above objection can have any force it must be proved that every creature (because he is a creature) is entitled to everlasting bliss, and that even though he falls into sin and becomes a rebel against his maker, God is morally obliged to save him. To such absurdities is the objector necessarily reduced.

"If eternal felicity be due to every man without exception, surely temporal felicity must be their due likewise: if they have a right to the greater their claim to the less can hardly be doubted. If the Omnipotent is bound, on penalty of becoming unjust, to do all He can to make every individual happy in the next life; He must be equally bound to render every individual happy in this. But are all men happy? Look around the world and say Yes if you can. Is the Creator therefore unjust? none but Satan would suggest it: none but his echoes will affirm it. The Lord is a God of truth, and without iniquity: just and right is He. . . . Is the constituted order of things mysterious? impenetrably so. Yet the mysteriousness of God's dispensations evinces, not the injustice of the sovereign dispenser, but the shallowness of human comprehension, and the shortness of human sight. Let us then, by embracing and revering the Scriptural doctrines of predestination and providence, give God credit for being infinitely wise, just, and good; though for the present His way is in the deep, and His footsteps are not known" (A. Toplady, author of "Rock of Ages").

Finally, let it be pointed out that God never refuses mercy to anyone who humbly seeks it. Sinners are freely invited to forsake their wicked ways and sue unto the Lord for pardon. The gospel feast is spread before them; if they refuse to partake thereof, if instead they loathe and turn away from it with disdain, is not their blood on their own heads? What sort of "justice" is it which requires God to bring to heaven those who hate Him? If God has performed a miracle of grace in you, my reader, and begotten in your heart a love for Him, be fervently thankful for the same, and disturb not your peace and joy by asking why He has not done the same for your fellow transgressors.

Third, the gospel offer is meaningless. Those who refuse to receive the truth of divine election are fond of saying that the idea of God having eternally chosen one and passed by another of His creatures would reduce evangelical preaching to a farce. They argue that if God has foreordained a part of the human race to destruction, it can contain no bona fide offer of salvation to them. Let it first be pointed out that this objection does not press upon Calvinism alone, but applies with the same force to Arminianism. Free-willers deny the absoluteness of the divine decrees, yet they affirm the divine presence. Then let us turn the question round upon him: How can God in good faith bid men to repent and believe the gospel, when He infallibly foreknows they will never do so? If he supposes the former objection to be irrefutable, he will find our question is unanswerable by his own principles.

Whatever difficulty may be presented at this point—and the writer has no thought of belittling it—one thing is clear: to whomsoever the gospel comes, God is sincere in bidding its hearers submit to its requirements, receive its glad tidings, and be saved thereby. Whether we can or cannot perceive how this is so, matters nothing; but the integrity of the divine character must be maintained at all costs. The mere fact that we are unable to discern the consistency and harmony between two distinct lines of truth, certainly does not warrant our rejecting either one of them. The doctrine of sovereign election is clearly revealed in the Scriptures; so too is the genuineness of the gospel offer to all who receive it: the one must be contended for as earnestly as the other.

But do we not create our own difficulty by supposing that the salvation of men is God's sole object, or even His principal design, in the sending forth of the gospel? But what other ends, it may be asked, are accomplished thereby? Many. God's first end in the gospel, as in everything else, is the honor of His own great name and the glory of His Son. In the gospel the character of God and the excellency of Christ are more fully revealed than anywhere else. That a worldwide testimony should be borne thereto is infinitely fitting. That men should have made known to them the ineffable perfections of Him with whom they have to do is certainly most desirable. God, then, is magnified and the matchless worth of His Son proclaimed, even though not one sinner ever believed and was saved thereby.

Again; the preaching of the gospel is the appointed instrument in the hands of the Holy Spirit whereby the elect are brought to Christ. God does not disdain instrumental agencies, but is pleased to employ them: He who ordained the end, also appointed the means thereto. Just because God's elect are "scattered abroad" (John 11:52) among all nations, He has commanded that "Repentance and remission of sins should be preached in His name among all nations" (Luke 24:47). It is by hearing the gospel they are called out of the world. By nature God's elect are the children of wrath "even as others": they are lost sinners needing a Savior, and apart from Christ there is no salvation for them. Therefore the gospel must be preached to and believed in by them before they can rejoice in the knowledge that their sins are forgiven. The gospel, then, is God's great winnowing fan, separating the wheat from the chaff, and gathering the former into His garner.

Moreover, the non-elect gain much from the gospel even though it effects not their eternal salvation. The world exists for the elect's sake, yet all share the benefits of it. The sun shines upon the evil as well as the good; refreshing showers fall upon the lands of the wicked as truly as on the ground of the righteous. So God causes the gospel to reach the ears of many of the non-elect, as well as those of His favored people. Why? Because it is one of His powerful agencies to hold in check the wickedness of fallen men. Millions who are never saved by it, are reformed: their lusts are bridled, their outward course improved, and society is made more suitable for the saints to live in. Compare the peoples without the gospel and those who have it: in the case of the latter it will be found that higher morality obtains even where there is no spirituality.

Finally, it should be pointed out that the gospel is made a real test of the characters of all who hear it. The Scriptures declare that man is a fallen, corrupt, and sin-loving creature. They insist that his mind is enmity against God, that he loves darkness rather than light, that he will not be subject to God under any circumstances. Yet who believes such humbling truths? But the response to the gospel by the non-elect demonstrates the verity of God's Word. Their continued impenitence, unbelief, and disobedience bears witness to their total depravity. God instructed Moses to go unto Pharaoh and make request that Israel should be allowed to worship Jehovah in the wilderness; yet in the next verse He told him, "I am sure that the king of Egypt will not let you go, not by a mighty hand" (Ex. 3:18, 19).Then why send Moses on such an errand? To make manifest the hardness of Pharaoh's heart, the stubbornness of his will, and the justice of God in destroying such a wretch.

Fourth, it destroys human responsibility. Arminians contend that to affirm God has unalterably decreed and fixed the history and destiny of every man, would be to demolish human accountability, that in such a case man would be no better than a machine. They insist that man's will must be free, free equally unto good and evil, or otherwise he would cease to be a moral agent. They argue that unless a person's actions are without compulsion, and are in accordance with his own desires and inclinations, he could not be justly held responsible for them. From this premise the conclusion is drawn that it is the creature and not the Creator who chooses and decides his eternal destiny, for if his acts are self-determined, they cannot be divinely determined.

Such an objection is really a descent into the dark regions of philosophy and metaphysics, a specious attempt of the Enemy to lead us away from the realm of divine revelation. So long as we abide by the Holy Scriptures, we are safe, but as soon as we resort to reasoning upon spiritual matters we are certain to err. God has already made known all that He deems well for us to know in this life, and any attempt to be wise above that which is written is naught but folly and impiety. From the Scriptures it is clear as a sunbeam that man—whether considered as unfallen or fallen—is a responsible being, that he is made to reap whatsoever he sows, that he will yet have to render unto God an account of all his deeds and be judged accordingly; and nothing must be allowed to weaken the impression of these solemn facts upon our minds.

The same line of reasoning has been employed by those who reject the verbal inspiration of the Scriptures. It is contended that such a postulate entirely eliminates the human element from the Bible, that if we insist (as this writer, for one, most emphatically does) that not only the thoughts and sentiments but the very language itself is divine, that every word and syllable of the original manuscripts was God-breathed then the human penman employed in transmitting the same were merely automatons. But this we know is false. In like manner, with as much show of reason might the objector declare that Christ cannot be both divine and human: that if He be God, He cannot be man, and that if He be truly man, it follows that He cannot be God. What is reasoning worth, my reader, upon such matters!

The books of the Bible were written by men, written by them under the free exercise of their natural faculties, in such a way that the impress of their personalities is clearly left upon their several contributions. Nevertheless, they originated nothing: they were "moved by the Holy Ghost" (2 Peter 1:21), and so completely were they controlled by Him, that not the slightest shadow of a mistake or error was made by them, and everything they wrote was "the words which . . . the Holy Ghost teacheth" (1 Cor. 2:13). The redeemer is the Son of man, who was "in all things . . . made like unto His brethren" (Heb. 2:17); yet because His humanity was taken into union with His divine person everything He did possessed a unique and infinite value. Man is a moral agent, acting according to the desires and dictates of his nature: he is at the same time a creature, fully controlled and determined by his Creator. In each of these cases the divine and human elements coalesce, but the divine dominates, yet not to the exclusion of the human.

"Woe unto the world because of offenses! for it must needs be that offenses come." Then surely, may an objector reply, there can be no guilt resting on him who introduces that which is inevitable. Different far was the teaching of Christ: "but woe to that man by whom the offense cometh" (Matt. 18:7). "When ye shall hear of wars and rumors of wars, be ye not troubled: for such things must needs be" (Mark 13:7). There is a must-be for these death-dealing scourges, yet that alters not the criminality of the instigators of them. There is a needs-be for "heresies" (I Cor. 11:19), yet the heretics themselves are blamable. Absolute necessity and human responsibility are, therefore, perfectly compatible, whether we can perceive their consistency or no.

Fifth, it is objected against the truth of predestination that it supersedes the use of means and renders all incentives to human endeavor negatory. It is asserted that if God has elected a man unto salvation that he will be saved although he remains utterly unconcerned and continues to take his fill of sin; that if he has not been elected, then no efforts to obtain eternal life would be of any use. It is said that for men to be told they have been divinely ordained either to life or death by an eternal and immutable decree, they will at once conclude that it makes no difference whatever how they conduct themselves, since no acts of theirs can to the slightest decree either impede or promote the foreordination of God. Thus, it is argued, all motives to diligence are effectually neutralized, that it is subversive of every exhortation to morality and spirituality.

Really this is the most senseless of all objections. It is not an objection at all against the Scriptural doctrine of predestination, but against an entirely different concept, one hatched in the brains of ignorance, or conceived by malignity in order to bring odium on the truth. The only sort of predestination to which this objection is applicable, would be an absolute pre-appointment to an end without any regard to the means. Stripped of all ambiguity, this objection presupposes that God secures His purposes without employing any instrumental agencies. Thus, when the objection is exposed in its nakedness we see at once what a sorry figure it cuts. Those whom God has elected to salvation He has chosen to it "through sanctification of the Spirit and belief of the Truth" (II Thess. 2:13).

The fact is that God decreed to bring His elect to glory in a way of sanctification, and in no other way than that; and throughout their entire course. He treats them as rational and accountable creatures, using suitable means and motives to draw out their hearts unto Himself. To affirm that if they are elected they will reach heaven whether sanctified or no, is just as silly as to say Abraham might have been the father of many nations although he had died in infancy, or that Hezekiah could have lived his extra fifteen years without food or sleep. Prior to the taking of Jericho it was divinely revealed to Joshua that he should be master of that place (6:2): the assurance was absolute. Did, then, Israel's leader conclude that no action was needed, that all might sit down and fold their arms? No; he arranged the procession around its walls in obedience to God's command, and the event was accomplished accordingly.

We turn now briefly to consider some of the principal Scriptures used by those who resist the Truth. "Because I have called, and ye refused; I have stretched out my hand, and no man regarded; but ye have set at naught all my counsel, and would none of my reproof" (Prov. 1:24, 25). "I have spread out my hands all the day unto a rebellious people which walketh in a way that was not good, after their own thoughts" (Isa. 65:2). "How often would I have gathered thy children together . . . and ye would not" (Matt. 23:37). We are told by Arminians that these declarations are irreconcilable with Calvinism, that they show plainly the will of God can be resisted and thwarted by men. But most certainly a disappointed and defeated God is not the God of Holy Writ. To draw from these verses the conclusion that the divine decrees fail of accomplishment is utterly erroneous: they have nothing whatever to do with God's eternal purpose, but instead, they respect only His external agencies, whereby He enforces man's responsibility, tests his character, and makes evident the wickedness of his heart.

"For God so loved the world that he gave his only begotten Son" (John 3:16). From these words it is urged that if God loves the world He desires the salvation of the whole human race, and that it was for this end He provided a Savior for them. Here it is a case of being misled by the mere sound of a word, instead of ascertaining its real import. To say that God gave His Son with the design of providing salvation for all of Adam's children is manifestly absurd, for half of them had already died before Christ was born, and the vast majority of them perished in heathen darkness. Where is there the slightest hint in the Old Testament that God loved the Egyptians, the Canaanites, the Babylonians? And where else in the New Testament is there any statement that God loves all mankind? The "world" in John 3:16 (as in many other places) is a general term, used in contrast from Israel, who imagined they had a monopoly on redemption. God's love extends far beyond the bounds of Judaism, embracing His elect scattered among all nations.

"And ye will not come to me, that ye might have life" (John 5:40). Strange to say this is one of the verses appealed to by those who will not have election at any price. They suppose it teaches the free will unto good of fallen man, and that Christ seriously intended the salvation of those who despise and reject Him. But what is there in these words which declares that Christ seriously intended their salvation? Do they not rather signify that He was here preferring a solemn charge against them? So far from our Lord's utterance implying that these men had the power within themselves to come to Him, they rather declare the perversity and stubbornness of their wills. Instead of any inclination for the Holy One, they hated Him.

"Who will have all men to be saved, and to come unto the knowledge of the truth . . . who gave Himself a ransom for all" (1 Tim. 2:4, 6). In order to understand these words they must not be considered separately, but in connection with their setting. From the context it is unmistakably evident that the "all men" God wills to be saved and for whom Christ died are all men without regard to national distinctions. Timothy's ministry was exercised chiefly among Jewish converts, many of whom still retained their racial prejudices, so that they were unwilling to submit to the authority of heathen rulers. This was why the Pharisees had sought to discredit Christ before all people when they asked Him whether it was lawful to pay tribute to Caesar. Paul here tells Timothy that Christians were not only to yield obedience unto Gentile rulers, but to pray for them as well (vv. 1, 2).

In 1 Timothy 2 Paul struck at the very root of the prejudice which Timothy was called upon to combat. That law of Moses was now set aside, the distinction which so long obtained between the lineal descendants of Abraham and the rest of mankind no longer obtained: God willed the salvation of Gentiles and Jews alike. Note particularly these details. First, "There is one God [see Rom. 3:29, 30], and one mediator between God and [not "the Jews" but] men" (v. 5). Second, "Who gave himself a ransom for all [indefinitely], to be testified in due time." (v. 6): when Christ was crucified it was not generally understood, not even among His disciples, that He gave Himself for Gentiles and Jews alike; but in "due time" (particularly under Paul's ministry), it was clearly "testified." Third, "whereunto I am ordained a preacher and an apostle . . . a teacher of the Gentiles" (v. 7). Fourth, "I [with apostolic authority] will therefore that men pray everywhere" (v. 8): those professing the faith of Christ must drop at once and forever their Jewish notions and customs—Jerusalem no longer possessed any peculiar sanctity.

"We see Jesus . . . that he by the grace of God should taste death for every man" (Heb. 2:9). Have you taken the trouble to ascertain how that expression is used elsewhere in the New Testament? "And then shall every man have praise of God" (1 Cor. 4:5). Does that mean all of Adam's race? How can it, when "depart from me, ye cursed" will be the portion of many? "The head of every man is Christ" (1 Cor. 11:3): was He the Head of Judas or Nero? "The manifestation of the Spirit is given to every man" (1 Cor. 12:7). But some are "sensual, having not the Spirit" (Jude v. 19 and cf. Rom. 8:9). It is "everyone in God's family" that is meant in all of these epistle passages: note how the "everyone" of Hebrews 2:9 are defined as "many sons" (v. 10), "brethren" (v. 11), "children" (vv. 12-14).

"There shall be false teachers among you who truly shall bring in damnable heresies, even denying the Lord that bought them" (1 Peter 2:1). This verse is often cited in an attempt to disprove that Christ died for the elect only, which only serves to show what desperate shifts our opponents are reduced to. Why the verse makes no reference unto Christ at all, still less to His death! The Greek word here is not kurios at all—the one commonly used when referring to the Lord Jesus; but despotes. The only places where it occurs, when applied to a divine person, are Luke 22:9; Acts 4:24; 2 Timothy 2:22; Jude 4; Revelation 6:10, in all of which God the Father is plainly intended, and in most of them as manifestly distinguished from Christ. "Buying" here has reference to temporal deliverance, being taken from Deuteronomy 32:6. Peter was writing to Jews, who boasted loudly they were a people purchased by the Lord, and therefore he used this expression to aggravate the impiety of these false teachers among the Jews.

"Not willing that any should perish, but that all should come to repentance" (2 Peter 3:9). Here again a false meaning is extracted by divorcing a snippet from its context. The key to this verse is found in the word "us-ward": "the Lord is . . . longsuffering to us-ward," for He is not willing that "any" of them should perish. And who are they? Why, the "beloved" of verse 1 (those mentioned at the beginning of the First Epistle, "elect according to the foreknowledge of God the Father, through sanctification of the Spirit"), and because He has purposed that "all" of them should come to repentance," He defers the second coming of Christ (vv. 3, 4). Christ will not return till the last of His people are safely in the Ark of Salvation.

Chapter 12
Its Publication

During the last two or three generations the pulpit has given less and less prominence to doctrinal preaching, until today—with very rare exceptions—it has no place at all. In some quarters the cry from the pew was, We want living experience and not dry doctrine; in others, We need practical sermons and not metaphysical dogmas; and yet others, Give us Christ and not theology. Sad to say, such senseless cries were generally heeded: "senseless" we say, for there is no other safe way of testing experience, as there is no foundation for practicals to be built upon, if they be divorced from Scriptural doctrine; while Christ cannot be known unless He be preached (1 Cor. 1:23), and He certainly cannot be "preached" if doctrine is shelved. Various reasons may be given for the lamentable failure of the pulpit: chief among them being laziness, desire for popularity, superficial and lop-sided "evangelism," love of the sensational.

Laziness. It is a far more exacting task, one which calls for much closer confinement in the study, to prepare a series of sermons on say the doctrine of justification, than it does to make addresses on prayer, missions, or personal-work. It demands a far wider acquaintance with the Scriptures, a more rigid disciplining of the mind, and a more extensive perusal of the older writers. But this was too exacting for most of the ministers, and so they chose the line of least resistance and followed an easier course. It is because of his proneness to this weakness that the minister is particularly exhorted, "Give attendance to reading . . . take heed unto thyself, and unto the doctrine; continue in them" (1 Tim. 4:13, 16); and again, "Study to show thyself approved unto God, a workman that needeth not to be ashamed" (2 Tim. 2:15).

Desire for popularity. It is natural that the preacher should wish to please his hearers, but it is spiritual for him to desire and aim at the approbation of God. Nor can any man serve two masters. As the apostle expressly declared, "For if I yet pleased men, I should not be the servant of Christ" (Gal. 1:10): solemn words are those. How they condemn them whose chief aim is to preach to crowded churches. Yet what grace it requires to swim against the tide of public opinion, and preach that which is unacceptable to the natural man. But on the other hand, how fearful will be the doom of those who, from a determination to curry favor with men, deliberately withheld those portions of the truth most needed by their hearers. "Ye shall not add unto the word which I command you, neither shall ye diminish ought from it" (Deut. 4:2). O to be able to say with Paul, "I kept back nothing that was profitable unto you. . . . I am pure from the blood of all" (Acts 20:20, 26).

A superficial and lop-sided "evangelism." Many of the pulpiteers of the past fifty years acted as though the first and last object of their calling was the salvation of souls, everything being made to bend to that aim. In consequence, the feeding of the sheep, the maintaining of a Scriptural discipline in the church, and the inculcation of practical piety, was crowded out; and only too often all sorts of worldly devices and fleshly methods were employed under the plea that the end justified the means; and thus the churches were filled with unregenerate members. In reality, such men defeated their own aim. The hard heart must be ploughed and harrowed before it can be receptive to the gospel seed. Doctrinal instruction must be given on the character of God, the requirements of His law, the nature and heinousness of sin, if a foundation is to be laid for true evangelism. It is useless to preach Christ unto souls until they see and feel their desperate need of Him.

Love of the sensational. In more recent times the current has changed. A generation arose which was less tolerant even of superficial evangelism, which demurred at hearing anything which was calculated to make them the least uneasy in their sins. Of course, such people must not be driven from the churches: they must be catered to and given something which would tickle their ears. The stage of public action afforded abundant material. The World-war and such characters as the Kaiser, Stalin, and Mussolini were much in the public eye, as Hitler and Abyssinia have been since. Under the guise of expounding prophecy the pulpit turned its attention to what was styled "the Signs of the Times" and the pew was made to believe that the "dictators" were fulfilling the predictions of Daniel and the Apocalypse. There was nothing in such preaching that pricked the conscience, yet tens of thousands were deluded into thinking that the very hearing of such rubbish made them religious; and thus the churches were enabled to "carry on."

Ere proceeding further, let it be pointed out that the objections most commonly made against doctrinal preaching are quite pointless. Take, first, the clamor for experimental preaching. In certain quarters—quarters which though very restricted, yet consider themselves the very champions of orthodoxy and the highest exponents of vital godliness—the demand is for a detailed tracing out of the varied experiences of a quickened soul both under the law and under grace, and any other type of preaching, especially doctrinal, is frowned upon as supplying nothing but the husk. But as one writer tersely put it, "Though matters of doctrine are by some considered merely as the shell of religion, and experience as the kernel, yet let it be remembered that there is no coming to the kernel but through the shell; and while the kernel gives value to the shell, yet the shell is the guardian of the kernel. Destroy that, and you injure this." Eliminate doctrine and you have nothing left to test experience by, and mysticism and fanaticism are inevitable.

In other quarters the demand has been for preaching along practical lines, such people supposing and insisting that doctrinal preaching is merely theoretical and impracticable. Such a concept betrays woeful ignorance. "All Scripture is given by inspiration of God, and is profitable [first] for doctrine, [and then] for reproof, for correction, for instruction in righteousness" (2 Tim. 3:16). Study the epistles of Paul and see how steadily that order is maintained. Romans 1-11 are strictly doctrinal; 12-16 practical exhortations. Take a concrete example: in 1 Timothy 1:9, 10 the apostle draws up a catalog of sins against which the denunciations of the law are imminently directed, and then he added "And if there be any other thing which is contrary to sound doctrine." What a plain intimation is this that error in principles fundamental has a most unfavorable influence on practicals, and that in proportion as the doctrine of God is disbelieved the authority of God is disowned. It is the doctrine which supplies motives for obedience to the precepts.

In connection with those who cry, preach Christ and not theology, we have long observed that they never preach Him as the One with whom God made a covenant (Ps. 89:3), nor as His "elect" in whom His soul delighteth (Isa. 42:1). They preach a "Christ" which is the product of their own imaginations, the creation of sentiment. If we preach the Christ of Scripture we must set Him forth as the servant of God's choice (1 Peter 2:4), as the Lamb "foreordained before the foundation of the world" (1 Peter 1:19, 20), as the One "set for the fall and the rising again of many in Israel" (Luke 2:34), as "the stone of stumbling and a rock of offense." Christ is not to be preached as separate from His members, but as the Head of His mystical body—Christ and those whom God chose in Him are one, eternally and immutably one. Then preach not a mutilated Christ. Preach Him according to the eternal counsels of God.

Now if doctrinal preaching generally be so unpopular, the doctrine of election is particularly and pre-eminently so. Sermons on predestination are, with very rare exceptions, hotly resented and bitterly denounced. "There seems to be an inevitable prejudice in the human mind against this doctrine, and although most other doctrines will be received by professing Christians, some with caution, others with pleasure, yet this one seems to be most frequently disregarded and discarded. In many of our pulpits it would be reckoned a high sin and treason to preach a sermon upon election" (C. H. Spurgeon). If that was the case fifty years ago, much more is it so now. Even in avowedly orthodox circles the very mention of predestination is like waving a red rag before a bull. Nothing so quickly makes manifest the enmity of the carnal mind in the smug religionist and self-righteous pharisees as does the proclamation of the divine sovereignty and His discriminating grace; and few indeed are the men now left who dare to contend valiantly for the truth.

Fearful beyond words are the lengths to which the horror and hatred of election have carried even avowedly evangelical leaders in their blasphemous speeches against this blessed truth: we refuse to pollute these pages by quoting from their ungodly speeches. Some have gone so far as to say that, even if predestination be revealed in the Scriptures it is a dangerous doctrine, creating dissent and division, and therefore it ought not to be preached in the churches; which is the self-same objection used by the Romanists against giving the Word of God to the common people in their own mother tongue. If we are to whittle down the truth so as to preach only that which is acceptable to the natural man, how much would be left? The preaching of Christ crucified is to the Jews a stumbling block and to the Greeks foolishness (1 Cor. 1:23): is the pulpit to be silent thereon? Shall the servants of God cease proclaiming the person, office and work of His beloved Son, merely because He is "a stone of stumbling and a rock of offense" (1 Peter 2:8) to the reprobate?

Many are the objections brought against this doctrine by those who desire to discredit it. Some say election should not be preached because it is so mysterious, and secret things belong unto the Lord. But it is not a secret, for God has plainly revealed it in His Word; and if it is not be to preached because of its mysteriousness, then for the same reason nothing must be said about the unity of the divine nature subsisting in a trinity of Persons, nor of the virgin-birth, nor of the resurrection of the dead. According to others, the doctrine of election cuts the nerve of all missionary enterprise, in fact stands opposed to all preaching, rendering it entirely negatory. Then in such a case the preaching of Paul himself was altogether useless, for it was full of this doctrine: read his epistles and it will be found that he proclaimed election continually, yet we never read of him ceasing to preach it because it rendered his labor useless.

Paul taught that "It is God which worketh in you both to will and to do of his good pleasure" (Phil. 2:13), yet we do not find that on this account he ceased to exhort men to will and endeavor those things which are pleasing to God, and to work themselves with all their might. If we are unable to perceive the consistency of the two things, that is no reason why we should refuse to believe and heed either the one or the other. Some argue against election because the preaching of it shakes assurance and fills the minds of men with doubts and fears. But in our day especially we should be thankful for any truth which shatters the complacency of empty professors and arouses the indifferent to examine themselves before God. With as much reason might it be said that the doctrine of regeneration should not be promulgated, for is it any easier to make sure that I have been truly born again than it is to ascertain that I am one of God's elect? It is not.

Still others insist that election should not be preached because the ungodly will make an evil use of it, that they will shelter behind it to excuse their unconcern and procrastination, arguing that if they are elected to salvation that in the meantime they may live as they please and take their fill of sin. Such an objection is puerile, childish in the extreme. But what truth is there that the wicked will not pervert? Why, they will turn the grace of God into lasciviousness, and use (or rather misuse) His very goodness, His mercy, His long sufferance, for continuance in a course of evil doing. Arminians tells us that to preach the eternal security of the Christian encourages slothfulness; while at the opposite extreme, hyper-Calvinists object to the exhorting of the unregenerate unto repentance and faith on the ground that it inculcates creature ability. Let us not pretend to be wise above what is written, but preach all the counsel of God and leave results to Him.

The servant of God must not be intimidated or deterred from professing and proclaiming the unadulterated truth. His commission today is the same as Ezekiel's of old: "Be not afraid of them, neither be afraid of their words, though briers and thorns be with thee, and thou dost dwell among scorpions: be not afraid of their words, nor be dismayed at their looks, though they be a rebellious house. And thou shalt speak my words unto them whether they will hear, or whether they will forbear: for they are most rebellious" (Ezek. 2:6, 7). He must expect to encounter opposition, especially from those making the loudest profession, and fortify himself against it. The announcement of God's sovereign choice of men has evoked the spirit of malice and persecution from earliest times. It did so as far back as the days of Samuel. When the prophet announced to Jesse concerning his seven sons "neither hath the Lord chosen these" (1 Sam. 16:10), the anger of his firstborn was kindled against David (1 Sam. 17:28). So too when Christ Himself stressed the distinguishing grace of God unto the Gentile widow of Zarephath and Naaman the Syrian, the synagogue worshippers were "filled with wrath" and sought to kill him (Luke 4:25-29). But the very hatred this solemn truth arouses is one of the most convincing proofs of its divine origin.

Election is to be preached and published, first, because it is brought forward all through the Scriptures. There is not a single book in the Word of God where election is not either expressly stated, strikingly illustrated, or clearly implied. Genesis is full of it: the difference which the Lord made between Nahor and Abraham, Ishmael and Isaac, and His loving Jacob and hating Esau are cases to the point. In Exodus we behold the distinction made by God between the Egyptians and the Hebrews. In Leviticus the atonement and all the sacrifices were for the people of God, nor were they bidden to go and "offer" them to the surrounding heathen. In Numbers Jehovah used a Balaam to herald the fact that Israel were "the people" who "shall dwell alone, and shall not be numbered among the nations" (23:9); and therefore was he constrained to cry "How goodly are thy tents, O Jacob, and thy tabernacles, 0 Israel" (24:5). In Deuteronomy it is recorded "The Lord's portion is his people; Jacob is the lot of his inheritance" (32:9).

In Joshua we behold the discriminating mercy of the Lord bestowed upon Rahab the harlot, while the whole of her city was doomed to destruction. In Judges the sovereignty of God appears in the unlikely instruments selected, by which He wrought victory for Israel: Deborah, Gideon, Samson. In Ruth we have Orpah kissing her mother-in-law and returning to her gods, whereas Ruth cleaves to her and obtained inheritance in Israel—who made them to differ? In 1 Samuel David is chosen for the throne, preferred to his older brethren. In 2 Samuel we learn of the everlasting covenant "ordered in all things, and sure" (23:5). In 1 Kings Elijah becomes a blessing to a single widow selected from many; while in 2 Kings Naaman alone, of all the lepers, was cleansed. In 1 Chronicles it is written "Ye children of Jacob, His chosen ones" (16:13); while in 2 Chronicles we are made to marvel at the grace of God bestowing repentance upon Manasseh. And so we might go on. The Psalms, Prophets, Gospels and Epistles are so full of this doctrine that he who runs may read.

Second, the doctrine of election is to be prominently preached because the gospel cannot be Scripturally proclaimed without it. Alas, so deep is the darkness and so widespread the ignorance which now prevails, that few indeed perceive that there is any vital connection between predestination and the evangel of God. Pause, then, for a moment and seriously ponder these questions: Is the success or failure of the gospel a matter of chance? or, to put it in another way, are the fruits of the most stupendous undertaking of all—the atoning work of Christ—left contingent upon human caprice? Could it be positively affirmed that the Redeemer shall yet "see of the travail of his soul, and...be satisfied" (Isa. 53:11) if all is left dependent upon the will of fallen man? Has God so little regard for the death of His son that He has left it uncertain as to how many shall be saved thereby?

"The gospel of God" (Rom. 1:1) can only be Scripturally presented as the Triune God is owned and honored therein. The attenuated "gospel" of our degenerate age confines the attention of its hearers to the sacrifice of Christ, whereas salvation originated in the heart of God the Father and is consummated by the operations of God the Spirit. All the blessings of salvation are communicated according to God's eternal counsels, and it was for the whole of election of grace (and none others) that Christ wrought salvation. The very first chapter of the New Testament announces that Jesus "shall save His people from their sins:" not "may," but "shall"; not shall offer to or try to, but actually "save" them. Again; not a single soul ever benefited from the death of Christ if the Spirit had not been given to apply its virtues to the chosen seed. Any man, then, who omits the Father's election, and the Spirit's sovereign and effectual operations, preaches not the gospel of God, no matter what be his reputation as a "soul winner.

We have exposed the senselessness of those objections which are made against doctrinal preaching in general and the arguments which are leveled against the proclamation of predestination in particular. Then we pointed out some of the reasons why this grand truth is to be published. First, because the Scriptures, from Genesis to Revelation, are full of it. Second, because the gospel cannot be Scripturally preached without it. The great commission given to the public servants of Christ, duly called and equipped by Him, reads thus, "preach the gospel" (Mark 16:15): not parts of it, but the whole of it. The gospel is not be preached piecemeal, but in its entirety, so that each person in the Godhead is equally honored. Just as far as the gospel is mutilated, just so far as any branch of the evangelical system is suppressed, is the gospel not preached. To begin at Calvary, or even at Bethlehem, is to begin in the middle: we must go right back to the eternal counsels of divine grace.

Rightly did a renowned reformer put it, "Election is the golden thread that runs through the whole Christian system . . . it is the bond which connects and keeps it together, which, without this, is like a system of sand ever ready to fall to pieces. It is the cement which holds the fabric together; nay, it is the very soul that animates the whole frame. It is so blended and interwoven with the entire scheme of gospel doctrine that when the former is excluded, the latter bleeds to death. An ambassador is to deliver the whole message with which he is charged. He is to omit no part of it, but must declare the mind of the sovereign he represents, fully and without reserve. He is to say neither more nor less than the instructions of his court require, else he comes under displeasure, perhaps loses his head. Let the ministers of Christ weigh this well" (J. Zanchius, 1562).

Moreover the Gospel is to be preached "to every creature," that is, to all who frequent the Christian ministry, whether Jew or Gentile, young or old, rich or poor. All who wait upon the ministrations of God's servants have a right to hear the gospel fully and clearly, without any part of it being kept back. Now an important part of the gospel is the doctrine of election: God's eternal, free, and irreversible choice of certain persons in Christ to everlasting life. God foreknew that if the success of the preaching of Christ crucified were left contingent upon the response made to it by fallen men, there would be a universal despising of the same. This is clear from, "They all with one consent began to make excuse" (Luke 14:18). Therefore did God determine that a remnant of

Adam's children should be the eternal monuments of His mercy, and accordingly He decreed to bestow upon them a saving faith and repentance. That is good news, indeed: all rendered certain and immutable by the sovereign will of God.

Christ is the supreme evangelist, and we find this doctrine was on His lips all through His ministry. "I thank Thee, O Father, Lord of heaven and earth, because thou hast hid these things from the wise and prudent, and hast revealed them unto babes. Even so, Father: for so it seemed good in thy sight"; "For the elect's sake those days shall be shortened"; "Come, ye blessed of my Father, inherit the kingdom prepared for you from the foundation of the world" (Matt. 11:25; 24:22; 25:34). "Unto you it is given to know the mystery of the kingdom of God: but unto them that are without [i.e., the pale of election] ,all these things are done in parables" (Mark 4:11). "Rejoice, because your names are written in heaven" (Luke 10:20). "All that the Father giveth me shall come to me"; "Ye believe not, because ye are not of my sheep"; "Ye have not chosen me, but I have chosen you" (John 6:37; 10:26; 15:16).

The same is true of the greatest of the apostles. Take the first and chiefest of his epistles, which is expressly devoted to an unfolding of "the Gospel of God" (Rom. 1:1). In Chapter 8 he describes those who are "the called according to God's purpose" (v. 28), and in consequence of which they were "foreknown" and "predestinated to be conformed to the image of his son" (v. 29). The whole of Chapter 9 is devoted thereto: there he shows the difference which God made between Ishmael and Isaac, between Esau and Jacob, the vessels of wrath and the vessels of mercy. There he tells us that God hath "mercy on whom he will have mercy, and whom he will he hardeneth" (v. 18). Nor were these things written to a few persons in some obscure corner, but addressed to the saints at Rome, "which was, in effect, bringing this doctrine upon the stage of the whole world, stamping an universal imprimatur upon it and publishing it to believers at large throughout the earth" (Zanchius).

The doctrine of election is to be preached, third, because the grace of God cannot be maintained without it. Things have now come to such a sorry pass that the remainder of this chapter should really be devoted to the elucidation and amplification of this important point; but we must content ourselves with some brief remarks. There are thousands of Arminian evangelists in Christendom today who deny predestination, either directly or indirectly, and yet suppose they are magnifying divine grace. Their idea is that God, out of His great goodness and love, has provided salvation in Christ for the whole human family, and that such is what He now desires and seeks. It is the view of these men that God makes an offer of His saving grace through the gospel message, makes it to the freewill of all who hear it, and that they can either accept or refuse it. But that is not "grace" at all.

Divine grace and human worthiness are as far apart as the poles, standing directly opposed the one to the other. But not so is the "grace" of the Arminian. If grace is merely something which is offered to me, something which I must improve if it is to do me any good, then my acceptance thereof is a meritorious act, and I have ground for boasting. If some refuse that grace and I receive it, then it must be (since it is wholly a matter of the freewill of the hearer) because I have more sense than they have, or because my heart is more tender than theirs, or because my will is less stubborn; and were the question put to me "Who maketh thee to differ?" (1 Cor. 4:7), then the only truthful answer I could make would be to say, I made myself to differ, and thus place the crown of honor and glory upon my own head.

To this it may be replied by some, We believe that the heart of the natural man is hard and his will stubborn, but God in His grace sends the Holy Spirit, and He convicts men of sin and in the day of His visitation melts their hearts and seeks to woo them unto Christ; yet they must respond to His "sweet overtures" and co-operate with His "gracious influence." Here the ground is forsaken that it is wholly a matter of man's will. Yet here too we have nothing better than a burlesque of divine grace. Those very men affirm that many of those who are the subjects of these influences of the Spirit, resist the same and perish. Thus, those who are saved, owe their salvation (in the final analysis) to their improving of the Spirit's overtures—they "cooperate" with Him. In such a case the honors would be divided between the Spirit's operations and my improvements of the same. But that is not "grace" at all.

There are still others who seek to blunt the sharp edge of the Spirit's sword by saying, We believe in the doctrine of predestination, though not as you Calvinists teach it. A. single word serves to untie this knot for us—"foreknowledge": Divine election is based upon divine foreknowledge. God foresaw who would repent of their sins and accept Christ as their Savior, and accordingly he chose them unto salvation. Here again human merits are dragged in. Grace is not free, hut tied by the "decision" of the creature. Such a carnal concept as this reverses the order of Scripture, which teaches that the divine foreknowledge is based upon the divine purpose—God foreknows what will be because He has decreed what shall be. Note carefully the order in Acts 2:23 and Romans 8:28 (last clause) and 29. Nowhere does Holy Writ speak of God foreseeing or foreknowing our repentance and faith: it is always foreknowledge of persons and never of acts—"whom He did foreknow" and not "what He did foreknow."

But does not Scripture say "whosoever will may come?" It does, and the all-important question is, where does the willingness come from in the case of those who respond to such an invitation? Men in their natural condition are unwilling: as Christ declared "ye will not come to me that ye might have life" (John 5:40). What, then, is the answer? This, "Thy people [says the Father to the Son—see context] shall be willing [to come] in the day of thy power" (Ps. 110:3). It is divine power, that and nothing else, which makes the unwilling willing, which overcomes all their enmity and obstinacy, which impels or "draws" them to the feet of the Lord Jesus. The grace of God, my readers, is far more than a lovely concept to sing about: it is an almighty power, an invincible dynamic, a principle victorious over all resistance. "My grace [says God] is sufficient for thee" (2 Cor. 12:9); it asks for no assistance from us. "By the grace of God [and not by my] co-operation, I am what I am" (1 Cor. 15:10), said the apostle.

Divine grace has done far more than make possible the salvation of sinners: it makes certain the salvation of God's chosen ones. It not only provides salvation for them, it brings salvation to them; and it does so in such a way that its honors are not shared by the creature. The doctrine of predestination batters down this dagon-idol of "freewill" and human merits, for it tells us that if we have indeed willed and desired to lay hold of Christ and salvation by Him, then that very will and desire are the effect of God's eternal purpose and the result of the efficacious workings of His grace, for it is God who worketh in us both to will and to do of His good pleasure; and therefore do we glory only in the Lord and ascribe all the praise unto Him. This writer sought not the Lord, but hated, opposed, and endeavored to banish Him from his thoughts; but the Lord sought him, smote him to the ground (like Saul of Tarsus), subdued his vile rebellion, and made him willing in the day of His power. That is Grace indeed—sovereign, amazing, triumphant grace.

Fourth, the doctrine of election is to be published because it abases man. Arminians imagine that they do so by declaring the total depravity of the human family, yet in their very next breath they contradict themselves by insisting on their ability to perform spiritual acts. The fact is that "total depravity" is merely a theological expression on their lips which they repeat like parrots for they understand not nor believe the terrible import of that term. The fall has radically affected, corrupted, every part and faculty of our being, and therefore if man be totally depraved it necessarily follows that unto sin our wills are completely enslaved. As man's apostasy from God resulted in the darkening of his understanding, the defiling of his affections, the hardening of his heart, so it brought his will into complete bondage to Satan. He can no more free himself than can a worm under the foot of an elephant.

One of the marks of God's people is that they have "no confidence in the flesh" (Phil. 3:3), and nothing is so well calculated to bring them into that state as the truth of election. Shut out divine predestination and you must bring in the doings of the creature, and that makes salvation contingent, and thus it is neither of grace alone nor of works alone, but a nauseating mixture. The man who thinks he can be saved without election must have some confidence in the flesh, no matter how strongly he may deny it. Just so long as we are persuaded that it lies in the power of our own wills to contribute anything, be it never so little, unto our salvation, we remain in carnal confidence, and therefore are not truly humbled before God. It is not until we are brought to the place of self-despair—abandoning all hope in our own abilities—that we truly look outside of ourselves for deliverance.

When the truth of election is divinely applied to our hearts we are brought to realize that salvation turns solely on the will of a sovereign God, that "it is not of him that willeth, nor of him that runneth, but of God that showeth mercy" (Rom. 9:16). When we are granted a feeling sense of those words of Christ's "without me ye can do nothing" (John 15:5), then our pride receives its death-wound. So long as we entertain the mad idea that we can lend a helping hand in the business of our salvation, there is no hope for us; but when we perceive that we are clay in the hands of the divine potter to be molded into vessels of honor or dishonor as pleaseth Him, then we shall renounce our own strength, despair of any self-assistance, and pray and submissively wait for the mighty operations of God; nor shall we pray and wait in vain.

Fifth, election is to be preached because it is a divinely appointed means of faith. One of the first effects produced in serious-minded hearers is to stir them unto earnestly inquiring, Am I one of the elect, and to diligently examine themselves before God. In many instances this leads to the painful discovery that their profession is an empty one, resting on nothing better than some "decision" made by them years before under emotional stress. Nothing is more calculated to reveal a sham conversion than a Scriptural setting forth of the birth-marks of God's elect. Those who are predestinated unto salvation are made the subjects of a miraculous work of grace in their hearts, and that is a vastly different thing from a creature-act of "deciding for Christ" or becoming a member of some church. Far more than a natural faith is required to unite the soul unto a supernatural Christ.

The preaching of election acts as a flail in separating the wheat from the chaff. "Faith cometh by hearing, and hearing by the Word of God" (Rom. 10:17), and how can "the faith of God's elect" (Titus 1:1) be begotten and strengthened if the truth of election be suppressed? Divine foreordination does not set aside the use of means, but ensures the continuation and efficacy of them. God has pledged Himself to honor those who honor Him, and that preaching which brings most glory unto the Lord is what He most blesses. That is not always apparent now, but it will be made fully manifest in the Day to come, when it will be seen that much which Christendom regarded as gold, silver, precious stones, was naught but wood, hay, and stubble. Salvation and the knowledge of the truth are inseparably connected (1 Tim. 2:4), but how can men arrive at a saving knowledge of the truth, if the most vital and basic part of it be withheld from them?

Sixth, election is to be preached because it incites to holiness. What can possibly be a more powerful incentive to piety than a heart which is overwhelmed by a sense of the sovereign and amazing grace of God! The realization that He set His heart upon me from all eternity, that He singled me out from many when I had no more claim upon His notice that they had, that He chose me to be an object of His distinguishing favor, giving me unto Christ, inscribing my name in the Book of life, and at His appointed time bringing me from death unto life and giving me vital union with His dear Son; this indeed will fill me with gratitude and cause me to seek to honor and please Him. God's electing love for us begets in us an endless love for Him. No motives so sweet or so potent as the love of God constraining us.

Seventh, election is to be preached because it promotes the spirit of praise. Said the apostle, "We are bound to give thanks always to God for you, brethren beloved of the Lord, because God hath from the beginning chosen you to salvation through sanctification of the Spirit and belief of the truth" (2 Thess. 2:13). How can it be otherwise? Gratitude must find vent in adoration. A sense of God's electing grace and everlasting love makes us bless Him as nothing else does. Christ Himself returned special thanks unto the Father for His discriminating mercy (Matt. 11:25). The gratitude of the Christian flows forth because of the regenerating and sanctifying operations of the Spirit; it is stirred afresh by the redemptive and intercessory work of Christ; but it must rise still higher and contemplate the first cause—the sovereign grace of the Father—which planned the whole of our salvation. As then election is the great matter of thanksgiving unto God, it must be freely preached to His people.

The value of this blessed doctrine appears in its suitability and sufficiency to stabilize and settle true Christians in the certainty of their salvation. When regenerated souls are enabled to believe that the glorification of the elect is so infallibly fixed in God's eternal purpose that it is impossible for any of them to perish, and when they are enabled to Scripturally perceive that they themselves belong to the people of God's choice, how its strengthens and confirms their faith. Nor is such a confidence presumptuous—though any other most certainly is so—for every genuinely converted person has the right to regard himself as belonging to that favored company, since the Holy Spirit quickens none but those who were predestinated by the Father and redeemed by the Son. This is a hope "which maketh not ashamed," for it cannot issue in disappointment when entertained by those in whose hearts the love of God is shed abroad by the Spirit (Rom. 5:5).

The holy assurance which issues from a believing apprehension of this grand truth is forcibly set forth by the apostle in the closing verses of Romans 8. There he assures us, "Whom He did predestinate, them he also called: and whom He called them He also justified: and whom he justified, them he also glorified" (v. 30). Such a beginning guarantees such an end: a salvation which originated in a past eternity must be consummated in a future eternity. From such grand premises Paul drew the blessed conclusion "If God be for us, who can be against us?" (v. 31). And again, "Who shall lay anything to the charge of God's elect?" (v. 33). And yet again, "Who shall separate us from the love of Christ?" (v. 35). If such precious streams issue from this fountain, then how great is the madness and how heinous the sin of those who desire to see it choked. The everlasting security of Christ's sheep cannot be presented in its full force until we base it upon the divine decree.

How apt the trembling believer is to doubt his final perseverance, for sheep (both natural and spiritual) are timid and self-distrustful creatures. Not so the wild and wayward goats: true to their type, they are full of carnal confidence and fleshly boasting. But the believer has such a sense of his own weakness, such a sight of his sinfulness, such a realization of his fickleness and stability, that he literally works out his own salvation in fear and trembling." Moreover, as he sees so many who did run well doing so no longer, so many who made such a fair and promising profession end by making shipwreck of the faith, the very sight of their apostasy causes him to seriously question his own state and latter end. It is to stabilize their hearts that God has revealed in His Word that those who are enabled to see in themselves the marks of election may rejoice in the certainty of their everlasting blessedness.

Let us also point out what a stabilizing effect the apprehension of this grand truth has upon the true servant of God. How much there is to dishearten him: the fewness of those who attend his ministry, and opposition made to those portions of the truth which most exalt God and abase man, the scarcity of any visible fruits attending his labors, the charge preferred by some of his officers or closest friends that if he continues along such lines he will have no one at all left to preach to, the whisperings of Satan that God Himself is frowning on such efforts, that he is a rank failure and had better quit; these and other considerations have a powerful tendency to fill him with dismay or tempt him to trim his sails and float along the tide of popular sentiment. We know whereof we write, for we have personally trod this thorny path.

Ah, but God has graciously provided an antidote for Satan's poison, and an effectual cordial to revive the drooping spirits of His sorely tried servants. What is this? The knowledge that their Master has not sent them forth to draw a bow at a venture, but rather to be instruments in His hand of accomplishing His eternal decree. Though He has commissioned them to preach the gospel unto all who attend their ministry, yet He has also made it plain in His Word that it is not His purpose that all or even that many should be saved thereby. He has made it known that His flock is (Greek) a "very little" one (Luke 12:32), that there is only "a remnant according to the election of grace" (Rom. 11:5), that the "many" would be found on the broad road that leadeth to destruction and that only a "few" would walk that narrow way that leadeth unto life.

It is for the calling out from the world of this chosen remnant and for the feeding and establishing of them that God chiefly employs His servants. It is the due apprehension and personal belief of this which tranquilizes and stabilizes the minister's heart as nothing else will. As he rests upon the sovereignty of God, the efficacy of His decrees, the absolute certainty that God's counsels shall be fully realized, then he is assured that whatever God has sent him forth to do must be accomplished, that neither man nor devil can prevent it. Appalled by the ruin all around him, humiliated by his own sad failures, yet he perceives that the outworking of the divine plan is infallibly ensured. Those whom the Father ordained will believe (Acts 13:48), those for whom the Son died must be saved (John 10:16), those whom the Spirit quickens shall be effectually preserved (Phil. 1:6).

When the minister receives a message to deliver in the name of his Master, he may rest with unshaken confidence on the promise, "So shall My Word be that goeth forth out of my mouth; it shall not return unto me void, but it [not "may"] shall accomplish that which I please, and it shall prosper in the thing whereto I sent it" (Isa. 55:11). It may not accomplish what the preacher wishes nor prosper to the extent which the saints desire, but no power on earth or in hell can prevent the fulfillment of God's will. If God has marked out a certain person to be brought into a saving knowledge of the truth under a particular sermon, then no matter how buried in sin that soul may be nor how hardly he may kick against the pricks of conscience, he shall (like Paul of old) be made to cry "Lord, what wouldest thou have me to do?" Here, then, is a sure resting place for the minister's heart. This was where Christ found consolation, for when the nation at large despised and rejected Him, He consoled Himself with the fact that "All that the Father giveth me shall come to me" (John 6:3 7).

The value of this doctrine appears again in that it provides real encouragement to praying souls. Nothing so promotes the spirit of holy boldness at the throne of grace as the realization that God is our God and that we are the people of His choice. They are His peculiar treasure, the very apple of His eye, and they above all people have His ear. "Shall not God avenge his own elect, which cry day and night unto him?" (Luke 18:7). Assuredly He shall do so, for they are the only ones who supplicate Him in meekness, presenting their requests in subjection to His sovereign pleasure. O my readers, when we are on our knees, how this fact that God set His heart upon us from everlasting must inspire fervency and faith. Since God chose to love us, can He refuse to hear us? Then let us take courage from our predestination to make more earnest supplication.

"But know that the Lord hath set apart him that is godly for himself: the Lord will hear when I call unto him" (Ps. 4:3). "'But know.' Fools will not learn, and therefore they must again and again be told the same thing, especially when it is such a bitter truth which is to be taught them, viz:—the fact that the godly are the chosen of God, and are, by distinguishing grace, set apart and separated from other men. Election is a doctrine which unrenewed man cannot endure, but nevertheless it is a glorious and well-attested truth, and one which should comfort the tempted believer. Election is the guarantee of complete salvation, and an argument for success at the throne of grace. He who chose us for Himself will surely hear our prayers. The Lord's elect shall not be condemned nor shall their cry be unheard. David was king by divine decree, and we are the Lord's people in the same manner; let us tell our enemies to their faces that they fight against God and destiny, when they strive to overthrow our souls" (C. H. Spurgeon).

Not only does a knowledge of the truth of election afford encouragement to praying souls, but it supplies important instruction and guidance therein. Our petitions ought ever to be framed in harmony with divine truth. If we believe in the doctrine of predestination we should pray accordingly. The language we use should be in agreement with the fact that we believe there are a company of persons chosen in Christ before the foundation of the world, and that it was for them, and them alone, He suffered and died. If we believe in particular redemption (rather than in a universal atonement) we should beg the Lord Jesus to have respect unto such as He has purchased by His soul's travail. This will be a means of keeping up right apprehensions in our own minds, as it will also be setting a proper example in this matter before others.

In the present day there are many deplorable expressions made use of in prayer, which are utterly unjustifiable, yea, which are altogether opposed to the will or Word of the Lord. How often the modern pulpit asks for the salvation of all present, and the head of the household requests that not one in the family miss eternal glory. To what purpose is this? Are we going to direct the Lord, who He shall save? Let us not be misunderstood: we are not against the preacher praying for his congregation, nor the parent for his family; that which we are opposed to is that praying which is in direct opposition unto the truth of the gospel. Prayer must be subordinated to the divine decrees, otherwise we are guilty of rebellion. When praying for the salvation of others, it should always be with the proviso "If they be thine elect" or "if it be thy sovereign will," or with some similar qualification.

The Lord Jesus has left us a perfect example in this, as in everything else. In His great high priestly prayer, recorded in John 17, we find Him saying, "I pray not for the world, but for them which Thou hast given Me; for they are Thine" (v. 9). Our Lord knew the whole of His Father's good will and pleasure towards the elect. He knew that the act of election was a sovereign and irreversible act in His mind. He knew that He Himself could not add one to the number of the chosen. He knew that He was sent from the Father to live and die for them, and them only. And in perfect agreement with this He declared, "I pray for them: I pray not for the world." If, then, Christ left out the world, if He prayed not for the non-elect, neither should we. We must learn of Him and follow His steps, and instead of resenting, be well pleased with the whole good pleasure of God's sovereign will.

To be submissive unto the divine will is the hardest lesson of all to learn. By nature we are self-willed and anything which crosses us is resented. The upsetting of our plans, the dashing of our cherished hopes, the smashing of our idols, stirs up the enmity of the flesh. A miracle of grace is required in order to bring us into acquiescence to God's dealing with us, so that we say from the heart "It is the Lord: let Him do what seemeth Him good" (1 Sam. 3:18). And in bringing this miracle to pass, God uses means. He impresses on our hearts, an effectual sense of His sovereignty, so that we are brought to realize that He has the unqualified right to do as He pleases with His creatures. And no other truth has such a powerful tendency to teach us this vital lesson as has the doctrine of election. A saving knowledge of the fact that God chose us unto salvation begets within us a readiness for Him to order all our affairs, till we cry "not my will, but thine be done."

Now in view of all these considerations, we ask the reader, ought not the doctrine of election to be plainly and freely proclaimed? If God's Word be full of it, if the gospel cannot be Scripturally preached without it, if the grace of God cannot be maintained when it is suppressed, if the proclamation of it abases man into the dust, if it be a divinely appointed means of faith, if it be a powerful incentive unto the promotion of holiness, if it stirs in the soul the spirit of praise, if it establishes the Christian in the certainty of his security, if it be such a source of stability to the servant of God, if it supplies encouragement to praying souls and affords valuable instruction therein, if it work in us a sweet submission to the divine will; then shall we refuse to give unto God's children this valuable bread merely because dogs snap at it or withhold from the sheep this vital ingredient of their food simply because the goats cannot digest it?

And now, in conclusion, a few words on how this doctrine should he published. First, it ought to be presented basically. This is not an incidental or secondary truth, but one of fundamental importance and therefore it is not to be crowded into a corner, nor spoken of with bated breath. Predestination lies at the very foundation of the entire scheme of divine grace. This is clear from Romans 8:30, where it is mentioned before effectual calling, justification, and glorification. It is clear again from the order followed in Ephesians 1, where election (v. 4) precedes adoption, our acceptance in the Beloved, and our having redemption through His blood (vv. 5-7). The minister must, therefore, make it clear to his hearers that God first chose a people to be His peculiar treasure, then sent His Son to redeem them from the curse of the broken law, and now gives the Spirit to quicken them and bring them to everlasting glory.

Second, it ought to be preached fearlessly. God's servants must not be intimidated by the frowns of men nor deterred from performing their duty by any form of opposition. The minister of the gospel is called upon to "endure hardness as a good soldier of Jesus Christ" (2 Tim. 2:3), and soldiers who fear the foe or take to flight are of no service to their king. The same holds good of those who are officers of the King of kings. How fearless was the apostle Paul! How valiant for the truth were Luther and Calvin, and the thousands of those who were burned at the stake because of their adherence to this doctrine. Then let not those whom Christ has called to preach the gospel conceal this truth because of the fear of man, for the Master has plainly warned them "Whosoever therefore shall be ashamed of me and of my words in this evil and adulterous generation; of him also shall the Son of man be ashamed" (Mark 8:38).

Third, it is to be preached humbly. Fearlessness does not require us to be bombastic. The holy Word of God must ever be handled with reverence and sobriety. When the minister stands before his people they ought to feel by his demeanor that he has come to them from the audience-chamber of the Most High, that the awe of Jehovah rests upon his soul. To preach upon the sovereignty of God, His eternal counsels, His choosing of some and passing by of others, is far too solemn a matter to be delivered in the energy of the flesh. There is a happy medium between a cringing, apologetic attitude, and adopting the style of a political tirader. Earnestness must not degenerate into vulgarity. It is "in meekness" we are to instruct those who oppose themselves "if God peradventure will give them repentance to the acknowledging of the truth" (2 Tim. 2:25).

Fourth, it is to be preached proportionately. Though the foundation be of first importance it is of little value unless a superstructure be erected upon it. The publication of election is to make way for the other cardinal truths of the gospel. If any doctrine be preached exclusively it is distorted. There is a balance to be preserved in our presentation of the truth; while no part of it is to be suppressed, no part of it is to be made unduly prominent. It is a great mistake to harp on one string only. Man's responsibility must be enforced as well as God's sovereignty insisted upon. If on the one hand the minister must not be intimidated by Arminians, on the other he must not be brow-beaten by hyper-Calvinists, who object to the calling upon the unconverted to repent and believe the gospel (Mark 1:15).

Fifth, it is to be preached experimentally. This is how the apostles dealt with it, as is clear from "give diligence to make your calling and election sure" (2 Peter 1:10). But how can this be done unless we are taught the doctrine of election, instructed in the nature and use of it? The truth of election can be small comfort to any man until he has a well-grounded assurance that he is one of God's chosen people; and that is possible only by ascertaining that he possesses (in some measure) the Scriptural marks of Christ's sheep. As we have already dealt with this aspect of our subject at some length, we will say no more. May it please the Lord to use these words unto His own glory and the blessing of His dear saints.

THE DOCTRINE
OF JUSTIFICATION

Contents

Chapter 1
Introduction

Our first thought was to devote an introductory chapter unto a setting forth the principle errors which have been entertained upon this subject by different men and parties, but after more deliberation we decided this would be for little or no profit to the majority of our readers. While there are times, no doubt, when it becomes the distasteful duty of God's servants to expose that which is calculated to deceive and injure His people, yet, as a general rule, the most effective way of getting rid of darkness is to let in the light. We desire, then, to pen these articles in the spirit of the godly John Owen, who, in the introduction to his ponderous treatise on this theme said, "More weight is to be put on the steady guidance of the mind and conscience of one believer, really exercised about the foundation of his peace and acceptance with God, than on the confutation of ten wrangling disputers. . .To declare and vindicate the truth unto the instruction and edification of such as love it in sincerity, to extricate their minds from those difficulties in this particular instance, which some endeavor to cast on all Gospel mysteries, to direct the consciences of them that inquire after abiding peace with God, and to establish the minds of them that do believe, are the things I have aimed at."

There was a time, not so long ago, when the blessed truth of Justification was one of the best known doctrines of the Christian faith, when it was regularly expounded by the preachers, and when the rank and file of church-goers were familiar with its leading aspects. But now, alas, a generation has arisen which is well-nigh totally ignorant of this precious theme, for with very rare exceptions it is no longer given a place in the pulpit, nor is scarcely anything written thereon in the religious magazines of our day; and, in consequence, comparatively few understand what the term itself connotes, still less are they clear as to the ground on which God justifies the ungodly. This places the writer at a considerable disadvantage, for while he wishes to avoid a superficial treatment of so vital a subject, yet to go into it deeply, and enter into detail, will make a heavy tax upon the mentality and patience of the average person. Nevertheless, we respectfully urge each Christian to make a real effort to gird up the loins of his mind and seek to prayerfully master these chapters.

That which will make it harder to follow us through the present series is the fact that we are here treating of the doctrinal side of truth, rather than the practical; the judicial, rather than the experimental. Not that doctrine is impracticable; no indeed; far, far from it. "All Scripture is given by inspiration of God, and is profitable (first) for doctrine, (and then) for reproof, for correction, for instruction in righteousness" (2 Tim. 3:16). Doctrinal instruction was ever the foundation from which the Apostles issued precepts to regulate the walk. Not until the 6th chapter will any exhortation be found in the Roman Epistle: the first five are devoted entirely to doctrinal exposition. So again in the Epistle to the Ephesians: not until 4:1 is the first exhortation given. First the saints are reminded of the exceeding riches of God's grace, that the love of Christ may constrain them; and then they are urged to walk worthy of the vocation wherewith they are called.

While it be true that a real mental effort (as well as a prayerful heart) is required in order to grasp intelligently some of the finer distinctions which are essential to a proper apprehension of this doctrine, yet, let it be pointed out that the truth of justification is far from being a mere piece of abstract speculation. No, it is a statement of Divinely revealed fact; it is a statement of fact in which every member of our race ought to be deeply interested in. Each one of us has forfeited the favor of God, and each one of us needs to be restored to His favor. If we are not restored, then the outcome must inevitably be our utter ruin and hopeless perdition. How fallen creatures, how guilty rebels, how lost sinners, are restored to the favor of God, and given a standing before Him inestimably superior to that occupied by the holy angels, will (D. V.) engage our attention as we proceed with our subject.

As said Abram Booth in his splendid work "The Reign of Grace" (written in 1768), "Far from being a merely speculative point, it spreads its influence through the whole body of divinity (theology), runs through all Christian experience, and operates in every part of practical godliness. Such is its grand importance, that a mistake about it has a malignant efficacy, and is attended with a long train of dangerous consequences. Nor can this appear strange, when it is considered that this doctrine of justification is no other than the way of a sinner's acceptance with God. Being of such peculiar moment, it is inseparably connected with many other evangelical truths, the harmony and beauty of which we cannot behold, while this is misunderstood. Till this appears in its glory, they will be involved in darkness. It is, if anything may be so called, a fundamental article; and certainly requires our most serious consideration" (from his chapter on "Justification").

The great importance of the doctrine of justification was sublimely expressed by the Dutch Puritan, Witsius, when he said, "It tends much to display the glory of God, whose most exalted perfections shine forth with an eminent luster in this matter. It sets forth the infinite goodness of God, by which He was inclined to procure salvation freely for lost and miserable man, 'to the praise of the glory of His grace' (Eph. 1:6). It displays also the strictest justice, by which He would not forgive even the smallest offense, but on condition of the sufficient engagement, or full satisfaction of the Mediator, 'that He might be just, and the Justifier of him which believeth in Jesus' (Rom 3:26). It shows further the unsearchable wisdom of the Deity, which found out a way for the exercise of the most gracious act of mercy, without injury to His strictest justice and infallible truth, which threatened death to the sinner: justice demanded that the soul that sinned should die (Rom. 1:32). Truth had pronounced the curses for not obeying the Lord (Deut. 28:15-68). Goodness, in the meantime, was inclined to adjudge life to some sinners, but by no other way than what became the majesty of the most holy God. Here wisdom interposed, saying, 'I, even I, am He that blotteth out thy transgressions for Mine own sake, and will not remember thy sins' (Isa. 43:25). Nor shall you, His justice and His truth have any cause of complaint because full satisfaction shall be made to you by a mediator. Hence the incredible philanthropy of the Lord Jesus shineth forth, who, though Lord of all, was made subject to the law, not to the obedience of it only, but also to the curse: 'hath made Him to be sin for us, who knew no sin; that we might be made the righteousness of God in Him" (2 Cor. 5:21).

Ought not the pious soul, who is deeply engaged in the devout meditation of these things, to break out into the praises of a justifying God, and sing with the church, "Who is a God like unto Thee, that pardoneth iniquity, and passeth by the transgression" (Micah 7:18). O the purity of that holiness which chose rather to punish the sins of the elect in His only begotten Son, than suffer them to go unpunished! O the abyss of His love to the world, for which He spared not His dearest Son, in order to spare sinners! O the depth of the riches of unsearchable wisdom, by which He exercises mercy towards the penitent guilty, without any stain to the honor of the most impartial Judge! O the treasures of love in Christ, whereby He became a curse for us, in order to deliver us therefrom! How becoming the justified soul, who is ready to dissolve in the sense of this love, with full exultation to sing a new song, a song of mutual return of love to a justifying

God.

So important did the Apostle Paul, under the guidance of the Holy Spirit, deem this doctrine, that the very first of his epistles in the New Testament is devoted to a full exposition thereof. The pivot on which turns the entire contents of the Epistle to the Romans is that notable expression "the righteousness of God"—than which is none of greater moment to be found in all the pages of Holy Writ, and which it behooves every Christian to make the utmost endeavor to clearly understand. It is an abstract expression denoting the satisfaction of Christ in its relation to the Divine Law. It is a descriptive name for the material cause of the sinner's acceptance before God. "The righteousness of God" is a phrase referring to the finished work of the Mediator as approved by the Divine tribunal, being the meritorious cause of our acceptance before the throne of the Most High.

In the succeeding chapters (D. V.) we shall examine in more detail this vital expression "the righteousness of God," which connotes that perfect satisfaction which the Redeemer offered to Divine justice on the behalf of and in the stead of that people which had been given to Him. Suffice it now to say that that "righteousness" by which the believing sinner is justified is called "the righteousness of God" (Rom. 1:17; 3:21) because He is the appointer, approver, and imputer of it. It is called "the righteousness of God and our Savior Jesus Christ" (2 Pet. 1:1) because He wrought it out and presented it unto God. It is called "the righteousness of faith" (Rom. 4:13) because faith is the apprehender and receiver of it. It is called "man's righteousness" (Job 33:26) because it was paid for him and imputed to him. All these varied expressions refer to so many aspects of that one perfect obedience unto death which the Savior performed for His people.

Yes, so vital did the Apostle Paul, under the guidance of the Holy Spirit, esteem this doctrine of Justification, that he shows at length how the denial and perversion of it by the Jews was the chief reason of their being rejected by God: see the closing verses of Romans 9 and the beginning of chapter 10. Again; throughout the whole Epistle to the Galatians we find the Apostle engaged in most strenuously defending and zealously disputing with those who had assailed this basic truth. Therein he speaks of the contrary doctrine as ruinous and fatal to the souls of men, as subversive of the cross of Christ, and calls it another gospel, solemnly declaring "though we, or an angel from heaven, preach any other gospel unto you... let him be accursed" (Gal. 1:8). Alas, that under the latitudinal liberty and false "charity" of our day, there is now so little holy abhorrence of that preaching which repudiates the vicarious obedience of Christ which is imputed to the believer.

Under God, the preaching of this grand truth brought about the greatest revival which the Cause of Christ has enjoyed since the days of the Apostles. "This was the great fundamental distinguishing doctrine of the Reformation, and was regarded by all the Reformers as of primary and paramount importance. The leading charge which they adduced against the Church of Rome was that she had corrupted and perverted the doctrine of Scripture upon this subject in a way that was dangerous to the souls of men; and it was mainly by the exposition, enforcement, and application of the true doctrine of God's Word in regard to it, that they assailed and overturned the leading doctrines and practices of the Papal system. There is no subject which possesses more of intrinsic importance than attaches to this one, and there is none with respect to which the Reformers were more thoroughly harmonious in their sentiments" (W. Cunningham).

This blessed doctrine supplies the grand Divine cordial to revive one whose soul is cast down and whose conscience is distressed by a felt sense of sin and guilt, and longs to know the way and means whereby he may obtain acceptance with God and the title unto the Heavenly inheritance. To one who is deeply convinced that he has been a life-long rebel against God, a constant transgressor of His Holy Law, and who realizes he is justly under His condemnation and wrath, no inquiry can be of such deep interest and pressing moment as that which relates to the means of restoring him to the Divine favor, remitting his sins, and fitting him to stand unabashed in the Divine presence: till this vital point has been cleared to the satisfaction of his heart, all other information concerning religion will be quite unavailing.

"Demonstrations of the existence of God will only serve to confirm and more deeply impress upon his mind the awful truth which he already believes, that there is a righteous Judge, before whom he must appear, and by whose sentence his final doom will be fixed. To explain the moral law to him, and inculcate the obligations to obey it, will be to act the part of a public accuser, when he quotes the statutes of the land in order to show that the charges which he has brought against the criminal at the bar are well founded, and, consequently, that he is worthy of punishment. The stronger the arguments are by which you evince the immortality of the soul, the more clearly do you prove that his punishment will not be temporary, and that there is another state of existence, in which he will be fully recompensed according to his desert" (J. Dick).

When God Himself becomes a living reality unto the soul, when His awful majesty, ineffable holiness, inflexible justice, and sovereign authority, are really perceived, even though most inadequately, indifference to His claims now gives place to a serious concern. When there is a due sense of the greatness of our apostasy from God, of the depravity of our nature, of the power and vileness of sin, of the spirituality and strictness of the law, and of the everlasting burnings awaiting God's enemies, the awakened soul cries out, "Wherewith shall I come before the Lord, and bow myself before the high God? shall I come before Him with burnt offerings, with calves of a year old? Will the Lord be pleased with thousands of rams, or with ten thousands of rivers of oil? shall I give my firstborn for my transgression, the fruit of my body for the sin of my soul?" (Micah 6:6, 7). Then it is that the poor soul cries out, "How then can man be justified with God? or how can he be clean that is born of a woman?" (Job 25:4). And it is in the blessed doctrine which is now to be before us that we are taught the method whereby a sinner may obtain peace with his Maker and rise to the possession of eternal life.

Again; this doctrine is of inestimable value unto the conscientious Christian who daily groans under a sense of his inward corruptions and innumerable failures to measure up to the standard which God has set before him. The Devil, who is "the accuser of our brethren" (Rev. 12:10), frequently charges the believer with hypocrisy before God, disquiets his conscience, and seeks to persuade him that his faith and piety are nought but a mask and outward show, by which he has not only imposed upon others, but also on himself. But, thank God, Satan may be overcome by "the blood of the Lamb" (Rev. 12:11): by looking away from incurably depraved self, and viewing the Surety, who has fully answered for the Christian's every failure, perfectly atoned for his every sin, and brought in an "everlasting righteousness" (Dan. 9:24), which is placed to his account in the high court of Heaven. And thus, though groaning under his infirmities, the believer may possess a victorious confidence which rises above every fear.

This it was which brought peace and joy to the heart of the Apostle Paul: for while in one breath he cried, "O wretched man that I am! who shall deliver me from the body of this death?" (Rom. 7:24), in the next he declared, "There is therefore now no condemnation to them which are in Christ Jesus" (Rom. 8:1). To which he added, "Who shall lay anything to the charge of God's elect? It is God that justifieth. Who is he that condemneth? It is Christ that died, yea rather, that is risen again, who is even at the right hand of God, who also maketh intercession for us. Who shall separate us from the love of Christ?" (vv. 33-35). May it please the God of all grace to so direct our pen and bless what we write unto the readers, that not a few who are now found in the gloomy dungeons of Doubting Castle, may be brought out into the glorious light and liberty of the full assurance of faith.

Chapter 2
Its Meaning

Deliverance from the condemning sentence of the Divine Law is the fundamental blessing in Divine salvation: so long as we continue under the curse, we can neither be holy nor happy. But as to the precise nature of that deliverance, as to exactly what it consists of, as to the ground on which it is obtained, and as to the means whereby it is secured, much confusion now obtains. Most of the errors which have been prevalent on this subject arose from the lack of a clear view of the thing itself, and until we really understand what justification is, we are in no position to either affirm or deny anything concerning it. We therefore deem it requisite to devote a whole chapter unto a careful defining and explaining this word "justification," endeavoring to show both what it signifies, and what it does not connote.

Between Protestants and Romanists there is a wide difference of opinion as to the meaning of the term "justify": they affirming that to justify is to make inherently righteous and holy; we insisting that to justify signifies only to formally pronounce just or legally declare righteous. Popery includes under justification the renovation of man's moral nature or deliverance from depravity, thereby confounding justification with regeneration and sanctification. On the other hand, all representative Protestants have shown that justification refers not to a change of moral character, but to a change of legal status; though allowing, yea, insisting, that a radical change of character invariably accompanies it. It is a legal change from a state of guilt and condemnation to a state of forgiveness and acceptance; and this change is owing solely to a gratuitous act of God, founded upon the righteousness of Christ (they having none of their own) being imputed to His people.

"We simply explain justification to be an acceptance by which God receives us into His favor and esteems us as righteous persons; and we say that it consists in the remission of sins and the imputation of the righteousness of Christ. . . Justification, therefore, is no other than an acquittal from guilt of him who was accused, as though his innocence has been proved. Since God, therefore, justifies us through the mediation of Christ, He acquits us, not by an admission of our personal innocence, but by an imputation of righteousness; so that we, who are unrighteous in ourselves, are considered as righteous in Christ" (John Calvin, 1559).

"What is justification? Answer: Justification is an act of God's free grace unto sinners, in which He pardoneth all their sins, accepteth and accounteth their persons righteous in His sight; not for anything wrought in them, or done by them, but only for the perfect obedience and full satisfaction of Christ, by God imputed to them, and received by faith alone" (Westminster Catechism, 1643).

"We thus define the Gospel justification of a sinner: It is a judicial, but gracious act of God, whereby the elect and believing sinner is absolved from the guilt of his sins, and hath a right to eternal life adjudged to him, on account of the obedience of Christ, received by faith" (H. Witsius, 1693).

"A person is said to be justified when he is approved of God as free from the guilt of sin and its deserved punishment; and as having that righteousness belonging to him that entitles to the reward of life" (Jonathan Edwards, 1750).

Justification, then, refers not to any subjective change wrought in a person's disposition, but is solely an objective change in his standing in relation to the law. That to justify cannot possibly signify to make a person inherently righteous or good is most clearly to be seen from the usage of the term itself in Scripture. For example, in Proverbs 17:15 we read, "He that justifieth the wicked, and he that condemneth the just, even they both are abomination to the LORD": now obviously he who shall make a "wicked" person just is far from being an "abomination to the LORD," but he who knowingly pronounces a wicked person to be righteous is obnoxious to Him. Again; in Luke 7:29 we read, "And all the people that heard Him, and the publicans, justified God": how impossible it is to make the words "justified God" signify any moral transformation in His character; but understand those words to mean that they declared Him to be righteous, and all ambiguity is removed. Once more, in 1 Timothy 3:16 we are told that the incarnate Son was "justified in (or "by") the Spirit": that is to say, He was publicly vindicated at His resurrection, exonerated from the blasphemous charges which the Jews had laid against Him.

Justification has to do solely with the legal side of salvation. It is a judicial term, a word of the law courts. It is the sentence of a judge upon a person who has been brought before him for judgment. It is that gracious act of God as Judge, in the high court of Heaven, by which He pronounces an elect and believing sinner to be freed from the penalty of the law, and fully restored unto the Divine favor. It is the declaration of God that the party arraigned is fully conformed to the law; justice exonerates him because justice has been satisfied. Thus, justification is that change of status whereby one, who being guilty before God, and therefore under the condemning sentence of His Law, and deserving of nought but an eternal banishment from His presence, is received into His favor and given a right unto all the blessings which Christ has, by His perfect satisfaction, purchased for His people.

In substantiation of the above definition, the meaning of the term "justify" may be determined, First, by its usage in Scripture. "And Judah said, What shall we say unto my lord? what shall we speak? or how shall we clear (this Hebrew word "tsadag" always signifies "justify") ourselves?" (Gen. 44:16). Here we have an affair which was entirely a judicial one. Judah and his brethren were arraigned before the governor of Egypt, and they were concerned as to how they might procure a sentence in their favor. "If there be a controversy between men, and they come unto judgment, that the judges may judge them; then they shall justify the righteous, and condemn the wicked" (Deut. 25:1). Here again we see plainly that the term is a forensic one, used in connection with the proceedings of law-courts, implying a process of investigation and judgment. God here laid down a rule to govern the judges in Israel: they must not "justify" or pass a sentence in favor of the wicked: compare 1 Kings 8:31, 32.

"If I justify myself, mine own mouth shall condemn me: if I say, I am perfect, it shall also prove me perverse" (Job 9:20): the first member of this sentence is explained in the second—"justify" there cannot signify to make holy, but to pronounce a sentence in my own favor. "Then was kindled the wrath of Elihu . . . against Job . . . because he justified himself rather than God" (Job 32:2), which obviously means, because he vindicated himself rather than God. "That Thou mightest be justified when Thou speakest, and be clear when Thou judgest" (Ps. 51:4), which signifies that God, acting in His judicial office, might be pronounced righteous in passing sentence. "But wisdom is justified of her children" (Matt. 11:19), which means that they who are truly regenerated by God have accounted the wisdom of God (which the scribes and Pharisees reckoned foolishness) to be, as it really is, consummate wisdom: they cleared it of the calumny of folly.

Second, The precise force of the term "to justify" may be ascertained by noting that it is the antithesis of "to condemn." Now to condemn is not a process by which a good man is made bad, but is the sentence of a judge upon one because he is a transgressor of the law. "He that justifieth the wicked, and he that condemneth the just, even they both are abomination to the LORD" (Prov. 17:15 and cf. Deut. 25:1). "For by thy words thou shalt be justified, and by thy words thou shalt be condemned" (Matt. 12:37). "It is God that justifieth. Who is he that condemneth?" (Rom. 8:33, 34). Now it is undeniable that "condemnation" is the passing of a sentence against a person by which the punishment prescribed by the law is awarded to him and ordered to be inflicted upon him; therefore justification is the passing of a sentence in favor of a person, by which the reward prescribed by the law is ordered to be given to him.

Third, That justification is not an experimental change from sin to holiness, but a judicial change from guilt to no-condemnation may be evidenced by the equivalent terms used for it. For example, in Romans 4:6 we read, "Even as David also describeth the blessedness of the man, unto whom God imputeth righteousness without works": so that legal "righteousness" is not a habit infused into the heart, but a gift transferred to our account. In Romans 5:9, 10 to be "justified by Christ's blood" is the same as being "reconciled by His death," and reconciliation is not a transformation of character, but the effecting of peace by the removal of all that causes offense.

Fourth, From the fact that the judicial side of our salvation is propounded in Scripture under the figures of a forensic trial and sentence. "(1) A judgment is supposed in it, concerning which the Psalmist prays that it may not proceed on the terms of the law: Psalm 143:2. (2) The Judge is God Himself: Isaiah 50:7, 8. (3) The tribunal whereon God sits in judgment is the Throne of Grace: Hebrews 4:16. (4) A guilty person. This is the sinner, who is so guilty of sin as to be obnoxious to the judgment of God: Romans 3:18. (5) Accusers are ready to propose and promote the charge against the guilty person; these are the law (John 5:45), conscience (Rom. 2:15), and Satan: Zechariah 3:2, Revelation 12:10. (6) The charge is admitted and drawn up in a 'handwriting' in form of law, and is laid before the tribunal of the Judge, in bar to the deliverance of the offender: Colossians 2:14. (7) A plea is prepared in the Gospel for the guilty person: this is grace, through the blood of Christ, the ransom paid, the eternal righteousness brought in by the Surety of the covenant: Romans 3:23, 25, Daniel 9:24. (8) Hereunto alone the sinner betakes himself, renouncing all other apologies or defensatives whatever: Psalm 130:2, 3; Luke 18:13. (9) To make this plea effectual we have an Advocate with the Father, and He pleads His own propitiation for us: 1 John 2:1, 2. (10) The sentence hereon is absolution, on account of the sacrifice and righteousness of Christ; with acceptation into favor, as persons approved of God: Romans 8:33, 34; 2 Corinthians 5:21" (John Owen).

From what has been before us, we may perceive what justification is not. First, it differs from regeneration. "Whom He called, them He also justified" (Rom. 8:30). Though inseparably connected, effectual calling or the new birth and justification are quite distinct. The one is never apart from the other, yet they must not be confounded. In the order of nature regeneration precedes justification, though it is in no sense the cause or ground of it: none is justified till he believes, and none believe till quickened. Regeneration is the act of the Father (James 1:18), justification is the sentence of the Judge. The one gives me a place in God's family, the other secures me a standing before His throne. The one is internal, being the impartation of Divine life to my soul: the other is external, being the imputation of Christ's obedience to my account. By the one I am drawn to return in penitence to the Father's house, by the other I am given the "best robe" which fits me for His presence.

Second, it differs from sanctification. Sanctification is moral or experimental, justification is legal or judicial. Sanctification results from the operation of the Spirit in me, justification is based upon what Christ has done for me. The one is gradual and progressive, the other is instantaneous and immutable. The one admits of degrees, and is never perfect in this life; the other is complete and admits of no addition. The one concerns my state, the other has to do with my standing before God. Sanctification produces a moral transformation of character, justification is a change of legal status: it is a change from guilt and condemnation to forgiveness and acceptance, and this solely by a gratuitous act of God, founded upon the imputation of Christ's righteousness, through the instrument of faith alone. Though justification is quite separate from sanctification, yet sanctification ever accompanies it.

Third, it differs from forgiveness. In some things they agree. It is only God who can forgive sins (Mark 2:7) and He alone can justify (Rom. 3:30). His free grace is the sole moving cause in the one (Eph. 1:7) and of the other (Rom. 3:24). The blood of Christ is the procuring cause of each alike: Matthew 26:28, Romans 5:9. The objects are the same: the persons that are pardoned are justified, and the same that are justified are pardoned; to whom God imputes the righteousness of Christ for their justification to them He gives the remission of sins; and to whom He does not impute sin, but forgives it, to them He imputes righteousness without works (Romans 4:6-8). Both are received by faith (Acts 26:18, Rom. 5:1). But though they agree in these things, in others they differ.

God is said to be "justified" (Rom. 3:4), but it would be blasphemy to speak of Him being "pardoned"—this at once shows the two things are diverse. A criminal may be pardoned, but only a righteous person can truly be justified. Forgiveness deals only with a man's acts, justification with the man himself. Forgiveness respects the claims of mercy, justification those of justice. Pardon only remits the curse due unto sin; in addition justification confers a title to Heaven. Justification applies to the believer with respect to the claims of the law, pardon with respect to the Author of the law. The law does not pardon, for it knows no relaxation; but God pardons the transgressions of the law in His people by providing a satisfaction to the law adequate to their transgressions. The blood of Christ was sufficient to procure pardon (Eph. 1:7), but His righteousness is needed for justification (Rom. 5:19). Pardon takes away the filthy garments, but justification provides a change of raiment (Zech. 3:4). Pardon frees from death (2 Sam. 12:13), but righteousness imputed is called "justification of life" (Rom. 5:18). The one views the believer as completely sinful, the other as completely righteous. Pardon is the remission of punishment, justification is the declaration that no ground for the infliction of punishment exists. Forgiveness may be repeated unto seventy times seven, justification is once for all.

From what has been said in the last paragraph we may see what a serious mistake it is to limit justification to the mere forgiveness of sins. Just as "condemnation" is not the execution of punishment, but rather the formal declaration that the accused is guilty and worthy of punishment; so "justification" is not merely the remission of punishment but the judicial announcement that punishment cannot be justly inflicted—the accused being fully conformed to all the positive requirements of the law in consequence of Christ's perfect obedience being legally reckoned to his account. The justification of a believer is no other than his being admitted to participate in the reward merited by his Surety. Justification is nothing more or less than the righteousness of Christ being imputed to us: the negative blessing issuing therefrom is the remission of sins; the positive, a title to the heavenly inheritance.

Beautifully has it been pointed out that "We cannot separate from Immanuel His own essential excellency. We may see Him bruised and given like beaten incense to the fire, but was incense ever burned without fragrance, and only fragrance being the result? The name of Christ not only cancels sin, it supplies in the place of that which it has canceled, its own everlasting excellency. We cannot have its nullifying power only; the other is the sure concomitant. So was it with every typical sacrifice of the Law. It was stricken: but as being spotless it was burned on the altar for a sweet-smelling savor. The savor ascended as a memorial before God: it was accepted for, and its value was attributed or imputed to him who had brought the vicarious victim. If therefore, we reject the imputation of righteousness, we reject sacrifice as revealed in Scripture; for Scripture knows of no sacrifice whose efficacy is so exhausted in the removal of guilt as to leave nothing to be presented in acceptableness before God" (B. W. Newton).

"What is placing our righteousness in the obedience of Christ, but asserting that we are accounted righteous only because His obedience is accepted for us as if it were our own? Wherefore Ambrose appears to me to have very beautifully exemplified this righteousness in the benediction of Jacob: that as he, who had on his own account no claim to the privileges of primogeniture, being concealed in his brother's habit, and invested with his garment, which diffused a most excellent odor, insinuated himself into the favor of his father, that he might receive the benediction to his own advantage, under the character of another; so we shelter ourselves under the precious purity of Christ" (John Calvin).

Chapter 3
Its Problem

In this and the following chapter our aim will be fourfold. First, to demonstrate the impossibility of any sinner obtaining acceptance and favour with God on the ground of his own performances. Second, to show that the saving of a sinner presented a problem which nought but omniscience could solve, but that the consummate wisdom of God has devised a way whereby He can pronounce righteous a guilty transgressor of His Law without impeaching His veracity, sullying His holiness, or ignoring the claims of justice; yea, in such a way that all His perfections have been displayed and magnified, and the Son of His love glorified. Third, point out the sole ground on which an awakened conscience can find solid and stable peace. Fourth, seek to give God's children a clearer understanding of the exceeding riches of Divine grace, that their hearts may be drawn out in fervent praise unto the Author of "so great salvation."

But let it be pointed out at the onset that, any reader who has never seen himself under the white light of God's holiness, and who has never felt His Word cutting him to the very quick, will be unable to fully enter into the force of what we are about to write. Yea, in all probability, he who is unregenerate is likely to take decided exception unto much of what will be said, denying that any such difficulty exists in the matter of a merciful God pardoning one of His offending creatures. Or, if he does not dissent to that extent, yet he will most likely consider that we have grossly exaggerated the various elements in the case we are about to present, that we have pictured the sinner's condition in far darker hues than was warranted. This must be so, for he has no experimental acquaintance with God, nor is he conscious of the fearful plague of his own heart.

The natural man cannot endure the thought of being thoroughly searched by God. The last thing he desires is to pass beneath the all-seeing eye of his Maker and Judge, so that his every thought and desire, his most secret imagination and motive, stands exposed before Him. It is indeed a most solemn experience when we are made to feel with the Psalmist, "O LORD, Thou hast searched me, and known me. Thou knowest my downsitting and mine uprising, Thou understandest my thought afar off. Thou compassest my path and my lying down, and art acquainted with all my ways. For there is not a word in my tongue, but, lo, O LORD, Thou knowest it altogether. Thou hast beset me behind and before, and laid Thine hand upon me" (Ps. 139:1-5).

Yes, dear reader, the very last thing which the natural man desires is to be searched, through and through by God, and have his real character exposed to view. But when God undertakes to do this very thing—which He either will do in grace in this life, or in judgment in the Day to come—there is no escape for us. Then it is we may well exclaim, "Whither shall I go from Thy Spirit? or whither shall I flee from Thy presence? If I ascend up into Heaven, Thou art there: if I make my bed in Hell, behold, Thou art there. If I take the wings of the morning, and dwell in the uttermost parts of the sea; Even there shall Thy hand lead me, and Thy right hand shall hold me. If I say, Surely the darkness shall cover me; even the night shall be light about me" (Ps. 139:7-11). Then it is we shall be assured, "Yea, the darkness hideth not from Thee; but the night shineth as the day: the darkness and the light are both alike to Thee" (v. 12).

Then it is that the soul is awakened to a realization of who it is with whom it has to do. Then it is that he now perceives something of the high claims of God upon him, the just requirements of His Law, the demands of His holiness. Then it is that he realizes how completely he has failed to consider those claims, how fearfully he has disregarded that law, how miserably he falls short of meeting those demands. Now it is that he perceives he has been "a transgressor from the womb" (Isa. 48:8), that so far from having lived to glorify His Maker, he has done nought but follow the course of this world and fulfill the lust of the flesh. Now it is he realizes that there is "no soundness" in him but, from the sole of the foot even unto the head, "wounds, and bruises, and putrifying sores" (Isa. 1:6). Now it is he is made to see that all his righteousness are as "filthy rags" (Isa. 64:6).

"It is easy for anyone in the cloisters of the schools to indulge himself in idle speculations of the merit of works to justify men; but when he comes into the presence of God, he must bid farewell to these amusements, for there the business is transacted with seriousness, and no ludicrous logomachy (dispute about words) practiced. To this point, then, must our attention be directed, if we wish to make any useful inquiry concerning true righteousness; how we can answer the celestial Judge, when He shall call us to an account. Let us place that Judge before our eyes, not according to the spontaneous imaginations of our minds, but according to the descriptions given of Him in the Scripture; which represents Him as one whose refulgence eclipses the stars, whose power melts the mountains, whose anger shakes the earth, whose wisdom takes the subtle in their own craftiness, whose purity makes all things appear polluted, whose righteousness even the angels are unable to bear, who acquits not the guilty, whose vengeance, when it is once kindled, penetrates even to the abyss of Hell" (John Calvin).

Ah, my reader, tremendous indeed are the effects produced in the soul when one is really brought into the presence of God, and is granted a sight of His awesome majesty. While we measure ourselves by our fellow men, it is easy to reach the conclusion that there is not much wrong with us; but when we approach the dread tribunal of ineffable holiness, we form an entirely different estimate of our character and conduct. While we are occupied with earthly objects we may pride ourselves in the strength of our faculty, but fix the gaze steadily on the midday sun and under its dazzling brilliance the weakness of the eye will at once become apparent. In like manner, while I compare myself with other sinners I can but form a wrong estimate of myself, but if I gauge my life by the plummet of God's Law, and do so in the light of His holiness, I must "Abhor myself, and repent in dust and ashes" (Job 42:6).

But not only has sin corrupted man's being, it has changed his relation to God: it has "alienated" him (Eph. 4:18), and brought him under His righteous condemnation. Man has broken God's Law in thought and word and deed, not once, but times without number. By the Divine tribunal he is pronounced an incorrigible transgressor, a guilty rebel. He is under the curse of his Maker. The law demands that its punishment shall be inflicted upon him; justice clamors for satisfaction. The sinner's case is deplorable, then, to the last degree. When this is painfully felt by the convicted conscience, its agonized possessor cries out, "How then can man be justified with God? or how can he be clean that is born of a woman?" (Job 25:4). How indeed! Let us now consider the various elements which enter into this problem.

The requirements of God's Law. "Every question therefore, respecting justification necessarily brings before us the judicial courts of God. The principles of those courts must be determined by God alone. Even to earthly governors we concede the right of establishing their own laws, and appointing the mode of their enforcement. Shall we then accord this title to man, and withhold it from the all-wise and almighty God? Surely no presumption can be greater than for the creature to sit in judgment on the Creator, and pretend to determine what should, or should not be, the methods of His government. It must be our place reverently to listen to His own exposition of the principles of His own courts, and humbly to thank Him for His goodness in condescending to explain to us what those principles are. As sinners, we can have no claim on God. We do have claim to a revelation that should acquaint us with His ways.

"The judicial principles of the government of God, are, as might be expected, based upon the absolute perfectness of His own holiness. This was fully shown both in the prohibitory and in the mandatory commandments of the law as given at Sinai. That law prohibited not only wrong deeds and wrong counsels of heart, but it went deeper still. It prohibited even wrong desires and wrong tendencies, saying, 'thou shalt not be concupiscent'—that is, thou shalt not have, even momentarily, one desire or tendency that is contrary to the perfectness of God. And then as to its positive requirements, it demanded the perfect, unreserved, perpetual surrender of soul and body, with all its powers, to God and to His service. Not only was it required, that love to Him—love perfect and unremitted—should dwell as a living principle in the heart, but also that it should be developed in action, and that unvaryingly. The mode also of the development through-out, was required to be as perfect as the principle from which the development sprang.

"If any among the children of men be able to substantiate a claim to perfectness such as this, the Courts of God are ready to recognize it. The God of Truth will recognize a truthful claim wher-ever it is found. But if we are unable to present any such claim—if corruption be found in us and in our ways—if in anything we have fallen short of God's glory, then it is obvious that however willing the Courts of God may be to recognize perfectness wherever it exists, such willingness can afford no ground of hope to those, who, instead of having perfectness, have sins and short-comings unnumbered" (B. W. Newton).

The indictment preferred against us. "Hear, O heavens, and give ear, O earth: for the LORD hath spoken, I have nourished and brought up children, and they have rebelled against me. The ox knoweth his owner, and the ass his master's crib: but Israel doth not know, My people doth not consider. Ah sinful nation, a people laden with iniquity, a seed of evildoers, children that are corrupters: they have forsaken the LORD, they have provoked the Holy One of Israel unto anger, they are gone away backward" (Isa. 1:2-4). The eternal God justly charges us with having broken all His commandments—some in act, some in word, all of them in thought and imagination.

The enormity of this charge is heightened by the fact that against light and knowledge we chose the evil and forsook the good: that again and again we deliberately turned aside from God's righteous Law, and went astray like lost sheep, following the evil desires and devices of our own hearts. Above, we find God complaining that inasmuch as we are his creatures, we ought to have obeyed Him, that inasmuch as we owe our very lives to His daily care we ought to have rendered Him fealty instead of disobedience, and have been His loyal subjects instead of turning traitors to His throne. No exaggeration of sin is brought against us, but a statement of fact is declared which it is impossible for us to gainsay. We are ungrateful, unruly, ungodly creatures. Who would keep a horse that refused to work? Who would retain a dog which barked and flew at us? Yet we have broken God's sabbaths, despised His reproofs, abused His mercies.

The sentence of the law. This is clearly announced in the Divine oracles, "Cursed is every one that continueth not in all things which are written in the book of the law to do them" (Gal. 3:10). Whoever violates a single precept of the Divine Law exposes himself to the displeasure of God, and to punishment as the expression of that displeasure. No allowance is made for ignorance, no distinction is made between persons, no relaxation of its strictness is permissible: "The soul that sinneth it shall die" is its inexorable pronouncement. No exception is made whether the trans-gressor be young or old, rich or poor, Jew or Gentile: "the wages of sin is death"; for "the wrath of God is revealed from heaven against all ungodliness and unrighteousness of men" (Rom. 1:18).

The Judge Himself is inflexibly just. In the high court of Divine justice God takes the law in its strictest and sternest aspect, and judges rigidly according to the letter. "But we are sure that the judgment of God is according to truth against them which commit such things. . .Who will render to every man according to his deeds" (Rom. 2:2, 6). God is inexorably righteous, and will not show any partiality either to the law or to its transgressor. The Most High has determined that His Holy Law shall be faithfully upheld and its sanctions strictly enforced.

What would this country be like if all its judges ceased to uphold and enforce the laws of the land? What conditions would prevail were sentimental mercy to reign at the expense of righteousness? Now God is the Judge of all the earth and the moral Ruler of the universe. Holy Writ declares that "justice and judgment," and not pity and clemency, are the "habitation" of His "throne" (Ps. 89:14). God's attributes do not conflict with each other. His mercy does not override His justice, nor is His grace ever shown at the expense of righteousness. Each of His perfections is given free course. For God to give a sinner entrance into Heaven simply because He loved him, would be like a judge sheltering an escaped convict in his own home merely because he pitied him. Scripture emphatically declares that God, "will by no means clear the guilty" (Ex. 34:7).

The sinner is unquestionably guilty. It is not merely that he has infirmities or that he is not as good as he ought to be: he has set at nought God's authority, violated His commandments, trodden His Laws under foot. And this is true not only of a certain class of offenders, but "all the world" is "guilty before God" (Rom. 3:19). "There is none righteous, no, not one: They are all gone out of the way, they are together become unprofitable; there is none that doeth good, no, not one" (Rom. 3:10, 12). It is impossible for any man to clear himself from this fearful charge. He can neither show that the crimes of which he is accused have not been committed, nor that having been committed, he had a right to do them. He can neither disprove the charges which the law preferred against him, nor justify himself in the perpetration of them.

Here then is how the case stands. The law demands personal, perfect, and perpetual conformity to its precepts, in heart and act, in motive and performance. God charges each one of us with having failed to meet those just demands, and declares we have violated His commandments in thought and word and deed. The law therefore pronounces upon us a sentence of condemnation, curses us, and demands the infliction of its penalty, which is death. The One before whose tribunal we stand is omniscient, and cannot be deceived or imposed upon; He is inflexibly just, and swayed by no sentimental considerations. We, the accused, are guilty, unable to refute the accusations of the law, unable to vindicate our sinful conduct, unable to offer any satisfaction or atonement for our crimes. Truly, our case is desperate to the last degree.

Here, then, is the problem. How can God justify the willful transgressor of His Law without justifying his sins? How can God deliver him from the penalty of His broken Law without compromising His holiness and going back upon His word that He will "by no means clear the guilty"? How can life be granted the guilty culprit without repealing the sentence "the soul that sinneth it shall die"? How can mercy be shown to the sinner without justice being flouted? It is a problem which must forever have baffled every finite intelligence. Yet, blessed be His name, God has, in His consummate wisdom, devised a way whereby the "chief of sinners" may be dealt with by Him as though he were perfectly innocent; nay more, He pronounces him righteous, up to the required standard of the law, and entitled to the reward of eternal life. How this can be will be taken up in the next chapter.

Chapter 4
Its Basis

In our last chapter we contemplated the problem which is presented in the justifying or pronouncing righteous one who is a flagrant violator of the Law of God. Some may have been surprised at the introduction of such a term as "problem": as there are many in the ranks of the ungodly who feel that the world owes them a living, so there are not a few Pharisees in Christendom who suppose it is due them that at death their Creator should take them to Heaven. But different far is it with one who has been enlightened and convicted by the Holy Spirit, so that he sees himself to be a filthy wretch, a vile rebel against God. Such an one will ask, seeing that the word of God so plainly declares "there shall in no wise enter into it anything that defileth, neither whatsoever worketh abomination" (Rev. 21:27), how is it possible that I can ever gain admission into the heavenly Jerusalem? How can it be that one so completely devoid of righteousness as I am, and so filled with unrighteousness, should ever be pronounced just by a holy God?

Various attempts have been made by unbelieving minds to solve this problem. Some have reasoned that if they now turn over a new leaf, thoroughly reform their lives and henceforth walk in obedience to God's Law, they shall be approved before the Divine Tribunal. This scheme, reduced to simple terms, is salvation by our own works. But such a scheme is utterly untenable, and salvation by such means is absolutely impossible. The works of a reformed sinner cannot be the meritorious or efficacious cause of his salvation, and that for the following reasons. First, no provision is made for his previous failures. Suppose that henceforth I never again transgress God's Law, what is to atone for my past sins? Second, a fallen and sinful creature cannot produce that which is perfect, and nothing short of perfection is acceptable to God. Third, were it possible for us to be saved by our own works, then the sufferings and death of Christ were needless. Fourth, salvation by our own merits would entirely eclipse the glory of Divine grace.

Others suppose this problem may be solved by an appeal to the bare mercy of God. But mercy is not an attribute that overshadows all the other Divine perfections: justice, truth, and holiness are also operative in the salvation of God's elect. The law is not set aside, but honored and magnified. The truth of God in His solemn threats is not sullied, but faithfully carried out. The Divine righteousness is not flouted, but vindicated. One of God's perfections is not exercised to the injury of any of the others, but all of them shine forth with equal clearness in the plan which Divine wisdom devised. Mercy at the expense of justice over-ridden would not suit the Divine government, and justice enforced to the exclusion of mercy would not befit the Divine character. The problem which no finite intelligence could solve was how both might be exercised in the sinner's salvation.

A striking example of mercy helpless before the claims of the law occurs in Daniel 6. There we find that Darius, the king of Babylon, was induced by his nobles to sign a decree that any subject within his kingdom who should pray, or "ask a petition of any God or man for thirty days" save the king himself, should be cast into the den of lions. Daniel knowing this, nevertheless, continued to pray before God as hitherto. Whereupon the nobles acquainted Darius with his violation of the royal edict, which "according to the law of the Medes and Persians altereth not," and demanded his punishment. Now Daniel stood high in the king's favor, and he greatly desired to show clemency unto him, so he "set his heart on Daniel to deliver him, and he labored till the going down of the sun to deliver him." But he found no way out of the difficulty: the law must be honored, so Daniel was cast into the lion's den.

An equally striking example of law helpless in the presence of mercy is found in John 8. There we read of a woman taken in the act of adultery. The scribes and Pharisees apprehended her and set her before Christ, charging her with the crime, and reminding the Savior that "Moses in the law commanded us that such should be stoned." She was unquestionably guilty, and her accusers were determined that the penalty of the law should be inflicted upon her. The Lord turned to them and said, "He that is without sin among you, let him first cast a stone at her"; and they, being convicted by their own conscience, went out one by one, leaving the adulteress alone with Christ. Turning to her, He asked, "Woman, where are thine accusers, hath no man condemned thee?" She replied, "No man, Lord," and He answered, "Neither do I condemn thee, go, and sin no more."

The two adverse principles are seen operating in conjunction in Luke 15. The "Father" could not have the (prodigal) son at His table clad in the rags of the far country, but He could go out and meet him in those rags: He could fall on his neck and kiss him in those rags—it was blessedly characteristic of His grace so to do; but to seat him at His table in garments suited to the swine-troughs would not be fitting. But the grace which brought the Father out to the prodigal "reigned" through that righteousness which brought the prodigal in to the Father's house. It had not been "grace" had the Father waited till the prodigal decked himself out in suitable garments of his own providing; nor would it have been "righteousness" to bring him to His table in his rags. Both grace and righteousness shone forth in their respective beauty when the Father said "bring forth the best robe, and put it on him."

It is through Christ and His atonement that the justice and mercy of God, His righteousness and grace, meet in the justifying of a believing sinner. In Christ is found the solution to every problem which sin has raised. In the Cross of Christ every attribute of God shines forth in its meridian splendor. In the satisfaction which the Redeemer offered unto God every claim of the law, whether preceptive or penal, has been fully met. God has been infinitely more honored by the obedience of the last Adam than He was dishonored by the disobedience of the first Adam. The justice of God was infinitely more magnified when its awful sword smote the beloved Son, than had every member of the human race burned for ever and ever in the lake of fire. There is infinitely more efficacy in the blood of Christ to cleanse, than there is in sin to befoul. There is infinitely more merit in Christ's one perfect righteousness than there is demerit in the combined unrighteousness of all the ungodly. Well may we exclaim, "But God forbid that I should glory, save in the cross of our Lord Jesus Christ" (Gal. 6:14).

But while many are agreed that the atoning death of Christ is the meritorious cause of His peoples' salvation, there are now few indeed who can give any clear Scriptural explanation of the way and manner by which the work of Christ secures the justification of all who believe. Hence the need for a clear and full statement thereon. Hazy ideas at this point are both dishonoring to God and unsettling to our peace. It is of first importance that the Christian should obtain a clear understanding of the ground on which God pardons his sins and grants him a title to the heavenly inheritance. Perhaps this may best be set forth under three words: substitution, identification, imputation. As their Surety and Sponsor, Christ entered the place occupied by His people under the law, so identifying Himself with them as to be their Head and Representative, and as such He assumed and discharged all their legal obligations: their liabilities being transferred to Him, His merits being transferred to them.

The Lord Jesus has wrought out for His people a perfect righteousness by obeying the law in thought and word and deed, and this righteousness is imputed to them, reckoned to their account. The Lord Jesus has suffered the penalty of the law in their stead, and through His atoning death they are cleansed from all guilt. As creatures they were under obligations to obey Gods' Law; as criminals (transgressors) they were under the death-sentence of the law. Therefore, to fully meet our liabilities and discharge our debts it was necessary that our Substitute should both obey and die. The shedding of Christ's blood blotted out our sins, but it did not, of itself, provide the "best robe" for us. To silence the accusations of the law against us so that there is now "no condemnation to them which are in Christ Jesus" is simply a negative blessing: something more was required, namely, a positive righteousness, the keeping of the law, so that we might be entitled to its blessing and reward.

In Old Testament times the name under which the Messiah and Mediator was foretold is, "THE LORD OUR RIGHTEOUSNESS" (Jer. 23:6). It was plainly predicted by Daniel that He should come here to "finish the transgression, and to make an end of sins, and to make reconciliation for iniquity, and to bring in everlasting righteousness" (9:24). Isaiah announced "Surely, shall one say, in the LORD have I righteousness and strength: even to Him shall men come; and all that are incensed against Him shall be ashamed. In the LORD shall all the seed of Israel be justified, and shall glory" (45:24, 25). And again, he represents each of the redeemed exclaiming, "I will greatly rejoice in the LORD, my soul shall be joyful in my God; for He hath clothed me with the garments of salvation, He hath covered me with the robe of righteousness" (61:10).

In Romans 4:6-8 we read, "David also describeth the blessedness of the man, unto whom God imputeth righteousness without works, Saying, Blessed are they whose iniquities are forgiven, and whose sins are covered. Blessed is the man to whom the Lord will not impute sin." Here we are shown the inseparability of the two things: God imputing "righteousness" and God not imputing "sins." The two are never divided: unto whom God imputes not sin He imputes righteousness; and unto whom He imputes righteousness, He imputes not sin. But the particular point which we are most anxious for the reader to grasp is, Whose "righteousness" is it that God imputes or reckons to the account of the one who believes? The answer is, that righteousness which was wrought out by our Surety, that obedience to the law which was vicariously rendered by our Sponsor, even "the righteousness of God and our Savior Jesus Christ" (2 Pet. 1:1). This righteousness is not only "unto all" but also "upon all them that believe" (Rom. 3:22). It is called "the righteousness of God" because it was the righteousness of the God-man Mediator, just as in Acts 20:28 His blood is call the blood of God.

The "righteousness of God" which is mentioned so frequently in the Roman epistle refers not to the essential righteousness of the Divine character, for that cannot possibly be imputed or legally transferred to any creature. When we are told in 10:3 that the Jews were "ignorant of God's righteousness" it most certainly does not mean they were in the dark concerning the Divine rectitude or that they knew nothing about God's justice; but it signifies that they were unenlightened as to the righteousness which the God-man Mediator had vicariously wrought out for His people. This is abundantly clear from the remainder of that verse: "and going about to establish their own righteousness"—not their own rectitude or justice, but performing works by which they hoped to merit acceptance with God. So tightly did they cling to this delusion, they, "submitted not themselves unto the righteousness of God": that is, they refused to turn from their self-righteousness and put their trust in the obedience and sufferings of the incarnate Son of God.

"I would explain what we mean by the imputation of Christ's righteousness. Sometimes the expression is taken by our divines in a larger sense, for the imputation of all that Christ did and suffered for our redemption whereby we are free from guilt, and stand righteous in the sight of

God; and so implies the imputation both of Christ's satisfaction and obedience. But here I intend it in a stricter sense, for the imputation of that righteousness or moral goodness that consists in the obedience of Christ. And by that obedience being imputed to us, is meant no other than this, that that righteousness of Christ is accepted for us, and admitted instead of that perfect inherent righteousness that ought to be in ourselves: Christ's perfect obedience shall be reckoned to our account, so that we shall have the benefit of it, as though we had performed it ourselves: and so we suppose, that a title to eternal life is given us as the reward of this righteousness" (Jonathan Edwards).

The one passage which casts the clearest light upon that aspect of justification which we are now considering is 2 Corinthians 5:21, "For He hath made Him to be sin for us, who knew no sin; that we might be made the righteousness of God in Him." Here we have the counter imputations: of our sins to Christ, of His righteousness to us. As the teaching of this verse is of such vital moment let us endeavor to consider its terms the more closely. How was Christ "made sin for us"? By God imputing to Him our disobedience, or our transgressions of the law; in like manner, we are made "the righteousness of God in Him" (in Christ, not in ourselves) by God imputing to us Christ's obedience, His fulfilling the precepts of the law for us.

As Christ "knew no sin" by inward defilement or personal commission, so we "knew" or had no righteousness of our own by inward conformity to the law, or by personal obedience to it. As Christ was "made sin" by having our sins placed to His account or charged upon Him in a judicial way, and as it was not by any criminal conduct of His own that He was "made sin," so it is not by any pious activities of our own that we become "righteous": Christ was not "made sin" by the infusion of depravity, nor are we "made righteous" by the infusion of holiness. Though personally holy, our Sponsor did, by entering our law-place, render Himself officially liable to the wrath of God; and so though personally unholy, we are, by virtue of our legal identification with Christ, entitled to the favor of God. As the consequence of Christ's being "made sin for us" was, that "the LORD laid on Him the iniquity of us all" (Isa. 53:6), so the consequence of Christ's obedience being reckoned to our account is that God lays righteousness "upon all them that believe" (Rom. 3:22). As our sins were the judicial ground of the sufferings of Christ, by which sufferings He satisfied Justice; so Christ's righteousness is the judicial ground of our acceptance with God, by which our pardon is an act of Justice.

Notice carefully that in 2 Corinthians 5:21 it is God who "made" or legally constituted Christ to be "sin for us," though as Hebrews 10:7 shows, the Son gladly acquiesced therein. "He was made sin by imputation: the sins of all His people were transferred unto Him, laid upon Him, and placed to His account and having them upon Him He was treated by the justice of God as if He had been not only a sinner, but a mass of sin: for to be made sin is a stronger expression than to be made a sinner" (John Gill). "That we might be made the righteousness of God in Him" signifies to be legally constituted righteous before God—justified. "It is a righteousness 'in Him,' in Christ, and not in ourselves, and therefore must mean the righteousness of Christ: so called, because it is wrought by Christ, who is God over all, the true God, and eternal life" (Ibid.).

The same counter-exchange which has been before us in 2 Corinthians 5:21 is found again in Galatians 3:13, 14, "Christ hath redeemed us from the curse of the law, being made a curse for us: for it is written, Cursed is every one that hangeth on a tree: That the blessing of Abraham might come on the Gentiles through Jesus Christ." As the Surety of His people, Christ was "made under the law" (Gal. 4:4), stood in their law-place and stead, and having all their sins imputed to Him, and the law finding them all upon Him, condemned Him for them; and so the justice of God delivered Him up to the accursed death of the cross. The purpose, as well as the consequence, of this was "That the blessing of Abraham might come on the Gentiles": the "blessing of Abraham" (as Rom. 4 shows) was justification by faith through the righteousness of Christ.

> "Upon a Life I did not live,
> Upon a Death I did not die;
> Another's death, Another's life
> I'd rest my soul eternally."

Chapter 5
Its Nature

Justification, strictly speaking, consists in God's imputing to His elect the righteousness of Christ, that alone being the meritorious cause or formal ground on which He pronounces them righteous: the righteousness of Christ is that to which God has respect when He pardons and accepts the sinner. By the nature of justification we have reference to the constituent elements of the same, which are enjoyed by the believer. These are, the non-imputation of guilt or the remission of sins, and second, of the investing of the believer with a legal title to Heaven. The alone ground on which God forgives any man's sins, and admits him into His judicial favor, is the vicarious work of his Surety—that perfect satisfaction which Christ offered to the law on his behalf. It is of great importance to be clear on the fact that Christ was "made under the law" not only that He might redeem His people "from the curse of the law" (Gal. 3:13), but also that they might "receive the adoption of sons" (Gal. 4:4, 5), that is, be invested with the privileges of sons.

This grand doctrine of Justification was proclaimed in its purity and clarity by the Reformers—Luther, Calvin, Zanchius, Peter Martyr, etc.; but it began to be corrupted in the seventeenth century by men who had only a very superficial knowledge of it, who taught that justification consisted merely in the removal of guilt or forgiveness of sins, excluding the positive admittance of man into God's judicial favor: in other words, they restricted justification unto deliverance from Hell, failing to declare that it also conveys a title unto Heaven. This error was perpetuated by John Wesley, and then by the Plymouth Brethren, who, denying that the righteousness of Christ is imputed to the believer, seek to find their title to eternal life in a union with Christ in His resurrection. Few today are clear upon the twofold content of Justification, because few today understand the nature of that righteousness which is imputed to all who believe.

To show that we have not misrepresented the standard teachings of the Plymouth Brethren on this subject, we quote from Mr. W. Kelly's "Notes on Romans." In his "Introduction" he states, "There is nothing to hinder our understanding 'the righteousness of God' in its usual sense of an attribute or quality of God" (p. 35). But how could an "attribute" or "quality" of God be "upon all them that believe" (Rom. 3:22)? Mr. Kelly will not at all allow that the "righteousness of God" and "the righteousness of Christ" are one and the same, and hence, when he comes to Romans 4 (where so much is said about "righteousness" being imputed to the believer) he evacuates the whole of its blessed teaching by trying to make out that this is nothing more than our own faith, saying of Abraham, "his faith in God's word as that which he exercised, and which was accounted as righteousness" (p. 47).

The "righteousness of Christ" which is imputed to the believer consists of that perfect obedience which He rendered unto the precepts of God's Law and that death which He died under the penalty of the law. It has been rightly said that, "There is the very same need of Christ's obeying the law in our stead, in order to the reward, as of His suffering the penalty of the law in our stead in order to our escaping the penalty; and the same reason why one should be accepted on our account as the other... To suppose that all Christ does in order to make atonement for us by suffering is to make Him our Savior but in part. It is to rob Him of half His glory as a Savior. For if so, all that He does is to deliver us from Hell; He does not purchase Heaven for us" (Jonathan Edwards). Should any one object to the idea of Christ "purchasing" Heaven for His people, he may at once be referred to Ephesians 1:14, where Heaven is expressly designated "the purchased possession."

The imputation to the believer's account of that perfect obedience which his Surety rendered unto the law for him is plainly taught in Romans 5:18, 19, "Therefore as by the offence of one judgment came upon all men to condemnation; even so by the righteousness of one the free gift came upon all men unto justification of life. For as by one man's disobedience many were made sinners, so by the obedience of one shall many be made righteous." Here the "offence" or "disobedience" of the first Adam is set over against the "righteousness" or "obedience" of the last Adam, and inasmuch as the disobedience of the former was an actual transgression of the law, therefore the obedience of the latter must be His active obedience unto the law; otherwise the force of the Apostle's antithesis would fail entirely. As this vital point (the chief glory of the Gospel) is now so little understood, and in some quarters disputed, we must enter into some detail.

The one who was justified upon his believing sustained a twofold relation unto God: first, he was a responsible creature, born under the law; second, he was a criminal, having transgressed that law—though his criminality has not canceled his obligation to obey the law any more than a man who recklessly squanders his money is no longer due to pay his debts. Consequently, justification consists of two parts, namely, an acquittal from guilt, or the condemnation of the law (deliverance from Hell), and the receiving him into God's favor, on the sentence of the law's approval (a legal title to Heaven). And therefore, the ground upon which God pronounces him just is also a double one, as the one complete satisfaction of Christ is viewed in its two distinct parts: namely, His vicarious obedience unto the precepts of the law, and His substitutionary death under the penalty of the law, the merits of both being equally imputed or reckoned to the account of him who believes.

Against this it has been objected, "The law requires no man to obey and die too." To which we reply in the language of J. Hervey (1750), "But did it not require a transgressor to obey and die? If not, then transgression robs the law of its right, and vacates all obligation to obedience. Did it not require the Surety for sinful men to obey and die? If the surety dies only, He only delivers from penalty. But this affords no claim to life, no title to a reward—unless you can produce some such edict from the Court of Heaven. Suffer this, and thou shalt live.' I find it written 'In keeping Thy commandments there is great reward' (Ps. 19:11), but nowhere do I read, 'In undergoing Thy curse, there is the same reward.' Whereas, when we join the active and passive obedience of our Lord—the peace-speaking Blood with the Life-giving righteousness—both made infinitely meritorious and infinitely efficacious by the Divine glory of His person, how full does our justification appear! How firm does it stand!"

It is not sufficient that the believer stand before God with no sins upon him—that is merely negative. The holiness of God requires a positive righteousness to our account—that His Law be perfectly kept. But we are unable to keep it, therefore our Sponsor fulfilled it for us. By the blood-shedding of our blessed Substitute the gates of Hell have been forever shut against all those for whom He died. By the perfect obedience of our blessed Surety the gates of Heaven are opened wide unto all who believe. My title for standing before God, not only without fear, but in the conscious sunshine of His full favor, is because Christ has been made "righteousness" unto me (1 Cor. 1:30). Christ not only paid all my debts, but fully discharged all my responsibilities. The law-Giver is my law-Fulfiller. Every holy aspiration of Christ, every godly thought, every gracious word, every righteous act of the Lord Jesus, from Bethlehem to Calvary, unite in forming that "best robe" in which the seed royal stand arrayed before God.

Yet sad to say, even so widely-read and generally-respected a writer as the late Sir Rob. Anderson, said in his book, "The Gospel and Its Ministry" (Chapter on Justification by Blood), "Vicarious obedience is an idea wholly beyond reason; how could a God of righteousness and truth reckon a man who has broken law to have kept law, because someone else has kept it? The thief is not declared to be honest because his neighbor or his kinsman is a good citizen." What a pitiable dragging down to the bar of sin-polluted human reason, and a measuring by worldly relations, of that Divine transaction wherein the "manifold wisdom of God" was exercised! What is impossible with men is possible with God. Did Sir Robert never read that Old Testament prediction wherein the Most High God declared, "Therefore, behold, I will proceed to do a marvelous work among this people, even a marvelous work and a wonder: for the wisdom of their wise men shall perish, and the understanding of their prudent men shall be hid" (Isa. 29:14)?

It is pointed out that, "In the human realm, both innocence and righteousness are transferable in their effects, but that in themselves they are untransferable." From this it is argued that neither sin nor righteousness are in themselves capable of being transferred, and that though God treated Christ as if He were the sinner, and deals with the believer as though he were righteous, nevertheless, we must not suppose that either is actually the case; still less ought we to affirm that Christ deserved to suffer the curse, or that His people are entitled to be taken to Heaven. Such is a fair sample of the theological ignorance of these degenerate times, such is a representative example of how Divine things are being measured by human standards; by such sophistries is the fundamental truth of imputation now being repudiated.

Rightly did W. Rushton, in his "Particular Redemption," affirm, "In the great affair of our salvation, our God stands single and alone. In this most glorious work, there is such a display of justice, mercy, wisdom and power, as never entered into the heart of man to conceive, and consequently, can have no parallel in the actions of mortals. 'Who hath declared this from ancient time? who hath told it from that time? have not I the LORD? and there is no God else beside Me; a just God and a Savior; there is none beside Me': Isaiah 45:21." No, in the very nature of the case no analogy whatever is to be found in any human transactions with God's transferring our sins to Christ or Christ's obedience to us, for the simple but sufficient reason that no such union exists between worldlings as obtains between Christ and His people. But let us further amplify this counter-imputation.

The afflictions which the Lord Jesus experienced were not only sufferings at the hands of men, but also enduring punishment at the hand of God: "it pleased the LORD to bruise Him" (Isa. 53:10); "Awake, O sword, against My Shepherd, and against the man that is My Fellow, saith the LORD of hosts: smite the shepherd" (Zech. 13:7) was His edict. But lawful "punishment" presupposes criminality; a righteous God had never inflicted the curse of the law upon Christ unless He had deserved it. That is strong language we are well aware, yet not stronger than what Holy Writ fully warrants, and things need to be stated forcibly and plainly today if an apathetic people is to be aroused. It was because God had transferred to their Substitute all the sins of His people that, officially, Christ deserved to be paid sin's wages.

The translation of our sins to Christ was clearly typed out under the Law: "And Aaron shall lay both his hands upon the head of the live goat, (expressing identification with the substitute), and confess over him all the iniquities of the children of Israel, and all their transgressions in all their sins, putting them upon the head of the goat (denoting transference), and shall send him away by the hand of a fit man into the wilderness: And the goat shall bear upon him all their iniquities unto a land not inhabited" (Lev. 16:21, 22). So too it was expressly announced by the Prophets: "The LORD hath laid on Him the iniquity of us all... He shall bear their iniquities" (Isa. 53:6, 11). In that great Messianic Psalm, the 69th, we hear the Surety saying, "O God, Thou knowest My foolishness;

and My sins are not hid from Thee" (v. 5) —how could the spotless Redeemer speak thus, unless the sins of His people had been laid upon Him?

When God imputed sin to Christ as the sinner's Surety, He charged Him with the same, and dealt with Him accordingly. Christ could not have suffered in the stead of the guilty unless their guilt had been first transferred to Him. The sufferings of Christ were penal. God by act of transcendent grace (to us) laid the iniquities of all that are saved upon Christ, and in consequence, Divine justice finding sin upon Him, punished Him. He who will by no means clear the guilty must strike through sin and smite its bearer, no matter whether it be the sinner himself or One who vicariously takes his place. But as G. S. Bishop well said, "When justice once strikes the Son of God, justice exhausts itself. Sin is amerced in an Infinite Object." The atonement of Christ was contrary to our processes of law because it rose above their finite limitations!

Now as the sins of him who believes were, by God, transferred and imputed to Christ so that God regarded and treated Him accordingly—visiting upon Him the curse of the law, which is death; even so the obedience or righteousness of Christ is, by God, transferred and imputed to the believer so that God now regards and deals with him accordingly—bestowing upon him the blessing of the law, which is life. And any denial of that fact, no matter by whomsoever made, is a repudiation of the cardinal principle of the Gospel. "The moment the believing sinner accepts Christ as his Substitute, he finds himself not only freed from his sins, but rewarded: he gets all Heaven because of the glory and merits of Christ (Rom. 5:17). The atonement, then, which we preach is one of absolute exchange (1 Pet. 3:18). It is that Christ took our place literally, in order that we might take His place literally—that God regarded and treated Christ as the Sinner, and that He regards and treats the believing sinner as Christ.

"It is not enough for a man to be pardoned. He, of course, is then innocent—washed from his sin—put back again, like Adam in Eden, just where he was. But that is not enough. It was required of Adam in Eden that he should actually keep the command. It was not enough that he did not break it, or that he is regarded, through the Blood, as though he did not break it. He must keep it: he must continue in all things that are written in the book of the law to do them. How is this necessity supplied? Man must have a righteousness, or God cannot accept him. Man must have a perfect obedience, or else God cannot reward him" (G. S. Bishop). That necessary and perfect obedience is to be found alone in that perfect life, lived by Christ in obedience to the law, before He went to the cross, which is reckoned to the believer's account.

It is not that God treats as righteous one who is not actually so (that would be a fiction), but that He actually constitutes the believer so, not by infusing a holy nature in his heart, but by reckoning the obedience of Christ to his account. Christ's obedience is legally transferred to him so that he is now rightly and justly regarded as righteous by the Divine Law. It is very far more than a naked pronouncement of righteousness upon one who is without any sufficient foundation for the judgment of God to declare him righteous. No, it is a positive and judicial act of God "whereby, on the consideration of the mediation of Christ, He makes an effectual grant and donation of a true, real, perfect righteousness, even that of Christ Himself unto all that do believe, and accounting it as theirs, on His own gracious act, both absolves them from sin, and granteth them right and title unto eternal life" (John Owen).

It now remains for us to point out the ground on which God acts in this counter-imputation of sin to Christ and righteousness to His people. That ground was the everlasting covenant. The objection that it is unjust the innocent should suffer in order that the guilty may escape loses all its force once the covenant-headship and responsibility of Christ is seen, and the covenant-oneness with Him of those whose sins He bore. There could have been no such thing as a vicarious sacrifice unless there had been some union between Christ and those for whom He died, and that relation of union must have subsisted before He died, yea, before our sins were imputed to Him. Christ undertook to make full satisfaction to the law for His people because He sustained to them the relation of a surety. But what justified His acting as their surety? He stood as their Surety because He was their substitute: He acted on their behalf, because He stood in their room. But what justified the substitution?

No satisfactory answer can be given to the last question until the grand doctrine of everlasting covenant-oneness comes into view: that is the great underlying relation. The federal oneness between the Redeemer and the redeemed, the choosing of them in Christ before the foundation of the world (Eph. 1:4), by which a legal union was established between Him and them, is that which alone accounts for and justifies all else. "For both He that sanctifieth and they who are sanctified are all of one: for which cause He is not ashamed to call them brethren" (Heb. 2:11). As the Covenant-Head of His people, Christ was so related to them that their responsibilities necessarily became His, and we are so related to Him that His merits necessarily become ours. Thus, as we said in an earlier chapter, three words give us the key to and sum up the whole transaction: substitution, identification, imputation—all of which rest upon covenant-oneness. Christ was substituted for us, because He is one with us—identified with us, and we with Him. Thus God dealt with us as occupying Christ's place of worthiness and acceptance. May the Holy Spirit grant both writer and reader such an heart-apprehension of this wondrous and blessed truth, that overflowing gratitude may move us unto fuller devotedness unto Him who loved us and gave Himself for us.

Chapter 6
Its Source

Let us here review, briefly, the ground which we have already covered. We have seen, first, that "to justify" means to pronounce righteous. It is not a Divine work, but a Divine verdict, the sentence of the Supreme Court, declaring that the one justified stands perfectly conformed to all the requirements of the law. Justification assures the believer that the Judge of all the earth is for him, and not against him: that justice itself is on his side. Second, we dwelt upon the great and seemingly insoluble problem which is thereby involved: how a God of truth can pronounce righteous one who is completely devoid of righteousness, how He can receive into His judicial favor one who is a guilty criminal, how He can exercise mercy without insulting justice, how He can be gracious and yet enforce the high demands of His Law. Third, we have shown that the solution to this problem is found in the perfect satisfaction which the incarnate Son rendered unto Divine Law, and that on the basis of that satisfaction God can truthfully and righteously pronounce just all who truly believe the Gospel.

In our last article we pointed out that the satisfaction which Christ made to the Divine Law consists of two distinct parts, answering to the twofold need of him who is to be justified. First, as a responsible creature I am under binding obligations to keep the law—to love God with all my heart and my neighbor as myself. Second, as a criminal I am under the condemnation and curse of that law which I have constantly transgressed in thought and word and deed. Therefore, if another was to act as my surety and make reparation for me, he must perfectly obey all the precepts of the law, and then endure the awful penalty of the law. That is exactly what was undertaken and accomplished by the Lord Jesus in His virtuous life and vicarious death. By Him every demand of the law was fulfilled; by Him every obligation of the believer was fully met.

It has been objected by some that the obedience of Christ could not be imputed to the account of others, for being "made under the law" (Gal. 4:4) as man, He owed submission to the law on His own account. This is a serious mistake, arising out of a failure to recognize the absolute uniqueness of the Man Christ Jesus. Unlike us, He was never placed under the Adamic Covenant, and therefore He owed nothing to the law. Moreover, the manhood of Christ never had a separate existence: in the virgin's womb the eternal Son took the seed of Mary into union with His Deity, so that whereas the first man was of the earth, earthy, "the second Man is the Lord from Heaven" (1 Cor. 15:47), and as such He was infinitely superior to the law, owing nothing to it, being personally possessed of all the excellence of Deity. Even while He walked this earth "in Him dwelleth all the fullness of the Godhead bodily."

It was entirely for His peoples' sake that the God-man Mediator was "made under the law." It was in order to work out for them a perfect righteousness, which should be placed to their account, that He took upon Himself the form of a servant and became "obedient unto death." What has been said above supplies the answer to another foolish objection which has been made against this blessed truth, namely, that if the obedience of the Man Christ Jesus were transferable it would be available only for one other man, seeing that every human being is required to obey the law, and that if vicarious obedience be acceptable to God then there would have to be as many separate sureties as there are believers who are saved. That would be true if the "surety" were merely human, but inasmuch as the Surety provided by God is the God-man Mediator, His righteousness is of infinite value, for the law was more "honored and magnified" by the obedience of "the Lord from Heaven" than had every member of the human race perfectly kept it. The righteousness of the God-man Mediator is of infinite value, and therefore available for as many as God is pleased to impute it unto.

The value or merit of an action increases in proportion to the dignity of the person who performs it, and He who obeyed in the room and stead of the believer was not only a holy man, but the Son of the living God. Moreover, let it be steadily borne in mind that the obedience which Christ rendered to the law was entirely voluntary. Prior to His incarnation, He was under no obligation to the law, for He had Himself (being God) formulated that law. His being made of a woman and made under the law was entirely a free act on His own part. We come into being and are placed under the law without our consent; but the Lord from Heaven existed before His incarnation, and assumed our nature by His spontaneous act: "Lo, I come... I delight to do Thy will" (Ps. 40:7, 8). No other person could use such language, for it clearly denotes a liberty to act or not to act, which no mere creature possesses. Placing Himself under the law and rendering obedience to it was founded solely on His own voluntary deed. His obedience was therefore a "free will offering," and therefore as He did not owe obedience to the law by any prior obligation, not being at all necessary for Himself, it is available for imputation to others, that they should be rewarded for it.

If, then, the reader has been able to follow us closely in the above observations, it should be clear to him that when Scripture speaks of God "justifying the ungodly" the meaning is that the believing sinner is brought into an entirely new relation to the law; that in consequence of Christ's righteousness being made over to him, he is now absolved from all liability to punishment, and is given a title to all the reward merited by Christ's obedience. Blessed, blessed truth for comforting the conscientious Christian who daily groans under a sense of his sad failures and who mourns because of his lack of practical conformity to the image of Christ. Satan is ever ready to harass such an one and tell him his profession is vain. But it is the believer's privilege to overcome him by "the blood of the Lamb" (Rev. 12:11)—to remind himself anew that Another has atoned for all his sins, and that despite his innumerable shortcomings he still stands "accepted in the Beloved" (Eph. 1:6). If I am truly resting on the finished work of Christ for me, the Devil cannot successfully lay anything to my charge before God, though if I am walking carelessly He will suffer him to charge my conscience with unrepented and unconfessed sins.

In our last chapter, under the nature of justification, we saw that the constituent elements of this Divine blessing are two in number, the one being negative in its character, the other positive. The negative blessing is the cancellation of guilt, or the remission of sins—the entire record of the believer's transgressions of the law, filed upon the Divine docket, having been blotted out by the precious blood of Christ. The positive blessing is the bestowal upon the believer of an inalienable title to the reward which the obedience of Christ merited for him—that reward is life, the judicial favor of God, Heaven itself. The unchanging sentence of the law is "the man which doeth those things shall live by them" (Rom. 10:5). As we read in Romans 7:10, "the commandment, which was ordained to life." It is just as true that obedience to the law secured life, as disobedience insured death. When the young ruler asked Christ "what good thing shall I do, that I may have eternal life?" He answered, "If thou wilt enter into life, keep the commandments" (Matt. 19:16, 17).

It was because His people had failed to "keep the commandments" that the God-man Mediator was "made under the law," and obeyed it for them. And therefore its reward of "life" is due unto those whose Surety He was; yea, due unto Christ Himself to bestow upon them. Therefore did the Surety, when declaring "I have glorified Thee on the earth: I have finished the work which Thou gavest Me to do" (John 17:4), remind the Father, "that He should give eternal life to as many as Thou hast given Him" (v. 2). But more, on the footing of justice, Christ demands that His people be taken to Heaven, saying, "Father, I will that they also, whom Thou hast given Me, be with Me where I am" (John 17:24)—He claims eternal life for His people on the ground of His finished work, as the reward of His obedience.

"Therefore as by the offence of one judgment came upon all men to condemnation; even so by the righteousness of One the free gift came upon all men unto justification of life" (Rom. 5:18). The offence of the first Adam brought down the curse of the broken law upon the whole human race; but the satisfaction of the last Adam secured the blessing of the fulfilled law upon all those whom He represented. Judgment unto condemnation is a law term intending eternal death, the wages of sin; the "free gift" affirms that a gratuitous justification is bestowed upon all its recipients—"justification of life" being the issue of the gift, parallel with "shall reign in life by one, Jesus Christ" (v. 17). The sentence of justification adjudges and entitles its object unto eternal life.

Having now considered the two great blessings which come to the believer at his justification—deliverance from the curse of the law (death) and a title to the blessing of the law (life)—let us now seek to take a view of the originating source from which they proceed. This is the free, pure sovereign grace of God: as it is written "Being justified freely by His grace" (Rom. 3:24). What is grace? It is God's unmerited and uninfluenced favor, shown unto the undeserving and hell-deserving: neither human worthiness, works or willingness, attracting it, nor the lack of them repelling or obstructing it. What could there be in me to win the favorable regard of Him who is of too pure eyes to behold evil, and move Him to justify me? Nothing whatever; nay, there was everything in me calculated to make Him abhor and destroy me—my very self-righteous efforts to earn a place in Heaven deserving only a lower place in Hell. If, then, I am ever to be "justified" by God it must be by pure grace, and that alone.

Grace is the very essence of the Gospel—the only hope for fallen men, the sole comfort of saints passing through much tribulation on their way to the kingdom of God. The Gospel is the announcement that God is prepared to deal with guilty rebels on the ground of free favor, of pure benignity; that God will blot out sin, cover the believing sinner with a robe of spotless righteousness, and receive him as an accepted son: not on account of anything he has done or ever will do, but of sovereign mercy, acting independently of the sinner's own character and deservings of eternal punishment. Justification is perfectly gratuitous so far as we are concerned, nothing being required of us in order to it, either in the way of price and satisfaction or preparation and meetness. We have not the slightest degree of merit to offer as the ground of our acceptance, and therefore if God ever does accept us it must be out of unmingled grace.

It is as "the God of all grace" (1 Pet. 5:10) that Jehovah justifies the ungodly. It is as "the God of all grace" He seeks, finds, and saves His people: asking them for nothing, giving them everything. Strikingly is this brought out in that word "being justified freely by His grace" (Rom. 3:24), the design of that adverb being to exclude all consideration of anything in us or from us which should be the cause or condition of our justification. That same Greek adverb is translated "without a cause" in John 15:25—"they hated Me without a cause." The world's hatred of Christ was "without a cause" so far as He was concerned: there was nothing whatever in Him which, to the slightest degree, deserved their enmity against Him: there was nothing in Him unjust, perverse, or evil; instead, there was everything in Him which was pure, holy, lovely. In like manner, there is nothing whatever in us to call forth the approbation of God: by nature there is "no good thing" in us; but instead, everything that is evil, vile, loathsome.

"Being justified without a cause by His Grace." How this tells out the very heart of God! While there was no motive to move Him, outside of Himself, there was one inside Himself; while there was nothing in us to impel God to justify us, His own grace moved Him, so that He devised a way whereby His wondrous love could have vent and flow forth to the chief of sinners, the vilest of rebels. As it is written, "I, even I, am He that blotteth out thy transgressions for Mine own sake, and will not remember thy sins" (Isa. 43:25). Wondrous, matchless grace! We cannot for a moment look outside the grace of God for any motive or reason why He should ever have noticed us, still less had respect unto such ungodly wretches.

The first moving cause, then, that inclined God to show mercy to His people in their undone and lost condition, was His own wondrous grace—unsought, uninfluenced, unmerited by us. He might justly have left us all obnoxious to the curse of His Law, without providing any Surety for us, as He did the fallen angels; but such was His grace toward us that "He spared not His own Son." "Not by works of righteousness which we have done, but according to His mercy He saved us, by the washing of regeneration, and renewing of the Holy Ghost; Which He shed on us abundantly through Jesus Christ our Savior; That being justified by His grace, we should be made heirs according to the hope of eternal life" (Titus 3:5-7). It was His own sovereign favor and good will which actuated God to form this wondrous scheme and method of justification.

Against what has been said above, it has been objected by Socinians and their echoists that this cannot be: if the believing sinner is justified upon the grounds of a full satisfaction having been made to God for him by a surety, then his discharge from condemnation and his reception into God's judicial favor must be an act of pure justice, and therefore could not be by grace. Or, if it be purely an act of divine grace, then no surety can have obeyed the law in the believer's stead. But this is to confound two distinct things: the relation of God to Christ the Surety, and the relation of God to me the sinner. It was grace which transferred my sins to Christ; it was justice which smote Christ on account of those sins. It was grace which appointed me unto everlasting bliss; it is justice to Christ which requires I shall enjoy that which He purchased for me.

Toward the sinner justification is an act of free unmerited favor; but toward Christ, as a sinner's Surety, it is an act of justice that eternal life should be bestowed upon those for whom His meritorious satisfaction was made. First, it was pure grace that God was willing to accept satisfaction from the hands of a surety. He might have exacted the debt from us in our own persons, and then our condition had been equally miserable as that of the fallen angels, for whom no mediator was provided. Second, it was wondrous grace that God Himself provided a Surety for us, which we could not have done. The only creatures who are capable of performing perfect obedience are the holy angels, yet none of them could have assumed and met our obligations, for they are not akin to us, possessing not human nature, and therefore incapable of dying. Even had an angel became incarnate, his obedience to the law could not have availed for the whole of God's elect, for it would not have possessed infinite value.

None but a Divine person taking human nature into union with Himself could present unto God a satisfaction adequate for the redemption of His people. And it was impossible for men to have found out that Mediator and Surety: it must have its first rise in God, and not from us: it was He that "found" a ransom (Job 33:24) and laid help upon One that is "mighty" (Ps. 89:19). In the last place, it was amazing grace that the Son was willing to perform such a work for us, without whose consent the justice of God could not have exacted the debt from Him. And His grace is the most eminent in that He knew beforehand all the unspeakable humiliation and unparalleled suffering which He would encounter in the discharge of this work, yet that did not deter Him; nor was He unapprised of the character of those for whom He did it—the guilty, the ungodly, the hell-deserving; yet He shrank not back.

> "O to grace how great a debtor,
> Daily I'm constrained to be!
> Let Thy grace, Lord, like a fetter,
> Bind my wandering heart to Thee."

Chapter 7
Its Objects

We have now reached a point in our discussion of this mighty theme where it is timely for us to ask the question, Who are the ones that God justifies? The answer to that question will necessarily vary according to the mental position we occupy. From the standpoint of God's eternal decrees the reply must be, God's elect: Romans 8:33. From the standpoint of the effects produced by quickening operations of the Holy Spirit the reply must be, those who believe: Acts 13:39. But from the standpoint of what they are, considered in themselves, the reply must be, the ungodly (Rom. 4:5). The persons are the same, yet contemplated in three different relations. But here a difficulty presents itself: If faith be essential in order to justification, and if a fallen sinner must be quickened by the Holy Spirit before he can believe, then with what propriety can a regenerated person, with the spiritual grace of faith already in his heart, be described as "ungodly"?

The difficulty pointed out above is self-created. It issues from confounding things which differ radically. It is the result of bringing in the experimental state of the person justified, when justification has to do only with his judicial status. We would emphasize once more the vital importance of keeping quite distinct in our minds the objective and subjective aspects of truth, the legal and the experimental: unless this be steadily done, nought but confusion and mistakes can mark our thinking. When contemplating what he is in himself, considered alone, even the Christian mournfully cries "O wretched man that I am"; but when he views himself in Christ, as justified from all things, he triumphantly exclaims, "who shall lay anything to my charge!"

Above, we have pointed out that from the viewpoint of God's eternal decrees the question "Who are the ones whom God justifies?" must be "the elect." And this brings us to a point on which some eminent Calvinists have erred, or at least, have expressed themselves faultily. Some of the older theologians, when expounding this doctrine, contended for the eternal justification of the elect, affirming that God pronounced them righteous before the foundation of the world, and that their justification was then actual and complete, remaining so throughout their history in time, even during the days of their unregeneracy and unbelief; and that the only difference their faith made was in making manifest God's eternal justification in their consciences. This is a serious mistake, resulting (again) from failure to distinguish between things which differ.

As an immanent act of God's mind, in which all things (which are to us past, present, and future) were cognized by Him, the elect might be said to be justified from all eternity. And, as an immutable act of God's will, which cannot be frustrated, the same may be predicated again. But as an actual, formal, historical sentence, pronounced by God upon us, not so. We must distinguish between God's looking upon the elect in the purpose of his grace, and the objects of justification lying under the sentence of the law: in the former, He loved His people with an everlasting love (Jer. 31:3); in the latter, we were "by nature the children of wrath, even as others" (Eph. 2:3). Until they believe, every descendant of Adam is "condemned already" (John 3:18), and to be under God' condemnation is the very opposite of being justified.

In his ponderous treatise on justification, the Puritan Thomas Goodwin made clear some vital distinctions, which if carefully observed will preserve us from error on this point. "1. In the everlasting covenant. We may say of all spiritual blessings in Christ, what is said of Christ Himself, that their 'goings forth are from everlasting.' Justified then we were when first elected, though not in our own persons, yet in our Head (Eph. 1:3). 2. There is a farther act of justifying us, which passed from God towards us in Christ, upon His payment and performance at His resurrection (Rom. 4:25, 1 Tim. 3:16). 3. But these two acts of justification are wholly out of us, immanent acts in God, and though they concern us and are towards us, yet not acts of God upon us, they being performed towards us not as actually existing in ourselves, but only as existing in our Head, who covenanted for us and represented us: so as though by those acts we are estated into a right and title to justification, yet the benefit and possession of that estate we have not without a farther act being passed upon us."

Before regeneration we are justified by existing in our Head only, as a feoffee (one who is given a grant), held in trust for us, as children under age. In addition to which, we "are to be in our own persons, though still through Christ, possessed of it, and to have all the deeds and evidences of it committed to the custody and apprehension of our faith. We are in our own persons made true owners and enjoyers of it, which is immediately done at that instant when we first believe; which act (of God) is the completion and accomplishment of the former two, and is that grand and famous justification by faith which the Scripture so much inculcates—note the 'now' in Romans 5:9, 11; 8:11... God doth judge and pronounce His elect ungodly and unjustified till they believe" (Ibid.)

God's elect enter this world in precisely the same condition and circumstances as do the non-elect. They are "by nature the children of wrath, even as others" (Eph. 2:3), that is, they are under the condemnation of their original sin in Adam (Rom. 5:12, 18, 19) and they are under the curse of God's Law because of their own constant transgressions of it (Gal. 3:10). The sword of divine justice is suspended over their heads, and the Scriptures denounce them as rebels against the Most High. As yet, there is nothing whatever to distinguish them from those who are "fitted to destruction." Their state is woeful to the last degree, their situation perilous beyond words; and when the Holy Spirit awakens them from the sleep of death, the first message which falls upon their ears is, "Flee from the wrath to come." But how and whither, they, as yet, know not. Then it is they are ready for the message of the Gospel.

Let us turn now to the more immediate answer to our opening inquiry, Who are the ones that God justifies? A definite reply is given in Romans 4:5: "Him that justifieth the"—whom? the holy, the faithful, the fruitful? no, the very reverse: "Him that justifieth the ungodly." What a strong, bold, and startling word is this! It becomes yet more emphatic when we observe what precedes: "But to him that worketh not, but believeth on Him that justifieth the ungodly." The subjects of justification, then, are viewed in themselves, apart from Christ, as not only destitute of a perfect righteousness, but as having no acceptable works to their account. They are denominated, and considered as ungodly when the sentence of justification is pronounced upon them. The mere sinner is the subject on which grace is magnified, toward which grace reigns in justification!

"To say, he who worketh not is justified through believing, is to say that his works, whatever they be, have no influence in his justification, nor hath God, in justifying him, any respect unto them. Wherefore he alone who worketh not, is the subject of justification, the person to be justified. That is, God considereth no man's works, no man's duties of obedience, in his justification; seeing we are justified freely by His grace" (John Owen). Those whom God, in His transcendent mercy, justifies, are not the obedient, but the disobedient; not those who have been loyal and loving subjects of His righteous government, but they who have stoutly defied Him and trampled His laws beneath their feet. Those whom God justifies are lost sinners, lying in a state of defection from Him, under a loss of original righteousness (in Adam) and by their own transgressions brought in guilty before His tribunal (Rom. 3:19). They are those who by character and conduct have no claim upon divine blessing, and deserve nought but unsparing judgment at God's hand.

"Him that justifieth the ungodly." It is deplorable to see how many able commentators have weakened the force of this by affirming that, while the subject of justification is "ungodly" up to the time of his justification, he is not so at the moment of justification itself. They argue that, inasmuch as the subject of justification is a believer at the moment of his justification and that believing presupposes regeneration—a work of divine grace wrought in the heart—he could not be designated "ungodly." This seeming difficulty is at once removed by calling to mind that justification is entirely a law matter and not an experimental thing at all. In the sight of God's law every one whom God justifies is "ungodly" until Christ's righteousness is made over to him. The awful sentence "ungodly" rests as truly upon the purest virgin as much as it does upon the foulest prostitute until God imputes Christ's obedience to her.

"Him that justifieth the ungodly." These words cannot mean less than that God, in the act of justification, has no regard whatever to anything good resting to the credit of the person He justifies. They declare, emphatically, that immediately prior to that divine act, God beholds the subject only as unrighteous, ungodly, wicked, so that no good, either in or by the person justified, can possibly be the ground on which or the reason for which He justifies him. This is further evident from the words "to him that worketh not": that this includes not only works which the ceremonial law required, but all works of morality and godliness, appear from the fact that the same person who is said to "work not" is designated "ungodly." Finally, seeing that the faith which belongs to justification is here said to be "counted for [or "unto"] righteousness," it is clear that the person to whom "righteousness" is imputed, is destitute of righteousness in himself.

A parallel passage to the one which has just been before us is found in Isaiah 43. There we hear God saying, "I, even I, am He that blotteth out thy transgressions for Mine own sake, and will not remember thy sins" (v. 25). And to whom does God say this? To those who had sincerely endeavored to please Him? To those who, though they had occasionally been overtaken in a fault, had, in the main, served Him faithfully? No, indeed; very far from it. Instead, in the immediate context we find Him saying to them, "But thou hast not called upon Me, O Jacob; but thou hast been weary of Me, O Israel. Thou hast bought Me no sweet cane with money, neither hast thou filled Me with the fat of thy sacrifices: but thou hast made Me to serve with thy sins, thou hast wearied Me with thine iniquities" (vv. 22, 24). They were, then, thoroughly "ungodly"; yet to them the Lord declared, "I, even I, am He that blotteth out thy transgressions"—why? Because of something good in them or from them? No, "for Mine own sake"!

Further confirmation of what has been before us in Romans 4:5 is found in both what immediately precedes and what follows. In verses 1-3 the case of Abraham is considered, and the proof given that he was not "justified by works," but on the ground of righteousness being imputed to him on his believing. "Now if a person of such victorious faith, exalted piety, and amazing obedience as his was, did not obtain acceptance with God on account of his own duties, but by an imputed righteousness; who shall pretend to an interest in the heavenly blessing, in virtue of his own sincere endeavors, or pious performances?--performances not fit to be named, in comparison with those that adorned the conduct and character of Jehovah's friend" (A. Booth).

Having shown that the father of all believers was regarded by the Lord as an "ungodly" person, having no good works to his credit at the moment of his justification, the Apostle next cited David's description of the truly blessed man. "And how does the royal Psalmist describe him? To what does he attribute his acceptance with God? To an inherent, or to an imputed righteousness? Does he represent him as attaining the happy state, and as enjoying the precious privilege, in consequence of performing sincere obedience, and of keeping the law to the best of his power?

No such thing. His words are, 'Blessed are they whose iniquities are forgiven, and whose sins are covered. Blessed is the man to whom the Lord will not impute sin' (vv. 7-9). The blessed man is here described as one who is, in himself, a polluted creature, and a guilty criminal. As one who, before grace made the difference, was on a level with the rest of mankind; equally unworthy, and equally wretched: and the sacred penman informs us that all his blessedness arises from an imputed righteousness" (A. Booth).

"Him that justifieth the ungodly." Here is the very heart of the Gospel. Many have argued that God can only pronounce just, and treat as such, those who are inherently righteous; but if this was so, what good news would there be for sinful men? Enemies of the Truth insist that for God to pronounce just those whom His law condemns would be a judicial fiction. But Romans 4:5 makes known a divine miracle: something only God could have achieved. The miracle announced by the Gospel is that God comes to the ungodly with a mercy that is righteous, and in spite of all their depravity and rebellion, enables them through faith (on the ground of Christ's righteousness) to enter into a new and blessed relation with Himself.

The Scriptures speak of mercy, but it is not mercy coming in to make up the deficiencies and forgive the slips of the virtuous, but mercy extended through Christ to the chief of sinners. The Gospel which proclaims mercy through the atonement of the Lord Jesus is distinguished from every religious system of man, by holding out salvation to the guiltiest of the human race, through faith in the blood of the Redeemer. God's Son came into this world not only to save sinners, but even the chief of sinners, the worst of His enemies. Mercy is extended freely to the most violent and determined rebel. Here, and here only, is a refuge for the guilty. Is the trembling reader conscious that he is a great sinner, then that is the very reason why you should come to Christ: the greater your sins, the greater your need of the Savior.

There are some who appear to think that Christ is a Physician who can cure only such patients as are not dangerously ill, that there are some cases so desperate as to be incurable, beyond His skill. What an affront to His power, what a denial of His sufficiency! Where can a more extreme case be found than that of the thief on the cross? He was at the very point of death, on the very brink of Hell! A guilty criminal, an incorrigible outlaw, justly condemned even by men. He had reviled the Savior suffering by his side. Yet, at the end, he turned to Him and said, "Lord remember me." Was his plea refused? Did the Physician of souls regard his as a hopeless case? No, blessed be His name, He at once responded "Today shalt thou be with Me in Paradise." Only unbelief shuts the vilest out of Heaven.

"Him that justifieth the ungodly." And how can the thrice holy God righteously do such a thing? Because "Christ died for the Ungodly" (Rom. 5:6). God's righteous grace comes to us through the law-honoring, justice-satisfying, sin-atoning Work of the Lord Jesus! Here, then, is the very essence of the Gospel: the proclamation of God's amazing grace, the declaration of divine bounty, altogether irrespective of human worth or merit. In the great Satisfaction of His Son, God has "brought near HIS righteousness" (Isa. 46:13). "We do not need to go up to Heaven for it; that would imply Christ had never come down. Nor do we need to go down to the depths of the earth for it; that would say Christ had never been buried and had never risen. It is near. We do not need to exert ourselves to bring it near, nor do anything to attract it towards us. It is near... The office of faith is not to work, but to cease working; not to do anything, but to own that all is done" (A. Bonar).

Faith is the one link between the sinner and the Savior. Not faith as a work, which must be properly performed to qualify us for pardon. Not faith as a religious duty, which must be gone through according to certain rules in order to induce Christ to give us the benefits of His finished work. No, but faith simply extended as an empty hand, to receive everything from Christ for nothing. Reader, you may be the very "chief of sinners," yet is your case not hopeless. You may have sinned against much light, great privileges, exceptional opportunities; you may have broken every one of the Ten Commandments in thought, word and deed; your body may be filled with disease from wickedness, your head white with the winter of old age; you may already have one foot in Hell; and yet even now, if you but take your place alongside of the dying thief, and trust in the divine efficacy of the precious blood of the Lamb, you shall be plucked as a brand from the burning. God "justifieth the ungodly." Hallelujah! If He did not, the writer had been in Hell long ago.

Chapter 8
Its Instrument

"Being justified freely by his grace" (Rom. 3:24); "being now justified by His blood" (Rom. 5:9); "being now justified by faith" (Rom. 5:1). A full exposition of the doctrine of justification requires that each of these propositions should be interpreted in their Scriptural sense, and that they be combined together in their true relations as to form one harmonious whole. Unless these three propositions be carefully distinguished there is sure to be confusion; unless all the three are steadily borne in mind we are sure to land in error. Each must be given its due weight, yet none must be understood in such a way as to make its force annul that of the others. Nor is this by any means a simple task, in fact none but a real teacher (that is, a spiritual theologian) who has devoted a lifetime to the undivided study of Scriptures is qualified for it.

"The righteousness of God which is by faith of Jesus Christ" (Rom. 3:22); "A man is justified by faith without the deeds of the law" (Rom. 3:28); "even we have believed in Jesus Christ, that we might be justified by the faith of Christ, and not by the works of the law" (Gal. 2:16). What is the precise place and influence which faith has in the important affairs of justification? What is the exact nature or character of justifying faith? In what particular sense are we to understand this proposition that we are "justified by faith"? and what is the connection between that proposition and the postulates that we are "justified by grace" and "justified by His blood"? These are matters which call for the utmost care. The nature of justifying faith requires to be closely defined so that its particular agency is correctly viewed, for it is easy to make a mistake here to the prejudice of Christ's honor and glory, which must not be given to another—no, not to faith itself.

Many would-be teachers have erred at this point, for the common tendency of human nature is to arrogate to itself the glory which belongs alone to God. While there have been those who rejected the unscriptural notion that we can be justified before God by our own works, yet not a few of these very men virtually make a savior of their own faith. Not only have some spoken of faith as though it were a contribution which God requires the sinner to make toward his own salvation—the last mite which was necessary to make up the price of his redemption; but others (who sneered at theologians and boasted of their superior understanding of the things of God) have insisted that faith itself is what constitutes us righteous before God, He regarding faith as righteousness.

A deplorable example of what we have just mentioned is to be found in the comments made upon Romans 4 by Mr. J. N. Darby, the father of the Plymouth Brethren: "This was Abraham's faith. He believed the promise that he should be the father of many nations, because God had spoken, counting on the power of God, thus glorifying Him, without calling in question anything that He had said by looking at circumstances; therefore this also was counted to him for righteousness. He glorified God according to what God was. Now this was not written for his sake alone: the same faith shall be imputed to us also for righteousness" ("Synopsis" vol. 4, p. 133--italics ours). The Christ-dishonoring error contained in those statements will be exposed later on in this chapter.

"How doth faith justify a sinner in the sight of God? Answer: Faith justifies a sinner in the sight of God, not because of those other graces which do always accompany it, nor of good works that are the fruits of it, nor as if the grace of faith, or any act thereof, were imputed to him for justification; but only as it is an instrument by which he receiveth and applieth Christ and His righteousness" (Westminster Confession of Faith). Though this definition was framed upwards of two hundred and fifty years ago, it is far superior to almost anything found in current literature on the subject. It is more accurate to speak of faith as the "instrument" rather than as the condition, for a "condition" is generally used to signify that for the sake whereof a benefit is conferred. Faith is neither the ground nor the substance of our justification, but simply the hand which receives the divine gift proffered to us in the Gospel.

What is the precise place and influence which faith has in the important affair of justification? Romanist answer, It justifies us formally, not relatively: that is, upon the account of its own intrinsic value. They point out that faith is never alone, but "worketh by love" (Gal. 5:6), and therefore its own excellency merits acceptance at God's hand. But the faith of the best is weak and deficient (Luke 17:5), and so could never satisfy the law, which requires a flawless perfection. If righteousness was given as a reward for faith, its possessor would have cause for boasting, expressly contrary to the Apostle in Romans 3:26, 27. Moreover, such a method of justification would entirely frustrate the life and death of Christ, making His great sacrifice unnecessary. It is not faith as a spiritual grace which justifies us, but as an instrument—the hand which lays hold of Christ.

In connection with justification, faith is not to be considered as a virtuous exercise of the heart, nor as a principle of holy obedience: "Because faith, as concerned in our justification, does not regard Christ as King, enacting laws, requiring obedience, and subduing depravity; but as a Substitute, answering the requirements of the divine Law, and as a Priest expiating sin by His own death on the cross. Hence, in justification we read of 'precious faith... through the righteousness of God and our Savior Jesus Christ' (2 Pet. 1:1) and of 'faith in His blood' (Rom. 3:25), and believers are described as 'receiving the atonement' and 'receiving the gift of righteousness' (Rom. 5:11, 17). Therefore it is evident that faith is represented as having an immediate regard to the vicarious work of Christ, and that it is considered not under the notion of exercising virtue or of performing a duty, but of receiving a free gift" (A. Booth).

What is the relation of faith to justification? The Arminian answer to the question, refined somewhat by the Plymouth Brethren, is, that the act of believing is imputed to us for righteousness. One error leads to another. Mr. Darby denied that Gentiles were ever under the law, hence he denied also that Christ obeyed the law in His people's stead, and therefore as Christ's vicarious obedience is not reckoned to their account, he had to seek elsewhere for their righteousness. This he claimed to find in the Christian's own faith, insisting that their act of believing is imputed to them "for righteousness." To give his theory respectability, he clothed it in the language of several expressions found in Romans 4, though he knew quite well that the Greek afforded no foundation whatever for that which he built upon it.

In Romans 4 we read "his faith is counted for righteousness" (v. 5), "faith was reckoned to Abraham for righteousness" (v. 9), "it was imputed to him for righteousness" (v. 22). Now in each of these verses the Greek preposition is "eis" which never means "in the stead of," but always signifies "towards, in order to, with a view to": it has the uniform force of "unto." Its exact meaning and force is unequivocally plain in Romans 10:10, "with the heart man believeth unto ["eis"] righteousness": that is, the believing heart reaches out toward and lays hold of Christ Himself. "This passage (Rom. 10:10) may help us to understand what justification by faith is, for it shows that righteousness there comes to us when we embrace God's goodness offered to us in the Gospel. We are then, for this reason, made just: because we believe that God is propitious to us through Christ" (J. Calvin).

The Holy Spirit has used the Greek prepositions with unerring precision. Never do we find Him employing "eis" in connection with Christ's satisfaction and sacrifice in our room and stead, but only "anti" or "huper," which means in lieu of. On the other hand, "anti" and "huper" are never used in connection with our believing, for faith is not accepted by God in lieu of perfect obedience. Faith must either be the ground of our acceptance with God, or the means or instrument of our becoming interested in the true meritorious ground, namely, the righteousness of Christ; it cannot stand in both relations to our justification. "God justifieth, not by imputing faith itself, the act of believing, but by imputing the obedience and satisfaction of Christ" (Westminster Catechism).

That faith itself cannot be the substance or ground of our justification is clear from many considerations. The "righteousness of God (i.e., the satisfaction which Christ rendered to the law) is revealed to faith" (Rom. 1:17) and so cannot be faith itself. Romans 10:10 declares "with the heart man believeth unto righteousness" so that righteousness must be a distinct thing from believing. In Jeremiah 23:6 we read "The LORD our righteousness," so faith cannot be our righteousness. Let not Christ be dethroned in order to exalt faith: set not the servant above the master. "We acknowledge no righteousness but what the obedience and satisfaction of Christ yields us: His blood, not our faith; His satisfaction, not our believing it, is the matter of justification before God" (J. Flavel). What alterations are there in our faith! what minglings of unbelief at all times! Is this a foundation to build our justification and hope upon?

Perhaps some will say, Are not the words of Scripture expressly on Mr. Darby's side? Does not Romans 4:5 affirm "faith is counted for righteousness"? We answer, Is the sense of Scripture on his side? Suppose I should undertake to prove that David was cleansed from guilt by the "hyssop" which grows on the wall: that would sound ridiculous. Yes; nevertheless, I should have the express words of Scripture to support me: "Purge me with hyssop, and I shall be clean" (Ps. 51:7). Yet clear as those words read, they would not afford me the least countenance imaginable from the sense and spirit of God's Word. Has the hyssop—a worthless shrub—any kind of fitness to stand in the stead of the sacrificial blood, and make an atonement for sin? No more fitness has faith to stand in the stead of Christ's perfect obedience, to act as our justifying righteousness, or procure our acceptance with God!!

An apology is really due many of our readers, for wasting their time with such puerilities, but we ask them to kindly bear with us. We hope it may please God to use this article to expose one of Darby's many grievous errors. For "grievous" this error most certainly is. His teaching that the Christian's faith, instead of the vicarious obedience of Christ, is reckoned for righteousness (Mr. W. Kelly, his chief lieutenant, wrote "his [Abraham's] faith in God's word as that which he exercised and which was accounted as righteousness"—see article 5) makes God guilty of a downright lie, for it represents Him as giving to faith a fictitious value—the believer has no righteousness, so God regards his poor faith as "righteousness."

"And he believed in the Lord; and He counted it to him for righteousness" (Gen. 15:6). The one point to be decided here is: was it Abraham's faith itself which was in God's account taken for righteousness (horrible idea!), or, was it the righteousness of God in Christ which Abraham's faith prospectively laid hold of? The comments of the Apostle in Romans 4:18-22 settle the point decisively. In these verses Paul emphasizes the natural impossibilities which stood in the way of God's promise of a numerous offspring to Abraham being fulfilled (the genital deadness both of his own body and Sarah's), and on the implicit confidence he had (notwithstanding the difficulties) in the power and faithfulness of God that He would perform what He promised. Hence, when the Apostle adds, "Therefore it was imputed to him for righteousness" (v. 22), that "therefore" can only mean: Because through faith he completely lost sight of nature and self, and realized with undoubting assurance the sufficiency of the divine arm, and the certainty of its working.

Abraham's faith, dear reader, was nothing more and nothing else than the renunciation of all virtue and strength in himself, and a hanging in childlike trust upon God for what He was able and willing to do. Far, very far, indeed, was his faith from being a mere substitute for a "righteousness" which he lacked. Far, very far was God from accepting his faith in lieu of a perfect obedience to His Law. Rather was Abraham's faith the acting of a soul which found its life, its hope, its all in the Lord Himself. And that is what justifying faith is: it is "simply the instrument by which Christ and His righteousness are received in order to justification. It is emptiness filled with Christ's fullness; impotency lying down upon Christ's strength" (J. L. Girardeau).

> "The best obedience of my hands
> Dares not appear before Thy throne;
> But faith can answer Thy demands,
> By pleading what my Lord has done."

What is the relation of faith to justification? Antinomians and hyper-Calvinists answer, Merely that of comfort or assurance. Their theory is that the elect were actually justified by God before the foundation of the world, and all that faith does now is to make this manifest in their conscience. This error was advocated by such men as W. Gadsby, J. Irons, James Wells, J.C. Philpot. That it originated not with these men is clear from the fact that the Puritans refuted it in their day. "By faith alone we obtain and receive the forgiveness of sins; for notwithstanding any antecedent act of God concerning us in and for Christ, we do not actually receive a complete soul-freeing discharge until we believe" (J. Owen). "It is vain to say I am justified only in respect to the court of mine own conscience. The faith that Paul and the other Apostles were justified by, was their believing on Christ that they might be justified (Gal. 2:15, 16), and not a believing they were justified already; and therefore it was not an act of assurance" (T. Goodwin, vol. 8).

How are we justified by faith? Having given a threefold negative answer: not by faith as a joint cause with works (Romanists), not by faith as an act of grace in us (Arminians), not by faith as it receives the Spirit's witness (Antinomians); we now turn to the positive answer. Faith justifies only as an instrument which God has appointed to the apprehension and application of Christ's righteousness. When we say that faith is the "instrument" of our justification, let it be clearly understood that we do not mean faith is the instrument wherewith God justifies, but the instrument whereby we receive Christ. Christ has merited righteousness for us, and faith in Christ is that which renders it meet in God's sight the purchased blessing be assigned. Faith unites to Christ, and being united to Him we are possessed of all that is in Christ, so far as is consistent with our capacity of receiving and God's appointment in giving. Having been made one with Christ in spirit, God now considers us as one with Him in law.

We are justified by faith, and not for faith; not because of what faith is, but because of what it receives. "It hath no efficacy of itself, but as it is the band of our union with Christ. The whole virtue of cleansing proceeds from Christ the object. We receive the water with our hands, but the cleansing virtue is not in our hands, but in the water, yet the water cannot cleanse us without our receiving it; our receiving it unites the water to us, and is a means whereby we are cleansed. And therefore is it observed that our justification by faith is always expressed in the passive, not in the active: we are justified by faith, not that faith justifies us. The efficacy is in Christ's blood; the reception of it is in our faith" (S. Charnock).

Scripture knows no such thing as a justified unbeliever. There is nothing meritorious about believing, yet it is necessary in order to justification. It is not only the righteousness of Christ as imputed which justifies, but also as received (Rom. 5:11, 17). The righteousness of Christ is not mine until I accept it as the Father's gift. "The believing sinner is 'justified by faith' only instrumentally, as he 'lives by eating' only instrumentally. Eating is the particular act by which he receives and appropriates food. Strictly speaking, he lives by bread alone, not by eating, or the act of masticating. And, strictly speaking, the sinner is justified by Christ's sacrifice alone, not by his act of believing in it" (W. Shedd). In the application of justification faith is not a builder, but a beholder; not an agent, but an instrument; it has nothing to do, but all to believe; nothing to give, but all to receive.

God has not selected faith to be the instrument of justification because there is some peculiar virtue in faith, but rather because there is no merit in it: faith is self-emptying—"Therefore it is of faith that it might be by grace" (Rom. 4:16). A gift is seen to be a gift when nothing is required or accepted of the recipient, but simply that he receive it. Whatever other properties faith may possess, it is simply as receiving Christ that it justifies. Were we said to be justified by repentance, by love, or by any other spiritual grace, it would convey the idea of something good in us being the consideration on which the blessing was bestowed; but justification by faith (correctly understood) conveys no such idea.

"Faith justifies in no other way than as it introduces us into a participation of the righteousness of Christ" (J. Calvin). Justifying faith is a looking away from self, a renouncing of my own righteousness, a laying hold of Christ. Justifying faith consists, first, of a knowledge and belief of the truth revealed in Scripture thereon; second, in an abandonment of all pretense, claim or confidence in our own righteousness; third, in a trust in and reliance upon the righteousness of Christ, laying hold of the blessing which He purchased for us. It is the heart's approval and approbation of the method of justification proposed in the Gospel: by Christ alone, proceeding from the pure grace of God, and excluding all human merits. "In the Lord have I righteousness and strength" (Isa. 45:24).

None will experimentally appreciate the righteousness of Christ until they have been experimentally stripped by the Spirit. Not until the Lord puts us in the fire and burns off our filthy rags, and makes us stand naked before Him, trembling from head to foot as we view the sword of His justice suspended over our heads, will any truly value "the best robe." Not until the condemning sentence of the law has been applied by the Spirit to the conscience does the guilty soul cry, "Lost, lost!" (Rom. 7:9, 10). Not until there is a personal apprehension of the requirements of God's Law, a feeling sense of our total inability to perform its righteous demands, and an honest realization that God would be just in banishing us from His presence forever, is the necessity for a precious Christ perceived by the soul.

Chapter 9
Its Evidence

In Romans 3:28 the Apostle Paul declared "that a man is justified by faith without the deeds of the law," and then produces the case of Abraham to prove his assertion. But the Apostle James, from the case of the same Abraham, draws quite another conclusion, saying, "Ye see then how that by works a man is justified, and not by faith only" (James 2:24). This is one of the "contradictions in the Bible" to which infidels appeal in support of their unbelief. But the Christian, however difficult he finds it to harmonize passages apparently opposite, knows there cannot be any contradiction in the Word of God. Faith has unshaken confidence in the inerrancy of Holy Writ. Faith is humble too and prays, "That which I see not teach Thou me" (Job. 34:32). Nor is faith lazy; it prompts its possessor unto a reverent examination and diligent investigation of that which puzzles and perplexes, seeking to discover the subject of each separate book, the scope of each writer, the connections of each passage.

Now the design of the Apostle Paul in Romans 3:28 may be clearly perceived from its context. He is treating of the great matter of a sinner's justification before God: he shows that it cannot be by works of the law, because by the law all men are condemned, and also because if men were justified on the ground of their own doings, then boasting could not be excluded. Positively he affirms that justification is by grace, through the redemption that is in Christ Jesus. His reasoning will appear the more conclusive if the whole passage (Rom. 3:19-28) be read attentively. Because the Jews had a high regard of Abraham, the Apostle proceeded to show in the 4th chapter of Romans that Abraham was justified in that very way—apart from any works of his own, by faith alone. By such a method of justification the pride of the creature is strained, and the grace of God is magnified.

Now the scope of the Apostle James is very different: his Epistle was written to counteract quite another error. Fallen men are creatures of extremes: no sooner are they driven out of the false refuge of trusting to their own righteousness, than they fly to the opposite and no less dangerous error of supposing that, since they cannot be justified by their own works, that there is no necessity whatever for good works, and no danger from ungodly living and unholy practice. It is very clear from the New Testament itself that very soon after the Gospel was freely proclaimed, there arose many who turned the grace of God into "lasciviousness": that this was not only quickly espoused in theory, but soon had free course in practice. It was therefore the chief design of the Apostle James to show the great wickedness and awful danger of unholy practice and to assert the imperative necessity of good works.

The Apostle James devoted much of his Epistle to the exposing of any empty profession. In his second chapter, particularly, he addresses himself unto those who rested in a notion which they called "faith," accounting an intellectual assent to the truth of the Gospel sufficient for their salvation, though it had no spiritual influence upon their hearts, tempers, or conduct. The Apostle shows their hope was a vain one, and that their "faith" was not a whit superior to that possessed by the demons. From the example of Abraham he proves that justifying faith is a very different thing from the "faith" of empty professors, because it enabled him to perform the hardest and most painful act of obedience, even the offering up of his only son upon the altar; which act took place many years after he had been justified by God, and which act manifested the reality and nature of his faith.

From what has been said above, it should be very evident that the "justification" of which Paul treats is entirely different from the "justification" with which James deals. The doctrine of the former is that nothing renders any sinner acceptable to God but faith in the Lord Jesus Christ; the doctrine of the latter is that such a faith is not solitary, but accompanied with every good work, and that where good works are absent, justifying faith cannot exist. James is insistent that it is not enough to say I have justifying faith, I must give proof of the same by exhibiting those fruits which love toward God and love toward men necessarily produce. Paul writes of our justification before God, James of our justification before men. Paul treats of the justification of persons; James, of the justification of our profession. The one is by faith alone; the other is by a faith which worketh by love and produces obedience.

Now it is of first importance that the above-mentioned distinctions should be clearly grasped. When Christian theologians affirm that the sinner is justified by faith alone, they do not mean that faith exists alone in the person justified, for justifying faith is always accompanied by all the other graces which the Spirit imparts at our regeneration; nor do they mean that nothing else is required in order to our receiving forgiveness from God, for He requires repentance and conversion as well as faith (Acts 3:19). No, rather do they mean that there is nothing else in sinners themselves to which their justification is in Scripture ascribed: nothing else is required of them or exists in them which stands in the same relation to justification as their faith does, or which exerts any casual influence or any efficacy of instrumentality in producing the result of their being justified (Condensed from Cunningham).

On the other hand, that faith which justifies is not an idle and inoperative principle, but one that purifies the heart (Acts 15:9) and works by love (Gal. 5:6). It is faith which can easily be distinguished from that mental faith of the empty professor. It is this which the Apostle James insists so emphatically upon. The subject of this Epistle is not salvation by grace and justification by faith, but the testing of those who claim to have faith. His design is not to show the ground on which sinners are accepted before God, but to make known that which evidences a sinner's having been justified. He insists that the tree is known by its fruits, that a righteous person is one who walks in the paths of righteousness. He declares that the man who is not a doer of the Word, but a "hearer only," is self-deceived, deluded. When God justifies a man, He sanctifies him too: the two blessings are inseparable, never found apart.

Unless the subject and scope of James' Epistle be clearly seen, the apprehension of many of its statements can only issue in God-dishonoring, grace-repudiating, soul-destroying error. To this portion of the Word of God, more than any other, have legalists appealed in their opposition to the grand truth of justification by grace, through faith, without works. To the declarations of this Epistle have they turned to find support for their Christ-insulting, man-exalting, Gospel-repudiating error of justification by human works. Merit-mongers of all descriptions cite James 2 for the purpose of setting aside all that is taught elsewhere in Scripture on the subject of justification. Romanists, and their half-brothers the Arminians, quote "Ye see then how that by works a man is justified, and not by faith only" (v. 24), and suppose that ends all argument.

We propose now to take up James 2:14-26 and offer a few comments thereon. "What doth it profit, my brethren, though a man say he hath faith, and have not works? can faith save him?" (v. 14). Observe carefully that the Apostle does not here ask, "What doth it profit a man though he hath faith and have not works?"—such a supposition is nowhere countenanced by the Word of God: it were to suppose the impossibility for wherever real faith exists, good works necessarily follow. No, instead he asks, "What doth it profit, my brethren, though a man (not "one of you"!) say he hath faith"? Professing to be a Christian when a man is not one, may secure a standing among men, improve his moral and social prestige, obtain membership in a "church," and promote his commercial interests; but can it save his soul?

It is not that those empty professors who call themselves Christians are all (though many probably are) conscious hypocrites, rather are they deceived souls, and the tragic thing is that in most places there is nothing in the preaching which is at all calculated to un-deceive them; instead, there is only that which bolsters them up in their delusion. There is a large class in Christendom today who are satisfied with a bare profession. They have heard expounded some of the fundamentals of the Christian faith, and have given an intellectual assent thereto, and they mistake that for a saving knowledge of the Truth. Their minds are instructed, but their hearts are not reached, nor their lives transformed. They are still worldly in their affections and ways. There is no real subjection to God, no holiness of walk, no fruit to Christ's glory. Their "faith" is of no value at all; their profession is vain.

"What doth it profit, my brethren, though a man say he hath faith, and have not works? Can faith save him?" By noting the emphasis upon the word "say," we perceive at once that James is arguing against those who substituted a theoretical belief of the Gospel for the whole of evangelical religion, and who replied to all exhortations and reproofs by saying, "We are not justified by our works, but by faith alone." He therefore begins by asking what profit is there in professing to be a believer, when a man is devoid of true piety? The answer is, none whatever. To merely say I have faith when I am unable to appeal to any good works and spiritual fruits as the evidence of it, profits neither the speaker nor those who listen to his empty talk. Ability to prate in an orthodox manner about the doctrines of Christianity is a vastly different thing from justifying faith.

"If a brother or sister be naked, and destitute of daily food, And one of you say unto them, Depart in peace, be ye warmed and filled; notwithstanding ye give them not those things which are needful to the body; what doth it profit?" (vv. 15, 16). Here the Apostle shows by an opposite illustration the utter worthlessness of fair talking which is unaccompanied by practical deeds: notice the "say unto them, depart in peace" etc. What is the use and value of feigning to be charitable when the works of charity are withheld? None whatever: empty bellies are not filled by benevolent words, nor are naked backs clothed by good wishes. Nor is the soul saved by a bare profession of the Gospel.

"Faith worketh by love" (Gal. 5:6). The first "fruit of the spirit," that is of the new nature in the regenerated soul, is "love" (Gal. 5:22). When faith has truly been wrought in the heart by the Holy Spirit, that faith is manifested in love—love toward God, love toward His commandments (John 14:23), love toward the brethren, love toward our fellow-creatures. Therefore in testing the "faith" of the empty professor, the Apostle at once puts to the proof his love. In showing the pretense of his love, he proves the worthlessness of his "faith." "But whoso hath this world's good, and seeth his brother have need, and shutteth up his bowels of compassion from him, how dwelleth the love of God in him?" (1 John 3:17)! Genuine love is operative; so is genuine faith.

"Even so faith, if it hath not works, is dead, being alone" (James 2:17). Here the Apostle applies the illustration he has employed to the case before him, proving the worthlessness of a lifeless and inoperative "faith." Even our fellow-men would promptly denounce as valueless a "love" which was gushing in words but lacking in works. Unregenerate people are not deceived by those who talk benignly to the indigent, but who refuse to minister unto their needs. And think you, my reader, that the omniscient God is to be imposed upon by an empty profession? Has He not said, "Why call ye Me, Lord, Lord, and do not the things which I say?" (Luke 6:46).

That "faith" which is only of the lips and is not confirmed by evidence in the life, is useless.

No matter how clear and sound may be my head-knowledge of the Truth, no matter how good a talker upon divine things I am, if my walk is not controlled by the precepts of God, then I am but "sounding brass and a tinkling symbol." "Faith, if it hath not works, is dead, being alone." It is not a living and fruitful faith, like the faith of God's elect, but a thing which is utterly worthless—"dead." It is "alone," that is, divorced from love to God and men and every holy affection. How could our holy Lord approve of such a "faith"! As works without faith are "dead" (Heb. 9:14), so a "faith" which is without "works" is a dead one.

"Yea, a man may say, Thou hast faith, and I have works: show me thy faith without thy works, and I will show thee my faith by my works" (Jam. 2:18). Here the true Christian challenges the empty professor: You claim to be a believer, but disgrace the name of Christ by your worldly walk, so do not expect the real saints to regard you as a brother till you display your faith in the good works of a holy life. The emphatic word in this verse is "show"—proof is demanded: demonstrate your faith to be genuine. Actions speak louder than words: unless our profession can endure that test it is worthless. Only true holiness of heart and life vindicates a profession of being justified by faith.

"Thou believest that there is one God; thou doest well: the devils also believe, and tremble" (v. 19). Here the Apostle anticipates an objection: I do actually believe in the Lord! Very well, so also do the demons, but what is the fruit of their "believing"? Does it influence their hearts and lives, does it transform their conduct Godward and manward? It does not. Then what is their "believing" worth! "But wilt thou know, O vain man, that faith without works is dead?" (v. 20): "vain" signifies "empty," exposing the hollowness of one who claims to be justified by faith yet lacks the evidence of an obedient walk.

"Was not Abraham our father justified by works, when he had offered Isaac his son upon the altar? Seest thou how faith wrought with his works, and by works was faith made perfect?" (vv. 21, 22). The faith which reposes on Christ is not an idle, but an active and fruitful principle. Abraham had been justified many years before (Gen. 15:6); the offering up of Isaac (Gen. 22) was the open attestation of his faith and the manifestation of the sincerity of his profession. "By works was faith made perfect" means, in actual obedience it reaches its designed end, the purpose for which it was given is realized. "Made perfect" also signifies revealed or made known (see 2 Cor. 10:9).

"And the Scripture was fulfilled which saith, Abraham believed God, and it was imputed unto him for righteousness: and he was called the Friend of God" (Jam. 2:23). The "Scripture" here is God's testimony to Abraham in Genesis 15:6: that testimony was "fulfilled" or verified when Abraham gave the supreme demonstration of his obedience to God. Our being informed here that Abraham was "called the friend of God" is in beautiful accord with the tenor of the whole of this passage, as is clear from a comparison with John 15:14: "Ye are my friends, if ye do whatsoever I command you."

"Ye see then how that by works a man is justified, and not by faith only" (Jam. 2:24). In the "ye see then" the Apostle draws his "conclusion" from the foregoing. It is by "works," by acts of implicit obedience to the divine command, such as Abraham exercised—and not by a mere "faith" of the brain and the lips—that we justify our profession of being believers, that we prove our right to be regarded as Christians.

"Likewise also was not Rahab the harlot justified by works, when she had received the messengers, and had sent them out another way?" (v. 25). Why bring in the case of Rahab? Was not the example of Abraham conclusive and sufficient? First, because "two witnesses" are required for the truth to be "established"—cf. Romans 4:3, 6. Second, because, it might be objected Abraham's case was so exceptional that it could be no criterion to measure others by. Very well: Rahab was a poor Gentile, a heathen, a harlot; yet she too was justified by faith (Heb. 11:31), and later demonstrated her faith by "works"—receiving the spies at the imminent risk of her own life.

"For as the body without the spirit is dead, so faith without works is dead also" (Jam. 2:26). Here is the summing up: a breathless carcass and a worthless faith are alike useless as unto all the ends of natural and spiritual life. Thus the Apostle has conclusively shown the worthlessness of the garb of orthodoxy when worn by lifeless professors. He has fully exposed the error of those who rest in a bare profession of the Gospel—as if that could save them, when the temper of their minds and the tenor of their lives was diametrically opposed to the holy religion they professed. A holy heart and an obedient walk are the scriptural evidence of our having been justified by God.

Chapter 10
Its Results

The justification of the believer is absolute, complete, final. "It is God that justifieth" (Rom. 8:33), and "I know that, whatsoever God doeth, it shall be forever: nothing can be put to it, nor any thing taken from it" (Eccl. 3:14). So absolute and inexorable is this blessed fact that, in Romans 8:30 we are told, "Whom He justified, them He also glorified": notice it is not simply a promise that God "will glorify," but so sure and certain is that blissful event, the past tense is used. "Them He also glorified" is speaking from the standpoint of the eternal and unalterable purpose of God, concerning which there is no conditionality or contingency whatsoever. To be "glorified" is to be perfectly conformed to the lovely image of Christ, when we shall see Him as He is and be made like Him (1 John 3:2). Because God has determined this, He speaks of it as already accomplished, for He "calleth those things which be not as though they were" (Rom. 4:17).

So far as the believer is concerned, the penal side of the sin question has been settled once and for all. His case has been tried in the supreme court, and God has justified him: in consequence thereof the Divine decision is "There is therefore now no condemnation to them which are in Christ Jesus" (Rom. 8:1). Once those very persons were under condemnation—"condemned already" (John 3:18); but now that their faith has united them to Christ there is no condemnation. The debt of their sin has been paid by their great Surety; the record thereof has been "blotted out" by His cleansing blood. "It is God that justifieth. Who is he that condemneth" (Rom. 8:33, 34). Who will reverse His decision! Where is that superior tribunal to which this cause can be carried? Eternal justice has pronounced her fiat; immutable judgment has recorded her sentence.

It is utterly and absolutely impossible that the sentence of the Divine Judge should ever be revoked or reversed. His sentence of justification results from and rests upon a complete satisfaction having been offered to His Law, and that in the fulfillment of a covenant engagement. Thus is effectually precluded the recall of the verdict. The Father stipulated to release His elect from the curse of the law provided the Son would meet the claims of justice against them. The Son freely complied with His Father's will: "Lo, I come." He was now made under the law, fulfilled the law, and suffered the full penalty of the law; therefore shall He see of the travail of His soul and be satisfied. Sooner shall the lightenings of omnipotence shiver the Rock of Ages than those sheltering in Him again be brought under condemnation.

How very, very far from the glorious truth of the Gospel is the mere conditional pardon which Arminians represent God as bestowing upon those who come to Christ—a pardon which may be rescinded, yea, which will be canceled, unless they "do their part" and perform certain stipulations! What a horrible and blasphemous travesty of the Truth is that!—an error which must be steadfastly resisted no matter who holds it: better far to hurt the feelings of a million of our fellow-creatures than to displease their august Creator. On no such precarious basis as our fulfilling certain conditions has God suspended the justification of His people. Not only is there "now no condemnation" resting upon the believer, but there never again shall me, for "Blessed is the man to whom the Lord will not impute sin" (Rom. 4:8).

The dread sentence of the law, "Thou shalt surely die," cannot in justice be executed upon the sinner's Surety and also upon himself. Hence by a necessity existing in the very nature of moral government, it must follow that the believing sinner be freed from all condemnation, that is, so cleared of the same that he is raised above all liability to punishment. So declared our blessed Savior Himself, in words too plain and emphatic to admit of any misunderstanding: "Verily, verily, I say unto you, He that heareth My word, and believeth on Him that sent Me, hath everlasting life, and shall not come into condemnation; but is passed from death unto life" (John 5:24). He, the habitation of whose throne is "justice and judgment," has sealed up this declaration forever, by affirming "I will never leave thee nor forsake thee." Sooner shall the sword of justice cleave the helmet of the Almighty than any Divinely pardoned soul perish.

But not only are the sins of all who truly come to Christ eternally remitted, but the very righteousness of the Redeemer passes over to them, is placed upon them, so that a perfect obedience to the law is imputed to their account. It is theirs, not by promise, but by gift (Rom. 5:17), by actual bestowment. It is not simply that God treats them as if they were righteous, they are righteous and so pronounced by Him. And therefore may each believing soul exclaim, "I will greatly rejoice in the LORD, my soul shall be joyful in my God; for He hath clothed me with the garments of salvation, He hath covered me with the robe of righteousness, as a bridegroom decketh himself with ornaments, and as a bride adorneth herself with her jewels" (Isa. 61:10). O that each Christian reader may be enabled to clearly and strongly grasp hold of this glorious fact: that he is now truly righteous in the sight of God, is in actual possession of an obedience which answers every demand of the law.

This unspeakable blessing is bestowed not only by the amazing grace of God, but it is actually required by His inexorable justice. This too was stipulated and agreed upon in the covenant into which the Father entered with the Son. That is why the Redeemer lived here on earth for upwards of thirty years before He went to the cross to suffer the penalty of our sins: He assumed and discharged our responsibilities; as a child, as a youth, as a man, He rendered unto God that perfect obedience which we owed Him. He "fulfilled all righteousness" (Matt. 3:15) for His people, and just as He who knew no sin was made sin for them, so they are now made "the righteousness of God in Him" (2 Cor. 5:21). And therefore does Jehovah declare, "For the mountains shall depart, and the hills be removed; but My kindness shall not depart from thee, neither shall the covenant of My peace be removed, saith the LORD that hath mercy on thee" (Isa. 54:10).

By actually believing with a justifying faith the sinner doth receive Christ Himself, is joined to Him, and becomes immediately an heir of God and joint-heir with Christ. This gives him a right unto and an interest in the benefits of His mediation. By faith in Christ he received not only the forgiveness of sins, but an inheritance among all them that are sanctified (Acts 26:18), the Holy Spirit (given to him) being "the earnest of our inheritance" (Eph. 1:13, 14). The believing sinner may now say "in the LORD have I righteousness" (Isa. 45:24). He is "complete in Him" (Col. 2:10), for by "one offering" the Savior hath "perfected forever them that are sanctified" (Heb. 10:14). The believer has been "accepted in the Beloved" (Eph. 1:6), and stands before the throne of God arrayed in a garment more excellent than that which is worn by the holy angels.

How infinitely does the glorious Gospel of God transcend the impoverished thoughts and schemes of men! How immeasurably superior is that "everlasting righteousness" which Christ has brought in (Dan. 9:24) from that miserable thing which multitudes are seeking to produce by their own efforts. Greater far is the difference between the shining light of the midday sun and the blackness of the darkest night, than between that "best robe" (Luke 15:22) which Christ has wrought out for each of His people and that wretched covering which zealous religionists are attempting to weave out of the filthy rags of their own righteousness. Equally great is the difference between the truth of God concerning the present and immutable standing of His saints in all the acceptability of Christ, and the horrible perversion of Arminians who make acceptance with God contingent upon the believer's faithfulness and perseverance, who suppose that Heaven can be purchased by the creature's deeds and doings.

It is not that the justified soul is now left to himself, so that he is certain of getting to Heaven no matter how he conducts himself—the fatal error of Antinomians. No Indeed. God also imparts to him the blessed Holy Spirit, who works within him the desire to serve, please, and glorify the One who has been so gracious to Him. "The love of Christ constraineth us... that they which live should not henceforth live unto themselves, but unto Him which died for them, and rose again" (2 Cor. 5:14, 15). They now "delight in the law of God after the inward man" (Rom. 7:22), and though the flesh, the world, and the Devil oppose every step of the way, occasioning many a sad fall—which is repented of, confessed, and forsaken—nevertheless the Spirit renews them day by day (2 Cor. 4:16) and leads them in the paths of righteousness for Christ's name's sake.

In the last paragraph will be found the answer to those who object that the preaching of justification by the imputed righteousness of Christ, apprehended by faith alone, will encourage carelessness and foster licentiousness. Those whom God justifies are not left in their natural condition, under the dominion of sin, but are quickened, indwelt, and guided by the Holy Spirit. As Christ cannot be divided, and so is received as Lord to rule us as well as Savior to redeem us, so those whom God justifies He also sanctifies. We do not affirm that all who receive this blessed truth into their heads have their lives transformed thereby—no indeed; but we do insist that where it is applied in power to the heart there always follows a walk to the glory of God, the fruits of righteousness being brought forth to the praise of His name. Each truly justified soul will say:

> "Let worldly minds the world pursue,
> It has no charms for me;
> I once admired its trifles too,
> But grace has set me free."

It is therefore the bounden duty of those who profess to have been justified by God to diligently and impartially examine themselves, to ascertain whether or not they have in them those spiritual graces which always accompany justification. It is by our sanctification, and that alone, that we may discover our justification. Would you know whether Christ fulfilled the law for you, that His obedience has been imputed to your account? Then search your heart and life and see whether a spirit of obedience to Him is daily working in you. The righteousness of the law is fulfilled only in those who "walk not after the flesh, but after the Spirit" (Rom. 8:4). God never designed that the obedience of His Son should be imputed to those who live a life of worldliness, self-pleasing, and gratifying the lusts of the flesh. Far from it: "If any man be in Christ, he is a new creature: old things are passed away; behold, all things are become new" (2 Cor. 5:17).

Summarizing now the blessed results of justification.

The sins of the believer are forgiven. "Through this Man is preached unto you the forgiveness of sins. And by Him all that believe are justified from all things" (Acts 13:38, 39). All the sins of the believer, past, present, and to come, were laid upon Christ and atoned for by Him. Although sins cannot be actually pardoned before they are actually committed yet their obligation to the curse of the law were virtually remitted at the Cross, antecedently to their actual commission. The sins of Christians involve only the governmental dealings of God in this life, and these are remitted upon a sincere repentance and confession.

An inalienable title unto everlasting glory is bestowed. Christ purchased for His people the reward of blessing of the law, which is eternal life. Therefore does the Holy Spirit assure the Christian that he has been begotten "to an inheritance incorruptible, and undefiled, and that fadeth not away, reserved in heaven for you" (1 Peter 1:4). Not only is that inheritance reserved for all the justified, but they are all preserved unto it, as the very next verse declares, "who are kept by the power of God through faith unto salvation ready to be revealed in the last time" (v. 5)--"kept" from committing the unpardonable sin, from apostatizing from the truth, from being fatally deceived by the Devil; so "kept" that the power of God prevents anything separating them from His love in Christ Jesus (Rom. 8:35-38).

Reconciliation unto God Himself. "Therefore being justified by faith, we have peace with God through our Lord Jesus Christ... we were reconciled to God by the death of His Son" (Rom. 5:1, 10). Until men are justified they are at war with God, and He is against them, being "angry with the wicked every day" (Ps. 7:11). Dreadful beyond words is the condition of those who are under condemnation: their minds are enmity against God (Rom. 8:7), all their ways are opposed to Him (Col. 1:21). But at conversion the sinner throws down the weapons of his rebellion and surrenders to the righteous claims of Christ, and by Him he is reconciled to God. Reconciliation is to make an end of strife, to bring together those at variance, to change enemies into friends. Between God and the justified there is peace—effected by the blood of Christ.

An unalterable standing in the favor of God. "Therefore being justified by faith, we have peace with God through our Lord Jesus Christ: by whom also we have access by faith into this grace wherein we stand" (Rom. 5:1, 2). Mark the word "also": not only has Christ turned away the wrath of God from us, but in addition He has secured the benevolence of God toward us. Previous to justification our standing was one of unutterable disgrace, but now, through Christ, it is in one of unclouded grace. God now has naught but good-will toward us. God has not only ceased to be offended at us, but is well-pleased with us; not only will He never afflict punishment upon us, but He will never cease to shower His blessings upon us. The throne to which we have free access is not one of judgment, but of pure and unchanging grace.

Owned by God Himself before an assembled universe. "But I say unto you, That every idle word that men shall speak, they shall give account thereof in the day of judgment. For by thy words thou shalt be justified" (Matt. 12:36, 37): yes, justified publicly by the Judge Himself! "These shall go away into everlasting punishment: but the righteous into life eternal" (Matt. 25:46). Here will be the final justification of the Christian, this sentence being declaratory unto the glory of God and the everlasting blessedness of those who have believed.

Let it be said in conclusion that the justification of the Christian is complete the moment he truly believes in Christ, and hence there are no degrees in justification. The Apostle Paul was as truly a justified man at the hour of his conversion as he was at the close of his life. The feeblest babe in Christ is just as completely justified as is the most mature saint. Let theologians note the following distinctions. Christians were decretively justified from all eternity: efficaciously so when Christ rose again from the dead; actually so when they believed; sensibly so when the Spirit bestows joyous assurance; manifestly so when they tread the path of obedience; finally so at the Day of Judgment, when God shall sententiously, and in the presence of all created things, pronounce them so.

THE DOCTRINE
OF MAN'S IMPOTENCE

Contents

Chapter 1
Introduction

The title of this second section of our book (Part II from Gleanings from the Scriptures; Man's Total Depravity) may occasion a raising of the eyebrows. That we should designate the spiritual helplessness of fallen man a "doctrine" is likely to cause surprise, for it is certainly not so regarded in most circles today. Yet this is hardly to be wondered at. Didactic preaching has fallen into such general disuse that more than one important doctrine is no longer heard from the pulpits. If on the one hand there is a deplorable lack of a clear and definite portrayal of the character of God, on the other there is also a woeful absence of any lucid and comprehensive presentation of the teaching of Scripture concerning the nature and condition of man. Such failure at either point leads to the most disastrous consequences. A study of this neglected subject is therefore timely and urgent.

Timely and Urgent Study

It is of the utmost importance that people should clearly understand and be made thoroughly aware of their spiritual impotence, for thus alone is a foundation laid for bringing them to see and feel their imperative need of divine grace for salvation. So long as sinners think they have it in their own power to deliver themselves from their death in trespasses and sins, they will never come to Christ that they might have life, for "the whole need not a physician, but they that are sick." So long as people imagine they labor under no insuperable inability to comply with the call of the gospel, they never will be conscious of their entire dependence on Him alone who is able to work in them "all the good pleasure of his goodness, and the work of faith with power" (2 Thess. 1:11). So long as the creature is puffed up with a sense of his own ability to respond to God's requirements, he will never become a suppliant at the footstool of divine mercy.

A careful perusal of what the Word of God has to say on this subject leaves us in no doubt about the awful state of spiritual serfdom into which the fall has brought man. The depravity, blindness and deafness of all mankind in things of a spiritual nature are continually inculcated and emphatically insisted on throughout the Scriptures. Not only is the total inability of the natural man to obtain salvation by deeds of the law frequently asserted, but his utter helplessness in himself to comply with the terms of the gospel is also strongly affirmed—not indirectly and occasionally, but expressly and continually. Both in the Old Testament and in the New, in the declarations of the prophets, of the Lord Christ, and of His apostles, the bondage of the natural man to Satan is often depicted, and his complete impotence to turn to God for deliverance is solemnly and unequivocally set forth. Ignorance or misconception on the matter is therefore inexcusable.

Nevertheless the fact remains that this is a doctrine which is little understood and rarely insisted upon. Notwithstanding the clear and uniform testimony of the Scriptures, the actual conditions of men, their alienation from God, their sinful inability to return to Him, are but feebly apprehended and seldom heard even in orthodox quarters. The fact is that the whole trend of modern thought is in the very opposite direction. For the past century, and increasingly so during the last few decades, the greatness of man—his dignity, his development and his achievements—has been the predominant theme of pulpit and press. The antiscriptural theory of evolution is a blank detail of the fall and its dire consequences, and even where the Darwinian hypothesis has not been accepted, its pernicious influences have been more or less experienced.

The evil effects from the promulgation of the evolutionary lie are far more widespread than most Christians realize. Such a philosophy (if it is entitled to be called that) has induced multitudes of people to suppose that their state is far different from, and vastly superior to, the fearful diagnosis given in Holy Writ. Even among those who have not accepted without considerable reservation the idea that man is slowly but surely progressing, the great majority have been encouraged to believe that their case is far better than it actually is. Consequently, when a servant of God boldly affirms that all the descendants of Adam are so completely enslaved by sin that they are utterly unable to take one step toward Christ for deliverance, he is looked upon as a doleful pessimist or a crazy fanatic. To speak of the spiritual impotence of the natural man is, in our day, to talk in an unknown tongue.

Not only does the appalling ignorance of our generation cause the servant of God to labor under a heavy handicap when seeking to present the scriptural account of man's total inability for good; he is also placed at a serious disadvantage by virtue of the marked distastefulness of this truth. The subject of his moral impotence is far from being a pleasing one to the natural man. He wants to be told that all he needs to do is exert himself, that salvation lies within the power of his will, that he is the determiner of his own destiny. Pride, with its strong dislike of being a debtor to the sovereign grace of God, rises up against it. Self-esteem, with its rabid repugnance of anything which lays the creature in the dust, hotly resents what is so humiliating. Consequently, this truth is either openly rejected or, if seemingly received, is turned to a wrong use.

Moreover, when it is insisted on that man's bondage to sin is both voluntary and culpable, that the guilt for his inability to turn to God or to do anything pleasing in His sight lies at his own door, that his spiritual impotence consists in nothing but the depravity of his own heart and his inveterate enmity against God, then the hatefulness of this doctrine is speedily demonstrated. While men are allowed to think that their spiritual helplessness is involuntary rather than willful, innocent rather than criminal, something to be pitied rather than blamed, they may receive this truth with a measure of toleration; but let them be told that they themselves have forged the shackles which hold them in captivity to sin, that God counts them responsible for the corruption of their hearts, and that their incapability of being holy constitutes the very essence of their guilt, and loud will be their outcries against such a flesh-withering truth.

However repellent this truth may be, it must not be withheld from men. The minister of Christ is not sent forth to please or entertain his congregation, but to declare the counsel of God, and not merely those parts of it which may meet with their approval and acceptance, but "all the counsel of God" (Acts 20:27). If he deliberately omits that which raises their ire, he betrays his trust. Once he starts whittling down his divinely given commission there will be no end to the process, for one class will murmur against this portion of the truth and another against that. The servant of God has nothing to do with the response which is made to his preaching; his business is to deliver the Word of God in its unadulterated purity and leave the results to the One who has called him. And he may be assured at the outset that unless many in his congregation are seriously disturbed by his message, he has failed to deliver it in its clarity.

A Resented Doctrine

No matter how hotly this doctrine of man's spiritual impotence is resented by both the profane and the religious world, it must not be withheld through cowardice. Christ, our supreme Exemplar, announced this truth emphatically and constantly. To the Pharisees He said, "O generation of vipers, how can ye, being evil, speak good things? For out of the abundance of the heart the mouth speaketh" (Matt. 12:34). Men's hearts are so vile, it is utterly impossible that anything holy should issue from them. They can no more change their nature by an effort of will than a leper might heal himself by his own volition. Christ further said, "How can ye believe, which receive honor one of another, and seek not the honor that cometh from God only?" (John 5:44). It is a moral impossibility—pride and humility are opposites. Those who seek to please self and those who sincerely aim at the approbation of God belong to two entirely different stocks.

On another occasion the Lord Christ asked, "Why do ye not understand my speech?" to which He Himself answered, "Even because ye cannot hear my word" (John 8:43). There is no mistaking His meaning here and no evading the force of His solemn utterance. The message of Christ was hateful to their worldly and wicked hearts and could no more be acceptable to them than would wholesome food to birds accustomed to feed on carrion. Man cannot act contrary to his nature; one might as well expect fire to burn downward or water flow upward. "Ye are of your father the devil, and the lusts of your father ye will do" (John 8:44) said the Savior to the Jews. And what was their response? "Say we not well that thou art a Samaritan, and hast a devil?" (v. 48). Sufficient for the servant to be as his Master.

Now if such is the case with the natural man that he can no more break the bonds which hold him in captivity to Satan than he could restore the dead to life, ought he not to be faithfully informed of his wretched condition? If he is so helpless and hopeless in himself that he cannot turn from sin to holiness, that he cannot please God, that he cannot take one step toward Christ for salvation, is it not a kindness to acquaint him with his spiritual impotence, to shatter his dreams of self-sufficiency, to expose the delusion that he is lord of himself? In fact, is it not positively cruel to leave him alone in his complacency and make no effort to bring him face to face with the desperateness of his depravity? Surely anyone with a vestige of charity in his heart will have no difficulty in answering such questions.

It is far from a pleasant task for a physician to tell an unsuspecting patient that his or her heart is organically diseased or to announce to a young person engaging in strenuous activities that his lungs are in such a condition he is totally unfit for violent exertions; nevertheless it is the physician's duty to break such news. Now if this principle holds good in connection with our mortal bodies, how much more so with regard to our never dying spirits. True, there are some doctors who persuade themselves that there are times when it is expedient for them to withhold such information from their patients, but a true physician of souls is never justified in concealing the more distasteful aspect of the truth from those who are under his care. If he is to be free from their blood, he must unsparingly expose the plague of their hearts.

The fact of fallen man's moral inability is indissolubly bound up with the doctrine of his total depravity, and any denial of the one is a repudiation of the other, as any attempt to modify the former is to vitiate the latter. In like manner, the fact of the natural man's impotence to deliver himself from the bondage of sin is inseparably connected with the truth of regeneration; for unless we are without strength in ourselves, what need is there for God to work a miracle of grace in us? It is, then, the reality of the sinner's helplessness which provides the dark background necessary for the gospel, and just in proportion as we are made aware of our helplessness shall we really value the mercy proffered us in the gospel. On the other hand, while we cherish the delusion that we have power to turn to God at any time, just so long we shall continue procrastinating and thereby despise the gracious overtures of the gospel.

William Shedd stated:

A sense of danger excites; a sense of security puts to sleep. A company of gamblers in the sixth story are told that the building is on fire. One of them answers, "We have the key to the fire escape," and all continue the game. Suddenly one exclaims, "The key is lost"; all immediately spring to their feet and endeavor to escape.

Just so long as the sinner believes—because of his erroneous notion of the freedom of his will—that he has the power to repent and believe at any moment, he will defer faith and repentance; he will not so much as beg God to work these graces in him.

The first office of the preacher is to stain the pride of all human glory, to bring down the high looks of man, to make him aware of his sinful perversity, to make him feel that he is unworthy of the least of all God's mercies. His business is to strip him of the rags of his self-righteousness and to shatter his self-sufficiency; to make him conscious of his utter dependence on the mere grace of God. Only he who finds himself absolutely helpless will surrender himself to sovereign grace. Only he who feels himself already sinking under the billows of a justly deserved condemnation will cry out, "Lord, save me, I perish." Only he who has been brought to despair will place the crown of glory on the only head entitled to wear it. Though God alone can make a man conscious of his impotence, He is pleased to use the means of the truth—faithfully dispensed, effectually applied by the Spirit—in doing so.

Chapter 2
Reality

The spiritual impotence of the natural man is no mere product of theological dyspepsia, nor is it a dismal dogma invented during the Dark Ages. It is a solemn fact affirmed by Holy Writ, manifested throughout human history, confirmed in the conscious experience of every genuinely convicted soul. The moral powerlessness of the sinner is not proclaimed in the pulpit today, nor is it believed in by professing Christians generally. When it is insisted that man is so completely the bondslave of sin that he cannot move toward God, the vast majority will regard the statement as utterly unreasonable and reject it with scorn. To tell those who consider themselves to be hale and hearty that they are without strength strikes them as a preposterous assumption unworthy of serious consideration.

Objections of Unbelief

When a servant of God does press this unwelcome truth on his hearers, the fertile mind of unbelief promptly replies with one objection after another. If we are totally devoid of spiritual ability, then assuredly we must be aware of the fact. But that is far from being the case. The skeptic says we are very much aware of our power to do that which is pleasing in God's sight; even though we do not perform it, we could if we would. He also contends that were we so completely the captives of Satan as is declared, we should not be free agents at all. Such a concept as that we will not allow for a moment. Another point of the skeptic is that if man has no power to do that which God requires, then obviously he is not a responsible creature, for he cannot justly be held accountable to do that which is beyond his powers to achieve.

We must establish the fact of man's spiritual impotence and show that it is a solemn reality; for until we do this, it is useless to discuss the nature of that impotence, its seat, its extent or its cause. And it is to the inspired Word of God alone that we shall make our appeal; for if the Scriptures of truth plainly teach this doctrine, then we are on sure ground and may not reject its testimony even though no one else on earth believed it. If the divine oracles affirm it, then none of the objections brought against it by the carnal mind can have any weight with us, though in due course we shall endeavor to show that these objections are as pointless as they are groundless.

In approaching more definitely the task now before us it should be pointed out that, strictly speaking, it is the subject of human depravity which we are going to write on; yet to have so designated this section would be rather misleading as we are going to confine ourselves to only one aspect of it. The spiritual impotence of the natural man forms a distinct and separate branch of his depravity. The state of evil into which the fall has plunged us is far more dreadful and its dire consequences far more wide-reaching than is commonly supposed. The common idea is that though man has fallen he is not so badly damaged but that he may recover himself, providing he properly exercises his remaining strength or with due attention improves the help proffered him. But his case is vastly more serious than that.

A. A. Hodge said:

The three main elements involved in the consequences entailed by the sin of Adam upon his posterity are these: First, the guilt, or just penal responsibility of Adam's first sin or apostatizing act, which is imputed or judicially charged upon his descendants, whereby every child is born into the world in a state of antenatal forfeiture or condemnation. Second, the entire depravity of our nature, involving a sinful innate disposition inevitably leading to actual transgression. Third, the entire inability of the soul to change its own nature, or to do anything spiritually good in obedience to the Divine Law.

God's Word on the Subject

Let us consider some of the solemn declarations of our Lord on the third of these dire consequences of the fall. "Verily, verily, I say unto thee, Except a man be born again, he cannot see the kingdom of God" (John 3:3). Until a man is born again he remains in his natural, fallen and depraved state and so long as that is the case it is utterly impossible for him to discern or perceive divine things. Sin has both darkened his understanding and destroyed his spiritual vision. "The way of the wicked is as darkness: they know not at what they stumble" (Prov. 4:19). Though divine instruction is supplied them, though God has given them His Word in which the way to heaven is plainly marked out, still they are incapable of profiting from it. Moses represented them as groping at noonday (Deut. 28:29), and Job declares, "They meet with darkness in the daytime, and grope in the noonday as in the night" (5:14). Jeremiah depicts them as walking in "slippery ways in the darkness" (23:12).

Now this darkness which envelops the natural man is a moral one, having its seat in the soul. Our Savior declared, "The light of the body is the eye: if therefore thine eye be single, thy whole body shall be full of light. But if thine eye be evil, thy whole body shall be full of darkness. If therefore the light that is in thee be darkness, how great is that darkness!" (Matt. 6:22-23). The heart is the same to the soul as the eye is to the body. As a sound eye lets in natural light, so a good heart lets in spiritual light; and as a blind eye shuts out natural light, so an evil heart shuts out spiritual light. Accordingly we find the apostle expressly ascribing the darkness of the understanding to the blindness of the heart. He represents all men as "having the understanding darkened, being alienated from the life of God through the ignorance that is in them, because of the blindness of their heart" (Eph. 4:18).

While sinners remain under the entire dominion of a wicked heart they are altogether blind to the spiritual excellence of the character, the works and the ways of God. "Hear now this, O foolish people, and without understanding; which have eyes, and see not; which have ears, and hear not" (Jer. 5:21). The natural man is blind. This awful fact was affirmed again and again by our Lord as He addressed hypocritical scribes thus: "blind leaders of the blind," "ye blind guides," "thou blind Pharisee" (Matt. 15:14; 23:24, 26). Paul said: "The god of this world hath blinded the minds of them which believe not" (2 Cor. 4:4). There is in the unregenerate mind an incompetence, an incapacity, an inability to understand the things of the Spirit; and Christ's repeated miracle in restoring sight to the naturally blind was designed to teach us our imperative need of the same divine power recovering spiritual vision to our souls.

A question has been raised as to whether this blindness of the natural man is partial or total, whether it is simply a defect of vision or whether he has no vision at all. The nature of his disease may best be defined as spiritual myopia or shortsightedness. He is able to see clearly objects which are nearby, but distant ones lie wholly beyond the range of his vision. In other words, the mind's eye of the sinner is capable of perceiving natural things, but he has no ability to see spiritual things. Holy Writ states that the one who "lacketh these things," namely, the graces of faith, virtue, knowledge, and so forth, mentioned in 2 Peter 1:5-7, is "blind, and cannot see afar off" (v. 9). The Book therefore urges him to receive "eyesalve" from Christ, that he may see (Rev. 3:18).

For this very purpose the Son of God came into the world: to give "deliverance to the captives, and recovering of sight to the blind" (Luke 4:18). Concerning those who are the subjects of this miracle of grace it is said, "Ye were sometimes darkness, but now are ye light in the Lord" (Eph. 5:8). This is the fulfillment of our Lord's promise: "I am the light of the world: he that followeth me shall not walk in darkness, but shall have the light of life" (John 8:12). God is light, therefore those who are alienated from Him are in complete spiritual darkness. They do not see the frightful danger to which they are exposed. Though they are led captive by Satan from day to day and year to year, they are totally unaware of his malignant influence over them. They are blind to the nature and tendency of their religious performances, failing to perceive that no matter how earnestly they engage in them, they cannot be acceptable to God while their minds are at enmity against Him. They are blind to the way and means of recovery.

The awful thing is that the natural man is quite blind to the blindness of his heart which is insensibly leading him to "the blackness of darkness forever" (Jude 13). That is why the vast majority live so securely and peacefully. It has always appeared strange to the godly why the ungodly can be so unconcerned while under sentence of death, and conduct themselves so frivolously and gaily while exposed to the wrath to come. John was surprised to see the wicked spending their days in carnality and feasting. David was grieved at the prosperity of the wicked and could not account for their not being in trouble as other men. Amos was astonished to behold the sinners in Zion living at ease, putting the evil day far from them, lying on beds of ivory. Nothing but their spiritual blindness can explain the conduct of the vast majority of mankind, crying peace and safety when exposed to impending destruction.

Man's Opposition

Since all sinners are involved in such spiritual darkness as makes them unaware of their present condition and condemnation, it is not surprising that they are so displeased when their fearful danger is plainly pointed out. Such faithful warning tends to disturb their present peace and comfort and to destroy their future hopes and prospects of happiness. If they were once made to truly realize the imminent danger of the damnation of hell, their ease, security and joy would be completely dispelled. They cannot bear, therefore, to hear the plain truth respecting their wretchedness and guilt. Sinners could not bear to hear the plain teachings of the prophets or Christ on this account; this explains their bitter complaints and fierce opposition. They regard as enemies those who try to befriend them. They stop their ears and run from them.

That the natural man—even the most zealous religionist—has no perception of this spiritual blindness, and that he is highly displeased when charged with it, is evident: "Jesus said, For judgment I am come into this world, that they which see not might see; and that they which see might be made blind. And some of the Pharisees which were with him heard these words, and said unto him, Are we blind also? And Jesus said unto them, If ye were blind, ye should have no sin: but now ye say, We see; therefore your sin remaineth" (John 9:39-41). God's Son became incarnate for the purpose of bringing to light the hidden things of darkness. He came to expose things, that those made conscious of their blindness might receive sight, but that they who had spiritual sight in their own estimation should be "made blind"—judicially abandoned to the pride of their evil hearts. The infatuated Pharisees had no desire for such an experience. Denying their blindness, they were left in their sin.

"Verily, verily, I say unto thee, Except a man be born again, he cannot see the kingdom of God" (John 3:3). He cannot see the things of God because by nature he is enveloped in total spiritual darkness; even though external light shine on him, he has no eyes with which to see. "The light shineth in darkness; and the darkness comprehended it not" (John 1:5). When the Lord of life and light appeared among them, men had no eyes to see His beauty, but despised and rejected

Him. And so it is still; every verse in Scripture which treats of the Spirit's illumination confirms this solemn fact. "For God, who commanded the light to shine out of darkness, hath shined in our hearts, to give the light of the knowledge of the glory of God in the face of Jesus Christ" (2 Cor. 4:6). This giving of light and knowledge is by divine power, being analogous to that power by which the light at the first creation was provided. As far as spiritual, saving knowledge of the truth is concerned, the mind of fallen man is like the chaos before God said "Let there be light." "Darkness was upon the face of the deep," and in that state it is impossible for men to understand the things of the Spirit.

Not only is the understanding of the natural man completely under the dominion of darkness, but his will is paralyzed against good; and if that is so, the sinner is indeed impotent. This fact was made clear by Christ when He affirmed, "No man can come to me, except the Father which hath sent me draw him" (John 6:44). And why is it that the sinner cannot come to Christ by his own unaided powers? Because he has no inclination to do so and, therefore, no volition in that direction. The Greek might be rendered "Ye will not come to me." There is not the slightest desire in the unregenerate heart to do so.

The will of fallen man is depraved, being completely in bondage to sin. There is not merely a negative lack of inclination, but there is a positive disinclination. The unwillingness consists of aversion: "The carnal mind is enmity against God: for it is not subject to the law of God, neither indeed can be" (Rom. 8:7). And not only is there an aversion against God, there is a hatred of Him. Christ said to His disciples, "If the world hate you, ye know that it hated me before it hated you" (John 15:18). This hatred is inveterate obstinacy: "The Lord said unto Moses, I have seen this people, and, behold, it is a stiffnecked people" (Exodus 32:9). "All day long I have stretched forth my hands unto a disobedient and gainsaying people" (Rom. 10:21). Man is incorrigible and in himself his case is hopeless. "Thy people shall be willing in the day of thy power" (Ps. 110:3) because they have no power whatever of their own to effect such willingness.

Since we have demonstrated from the Scriptures of truth that the natural man is utterly unable to discern spiritual things, much less to choose them, there is little need for us to labor the point that he is quite incompetent to perform any spiritual act. Nor is this only a logical inference drawn by theologians; it is expressly affirmed in the Word: "So then they that are in the flesh cannot please God" (Rom. 8:8). There is no denying the meaning of that terrible indictment, as there is no likelihood of its originating with man himself. Jeremiah said, "O Lord, I know that the way of man is not in himself: it is not in man that walketh to direct his steps" (10:23). All power to direct our steps in the paths of righteousness was lost by us at the fall, and therefore we are entirely dependent on God to work in us "both to will and to do of his good pleasure" (Phil. 2:13).

Little as this solemn truth of man's moral impotence is known today and widely as it is denied by modern thought and teaching, there was a time when it was generally contended for. In the Thirty nine Articles of the Church of England (to which all her ministers must still solemnly and formally subscribe) the Tenth reads thus:

The condition of man after the fall of Adam is such, that he cannot turn and prepare himself, by his own natural strength and good works to faith and calling upon God. Wherefore we have no power to do good works pleasant and acceptable to God.

In the Westminster Confession of Faith chapter 6 begins thus:

Our first parents being seduced by the subtlety and temptation of Satan, sinned in eating the forbidden fruit. This their sin God was pleased, according to His wise and holy counsel, to permit, having purposed to order it to His own glory. By this sin they fell from their original righteousness and communion with God, and so became dead in sin, and wholly defiled in all the faculties and parts of soul and body. They being the root of all mankind, the guilt of this sin was imputed, and the same death in sin and corrupted nature conveyed to all their posterity, descending from them by ordinary generation. From this original corruption, whereby we are utterly indisposed, disabled, and made opposite to all good, and wholly inclined to all evil, do proceed all actual transgressions.

Chapter 3
Nature

The doctrine we are now considering is a most solemn and forbidding one. Certainly it is one which could never have been invented by man, for it is far too humbling and distasteful. It is one which is most offensive to human pride, and at complete variance with the modem idea of the progress of the human race. Nevertheless, if we accept the Scriptures as a divine revelation, we have no choice but to uncomplainingly receive this truth. The ruined and helpless state of the sinner is fully attested by the Bible. There fallen man is represented as so utterly carnal and sold under sin as to be not only "without strength" (Rom. 5:6) but lacking the least inclination to move toward God. Very dark indeed is this side of the truth, but its supplement is the glory of God in rich grace, for it furnishes a real but necessary background to the blessed contents of the gospel.

Clear Teaching of Scripture
The Scriptures plainly teach that man is a fallen being, that he is lost (Luke 19:10), that he cannot recover himself from his ruin, that despite the fact of an all-sufficient Savior presented to him, he cannot come to Him until he is moved upon by the Spirit of God. Thus it is quite evident that if a sinner is saved, he owes his salvation entirely to the free grace and effectual power of God, and not to any good in or from or by himself. "Not unto us, O Lord, not unto us, but thy name give glory, for thy mercy" (Ps. 115:1) is the unqualified acknowledgment of all the redeemed. Scripture speaks in no uncertain language on this point. If one man differs from another on this all-important matter of being saved, then it is God who has made him to differ (1 Cor. 4:7) and not himself.

Nor is the sinner's salvation to be in any way attributed to either pliability of heart or diligence in the use of means. "So then it is not of him that willeth, nor of him that runneth, but of God that showed mercy." "Therefore hath he mercy on whom he will have mercy" (Rom. 9:16, 18). The context of John 6:44 indicates that our Lord was thus accounting for the enmity of the murmuring Jews: "No man can come to me, except the Father which hath sent me draw him." By those words Christ intimated that, considering what fallen human nature is, the conduct of His enemies is not to be wondered at; that they acted in no other way than will all other men when left to themselves; that His own disciples would never have obeyed and followed Him had not a gracious divine influence been exercised on them.

Man's Strong Objection
But as soon as this flesh-withering truth is pressed upon the unregenerate, they raise an outcry and voice their objections against it. If the spiritual condition of fallen man is one of complete helplessness, then how can the gospel ask him to turn from his sins and flee to Christ for refuge? If the natural man is unable to repent and believe the gospel, then how can he be justly punished for his impenitence and unbelief? On what ground can man be blamed for not doing what is morally impossible? Notwithstanding these difficulties the point of doctrine which we shall insist upon is that no one is able to comply with the terms of the gospel until he is made the subject of the special and effectual grace of God, that is, until he is divinely quickened, made willing, so that he actually does comply with its terms.

Nevertheless, we shall endeavor to show that sinners are not unjustly condemned for their depravity, but that their inability is blameworthy. Great care needs to be taken in stating this doctrine accurately. Otherwise men will be encouraged to put it to wrong use, making it a comfortable resting place for their corrupt hearts. By a misrepresentation of this doctrine more than one preacher has "strengthened the hands of the wicked, that he should not return from his wicked way" (Ezek. 13:22). The truth of man's spiritual impotence has been so distorted that many sinners have been made to feel that they are to be pitied, that they are sincere in desiring a new heart— which has not yet been granted them. Many, while excusing their helplessness, suppose this to be consistent with a genuine longing to be renewed. It is the duty of the minister to make his hearers realize they are under no inability except the excuseless corruption of their own hearts.

Need for Understanding the Doctrine

There is a real need for us to look closely at the precise nature of man's spiritual inability, as to why he cannot come to Christ unless he be divinely drawn. But first let us notice some of the tenets of others on this point. These fall into two main classes, Pelagians and Semi-Pelagians— Pelagius being the principal opponent of the godly Augustine in the fifth century.

A. A. Hodge in his Outlines of Theology has succinctly summarized the Pelagian dogmas on the subject of man's ability to fulfill the law of God. Here is the essence of his four points: (1) Moral character can be predicated only of volitions. (2) Ability is always the measure of responsibility. (3) Hence every man has always plenary power to do all that it is his duty to do. (4) Hence the human will alone, to the exclusion of the interference of any internal influence from God, must decide human character and destiny. The only divine influence needed by man or consistent with his character as a self-determining agent is an external, providential and educational one.

Semi-Pelagians believe thus: (1) Man's nature has been so far weakened by the fall that it cannot act right in spiritual matters without divine assistance. (2) This weakened moral state which infants inherit from their parents is the cause of sin, but not itself sin in the sense of deserving the wrath of God. (3) Man must strive to do his whole duty, when God meets him with cooperative grace and makes his efforts successful. (4) Man is not responsible for the sins he commits until after he has enjoyed and abused the influences of grace.

Arminians are Semi-Pelagians, many of them going the whole length of the error in affirming the freedom of fallen man's will toward good. But their practical contention may fairly be stated thus: Man has certainly suffered considerably from the fall, so much so that sinners are unable to do much, if anything, toward their salvation merely of themselves. Nevertheless sinners are able, by the help of common grace (supposed to be extended by the Spirit to all who hear the gospel) to do those things which are regarded as fulfilling the preliminary conditions of salvation (such as acknowledging their sins and calling on God for help to forsake them and turn to Christ). And if sinners will thus pray, use the means of grace, and put forth what power they do have, then assuredly God will meet them halfway and renew their hearts and pardon their iniquities.

We object to this belief. First, far from the Scriptures representing man as being partially disabled by the fall, they declare him to be completely ruined—not merely weakened, but "without strength" (Rom. 5:6). Second, to affirm that the natural man has any aspiration toward God is to deny that he is totally depraved, that "every imagination of the thoughts of his heart . . .[is] only evil continually" (Gen. 6:5; cf. 8:21), that "there is none that seeketh after God" (Rom. 3:11). Third, if it were true that God could not justly condemn sinners for their inability to comply with the terms of the gospel, and that in order to give every man a "fair chance" to be saved He extends to all the common help of His Spirit, that would not be "grace" but a debt which He owed to His creatures. Fourth, if such a God-insulting principle were granted, the conclusion would inevitably follow that those who improved this "common grace" could lawfully boast that they made themselves to differ from those who did not improve it.

But enough of these shifts and subterfuges of the carnal mind. Let us now turn to God's own Word and see what it teaches us concerning the nature of man's spiritual impotence. First, it represents it as being a penal one, a judicial sentence from the righteous Judge of all the earth. Unless this is clearly grasped at the outset we are left without any adequate explanation of this dark mystery. God did not create man as he now is. God made man holy and upright, and by man's own apostasy he became corrupt and wicked. The Creator originally endowed man with certain powers, placed him on probation, and prescribed a rule of conduct for him. Had our first parents preserved their integrity, had they remained in loving and loyal subjection to their Maker and Ruler, all would have been well, not only for themselves but also for their posterity. But they were not willing to remain in the place of subjection. They took the reins into their own hands, rebelling against their Governor. And the outcome was dreadful.

The sin of man was extreme and aggravated. It was committed contrary to knowledge and, through the beneficence of the One against whom it was directed, in the face of great advantages. It was committed against divine warning, and against an explicit declaration of the consequence of man's transgression. In Adam's fearful offense there were unbelief, presumption, ingratitude, rebellion against his righteous and gracious Maker. Let the dreadfulness of this first human sin be carefully weighed before we are tempted to murmur against the dire consequences which accompanied it. Those dire consequences may all be summed up in the fearful word "death," for "the wages of sin is death." The full import of that statement can best be ascertained by considering all the evil effects which have since come to man. A just, holy, sin-hating God caused the punishment to fit the crime.

Probation of Human Race in Adam

When God placed Adam on probation it pleased Him to place the whole human race on probation, for Adam's posterity were not only in him seminally as their natural head, but they were also in him legally and morally as their legal and moral head. In other words, by divine constitution and covenant Adam stood and acted as the federal representative of the whole human race. Consequently, when he sinned, we sinned; when he fell, we fell. God justly imputed Adam's transgression to all his descendants, whose agent he was: "By the offence of one judgment came upon all men to condemnation" (Rom. 5:18). By his sin Adam became not only guilty but corrupt, and that defilement of nature is transmitted to all his children. Thomas Boston said, "Adam's sin corrupted man's nature and leavened the whole lump of mankind. We putrefied in Adam as our root. The root was poisoned, and so the branches were envenomed."

"Wherefore, as by one man sin entered into the world, and death by sin; and so death passed upon all men, for that all sinned" (Rom. 5:12). We repeat that Adam was not only the father but the federal representative of his posterity. Consequently justice required that they should be dealt with as sharing in his guilt, that therefore the same punishment should be inflicted on them, which is exactly what the vitally important passage in Romans 5:12-21 affirms. "By one man [acting on behalf of the many], sin entered [as a foreign element, as a hostile factor] into the world [the whole system over which Adam had been placed as the vicegerent of God: blasting the fair face of nature, bringing a curse upon the earth, ruining all humanity], and death by sin [as its appointed wages]; and so death [as the sentence of the righteous Judge] passed upon all men [because all men were seminally and federally in Adam]."

It needs to be carefully borne in mind that in connection with the penal infliction which came upon man at the fall, he lost no moral or spiritual faculty, but rather the power to use them right. In Scripture "death" (as the wages of sin) does not signify annihilation but separation. As physical death is the separation of the soul from the body, so spiritual death is the separation of the soul from its Maker. Ephesians 4:18 expresses it as "being alienated from the life of God." Thus, when the father said of the prodigal, "This my son was dead" (Luke 15), he meant that his son had been absent from him—away in the "far country." Hence when, as the Substitute of His people, Christ was receiving in their stead the wages due them, He cried, "My God, my God, why hast thou forsaken me?" This is why the lake of fire is called "the second death"—because those cast there are "punished with everlasting destruction from the presence of the Lord" (2 Thess. 1:9).

We have said that all of Adam's posterity shared in the guilt of the great transgression committed by their federal head, and that therefore the same punishment is inflicted on them as on him. That punishment consisted (so far as its present character is concerned) in his coming under the curse and wrath of God, the corrupting of his nature, and the mortalizing of his body. Clear proof of this is found in that inspired statement "And Adam lived a hundred and thirty years, and begat a son in his own likeness, after his image" (Gen. 5:3), which is in direct antithesis to his being created "in the image of God" (Gen. 1:27). That Adam's first son was morally depraved was clearly evidenced by his conduct; and that his second son was also depraved was fully acknowledged by the sacrifice which he brought to God.

As a result of the fall man is born into this world so totally depraved in his moral nature as to be entirely unable to do anything spiritually good; furthermore, he is not in the slightest degree disposed to do good. Even under the exciting and persuasive influences of divine grace, the will of man is completely unfit to act right in cooperation with grace until the will itself is by the power of God radically and permanently renewed. The tree itself must be made good before there is the least prospect of any good fruit being borne by it. Even after a man is regenerated, the renewed will always continue dependent on divine grace to energize, direct and enable it for the performance of anything acceptable to God, as the language of Christ clearly shows: "Without me ye can do nothing" (John 15:5).

But let it be clearly understood that though man has by the fall lost all power to do anything pleasing to God, yet his Maker has not lost His authority over him nor forfeited His right to require that which is due Him. As creatures we were bound to serve God and do whatever He commanded; and the fact that we have, by our own folly and sin, thrown away the strength given to us cannot and does not cancel our obligations. Has the creditor no right to demand payment for what is owed him because the debtor has squandered his substance and is unable to pay him? If God can require of us no more than we are now able to give Him, then the more we enslave ourselves by evil habits and still further incapacitate ourselves the less our liabilities; then the deeper we plunge into sin the less wicked we would become. This is a manifest absurdity.

Even though by Adam's fall we have become depraved and spiritually helpless creatures, yet the terrible fact that we are enemies to the infinitely glorious God, our Maker, makes us infinitely to blame and without the vestige of a legitimate excuse. Surely it is perfectly obvious that nothing can make it right for a creature to voluntarily rise up at enmity against One who is the sum of all excellence, infinitely worthy of our love, homage and obedience. Thus, for man—whatever the origin of his depravity—to be a rebel against the Governor of this world is infinitely evil and culpable. It is utterly vain for us to seek shelter behind Adam's offense while every sin we commit is voluntary and not compulsory—the free, spontaneous inclination of our hearts. This being the case, every mouth will be stopped, and all the world stand guilty before God (Rom. 3:19).

To this it may be objected that the writer of Romans argued that he was not personally and properly to blame for the corruptions of his heart: "It is no more I that do it, but sin that dwelleth in me" (7:17, 20). But there is no justification for perverting the language in that passage. If the scope of the words is noted, such a misuse of them is at once ruled out. The writer was showing that divine grace and not indwelling sin was the governing principle within him—as he had affirmed previously: "Sin shall not have dominion over you: for ye are not under the law, but under grace" (6:14). Far from insinuating that he did not feel wholly blamable for his remaining corruption, he declared, "I am carnal, sold under sin" (7:14), and cried as a brokenhearted penitent, "O wretched man that I am!" (v. 24). It is perfectly obvious that he could not have mourned for his remaining corruption as being sinful if he had not felt he was to blame for them.

Man's spiritual impotence is not only penal but moral, by which we mean that he is now unable to meet the requirements of the moral law. We employ this term "moral," first of all, in contrast with "natural," for the spiritual helplessness of fallen man is unnatural, inasmuch as it does not pertain to the nature of man as created by God. Man (in Adam) was endowed with full ability to do whatever was required of him, but he lost that ability by the fall. We employ this term "moral," in the second place, because it accurately defines the character of fallen man's malady. His inability is purely moral, because while he still possesses all moral as well as intellectual faculties requisite for right action, yet the moral state of his faculties is such as to render right action impossible. A. A. Hodge said, "Its essence is in the inability of the soul to know, love, or choose spiritual good; and its ground exists in that moral corruption of soul whereby it is blind, insensible, and totally averse to all that is spiritually good."

The affirmation that fallen man is morally impotent presents a serious difficulty for many. They suppose that to assert his inability to will or do anything spiritually good is utterly incompatible with human responsibility or the sinner's guilt. These difficulties are later considered at length. But it is necessary for us to allude to these difficulties at the present stage because the effort to show the reconcilability of fallen man's inability with his responsibility has led not a few defenders of the former truth to make predications which were unwarrantable and untrue. They have felt that there is, there must be, some sense or respect in which even fallen man may be said to be able to will and do what is required of him; and they have labored to show in what sense this ability exists, while at the same time man is, in another sense, unable.

Many Calvinists have supposed that in order to avoid the awful error of Antinomian fatalism it was necessary to ascribe some kind of ability to fallen man, and therefore they have resorted to the distinction between natural and moral inability. They have affirmed that though man is now morally unable to do what God requires, yet he has a natural ability to do it, and therefore is responsible for not doing it. In the past we ourselves have made use of this distinction, and we still believe it to be a real and important one, though we are now satisfied that it is expressed faultily. There is a radical difference between a person being in possession of natural or moral faculties, and his possessing or not possessing the power to use those faculties right. And in the accurate stating of these considerations lies the difference between the preservation of the doctrine of man's depravity and moral impotence, and the repudiation or at least the whittling down of it.

At this very point many have burdened their writings with a metaphysical discussion of the human will, a discussion so abstruse that comparatively few of their readers possessed the necessary education or mentality to intelligently follow it. We do not propose to discuss such questions as Is the will of fallen man free? If so, in what sense? To introduce such an inquiry here would divert attention too much from the more important query, Can man by any efforts of his own recover himself from the effects of the fall? Suffice it, then, to insist that the sinner's unwillingness to come to Christ is far more than a mere negation or a not putting forth of such a volition. It is a positive thing, an active aversion to Him, a terrible and inveterate enmity against Him.

Impossibility of Moral Obedience

The term "ability," or "power," is not easy to define, for it is a relative term, having reference to something to be done or resisted. Thus when we meet with the word, the mind at once asks, Power to do what? Ability to resist what? The particular kind of ability necessary is determined by the particular kind of action to be performed. If it is the lifting of a heavy weight, physical ability is needed; if the working out of a sum in arithmetic, mental power; if the choosing between good and evil, moral power. Man has sufficient physical and intellectual ability to keep many of the precepts of the moral law, yet no possible expenditure of such power could produce moral obedience. It may be that Gabriel has less natural and intellectual power than Satan. Suppose it is so, then what? The conclusion is simply that no amount of ability can go beyond its own kind. Love to God can never proceed from the powers possessed by Satan.

Let us now consider what the Scriptures teach concerning the bodily, mental and moral abilities of fallen man. First, they teach that his bodily faculties are in a ruined state, that his physical powers are enfeebled, and this as a result of sin. "By one man sin entered into the world, and death by sin" (Rom. 5:12). None of our readers is likely to deny that this includes physical death. Now death necessarily implies a failure of the powers of the body. Sickness, feebleness, the wasting of the physical energies and tissues are included. And all of these originate in sin as their moral cause, and are the penal results of it. Every aching joint, every quivering nerve, every pang of pain we experience, is a reminder and mark of God's displeasure on the original misuse of our bodily powers in the garden of Eden.

Second, man's intellectual powers have suffered by the fall. "Having the understanding darkened, being alienated from the life of God through the ignorance that is in them, because of the blindness of their heart" (Eph. 4:18). A very definite display of this ignorance was made by our first parents after their apostasy. Their sin consisted in allowing their affections to wander after a forbidden object, seeking their happiness not in the delightful communion of God but in the suggestion presented to them by the tempter. Like their descendants ever since, they loved and served the creature more than the Creator. Their conduct in hiding from God showed an alienation of affections. Had their delight been in the Lord as their chief good, then desire for concealment could not have possessed their minds. That foolish attempt to hide themselves from the searching eye of God betrayed their ignorance as well as their conscious guilt. Had not their foolish hearts been darkened, such an attempt would not have been made. "Professing themselves to be wise, they became fools" (Rom. 1:22).

This mental darkness, this ignorance of mind, is insuperable to man unaided by supernatural grace. Fallen man never would, never could, dispel this darkness, overcome this ignorance. He labors under mental paucity to such a degree as to make it impossible for him to attain to the true knowledge of God and to understand the things of the Spirit. He has an understanding by which he may know natural things: he can reason, investigate truth, and learn much of God's wisdom as it is displayed in the works of creation. He is capable of knowing the moral truths of God's Word as mere abstract propositions; but a true, spiritual, saving apprehension of them is utterly beyond his unaided powers. There is a positive defect and inability in his mind. "The natural man receiveth not the things of the Spirit of God: for they are foolishness unto him: neither can he know them, because they are spiritually discerned" (1 Cor. 2:14).

The Natural Man

By the "natural man" is unquestionably meant the unrenewed man, the man in whom the miracle of regeneration and illumination has not been effected. The context makes this clear: "Now we [Christians] have received, not the spirit of the world, but the Spirit which is of God" (v.

12). And for what end had the Spirit been given to them? That they might be delivered from their chains of ignorance, that their inability of mind might be removed so that they "might know the things that are freely given to us of God." "Which things [of the Spirit] also we speak, not in the words which man's wisdom teacheth, but which the Holy Ghost teacheth; comparing spiritual things with spiritual" (v. 13). Here is a contrast between man's wisdom and its teachings, and the Spirit's wisdom and His teachings. That the natural man" of verse 14 is unregenerate is further seen from contrasting him with the "spiritual" man in verse 15.

A divine explanation is here given as to why the natural man does not receive the things of the Spirit of God. It is a most cogent and solemn one: "For they are foolishness unto him." That is, he rejects them because they are absurd to his apprehension. It is contrary to the very nature of the human mind to receive as truth that which it thinks is preposterous. And why do the things of the Spirit of God appear as foolishness to the natural man? Are they not in themselves the consummation of wisdom? Wisdom is not folly; no, yet it may appear as such and be so treated, even by minds which in other matters are of quick and accurate perception. The wisdom of the higher mathematician is foolishness to the illiterate. Why? Because he cannot understand it; he does not have the power of mind to comprehend the mighty thoughts of a Newton.

Why are the things of the Spirit of God beyond the comprehension of the natural man? Do not many of the unregenerate possess vigorous and clear-thinking minds? Can they not reason accurately when they have perceived clearly? Have not some of the unconverted given the most illustrious displays of the powers of the human intellect? Why, then, cannot they know the things of the Spirit? This too is answered by 1 Corinthians 2:14. Those things require a peculiar power of discernment, which the unrenewed have not: "They are spiritually discerned." And the natural man is not spiritual. Until the natural man is taught of God—until the eyes of his understanding are enlightened (Eph. 1:18)—he will never see any beauty in the Christ of God or any wisdom in the Spirit of God.

If further proof of the mental inability of the natural man is needed, it is furnished in those passages which speak of the Spirit's illumination. "God, who commanded the light to shine out of darkness, hath shined in our hearts, to give the light of the knowledge of the glory of God in the face of Jesus Christ" (2 Cor. 4:6). Hence, "the spirit of wisdom and revelation in the knowledge of him" is said to be the gift of the Father (Eph. 1:17). Previous to that gift, "ye were sometimes darkness, but now are ye light in the Lord" (Eph. 5:8). "But the anointing which ye have received of him abideth in you, and ye need not that any man teach you" (1 John 2:27). From these passages it is evident (1) that the mind of man is in a state of spiritual darkness; (2) that it continues, and will continue so, until the Spirit of God gives it light or knowledge; (3) that this giving of light or knowledge is by divine power, a miracle of grace, as truly a miracle as when at the beginning the Lord said, "Let there be light."

Some have objected that man possesses the organ of vision, and therefore he has the ability to see, although he does not have the light. Simply remove the obstructing shutters and the prisoner in his dungeon will see. But let us not be deceived by such sophistry. It is not true that man having a sound eye has the ability to see. It is often contrary to facts, both naturally and spiritually. Without light he cannot see, he has not the ability to do so. Indeed, those with sound eyes and light cannot see all things, even things which are perceptible to others; myopia, or nearsightedness, hinders. A man who may be able to see with the mind's eye a simple proposition cannot see the force of a profound argument.

Third, the moral powers of man's soul are paralyzed by the fall. Darkness on the understanding, ignorance in the mind, corruption of the affections, must of necessity radically affect motives and choice. To insist that either the mind or the will has a power to act contrary to motive is a manifest absurdity, for in that case it would not be a moral act at all. The very essence of morality is a capacity to be influenced by considerations of right and wrong. Were a rational mind to act without any motive—a contradiction in terms—it certainly would not be a moral act. Motives are simply the mind's view of things, influencing to action; and since the understanding has been blinded by sin and the affections so corrupted, it is obvious that until man is renewed he will reject the good and choose the evil.

Man's Bias Toward Evil

As we have already pointed out, man is unwilling to choose the good because he is disinclined to it, and he chooses evil because his heart is biased toward it. Men love darkness rather than light. Surely no proof of such assertions is needed; all history too sadly testifies to their verity. It is a waste of breath to ask for evidence that man is inclined to evil as the sparks fly upward. Common observation and our own personal consciousness alike bear witness to this lamentable fact. It is equally plain that it is the derangement of the mind by sin which affects the moral power of perceiving right and wrong enfeebling or destroying the force of moral motives.

An unregenerate and a regenerate man may contemplate the same subject matter, view the same objects; but how different their moral perceptions! Therefore their motives and actions will be quite different. The things seen by their minds being different, diverse effects are necessarily produced on them. The one sees a "root out of a dry ground" in which there is "no form nor comeliness," whereas the other sees One who is "altogether lovely." In consequence, our Lord is despised and rejected by the former, whereas He is loved and embraced by the latter. While such are the views (perceptions) of the two individuals, respectively, such must be their choice and conduct. It is impossible to be otherwise. Their moral perception must be changed before it is possible for their volitions to be altered.

Such is the ruined condition of the fallen creature. No human power is able to effect any alteration in the moral perceptions of sinful men. "Can the Ethiopian change his skin, or the leopard his spots? Then may ye also do good, that are accustomed to do evil" (Jer. 13:23). Nothing short of the sinner, mentally and morally blind to divine light. Here, then, lies the moral inability of the natural man: it consists in the lack of adequate powers of moral perception. His moral sense is prostrated, his mind unable to properly discern between good and evil, truth and falsehood, God and Mammon, Christ and Belial. Not that he can perceive no difference, but that he cannot appreciate in any tolerable degree the excellence of truth or the glory of its Author. He cannot discern the real baseness of falsehood or the degradation of vice.

It is a great mistake to suppose that fallen man possesses adequate faculties for such moral perception, and lacks only the necessary moral light. The very opposite is the actual case. Moral light shines all around him, but his powers of vision are gone. He walks in darkness while the midday splendors of the sun of righteousness shine all around him. Fables are regarded as truth, but the truth itself is rejected. Shadows are chased, but the substance is ignored. The gospel is "hid to them that are lost" (2 Cor. 4:3). When the Lord is presented to sinners, they "see in him no beauty that they should desire him." So blind is the natural man that he gropes in the noonday and stumbles over the rock of ages. And unless a sovereign God is pleased to have mercy on him, his moral blindness continues until he passes out into the "blackness of darkness forever."

The deprivation of our nature consists not in the absence of intelligence, but in the ability to use our reason in a wise and fit manner. That which man lost at the fall was not a faculty but a principle. He still retains everything which is requisite to constitute him a rational, moral and responsible being; but he threw away that uprightness which secured the approbation of God. He lost the principle of holiness and, with it, all power to keep the moral law. Nor is this all; a foreign element—an element diametrically opposed to God—entered into man, corrupting his whole being. The principle of holiness was supplanted by the principle of sin, and this has rendered man utterly unable to act in a spiritual manner. True, he may mechanically or imitatively perform spiritual acts (such as praying), yet he cannot perform them in a spiritual manner—from spiritual motives and for spiritual ends. He has no moral ability to do so. True, he can do many things, but none rightly—in a way pleasing to God.

Spiritual good is holiness, and holiness consists in supreme love of God and equal love of men. Fallen man, alone and of himself, is utterly unable to love God with all his soul and strength, and his neighbor as himself. This principle of holy love is completely absent from his heart, nor can he by any effort beget such an affection within himself. He is utterly unable to originate within his will any inclination or disposition that is spiritually good; he has not the moral power to do so. Moral power is nothing more nor less than a holy nature with holy dispositions; it is the perception of the beauty of God and the response of the heart to the excellence and glory of God, with the consequent subjection of the will to His royal law of liberty. J. Thornwell said, "Spiritual perceptions, spiritual delight, spiritual choice, these and these alone, constitute ability to good."

In our efforts to carefully define and describe the precise character of fallen man's inability to do anything which is pleasing to God, we have shown, first, that the impotence under which he now labors is a penal one, judicially inflicted upon him by the righteous Judge of all the earth, because of his misuse of the faculties with which he was originally endowed in Adam. Second, we noted that his spiritual helplessness is a moral one, having its seat in the soul or moral nature. The principle of holiness was lost by man when he apostatized from his Maker and Governor, and the principle of sin entered his soul, corrupting the whole of his being, so that he is no longer capable of rendering any spiritual obedience to the moral law; that is, he is incapable of obeying it from spiritual motives and with spiritual designs.

We pass on now to show, third, that fallen man's inability is voluntary. Some of our readers who have had no difficulty in following us through the first two sections are likely to demur here. We refer to hyper-Calvinists who have such a one-sided conception of man's spiritual helplessness that they have lapsed into serious error. They look upon the condition and case of the sinner much as they do those people who have suffered a stroke which has paralyzed their limbs: as a calamity and not the result of a crime, as something which necessitates a state of inertia and inactivity, as something which annuls their responsibility. They fail to see that the moral impotence of the natural man is deliberate and therefore highly culpable.

Before appealing to the Scriptures for proofs of this third point, we must explain the sense in which we use our term. In affirming that the moral and sinful inability of fallen man is a voluntary one, we mean that he acts freely and spontaneously, unforced either from within or without. This is an essential element of an accountable being, everywhere recognized and acknowledged among men. Human law (much less divine) does not hold a person to be guilty if he has been compelled by others to do wrong against his own will and protests. In all moral action the human will is self-inclined, acting freely according to the dictates of the mind, which are in turn regulated by the inclination of the heart. Though the mind be darkened and the heart corrupted, nevertheless the will acts freely and the individual remains a voluntary agent.

Some of the best theologians have drawn a distinction between the liberty and ability of the sinner's will, affirming the former but denying the latter. We believe this distinction to be accurate and helpful. Unless a person is free to exercise volitions as he pleases, he cannot be an accountable being. Nevertheless, fallen man cannot, by any exercise of will, change his nature or make any choice contrary to the governing tendencies of indwelling sin. He totally lacks any disposition to meet the requirements of the moral law, and therefore he cannot make himself willing to do so. The affections of the heart and the perceptions of the mind regulate our volitions, and the will has no inherent power to change our affections; we cannot by any resolution, however strong or prolonged, make ourselves love what we hate or hate what we love.

Because the sinner acts without any external compulsion, according to his own inclinations, his mind is free to consider and weigh the various motives which come before it, making its own preferences or choices. By motives we mean those reasons or inducements which are presented to the mind tending to lead to choice and action. The power or force of these inducements lies not in themselves (abstractedly considered), but in the state of the person who is the subject of them; consequently that which would be a powerful motive in the view of one mind would have no weight at all in the view of another. For example, the offer of a bribe would be a sufficient motive to induce one judge to decide a case contrary to law and against the evidence; whereas to another such an offer, far from being a motive to such an evil course, would be highly repulsive.

Let this be clearly grasped by the reader: Those external inducements which are presented to the mind affect a person according to the state of his or her heart. The temptation presented by Potiphar's wife, which was firmly refused by Joseph, would have been a motive of sufficient power to ruin many a youth of less purity of heart. External motives can have no influence over the choice and conduct of men except as they make an appeal to desires already existing in the mind. Throw a lighted match into a barrel of gunpowder and there is at once an explosion; but throw that match into a barrel of water and no harm is done. "The prince of this world cometh, and hath nothing in me" (John 14:30) said the holy One of God. None among the children of men can make such a claim.

Freedom of Human Will

All the affections of the human heart are, in their very nature, free. The idea of compelling a man to love or hate any object is manifestly absurd. The same holds good of all his faculties. Conscience may be enlightened and made more sensitive, or it may be resisted and hardened; but no man can be compelled to act contrary to its dictates without depriving him of his freedom, and at the same time of his responsibility. So of his will or volition: two or more alternatives confront a man, conflicting motives are presented to his mind, and his will is quite free in making a preference or choice between them. Nevertheless, it is the very nature of his will to choose that which is preferable, that which is most agreeable to his heart. Consequently, though the will acts freely, it is biased by the corruptions of the heart and therefore is unable to choose spiritual good. The heart must be changed before the will chooses God.

Against our assertion that the spiritual impotence of fallen man is a voluntary one, it may be objected that the sinner is so strongly tempted, so powerfully influenced by Satan and so thoroughly under his control that (in many instances, at least) he cannot help himself, being irresistibly drawn into sinning. That there is some force in this objection is readily granted, but we can by no means allow the length to which it is carried. However subtle the craft, however influential the sophistry, however great the power of the devil, these must not be used to repudiate our personal responsibility and criminality in sinning, nor must we construe ourselves into being his innocent dupes or unwilling victims. Never does Scripture so represent the matter; rather, we are told "Resist the devil, and he will flee from you" (Jam. 4:7). And if we seek grace to meet the conditions (specified in 1 Pet. 5:8-9), God will assuredly make good His promise.

Satan's power is not physical but moral. He has intimate access to the faculties of our souls, and though he cannot (like the Holy Spirit) work at their roots so as to change and transform their tendencies, he can ply them with representations and delusions which effectually incline them to will and do according to his good pleasure. He can cheat the understanding with appearances of truth, fascinate the fancy with pictures of beauty, and mock the heart with semblances of good. By a secret suggestion he can give an impulse to our thoughts and turn them into channels which serve the purposes of his malignity. But in all of this he does no violence to the laws of our nature. He disturbs neither the spontaneity of the understanding nor the freedom of the will. He cannot make us do a thing without our own consent, thus in consenting to his evil suggestions lies our guilt.

That sinners act freely and voluntarily in all their wrongdoing is taught throughout the Scriptures. Take, first of all, the horrible state of the heathen, a dark picture of whom is painted for us in Romans 1. There we see the consummation of human depravity. Heathenism is the full development of the principle of sin in its workings upon the intellectual, moral and religious nature of man. In Romans 1 we are shown that the dreadful condition in which the heathen now lie (and missionaries bear clear witness that what comes before their notice accurately corresponds to what is here stated) is the consequence of their own voluntary choice. "When they knew God, they glorified him not as God" (v. 21). They "changed the glory of the uncorruptible God into an image made like to corruptible man" (v. 23). They "changed the truth of God into a lie" (v. 25). They "did not like to retain God in their knowledge" (v. 28).

Nor was it any different with the favored people of Israel. So averse were they to God and His ways that they hated, persecuted and killed those messengers whom He sent to reclaim them from their wickedness. "They kept not the covenant of God, and refused to walk in his law" (Ps. 78:10). They said, "I have loved strangers, and after them will 1 go" (Jer. 2:25). "Thus saith the Lord, Stand ye in the ways, and see, and ask for the old paths, where is the good way, and walk therein, and ye shall find rest for your souls. But they said, We will not walk therein. Also I set watchmen over you saying, Hearken to the sound of the trumpet. But they said, We will not hearken" (Jer. 6:16-17). The Lord called to them, but they "refused." He stretched forth His hand, but "no man regarded." They set at nought all His counsel, and would heed none of His reproofs (Prov. 1:24-25). "The Lord God of their fathers sent to them by his messengers, rising up betimes, and sending.

But they mocked the messengers of God, and despised his words, and misused his prophets, until the wrath of the Lord rose against his people, till there was no remedy" (2 Chron. 36:15-16). God's blessed Son did not receive any better treatment at their hands. Though He appeared before them in "the form of a servant," He did not appeal to their proud hearts. Though He was "full of grace and truth," they despised and rejected Him. Though He sought only their good, they returned Him nought but evil. Though He proclaimed glad tidings for them, they refused to listen. Though He worked the most wonderful miracles before them, yet they would not believe Him. "He came unto his own, and his own received him not" (John 1:11). Their retort was "We will not have this man to reign over us" (Luke 19:14). It was a voluntary and deliberate refusal of Him. It is this very voluntariness of their sin which shall be charged against them in the day of judgment, for then shall He give order thus: "But those mine enemies, which would not that I should reign over them, bring hither, and slay them before me" (Luke 19:27).

And from whence did such wicked treatment of the Son of God proceed? From the vile corruptions of their own hearts. "They hated me without a cause" (John 15:25) declared the incarnate Son of God. There was absolutely nothing whatever either in His character or conduct which merited their wicked contempt and enmity. Did anyone force them to be of such an abominable disposition? Surely not; they were hearty in it. Were they of such bad temper against their wills? No indeed. They were voluntary in their wicked hatred of Christ. They loved darkness. They were infatuated by their corruptions and delighted in gratifying them. They were highly pleased with false prophets, because they preached in their favor, flattering them and gratifying their evil hearts. But they hated whatever was disagreeable to their evil ways.

Mistreatment of Christ's Followers

It was the same with those who heard the ambassadors of Christ, except for those in whom the sovereign God wrought a miracle of grace. Jews and Gentiles alike willfully opposed and rejected the gospel. In some cases their hatred of the truth was less openly manifested than in others; nevertheless, it was just as real. And the disrelish of and opposition to the gospel was entirely voluntary on the part of its enemies. Did not the Jewish leaders act freely when they threw Peter and John into prison? Did not the murderers of Stephen act freely when they "stopped their ears, and ran upon him with one accord" (Acts 7:57)? Did not the Philippians act freely when they "rose up together" against Paul and Silas, beat them, and cast them into prison?

The same thing obtains everywhere today. If the gospel of Christ is preached in its purity and all its glory, it does not gain the regard of the masses who hear it. Instead, as soon as the sermon is over, like the generality of the Jews in our Lord's day, they make light of it and go their ways, "one to his farm, another to his merchandise" (Matt. 22:5). They are too indifferent to seek after obtaining even a doctrinal knowledge of the truth. There are many who regard this dullness of the unsaved as mere indifference, but it is actually something far worse: it is dislike of the heart for God, deliberate opposition to Him. "They are like the deaf adder that stoppeth her ear; which will not hearken to the voice of charmers, charming never so wisely" (Ps. 58:4-5). As Paul declared in his day, "The heart of this people is waxed gross, and their ears are dull of hearing, and their eyes have they closed; lest they should see with their eyes, and hear with their ears, and understand with their heart, and should be converted" (Acts 28:27).

"They say unto God, Depart from us; for we desire not the knowledge of thy ways" (Job 21:14). Such is the desperately wicked state of man's heart, diametrically opposite to the divine excellences. Yet when this solemn truth is pressed on the unregenerate, many of them will strongly object, denying that there is any such contrariety in their hearts, saying, "I have never hated God, but have always loved Him." Thus they flatter themselves and seek to make themselves out to be far different from what they are. Nor are they wittingly lying when they make such a claim; rather, they are utterly misled by their deceitful hearts. The scribes and Pharisees truly thought that they loved God and that, had they lived in the days of their forefathers, they would not have put the prophets to death (Matt. 23:29-30). They were altogether insensible to their fearful and inveterate enmity against God; nevertheless it was there, and it later unmistakably displayed itself when they hounded the Son of God to death.

Why was it that the scribes and Pharisees were quite unconscious of the opposition of their hearts to the divine nature? It was because they had erroneous notions of the divine Being and loved only that false image which they had framed in their own imaginations; therefore they had false conceptions of the prophets which their fathers hated and murdered, and hence supposed they would have loved them. But when God was manifested in Christ, they hated Him with bitter hatred. In like manner there are multitudes of sinners today, millions in Christendom who persuade themselves that they truly love God, when in reality they hate Him; and the hardest of all tasks confronting the ministers of Christ is to shatter this cherished delusion and bring their unsaved hearers face to face with the horrible reality of their unspeakably vile condition.

Loudly as our deluded fellow creatures may boast of their love of the divine nature, as soon as they pass out of time into eternity and discover what God is, their spurious love immediately vanishes and their enmity bursts forth in full force. Sinners today do not perceive their contrariety to the divine nature because they are utterly ignorant of the true God. It must be so, for a sinful nature and a holy nature are diametrically opposite. Christendom has invented a false "God," a "God" without any sovereign choice, a "God" who loves all mankind, a "God" whose justice is swallowed up in His mercy. Were they acquainted with the God of Holy Writ—who "hatest all workers of iniquity" (Ps. 5:5), who will one day appear "in flaming fire taking vengeance on them that know not God, and that obey not the gospel of our Lord Jesus Christ: who shall be punished with everlasting destruction from the presence of the Lord" (2 Thess. 1:8-9)—they, if they honestly examined their hearts, would be conscious of the hatred they bear Him.

Guilt of Natural Man

The spiritual inability of the natural man is a criminal one. This follows inevitably from the fact that his impotence is a moral and voluntary one. It is highly important that we should be brought to see, feel and own that our spiritual helplessness is culpable, for until we do so we shall never truly justify God nor condemn ourselves. To realize oneself to be equally "without strength" and "without excuse" is deeply humiliating, and fallen man will strive with all his might to stifle such a conviction and deny the truth of it. Yet until we place the blame of our sinfulness where it really belongs, we shall not, we cannot, either vindicate the righteousness of the divine law or appreciate the marvelous grace made known in the gospel. To condemn ourselves as God condemns us is the one prerequisite to establish our title to salvation in Christ.

John Newton wrote:

We cannot ascribe too much to the grace of God; but we should be careful that, under a semblance of exalting His grace, we do not furnish the slothful and unfaithful (Matt. 25: 16) with excuses for their willfulness and wickedness. God is gracious; but let man be justly responsible for his own evil and not presume to state his case so as would, by just consequence, represent the holy God as being the cause of the sin which He hates and forbids.

That was indeed a timely word. Unfortunately, some who claim to be great admirers of Newton's works have sadly failed to uphold the responsibility of the sinner, and have so expressed his spiritual inability as to furnish him with much excuse for his sloth and infidelity. Only by insisting on the criminality of fallen man's impotence can such a deplorable snare be avoided. Inexorably as man's criminality attaches to his free agency in the committing of sin, yet the sinner will strive with might and main to avoid such a conclusion and seek to throw the blame on someone else. He will haughtily ask, "Would any right-minded person blame a man whose arms had been broken because he could no longer perform manual labor, or condemn a blind man because he did not read? Then why should I be held guilty for not performing spiritual duties which are altogether beyond my powers?"

To this difficulty several replies may be made: (1) There is no analogy in the cases advanced. Broken arms and sightless eyes are incompetent members; but the intellectual and moral faculties have not been destroyed, and it is because of misuse of these that the sinner is justly held culpable. (2) Not only does he fail to use his moral faculties in the performing of spiritual good, but he employs them in the doing of moral evil; and the excuse that he cannot help himself is an idle one.

Apply that principle to the commercial transactions of society, and what would be the result? A man contracts a debt within the compass of his present financial ability to meet. He then perversely and wickedly squanders his money and gambles away his property, so that he is no longer able to pay what he owes. Is he therefore not bound to pay? Has his reckless prodigality freed him from all moral obligation to discharge his debts? Must justice break her scales and no more hold an equal balance because he chooses to be a villain? No indeed; unregenerate men would not allow such reasoning.

To this it may be objected, "I did not bring this depravity upon myself, but was born with it. If my heart is altogether evil and I did not make it so, if such a heart was given me without my choice and consent, then how can I be to blame for its inevitable issues and actions?" Such a question betrays the fact that a wicked heart is regarded as a calamity which man did not choose, but which must be endured. It is contemplated as a thing not at all faulty in its own nature; if there is any blame attaching to it, it must be for something previous to it and of quite another kind. A person born diseased is not personally to blame, but if the disease is the result of his own indiscretion it is a just retribution. But to reason thus about sin is utterly erroneous, as if it were no sin to be a sinner or to commit sin when one has an inclination to do so, but to bring a sinful predisposition upon oneself would be a wicked thing.

Stripped of all disguise and ambiguity, the above objection amounts to this: Adam was in reality the only sinner; and we, his miserable offspring, being by nature depraved, are under a necessity of sinning, therefore cannot be to blame for it. The fact that sin itself is sinful is lost sight of. Scripture traces all our evil acts back to a sinful heart, and teaches that this is a blamable thing in itself. A depraved heart is a moral thing, being something quite different from a weak head, a bad memory or a frail constitution. A man is not to blame for these infirmities, providing he has not brought them upon himself. To say that I cannot help hating God and opposing my neighbor, and that therefore I am not to blame for doing so, certainly makes me out to be a vile and insensible scoundrel.

In order for a fallen creature to be blameworthy for his evil tendencies, it is not necessary that he should first be virtuous or free from moral corruption. If a person now finds that he is a sinner, and that from the heart he approves and chooses rebellion against God and His law, he is not the less a sinner because he has been of the same disposition for many years and has always sinned from his birth. His having sinned from the beginning, and having done nothing else, cannot be a legitimate excuse for sinning now. Nor is man's guilt the less because sin is so deeply and so thoroughly fixed in his heart. The stronger the enmity against God, the greater its heinousness. Disinclination Godward is the very essence of depravity. When we rightly define the nature of man's inability to do good—namely, a moral and a voluntary inability (not the absence of faculties, but the misuse of them) —then this excuse of blamelessness is at once exposed.

But the carnal mind will still object. We are natively no other way than God has made us; therefore if we are born sinful and God has created us thus, then He, not ourselves, is the Author of sin. To such awful lengths is the enmity of the carnal mind capable of going: shifting the onus from his own guilty shoulders and throwing the blame upon the thrice holy God. But this objection was earlier obviated. God made man upright, but he apostatized. Man ruined himself. God endowed each of us with rationality, with a conscience, with a will to refuse the evil and choose the good. It is by the free exercise of our faculties that we sin, and we have no more justification for transferring the guilt from ourselves to someone else than Adam had to blame Eve or Eve the serpent.

But is it consistent with the divine perfections to bring mankind into the world under such handicapped and wretched circumstances? "Nay but, O man, who art thou that repliest against God? Shall the thing formed say to him that formed it, Why hast thou made me thus?" (Rom. 9:20). It is blasphemous to say that it is not consistent with the divine perfections for God to do what in fact He does. It is a matter of fact that we are born into the world destitute of the moral image of God, ignorant of Him, insensible of His infinite glory. It is a plain matter of fact that in consequence of this deprivation we are disposed to love ourselves supremely, live to ourselves ultimately, and wholly delight in what is not of God. And it is clearly evident that this tendency is in direct contrariety to God's holy law and is exceedingly sinful. Whether or not we can see the justice and wisdom of this divine providence, we must remember that God is "holy in all his ways, and righteous in all his works."

But how can the sinner possibly be to blame for his evil inclination when it was Adam who corrupted human nature? The sinner is an enemy to the infinitely glorious God, and that voluntarily; therefore he is infinitely to blame and without excuse, for nothing can make it right for a creature to be deliberately hostile to his Creator. Nothing can possibly extenuate such a crime. Such hostility is in its own nature infinitely wrong, and therefore the sinner stands guilty before God. The very fact that in the day of judgment every mouth will be stopped (Rom. 3:19) shows there is no validity or force to this objection. It is for the acting out of his nature-instead of its mortifying—that the sinner is held accountable. The fact that we are born traitors to God cannot cancel our obligation to give Him allegiance. No man can escape from the righteous requirements of law by a voluntary opposition to it.

The fact that man's sinful nature is the direct consequence of Adam's transgression does not in the slightest degree make it any less his own sin or render him any less blameworthy. This is clear not only from the justice of the principle of representation (Adam's acting as our federal head), but also from the fact that each of us approves of Adam's transgression by emulating his example, joining ourselves with him in rebellion against God. That we go on to break the covenant of works and disobey the divine law demonstrates that we are righteously condemned with Adam. Because each descendant of Adam voluntarily prolongs and perpetuates in himself the evil inclination originated by his first parents, he is doubly guilty. If not, why do we not repudiate Adam and refuse to sin—stand out in opposition to him, and be holy? If we resent our being corrupted through Adam, why not break the involvement of sin?

But let us turn from these objections to the positive side of our subject. The Scriptures uniformly teach that fallen man's moral and voluntary inability is a criminal one, that God justly holds him guilty both for his depraved state and for all his sinful actions. So plain is this, so abundantly evidenced, that there is little need for us to labor the point. The first three chapters of Romans are expressly devoted to this solemn theme. There it is declared, "The wrath of God is revealed from heaven against all ungodliness and unrighteousness of men, who hold the truth in unrighteousness" (1:18). The reason for this is given in verses 19-20, ending with the inexorable sentence "They are without excuse." Chapter 2 opens with "Therefore thou art inexcusable, O man," and in 3:19 the apostle shows that the ruling of the divine law is such that, in the day to come, "every mouth may be stopped, and all the world may become guilty before God."

The criminality of the sinner's depravity and moral impotence is clearly brought out in Matthew 25:14-30. The general design of that parable is easily perceived. The "lord" of the servants signifies the Creator as the Owner and Governor of this world. The "servants" represent mankind in general. The different "talents" depict the faculties and powers with which God has endowed us, the privileges and advantages by which He distinguishes one person from another. The two servants who faithfully improved their talents picture the righteous who serve God with fidelity. The slothful and unfaithful servant portrays the sinner, who entirely neglects the service of God and blames Him rather than himself for his negligence. His grievance in verses 24-25 expresses the feelings of every impenitent sinner, who complains that God requires from him (holiness) what He has not given to him (a holy heart). This servant's condemnation was on the ground that he did not improve what he did have (v. 27)—his rational faculties and moral powers. "Cast ye the unprofitable servant into outer darkness" (v. 30) shows the justice of his condemnation.

Excuses of Natural Man

The excuse that we cannot help being so perverse is further ruled out of court by Christ's declarations to the scribes and Pharisees. They had no heart either for Christ or His doctrine. He told them plainly, "Why do ye not understand my speech? Even because ye cannot hear my word" (John 8:43). But their inability was no excuse for them in His accounting, for He affirmed that all their impotence rose from their evil hearts, their lack of a holy makeup: "Ye are of your father the devil, and the lusts of your father ye will [desire to] do" (v. 44). Though they had no more power to help themselves than we have, and were no more able to transform their hearts than we are, nevertheless our Lord judged them to be wholly to blame and altogether inexcusable, saying of them, "If I had not come and spoken unto them, they had not had sin: but now they have . . . [no excuse] for their sin (John 15:22).

Let it be specifically pointed out that when Scripture affirms the inability of a man to do good, it never does so by way of excuse. Thus, when Jehovah asked Israel, "Can the Ethiopian change his skin, or the leopard his spots? Then may ye also do good, that are accustomed to do evil" (Jer. 13:23), it was not for the purpose of mitigating their guilt, but with the object of showing how it aggravated their obstinacy of heart and to evince that no external means could affect their recovery. Just as likely was an Ethiopian to be moved by exhortation to change the color of his skin as were rebels against God to be moved by appeals to renounce their iniquities.

"Because I tell you the truth, ye believe me not. Which of you convinceth me of sin? And if I say the truth, why do ye not believe me? He that is of God heareth God's words: ye therefore hear them not, because ye are not of God" (John 8:45-47). Those cutting interrogations of our Lord proceeded on the supposition that His listeners could have received the teaching of Christ if it had been agreeable to their corrupt nature; it being otherwise, they could not understand or receive it. In like manner, when He affirmed, "No man can come to me, except the Father which hath sent me draw him," Christ did not intimate that any natural man honestly desired to come to Him, but was deterred from doing so against his will; rather, He meant that man is incapable of freely doing that which is inconsistent with his corruptions. They were averse to come to the holy Redeemer because they were in love with sin.

The excuse that I cannot help doing wrong is worthless. To plead my inability to do good simply because I lack the heart to do it would be laughed out of court even among men. Does anyone suppose that only the lack of a will to earn his living excuses a man from doing so, just as bodily infirmity does? Does anyone imagine that the covetous miser, who has no heart to give a penny to the poor, is for that reason excused from deeds of charity as one who has nothing to give? A man's heart being fully set to do evil does not render his wicked actions the less evil. If it did, it would necessarily follow that the worse any sinner grows, the less he is to blame. Nothing could be more absurd.

Let us show yet further the utter worthlessness of those evasions by which the sinner seeks to deny the criminality of his moral impotence. Men never resort to such silly reasonings when they are wronged by others. When treated with disrespect and animosity by their associates, they never offer the excuses for them behind which they seek to hide their own sins. If someone deliberately robbed me, would I say, "Poor fellow, he could not help himself; Adam is to blame"? If someone wickedly slandered me, would I say, "This person is to be pitied, for he was born into the world with this evil disposition"? If someone whom I had always treated honorably and generously returned my kindness by doing all he could to injure me, and then said, "I could not help hating you," far from accepting that as a valid extenuation, I would rightly consider that his enmity made him all the more to blame.

When a sinner is truly awakened, humbled and broken before God, he realizes that he deserves to be damned for his vile rebellion against God, and freely acknowledges that he is what he is voluntarily and not by compulsion. He realizes that he has had no love for God, nor any desire to love Him. He admits that he is an enemy to Him in his very heart, and voluntarily so; that all his fair pretenses, promises, prayers and religious performances were mere hypocrisy, arising only from self-love, guilty fears and mercenary hopes. He feels himself to be without excuse and owns that eternal judgment is His just due. When truly convicted of sin by the Holy Spirit, the sinner is driven out of all his false refuges and owns that his inability is a criminal one, that he is guilty.

Chapter 4
Root

As no heart can sufficiently conceive, so no voice or pen can adequately portray the awful state of wretchedness and woe into which sin has cast guilty man. It has separated him from God and so has severed him from the only Source of holiness and true happiness. It has ruined him in spirit and soul and body. By the fall man not only plunged himself into a state of infinite guilt from which there is no deliverance unless sovereign grace unites him with the Mediator; by his apostasy man also lost his holiness and is wholly corrupt and under the dominion of dispositions or lusts which are directly contrary to God and His law (Rom. 8:7). The fall has brought man into love of sin and hatred of God. The corruption of man's being is so great and so entire that he will never truly repent or even have any right responses toward God and His law unless and until he is supernaturally renewed by the Holy Spirit.

Corruption of Human Nature

If any reader is inclined to think we have painted too dark a picture or have exaggerated the case of the fallen creature, we ask him to carefully ponder the second half of Romans 7 and note how human nature is there represented as so totally depraved as to be utterly unable not merely to keep God's law perfectly, but to do anything agreeable with it. "The law is spiritual: but I am carnal, sold under sin. For I know that in me (that is, in my flesh,) dwelleth no good thing: for to will is present with me; but how to perform that which is good I find not. But I see another law in my members, warring against the law of my mind, and bringing me into captivity to the law of sin which is in my members" (vv. 14, 18, 23). How completely at variance is that language from the sentiments which prevail in Christendom today. Paul, that most eminent Christian, nothing behind the chief apostles, when he considered what he was in himself, confessed that he was "sold under sin."

The apostle's phrase "in my flesh," as may be seen by tracing it through the New Testament, means "in me by nature." He was saying, "There is nothing in me naturally good." But before proceeding further let us seek to carefully define what is signified by the term "the natural man," or "man by nature." It does not mean the human nature itself, or man as a tripartite being of spirit and soul and body, for then we should include the Lord Jesus Christ, who truly and really assumed human nature, becoming the Son of Man. No, this term connotes not man as created, but man as corrupted. God did not in creation plant in us a principle of contrariety to Himself, for He fashioned man after His own image and likeness. He made him upright, holy. It was our defection from Him which plunged us into such immeasurable wretchedness and woe, which polluted and defiled all the springs of our being and corrupted all our faculties.

As a result of the fall man is the inveterate enemy of God, not only because of what he does, but because of what he now is in himself. Stephen Charnock said:

What kind of enmity this is. First, I understand it of nature, not of actions only. Every action of a natural man is an enemy's action, but not an action of enmity. A toad doth not envenom every spire of grass it crawls upon nor poison everything it toucheth, but its nature is poisonous. Certainly every man's nature is worse than his actions: as waters are purest at the fountain, and poison most pernicious in the mass, so is enmity in the heart. And as waters partake of the mineral vein they run through, so the actions of a wicked man are tinctured with the enmity they spring from, but the mass and strength of this is lodged in his nature. There is in all our natures such a diabolical contrariety to God, that if God should leave a man to the current of his own heart, it would overflow in all kinds of wickedness.

It is quite true that their deep enmity against God is less openly displayed by some than others, but this is not because they are any better in themselves than those who cast off all pretenses of decency. Their moderation in wickedness is to be attributed to the greater restraints which God places upon them either by the secret workings of His Spirit upon their hopes and fears or by His external providences—such as education, religious instruction, the subduing influence of the pious. But none is born into this world with the slightest spark of love to God in him. "The wicked are estranged from the womb: they go astray as soon as they be born, speaking lies. Their poison is like the poison of a serpent" (Ps. 58:3-4). The poison of a serpent is radically the same in all of its species.

"That which is born of the flesh is flesh" (John 3:6). These words make it clear that inherent corruption is imparted to us by birth. This is evident from the remainder of the verse: "and that which is born of the Spirit is spirit." The "spirit" which is begotten differs from the Spirit who is the Begetter, and signifies that new creation of holiness which is effected and inbred in the soul and therefore is called "the seed of God" (1 John 3:9). As the spirit here unquestionably denotes the new nature or principle of holiness, so the flesh in John 3:6 stands for the old nature or principle of sin. This is further established by Galatians 5:17: "For the flesh lusteth against the Spirit, and the Spirit against the flesh: and these are contrary the one to the other: so that ye cannot do the things that ye would." Flesh and spirit are there put as two inherent qualities conveyed by two several births, and so are in that respect opposed. That the flesh refers to our very nature as corrupt is seen from the fact that it has works or fruits. The flesh is a principle from which operations issue, as buds from a root.

The scope of Christ in John 3 shows that flesh has reference to the corruption of our nature. His evident design in those verses was to show what imperative need there is for fallen man to be regenerated. Now regeneration is nothing else but a working of new spiritual dispositions in the whole man, called there "spirit," without which it is impossible that he should enter the kingdom of God. Christ said, "That which is born of the flesh is flesh" (v. 6), by which statement He made it the direct opposite of the spirit of holiness which is wrought in the soul by the Holy Spirit. Had we derived only guilt from Adam we would need only justification; but since we also derived corruption of nature we need regeneration too.

There is, then, in every man born into this world a mass of corruption which inheres in and clings to him and which is the principle and spring of all his activities. This may justly be termed his nature, for it is the predominant quality which is in all and which directs all that issues from him. Let us now proceed to the proof of this compound assertion. First, it is a mass of corruption, for that which our Lord called flesh in John 3:6 is called "the old man, which is corrupt" by His apostle in Ephesians 4:22. Observe carefully what is clearly implied by this term, and see again how perfectly one part of Scripture harmonizes with another. Corruption necessarily denotes something which was previously good, and so it is with man. God made him righteous; now he is defiled. Instead of having a holy soul, it is depraved; instead of an immortal body, it has within it even now the seeds of putrefaction.

Second, we have said that this corruption cleaves to man's very nature. It is expressly said to be within him: "Now then it is no more I that do it, but sin that dwelleth in me. For I know that in me (that is, in my flesh,) dwelleth no good thing" (Rom. 7:17-18). Man, then, has not only acts of sin which are transient, which come from him and go away, but he has a root and spring of sin dwelling with him, residing in him, not only adjacent to but actually inhabiting him. Not simply our ways and works are corrupt; "the heart is deceitful above all things, and desperately wicked" (Jer. 17:9). Nor is this something which we acquire through association with the wicked; rather it is that which we bring with us into the world: "Foolishness is bound in the heart of a child" (Prov. 22:15).

Third, we have stated that this indwelling corruption is the predominant principle of all the actions of unregenerate man, that from which all proceeds. Surely this is clear from "Now the works of the flesh are manifest, which are these: adultery, fornication, uncleanness, lasciviousness, idolatry, witchcraft, hatred, variance, emulations, wrath, strife" (Gal. 5:19-21). The flesh is here said to have works or fruits, and this quality of fruit-bearing exists in man's nature. Note that hatred and wrath are not deeds of the body, but dispositions of the soul and affections of the heart; thus the flesh cannot be restricted to our physical structure. This evil principle or corruption is divinely labeled a root: "Lest there should be among you a root that beareth gall and wormwood" (Deut. 29:18; cf. Heb. 12:13). It is a root which brings forth "gall and wormwood," that is, the bitter fruits of sin; in fact, it is said to "bring forth fruit unto death" (Rom. 7:5).

Fourth, we have affirmed that there is a mass of this corruption which thoroughly affects and defiles man's being. This is confirmed by the fact that in Colossians 2:11 it is called a body, which has many members: "In whom also ye are circumcised with the circumcision made without hands, in putting off the body of the sins of the flesh by the circumcision of Christ." This body of the sins of the flesh is of abounding dimensions, a body which has internal and external manifestations, gross and more secret lusts. Among these are atheism and contempt or hatred of God, which is not fully perceived by man until the Holy Spirit pierces him to the dividing asunder of soul and spirit. That this corruption lies in the very nature of man appears from the psalmist's statement "Behold, I was shapen in iniquity; and in sin did my mother conceive me" (51:5). David was there confessing the spring from which his great act of sin sprang. In essence he said, "I have not only committed the awful act of adultery, but there is sin even in my inward parts, defiling me from the moment I was conceived" (cf. v. 6).

Finally, we have declared that this corruption may in a very real sense be termed the nature of man. Once more we appeal to John 3:6 in proof, for there it is predicated in the abstract, which implies more than a simple quality, even that which explains the very definition and nature of man. The Lord Jesus did not say merely, "That which is born of the flesh is fleshly"; He said it "is flesh." In that statement Christ framed a new definition of man, beyond any the philosophers have framed. Philosophers define man as a rational animal; the Son of God announces him to be flesh, that is, sin and corruption contrary to grace and holiness, this being his very nature as a fallen creature in the sight of God. The very fact that this definition of man's nature is, as it were, in the abstract argues that it is a thing inherent in us. But let us enlarge a little on this point.

Definitions are taken from things brought out in nature, and none but essential properties are ingredients in definitions. Definitions are taken from the most predominant qualities. Sinful corruption is a more predominant principle in man's nature than is reason itself, for it not only guides reason, but it resides in every part and faculty of man, while reason does not. This corruption is so inbred and predominant and so diffused through the whole man that there is mutual expression between man and it. In John 3:6 the whole of man's nature is designated flesh; in Ephesians 4:22 this corruption is called man: "Put off . . . the old man, which is corrupt." Obviously we cannot put off our essential substance or discard our very selves, only that which is sinful and foul. It is called the old man because it is inherited from Adam, and because it is contrasted with our new nature.

Bondage of Corruption

Man's nature, then, which has become corrupt and termed flesh, is a bundle of foolishness and vileness, and it is this which renders him totally impotent to all that is good. Thus Scripture speaks of "the bondage of corruption" (Rom. 8:21) and declares men to be "the servants [Greek, 'slaves'] of corruption" (2 Pet. 2:19). Reluctant as any are to acknowledge this humbling truth, the solemn fact that the very nature of man is corrupt and that it defiles everything which issues from him is clearly and abundantly demonstrated. First, the human creature sins from earliest years. The first acts which evidence reason have sin also mingled with them. Take any child and observe him closely, and it will be found that the first dawnings of reason are corrupt. Children express reason selfishly—as in rebellion when thwarted, in readiness to please themselves, in doing harm to others, in excusing themselves by lying, in pride of apparel.

John Bunyan said:

To speak my mind freely: I do confess it is my opinion that children come polluted with sin into the world, and that oftentimes the sins of their youth—especially while they are very young—are rather by virtue of indwelling sin than by examples that are set before them by others: not but what they learn to sin by example too, but example is not the root but rather the temptation to wickedness.

How can we believe otherwise when our Lord has expressly affirmed, "For from within, out of the heart of .men [and not from association with degenerates], proceed evil thoughts, adulteries, fornications, murders, thefts, covetousness, wickedness, deceit, lasciviousness, an evil eye, blasphemy, pride, foolishness: all these things come from within, and defile the man" (Mark 7:21-23). It is true that evil habits may be acquired through contact with evildoers, but they are the occasion and not the radical cause of the habits.

This pollution of our very nature, this indwelling corruption, holds men in complete bondage, making them utterly impotent to do that which is good. In further proof of this, let us turn again to Romans 7. In his explanation of why he was unable to perform that obedience which God required, the apostle said, "I find then a law, that, when I would do good, evil is present with me. For I delight in the law of God after the inward man: but I see another law in my members, warring against the law of my mind, and bringing me into captivity to the law of sin which is in my members" (vv. 21-23). Indwelling sin is here called a law. Literally, a law is a moral rule which directs and commands, which is enforced with rewards and penalties, which impels its subjects to do the things ordered and to avoid the things forbidden. Figuratively, law is an inward principle that moves and inclines constantly to action. As the law of gravity draws all objects to their center, so sin is an effectual principle and power inclining to actions according to its own evil nature.

When the apostle says, "I see another law in my members" (that is, in addition to the principle of grace and holiness communicated at the new birth), he refers to the presence and being of indwelling sin; when he adds "bringing me into captivity" he signifies its power and efficacy. Indwelling sin is a law even in believers, though not to them. Paul said, "I find, then. . . a law of sin." It was a discovery which he had made as a regenerate man. From painful experience he found there was that in him which hindered his communion with God, which thwarted his deepest longings to live a sinless life. The operations of divine grace preserve in believers a constant and ordinarily prevailing will to do good, notwithstanding the power and efficacy of indwelling sin to the contrary. But the will in unbelievers is completely under the power of sin—their will of sinning is never taken away. Education, religion and convictions of conscience may restrain unbelievers, but they have no spiritual inclinations of will to do that which is pleasing to God.

That the very nature of man is corrupt, that it defiles everything which issues from him, is apparent not only by his sinning from earliest youth. Second, it is apparent by his sinning constantly. Not only is his first act sinful; all his subsequent actions are such. "And God saw that the wickedness of man was great in the earth, and that every imagination of the thoughts of his heart was only evil continually" (Gen. 6:5)—nor has man improved the slightest since then. Not that everything done by the natural man is in its own nature sinful; but as the acts are those of a sinner, they cannot be anything else than sinful. The act itself may be the performance of duty; yet if there is no respect for the commandment of God, it is sinful. To provide food and raiment is a duty, but if this duty is done from no spiritual motive (out of subjection to God's authority or the desire to please Him) or end (that God may be glorified), it is sinful. "The plowing of the wicked is sin" (Prov. 21:4); plowing is a duty in itself; nevertheless it is sinful as being the action of a sinner.

Third, it is not thus with a few, but with every member of Adam's fallen race. This further demonstrates that all evil proceeds from the very nature of man. "All flesh had corrupted his way upon the earth" (Gen. 6:12). "There is none righteous, no, not one. . . . They are all gone out of the way, they are together become unprofitable; there is none that doeth good" (Rom. 3:10-12). All members of the human race sin thus of their own accord. "A child left to himself bringeth his mother to shame" (Prov. 29:15). A child does not have to be taught to sin; he has only to be left to himself, and he will soon bring his parents to shame. Things which are not natural have to be taught us and diligently practiced before we learn them. Throw a child into the water, and it is helpless; throw an animal in, and it will at once begin to swim, for its nature teaches it to do so. "Train up a child in the way he should go" (Prov. 22:6). Much diligence and patience are required in those who would thus train the child; but no instructors are needed to inform him of the way in which he should not go. His depraved nature urges him into forbidden paths; indeed, it makes him delight in them.

Chapter 5
Extent

When seeking to uphold some other great truths of Scripture by means of contemplating separately their component parts, we reminded the reader how very difficult it was to avoid some overlapping. The same thing needs to be pointed out here in connection with the subject we are now considering. A river has many tributaries and a surveyor must necessarily trace out each one separately, yet he does so with the knowledge that they all run out of or into the same main stream. A tree has many boughs which, though distinct members of it, often interweave. So it is with our present theme, and as we endeavor to trace its various branches there is of necessity a certain measure of repetition. Though in one way this is to be regretted, being apt to weary the impatient, yet it has its advantages, for it better fixes in our minds some of the principal features.

We began by showing the solemn reality of man's spiritual impotence, furnishing clear proofs from Holy Writ. Next, we endeavored to delineate in detail the precise nature of man's inability: that it is penal, moral, voluntary and criminal. Then we considered the root of the awful malady, evidencing that it lies in the corruption of our very nature. We now examine the extent of the spiritual paralysis which has attacked fallen man's being. Let us state it concisely before elaborating and offering confirmation. The spiritual impotence of the natural man is total and entire, irreparable and irremediable as far as all human efforts are concerned. Fallen man is utterly indisposed and disabled, thoroughly opposed to God and His law, wholly inclined to evil. Sooner would thistles yield grapes than fallen man originate a spiritual volition.

Reign of Sin in Unregenerate
We have supplied a number of proofs that man's nature is now thoroughly corrupt. This is seen in the fact that he is sinful from his earliest years; the first dawnings of reason in a child are fouled by sin. It appears too in that men sin continually. As Jeremiah 13:23 expresses it, they are "accustomed to do evil." It is also evidenced by the universal prevalence of this disease; not only some, nor even the great majority, but all without exception are depraved. It is demonstrated by their freedom in this state. All sin continually of their own accord. A child has only to be left to himself and he will quickly put his mother to shame. Moreover, men cannot be restrained from their sin. Neither education nor religious instruction, neither expostulation nor threatening (human or divine) will deter them; that which is bred in the bone comes out in the flesh. Corruption can neither be eradicated nor moderated. The tongue is a little member, yet God Himself declares it is one which no man can tame (Jam. 3:8).

"The law of sin which is in my members" (Rom. 7:23). The first thing which attends every law as such is its rule or sway: "The law hath dominion over [literally 'lords it over'] a man as long as he liveth" (Rom. 7:1). The giving of law is the act of a superior, and in its very nature it exacts obedience by way of dominion. The law of sin possesses no moral authority over its subjects, but because it exerts a powerful and effectual dominion over its slaves it is rightly termed a law. Though it has no rightful government over men, yet it has the equivalent, for it dominates as a king: "Sin hath reigned unto death" (Rom. 5:21). Because believers have been delivered from the complete dominion of this evil monarch, they are exhorted, "Let not sin therefore reign in your mortal body, that ye should obey it in the lusts thereof" (Rom. 6:12). Here we learn the precise case with the unregenerate: Sin reigns undisputedly within them, and they yield ready and full obedience to it.

The second thing which attends all law as such is its sanctions, which have efficacy to move those who are under the law to do the things it requires. In other words, a law has rewards and penalties accompanying it, and these serve as inducements to obedience even though the things commanded are unpleasant. Speaking generally, all laws owe their efficacy to the rewards and punishments annexed to them. Nor is the "law of sin"—indwelling corruption—any exception. The pleasures and profits which sin promises its subjects are rewards which the vast majority of men lose their souls to obtain. A striking biblical illustration of this is the occasion when the law of sin contended against the law of grace in Moses, who chose "rather to suffer affliction with the people of God, than to enjoy the pleasures of sin for a season; esteeming the reproach of Christ greater riches than the treasures in Egypt: for he had respect unto the recompense of the reward" (Heb. 11:25-26).

In the above example we see the conflict in the mind of Moses between the law of sin and the law of grace. The motive on the part of the law of sin, by which it sought to influence him and with which it prevails over the majority, was the temporary reward which it set before him, namely, the present enjoyment of the pleasures of sin. By that it contended with the eternal reward annexed to the law of grace, called here "the recompense of the reward." By this wretched reward the law of sin keeps the whole world in obedience to its commands. Scripture, observation and personal experience teach us how powerful and potent this influence is. This was what induced our first parents to taste the forbidden fruit, Esau to sell his birthright, Balaam to hire himself to Balak, Judas to betray the Savior. This is what now moves the vast majority of our fellowmen to prefer Mammon to God, Belial to Christ, the things of time and sense to spiritual and eternal realities.

The law of sin also has penalties with which it threatens any who are urged to cast off its yoke. These are the sneers, the ostracism, the persecutions of their peers. The law of sin announces to its votaries that nothing but unhappiness and suffering is the portion of those who would be in subjection to God, that His service is oppressive and joyless. It represents the yoke of Christ as a grievous burden, His gospel as quite unsuited to those who are young and healthy, the Christian life as a gloomy and miserable thing. Whatever troubles and tribulations come on the people of God because of their fidelity to Him, whatever hardships and self-denial the duties of mortification require, are represented by the law of sin as so many penalties following the neglect of its commands. By these it prevails over the "fearful, and unbelieving," who have no share in the life eternal (Rev. 21:8). It is hard to say where its greater strength lies: in its pretended rewards or in its pretended punishments.

The power and effect of this law of sin appears from its very nature. It is not an outward, inoperative, directing law, but an inbred, working, effectual law. A law which is proposed to us cannot be compared for efficacy with a law bred in us. God wrote the moral law on tables of stone, and now it is found in the Scriptures. But what is its efficacy? As it is external to men and proposed to them, does it enable them to perform the things which it requires? No indeed. The moral law is rendered "weak through the flesh" (Rom. 8:3). Indwelling corruption makes it impossible for man to meet its demands. And how does God deliver from this awful bondage? In this present life by making His law internal for His elect, for at their regeneration He makes good that promise "I will put my law in their inward parts, and write it in their hearts" (Jer. 31:33). Thus His law becomes an internal, living, operative and effectual principle within them.

Now the law of sin is an indwelling law. It is "sin that dwelleth in me"; it is "in my members."

It is so deep in man that in one sense it is said to be the man himself: "I know that in me (that is, in my flesh,) there dwelleth no good thing" (Rom. 7:18; cf. vv. 20, 23). From this reasoning we may perceive the full dominion it has over the natural man. It always abides in the soul, and is never absent. It "dwelleth," has its constant residence, in us. It does not come upon the soul only at certain times; if that were so, much might be accomplished during its absence, and the soul might fortify itself against it. No, it never leaves. Wherever we are, whatever we are engaged in, this law of sin is present. Whether we are alone or in company, by night or by day, it is our constant companion. A ruthless enemy indwells our soul. How little this is considered by men! O the woeful security of the unregenerate: a fire is in their bones, fast consuming them. The watch-fulness of most professing Christians corresponds little to the danger of their state.

Being an indwelling law, sin applies itself to its work with great facility and ease. It needs not force open any door nor use any stress whatever. The soul cannot apply itself to any duty except by those very faculties in which this law has its residence. Let the mind or understanding be directed to anything, and there are ignorance, darkness, madness to contend with. As for the will, in it are spiritual deadness, mulish stubbornness, devilish obstinacy. Shall the affections of the heart be set on divine objects? How can they be, when they are wholly inclined toward the world and present things and are prone to every vanity and defilement? Water never rises above its own level. How easy it is, then, for indwelling sin to inject itself into all we do, hindering whatever is good and furthering whatever is evil. Does conscience seek to assert itself? Then our corruptions soon teach us to turn a deaf ear to its voice.

The Scripture everywhere declares the seat of this law of sin to be the heart. "Out of the heart are the issues of life" (Prov. 4:23). It is there that indwelling corruption keeps its special residence; it is there this evil monarch holds court. It has invaded and possessed the throne of God within us. "The heart of the sons of men is full of evil, and madness is in their heart while they live" (Eccles. 9:3). Here is the source of all the madness which appears in men s lives. "All these evil things [mentioned in vv. 21-22] come from within, and defile the man" (Mark 7:23). There are many outward temptations and provocations which befall man, which excite and stir him up to many evils; yet they merely open the vessel and let out what is stored within it. "An evil man out of the evil treasure of his heart bringeth forth that which is evil: for of the abundance of the heart his mouth speaketh" (Luke 6:45). This "evil treasure" or store is the principle of all moral action on the part of the natural man. Temptations and occasions put nothing into men; they only draw out what was in them before. The root or spring of all wickedness lies in the center of our corrupt being.

Enmity of Carnal Mind Against God

Let us next consider the outstanding property of indwelling sin. "The carnal mind is enmity against God: for it is not subject to the law of God, neither indeed can be" (Rom. 8:7). That which is here called the carnal mind is the same as the law of sin. It is to be solemnly noted that the carnal mind is not only an enemy, for as such there would be a possibility of some reconciliation with God; it is enmity itself, thus not disposed to accept any terms of peace. Enemies may be reconciled, but enmity cannot. The only way to reconcile enemies is to destroy their enmity. So the apostle tells us, "When we were enemies, we were reconciled to God by the death of his Son" (Rom. 5:10); that is, a supernatural work has been accomplished in the elect on the ground of the merits of Christ's sacrifice, which results in the reconciliation of those who were enemies. But when the apostle came to speak of enmity there was no other way but for it to be destroyed: "Having abolished in his flesh the enmity" (Eph. 2:15).

Let it also be duly considered that the apostle used a noun and not an adjective: "The carnal mind is enmity against God" (Rom. 8:7). He did not say that it merely is opposed to God, but that it is positive opposition itself. It is not black but blackness; it is not an enemy but enmity; it is not corrupt but corruption itself; not rebellious but rebellion. As C. H. Spurgeon so succinctly expressed it, "The heart, though it be deceitful, is positively deceitful: it is evil in the concrete, sin in the essence: it is the distillation, the quintessence of all things that are vile; it is not envious against God, it is enmity itself—not at enmity, it is actual enmity." This is unspeakably dreadful. To the same effect are those fearful words of the psalmist: "Their inward part is very wickedness" (5:9). Beyond that human language cannot go.

This carnal mind is in every fallen creature, not even excluding the newborn infant. Many who have had the best of parents have turned out the worst of sons and daughters. This carnal mind is in each of us every moment of our lives. It is there just as truly when we are unconscious of its presence as when we are aware of the rising of opposition in us to God. The wolf may sleep, but it is a wolf still. The snake may rest among the flowers, and a boy may stroke its back, but it is a snake still. The sea is the house of storms even when it is placid as a lake. And the heart, when we do not see its seethings, when it does not spew out the hot lava of its corruption, is still the same dread volcano.

The extent of this fearful enmity appears in the fact that the whole of the carnal mind is opposed to God: every part, every power, every passion of it. Every faculty of man's being has been affected by the fall. Take the memory. Is it not a solemn fact that we retain evil things far more easily than those which are good? We can recollect a foolish song much more readily than we can a passage of Scripture. We grasp with an iron hand things which concern our temporal interests, but hold with feeble fingers those which respect our eternal welfare. Take the imagination. Why is it that when a man is given that which intoxicates him, or when he is drugged with opium, his imagination soars as on eagles' wings? Why does not the imagination work thus when the body is in a normal condition? Simply because it is depraved; and unless our body enters a sordid environment the fancy will not hold high carnival. Take the judgment. How vain—often mad—are its reasonings even in the wisest of men.

This fearful enmity is irremediable. "It is not subject to the law of God, neither indeed can be" (Rom. 8:7). Even though divine grace intervenes and subdues its force, yet it does not affect the slightest change in its nature. It may not be so powerful and effectual in operation as when it had more life and freedom, yet it is enmity still. As every drop of poison is poison and will infect, as every spark of fire is fire and will burn, so is every part and degree of the law of sin enmity—it will poison, it will burn. The Apostle Paul can surely be regarded as having made as much progress in the subduing of this enmity as any man on earth, yet he exclaimed, "O wretched man that I am!" (Rom. 7:24) and cried for deliverance from this irreconcilable enmity. Mortification abates its awful force, but it does not affect any reformation in it. Whatever effect divine grace may work upon it, no change is made in it; it is enmity still.

Not only is this awful enmity inbred in every one of Adam's fallen race, not only has it captured and dominated every faculty of our beings, not only is it present within us every moment of our lives, not only is it incapable of reconciliation. Most frightful of all, this indwelling sin is "enmity against God." In other passages it is exhibited as our own enemy: "Abstain from fleshly lusts, which war against the soul" (1 Pet. 2:11): those indwelling corruptions are constantly seeking to destroy us. This deadly poison of sin, this ruinous law of indwelling evil, consistently opposes the new nature or law of grace and holiness in the believer: "The flesh lusteth against the Spirit" (Gal. 5:17); that is, the principle of sin fights against and seeks to vanquish the principle of spirituality. It is dreadful to relate that its proper formal object is God Himself. It is "enmity against God."

This frightful enmity has, as it were, received from Satan the same command which the Assyrians had from their monarch: "Fight neither with small nor great, save only with the king" (1 Kings 22:31). Sin sets itself not against men but against the King of heaven. This appears in the judgments which men form of God. What is the natural man's estimate of the Creator and Ruler of this world? For answer let us turn to the regions of heathendom. Consider the horrible superstitions, the disgusting rites, the hideous symbols of Deity, the cruel penances and gross immoralities which everywhere prevail in lands without the gospel. Consider the appalling abominations which for so long passed, and which in numerous instances still pass, under the sacred name of divine worship. These are not merely the products of ignorance of God; they are the immediate fruits of positive enmity against Him.

But we need not go so far afield as heathendom. The same terrible feature confronts us in so-called Christendom. Witness the multitudinous and horrible errors which prevail on every side in the religious realm today, the degrading and insulting views of the Most High held by the great majority of church members. And what of the vast multitudes who make no profession at all? Some think of and act toward the great Jehovah as One who is to be little regarded and respected. They consider Him as One entitled to very little esteem, scarcely worthy of any notice at all. "Therefore they say unto God, Depart from us, for we desire not the knowledge of thy ways. What is the Almighty, that we should serve him? And what profit should we have, if we pray unto him?" (Job 21:14-15). Such is the language of their hearts and lives, if not of their lips. Countless others flatly deny the existence of God.

The most solemn and dreadful aspect of the subject we are here contemplating is that the outstanding property of the "flesh" or indwelling sin consists of enmity against God Himself, such enmity that "is not subject to the law of God, neither indeed can be" (Rom. 8:7). This frightful and implacable enmity is entire and universal, being opposed to all of God. If there were anything of God—His nature, His character or His works—that indwelling corruption was not enmity against, then the soul might have a retreat within itself where it could shelter and apply itself to that which is of God. Unfortunately, such is the enmity of fallen man that it hates all that is of God, everything wherein or whereby we have to do with Him.

Sin is enmity against God, and therefore against all of God. It is enmity against His law and against His gospel alike, against every duty to Him, against any communion with Him. It is not only against His sovereignty, His holiness, His power, His grace, that sin rears its horrible head; it abhors everything of or pertaining to God. His commandments and His threatenings, His promises and His warnings, are equally disliked. His providences are reviled and His dealings with the world blasphemed. And the nearer anything approaches to God, the greater is man's enmity against it. The more of spirituality and holiness manifested in anything, the more the flesh rises up against it. That which is most of God meets with most opposition. "Ye have set at naught all my counsel and would none of my reproof" (Prov. 1:25) is the divine indictment. The wicked heart of man is opposed to not merely some parts of God's counsel but the whole of it.

Not only is this fearful enmity opposed to everything of God, but it is all-inclusive in the soul. Had indwelling sin been content with partial dominion, had it subjugated only a part of the soul, it might have been more easily and successfully opposed. But this enmity against God has invaded and captured the entire territory of man's being; it has not left a single faculty of the soul free from its tyrannical yoke; it has not exempted a single member from its cruel bondage. When the Spirit of God comes with His gracious power to conquer the soul, He finds nothing whatever in the sinner's soul which is in sympathy with His operations, nothing that will cooperate with Him. All within us alike opposes and strives against His working. There is not the faintest desire for deliverance within the unregenerate: "The whole head is sick, and the whole heart faint" (Isa. 1:5). Even when grace has made its entrance, sin still dwells in all its coasts.

Distasteful and humiliating as this truth may be, we must dwell further on it and amplify what has been merely affirmed. We showed how this fearful enmity is evidenced by the judgments or concepts which men form of God. Sin has so perverted the human mind that distorted views and horrible ideas are entertained of the Deity. Nor is this all. Sin has so inflated the creature that he considers himself competent to comprehend the incomprehensible. Filled with pride, he refuses to acknowledge his limitations and dependence; and in his flight after things which are far beyond his reach, he indulges in the most impious speculations. When he cannot stretch himself to the infinite dimensions of truth, he deliberately contracts the truth to his own little measure. This is what the apostle meant by fallen man's "vanity of mind."

The natural man's enmity against God appears in his affections. As the superlatively excellent One, God has paramount claims on man's heart. He should be the supreme object of his delight. But is He? Far from it. The smallest trifles are held in greater esteem than is God, the fountain of all true joy. The unregenerate see in Him no beauty that they should desire Him. When they hear of His sublime attributes they dislike them. When they hear His Word quoted it is repugnant to them. When invited to draw near to His throne of grace they have no inclination to do so. They have no desire for fellowship with God; they would rather think and talk about anything other than the Lord and His government. They secretly hate His people, and will only tolerate their presence so long as they conform to their wishes. The pleasures and baubles of this world entirely fill their hearts. Corrupted nature can never give birth to a single affection which is really spiritual.

The natural man's enmity appears in his will. Inevitably so, for God's will directly crosses His. God is infinitely holy; man is thoroughly evil; therefore God commands the things which man hates and forbids the things man likes. Hence man despises His authority, refuses His yoke, rebels against His government and goes his own way. Men have no concern for God's glory and no respect for His will. They will not listen to His reproofs nor be checked in their defiant course by His most solemn threatenings. They are as intractable as a wild ass' colt. They are like a bullock unaccustomed to the yoke. They prate of the freedom of their wills, but their wills are active against God and never toward Him. They are determined to have their own way no matter what the cost. When Christ is presented to them they will not come to Him that they might have life. Sooner will water flow uphill of its own accord than the will of man incline itself to God.

The enmity of the natural man against God appears in his conscience. Because he is anxious to be at peace with himself in the reflections which he makes upon his own life and character, it is obvious that his conscience must be a perpetual source of false representations of God. When guilt rankles in his breast, man will blaspheme the justice of his Judge. And self-love prompts him to denounce the punishment of himself as remorseless cruelty. A guilty conscience, unwilling to relinquish its iniquities and yet desirous of being delivered from fears of punishment, prompts men to represent Deity as subject to the weaknesses and follies of humanity. God is to be flattered and bribed with external marks of submission and esteem, or else insulted when the worshiper regards Him as cruel. Conscience fills the mind with prejudices against the nature and character of God, just as a human insult fills our heart with prejudice against the one who mortifies our self-respect. Conscience cannot judge rightly of one whom it hates and dreads.

The enmity of the natural man against God evidences itself in his practice. This dreadful hatred of God is not a passive thing, but an active principle. Sinners are involved in actual warfare against their Maker. They have enlisted under the banner of Satan and they deliberately oppose and defy the Lord. They scoff at His Word, disregard His precepts, flout His providences, resist His Spirit, and turn a deaf ear to the pleas of His servants. Their hearts are fully set to do wickedness. "Their throat is an open sepulcher; with their tongues they have used deceit: the poison of asps is under their lips: Whose mouth is full of cursing and bitterness: Their feet are swift to shed blood: destruction and misery are in their ways: and the way of peace have they not known: there is no fear of God before their eyes" (Rom. 3:13-18). There is in every sinner a deeply rooted aversion for God, a seed of malice. While God leaves sinners alone, their malice may not be clearly revealed; but let them feel a little of His wrath upon them, and their hatred is swiftly manifest.

The sinner's enmity against God is unmixed with any love at all. The natural man is utterly devoid of the principle of love for God. As Jonathan Edwards solemnly expressed it, "The heart of the sinner is as devoid of love for God as a corpse is of vital heat." As the Lord Jesus expressly declared, "I know you, that ye have not the love of God in you" (John 5:42). And remember, that fearful indictment was made by One who could infallibly read the human heart. Moreover that indictment was passed on not the openly vicious and profane but on the strictest religionists of His day. Reader, you may have a mild temper, an amiable disposition, a reputation for kindness and generosity; but if you have never been born again you have no more real love in your heart for God than Judas had for the Savior. What a frightful character—the unmitigated enemy of God!

The power of man's enmity against God is so great that nothing finite can break it. The sinner cannot break it himself. Should an unregenerate person read this and be horrified at the hideous picture which it presents of himself, and should he earnestly resolve to cease his vile enmity against God, he cannot do so. He can no more change his nature than the Ethiopian can change the color of his skin. No preacher can persuade him to throw down the weapons of his rebellion and become a friend of God. One may set before him the excellence of the divine character and plead with him to be reconciled to God, but his heart will remain as steeled against Him as ever. Even though God Himself works miracles in the sight of sinners, no change is effected in their hearts. Pharaoh's enmity was not overcome by the most astonishing displays of divine power, nor was that of the religionists of Palestine in Christ's day.

Indwelling sin may be likened to a powerful and swiftly flowing river. So long as its tributaries are open and waters are continually supplied to its streams, though a dam is set up, its waters rise and swell until it bears down on all and overflows the banks about it. Thus it is with the enmity of the carnal mind against God. While its springs and fountains remain open, it is utterly vain for man to set up a dam of his convictions and resolutions, promises and penances, vows and self-efforts. They may check it for a while, but it will rise up and rage until sooner or later it breaks down all those convictions and resolutions or makes itself an underground passage by some secret lust which will give full vent to it. The springs of that enmity must be subdued by regenerating grace, the streams abated by holiness, or the soul will be drowned and destroyed. Even after regeneration, indwelling sin gives the soul no rest, but constantly wages war upon it.

The Christian is, in fact, the only one who is conscious of the awful power and ragings of this principle of enmity. How often he is made aware that when he would do good, evil is present with him, opposing every effort he makes Godward. How often, when his soul is doing quite another thing, engaged in a totally different design, sin starts something in his heart or imagination which carries it away to that which is evil. Yes, the soul may be seriously engaged in the mortification of sin, when indwelling corruption will by some means or other lead the soul into trifling with the very sin which it is endeavoring to conquer. Such surprisals as these are proofs of the habitual propensity to evil of that principle of enmity against God from which they proceed. The ever abiding presence and continual operation of this principle prevent much communion with God, disturb holy meditations and defile the conscience.

But let us return to our consideration of the enmity of the unregenerate. This enmity in the heart of the sinner is so great that he is God's mortal enemy. Now a man may feel unfriendly toward another, or he may cherish ill will against him, yet not be his mortal enemy. That is, his enmity against the one he hates is not so great that nothing will satisfy him but his death. But it is far otherwise with sinners and God. They are His mortal enemies. True, it does not lie in their power to kill Him, yet the desire is there in the heart. There is a principle of enmity within fallen man which would rejoice if Deity could be annihilated. "The fool hath said in his heart, There is no God" (Ps. 14:1). In the Bible the words "there is" are in italics—supplied by the translators for clarity. But the original has it, "The fool hath said in his heart, No God." It is not the denial of God's existence, but the affirmation that he desires no contact with Him: "I desire no God; I would that He did not exist."

Here is the frightful climax: The carnal mind is enmity with the very being of God. Sin is destructive of all being. Man is suicidal—he has destroyed himself. He is homicidal—his evil influence destroys his fellowmen. He is guilty of Deicide(the act of killing a divine being)—he wishes he could annihilate the very being of God. But the sinner does not regard himself as being so vile. He does not consider himself to be the implacable and inveterate enemy of God. He has a far better opinion of himself than that. Consequently, if he hears or reads anything like this, he is filled with objections: "I do not believe I am such a dreadful creature as to hate God. I do not feel such enmity in my heart. I am not conscious that I harbor any ill will against Him. Who should know better than myself? If I hate a fellowman I am aware of it; how could I be totally unconscious of it if there is in my soul such enmity against God?"

Several answers may be given to these questions. First, if the objector would seriously examine his heart and contemplate himself, unless he were strangely blinded, he would certainly discover in himself those very elements in which enmity essentially consists. He loves and respects his friends, he is fond of their company, he is anxious to please them and promote their good. Is this his attitude toward God? If he is honest with himself, he knows it is not. He has no respect for His authority, no concern for His glory, no desire for fellowship with Him. He gives God none of his time, despises His Word, breaks His commandments, rejects His Son. He has been opposed to God all his life. These things are the very essence of enmity.

Second, the sinner's ignorance and unconsciousness of his enmity against God are due to the false conceptions which he entertains of His nature and character. If he were better acquainted with the God of Holy Writ, he would be more aware of his hatred of Him. But the God he believes in is merely a creation of his own fancy. The true God is ineffably holy, inflexibly just. His wrath burns against sin and He will by no means clear the guilty. If mankind likes the true God, why is it that they have set up so many false gods? If they admire the truth, why have they invented so many false systems of religion? The contrariety between the carnal mind and God is the contrariety between sin and holiness. The divine law requires man to love God supremely; instead, he loves himself supremely. It requires him to delight in God superlatively; instead, he wholly delights in all that is not of God. It requires him to love his neighbor as himself; instead, his heart is inordinately selfish.

Third, we have said that the enmity of the natural man against God is a mortal one. This the sinner will not admit. But indubitable proof of the assertion is found in man's treatment of God when, in the person of His Son, He became incarnate. When God brought Himself as near to man as Infinity could approach, man saw in Him "no beauty" that he should desire Him; rather was He despised and rejected by him. Not only did man dislike Him (Isa. 53:2-3), but he hated Him "without a cause" (John 15:25). So bitter and relentless was that hatred that man exclaimed, "This is the heir: come, let us kill him" (Luke 20:14). And what form of death did man select for Him? The most painful and shameful his malignity could devise. And the Son of God is still despised and rejected. Remember His words "He that hateth me hateth my Father also" (John

15:23). Our proof is complete.

What bearing on our subject has this lengthy discourse on man's enmity? Why take up the total depravity of fallen man when we are supposed to be considering his spiritual impotence? We have not wandered from our theme at all. Instead, while dealing with the root and extent of man's impotence, we have followed strictly the order of Scripture. What is the very next word of the apostle's after Romans 8:7? This: "So then they that are in the flesh cannot please God" (v. 8). It is just because man is corrupt at the very center of his being, because indwelling sin is a law over him, because his mind (the noblest part of his being) is enmity against God, that he is completely incapable of doing anything to meet with the divine approbation.

Here is inevitable inference, the inescapable conclusion: "So then"—because fallen man's mind is enmity with God and incapable of subordination to His law—"they that are in the flesh cannot please God" (Rom. 8:8). To be "in the flesh" is not necessarily to live immorally, for there is the religiousness as well as the irreligiousness of the flesh. So great, so entire, so irremediable is this impotence of fallen man that he is unable to effect any change in his nature, acquire any strength by his own efforts, prepare himself to receive divine grace, until the Spirit renews him and works in him both to will and to do of God's good pleasure. He is unable to discern spiritual things (1 Cor. 2:14), incapable of believing (John 8:47), powerless to obey (Rom. 8:7). He cannot think a good thought of himself (2 Cor. 3:5), he cannot speak a good word; indeed, without Christ he "can do nothing" (John 15:5). Thus, the sinner is "without strength," wholly impotent and unable to turn himself to God.

Chapter 6
Problem

We have now arrived at the most difficult part of our subject, and much wisdom from above is needed if we are to be preserved from error. It has been well said that truth is like a narrow path running between two precipices. The figure is an apt one, for fatal consequences await those who depart from the teaching of God's Word, no matter which direction that departure may take. It is so with the doctrine of man's impotence. It matters little whether the total bondage of the fallen creature and his utter inability to perform that which is good in the sight of God are repudiated and the freedom of the natural man is insisted on, or whether his complete spiritual impotence is affirmed and at the same time his responsibility to perform that which is pleasing to God is denied. In either case the effect is equally disastrous. In the former, the sinner is given a false confidence; in the latter, he is reduced to fatalistic inertia. In either case the real state of man is grossly misrepresented.

Man's Inability and God's Demands

The careful reader must have felt the force of the difficulties which we shall now examine. May God's Spirit enable us to throw some light on them. If the carnal mind is such fearful enmity against God that it is not subject to His law, "neither indeed can be," then why does He continue to press its demands on us and insist that we meet its requirements under pain of eternal death? If the fall has left man morally helpless and reduced him to the point where he is "without strength," then with what propriety can he be called on to obey the divine precepts? If man is so thoroughly depraved that he is the slave of sin, wherein lies his accountability to live for the glory of God? If man is born under "the bondage of corruption," how can he possibly be "without excuse" in connection with the sins he commits?

In seeking to answer these and similar questions we must of necessity confine ourselves to what is clearly revealed on them in Holy Writ. We say "of necessity," for unless we forsake our own thoughts (Isa. 55:7) and completely submit our minds to God's, we are certain to err. In theory this is granted by most professing Christians, yet in practice it is too often set aside. In general it is conceded, but in particular it is ignored. A highly trained intellect may draw what appear to be incontestable conclusions from a scriptural premise; yet, though logic cannot refute them, the practices of Christ and His apostles prove them to be false. On the one hand we may take the fact that the Lord has given orders for His gospel to be preached to every creature. Then must we not infer that the sinner has it in his own power to either accept or reject that gospel? Such an inference certainly appears reasonable, yet it is erroneous. On the other hand take the fact that the sinner is spiritually impotent. Then is it not a mockery to ask him to come to Christ? Such an inference certainly appears reasonable; yet it is false.

It is at this very point that most of Christendom has been deluged with a flood of errors. Most of the leading denominations began by taking the Word of God as the foundation and substance of their creed. But almost at once that foundation was turned into a platform on which the proud intellect of man was exercised, and in a very short time human reason—logical and plausible—supplanted divine revelation. Men attempted to work out theological systems and articles of faith that were thoroughly "consistent," theories which—unlike the workings of both nature and providence—contained in them no seeming "contradictions" or "absurdities," but which commended themselves to their fellowmen. But this was nothing less than a presumptuous attempt to compress the truth of God into man-made molds, to reduce that which issued from the Infinite to terms comprehensible to finite minds. It is another sad example of that egotism which refuses to receive what it cannot understand.

Biblical Harmony

It is true that there is perfect harmony in all parts of divine truth. How can it be otherwise, since God is its Author? Yet men are so blind that they cannot perceive this perfect harmony. Some cannot discern the consistency between the infinite love and grace of God and His requiring His own Son to pay such a costly satisfaction to His broken law. Some cannot see the consistency between the everlasting mercy of God and the eternal punishment of the wicked, insisting that if the former be true the latter is impossible. Some cannot see the congruity of Christ satisfying every requirement of God on behalf of His people and the imperative necessity of holiness and obedience in them if they are to benefit thereby; or between their divine preservation and the certainty of destruction were they to finally apostatize. Some cannot see the accord between the divine foreordination of our actions and our freedom in them. Some cannot see the agreement between efficacious grace in the conversion of sinners and the need for the exercise of their faculties by way of duty. Some cannot see the concurrence of the total depravity or spiritual impotence of man and his responsibility to be completely subject to God's will.

As a sample of what we have referred to in the last two paragraphs, note the following quotation:

We deny duty-faith, and duty-repentance—these terms signifying that it is every man's duty to spiritually and savingly repent and believe (Gen. 6:5; 8:21; Matt. 15:19; Jer. 17:9; John 6:44, 65). We deny also that there is any capability in man by nature to any spiritual good whatever. So that we reject the doctrine that men in a state of nature should be exhorted to believe in or turn to God (John 12:39, 40; Eph. 2:8; Rom. 8:7, 8; 1 Cor. 4:7). We believe that it would be unsafe, from the brief records we have of the way in which the apostles, under the immediate direction of the Lord, addressed their hearers in certain special cases and circumstances, to derive absolute and universal rules for ministerial addresses in the present day under widely-different circumstances. And we further believe that an assumption that others have been inspired as the apostles were has led to the grossest errors amongst both Romanists and professed Protestants. Therefore, that for ministers in the present day to address unconverted persons, or indiscriminately all in a mixed congregation, calling upon them to savingly repent, believe, and receive Christ, or perform any other acts dependent upon the new creative power of the Holy Ghost, is, on the one hand, to imply creature power and on the other, to deny the doctrine of special redemption.

It may come as a surprise to many of our readers to learn that the above is a verbatim quotation from the Articles of Faith of a Baptist group in England with a considerable membership, which will permit no man to enter their pulpits who does not solemnly subscribe to and sign his name to the same. Yet this is the case. These Articles of Faith accurately express the belief of the great majority of certain Baptist groups in the United States on this subject. In consequence, the gospel of Christ is deliberately withheld from the unsaved, and no appeals are addressed to them to accept the gospel offer and receive Christ as their personal Lord and Savior. Need we wonder that fewer and fewer in their midst are testifying to a divine work of grace in their hearts, and that many of their churches have ceased to be.

It is a good thing that many of the Lord's people are sounder of heart than the creeds held in their heads, yet that does not excuse them for subscribing to what is definitely unscriptural. It is far from a pleasant task to expose the fallacy of these Articles of Faith, for we have some friends who are committed to them; yet we would fail in our duty to them if we made no effort to convince them of their errors. Let us briefly examine these Articles. First, they deny that it is the duty of every man who hears the gospel to spiritually and savingly repent and believe, notwithstanding the fact that practically all the true servants of Christ in every generation (including the Reformers and nine-tenths of the Puritans) have preached that duty. It is the plain teaching of Holy Writ. We will not quote from the writings of those used of the Spirit in the past, but confine ourselves to God's Word.

God Himself "now commandeth all men everywhere to repent" (Acts 17:30). What could possibly be plainer than that? There is no room for any quibbling, misunderstanding or evasion. It means just what it says, and says just what it means. The framers of those Articles, then, are taking direct issue with the Most High. It is because of his "hardness and impenitence of heart" that the sinner treasures up to himself "wrath against the day of wrath" (Rom. 2:5). "He that believeth on him is not condemned: but he that believeth not is condemned already, because he hath not believed in the name of the only begotten Son of God. And this is the condemnation, that light is come into the world, and men loved darkness rather than light, because their deeds were evil" (John 3:18-19). Here too it is impossible to fairly evade the force of our Lord's language. He taught that it is the duty of all who hear the gospel to savingly believe on Him, and declared that rejecters are condemned because they do not believe. When He returns it will be "in flaming fire taking vengeance on them that know not God, and that obey not the gospel" (2 Thess. 1:8).

Next, note that the framers of these Articles follow their denial by referring to six verses of Scripture, the first four of which deal with the desperate wickedness of the natural man's heart and the last two with his complete inability to turn to Christ until divinely enabled. These passages are manifestly alluded to in support of the contention made. Each reader must decide their pertinence for himself. The only relevance they can possess is on the supposition that they establish a premise which requires us to draw the conclusion so dogmatically expressed. We are asked to believe that since fallen man is totally depraved we must necessarily infer that he is not a fit subject to be exhorted to perform spiritual acts. Thus, when analyzed, this Article is seen to consist of nothing more than an expression of human reasoning.

Not only does the substance of this Article of Faith consist of nothing more substantial and reliable than a mental inference, but when weighed in the balances of the sanctuary it is found to clash with the Scriptures, that is, with the practice of God's own servants recorded in them. For example, we do not find the psalmist accommodating his exhortations to the sinful inability of the natural man. Far from it. David called on the ungodly thus: "Be wise now therefore, O ye kings: be instructed, ye judges of the earth. Serve the Lord with fear, and rejoice with trembling. Kiss the Son, lest he be angry, and ye perish from the way, when his wrath is kindled but a little. Blessed are all they that put their trust in him" (Ps. 2:10-12). David did not withhold these warnings because the people were such rebels that they would not and could not give their hearts' allegiance to the King of kings. He uncompromisingly and bluntly commanded them to do so whether they could or not.

It was the same with the prophets. If ever a man addressed an unregenerate congregation it was when Elijah the Tishbite spoke to the idolatrous Israelites: "Elijah came unto all the people, and said, How long halt ye between two opinions? If the Lord be God, follow him: but if Baal, then follow him" (1 Kings 18:21). That exhortation was not restricted to the remnant of renewed souls, but was addressed to the nation indiscriminately. It was a plain call for them to perform a spiritual duty, for them to exercise their will and choose between God and the devil. In like manner Isaiah called on the debased generation of his day: "Wash ye, make you clean; put away the evil of your doings from before mine eyes; cease to do evil; learn to do well" (1:16-17). One prophet went so far as to say to his hearers, "Make you a new heart and a new spirit" (Ezek. 18:31), yet he was in perfect accord with his fellow prophet Jeremiah who taught the helplessness of man in those memorable questions "Can the Ethiopian change his skin? Or the leopard his spots?" These men, then, did not decide they must preach only that which lay in the power of their hearers to comply with.

The words "We deny also that there is any capability in man by nature to any spiritual good whatever" will strike the vast majority of God's people as far too sweeping. They will readily agree that fallen man possesses no power at all to perform any spiritual acts; yet they will insist that nothing prevents the spiritual obedience of any sinner except his own unwillingness. Man by nature—that is, as he originally left the hands of his Creator—was endowed with full capability to meet his Maker's requirements. The fall did not rob him of a single faculty, and it is his retention of all his faculties which constitutes him still a responsible creature. Of the last four passages referred to in the Article (John 12:39, 40, etc.) two of them relate to the spiritual impotence of fallen man and the other two to divine enablement imparted to those who are saved.

With regard to the other Articles affirming that it "would be unsafe" for us now to derive rules for ministerial address from the way in which the apostles spoke to their hearers, this is their summary method of disposing of all those passages in the Old and New Testaments alike which are directly opposed to their theory. Since the Lord Jesus Himself did not hesitate to say to the people, "Repent ye, and believe the gospel" (Mark 1:15), surely His servants today need not have the slightest hesitation in following His example. If ministers of the Word are not to find their guidance and rules from the practice of their Master and His apostles, then where shall they look for them? Must each one be a rule unto himself? Or must they necessarily place themselves under the domination of self-made popes? These very men who are such sticklers for "consistency" are not consistent with themselves, for when it comes to matters of church polity they take the practice of the apostles for their guidance! Lack of space prevents further comment on this.

To human reason there appears to be a definite conflict between two distinct lines of divine truth. On the one hand, Scripture plainly affirms that fallen man is totally depraved, enslaved by sin, entirely destitute of spiritual strength, so that he is unable of himself to either truly repent or savingly believe in Christ. On the other hand, Scripture uniformly addresses fallen man as a being who is accountable to God, responsible to forsake his wickedness and serve and glorify his Maker. He is called on to lay down the weapons of his warfare and be reconciled to God. The Ruler of heaven and earth has not lowered the standard of holiness under which He placed man. He declares that notwithstanding man's ruined condition, he is "without excuse" for all his iniquities. The gospel depicts man in a lost state, "dead in trespasses and sins"; nevertheless it exhorts all who come under its sound to accept Christ as their Lord and Savior.

Such in brief is the problem presented by the doctrine we are here considering. The unregenerate are morally impotent, yet are they fully accountable beings. They are sold under sin, yet are they justly required to be holy as God is holy. They are unable to comply with the righteous requirements of their Sovereign, yet they are exhorted to do so under pain of eternal death. What, then, should be our attitude to this problem? First, we should carefully test it and thoroughly satisfy ourselves that both of these facts are plainly set forth in Holy Writ. Second, having done so, we must accept them both at their face value, assured that however contrary they may seem to us, yet there is perfect harmony between all parts of God's Word. Third, we must hold firmly to both these lines of truth, steadfastly refusing to relinquish either of them at the dictates of any theological party or denominational leader. Fourth, we should humbly wait on God for fuller light on the subject.

But such a course is just what the proud heart of man is disinclined to follow. Instead, he desires to reduce everything to a simple, consistent and coherent system, one which falls within the compass of his finite understanding. Notwithstanding the fact that he is surrounded by mystery on every side in the natural realm, notwithstanding the fact that so very much of God's providential dealings both with the world in general and with himself in particular are "past finding out," he is determined to philosophize and manipulate God's truth until it is compressed into a series of logical propositions which appear reasonable to him. He is like the disciples whom our Lord called "fools" because they were "slow of heart to believe all that the prophets have spoken" (Luke 24:25). Those disciples were guilty of picking and choosing, believing what appealed to their inclination and rejecting that which was distasteful and which appeared to them to clash with what they had been taught.

Antinomian-Pelagian Debate

The testimony of the prophets did not seem to the disciples to be harmonious; one part appeared to conflict with another. In fact, there were two distinct lines of Messianic prediction which looked as though they flatly contradicted each other. The one spoke of a suffering, humiliated and crucified Messiah; the other of an all-powerful, glorious and triumphant Messiah. And because the disciples could not see how both could be true, they held to the one and rejected the other. Precisely the same capricious course has been followed by theologians in Christendom. Conflicting schools or parties among them have, as it were, divided the truth among themselves, one party retaining this portion and jettisoning that, and another party rejecting this and maintaining that. They have ranged themselves into opposing groups, each holding some facets of the truth, each rejecting what the opponents contend for. Party spirit has been as rife and as ruinous in the religious world as in the political.

On the one side Arminians have maintained that men are responsible creatures, that the claims of God are to be pressed upon them, that they must be called on to discharge their duty, that they are fit subjects for exhortation. Yet while steadfastly adhering to this side of the truth, they have been guilty of repudiating other aspects which are equally necessary and important. They have denied—in effect if not in words—the total depravity of man, his complete spiritual helplessness, the bondage of his will under sin, and his utter inability to cooperate with the Holy Spirit in the work of his salvation. On the other side Antinomians, while affirming all that the Arminians deny, are themselves guilty of repudiating what their opponents contend for, insisting that since the unregenerate have no power to perform spiritual acts it is useless and absurd to call on them to do so. Thus they aver that gospel offers should not be made unto the unregenerate.

These Antinomians consider themselves to be towers of orthodoxy, valiant defenders of the truth, sounder in the faith than any other section of Christendom. Many of them wish to be regarded as strict Calvinists; but whatever else they may be, they certainly are not that, for Calvin himself taught and practiced directly the contrary. In his work The Eternal Predestination of God the great Reformer wrote:

It is quite manifest that all men without difference or distinction are outwardly called or invited to repentance and faith; . . . the mercy of God is offered to those who believe and to those who believe not, so that those who are not Divinely taught within are only rendered inexcusable, not saved.

In his Secret Providence of God he asked:

And what if God invites the whole mass of mankind to come unto Him, and yet knowingly and of His own will denies His Spirit to the greater part, "drawing" a few only unto obedience unto Himself by His Spirit's secret inspiration and operation—is the adorable God to be charged, on that account, with inconsistency?

In the same work Calvin stated:

Nor is there any want of harmony or oneness of truth when the same Savior, who invites all men unto Him without exception by His external voice, yet declares that "A man can receive nothing except it be given him from above:" John 19:11.

Many regarding themselves as Calvinists have departed far from the teaching and practice of that eminent servant of God.

There is no difference in principle between the unregenerate being called on to obey the gospel and accept its gracious overtures, and the whole heathen world being required to respond to the call of God through nature before His Son became incarnate. In his address to the Athenians the apostle declared on Mars Hill, "God that made the world and all things therein, seeing that he is Lord of heaven and earth, dwelleth not in temples made with hands; neither is worshipped with men's hands, as though he needed anything, seeing he giveth to all life, and breath, and all things; and hath made of one blood all nations of men for to dwell on all the face of the earth, and hath determined the times before appointed, and the bounds of their habitation; that they should seek the Lord, if haply they might feel after him, and find him" (Acts 17:24-27). The force of that statement is this: Seeing God is the Creator, the Governor of all, He cannot be supposed to inhabit temples made by men, nor can He be worshiped with the products of their hands; and seeing that He is the universal Benefactor and Source of life and all things to His creatures, He is on that account required to be adored and obeyed; and since He is sovereign Lord appointing the different ages of the world and allotting to the nations their territories, His favor is to be sought after and His will submitted to.

The voice of nature is clear and loud. It testifies to the being of God and tells of His wisdom, goodness and power. It addresses all alike, bidding men to believe in God, turn to Him and serve Him. "The heavens declare the glory of God; and the firmament showed his handywork" (Ps. 19:1). These are the preachers of nature to all nations alike. They are not silent, but vocal, speaking to those in every land: "Day unto day uttereth speech, and night unto night showed knowledge. There is no speech nor language, where their voice is not heard. Their line is gone out through all the earth, and their words to the end of the world" (vv. 2-4). In view of these and similar phenomena the apostle declares, "That which may be known of God is manifest in them; for God hath showed it unto them. For the invisible things of him from the creation of the world are clearly seen, being understood by the things that are made, even his eternal power and Godhead; so that they are without excuse" (Rom. 1:19-20).

Now why do not Antinomians object to nature addressing men indiscriminately? Why do not these hyper-Calvinists protest against what we may designate the theology of the sun and the moon? Why do they not exclaim that there is no proper basis for such a call as nature makes? This view not only mocks the unregenerate, but belittles God, seeing that it is certain to prove fruitless, for He has not purposed that either savage or sage should respond to nature's call. But with the sober and the spiritual this branch of the divine government needs no apology. It is in all respects worthy of Him who is wonderful in counsel and excellent in working. Those groups of mankind who do not have the sacred Scriptures are as truly rational and accountable beings as those who are reared with God's written Word. Their having lost the power to read God's character in His works, as well as the inclination to seek after and find Him, does not in the least divest the Lord of His right to require of them both that inclination and power, and to deal with them by various methods of providence according to their several advantages.

It is altogether reasonable that intelligent creatures who, by falling into apostasy, have become blind to God's excellences and enemies to Him in their minds, should yet be commanded to yield Him the homage which is His due and should be urged and exhorted by a thousand tongues, speaking from every quarter of the heaven and the earth, to turn to Him as their supreme good, although it is absolutely certain that without gifts they do not possess, without a supernatural work of grace being wrought in their hearts, not one of them will ever incline his ear. Who does not perceive that this is an unimpeachable arrangement of things, in every respect worthy of the character of Him who is "righteous in all his ways, and holy in all his works" (Ps. 145:17)? The light of nature leaves all men without excuse, and God has a perfect right to require them to seek Him without vouchsafing the power of doing so, which power He is under no obligation to grant.

Exactly analogous to this is the case of those who come under the sound of the gospel, yet without being chosen to salvation or redemption by the precious blood of the Lamb. The love of God in Christ to sinners is proclaimed to them, and they are exhorted and entreated by all sorts of arguments to believe in Christ and be saved. Let it be clearly pointed out that no obstacle lies in the way of the reprobates' believing but what exists in their own evil hearts. Their minds are free to think and their wills to act. They do just as they please, unforced by anyone. They choose and refuse as seems good to themselves. The secret purpose of God in not appointing them to everlasting life or in withholding from them the renewing operations of His Spirit has no causal influence on the decision to which they come. Their advantages are vastly superior to the opportunities of those who enjoy only the light of nature.

The manifestation of the divine character granted to those living in Christendom is incomparably brighter and more impressive than that given to those born in heathendom, and consequently their responsibility is proportionately greater. Much more is given the former, and, on the ground of equity, much more will certainly be required of them (Luke 12:48). What, then, shall we say of the conduct of the Most High in His dealings with such persons? Shall we presumptuously question His sincerity in exhorting them by His Word or His sincerity in urging them by the general operations of His Spirit (Gen. 6:3; Acts 7:51)? With equal propriety we might question the sincerity of nature, when it bears witness to God's power in the shaking of the earth and the kindling of the volcano; or we might doubt God's goodness in clothing the valleys with corn and filling the pastures with flocks, leaving Himself "not . . . without witness" (Acts 14:17), in order that men "should seek the Lord, if haply they might feel after him, and find him" (Acts 17:27).

We by no means affirm that what we have pointed out entirely removes the difficulty felt by those who do not perceive the justice in exhorting sinners to perform acts altogether beyond their power. But we do insist that, in the light of God's method of dealing with the vast majority of men in the past, withholding the gospel effectually blunts its point. Ministers err grievously if they allow their hands to be tied or their mouths muzzled, thus disobeying Christ. The only difference between those living under the gospel and those who have only the light of nature seems to be that the grace of the one allotment is far greater than that of the other, that the responsibility is higher in proportion, and that the condemnation which results from disobedience must therefore be more severe in the one case than in the other in the great day of accounts. To those divinely called to preach the gospel the course is clear. They are to go forth in obedience to their commission, appealing to "every creature," urging their hearers to be reconciled to God.

Speaking for himself, the writer (who for more than twenty years was active in oral ministry) never found any other consideration to deter him from sounding forth the universal call of the gospel. He knew there might well be some in his congregation who had sinned that sin for which there is no forgiveness (Matt. 12:31-32), others who had probably sinned away their day of grace, having quenched the Spirit (1 Thess. 5:19) till it was no longer possible to renew them again to repentance (Luke 13:24-25; 19:48). Yet since this was mercifully concealed from him, he sought to cry aloud and spare not. He knew that the gospel was to be the savior of death unto death to some, and that God sometimes sends His servants forth with a commission similar to that of Isaiah's (6:9-10). Still that furnished no more reason why he should be silent than that the sun and moon should cease proclaiming their Creator's glory merely because the world is blind and deaf.

In this same connection it is pertinent to consider the striking and solemn case of Pharaoh. It indeed presents an awe—inspiring spectacle, yet that must not hinder us from looking at it and ascertaining what light it throws on the character and ways of the Most High. It is the case not merely of an isolated individual, but of a fearfully numerous class—the vessels of wrath fitted to destruction. It is true that Pharaoh was not called on to believe and be saved, he was not exhorted to yield himself to the constraining love of God as manifested in the gift of His Son; but he was required to submit himself to the authority of God and to accede to His revealed will. He was ordered to let Jehovah's people go that they might serve Him in the wilderness, and he was required to comply with the divine command not sullenly or reluctantly, not as a matter of necessity, but with his whole heart.

A Promise for Every Command of God

Let it not be overlooked that every divine command virtually implies a promise, for our duty and our welfare are in every instance inseparably joined (Deut. 10:12-13). If God is truly obeyed He will be truly glorified, and if He is truly glorified He will be truly enjoyed. Had the king of Egypt obeyed, certainly his fate would have been different. He would have been regarded not with disapproval but with favor; he would have been the object not of punishment but rather of reward. Nevertheless, it was not intended that he should obey. The Most High had decreed otherwise. Before Moses entered the presence of Pharaoh and made known Jehovah's command, the Lord informed His servant, "I will harden his heart that he shall not let the people go" (Ex. 4:21). This is unspeakably awful, yet it need not surprise us. The same sun whose rays melt the wax hardens the clay—an example in the visible realm of what takes place in the hearts of the renewed and of the unregenerate.

Not only was it God's intention to harden Pharaoh's heart so that he should not obey His command, but He plainly declared, "In very deed for this cause have I raised thee up; for to show in thee my power; and that my name may be declared throughout all the earth" (Ex. 9:16). The connection in which that solemn verse is quoted in Romans 9:17 makes it unmistakably plain that God ordained that this haughty monarch should be an everlasting monument to His severity. Here we witness the Ruler of this world dealing with men—for Pharaoh was representative of a large class—dealing with them about what concerns their highest interests, their happiness or their woe throughout eternity, not intending their happiness, not determining to confer the grace which would enable them to comply with His will, yet issuing commands to them, denouncing their threatenings, working signs and wonders before them, enduring them with much long-suffering while they add sin to sin and ripen for destruction. Yet let it be remembered that there was nothing which hindered Pharaoh from obeying except his own depravity. Whatever objection may be brought against the Word calling on the non-elect to repent and believe may with equal propriety be brought against the whole procedure of God with Pharaoh.

In their Articles of Faith the hyper-Calvinists declare, "We deny duty-faith and duty-repentance—these terms signifying that it is every man's duty to spiritually and savingly repent and believe." Those who belong to this school of theology insist that it would be just as sensible to visit our cemeteries and call on the occupants of the graves to come forth as to exhort those who are dead in trespasses and sins to throw down the weapons of their warfare and be reconciled to God. Such reasoning is unsound, for there is a vast and vital difference between a spiritually dead soul and a lifeless body. The soul of Adam became the subject of penal and spiritual death; nevertheless it retained all its natural powers. Adam did not lose all knowledge nor become incapable of volition; nor did the operations of conscience cease within him. He was still a rational being, a moral agent, a responsible creature, though he could no longer think or will, love or hate, in conformity to the law of righteousness.

It is far otherwise with physical dissolution. When the body dies it becomes as inactive, unintelligent and unfeeling as a piece of unorganized matter. A lifeless body has no responsibility, but a spiritually dead soul is accountable to God. A corpse in the cemetery will not "despise and reject" Christ (Isa. 53:3), will not "resist the Holy Ghost" (Acts 7:51), will not disobey the gospel (2 Thess. 1:8); but the sinner can and does do these very things, and is justly condemned for them. Are we, then, suggesting that fallen man is not "dead in trespasses and sins"? No indeed, but we do insist that those solemn words be rightly interpreted and that no false conclusions be drawn from them. Because the soul has been deranged by sin, because all its operations are unholy, it is correctly said to be in a state of spiritual death, for it no more fulfills the purpose of its being than does a dead body.

The fall of man, with its resultant spiritual death, did not dissolve our relation to God as the Creator, nor did it exempt us from His authority. But it forfeited His favor and suspended that communion with Him by which alone could be preserved that moral excellence with which the soul was originally endowed. Instead of attempting to draw analogies between spiritual and physical death and deriving inferences from them, we must stick very closely to the Scriptures and regulate all our thoughts by them. God's Word says, "You hath he quickened, who were dead in trespasses and sins: wherein in times past ye walked" (Eph. 2:1-2). Thus the spiritual death of the sinner is a state of active opposition against God—a state for which he is responsible, the guilt and enormity of which the preacher should constantly press upon him. Why do we speak of active opposition against God as being dead in sins? Because in Scripture "death" does not mean cessation of being, but a condition of separation and alienation from God (Eph. 4:18).

The solemn and humbling fact that fallen man is fully incapable of anything spiritually good or of turning to God is clearly revealed and insisted on in His Word (John 6:44; 2 Cor. 3:5, etc.), yet the majority of professing Christians have rejected that fact. It is important to note that the grounds and reasons for which it has been opposed by some are not scriptural. They do not allege that there is any specific statement of Holy Writ which directly contradicts it. They do not affirm that any passage can be produced from the Word which expressly tells us that fallen man has the power of will to do anything spiritually good, or that he is able by his own strength to turn to God, or even prepare himself to do so. Instead, they are obliged to fall back on a process of reasoning, making inferences and deductions from certain general principles which the Scriptures sanction. It is at once apparent that there is a vast difference in point of certainty between these two things.

Principle of Exhortation in Scripture

The principal objection made against the doctrine of fallen man's inability is drawn from the supposed inconsistency between it and the principle of exhortation which runs all through Scripture. It is pointed out that commands and exhortations are addressed to the descendants of Adam, that they are manifestly responsible to comply with them, that they incur guilt by failure to obey. Then the conclusion is drawn that, therefore, these commandments would never have been given, that such responsibility could not belong to man, and such guilt could not be incurred, unless they were able to will and to do the things commanded. Thus their whole argument rests not on anything actually stated in Scripture, but on certain notions respecting the reasons why God issued these commands and exhortations, and respecting the ground upon which moral responsibility rests.

In like manner we find the hyper-Calvinists pursuing an identical course in their rejection of the exhortation principle. Though at the opposite pole in doctrine—for they contend for the spiritual impotence of fallen man—yet they concur with others in resorting to a process of reasoning. They cannot produce a single passage from God's Word which declares that the unregenerate must not be urged to perform spiritual duties. They cannot point to any occasion on which the Savior Himself warned His apostles against such a procedure, not even when He commissioned them to go and preach His gospel. They cannot even discover a word from Paul cautioning either Timothy or Titus to be extremely careful when addressing the unsaved lest they leave their hearers with the impression that their case was far from being desperate.

Not only are the hyper-Calvinists unable to produce one verse of Scripture containing such prohibitions or warnings as we have mentioned above, but they are faced with scores of passages both in the Old and the New Testaments which show unmistakably that the servants of God in biblical times followed the very opposite course to that advocated by these twentieth century theorists. Neither the prophets, the Savior, nor His apostles shaped their policy by the state of their hearers. They did not accommodate their message according to the spiritual impotence of sinners, but plainly enforced the just requirements of a holy God. How, then, do these men dispose of all those passages which speak directly against their theories? By what is called (in some law courts) a process of "special pleading." We quote again from their Articles of Faith:

We believe that it would be unsafe, from the brief records we have of the way in which the apostles, under the immediate direction of the Lord, addressed their hearers in certain special cases and circumstances, to derive absolute and universal rules for ministerial addresses in the present day under widely-different circumstances.

Thus they naively attempt to neutralize and set aside the practice of our Lord and of His apostles. It is very much like the course followed by the Pharisees, who drew up their own rules and regulations, binding them upon the people, against whom Christ preferred the solemn charge of "making the word of God of none effect through your tradition" (Mark 7:13). The statement "We believe it would be unsafe" is lighter than chaff when weighed against the authority of Holy Writ. If God's servants today are not to be regulated by the recorded examples of their Master and His apostles, where shall they turn for guidance?

And why do the framers of these Articles of Faith consider it "unsafe" to follow the precedents furnished by the Gospels and the Acts? Their next Article supplies the answer:

Therefore, that for ministers in the present day to address unconverted persons, or indiscriminately all in a mixed congregation, calling upon them to savingly repent, believe, and receive Christ, or perform any other acts dependent upon the new-creative power of the Holy Ghost, is, on the one hand, to imply creature power, and, on the other, to deny the doctrine of special redemption.

Here they come out into the open and show their true colors, as mere rationalizers. They object to indiscriminate exhortations because they cannot see the consistency of such a policy with other doctrines. Just as extreme Arminians reject the truth of fallen man's moral impotence because they are unable to reconcile it with the exhortation principle, so Antinomians throw overboard human responsibility because they consider it out of harmony with the spiritual helplessness of the sinner.

Witness the consistency of man. As God Himself tells us, "Verily, every man at his best estate is altogether vanity" (Ps. 39:5). No wonder, then, that He bids us "Cease ye from man, whose breath is in his nostrils: for wherein is he to be accounted of?" (Isa. 2:22). Yes, "Cease ye from man"—religious man as much as irreligious man; cease placing any confidence in or dependence on him, especially in connection with spiritual and divine matters, for we cannot afford to be misdirected in these. Then what should the bewildered reader do? He must weigh everything he hears or reads in the balances of the Lord, testing it diligently by Holy Writ: "Prove all things; hold fast that which is good" (1 Thess. 5:21). And what is the servant of Christ to do? He must execute the commission his Master has given him, declare all the counsel of God (not mangled bits of it), and leave the Lord to harmonize what may seem contradictory to him—just as Abraham proceeded to obediently sacrifice Isaac, even though he was quite incapable of harmonizing God's command with His promise "In Isaac shall thy seed be called" (Gen. 21:12).

It will be no surprise to most of our readers that those ministers who are restricted from calling on the unsaved to repent and believe the gospel are also very slack in exhorting professing Christians. The divine commandments are almost entirely absent from their ministry. They preach a lot on doctrine, often on experience, but life conduct receives the scantiest notice. It is not too much to say that they seem to be afraid of the very word "duty." They preach soundly and beneficially on the obedience which Christ gave to God on behalf of His people, but they say next to nothing of that obedience which the Lord requires from those He has redeemed. They give many comforting addresses from God's promises, but they are woefully remiss in delivering searching messages on His precepts. If anyone thinks this charge is unfair, let him pick up a volume of sermons by any of these men and see if he can find a single sermon on one of the precepts.

As an example of what we have just mentioned we quote at some length from a series of "Meditations on the Preceptive part of the Word of God" by J. C. Philpot. Note that these were not the casual and careless utterances of the pulpit, but the deliberate and studied products of his pen. In his first article on the precepts of the Word of God, Mr. Philpot said:

It is a branch of Divine revelation which, without wishing to speak harshly or censoriously, has in our judgment been sadly perverted by many on the one hand, and we must say almost as sadly neglected, if not altogether ignored and passed by, by many on the other. . . . It is almost become a tradition in some churches professing the doctrines of grace to disregard the precepts and pass them by in a kind of general silence.

This declaration was sadly true, for the charge preferred characterized the greater part of his own ministry and applied to the preachers in his own denomination. That Mr. Philpot was fully aware of this sad state of affairs is clear from the following:

Consider this point, ye ministers, who Lord's day after Lord's day preach nothing but doctrine, doctrine, doctrine; and ask yourselves whether the same Holy Spirit who revealed the first three chapters of the epistle to the Ephesians did not also reveal the last three? Is not the whole epistle equally inspired, a part of that Scripture of which we read, "All Scripture is given by inspiration of God and is profitable for doctrine, for reproof, for correction, for instruction in righteousness, that the man of God may be perfect, thoroughly furnished unto all good works" (2 Tim. 3:16, 17)? How, then, can you be "a man of God perfect" (that is, complete as a minister) and "thoroughly furnished unto all good works," if you willfully neglect any part of that Scripture which God has given to be profitable to you, and to others by you? . . . Can it be right, can it be safe, can it be Scriptural, to treat all this fullness and weight of precept with no more attention than an obsolete Act of Parliament?

To the same effect, he declared:

To despise, then, the precept, to call it legal and burdensome, is to despise not man, but God, who hath given unto us His Holy Spirit in the inspired Scriptures for our faith and obedience. .

. . Nothing more detects hypocrites, purges out loose professors, and fans away that chaff and dust which now so thickly covers our barn floors than an experimental handling of the precept. A dry doctrinal ministry disturbs no consciences. The loosest professors may sit under it, nay, be highly delighted with it, for it gives them a hope, if not a dead confidence, that salvation being wholly of grace they shall be saved whatever be their walk of life. But the experimental handling of the precept cuts down all this and exposes their hypocrisy and deception.

In developing his theme Mr. Philpot rightly began by discussing its importance, and this at considerable length. First, he called attention to its "bulk," or the large place given to precepts in the Word:

The amount of precept in the epistles, measured only by the test of quantity would surprise a person whose attention had not been directed to that point, if he would but carefully examine it. But it is sad to see how little the Scriptures are read amongst us with that intelligent attention, that careful and prayerful studiousness, that earnest desire to understand, believe, and experimentally realize their Divine meaning, which they demand and deserve, and which the Word of God compares to seeking as for silver, and searching "as for hid treasure" (Prov. 2:4).

How much less are the Scriptures read today than they were in Mr. Philpot's time!

Next, he pointed out the following:

Were there no precepts in the New Testament we should be without an inspired rule of life, without an authoritative guide for our walk and conduct before the Church and the world. . . . But mark what would be the consequence if the preceptive part of the New Testament were taken out of its pages as so much useless matter. It would be like going on board of a ship bound on a long and perilous voyage, and taking out of her just before she sailed, all her charts, her compass, her sextants, her sounding line, her chronometer; in a word, all the instruments of navigation needful for her safely crossing the sea, or even leaving her port.

He disposed of the quibble that if there were no precepts, the church would still have the Holy Ghost to guide her by saying, "If God has mercifully and graciously given us rules and directions whereby to walk, let us thankfully accept them, not question and cavil how far we could have done without them."

Under his third reason for showing the importance of the precepts are some weighty remarks from which we select the following:

Without a special revelation of the precepts in the word of truth we should not know what was the will of God as regards all spiritual and practical obedience, so, without it as our guide and rule, we should not be able to live to His glory. . . . Be it, then, observed, and ever borne in mind that, as the glory of God is the end of all our obedience, it must be an obedience according to His own prescribed rule and pattern. In this point lies all the distinction between the obedience of a Christian to the glory of God and the self-imposed obedience of a Pharisee to the glory of self. . . . Thus we see that if there were no precepts as our guiding rule, we could not live to the glory of God, or yield to Him an acceptable obedience; and for this simple reason, that we should not know how to do so. We might wish to do so; we might attempt to do so; but we should and must fail.

This section on the importance of the precepts was denied by pointing out: "On its fulfillment turns the main test of distinction between the believer and the unbeliever, between the manifested vessel of mercy and the vessel of wrath fitted to destruction." At the close of this division he said, "Take one more test from the Lord's own lips. Read the solemn conclusion of the Sermon on the Mount—that grand code of Christian precepts."

After quoting Matthew 7:24-27 Mr. Philpot asks:

What is the Lord's own test of distinction between the wise man who builds on the rock, and the foolish man who builds on the sand? The rock, of course, is Christ, as the sand is self. But the test, the mark, the evidence, the proof of the two builders and the two buildings is the hearing of Christ's sayings and doing them, or the hearing of Christ's sayings and doing them not. We may twist and wriggle under such a text, and try all manner of explanations to parry off its keen, cutting edge; we may fly to arguments and deductions drawn from the doctrine of grace to shelter ourselves from its heavy stroke, and seek to prove that the Lord was there preaching the law and not the gospel, and that as we are saved by Christ's blood and righteousness, and not by our own obedience or our good works, either before or after calling, all such tests and all such texts are inapplicable to our state as believers. But after all our questionings and cavillings, our nice and subtle arguments, to quiet conscience and patch up a false peace, there the word of the Lord stands.

It is disastrous that such cogent arguments have carried little weight and that the precepts are still sadly neglected by many of the Lord's servants.

Chapter 7
Complement

Let us begin by defining our term. The "complement" of a thing is that which gives it completeness. In contemplating the natural condition of Adam's children we obtain a one-sided and misleading view if we confine our attention to their spiritual helplessness. That they are morally impotent, that they are totally depraved, that they are thoroughly under the bondage of sin, has been amply demonstrated. But that does not supply us with a complete diagnosis of their present state before God. Though fallen man is a wrecked and ruined creature, nevertheless he is still accountable to his Maker and Ruler. Though sin has darkened his understanding and blinded his judgment, he is still a rational being. Though his very nature is corrupt at its root, this does not exempt him from loving God with all his heart. Though he is "without strength," yet he is not "without excuse." And why not? Because side by side with fallen man's inability is his moral responsibility.

Moral Responsibility of Man

It is at this very point that the people of God, and especially His ministers, need to be much on their guard. If they appropriate one of the essential parts of the doctrine of Scripture but fail to lay hold of the equally essential supplementary part, then they will necessarily obtain a distorted view of the doctrine. "The word of God is quick, and powerful, and sharper than any two-edged sword" (Heb. 4:12). The word emphasized in the above quotation is of paramount importance, though its significance seems to be discerned by few today. Truth is twofold. Every aspect of truth presented in the Word is balanced by a counterpart aspect; every element of doctrine has its corresponding obligation. These two sides of the truth do not cross each other, but run parallel. They are not contradictory but complementary. The one aspect is just as essential as the other, and both must be retained if we are to be preserved from dangerous error. It is only as we hold firmly to "all the counsel of God" that we are delivered from the fatal pitfalls of false theology.

God Himself has illustrated this duality of truth by communicating the same concept to us in the form of the two Testaments, the Old and the New, the contents of which, broadly speaking, exemplify those two summaries of His nature and character: "God is light" (1 John 1:5); "God is love" (1 John 4:8). This same fundamental feature is seen again in the two principal communications which God has made, namely, His law and His gospel. That which characterizes the divine revelation in its broad outlines also holds equally good in connection with its details. Promises are balanced by precepts, the gifts of grace with the requirements of righteousness, the bestowments of abounding mercy with the exactions of inflexible justice. Correspondingly, the duties placed upon us answer to this twofold revelation of the divine character and will; as light and the Giver of the law, God requires the sinner to repent and the saint to fear Him; as love and the Giver of the gospel, the one is called upon to believe and the other to rejoice.

The doctrine of man's accountability and responsibility to God is set forth so plainly, so fully and so constantly throughout the Scriptures that he who runs may read it, and only those who deliberately close their eyes to it can fail to perceive its verity and force. The entire volume of God's Word testifies to the fact that He requires from man right affections and right actions, and that He judges and treats him according to these. "So then every one of us shall give account of himself to God" (Rom. 14:12) that the rights of God may be enforced upon moral agents. In the day of the revelation of His righteous judgment, God "will render to every man according to his deeds" (Rom. 2:5-6). Then will be fulfilled that word of Christ's "He that rejecteth me, and receiveth not my words, hath one that judgeth him: the word that I have spoken, the same shall judge him in the last day" (John 12:48). Men are responsible to employ in God's service the faculties He has given them (Matt. 25:14-30; Luke 12:48). They are responsible to improve the opportunities God has afforded them (Matt. 11:20-24; Luke 19:41-42).

Thus it is clear that—in keeping with the Word of God as a whole and with all His ways both in creation and providence—the doctrine of man's inability has a complementary and balancing doctrine, namely, his responsibility; and it is only by maintaining both in their due proportions that we shall be preserved from distorting the truth. But man is a creature of extremes, and his tendency to lopsidedness is tragically evidenced all through Christendom. The religious world is divided into opposing parties which contend for bits of the truth and reject others. Where can be found a denomination which preserves a due balance in its proclamation of God's law and God's gospel? In the presentation of God as light and God as love? In an equal emphasis on His precepts and His promises? And where shall we find a group of churches, or even a single church, which is preserving a due proportion in its preaching on man's inability and man's responsibility?

On every side today men in the pulpits pit one part of the truth against another, overstressing one doctrine and omitting its complement, setting those things against each other which God has joined together, confounding what He has separated. So important is it that God's servants should preserve the balance of truth, so disastrous are the consequences of a one-sided ministry, that we feel impressed to point out some of the more essential balancing doctrines which must be preserved if God is to be duly honored and His people rightly edified. We shall later resume the subject of human responsibility in order to throw light on the problem raised by the doctrine of man's impotence.

Means of Salvation

First, let us consider the causes and the means of salvation. There are no less than seven things which do concur in this great work, for all of them are said, in one passage or another, to "save" us. Salvation is ascribed to the love of God, to the atonement of Christ, to the mighty operations of the Spirit, to the instrumentality of the Word, to the labors of the preacher, to the conversion of a sinner, to the ordinances, or sacraments. The view of salvation entertained today by the majority of professing Christians is so superficial, so cramped, so inadequate. Indeed, so great is the ignorance which now prevails that we had better furnish proof texts for each of these seven concurring causes lest we be charged with error on so vital a subject.

Salvation is ascribed to God the Father "Who hath saved us, and called us with an holy calling" (2 Tim. 1:9)—because of His electing love in Christ. To the Lord Jesus: "He shall save his people from their sins" (Matt. 1:21)— because of His merits and satisfaction. To the Holy Spirit: "He hath saved us, by the renewing of the Holy Spirit" (Titus 3:5)—because of His almighty efficacy and operations. To the instrumentality of the Word, "the engrafted word, which is able to save your souls" (Jam. 1:21) —because it discovers to us the grace whereby we may be saved. To the labors of the preacher: "In doing this thou shalt both save thyself, and them that hear thee" (1 Tim. 4:16)—because of their subordination to God's work. To the conversion of a sinner in which repentance and faith are exercised by us: "Save yourselves from this untoward generation"—by the repentance spoken of in verse 38 (Acts 2:40); "By grace are ye saved through faith" (Eph. 2:8). To the ordinances, or sacraments: "Baptism doth also now save us" (1 Peter 3:21)— because it seals the grace of God to the believing heart.

Now these seven things must be considered in their order and kept in their place, otherwise incalculable harm will be done. For instance, if we elevate a subsidiary cause above a primary one, all sense of real proportion is lost. The love and wisdom of God comprise the prime cause, the first mover of all the rest of the causes which contribute to our salvation. Next are the merit and satisfaction of Christ, which are the result of the eternal wisdom and love of God and also the foundation of all that follows. The omnipotent operations of the Holy Spirit work in the elect those things which are necessary for their participation in and application of the benefits purposed by God and purchased by Christ. The Word is the chief means employed in conversion, for faith comes by hearing (Rom. 10:17). As the result of the Spirit's operations and His application of the Word, we are brought to repent and believe. In this it is the Spirit's general custom to employ the ministers of Christ as His subordinate agents. Baptism and the Lord's Supper are to confirm repentance and faith in us.

Not only must these seven concurring causes of salvation be considered in their proper order and kept in their due place, but they must not be confounded with one another so that we attribute to a later one what belongs to a primary one. We must not attribute to the ordinances that which belongs to the Word; the Word is appointed for conversion, the ordinances for confirmation. A legal contract is first offered and then sealed (ratified) when the parties are agreed: "Then they that [1] gladly received his word were [2] baptized" (Acts 2:41). Nor must we ascribe to the ordinances that which belongs to conversion. Many depend on their outward hearing of the Word as ground for partaking of the Lord's Supper: "We have eaten and drunk in thy presence, and thou hast taught in our streets" (Luke 13:26). But sound conversion, not frequenting the means of grace, is our title to pardon and life: "Be ye doers of the word, and not hearers only" (Jam. 1:22).

Again, we must not ascribe to conversion what belongs to the Spirit. Our repentance and faith are indispensable for the enjoyment of the privileges of Christianity, yet these graces do not spring from mere nature but are wrought in us by the Holy Spirit. Nor must we ascribe to the Spirit that honor which belongs to Christ, as if our conversion were meritorious, or that the repentance and faith worked in us deserved the benefits we have come to possess. No, that honor pertains to the Lamb alone, who merited and purchased all for us. Neither must we ascribe to Christ that which belongs to the Father, for the Mediator came not to take us away from God, but to bring us to Him: "Thou . . . hast redeemed us to God" (Rev. 5:9). Thus all things pertaining to our salvation must be ranged in their proper place, and we must consider what is peculiar to the love of God, the merit of Christ, the operations of the Spirit, the instrumentality of the Word, the labors of the preacher, the conversion of a sinner, the ordinances.

Unless we observe the true order of these causes and rightly predicate what pertains to each, we fall into disastrous mistakes and fatal errors. If we ascribe all to the mercy of God so as to shut out the merit of Christ, we exclude God's great design in the cross—to demonstrate His righteousness (Rom. 3:24-26). On the other hand, if we proclaim the atonement of Christ in a manner that lessens esteem of God's love, we are apt to form the false idea that He is all wrath and needed blood to appease Him; whereas Christ came to demonstrate His goodness (2 Cor. 5:19). If we ascribe to the merits of Christ that which is proper to the work of the Spirit, we confound things that are to be distinguished, as if Christ's blood could take us to heaven without a new nature being wrought in us. If we ascribe our conversion to the exercise of our own strength, we wrong the Holy Spirit. If, upon pretended conversion, we neglect the means and produce no good works, we err fatally.

Not only must these seven things not be confounded, but they must not be separated from one another. We cannot rest on the grace of God without the atonement and merits of Christ, for God does not exercise His mercy to the detriment of His justice. Nor can we rightly take comfort in the sacrifice of Christ without regeneration and true conversion wrought in us by the Spirit, for we must be vitally united to Christ before we can receive His benefits. Nor must we expect the operations of the Spirit without the instrumentality of the Word, for of the church it is said that Christ (by the Spirit) would "sanctify and cleanse it with the washing of water by the word" (Eph. 5:26). Nor must we conclude that we are regenerated by the Spirit without repentance and faith, for these graces are evidences of the new birth. Nor must the ordinances of baptism and the Lord's Supper be slighted; otherwise we dislocate the method by which God dispenses His grace.

Second, Christ must not be divided, either in His natures or His offices. There may be an abuse of the orthodox assertion of His deity, for if we reflect exclusively on that and neglect His great condescension in becoming flesh, we miss the chief intent of His incarnation—to bring God near to us in our nature. On the other hand, if we altogether consider Christ's humanity and overlook His Godhead, we are in danger of denying His super-eminent dignity, power and merit. Man is always disturbing the harmony of the gospel and setting one part against another. Unitarians deny that Christ is God and so impeach His atonement, pressing only His doctrine and example. Carnal men reflect only on Christ's redemption as the means of our atonement with God, and so overlook the necessary doctrine of His example, of Christ's appearing in order to be a pattern of obedience in our nature—so often pressed in Scripture (John 13:15; 1 Pet. 2:21; 1 John 2:6). Let us not put asunder what God has joined together.

So with Christ's offices. His general office is but one, to be Mediator, or Redeemer, but the functions which belong to it are three: prophetic, priestly and royal, one of which concerns His mediation with God, the other His dealings with us. We are to reflect on Him in both parts: "Consider the Apostle and High Priest of our profession, Christ Jesus" (Heb. 3:1). The work of an apostle has to do with men, that of a high priest with God. But some are so occupied with Christ's mediation with God that they give little thought to His dealings with men; others so consider His relation to men that they overlook His mediation with God. Regarding His very priesthood, some are so concerned with His sacrifice that they ignore His continual intercession and thus fail to appreciate what a comfort it is to present our requests by such a worthy hand to God; yet both are acts of the same office.

Great harm has been done by so preaching the sacrifice and intercession of Christ that His doctrine and government have been made light of. This is one of the most serious defects today in a considerable section of Christendom which prides itself on its orthodoxy. They look so much to the Savior that they have scarcely any eyes for the Teacher and Master. The whole religion of many professing Christians consists in depending on Christ's merits and trusting in His blood, without any real concern for His laws, by believing and obeying of which we are interested in the fruits of His righteousness and sacrifice. But the Word of God sets before us an entirely different sort of religion and does not make one office of the Redeemer disturb another. None find true rest for their souls until they take Christ's yoke upon them. He is the Savior of none unless He is first their Lord.

The Scriptures of truth set forth Christ under such terms as not only intimate privilege to us, but speak of duty and obedience as well. "God hath made that same Jesus . . . both Lord and Christ" (Acts 2:36). He is Lord, or supreme Governor, as well as Christ the anointed Savior; not only a Savior to redeem and bless, but a Lord to rule and command. "Him hath God exalted . . . to be a Prince and a Savior, for to give repentance to Israel, and forgiveness of sins" (Acts 5:31). Here again the compound terms occur because of His double work—to require and to give. Christ is such a Prince that He is also a Savior, and such a Savior that He is also a Prince; and as such He must be apprehended by our souls. Woe be to those who divide what God has joined. Also, "Christ is the head of the church: and he is the Savior of the body" (Eph. 5:23). On the one side, as Christ saves His people from their sins, so He also governs them; on the other side, His dominion over the church is exercised in bringing about its salvation.

The carnal segment of the religious world snatches greedily at comforts but has no heart for duties; it is all for privileges but wants nothing of obligations. This libertine spirit is very natural to all of us: "Let us break their bands asunder, and cast away their cords from us" (Ps. 2:3). It was thus with men when Christ was in their midst: "We will not have this man to reign over us" (Luke 19:14). Had He presented Himself to them simply as Redeemer He would have been welcome, but they had no desire for a Sovereign over them. Christ is wanted for His benefits, such as pardon, eternal life and everlasting glory; but the unregenerate cannot endure His strict doctrine and righteous laws—submission to His scepter is foreign to their nature.

On the other hand there are some who so extol the mediation of Christ with men that they ignore His mediation with God. Some are so absorbed with the letter of His doctrine that they overlook the necessity of the Holy Spirit to interpret it for them and apply it to their hearts. Men are such extremists that they cannot magnify one thing without deprecating another. They rejoice in the Spirit's communicating the Scriptures, but they deprecate His equally important work of opening hearts to receive them (Acts 16:14). Others so urge Christ as Lawgiver that they neglect Him as the fountain of grace. They are all for His doctrine and example, but despise His atonement and continued intercession. It is this taking of the gospel piecemeal instead of whole which has wrought such damage and corrupted the truth. Oh, for heavenly wisdom and grace to preserve the balance and to preach a full gospel.

We have pointed out that side by side with the fact of fallen man's spiritual impotence must be considered the complementary truth of his moral responsibility. We have sought to show the vital importance of holding fast to both and presenting them in their due proportions, thereby preserving the balance between them. In order to make this the more obvious and impressive, and at the same time to demonstrate the disastrous consequences of failing to do this, we have enlarged on the general principle of maintaining the gospel in its fullness instead of taking it piecemeal. We have endeavored to enforce the necessity for adhering to what God has joined together and of not confounding what He has separated, illustrating the point by a presentation of the seven concurring causes of salvation and of the natures and offices of Christ. We now resume that line of thought.

Third, the order of the covenant must not be disturbed. Said David of the Lord, "He hath made with me an everlasting covenant, ordered in all things, and sure" (2 Sam. 23:5). Certain writers have expressed themselves quite freely on the everlastingness of this covenant, and also on its sureness; but they have said very little on the ordering of it, and still less on the necessity of our abiding by its arrangements. No one will have any part in this covenant unless he is prepared to take the whole compact. Within the contract God has so arranged things that they may not and do not hinder one another. This order of the covenant appears chiefly in the right statement of privileges and conditions, means and ends, duties and comforts.

1. Privileges and conditions. "Through this man is preached unto you the forgiveness of sins: and by him all that believe are justified from all things" (Acts 13:38-39). Do not those words state a condition which excludes the infidel and includes the penitent believer? "If I wash thee not, thou hast no part with me," declared the holy Savior (John 13:8). Unless we are cleansed by Him we can have no part with Him in His benefits. "He became the author of the eternal salvation unto all them that obey him" (Heb. 5:9). Christ would act contrary to His divine commission, contrary to the covenant agreed upon by Him, were He to dispense His grace upon any other terms. Some men trust in their own external and imperfect righteousness, as if that were the only plea to make before God; whereas others look at nothing in themselves—either as conditions,

evidence or means-and think their only plea is Christ's merits.

But neither those who trust in their own works nor those who think that no consideration is to be had for repentance, faith and new obedience adhere to the covenant of grace. Those who preach such a course offer men a covenant of their own modeling, not the covenant of God which is the sole charter and sure ground of the Christian's hope. The blood of Christ accomplishes its work, but repentance and faith must also do theirs. True, they have not the least degree of that honor which belongs to the love of God, the sacrifice of Christ or the operations of the Spirit; nevertheless repentance, faith and new obedience must be kept in view in their place. Is it not self-evident that none of the privileges of the covenant belong to the impenitent and unbelieving? It is the Father's work to love us, Christ's to redeem, and the Spirit's to regenerate; but we must accept the grace offered—that is, repent, believe and live in obedience to God.

2. Means and ends. There is a right order of means and ends, that by the former we may come to the latter. The greater end of Christianity is our coming to God, and the prime and general means are the office and work of Christ: "For Christ hath also once suffered for sins, the just for the unjust, that he might bring us to God" (1 Pet. 3:18). The subordinate means are the fruits of Christ's grace in sanctifying us and enabling us to overcome temptations—more expressly by patient suffering and active obedience. By patient suffering: "If so be that we suffer with him, that we may be also glorified together" (Rom. 8:17). "Wherefore let them that suffer according to the will of God commit the keeping of their souls to him in well doing, as unto a faithful Creator" (1 Pet. 4:19). By obedience: "Know ye not, that to whom ye yield yourselves servants to obey, his servants ye are to whom ye obey; whether of sin unto death, or of obedience unto righteousness?" (Rom. 6:16). "He that saith, I know him, and keepeth not his commandments, is a liar, and the truth is not in him" (1 John 2:4).

Now the great difficulty in connection with our salvation (1 Pet. 4:18) lies not in a respect to the end but the means. There is some difficulty about the end, namely, to convince men of an unseen bliss and glory; but there is far more about the means. There is not only greater difficulty in convincing their minds, but in gaining their hearts and bringing them to submit to that patient, holy, self-denying course whereby they may obtain eternal life. Men wish the end, but refuse the means. Like Balaam (Num. 23:10) they want to die the death of the righteous, but are unwilling to live the life of the righteous. When the Israelites despised the land of Canaan (Ps. 106:24-25) it was because of the difficulty of getting to it. They were assured that Canaan was a land flowing with milk and honey, but when they learned there were giants to be overcome first, walled towns to be scaled and numerous inhabitants to be vanquished, they demurred. Heaven is a glorious place, but it can only be reached by the way of denying self; and this few are willing to do. But the covenant expressly urges this upon us (Matt. 16:24; Luke 14:26).

3. Duties and comforts. Also there is a right order of duties and comforts. "Come unto me, all ye that labour and are heavy laden, and I will give you rest. Take my yoke upon you, and learn of me; for I am meek and lowly in heart: and ye shall find rest unto your souls" (Matt. 11:28-29). Observe carefully how commands and comforts, precepts and promises are here interwoven, and let us not separate what God has joined together. We must diligently attend to both in our desires and practices alike. We must not pick and choose what suits us best and pass by the rest, but earnestly seek after God and diligently use all His appointed means that He may "fulfill all the good pleasure of his goodness, and the work of faith with power" (2 Thess. 1:11). But of how many must God say, as He did of old, "Ephraim is as a heifer that is taught and loveth to tread out the corn, but will not break the clods" (Hosea 10:11, an ancient translation). People desire privileges but neglect duties; they are all for wages but reluctant to work for them.

So it is even in the performance of duties: some are welcomed and done, others are disliked and shirked. But every duty must be observed in its place and season, and one must never be set against another. In resisting sin some avoid sensuality but yield to worldliness, deny fleshly lusts but fall into deadly errors. So with graces: Christians look so much to one that they forget the others. We are told to take unto ourselves "the whole armor of God" (Eph. 6:11), not simply a breastplate without a helmet. We must not play up knowledge so as to neglect practice, nor fervor of devotion so as to mislead us into ignorance and blind superstition. Some set their whole hearts to mourn for sin and think little of striving after a sense of their Savior's love; others prattle of free grace but are not watchful against sin nor diligent in being fruitful.

Lest some imagine that we have departed from the landmarks of our fathers and have inculcated a spirit of legality, we propose to supply a number of quotations from the writings of some of the most eminent of God's servants in the past, men who in their day lifted up their voices in protest against the lopsided ministry which we are decrying, and who stressed the vital importance of preserving the balance of truth and of according to each segment its due place and emphasis. For the evil we are resisting is no new thing, but one that has wrought much havoc in every generation. The pendulum has ever swung from one extreme to the other, and few have been the men who preserved the happy mean or who faithfully declared all the counsel of God.

We begin with a portion of Bishop J. C. Ryle's Estimate of Manton, the Puritan:

Manton held strongly the need of preventing and calling grace; but that did not hinder him from inviting all men to repent, believe, and be saved. Manton held strongly that faith alone lays hold on Christ and appropriates justification; but that did not prevent him urging upon all the absolute necessity of repentance and turning from sin. Manton held strongly to the perseverance of God's elect; but that did not hinder him from teaching that holiness is the grand distinguishing mark of God's people, and that he who talks of "never perishing" while he continues in willful sin, is a hypocrite and a self-deceiver. In all this I frankly confess I see much to admire. I admire the Scriptural wisdom of a man who, in a day of hard and fast systems, could dare to be apparently inconsistent in order to "declare all the counsel of God." I firmly believe that this is the test of theology which does good in the church of Christ. The man who is not tied hand and foot by systems, and does not pretend to reconcile what our imperfect eyesight cannot reconcile in this dispensation, he is the man whom God will bless.

If Manton were on earth today we do not know where he would be able to obtain a hearing. One class would denounce him as a Calvinist, while another would shun him as an Arminian. One would accuse him of turning the grace of God into lasciviousness, while another would charge him with gross legality. All would say he was not consistent with himself, that one of his sermons contradicted another; that he was a "yea and nay preacher," one day building up and the next day tearing down what he had previously erected. So long as he confined himself to what their Articles of Faith expressed, Calvinists would allow him to address them; but as soon as he began to press duties upon them and exhort to performance of those duties, he would be banished from their pulpits. Arminians would tolerate him just so long as he kept to the human responsibility side of the truth, but the moment he mentioned unconditional election or particular redemption they would close their doors against him.

That prince of theologians, John Owen, in his work "The Causes, Ways, and Means of Understanding the Mind of God," after fully establishing "the necessity of an especial work of the Holy Spirit in the illumination of our minds to make us understand the mind of God as revealed in the Scriptures," and before treating of the means which must be used and the diligent labors put forth by us, began his fourth chapter by anticipating and disposing of an objection. A certain class of extremists (termed enthusiasts in those days) argued that, if our understanding of the Scriptures was dependent upon the illuminating operations of the Holy Spirit, then there was no need for earnest effort and laborious study on our part. After affirming that the gracious operations of the Spirit "do render all our use of proper means for the right interpretation of the Scripture, in a way of duty, indispensably necessary," Mr. Owen went on to point out:

But thus it hath fallen out in other things. Those who have declared anything either of doctrine or of the power of the grace of the Gospel, have been traduced as opposing the principles of morality and reason, whereas on their grounds alone, their true value can be discovered and their proper use directed. So the apostle preaching faith in Christ with righteousness and justification thereby, was accused to have made void the law, whereas without his doctrine the law would have been void, or of no use to the souls of men. So he pleads "Do we then make void the law through faith? God forbid: yea, we establish the law" (Rom. 3:31). So to this day, justification by the imputation of the righteousness of Christ and the necessity of our own obedience, the efficacy of Divine grace in conversion and the liberty of our wills, the stability of God's promises and our diligent use of means, are supposed inconsistent.

It will be seen from the closing sentences of the above quotation that there were some in the days of the Puritans who made a god of consistency, or rather of what they considered to be consistent, and that they pitted parts of the truth against their own favorite doctrines, rejecting anything which they considered to be inharmonious or incongruous. But Owen refused to accede to them and preferred to be regarded as inconsistent with himself rather than withhold those aspects of the gospel which he well knew were equally glorifying to God and profitable for His people. It is striking to note that the particular things singled out by him for mention are the very ones objected to by the hyper-Calvinists today, which shows how far astray they are from what Owen taught. We continue to quote from him:

So it is here also. The necessity of the communication of spiritual light unto our minds to enable us to understand the Scriptures, and the exercise of our own reason in the use of external means, are looked on as irreconcilable. But as the apostle saith, "Do we make void the law by faith? yea, we establish it;" though he did it not in that place, nor unto those ends that the Jews would have had and used it. So we may say, do we by asserting the righteousness of Christ make void our own obedience, by the efficacy of grace destroy the liberty of our wills, by the necessity of spiritual illumination take away the use of reason? yea, we establish them. We do it not, it may be, in such a way or in such a manner as some would fancy and which would render them all on our part really useless, but in a clear consistency with and proper subservience unto the work of God's Spirit and grace.

"The people answered him, We have heard out of the law that Christ abideth for ever: and how sayest thou, The Son of man must be lifted up?" (John 12:34). In his comments upon this verse, that grand old commentator Matthew Henry said:

They alleged those scriptures of the O.T. which speak of the perpetuity of the Messiah, that He should be so far from being cut off in the midst of His days, that He should be a "Priest forever" (Psa. 110:4) and a King "forever" (Psa. 89:29, etc.). That He should have length of days forever and ever, and His years "as many generations" (Psa. 61:6); from all this they inferred the Messiah should not die. Thus great knowledge in the letter of the Scripture, if the heart be unsanctified, is capable of being abused to serve the cause of infidelity and to fight Christianity with its own weapons. Their perverseness will appear if we consider that when they vouched the Scripture to prove that the Messiah "abideth forever," they took no notice of those texts which speak of the Messiah's death and sufferings: they had heard out of the law that He "abideth forever," but had they never heard out of the law that Messiah "shall be cut off" (Dan. 9:26), that He shall "pour out His soul unto death" (Isa. 53:12), and particularly that His "hands and feet" should be pierced? Why then do they make so strange of His being "lifted up?"

The folly of these skeptical Jews was not one whit greater than that of rationalistic Calvinists. The one group refused to believe one part of Messianic prophecy because they were unable to harmonize it with another; the latter reject the truth of human responsibility because they cannot perceive its consistency with the doctrine of fallen man's spiritual impotence. Aptly did Matthew Henry follow up the above remarks by immediately adding:

We often run into great mistakes, and then defend them with Scripture arguments, by putting those things asunder which God in His Word has put together, and opposing one truth under the pretence of supporting another. We have heard out of the Gospel that which exalts free grace, we have heard also that which enjoins duty, and we must cordially embrace both, and not separate them, or set them at variance.

Divine grace is not bestowed with the object of freeing men from their obligations but rather with that of supplying them with a powerful motive for more readily and gratefully discharging those obligations. To make God's favor a ground of exemption from the performance of duty comes perilously near to turning His grace into lasciviousness.

In his "Precious Remedies Against Satan's Devices," Thomas Brooks wrote:

The fourth device Satan hath to keep souls off from holy exercises, is by working them to make false inferences on those blessed and glorious things that Christ hath done. As that Jesus Christ hath done all for us, therefore there is nothing for us to do but to joy and rejoice. He hath perfectly justified us, fulfilled the law, satisfied Divine justice, pacified His Father's wrath, and is gone to Heaven to prepare a place for us, and in the meantime to intercede for us; and therefore away with praying, mourning, hearing, etc. Ah! what a world of professors hath Satan drawn in these days from religious services by working them to make such sad, wild and strange inferences from the excellent things the Lord Jesus hath done for His beloved ones.

The Puritan named one remedy for this:

To dwell as much on those scriptures that show you the duties and services that Christ requires of you, as upon those scriptures that declare to you the precious and glorious things Christ hath done for you. It is a sad and dangerous thing to have two eyes to behold our dignity and privileges, and not one to see our duties and services. I should look with one eye upon the choice things Christ hath done for me to raise up my heart to love Christ with the purest love and to joy in Him with the strongest joy, and to lift up Christ above all who hath made Himself to be my all; and I should look with the other eye upon those services and duties that the scriptures require of those for whom Christ hath done such blessed things, as 1 Cor. 6:19, 20; 15:58; Gal. 6:9; 1 Thess. 5:16, 17; Phil. 2:12; Heb. 10:24, 25. Now a soul that would not be drawn away by this device of Satan must not look with a squint eye upon these blessed scriptures, and many more of like import, but he must dwell upon them, make them to be his chiefest and choicest companions, and this will be a happy means to keep him close to Christ.

Our principal design in writing further on the fact that man's spiritual impotence is his moral responsibility is to make plainly manifest the tremendous importance of preserving the balance of truth, which is mainly a matter of setting forth each element of it in its scriptural proportions. Almost all theological and religious error consists of truth perverted, truth wrongly divided, truth misapplied, truth overemphasized, truth viewed in a wrong perspective. The fairest face on earth, possessed of the most comely features, would soon become ugly and unsightly if one feature continued growing while the others remained undeveloped. Physical beauty is mainly a thing of due proportion. And thus it is with the Word of God: Its beauty and blessedness are best perceived when it is presented in its true proportions. Here is where so many have failed in the past; some favorite doctrine has been concentrated on, and others of equal importance neglected.

Need for Balanced Teaching

It is freely granted that in these degenerate days the servant of God is often called upon to give special emphasis to those verities of Holy Writ which are now so generally ignored and denied. Yet even here much wisdom is needed lest our zeal run away with us. The requirements of that phrase meat in due season" must ever be borne in mind. When working among Arminians we should not altogether omit the human responsibility side of the truth, yet the main emphasis ought to be placed on the divine sovereignty and its corollaries, which are so sadly perverted, if not blankly denied, by free-willers. Contrariwise, when ministering to Calvinists our chief aim should be to bring before them not those things they most like to hear, but those which they most need—those aspects of truth they are least familiar with. Only thus can we be of the greatest service to either group.

To illustrate what we have just said, take the subject of prayer. In preaching on it to Arminians, it would be well to define very clearly what this holy exercise is not designed to accomplish and what is its spiritual aim, showing that our prayers are not intended for the overcoming of any reluctance in God to grant the mercies we need, still less our supplications meant to effect any change in the divine purpose. "The counsel of the Lord standeth forever, the thoughts of his heart to all generations" (Ps. 33:11). Rather the purpose of prayer is the subjecting of ourselves to God in asking for those things which are according to His will. In preaching to Calvinists we should warn against that fatalistic attitude which assumes that it will make no difference to the event whether we petition God or not, reminding them that "the effectual fervent prayer of a righteous man availeth much" (Jam.5:16). Some Arminians need rebuking for irreverence and unholy familiarity in addressing the Most High, while some Calvinists should be encouraged to approach the throne of grace with holy boldness, with the liberty of children petitioning their father.

The same course needs to be followed when expounding the great subject of salvation. Discrimination must be used as to which aspects most need to be set before any particular congregation. The manner in which this most blessed theme should be presented calls for much understanding, not only of the subject itself but also of the truth. Some doctrines are more difficult to apprehend than others (2 Peter 3:16), and they need to be approached gradually and given out "here a little, there a little." We are well aware that in offering such counsel we lay ourselves open to the charge of acting craftily; in reality we are simply advocating the very policy pursued by Christ and His apostles. Of the Savior it is recorded that "with many such parables spoke he the word unto them, as they were able to hear it" (Mark 4:33); and addressing His apostles He said, "I have yet many things to say unto you, but ye cannot bear them now" (John 16:12; cf. 1 Cor. 3:1-2; 9:19-22).

What we have advocated above is simply adopting our presentation of the truth according to the state of our congregation. There is a vast difference between presenting the way of salvation to the unconverted and expounding the doctrine of salvation to those who are converted, though too many preachers make little distinction here. Great care needs to be exercised when preaching from one of the Epistles to a general congregation, lest on the one hand the children's bread be cast to the dogs or, on the other, seekers after the Lord be stumbled. While it is true that, in the absolute sense, no sinner can save himself or even contribute anything toward his salvation by any physical or mental act of his own, yet he must be constantly reminded that the gospel sets before him an external Savior (rather than One who is working secretly and invincibly in him) whom he is responsible to promptly receive on the terms by which He is offered, to him.

It is most important that pulpit and pew alike should have a right conception of the relation of faith to salvation—a full-orbed conception and not a restricted and one-sided view. Believing is not only an evidence of salvation and a mark of regeneration, but it is also necessary in order to obtain salvation. True, the sinner is not saved for his faith; yet it is equally true that he cannot be saved without it. That believing is in one sense a saving act is clearly affirmed: "But we are not of them who draw back unto perdition; but of them that believe to the saving of the soul" (Heb. 10:39). Take the case of Cornelius. It is plain from Acts 10:2, 4 that a work of grace had been wrought in his heart before Peter was sent to him; yet Acts 11:14 makes it equally clear that it was necessary for the apostles to go and speak words "whereby he and his house should be saved." One of those "words" was "To him give all the prophets witness, that through his name whosoever believeth in him shall receive remission of sins" (10:43). Let it not be objected that we are hereby making a savior of faith, for Christ did not hesitate to say "Thy faith hath saved thee" (Luke 7:50).

As an example of how well Calvin himself preserved the balance of truth we quote the following from his Institutes:

Yet at the same time a pious man will not overlook inferior causes. Nor, because he accounts those from whom he has received any benefit, the ministers of the Divine goodness, will he therefore cast them by unnoticed, as though they deserved no thanks for their kindness; but will feel and readily acknowledge his obligation to them, and study to return it as ability and opportunity may permit. Finally, he will reverence and praise God as the principal Author of benefits received, will honor men as His ministers; and will understand, what, indeed, is the fact, that the will of God has laid him under obligations to those persons by whose means the Lord has been pleased to communicate His benefits.

While ascribing supreme honor and glory to the Author of every blessing, we must not despise the instruments He may design to employ in the imparting of them.

The great Reformer went on:

If He suffer any loss either through negligence or through imprudence, he will conclude that it happened according to the Divine will, but will also impute the blame of it to himself. If any one be removed by disease, whom, while it was his duty to take care of him, he has treated with neglect,—though he cannot be ignorant that that person had reached those limits which it was impossible for him to pass, yet he will not make this a plea to extenuate his guilt; but, because he has not faithfully performed his duty towards him, will consider him as having perished through his criminal negligence. Much less, when fraud and preconceived malice appear in the perpetration either of murder or of theft, will he excuse those enormities under the pretext of the Divine Providence: in the same crime he will distinctly contemplate the righteousness of God and the iniquity of man, as they respectively discover themselves.

How far was Calvin from the squint-eyed vision of many who claim to be his admirers! Writing on "the conducting of prayer in a right and proper manner," he stated:

The fourth and last rule is, That thus prostrate with true humility, we should nevertheless be animated to pray by the certain hope of obtaining our requests. It is indeed an apparent contradiction to connect a certain confidence of God's favor with a sense of His righteous vengeance, though these two things are perfectly consistent if persons oppressed by their own guilt be encouraged solely by the Divine goodness. For as we have before stated that repentance and faith, of which one terrifies and the other exhilarates, are inseparably connected, so their union is necessary in prayer. And this agreement is briefly expressed by David: "I will come into Thy house in the multitude of Thy mercy: and in Thy fear will I worship toward Thy holy temple" (Psa. 5:7). Under the goodness of God he comprehends faith, though not to the exclusion of fear, for His majesty not only commands our reverence, but our own unworthiness makes us forget all pride and security and fills us with fear. I do not mean a confidence which delivers the mind from all sense of anxiety, and soothes it into pleasant and perfect tranquility, for such a placid satisfaction belongs to those whose prosperity is equal to their wishes, who are affected by no care, corroded by no anxiety and alarmed by no fear. And the saints have an excellent stimulus to calling upon God when their needs and perplexities harass and disquiet them and they are almost despairing in themselves, till faith opportunity relieves them; because amid such troubles the goodness of God is so glorious in their view, that though they groan under the pressure of present calamities and are likewise tormented with the fear of greater in future, yet a reliance on it alleviates the difficulty of bearing them and encourages a hope of deliverance.

Here we have brought together two radically different exercises of the mind, which are totally diverse in their springs, their nature and their tendency—fear and confidence, perturbation and tranquility: two spiritual graces which some imagine neutralize each other—humility and assurance. A sight of God's ineffable holiness fills a renewed heart with awe; and when it is coupled with a sense of His high majesty and inflexible righteousness, the soul—conscious of its excuseless sins, its defilement and its guilt—is made to fear and tremble, feeling utterly unfit and unworthy to address the Most High. Yes, but if the humbled saint is able to also contemplate the goodness of God, view Him as the Father of mercies and consider some of His exceeding great and precious promises which are exactly suited to his dire needs, he is encouraged to hope. And while his humility does not then degenerate into presumption, yet is he constrained to come boldly to the throne of grace and present his petitions.

Calvin spoke clearly on this point:

The prayers of a pious man, therefore, must proceed from both these dispositions, and must also contain and discover them both: though he must groan under present evils and is anxiously afraid of new ones, yet at the same time he must resort for refuge to God, not doubting His readiness to extend the assistance of His hand. For God is highly displeased by our distrust, if we supplicate Him for blessings which we have no expectation of receiving. There is nothing, therefore, more suitable to the nature of prayers, than that they be conformed to this rule:—not to rush forward with temerity, but to follow the steps of faith. "If any of you lack wisdom, let him ask of God, that giveth to all men liberally, and upbraideth not. But let him ask in faith, nothing wavering" (Jam. 1:5, 6). Where, by opposing "faith" to "wavering" he very aptly expresses its nature. And equally worthy of attention is what he adds, that they avail nothing who call upon God in unbelief and doubt, and are uncertain in their minds whether they shall be heard or not.

The charge preferred by God against Israel's priests of old—"Ye have not kept my ways, but have been partial in the law" (Mal. 2:9)—applies to many preachers today. Some have gone to such extremes that they have denied there is any such thing as God chastising His own dear children. They argue that since "he hath not beheld iniquity in Jacob, neither hath he seen perverseness in Israel" (Num. 23:21), and since He has declared of His bride, "Thou art all fair, my love; there is no spot in thee" (Song of Sol. 4:7), there remains no occasion for the rod. It is this dwelling on favorite portions of truth to the exclusion of others which has led many into grievous errors. The non-imputation of sin to believers and the chastising of sin in believers are both plainly taught in the Scriptures (e.g., 2 Sam. 12:13-14 where both facts are mentioned side by side). Whether or not they can be reconciled to mere human reason, both must be firmly held by us.

As Matthew Henry tersely expressed it, "In the doctrine of Christ there are paradoxes which to men of corrupt mind are stumblingstones." It is the twofoldness of truth which has (in part) furnished occasion for infidels to declare that the Bible is full of contradictions; being blind spiritually, they are unable to perceive the perfect harmony of the whole. To what a sorry pass have things come, then, when some who wish to be regarded as the very champions of orthodoxy make the same charge against those who contend for the entire faith once delivered to the saints. The truth, the whole truth, and nothing but the truth, is the standard which must be applied to the pulpit as well as the lawcourt. One element of truth must not be pressed to such an extreme that another is denied; each must be given its due and distinctive place.

It is a favorite device of Satan's to drive us from one extreme to another. This may be seen by observing the order of the temptations which he set before the Savior. First he sought to over-throw Christ's faith, to bring Him to doubt the Word of God and His goodness to Him. He said something like this: "God has proclaimed from heaven that Thou art His beloved Son, yet He is allowing Thee to starve to death here in the wilderness," as is clear from his "If thou be the Son of God, command that these stones be made bread." Failing to prevail by such an assault, Satan then took a contrary course in his next attack, seeking to bring the Lord Jesus to act presump-tuously: "If thou be the Son of God, cast thyself down: for it is written, He shall give his angels charge concerning thee: and in their hands they shall bear thee up, lest at any time thou dash thy foot against a stone." The force of this was: "Since Thou art so fully assured of the Father's loving care, demonstrate Thy confidence in His protection; since Thy faith in His Word is so unshakable, count upon His promise that no harm shall befall Thee even though Thou castest Thyself from the pinnacle of the temple."

The above has been recorded for our learning, for it shows us the guile of the devil and the cunning tactics which he employs, especially that of swinging from one extreme to another. Let it be borne in mind that as he dealt there with Christ the Head, so Satan continues to act with all Christ's members. If he cannot bring them to one extreme, he will endeavor to drive them to another. If he cannot bring a man to covetousness and miserliness, he will attempt to drive him to prodigality and thriftlessness. If a man is of the sober and somber type, let him beware lest the devil, in condemning him for this, lead him into levity and irreverence. The devil cannot endure one who turns neither to the right hand nor to the left; nevertheless, we must seek to keep the golden mean, neither doubting on the one hand nor presuming on the other, giving way neither to despair nor to recklessness.

Let us not forget that truth itself may be misused (2 Pet. 3:16), and the very grace of God may be turned into lasciviousness (Jude 4). Solemn warnings are these. "Commit thy way unto the Loan; trust also in him; and he shall bring it to pass" (Ps. 37:5). That is a blessed promise, yet I altogether pervert it if I use it to the neglect of duty and sit down and do nothing. "Stand fast therefore in the liberty wherewith Christ hath made us free" (Gal. 5:1). That is an important precept, yet I put it to wrong use if I so stand up for my own rights that I exercise no love for my brothers in Christ. "Who are kept by the power of God through faith unto salvation ready to be revealed in the last time" (1 Pet. 1:5). That too is a blessed promise, yet it does not exempt me from using all proper means for my preservation. The Christian farmer knows that unless God is pleased to bless his labors he will reap no harvest, but that does not hinder him from plowing and harrowing.

Let us close these remarks by a helpful quotation from one who showed the perfect consis-tency between Romans 8:38-39 and 1 Corinthians 9:27: "But I keep under my body, and bring it into subjection: lest that by any means, when I have preached to others, I myself should be a castaway."

Charles Hodge stated:

The reckless and listless Corinthians thought they could safely indulge themselves to the very verge of sin; while this devoted apostle considered himself as engaged in a life-struggle for his salvation. The same apostle, however, who evidently acted on the principle that the righteous scarcely are saved and that the kingdom of heaven suffereth violence, at other times breaks out in the most joyous assurance of salvation, and says that he was persuaded that nothing in heaven, earth or hell could ever separate him from the love of God. The one state of mind is the necessary condition of the other. It is only those who are conscious of this constant and deadly struggle with sin, to whom this assurance is given. In the very same breath Paul says, "O wretched man that I am" and "thanks be to God who giveth us the victory" (Rom. 7: 24, 25). It is the indolent and self-empty professor who is filled with a carnal confidence.

Chapter 8
Elucidation

Had we followed a strictly logical order, this branch of our subject would have immediately followed our discussion of the problem which is raised by this doctrine. But we considered it better to first build a broader foundation for our present remarks by considering its "complement." We showed (1) that there is a twofoldness of truth which characterizes the whole of divine revelation; (2) that parallel with the fact of man's spiritual impotence runs his full responsibility; (3) that the acid test of sound theology consists in preserving the balance of truth or presenting its component parts in their proper perspective; (4) that the servant of God must always strive to set forth each aspect of the gospel in its fair proportions, being impervious to the charge of inconsistency which is sure to be hurled at him by extremists.

God's Requirements Versus Man's Impotence

Let us now restate the problem to which this and the following chapters endeavor to present a solution. How can fallen man be held responsible to glorify God when he is incapable of doing so? How can it conform with the mercy of God for Him to require the debt of obedience when we are unable to pay it? How can it consist with the justice of God to punish with eternal suffering for the neglect of what lies altogether beyond the sinner's power? If fallen man be bound fast with the cords of sin, with what propriety can God demand of him the performance of a perfect holiness? Since the sinner is the slave of sin, how can he be a free agent? Can he really be held accountable for not doing what it is impossible for him to do? If the fall has not annulled human responsibility, must it not to a considerable extent have modified it?

It is not for the benefit of the carping critic or the objecting infidel that we take up such questions as these, but with the desire to help our fellow Christians. Though such problems do not to the least degree shake their confidence in the character of the Lord or the integrity of His Word, some believers are at a loss to see how His ways can be equal. On the one hand Scripture declares, "The carnal mind is enmity against God: for it is not subject to the law of God, neither indeed can be." Therefore it is incapable of doing anything else but sin: "So then they that are in the flesh cannot please God" (Rom. 8:7-8). Yet on the other we are informed that "the wrath of God is revealed from heaven against all ungodliness and unrighteousness of men" (Rom. 1:18) and that "every transgression and disobedience" shall receive "a just recompense of reward" (Heb. 2:2). Nor is any deliverance from God's wrath obtainable through the gospel except on such conditions as no natural man can comply with; nevertheless, noncompliance with those conditions brings additional condemnation.

To those who give serious thought to this subject it almost seems to make out the Most High to be what the slothful servant said: "Reaping where thou hast not sown, and gathering where thou hast not strewed" (Matt. 25:24). That this is far from being the case every regenerate heart is fully assured, yet the removal of this God-dishonoring suspicion is earnestly desired by those who are perplexed by it. These points have engaged our mind for many years, and it is our desire to pass on to other members of the household of faith what has been a help to us. How fallen man can be morally impotent yet morally responsible is the matter we shall try to elucidate.

In seeking the solution to our problem we shall first aim to cast upon it the light furnished by the relationship which exists between the Creator and the creature, between God and fallen man. When facing the difficulties raised by the truth of the moral impotence of fallen man, it is of vast importance that we clearly recognize and tenaciously hold the fact that God has not forfeited His right over the creature even though the creature has lost his power to meet God's requirements. At this point, especially, much of the difficulty is removed. Further light is thrown upon the nature of human responsibility when we obtain a right view of man's moral agency. By far the greater part of the difficulty vanishes when we correctly define and state the nature of man's impotence: what it is not, and what it does consist of. Finally, it will be found that man's own conscience and consciousness bear witness to the fact of his accountability.

In seeking to show the relationship which exists between the Creator and the creature, between God and the fallen man, let us inquire, What is the foundation of moral obligation? What is the rule of human duty? It should be evident to any anointed eye that there can be only one answer to these questions: The will of God, the will of God as revealed to us. God is our Maker and as such He has the right to unlimited control over the creatures of His hands. That right of God is absolute, uncontrolled and without any limitation. It is the right of the potter over the clay. Moreover, the creature is entirely dependent upon the Creator: "In him we live, and move, and have our being" (Acts 17:28). He that "formeth the spirit of man within him" sustains that spirit and the body which it inhabits. In reference to our bodies we have no self-sustaining power; let God's hand be withdrawn, and we return to the dust. The soul of man is equally dependent upon the sustaining power of God.

Man's Obligation

Because God is who He is and because man is the work of His hands, the will of God must be the foundation of moral obligation. "All things were created by him, and for him" (Col. 1:16). "Thou hast created all things, and for thy pleasure they are and were created" (Rev. 4:11). But God is not only our Creator. He is also our Ruler and Governor, and His rights over us are made known by His will, by His expressed will. Man is bound to do what God commands and to abstain from what He forbids, simply because He commands and forbids. Beyond that there is no reason. Direct reference to the divine will is essential to any moral virtue. When an action is done regardless of God's will, no honor is shown Him and no virtue pertains to it. Such is the clear and definite teaching of Holy Writ; it knows no foundation of right or wrong, no obligation, except the will of the Most High.

It therefore follows that the will of God revealed is the rule of duty. It is self-evident that the will of God cannot direct and govern us except as it is made known to us, and in His Word it is made known. God's own rule of action is His will, for there can be no higher or holier rule. "He doeth according to his will in the army of heaven, and among the inhabitants of the earth" (Dan. 4:35); "He saith to Moses, I will have mercy on whom I will have mercy, and I will have compassion on whom I will have compassion" (Rom. 9:15). To the will of God our blessed Redeemer uniformly referred as both the obligation and rule of His own action. "I delight to do thy will, o my God: yea, thy law is within my heart" (Ps. 40:8); "I seek not mine own will, but the will of the Father which hath sent me" (John 5:30). Even when the desire of His sinless humanity was for an escape from the awful cup, His holy soul felt the binding obligation of the divine will: "Not as I will, but as thou wilt." Does not that settle the question once for all? If the incarnate Son looked no higher, no lower, no farther, why should we? Compliance with the will of God because it is the will of God is the perfection of moral virtue.

It is a striking fact that whenever the heart of man is pierced by the arrows of the Almighty and his soul is bowed down before the Majesty of heaven, whenever he begins to feel the awful burden of his guilt and his conscience is agitated over his fearful accountabilities and how they are to be met, his inquiry always is "Lord, what wilt Thou have me to do?" Everyone who has been taught of God knows this to be true. There is therefore a revealed testimony in every renewed heart to the righteousness of God's rule and the reality of its obligation. This is the basic principle of Christian fidelity and fortitude. Under its influence the regenerate soul has only one inquiry in reference to any proposed enterprise: Is it the will of God? Satisfied with this, his heart tells him it must be done. Difficulties, hardships, dangers, death present no obstacle; onward he presses in the path marked out for him by the will of his Father. Obedience to that is his only responsibility.

The whole question of man's responsibility is resolved thus: Has God revealed, has God commanded? It must be grounded on the simple authority of the Most High. God neither reveals what is untrue nor commands what is unjust; therefore the first principle of our moral duty is to know, acknowledge and perform the divine will as the ultimate fact in the government of God over us. This question must be resolved altogether irrespective of the state into which the fall has brought man; otherwise God must cease to be God and the creature must sit in judgment on his Creator. But men in the enmity of their carnal mind and the pride of their heart dare to sit in judgment upon the rule God has given them, measuring it by how far they consider it suitable to their condition, how far it complies with their ability, how far it commends itself to their reason—which is the very essence of unbelief and rebellion, the opposite of faith and obedience. Responsibility rests not upon anything in the creature, but on the authority of God who has made known His will to us. Responsibility is our obligation to respond to God's will.

We turn next to consider the moral agency of man. Since God supplied all other creatures with faculties suited to them and abilities to fill their several purposes and to attain their different ends (as fish to swim in water, and birds to fly in the air), so He was no less gracious to man. He who did not deny capacity to His lower creatures did not withhold it from the noblest of His earthly works. How could God have pronounced him "very good" (Gen. 1:31) if he lacked the natural capacity to fulfill the end of his creation? As he was to be subject to moral government, man was endowed with moral agency. Man then has been fitted to serve his Maker, because he has been invested with faculties suited to the substance of the divine commands; therefore it is our certain duty to obey whatever laws God gives us.

In amplifying what has just been said, we must consider the question What is the essence of moral agency? The answer is rational intelligence. If man was incapable of comparing ideas, of marking their agreement or difference to draw conclusions and infer results of conduct, he would not be a moral agent. That is to say, he would not be under a law or revealed will and liable to punishment for its violation or reward for its obedience. We do not treat infants or idiots as subjects of moral government, nor do we regard brute beasts as responsible moral agents. The unhappy maniac is pitied, not blamed. But something more than a capacity to reason is included in the idea of moral agency; there are processes of reason, such as a mathematical demonstration, which contain no moral character.

Man's Power of Choice

To will is an act of the mind directing its thoughts to the production of an action and thereby exerting its power to produce it. The faculty of the will is that power or principle of the mind by which it is capable of choosing. An act of the will is simply a choice. When the herdsmen of Abraham and his nephew quarreled, the patriarch proposed a separation and graciously offered the young man his choice of the whole land. "Then Lot chose him all the plain of Sodom." What does that choice signify? He took a view of the different localities, observed their relative features, balanced in his mind their respective advantages and disadvantages; and that which pleased him best offered the most powerful motive or incentive, and so was his choice. Such power of choice is necessary to constitute moral agency. Anyone who is physically forced to perform an act contrary to his desires, be it good or bad, is not accountable for it.

Conscience is a moral sense which discerns between moral good and evil, perceiving the difference between worthiness and blamableness, reward and punishment. A moral agent is one who has a capacity for being influenced in his actions by moral inducements or motives exhibited to the understanding or reason, so as to engage to a conduct agreeable to the moral faculties. That such a faculty exists within us is witnessed to by the consciousness of men the world over. There is an inward monitor from whose authority there is no escape, ever accusing or excusing. When its authority is defied, sooner or later conscience smites the transgressor with deep remorse and causes him to shrink from the anticipation of a reckoning to come. In a healthy state man recognizes the claims made by his moral faculty to supreme dominion over him. Thus the Creator has placed within our own beings His vice-regent, ever testifying to our responsibility to render obedience to Him.

Man's responsibility does not rest on anything within himself, but is based solely upon God's rights over him—His right to command, His right to be obeyed. The faculties of intelligence, volition and conscience merely qualify man to discharge his responsibility. In addition to these faculties of his soul, man has also been given strength or power to meet the requirements of his Maker. God originally made him "upright" (Eccles. 7:29) and placed within him holy tendencies which perceived the glory of God, a heart which responded to His excellence. Man was made in the image of God, after His likeness (Gen. 1:27); in other words, he was "created in righteousness and true holiness" (Eph. 4:24). Man's understanding was spiritually enlightened, his will rightly inclined; therefore he was capacitated to love the Lord his God with all his faculties and to render Him sinless obedience. Thus was he fitted to discharge his responsibility.

How was it possible for such a creature—so richly endowed by his Creator, so "very good" in his being, so capacitated to love and serve his Maker—to fall? It was possible because he was not constituted immutable, that is, incapable of any change. Creaturehood and mutability (liability to change) are correlated terms. Having been given everything necessary to constitute him a moral agent, everything which fitted him to meet the divine requirements, man was made the subject of moral government. A rule of action was set before him, a rule which was vested with sanctions: reward for obedience, punishment for disobedience. Man then was put on probation under a covenant of works. He was duly tried, his fealty to God being tested by Satan. Man deliberately cast off his allegiance to God, rejected His authority, preferred the creature to his Creator and thereby fell from his original estate.

It needs to be pointed out—for in some circles of professing Christians it is quite unknown—that when God placed Adam under the covenant of works and put him on probation, he acted not simply as a private individual but as a public person, as the federal head, as the legal representative and father of all his posterity. Such was the constitution which it pleased the Lord to appoint to the human race at the beginning of its history; and whether we can or cannot perceive the propriety and righteousness of such an arrangement, no spiritual mind will doubt its wisdom or justice once he is satisfied it is definitely revealed in Holy Writ. Had Adam survived his testing and remained loyal to his Ruler, the whole of his posterity would have shared his reward. Instead, he rebelled and sinned; in consequence, "by the offence of one judgment came upon all men to condemnation; . . . by one man's disobedience many were made sinners" (Rom. 5:18-19); "in Adam all die" (1 Cor. 15:22).

As the result of our federal head's transgression, we are born into this world depraved creatures, unable to render acceptable obedience to the divine law. But the fall has neither changed man's relationship to God nor canceled his responsibility. He is still a subject of the divine government, still a moral agent, still accountable for his actions, still required to love and serve the Lord his God. God has not lost His right to enforce His just demands, though man has lost his power to meet them; depravity does not annul obligation. A human creditor may without the slightest injustice sue a prodigal debtor who has squandered his substance in riotous living. How much more so the divine Creditor! The entrance of sin has neither weakened God's right to demand subjection from His creatures nor invalidated their obligation to discharge their duty.

In seeking to supply solution to the problem of how one who is morally impotent can be justly held to be fully accountable to God, before we endeavor to point out more clearly the exact nature of that impotence (what it does not and what it does consist of), we feel it necessary to further amplify the fact that we must first throw upon this problem the light which is furnished by the relationship which exists between the Creator and the creature, between God and fallen man. Unless we follow this order we are certain to go wrong. It is only in God's light we can ever "see light." God inhabits eternity; man is but a thing of time. Since God is both before and above man, we must start with God in our thoughts and descend to man, and not start with the present condition of fallen man and then seek to think backward to God.

Rights of God over Man

That upon which we must first concentrate is not the rights of man but the rights of God, the rights of God over man. The relation in which the Creator stands to His creatures makes them, in the strictest sense, His property. The Almighty has an absolute right to appropriate and control the products of His own omnipotence and will. Observe how the psalmist ascribes the supremacy of God to the dependence of all things upon Him for their original existence. "For the Lord is a great God, and a great King above all gods. In his hand are the deep places of the earth: the strength of the hills is his also. The sea is his, and he made it: and his hands formed the dry land. O come, let us worship and bow down: let us kneel before the Lord our maker. For he is our God; and we are the people of his pasture, and the sheep of his hand" (Ps. 95:3-7).

Since creation itself gives the Most High an absolute right to the disposal of His creatures, His constant preservation of them continually augments His title. To keep in being calls for the exercise of power no less than to create out of nothing. To God as Creator we owe our original existence; to God as Preserver we are indebted for our continued existence. Upon this sure foundation of creation and preservation God possesses an unquestionable and inalienable propriety in all His creatures, and consequently they are under a corresponding obligation to acknowledge His dominion. Their dependence upon Him for past, present and continued existence makes it a matter of imperative duty to submit to His authority. From the fact that we are His property it follows that His will is our law. "Shall the thing formed say to him that formed it, Why hast thou made me thus?" (Rom. 9:20). God's right to govern us is the necessary consequence of the mutual relations existing between Creator and creatures.

The dominion of God was not adjusted with reference to man, but man was constituted with reference to it. That is to say, it pleased the Lord to appoint and institute a system of moral government, and accordingly He constituted man a moral agent, fitted to His requirements. Man was endowed with understanding, conscience, affections and will, capable of bearing the image of his Maker's holiness, of appreciating the distinctions between right and wrong, of feeling the supremacy of moral law. To such beings God sustains the relation of Ruler, for a moral creature is necessarily the subject of obligation. It must seek the law of its being beyond itself; the ultimate standard of its conduct must be found in a superior will to which it is responsible. To all created intelligences the authority of their Creator is absolute, complete and final. Thus the will of God, now expressed, is to them the sole standard of moral obligation. To deny this would be to make the creature independent.

The essential elements which constitute all true government were present when God placed man in Eden: there was competent authority, a rule of action proclaimed, and a suitable sanction to enforce that rule. As we have pointed out, the relationship obtaining between God and His creatures is such as to invest Him with an absolute right to exact obedience from them. As dependence is the very condition of his being, man possesses no authority to move, to exert a single faculty or to lose a single quality without evoking the divine displeasure. So absolutely is the creature the property of its Maker that it has no right to think its own thoughts or indulge its own inclinations. Moral agents must act, but their actions must be determined and regulated by the will of their Maker. "And the Lord God commanded the man, saying, Of every tree of the garden thou mayest freely eat" (Gen. 2:16); without the grant, it would have been an act of theft for Adam to partake of any of them!

J. H. Thornwell stated:

A creature has no more right to act than it has power to be, without the consent of the Almighty. Dependence, absolute, complete, inalienable is the law of its existence. Whatever it performs must be in the way of obedience; there can be no obedience without an indication of the will of a ruler, and no such indication without a government. It is, therefore, undeniably necessary that to justify a creature in acting at all there must be some expression, more or less distinct, direct or indirect of the will of its Creator. As, then, the Almighty, from the very necessity of the case, must will to establish some rule, we are prepared to inquire what kind of government He was pleased to institute.

As we mentioned previously, it was a moral government, of moral creatures, who were placed under revealed law. It was law to which was attached penal sanction, and this in the very nature of the case. In order to enforce His authority as Ruler, in order to make manifest the estimate He places upon His law, God determined that disobedience to that law must be visited with summary punishment. How else could God's hatred of sin be known? Since the moral conduct of a creature is to be regulated with a specific reference to God's authority, unless He allowed it to be a god—uncontrolled, independent—there must be a recognition of His right to command. The actions of a moral creature must proceed from a sense of obligation corresponding to the rights of the Ruler. But there could be no such sense of obligation unless the law was enforced by a penal sanction; for without such, the obedience of the creature would be merely the result of persuasion rather than authority.

Precept without penalty is simply advice, or at most a request; and rewards without punishment are nothing but inducements. Had Adam and Eve been placed under such principles, the result would evidently have been but a system of persuasion and not of authoritative rule (which is precisely what most human government, in the home, the church and the state, has now degenerated into). In such a case their obedience would have been nothing more than pleasing themselves, following the impulse of their own desires, and not submitting to the rightful demands of their Creator; they would have been acting out their own wills and not the will of the Most High. It should be quite plain to the reader that such an (inconceivable) arrangement would have vested the creature with absolute sovereignty, making it a law unto itself, entirely independent of its Maker. The essence of all morality is compliance with the will of God, not because it commends itself to our reason or is agreeable to our disposition, but simply because it is His will.

In order that the will of God may be felt as law and may produce in the creature a corresponding sense of obligation, it must be enforced by a penal sanction. Declared penalty for disobedience upholds the authority of the Creator and keeps prominently in view the responsibility of the creature. It makes clear the just supremacy of the One and the due subordination of the other. The moral sense in man, even in fallen man, bears witness to the rightness of this basic fact. Conscience is a prospective principle; its decisions are by no means final, but are only the prelude of a higher sentence to be pronounced in a higher court. Conscience derives its power from anticipations of the future. It brings before its possessor the dread tribunal of eternal justice and almighty power; it summons us into the awful presence of a right-loving and sin-hating God. It testifies to an ultimate reward for right doing and an ultimate punishment for wrongdoing.

We again quote Thornwell:

When a man of principle braves calumny, reproach and persecution, when he stands unshaken in the discharge of duty and public opposition and private treachery, when no machinations of malice or seductions of flattery can cause him to bend from the path of integrity,—that must be a powerful support through which he can bid defiance to the "storms of fate." He must feel that a strong arm is underneath him; and though the eye of sense can perceive nothing in his circumstances but terror, confusion, and dismay, he sees his mountain surrounded by "chariots of fire and horses of fire," which sustain his soul in unbroken tranquility. In the approbation of his conscience there is lifted up the light of the Divine countenance upon him, and he feels the strongest assurance that all things shall work together for his ultimate good. Conscience anticipates the rewards of the just, and in the conviction which it inspires of Divine protection lays the foundation of heroic fortitude.

When, on the contrary, the remembrance of some fatal crime rankles in the breast, the sinner's dreams are disturbed by invisible ministers of vengeance and the fall of a leaf can strike him with horror; in every shadow he sees a ghost: in every tread he hears an avenger of blood; and in every sound the trump of doom. What is it that invests his conscience with such terrible power to torment? Is there nothing here but the natural operation of a simple and original instinct? Who does not see that the alarm and agitation and fearful forebodings of the sinner arise from the terrors of an offended Judge and insulted Lawgiver. An approving conscience is the consciousness of right, of having done what has been commanded, and of being now entitled to the favor of the Judge. Remorse is the sense of ill-desert. The criminal does not feel that his present pangs are his punishment; it is the future, the unknown and portentous future, that fills him with consternation. He deserves ill, and the dread of receiving it makes him tremble.

Let there be no uncertainty on this point. Were it possible to remove the penalty from the divine law, we should be wresting the scepter from the hands of Deity, divesting Him of power to enforce His just demands, denuding Him of the essential dignity of His character, reducing Him to a mere suppliant at the feet of His creatures. Modern theology (if it deserves to be called theology) presents to men a parody of God, who commands the respect of none, who is disrobed of His august and glorious majesty, who, far from doing His will in the army of heaven and among the inhabitants of the earth, is pictured as a kindly petitioner seeking favors at the hands of worms of the dust. Such a "god" has no powerful voice which shakes the earth and makes guilty rebels quail, but only offers entreaties which may be despised with impunity. Unless God is able to enforce His will He ceases to be God. If He speaks with authority, resistless power stands ready to support His command.

"And the Lord God commanded the man, saying, Of every tree of the garden thou mayest freely eat: but of the tree of the knowledge of good and evil thou shalt not eat of it" (Gen. 2:16-17). There was the original command given to man at the dawn of human history. It surely was uttered in a tone which carried the conviction that it must be obeyed. "For in the day that thou eatest thereof thou shalt surely die." There was the penal sanction enforcing the authority of the Lawgiver, the plainly announced penalty for transgression. Man was not left in ignorance or uncertainty of what would follow the forbidden act. The loss of God's favor, the incurring of His sore displeasure, certain and inescapable destruction would be the portion of the disobedient. And that awful threat was no isolated and exceptional one, but the enunciation of an abiding principle which God has constantly pressed upon men all through His Word: "The soul that sinneth, it shall die"; "The wages of sin is death." Even when the Savior commissioned His servants to go forth and preach the gospel to every creature, He expressly told them to make known that "he that believeth not shall be damned." Such a God is not to be trifled with!

Let us digress for a moment. In view of what has been said above, the discerning reader will hardly need for us to point out to him the unspeakable solemnity, the immeasurable awfulness, the consummate folly of the course followed in the vast majority of the pulpits for many years. Even where the requirements of the moral law have been insisted on, its fearful penal sanction scarcely ever has been pressed. It has either been flatly denied that God will consign to everlasting woe all who have trampled on His commandments and died impenitent of their rebellion, or else a guilty silence has been maintained and in its stead a one-sided portrayal of the divine character presented, all the emphasis being placed on His love and mercy. Disastrous indeed must be the consequence of such a course, and disastrous indeed has it proved. An insulted Deity is now allowing us to reap what we have sown.

Problem of Lawlessness

A law which is not enforced by penalties will not be obeyed. True alike of God's law or man's, God's law will exert very little restraining influence upon the unregenerate if fear of the wrath to come is not definitely before their minds; and the multitude will have little respect for the statutes of the realm once they cease to regard the magistrate with "terror" (Rom. 13:2-4). For generations past there has been scarcely anything from the pulpit to inspire fear of God, and now there is practically no fear of magistracy left. Respect for the divine authority has not been faithfully proclaimed and enforced, and now there is only a mere pretense of respect for human authority. The terrible penalty for disobeying God's law—endless suffering in the lake of fire— has not been plainly and frequently held before those in the pew, and now we are witnessing a miserable parody, a mere formal pretense of enforcing the prescribed penalties for violations of human laws.

During the course of the last century, churchgoers grew less and less afraid of the consequences of breaking God's precepts; now the masses, even children, are less and less afraid of transgressing the laws of our country. Witness not merely the leniency but the utter laxity of most of our magistrates in dismissing offenders either with a warning or a trifling fine; witness the many murderers sentenced to death "with strong recommendation for mercy" and the increasing number of those whose capital punishment is remitted; witness the pathetic spectacle of governments afraid to act firmly, making "appeals" and "requests," instead of using their authority. And what we are now seeing in the civil realm is the inevitable repercussion of what took place in the religious. We sowed the wind; a righteous God is now allowing us to reap the whirlwind. Nor can there be any hope of a return to law and order, either between the nations or in our civil life, until the law of God is again given its proper place in our homes and churches, until the authority of the Lawgiver is respected, until the penalty for breaking His law is proclaimed.

Returning to our more immediate discussion, it should be pointed out that the fall did not to the slightest degree cancel man's responsibility. How could it? Man is just as much under the authority of God now as he was in Eden. He is still as truly the subject of divine command as he ever was, and therefore as much responsible to render perfect and ceaseless obedience to the divine law. The responsibility of man, be he unfallen or fallen, is that of a subject to his sovereign. They who imagine that man's own willful sin has canceled his obligation show how completely darkened is their judgment. Since God continues to be man's rightful Lord and man is His lawful subject, since He still possesses the right to command and we are still under obligation to obey, it should not be thought strange that God deals with man according to this relationship, and actually requires obedience to His law though man is no longer able to give it.

No, the fall of man most certainly has neither annulled nor impaired man's responsibility. Why should it? It was not God who took from man his spiritual strength and deprived him of his ability. Man was originally endowed with power to meet the righteous requirements of his Maker; it was by his own madness and wickedness that he threw away that power. Does a human monarch forfeit his right to demand allegiance from his subjects as soon as they turn rebels? Certainly not. It is his prerogative to demand that they throw down the weapons of their warfare and return to their original loyalty. Has then the King of kings no such right to require that lawless rebels become loyal subjects? We repeat, it was not God who stripped man of original righteousness, for he had lost it before God passed sentence upon him, as his "I was naked" (Gen. 3:10) acknowledged. If inability canceled man's obligation, there would be no sin in the world, and consequently no judgment here or hereafter. For God to allow that fallen creatures be absolved from loving Him with all their hearts would be to abrogate His government.

God's sovereignty and man's responsibility are never confounded in the Scriptures but, from the two trees in the midst of Eden's garden (the "tree of life" and "the tree of knowledge of good and evil" [Gen. 2:9]) onward, are placed in juxtaposition. Human responsibility is the necessary corollary of divine sovereignty. Since God is the Creator, since He is sovereign Ruler over all, and since man is simply a creature and a subject, there is no escape from his accountability to his Maker. For what is man responsible? Man is obligated to answer to the relationship which exists between him and his Creator. He occupies the place of creaturehood, subordination, complete dependence; therefore he must acknowledge God's dominion, submit to His authority, and love Him with all his heart and strength. The discharge of human responsibility is simply to recognize God's rights and act accordingly, rendering His unquestionable due.

Man's Accountability to God
Responsibility is entirely a matter of relationship and the discharge of those obligations which that relationship entails. When a man takes a wife he enters into a new relationship and incurs new obligations, and his marital responsibility lies in the fulfillment of those obligations. If a child is given to him a further relationship is involved with added obligations (to both his wife and child), and his parental responsibility consists of the faithful meeting of those obligations. Once it is known who God is and what is man's relationship to Him, the question of his responsibility is settled once for all. God is our Owner and Governor, possessed of absolute authority over us, and this must be acknowledged by us in deed as well as word. Thus we are responsible to be in complete subjection to the will of our Maker and Lord, to employ in His service the faculties He has given us, to use the means He has appointed, and to improve the opportunities and advantages He had provided us. Our whole duty is to glorify God.

From the above definition it should be crystal clear that the fall did not and could not to the slightest degree cancel or impair human responsibility. The fall has not altered the fundamental relationship subsisting between Creator and creature. God is the Owner of sinful man as truly and as fully as He was of sinless man. God is still our Sovereign and we are still His subjects. God's absolute dominion over us pertains as strictly now as it did in Eden. Though man has lost his power to obey, God has not lost His right to demand. To argue that inability cancels responsibility is the height of absurdity. Because an intoxicated employee is incapable of performing his duties, is his master deprived of the right to demand their accomplishment? Man cannot blame God for the wretched condition in which he now finds himself. The entire onus rests on the creature, for his moral impotence is the immediate effect of his own wrongdoing.

God's right to command and man's obligation to give perfect and perpetual obedience remain unshaken. God gave man his "substance" (Luke 15), but he spent it in riotous living; nevertheless God may justly challenge His own. If an earthly master gives a servant money and sends him to purchase supplies, may he not lawfully demand those supplies even if that servant spends the money in debauchery and gambling? God supplied Adam with a suitable stock, but he trifled it away. Surely then God is not to suffer because of the creature's folly; He should not be deprived of His right because of man's crime. The fact that man is a spiritual embezzler cannot destroy God's authority to require what the creature cannot be excused from. A debtor who cannot pay the debts which he has incurred remains under the obligation of paying. God not only possesses the right to demand from man the debt of obedience; from Genesis 3 to the last chapter of the New Testament He exercises and enforces that right and will yet make it publicly manifest before the assembled universe.

Though it be true that man himself is entirely to blame for the wretched spiritual condition in which he now finds himself, that the guilt of his depravity and powerlessness lies at his own door, yet we must not lose sight of the fact that his very impotence is a penal infliction, a divine judgment upon his original rebellion. Moral inability is the necessary effect of disobedience, for sin is essentially destructive, being opposed to all that is holy. God has so ordered it that the effects which sin has produced in man furnish a powerful witness to and an unmistakable demonstration of the exceeding sinfulness of sin and the dreadfulness of the malady which it produces. Sin not only defiles but enervates. It not only makes man obnoxious in the pure eyes of his Maker, but it saps man of his original strength to use his faculties right; and the more he now indulges in sin the more he increases his inability to walk uprightly.

Further light is cast on the problem of fallen man's responsibility by obtaining a right view of the precise nature of his inability. Let us begin by pointing out what it does not consist of. First, the moral inability of fallen man does not lie in the absence of any of those faculties which are necessary to constitute him a moral agent. By his transgression man lost both his spiritual purity and power, but he lost none of his original faculties. Fallen man possesses every faculty with which unfallen man was endowed. He is still a rational creature. He has an understanding to think with, affections capable of being exercised, a conscience to discern between right and wrong, a will to make choice with. Because man is in possession of such capacities he has faculties suited to the substance of the divine commands. Because he is a moral agent he is under moral government, and must yet render an account to the supreme Governor.

At this point notice must be taken of an error which obtains in the minds of some, tending to obscure and undermine the truth of fallen man s unimpaired responsibility. God declared that in the day Adam ate of the forbidden fruit he should "surely die," which has been wrongly understood to mean that his spirit would be extinguished and that, consequently, while the natural man possesses a soul he has no spirit, and cannot have one until he is born again. This is quite wrong. In Scripture "death" signifies separation and never annihilation. At physical death the soul is not exterminated but separated from the body. The spiritual death of Adam was not the extinction of any part of his being, but the severance of his fellowship with a holy God. In consequence Adam's descendants are born into this world "dead in trespasses and sins," which is defined as "being alienated from the life of God through the ignorance that is in them, because of the blindness of their heart" (Eph. 4:18).

When the prodigal's father said, "This my son was dead, and is alive again" (Luke 15:24), he most certainly did not mean that the son had ceased to exist, but simply that the prodigal had been "in the far country" and had now returned. The lake of fire into which the wicked are cast is termed the second death (Rev. 20:14) because they are "punished with everlasting destruction from the presence of the Lord, and from the glory of his power" (2 Thess. 1:9). That the natural man is possessed of a spirit is clear from "the Lord which . . . formeth the spirit of man within him" (Zech. 12:1); "What man knoweth the things of a man, save the spirit of man which is in him?" (1 Cor. 2:11); "The spirit shall return unto God who gave it" (Eccles. 12:7). It is a serious mistake to say that when Adam died in Eden any portion of his tripartite nature ceased to exist. Fallen man, we repeat, possesses all the faculties which unfallen man had.

When the Scriptures affirm "They that are in the flesh cannot please God" (Rom. 8:8) it is not because these lack the necessary faculties. That "cannot" must be understood in a way which comports fully with fallen man's responsibility, otherwise we should be guilty of making one verse contradict another. The "cannot" of Romans 8:8 (and similar passages) is in no way analogous to the "cannot walk" of a man who has lost his legs, or the "cannot see" of one who is deprived of his eyes. In such cases the individuals "cannot" because they do not have the requisite faculties or organs. A person who was devoid of such members at his birth could not possibly be held accountable for the non-exercise of them. But the moral impotence of the sinner is far otherwise. He does possess moral faculties, and the reason he fails to use them for the glory of God is solely because of his hatred of Him, because of the corruption of his nature, the enmity of his mind, the perversity of his will; and for these he is responsible.

For a man to be so enslaved by strong drink that he cannot help getting inebriated, far from excusing him, adds to his condemnation. For a man to give way to speaking what is untrue, forming the habit of telling falsehoods until he becomes such a confirmed liar that he is incapable of uttering the truth, only evidences the awful depths of his depravity. But ponder carefully the nature of his incapability. It is not because he has lost any faculty, for he still possesses the organs of speech, but because he has sunk so low that he can no longer use those organs to good purpose. Thus it is with the natural man and his incapability of pleasing his Maker. Man is endowed with moral faculties but he perverts them, puts them to wrong use. He has the same heart for loving God as for hating Him, the same members for serving Him as for disobeying Him.

Stephen Charnock said:

It is strange if God should invite the trees or beasts to repent, because they have no foundation in their nature to entertain commandments and invitations to obedience and repentance; for trees have no sense and beasts have no reason to discern the difference between good and evil. But God addresseth Himself to men that have senses open to objects, understanding to know, wills to move, affections to embrace objects. These understandings are open to anything but that which God doth command, their wills can will anything but that which God doth propose. The commandment is proportioned to their rational faculty and the faculty is proportioned to the excellency of the command.

We have affections, as love and desire. In the commands of loving God and loving our neighbor there is only a change of the object of our affections required; the faculties are not weakly but by viciousness of nature, which is of our own introduction. It is strange, therefore, that we should excuse ourselves and pretend we are not to be blamed because God's command is impossible to be observed, when the defect lies not in the want of a rational foundation, but in our own giving up ourselves to the flesh and the love of it, and in willful refusal of applying our faculties to their proper objects, when we can employ those faculties with all vehemence about those things which have no commerce with the Gospel.

This is a suitable place for us to mention and correct a mistake which occurs in some of our earlier writings. Lacking the light which God has now vouchsafed us, we then taught (1) that fallen man still possessed a natural ability to render to God the obedience which He requires, though he lacks the necessary moral ability; and (2) that because man is possessed of such natural ability he is a responsible creature. The first mistake was really more a matter of terms than anything else, for all that we meant to signify by "natural ability" was the possession of faculties which capacitated man to act as a moral agent; nevertheless, as wrong terms conduce to wrong ideas we must correct them. The second was an error in doctrine, due to our ignorance. In this present work we have shown that the basis of human responsibility consists not in anything in man, but rather in his relationship to God, and that the faculties which make him a moral agent merely equip him to discharge his responsibility.

Chapter 9
Affirmation

Many able writers, in their efforts to solve the problem presented by the moral impotence and yet the moral responsibility of fallen man, have stressed the distinction between natural and moral ability and inability. They have not seen how a man could be held accountable for his actions unless he was, in some sense, capable of performing his duty. That capability they have ascribed to his being in possession of all the faculties requisite for the performance of obedience to the divine law. But it is now clear to us that these men employed the wrong term when they designated this possession of faculties a "natural ability," for the simple but sufficient reason that fallen man has lost the power or strength to use those faculties right; it is surely a misuse of terms to predicate "ability" in one who is without strength. To affirm that the natural man possesses ability of any sort is really a denial of his total depravity.

In the second place, it should be pointed out that the moral inability of the natural man is not brought about by any external compulsion. It is an utterly erroneous idea to suppose that the natural man possesses or may possess a genuine desire and determination to do that which is pleasing to God and to abstain from what is displeasing to Him, but that a power outside himself thwarts him and obliges him to act contrary to his inclinations. Were such the case, man would be neither a moral agent nor a responsible creature. If some physical law operated upon man (like, that which regulates the planets), if some external violence (like the wind) carried men forward where they did not desire to go, they would be exempted from guilt. Those who are compelled to do what they are decidedly averse to cannot be justly held accountable for such actions.

Influence of Motives on the Will
One of the essential elements of moral agency is that the agent acts without external compulsion, in accord with his own desires. The mind must be capable of considering the motives to action which are placed before it and of choosing its own course—by "motives" we mean those reasons or inducements which influence to choice and action. Thus that which would be a powerful motive in the view of one mind would be no motive at all in the view of another. The offer of a bribe would be sufficient inducement to move one judge to decide a case contrary to evidence and law; to another such an offer, far from being a motive for wrongdoing, would be highly repellent. The temptation presented by Potiphar's wife, which was firmly resisted by Joseph, would have been an inducement sufficiently powerful to ruin many a youth of less purity of heart.

It should be quite evident that no external motive (inducement or consideration) can have any influence over our choices and actions except so far as they make an appeal to inclinations already existing within us. The affections of the heart act freely and spontaneously: in the very nature of the case we cannot be compelled either to love or to hate any object. Neither an infant nor an idiot is capable of weighing motives or of discerning moral values; therefore they are not accountable creatures, amenable to law. But because man, though fallen and under the dominion of sin, is still a rational being, possessed of the power to ponder the motives set before his mind and to decide good and evil, he is fully accountable, for he freely chooses that which, on the whole, he most prefers. Moral agency can only be destroyed by a force from without obliging man to act contrary to his nature and inclinations.

There is nothing outside of man which imposes on him any necessity of sinning or which prevents his turning from sin to holiness. There is no force brought to bear immediately on man's power of volition, or even on the connection between his volitions and his actions, which obliges him to follow the course he does. No, what man does ordinarily he does voluntarily or spontaneously in the uncontrolled exercise of his own faculties. No compulsion whatever is imposed on him. He does evil, nothing but evil, simply because he chooses to do so; the only immediate and direct cause of his doing evil is that he so wills it. Therefore since man is a responsible creature who, without any external power forcing him to act contrary to his desires, freely rejects the good and chooses the evil, he must be held accountable for his criminal conduct.

What has been pointed out considerably relieves the difficulty presented by the impotence of fallen man to meet the just requirements of God. If the reader will carefully ponder the case it should be apparent to him that the problem of human inability and accountability is by no means so formidable as it appears at first sight. The case of the fallen creature is vastly altered once it is clear what his impotence does not consist of. It makes a tremendous difference that his inability to obey his Maker does not lie in the absence of those faculties by which obedience is performed. So too the complexion of the case is radically changed when we perceive that man is not the victim of a hostile power outside himself which forces him to act contrary to his own desires and inclinations.

Grounds for Man's Blame

It will thus be evident that far from fallen man being an object of pity because of his moral impotence, he is justly to be blamed for the course which he pursues. We do not condemn a legless man because he is unable to walk, but rightly commiserate with him. We do not censure a sightless man for not admiring the beauties of nature; rather our compassion goes out to him. But how different is the case of the natural man in connection with his firm obligations to serve and glorify his rightful Lord! He is in possession of all the requisite faculties, but he voluntarily misuses them, deliberately following a course of madness and wickedness; for that he is most certainly culpable. His guiltiness will appear yet more plainly in what follows, when we understand what his moral impotence does consist of, when we consider the several elements which comprise it.

A further word needs to be added on the error of affirming that fallen man possesses a natural "ability" to obey God. Most of the writers who affirm this (Calvinists) take the ground that all the natural man lacks in order to perform that which is pleasing to God is a willingness to do so; that since his mental and moral endowments are admirably suited to the substance of the divine commandments, and since he is still possessed of every faculty which is required for the discharge of his duty, he could obey God if he would. But this is far from being the case. The condition of fallen man is much worse than that. He not only will not, but he cannot please God. Such is the emphatic and unequivocal teaching of Holy Writ, and it must be held fast by us at all costs, no matter what difficulties it may seem to involve. Yet we are fully convinced that this cannot, does not in the least, annul man's responsibility or make him any less blameworthy than was sinless Adam in committing his first offense.

"Unto them that are defiled and unbelieving is nothing pure; but even their mind and conscience is defiled" (Titus 1:15). In the unregenerate the mind and conscience are under an inherent and universal incapacity to form a right judgment or come to a right decision in regard to things pertaining to God, and as pertaining to Him. It is not merely that they are in the condition of one with a thick veil before his eyes, while the eyes themselves are sound and whole; rather they are like one whose eyes are diseased—weakened, decayed in their very internal organism. A diseased physical eye may be incapable of giving safe direction. But the eyes of fallen man's heart and understanding are so seriously affected that they cannot receive or even tolerate any spiritual light at all, until the great Physician heals them.

The solemn and terrible fact is that the brighter and more glorious is the divine light shed on the unregenerate, the more offensive and unbearable it is to them. The eyes of our understanding are radically diseased, and it is the understanding—under false views and erroneous estimates of things— which misleads the affections and the will. How, then, can we with the slightest propriety affirm that man still possesses a "natural ability" to receive God's truth to the saving of his soul? In man as created there was a perfect adaptation of faculties and a capability of receiving the divine testimony. But in fallen man, though there is a suitableness in the essential nature of his faculties to receive the testimony of God—so that his case is far superior to that of the brute beast—yet his ability to use those faculties and actually to receive God's testimony for suitable ends is completely deranged and destroyed.

Disorganization of Man's Being

The entrance of sin into man has done far more than upset his poise and disorder his affections. It has corrupted and disorganized his whole being. His intellectual faculties are so impaired and debased that his understanding is quite incapable of discerning spiritual things in a spiritual manner. His heart (including the will), which is the practical principle of operation, is "desperately wicked" and in a state of "blindness" (Eph. 4:18). The mind of fallen man is not only negatively ignorant, but positively opposed to light and convictions. To say that the natural man could please God if he would is false. His impotence is insurmountable, for he lacks the nature or disposition to will good. Therefore many men have greatly erred in supposing that the faculties of man are as capable now of receiving the testimony of God as they were before the fall.

Unwillingness is not all that the Scriptures predicate of fallen man. They declare sin has so corrupted his being that he is completely incapable of holy perceptions; it has utterly disabled him to perform spiritual acts. Moses told the people of Israel, "Ye have seen all that the Lord did before your eyes in the land of Egypt unto Pharaoh, and unto all his servants, and unto all his land; the great temptations which thine eyes have seen, the signs, and those great miracles: yet the Lord hath not given you a heart to perceive, and eyes to see, and ears to hear, unto this day" (Deut. 29:2-4). The faculties were there, but the people had not obtained power from God to perceive. Earlier Moses had said, "And the Lord heard the voice of your words, when ye spoke unto me; and the Lord said unto me, I have heard the voice of the words of this people, which they have spoken unto thee: they have well said all that they have spoken. O that there were such an heart in them, that they would fear me, and keep all my commandments always, that it might be well with them, and with their children forever" (Deut. 5:28-29). The faculties were there, but they lacked the spiritual power to use them. The unregenerate man is utterly disabled by indwelling sin in all the faculties of his spirit and soul and body from thinking, feeling or doing any spiritual good toward God.

Yet these facts do not to the slightest degree destroy or even lessen man s responsibility to glorify his Maker. This will more fully appear as we now consider what man's inability actually consists of. First, it is a voluntary inability. It was so originally. Adam acted freely when he ate of the forbidden fruit, and in consequence he lost his native holiness and became in bondage to evil. Nor can his descendants justly murmur at their inheriting the depravity of their first parents and being made answerable for their inability to will or to do good, as part of the forfeiture penalty due the first transgression; their moral impotence consists of their own voluntary continuation of Adam's offense. The entire history of sin lies in inclination and self-determination. It must not be supposed for a moment that after the first sin of Adam all self-determination ceased.

W. G. Shedd stated:

Original sin, as corruption of nature in each individual, is only the continuation of the first inclining away from God. The self-determination of the human will from God the creature, as an ultimate end, did not stop short with the act in Eden, but goes right onward to every individual of Adam's posterity, until regeneration reverses it. As progressive sanctification is the continuation of that holy self-determination of the human will which begins in its regeneration by the Holy Spirit, so the progressive depravation of the natural man is the continuation of that sinful self-determination of the human will which began in Adam's transgression.

The very origin and nature of man's inability for good demonstrates that it cannot annul his responsibility; it was self-induced and is now self-perpetuated. Far from human depravity being a calamity for which we are to be pitied, it is a crime for which we are rightly to be blamed. Far from sin being a weakness or innocent infirmity rising from some defect of creation, it is a hostile power, a vicious enmity against God. The endowments of the creature placed him under lasting obligation to his Creator, and that obligation cannot be canceled by any subsequent action of the creature. If man has deliberately destroyed his power, he has not destroyed his obligation. God does no man wrong in requiring from him what he cannot now perform, for by his own deliberate act of disobedience man deprived himself and his posterity of that power; and his posterity consent to Adam's act of disobedience by deliberately choosing and following a similar course of wickedness.

But how can man be said to act voluntarily when he is impelled to do evil by his own lusts? Because he freely chooses the evil. This calls for a closer definition of freedom or voluntariness of action. A free agent is one who is at liberty to act according to his own choice, without compulsion or restraint. Has not fallen man this liberty? Does he, in any instance, break God's law by compulsion, against his inclinations? If it were true that the effect of human depravity is to destroy free agency and accountability, it would necessarily follow that the more depraved or vicious a man becomes the less capable he is of sinning, and that the most depraved of all commit the least sin of any. This is too absurd to need refutation.

Though on the one hand it is a fact that fallen man is the slave of sin and the captive of the devil, yet on the other it is equally true that he is still a voluntary and accountable agent. Man has not lost the essential power of choice, or he would cease to be man. Though in one sense he is impelled hellward by the downward trend of his depravity, yet he elects to sin, consenting to it. Though the rectitude of our will is lost, nevertheless we still act spontaneously. "The soul of the wicked desireth evil" (Prov. 21:10), and for that he is to be blamed. If a man picked your pocket and, when arrested, said, "I could not help myself; I have a thieving disposition, and I am obliged to act according to my nature," his judge would reply, "All the more reason why you should be in prison."

Because fallen man possesses the power of choice and is a rational creature, he is obligated to make a wise and good choice. The fault lies entirely at his own door that he does not do so, for he deliberately chooses the evil. "They have chosen their own ways, and their soul delighteth in their abominations. I also will choose their delusions, and will bring their fears upon them; because when I called, none did answer; when I spoke, they did not hear: but they did evil before mine eyes, and chose that in which I delighted not" (Isa. 66:3-4). The bondage of the will to sinful inclinations neither destroys voluntariness nor responsibility, for the enslaved will is still a self-determining faculty and, therefore, under inescapable obligations to choose what man knows to be right. That very bondage is culpable, for it proceeds from self and not from God. Though man is the slave of sin it is a voluntary servitude, and therefore it is inexcusable.

The will is biased by the disposition of the heart: as the heart is, so the will acts. A holy will has a holy bias and therefore is under a moral necessity of exerting holy volitions: "A good tree cannot bring forth evil fruit." But a sinful will has a sinful bias because it has an evil disposition and therefore is under a moral necessity of exerting sinful volitions. But let it be pointed out once more that the evil disposition of man's will is not the effect of some original defect in the creature, for God made man "upright." No, his sinful disposition is the abiding self-determination of the human will. Its origin is due to the misuse Adam made of his freedom, and its continuation results from the unceasing self-determination of every one of his posterity. Each man perpetuates and prolongs the evil started by his first parents.

Because man must act according to the state of his heart, does this destroy his freedom? Certainly not, for acting according to his heart simply means doing as he pleases. And doing as we please is the very thing in which all free agency consists. The pulse can beat and the limbs can act in bodily disorders, whether we will or no. We would, with good reason, consider ourselves unfairly dealt with if we were blamed for such actions; nor does God hold us accountable for them. A good man's pulse may beat as irregularly in sickness as the worst villain's in the world; his hands may strike convulsively those who seek to hold him still. For such actions as these we are not accountable because they have no moral value. No evil inclination of ours nor the lack of a good one is necessary in order to do them; they are independent of us.

If all our actions were involuntary and out of our power, in no way necessarily connected with our disposition, our temper of mind, our choice, then we should not be accountable creatures or the subjects of moral government. If a good tree could bring forth evil fruit and a corrupt tree good fruit, if a good man out of the good treasure of his heart could bring forth evil things, and an evil man out of his evil treasure good things, the tree could never be known by its fruit. In such a case, all moral distinctions would be at an end and moral government would cease to be, for men could no longer be dealt with according to their works—rewarded for the good and punished for the evil. The only man who is justly held accountable, rewardable or punishable is one whose actions are properly his own, dictated by himself and impossible without his consent.

Here, then, is the answer to the objection that if fallen man is obliged to act according to the evil bias of his heart, he cannot rightly be termed a free agent. Necessity and choice are incompatible. Any inability to act otherwise than agreeably to our own minds would be an inability to act other than as free agents. But that necessity which arises from, or rather consists in, the temper and choice of the agent himself is the very opposite of acting against his nature and freedom. The sinner acts freely because he consents, even when irresistibly influenced by his evil lusts. Of Christ we read, "The spirit driveth him into the wilderness" (Mark 1:12), which indicates a forcible motion and powerful influence; yet of this same action we are also told, "Then was Jesus led up of the spirit into the wilderness" (Matt. 4:1), which plainly signifies His freedom of action. So too the Christian is both drawn and taught of God (John 6:44-45). Liberty of will and the victorious efficacy of divine grace are united together.

Second, fallen man's inability is moral, not physical or constitutional. Unless this is clearly perceived we shall be inclined to turn our impotence into an excuse or ground of self-extenuation. Man will be ready to say, "Even though I possess the requisite faculties for the discharge of my duty, if I am powerless I cannot be blamed for not doing it." A person who is paralyzed possesses all the members of his body, but he lacks the physical power to use them; and no one condemns him for his helplessness. It needs to be made plain that when the sinner is said to be morally and spiritually "without strength," his case is entirely different from that of one who is paralyzed physically. The normal or ordinary natural man is not without either mental or physical strength to use his talents. What he lacks is a good heart, a disposition to love and serve God, a desire to please Him; and for that lack he is justly blamable.

The mental and moral faculties with which man is endowed, despite their impaired condition, place him under moral obligation to love and serve his Creator. The illustrious character and perfections of God make it unmistakably clear that He is infinitely worthy of being loved and served; therefore we are bound to love Him, which is what a good heart essentially does. There is no way of evading the plain teaching of Christ on this subject in the parable of the talents: "Thou oughtest therefore to have put my money to the exchangers, and then at my coming I should have received mine own with usury" (Matt. 25:27). In the light of the immediate context, this clearly means that man ought to have had a heart to invest to the best advantage (use right) the talents which were committed to him.

The inability of the natural man to meet the holy and just requirements of God consists in the opposition of his heart to Him because of the presence and prevalence of a vicious and corrupt disposition. Men know that God does not desire from them a selfish and wicked heart, and they also know that He has the right to require from them a good and obedient heart. To deny that God has the right to require a holy and good heart from fallen man would be tantamount to saying He had no right to require anything from them; then it would follow that they were incapable of sinning against Him. For if God had no right to require anything from man, he would not be guilty of disobedience against Him. If God has no right to require a good heart from man, then He has no right to require him to do anything which he is unwilling to do, which would render him completely innocent.

A child has no right to complain against a parent for requiring him to do that which he has faculties to perform, but for which he has no heart. A servant has no right to murmur against a master for reasonably requiring him to do that which his endowments fit him to perform, but for which he is unwilling. A subject has no right to find fault with a ruler for requiring him to perform that which the good of his country demands, and which he is capacitated to render, merely because he lacks the disposition to do it. All human authority presupposes a right to require that of men which they are qualified to perform, even though they may have no heart for it. How much less reason, then, have those who are the subjects of divine authority to complain of being required to do that which their faculties fit them for but which their hearts hate. God has the same supreme right to command cordial and universal obedience from Adam's posterity as He has from the holy angels in heaven.

For the sake of those who desire additional insight on the relation of man's inability to his responsibility, we feel we must further consider this difficult but important (perhaps to some, abstruse and dry) aspect of our subject. Light on it has come to us "here a little, there a little"; but it is our duty to share with others the measure of understanding vouchsafed us. We have sought to show that the problem we are wrestling with appears much less formidable when once the precise nature of man's impotence is properly defined. It is due neither to the absence of requisite faculties for the performance of duty nor to any force from without which compels him to act contrary to his nature and inclinations. Instead, his bondage to sin is voluntary; he freely chooses the evil. Second, it is a moral inability, and not physical or constitutional.

In saying that the spiritual impotence of fallen man is a moral one, we mean that it consists of an evil heart, of enmity against God. The man has no affection for his Maker, no will to please Him, but instead an inveterate desire and determination to please himself and have his own way, at all costs. It is therefore a complete misrepresentation of the facts to picture fallen man as a being who wishes to serve God but who is prevented from doing so by his depraved nature; to infer that he genuinely endeavors to keep His law but is hindered by indwelling sin. The fact is that he always acts from his evil heart and not against it. Man is not well disposed toward his

Creator, but ill disposed. No matter what change occurs in his circumstances, be it from poverty to wealth, sickness to health, or vice versa, man remains a rebel—perverse, stubborn, wicked—with no desire to be any better, hating the light and loving the darkness.

It therefore follows that man's voluntary and moral inability to serve and glorify God is, third, a criminal one. As we have pointed out, a wicked heart is a thing of an entirely different order from weak eyesight, a bad memory or paralyzed limbs. No man is to blame for physical infirmities, providing they have not been self-induced by sinful conduct. But a wicked heart is a moral evil, indeed the sum of all evil, for it hates God and is opposed to our neighbors, instead of loving them as we are required. To say that a sinner cannot change or improve his heart is only to say he cannot help being a most vile and inexcusable wretch. To be unalterably in love with sin, far from rendering it less sinful, makes it more so. Surely it is self-evident that the more wicked a man's heart is, the more evil and blameworthy he is. The only other possible alternative would be to affirm that sin itself is not sinful.

It is because the natural man loves sin and hates God that he has no inclination and will to keep His law. But far from excusing him, that constitutes the very essence of his guilt. We are told that Joseph's brothers "hated him, and could not speak peaceably unto him" (Gen. 37:4). Why was it that they were unable to speak peaceably to him? Not because they lacked vocal organs, but because they hated him so much. Was such inability excusable? No, in that consisted the greatness of their guilt. An apostle makes mention of men "having eyes full of adultery, and that cannot cease from sin" (2 Pet. 2:14). But was not their impotence culpable? Surely it was; the reason they could not cease from sin was that their eyes were "full of adultery." Far from such an inability being an innocent one, it constituted the enormity of their crime; far from excusing them, it made their sin greater. Men must indeed be blind when they fail to see it is their moral impotence, their voluntary slavery to sin, which makes them obnoxious in the sight of the holy One.

A man's heart being fully set in him to do evil does not render his sinful actions the less criminal, but the more so. Consider the opposite: Does the strength of a virtuous disposition render a good action less or more praiseworthy? God is no less glorious because He is so infinitely and unchangeably holy in His nature that He "cannot be tempted with evil" (Jam. 1:13) nor act otherwise than in the most righteous and perfect manner. Holiness constitutes the very excellence of the divine character. Is Satan any less sinful and criminal because he is of such a devilish disposition, so full of unreasonable malice against God and men, as to be incapable of anything but the most horrible wickedness? So of humanity. No one supposes that the want of a will to work excuses a man from work, as physical incapacity does. No one imagines that the covetous miser, with his useless hoard of gold, with no heart to give a penny to the poor, is for that reason excused from deeds of charity as though he had nothing to give.

God's Just Rights

How justly, then, may God still enforce His rights and demand loyal allegiance from men. God will not relinquish His claims because the creature has sinned nor lower His requirements because he has ruined himself. Were God to command that which we ardently desired and truly endeavored to do, but for which we lacked the requisite faculties, we should not be to blame. But when He commands us to love Him with all our hearts and we refuse to do so, we are most certainly to blame, notwithstanding our moral impotence, because we still possess the necessary faculties for the exercise of such love. This is precisely what sin consists of: the want of affection for God with its suitable expression in obedient acts, the presence of an inveterate enmity against Him with its works of disobedience. Were God to grant rebels against His government the license to freely indulge their evil proclivities, that would be to abandon the platform of His holiness and to condone if not endorse their wickedness.

William Cunningham said:

There is no difficulty in seeing the reasons why God might address such commands to fallen and depraved men. The moral law is a transcript of God's moral perfections, and must ever continue unchangeable. It must always be binding, in all its extent, upon all rational and responsible creatures, from the very condition of their existence, from their necessary relation to God. It constitutes the only accurate representation of the duty universally and at all times incumbent upon rational beings,—the duty which God must of necessity impose upon and require of them. Man was able to obey this law, to discharge this whole duty, in the condition in which he was created. If he is now in a different condition—one in which he is no longer able to discharge this duty—this does not remove or invalidate his obligation to perform it; it does not affect the reasonableness and propriety of God, on the ground of His own perfections, and of the relation in which He stands to His creatures, proclaiming and imposing this obligation—requiring of men to do what is still as much as ever incumbent upon them.

It has generally been lost sight of that the moral law is not only the rule of our works but also of our strength. Inasmuch as well-being is the ground of well doing—the tree must be good before the fruit can be—we are obliged to conclude that the law is the rule of our nature as truly as it is of our deeds. "Thou shalt love the Lord thy God with all thine heart, and with all thy soul, and with all thy might" (Deut. 6:5). That was said not only to unfallen Adam but also to his fallen descendants. The Savior repeated it: "Thou shalt love the Lord thy God with all thy heart, and with all thy soul, and with all thy strength" (Luke 10:27). The law not only requires us to love, but to have minds equipped with all strength to love God, so that there may be life and vigor in our love and obedience to Him. The law requires no more love than it does strength; if it did not require strength to love, it would require no love either. Thus it is plain that God not only enforces His rightful demands upon fallen man, but also has not abated one iota of His requirements because of the fall.

If the divine law said nothing more to the natural man today than "Thou shalt love the Lord thy God with what strength thou now hast"—rather than with the strength He requires him to have and which He first gave to him, so that both strength and faculty, love and its manifestation, came under the command—it would amount to "Thou needest not love the Lord thy God at all, for thou art now without strength and therefore incapable of loving and serving Him, and art not to be blamed for having none." But as we have shown, man is culpable for his impotence. The only reason why he does not love God is because his heart holds enmity against Him. Did a murderer ever plead at the bar of justice that he hated his victim so intensely that he could not go near him without killing him? If such were his acknowledgment, it would only aggravate his crime; he would stand condemned by his own word. Hell, then, must be the only final place for inalienable rebels against God.

We should also call attention to the propriety of the divine law being pressed upon fallen man, in all the length and breadth of its requirements, both as a means of knowledge and a means of conviction, even though no longer available as a standard which he is able to measure up to. In spite of man's inability to obey it, the law serves to inform him of the holy character of God, the relation in which he stands to Him, and the duty which He still requires of him. Also it serves as an essential means of convicting men of their depravity. Since they are sinners, it is most important that they should be made aware of the fact. If their duty is made clear, if they are told to do that which is incumbent upon them, they are more likely to perceive how far short they come. If they are stirred up to compliance with God's requirements, to a discharge of their obligations, they will discover their moral helplessness in a way more forcible than any sermons can convey.

In the next place let us point out that fallen man is responsible to use means both for the avoidance of sin and the performance of holiness. Though the unregenerate are destitute of spiritual life, they are not therefore mere machines. The natural man has a rational faculty and a moral sense which distinguish between right and wrong, and he is called upon to exert those faculties. Far from being under an inevitable necessity of living in known and gross sins, it is only because of deliberate perversity that any do so. The most profane swearer is able to refrain from his oaths when in the presence of someone whom he fears and to whom he knows it would be displeasing. Let a drunkard see poison put into his liquor, and it would stand by him untasted from morning until night. Criminals are deterred from many offenses by the sight of a policeman, though they have no fear of God in their hearts. Thus self-control is not utterly outside man's power.

"Enter not into the path of the wicked, and go not in the way of evil men. Avoid it, pass not by it, turn from it, and pass away" (Prov. 4:14-15). Is not the natural man capable of heeding such warnings? It is the duty of the sinner to shun everything which has a tendency to lead to wrongdoing, to turn his back on every approach to evil and every custom which leads to wickedness. If we deliberately play with fire and are burned, the blame rests wholly on ourselves. There is still in the nature of fallen man some power to resist temptation, and the more it is asserted the stronger it becomes; otherwise there would be no more sin in yielding to an evil solicitation than there is sin in a tree being blown down by a hurricane. Moreover, God does not deny grace to those who humbly and earnestly seek it from Him in His appointed ways. When men are influenced to passion, to allurements, to vice, they are blamable and must justly give account to God.

No rational creature acts without some motive. The planets move as they are driven, and if a counter-influence supervenes, they have no choice but to leave their course and follow it. But man has a power of resistance which they do not have, and he may strengthen by indulgence or weaken by resistance the motives which induce him to commit wrong. How often we hear of athletes voluntarily submitting to the most rigorous discipline and self-denial; does not that evince that the natural man has power to refrain from self-indulgence when he is pleased to use it. Highly paid vocalists, abstaining from all forms of intemperance in order to keep themselves physically fit, illustrate the same principle. Abimelech, a heathen king, took Sarah for himself; but when God warned him that she was another man's wife, he did not touch her. Observe carefully what the Lord said to him: "I know that thou didst this in the integrity of thine heart; for I also withheld thee from sinning against me: therefore suffered I thee not to touch her" (Gen. 20:6). Abimelech had a natural "integrity" which God acknowledged to be in him, though He also affirmed His own power in restraining him. If men would nourish their integrity, God would concur with them to preserve them from many sins.

Not only is man responsible to use means for the avoidance of evil, but he is under binding obligation to employ the appointed means for the furtherance of good. It is true that the efficacy of means lies in the sovereign power of God and not in the industry of man; nevertheless He has established a definite connection between the means and the end desired. God has appointed that bodily life shall be sustained by bodily food, and if a man deliberately starves himself to death he is guilty of self-destruction. Men still have power to utilize the outward means, the principal ones of which are hearing the Word and practicing prayer. They have the same feet to take them to church as conduct them to the theater, the same ability to pray to God as the heathen have to cry to idols. Slothfulness will be reproved in the day of judgment (Matt. 25:26). The sinner's plea that he had no heart for these duties will mean nothing. He will have to answer for his contempt of God.

Because he is a rational creature, man has the power to exercise consideration. He does so about many things; why not about his soul? God Himself testifies to this power even in a sinful nation. To His prophet He said, "Thou shalt remove from thy place to another place in their sight: it may be they will consider, though they be a rebellious house" (Ezek. 12:3). Christ condemned men for their failure at this very point: "Ye hypocrites, ye can discern the face of the sky and of the earth; but how is it that ye do not discern this time? Yea, and why even of yourselves judge ye not what is right?" (Luke 12:56-57). If men have the ability to take an inventory of their business, why not of their eternal concerns? Refusal to do so is criminal negligence. "All the ends of the world shall remember and turn unto the Lord" (Ps. 22:27). The natural man possesses the faculty of memory and is obligated to put it to the best use. "Let us search and try our ways, and turn again to the Lord" (Lam. 3:40). Failure to do so is willful negligence.

Man has not only physical organs but affections, or passions. If Esau could weep for the loss of his blessing, why not for his sins? Observe the charge which God brought against Ephraim: "They will not frame their doings to turn unto their God" (Hosea 5:4). They would entertain no thoughts nor perform any actions that had the least prospect toward reformation. The unregenerate are capable of considering their ways. They know they shall not continue in this life forever, and most of them are persuaded in their conscience that after death there is an appointed judgment. True, the sinner cannot save himself, but he can obstruct his own mercies. Not only do men refuse to employ the means which God has appointed but they scorn His help by fighting against illumination and conviction. Remember Joseph's brothers: "We are verily guilty concerning our brother, in that we saw the anguish of his soul, when he besought us, and we would not hear" (Gen. 42:21). "Ye do always resist the Holy Ghost" (Acts 7:51).

Summary of Man's Liability to God

How can the natural man be held responsible to glorify God when he is incapable of doing so? Let us summarize our answers. First, sin has not produced any change in the essential relation between the creature and the Creator; nothing can alter God's right to command and to be obeyed. Second, sin has not taken away the moral agency of man, consequently he is as much a subject of God's moral government as he ever was. Third, since man still possesses faculties which are suited to the substance of God's commands, he is under binding obligations to serve his Maker. Fourth, the moral inability of man is not brought about by any external compulsion, for nothing outside of man can impose upon him any necessity of sinning; because all sin issues out of his own heart, he must be held accountable for it. Fifth, man's servitude to sin was self-induced and is self-perpetuated, and since he freely chooses to do evil he is inexcusable. Sixth, man's inability is moral and not constitutional, consisting of enmity against and opposition to God; therefore it is punishable. Seventh, because man refuses to use those means which are suited to lead to his recovery and scorns the help which is proffered him, he deliberately destroys himself.

It should be pointed out that, in spite of all the excuses offered by the sinner in defense of his moral impotence, in spite of the outcries he makes against the justice of being required to render to God that which lies altogether beyond his power, the sentence of his condemnation is articulated within his own being. Man's very consciousness testifies to his responsibility, and his conscience witnesses to the criminality of his wrongdoing. The common language of man under the lashings of conscience is "I might have done otherwise; O what a fool I have been! I was faithfully warned by those who sought my good, but I was self-willed. I had convictions against wrongdoing, but I stifled them. My present wretchedness is the result of my own madness. No one is to blame but myself." The very fact that men universally blame themselves for their folly establishes their accountability and evinces their guilt.

If we are to attain anything approaching completeness of this aspect of our subject it is necessary to consider the particular and special case of the Christian's inability. This is a real yet distinct branch of our theme, though all the writers we have consulted appear to have studiously avoided it. This is in some respects admittedly the most difficult part of our problem, yet that is no reason why it should be evaded. If Holy Writ has nothing to say on the subject, then we must be silent too; but if it makes pronouncement, it is our duty to believe and try to understand what that pronouncement signifies. As we have seen, the Word of God plainly and positively affirms the moral impotence of the natural man to do good, yet at the same time teaches throughout that his depravity does not supply the slightest extenuation for his transgression against the divine law. But the question we now desire to look squarely in the face is How is it with the one who has been born again? Wherein does his case and condition differ from what it was previously, both with respect to his ability to do those things which are pleasing to God and with respect to the extent of his responsibility?

Are we justified in employing the expression "the Christian's spiritual impotence?" Is it not a contradiction in terms? Scripture does warrant the use of it. "Without me ye can do nothing" (John 15:5) connotes that the believer has no power of his own to bring forth any fruit to the glory of God. "For to will is present with me; but how to perform that which is good I find not" (Rom. 7:18). Such an acknowledgment from the most eminent of the apostles makes it plain that no saint has strength of his own to meet the divine requirements. "Not that we are sufficient of ourselves to think any thing as of ourselves" (2 Cor. 3:5). If insufficient of ourselves to even think a good thought, how much less can we perform a good deed. "For the flesh lusteth against the Spirit, and the Spirit against the flesh: and these are contrary the one to the other: so that ye cannot do the things that ye would" (Gal. 5:17). That "cannot" clearly authorizes us to speak of the Christian's inability. Every prayer for divine succor and strength is a tacit confirmation of the same truth.

Then if such be the case of the Christian, is he in this regard any better off than the non-Christian? Does not this evacuate regeneration of its miraculous and most blessed element? We must indeed be careful not to disparage the gracious work of the Spirit in the new birth, nevertheless we must not lose sight of the fact that regeneration is only the beginning of His good work in the elect (Phil. 1:6), the best of whom are but imperfectly sanctified in this life (Phil. 3:12). That there is a real, radical difference between the unregenerate and the regenerate is gloriously true. The former are dead in trespasses and sins; the latter have passed from death to life. The former are the subjects and slaves of the devil; the latter have been delivered from the power of darkness and translated into the kingdom of God's dear Son (Col. 1:13). The former are completely and helplessly under the dominion of sin; the latter have been made free from sin's dominion and have become the servants of righteousness (Rom. 6:14, 18). The former despise and reject Christ; the latter love and desire to serve Him.

In seeking to grapple with the problem of the Christian's spiritual inability and the nature and extent of his responsibility, there are two dangers to be avoided, two extremes to guard against: (1) practically reducing the Christian to the level of the unregenerate, which is virtually a denial of the reality and blessedness of regeneration; (2) making out the Christian to be very nearly independent and self-sufficient. We must aim at preserving the balance between "Without me ye can do nothing" (John 15:5) and "I can do all things through Christ which strengtheneth me" (Phil. 4:13). What we are now discussing is part of the Christian paradox, for the believer is often a mystery to himself and a puzzle to others because of the strange and perplexing contrarieties meeting in him. He is the Lord's free man, yet declares, "I am carnal, sold under sin" (Rom. 7:14). He rejoices in the law of the Lord, yet cries, "O wretched man that I am!" (Rom. 7:24). He acknowledges to the Lord "I believe," yet in the same breath prays, "Help Thou my unbelief." He declares, "When I am weak then am I strong." One moment he is praising his Savior and the next groaning before Him.

Wherein does the regenerate differ from the unregenerate? First, the regenerate has been given an understanding that he may know Him who is true (1 John 5:20). His mind has been supernaturally illumined; the spiritual light which shines in his heart (2 Cor. 4:6) capacitates him to discern spiritual things in a spiritual and transforming manner (2 Cor. 3:18); nevertheless its development may be hindered by neglect and sloth. Second, the regenerate has a liberated will, so that he is capacitated to consent to and embrace spiritual things. His will has been freed from that total bondage and dominion of sin under which he lay by nature; nevertheless he is still dependent upon God's working in him both to will and to do of His good pleasure. Third, his affections are changed so that he is capacitated to relish and delight in the things of God; therefore he exclaims, "O how love I Thy law." Before, he saw no beauty in Christ, but now He is "altogether lovely." Sin which was formerly a spring of pleasure is now a fountain of sorrow. Fourth, his conscience is renewed, so that it reproves him for sins of which he was not previously aware and discloses corruptions which he never suspected.

But if on the one hand there is a radical difference between the regenerate and the unregenerate, it is equally true that there is a vast difference between the Christian in this life and the Christian in the life to come. While we must be careful not to belittle the Spirit's work in regeneration, we must be equally on our guard lest we lose sight of the believer's entire dependence on God. Although a new nature is imparted at regeneration, the believer is still a creature (2 Cor. 5:17); the new nature is not to be looked to, rested in or made an idol. Though the believer has had the principle of grace communicated to him, yet he has no store of grace within himself from which he may now draw. He is but a "babe" (1 Pet. 2:2), completely dependent on Another for everything. The new nature does not of itself empower or enable the soul for a life of obedience and the performance of duty; it simply fits and makes it compatible to these. The principle of spiritual life requires its Bestower to call it into operation. The believer is, in that respect, like a becalmed ship—waiting for a heavenly breeze to set it in motion.

Yet in another sense the believer resembles the crew of the ship rather than the vessel itself, and in this he differs from those who are unrenewed. Before regeneration we are wholly passive, incapable of any cooperation; but after regeneration we have a renewed mind to judge aright and a will to choose the things of God when moved by Him; nevertheless we are dependent on His moving us. We are daily dependent on God's strengthening, exciting and directing the new nature, so that we need to pray "Incline my heart unto thy testimonies . . . and quicken thou me in thy way" (Ps. 119:36-37). The new birth is a vastly different thing from the winding of a clock so that it will run of itself; rather the strongest believer is like a glass without a base, which cannot stand one moment longer than it is held. The believer has to wait upon the Lord for his strength to be renewed (Isa. 40:31). The Christian's strength is sustained solely by the constant operations and communications of the Holy Spirit, and he lives spiritually only as he clings close to Christ and draws virtue from Him.

There is a suitableness or answerableness between the new nature and the requirements of God so that His commands "are not grievous" to it (1 John 5:3), so that Wisdom's ways are found to be "pleasant" and all her paths "peace" (Prov. 3:17). Nevertheless the believer stands in constant need of the help of the Spirit, working in him both to will and to do, granting fresh supplies of grace to enable him to perform his spiritual desires. A simple delight in the divine law is not of itself sufficient to produce obedience. We have to pray, "Make me to go in the path of thy commandments" (Ps. 119:35). Regeneration conveys to us an inclination and tendency for that which is good, thereby fitting us for the Master's use; nevertheless we have to look outside ourselves for enabling grace: "Be strong in the grace that is in Christ Jesus" (2 Tim. 2:1). Thereby God removes all ground for boasting. He would have all the glory given to His grace: "By the grace of God I am what I am" (1 Cor. 15:10).

If enough rain fell in one day to suffice for several years we would not so clearly discern the mercies of God in His providence nor be kept looking to Him for continued supplies. So it is in connection with our spiritual lives: we are daily made to feel that "our sufficiency is of God." The believer is entirely dependent on God for the exercise of his faith and for the right use of his knowledge. Said the apostle: "I live; yet not I, but Christ liveth in me" (Gal. 2:20), which gives the true emphasis and places the glory where it belongs. But he at once added, "And the life which I now live in the flesh I live by the faith of the Son of God [by the faith of which He is its Object], who loved me, and gave himself for me." That preserves the true balance. Though it was Christ who lived in and empowered him, yet he was not passive and idle. He put forth acts of faith in Him and thereby drew virtue from Him; thus he could do all things through Christ strengthening him.

Responsibility of the Christian

It is at that very point the responsibility of the Christian appears. As a creature his responsibility is the same as pertains to the unregenerate, but as a new creature in Christ Jesus (2 Cor. 5:17) he has incurred increased obligations: "Unto whomsoever much is given, of him shall be much required" (Luke 12:48). The Christian is responsible to walk in newness of life, to bring forth fruit for God as one who is alive from the dead, to grow in grace and in the knowledge of the Lord, to use his spiritual endowments and to improve or employ his talents. The call comes to him "Stir up the gift of God, which is in thee" (2 Tim. 1:6). Isaiah the prophet complained of God's people, "There is none that stirreth up himself to lay hold of thee" (64:7), which condemns slothfulness and spiritual lethargy. The Christian is responsible to use all the means of grace which God has provided for his wellbeing, looking to Him for His blessing upon them. When the Scripture says, "The Spirit also helpeth our infirmities" (Rom. 8:26), the Greek verb is "helpeth together"—He cooperates with our diligence not our idleness.

The Christian has received spiritual life, and all life is a power to act by. Inasmuch as that spiritual life is a principle of grace animating all the faculties of the soul, he is capacitated to use all means of grace which God has provided for his growth and to avoid everything which would hinder or retard his growth. He is required to keep the heart with all diligence (Prov. 4:23), for if the fountain is kept clean, the springs which issue from it will be pure. He is required to "make not provision for the flesh, to fulfill the lusts thereof" (Rom. 13:14), not allowing his mind and affections to fix themselves on sinful or unlawful objects. He is required to deny himself, take up his cross and follow the example which Christ has left him. He is commanded to "love not the world, neither the things that are in the world" (1 John 2:15), and therefore he must conduct himself as a stranger and pilgrim in this scene of action, abstaining from fleshly lusts which war against the soul (1 Pet. 2:11) if he would not lose the heavenly inheritance (1 Cor. 9:27). And for the performance of these difficult duties he must diligently and earnestly seek supplies of grace counting on God to bless the means to him.

No small part of the Christian's burden and grief is the inward opposition he meets, thwarting his aspirations and bringing him into captivity to that which he hates. The believer's "life" is a hidden one (Col. 3:3), and so also is his conflict. He longs to love and serve God with all his heart and to be holy in every detail of his life, but the flesh resists the spirit. Worldliness, unbelief, coldness, slothfulness exert their power. The believer struggles against their influence and groans under their bondage. He desires to be clothed with humility, but pride is constantly breaking forth in some form or other. He finds that he cannot attain to that which he desires and approves. He discovers a wide disparity between what he knows and does, between what he believes and practices, between his aims and realizations. Truly he is "an unprofitable servant." He is so often defeated in the conflict that he is frequently faint and weary in the use of means and in performance of duty; he may question the genuineness of his profession and be tempted to give up the fight.

In seeking to help distressed saints concerning this acute problem, the servant of God needs to be very careful lest he foster a false peace in those who have a historical faith in the gospel but are total strangers to its saving power. God's servant must be especially watchful not to bolster the false hopes of those who delight in the mercy of God but hate His holiness, who misappropriate the doctrine of His grace and make it subservient to their lusts. He must therefore call upon his hearers to honestly and diligently examine themselves before God, that they may discover whence the inward oppositions arise and what are their reactions to them. They must determine whether these inconsistencies spring from an unwillingness to wear the yoke of Christ, their whole hearts accompanying and consenting to such resistances to God's righteous requirements, or whether these oppositions to God's laws have their rise in corruptions which they sincerely endeavor to oppose, which they hate, which they mourn over, which they confess to God and long to be released from.

When describing the conflict in himself between the flesh and the spirit— between indwelling sin and the principle of grace he had received at the new birth—the Apostle Paul declared, "For that which I do [which is contrary to the holy requirements of God] I allow not [I do not approve of it; it is foreign to my real inclinations and purpose of heart]: but what I hate, that do I" (Rom. 7:15). Paul detested and yearned to be delivered from the evil which rose up within him. Far from affording him any satisfaction, it was his great burden and grief. And thus it is with every truly regenerated soul when he is in his right mind. He may be, yes is, frequently overcome by his carnal and worldly lusts; but instead of being pleased at such experience and contentedly lying down in his sins, as a sow delights to wallow in the mire, he cries in distress, confesses such failures as grievous sins, and prays to be cleansed from them.

"If I were truly regenerate, how could sin rage so fiercely within and so often obtain the mastery over me?" This question deeply exercises many of God's people. Yet the Scripture declares, "A just man falleth seven times" (Prov. 24:16); but it at once adds "and riseth up again." Did not David lament, "Iniquities prevail against me" (Ps. 65:3)? Yet if you are striving to mortify your lusts, looking daily to the blood of Christ to pardon, and begging the Spirit to more perfectly sanctify you, you may add with the psalmist, "As for our transgressions, thou shalt purge them away." Indeed, did not the highly favored apostle declare, "For we know that the law is spiritual: but I am carnal, sold [not 'unto' but] under sin" (Rom. 7:14). There is a vast difference between Paul and Ahab, of whom we read that he "did sell himself to work wickedness in the sight of the Lord" (I Kings 21:25). It is the difference between one who is taken captive in war, becoming a slave unwillingly and longing for deliverance, and one who voluntarily abandons himself to a course of open defiance of the Almighty and who so loves evil that he would refuse release.

We must distinguish between sin's dominion over the unregenerate and sin s tyranny and usurpation over the regenerate. Dominion follows upon right of conquest or subjection. Sin's great design in all of us is to obtain undisputed dominion; it has it in unbelievers and contends for it in believers. But every evidence the Christian has that he is under the rule of grace is that much evidence he is not under the dominion of sin. "For I delight in the law of God after the inward man: But I see another law in my members, warring against the law of my mind, and bringing me into captivity to the law of sin which is in my members" (Rom. 7:22-23). That does not mean that sin always triumphs in the act, but that it is a hostile power which the renewed soul cannot evict. It wars against us in spite of all we can do. The general makeup of believers is that, notwithstanding sin being a "law" (governing force) not "to" but "in" them, they "would [desire and resolve to] do good," but "evil is present" with them. Their habitual inclination is to good, and they are brought into captivity against their will. It is the "flesh" which prevents the full realization of their holy aspirations in this life.

But if the Son has "made us free" (John 8:36), how can Christians be in bondage? The answer is that Christ has already freed them from the guilt and penalty, love and dominion of sin, but not yet from its presence. As the believer hungers and thirsts after righteousness, pants for communion with the living God, and yearns to be perfectly conformed to the image of Christ, he is "free from sin"; but as such longings are more or less thwarted by indwelling corruptions, he is still "sold under sin." Then let prevailing lusts humble you, cause you to be more watchful and to look more diligently to Christ for deliverance; then those very exercises will evidence a principle of grace in you which desires and seeks after the destruction of inborn sin. Those who have hearts set on pleasing God are earnest in seeking enabling grace from Him, yet they must remember He works in them both to will and to do of His good pleasure, maintaining His sovereignty in this as in everything else. Bear in mind that it is allowed sin which paralyzes the new nature.

Thus God has not yet uprooted sin from the soul of the believer, but allows him to groan under its uprisings, that his pride may be stained and his heart made to constantly feel he is not worthy of the least of God's mercies. To produce in him that feeling of dependence on divine power and grace. To exalt the infinite condescension and patience of God in the apprehension of the humbled saint. To place the crown of glory on the only head worthy to wear it: "Not unto us, O Lord, not unto us, but unto thy name give glory, for thy mercy, and for thy truth's sake" (Ps. 115:1).

Chapter 10
Opposition

In bringing this study to a close it seems desirable that we should consider the opposition made against this truth before giving an exposition of it. This subject of the moral inability of fallen man for good is peculiarly repugnant to his pride, and therefore it is not surprising that his outcry against it is so loud and prolonged. The exposure of human depravity, the disclosure of the fearful ruin which sin has wrought in our constitution, cannot be a pleasant thing to contemplate and still less to acknowledge as a fact. To heartily own that by nature I am devoid of love for God, that I am full of inveterate enmity against Him, is diametrically opposed to my whole makeup. It is only natural to form a high estimate of ourselves and to entertain exalted views of both our capabilities and our good intentions. To be assured on divine authority that our hearts are incurably wicked, that we love darkness rather than light, that we hate alike the law and the gospel, is revolting to our whole being. Every possible effort is put forth by the carnal mind to repudiate such a flesh-withering and humiliating description of human nature. If it cannot be refuted by an appeal to facts, then it must be held up to ridicule.

Man's Refusal to Accept the Doctrine

Such opposition to the truth should neither surprise nor discourage us, for it has been plainly announced to us: "The natural man receiveth not the things of the Spirit of God: for they are foolishness unto him" (1 Cor. 2:14). The very fact that they are foolishness to him should lead us to expect he will laugh at and scorn them. Nor must we be alarmed when we find this mocking of the truth is far from being confined to avowed infidels and open enemies of God; this same antagonism appears in the great majority of religious persons and those who pose as the champions of Christianity. Passing through a seminary and putting on the ministerial garb does not transform the unregenerate into regenerate men. When our Lord announced, "The truth shall make you free," it was the religious leaders of the Jews who declared they were never in bondage; and when He affirmed, "Ye are of your father the devil, and the lusts of your father ye will do," they replied, "Say we not well that thou art a Samaritan, and hast a devil?" (John 8).

Principal Objections

It is just because the fiercest opposition to this truth comes from those inside Christendom, not from those outside, that we consider it wise to face the principal objections. We do so to place the Lord's people on their guard and to let them see there is no weight in such criticism. We would not waste time in seeking to close the mouths of those whom God Himself will deal with in due time, but we desire to expose their sophistries so that those with spiritual discernment may perceive that their faith rests on a foundation which no outbursts of unbelief can shake. Every objection against the doctrine of man's spiritual impotence has been overthrown by God's servants in the past, yet each fresh generation repeats the arrogance of its forebears. We have already refuted most of these objections in the course of this study, yet by now assembling them together and showing their pointlessness we may render a service which will not be entirely useless.

1. If fallen man is unable to keep God's law, he cannot be obligated to keep it. Impotence obvi-

ously cancels responsibility. A child three or four years of age ought not to be whipped because it does not read and write. A legless man should not be sent to prison because he does not walk. Surely a just and holy God does not require sinful creatures to render perfect obedience to a divine and spiritual law.

How is this objection to be met? First, by pointing out that it is not based upon Holy Writ but is merely human reasoning. Scripture affirms again and again that fallen man is spiritually impotent, "without strength," and that he "cannot please God"; from that nothing must move us. Scripture nowhere states that spiritual helplessness releases man from God's claims upon him; therefore no human reasoning to the contrary, however plausible or pleasing, is entitled to any consideration from those who tremble at God's Word. Scripture reveals that God does hold fallen man responsible to keep His law, for He gave it to Israel at Sinai and pronounced His curse upon all transgressors of it.

What has been pointed out should be sufficient for any simple soul who fears the Lord. But lest it be thought that this is all which can be said by way of refutation, lest it be supposed that this objection is so forceful that it cannot be met in a more direct rebuttal, we add the following: To declare that man cannot be obligated to keep the law if he is unable to do so demands an inquiry into both the nature and the cause of his inability. Once that investigation is entered into, the sophistry of the objection will quickly appear. Wherein lies man's inability to keep God's law? Is it the absence of the requisite faculties or his unwillingness to use aright the faculties with which he is endowed? Were fallen man devoid of reason, conscience, will, there would be some force in this objection; but since he is possessed of all those faculties which constitute a moral being, it is quite inane and invalid. There is no analogy whatever between the sinner's inability to travel the highway of holiness and the inability of a legless man to walk.

The worthlessness of this objection is made evident not only when we examine the nature of man's spiritual impotence; it equally appears void when we diagnose its cause. Why is fallen man unable to keep God's law? Is it because he is worked upon by some almighty being who prevents him from rendering obedience? Were fallen man truly desirous of serving and pleasing God, were it a case of his ardently longing to do so but being thwarted because another more powerful than himself hindered him, there would be some force to this objection. But God, far from placing any obstacle in our way, sets before us every conceivable inducement to comply with His precepts. If it be argued that the devil is more powerful than man and that he is continually seeking to turn him from the path of rectitude, the answer is that Satan can do nothing without our own consent. All he can do is to tempt to wrongdoing; it is man's own will which either yields or refuses.

In reply to what has last been pointed out, someone may say, "But fallen man has no sufficient power of his own with which to successfully resist Satan's evil solicitations." Suppose that be so, then what? Does that oblige us to take sides with the enemies of the truth and affirm that therefore man is to be excused for his sinful deeds, that he is not obligated to render perfect obedience to the law merely because he does not have the power to cope with his adversary? Not at all. Once more we must inquire as to the cause. Why is it that man cannot put the devil to flight? Is it because he was originally vested with less moral strength than his foe possesses? No indeed, for he was made in the image and likeness of God. Man's present inability has been brought about by an act of his own and not by any stinginess or oversight of his Creator. "Thou hast destroyed thyself" (Hosea 13:9) is the divine verdict. Though man is unable to recover what he lost, he has none but himself to blame for his willful and wicked destruction of his original strength.

It is at this very point man twists and wriggles most, seeking to get from under the onus which righteously rests on him. When Adam offended against the divine law he sought to throw the blame upon his wife, and she in turn upon the devil; ever since then the great majority have attempted to cast it on God Himself, on the pretext that He is the One who gave them being and sent them into the world in their present handicapped condition. It must be kept steadily in mind that original ability destroyed by self-determination does not and cannot destroy the original obligation any more than weakened moral strength by self-indulgence and the formation of evil habits destroys or diminishes obligation. To say otherwise would be to declare that the result of sin excuses sin itself, which is a manifest absurdity. Man's wrongdoing certainly does not annul God's rights. God is no Egyptian taskmaster .requiring men to make bricks without straw. He endowed man with everything requisite for the discharge of his duty, and though man has squandered his substance in riotous living, that does not free him from God's just claims upon him.

The drunkard is certainly less able to obey the law of temperance than the sober man is, yet that law has precisely the same claims upon the former as it has upon the latter. In commercial life the loss of ability to pay does not release from obligation; the loss of property does not free man from his indebtedness. A man is as much a debtor to his creditors after his bankruptcy as he was previously. It is a legal maxim that bankruptcy does not invalidate contracts. Someone may point out that an insolvent debtor cannot be sued in the courts. Nevertheless, even if human law declares it equitable to free an insolvent debtor, the law of God does not. And that verdict is righteous, for the sinner's inability to give God His due is voluntary—he does not wish to pay because he hates Him. Thus both the nature and the cause of man's inability demonstrate that he is "without excuse."

2. When inquiry is made as to the cause of man's spiritual impotence and when it has been shown that this lies not in the Creator but in man's own original rebellion, the objector, far from being silenced, will demur against his being penalized for what his first parents did. He may ask, "Is it just that I should be sent into this world in a state of spiritual helplessness because of their offense? I did not make myself; if I was created with a corrupt nature, why should I be held to blame for its inevitable fruits?" First, let it be pointed out that it is not essential in order for a fallen creature to be blamable for his evil dispositions and acts that he must first be inherently holy. A person who is depraved, who from his heart hates God and despises His law, is nonetheless a sinner because he has been depraved from his birth. His having sinned from the beginning and throughout his existence is surely no valid excuse for his sinning now. Nor is his guilt any the less because his depravity is so deeply rooted in his nature. The stronger his enmity against God the greater its heinousness.

But how can man be condemned for his evil heart when Adam corrupted human nature? Fallen man is voluntarily an enemy to the infinitely glorious God and nothing can extenuate such vile hostility. The very fact that in the day of judgment "every mouth will be stopped" (Rom. 3:19) demonstrates there can be no force in this objection. It is the free and self-determined acting out of his nature for which the sinner will be held accountable. The fact that we are born traitors to God cannot cancel our obligation to give Him allegiance. None can escape the righteous requirements of the law by deliberate opposition to it. That man's nature is the direct consequence of Adam's transgression does not to the slightest degree mitigate his own sins. Is it not a solemn fact that each of us has approved Adam's transgression by following his example and joining with him in rebellion against God? That we go on to break the divine law demonstrates that we are justly condemned with Adam. If we resent our being corrupted through Adam, why not repudiate him and refuse to sin, stand out in opposition to him and be holy?

Yet still the carnal mind will ask, "Since I lost all power to love and serve God even before I was born, how can I be held accountable to do what I cannot? Wherein is the justice in requiring from me what it is impossible to render?" Exactly what was it that man lost by the fall? It was a heart that loved God. And it is the possessing of a heart which has no love for God that is the very essence of human depravity. It is this in which the vileness of fallen man consists: no heart for God. But does a loveless heart for God excuse fallen man? No indeed, for that is the very core of his wickedness and guilt. Men never complain of their lack of power for loving the world. And why are they so thoroughly in love with the world? Is it because the world is more excellent and glorious than God is? Certainly not. It is only because fallen man has a heart which naturally loves the world, but he has no heart with which to love God. The world suits and delights him, but God does not; rather, His very perfections repel him.

Now let us put it plainly and honestly: Can our being devoid of any true love for God free us from our obligation to love Him? Can it to the slightest degree lessen our blame for not loving Him? Is He not infinitely worthy of our affections, our homage, our allegiance? None would argue in any other connection as does the objector here. If a king rules wisely and well, is he not entitled to the honor and loyalty of his subjects? If an employer is merciful and considerate, has he not the right to expect his employees to further his interests and carry out his orders? If I am a kind and dutiful parent, shall I not require the esteem and obedience of my children? If my servant or child has no heart to give what is due, shall I not justly consider him blamable and deserving of punishment? Or shall we reason so insanely that the worse man grows the less he is to blame? "A son honoreth his father, and a servant his master: if then I be a father, where is mine honor? And if I be a master, where is my fear? saith the Lord of hosts" (Mal. 1:6).

3. It is objected that if the sinner is so enslaved by sin that he is impotent to do good, his free agency is denied and he is reduced to a mere machine. This is more a metaphysical question than a practical one, being largely a matter of terms. There is a real sense in which the natural man is in bondage; nevertheless within certain limits he is a free agent, for he acts according to his own inclinations without compulsion. There is much confusion on this subject. Freedom of will is not freedom from action; inaction of the will is no more possible than is inaction of the understanding. Nor is freedom of will a freedom from the internal consequences of voluntary action; the formation of a habit is voluntary, but when formed it cannot be eradicated by volition. Nor is freedom of will a freedom from the restraint and regulation of law; the glorified saints will be completely delivered from sin yet regulated by the divine will. Nor is freedom of will a freedom from bias; Christ acted freely, yet being the holy One He could not sin. The unregenerate act freely, that is, spontaneously, agreeably to their desires; yet being depraved, they can neither will nor do anything which is spiritual.

4. If man is spiritually impotent, all exhortations to the performance of spiritual duties are needless and useless. This objection assumes that God would not address His commands to men unless they were able to obey them. This idea is most presumptuous, for in it man pretends to be capable of judging the reasons which regulate the divine procedure. Has God no right to press His claims because man has wickedly squandered his power to meet them? The divine commands cover not what we can do, but what we should do; not what we are able to do, but what we ought to do. The divine law is set before us, in all the length and breadth of its holy requirements, as a means of knowledge, revealing to us God's character, the relation in which we stand to Him, and the duty which He justly requires of us. It is also a means of conviction, both of our sin and inability. If men are sinners it is important that they should be made aware of the fact—by setting before them a perfect standard that they may see how far short they come of it. If men are unable to discharge the duties incumbent upon them, it is necessary that they should be made aware of their woeful condition—that they should be made to realize their need of salvation.

5. To teach men they are spiritually impotent is to cut the nerve of all religious endeavor. If man is helpless, what is the use of urging him to strive? Necessity is a sufficient reason to act without further encouragement. A man in the water who is ready to drown will try to save his life, even

though he cannot swim and some on the banks tell him it is impossible. Again we would press the divine side. There is a necessity on us whenever there is a command from God. If He requires, it behooves man to use the means and leave the issue with Him. Again, spiritual inability is no excuse for negligence and inertia, because God does not refuse strength to perform His bidding if it is humbly, contritely and trustfully sought. When did He ever deny grace to the sinner who waited upon Him in earnest supplication and in consistent use of the means for procuring it? Is not His Word full of promises to seeking souls? If a man has hands and food is set before him, is it not an idle excuse for him to say he cannot eat because he is not moved from above?

6. If the sinner is spiritually powerless, it is only mocking him to tell him to repent of his sins and believe the gospel. To call on the unregenerate to savingly receive Christ as his Lord and Savior is far from mocking him. Did the Son of God mock the rich young ruler when He told him to sell all that he had and follow Him and then he should have treasure in heaven? Certainly not. Had the ruler no power to sell his possessions? Was it not rather lack of inclination, and for such lack was he not justly blamable? Such a demand served to expose the state of his heart. He loved money more than Christ, earthly things above heavenly. The exhortations, warnings and promises set down in the Word are to be pressed on the ungodly so as to make them more inexcusable, so that they may not say in the day to come that, had they been invited to receive such good things, they would have embraced them; that, had they been admonished for their sins, they would have forsaken them. Their own conscience will convict them, and they will know a prophet of God spoke to them.

7. Finally, it is objected that the doctrine of man's spiritual impotence stifles all hope. To tell a man his condition is irremediable, that he can do nothing whatever to better himself, will drive him to despair. This is precisely what is desired. One principal end which must be kept before the preacher is to shatter the self-sufficiency of his hearer. His business is to undermine the spirit of self-righteousness, to break down self-satisfaction, to sweep away those refuges of lies in which men shelter, to convince them of the utter futility of seeking to win heaven by their own endeavors. His business is to bring before them the exalted claims of God's law and to show how far short we come of it, to expose the wickedness of the human heart, to reveal the ruin which sin has wrought, to bring the sinner face to face with the thrice holy God and to make him realize he is utterly unfit to stand before Him. In a word, the business of God's servant is to make his hearer conscious that unless a miracle of grace is performed in him he is lost forever. Not until the sinner feels that he is helpless and hopeless in himself is he prepared to look outside of himself. Despair opens the door of hope! "Thou hast destroyed thyself, but in me is thine help" (Hosea 13:9).

Chapter 11
Exposition

(Intended chiefly for preachers)

THE PRECEDING CHAPTERS should have made it clear that the subject of the sinner's moral impotence is far more than an academic one, more than a flight into theological metaphysics. Rather is it a truth of divine revelation—a unique one—for it will not be found enunciated in any of the leading religions of antiquity, like Zoroastrianism, Buddhism or Confucianism. Nor do we remember finding any trace of it in the poets and philosophers of early Greece. It is truth which is made prominent in the Scriptures, and therefore must be given a place in the pulpit if it is to declare "all the counsel of God." It is closely bound up with the law and the gospel, the great end of the former being to demonstrate its reality, of the latter to make known the remedy. It is one of the chief battering rams which the Spirit directs against the insensate pride of the human heart, for belief in his own capabilities is the foundation on which man's self-righteousness rests. It is the one doctrine which above all others reveals the catastrophic effects of the fall and shuts up the sinner to the sovereign mercy of God as his only hope.

Generalization Not Sufficient

It is not sufficient for the preacher to generalize and speak of "the ruin which sin has wrought" and affirm that man is "totally depraved"; such expressions convey no adequate concept to the modern mind. It is necessary that he should particularize and show from Holy Writ that "they that are in the flesh cannot please God." His task is to paint fallen human nature in its true colors and not deceive by flattery. The state of the natural man is far, far worse than he has any consciousness of. Though he knows he is not perfect, though in serious moments he is aware that all is not well with him, yet he has no realization whatever that his condition is desperate and irremediable so far as all self-help is concerned. A great many people regard religion as a medicine for the soul, and suppose that if it is taken regularly it will ensure their salvation; that if they do this and that and avoid the other, all will be well in the end. They are totally oblivious to the fact that they are "without strength" and can no more perform spiritual duties than the Ethiopian can change his skin or the leopard his spots.

It is a matter of first importance that the moral inability of fallen man should be understood by all. It concerns both young and old, illiterate and educated; therefore each should have right views on the issue. It is most essential that the unsaved should be made aware not only that they are unable to do what God requires of them, but also why they are unable. They should be told the fact that it is impossible for them to "fulfill all righteousness," but also the cause of this impossibility. Their - self-sufficiency cannot be undermined while they believe they have it in their own power to perform God's commands and to comply with the terms of His gospel. Nevertheless they must not be left with the impression that their impotence is a calamity for which they are not to blame, a deprivation for which they are to be pitied; for they are endowed with faculties suited to respond to law and gospel alike. A mistake concerning either of these truths—man's impotence and man's responsibility—is likely to have a fatal consequence.

On the other hand, as long as men imagine they have it in their own power to perform their whole duty or do all that God requires of them in order for them to obtain pardon and eternal life, they feel at ease and are apt to neglect to diligently apply themselves to the performance of that duty. They are not at all likely to pray in earnest or to watch against sin with any anxiety. They neither see the need of God's working in them "both to will and to do of his good pleasure" nor the necessity of their "working out their own salvation with fear and trembling." To wake men out of this dream of self-sufficiency the Savior has given such alarming declarations as these: "Except a man be born again, he cannot see the kingdom of God" (John 3:3); "No man can come to me, except the Father which hath sent me draw him" (John 6:44). And to cut off effectually from the unregenerate all hope of obtaining mercy on the ground of the supposed acceptableness of anything they have done or can do until created in Christ Jesus unto good works, His apostle declared, "They that are in the flesh cannot please God" (Rom. 8:8).

On the other hand, should the unregenerate be allowed to suppose they are devoid of those faculties which are necessary for knowing God's will and doing those things which are pleasing in His sight, such a delusion is likely to prove equally fatal to them. For in that case how could they ever be convinced of either sin or righteousness: of sin in themselves and of righteousness in God? How could they ever perceive that the ways of the Lord are just and their own unjust? If in fact the natural man had no kind of capacity any more than has the horse or mule to love and serve God, to repent and believe the gospel, then the pressing of such duties upon him would be most unreasonable, nor could their noncompliance be at all criminal. Accordingly we find that after our Lord informed Nicodemus of the necessity of man's being born again before he could "see" or believe to the saving of his soul, He declared that he was "condemned already" for not believing (John 3:18). Then He cleared up the whole matter by saying, "This is the condemnation, that light is come into the world, and men loved darkness rather than light, because their deeds were evil. For every one that doeth evil hateth the light, neither cometh to the light, lest his deeds should be reproved" (vv. 19-20).

Clear Distinctions Necessary

From these and similar verses well-instructed scholars of the Word of God have been led to draw a sharp distinction between the absence of natural faculties and the lack of moral ability, the latter being the essence of moral depravity. The absence of natural faculties clears one from blame, for one who is physically blind is not blameworthy because he cannot see, nor is an idiot to be condemned because he is devoid of rationality. Moral inability is of a totally different species, for it proceeds from an evil heart, consisting of a culpable failure to use in the right way those talents with which God has endowed us. The unregenerate man who refuses to obtain any knowledge of God through reading His Word is justly chargeable with such neglect; but the saint is not guilty because he fails to arrive at a perfect knowledge of God, for such an attainment lies beyond the reach of his faculties.

Some may object to what has just been pointed out and say that this is a distinction of no consequence; inability is inability; what a man cannot do he cannot do; whether it be owing to a lack of faculties or the absence of a good heart, it comes to the same thing. All this is true so far as the end is concerned, but not so far as the criminality. If an evil disposition were a valid excuse, then all the evil in the world would be excusable. Because sin cannot be holiness, is it the less evil? Because the sinner cannot, at the same time, be a saint, is he no more a sinner? Because an evil-minded man cannot get rid of his evil mind while he has no inclination to do so, is he only to be pitied like one who labors under a misconception? True also, this distinction affords no relief to one who is dead in sin, nor does it inform him how he can by his own effort become alive to God; nevertheless, it adds to his condemnation and makes him aware of his awful state.

For vindicating the justice of God, for magnifying His grace, for laying low the haughtiness of man, moral inability is a distinction of vital consequence, however hateful it may be to the ungodly. Unless the line is drawn between excusing a wicked heart and pitying a palsied hand, between moral depravity and the lack of moral faculties, the whole Word of God and all His ways with man must appear invalid, shrouded in midnight darkness. Deny this distinction, and God's requiring perfect obedience from such imperfect creatures must seem altogether unreasonable, His condemning to everlasting misery everyone who does evil (when doing evil is what no man can avoid) excessively harsh. But let men be made aware of the horrible plague of their hearts, let the distinct difference between the absence of moral faculties and the sinful misuse of them be seen and felt, and every mouth will be stopped and all the world become guilty before God.

Though at first it may seem to the preacher that the proclamation of human impotence defeats his ends and works against the highest interest of his hearers, yet if God is pleased to bless his fidelity to the truth (and faith may always count upon such blessing), it will do the hearer good in his latter end, for it will drive him out from the hiding place of falsehood, it will bring him to realize his need of fleeing for refuge to the glorious hope set before him in the gospel. By pulling down strongholds, casting down imaginations and every high thing that exalts itself against God, the way is paved for bringing into captivity every thought to the obedience of Christ. To see oneself "without strength" and at the same time "without excuse" is indeed humiliating, yet this must be seen by the sinner—before either the justice of the divine law or one's utter helplessness and conviction of guilt—as the chief prerequisite for embracing Christ as one's all-sufficient Savior.

It will thus be seen that there are two chief dangers concerning which the preacher must be on his guard while endeavoring to expound this doctrine. First, while pressing the utter inability of the natural man to meet the just claims of God or even so much as perform a single spiritual duty, he must not overthrow or even weaken the equally evident fact of man's moral responsibility. Second, in his zeal to leave unimpaired the moral agency and personal accountability of the sinner, he must not repudiate his total depravity and death in trespasses and sins. This is no easy task, and here as everywhere the minister is made to feel his need of seeking wisdom from above. Yet let it be pointed out that prayer is not designed as a substitute for hard work and study, but rather as a preparative for the same. Difficulties are not to be shunned, but overcome by diligent effort; but diligent effort can only be rightly directed and effectually employed as divine grace enables, and that grace is to be expectantly sought.

Probably it is best to begin by considering the fact of man's impotence. At first this may be presented in general terms and in its broad outlines by showing that the thrice holy God can require nothing less than holiness from His creatures, that He can by no means tolerate any sin in them. The standard which God has set before men is the moral law which demands perfect and perpetual obedience; being spiritual it enjoins holiness of character as well as conduct, purity of heart as well as acts. Such a standard fallen man cannot reach, such demands he cannot meet, as is demonstrated from the entire history of the Jews under that law.

Next it should be pointed out that the Lord Jesus did not lower that standard or modify God's commands, but uniformly and insistently upheld the one and pressed the other, as is unmistakably clear in Matthew 5:17-48; nevertheless He repeatedly affirmed the moral impotence of fallen man (John 5:44; 6:44; 8:43). This same twofold teaching is repeated by the apostles, especially in the epistles to the Romans and Corinthians.

From the general we may descend to the particular and show the extent of man's impotence and depravity. Sin has so ruined the whole of his being that the understanding is darkened, the heart corrupted, the will perverted, each detail being proved and illustrated from Scripture. Then in summing up this solemn aspect, appeal may be made to that word of Christ's where He declared not merely that there were many things (or even some things) man could not do without His enablement, but that without Him man could do nothing" (John 15:5)—nothing good, nothing acceptable to God. If man could prepare himself to turn to God, or turn of himself after the Holy Spirit has prepared him, he could do much. But since it is God who works in us "both to will and to do of his good pleasure" (Phil. 2:13), He is the One who first implants the desire and then gives the power to fulfill it. Not only must the understanding be so enlightened as to discern the good from the evil, but the heart has to be changed so as to prefer the good before the evil.

Next it is well to show clearly the nature of man's inability: what it does not consist of (the lack of faculties suited to the performance of duty) and what it does consist of. Care needs to be taken and arguments given to show that man's inability is moral rather than physical, voluntary rather than compulsory, criminal rather than innocent. After this has been done at some length, confirmation may be obtained by an appeal to the hearer's own experience. If honest he must acknowledge that his own consciousness testifies to the fact that he sins willingly and therefore willfully, and that his conscience registers condemnation upon him. The very facts that we sin freely and that conscience accuses us show we ought to have avoided it. Whatever line a man takes in attempting to justify his own wrongdoing, he promptly forsakes it whenever his fellowmen wrong him. He never argues that they were unable to do otherwise, nor does he excuse them on the ground of their inheriting a corrupt nature from Adam! Moreover, in the hour of remorse, the man who has squandered his substance and wrecked his health does not even excuse himself, but freely owns "What a fool I have been! There is no one to blame but myself."

The impotence of the natural man to choose God for his portion is greater than that of an ape to reason like an Isaac Newton, yet there is this vital difference between the two: the inability of the former is a criminal one, that of the latter is not so because of its native and original incapacity. Man's moral inability lies not in the lack of capacity but in lack of desire. One incurs no guilt when there is a willingness of mind and a desire of heart to do the thing commanded but no capacity to carry it out. But where there is capacity (competent faculties) but unwillingness, there is guilt—wherever disaffection for God exists so does sin. Man's moral inability consists of an inveterate aversion for God, and it is this corruption of heart which alone has influence to prevent the proper use of the faculties with which he is endowed, and issues in acts of sin and rebellion against God. Even the bare knowledge of duty in all cases renders moral agents under obligation to do it: "To him that knoweth to do good, and doeth it not, to him it is sin" (Jam. 4:17).

It is very necessary that the preacher should be perfectly clear in his own mind that the moral impotence of the natural man is not of such a nature as to exempt him from God's claims or excuse him from the discharge of his duties. Some have drawn the erroneous conclusion that it is incongruous to call upon the unregenerate to perform spiritual duties. They say that only exhortations suited to the state of the unregenerate, such as the performance of civil righteousness, should be addressed to them. The truth is that a perfect heart and a perfect life are as much required as if men were not fallen creatures, and required of the greatest sinner as much as of the best saint. The righteous demands of the Most High must not be whittled down because of human depravity. David did not trim his exhortations to meet the inability of man: "Kiss the Son, lest he be angry, and ye perish from the way" (Ps. 2:12). Isaiah did not keep back the command "Wash you, make you clean; put away the evil of your doings from before mine eyes" (1:16) though he knew the people were so corrupt they would not and could not comply.

Urgent Invitation Obligatory

Nor should the preacher have the slightest hesitation in urging the unregenerate to use the means of grace and in declaring it is men's certain duty to employ them. The divine ordinances of hearing and reading the Word, of praying and conversing with God's people, are thereby made a real test of men's hearts—as to whether they really desire salvation or despise it. Though God does renew men by His Spirit, yet He appoints the means by which sinners are to be subservient to such a work of grace. If they scorn and neglect the means, the blame is in themselves and not in God. If we are not willing to seek salvation, it proves we have no desire to find it; then in the day to come we shall be reproved as wicked and slothful servants (Matt. 25:26). The plea that man has no power will then mean nothing, for then the fact that his lack of power consists only in a lack of heart will appear with sunlight clearness, and he will be justly condemned for contempt of God's Word; his blood will be upon his own head for disregarding the warnings of God's servants.

Yet so perverse is fallen human nature that men will argue, "What is the good of using the means when it does not lie in our power to give effect to them?" Even if there were no hope of success, God's command for us to use the means is sufficient to demand our compliance: "Master, we have toiled all the night, and have taken nothing: nevertheless at thy word I will let down the net" (Luke 5:5). I cannot infallibly promise a farmer who plows and sows that he will have a good crop, yet I may assure him that it is God's general way to bless the prudent and diligent. I cannot say to everyone who desires posterity, "Marry and you shall have children." But I may point out that if people refuse the ordinance of marriage they will never have any lawful children. The preacher needs to point out the grave peril incurred by those who spurn the help God proffers. Felix "trembled" (Acts 24:25), but he failed to act on his convictions. Unless the Lord is sought while He is "near" us (Isa. 55:6), He may finally abandon us. Every resistance to the impressions of the Spirit leaves the heart harder than it was before.

After all that has been said it is scarcely necessary for us to press upon the preacher the tremendous importance of this doctrine. It displays as no other the perfect consistency of divine justice and grace. It reveals to the believer that his infirmities and imperfections are not the comforting cover-up of guilt that he would like to think they are. All moral infirmity, all lack of perfect holiness, is entirely his own fault, for which he should be deeply humbled. It shows sinners that their perdition is really altogether of themselves, for they are unwilling to be made clean. The kindest thing we can do for them is to shatter their self-righteous hopes, to make them realize both their utter helplessness and their entire inexcusableness. The high demands of God are to be pressed upon them with the design of bringing them to cry to Him to graciously work in them that which He requires. Genuine conviction of sin consists in a thorough realization of responsibility and guilt, of our inability and dependence upon divine grace. Nothing is so well calculated to produce that conviction, under the Spirit's blessing, as the faithful preaching of this unpalatable truth.

THE DOCTRINE
OF RECONCILIATION

Contents

Introduction

Three considerations have influenced us in the selection of this theme. First, a desire to preserve the balance of Truth. In order to do this it is desirable that there should be an alternation between and a proportionate emphasis upon both the objective and the subjective sides of the Truth. After we had completed our exposition of the doctrine of Justification we followed the same with a series on the doctrine of Sanctification: the former treats entirely of the righteousness which Christ has wrought or procured for His people, being something wholly outside of themselves and independent of their own efforts; whereas the latter speaks not only of the perfect purity which the believer has in Christ, but also of the holiness which the Spirit actually communicates to the soul and which is influential on his conduct. Then we took up the doctrine of Predestination which is concerned entirely with the sovereignty of God, and therefore we followed that with a series of man's Impotency and the Saint's Perseverance, where the principal emphasis was upon human responsibility. It will be well for us now to turn our attention back again to the Divine operations and the wondrous provisions of Divine grace for the recovery of rebels against God.

Second, because of a felt need of again bringing conspicuously before our readers "the cross of our Lord Jesus Christ." It is His sacrificial work which is prominent, yea, dominant in the reconciling of God to His people. It was by the shedding of Christ's precious blood that God was placated and His wrath averted. It was by Christ's being chastised that peace has been made for us. And it is by the preaching of the Cross that our awful enmity against God is slain and that we are moved to abandon our vile warfare against Him. As it is upwards of twelve years since we completed the rather lengthy series of articles we wrote upon the Atonement, under the title "The Satisfaction of Christ," it seems high time that we once more contemplated the greatest marvel and miracle of all history, namely, the Lamb of God being slain for the redemption of sinners. The doctrine of reconciliation has much to do with what took place at Calvary, yea apart from that no reconciliation with God had been possible. It is therefore a subject which should warm the hearts of the saints and bow them in adoration at the feet of the Redeemer.

Third, because it treats of an aspect of the Gospel which receives scant attention in the modern pulpit. Nor has it ever, so far as we have been able to ascertain, been made very prominent. This doctrine has failed to command the notice which it merits even from God's own servants and people. Far less appears to have been preached on it than on either justification or sanctification. For one book written on this subject probably fifty have been published on either of the others. Why this should be is not easy to explain: it is not because it is more obscure or intricate. In our judgment, much to the contrary. Certainly it is of equal importance and value, for it treats of an aspect of our relationship and recovery to God as essential as either of the others. Our need of justification lies in our failure to keep the Law of God; of sanctification, because we are defiled and polluted by sin, and therefore unfit for the presence of the, Holy One; our reconciliation, because we are alienated from God, rebels against Him, with no heart for fellowship with Him. Though the terms justify and sanctify occur more frequently in the New Testament than does "reconcile," yet the correlative "God of peace" and other expressions must also be duly noted.

Not only has this doctrine been more or less neglected, but it has been seriously perverted by some and considerably misunderstood by many others. Both Socinians (who repudiate the Triunity of the Godhead and the Atonement of Christ) and Arminians deny the twofoldness of reconciliation, declaring it to be only on one side. They insist that it is man who is alienated from God, and so in need of reconciliation, that God never entertained enmity toward His fallen creatures, but has ever sought their recovery. They argue that since it was man who made the breach by departing from his Maker, he is the one who needs to be reconciled and restored to Him. They refuse to allow that sin has produced any change in God's relationship or attitude unto the guilty, yea, so far from doing so that His own love moved Him to take the initiative and provide a Savior for rebels, and that He now beseeches them to throw down the weapons of their opposition, assuring them of a Father's welcome when they return unto Him.

Such is the view of the Plymouth Brethren. In his work "The Ministry of Reconciliation" C. H. Macintosh (one of the most influential of their early men) declares: "We often hear it said that 'the death of Christ was necessary in order to reconcile God to man.' This is a pious mistake, arising from inattention to the language of the Holy Spirit and indeed to the plain meaning of the word 'reconcile.' God never changed, never stepped out of His normal and true position. He abides faithful. There was, and could be, no derangement, no confusion, no alienation, so far as He was concerned; and therefore there could be no need of reconciling Him to us. In fact it was exactly the contrary. Man had gone astray; he was the enemy, and needed to be reconciled... Wherefore, then, as might be expected, Scripture never speaks of reconciling God to man. There is no such expression to be found within the covers of the New Testament." This is something he calls a "point of immense importance," and consequently all who have succeeded him in that strange system have echoed his teaching: how far it is removed from the Truth will be shown in the articles that follow.

Some hyper-Calvinists are also much confused on this doctrine. Through failing to see that God's being reconciled to sinners who believe concerns His official relationship and not His essential character, they have demurred at the expression "a reconciled God," supposing it connotes some charge within Himself. They argue that since God has loved His elect with an everlasting love (Jer. 31:3) and that since He changes not (Mal. 3:6), it is wrong for us to suppose that reconciliation to anything more on our side only. They insist that to speak of God's being reconciled unto us implies an alteration either in His affections or purpose, and that neither of these can stand with His immutability. To speak of God's first loving His people, then hating then, and then again loving them, appears to them as imputing fickleness to Him. So it would be if these predictions of God were made of Him considered in the same character and relationship. But they are not. As their Father God has loved His people with an unalterable love, but as the Moral Governor of this world and the Judge of all the earth He has a legal enmity against those who trample His Law beneath their feet.

The following question was submitted to Mr. J. C. Philpot:—"What is meant by 'a reconciled God,' an expression which some of the Lord's children, even great and good men, have made use of? I believe that the Lord Jehovah from all eternity foresaw the fall, and provided means to save those whom He had chosen in Christ, consistent with all His attributes, holiness, justice, etc. Now, as love was the moving cause, how can the word 'reconcile' be correctly used in respect of God? Does it not imply a change? If it does, how can it be correctly used in reference to God?" His answer to this appears in the March 1856 issue of "The Gospel Standard," and though it will make a rather lengthy quotation, yet we might be doing him an injustice not to give it in full.

"We do not consider the expression 'A reconciled God' strictly correct. The language of the New Testament is not that God is reconciled to us, but that we are reconciled to God. 'And all things are of God, who has reconciled us unto Himself by Jesus Christ, and has given to us the ministry of reconciliation— that God was in Christ reconciling the world to Himself, not imputing their trespasses to them; and that He has committed to us the word of reconciliation. Now we are ambassadors for Christ, as though God did beseech you by us. We beg you in Christ's stead, be reconciled to God.' (2 Cor. 5:18-20). And again 'And, having made peace through the blood of His cross, it pleased the Father to reconcile all things by Him unto Himself—by Him, whether things in earth or things in Heaven. And you, who were once alienated and enemies in your mind by wicked works, yet now He has reconciled in the body of His flesh through death to present you holy and unblameable and unreprovable in His sight,' (Col. 1:20-22). See also Romans 5:10.

"The very nature of God, His very being and essence, is to be unchanging and unchangeable, as James beautifully speaks: 'With Him there is no variableness, neither shadow of turning.' But reconciliation on God's part to us, would seem to imply a change of mind, an alteration of purpose in Him, and is therefore, so far, inconsistent and incompatible with the unchangeableness of the Divine character. It is also, strictly speaking, inconsistent, as our correspondent observes, with the eternal love of God, and seems to represent the atonement as influencing His mind, and turning it from wrath to love, and from displeasure to mercy and grace. Now, the Scripture represents the gift of Christ, and consequently the sufferings and blood-shedding for which and unto which He was given, not, as the procuring cause, but as the gracious effect of the love of God. 'Herein is love, not that we loved God, but that He loved us, and sent His Son to be a propitiation for our sins' (1 John 4:10). See also John 3:16, Romans 8:32, 1 John 4:9.

"But though the Scripture speaks of reconciliation, not of God to man, but of man to God, and that through the blood of the cross alone (Col. 1:20); yet it holds forth, in the plainest, strongest language, a real and effective 'sacrifice,' 'atonement,' and 'propitiation,' offered to God by the Lord Jesus; all which terms express or imply an actual satisfaction rendered to God for sin, and such a satisfaction, as that without it there could be no pardon. It is especially needful to bear this in mind, because the Socinians and other heretics who deny or explain away the atonement, insist much on this point, that the Scripture does not speak of a reconciled God. Therefore, though we do not believe that the atonement produced a change in the mind of God, so as to turn Him from hatred to love, for He loved the elect with an everlasting love, (Jer. 31:3), or that it was a price paid to procure His favor, still, there was a sacrifice offered, a propitiation made, whereby, and whereby alone, sin was pardoned, blotted out, and forever put away.

"By steadily bearing these two things in mind, we shall be the better prepared to understand in what reconciliation through the blood of the cross consists. Against the persons of the elect there was, in the mind of God, no vindictive wrath, no penal anger (Isa. 27:4); but there was a displeasure against their sins, and so far with them for their sins. So God was angry with Moses (Deut. 1:37), with Aaron (Deut. 9:20), with David (2 Sam. 11:27; 1 Chron. 21:7), with Solomon (1 Kings 11:9) for their personal sins, though all of them were in the covenant of grace, and loved by Him with an everlasting love. Thus the Scriptures speak of the anger and wrath of God, and of that wrath being turned away and pacified (Isa. 12:1; Ezek. 16:63), which it could only be by the blood of the Lamb.

"Again, sin is a violation of the justice of God, a breaking of His holy Law, an offence against His intrinsic purity and holiness, which He cannot pass by. Adequate satisfaction must, therefore, be made to His offended justice, or pardon cannot be granted. Now, here we see the necessity and nature of the sufferings and obedience, blood-shedding and death of the Lord Jesus, as also why reconciliation was needed, and what reconciliation effected. By the active and passive obedience of the Son of God in the flesh, by His meritorious life and death, by His offering Himself as a sacrifice for sin, a full and complete satisfaction was rendered to the violating justice of God, the Law was perfectly obeyed and everlasting righteousness brought in. Satisfaction being rendered to His infinite justice, now God can be just and yet the Justifier of him which believes in Jesus.'

Now the jarring perfections of mercy and justice are harmonized and reconciled, so that mercy and truth meet together, righteousness and peace kiss each other. Now God can not only be gracious, but 'faithful and just to forgive us our sins and to cleanse us from all unrighteousness.' There is, then, no such reconciliation of God as to make Him love those whom He did not love before, for He loved the elect from all eternity in Christ, their covenant—head. But a breach being made by the fall, and sin having, as it were, burst in to make a separation between God and them (Isa. 59:2), that love could not flow forth till satisfaction was made for sin, and that barrier removed, which it was in one day (Zech. 3:9). And not only so, but the persons of the elect were defiled with sin (Ezek. 16:5,6), and therefore needed washing, which they were in the blood of the Lamb (Rev. 1:5, etc.). In this way not only was the reconciliation of the Church effected, but she, the bride and spouse of Christ, was brought near unto God, from whom sin had separated her.

"But reconciliation has a further aspect. It comprehends our reconciliation to God not merely as a thing already effected by the blood-shedding of God's dear Son, but as a present experience in the soul. The apostle says 'By whom we have now received the atonement' (Rom. 5:11); and again, 'we pray you, in Christ's stead, be reconciled to God' (2 Cor. 5:20), that is, by receiving into your hearts the reconciliation already made by His blood. It is with reference to this experience that much is spoken in the Scriptures which has led to the idea of 'a reconciled God. ' Thus the Church complains of God's being angry with her (Isa. 12:1), of being 'consumed by His anger and troubled by His wrath' (Ps. 90:7), of His 'shutting up in anger His tender mercies' (Ps. 77:9), and again of His 'turning away from the fierceness of His anger and causing it to cease' (Ps. 85:3, 4), of His 'not keeping anger forever' (Ps. 103:9), of His being pacified (Ezek. 16:63) of His 'anger being turned away' (Ps. 78:38; Hos. 14:4). All these expressions are the utterance of the Church's experience. When God's anger is sensibly felt in the conscience He is viewed as angry, and His wrathful displeasure is dreaded and deprecated; when He manifests mercy this anger is felt to be removed, to be turned away; and it is now as if He were reconciled to the sinner.

"Putting all these things together we seem to arrive at the following conclusions: (1) That it is not God who is reconciled to the Church, but that it is the Church which is reconciled to God. (2) That this reconciliation was effected by the incarnation, obedience, sacrifice and death of the Lord Jesus. (3) That till this reconciliation be made experimentally known the awakened conscience feels the anger of God on account of sin. (4) That when the atonement is received and the blood of Christ sprinkled on the conscience, then the soul is really and truly reconciled to God."

What satisfaction this reply gave to the original inquirer, or how lucid it appears to our readers (even after a second or third perusal), we know not, but to us it seems a strange medley, lacking in perspicuity and betraying confusion of thought in the mind of its composer. First, Mr. Philpot considered that the language of the New Testament does not warrant the expression "A reconciled God." Second, he felt that to affirm a reconciliation on God's part to us would imply an alteration of purpose in Him and as though the Atonement changed His mind "From displeasure to mercy and grace." Then he evidently feared he was coming very close to the ground occupied by the Socinians; so, third, he allowed that the work of Christ was both a "sacrifice" and a "propitiation." But "a propitiation" is the very thing which is needed to conciliate one who is offended! To aver there was "rendered to God for sin an actual satisfaction, and such a satisfaction as that without which there could be no pardon," is only another way of saying that God was alienated and needed placating before He could be reconciled to His enemies.

In his next paragraph he virtually or in effect contradicts what he had advanced in the previous one, for he expressly declares "Against the persons of the elect there was in the mind of God no vindictive wrath, no penal anger." Then wherein lay the need of a "propitiation?" "Penal" means "relating to punishment. "if there was no judicial anger on God's part as Governor and Judge and if His elect were not exposed to the punishment of the Law because of their sins, then why the sacrifice of Christ for them? Clearly Mr. P. felt the shoe pinching him there, for in his next paragraph he brings in the violation of the justice of God and the "satisfaction" this required. Yet toward the end he wavers again by saying "sin having, as it were, burst in to make a separation between God and them." Why such hesitating qualification? Sin did cause a breach on both sides, and the one Party needed to be "propitiated," and the other "converted" before the breach could be healed. Our purpose in quoting form C.H. Machintosh and J.C. Philpot (whose writings served to mould the views of many thousands) is to demonstrate the need for a Scriptural exposition of this doctrine.

We are glad to say that in his last years Mr. Philpot was granted a clearer grasp of the truth, as appears from his helpful exposition of Ephesians 2.

Chapter 1
Its Distinctions

Before taking up our subject in a positive and constructive manner it seems advisable that we should endeavor to remove a misapprehension under which a number of our readers are laboring, and which requires to be cleared up before they will be in a fit condition to weigh without bias and thus be enabled to receive what we hope to present in later articles. It is for their special benefit this one is composed, and we trust that other friends will kindly bear with us if they find it rather wearisome to follow a labored discussion of that which presents no difficulty to them. To enter into a consideration of this particular point at such an early stage in the series will oblige us to somewhat infringe upon other aspects of our subject which will be taken up later, but, this appears necessary if we are to "clear the decks for action," or to change the figure, if we are to rid the ground of superfluous encumbrances and fit it for a sowing of the seed.

That which presents a difficulty to those who have been brought up in some Calvinistic circles is, how can God be said to be reconciled to His elect, seeing that He has loved them with an everlasting and unchanging love? Much of our opening article was devoted to a particular answer to such an inquiry, but as we deem that answer far from being a satisfactory one, we shall here confine ourselves to its elucidation. To us it appears that the explanation furnished by Mr. Philpot was confused and faulty, and that is was so through failure to distinguish between things that differ—therefore the title we have accorded this article. If we are to avoid becoming hopelessly muddled on this point, we must discriminate sharply between what the elect are as viewed only in the eternal purpose of God, and what they are in themselves by nature. And further, we must carefully differentiate between God considered as their Father and God considered as the Moral Governor and Judge of all mankind.

That it may appear we do not advance anything in the remainder of this article which clashes with or deviates from the teaching of sound theologians in the past, we will make brief quotations from four .of the best-known Puritans. "We are actually justified, pardoned and reconciled when we repent and believe. Whatever thoughts and purposes of grace God may have towards us from eternity, we are under the fruits of sin till we become penitent believers" (T. Manton). In his treatise on "The Work of the Holy Spirit in our Salvation" Thos. Goodwin points out: "There are two different states or conditions which the elect of God, who are saved, pass through, between which regeneration is the passage. The one is their first state in which they are born: a state of bondage to sin, and obnoxious to instant damnation while they remain in it.. .The other of grace and salvation, therefore opposite to the former state."

"God does hate His elect in some sense before their actual reconciliation. God was placable before Christ, appeased By Christ. But until there be such conditions which God has appointed in the creature, he has no interest in this reconciliation of God, and whatever person he be in whom the condition is not found, he remains under the wrath of God, and therefore in some sense under God's hatred" (Stephen Charnock, vol. 3, p. 345). When writing on "The Satisfaction of Christ" John Owen said: "This then is what we ascribe to the death of Christ, when we say that as a sacrifice we were reconciled to God or that He made reconciliation for us. Having made God our Enemy by sin, Christ by His death turned away His anger, appeased His wrath, and brought us into favor again with God." How far Mr. Philpot digressed from the teaching of these men we must leave his friends to judge for themselves. But we appeal now to an infinitely higher authority, namely, the Word of God.

Nothing is more plainly taught in Scripture than that all men without exception are before actual regeneration in a like state and condition, and occupy the same standing or status before the Divine Law. Whatever distinguishing design God has purposed in Himself to afterward effect as a change in His own elect by the operations of His free grace, until those operations take place they are in precisely the-same case as the non-elect. "We have before proved both Jews and Gentiles that they are all under sin"—guilty, beneath sentence of condemnation. "There is none righteous, no not one"—not one who has met the requirements of the Divine Law. "That every mouth may be stopped and all the world may become guilty before God"— that is, obnoxious to the Divine Judgment. "There is no difference for all have sinned and come short of the glory of God" (Rom. 3:9, 10, 19, 22, 23). The condition and position of every one relative to the Law is one and the same before his regeneration and justification, and the decree of God concerning any difference that is yet to be made in some in nowise modifies that solemn fact. This is one chief reason why the Gospel is to be preached to every creature.

The Scriptures are equally explicit in describing the effects and consequences of lying under God's wrath. Before conversion the elect equally with the non—elect are in a state of alienation from God (Eph. 4:18), and therefore none of their services or performances can be acceptable to Him. He will receive naught at their hands: "he who turns away his ear from hearing the Law (an in the case with every unregenerate soul), even his prayer is a hateful thing" (Prov. 28:9). They are all under the power of the Devil (Col. 1:13), who rules at his pleasure in the children of disobedience (Eph. 2:2). They are "without Christ. . . having no hope, and without God in the world" (Eph. 2:12). They are under the curse or condemning power of the Law (Gal. 3:13). They are "children in whom is no faith" (Deut. 32:20) and therefore utterly unable to do a single thing which can meet with God's approval, for "without faith it is impossible to please God" (Heb. 11:6). They are therefore "ready to perish" (Deut. 26:5).

"He who does not the Son shall not see life, but the wrath of God abides upon him" (John 3:36). What could be plainer than that? Is not an elect soul an unbeliever until the moment God is pleased to give faith unto him? Assuredly: then equally sure is it that he is also under the wrath of God so long as he remains an unbeliever. Not only so, but the Word of God solemnly declares that the elect are "by nature the children of wrath even as others" (Eph. 2:3), and no Papish priest can make them otherwise by sprinkling a few drops of "holy water" upon them. But "children of wrath" they could not be had they come into this world in a justified and reconciled state. No person can be in two contrary states at the same time, obnoxious to wrath, and yet God at pcacc with him, under the guilt of sin and yet justified. Wrath is upon them from the womb (because of their sinning in Adam), and that wrath remains Oft them so long as they continue unbelievers. Though they were (in God's purpose) in Christ from eternity, that did not prevent them being in Adam in time and suffering the penal effects of this fall.

There is an appointed hour in their earthly history when the- elect pass from under the penal wrath of God and are justified by Him and reconciled to Him. Justification is an act of God, an act in time, an external act. It is an act of God in a way of judicial process—His declaration as supreme Judge. It is opposed to condemnation, the granting a full discharge therefrom (Rom. 8:33-35). It is not an internal decision in God, which always remains in Him, and effects change in the status of the person justified; but is a temporal act of His power which makes a relative change in the person's standing before Him. It is upon the person's believing in Christ that God justifies him and that he passes from a state of guilt and alienation to one of righteousness and reconciliation: he that believes on Him is not condemned (that is, he is justified), but he that believes not is condemned already (John 3:18). "He who believes on Him that sent Me but has everlasting life (by regeneration), and shall not come into condemnation, but is passed from death unto life"—that is, the life of justification (John 5:24).

If persons are justified in a proper sense by faith, then they are not justified from eternity, for we believe in time, not eternity. That we are justified by faith, is the doctrine of the Gospel, as is apparent from the whole current of God's Word. To cite but one verse: "Knowing that a man is not justified by the works of the Law, but by faith of Jesus Christ, even we have believed in Jesus Christ," (Gal. 2:16). That the apostle is there speaking of being justified in the sight of God, and not merely in the court of conscience, is beyond all doubt to any that will duly and fairly consider the scope of the Holy Spirit in that passage. Being justified by faith in Jesus Christ is there placed in opposition to being "justified by the works of the Law" which shows that something more fundamental than our own assurance is in view. "By the deeds of the Law shall no flesh be justified in His sight" (Rom. 3:19) makes it clear that none can obtain sentence of acquittal in the court of Divine adjudication by their own deeds. It is before God and not in the believer's consciousness that justification takes place.

"And the Scripture foreseeing that God would justify the heathen through faith, preached before the Gospel unto Abraham, saying, In you shall all nations be blessed" (Gal. 3:8). It is to be noted that there are two words here which lie directly against justification before believing: that God would justify the heathen—which must needs respect time to come; and "shall all nations be blessed" or justified—a "shall be" cannot be put for a thing already done. To this agrees "in the Lord shall all the seed of Israel be justified" (Isa. 45:25): by union with Christ through faith shall they be pronounced righteous. Again; "For as by one man's disobedience many were made sinners, so by the obedience of One shall many be made righteous" (Rom. 5:19). Upon which the Puritan Win. Bridge said, "It is remarkable. that when the Holy Spirit speaks of Adam's sin condemning his posterity, He speaks of it as already past; but when He speaks of Christ's righteousness for the justification of sinners He changes to the future tense—as if He purposely designed to prevent our thoughts running after justification before believing."

What has been said above about the justification of God's elect upon their believing, holds equally good concerning His reconciliation to them when they throw down the weapons of their warfare against Him. Not only was their reconciliation decreed from everlasting but peace was actually made by Christ when He shed His blood (Col. 1:20); nevertheless, reconciliation itself is not effected until the Holy Spirit has so wrought within them as to bring about their conversion. This is conclusively established by the following passages: "For if, when we were enemies we were reconciled to God by the death of His Son, much more being reconciled, we shall be saved by His life. And not only so, but we also joy in God through our Lord Jesus Christ, by whom we have now received the reconciliation" (Rom. 5:10, 11)— that "now" would be meaningless if we were reconciled only in the eternal decree of God: what God decreed for us is here received by us! So again, "And you that were sometime alienated and enemies in your mind by wicked works, yet NOW has He reconciled" (Col. 1:21).

It would obviate considerable misunderstanding if it were clearly perceived that the everlasting love of God toward His elect is mainly an act of His will, the exercise of His good pleasure, the purpose of His grace, whereby He determined to do certain things for them and instate them in glory in His own good time and way. But that purpose effects nothing for them nor puts anything into them—for these there must be external acts of God's power making good His purpose. From all eternity God determined to make this earth, yet six thousand years ago it did not exist! He had ordained a final Day of Judgment but it has not yet arrived. God has purposed that in and through Christ He will justify and save certain persons, but they are not thereby justified because God has purposed it. It is true they will be in due time, but not before they have been enabled to believingly appropriate the atoning work of Christ in their behalf. We must therefore draw a line between the absolute certainty of the fruition of anything God has eternally purposed, and its actual accomplishment or bringing it to pass in His appointed time.

What has been pointed out in the last paragraph should make it easier for the reader to grasp that God's eternal love unto His own (which is an imminent act of His will or good pleasure, entirely within Himself) does not exempt them from coming beneath His anger (which is not any passion in God, but the outward visitation of His displeasure— because of sin; nor does it prevent their lying beneath the dispensations of His judicial wrath, until by some interpositions of His grace in time, when He actually changes their personal state (by regeneration) and legal status (by justification), freeing them from condemnation and instating them into His favor. In other words, much may occur in the interval between God's eternal purpose and the actual working out of the same—though nothing which can in anywise jeopardize His purpose, and nothing that was not foreseen when He framed it.

But it is objected by hyper-Calvinists, If the elect were not justified in Christ from all eternity then when God pronounces them just there is an alteration in His will and love toward them. Not so, God is no more mutable because He justifies His people in time, than He is because He regenerates them in time. God is no more chargeable with change of purpose when He produces a change in a person's standing upon his believing, than He is when He produces a change in a person's condition by the miracle of the new birth. All the change is in the creature. Though God absolutely decrees, and that from everlasting, to regenerate, to justify and to reconcile all His chosen, with the alteration of His governmental attitude toward them which that involves, yet this argues not the least shadow of change in God Himself when at the predestinated hour that great change is affected. Do but distinguish between the grace decreeing and the power of God executing, and all is plain. "Whom He did predestinate, them He also called, and whom He called, them He also justified" (Rom. 8:30) —the calling and justifying are the fruits of His electing love.

But again it is objected, the elect are designated "sheep" before they believe (John 10:16), and in God's esteem they are then in a justified state. Answer: they are called "sheep" according to the immutability of the Divine decree, which cannot be frustrated, and on that account God calls "things which are not as though they were" (Rom. 4:17), nevertheless, that verse affirms they "are not" that is, they have no actual existence. They are "sheep" in the purpose of God, but not so as touching the accomplishment of the same until they are regenerated. Paul was a sheep in the decree of God even when he was wolf-like in preying upon the flock of Christ. Surely none will say he was actually a sheep while he was "breathing out threatenings and slaughter against the disciples of the Lord" (Acts 9:1). From the decree of God we may safely conclude the certainty of its accomplishment; but to argue that a thing is actually accomplished because Divinely foreordained is a most foolish and dangerous way of reasoning.

The love of God's purpose and good pleasure has not the least inconsistency with those hindrances to the peace and friendship of God which sin has interposed, for though the holiness of His Law, the righteousness of His government and the veracity of His Word, stood in the way of His taking a sinner into friendship and fellowship with Himself, until full satisfaction has been made to His broken Law and insulted Majesty; nevertheless His love determined and His wisdom devised a way where His sovereign good will should recover His people, and that, without sullying the Divine character to the slightest degree, yea, in magnifying those attributes which sin had affronted. God's love has proven efficacious by the means He devised "that His banished one may not be cast out from Him" (2 Sam. 14:14).

From all that has been pointed out above it should be quite evident that this doctrine of reconciliation does not teach that God loved and hated His elect at the same time and in the same respect. He loved them in respect of the free purpose of His sovereign will; but His wrath was upon them in respect of His violated Law and provoked justice by their sin. But His love gave Christ to satisfy for their sins and to redeem them from the curse of the Law, and in due time He sends His Spirit to regenerate them, which lays the foundation for their conversion and restoration to Him.

The following distinctions must, then, be kept steadily in mind:

Between God's looking upon His elect in the purpose of His grace and as under the sentence of His Law: though the elect are born under the dispensation of His wrath, yet it is not executed upon them personally.

Between there being no change in God and a change in His outward dealings with us.

Between God's purpose concerning His elect in eternity and the accomplishment of that purpose in a time state.

Between God's viewing the elect in Christ their Covenant—Head and as the depraved descendants of fallen Adam. In the one cause, as "His dear children" in the other; as being "by nature the children of wrath."

Between God's unchanging love for us as our Father, and His official displeasure as our moral Governor and Judge. This distinction is illustrated in the case of Christ. He was the Beloved of the Father and never ceased to be so, yet Divine wrath was visited upon Him at the cross. He was dealt with not as the Son (as such) but as the Surety of His guilty people, by the Father, not as such, but as the supreme Judge.

Chapter 2
Its Need

The word reconciliation means to unite two parties who are estranged. It denotes that one has given offence and the other has taken umbrage or is displeased by it, in consequence of which there is a breach between them. Instead of friendship there is a state of hostility existing, instead of amity there is enmity, which results in separation and alienation between them. This it is which makes manifest the need for peace to be made between the estranged parties, that the wrong may be righted, the cause of the displeasure be removed, the ill-feeling cease, the breach be healed and reconciliation accomplished. The parties at variance are man and God. Man has grievously offended the Most High. He has cast off allegiance to Him, revolted from Him, despised His authority, trampled upon His commandments. The enormity of such an offence it is impossible for us to fully conceive. The heinousness of it can only be measured by the exalted dignity of the One against whom it is committed. It has been committed against the Almighty against One who is infinite in majesty, infinite in excellency, infinite in His sovereign rights over the creature of His own hands; and therefore it is an offence of infinite magnitude and turpitude.

The original offence was committed by Adam in Eden, but that fearful transgression can only be rightly understood as we recognize that Adam acted there not as a private individual but as a public person. He was Divinely constituted to be not only the father but also the federal head of the human race. He stood as the legal representative of all mankind, so that in the sight of the Divine Law what he did they did, the one transacting on the behalf of the many. The whole human race was placed on probation in the person of the first man. His trial was their trial. While he stood they stood. While he retained the approbation of God and remained in fellowship with Him, they did the same. Had he survived the trial, had he fitly discharged his responsibility, had he continued in obedience to God, his obedience had been reckoned to their account, and they had entered into the reward which had been bestowed upon him. Contrariwise, if he failed and fell, they failed and fell in him. If he disobeyed God his disobedience is imputed unto all those whom he represented and the just but fearful curse pronounced upon him falls likewise on all for whom he transacted.

What has just been pointed out by us above, was amplified at some length in our articles on the Adamic Covenant, which appeared in this magazine some ten years ago, but as many of our present readers have never seen them it will be necessary for us now to give a brief summary of what was then said. The legal relation between Adam and his posterity may be illustrated thus. God did not deal with mankind as with a field of corn, where each stalk stands upon its own individual root; but He dealt with it as a tree, all the branches of which have one common root and trunk. If you strike with an axe at the root of a tree, the whole tree falls—not only the trunk, but also the branches and even the twigs on the branches. All wither and die. So it was with Adam in Eden. God permitted Satan to lay the axe at the root of humanity and when he fell all his posterity fell with him. At one fatal stroke Adam was severed from communion with his Maker, and as the consequence "death passed upon all men." This is not a theory of human speculation but a fact of Divine revelation.

That Adam was the federal head of the human race, that he did act and transact in a representative character, and that the judicial consequences of his act was imputed to all those for whom he stood, is clearly taught in Romans 5. "Wherefore as by one man sin entered into the world, and death by sin, and so death passed upon all men, in whom all sinned" (v. 12). "Through the offence of one many be dead" (v. 15). "The judgment was by one to condemnation . . . By one man's offence death reigned . . . By the offence of one judgment came upon all men to condemnation . . . By one man 's offence many were made sinners" (vv. 16, 17, 18, 19). Such repetition and emphasis intimates the basic importance of the truth here revealed and also hints at our slowness or rather reluctance to receive the same. The meaning of these declarations is too plain for any unprejudiced mind to misunderstand. It pleased God to deal with the human race as represented in and by Adam. "In Adam all die" (1 Cor. 15:22). There is the plainly-revealed fact, and they who deny it make God a liar.

Here, then, we learn what is the formal ground of man's judicial condemnation before God. The popular idea of what it is which renders man a sinner in the sight of Heaven is altogether inadequate and erroneous. The prevailing conception is that a sinner is one who commits and practices sin. It is true that this is the character of the sinner, but it certainly is not that which primarily constitutes him such before the Divine Law. The truth is that every member of our race enters into this world a guilty sinner, alienated from God, before ever he commits a single transgression. It is not only that he possesses a depraved nature but that he is directly "under condemnation" the curse of the broken Law resting upon him, and from God he is "estranged from the womb" (Ps. 58:3). We are legally constituted sinners neither by what we are nor by what we are doing, but by the disobedience of our federal head, Adam. Adam acted not for himself alone, but for all who were to spring from him, so that his act, was forensically, our act.

Here also is the only key which satisfactorily opens to us the meaning of human history and explains the universal prevalence of sin. The human race is suffering for the sin of Adam, or it is suffering for nothing at all. There is no escape from that alternative. This earth is the scene of a grim and awful tragedy. In it we behold misery and wretchedness, strife and hatred, pain and poverty, disease and death on every side. None escape the fearful entail. That "man is born unto trouble as the sparks fly upward" is an indisputable fact. But what is the explanation of it? Every effect must have a previous cause. If we are not being punished for Adam's sin, then, coming into this world we are "children of wrath" (Eph. 2:3), beneath the Divine judgment, corrupt and defiled, on the broad road which leads to destruction, for nothing at all! Who would contend that this was better, more satisfactory, more illuminative, than the Scriptural explanation of our ruin? Genesis 3 alone explains why human history is written in the ink of blood and tears.

The objection that such an arrangement is unjust is invalid. The principle of representation is a fundamental one in human society. The father is the legal head of his children during their minority. What he does binds the family. A business house is held responsible for the transactions of its agents. Every popular election illustrates the fact that a constituency will act through its representative and be bound by his acts. The heads of a state are vested with such authority that the treaties they make are binding upon the whole nation. This principle is so basic it cannot be set aside. Human affairs could not continue nor society exist without it. This is the method by which God has acted all through. The sins of the fathers are visited upon the children. The posterity of Canaan were cursed for the single transgression of their parent (Gen. 9), the whole of his family stoned for Achan's sin (Joshua 7). Israel's high priest acted on behalf of the whole nation. One acting for others is a basic principle both of human and Divine government.

Finally, let it be pointed out that the sinner's salvation is made to depend upon this very same method. Beware, then, my reader, of quarrelling with the justice of this principle of representation—the one standing for the many. On this principle we were wrecked, and by this principle only can we be rescued. If on the one hand, the disobedience of the first Adam was the judicial ground of our condemnation, on the other hand the obedience of the last Adam is the legal basis on which God justifies sinners. The substitution of Christ in the place of His people, the imputation of their sins to Him and of His righteousness to them, is the central fact of the Gospel. But the principle of being saved by what Another has done is only possible on the ground that we were lost through what another did. The two stand or fall together. If there had been no Covenant of Works there would have been no Covenant of Grace. If there had been no death in Adam there had been no life in Christ. The Christian knows that such an arrangement is just because it is part of the revealed ways of Him who is infinitely holy and righteous.

Here, then, is the Divinely-revealed fact: "by the offence of one judgment came upon all men to condemnation" (Rom. 5:19). Here is cause of humiliation which few think about. We are members of an accursed race, the fallen children of a fallen parent, and as such we enter this world "alienated from the life of God" (Eph. 4:18), exposed to His judicial displeasure. In the day that Adam fell the frown of the Most High came upon His children. The holy nature of God abhorred the apostate race. The curse of His broken Law descended upon all of Adam's posterity. It is only thus we can account for the universality of human depravity and suffering. The corruption of human nature which we inherit from our first parents is a great evil, for it is the source of all our personal sins. For God to allow this transmission of depravity is to inflict a punishment. But how can God punish all, unless all were guilty? The fact that all do share in this common punishment is proof that all sinned in Adam. Our depravity and misery are not, as such, the infliction of the Creator, but are the retribution of the Judge.

If we now repeat some of the statements made above it is that the reader may not form a wrong conception or draw a false conclusion. We are very far from teaching here that the human race is suffering for an offence in which they had no part, that innocent creatures are being condemned for the action of another which could not fairly be laid to their account. Let it be clearly understood that God punishes none for Adam's sin (if considering him as a private person), but only for his own sin in Adam. The whole human race had a federal standing in Adam. Not only was each of us seminally in his loins when God created him, but each of us was legally represented by him when God made with him the Covenant of Works. Adam acted and transacted in that Covenant as a public person, not simply as a private individual, but as the surety and sponsor of his race. The very fact that we continue breaking the Covenant of Works and disobeying the Law of God demonstrates our oneness with Adam under the Covenant. Our complicity with Adam in his rebellion is evidenced every time that we personally sin against God.

It is nothing short of downright hypocrisy for us to murmur against the justice of this arrangement of constitution while we follow in the steps of Adam. If we have nothing to do with him and are not in bondage through him, why do we not repudiate him—refuse to sin, break the chain, stand out in opposition to him, and be holy? This brings us to the second chief count in the fearful indictment against us. We take sides with Adam. We perpetuate his evil course. We make him are exemplar. The life of the unregenerate is one unbroken curse of rebellion against God. There is no genuine submission to Him, no concern for His glory, no disinterested love for Him. Self-will is our governing principle and self-pleasing our goal. Whatever religious deference may apparently be shown God, it is rendered out of self-interest—either to curry favor with Him, or to appease His anger. The things of time and sense are preferred before Him, the lies of Satan are heeded rather than the Word of Truth, and instead of humbling ourselves before Him because of our original offence in Eden, we multiply transgressions against Him.

However unpalatable it may be to proud flesh and blood the fact is that the natural man is engaged in a warfare against God. He hates the things God loves, and loves the things He hates. He scorns the things God enjoins and pursues the things He has forbidden. He is a rebel against the Divine government, refusing to be in subjection to the Divine will. The moment his own will is crossed by the dispensations of Providence he murmurs. He is unthankful for the mercies of which he is the daily recipient, and less mindful of the Hand that so freely ministers to him than the horse or the mule to the one who feeds him. He continually growls at his lot, constantly grumbles at the weather, and is a stranger to contentment. In short "the carnal mind is enmity against God and is not subject to the Law of God, neither indeed can be" (Rom. 8:7). "The natural man does not receive the things of the Spirit of God, for they are foolishness unto him" (1 Cor. 2:14)—contrary to his corrupted mind, at variance with his vitiated desires. "There is none that seeks after God" (Rom. 3:11).

There is then a breach—a real, a broad, a fearful breach—between God and man. In the very nature of the cause it cannot be otherwise. That breach has been made by sin. God is holy, so holy that He is "of purer eyes than to behold evil and cannot look on iniquity" (Hab. 1:13). Sin has given infinite offence unto God, for it is that "abominable thing" which He hates (Jer. 44:4). Sin is a species of spiritual anarchy, a defiance of the triune Jehovah. It is a saying in actions "Let us break Their bands, and cast away Their cords from us" (Ps. 2:3)—let us disregard the Divine laws and be lords of ourselves. Not only is sin highly obnoxious to the infinitely-pure nature of God, but it is flagrant affront to His government, being rebellion against it, and therefore as the moral Rector of the universe He declares His displeasure against the same "For the wrath of God is revealed from heaven against all ungodliness and unrighteousness of men" (Rom. 1:18)—an open display of which was made of old when the flood swept the earth clean of His enemies.

Here then is the black background which discovers to us the need for reconciliation. "your iniquities have separated between you and your God, and your sins have hid His face from you" (Isa. 59:2). He is displeased with us and His justice cries out for our destruction. "They rebelled and vexed His Holy Spirit; therefore He was turned to be their Enemy" (Isa. 63:10). Unspeakably solemn is that, the terrible import of which is utterly beyond our powers to conceive. That the great I am, the Creator and Sustainer of the universe has become man's "Enemy" so that His anger burns against him. This was evidenced at the beginning, for right after God had arraigned the guilty culprits in Eden, we are told that "He drove out the man. And He placed cherubims at the east of the garden of Eden, and a flaming sword which turned every way—to keep the way of the tree of life" (Gen. 3:24). Man was now cut off from access to the One whom he had so grievously offended and turned to be his Enemy. And man is also at enmity with Him.

How little is it realized that there is an immeasurable gulf between God and sinner. And little wonder that so few have even the vaguest idea of the same. All human religion is an attempt to gloss over this fearful fact. And with exceedingly rare exceptions the religion of present-day Christendom is but a studied effort to hide the awful truth that man has forfeited the favor of God and is barred from His holy presence, yea that "the Lord is far from the wicked" (Prov. 15:29). The religion of the day proceeds on the assumption that God is favorably disposed even unto those who spend most of their time trampling His commandments beneath their feet. That providing they will assume an outwardly devout demeanor, they have but to petition Him and their supplications are acceptable unto Him. Priests and parsons who encourage such a delusion are but throwing dust in the eyes of the people: "the sacrifice of the wicked is an abomination unto the Lord" (Prov. 15:8).

The religion of our day deliberately ignores the fact of sin, with its terrible implications and consequences. It leaves out of sight that sin has radically changed the original relationship which existed between God and His creatures. It conceals the truth that man is outlawed by God and is "far off" (Eph. 2:11) from Him. It tacitly denies that "they that are in the flesh cannot please God" (Rom. 8:8), that He "hears not sinners" (John 9:3 1). Yea it insists that they can please Him with their hypocritical piety and sanctimonious playacting. But the Holy One cannot be deceived by their pretenses nor bribed by their offerings. Nor can they so much as draw nigh unto Him while they despise and reject the One who is the only Way of approach to Him. Make no mistake upon this point, my reader. Until that awful breach which sin has made be healed, you can have no fellowship with God; until He be reconciled to you and you to Him, He will accept nothing at your hands not can you obtain audience with Him. Unless reconciliation is affected you will be "punished with everlasting destruction from the presence of the Lord"(2 Thess. 1:9).

The need for reconciliation is unmistakable. A fearful breach exists, brought about by the entrance of sin, and continued by the perpetuation of man to God. Not only had man now forfeited His favor but he had incurred His wrath. God could no longer view him with approbation, but instead regarded him with detestation; while man ceased to be a loyal and loving subject, becoming a rebellious outlaw. And "what fellowship has righteousness with unrighteousness?"

"And what communion has light with darkness?" None. They are opposite, the one antagonistic to the other. That breach between God and man, between righteousness and unrighteousness, will be demonstrated in the distance between Heaven and Hell. Therefore did Christ represent Abraham as saying to Dives in the place of torment, "between us and you there is a great gulf fixed, so that they which would pass from here to you cannot; neither can they pass to us" (Luke 16:26). It is only by God's reconciliation to us and of our reconciliation to God the fearful breach can be healed. How that is effected we hope to show in future articles.

Chapter 3
Its Need-Continued

In our last we dwelt chiefly upon the fearful breach which the entrance of sin made between the thrice Holy One and His fallen and rebellious creatures. In this we must point out some of the consequences and evidences of that breach, thereby showing in more detail the urgency of the sinner's case. By his act of disobedience in Eden man invaded God's right of sovereignty, spurning as he did His authority, throwing off the yoke of submission, determining to be his own lord. The outcome of such revolt we are not left to guess at. It is plainly made known in the Scriptures. By his fearful offence man lost the favor and friendship of God and incurred His holy displeasure and righteous indignation. The Creator became the punishing Judge. Our first parents were promptly arraigned and sentence was passed upon the guilty culprits. Man had fallen into sin and the Divine wrath now fell upon him. God drove man out of Paradise and unsheathed the flaming sword (Gen. 3:24), thereby making it manifest that Heaven and earth were at variance. As the result of the fall sin became man's delight and henceforth he was an enemy to all holiness and consequently of the Holy One.

1. Fallen man became separated from God. It is easy to write or read those words, but who is competent to fathom their fearful import! Separated from God, the Fountain and Giver of all blessedness! Cast out of His favor. Severed from communion with Him. Cut off from the enjoyment of Him. Devoid of His life, of His holiness, of His love. Such is the terrible and inevitable consequence of sin. Sin snapped the golden cord which had united man to his Maker. Sin broke the happy relationship which originally existed between man and his rightful Lord. Sin made a breach between its committer and the Holy One. Not only did sin conduct man to a guilty distance from God, but sin necessarily placed God at a holy distance from man. God will not suffer those who are hostile to Him and offensive to His absolute purity to dwell in His presence. Therefore do we read that "God spared not the angels that sinned, but cast them down to Hell, and delivered them into chains of darkness, to be reserved unto judgment" (2 Pet. 2:4). They were banished from Heaven, excluded from the company of the Most High, imprisoned in the place of unutterable woe.

God had plainly made known unto our federal head the penalty of his disobedience: "But you shall not eat of the tree of knowledge of good and evil—for in the day that you eat of it, you shall surely die" (Gen. 2:17). Thus at the very beginning of human history the Lawgiver announced that "the wages of sin is death"—death spiritual, death judicial, death eternal if pardon was not obtained. And death is not annihilation but separation. Physical death is the separation of the soul from the body, expulsion from this earth. So spiritual death is the separation of the soul from God, expulsion from His favor. In that tragic yet hope-inspiring parable of the prodigal son our Lord represented the sinner as being in "the far country" a "great way off" from the Father's house (Luke 15:13,20), and when he returned in penitence the Father said, "this My son was dead (separated from Me) and is alive again (restored to Me); he was lost and is found." When Christ as the Substitute and Surety of His people bore their sins in His own body on the Tree (1 Pet. 2:24) He received the wages of sin, crying to God "why have You forsaken Me!"

But the death inflicted upon Adam and all whom he represented was also judicial. Fallen man is a malefactor, dead in Law, lying under its sentence, a criminal in chains of guilt, held fast in fetters until the day of execution, unless he obtains a pardon from God. If no pardon is obtained, then he shall be cast into "the lake which burns with fire and brimstone," and that is expressly denominated "the second death" (Rev. 21:8), because it is a being "punished with everlasting destruction from the presence of the Lord" (2 Thess. 1:9). Man then, every man while unregenerate, is living "without God in the world" "far off" from Him (Eph. 2:12,13). Being "dead in trespasses and sins" he is cut off from God, having no access to Him. He is a castaway from the Divine presence. God will have no commerce with him, nor receive any offering at his hands. He is outside the kingdom of God, and cannot enter it save by the new birth (John 3:5). He is born into the world alienated from the life of God (Eph. 4:18). When the Lord came down upon Sinai Israel was not suffered to draw near Him (Ex. 19). Sin had imposed an effectual barrier.

2. Fallen man became an object of abhorrence to God. Once more we use language the meaning of which no mortal is capable of fully entering into. It is not that we have employed terms which the case does not warrant, for we have but paraphrased the words of Holy Writ. Nor can it be otherwise if God is what Scripture affirms and if man has become what he is represented to be. God is light (1 John 1:5) and man is darkness (Eph. 5:8). God is holy, man totally depraved. God is our rightful Lord and King, man is an insurrectionist, a defiant rebel. God is immaculately pure, man a loathsome leper. If man saw himself as he appears to the Divine eye or even as he is portrayed by the Divine pencil, it would be evident that he must be an object of repugnance unto Him who sits enthroned on high. "From the sole of the foot even unto the head there is no soundness in it, but wounds and bruises, and putrefying sores. They have not been closed, neither bound up, neither soothed with oil" (Isa. 1:6). What a repulsive object! Yet that is precisely what you and I (by nature) look like in the eyes of God.

"You hate all workers of iniquity" (Ps. 5:5). In this Psalm God's alienation from and detestation of the wicked is set forth in six steps. First: He has no delight in them. "You are not a God that has pleasure in wickedness" (v. 4). Second: they cannot reside in His presence "neither shall evil dwell with You" (v. 4). Third: they have no status before Him. "The foolish shall not stand in Your sight" (v. 5). Fifth: He will pour upon them the fury of His indignation. "You shall destroy them that speak leasing" or "lies" (v. 6). Sixth: they will for all eternity be abhorred by Him. "The Lord will abhor the bloody and deceitful man" (v. 6). None would be shocked at such frightful declarations as these if he had anything like an adequate conception of the exceeding sinfulness of sin and of the infinite holiness of God. Though they are scarce ever heard from any pulpit today, whether we believe them or not, they are the words of Him who cannot lie and throughout eternity their verity will be borne amply witness to. "You hate all workers of iniquity." Not merely their evil works, but the workers themselves; not some of the most notorious of the workers but all of them. My reader, if you are out of Christ, still unregenerate, whether you are British, American, or Australian, you are an object of God's hatred. Rightly did C. H. Spurgeon point out from these words, "It is not a little dislike, but thorough hatred which God bears to workers of iniquity. To be hated of God is an awful thing. O let us be very faithful in warning the wicked around us, for it will be a terrible thing for them to fall into the hands of an angry God. . .How forcible is the word 'abhor' (in the next verse). Does it not show us how powerful and deep-seated is the hatred of the Lord against the workers of iniquity!" It is the very nature of righteousness to hate unrighteousness. Those who are so corrupt and abominable must be loathed by One who is ineffably holy. It is the very perfection of the Divine character to hate the totally depraved.

3. Fallen man came under the condemnation and curse of the Divine Law. "It is written, Cursed is everyone that continues not in all things which are written in the Book of the Law to do them"

(Gal. 3:10). Those words are a quotation from Deuteronomy 17:26—a verse which contains the conclusion of the maledictions pronounced upon the disobedient of the context, being really the sum and substance of them all. It is the solemn declaration that those who have despised God's authority and trampled His commandments beneath their feet are exposed to the Divine displeasure and to condign punishment as the expression of that displeasure. The "curse of the Law" is that sentence and penalty which is due unto sin. Sin and the curse are inseparable. Wherever the one is, the other must be. Therefore the unrestricted "every one," and that not only for multiplied transgressions but for a single offence. The Divine Law is perfect, and demands perfect and perpetual conformity to it. A single transgression brings down upon its perpetrator the Divine curse, as was evidenced in Eden, and in consequence of our representative participation therein, all of us entered this world under the maledictions of God's Law.

"Cursed is every one." Those solemn words, so little known, so faintly apprehended even by those who are acquainted with them, reveal the fearful situation of every soul out of Christ. They are under sentence of execution. Their position is identical with the convicted murderer in the condemned cell, awaiting the dread summons of vindictive justice. If you are unregenerate, my reader, at this very moment you are under sentence of death: "condemned already." Since the curse of the Law falls upon men for a single sin, then what must be the punishment that will be meted out upon those with multiplied transgressions to their account! "The curse of the Lord is in the house of the wicked" (Prov. 3:33). That unspeakable malediction rests upon all that he has and all that he does. "You shall be cursed in the city and you shall be cursed in the field. You shall be cursed in your basket and your store," (Deut. 28:17). Nay, God has said "I will curse your blessings; yea, I have cursed them already" (Mal. 2:2). To those out of Christ He will yet say. "Depart from Me you cursed into everlasting fire" (Matthew 25:41).

4. Fallen man came under the wrath of God. This follows inevitably from what has already been pointed out. Since a rebel against the Divine government is necessarily an object of abhorrence unto his holy Lord, since he has come beneath the curse and condemnation of the Divine Law, justice cries aloud for vengeance. The Maker of heaven and earth is no indifferent Spectator of the conduct of His creatures. He was not of Adam's. The father and head of the race was summoned before His judgment bar, fairly tried, justly condemned, and made to experience the beginnings of God's wrath, for the full measure thereof is reserved for the transgressor in the next life. As the consequence of their sin and fall in the person of their representative all of Adam's posterity are "by nature the children of wrath" (Eph. 2:3). Not only defiled and corrupt, but the objects of God's judicial indignation. "The children of wrath." Those words should be to the ungodly reader as the handwriting on Belshazzar's wall (Dan. 5:5, 6). They should blanch his countenance, trouble his thoughts, and make his knees smite together.

This fearful expression "the children of wrath" is more forceful than many conclude. In the previous verse we read of "children of disobedience," which means more than disobedient children, for such may the regenerate be. It means such as are addicted to disobedience, who make a trade of it. So "children of wrath" signifies more than to be liable to wrath. It connotes the objects of God's wrath, wholly devoted thereto, born to it as their portion and heritage—the corruptions of their nature being its fuel. When the angels sinned the wrath of God was visited upon them (2 Pet. 2:4), thereby evidencing that no natural excellence in the creature can exempt it from the judgment of God. Further demonstrations of His wrath were given when the flood was sent to drown the antediluvian world, when fire and brimstone destroyed Sodom and Gomorrah, and when Pharaoh and his hosts were overwhelmed at the Red Sea. And the execution of God's wrath upon you, my unsaved reader, is hourly drawn nearer. Ignorance cannot shield you from it. Outward privileges will not save you from it. Nor will a mere profession of religion. The only way of deliverance is for you to "flee from the wrath to come" by betaking yourself to Christ for refuge.

"God is angry with the wicked every day" (Ps. 7:11), on which Spurgeon remarks, "He not only detests sin, but is angry with those who continue to indulge in it. We have no insensible and stolid God to deal with. He can be angry, nay, He is angry today and every day with you, you ungodly and impenitent sinners. The best day that ever dawned on a sinner brings a curse with it. Sinners may have many feast days, but not safe days. From the beginning of the year even to its ending, there is not an hour in which God's oven is not hot and burning in readiness for the wicked, who shall be as stubble." And on the words of the verse which immediately follows—"If He turn not, He will whet His sword" —that faithful preacher declared: "What blows are those which will be dealt by that long uplifted arm! God's sword has been sharpening upon the revolving stone of our daily wickedness, and if we will not repent, it will speedily cut us to pieces. Turn or burn is the sinner's alternative."

Fallen man is the subject and slave of Satan, under a more terrible bondage than ever the Hebrews were to Pharaoh, for it is a bondage of the soul. Yet this is justly inflicted. At the beginning our first parents preferred Satan's lie to God's truth, and therefore did He allow Satan to obtain dominion over them. Yet with each of his descendants it is a willing bondage therein. As the Jews desired Barabbas rather than Christ, so we entered this world with a nature that is in harmony with Satan's. Yes, without a single exception, every member of our race is born so depraved that he voluntarily serves and obeys the arch enemy of God. There are but two spiritual kingdoms in this world: that of Christ's (Col. 1:13) and that of Satan's (Matthew 12:26), and every human being is a subject of the one or the other. Those who have not come to Christ and surrendered to His scepter are ruled by Satan and are fighting under his banner against God. Therefore when Paul was sent forth to preach the Gospel it was in order to open the eyes of men "to turn them from darkness to light and from the power of Satan unto God" (Acts 26:18).

The Devil is the sinner's master, as he was the Christian's before Divine grace regenerated him. "And He has made you alive who were dead in trespasses and sins—in which you once walked according to the course of this world, according to the Prince of the power of the air, the spirit that now works in the children of disobedience" (Eph. 2:1, 2). He not only tempts from without but dominates them from within. As God works in His people "both to will and to do of His good pleasure" (Phil 2:13) so the devil operates in the hearts of his subjects to perform his fiendish pleasure. He "put into the heart" of Judas to betray Christ (John 13:2). He made Pilate and Herod condemn Him to death, for it was "their hour and the power of darkness" (Luke 22:53). He "filled the heart" of Ananias to lie to the Holy Spirit (Acts 5:3). Yet each of them acted freely and according to the inclinations of his own evil nature. Satan's subjects render him a voluntary and cordial obedience. "You are of your father the Devil, and the lusts of your father you will do" (John 8:44).

6. Fallen man is under the reigning power of sin. This abominable thing which God hates has entered the human constitution like a deadly poison that has completely corrupted our whole being. Sin has full dominion and undisputed sway over the human soul. The mind makes no opposition to it, for it is sin's servant (John 8:34) and not captive. It exerts a determining power on the will. Sin so reigns in the heart of the unregenerate that it directs their affections and controls all the motives and springs of their actions, causing them to walk after their own evil imaginations and devisings. As the air is the native element of the birds, so sin is the natural element of fallen man. "Abominable and filthy is man, who drinks in iniquity like water" (Job 15:16). Like a parched traveler in the desert who craves water, seeks after it, and greedily swallows it when found, so is iniquity unto the sinner.

The course of the natural man is described as "serving divers lusts and pleasures" (Titus 3:3), as "bringing forth evil fruits" (Matthew 7:17), as yielding his members "servants to uncleanness and to iniquity" (Rom. 6:19). The service rendered by the unregenerate to sin is a whole-hearted one, voluntary, and cordial. Man is in love with sin, preferring darkness to light, this world to Heaven. His lusts are his idols. Therefore does he persist in sin despite all pleadings, warnings, threatenings, chastisements. While he is unregenerate he does nothing but sin in thought and word and deed. Solemn it is to think that everyone is in continual remembrance with God, set in the light of His countenance, recorded in that book which will be opened in the day of judgment. Not one of them is pardoned, or can be, while he is out of Christ. So much guilt lies upon his soul as is sufficient to sink it into the lowest Hell, and will do so unless blotted out by atoning blood.

7. Fallen man hates God. "The carnal mind is enmity against God, and is not subject to the Law of God"—and so inveterate is that "enmity" it is at once added—"neither indeed can be" (Rom. 8:7). We may not believe it, or be conscious of it, but there is the Divinely-revealed fact. God is an Object of aversion unto the natural man. The language of the hearts of sinners unto the Almighty is, "Depart from us; we desire not the knowledge of your ways," (Job 21:14). They do not hate Him as their Provider and Preserver, but as a Being who is infinitely holy and who therefore hates sin and is "angry with the wicked every day." They detest Him as a sovereign Being, who dispenses His favors according to His absolute pleasure. They abominate Him as the Moral Governor of the world, demanding obedience to His Law, and pronouncing cursed all who break it. They abhor Him as the Judge, who shall yet cast all His enemies into the Lake of Fire. Proof of this was furnished when God became incarnate and was manifested unto men. They crucified Him.

"Can two walk together except they be agreed?" (Amos 3:3). Obviously not; then how much less could rebels dwell together with a holy God for all eternity! For that reconciliation must be effected. But how is peace possible? How are alienated sinners to be restored to friendship with God without Him denying His own perfections? Some grand provision must be made whereby the wrath of God is appeased, whereby His Law is magnified, His honor vindicated, His justice satisfied. Some wondrous redemption is imperative if sinners are to be delivered from that dreadful state of enmity, darkness, and slavery into which the Fall conducted them. Some marvel of wisdom and miracle of grace is necessary if those so far off are to be made nigh, if the unholy are to be made holy, if those dead in sin are to be quickened into newness of life. Some unique Mediator is indispensable if the breach between an offended God and offended creatures is to be healed. A Mediator who is capable of conserving the interests and promoting the glory of God, and who also can win the hearts of those in revolt. The needs be for reconciliation is crystal clear; the effectuation of it is the grand subject of the Gospel, the wonder of angels, and will be the theme of the song of the redeemed throughout the unending ages of the future.

Chapter 4
Its Need-Continued

This doctrine of Reconciliation presents to our view that which is both indescribably horrible and also that which is inexpressibly blessed. The dark background of it is formed by the fearful calamity of Eden, when the entrance of sin into the world involved the ruination of our race and its alienation from God. The sin of Adam (and of ours in him) was a revolt against God's authority, a contempt of His government, a declaration of war against Him. Man is a rebel, an outlaw, an enemy of God, cut off from access to Him. This has already been before us in previous articles. Now we turn to contemplate the blessed contrast wherein God determined to deliver a part of Adam's descendants from the effects of the fall, and this in such a way that His absolute sovereignty, His free grace, His inexorable justice, unsearchable wisdom, ineffable holiness, all-mighty power, infinite goodness and rich mercy, might be equally honored. This is actually accomplished in the saving of His elect by Jesus Christ.

The Author of reconciliation is God. Most distinctly, it is God the Father, for there is an order of the Divine Persons in this work, as in all others. "But to us there is but one God, the Father, of whom are all things, and we by Him" (1 Cor. 8:5). "God who created all things by Jesus Christ" (Eph. 3:9). As that was the order of Their operation in connection with the old creation, so it is with regard to the new creation—the Father has effected reconciliation by the death of His Son (Rom. 5:10). Distinct offices are ascribed to each of the Eternal Three. The Father is the Deviser, the Son transacts the part of Mediator, being the One by whom the work of reconciliation is performed; the Holy Spirit is the Recorder of the Father's plan and of the satisfaction offered by the Son and of the peace He has made, and is also the One who sheds abroad Their love in the hearts of the redeemed.

The order pointed out above is still more observable in connection with our approach to God. It is through Christ and by the Holy Spirit that we have access unto the Father (Eph. 2:18). All the spiritual blessings we have in Christ are expressly attributed unto the Father (Eph. 1:3), by no means the least of which is reconciliation. Our election is ascribed particularly unto the Father (Eph. 1:3, 4) and so is our regeneration (James 1:17, 18). It is the Father who has made us meet to be partakers of the inheritance of the saints in light, having delivered us from the power of darkness and translated us into the kingdom of His dear Son (Col. 1:13). In accord with this Divine order we find the opening salutation in the Epistles is "grace unto you and peace from God the Father, and the Lord Jesus Christ." Therefore the Father is due the same honor and love from us for the sending of His Son, as the Son is for His willingness in being sent. Scripture represents the Father as the One directly wronged by sin, for we are told that Jesus Christ is "an Advocate with the Father"(1 John 2:1).

1. His will. When accountable creatures rebel against their Maker and King, they cut themselves off from all right to claim any blessing or benefit at His hands, for they deserve nothing from Him but wrath and punishment. If they are recovered from the ruin which they have brought upon themselves and are made partakers of Divine salvation, it is solely from the good pleasure of His will, and must be in a way that does not injure any of His perfections; but if they are left

to suffer the direful consequences of their apostasy, God is in nowise unjust, for He inflicts no more upon them than they deserve. When a large company of the angels and their chiefs, under Satan's lead, conspiring against the Most High, proudly aspiring to a higher position than had been allotted them, God promptly cast them down from their exalted state, banished them from His presence, and doomed them to suffer everlasting woe (2 Pet. 2:4). He had not a thought of mercy toward those celestial creatures when they revolted against Him.

In view of that unspeakably solemn example, it ought to be unmistakably clear to each of us that God might, without the slightest stain upon His own honor, without any unbecoming severity, have left the whole of Adam's guilty race to suffer eternal destruction, for certainly they had no more claim upon His favor than had the fallen angels. That He did not immediately consign the entire family of fallen mankind to irremediable woe, was due alone to His imperial will. That He was pleased to appoint a remnant of them to obtain salvation and eternal glory, is to be attributed solely to His sovereign and amazing grace. That such a concept is no invention of harsh theologians, but is plainly taught by the Word of God, is clear from His own declarations. "Having predestinated us unto the adoption of children by Jesus Christ to Himself according to the good pleasure of His will, to the praise of the glory of His grace" (Eph. 1:5, 6). "Who has saved us, and called us with a holy calling, not according to our works, but according to His own purpose and grace" (2 Tim. 1:9).

"Having made known unto us the mystery of His will, according to His good pleasure, which He has purposed in Himself" (Eph. 1:9). The mystery refers to the everlasting covenant in which God arranged and provided for the recovery and salvation of His people who fell in Adam. In proof of which assertion we cite 1 Corinthians 2:7: "But we speak the wisdom of God in a mystery, even the hidden wisdom, which God ordained before the world unto our glory" amplified in verses 9 and 10. Now that which is germane to our present design is, that God "purposed in Himself" or resolved to reconcile some of the sons of men to Himself, even though they had become guilty rebels against Him, and this purpose He purposed "before the world began" (2 Tim. 1:9). One portion or aspect of that purpose is expressly stated in what immediately follows. "That in the dispensation of the fullness of times He might gather together in one all things in Christ, both which are in heaven, and which are on earth, even in Him" (Eph. 1:10). Sin alienates and separates, but the putting away of sin by Christ healed the breach between God and man, between believing Jews and Gentiles, and between them and the holy angels. Now "The whole family in heaven and in earth" (Eph. 3:15) is one —see Revelation 5:11, 12.

The restoration and reconciliation of His guilty and alienated people is attributed to God's "good pleasure" whereof no reason is given save that He purposed it in Himself which means that the idea was suggested by none other and that no external motive influenced Him. There was no necessity put upon Him for this resolution. Without the least dishonor to Himself He might have destroyed the entire apostate race, yea, and have been glorified in their destruction. He who was able out of stones "to raise up children unto Abraham" (Matthew 3:9), could have consigned Adam and Eve to eternal woe before they produced any children, and have made a pair from the dust of the ground. There was nothing whatever in the creature that moved God to show mercy unto him. But there is another concept conveyed by this expression, namely, the certainty and powerful efficacy of what He has decided upon. God cannot possibly be disappointed in the accomplishment of His purpose, for none can overthrow it; nor will He ever alter it. "My counsel shall stand and I will do all My pleasure" (Isa. 46:10); "I am the Lord. I change not" (Mal. 3:6).

Here is sure and solid comfort for the spiritually awakened sinner. The simple fact that God is merciful in His nature is not sufficient. Satan knows that, but such knowledge affords him no peace! But the Divine assurance "I will show mercy" (Ex. 33:19) opens a real door of hope.

Suppose that Christ had died and there had been no Gospel revelation and proclamation of the Divine purpose of His death. The mere knowledge of His crucifixion avails me nothing unless I am assured that it was the will of God to accept Christ's death in lieu of the death of believing sinners: "by which will we are sanctified through the offering of the body of Jesus Christ once for all" (Heb. 10:10). The will of God is not only the foundation of the mystery or plan of redemption, but it is also its blessedness. This is the very pith and preciousness of the Gospel. That it is the revealed will of God to save and accept every sinner who puts his or her trust in the atoning blood of Christ. "Who gave Himself for our sins, that He might deliver us from (the corruption and doom) of this present evil world, according to the will of God and our Father" (Gal. 1:4).

2. His love. A few may be surprised that we should distinguish between the will and love of God, but probably a far greater number will wonder why any explanation should be required from us for so doing. Yet John Owen in his "Arguments against Universal Redemption" (chap. 8, para. 5) said, "The eternal love of God towards His elect is nothing by His purpose, good pleasure a pure act of His will, whereby He determines to do such and such things for them in His own time and way." And again, in his "Vindiciae Evangelicae" (chap. 29), after referring to John 3:16 and other passages: "Now the love of God is an eternal free act of His will, His purpose." Such a cold and bare definition may suit philosophers, and metaphysicians, but it will scarcely appeal to the hearts of the regenerate. When Scripture affirms that Christ is the "Son of His love" (Col. 1:13) we are surely to understand something more than that the Son is merely the Object on which the Divine will is set. Rather do we believe, with many others, that the Son is the Darling of the Father's heart. How, too, are we to understand the Savior's representation of the Father in His welcome of the returning prodigal. He "ran, and fell on his neck, and kissed him" (Luke 15:20). While we are far from believing that God's unfathomable love in anywise resembles ours, as an emotion or passion, subject to fluctuation, yet we refuse to regard it as a mere principle. When the voice of the Father audibly declared "this is My beloved Son in whom I am well pleased," He gave expression to the language of deep and warm affection. When the Lord Jesus affirmed "The only begotten Son which is in the bosom of the Father, He has declared Him" (John 1:18), we grant that He employed an anthropomorphism (ascribing to God what pertains properly to man), nevertheless we cannot allow that it was a mere figure of speech devoid of real meaning. "God is love" (1 John 4:8), and no refinements of the most eminent theologians must be suffered to rob us of the blessedness and preciousness of that fundamental truth. All things issue from the will of God (Eph. 1:11), but Scripture nowhere tells us that all things proceed from God's love. The non-elect are the subjects of His will, but they are not the objects of His love. Thus there is a clear distinction between the two things.

We greatly prefer the statement of Thos. Goodwin. Near the beginning of his massive work on "Christ the Mediator," he shows what was done by God the Father from all eternity in connection with our salvation. First, He points out His eternal purpose and grace, and then inquires "If you would further know, What should be the reason of this strange affection in our God (that is, exercised unto those who had rebelled against Him): why the Scripture gives it. Our God being love, even love itself." Love is an essential perfection in God's very nature, and as it has pleased Him to exercise the same unto His elect. It is an act of His will, yet not of His will absolutely considered but of "the good pleasure of His will" toward them. All the acts of God unto His people in Christ; all the blessings which He has bestowed upon them in Christ, all His thoughts concerning them, all the operations of His grace in them, and the workings of His providence for them, all the manifestations of His kindness and mercy unto them, proceed from His love for them. Love is the fountain from which flows every stream of His goodness unto them.

The wondrous love of God for His people can only be known by its blessed manifestations toward them. As the effects which it produces discovers to us the nature of the cause which produces them, so the love which God bears unto His elect is revealed by His acts unto them and bestowments upon them. God's love for us does not commence when we first respond to His gracious overtures unto us through the Gospel, nor even when He capacitates us to respond by first quickening us into newness of life, for His very calling of us out of darkness into His own marvelous light proceeds from His love for us. Nor did God's love for the Church begin when Christ died for her and put away her sins, for it was because God so loved her that He gave up His beloved Son to die in her room and stead. "I have loved you with an everlasting love" (Jer. 31:2) is God's own ringing declaration. Therefore it was in love that He "predestinated us unto the adoption of children by Jesus Christ unto Himself" (Eph. 1:4, 5), which is the foundation of all our blessings. Nor did our fall in Adam produce the slightest change of God's love unto His elect.

Though our sin in Eden did not quench God's love for His people nor even chill it to the slightest degree, yet that horrible disobedience of theirs raised such formidable obstacles from the holiness of His nature and the righteousness of His government, yea opposed such a barrier against us as appeared to all finite intelligences, an insuperable one to prevent the exercise of God's compassion unto His guilty and corrupted people. In a word, the Law of God with its inexorable demand for satisfaction, seemed to effectually prevent the operation and manifestation of His love toward its transgressors. Consider carefully an example on the human plane. Darius was induced to sign a decree, that if any person asked a petition during the next thirty days from any save himself, he should forfeit his life (Dan. 6). Daniel himself defied that decree, making supplication of his God as before. His watchful enemies promptly reported this to the king and demanded that Daniel should be cast into the den of lions. Darius was displeased with himself "and set his heart on Daniel to deliver him, and labored till the going down of the sun to deliver him" (v. 14). But in vain. The honor of his law barred the outflow of his love; justice triumphed over mercy.

Consider still another case. Absalom committed a grievous offence against his father, for he sought to rob him of his scepter and wrest the kingdom from his hands, and furthermore, murdered another of his sons. His attempt to gain the kingdom failed, and he fled the country, and remained an exile for three years. David mourned for his son every day and "longed to go forth unto him" (2 Sam. 13:39), but the honor of his throne clearly prohibited such an action. When Joab perceived "that the king's heart was toward Absalom" (14:1) and that he knew not how to make an advance toward him without disgracing his character and government he decided to further his own plans. Accordingly the unscrupulous Joab resorted to guile and employed a woman to speak to David, pleading that Absalom's crime might be pardoned, his attainder reversed, and be released from banishment. Strangely enough she reminded the king that God "doth devise means whereby His banished be not expelled from Him" (v. 14). But such a task of restoring his son without sullying his own honor was quite beyond David. The best he could devise was "Let him turn to his own house; and let him not see my face" (v. 24).

3. His wisdom. Where the wit of Darius completely failed before the requirements of human law, the wisdom of God gloriously triumphed over the obstacles interposed by the Divine Law. Where the wit of David could contrive nothing better than a wretched compromise, for which he later paid dearly, the omniscience of Deity found a way whereby His banished sons are restored and which redounds unto His everlasting honor. In pursuance of His gracious design to recover and reconcile His elect from their fall and alienation, the love of God set His consummate wisdom to work in contriving the fittest means for accomplishing the same. Therefore it is that we read in connection with God's grand purpose concerning our salvation that He "works all things after the counsel of His own will" (Eph. 1:11). "He works all by counsel to effect and bring to pass what His will is pitched upon, and the stronger His will is in a thing, the deeper are His counsels as to it" (Thos. Goodwin).

Chapter 5
Its Need-Concluded

In our last we were only able to barely mention that the wisdom of God was engaged in the salvation of His people. Before we attempt to illustrate this particular aspect let us point out that it was in His character of Judge that the Father then acted. It is most important that this should be recognized, yea, essential if we are to view our subject from the correct angle, for reconciliation was entirely a judicial procedure. In Hebrews 12:23 God the Father is expressly spoken of as "the Judge of all," which is an official title. He it was who passed sentence upon sinning Adam and all whom he represented as a federal head. None but "the Judge of all," could have "made Christ to be sin" for His people, or them to be "the righteousness of God in Him"(2 Cor. 5:21). "It is God that justifies" (Rom. 8:33). That is, it is the Father as the Judge who actually and formally pronounces righteous in His sight the sinner who believes on Christ. It is on this two-fold ground that the apostle there argues the irreversibility of our justification: that the sentence of justification is pronounced by the Supreme Judge, and that, on the basis of the full satisfaction which has been made to Him by Christ.

We closed our last by calling attention to the fact that the determination of the Father to recover His lapsed people is described as the purpose of Him who works all things after the counsel of His own will which signifies there was an exercise of His infinite understanding in devising how that resolve should be made good to His own glory. To speak after the manner of men, the Father consulted with Himself, called His omniscience into play, and drew up a plan in which His "manifold wisdom" (Eph. 3:10) is exemplified. That many sided plan is termed the mystery because it has to do with the deep things of God (1 Cor. 2:7, 10). "There is variety in the mystery and mystery in every part of the variety. It was not one single act, but a variety of counsels met in it: a conjunction of excellent ends and means" (Charnock). What those excellent ends and means were we shall now try to set forth, yet knowing full well that our utmost efforts can convey only a most inadequate and fragmentary idea of what will be our wonderment and admiration for all eternity. God's consummate and manifold wisdom is seen.

1. In Love's triumph over the Law. We begin here because it the better links up with the closing paragraph of our last and the opening one of this. Continuing that line of thought, be it said, the solution to the problems raised by sin and the harmonization of Love and Law is termed a "mystery" because it transcends human reason and can only be known by Divine revelation. it is called "the hidden wisdom" of God because it remained an impenetrable secret until He was pleased to disclose it. No discovery of it was made in creation. Though "the heavens declare the glory of God and the firmament shows His handiwork" yet they gave no indication it is His will to show mercy unto rebels: rather does the universe exhibit an inexorable reign of law. If a devoted mother gives her child medicine from the wrong bottle, the result would be the same as if an enemy poured poison down its throat. Break one of Nature's laws, even in ignorance, and no matter how deep our regret, there is no escaping the penalty. Divine Love has triumphed over the Law not by trampling upon it, but by fully meeting its demands and rendering it honorable. Divine wisdom contrived a way in which there was no compromise between Love and Law, but

each was given fullest expression.

The way in which God has dealt with what to human wit appears insolvable, both manifests His perfect wisdom and greatly redounds to His glory. He has dealt with the problem raised by sin by taking it into the court of His Law and settling it on a righteous basis. The needs-be for that is evident. Sin is far too great an evil for man to meddle with and every attempt he assays in that direction only makes bad matters worse—as appears in both the social and international spheres. Still more is this the case when man attempts to treat with God. His very efforts to remove sin do but aggravate it, and any attempt to approach God in spite of it only serves to increase his guilt. None but God is capable of dealing with sin, either as a crime or as pollution, as that which is a dishonor to Him or as it is a barrier to our access to Him. Moreover as sin is too great an evil for us to deal with, so righteousness is too high for the fallen creature to reach unto, yea too high for holy creatures to bring down to us. Only God Himself can bring near His righteousness (Isa. 46:13).

Yes, God has dealt with the momentous issue raised by sin by taking it into the court of His Law. For fallen man to have taken it there would have inevitably meant the losing of his case, for he is a transgressor of the Divine statute and a moral bankrupt utterly unable to make any reparation for his offence. But His consummate wisdom enabled the Judge of all to deal with it in such a manner that the honor of His Law has been maintained unimpeached, and yet the case has been settled on a basis equally favorable to God and the sinner! Settled in such a way that the wondrous love of God is free to flow forth unto His elect, children of disobedience though they be in themselves, without ignoring or condoning their disobedience, and so that His love remains a holy love. It is on that judicial settlement that an all sufficient and final answer has been furnished to man's anguished and age-long questions, "How then can man be justified before God? Or how can he be clean that is born of a woman?" (Job 25:4). "Wherewith shall I come before the Lord?" (Micah 6:6).

2. In exercising two Contrary principles in Redemption. This is an achievement worthy of Omniscience. God is love, nevertheless, He is "light" (1 John 1:5) as well. Not only is He full of kindness and benevolence, but He is immaculately pure and holy. God is abundant in mercy, but He is also just and "will by no means clear the guilty." Here then are two of the Divine perfections moving in opposite directions. How can such contraries be reconciled? Love goes out unto the prodigal, but Light cannot look upon iniquity (Hab. 1:13). Mercy would fain spare the offender, but justice demands his punishment. Grace is ready to bestow a gratuitous salvation, but righteousness insists that the defaulter cannot be released until he has "paid the uttermost farthing" (Matthew 5:26). Shall then the tenderness of the Father yield to the severity of the Judge? Or shall the rights of the Judge give place to the desires of the Father? Each must be satisfied. But how? Admire and adore that wondrous wisdom which devised a means whereby "Mercy and Truth have met together, Righteousness and Peace have kissed each other" (Ps. 85:10).

It is said God loves the sinner, but hates his sin. Yet that provides no solution to the problem. For the question still returns, Will God sink His love to the sinner in His hatred of his sin or allow His love for the sinner to override His hatred for sin? God has sworn "The soul that sins it shall die" (Ezek. 18:4). But He has also sworn "I have no pleasure in the death of the wicked, but that the wicked turn from his way and live" (Ezek. 33:11). The oath of justice and the oath of pity appear irreconcilable. Must then one yield to the other? No, both must stand. But how? In redemption God has manifested two opposite perfections at the same time, and in one action, in which there is shown supreme hatred of sin and superlative love of the sinner. Justice and mercy are alike maintained its ground without compromise, yea, has issued from the conflict honorable and glorious. Divine wisdom contrived a plan whereby God has punished transgression without scourging the transgressors, and has repaired the ruin of the sinner without condoning his sin.

3. In appointing a suitable Mediator. Clearly this was the first step necessary in order to a solution of the intricate problems to which we have alluded. The fall of man placed him at an immeasurable distance from God—"your iniquities have separated between you and your God" (Isa. 55:2). Not only so but the fall produced an infinite moral difference, man becoming polluted and a hater of God, God Himself ineffably holy and at legal enmity with man. Such a breach appeared unbridgeable, for on the one hand it became not the glory of His nature nor the honor of His government for God to make any direct advance towards rebellious subjects; and on the other hand, man had no desire to be restored to His image of favor, and even if he had, was barred from any, access to Him. Thus all intercourse between God and men was at an end, an impasse was created, an utterly hopeless situation seemed to exist. "Our God is a consuming fire" and who was there that could interpose himself between Him and us? But Divine wisdom provided a means and remedy, decreeing there should be a Mediator who would bridge the distance and heal the difference between them, affecting a mutual reconciliation.

But where was such an one to be found? One capable of laying his hand upon both (Job 9:33). He must be entirely clear of any participation in the offence. He must, on account of his personal excellence, stand high in the esteem of the injured One. He must be a person of exalted dignity if the weight of his mediation was to bear any proportion to the magnitude of the crime and the value of the favor he would confer. He must be able to fully maintain the interests and subserve the honor of God. He must also possess a tender compassion towards the wretched offenders or he would not cordially interest himself on their behalf. And to give greater fitness to such a procedure it would be eminently proper that he should be intimately related to each of the parties. But where was one with so many and so necessary qualifications to be found? There was no creature worthy of so high office and so honorable an undertaking, no, not "in heaven, nor in earth, neither under the earth" (Rev. 5:3). None but Omniscience had ever thought of appointing God's own beloved and co-equal Son to take upon Him our nature.

4. In the union of such diverse natures in the person of Christ. It was necessary that the Mediator should be a Divine person in order that He might be independent and not the mere creature of either party; in order that He might reveal the Father (John 1:18; 14:9), in order to render unto the Law an obedience He did not owe for Himself (as all creatures do) and be one of infinite value. And in order that He might be capacitated to administer the realms of providence and grace, which are committed to Him as Mediatorial Prince (Matthew 28:18; John 17:2). None other than God can forgive sins, impart eternal life, restore the fallen creature to true liberty, or bestow .the Holy Spirit. Yet it was equally necessary that the Mediator should be Man. In order that He might truly represent men as "the last Adam," in order that He might be "made under the law" to obey it, in order that He could suffer its death-penalty, and in order that, in His glorified humanity, He might be Head of the Church. He was to be "The Apostle and High Priest" (Heb. 3:1). God's Apostle unto us, our "High Priest" with God, for He must both pacify God's wrath and remove our enmity.

But how furnish the Son for His office? How become partaker of human nature without contracting its corruption? How unite Godhood and manhood, the Infinite with the finite, Immortality with mortality, Almightiness with weakness? How produce such a union that the two natures were perfectly wedded in one Person and yet preserve their distinctness, conjoined yet not confounded? So that the Deity was not changed into flesh nor flesh transformed into God? Before the Word's becoming flesh, must we not exclaim "O the depth of the riches both of the wisdom and knowledge of God" (Rom. 11:33)! By that unique and wondrous union Christ was fitted to be "the Mediator of a better covenant" (Heb. 8:6). There was nothing that belonged to Deity which

He did not possess, and nothing that pertained to humanity but He was clothed with (Heb. 2:17). He had the nature of Him that was offended by sin, and of him that offended. "As sin was our invention (Eccl. 7:29) so Christ alone is God's and therefore is He called 'The Wisdom of God' (1 Cor. 1:24), which is not spoken of Him essentially as Second Person, but as Mediator, because in Him God's wisdom to the utmost is made manifest" (Thos. Goodwin).

5. In constituting Christ the federal Head of His people. "When God in wisdom had found a suitable Person, yet since thus must be His only Son, here was a greater difficulty to be overcome: how to give Him for us" (Thos. Goodwin). To satisfy both the requirements of His justice and the abundance of His mercy, God determined that a full satisfaction should be made unto His Law, and such a satisfaction that it was thereby more honored than if it had never been broken, or the whole race damned. In order thereto, He appointed that Christ should serve as the Surety and Substitute of His people. He must stand as their Representative and both fulfill all righteousness for them and endure the curse in their stead, so that they might be legally reckoned to have obeyed and suffered in Him. By transferring their guilt to the Surety, God both punishes sin and pardons the sinner. In the same stupendous Sacrifice God has upheld the claims of His Law and lavished His kindness on His people. "The depths of God's love are seen here, as of His wisdom before, in not sparing His own Son, but exposing Him to all the rigors of justice, which Would not make the least abatement" (Thos. Goodwin).

Christ then was made the "Surety of a better covenant" (Heb. 7:22). There could be no thought of reconciliation between a holy God and polluted rebels until sin had been put away and everlasting righteousness brought in, and as our Surety the Lord Jesus accomplished both. But O my reader, marvel at and stand in awe before what that involved. It involved that He who was in the form of God should take upon Him the form of a Servant. That the Lord of angels should be laid in a manger. That the Maker of the universe should not have anywhere to lay His head. That He should be constantly engaged in doing good and injuring none, yet be cast out by the world and deserted by His own followers. That the Lord of glory should be condemned as a malefactor, His own holy face fouled by the vile spittle of men and His back scourged by them. That the King of kings should be nailed hand and foot to a convict's gibbet. That the Beloved of the Father should be smitten and forsaken for Him. Such contrasts transcend the wit of man and could never have been invented by him. Must we not exclaim "O Lord, how great are Your works! Your thoughts are very deep" (Ps. 92:5).

6. In overruling sin to our gain. What a marvel of Divine wisdom is this: that God has not only removed the reproach which the entrance of sin brought upon His government, but that He made sin to be the foil for the greatest and grandest display of His perfections, and that He has not only devised a plan whereby His people are completely recovered from all the direful consequences and effects of the fall, but that they obtain a vastly superior inheritance than was the portion of unfallen Adam. God would have His people not only saved from Hell, but also brought into Heaven, yet in such a way as should be to the most honor of Himself and of His Son. The apostle speaks of "the salvation which is in Christ with eternal glory" (2 Tim. 2:10). Not only salvation, but a glorious one: one that is to the glory of Him who contrived it, of Him who purchased it, of Him who applies it, and of them who enjoy it. What a truly amazing thing is this that shame should be the path to glory, that fallen sinners are enriched by the Redeemer's poverty, that those groveling in the mire of sin should be advanced to the highest dignities by Christ's making Himself "of no reputation."

What honor it brings to God's wisdom not only to restore fallen men, but to make the fall issue in their superior excellence. If they had only been restored to their forfeited estate and the enjoyment of that happiness which they had lost, it had been a remarkable triumph of grace, but to make them "joint-heirs with Christ" (Rom. 8:17) and partakers of His glory (John 17:24) leaves us lost in amazement. It is a mystery of nature that the corruption of one thing is made to minister to the generation of another (as the bones of animals fertilize vegetation), but it is a grander mystery of grace that our fall in Adam should occasion a nobler restitution. Innocence was not our last end. A superior felicity awaits us on High. Human nature is raised to a far higher degree of honor than had man retained his innocence, for through redemption and regeneration the elect are vitally united to the God-man Mediator and made members of His Body. The devil's empire is overthrown by the very same nature as he overthrew (Gen. 3:15; Rom. 16:20).

7. In winning rebels unto Himself. Having contemplated something of the wisdom and love of the Father, the willingness and work of the Son, here we are to behold (more distinctively) the power and grace of the Holy Spirit. When He first draws near to the elect in their unregenerate state He finds them in a most deplorable condition. Their understandings are darkened by sin, their hearts are filled with enmity toward God, their wills are steeled against Him. Not only have they no regard for His glory, but they are without any desire for His so-great salvation, yea positively and strongly averse to it. Here too are obstacles which need removing, obstacles so formidable that nothing short of omniscience and omnipotence could overcome the same. How shall captives be delivered who are thoroughly satisfied with their prison? How shall slaves be freed who are in love with their bonds? Particularly, how shall that be effected while treating them as rational and responsible beings, without offering violence to their wills and reducing them to mere machines?

Some may regard the above as a very exaggerated statement of the case, supposing that a complete solution is found by presenting the Gospel to them. But Scripture teaches, and experience and observation verifies it, that the natural man has no eyes capable of beholding the beauty of the Gospel, and that his heart is so desperately wicked he will not receive the Savior that it offers him. How then are such creatures to be saved from themselves? How shall those who detest holiness be brought to desire it? The dead in sins made to walk in newness of life? That such a miracle is performed we know, but how it is wrought we know not. Christ Himself declares it is a mystery as inscrutable to man as the workings of the wind (John 3:8). All we know is that life, light, love and supernaturally communicated, by which the unwilling are made willing. Not by compelling them to do what they abhor, but by sweetly overcoming their aversion. "With lovingkindness have I drawn you" (Jer. 31:3).

8. In making our holiness and happiness conserve each other. This is yet another of the marvels of God's wisdom: that He has contrived that the same Gospel which secures our everlasting felicity shall also promote our present purity. The sanctity of God Is not comprised by His clemency to sinners, for the Redeemer is Himself both the principle and pattern of holiness unto all who are saved by Him. Moreover, the same grace to send His Son to die for us gives the Holy Spirit to renew us according to the Divine image and thereby make us meet for communion with Him. What a wonder of Divine wisdom to so highly exalt those who are so utterly unworthy in themselves and yet at the same time effectually humble that they cry "Not unto us, O Lord, not unto us, but unto Your name give glory, for Your mercy and for Your truth's sake" (Ps. 115:1). God's lovingkindness unto His people neither loosens the bonds of duty nor breaks that relation in which they stand to Him as their sovereign Lord and Governor. The Gospel does not permit its beneficiaries to return hatred for love nor contempt for benefit, but lays them under deeper obligations of gratitude to obedience. Those chosen to salvation are also "predestinated to be conformed unto the image of God's Son." The law of faith requires us to submit to Christ's scepter as well as depend upon His sacrifice.

Chapter 6
Its Arrangement

In our last we dwelt upon God's decision to redeem and reconcile fallen rebels. His love originating, His will determining, and His wisdom planning the outworking of the same. In illustrating how the Divine wisdom found a solution to all the formidable problems which stood in the way, we unavoidably anticipated somewhat the ground which we hoped to cover in future articles. That Divine decision and scheme was "eternally purposed in Christ Jesus our Lord" (Eph. 3:11.), for God's purpose to reconcile and His provision for the same are inseparable. That purpose respected not simply the exercise of mercy unto His lapsed people, but also the exercise of it in such a way that His Law was honored. Yet it must not be supposed that God was under any moral necessity of saving His people, or that redemption was an expedient to deliver the Divine character from reproach on account of the strictness of the Law in condemning all transgressors—no atonement was provided for the fallen angels! Rather has redemption vindicated the Law, and that in such a way that no transgressor is exempted from suffering its curse, either in himself or in a Substitute.

Reconciliation has been procured by the incarnate Son, the Lord Jesus Christ, for He is the grand and all-sufficient Provision of God for the accomplishing of His purpose. But it was effected by the Lord Jesus in fulfillment of a Covenant agreement. Unless that be clearly perceived we are without the principal key to the understanding of this stupendous undertaking. There was a time when Christians generally were well instructed in Covenant truth, but alas, a generation has grown up the great majority of which have heard nothing or next to nothing on it. It will therefore be necessary for us to proceed slowly in connection with this fundamental aspect of our subject and enter into considerable detail, for we do not ask the reader to receive ought from our pen until clearly convinced it is in full accord with and has the definite backing of God's Word. A few of our readers are more or less familiar with what we shall advance, yet it will do them no harm to have brought before them again the foundation on which faith should rest and to ponder the proofs which we now bring forward. The great majority of our readers know that "it is the blood (and that alone, plus nothing from us) that makes an atonement for the soul" (Lev. 17:11), but we wonder how many of them have pondered and grasped the purport of that blessed and remarkable statement "The God of peace that brought again from the dead our Lord Jesus, that great Shepherd of the sheep, through the blood of everlasting covenant" (Heb. 13:20). That implies, first, that there was a covenant-agreement between God and our Lord Jesus; second, that it was a covenant made with Him as the Head of His people—"that great Shepherd of the sheep;" third, that Christ performed the condition of the covenant; fourth, that it was as the propitiated and reconciled One that God here acted; fifth, that it was in fulfillment of covenant purpose that He raised Christ; sixth, that Christ's blood was the meritorious ground on which He (and all the saints in Him) was delivered from the prison of the grave; seventh, that hereby the Church has Divine assurance of its complete redemption and salvation. We cannot dwell upon these points but would request a careful weighing of them as introductory to what follows.

Three things are necessary in order to a "covenant" the parties, the terms, the agreement. A "covenant" is a solemn pact or contract in which there are certain "articles" or conditions to be performed, in return for which performance an agreed award is promised and assured. It is a mutual agreement in which one party guarantees a stipulated return for the other's fulfillment of the work he had pledged himself to undertake. It is an agreement entered into voluntarily by both parties (see Matthew 26:15). The two parties in "the everlasting covenant" were the Father and the Son—the Holy Spirit concurring therein, being the Witness, and agreeing to co-operate in the same. In Scripture the Father is represented as taking the initiative in this matter, proposing to His Son the terms of the covenant. The Father proposed a federal transaction in which the Son should take upon Him the Mediatorial office and serve as the Head of His people, thereby assuming and discharging their liabilities and bringing in an everlasting righteousness for them. The Son is represented as freely and gladly consenting to it.

It needs to be pointed out and emphatically insisted upon that the Son was not so circumstanced antecedently to His susception of the Mediatorial office that He could not have avoided the humiliation and sufferings which He endured. We shall explain later the precise meaning of His words "My Father is greater than I" (John 14:28), "neither came I of Myself but He sent Me" (John 8:42), "this commandment (to lay down His life) have I received of My Father" (John 10:18); sufficient now to point out they have no reference whatever to His condition and position prior to the Covenant, for He then enjoyed absolute equality with the Father in every way. The Son might have resigned the whole human race to the dire consequences of their apostasy and have remained Himself everlastingly blessed and glorious. It was by His own voluntary consent that He entered into covenant engagement with the Father. In that free consent lay the excellency of it. It was His willing obedience and personal merits which gave infinite value to His oblation. Behind that willingness lay His love for the Father and His love for the Church.

On the other hand it is equally true that though the Son had pitied, yea to loved the elect (fore viewed as fallen) that He was willing to become their Surety and Substitute, yet He could not have redeemed them without the Father's acceptance of His sacrifice. The Father too must consent to such an undertaking. Thus, there must be a mutual agreement between Them. The relation which Christ assumed to His people and the work He did for them presupposed the Father's willingness to it. Before passing on it must also be pointed out that in consenting to become Mediator and Servant, and as such in subjection to the Father, the Son did not surrender any of His perfections not relinquish any of His Divine rights, but He agreed to assume an inferior office and for a season to be subordinate to the Father's will. This was for the glory of the whole Godhead and the salvation of His people. After He became incarnate He was still in possession of His essential glory, though He was pleased to veil it in large measure from men and make Himself of "no reputation" in the world.

Before adducing proof-texts of the covenant made between the Father and the Son, let us call attention to a number of passages which clearly imply it and which otherwise are not fully intelligible. Take Christ's very first recorded utterance after He became incarnate: "Do you not know that I must be about My Father's business" (Luke 2:49). Did not that intimate He had entered this world with a clearly defined and Divinely designed task before Him? "I came clown from heaven not to do Mine own will, but the will of Him that sent Me" (John 6:38) is even more explicit. Such subordination of one Divine person to another argues a mutual agreement between Them, and that, for some unique end. "Say you of Him whom the Father has sanctified and sent into the World; You blaspheme, because I said, I am the Son of God?" (John 10:36). Observe carefully the order of the two verbs: Christ was "sanctified" by the Father—that is, set apart and consecrated to His mediatorial office—before He was "sent" into the world! "Other sheep I have . . . them also I must bring" (John 10:16)—why "must" unless He was under definite engagement to do so?

That Christ went to the cross in fulfillment of a covenant-agreement may be gathered from His own words: "truly the Son of man goes as it was determined" (Luke 22:22), with which should be linked "Of a truth against Your holy child Jesus, whom You have anointed, both Herod and Pontius Pilate with the Gentiles and the people of Israel, were gathered together, for to do whatsoever Your hand and Your counsel determined before to be done" (Acts 4:27, 28). When you stand before the cross and gaze by faith upon its august Sufferer recognize that He was there fulfilling the compact into which He entered with the Father before the world was. His blood shedding was necessary—"ought not Christ to have suffered these things!" (Luke 24:26). He asked—because of the relation He sustained to His people as their Surety. He was pledged to secure their salvation in such a way as glorified God and magnified His Law, for that had been Divinely "determined" and mutually agreed upon in the everlasting Covenant. Had not Christ died there had been no atonement, no reconciliation to God; equally true is it that had there been no covenant, Christ had never died!

Every passage where Christ own the Father as His God witnesses to the same truth. When Jehovah established His covenant with Abraham He promised "I will. . .be a God unto You and to your seed" (Gen. 17:8), and therefore when He "remembered His covenant with Abraham, with Isaac and with Jacob" (Ex. 2:25) and revealed Himself to Moses at the burning bush preparatory to delivering His people from Egypt, He declared Himself to be "The Lord God of your fathers: the God of Abraham, the God of Isaac, and the God of Jacob: this is My name forever and this is My memorial to all generations" (Ex. 3:15). This is My covenant title and the guarantee of My covenant faithfulness. So too the grand promise of the new covenant is "I . . .will be their God" (Jer. 31:33 and Heb. 8:10). If then the Father had entered into covenant with His Son we should expect to find Him owning Him as His God during the days of His flesh. And this is exactly what we do find. "My God, My God, why have You forsaken Me" was not only a cry of agony, but an acknowledgement of covenant relationship. "I ascend to My Father and your Father, and to My God and your God" (John 20:17). So also after His ascension. He declared, "Him that overcomes will I make a pillar in the Temple of My God. . .and I will write upon Him the Name of My God, and the name of the city of My God" (Rev. 3:12).

Turning to the Epistles we find many passages which presuppose the Father's covenant with Christ before creation on behalf of His people. "Who has saved us. . .according to His own purpose and grace which was given us in Christ Jesus before the world began" (2 Tim. 1:9). Even at that time, if time it may be called, there was a federal relationship subsisting between Christ and the Church, though it was not made fully manifest until He became incarnate. That subsisting relationship formed the basis of the whole economy of Divine grace toward them after the fall, as it was the ground on which God pardoned the O. T. saints and bestowed spiritual blessings upon them. "In hope of eternal life which God, that cannot lie, promised before the world was" (Titus 1:2). Does not that "promised" imply an agreement that God made promise to Christ as the Covenant Head and to His people in Him? Christ was faithful to Him that appointed Him (Heb. 3:2). As "obedience" implies a precept, so "faithfulness" connotes a trust, and a trust wherein one has engaged himself to perform that trust according to directions given him.

Passing now from indirect allusions to what is more specific, we begin with Psalm 89:3. "I have made a covenant with My chosen, I have sworn unto David My Servant." The immediate allusion is to the historical David, but the spiritual reference is to David's Son and Lord. This is clear from many considerations. First, the striking and lofty manner in which this Psalm opens intimates that its leading theme must be one of great weight and value. "I will sing of the mercies of the Lord forever, with my mouth will I make known Your faithfulness to all generations. For I have said, Mercy shall be built up forever, Your faithfulness shall You establish in the very heavens" (vv. 1, 2). Such language denotes that no ordinary or common "mercies" are in view, but those which when apprehended fill the hearts of the redeemed with holy songs and cause them to magnify the fidelity of Jehovah as nothing else does. Thus, such an introduction should prepare us to expect Divine revelation of extreme importance and blessedness.

Second, "I have made a covenant with My Chosen" (same word as My Elect in Isa. 42:1). I have sworn unto David (which means Beloved) My Servant. In the following passages it may be seen that Christ is expressly referred to as "David" by the prophets (Jer. 30:9; Ezek. 34:23; 37:24; Hosea 3:5) and let it be duly borne in mind that all those predictions were made long after the historical David had passed away from this scene. "You spoke in vision to Your Holy One and said: I have laid help upon One that is mighty, I have exalted One chosen out of the people (Deut. 18:15), 1 have found David My Servant, with My holy oil have I anointed Him" (vv. 19, 20). Who can doubt that a greater than the son of Jesse is here before us? But more: God goes on to say "I will make Him My Firstborn higher than the kings of the earth.. .My covenant shall stand fast with Him" (vv. 27, 28)—does not that establish beyond a doubt the identity of the One with whom Jehovah made the covenant! Such declarations pertain to no mere human being.

Third, the covenant promises here made establish the same fact. "His seed will I make to endure forever and His throne as the days of heaven" (v. 29)—the throne of the historical David perished over two thousand years ago! That this promise was to be fulfilled in Christ is clear from Luke 1:31-33, where it was said to Mary. You "shall call His name Jesus. He shall be great and shall be called the Son of the Highest; and the Lord God shall give unto Him the throne of His father David, and He shall reign over the house of Jacob forever and of His kingdom there shall be no end." Another proof that it is not the typical David who is viewed in this Psalm appears in "If His children forsake My Law . . . then will I visit their transgression with the rod" (vv. 30-32). Had it been the successor of Saul who was the subject of this Psalm it had said "If he shall break My Law. . .! will visit his transgression with the rod" —as he was sorely chastised for so grievously wronging Uriah. No, it is Christ and His spiritual children who are referred to, and it is because of God's covenant with Him that He casts then not off. (See vv. 33-36).

Fourth, in Acts 13:34 Paul proved the resurrection of Christ thus: "As concerning that He raised Him from the dead to return no more to corruption, He said on this wise: I will give you the sure mercies of David." But in what did that quotation from Isaiah 55:3 provide proof? By the resurrection of Christ the "sure mercies of David" are confirmed unto His children. If they are in possession of them, then Christ must have risen! That word of Paul's looks back beyond Isaiah 55 to Psalm 89, which, as we have seen, begins thus: "I will sing of the mercies of the Lord forever." The principal mercies are "I have made a covenant with My chosen . . . Your seed will I establish forever, and build up Your throne for all generations" (vv. 3, 4). Here then are "the sure mercies of David:" that God has covenanted to raise up Christ and set Him at His own right hand from where, on His mediatorial throne, He communicates those mercies to His seed. All doubt on this point is removed by Peter's avowal that through David God had sworn that "Of the fruit of his loins . . . He would raise up Christ to sit on His throne" (Acts 2:30 and see v. 33).

On Psalm 89:3, 4 the immortal Toplady said, "Do you suppose that this was spoken to David in his own person only? No, indeed; but to David as the type, figure, and forerunner of Jesus Christ. 'I have sworn unto David My Servant' unto the Messiah, who was typified by David, unto My co-equal Son, who stipulated to take upon Himself 'the form of a servant.' 'Your seed' all those that I have given unto you in the decree of election; all those whom you shall live and die to redeem. Those 'will I establish forever,' so as to render their salvation irreversible and inadmissible. 'And build up Your Throne:' Your mediatorial throne, as King of saints and covenant Head of the elect.

'To all generations:' there shall always be a succession of favored sinners to be called and sanctified, in consequence of Your federal obedience unto death, and every period of time shall recompense Your covenant sufferings with an increasing revenue of converted souls, until as many as
were ordained to eternal life shall be gathered in" (Author of that precious hymn "Rock of Ages").

Chapter 7
Its Arrangement-Continued

A solemn covenant was entered into between the Father and the Son before ever the world was. A compact was made in which the Father assigned the Son to be the Head and Savior of His elect, and in which the Son consented to act as the Surety and Sponsor of His people. There was a mutual agreement between Them, of which the Holy Spirit was both the Witness and Recorder. It was in there that the Son was appointed unto the Mediatorial office, when He was "set up" (or anointed as the Hebrew signifies), when He was "brought forth" from the eternal decree (Prov. 8:23,24) and given a covenant subsistence as the God-man. It was then that Christ as a lamb without blemish and without spot "verily was foreordained before the foundation of the world" (1 Pet. 1:18, 19). It was then that everything was arranged between the Father and, the Son, concerning the redemption of the Church. It is this which throws such a flood of light upon many passages in the N.T. which otherwise are shrouded in mystery.

As the One more especially offended (1 John 2:1) the Father is represented as taking the initiative in this matter: "I have made a covenant with My Chosen" (Ps. 89:3), yet the very fact that it was a "covenant" necessarily implied the willing concurrence of the Son in it. Before the covenant was settled there was a conference between Them. As there was a conferring together of the Divine Persons concerning our creation (Gen. 1:26), so there was a consultation together over our reconciliation, as to how peace could be righteously made between God and His enemies and as to how their enmity against Him might be slain; and thus we are told "the counsel of peace shall be between Them both" (Zech. 6:13). The terms which the Father proposed unto the Son may be gathered from the office He assumed and the work He performed, for the relation into which He entered and the task He discharged were but the actual fulfilling of the conditions of the covenant. The Son's acceptance of those terms, His willingness in entering office and discharging its duties, is clearly revealed in both Testaments.

This covenant was made by the Father with Christ on behalf of His people: "Your seed will I establish forever" follows immediately after Psalm 89:3. So again "My covenant shall stand fast With Him: His seed also will I make to endure forever" (vv. 28,29). In the next verses His seed are termed "His children" and should they be unruly God says "I will visit their transgression with the rod, nevertheless My lovingkindness will I not take from Him"— showing their covenant oneness with Him. The elect were committed to Christ as a charge or trust so that He is held accountable for their eternal felicity: "Of them which You gave Me have I lost none" (John 18:9). Since the covenant was made with Christ as the Head of the elect it was virtually made with them in Him, they having a representative concurrence therein.

The terms of the covenant may be summed up thus. First, it was required that Christ should take upon Him the form of a Servant, be made in the likeness of men, and act as the Surety of His people. Second, it was required of Him that He should render a full and perfect obedience to the Law and thereby provide the meritorious means of their justification. Third, it was required of Him that He should make full satisfaction for their sins, by serving as their Substitute and having visited upon Him the entire curse of the Law. In consideration of His acceptance of those terms the Father promised Him adequate supports; and on fulfillment of the task prescribed, specified rewards were promised Him. Let us briefly amplify these points. Little needs to be said on the first, for it should be clear to the reader that in order for the Son to render obedience to the Law He must become a subject of it and be under its authority. Equally evident is it that to be the Substitute of His people and suffer the penalty of their sins. He must become partaker of their nature—yet without sharing its defilement.

It was required from our Surety that He should comply in every respect with the precepts of the Divine Law. Such obedience was required of man originally under the Adamic covenant, and since the nature of God and His relation to the creature changes not, that requirement holds good forever. If then a Surety engages to discharge all the obligations of God's elect then He must necessarily meet that requirement on their behalf, which is only another way of saying that He would thereby provide or bring in an everlasting righteousness for them. "There was no possibility that man could obtain happiness unless this obedience was performed by him, or by another whom the Law should admit to act in his name. 'If you will enter into life, keep the commandments' (Matthew 19:17) is the answer which the Law returns to the sinner who asks what he shall do to inherit eternal life. It is evident the same obedience was required from our Savior when acting as our federal Head" (J. Dick).

The Father required from our Surety full satisfaction for the sins of His people. Since they had broken the Divine Law its penalty must be inflicted, either on them or on One who was prepared to suffer in their room. But before the penalty could be inflicted the guilt of the transgressors must be transferred to Him. That is to say, their sins must be judicially imputed to Him. To that arrangement the Holy One willingly consented, so that He who "knew no sin" was legally "made sin" for His people. God laid on Him the iniquities of them all, and therefore the sword of Divine justice smote Him and exacted satisfaction. Without the shedding of blood there was no remission of sins. The blotting out of transgressions, procuring for us the favor of God, the purchase of the heavenly inheritance, required the death of Christ.

The Son's free acceptance of those terms is revealed in Psalm 40. All the best of the commentators from Calvin to Spurgeon have expounded this Psalm throughout of Christ as the Head of His Church. Its opening verses contain His personal thanksgiving for deliverance from death and the grave, but in His new song He makes mention of "our God" (v. 3)—His people sharing His glorious triumph. In verse 5 Christ owns Jehovah as "My God" and speaks of His thoughts to "Usward," that is, to the elect as one with Himself. But it is in verses 6-10 we have that which is most germane to our present subject—a passage quoted in Hebrews 10, and which looks back to the far distant past. The force of "sacrifice and offering You did not desire" (v. 6) is given us in "it is not possible that the blood of bulls, and goats should take away sins" (Heb. 10:4). "My ears have You dug" speaks in the type of Exodus 21:5, 6 and tells of our Lord's readiness to serve and His love to His Father and His children. "A body have You prepared Me" (Heb. 10:5) announces the Son's coming into this world equipped for His arduous undertaking.

"Then said I:" when alternatives had been discussed and it was agreed that animal sacrifices were altogether inadequate for satisfying Divine justice. "Lo, I come" willingly of My own volition—from the ivory palaces to the abodes of misery. Those words signified His cheerful acceptance of the terms of the covenant. "In the volume of the book it is written of Me:" thus it was recorded at the very beginning of the Divine decrees—of which the Scriptures are a faithful transcript—that I should make My advent to earth. Thus it was registered by the Holy Spirit who witnessed My solemn engagement with the Father so to do. Thus it was formally and officially inscribed that in the fullness of time I should become incarnate and accomplish a purpose which lay beyond the capacity of all the holy angels. "I delight to do You will, O My God" tells us first of the object for which He came—to make good the Father's counsels; second, His freeness and joy in it; third, the character in which He acted—as covenant Head: "My God."

"I delight to do Your will, O My God." Here consists the very essence of obedience: the soul's cheerful and loving devotion to God. Christ's obedience, which is the righteousness of His people, was pre-eminent in this quality. Notwithstanding unparalleled sorrows and measureless griefs our Lord found delight on His work. "Who for the joy that was set before Him endured the cross, despising the shame" (Heb. 12:2). "Yea, Your Law is within My heart" He declared. No mere outward and formal subjection to the Divine will was His. That Law which is "holy, just and good" (Rom. 7:12) was enshrined in His affections. "O how love I Your Law" (Ps. 119:97) He averred. The Law did not have to be written on His heart, as it has on ours (Heb. 8:10), for it was one with the holiness of His nature. Then what a horrible crime for any to speak disparagingly of or want to be delivered from that Law which Christ loved!

The two things—the Father's proposing the terms of the covenant and the Son's free acceptance of them—are brought together in a striking yet rarely considered passage. "And their Noble (the Hebrew is in the singular number) shall be of themselves and their Governor shall proceed from the midst of them, and I will cause Him to draw near, and He shall approach Me: for Who is this that engaged His heart to approach Me, says the Lord" (Jer. 30:21). That is one of the great Messianic prophecies, and it is closely parallel with Psalm 89:19, 20, 27. In it we see the Father taking the initiative, and equally so the Son's cheerful compliance. The Son is to become incarnate, for He was to "proceed from the midst of" the people of Israel. He was to be their "Governor," and in order thereto is seen "approaching" the Father, or voluntarily presenting Himself to serve in that capacity. His free consent and heartiness so to act appears in His "that engaged His heart to approach Me."

We cannot now enter into the connections of the above verse, but if the reader compares verse 9 of the same chapter and ponders what follows, he will rind confirmation of our interpretation. There the Father announced, "They shall serve the Lord their God and David their King, whom I will raise up (not from the grave, but exalt to office, as in Deut. 18:15; Luke 1:69 etc.) unto them." That can be meant of none other than Christ, the antitypical David, for "serve" includes rendering Divine homage (Matthew 4:10), and worship will never be performed to the resurrected son of Jesse. Now it is the antitypical David, the Father's "Beloved," who is the King and Governor of the spiritual Israel and to whom Divine honors are paid. And He is the One who before earth's foundation was laid "engaged His heart," or as the Heb. signifies "became a Surety in His heart" (for so the word is rendered in Gen. 44:32, Prov. 6:1 etc.,) and that is the ground of the covenant which follows: "and you shall be My people and I will be your God" (v. 22).

Before looking at some of the assurances made by the Father of adequate assistance to His incarnate Son in the discharge of His covenant engagements, we must consider closely the office in which He served. In previous articles we pointed out the needs be for a Mediator if God and His people were to be reconciled in a way that honored His Law, as we also intimated His consummate wisdom in such an arrangement, and showed the perfect fitness of Christ for such an office. As the Mediator He was to serve as our Surety and also fulfill the functions of Prophet, Priest and King. As the Mediator He was "set up" or "anointed" from the beginning (Prov. 8:23): that is, was given a covenant subsistence as such before God, in which He acted all through the O.T. era. The prophets (equally with the apostles) were His ministers, and therefore the Spirit who spoke in them is termed "the Spirit of Christ" (1 Pet. 1:11). In Zechariah 1:11, 12 and 3:2 we find Him interceding: and in anticipation of the incarnation He appeared as "Man" (Josh 5:13, 14; Dan. 12:6, 7).

Christ is Mediator in respect of His person as well as office. Only thus could He be the Representative of God unto us, the Image of the invisible God, the One in whom He is seen (John 14:9), the light of whose glory shines in His face (2 Cor. 4:6). It must be ever remembered that it was a Divine person who became flesh, and it is equally necessary to insist that the whole of His mediatory work is inseparably founded on the exercise of both of His natures. It is quite unwarrantable to predict certain things of His Divine nature and others of His human, for though not confounded there is perfect oneness between them. It was the God-man who was tempted, suffered and died— "the Lord's death" (1 Cor. 11:26). This is indeed a subject beyond human comprehension, nevertheless, thought "great is the mystery of godliness" yet it is "without controversy" (1 Tim. 3:16) unto all those who bow to the all-sufficient authority of Divine revelation and receive the same as "little children."

As the Mediator Christ became the Father's "Servant" (Isa. 42:1; Phil. 2:7). Yet in so doing He ceased not to be a Divine person, but rather the God-man in whom "dwells all the fullness of the Godhead bodily" (Col. 2:9). As our Surety Christ became subordinate to the Father's will, nevertheless He still retained all His Divine perfections and prerogatives. When the Holy Spirit announced that unto a Child should be born and a Son given, He was careful to declare that such an One was none other than "the mighty God" (Isa. 9:6). When the Father brought His Firstbegotten into the world He gave orders "Let all the angels of God worship Him" (Heb. 1:6). Yet as our Surety and the Father's Servant He was sent into the world, received commandment from His Father and became obedient unto death. Retaining as He did His Divine perfections He could rightly say "I and My Father are one" (John 10:30), co-equal and co-glorious; yet as the Servant "My Father is greater than I" (John 4:28)—not essentially so but officially, not by nature but by virtue of the place which He had taken. This distinction throws a flood of light upon many passages.

To be Himself "the true God" (John 5:20) and yet subject to God—owning Him as "My God;" to be the Law-Giver and yet "under the Law" (Gal. 4:4), to be one with the Father and yet inferior to Him, to be "The Lord of glory" (1 Cor. 2:8) and yet "made both Lord and Christ" (Acts 2:36), are, according to all human reason and logic, inconsistent properties: nevertheless Scripture itself expressly predicates these very things of one and the same Person—yet looked at in different relationships! In the days of His flesh Christ was "over all, God blessed forever" (Rom. 9:6), yet as our Surety "the Head of Christ is God" (1 Cor. 11:3). While walking this earth as the Man of sorrows the disciples beheld His glory "as of the Only-begotten of the Father" (John 1:4), yet as our Substitute He was "crucified through weakness" (2 Cor. 3:4). As God manifest in flesh He both laid down His life and took it again (John 10:18). but as our Shepherd God "brought again from the dead our Lord Jesus" (Heb. 3:20). There is perfect harmony amid wondrous variety.

Christ's entrance into covenant engagement was entirely voluntary on His part: there existed no prior obligation, nor was there any authority by which He could be compelled to it. As the Father's "Fellow" He was subject to no law and acknowledged no superior, supreme dominion was Him, and He "thought it not robbery to be equal with God" (Phil. 2:6). But having freely entered into the covenant and agreed to fulfill its terms, the Son became officially subordinate to the Father, and as our Surety He "sent Him into the world" (John 13:7), and as our Surety he was "anointed" with the Holy Spirit and with power (Acts 10:38), was "delivered up for us all" (Rom. 8:32), was raised from the dead (Acts 2:24), was "given all power" (Matthew 28:18), was elevated to the right hand of the Majesty on high (Heb. 1:3), was exalted "to be a Prince and a Savior, for to give repentance to Israel and forgiveness of sins" (Acts 5:31), and was "ordained of God to be the Judge of quick and dead" (Acts 10:42). Thus, the very passage over which "Unitarians" have stumbled and broken their necks speak of Christ not in His essential Person but in His mediatorial office: the former giving value to the latter, the latter endearing the former to our hearts.

Chapter 8
Its Arrangement-Continued

Upon the Son's cheerful acceptance of the terms proposed to Him concerning the federal undertaking He was to engage in, the Father in turn bound Himself to do certain things for and unto the Son. This it was which constituted the very essence of that compact which was made by Them, for a covenant is an agreement between two parties who come under mutual engagements. Something is to be done by one party, in consequence of which the other party binds himself to do another thing in return. As there must be two parties to a covenant, so there must be two parts in a covenant—a condition and a promise. It is the performing of the condition or terms of the covenant—the work or service specified—which gives the first party the right to the promised reward. Having already shown what Christ consented to do, we turn now to consider what the Father promised to bestow. First, He agreed to make all needful preparations for the incarnation of His Son. Second, to give Him all requisite assistance in the performing of His work. Third, to bestow upon Him a meet reward.

The promise to make all needful preparation for the incarnation of His Son comprehended the whole of the Father's providences or governance of this world from the creation of man until Christ began His public ministry: "My Father works until this time, and (now) I work" (John 5:17). The Father's "work" included the ordering of human history, and particularly His dealings with Abraham and his descendants and the separation of Israel from the rest of the nations, for it was from Israel that Christ, according to the flesh, would issue. The Father's "work" included the giving of a written revelation, in which the covenant was made known and the advent of His Son promised, so that an expectation of His appearing was created and a foundation was laid for His mission. The Father's "work" also involved the "preparation of a body" for His Son, which was accomplished by the miracle of the virgin birth. When "the fullness of time was come—when all the necessary preparations were completed—God sent forth His Son, made of a woman" (Gal. 4:4).

The Father promised to give His Son all requisite help for the performing of His work. First, in order for the discharge of His mediatorial office there was that which fitted Him to it. "There shall come forth a Rod out of the stem of Jesse and a Branch shall grow of his roots. And the Spirit of the Lord shall rest upon Him: the spirit of wisdom and understanding and spirit of counsel and might, the spirit of knowledge and of the fear of the Lord" (Isa. 11:1, 2). Upon which the Puritan Charnock said, "All the gifts of the Spirit should reside in Him as in a proper habitation, perpetually. The human nature being a creature could not beautify and enrich itself with needful gifts. This promise of the Spirit was therefore necessary. His humanity could not else have performed the work it was designed for. So that the habitual holiness residing in the humanity of Christ was a fruit of this eternal covenant. Though the Divine nature of Christ, by virtue of its union, might sanctify the human nature, yet the Spirit was promised Him because it is His proper office to confer those gifts which are necessary for any undertaking in the world; and the personal operations of the Trinity do not interfere. It might also be because every person in the Trinity should plainly have a distinct hand in our redemption."

The Father, then, furnished and equipped Christ for His arduous work by a plentiful effusion of the graces and gifts of the Holy Spirit. Thus He declared "Behold My Servant whom I uphold, My Elect in whom My soul delights: I have put My Spirit upon Him" (Isa. 42:1,2). Those promises were fulfilled at His baptism, when the Spirit descended upon Him (Matthew 3:16), for it was then that "God anointed Jesus of Nazareth with the Holy Spirit and with power" (Acts 10:38). This was freely owned by the Savior Himself, for in the synagogue He read "The Spirit of the Lord is upon Me, because He has anointed Me to preach the Gospel to the poor, He has sent Me to heal the brokenhearted, to preach deliverance to the captive, and recovering of sight to the blind, to set at liberty them that are bruised" and then declared "This day is this Scripture fulfilled in your ears" (Luke 4:18,21). So too we find Him acknowledging "I cast out demons by the Spirit of God" (Matthew 12:27).

Second, the Father promised to invest His Son with a threefold office. In order to the saving of His people it was most requisite that whatever Christ did He should act by the authority of the Father, by a commission under the broad seal of Heaven. Accordingly He said "I will raise them up a Prophet from among their brethren" (Deut. 18:15,18 and see Acts 3:22). Christ did not run without being sent. It was God who "anointed Him to preach." Again, "Christ glorified not Himself to be made an High Priest (He did not intrude Himself into that office), but He that said unto Him, You are My Son" (Heb. 5:5); Christ was "made a High Priest forever after the order of Melchizedek" (Heb. 6:20). So also God the Father invested Him with the royal office: "yet have I set My King upon My holy hill of Zion" (Ps. 2:6). "I will raise unto David a righteous Branch and a King shall reign and prosper" (Jer. 23:5), for the "the Father loves the Son and has given all things into His hand" (John 3:35); and therefore has He made Him "higher than the kings of the earth" (Ps. 89:27).

Third, the Father promised Christ strength, support and protection to execute the great work of redemption. His undertaking would be attended with such difficulties that creature power, though unimpaired by sin, would have been quite inadequate for it. It was to be performed in human nature, and that had failed in a much easier task, even when possessed of untainted innocence. Therefore did the Father assure Him of help and succor, to carry Him through all the obstacles and dangers, trials and opposition He would meet with. "Behold My Servant whom I uphold.. . .I the Lord have called You in righteousness and will hold Your hand and keep You, and give You for a covenant of the people, for a light to the Gentiles" (Isa. 42:1,6). "The work of redemption was so high and so hard that it would have broken the hearts and the backs of all the glorious angels and mighty men on earth had they entered on it; therefore the Father engaged Himself to stand close to Jesus Christ and mightily assist and strengthen Him in all His mediatorial administrations" (Thos. Brooks, Puritan).

Christ is said to be "The Son of man whom You made strong for Yourself" (Ps. 80:17), for He had sworn "My arm also shall strengthen Him" (Ps. 89:21). It is blessed to see how that the Redeemer, in the days of His flesh, acknowledged these promises. "I was cast upon You from the womb, You are My God from My mother's belly"! (Ps. 22:10). "Listen O isles unto Me, and hearken your people from afar: The Lord has called Me from the womb, from the bowels of My Mother (see Matthew 1:21, 22) has He made mention of My name. And He has made My mouth like a sharp sword, in the shadow of His hand has He hid Me" (Isa. 49:1,2). "The Lord God has given Me the tongue of the learned . . . the Lord God will help Me . . . and I know that I shall not be ashamed" (Isa. 59:4-7). In unshaken confidence, when His enemies were conspiring against Him and His friends were on the point of forsaking Him, He declared "yet I am not alone, because the Father is with Me" (John 16:32).

Those promises of the Father were the support of His soul in the hour of His supreme crisis. His heart laid hold of them, acted faith on them, and received comfort and strength therefrom.

"Preserve Me, O God, for in You do I put My trust" (Ps. 16:1), was His petition and plea. "I gave My back to the smiters and My cheeks to those that plucked off the hair. I hid not My face from shame and spitting, for the Lord God will help Me therefore shall I not be confounded, and therefore I set My face like a flint, and I know that I shall not be ashamed" (Isa. 50:6,7). When He was denounced by the Jews and condemned by Pilate, He consoled Himself with the assurance "He is near that justifies Me" (Isa. 50:8). "I have set the Lord always before Me: because He is at My right hand I shall not be moved. Therefore My heart is glad and My glory rejoices; My flesh also shall rest in hope, for You will not leave My soul in Sheol, neither will You suffer Your holy One to see corruption. You will show Me the path of life" (Ps. 16:8-11). In the prospect of death, He rejoiced in the sure knowledge of resurrection.

Fourth, the Father promised Him a glorious reward. First, a glory for Himself personally, as the God-man Mediator. As He was to endure the cross, so He was also to receive the crown. The enduring of the cross was a covenant engagement on His part, and the bestowing of the crown was a covenant engagement on the Father's part. That was plainly borne witness to by His prophets, for the Spirit in them "testified beforehand the sufferings of Christ and the glory which should follow." (1 Pet. 1:11). That glory consisted in His being fully invested with His priestly and royal offices. As it was with the type, so with the Antitype. David was anointed incipiently and privately before he slew Goliath (1 Sam. 16:13), but formally and publicly after his victories (2 Sam. 5:13). The antitypical David was indeed "anointed with the Holy Spirit" at the Jordan, but not until after He had triumphed over sin, Satan and the grave, did God anoint Him "with the oil of gladness above His fellows" (Heb. 1:9) and publicly make Him to be "both Lord and Christ" (Acts 2:36).

"The solemn inauguration into all His offices was after His making reconciliation: making an end of sin, bringing in everlasting righteousness, and thereby shutting up all prophecy and vision, because all the prophecies tended to Him and were accomplished in Him; and then as manifesting Himself the most holy, He was to be anointed—that is, fully invested in all the offices of Prophet, Priest and King (Dan. 9:24). The compact ran thus: Do this, suffer death for the vindication of the honor of My Law, and You shall be a Priest and King forever. He could not, therefore, be solemnly installed till He had performed the condition on His part (for the promise was made to Him considered as Mediator or God-man); then it was that He was advanced, for the ground of His exaltation is pitched wholly upon His sufferings. Therefore God has given Him a glory as a just debt due to the price paid, the sufferings undergone, and the obedience yielded to the mediatory Law" (S. Charnock). Therefore it is that the general assembly of Heaven say with a loud voice "Worthy is the Lamb that was slain to receive power, and riches, and wisdom, and strength, and honor, and glory, and blessing" (Rev. 5:12).

Subsidiary to that glorious investiture was the Father's promise to raise Christ from the dead. "He asked life of You, and You gave it Him, even length of days forever and ever" (Ps. 21:5). Beautifully does that link up with Ps. 102:23-27 —quoted by the apostle in Heb. 1:12 as the words of the Father to the Son. In Psalm 102:23, 24 we hear the incarnate Son saying, "He shortened My days: I said, O My God, take Me not away in the midst of My days," to which the Father made answer, "Your years are throughout all generations . . . Your years shall have no end" (v. 27). So again, He received assurance "He shall prolong His days!" (Isa. 53:10). The Father made promise that the One who had been bruised by Him and whose soul He had made "an offering for sin" should have a glorious deliverance and should reign in life. It was in fulfillment of such promises as these that "The God of peace (the reconciled One) brought again from the dead our Lord Jesus, that great Shepherd of the sheep, through the blood of the everlasting covenant" (Heb. 13:20).

In like manner subsidiary to Christ's glorious investiture of His full priestly and kingly offices was His ascension, for though He was born King and acted as Priest at the cross when He "offered

Himself to God" and "made intercession for the transgressors," yet not until He had completely performed His part of the covenant could He enter into His rightful reward. Accordingly we find promise of ascension made unto Him. It was clearly implied in "I will make Him My Firstborn, higher than the kings of the earth" (Ps. 89:27). It was revealed in "Who shall ascend into the Hill of the Lord? Who shall stand in His Holy Place?" answered by "Lift up your heads 0 you gates and be lifted up you everlasting doors, and the King of glory shall come in" (Ps. 24:3,7). It was plainly announced in "You have ascended on high, You have led captivity captive" (Ps. 68:18). It was such promises as these the Savior had in mind when He said "Ought not Christ to have suffered and to enter into His glory" (Luke 24:26).

"Behold, My Servant shall deal prudently. He shall be exalted and extolled, and by very high" (Isa. 52:13). The 53rd of Isaiah—that wondrous chapter in which we have so solemnly, so strikingly, and so evangelically depicted, the vicarious sufferings of Christ—closes with that blessed promise of the Father: "Therefore will I divide Him a portion with the great and He shall divide the spoil with the strong, because He has poured out His soul unto death" (v. 12). The similitude used there is taken from the honoring of military conquerors who, having in fight defeated and routed their enemies, gained a great victory and in consequence are suitably rewarded by their princes, being exalted by them and given a share of the spoils or fruits of war. It was as though God the Father said: This My incarnate and successful Son shall receive such honor, glory, renown and riches after His toils and conflicts as are meet for His triumphs. He shall have a glorious recompense for all His humiliation and sufferings at the hands of men, for His opposition from Satan, and for His enduring of My wrath. For nothing less is due Him. The fulfillment of Isaiah 53:12 is seen in Ephesians 4:8, Colossians 2:15, etc. "The obedience of Christ bears to these blessings not only the relation of antecedent to consequent, but of merit to reward, so that His obedience is the cause: and the condition being fulfilled by virtue of obedience, He has a right to the reward" (H. Witsius—the Dutch Puritan). That is the precise force of the "Wherefore" in the above verse, as it is also in "You love righteousness and hate wickedness, therefore God, Your God, has anointed You with the oil of gladness above Your fellows" (Ps. 45:7).It was not only that justice required it, but the covenant fidelity of the Father was involved therein. Therefore His assurance "My faithfulness and My mercy shall be with Him, and in My name shall His horn be exalted" (Ps. 89:24). Thus also the N. T., Christ "became obedient unto death, even the death of the cross, wherefore God also has highly exalted Him and given Him a name which is above every name" (Phil. 2:8,9). It was Christ's meriting the reward for Himself which was the ground of His meriting life and glory for us.

"Therefore let all the house of Israel know assuredly that God has made that same Jesus, whom you have crucified, both Lord and Christ" (Acts 2:36). That was the whole burden or theme of Peter's Pentecostal sermon, the grand truth proclaimed therein and enforced by Scripture: that He whom the Jews had vilified God had glorified. Having faithfully fulfilled the terms of the everlasting covenant, the Savior was elevated to dominion and empire over the world. God's exaltation of Him in His human nature to His own right hand (v. 33) was a full confirmation and demonstration of what He had acquired by His death. He made Him "both Lord and Christ," seating "Messiah the Prince" (Dan. 9:25) upon the throne of the universe. This is an economical Lordship, a dispensation committed to Him as God-man by the Father— just as He has "given Him authority to execute judgment also" (John 5:27). The One whom His enemies crowned with thorns God has "crowned with glory and honor" (Heb. 2:9). He must be received by us as "Lord" before we can have Him for our "Christ." He must have the throne of our hearts if we are to receive His benefits.

It was promised Christ that "He should have dominion from sea to sea and from river unto the ends of the earth.. . yea all kings shall fall down before Him, all nations shall serve Him. For He shall deliver the needy when he cries, the poor also, and him that has no helper" (Ps. 72:8, 11, 12). All of this in consequence of, "The Lord (the Father) said unto My Lord, Sit You at My right hand, until I make Your enemies Your footstool . . . The Lord has sworn and will not repent, You are a Priest forever, after the order of Melchizedek" (Ps. 110:1, 4); that is, a royal Priest—"He shall be a Priest upon His throne" (Zech. 6:13). A regal inheritance was assured Him. Not only has He acquired the mundane inheritance forfeited by the first Adam, but as the risen Redeemer declared, "all power is given unto Me in heaven and in earth" (Matthew 28:18), for the Father "has appointed (Him) Heir of all things," so that now He is "upholding all things by the word of His power" (Heb. 1:2,3), wielding the scepter or universal dominion. The "government" is upon "His shoulder" (Isa. 9:6).

It was promised that a blessed harvest should crown His undertaking, that He should reap the fruit of His sufferings. "The pleasure of the Lord shall prosper in His hand" (Isa. 53:10). What that signifies is intimated in such passages as the following: "I will preserve You and give You for a covenant of the people to establish the earth, to cause to inherit the desolate heritages, that You may say to the prisoners, Go forth" (Isa. 49:8,9). "Behold You shall call a nation that You know not and nations that know not You shall turn unto You, because of the Lord Your God, and the Holy One of Israel, for He has glorified You" (Isa. 55:5). The Gentiles shall come to Your light and kings to the brightness of Your rising (Isa. 60:3). To the One who came forth from Bethlehem it was promised "He shall be great unto the ends of the earth" (Micah 5:2, 4). How fully these promises have yet been fulfilled or how much longer human history must yet continue we do not profess to know, but even now "angels and authorities and powers" are "subject unto Him" (1 Pet. 3:22).

Chapter 9
Its Arrangement-Concluded

Consider now Christ's relation to the covenant. 1. He is the very substance of it. "I will give Him for a covenant of the people" (Isa. 49:8): as He is our "propitiation" (1 John 2:1) and "peace" (Eph. 2:14) so He is our covenant. 2. He is the Witness of the covenant (Isa. 55:3,4) for He saw, heard and testified it all, and therefore is He termed "the faithful and true Witness" (Rev. 3:14). 3. He is "the Prince of the covenant" (Dan. 11:22), called "Messiah The Prince" (Dan. 9:25), because He is given the royal right to administer it. 4. He is "the Messenger of the Covenant" (Dan. 9:25), because He is given the royal right to administer it. 4. He is "the Messenger of the covenant" (Mal. 3:1), acting as God's "Apostle" to us (Heb. 3:1) and our Representative before God. 5. He is the "Surety of the covenant" —"testament" is the same Greek word (Heb. 7:26)—because He engaged Himself to discharge the obligations of His people, its coventees. 6. He is "the Mediator of the covenant" (Heb. 8:6) because He stands between and serves both parties—God and His people. 7. He is the Testator of the covenant (Heb. 9:16, 17) because He has sealed it with His blood.

Consider its various and descriptive designations. 1. It is an "everlasting covenant" (Heb. 13:20) because it was entered into before all worlds and because its blessings shall be administered and enjoyed in perpetuity. 2. It is a "covenant of salt" (Num. 18:19; 2 Chron. 13:5) because it is incorruptible, inviolable, perpetual; because its provisions season us and makes all our services savory to God. 3. It is a "covenant of peace" (Isa. 54:10) for therein Christ engaged to pacify the Divine Judge, remove the enmity of His people, and effect a mutual reconciliation. 4. It is a "new covenant" (Jer. 31:31) for it secures for His people a new standing before God, makes them new creatures in Christ and puts a new song m their mouths. 5. It is a "covenant of life" (Mal. 2:5) for by its terms life is promised, restored and given more abundantly 6. It is a "holy covenant" (Luke 1:72) manifesting the ineffable purity of God in all its arrangements. 7. It is a covenant "of promise" (Eph. 2:12) both to Christ and His seed.

In view of what has just been pointed out well may we adopt the language of O. Winslow and say, "This covenant must be rich in its provisions of mercy, seeing it is made by Jehovah Himself, the Fountain of all holiness, goodness, mercy and truth whose very essence is 'Love.' It must be glorious, because the second Person in the blessed Trinity became its Surety. It must be stable, because it is eternal. It must meet all the circumstances of a necessitous Church, because it is 'ordered in all things.' ' It must be sure, seeing its administration is in the hands of an infinitely glorious Mediator, who died to secure it, rose again to confirm it, and ever lives to dispense its blessings as the circumstances of the saints require." To which might be added, it must be inviolable, since the eternal God is its Author, and the precious blood of Christ has sealed it. And therefore it should be "all my salvation and all my desire" (2 Sam. 23:5), for what more could I ask or wish!

Returning now to the covenant promises which the Father made unto the Mediator. In addition to those considered in our last, Christ was assured of a "seed." "When You shall make His soul an offering for sin, He shall see His seed" (Isa. 53:10). In the previous verses we are shown what was required from Christ in the discharge of His covenant engagements; here we have revealed the reward which the Father bestowed upon Him because of His fidelity. In the last three verses of this wonderful chapter we also behold the prophet replying to the Jews, who regarded the cross as a "stumblingblock," being scandalized at the idea of their Messiah suffering such an ignominious death. But it is here pointed out that Christ's crucifixion is not to be accounted an infamy to Him because it was the very means, ordained by God, whereby He propagated unto Himself a spiritual seed. He had Himself pointed out, "except a corn of wheat fall into the ground and die, it abides alone; but if it die, it brings forth much fruit" (John 12:24).

Observe well that in Isaiah 53:10 it was promised Him "He shall see His seed" which, coming immediately after "when You shall make His soul an offering for sin," clearly implied His resurrection; accordingly this is more explicitly stated in what at once follows: "He shall prolong His days." The figure is used again in the next verse. "He shall see of the travail of His soul and be satisfied." "A woman when she is in travail has sorrow because her hour is come. But as soon as she is delivered of the child, she remembers no more her travail, for joy that a man is born into the world" (John 16:21), considering her sufferings to be more than recompensed by the happy issue of them. So the Redeemer deems Himself richly rewarded for all His pains by the children which are His as the result of His dying travail. He is "satisfied" and "rejoices" (Luke 15:7) as each one of them is brought forth.

"This seed" which was promised Christ occupies a prominent place in the great Covenant Psalm—the 89th. There we hear the Father saying, "I have made a covenant with My Chosen, I have sworn unto David My Servant, Your seed will I establish forever" (vv. 3, 4). And again, "I will make Him My Firstborn, higher than the kings of the earth. My mercy will I keep for Him for evermore and My covenant shall stand fast with Him. His seed will I make to endure forever" (vv. 27-29). In the verses that follow His "seed" are termed "His children," and assurance is given that though they be wayward and the rod be visited upon their transgressions, yet God's covenant faithfulness shall be seen in their preservation (vv. 31-36). In the Cross Psalm it was declared "A seed shall serve Him, it shall be accounted to the Lord for a generation" (22:30). It was to be a perpetual seed. "His name shall be continued as long as the sun" (Ps. 72:17).

Christ then was assured by the Father from the beginning of the success of His undertaking and promised a seed which should bear His image, serve Him, and show forth His praises. "I will bring Your seed from the east and gather You from the west. I will say to the north to give up, and to the south keep not back; bring My sons from far and My daughters from the ends of the earth" (Isa. 43:5,6). Though they are born into this world in a state of unregeneracy, God promised they should be born again and savingly drawn to embrace Christ as their Lord and Savior. "Your people (said the Father to the Mediator—see v. 1) shall be willing in the day of Your power, in the beauties of holiness from the womb of the morning You have the dew of Your youth" (Ps. 110:3). Yet again, Christ is represented as saying "Behold I and the children whom the Lord has given Me" (quoted by the apostle of Christ in Heb. 2:13) are for signs and for wonders in Israel, for the Lord of hosts which dwells in mount Zion (Isa. 8:18). As there are two parts of the covenant so the elect were given to Christ in a twofold manner. As He was to fulfill the terms of the covenant they were entrusted to Him as a charge, but in fulfillment of it the Father promised to Christ to bestow them upon Him as a reward. The elect are to be regarded, first, as those who were beloved of the Father before time began. They are designated "God's own elect" (Greek of Luke 18:9), which signifies both His delight with and singular propriety in them. He chose them before all others: He preferred them above all others, and set His heart upon them. As such the Father gave them to Christ as God-man Mediator—"set up" in the Divine councils and therefore having a real subsistence—as a choice expression of His love for Him. Second, they are to be regarded as God fore-viewed them under their defection in Adam, and as such God gave them as a charge to Christ to be raised up from all the ruins of the fall, and also as a reward for His work on their behalf. The twofoldness of Truth needs ever to be borne in mind.

Viewed as fallen the elect were given to Christ as a charge for whose salvation He was held responsible. They were committed to Him as "prisoners" (Isa. 49:9), whose lawful discharge He must obtain. They were committed to Him as desperate patients, whom He must bind up and heal (Isa. 61:1). They were committed to Him as straying and lost sheep (Isa. 53:6), whom He must seek out and bring into the fold (John 10:16). God placed His elect in the hands of the Mediator and made them His care. How graciously and tenderly He discharged His trust appears in that touching word "He shall feed His flock like a Shepherd, He shall gather the lambs with His arm and carry them in His bosom, and shall gently lead those that are with young" (Isa. 40:10,11). It appears again in that wonderful word "And when He has found it, He lays it on His shoulders rejoicing" (Luke 15:5). Finally, it was evidenced at the moment of His arrest. "If therefore you seek Me, let those go their way, that the saying might be fulfilled which He spoke, Of them which You gave Me have I lost none" (John 18:8, 9).

On the fulfillment of His covenant engagement that people were given to Christ as His reward, as the fruit of His travail, as the trophies of His glorious victory over sin, Satan and death, as His crown of rejoicing in the day when all the inhabitants of the universe shall be assembled together, as His beloved and glorious Bride when the marriage of the Lamb is come. In contemplation of this God made certain promises to the Surety concerning them. He promised to bestow upon them the gift of eternal life. "Paul a servant of God and an apostle of Jesus Christ, according to the faith of God's elect and the acknowledging of the Truth which is after godliness, in hope of eternal life which God, that cannot lie, promised before the world began" (Titus 1:1 ,2). As the elect then had no actual existence, that promise must have been made in their name to the Surety. That particular promise virtually included all the benefits which Christ procured for His people, for as "eternal death" contains the essence of all evils, so "eternal life" contains the essence of all blessings.

"The Lord commanded the blessing, even life for evermore" (Ps. 133:3). "This is the promise that He has promised us, even eternal life" (1 John 2:25)—how perfect is the harmony between the Two Testaments! If we break up that promise into its component parts we may say that, first, God promised to regenerate His people or bestow upon them a spiritual nature which delights in His Law: "I will put My laws into their minds, and write them upon their hearts" (Heb. 8:10). Second, He promised to justify them, the negative part of which is to remit their transgressions. "For I will be merciful to their righteousness and their sins and iniquities will I remember no more" (Heb. 8:12). Third, He promised to sanctify them. "I will sprinkle clean water upon you and you shall be clean. From all your filthiness and from all your idols will I cleanse you" (Ezek. 36:25). Fourth, He promised to preserve them. "I will not turn away from them to do them good, but I will put My fear in their hearts that they shall not depart from Me" (Jer. 32:40). Fifth, He promised to glorify them. "They shall obtain joy and gladness and sorrow and sighing shall flee away" (Isa. 35:10).

Finally, God made promise of the Holy Spirit to Christ. What we are now to contemplate is admittedly one of the deep things of God and therefore requires to be handled with prayerful concern and godly caution. But if on the one hand we are certain to err should we deviate one iota from the Scriptures, on the other hand it is to the glory of God and His Christ and to the needful instruction of our souls that faith humbly receives all that is revealed to us in Holy Writ. Now Scripture teaches not only that the Spirit of the Lord rested upon Christ (Isa. 11:1, 2) during the days of His earthly ministry, that God put His Spirit upon Him to furnish Him for His great work (Isa. 42:10), that He was anointed with the Spirit in order to preach the Gospel (Isa. 61:1) and work miracles (Acts 10:38; Matthew 12:28), but the oracles of Truth make it very clear after Christ received the Spirit in another manner and for a different purpose after His ascension to heaven, namely, that to the God-man Mediator has been given the administration of the Spirit's activities and operations; and this both in the sphere of grace Churchward, and in the sphere of providence worldward.

In John 7:39 we read that "the Holy Spirit was not yet (given) because Jesus was not yet glorified," but He was both promised to Christ (Ps. 45:7) and by Christ. Let us seek to attentively consider some of His statements concerning the Holy Spirit's relation upon Himself. "But the Comforter, the Holy Spirit, whom the Father will send in My name" (John 14:26), the force of which is intimated in "whatsoever you shall ask the Father in My name He will give it you" (John 16:23). Again, "But when the Comforter is come, whom I will send unto you from the Father" (John 15:26) — which is parallel with Christ's being "sent" by Him (John 3:17). And again, "It is expedient for you that I go away, for if I go not away the Comforter will not come unto you; but if I depart, I will send Him unto you" (John 16:7). Such repetition argues both the importance of this truth and our slowness to receive it.

To the writer three things are clear concerning the above passages. First, each was spoken by the God-man Mediator, for they were the utterances of the Word made flesh. Second, from John 8:39 and 16:7 it is apparent that the advent of the Spirit was dependent upon the ascension of Christ, Third, from His repeated "whom I will send unto you" we learn that in this present era the activities of the Spirit are regulated by the will of the Lord Christ. That the Spirit is at the economical disposal of the Redeemer was evidenced after His resurrection and before His ascension, for to the apostles He said, "Peace be unto you. As My Father has sent Me, even so send I you," and then we are told "when He had said this He breathed on them and said unto them, Receive the Holy Spirit" (John 20:22; Gen. 2:7). And as He was on the point of leaving them the Savior said "Behold, I send the promise of My Father upon you" (Luke 24:49), which was duly accomplished ten days later.

In Acts 2, when Peter explained the supernatural phenomena of the day of Pentecost he said, "This Jesus has God raised up, of which we all are witnesses. Therefore being by the right hand of God exalted, and having received of the Father the promise of the Holy Spirit, He has shed forth this which you now see and hear" (vv. 32,33)—the glorified Savior has poured forth this effusion of the Spirit's gifts. On which the Puritan Thos. Goodwin, after quoting Psalm 45:7 and explaining it by Acts 2:36 and said on verse 33 "which receiving is not to be only understood of His bare and single receiving the promise of the Holy Spirit for us, by having power given Him to shed Him down upon them, as God has promised, though this is a true meaning of it; but further, that He had received Him first as poured forth on Himself, and so shed Him forth on them, according to that rule that whatever God does unto us by Christ, He first does it unto Christ" (Vol. 4, pg. 121). It was the Savior's outpouring of the Spirit's gifts which demonstrated He had been "made both Lord and Christ" (v. 36).

From the passages quoted above it seems plain that upon the completion of His covenant work the Father bestowed the Spirit on Christ to administer from His mediatorial throne. In full. accord with that we hear the Lord Jesus saying from heaven, "These things says He that has the seven Spirits of God" (Rev. 3:1), that is, has to administer the Holy Spirit in the plenitude of His power and the diversity of His manifestations—compare the seven-branched candlestick in Exodus 25:30, 31 and the sevenfold gift of the Holy Spirit to Christ in the days of His flesh (Isa. 11:1, 2). On the words "He that has the seven Spirits of God" (Rev. 3:1) Thos. Scott says, "that is, the Divine Savior, through whom the Holy Spirit, in the variety and abundance of His precious gifts and graces was communicated to all the churches." So again, in Revelation 5:6 we read "I beheld and in the midst . . . stood a Lamb as it had been slain, having seven horns and seven eyes, which are the seven Spirits of God sent forth into all the earth" (Compare Matthew 28:18). Here it is Christ exercising His governmental power and administering the Spirit toward the world—as in 3:1 it was toward the Church. Thus, if on the one hand none other ever suffered such ignominy as did the Mediator, on the other hand none other ever has received or ever will such marks of honor as He has.

Chapter 10
Its Effectuation

To refresh your memories we will here epitomize what has been presented in previous chapters. First, we pointed out the distinctions which require to be recognized if confusion is to be avoided. (1) That in connection with reconciliation God acts both as a loving Father and as an inflexible Judge. (2) That His elect are viewed both in the purpose of His grace and under the condemnation of His Law. (3) That they are viewed by Him both in Christ as their covenant-Head and as the depraved descendants of fallen Adam: in the one case as "His dear children," and in the other as being "by nature the children of wrath" (4) That though there is no change in God yet there is in His attitude unto and His dealings with them. (5) That God's purpose concerning His elect in eternity and the actual accomplishment of that purpose in a time-state must not be confused. Failure to observe these distinctions has caused many to err in their preaching and writing on this important subject.

Next, we demonstrated the need for reconciliation. Therein we dwelt upon the fearful breach which the entrance of sin made between God and man, the creature casting off all allegiance to his Maker, revolting from his rightful Lord, despising His authority, trampling under foot His commandments. We showed that while the original offence was committed by Adam, yet he was acting as the federal bead of his race, and therefore that the guilt and consequences of his transgression are justly imputed to all his descendants. Moreover, they take sides with him by perpetuating his evil course. The life of the unregenerate is one unbroken course of rebellion against God. The consequences of that breach are that fallen man is separated from God, he is an object of abhorrence to God, he is under the wrath of God, he is in bondage to Satan and so under the reigning power of sin that he hates God. Obviously such an one is in urgent need of being restored to His favor and having his vile enmity removed.

Then, we saw that the Author of reconciliation is God, and more particularly, God the Father. In the development of which we pointed out that the recovery of His fallen elect proceeds from the good pleasure of His will or "the eternal purpose which He purposed in Himself" That gracious design was suggested by none other, and no external motive influenced Him. No necessity was put upon Him to form such a resolution: it was simply His own sovereign design—"I will show mercy" Yet it was His own nature which prompted His decision: it originated in the everlasting love which God bore to His elect—a love so great that even their awful sins could not quench nor produce any change in it. Nevertheless, since the Divine holiness was infinitely antagonized by sin, Divine justice required that full satisfaction should be made for the dishonor it had wrought. Naught but Divine wisdom could find a way in which Love and Law were perfectly harmonized and solve the problem of how mercy and justice might alike maintain its ground without the slightest compromise, yea, issue from the conflict honorable and glorious.

Under the last division of our subject we turned our attention to the Divine arrangement for the accomplishment of reconciliation, namely, "The Everlasting Covenant," in which is displayed the Divine perfections in their blessed unity. In that covenant God gave His elect to Christ as a trust or charge, holding Him responsible for their everlasting felicity. In that covenant all the details of the wondrous plan of redemption were drawn up and settled. In that covenant the Father made known unto the Son the terms which He must fulfill and the task He must perform in order to the saving of "that which was lost;" while the Son voluntarily concurred therein and gladly consented to carry out its stipulations. In that covenant we have revealed the office which Christ was to assume and the nature of the work He was to do, namely, to serve as the Substitute and Surety of His people in the full discharge of all their obligations unto the Divine Law. In that covenant the Father gave assurance of rendering adequate assistance to the Mediator in the performing of His engagement and the guarantee of the glorious reward upon the successful completion thereof.

We are now to see how the eternal purpose of God was effected, how the mutual engagements of the everlasting covenant were fulfilled. "When the fullness of time was come, God sent forth His Son, made of a woman, made under the Law, to redeem them that were under the Law, that we might receive the adoption (or "status") of sons" (Gal. 4:4,5). The "fullness of time" means more than that the ordained hour had arrived: it signifies when all the preliminary operations of Divine providence had been completed, when the stage was thoroughly prepared for this unparalleled event, when the world's need had been fully demonstrated. The advent of God's Son to this earth was no isolated event, but the climax of a lengthy preparation. That He was now "made of a woman" was the fulfillment of the Divine announcement in Gen. 3:14 and Isa. 7:14. That He was "made under the Law" which His people had broken is what supplies the key to that which is otherwise an inexplicable mystery, in fact, throws a flood of light upon the experiences through which He passed from Bethlehem to Calvary.

The very circumstances of Christ's birth at once made unmistakably manifest that God had sent forth none other than His own Son and clearly intimated the unique mission upon which the Beloved of the Father had then entered. Nothing less than a supernatural birth befitted so august a Person, and such was accomplished by the miraculous conception of His virgin mother, by means of which a "holy" humanity became His (Luke 1:35)—a real human spirit, and soul and body, yet without the slightest taint of our corruption. The amazing event of the Incarnation and the Divine dignity of the One who had become flesh was signalized by the appearing again of "the Shekinah" (which had left Israel in the days of Ezekiel—10:4,18; 11:23), for "the glory of the Lord (namely, the Shekinah) shone round about" the shepherds on Bethlehem's plains, so that they were "sore afraid;" and an angel announced to them that the One just born was none other than "Christ the Lord;" while suddenly there was with the angel a multitude of the "heavenly host" praising God and saying "glory to God in the highest, and on earth, peace, good will toward men" (Luke 2:9.14).

But, if what we have just alluded to were clear proofs that God had indeed "sent forth His Son, made of a woman," there were other attendant circumstances which no less plainly intimated (to an anointed eye) that His Son was also "made under the Law," and that, as the Surety of His people, as the One who had entered their Law-place, He must receive what is due them. This has not been sufficiently recognized. In that same second of Luke we read that Mary "brought forth her firstborn son, and wrapped Him in swaddling clothes and laid Him in a manger, because there was no room for them in the inn" (v. 7). The force of that is better perceived if it be linked with "so He drove out the man" (Gen. 3:24) from Eden, for he had become an outcast from his Maker. Do we not behold then in His exclusion from the inn and birth in a cattle shed a definite shadowing forth of the fact that Christ had vicariously entered the place of His outcast people! In the circumcising of Him on the eight day (v. 21) there was an evident prefigurement that He had been made "in the likeness of sinful flesh" (Rom. 8:3). That was unspeakably solemn, but amazingly wonderful.

A little later it was made evident that the One cradled in the manger was more than human.

The wise men saw "His star in the east" and came to Jerusalem inquiring "Where is He that is born King of the Jews?" That extraordinary star "went before them until it came and stood over where the young Child was." Entering the house where He abode, they "fell down and worshipped Him" (Matthew 2:11), presenting gifts of gold, frankincense, and myrrh — thus were Divine honors paid Him. Yet immediately after a determined effort was made by Herod to slay Him, as though to show us from the beginning that His life was forfeit and that a death by violence awaited Him! But His hour had not then arrived and Joseph was warned to flee with Him. His sojourn in Egypt was not without significance, for it intimated that as the Surety of His people He had taken His place alongside of them in the typical house of bondage. With what awe and astonishment should we contemplate these things!

What we sought to point out unmistakably opens up to us the deeper meaning of much that is recorded in the Gospels, supplying the key to the strange mingling of the lights and shadows in the earthly career of our Lord. That key lies in the distinction which must ever be drawn between the adorable Person and the awful place which He took, between the Son of God incarnate and the office He was discharging. Though His essential glory was veiled by flesh, yet that glory frequently broke forth in splendor. Or to put it in another way: God had suffered His Beloved to "make Himself of no reputation" in this world, yet He was so jealous of His honor that again and again He afforded proof that the despised One was Immanuel. Thus if Christ—to the amazement of His forerunner—submitted to the ordinance of baptism, yet at that very time the heavens were "opened unto Him," and the Spirit descended like as a dove upon Him and the voice of the Father was heard saying "This is My beloved Son in whom Jam well pleased."

Yes, the key to the deeper meaning of much in the Gospels is found in keeping before us the distinction between the Person and the place He took. He was the Holy One, but He took the place of His sinful people. As the Holy One ineffable joy, unclouded blessedness, the love and homage of all creatures was His legitimate due. Treading the path of obedience, the smile of God and the ordering of His providences accordingly was what He was justly entitled to. Wisdom's ways are "ways of pleasantness, and all her paths are peace," and Christ ever trod Wisdom's ways without any deviation—why then did He encounter so much unpleasantness and opposition? "When a man's ways please the Lord, He makes even his enemies to be at peace with him" (Prov. 16:7), and Christ always pleased Him (John 8:29); yet the Father was far from making His enemies at peace with Him. Why? Ignore the office which Christ had taken (and was discharging from Bethlehem onwards!) and we are left without any possible solution.

"The foxes have holes, and birds of the air have nests; but the Son of man has nowhere to lay His head" (Matthew 8:20). The real force of that pathetic statement can best be perceived by grasping the meaning of the particular title which the Savior here employed. It has its roots in the following O. T. passages: "The stars are not pure in His sight. How much less man that is a worm, and the son of man which is a worm!" (Job 25:5,6); "What is man that You are mindful of him, and the son of man that You visit him" (Ps. 8:4; and cf. 146:3), from which it will be seen that it is a term of abasement and ignominy, expressive of lowly condition. In its application to Christ it connotes not only His true humanity, but also the humiliation and shame into which He descended. It is descriptive of His person, but more especially of His office; in other words, it points to Him as "the Second Man," the "last Adam," and as such, entering our lot, sharing our misery, serving as our Surety. Christ appropriated this title unto Himself as marking His condescending grace and as displaying the condition which He had taken to Himself.

A certain scribe had offered to follow Jesus wherever He went, and "the Son of man has nowhere to lay His head" was His response. It was not only a word bidding him count the cost, but an announcement that His path led to the place where none could accompany Him. It was more than a declaration that He who was rich for our sakes became poor in order to reinstate us: it was an intimation that He had voluntarily subjected Himself to the consequences of sin, that He would therefore be treated as a sinner both by God and by men, that He had entered the place of His disinherited people (driven out: Gen. 3:24) and therefore that He had no claim to ought in this world. "The Son of man came not to be ministered unto, but to minister, and to give His life a ransom for many" (Matthew 20:28). Thus it is clear that this "Son of man" title contemplates Christ as the humbled One. Confirmatory of this it is the fact that He is never referred to by it after His resurrection, though as "the Son of man" He appropriately receives His reward (Dan. 7:13; Matthew 26:64; John 5:27).

Justice demands that each one shall receive his due. Now the Lord Jesus was "holy, harmless, undefiled, separate from sinners:" then to what was He lawfully entitled at the hands of a righteous God? Does not the Judge of all the earth do right! then how shall He order His governmental dealings toward the One who eminently honored and glorified Him? Must He not show Himself strong on His behalf? Must He not shower upon Him the ceaseless tokens of His favor? Must He not turn the hearts of all men unto Him in loving homage? Certainly—but for one thing! Though personally holy, yet officially the guilt of His people rested upon Him. In view of Psalm 37:25 how can we possibly account for the righteous One Himself being forsaken by God in the hour of His acutest extremity? Only one answer is possible, and that is furnished by what we have sought to set before the reader.

> "Bearing the shame and scoffing rude
> In my place condemned He stood."

Blessed be God if the reader can, by sovereign grace, respond with us

> "Sealed my pardon with His blood,
> Hallelujah, what a Savior!"

If we shut our eyes to the solemn fact that the Son of God entered this world charged with the guilt of His people, then are we confronted with the supreme anomaly, the most flagrant injustice of all history. For on the one hand, we have the Personification of all virtue and moral excellency; and on the other, God suffering Him to be traduced as One possessed of a "demon" (John 10:20). On the one hand we have the supreme Benefactor of mankind ever going about and doing good, and yet God so ordering His lot that He "had nowhere to lay His head." On the one hand we have Him preaching glad tidings to the poor and binding up the broken hearted, and on the other hand God allowing Him to be so dealt with by those whom He befriended that He cried "reproach has broken My heart" (Ps. 69:20). On the one hand we have Him manifested as Love incarnate, yet on the other, God permitting His enemies to vent their bitterest hatred upon Him. In the case of all others we discern the principle of sowing and reaping, of the connection between conduct and the consequences which it righteously entails; but in the case of our Lord there was not, so far as He personally acted and was treated. Yet bring into account the relation which He sustained to His guilty people and the anomaly and seeming injustice vanishes.

Perhaps some readers are inclined to say: I can see why it was necessary for Christ as our Substitute to endure the wrath of God, but I am rather at a loss to understand why He should have to suffer such cruel treatment at the hands of men; true, their vile conduct against the Lord of glory demonstrated as nothing else has the fearful depravity of human nature, but why did the Father, under His righteous government of the world, permit His Son to be so unjustly dealt with by Jews and Gentiles alike? Though it was ordained that He should be crucified and slain by wicked hands (Acts 2:23), yet wherein lay the necessity for Him to be so mistreated by His own creatures? and that not only during "the Passion week" but throughout the whole course of His ministry? In the light of what we have sought to point out, there should surely be no difficulty at this point: it is only a matter of giving a wider application to that basic and illuminating principle.

As the Surety of His people Christ entered this world charged with all their guilt, and therefore He had to suffer not only for their sins against God but also against their fellows. We have broken both tables of the Law, and therefore the Redeemer must endure the penalty of both. See then in the treatment meted out to Him by men, what we deserve because of our woeful failure to love our neighbor as ourselves. As our Substitute a life of reproach among men was His due. Therefore "He came unto His own and His own received Him not," but instead, despised and rejected Him. Therefore was He, throughout His course, "a Man of sorrows and acquainted with grief" subjected to contempt, constantly persecuted by His enemies. The very next verse in Isaiah 53 explains why He was the Man of sorrows: "surely He has borne our griefs and carried our sorrows." Therefore was the sin-Bearer deserted by all His apostles (Matthew 26:56) as well as forsaken by God.

It is indeed in the closing scenes of "the days of His flesh" that we may perceive most clearly Christ occupying the place of His people and receiving both from man and God that which was due unto us. As we view Him before Caiaphas and Herod we must not be occupied only with the human side of things, but look higher and see Divine justice directing all. The Romans were renowned for their respect of law, their equity of dealings, and their mild treatment of those they conquered. Then how shall we account for the conduct of Pilate and his soldiers? and especially, why did God require His Son to be mocked with a trial that appears worse than a farce. Because though personally innocent, He was officially guilty.

Chapter 11
Its Effectuation-Continued

That which is here to engage our attention is the work performed by the Mediator in order to heal the breach between a righteous God and His sinful people and thus effect a mutual reconciliation. This will bring before us the most wonderful, awe-inspiring and glorious events in all the ways and works of God. It will conduct us to ground which is ineffably holy, and on which it becomes to tread with the utmost reverence and circumspection. The work of Christ is absolutely unique, being without precedent or parallel. Nothing whatever can be known about it save that which is revealed on it in Holy Writ. Neither philosophy, science, nor metaphysics can afford us the slightest assistance in the understanding of it. Carnal reasoning concerning it is utterly worthless and highly presumptuous. The great mystery of godliness is made known unto faith. Yet the utmost diligence and earnest prayer for the Holy Spirit's aid are called for in our searching of the Scriptures and in carefully weighing all they make known on the Death Divine, that faith may lack no part of the foundation on which it is to rest and none of the materials on which it is to feed.

In our last we sought to present more or less a general survey of the ground we hope to cover under this particular aspect of our subject. Now we must proceed to more detail. This will require us to examine closely what the Incarnate Son did in order to "make peace" between an offended God and His law-breaking people, which was the relation. Christ bore to them, the character in which He acted in that stupendous undertaking, and what was the office He discharged. It is all important at the outset to recognize that the Person we are to be occupied with was none other than Jehovah's "Fellow" (Zech. 13:7), co-essential and co-equal with the Father and the Spirit. Though God the Son took upon Him human nature and became the Son of man, yet in so doing He did not cease to be a Divine Person. It was the theanthropic (Divine-human) constitution of His person which qualified Him for His mediation, for as the God-man nothing could be too difficult for Him to effect or too great for Him to accomplish. The dignity of His person gave infinite value to His work.

The wrong done by sin unto God was so incalculably enormous and His hatred of the same is so great that only a perfect and infinitely meritorious satisfaction could appease Him, and obviously such a satisfaction could be rendered by none but a person of infinite dignity and worth. Our sins are committed against the infinite Majesty of Heaven and therefore are they infinitely culpable, and unless an atonement of infinite value is made for us, our sins must entail infinite suffering—therefore the punishment of the wicked is necessarily eternal. Sin, so far as it could do so, struck at the very throne of God. It was an act of high treason, a disowning of His authority, an attempt on the part of the creature to overthrow the Divine government. Sin has made such a breach in the order of things appointed by God that no mere creature could possibly repair it—least of all man, for he is the culprit, guilty and defiled. If then .the breach is to be healed, God must "lay help upon One that is mighty" (Ps. 89:19).

Writing on "The heinousness of human guilt" Jas. Hervey said, "Ten thousand volumes, written on purpose to display the aggravations of my various acts of disobedience, could not so effectually convince me of their inconceivable enormity as the consideration of that all-glorious Person, who, to make an atonement for them, spilt the last drop of His blood. I have sinned, may every child of Adam say; and what shall I do unto you, O You Observer of men? Shall I give my firstborn for my transgression, the fruit of my body for the sin of my soul? Vain commutation, and such as would be rejected by the blessed God with the utmost abhorrence. Will all the potentates, that sway the scepter in a thousand kingdoms, devote their royal and honored lives to rescue an obnoxious creature, from the stroke of vengeance? Alas, it must cost more, incomparably more, to expiate the malignity of sin and save a guilty wrath from Hell. Will all the principalities of Heaven be content to assume my nature and resign themselves to death for my pardon? Even this would be too mean a satisfaction for inexorable Justice, too scanty a reparation of God's injured honor.

"So flagrant is human guilt that nothing but a victim of infinite dignity could constitute an adequate propitiation. He who said 'Let there be light, and there was light,' let there be a firmament, and immediately the blue curtains floated in the sky; He must take flesh, He must feel the fierce torments of crucifixion and pour out His soul in agonies, if ever such transgressors are pardoned." There could be no satisfaction for the sinner without atonement, for God has declared He "will by no means clear the guilty" (Ex. 34:7). Equally evident is it that no atonement can be made by the violator of God's Law, for he can neither provide reparation for past offences—being a moral bankrupt, devoid of any merit; nor render perfect obedience in the present—being a depraved creature. God's Law requires righteousness of character before it will receive righteousness of conduct, and therefore a fallen creature is utterly disqualified to render acceptable obedience. The Law will not compound with our sinfulness by modifying its holy requirements. "Pay that which you owe" is its unchanging demand.

After what has been pointed out it should be quite clear that first, in order to save His people from their sins the incarnate Son of God must serve as their Substitute, acting in their stead and rendering satisfaction to the Law for them. By substitution is meant the transference of obligation from those who incurred it to One who willingly shouldered the same in their stead. The substitutionary death of Christ means far more than that He died for the benefit of all who savingly believe in Him. It signifies that He entered their Law-place and received what was due them and that through His sacrificial death He so expiated their sins that nothing can be laid to their .charge, that they stand "unblameable and unreproveable" in God's sight (Col. 1:22). "He was wounded for our transgressions, He was bruised for our iniquities; the chastisement of our peace was upon Him, and with His stripes we are healed" (Isa. 53:4). "For Christ also has suffered for sins, the Just for the unjust, that He might bring us to God" (1 Pet. 3:18).

Though there is no parallel to the greatest transaction in all history, though there is no analogy to the relations sustained to God and to His people in any of the relations of mere creatures to one another, yet God has graciously adapted a series of types, historical and ceremonial, to the illustration of His grand plan of redemption and to adumbrate various aspects of the office and work of Christ, and in them the wisdom of God is signally displayed. Of the first person to whom the Holy Spirit ascribes faith it is recorded that, "Abel offered unto God a more excellent sacrifice than Cain. by which he obtained witness that he was righteous" (Heb. 11:4). Cain brought of the fruit of the ground (the product of his own toil) an offering unto the Lord, but unto it He "had not respect. "But Abel brought "of the firstborn of his flock and the fat of it"—showing it had been slain. Realizing that death was his due, but that God graciously accepted a substitute in his place, he put a bleeding lamb between his sinful self and the Holy God.

The same elementary yet fundamental truth was taught the Hebrews on that most memorable night in their history. Jehovah had declared, "about midnight will I go out into the midst of Egypt, and all the firstborn in the land of Egypt shall die" (Ex. 11:4, 5). Sufficient attention had not been paid to the words "all, in." There were to be no exceptions: the firstborn sons of Israel equally with the Egyptians were to be slain. But though no exception was made, a difference was drawn: a substitute was provided for the former, though not for the latter. The Israelites were bidden to take a male lamb, without blemish, to slay it, and sprinkle its blood on the posts of their doors, and the Lord promised, "when I see the blood, I will pass over you" (Ex. 12). The angel of death entered not their houses, for judgment had already been executed there, the Lamb being slain as the substitute. In the light of that we are to understand "Christ our Passover is sacrificed for us." (1 Cor. 5:7).

But it was in the wilderness, after the Levitical priesthood was appointed and the tabernacle had been erected, that the Lord taught His people more fully the grand truth of pardon and cleansing, acceptance and blessing, through a substitute. A wide field of study is here opened to us, but we can only now briefly mention its outstanding lessons. First, in the unblemished animal required for sacrifice, God showed His people the perfections of the substitute in the room of their imperfections. Second, in their being required to bring such an offering, the claims of God were enforced. Third, in the words "he shall put his hand upon the head of the burnt offering, and it shall be accepted for him to make atonement for him" (Lev. 1:4) there was an identifying of the offerer with his offering. Fourth, on the great day of atonement, Aaron was required to "lay both his hands upon the head of the live goat, and confess over him all the iniquities of the children of Israel and all their transgressions in all their sins, putting them upon the head of the goat" (Lev. 16:21), thereby a transfer of guilt being signified.

Fifth, an Israelite was not only required to furnish the offering, but "he will kill the bull before the Lord" (Lev. 1:5) was the order: in this way he acknowledged that death was his own due and proof was furnished of God's displeasure against sin. Sixth, "and there came fire out from before the Lord and consumed upon the altar the burnt offering and the fat: which when all the people saw, they shouted, and fell on their faces" (Lev. 9:24 and compare 1 Kings 18:38; 2 Chron. 7:1). In that fire we see the holy wrath of the Judge consuming the victim in the sinner's room. Seventh, "And a man that is clean will gather up the ashes of the heifer, and lay them up without the camp in a clean place, and it will be kept for the congregation of the children of Israel for a water of separation. It is a purification for sin" (Num. 19:9). "In the ashes we have the proof that the wrath had spent itself, that the penalty was paid, that the work was done. 'It is finished' was the voice of the ashes" (H. Bonar). Thus was God's mercy expressed in a righteous way.

The main thing to grasp m connection with the sacrifices to which we have all too briefly alluded is, that they were not eucharistic but expiatory - not tokens of thanksgiving, but vicarious oblations. The animal or bird was put in the place of the one who brought it and is termed an "offering unto the Lord for his sin" and it would "make an atonement for him concerning his sin" (Lev. 5:6). It was then, a substitutionary sacrifice, slain in the stead of the offerer, to signify what he deserved and by which he was personally saved from undergoing the penalty. It was literally and specifically a life for a life, a life devoted to God in sacrifice. "For the life of the flesh is in the blood, and I have given it to you upon the altar to make an atonement (a propitiation or appeasement) for your souls. It is the blood that makes an atonement for the soul" (Lev. 17:11). Therefore did God enjoin upon His people "No soul of you will eat blood" (v. 5), it was to be held sacred by them.

Should it be asked, Why did God appoint the slaying of animals, the bringing of so many costly offerings to His altar, which were so frequently repeated? The answer is simple and conclusive, though it may be stated in a variety of ways. It was to signify that, in the purpose of God, the antitypical Lamb was slain from the foundation of the world. It was to inform His people that they must look outside themselves for salvation. It was thus to keep before them a continual reminder of His righteousness and what sin called for at His hands. It was to educate men for "the good things to come" by shadowing forth the great sacrifice. It was to furnish the N. T. saints with an infallible dictionary, for if we would understand the language which Christ and His apostles used in connection with the Sacrifice of Calvary we must needs define the terms employed of the grand Antitype by the meaning they obviously bear in the types—as 1 Corinthians 5-7 is to be interpreted in the light of Exodus 12.

It is the light of the Levitical offerings we should read "the Gospel of Isaiah 53" and regard the N. T. references to the atoning sacrifice of our Savior. Who can fail to see that the words "The Lord has laid on Him the iniquities of us all" (Isa. 53:6) look back to "Aaron shall lay both his hands on the head of the live goat and confess over him all the iniquities of the children of Israel. ..and the goat shall bear upon him all their iniquities unto a land not inhabited" (Lev. 16:21,22), and that "who His own self bear our sins in His own body on the tree" (1 Pet. 2:24) is an echo of the same language. When we read that "Christ died for our sins according to the Scriptures" (1 Cor. 15:3) are we not to regard the reference as being both' the types and the prophecies of the O. T. When we are told that "while we were yet sinners, Christ died for us" (Rom. 5:8) can it signify anything else than, that as a sacrificial offering was slain in the stead of the offerer, so Christ endured the penalty which our sins call for!

It needs to be insisted upon that the death of Christ was something more than an unparalleled act of benevolence, enduring crucifixion for the good of others. It was a penal death, in which He vicariously endured the penalty of the Law in the stead of others. The suffering of martyrs for the good of their cause, of patriots for their country, of philanthropists for mankind, are not "vicarious" for they are not substitutionary. Vicarious suffering is suffering endured in the place of others. Christ's sufferings were vicarious in precisely the same way that the death of animals in the O. T. sacrifices was in lieu of the death of the transgressors offering them. While in many passages of the N. T. the Holy Spirit has used the Greek "huper" which is rendered "for" yet in Mark 10:45 He has employed the decisive "anti." He gave his life a ransom for (anti—in the stead of), many. In Matthew 2:22 "anti" is rightly rendered "in the room of." Compare Matthew 5:38, Luke 11:11, Romans 12:17 where anti is rendered "For."

But does not the substitutionary sufferings of Christ raise a difficulty even in the minds of the reverent. Let us face it squarely and state it frankly. Was it altogether just that an innocent person should suffer in the stead of the guilty? At the back of many minds there lurks the suspicion that, though it was amazing grace and surpassing love which gave the Lord of glory to die for poor sinners, yet was it not, strictly speaking, a breach of equity? Was it right that One who perfectly honored God and illustriously magnified His Law by a flawless and perpetual obedience, should have to suffer its penalty and endure its awful curse? To answer, It had to be. There was no other way of saving Os, supplies no direct answer to the question. It is merely arguing on the Jesuitical basis that "the end justifies the means." Far better to remain silent in token of our ignorance than thus to sully the character of God. But such a suspicion is groundless and such ignorance causeless as we hope to yet show.

To say that sin must be punished that the penalty of the broken law could not be revoked, is but to repeat what Scripture clearly affirms. But to draw the conclusion that therefore an innocent Substitute had to be penalized in the Stead of the guilty is to impeach the Divine justice. Every regenerate person must feel that it had been infinitely better for the whole of Adam's race to have suffered eternally in Hell, rather than that God should act unrighteously in delivering His people from there. Such a thing could not be, for God "cannot deny Himself" that is act contrary to His own perfections. "The Lord is righteous in all His ways and holy in all His works" (Ps. 145:17), and most certainly the greatest and grandest of His works, that which supremely manifested and promoted His glory, is no exception to that rule. He has declared Himself to be "a just God and a Savior" (Isa. 45:21) and never was His justice more gloriously displayed than at the Cross.

Of old the question was asked, "Whoever perished being innocent?" (Job 4:7) and surely we may unhesitatingly reply, No one ever did under the righteous government of God. He who "will by no means clear the guilty" (Ex. 34:7) will by no means afflict the innocent. Startling as it must sound, it was not the innocent whom the sword of Divine justice smote at Calvary. And this brings us to say, second, in order to be our Savior Christ had to act as the Substitute of His people, and in order to be their Substitute He first assumed the office of Surety. As their Surety, as their legal Representative, Christ took upon Him their legal obligations—as the husband assumes the debts of the woman he marries. The guilt of His people's sins were charged to Christ's account, and therefore justice legally and righteously exacted payment from him. Though personally innocent, Christ was officially guilty when He suffered "the Just for the unjust." Much remains yet to be said but here we must stop.

Chapter 12
Its Effectuation-Continued

In our last we showed, first, that in order to satisfy the requirements of Divine justice the incarnate Son was "made under the Law" and that the work He did and the sufferings He endured in order to heal the break between an offended God and His offending people was performed and undergone by Him while acting as their Substitute. Then, second, in the concluding paragraphs we briefly pointed out that in order to be the Substitute of His people Christ had taken upon Him the office of Suretyship. It is of great importance that we should be quite clear upon the latter, for much harm has been done by novices who have grievously misrepresented the Atonement by their crude and carnal conceptions, and the cause of Truth has been much injured by their unwarrantable attempts to illustrate the central fact of the Gospel from supposed analogies in human relations. It cannot be insisted upon too emphatically that the plan of redemption, the office sustained by Christ, and the satisfaction which He rendered to the claims of justice against us, have no parallel in the relations of men to one another.

But how often has a popular preacher pictured a criminal, in whose character was no relieving feature, condemned to death for his aggravated crimes. While lying in the condemned cell, or perhaps as he stands upon the scaffold itself, the reigning monarch is supposed to send his or her own son and heir to die in the villain's stead, and then turn him loose on society. Such a monstrous supposition has frequently been offered as an illustration of the amazing fact that "God so loved the world that He gave His only begotten Son, that whosoever believes in Him should not perish, but have everlasting life." Not only is that imaginary illustration a gross misrepresentation of the Truth, but it is utterly revolting to serious minds and those who love righteousness. It is, too, a horrible degrading of the Gospel and a denial of the uniqueness of the Atonement. The Atonement carries us far above the sphere of the highest relations of created beings into the august counsels of the eternal and incomprehensible God, and it is nothing but a species of impiety for us to bring our petty line to measure counsels in which the "manifold wisdom" of Omniscience is contained.

Here as everywhere in connection with the things of God, spiritual things must be compared "with spiritual things" (1 Cor. 2:13) and not with carnal. One part of the Truth must be interpreted by—not drawing upon our imagination, but—by another part of the Truth. It is only in the light of the Word itself—our hearts being opened to receive the same—that we can see light. It is only as "we speak, not in the words which man's wisdom teaches but which the Holy Spirit teaches" that we can accurately express the grand mysteries of our Faith. Now the term "Surety" is one of the words the Holy Spirit has used of Christ Himself to enable us to understand the better the relation He sustained toward those on whose behalf He transacted and the special office He discharged for their sakes. Now a "surety" is one who is legally obligated to answer for another. A "surety" is one who undertakes for another or for others and who thereby makes himself responsible to render what is due from them or to suffer what is due to them.

"I have done judgment and justice. Leave me not to my oppressors. Be Surety for your servant for good. Let not the proud oppress me." (Psa. 119:121, 122) In like manner we find the godly Hezekiah praying, "O Lord, I am oppressed. Be Surety for me." Isaiah 38:14—the Hebrew rendered "undertake for me" is the same as translated "be Surety for me" in Psalm 119:122. Thus, in each instance believers made a request that the Lord would not barely bestow some favor on or confer some privilege on them, but do so under the particular character of a "Surety." By addressing themselves unto their Deliverer under that character it is clear they had knowledge that He had agreed to act in this office for His people. Since the O. T. saints, equally with the N. T. ones, were to benefit from the mediatorial work of the incarnate Son, they were not left in ignorance of the grand truth that He was appointed by the Father, and by His own consent, to serve as the Surety of His people.

On Psalm 119:122, John Gill pointed out, "What David prays to God to be for him, that Christ is for all His people. He drew near to God, struck hands with Him, gave His word and bond to pay the debts of His people. He put Himself in their law-place and stead and became responsible to Law and Justice for them. He engaged Himself to make satisfaction for their sins and bring in everlasting righteousness for their justification, and to preserve and keep them and bring them safe to eternal glory and happiness, and thus was being a 'Surety for good' for them." It is worthy of special notice that this particular verse wherein the Lord is besought to act as "Surety" is the only one in the 176 of this Psalm wherein the Word of God is not mentioned under the name of "Law" "Commandments," "statutes," "judgments" etc., thereby intimating that Christ as the Surety of His people met all their obligations and thereby fulfilled the Law in their stead.

In the O.T. is found a most striking and blessed type of N. T. teaching on this subject, and, as we might expect, it is found in connection with its initial occurrence. It is an almost if not an entirely unvarying rule that the first mention of anything in Scripture more or less defines its meaning and scope—from the way in which it is employed and the connections in which it is found—and forecasts it's subsequent significance. Such is the case here. When seeking to persuade Jacob to allow his beloved Benjamin to accompany his brethren on their journey into Egypt, Judah said, "Send the lad with me. . . I will be surety for him, of my hand shall you require him. If I bring him not unto you, then let me bear the blame forever." (Gen. 43:8,9). That was no idle boast on the part of Jacob's son, as the sequel shows, for he remained true to his promise, though God intervened and spared him from actually fulfilling his trust.

The reader will remember how that Joseph's cup was found in Benjamin's sack while they were returning home with the sorely-needed grain and how the whole company went back to Egypt and were brought before its governor. Joseph said, "The man in whose hand the cup is found, he shall be my servant, and as for you, get you up in peace unto your father." Whereupon Judah interposed and after explaining the situation in a most touching way, declared, "Thy servant became surety for the lad to my father saying, if I bring him not unto you, then I shall bear the blame of my father forever. Now therefore, I pray you, let your servant abide instead of the lad a bondman to my lord, and let the lad go up with his brethren." (Gen. 44:17, 18, 32, 33). Equally beautiful is the sequel and equally striking in completing the type: "Then Joseph could not refrain himself . . . he kissed all his brethren and wept upon them, and after that his brethren talked with him" (Gen. 45:1, 15).

It seems strange that no writer—of the many we are acquainted with—has made any attempt to "develop" this blessed evangelical picture and bring out the wondrous details of the type. First, observe the occasion of this incident. It was a matter of life and death, when Jacob and his household were faced with the prospect of starvation, that this proposal was made (Gen. 43:1-8). In like manner, unless Christ has interposed as the Surety of His people they had received the wages of sin. Second, it was not Reuben, Jacob's firstborn, but Judah who offered to act as "bondman" for Benjamin. Surely it is not without Divine design that in the only chapter in the N. T. where

Christ is specifically designated "Surety" we are therein reminded that "our Lord sprang out of Judah" (Heb. 7:14,22). Third, it is to be particularly noted that this office was not compulsorily thrust upon Judah, but that he freely and voluntarily assumed it, as did the antitypical Surety.

Fourth, let it also be duly observed that it was not for one unrelated to him but for his own brother that Judah proposed to serve—with which should be linked "he that is surety for a stranger shall smart for it" (Prov. 11:15). Fifth, it was in order to satisfy his father that Judah proposed to act. This at once refutes the error of the Socinians on Hebrews 7:22. Christ was not God's Surety unto us, rather did He serve as the Surety of His people to satisfy the justice of His Father. This is made very clear in the type: "your servant became surety for the lad unto my father." Sixth, the nature of suretyship is here clearly defined, namely, serving as a bondman in the room of another, discharging his obligations, "let your servant abide instead of the lad a bondman to my lord" (Gen. 44:33). Seventh, the result of this typical suretyship was that reconciliation was effected between Joseph and his estranged brethren. So the antitypical Surety secured reconciliation between an estranged God and his alienated people.

How very much better, then, is it to take our illustrations of any aspect of Divine Truth from the Word itself, rather than draw upon our imagination or stoop to human history for incidents which supply no analogy! They must indeed be devoid of spiritual vision who fail to see in what has been brought out above a truly remarkable foreshadowment of the Suretyship of Christ. If any regard as 'farfetched' the seven details to which we have called attention, they are to be pitied. It is true that at the last moment God intervened on Judah's behalf, as He did on Isaac's when his father had bound him to the altar and took a knife to slay him—God accepting the will for the deed. Yet just as surely as Abraham "received Isaac in a figure" from the dead (Heb. 11:19), so did Judah in a "figure" and literally so in intention, serve as surety for Benjamin. That God interposed both in Abraham's and Judah's case, exempting them from finalizing their intentions, only serves to emphasize the contrast that He "spared not His own Son" (Rom. 8:32).

That which is most relevant to our present subject is the result obtained by Judah's suretyship, namely, healing the breach which had for so long obtained between Joseph and his brethren—the type turning from Judah's relation to his father and the bringing in of Joseph and its effect upon him, being parallel to the type in Genesis 22 turning from Isaac, the willing victim on the altar, to the "ram" caught in the thicket and being slain in his stead. For many years Joseph had been separated from his brethren and they alienated in spirit from him. When they came into his presence the first time, he "made himself strange" to them and "spoke roughly to them" (Gen. 42:7)—as God did to us through His Law prior to our conversion. Though the heart of Joseph yearned toward them, he made not himself known to them. It was not until Judah stepped forward as the surety of Benjamin that everything was changed. "Then Joseph could not refrain himself" (45:1) and reconciliation was at once effected!

Now it is in the light of all that has been before us above that we are to interpret that blessed declaration "By so much (as the Melchizedek priesthood excelled the Levitical) was Jesus made a Surety of a better testament or covenant" (Heb. 7:22)—the contrast being not between an inferior "surety" and Christ, but the more excellent covenant. Christ is the Surety provided by the Everlasting Covenant, which was administered under the O. T. era (the "old covenant") beneath shadows and figures, but now (in this N. T. era) under the "new covenant" His Suretyship is fully revealed in its actual and historical fulfillment. The typical case of Judah exhibits every essential feature of the Suretyship of Christ and the more clearly it is fixed in our minds the better shall we be able to understand the Antitype. As the Surety of His people Christ undertook to yield that obedience to the Law which they owed and to make reparation to Divine justice for their sins—to discharge their whole debt both of obedience and suffering.

"God did not mince the matter and say, Son, if you will take flesh and die by the hands of wicked men, I will pardon all you die for, for your sake, and you will have an easy task of it. It shall be only enduring the corporeal pains of death, which thousands have undergone in a more terrible manner. But God says this, 'If you will be their Savior, you must be their Surety. You must pay all the debt of doing the Law and suffering for the breach of the Law. You must bear all their sins. You must suffer all their direful pains of body and soul, all the terrors and horrors due to them for sin from the wrath of God. I will make their sins fall on you with all the weight which would press all the elect into the vengeance of Hell-fire forever,' Those are the terms. Hard enough indeed, but if sinners be saved by My free grace in giving you for them, My righteousness and holiness must be satisfied and glorified. Do you have such a love to My glory and to their poor souls as to undergo all that for them? Yes, said our blessed Lord. I am content, Lo, I come to do your will, O God" (S. Crisp 1691).

Third, we have seen that in order to be our Savior Christ had to be our Substitute. We have shown that to legally act as our Substitute He had to take upon Him the office of Surety. We now push our inquiry still further back, and ask, What was it that justified the Holy One serving as our Surety and the government of a righteous God taking vengeance upon Him for our sins? Not until we obtain the Scriptural answer to this question do we arrive at bedrock and find a sure foundation for faith to rest upon—such a foundation as none of the sophistical reasonings of the carnal mind can shake, and against which the objections of skepticism are shattered into nothing, like the spray of the sea as its proud waves spend themselves upon the granite cliff. Nor do we have far to seek if we attend closely to Hebrews 7:22 federal relationship or covenant oneness is what makes manifest the righteousness of the Great Transaction. There is reciprocal identification between the covenant-Head and the Covenantees. Christ transacted for His people because He was one with them.

That Christ acted as the covenant-Head or federal Representative of His people is clear from 1 Corinthians 15:45 and 47, where He is designated "The last Adam" and "the second Man," the one expression explaining the other. Christ was not "the second man" in order of time and number, for such was Cain, but He was in the sense that He sustained the same relation to His people as the first man did to the whole of his posterity. As the margin of Hosea 6:7 shows, God made a "covenant" with the first Adam, in which he acted and transacted for all his natural seed as their legal head and representative, and therein was "the figure of Him that was to come" (Rom. 5:14), for Christ acted and transacted for all His spiritual seed as their legal Head and Representative. Thus in that sense there have been but two men who have sustained this special relation to others before the Divine Law: that each served as a public person, and that thereby a foundation was laid for the judicial consequences of the acts of each to be righteously charged to the account of all for whom each stood.

It has been well said that "The Atonement is founded upon the unity of Christ and His people, with whom He took part in flesh and blood" (Jas. Haldane). It is indeed true that all mankind are partakers of flesh and blood, but Christ "took part" only with the children whom God had given Him. This is brought out very clearly in the language of Heb. 2. "For both He that sanctifies and they who are sanctified are all of one, for which cause He is not ashamed to call them brethren" (v. 11). And again, "Behold I and the children which God has given Me. For as much as the children are partakers of flesh He also Himself likewise took part of the same. . . He took on Him the seed of Abraham"—not of Adam. "Therefore in all things it behooved Him to be made like unto His brethren" (vv. 13, 14, 15, 17). It was that unity between the Sanctifier and the sanctified which laid the foundation for Christ to "make reconciliation" (or rather) "propitiation for the sins of the people" (v. 17).

Under human governments there may be expedients by which the innocent are penalized in order that the guilty may escape, but such a device and arrangement is impossible under the righteous government of God. "Such is the perfection of the Divine government that under it no innocent person every suffered and no guilty person ever escaped" (Jas. Haldane 1847). It was not that a stranger, unrelated to the elect, had imposed upon Him their obligations, but that the Head of the body of which they are members—and the unity of the head and the members of our physical body (when any member suffers it is registered in the brain, and when the head is severed all the members at once die) is no closer than of Christ and His people (see Eph. 5:32). Just as every member of the human race has been made responsible for the original offence of the first Adam, so Christ is made responsible for the offences of His people and suffered accordingly. Furthermore, they themselves (legally considered) suffered in Him and with Him.

"Were it not for the unity of Christ and His people, justice, instead of being magnified, would have been violated in His substitution. However great the dignity of the sufferer, however deep his voluntary humiliation, it would have been no atonement for us. In order to purge our sins, in order to ransom His Church, Christ must so entirely unite Himself with His people, that their sins should become His sins, that His sufferings should be their sufferings, and His death their death" ("The Atonement" by Jas. Haldane). And this is indeed what took place. Christ not only bore our sins in His own body on the tree, but each believer can say, "I am crucified with Christ" (Gal. 2:20). Christ not only suffered for us, but we suffered in Him, for we were legally one with Him. He was substituted for us, because He was and is one with us and we are one with Him.

Chapter 13
Its Effectuation-Concluded

In seeking to show what Christ did in order to effect reconciliation between God and His people two methods of presentation were open to us—each warranted by the analogy of Scripture. To begin with the work of Christ as it is usually apprehended by us, working back to its ordination by God; or to start with the Divine appointment and trace out the progressive accomplishment of the same on the plane of human history. In the last three articles we followed the former plan. Now, to aid the reader still further, we will reverse the process. Under our fifth main division we saw how that a Covenant was entered into between the Father and the Son, in which everything necessary for the redemption of His elect was mutually agreed upon and settled; here we are to contemplate what was actually done in fulfillment of that covenant engagement.

First, having agreed to become the Mediator or Daysman between God and His people, the Beloved of the Father became incarnate. Oneness of nature was indispensable, for there must be a conjunction effected between the Redeemer and the redeemed if He was to be identified with those on whose behalf He acted. Accordingly, "He took not on Him the nature of angels, but He took on Him the seed of Abraham" (Heb. 2:16) that He might have a right of property in us as Man as well as God. In Galatians 4:4, 5 we are told that the Son became incarnate "to redeem them that were under the Law." By the law of Israel the right of redemption belonged to him that was next of blood (Lev. 25:25; Ruth 2:20). It was by being made like His brethren that Christ acquired the human and legal title to pay the ransom-price for His Church.

The obedience of man to the Divine Law is that to which "life" is promised (Matthew 19:17; Rom. 7:10). An angel's obeying in our stead would not have been the establishment of the original law, nor could life for men be claimed as the reward of angelic obedience. By man came death, and consequently, by man must come the resurrection from the dead (1 Cor. 15:21,22). It was essential that the Son of God should become incarnate and be in full possession of our humanity that He might obey the Law and bring in everlasting righteousness for His people. It was His becoming flesh which laid the foundation for the imputation of our liabilities unto Christ and His merits, obedience, and sufferings unto us.

Second, in becoming incarnate the Son of God "took upon Him (voluntary action!) the form of a servant" (Phil. 2:7)—God's Servant, but on our behalf. That service consisted of His entering into the office of Surety. "Suretyship is a relation constituted by covenant engagement, by which parties become legally one so that they can be dealt with as such in law" (J. Armour). Or to state it in other words, a surety is one who gives security for another that he will perform something which the other is bound to do, so that in case of the failure of the first party he will perform it for him. It was His natural union with His people that made possible and proper Christ's federal oneness with them. Thus, Christ as "the Surety of the covenant" came under obligation to perform the condition of the covenant in lieu of and behalf of His elect.

It must be carefully borne in mind that the Covenant was made with the covenantees (the saints) in the person of their Head. Thus when Christ came forth as the Surety of the covenant He appeared as the Representative of His people, assuming their liabilities and discharging their responsibilities, making satisfaction for their sins and bringing in an everlasting righteousness, and that in such a way that the Law was "magnified and made honorable" (Isa. 42:21) and that He (and His people in Him) became entitled to the award of the Law. We shall devote a disproportionate space to this essential point.

Third, in becoming our Surety Christ engaged to do all that was necessary m order to restore His people unto the favor of God and to secure for them the right of everlasting felicity. The first of those engagements or terms was His meeting the original and righteous demands which God made of them and in Adam under the Covenant of Works, namely, to render in their place perfect and perpetual obedience to the Divine Law. The second of those terms was that He should endure the penalty of the Law which they had broken, and this He did when He was "made a curse" for them and suffered the wrath of God on their behalf. From the first Adam the law demanded nothing but full conformity to its precept, but from the last Adam it necessarily demanded not only holy obedience but also penal suffering, that He might atone for our sins and blot out our iniquities.

It has been rightly pointed out that "In the original institute the whole substance of moral obedience was summed up in the single precept, relative to the fruit forbidden. As the Law is a unity, and he who offends in one point is guilty of all; so when the spirit of obedience is tested in a single point only, and confined to that point, a failure here, brings upon man the guilt of the whole—he is liable to the whole penalty. Now this was the sum total of the Law, as a covenant given to Adam, that he should obey, and as the reward of obedience should receive life. This glorious reward was held up as the motive prompting to choice on the side of law and right. The law was ordained unto life (Rom. 7:10). This is its object, and to this it was adapted. But it failed in the hands of the first Adam, and the last Adam comes in to make it good, to establish its principle and secure its object" (G. Junkin, on "Justification").

When Christ appeared as the Surety of His people it was with the affirmation "Lo, I come, to do Your will, O God" (Heb. 10:7). Note well the word to "do" God's will (before He suffered His wrath for our sins)—to "do" what the first Adam failed to perform. The fundamental nature of God's government must needs have been changed had He granted to men "life" on any other terms than what He had presented under the Covenant of Works, and to which man agreed. The Gospel contains no substitute for the Law, but reveals that remedial scheme by which is confirmed and made good the principles of righteousness originally laid down by God to Adam. "Do we then make void the Law through faith (in the gospel)? God forbid. Yea, (is the triumphant answer) we establish the Law" (Rom. 3:31).

The unchanging terms of the Covenant of Works is "This do (obey the Law) and you shall live" (Luke 10:28). And since I have broken the Law and am incapable of keeping it, then "life"—the reward of the Law—could never be mine unless the Surety had "this" done on my behalf. Therefore was He "made under the Law" for His appointed and agreed-upon task was not only to "make an end of sins" but also to "bring in everlasting righteousness" (Dan. 9:24), that is, a justifying righteousness for the whole election of grace. The Lord Jesus freely consented to pay His people's debts, both in making satisfaction to the Law which they had broken and in rendering perfect obedience in their stead. That "righteousness" Christ was working out for us from the moment of His birth until upon the cross He cried "It is finished."

In executing the great work of our redemption and reconciliation the incarnate Son paid homage to the Divine Law. He was not only "made under" it, but as He declared "Your Law is within My heart" (Ps. 40:8)—enshrined in His affections, and His whole life was one of complete subjection to it. Christ as the Sin-bearer and Sin-expiator only gives one side of His work. The other is His holy obedience—the two together furnishing us a complete view of the satisfaction which

He rendered to God. Christ's obedience was equally the work of the One for the many, the Head for His body, and equally essential as His death. His first recorded utterance "Do you not wish that I must be about My Father's business!" (Luke 2:49) shows clearly that He had entered this world on a special errand, that He was engaged in a specific work unto the Father, that He owed obedience to Him—as the "must" plainly intimates.

His first utterance on emerging from His private life struck the same note. When presenting Himself for baptism John demurred, for to comply made Christ appear to be a sinner, for it was "the baptism of repentance for the remission of sins" (Luke 3:3). But it was not as a private person Christ presented Himself, but as "the Lamb of God which takes (or "bears"), away the sin of the world" (John 1:29-31). To His forerunner's objection the Savior replied, "Suffer it to be so now, for thus it becomes us to fulfill all righteousness" (Matthew 3:15). The "now" is emphatic in the Greek. Now that I have "made Myself of no reputation," now that I am discharging My suretyship. It "became" Him to fulfill His engagement. As the One obeying for the many ("us!") it was requisite that He "fulfill the righteousness"—submit to God's positive, institutions or ordinances as well as the moral Law.

In His first public address Christ declared "Think not that I am come to destroy the Law or the Prophets. I am not come to destroy, but to fulfill" (Matthew 5:17). Those words supply us with a clear-cut definition of His mission and the character of the work in which He was engaged. In what way did He "fulfill" the Prophets? Why, by doing those things which they had foretold—such as preaching good tidings (Isa. 61:1) and healing the sick (Isa. 35:4-6)—and by suffering the indignities and pains which they had announced. In precisely the same way He "fulfilled" the Law, namely, by rendering the obedience which its precepts required, and by enduring the punishment which its penalty demanded. The grand end of the incarnation was that Christ should provide for His people a righteousness which excelled that of the scribes and Pharisees (Matthew 5:20).

"To satisfy both the requirements of His justice and the abundance of His mercy, God determined that a full satisfaction should be made unto His Law, and such a satisfaction that it was in that way more honored than if it had never been broken, or the whole race damned. In order to do this He appointed that Christ should serve as the Substitute and Surety of His people. He must stand as their Representative and fulfill all righteousness for them and endure the curse in their stead, so that they might be legally reckoned to have obeyed and suffered in Him" (Thos. Goodwin, Puritan). Accordingly we find Christ saying "My meat is to do the will of Him that sent Me and to finish His work" (John 4:34). The single principle that guided His holy life was obedience to God. In this way He not only left us an example to follow, but was working out for us a righteousness to be imputed to our account and by which we are justified and entitled to the reward of the Law. Calvary was not the beginning but the end of His life of perfect obedience—as the "unto death" of Philippians 2:8 testifies.

Fourth, God transferred the sins of His people and placed them upon their Surety the moment He assumed the office. "The Lord has laid on Him the iniquities of us all" (Isa. 53:6). Not experimentally, but legally; not the corruption of them, but the guilt; not that He was defiled by them, but that He became subject to their penalty. The sins of His people were charged to the account of the Holy One. So truly was this the case that He acknowledged the actuality of it crying, "For innumerable evils have compassed Me about. My iniquities have taken hold upon Me" (Ps. 40:12); and again, "O God, You know My foolishness, and My sins are not hid from You" (Ps. 69:5). That was the language of the Surety, as the context clearly shows.

Fifth, because Christ entered this world charged with the guilt of His people, Divine justice dealt with Him accordingly—as was shown under the first article on Christ effectuating reconciliation as our Substitute. Because Christ had shouldered the awful burden of His people's sins, He must be paid sin's wages. Because the Just had so united Himself to the unjust, He must suffer "the due reward of their iniquities." He must, accordingly, be wounded for our transgressions and bruised for our iniquities. The chastisement of our peace must be upon Him, if by our His stripes we are to be healed (Isa. 53:4,5). It was fore-announced "He shall bear their iniquities" (v. 11) and iniquities and guilt are inseparable, and since guilt signifies liability to punishment, Christ must be penalized in our stead. O that this article may be so blest to some reader that he may, for the first time, be able to truly say: "Upon a life I did not live, upon a death I did not die—Another's life, Another's death, I rest my soul eternally."

Sixth, because Christ was "made sin" for His people (2 Cor. 5:21) He was "made a curse" for them (Gal. 3:13)— that curse consisted of the avenging wrath of God. The Sinbearer was "numbered with the transgressors" (Isa. 53:12). The august dignity of Christ's person did not avail to any abatement of the Divine curse. God "spared not His own Son" (Rom. 8:32). So far from sparing Him, the Judge of all the earth, the moral Governor of this world, the Administrator of law cried, "Awake 0 sword, against My Shepherd, and against the Man that is My Fellow, says the Lord of hosts. Smite the Shepherd" (Zech. 13:7). Though He had done no violence, neither was any deceit in His mouth, yet it "pleased Jehovah to bruise Him. He has put Him to grief" (Isa. 53:9,10). The wages of sin is death, and as physical death consists of the severance of the soul from the body so spiritual death is the separation of the soul from God, and on the cross Christ was forsaken by God.

We must therefore look higher than the "band of men and officers" as the servants of the chief priests and Pharisees sent to apprehend Christ in the Garden, and see in them the agents of Divine justice, though they knew not what they did. We must needs direct our eyes above the Roman soldiers as they "plaited a crown of thorns and placed it on Christ's head" and see in them the executives of the Divine Law, branding our Surety with the marks of the curse (see Gen. 3:17, 18). We are required to exercise the vision of faith and behold in Caiaphas, Herod and Pilate doing "whatsoever God's hand and counsel determined before to be done" (Acts 4:28) in order that the terms of the Everlasting Covenant should be carried out, the requirements of righteousness satisfied, the holy wrath of God appeased, and the sins of His people forever removed from before Him, "as far as the east is from the west."

Seventh, because Christ rendered full satisfaction to Divine justice, He redeemed His people unto Himself, and they are not only absolved from all guilt but are reconciled to God. Not only are they no longer under the frown of the Divine Judge, but His smile rests upon them. Not only are they freed from His displeasure, but they are restored to His favor. Not only do they stand "unblameable and unreproveable in God's sight," but they have an inalienable title to everlasting felicity. There cannot be a substitution without a dual imputation. If the debt of the debtor is charged to the surety, then upon his discharge of the same the payment of the surety must be credited to the debtor. Accordingly we are told, "For He has made Him (legally) to be sin for us who knew no sin, that we might be made (legally) the righteousness of God in Him" (2 Cor. 5:21)—there is the counter-imputation. Christ's righteousness is reckoned to the account of His people.

"As by one man's disobedience many were made sinners (legally constituted so, and then as the consequence, experimentally became such) so by the obedience of One shall many be made (legally constituted so, and then as the consequence, experimentally become such) righteous" (Rom. 5:19). Christ took our place that we might take His. Christ removed our sins that we might be clothed with His merits. Because Christ kept the Law for us, we are entitled to "reign in life" (Rom. 5:17). "The Forerunner is for us entered into Heaven" (Heb. 6:20). Observe well how Christ demanded this as His legal right. "Father, I will that they also whom You have given Me, be with Me where I am" (John 17:24). I have fully discharged their obligations, I have wrought out for them an everlasting righteousness, now give them that which, for My sake, they are justly entitled to.

"The moment the believing sinner accepts Christ as his Substitute, he finds himself not only cleared from his guilt, but rewarded—he gets all heaven because of the glory and merits of Christ. The Atonement we preach is one of absolute exchange. It is that Christ took our place literally, in order that we might take His place literally—that God regarded and treated Christ as the sinner, and that He regards and treats the believing sinner, as Christ. From the moment we believe, God looks upon us as if we were Christ. He takes it as if Christ's atonement had been our atonement, and as if Christ's life had been our life; and He beholds, accepts, blesses, and rewards on the ground that all Christ was and did is ours" (G. S. Bishop "Doctrines of Grace"). What a glorious Gospel! Then proclaim it freely and boldly ministers of Christ.

From all that has been pointed out it should, we think, be more or less clear to the simplest reader that the breach between God and His sinning people has been righteously healed. That is to say, reconciliation has been effected in a way both gracious and legal. To have brought this suit into the court of Divine Law had availed nothing unless provision had been made for so ordering its process and judgment that the sinner might be honorably accepted and that God might be both "just and the Justifier of him which believes in Jesus" (Rom. 3:26). The Law must be on the sinner's side. His absolver and not his condemner, his justifier and not his accuser. That provision has been made by means of the Surety-Substitute, by the transference of total indebtedness from those who incurred it to One to incurred it not and fully discharged the same.

It is by the principle and on the ground of Suretyship hind Substitution that God's justice is displayed in all His transactions with the believing sinner. It is this which is the climacteric in the rood news proclaimed by the heralds of Christ. The grand Evangel not only exhibits the knowledge-surpassing love of God, but as the apostle declares "therein is the righteousness of God revealed." Grace indeed reigns, but it does so "through righteousness" (Rom. 1:17; 5:21). "Christ bears the sins of many because in His covenanted identification with those 'many' their sins are sinlessly and truly His. And unto the many sons and daughters of the covenant, the Father imputes the righteousness of the Son, because, in their covenant oneness with the Son, His righteousness is undeservedly but truly their own righteousness. And all throughout 'the judgment of God is according to truth' and equity" (H. Martin, on "The Atonement"). Thus we behold once more that, at the cross, Mercy and Truth met together, Righteousness and Peace have kissed each other (Ps. 85:10). It is not a peace at any price, a peace wherein justice is sacrificed and the law is flouted, but it righteous peace, one that glorifies all the Divine perfections. Such is the wondrous and blessed message of the Gospel.

Chapter 14
Its Meaning

It may seem strange to some that we have deferred until now a consideration of the meaning of "reconciliation," and to the critical reader it must appear as a real defect. Ordinarily a writer should define the terms which he uses at the beginning of his treatise, but in this case we wish to do very much more than furnish a mere definition of the word itself. Under the present division of our subject we desire to consider. more closely and definitely the thing itself. We have dwelt upon the need of reconciliation, its Author, its arrangement, and its effectuation, now we must describe more particularly what reconciliation actually is, as it concerns both God and His people. The previous chapters have been paving the way for this, and in measure furnishing materials for the same, and after what has already been presented the reader should be able to follow more easily our present discussion than if we had introduced it at an earlier stage, as it also relieves the writer from taking anything for granted. It is on the foundations already laid we now propose to build.

It is also because that what we are to be engaged with concerns the more controversial aspect of our theme, that we sought to first make clear and establish from Scripture what must be regarded as the essential elements which into the equation. In seeking to ascertain more precisely the nature and character of reconciliation we must carefully distinguish between cause and effect, between the means and end. Many are confused at this point, supposing that "atonement" and "reconciliation" are one and the same—the sound of the English word "at-one-ment" leading them to miss its true sense. Unfortunately this confusion is fostered by the only verse in the Authorized Version of the N. T. where it occurs: "by whom (namely, Jesus Christ) we have received the atonement" (Rom 5:11)—unhappily few avail themselves of the marginal alternative (generally the better rendition) where it is rightly given as "reconciliation." To speak of our "receiving" the Atonement does not make sense, for it was God and not ourselves who required an atonement or satisfaction, but it is correct to say that believers "receive" the reconciliation which Christ effected for them.

To "atone" is to placate or appease, to make reparation for injury or amends for wrong done another. "Atonement" simply signifies that a satisfaction has been made, that the demands of the Divine Law have been met, that justice has been honored, that God has been propitiated. The literal force of the Heb. "kaphar" (generally rendered atonement in the O. T.) is a "covering," and thus its appropriateness for this usage is clear—the sacrificial blood covered what was an affront to the offended eye of God by means of an adequate compensation. The term is applied to the "mercy-seat" which was the lid or cover of the ark of the covenant—and therefore a Divinely-appointed symbol closely connected with the presentation of sacrifices on the day of expiation. Thus there can be no objection to rendering "Christ Jesus: whom God has set forth a mercy-seat through faith in His blood" (Rom. 3:25) so long as its purport be explained and the "blood" be duly emphasized.

The principal idea, then, expressed by the word "kaphar"—"atonement" is that of averting vengeance by means of a placating offering. It is rendered "appease" in Genesis 32:20. When Jacob was about to make the dreaded meeting with Esau, he sent his servants with droves of animals before him, saying, "I will appease ("kaphar") him with this present that goes before me!" In Numbers 16:31 it is written, "He shall take no satisfaction (no "kaphar") for the life of a murderer which is guilty of death. But he shall surely be put to death," which again helps us to ascertain the force of this most-important Hebrew word, the word "satisfaction" meaning, of course, a legal compensation—none such being allowed in case of murder. Vengeance must take its course. "Moses said unto Aaron, Take a censer and put fire in it from off the altar and put on incense, and go quickly unto the congregation and make an atonement for them, for there is wrath gone out from the Lord, the plague is begun" (Num. 16:46)—here we see that "atonement" was plainly the means for propitiating Jehovah, for turning away His vengeance.

Now such was the Atonement made unto God by the Lord Jesus Christ. His sacrifice was offered for the satisfying of Divine justice, for the averting of Divine wrath from His people. God sent His Son to be "the propitiation for our sins" (1 John 4:10). The judicial displeasure of God was turned away from His Church by means of the substitutionary interposition of the Lamb, who was slain in their stead. The righteous vengeance of God was appeased by the Surety, pouring out His soul unto death. Certain effects or results followed from that. The sins of God's elect were blotted out, they were redeemed from the curse of the Law, God was reconciled to them. The Atonement was the cause, the means, the root; reconciliation was the effect, the end, the fruit. Thus the two things are clearly distinguished and should never be confounded. The very fact that the N. T. employs two entirely different words ("hilasmos" 1 John 2:2; 4:10 and "katallage" Rom. 5:11) shows plainly they are not the same—the latter resulting from the former.

It is a pity that the honorable translators of the A. V. did not always preserve that important distinction. Another verse which has served to cloud the judgment of English readers is Hebrews 2:17, where we are told the Son became incarnate that "He might be merciful and faithful High Priest in things pertaining to God, to make reconciliation for the sins of the people," which is correctly rendered (as Owen and others of the Puritans long ago insisted that it should be) in the R.V. that is, "make propitiation for the sins of the people." Because Christ made propitiation for their sins, the wrath of God was turned away from them and reconciliation was the outcome: "having made peace through the blood of His cross" (Col. 1:20) sums it up, and shows both the end and the means by which it was accomplished. That our English word "at-one" signifies to reconcile and not to "propitiate" is evident from Acts 7:26—"Moses would have set them at one again" that is, restore them to amity—the Greek word being rendered "peace" elsewhere.

But at this point we need to be careful in guarding against a misconception and the drawing of a wrong conclusion. While the atonement of Christ was an appeasement, it must not be regarded as an inducement. That is, as a price which the Redeemer had to pay in order to incline God to love His people. Yet it is right here that the enemies of the Gospel have made their main attack upon that aspect of it which we are now considering. They have accused those who maintain the Scriptural doctrine of propitiation in order to reconciliation as denying the Divine benevolence, as arguing that Christ shed His precious blood in order to induce God to love sinners, that those who insist God required an appeasing sacrifice before He would be gracious unto transgressors, are guilty of grievously misrepresenting the Divine character. But Socinians are the ones who wretchedly pervert the teachings of sound theologians when they charge them with portraying the cross of Christ as the means of changing God from a merciless Tyrant into a benevolent Being.

Socinians grievously wrest the Truth when they argue that those who proclaim the propitiatory character of Christ's death teach that His death wrought a change in God, that He produced a different feeling within Him with regard to sinners. So far from that, the very men who have most faithfully and fearlessly magnified the ineffable holiness of God in its antagonism against sin and His inexorable justice in punishing it, have been the ones who also made it crystal clear that love to sinners, a determination to save His people from the curse of the Law, existed eternally in the Divine mind, that it was the love of God for His Church, His compassion for its members, which moved Him to devise and execute the plan of salvation and to send His beloved to save them by making an atonement for their sins. Christ the Atoner was provided and given by the Father for His people! It was at His own tremendous cost — by not sparing His Son, but delivering Him up for them all—that the Father supplied that very compensation which His holiness and justice demanded.

We must not for a moment suppose that the atonement was in order to change the good-will of the Father toward those on whose behalf it was offered. No, He gave His elect—the objects of His everlasting and unchanging love— to the Son, and He gave the Son of His love to and for them. All that we owe unto Christ we owe unto God who gave Him. "Thanks be unto God for His unspeakable Gift" Nevertheless, the atonement was essentially necessary in order that God's love might flow to them in an honorable channel; that, so far from the glory of God being tarnished by their salvation, so far from His evidencing the slightest complicity in their sin, every Divine attribute might be placed in a more conspicuous view. So that in clothing His Church with the everlasting righteousness of His Son and adorning them with all the beauties of holiness, unto the enjoyment of an exceeding, even eternal weight of glory, God might appear "glorious in holiness, fearful in praises, doing wonders" (Ex. 15:11)—let it be noted that verse is taken from Israel's song of redemption (v. 13) after the destruction of their enemies at the Red Sea.

Nowhere does the love of God shine so illustriously as at the Cross. To die for a friend is the highest instance of love among mankind—an instance but rarely found. But God commends His love to men in that while they were sinners, Christ died for them—died for those who were "alienated and enemies in their mind by wicked works" (Col. 1:21). This is the most amazing feature of it. It may then be reasonably inferred that God loves whatever is lovely; but it may with equal certainty be inferred that whatever is not amiable displeases Him. Human reason, then, could never have discovered a way in which sinners should be the proper objects of Divine love. But the Scriptures reveal how God's wisdom found a way by which He has made the loathsome objects worthy of His love! In the atoning death of Christ all their pollutions are washed away, and in His perfect righteousness they stand graced before God with all the merits of their Surety—more worthy than the highest of the holy angels.

So far from teaching that the atonement of Christ was the procuring cause of God's love unto His people, we emphatically insist that God's love for them was the moving cause of giving Christ to suffer and die for them, that their sins might be atoned for. It is not that there was insufficient love in God to save sinners without the death of His Son, but that He determined to save them in such a way as gloriously exhibited His righteousness too. The love of God wrought in a way of holiness and justice. He did not choose to receive sinners into His favor without giving public expression to His detestation of their iniquities, but, as the entire universe will yet learn, cried, "Awake O sword against My Shepherd and against the Man that is My Fellow says the Lord of hosts, smite the Shepherd" (Zech. 13:7), so that "He might be just and the Justifier of him that believes in Jesus" (Rom. 3:26). God's love triumphed at the cross, yet not at the expense of Law! Let the reader judge, then, whether the Socinian or the Calvinist furnishes the most Scriptural and blessed exhibition of the Divine character and government.

The main objection made by those who formally reject the Atonement is, that it is inconsistent with the love of God. God needed nothing, they say, but His own goodness to incline Him to show mercy unto sinners, or if He did, it could not be of grace, since a price was paid to obtain it. But in the light of what has been pointed out above it should be quite evident that such an objection is utterly pointless, confusing the moving cause of mercy unto sinners with the manner of showing it. The sacrifice of Christ was not the cause but the effect of God's love. The love of God was amply sufficient to have pardoned the vilest sinner without any atonement, had God deemed it consistent with the holiness of his character and the righteousness of His government. David was not wanting in love for his son Absalom, for "his soul longed to go forth unto him," but he felt for his own honor as the head of the family and the nation, which, had he admitted him immediately to his presence, would have been compromised and the crime of murder connived at. Therefore, for a time he kept him at a distance, and when introduced, it must be by a mediator.

As Winslow so sublimely expressed it:

"It is a self-evident truth that, as God only knows, so He only can reveal His love. It is a hidden love, veiled deep within the recesses of His infinitude, yea, it seems to comprise His very essence, for 'God is love.' Not merely loving and lovely, but love itself, essential love. Who, then, can reveal it but Himself? 'In this was manifested the love of God toward us, because that God sent His only-begotten Son into the world that we might live through Him. Herein is love, not that we loved God, but that He loved us and sent His Son to be the propitiation for our sins' (1 John 4:9,10). But behold God's love! See how He has inscribed this glorious perfection of His nature in letters of blood drawn from the heart of Jesus. His love was so great that nothing short of the death of His beloved Son could give an adequate expression of its immensity.

'God so loved the world that He gave His only begotten Son, that whosoever believes in Him should not perish, but have everlasting life' (John 3:16). Here was the great miracle of love. Here was its most stupendous acknowledgment —here its most brilliant victory—and here its most costly and precious offering. 'Herein is love.' as though the apostle would say 'and nowhere but here.' That God should punish the (intrinsically) Innocent for the guilty—that He should exact His co-equal Son to cancel the guilt of rebels—that He should lay an infinite weight of wrath on His soul, in order to lay an infinite value of love on ours—that He should sacrifice His life of priceless value for ours, worthless, forfeited and doomed—that the Lord of glory should become the Man of sorrows—the Lord of life should die and the Heir of all things be as 'He that serves.' O the depths of love unfathomable! O the height of love unsearchable! O the length and breadth of love unmeasureable! O the love of God which passes knowledge!"

"Great is the mystery of godliness" is the Spirit's own express declaration. Therefore the finite mind, especially in its present condition (impaired by sin and clouded by prejudice) must expect to encounter features that are beyond its comprehension. Nevertheless, it is both our privilege and duty to receive all that Holy Writ reveals on it and beg God for a spiritual understanding of the same, and refuse to reject any aspect of the Truth, because, we no doubt, are unable to perceive its harmony with some other aspect. The Scriptures plainly teach that the Atonement of Christ was an appeasement of the wrath of God against His people, yet they are equally clear in making known that the Atonement was not made as an inducement of the love of God unto His people. The Savior did not shed His blood in order to procure God's love for His Church, rather, was God's gift of the Redeemer the supreme expression of His love for it. The Atonement appeased the wrath of God in His official character as the Judge of all; the love of God is His goodwill unto the elect as the covenant God and Father of our Lord Jesus Christ.

Chapter 15
Its Meaning-Continued

In our last chapter we pointed out the needs-be for and the importance of making a clear distinction between the Atonement and reconciliation, that the sacrifice of Christ was the cause and the means of which reconciliation was the effect and end. Some theologians, and good ones too, have demurred against terming the offering of Christ a "means," insisting that it was the procuring cause of our salvation. The fact is, it was both a means and a cause according as we view it in different relations. It was the meritorious cause of re-instating us in the favor of God and of procuring for us the Holy Spirit; the means by which God's mercy is exercised in a way of justice. "Being justified freely by His grace through the redemption that is in Christ Jesus" (Rom. 3:24). It may be regarded as a mean or medium in respect of the originating cause: thus grace is presented as the source from which it sprang, the redemptive work of Christ the channel by which it flows. In Hebrews 9:15 Christ's death is expressly termed the "means." Some may be inclined to chafe at the "distinctions" we frequently call attention to, considering we are too prone to confuse the minds of the simple by introducing "theological niceties." But did not the apostle pray that the Philippian saints might be moved by God to "try things that differ." We rather fear that such disrelish of these distinctions is a sign of mental slovenliness and spiritual slothfulness. Is it of no significance, or of no importance to us, to take notice of the fact that while the Scriptures speak of "the wrath of the Lamb" and of the "wrath of God" being upon both the non-elect and elect in a state of nature, they never once make reference to "the wrath of the Father!" If any of our readers sneer or shrug their shoulders at that as a mere "splitting of hairs," we are very sorry for them. God's Word is made up of words, and it behooves us to weigh every one of them attentively. If we do not, we shall obtain little more than a blurred impression rather than a clear-cut view of the Truth.

The work of Christ was indeed one and indivisible, nevertheless, it is capable of and requires to be viewed from various angles. For that reason, among others, the typical altar was not round but "foursquare" (Ex. 27:1). The nature of Christ's work was fourfold in its character: being a federal work—as the Representative of His people, a vicarious work—as their Surety and Substitute, a penal work—as He took their Law-place, a sacrificial work—offering Himself unto God on their behalf. The work of Christ accomplished four chief things. It propitiated God Himself, it expiated the sins of His people, it reinstated them in the Divine favor, and it estated them an everlasting inheritance of glory. There is also a fourfold consequence of Christ's work so far as His people are concerned. The guilt of their transgressions is cancelled so that they receive remission of sins; they are delivered from all bondage — redeemed, they are made legally and experimentally righteous; all enmity between God and them is removed—they are reconciled.

In our last we also exposed the sophistry of the Socinian contention that if the propitiatory character of Christ's sacrifice be insisted upon, then we repudiate the uncaused love and free grace of God. We sought to show that while the shedding of Christ's blood was an appeasement of the Divine wrath against God's people, it was not an inducement of His love unto them. Thus, in the latter half of our foregoing chapter we dealt more with the negative side in showing what the oblation of Christ was not designed to accomplish, namely, to procure God's good will unto sinners. Now we must turn to the positive side and point out what the Atonement was designed to effect. We need to be constantly on our guard against exalting the wondrous love of God to the deprecation of His ineffable holiness. If on the one hand it is blessed to continually bear in mind that never has there been such love as the love of God—so pure, so intense, so satisfying; it is equally necessary not to forget there has never been a law like unto the Law of God—so spiritual, so holy, so inexorable.

Divine love unto sinners originated reconciliation, but the Divine Law required that love to flow in a righteous channel. The method which it has pleased God to employ is one in which there is no compromise between love and law, but rather one where each has found full expression. At the cross we see the exceeding sinfulness of sin, the spotless purity of the Law, the unbending character of God's government, and the righteous outflow of His mercy unto Hell-deserving transgressors. The same conjunction of Divine light and love appears in connection with our receiving blessings in response to Christ's intercession, as is clear from His words, "I say not unto you that! will pray the Father for you, for the Father Himself loves you" (John 16:26, 27)—which was to assure us that we not only have the benefit of Christ's prayers but the Father Himself so loves us that that alone is sufficient to obtain anything at His hands. Think not that the Father is hard to be exhorted and that blessings have to be wrung from Him by My supplications. No, they issue from His love, but in an honorable way, and that we may appreciate them the more.

But in our day it is necessary to consider reconciliation more from the standpoint of God's holiness and justice, for during the last two or three generations there has been an entirely disproportionate emphasis on His love. While it is true that at the cross we behold the highest expression of God's love to sinners, yet it is equally true that there we also witness the supreme manifestation of God's hatred of sin, and the one should never be allowed to crowd out or obscure the other. The apostle hesitated not to affirm that God "set forth (His Son) to be a propitiation through faith in His blood, to declare (or demonstrate) His righteousness" (Rom. 3:25)—observe well how those words "to declare His righteousness" are repeated in the very next verse. If the question is asked, Why did God give His Son to die for sinners rather than have them to perish in their sins? the answer is, Because He loved them. But the answer to: Why did He give His Son to be a propitiation for sinners rather than save them without one? is Because He loved righteousness and hated iniquity.

To any who have followed us closely through these chapters up to the present point it should be quite clear, we think, that they err gravely who contend that reconciliation is entirely one-sided, that it is sinners who need to be reconciled to God, that in nowise did God require reconciling to His people, seeing that He changes not, that He loves them with an everlasting love, and that it was entirely His good-will and benevolence which provided the Atonement for them. Yet since it is at this very point that so many have departed from the Truth, we must labor it and enter into more detail. It is sin which has caused the breach between the Holy One and His fallen creatures, and since He was the One wronged and injured by sin, surely it is self-evident that reparation must be made unto Him for that offence and outrage. Why, every passage in which "propitiation" occurs is proof that God needed to be reconciled to sinners, that His wrath must be averted before peace could be made.

It is of first importance to recognize that "reconciliation" necessarily implies alienation, and that both reconciliation and alienation connote a relationship between God and us. Alienation signifies that a state of enmity and hostility exists between two parties, reconciliation that the cause and ground of the alienation has been removed, so that amity now obtains between them. It is therefore essential that we define carefully and accurately the changed relationship between

God and His people which was brought about by the entrance of sin. Though the everlasting objects of God's eternal favor have been chosen in Christ from all eternity and blest with all spiritual blessings in Him, nevertheless the elect (in Adam) apostatized from God, and in consequence of the Fall fell under the curse of His Law. Considered as the Judge of all, God became antagonistic to them; considered as fallen creatures (what they were in themselves) they were by nature enmity against Him. The entrance of sin into this world brought the Church into a condition of guilt before the Holy One, yet because of the Lamb being slain in the purpose of God, the Father's love never ceased unto His people, without any injury unto His justice.

There could be no thought of reconciliation between a holy God and a polluted rebel until full satisfaction had been made to His broken Law. Sin raised a barrier between God and us which we could in no wise surmount. "Your iniquities have separated between you and your God, and your sins have hid His face from you" (Isa. 59:2). Sin resulted in alienation between God and man. This was made unmistakably plain right after the Fall, in Eden itself, for we are told, "God drove out the man: and He placed at the east of the garden of Eden cherubim, and a flaming sword which turned every way, to keep the way of the tree of life" (Gen. 3:24). Let it be carefully remembered that God was not there dealing with Adam simply as a private person, but as the federal head of the race, as the legal representative of all his posterity—both of the elect and the non-elect. The "flaming sword" was emblematic of the vindictive justice of God. The natural man as such was excluded from Paradise and effectually barred from the tree of life. That it turned "every way" precluded any avenue of approach. The reconciliation must be mutual because the alienation was mutual. Christ had to remove God's wrath from us, as well as our sins from before God. If God were not reconciled to us, it would avail us nothing to lay aside our enmity against Him. The fact that the flaming sword "turned every way" to bar man's access to the tree of life signified that by no effort of his could the sinner repair the damage which his capital offence had wrought, and declared in the language of the N.T. that "they that are in the flesh cannot please God" (Rom. 8:8). By nature we are "the children of wrath" (Eph. 2:3), and by practice "alienated and enemies in our mind by wicked works" (Col. 1:21), and unless peace be made and reconciliation effected we should neither have any encouragement to go to Him for mercy nor any hope for acceptance with Him. The throwing down of the weapons of our rebellion would avail nothing while we were obnoxious to the curse of the Divine Law. How then shall we be delivered from the wrath to come is thus the all-important question, for His wrath is "revealed from heaven against all ungodliness and unrighteousness of men" (Rom. 1:18).

The fallen sons of men have not only removed themselves to a guilty distance from God, but He has judicially and morally removed Himself from them. "The Lord is far from the wicked" (Prov. 15:29). And men have wickedly departed from Him, God has righteously withdrawn from them, and thus the distance is mutual, and ever increasing. While Adam remained obedient, his Creator admitted him to near communion with Him, as is intimated by His "walking in the garden in the cool of the day," but when he transgressed the commandment, He withdrew His favor and thrust him out of Paradise. Had no Atonement been provided there had never again been any communion with God—any more than there is between Him and the fallen angels. This awful state of distance from God is still the condition of all the unregenerate—elect or non-elect, the interposition of Christ availing them not while they continue rejecting Him, as is made unmistakably plain by "he that believes not the Son shall not see life, but the wrath of God abides on him" (John 3:36).

While they remain in a state of nature the elect, equally with the non-elect lie under the guilt of sin and the condemnation of the Law, and are therefore obnoxious to God—considered as the moral Governor and Judge of all. "God hates sinners as they hate Him, for we are children of wrath from the womb, and that wrath abides on us till we enter into God's peace; and the more wicked we are, the more we increase His wrath. 'He is angry with the wicked every day' (Ps. 7:11); they are under His curse. Whatever be the secret purposes of His grace, yet so they are by the sentence of His Law, and according to that we must judge of our condition" (Manton vol. 13, p. 257). So too, J. Owen: "Reconciliation is the renewing of friendship between parties before at variance: both parties being properly said to be reconciled, even both he that offended and he that was offended. God and man were set at distance, at enmity, and variance by sin, man was the party offending, God offended, and the alienation was mutual on every side" ("The Death of Death" chap. 6, 2nd para.).

But how may God be said to love or hate believers before their reconciliation since He is the Author of it? Let us give a condensation of Charnock's reply. "First, God loves them with a love of purpose or election, but till grace be wrought in them not with a love of acceptation. We are within the love of His purpose as we are designed to be the servants of Christ, but not within the love of His acceptance till we are actually His servants—'He that in these things serves Christ is acceptable to God' (Rom. 14:18). They are alienated from God while in a state of nature and not accepted by God till in a state of grace. There is in God a love of good-will and a love of delight. The love of good-will is the root, the love of delight is love in the flower. The love of good-will looks upon us as afar off, the love of delight is itself in us, draws near to us. By peace with God we have access to Him, by His love of delight He has access to us. God wills well to them before grace, but is not well pleased with them till grace.

"Second, God does hate His elect in some sense before their actual reconciliation. (A) Not their persons, though He takes no pleasure in them, neither their persons nor services. (B) But He hates their sins. Sin is always odious to God, let the person be what it will. God never hated, nor ever could, the person of Christ, yet He hated and testified in the highest measure His hatred of those iniquities He stood charged with as our Surety. He hates the sins of believers, though pardoned and mortified. (C) God hates their state. The elect before conversion are in a state of enmity, of darkness, of slavery, and that state is odious to God, and makes them incapable while in that state to 'inherit the kingdom of God' (1 Cor. 6:9-11). The state of the elect before actual reconciliation is odious because it is a state of alienation from God. Whatever grows up from the root of the old Adam cannot be delightful to Him. (D) God hates them as to withholding the effects of His love. His frown rather than His smile is upon them."

In Eph. 2 the apostle informs us how this mutual alienation is removed, namely, by Christ "Having abolished in His flesh the enmity, even the law of commandments contained in ordinances, for to make in Himself of twain one new man, so making peace, and that He might reconcile both unto God in one body by the cross, having slain the enmity by that means" (vv. 15, 16). As Owen pointed out, "It is evident the reconciliation here mentioned consists in slaying the enmity so making peace. Now what is the enmity intended? Not that in our hearts to God, but the legal enmity that lay against us on the part of God." This passage will come before us again when we consider the scope of reconciliation, suffice it now to point out while verses 14, and 15 refer to that which was effected between believing Jews and Gentiles, verse 16 has in view that which relates to God Himself, and as Owen well pointed out this enmity of God against Jews and Gentiles alike was a legal one, that which the Divine Law entailed.

"And having made peace through the blood of His cross to reconcile all things unto Himself., and you, that were sometime alienated and enemies in your mind by wicked works, yet now has He reconciled in the body of His flesh through death, to present you holy and unblameable and unreproveable in His sight" (Col. 1:20-22). Since "peace" was made, there must have been enmity or hostility, and since the peace was made "through the blood of His cross" then the shedding of it was in order to the placating of God, by offering a satisfaction to His outraged Law. Thus, when theologians use the expression "a reconciled God" they signify that a change in His relationship and attitude toward us has been effected, from one of wrath to favor. It is the removal of that estrangement which was produced by our offence. In consequence of His atonement Christ has pacified God toward all who believe and brought them to God. Our reconciliation unto God is the same thing as our conversion, when we surrendered to His just claims upon us, and in heart desired and purposed to forsake all that is opposed to Him.

Chapter 16
Its Meaning-Continued

In our last chapter we pointed out that reconciliation is an attitude or relation, and dwelt upon the fact that it is a mutual affair. This is so obvious that it should need no arguing, yet since so many have denied that God required to be reconciled unto sinners, we must perforce dwell upon it. Where one has wronged another and a break ensues between then, then just as surely as "it takes two to make a quarrel" so it takes two for a friendship to be restored again. If the one who committed the injury confesses his fault and the other refuses to accept his apology and forgive him, there is no reconciliation effected between them; equally so if the injured party be willing to overlook the fault, desiring peace at any price, yet if the wrong-doer continues to bear enmity against the other, the breach still remains. There must be a mutual good-will before a state of amity prevails. That holds good in connection with God and His sinning creatures.

We dwelt upon the fact that the entrance of sin brought about a changed relationship between God and man. Since Adam stood as the federal head of the race and transacted as the legal representative of all his posterity, when he fell, the whole of mankind apostatized from God. In consequence of the fall, all mankind came under the curse of the Law, and therefore the elect equally with the non-elect are "by nature the children of wrath, even as others" (Eph. 2:3). Loved by God with regard to His eternal good-will, but born under His wrath in regard of His Law and its administration—let those words be carefully pondered. "Accepted in the Beloved" (Eph. 1:6) from all eternity, yet entering this time-state under Divine condemnation. Holy and without blame in Christ by election, yet guilty and depraved in ourselves by sin. We must distinguish, as Scripture does, between how God viewed His people in Christ in the glass of His decrees, and how He regards them as in Adam, participating in the consequences of his transgression and continuing in sin by their own course of constant rebellion against Him until they are regenerated.

"There is therefore now no condemnation to them which are in Christ Jesus" (Rom. 8:1) clearly implies that before they came to be "in Christ Jesus" the elect were under condemnation. As Romans 5:18 declares "by the offence of one judgment came upon all men to condemnation." If it is asked, But were not the elect "in Christ" from all eternity? The Answer is, In one sense yes, in another sense no. "In Christ" always has reference to union with Him. The elect were mystically united to Christ, being "chosen in Him before the foundation of the world" (Eph. 1:4), yet until that decree is actualized, they are "without Christ" (Eph. 2:13). At regeneration the elect are vitally united to Christ: "he that is joined to the Lord is one spirit" (1 Cor. 6:19 and 2 Cor. 5:17). Therefore Paul speaks of those who "were in Christ before me" (Rom. 16:7). Having been brought from death unto life, the elect embrace the Gospel offer and become fiducially united to Christ ("fiducial" is from the Latin "fido" to trust) for they then savingly "believe in Him" (John 3:15). "But He that believes is not condemned already" (John 3:18). The members of Christ's body the Church, are in a state of guilt and condemnation until they personally exercise faith in the atoning blood of Christ. We have labored this point because some of our readers have been taught the contrary.

It was the entrance of sin which caused the breach between God and us, but in this connection particularly it is important to remember what sin essentially consists of. While in some passages sin is regarded as a "debt" and God in connection with it as the Creditor, in other places as an "offence" and God in connection with it as the injured Party, and in still other verses as a "disease" and God in connection with it as the great Physician, yet none of those terms bring before us the primary element in and basic character of sin. The fundamental idea of sin is that it is "a transgression of God's Law"(1 John 3:4) the Rule which He has commanded us to observe, and this should therefore be the leading aspect in which it is contemplated when we consider how God deals with it. Proof of that is found in connection with the origin of human sin, in Genesis 2 and 3. God gave man a commandment which he transgressed: "by one man's disobedience many were made sinners" (Rom. 5:19).

Now as the essential idea of sin is not that it is merely a debt or injury, but a violation of our Rule of conduct, then it follows that the particular character in which God ought to be contemplating when we consider Him dealing with sin is not that of a Creditor or injured Party, who may remit the debt or forgive the injury as He pleases, but in His office as supreme Lord. Sin as transgression of the Divine Law has for its necessary corollary God as the Judge. Since He has promulgated a Divine Law which prohibits sin under pain of death, He is bound by His veracity to maintain the honor of His Law and establish His government by strict justice, and thus He cannot pardon sin unless adequate provision is made for accomplishing those objects. As the Judge of all the earth and Rector of the universe, His own perfections require Him to insist that if the penalty of the Law is remitted it must be by another suffering it vicariously, in that way meeting the claims of His Law.

There could be no reconciliation between an offended God and His apostate people until the breach between them had been healed, until His righteous wrath as the Governor of this world had been appeased, and until they also throw down the weapons of their warfare against Him. As the Judge of all, His honor required that His Law should receive full satisfaction, and since His fallen people were unable to make reparation, He graciously provided a Surety for them, who magnified His Law by rendering to it a perfect obedience and by dying in their stead, and thus enduring for them its unmitigated curse. In this way God's legal "enmity" or wrath was appeased and the sins of His people were blotted out, so God was propitiated and their guilt expiated. Though His atoning sacrifice Christ removed every legal obstacle which stood in the way of God's being merciful unto transgressors and receiving them into His favor, and by His merits Christ procured the Holy Spirit (Acts 2:33) who, by His effectual operations in the elect, slays their enmity against God, and brings them into loving and loyal subjection to Him, and thus (at their conversion) they are reconciled to God.

Socinians have objected that it was neither necessary nor just that Christ should both obey the Law in His people's stead and yet suffer punishment on the account of their transgressions, seeing that obedience is all that the Law requires. Such a demur would be valid had Christ been acting as the Surety of an innocent people who were under probation, but since He entered the Law-place of transgressors the objection is entirely without point. Obedience is not all that the Law requires of guilty creatures, for they are not only obliged to be obedient for the future, but to make satisfaction for the last. the covenant which the Lord God made with Adam had two branches: obey and live ["the commandment which was ordained to life" (Rom. 7:10)]: sin and die (Gen. 2:17). And therefore since Christ was "made under the law" (Gal. 4:4)—which, in the final analysis, signified "under the Covenant of Works"—and since He was acting and transacting as "the last Adam" and "the Second Man" (1 Cor. 15:45, 47) it devolved upon Him to meet the requirements of both branches of the Covenant. As we discussed that at length earlier there is no need to further enlarge upon it.

Since the will of God changes not and the requirements of His government remain the same forever, then if a Surety engaged Himself to discharge all the obligations of God's elect, He must necessarily meet all those requirements on their behalf. The Son therefore became incarnate and subjected Himself unto the full demands of the Law and was dealt with according to its high spirituality and rigorous justice. First He honored the perceptive part of the Covenant by rendering a perfect obedience to every detail. But that of itself would make no satisfaction for His people's transgressions nor afford ally expression of the Divine displeasure against sin; and therefore after a life spent in unremittingly doing the will of God, must also needs lay down His life. "Such a high Priest became us, who is holy, harmless, undefiled and separate from sinners" (Heb. 7:24). His compliance with the precepts was preparatory to His enduring the penalty of the Law, when He stood at the bar of Cod in the room of the guilty, and before God as the offended Lawgiver and angry Judge, executing upon Him what was due them.

Some are likely to still have a difficulty at this point. How could Christ be the gift of God's love if that Gift had for its first end the removing of His judicial "enmity" and the placating of His wrath? But such a difficulty arises from failure to distinguish between things that differ: between God in His essential and in His official character, between the elect as He views them in Christ and as He sees them as the fallen descendants of Adam. To affirm that God both loved and hated them at the same time and in the same respect, would indeed be a palpable contradiction; but this we do not. God loved His people in respect of His eternal purpose, but He was angry against them with respect to His violated Law and provoked justice by sin. There is no inconsistency whatever between God's loving the saints with a love of good-will and the hindrances to the outflow and the effects of it which their sins and His holiness interposed in the way of peace and friendship. Though the holiness of God's nature, the righteousness of His government, and the veracity of His Word, placed barriers in the way of His taking sinners into communion with Himself without full satisfaction being made to His Law, yet they did not hinder His love from providing the means to remove those barriers, and they were recovered from their apostasy.

"I have loved you with an everlasting love, therefore with lovingkindness have I drawn you" (Jer. 31:3); "I will call them My people, which were not My people; and her, Beloved, which was not beloved" (Rom. 9:25). It should be quite evident to every candid reader that if we are to avoid a contradiction in those two passages we must make a distinction in the interpretation of them, that in them the love of God is viewed in entirely different aspects. In other words, we must ascertain the precise meaning of the terms used. The former speaks of His paternal love or good-will towards them, the latter of His judicial favor or love of acceptance; the one concerns His eternal counsels, the other relates to His dealings with us in a time-state. The former is His love of philanthropy or benevolence, the latter of His love of approbation. The one has to do with His loving us in Christ, the other with His loving us for our own sakes—because of what the Holy Spirit wrought in us at regeneration and conversion. The one concerns our predestination, the other our reconciliation. That distinction reveals the confusion in the piece from Mr. Philpot, quoted in "The Introduction" of this series.

The same distinction has to be observed again when we contemplate God's dual attitude toward Christ, the Son of His love, whom He both loved and poured out His wrath upon — yes, and at the same time, though in entirely different relations. When the Father declared, "This is My beloved Son, in whom I am well pleased" (Matthew 3:17), He was expressing Himself paternally, as well as testifying to His approbation of both Christ's person and work. But when we are told that "It pleased the Lord to bruise Him" (Isa. 53:10) and cried "Awake, O sword, against My Shepherd and against the Man that is My Fellow, says the Lord of Hosts" (Zech. 13:7), it was as the Law-administrator or Judge He was acting. Never was God more "well pleased" with His beloved Son than when He hung upon the cross in obedience to Him (Phil 2:10), yet He withdrew from Him every effect or manifestation of His love during those three hours of awful darkness, yea, poured out His wrath upon Him as our sin-bearer, so that He exclaimed "Your wrath lies hard upon Me and You have afflicted Me with all Your waves" (Ps. 88:7).

The very men who object to God's loving and yet being antagonistic to the same person at one and the same time, perceive no antagonism between those things when they are adumbrated before their eyes and illustrated in their own experience on this lower plane. Love and anger are perfectly consistent at the same moment and may in different respects be terminated on the same subject. A father should feel a double affection or emotion toward a rebellious son. He loves him as his offspring, but is angry with him as disobedient. Have we not read of a judge who was called upon to pass sentence on his own child? Or of a military officer who was required to court-martial his son for insubordination in the ranks? Why then should we have difficulty in perceiving that, while in their lapsed state, God loved His people with a love of good-will, yet loathed and was angry with them as rebels against His government. As the injured Father He laid aside His anger, but as the Preserver of Justice He demanded full satisfaction from them or their Surety.

Equally pointless is another objection made by Socinians and Arminians, namely, that such a doctrine as we are propounding represents God as changeable, as a fickle Being—first angry and then pacified. But precisely the same objection might be well brought against repentance! If it be granted that sin is displeasing to God, then obviously He is no longer displeased when the sinner repents and He forgives him! "The atonement did not make God hate sin less than He did before, or excite feelings of compassion towards us which did not formerly exist. He loved us before He gave His Son; and sin still is, and ever will be, the object of His utmost aversion. The effect of the atonement was a change of dispensation, which is consistent with immutability of nature" (J. Dick). The fact is that God demanded an atonement because He does not change, and would not rescind or modify His Law, revoke His threatening, nor lay aside His abhorrence of sin. They who represent God as being mutable are the very ones who assert that He pardons sin without satisfaction to His justice. The precise nature of "reconciliation" can be ascertained clearly from the Levitical offerings. Unless those O. T. types were misleading, then they definitely exhibited the fact that the sacrifice of Christ pacified God, made peace and procuring His favor.. Personally we unhesitatingly adopt the words of Principal Cunningham when he said, "The whole institution of Levitical sacrifices and the place which they occupied is the Mosaic economy, were regulated and determined by a regard to the one sacrifice of Christ." Those sacrifices set forth the principles on which the effects of the Redeemer's work depended, and provide the surest and best materials for interpreting and illustrating the character and bearing of the Atonement. Those typical sacrifices demonstrated beyond any doubt that the sacrifice of Christ was vicarious and expiatory, that it was presented and accepted in the room and stead of others, that it propitiated God and averted His wrath, and therefore that it procured the exemption of His people from the penal consequences of their sins and effected their reconciliation unto God.

Earlier we quoted Numbers 16:46 in proof that "an atonement" is made in order to turn away the "wrath of the Lord;" let us now allude to further examples. "And David built there an altar unto the Lord and offered burnt offerings and peace offerings. So the Lord was entreated for the land and the plague was stayed from Israel" (2 Sam. 24:25)—the occasion being when "the anger of the Lord was kindled against Israel" because David had numbered the people (v. 1). The same incident is mentioned again in 1 Chronicles 21, where we are told that "God sent an angel unto Jerusalem to destroy it" (v. 15), which was in addition to the "pestilence" or "plague" which slew seventy thousand Israelites mentioned in 2 Samuel 24. Then, after David had built an altar there unto the Lord and had offered appropriate sacrifices and "called upon the Lord," and He had "answered him from heaven by fire upon the altar" (in token of His acceptance of the same), we read that "the Lord commanded the angel, and he put up His sword again into the sheath" (vv. 26, 27). What anointed eye can fail to see in that incident a vivid anticipation and adumbration of what occurred at Calvary. There is a striking case of alienated friends being reconciled by means of sacrifice recorded in Job 42. "The Lord said to Eliphaz the Temanite, My wrath is kindled against you and against your two friends, for you have not spoken of Me the thing that is right, as My servant Job has. Therefore take unto you now seven bulls and seven rams and go to My servant Job and offer up for yourselves a burnt offering, and My servant Job shall pray for you, for him will I accept, lest I deal with you after your folly" (vv. 7, 8). Upon which Owen pointed out:

"The offenders are Eliphaz and his two friends, the offence is their folly in not speaking aright of God. The issue of the breach is, that the wrath or anger of God was towards them; reconciliation is the turning away of that wrath; the means by which this was done, appointed by God, is the sacrifice of Job for atonement. This then is that which we ascribe to the death of Christ when we say that as a sacrifice we were reconciled to God. Having made God our Enemy by sin, Christ by His sacrifice appeased His wrath and brought us into favor again with God."

The more closely that example in Job 42:7, 8 is examined the more clearly should we perceive the meaning and significance of the antitype. There was a declaration of God's anger against those three men, yet also a revelation of His love to them, by directing them to the means by which His anger might be put away and they restored to His favor. Clearly, He had good-will unto them before He directed them what to do, yet He was not then reconciled to them—otherwise there was no need of an atonement for appeasing Him. There was a cloud upon God's face, yet the sun of mercy peeped out through that cloud: as He acquaints them with His anger, so He also shows them the way to pacify it. Though His wrath was truly kindled, yet He was ready for it to be quenched by the means of His prescribing. God could not find complacency in them till He was reconciled to them. In acting on their behalf, Job was a type of Christ, whose propitiatory sacrifice God both appointed and accepted.

Chapter 17
Its Meaning-Concluded

A beautiful type of what we have contended for in these articles is found in Genesis 8. In the preceding chapter we behold the fearful judgment of God under the antediluvian world because of its wickedness—solemn figure of what our Sinbearer endured for us as He was "made a curse," when He cried "deep calls unto deep at the noise of Your waterspouts. All Your waves and billows are gone over Me" (Ps. 42:7). After the storm of wrath had done its awful work, Noah (who represented the company of God's elect in the place of safety, exempted from the Divine vengeance) opened the window of the ark and "sent forth a dove." Later, he sent her forth again, and "the dove came unto him in the evening, and lo, in her mouth was an olive leaf"—"the emblem of peace" (v. 11). Christ was the Pacifier of God and He is "our Peace" (Eph. 2:14). He is the former, because He is "to make reconciliation for iniquity" (Dan. 9:24). He is the latter, because He has satisfied every claim of God upon us. Therefore He designated "shiloh" (Gen. 49:10)—an appellation which signifies "the Peacemaker"—and "the Prince of peace" (Isa. 9:6).

Reconciliation was one of the effects which resulted from the atonement which Christ made unto God, and in our last we pointed out that the simplest and surest way of ascertaining the significance of the antitype is to attend closely to the types. Now the Levitical offerings were not designed to produce any change within the offerer, but were presented for the express purpose of placating and propitiating God Himself. The Israelites did not offer them with the object of turning away their own enmity from Jehovah, but rather to turn away His anger from them, and since the sacrifices which they presented were emblems of the one great Sacrifice of Christ, it necessarily follows that the chief end of His oblation was to divert God's wrath from those on whose behalf it was made. The great fact—the terrible thing—brought out by this doctrine is, that God is the offended Party; while the central fact—the grand thing—proclaimed by it is, that Christ is the all-sufficient Pacifier of God.

We are afraid that some of our friends will feel that we have drawn out these articles on the meaning of Reconciliation to a rather wearisome length, and for their sakes we regret that it was necessary for us to do so. But while they may not have been troubled by the errors we have refuted or the objections answered, yet a considerable number of our readers have been much bewildered by them, and therefore as a servant of God it was part of our duty to "prepare a way, take up the stumbling-block out of the way of My people" (Isa. 57:14). At the beginning of our first article on this branch of the subject we stated that we proposed to do much more than barely furnish a definition of the word reconciliation. Having sought to make good that promise, we must now look more closely at the term itself and ponder carefully how it is used in Scripture.

Reconciliation presupposes alienation and therefore it results from the removal of hindrance to concord, and is the act of uniting parties which have been at variance. It is the putting an end to strife and changing enemies into friends. Sin has placed God and man apart from one another—all harmony between them being disrupted. Therefore satisfaction must be made for sin before peace can be restored. Consequently, to be "reconciled to God by the death of His Son" is to be restored to His favor. It is the reconciliation of the King to His rebellious subjects, of the Judge to offenders against Himself. To reconcile is to bring to agreement, to unite those who were divided, to restore to unity and amity. Reconciliation is a relation, a mutual one. On God's part it denotes a change from wrath to favor; on ours, from one of contempt and opposition to loyal and loving obedience. It is therefore a change from hostility to tranquility, from strife to fellowship.

The "peace" which Christ procured for His people was effected through chastisement. "But He was wounded for our transgressions, He was bruised for our iniquities: the chastisement of our peace was upon Him, and with His stripes we are healed" (Isa. 53:5). There are three things here. First, the history of Christ's sufferings: set out by wounds, bruises, chastisements and stripes—the expressions being multiplied to impress our hearts more deeply. The cause of those sufferings: our transgressions and iniquities—the difference between sins of commission and omission. The fruits or benefits of them: peace and healing—a summary of the objective and subjective results of them. The punishment due our sins was borne by Christ that we might have "peace with God." "He, by submitting to those chastisements, slew the enmity and settled an amity between God and man; He made peace by the blood of His cross. Whereas by sin we were become odious to God's holiness and obnoxious to His justice, through Christ God is reconciled to us, and not only forgives our sins and saves us from ruin, but takes us into friendship and fellowship with Himself" (Matt. Henry).

"The chastisement of our peace was upon Him" is explained by "therefore being justified by faith we have peace with God through our Lord Jesus Christ" (Rom. 5:1), where the reference is not to a state of heart, but to a relation with God. "Peace with God" does not have reference to anything that is subjective, but only to what is objective: not to an inward peace of conscience (though that follows if repentance and faith are in exercise), nor to that "peace of God which passes all understanding" which keeps our hearts and minds through Christ Jesus (Phil. 4:7), but to "peace with God"—in other words, to reconciliation. It means we are no longer the objects of His displeasure, and have no more reason to dread the Divine vengeance. It is that blessed relation which results from the expiation of our sins: because Christ endured the penalty of them, we are no longer God's enemies in the objective sense, but the subjects of His favor. Every one that is "justified" does not enjoy peace of conscience (though he should); but every justified person has "peace with God" (whether he knows it or not) for His quarrel against him is ended, Christ having made God (judicially) his Friend.

There is an interesting passage in 1 Samuel 29 which makes quite clear the meaning of this controverted word and shows it signifies the very opposite of what the Socinians understand by it. While a fugitive from Saul, David and a company of his devoted followers found refuge in Gath of Philistia, where Achish its "king" ("lord" or "chief") showing' kindness to him (1 Sam. 27:2,3). While he was there, the Philistines planned a concerted attack upon Israel, and Achish proposed that David and his men should accompany him (28:1,2), to which he acceded. But when the other lords of the Philistines discovered the presence of David and his men among the forces of Achish they were angry, for they feared he would not be loyal to their cause, saying "Let him not go down to battle with us, lest in the battle he be an adversary to us, for wherewith shall he reconcile himself unto his master? Shall it not be with the heads of these men?" (29:4). "Reconcile" there means not, How shall he remove his own anger against Saul, but Saul's against him. How shall he restore himself again to his master's favor.

The great thing to be clear upon in connection with reconciliation is, that it is objective in its significance and action. In other words, it terminates upon the object and not upon the subject. The offender does not reconcile himself, but the person whom he has wronged, and that, by making suitable amends or reparation. Socinians and Arminians have sought to make capital out of the fact that in the Scriptures it is never said in so many words that "God is reconciled to us," but that they uniformly speak of "our being reconciled to Him." The explanation of that is very simple. God is the Party offended, we the parties offending, and it is always the offending party who is said to be the one reconciled and not the offended. Another clear proof is found in Matthew 5:23 and 24, "Therefore if you bring your gift to the altar and there remember that your brother has aught against you, Leave there your gift before the altar and go your way, first be reconciled to your brother, and then come and offer your gift."

There we have a brother offended, a grievance against one who has injured him. Aware of that, the duty of the wrong-doer is clear, he must do all in his power to right the wrong, remove the ground of grievance and secure amity between them, for until that is done a holy God will not receive his worship. "Be reconciled to your brother" does not refer to any state of mind or feeling in the emotions of the wrong-doer, but signifies, makes reparation to him, pacify him. The offender is not bidden to lay aside his own enmity, though that is understood, but is to go to the aggrieved one and seek to turn away his wrath from him, by means of an humble and frank confession of his sin, in that way gaining an entrance again into his good-will and favor. Nothing could be plainer. "Be reconciled to your brother" means, put right what is wrong, conciliate him and thus heal the breach between you which is hindering your communion with God.

Before going further we want the reader to be thoroughly clear upon what has been said. At first sight "with which he shall reconcile himself unto his master?" (1 Sam. 29:4) seems to mean David's laying aside his own ill-will and healing a breach he had made. Yet the very opposite is Its actual sense. It was Saul who hated him! The Philistines feared that David and his men would slay them and take their heads to Saul and thus cause him to look favorably again on David. So too a careless reader of Matthew 5:24 would conclude "be reconciled to your brother" signifies that the one addressed was the offended party, who needed to change his own feelings toward the other. But again, the very opposite is the case. It. was the brother who had something against him, because of a wrong he had done him, and thus the one addressed is the offender and so "be reconciled to your brother" means, go and confess your fault and appease him. The sense of the words is the reverse of their sound.

Matthew 5:24 contains the initial occurrence of our term, and in accordance with the law of first mention intimates how the word is used throughout the N. T. It definitely establishes the fact that to be reconciled to another connotes the pacifying of the offended party so that a state of concord is the result, and it has precisely the same force Whenever it is used in connection with God. We are reconciled to Him as we are to an injured brother—reparation having been made to Him, we are restored to His favor. This is plain, again, from the next occurrence of the word in Romans 5:10. There the whole context makes it plain that God is the offended one, that the cause of His indignation against us was our sins, that Christ offered a sufficient satisfaction unto Him, thereby removing His wrath and conciliating Him unto us. Christ's sacrifice averted God's displeasure as our Governor and Judge. His relation and judicial attitude toward us was changed by a great historical transaction. "For if, when we were enemies, we were reconciled to God by the death of His Son, much more, being reconciled, we shall be saved by His life."

Here then is the issue. Do those words "reconciled to God by the death of His Son" signify that Christ pacified God so that He has laid aside His judicial wrath against His people, or, that Christ moves us to lay aside our enmity and hostility against God? We contend that it means the former, that, in the language of Wm. Shedd, "Here the reconciliation is described from the side of the offending party—man is said to be reconciled. Yet this does not mean the subjective reconciliation of the sinner toward God, but the objective reconciliation of God towards the sinner. For the preceding verse speaks of God as a Being from whose wrath the believer is saved by the death of Christ. This shows that the reconciliation effected by Christ's atoning death is that of the

Divine anger against sin." The reconciliation which is here mentioned is prior to conversion and therefore quite distinct from conversion (which is when we lay aside our enmity), for occurred when Christ laid down His life for us and not when the Holy Spirit quickened us.

We submit that, from the following considerations, "reconciled to God by the death of His Son" refers to God's reconciliation to His people. First, from the relation which that clause bears to "while we were yet sinners Christ died for us" (v. 8). The one being parallel with the other. Why did Christ die for sinners? Was it not in order to deliver them from the curse of God and to secure everlasting felicity for them! Second, from the fact that the same expression is described as "being justified by His blood" (v. 9), for in the previous verse the apostle speaks of Christ's dying for sinners or rebels against God. The consequence of His death is that believers are "justified by His blood" and, as every Scripturally-enlightened person knows, to be "justified" is to be received into God's favor (being His acceptance of us, and not ours of Him), which is precisely what "reconciliation" is. Third, from the fact that the "when we were enemies" refers to the relation we stood in to God—the objects of His displeasure. "Sinners . . . justified by His blood" and "enemies . . . reconciled to God by Christ's death" correspond exactly the one to the other.

Fourth, from the obvious sense of the verse the apostle is arguing (as his "if" and "much more" shows) from the less to the greater. If when we had no love for God, Christ's sacrifice procured His favor, much more, now that we are converted, will His mediation on high deliver us from our sins as Christians. Fifth, from the reconciliation being ascribed to Christ's death, which was definitely and solely Godward. Had it been the removing of our enmity and turning us to love God, it had been attributed to Christ's Spirit. Sixth, from the obvious meaning of the term: as we have shown from 1 Samuel 29:4 and Matthew 5:23,24, it is the injured party who is the one needing to be reconciled to the offender. Seventh, from the fact that our reconciliation is something which is tendered to us. "we have now received the reconciliation" (v. 11): we received the reconciliation effected by Christ and then presented for our acceptance in the Gospel. It would be the height of absurdity to say that we "received" the laying down of the weapons of our warfare against God. "All things are of God, who has reconciled us to Himself by Jesus Christ, and has given us the ministry of reconciliation. To wit, that God was in Christ reconciling the world unto Himself, not imputing their trespasses unto them" (2 Cor. 5:18,19). That His reconciling of "us" "the world" unto Himself refers to God's placation unto and favor toward us is clear. First, because it was effected by "Jesus Christ" and therefore signifies the removing of God's anger. Second, because had it meant His work of grace within us, subduing our enmity, it had said "God is in Christ" or more precisely "God by His Spirit is reconciling the world unto Himself." Third, because "God was in Christ reconciling the world unto Himself" means, God appointed and anointed Christ to procure His reconciliation. He was in Christ as the Surety—God out of Christ is "a consuming fire" to the wicked. Fourth, because the term is here formally defined as "not imputing their trespasses unto them," which is God's act and not the creature's—"not imputing" etc. means, not dealing with us as justice required for our sins, on account of Christ's atonement. Fifth, because the "ministry" and "word of reconciliation" was committed to the apostles—that is, the Atonement was the grand theme of their preaching (1 Cor. 2:2). Sixth, because on that ground sinners are exhorted to be "reconciled to God" (v. 20). Since God has changed His attitude unto you, change yours toward Him. Seventh, because our sins were imputed to Christ, and since He atoned for them His righteousness is imputed to us (v. 21).

"And that He (Christ Jesus) might be reconciled both unto God in one body by the cross, having slain the enmity by it, and came and preached peace to you" (Eph. 2:16,1 7). As these verses and their context will come before us again we will confine ourselves now to that which concerns our present purpose. The "both" refers to Jews and Gentiles "in one body" signifies the Savior's humanity—compare "in the body of His flesh" (Col. 1:22). "By the cross" speaks of a definite historical action in the past, and not a protracted process throughout the whole Gospel era. "Having slain the enmity by it" signifies not that between Jew and Gentile (which is mentioned in the former verse), but of God's judicial disapprobation against both. This is confirmed in the next verse, where the "preached peace" means preached the peace made with God, as the "access" in v. 18 clearly indicates. Having effected peace, Christ, after His resurrection, ministerially (2 Cor. 5:18-20) announced it.

"And having made peace through the blood of His cross, by Him to reconcile all things unto Himself" (Col. 1:20). This passage we also hope to enter into more fully in a later chapter, suffice it now to point out that: since peace was "made" there must previously have been hostility, and since that peace was made through "the blood of His cross," then the shedding of it was the placating of God, by offering a satisfaction to His violated Law. In Scripture man is never represented as making reconciliation Godward. It is what he experiences or embraces, and not what he makes. It should also be pointed out that never is reconciliation ascribed to the risen Christ, any more than that we are "justified in a risen Christ." It is His blood that justifies (Rom. 5:9), which brings redemption (Eph. 1:7), by which we are brought nigh (Eph. 2:13), which sanctifies (Heb. 13:12), which gives us the right of approach to God (Heb. 10:19).

We have been contending for a great truth and not merely for a word or syllable. When Socinians object that Scripture nowhere says in so many words that "God is reconciled to us," they are guilty of mere trifling, for equivalent expressions most certainly do occur. If it be admitted that sin is displeasing to God and that His vengeance is proclaimed against the sinner, it must also be admitted that if God's anger has been turned away from sinners by a propitiatory sacrifice, then He must have been reconciled to them. "He who once threatened to punish another but has since pardoned him and now treats him with kindness, has certainly been reconciled to him" (J. Dick). The emphasis is thrown upon our reconciliation to God because we were first in the breach. We fell out with God, before He fell out with us; and because the averseness is on our side. The Gospel makes known His willingness to receive us (because of Christ's sacrifice) if we are prepared to cease our fighting against Him.

If it be asked, Was God reconciled to all the elect and they to Him the moment Christ cried "it is finished," the answer is both yes and no. We must distinguish between (1) reconciliation in the eternal purpose of God (2) as it was effected by Christ (3) as it is offered to us in the Gospel (4) as it actually becomes ours when we believe.

Chapter 18
Its Scope

Who are the ones from whom the wrath of God has been turned away and to whom He is reconciled? Who are they whose enmity against God has been slam and are actually reconciled to Him? Though those questions are quite distinct, yet are they intimately allied the one to the other; though they relate to separate transactions, yet really they are but parts of one whole. Those inquiries signify much the same as though we asked, On whose behalf did Christ satisfy God? Who are the ones who must eventually partake of the saving benefits of His mediation? Theologians have been by no means agreed in the answers they have returned, for those questions necessarily raise the fundamental issues which have divided Christendom into Calvinists and Arminians. That issue may be more clearly drawn if we make our question yet more definite and specific. For whom did Christ act as Surety and Substitute? For all the human race, or for the Church only? What was the scope of the Everlasting Covenant? Did it embrace the whole of Adam's posterity or did it respect only a chosen remnant of them? Who are the ones who will eternally benefit from the great Propitiation? Probably most of our readers would reply, all who truly exercise faith in the blood of Christ. Nor would their answer be incorrect, though it would be more satisfactory to frame it from the Divine side of things rather than from the human side. As it is made from the latter, we have to push the inquiry further back and ask, Who are the ones who savingly trust in the blood of Christ? Not all who hear the Gospel, for even the majority of them turn a deaf ear unto it, so that its preachers have to exclaim "who has believed our report?" (Isa. 53:1). Perhaps the reader will return answer to this last inquiry, Those who are willing to receive Christ as their Lord and Savior. Correct: but who are they? By nature none are willing to do that. "No man can come to Me except the Father which has sent Me draw him" (John 6:44) that is overcome his reluctance. "Your people shall be willing in the day of Your power" (Ps. 110:3) gives the Scriptural answer. From the Divine side, the reply to our opening question is, Those on whose behalf the great propitiation was made— God's people.

If there were no explicit statements in Scripture there are many implicit ones in it from which we may determine with certainty the precise scope of reconciliation. The ordination, impetration, (accomplishment) and application (bestowal of the benefits) of Christ's work must of necessity be coextensive. We say "of necessity" for otherwise we should be affirming that the ways of God were "unequal"—inconsistent, inharmonious. What God the Father purposed that God the Son effected, and what He effected God the Spirit applies and bestows. The only other possible alternative is to predicate a defeated Father, a disappointed Christ, and a disgraced Holy Spirit—which is the kind of "God" the Arminians believe in. But there are clear and decisive statements in Scripture which reveal to us the extent of the Father's purpose and the scope of the Son's purchase.. Says the Father concerning His Son, "for the transgression of My people was He stricken" (Isa. 53:8). "You shall call His name Jesus for He shall save His people from their sins" (Matthew 1:21). Said the Son "the good Shepherd gives His life for the sheep" (John 10:11)—and not the goats.

The idea of a mere conditional "provision" for the reconciliation of all mankind is a theory which sets aside the absolute purpose of God respecting the work of Christ. That theory renders of no account the promises of God concerning the death of His Son, for by pleading that it made the salvation of all men possible, in actuality it denies that it made the salvation of any man certain. God the Father promised His Son a definite reward upon the successful accomplishment of His work. "He shall see His seed, He shall prolong His days, and the pleasure of the Lord shall prosper in His hands. He shall see of the travail of His soul, and shall be satisfied" (Isa. 53:10,11). How could He be satisfied if any of those for whom He was their sin-offering were finally lost? "By the blood of Your covenant I have sent forth Your prisoners out of the pit in which is no water" (Zech. 9:11). But what security could there be for the fulfillment of those promises if no infallible provision was made for the regeneration of those persons, and instead, everything was left contingent on the wills of men!

Consider the special character in which Christ died. "Now the God of peace that brought again from the dead that great Shepherd of the sheep through the blood of the everlasting covenant make you perfect in every good work to do His will, working in you that which is well pleasing in His sight through Jesus Christ" (Heb. 13:20, 21). In serving as the Shepherd Christ died for the sheep and not for the goats. Said He "I am the good Shepherd, the good Shepherd gives His life for the sheep" (John 10:11), and mark it well, they are represented as being His "sheep" before they believe. "And other sheep I have (as the Father's gift and charge), which are not of this (Jewish) fold. Them also I must bring, and they shall hear My voice (when the Spirit quickens them) and they shall be one fold, one Shepherd" (John 10:16). But all men pertain not to the "sheep" of Christ: said He to those who rejected Him "you believe not, because you are not of My sheep" (John 10:26). The "sheep" are the elect, God's chosen people. Christ Himself declared that His "flock" is a little one (Luke 12:32), and therefore not the whole human race.

Christ laid down His life as a Husband. "Your Maker is your Husband, The Lord of hosts is His name, and your Redeemer the Holy One of Israel, The God of the whole earth shall He be called" (Isa. 54:5). Note this comes right after Isaiah 53! Equally clear is the teaching of the N. T.: "Husbands love your wives even as Christ also loved the Church and gave Himself for it, that He might sanctify and cleanse it with the washing of water by the Word, that He might present it to Himself a glorious Church" (Eph. 5:25-27). As the Husband He died for His Wife (Rev. 19:7). It was His love which caused Him to do so, and it was a discriminating love—set upon a definite object. And again we say, note this well, that the Church for whom Christ gave Himself is not here viewed as a regenerated and believing company, but as one whose members needed to be "sanctified and cleansed." He died not for believers as such, but "while we were yet enemies" (Rom. 5:10). Nor can Christ be foiled of His design, for He will yet present the Church to Himself "a glorious Church" and not a mutilated one—as it would be if any of its members were finally missing.

Christ served as a Surety. He is expressly denominated the "Surety" of a better covenant (Heb. 7:22), and unless we are prepared to believe that Christ is defeated in His undertaking, then we cannot extend the persons for whom He was Sponsor beyond those who are finally saved. To speak of a "surety" failing is surely a contradiction in terms. If he does not, with certainty, prevent loss how can he be a "surety!" To remove any doubt on this point Scripture declares "He shall not fail" (Isa. 42:4). He shall yet triumphantly exclaim, "Behold land the children which God has given Me" (Heb. 2:13). Christ's suretyship was no fictitious one, but real. Under that office He engaged Himself to make satisfaction for certain people, and by His engagement to cancel all their debt and fulfill all righteousness in their stead, and since He has perfectly performed this, as much and as truly as though those for whom He acted had themselves endured all the punishment due their sins and had rendered to the Law all the obedience it required, the consequence is clear and inescapable. Those for whom He engaged and satisfied are they who are actually saved from their sins and pronounced righteous by God, and none else.

The very nature of Christ's satisfaction determines to a demonstration those who are the beneficiaries of it. It was a federal work. There was both a covenant and legal oneness between Christ and those for whom He transacted. The Savior stood as the Bondsman of a particular people, and if a single one of those whose obligations He assumed received not a full discharge, then Divine justice would be reduced to a farce. It was a substitutionary work. Christ acted not only on the behalf of, but in the stead of, those who had been given to Him by the Father; therefore all those whose sins He bore must of necessity have their sins remitted—God cannot punish twice. First the Substitute and then the subject. It was a legal work. Every requirement of the Divine law, both perceptive and punitive was fulfilled by Christ. Therefore all for whom He acted must receive the reward of His obedience, which is everlasting life. It was a priestly work: He presented Himself as an offering to God, and since God accepted His sacrifice its efficacy and merits must be imputed unto all those for whom it was offered.

The intercession of Christ defines the scope of His atoning sacrifice. The death and intercession of Christ are co-extensive. Define the extent of the one and you determine the extent of the other. That must be so, for the latter is based upon the former and is expressive of its grand design. Scripture is too plain on this point to allow of any uncertainty or mistake. "Who shall lay anything to the charge of God's elect? It is God that justifies. Who is he that condemns? It is Christ that dies, yea rather that is risen again, who is even at the right hand of God, who also makes intercession for us" (Rom. 8:33,34). "Wherefore He is able also to save those to the uttermost that come unto God by Him, seeing He ever lives to make intercession for them" (Heb. 7:25). To make assurance doubly sure on this important matter our great High Priest has expressly declared "I pray not for the world" (John 17:9). Thus there must be a "world" for whom He did not die. For whom did He say He prays? "But for them which You have given Me, for they are Yours."

There are those who suppose that the doctrine of particular redemption detracts from the goodness and grace of God and from the merits of Christ, and therefore conclude it cannot be true. But this mistake becomes manifest if we examine the alternative view. Surely it is not honoring the goodness and grace of God to affirm that the whole human race has nothing but a bare possibility of salvation, yea, a great probability of perishing, notwithstanding all that He has done to save them. Yet that is exactly what is involved in the Arminian scheme, which avers that Christ died to make the salvation of all men possible. That love and grace must indeed be greater which infallibly secures the salvation of some, even though a minority, than that which only provides a mere contingency for all. To us it seems to indicate coldness and indifference for God to leave it a second time to the mutable will of man to secure his salvation, when man's will at its best estate ruined Adam and all his posterity.

If infinite love and goodness was shown to all men in giving Christ to die for them, would it not also give the Holy Spirit to all of them to effectually apply salvation—to subdue their lusts, overcome their enmity, make them willing to comply with the terms of the Gospel and fix their adherence to it? The Scriptures set forth the love and kindness of God as one which makes not merely a bare offer of salvation to sinners, but as actually saving "by the washing of regeneration and renewing of the Holy Spirit" (Titus 3:4,5). The Word of Truth declares that the "God who is rich in mercy, for His great love with which He loved us, even when we were dead in sins, has quickened us together with Christ. By grace you are saved" (Eph. 2:4,5). How would God's love and mercy toward men appear if He gave Christ for all only to make it possible that they might be saved, and then left by far the greater part of them ignorant of even the knowledge of salvation, and a large number of those who are acquainted with it, not made willing to embrace it in a day of His power?

But over against all that has been set forth in the above paragraphs some will quote "God was in Christ reconciling the world unto Himself" (2 Cor. 5:19), and suppose that by so doing they have completely overthrown the whole of what has been brought out. But surely the candid reader can perceive for himself that what has been presented in the whole of the foregoing is not the theories of Calvinistic theologians, nor the subtle reasoning of metaphysicians, but rather the plain and simple teaching of Holy Writ itself. Thus, whatever 2 Corinthians 5:19 does or does not mean, it cannot annul all the other passages which have been appealed to. God's Word does not contradict itself, and it is positively sinful for any of us to pit those verses we like against those we dislike. If we humbly look to God for wisdom and patiently search His Word, it should be found that 2 Corinthians 5:19 can be interpreted in perfect harmony with all other Scripture, and that, without any wresting or straining, namely, by the same principles of exegesis which we apply to all other passages.

Like every other portion of the Word 2 Corinthians 5:29 needs interpreting, by which is meant, its terms explained. Perhaps some demur and say, No explanation is necessary. The verse says what it means and means what it says. We fully agree that it means what it says, but are we sure that we understand what it means? The meaning of a verse is not obtainable from the sound of its words, but rather from the sense of them, and that can only be ascertained from the way in which they are used and by comparing other passages where the same subject is in view. If we take general and indefinite terms and understand them in an unlimited sense, then we soon land ourselves in the grossest absurdities. For instance, when the apostle said, "I am made all things to all men that I might by all means save some" (1 Cor. 9:22), he surely did not include duplicity, unfaithfulness, or the use of carnal means. When we are exhorting "in everything give thanks" (1 Thess. 5:18) we must exclude a course of sinning, for God condemns the one who blesses himself in a wicked way (Deut. 29:19).

Now just as all things and all means in 1 Corinthians 9:22 are general expressions, which other passages (and considerations), require us to qualify, so the term "world" in 2 Corinthians 5:19 is an indefinite one, and its scope is to be determined by the tenor of the passage in which it occurs and its meaning understood in a way harmonious with the teaching of Holy Writ. Anyone who has taken the trouble to make a concordant study of the word "world" will have discovered that it is a most ambiguous term, that it has widely different significations in Scripture, and therefore no definition of its extent can be framed from the bare mention of the term itself. Sometimes the "world" has reference to the material world, and sometimes to its inhabitant; it is used in both these senses in John 1:10. In some cases it refers to only a very small part of its inhabitant, as in "show Yourself to the world" (John 17:4) and "the world is gone after Him" (John 12:19), where the references are to only a portion of Judea, and cannot signify "all mankind." Other passages will be noticed in the article which immediately follows, where further proof is given that the term "world" is far from being used with one uniform significance, and that it rarely means the whole human race.

Chapter 19
Its Scope-Continued

Sometimes the "world" signifies the Gentiles in general, in contrast from the Jews in particular, as in "If the fall of them (unbelieving Israel) be the riches of the world," which is explained in the next clause—"and the diminishing of them (Jews) the riches of the Gentiles," and "if the casting away of them be the reconciling of the world" (Rom. 11:12,15). In other places the "world" refers to the non-elect, as in "the Spirit of truth whom the world cannot receive, because it sees Him not, neither knows Him" (John 14:17), and "I pray not for the world." In Luke 2:1 it is the profane world that is in view: "there went out a decree from Caesar Augustus that the world should be taxed"—yet even that included only those parts of the earth which were subject to the Romans: whereas in John 15:18-25 it is the professing world—it was the religious sections of Judaism Christ alluded to when He said "if the world hate you, you know that it hated Me before it hated you."

In Romans 4:13 the "world" signifies the Church, for when Abram is there said to be "the heir of the world" it manifestly expresses the same idea as when he is termed "the father of all them that believe" and "the father of many nations" (Rom. 4:11,18). When Christ said of Himself "the Bread of God is He which comes down from heaven and gives (not merely offers) life unto the world" (John 6:33). He must have meant His Church, for all who are not members of it remain dead in sins until the end of their careers. We have just as much right to cite the words "the world knew Him not" (John 1:10) as a proof that not a single member of Adam's race knew Christ—when aged Simeon did (Luke 1:28-30)—as we have to argue that "Behold the Lamb of God, which takes away the sin of the world" (John 1:29) means the sin of all mankind. When it is said "the whole world lies in the Wicked one" (1 John 5:19) it cannot mean every one alive on earth, for all the saints are excluded; and "all the world wondered after the Beast" (Rev. 13:4) excepts the faithful remnant!

It should be quite clear to any candid and careful reader that, taken by itself, the word "world" in 2 Corinthians 5:19 supplies no proof and furnishes nothing decisive in enabling us to determine the scope or extent of reconciliation, for that term is an indefinite and general one: more so than usual here, for in the Greek there is no definite article—literally "reconciling world unto Himself." It should also be obvious that this verse calls for a careful and detailed exposition: pointing out its relation to what precedes and its connection with what follows, seeking also to define each separate expression in it. To the best of our ability we will now set ourselves to this task, and in so doing seek to show that everything in it and the setting in which it is found obliges us to regard the "world" reconciled to God as connoting His Church, and not the entire human family.

Under our next main division when we shall deal with our reception of the Reconciliation, or our response to the Gospel call "Be reconciled to God" (2 Cor. 5:20), we hope to enter more fully into the scope of the whole context (from v. 11 onwards): suffice it now to begin at verse 17. Nor shall we even attempt an exposition of that much misunderstood verse, rather will we limit ourselves to its central truth, namely, that of regeneration. "Therefore if any man is in Christ he is a new creature"—literally "a new creation" (v. 17). That is, if anyone is favored to be "in Christ," first, by federal constitution or legal representation, then it will sooner or later follow that he is "in Christ," second, by vital union or regeneration. Whatever is meant by "old things are passed away; behold, all things are become new" no explanation of those words can possibly be right if it clashes with Romans 7:21-25 and Galatians 5:17, for Scripture is perfectly harmonious. "And all things are of God who has reconciled us to Himself by Jesus Christ." When expounding the "all things are of God" Chas. Hodge rightly pointed out that, "this is not spoken of the universe as proceeding from God as its Author, nor does it refer to the providential agency of God by which all events are controlled. The meaning is: 'but all is of God,' that is the entire change of which he had been speaking. The new creation experienced by those in Christ is 'out of God' (Greek), proceeding from Him as its efficient cause. It is His work." Proof that it is His work and that "God" here refers to the Father in His official character, appears in what immediately follows: "who has reconciled us to Himself by Jesus Christ." But that last clause does something more than supply evidence that the glorious work of regeneration issues from the Father as its originating source. It also explains to us the meritorious cause by which the new creation is brought into existence— regeneration is the effect of reconciliation.

The connection then between verses 17 and 18 is plain. Having spoken of the new creation in the former, the apostle proceeded to point out the legal foundation on which that new creation rests, namely, God's having been pacified by the work of His Son and that work having purchased rich blessings for His people. It is not simply as our Maker, but as a reconciled God, that He quickens His people into newness of life. On verses 17 and 18 the eminent Puritan, Stephen Charnock declared, "God is first the God of peace before He is the God of sanctification: 'and the very God of peace sanctify you wholly' (1 Thess. 5:23). The destruction of the enmity of our nature (against Him) was founded upon the removing of enmity in God (against us). There had been no sanctification of our natures had there not been a reconciliation of our persons." Thus, there had been no regenerating of us by God until He had been reconciled to us. "All the powerful effects and operations of the Gospel in the hearts of men are from God as reconciled by Christ, not from God as Creator" (Charnock).

What has just been before us in the immediate context of 2 Corinthians 5:19 provides a clear index to the scope of reconciliation, being of equal extent with the new creation! It may be stated either way: the ones whom God regenerates are those to whom He has been reconciled; all to whom He was reconciled, in due course He makes new creatures. If the one is universal, the other is; if the one is limited, the other must be. "And has given us the ministry of reconciliation" (v. 18). The "us" refers first to the apostles, and second to all whom God has specially called and qualified to-act as His heralds. "The ministry of reconciliation" is but another name for the proclamation of the Gospel, except that it is more specific, having in view that particular aspect of the Gospel which is concerned with the doctrine of reconciliation. Exactly what that consists of in its essential elements is stated in verses 19-21. First, "To wit (or 'namely') that God was in Christ reconciling the world unto Himself" (v. 19).

The relation of verse 19 to verse 18 is also quite clear. In the former the apostle said "All things are of God, who has reconciled us to Himself by Jesus Christ," which signifies (as shown in an earlier article) has turned away His wrath from His fallen people and received them into His favor by virtue of the mediation of His Son. But here he informs us, that transaction was not one which began of late to be done by Him, but rather had engaged His mind and will in His eternal counsels. "God was in Christ reconciling the world unto Himself." As the Church was in Christ from everlasting, as her Surety and Head, so God was in Him from everlasting as His ambassador, making peace for those who had revolted against Him. The reference is not to a present process by which God is little by little winning the world back into allegiance with Himself, but to something actually accomplished. God is already propitiated. "God in Christ" signifies the covenant-God of His people, for out of Christ "our God is a consuming fire" (Heb. 12:29). "God was in Christ" speaks then in the language of the "everlasting covenant," and that embraced none but the elect.

Definite light is thrown upon what "world" it was unto which God is reconciled by ascertaining the force of that clause "God was in Christ reconciling" it. In His ancient designs He formed the purpose of reconciliation in, by and through the Mediator. The identical idea is conveyed whether it be said we are "in Christ" or God was "in Christ acting toward us," namely that He designed to show favor unto us as a covenant God. God never was and never will be "in Christ" toward any other persons but His Church. Redemption was not the work of the Son only. The Father appointed the Mediator, receiving the stipulated price from Him, and imputes the full value of it to His believing people. The Savior distinctly affirmed "the Father is in Me" (John 10:38). As the elect were in Christ mystically, federally, legally, the Father was in Him authoritatively and efficiently as His Plenipotentiary. Yet the ultimate reference is to God's being in Christ imminently by His eternal decree.

"God was in Christ reconciling the world unto Himself, not imputing their trespasses unto them." It is in that last clause we have the most decisive proof of all that the "world" there cannot possibly signify mankind in general, for most certainly God does impute their trespasses unto all who are without Christ. The great problem which confronted the Divine government was how sin could be remitted without righteousness being compromised, but since God has received full satisfaction to His broken law, He has laid aside His official wrath and justice can no longer clamor for punishment. The pardon of sin is one of the main branches and fruits of reconciliation. Not to impute sin is to forgive it. "Blessed is he whose transgression is forgiven whose sin is covered. Blessed is the man unto whom the Lord imputes not iniquity" (Ps. 32:1,2). Here then is the "world" to which God is reconciled—the pardoned, the justified, the elect (Rom. 8:33).

Not only do the verses preceding, not only do all the terms used in 2 Corinthians 5:19 oblige us to understand the "world" there as an indefinite term, including all "the children of God that were scattered abroad" (John 11:52), but the closing words of the passage compel us to take the same view. "For He has made Him to be sin for us who knew no sin, that we might be made the righteousness of God in Him" (v. 21). Here we learn why God does not impute their trespasses unto His believing people. It is because they were transferred and imputed to their Surety, and accordingly vengeance was executed upon Him. Here too we learn that not only is there no charge laid to the account of God's elect, but that, positively, they are constituted the righteousness of God in Christ—all the merits of His obedience being charged to them. Thus the "reconciled us" of verse 18, the "their" of verse 19, and the "us" and "we" of verse 21 all refer to the same company, and that company is one and the same as "world" in verse 19.

If it is inquired, since it is the Church, the mystical body of Christ, that is in view in 2 Corinthians 5:19, why did the Holy Spirit designate her by the term "world?" First, to show it was not the fallen angels. No Mediator nor Reconciler was provided for them. Second, to show that the love of God in Christ was not restricted unto the Jews (as they supposed) but included also a people to be "taken out of the Gentiles for His name" (Acts 15:14). Third, to represent the freeness of God's grace. "The whole world lies in the Wicked one" (1 John 5:19). "In themselves God's elect differ nothing from the rest of the world till grace prevent them. They were as bad as any in the world, of the same race as cursed mankind." Fourth, "to awaken all that are concerned to look after their privilege, which is come to all nations. The offer is made indifferently to all sorts of persons where the Gospel comes, and this grace is effectually applied to all the elect of all nations" (T. Manton).

None should be stumbled by a particular redemption which pertains only to the Church of God being expressed in such extended terms as "the world" and "all men" in the N. T. The employment of such language is fully accounted for by the change of dispensation, from the local religion of Judaism to the international reach of Christianity. The Mosaic economy was entirely exclusive, whereas that of the Gospel is inclusive. In anticipation of that, we should note the indefinite language used by the Prophets when predicting the blessings of Messiah, as extending beyond Judea and bestowing indiscriminately. "The Desire of all nations shall come" (Hag. 2:8). "All kings shall fall down before Him and all nations shall serve Him" (Ps. 72:1). "O You that hear prayer, unto You shall all flesh come" (Ps. 65:2). "I will pour out My Spirit upon all flesh" (Joel 2:25)—interpreted by Peter as accomplished on the day of Pentecost (Acts 2:16)! Such language was as universal as any employed by Christ and His apostles, yet it certainly did not signify that every individual the earth over would become a subject of Christ's kingdom and a partaker of His saving benefits.

There are other general terms used in the N. T. besides "world" which cannot be taken in an unlimited sense. For example "every man." We read of one to whom the Lord gave sight that he "saw every man clearly" (Mark 8:28). The kingdom of God was preached "and every man presses into it" (Luke 16:16). The early Christians sold their possessions and goods "and parted them to all, as every man had need" (Acts 2:45). "God has dealt to every man the measure of faith" (Rom. 12:3 but see 2 Thess. 3:2). "Then shall every man have praise of God" (1 Cor. 4:5). Other passages could be quoted where "every man" cannot be understood without qualification. "The Gentiles" is another general expression which is restricted by what is predicated of them in each case. For instance "on the Gentiles also was poured out the gift of the Holy Spirit" (Acts. 10:45). And again "God also to the Gentiles granted repentance unto life "(Acts 11:18). "Declaring the conversion of the Gentiles" (Acts 15:3). "The salvation of God is sent unto the Gentiles, and they will hear it" (Acts 28:28). Let those who say of John 3:16 or 2 Cor. 5:19 "we keep by the plain declaration of the passage," apply the same principle to the verses quoted in this paragraph!

"And having made peace through the blood of His cross, by Him to reconcile all things unto Himself; by Him, whether they are things in earth or things in heaven" (Col. 1:20). These words bring before us another aspect of our theme, and one which has been generally overlooked by writers on this subject. By means of His mediatory work Christ has not only effected a reconciliation between God and the whole election of grace, but He has also closed the breach which existed between the celestial hosts and the Church. At the creation of the world the holy angels sang together and even shouted for joy (Job 38:7), "because though it was not made for them, but for the children of men, and though it would increase their work and service, yet they knew that the eternal Wisdom and Word whom they were to worship (Heb. 1:6), would 'rejoice in the habitable parts of the earth' and that a large part of 'His delight would be with the sons of men'" (Prov. 8:31) [Matt. Henry]. Likewise, when the grand foundation of the new creation was laid, we read of "the heavenly host praising God, and saying, Glory to God in the highest, and on earth, peace, good will toward men" (Luke 2:13,14).

When God made the earth and placed man in it the angels rejoiced in the work of their Creator's hands, and so far from being jealous at the appearing of a further order of beings, they took delight in them. But upon man's revolt from his Maker and Lord, they would be filled with disgust and holy indignation. The sin of Adam (and of the race in him) not only alienated man from God, but also from the holy ones on high. No sooner did our first parents fall from their original state, followed by their expulsion from Paradise, than God employed the holy angels as the executors of His vengeance against them: represented by the cherubim with the flaming sword [for

He "makes His angels spirits and His ministers a flame of fire" (Heb. 1:7)] to keep them out of Eden and from the tree of life (Gen. 3:24). Yet now they are "all ministering spirits, sent forth to minister for them who shall be heirs of salvation" (Heb. 1:14). And, my reader, it is the blood of the cross which has brought about that blessed change. The atonement of Christ has made the celestial hosts the friends and helpers of His people.

It was not that "the things in heaven" were alienated from God, but that Adam's fall introduced disruption into the universe, so that the inhabitants of heaven were alienated from those on earth; but Christ has restored perfect concord again. His sacrifice has repaired the breach between the elect and the holy angels; He has restored the broken harmony of the universe. As one has well pointed out, "If Paul could address the Corinthians concerning one of their excluded members, who had been brought to repentance, 'To whom you forgive anything, I also' (2 Cor. 2:10), much more would the friends of righteousness (the angels) say in their addresses to the great Supreme, concerning an excluded member from the moral system, 'to whom You forgive anything, we also.'" For this reason we find "there is joy in the presence of the angels of God over one sinner that repents" (Luke 15:10), for another has been joined to their company as worshippers of the Most High.

Chapter 20
Its Scope-Continued

"And having made peace through the blood of His cross, by Him to reconcile all things unto Himself, whether things in earth or things in heaven" (Col. 1:20). In the final paragraphs of our last we touched upon this aspect of our subject, pointing out that the mediatory work of Christ not only effected a reconciliation between God and the whole election of grace, but also closed the breach which existed between the celestial hosts and the Church. But our remarks on it were all too brief for a subject so blessed, so important, so honoring to Christ, yet so little understood. The relation which exists between the holy angels and the Church which is the mystical body of Christ has not received the attention that it deserves, and failure to perceive that the basis of this fellowship lies in the person and work of Christ obscures one of the distinctive honors which God has placed upon His beloved Son and loses sight of one of His mediatorial glories. "On His head are many crowns" (Rev. 19:12), and that which is now engaging our attention is by no means the least of them.

According to the principle of "the process of doctrine" or the orderly unfolding of the Truth (first the blade, then the ear, etc.), in the earlier epistles of Paul (Thess., Rom., Cor., Gal.,) we see more the individual effects and blessings of Redemption. The truth of justification, so prominent in it, brings each person face to face with his own sin and salvation. In that supreme crisis of the soul, the crisis of spiritual life and death, there is consciousness of but two existences—God and self. But when we come to the prison epistles (Eph., Phil., Col., etc.), it is no longer the individual as such which is prominent, but rather as he is part of a greater whole—a member of the body of Christ. True, in the earlier epistles the Church is recognized, as in later epistles the individual believer is never for a moment ignored. But the proportion of the two aspects is changed—what is prominent in the first becomes secondary in the other. This is the natural order in the development of Truth. The Christian unity is directly the unity of each soul with Christ, the Head, and indirectly the unity of the various members in the one Body.

When the Gospel of salvation speaks it must speak to the individual, but when the Savior has been found by each soul as the Christ "who lives in me" (Gal. 2:20), then the question arises, What is my relation to other believers? The answer to which is, fellow-members of the Church, fellow-members of the family of God. Accordingly, when taking up the doctrine of reconciliation, the apostles first placed the emphasis upon "be reconciled to God" (2 Cor. 5:20), though even there he indicated the basis on which the call is made. But it was reserved for his later epistles to bring out the reconciliation or unity which Christ has effected between believing Jews and Gentiles—which he shows at some length in Ephesians 2; while in Colossians he goes still further and presents Christ as the Head of all created beings and the new relation which He has established between the Church and the celestial hosts. It is much to their loss that so many Christians advance no further than the epistle to the Romans in their apprehension of the Truth; I must beware of being so wrapped up in what Christ has done for me, that I fail to glory in the wider results of His work.

There was a particular reason why this reference to the larger scope of reconciliation was made in the epistle to the Colossians (rather than in Eph. or Phil.) for as the Judaisers were corrupting the Galatians, so the Gnostics were seeking to seduce the saints at Colosse. The word Gnostic means "one who knows" (the opposite of agnostic) and that which characterized this sect (which to a considerable extent exerted a powerful and pernicious influence upon early Christianity) was an Orientalized form of Grecian philosophy—a modern though more Buddhistic species of which is "Theosophy." Gnosticism was an attempt of carnal reason to show the relation between the Infinite and the finite, the Absolute and the phenomenal, the "first Cause" and the universe. They argued that the gulf could only be bridged by a series of creatures rising in the scale of being, the highest of them being semi-personal emanations, of which Christ was the first (yet only a creature), and then many orders of angels which intervened between God and men.

Therefore it was that in the Colossian epistles the apostle insisted that by Christ "were all things created that are in heaven and that are in earth, visible and invisible, whether thrones or dominions, or principalities or powers, all things were created by Him and for Him. And He is before all things, and by Him all things consist" (1:16, 17), and that he bids the saints there "beware lest any man spoil you through philosophy and vain deceit" (2:8). Here too he insisted that "in Christ dwells all the fullness of the Godhead bodily," and again warned them "that no man beguile you of your reward in a voluntary humility and worshipping of angels, intruding into those things which he has not seen, vainly puffed up by his fleshly mind" (2:9, 18). Having stated in 1:16 that the angels were created by Christ, he then went on to show how they were also the gainers by the blood of His cross, for that blood had "made peace" not only with God, but it had also restored to amicable relationship the two great branches of His family—the angelic hosts and the Church.

There was originally a union between the holy angels and unfallen men, for they existed as fellow-citizens in the kingdom of God, but upon Adam's apostasy that union was broken. Sin is rebellion, and the holy angels could have no fellowship with rebels against their God. "Things in earth" and "things in heaven" became at variance through sin. When men became the enemies of God, they became at the same time the enemies of all His faithful subjects. Take this analogy on a lower plane. Suppose that one country in England should cast off allegiance to King George and disown his government at Westminster, then all lawful communion between the inhabitants of that country and the loyal subjects of the crown in all other parts of the country would be at an end. A line of moral and patriotic separation would at once be drawn between the two companies, and all friendly intercourse would be forbidden. Nor would it less accord with their inclination than the duty of all the friends of the throne to withdraw their communion and connection from those who were in revolt against the supreme authority and the general good.

But now suppose one possessing the necessary dignity and qualifications, say a member of the royal house, should voluntarily undertake to make adequate reparation unto his majesty for the injury done him by the rebellious country, and that he was pleased to acknowledge that reparation as a full satisfaction to his honor. And suppose that his plenipotentiary succeeded in removing all enmity against their king from the members of that county, so that they sincerely repented of their insubordination and threw down the weapons of their hostility against the throne and government; as soon as it became generally known that company had been restored to reality, would not the remainder of the country rejoice and all the loyal subjects of the crown be ready to resume fellowship with them again? That is as close a parallel as we can think of. Having made peace between God and the Church by the blood of His cross, Christ has also united the Church unto all who love God throughout the whole extent of creation. Things or creatures on earth have been reconciled to things or creatures in heaven.

The redemptive work of Christ has done something more than "gather together in one the children of God that were scattered abroad" by the fall (John 11:52). It has also united a disrupted universe. As we are informed in Ephesians 1:9, 10 it was God's eternal purpose "that in the dispensation of the fullness of times He might gather together in one (kingdom and family) all things in Christ, both which are in heaven and which are on earth, in Him." It was unto the accomplishment of this end that God was working all through the preceding dispensations. He had ordained that unto the last Adam should pertain the honor and glory of repairing the great breach made by the first Adam's sin. Christ could say "I restored that which I took not away" (Ps. 69:4). He restored honor to God in the scene where He had been so grievously dishonored, He restored glory to the Law in the very place where it had been trampled underfoot. He brought blessing to the fallen Church by restoring it to the judicial favor of the Judge of all, He restored harmony to the broken universe by reconciling the two most important sections or members of it.

Ephesians 1:9 and 10 makes known to us the entire range of God's eternal purpose of grace. It was to gather together in Christ not only the elect from the sons of men on earth, but also the elect from among the angels in heaven, uniting all into one harmonious whole, and this with the grand design of making more manifest the glory of the God-man Mediator. Under His eternal foreview of the entrance of sin, God purposed the reunion of the two great portions of the moral universe, bringing them into one holy and happy commonwealth under Christ as their glorious Sovereign. If it is asked, Why are the persons of angels and men referred to as "things?" The answer is, This is the Scriptural form of expressing them. As when the apostle said "all things are yours whether Paul or Apollos or Cephas" (1 Cor. 3:21,22), or, "the Scripture shuts up all things under sin" (Gal. 3:22) which is explained by "God has shut them all up in unbelief" (Rom. 11:32). As the "all men" of 2 Timothy 2:1, 2 signifies men of all stations, so the "all things in heaven" of Ephesians 1:10 means angels of all ranks—"thrones or dominions, or principalities or powers," etc. (Col. 1:16).

The word for "dispensation" (oikonomia) contains no time element and has no reference to an age or era. Literally it means "the arrangement of a house" (Young's Concordance), or as we should say today, the administration or management of a household. Its force may be clearly ascertained from its first occurrence in the N. T.: "give an account of your stewardship" (Luke 16:2), that is of your administration of my household—the same Greek word is again translated "stewardship" in the next two verses. Thus the "Dispensationalists" have no warrant whatever for their arbitrary partitioning of the Scriptures. When Paul said "a dispensation of the Gospel is committed unto me" (1 Cor. 9:17), obviously he is to be understood as meaning, an administration or dispensing of the Gospel is entrusted to me in my apostolic labors. The "fullness of times" signifies the termination of the times or "seasons," namely, this final Christian season, which is the culmination and termination of all preceding ones—as Hebrews 1:1, 2; 1 John 2:18 make evident.

The "gathering together of one" is a single (compound) word in the Greek occurring nowhere else in the N.T. except Romans 13:8, where it is rendered "briefly comprehended." There, after quoting several of the Commandments—"You shall not commit adultery, you shall not steal," etc., —the apostle added and if any other commandment, it is briefly comprehended in this saying namely, "you shall love your neighbor as yourself," that is, all these precepts of the second table are summed up in that single injunction. It is an arithmetical term, where many items are added together in one total sum. It is also a rhetorical term, to recapitulate, as an orator does at the close of his discourse. Thus it contains (in its prefix) the idea of repetition, as "gathering together" implies an original unity and then a scattering, before the unity is restored. In Christ God has re-gathered and re-established in a new condition of stability and blessedness the previously disrupted elements, forming them into one kingdom, under one Head, having restored to harmony and mutual love the alienated portions of His empire.

Christ is not only "the Head of the Church" (Eph. 4:23), but He is also "the Head of all principality and power" (Col. 2:10), "angels and authorities and powers being made subject unto Him" (1 Pet. 3:22). Thus He is "the Head over all" (Eph. 1:22). Christ is the gathering Center of all holy creatures, they being united into one great commonwealth under His sovereignty. Elect angels and elect men make up one household. This is clearly brought out in, "I bow my knees unto the Father of our Lord Jesus Christ, of whom the whole family in heaven and earth is named" (Eph. 3:14, 15). Since Christ is the Head of all (Eph. 1:22), the whole family receive its name from Him. They all own Him, and He owns them all. So too, together they make up one City, the new Jerusalem, of which Christ is the Governor and King. "You are come unto Zion and unto the City of the living God, the heavenly Jerusalem" (Heb. 12:22). There is the general description, but who are the inhabitants? The same verse goes on to tell us "and to an innumerable company of angels, to the General Assembly and Church of the Firstborn" they all make up one united company of worshippers, for the angels worship Christ as the redeemed do.

As Goodwin showed at length in his masterly exposition of Ephesians 1:10, this honor was due Christ. First, as the God-man and "Heir of all things" (Heb. 1:2) it was right that He should be the Head over the highest of God's creatures—of the celestial hosts as well as the Church. Second, this unity of the holy angels with the redeemed into one family and commonwealth is greatly to the honor and splendor of the Church. Third, angels and men are capable of being thus knit together under one Head, for they each have an understanding, affection, will and spiritual nature, and therefore are suited to the same happiness, dwelling together in the same place. As Matthew 22:30 tells us "In the resurrection they.. .are as the angels of God in heaven!" Fourth, by this arrangement there is constituted a complete parallel in opposition to Satan, who is the head both of wicked men and demons. The Devil is the head of the evil angels (Rev. 12:7), called "the Prince of the Demons" (Matthew 12:24), and he is the head of the wicked (1 John. 5:19) and termed "the Prince of this world" (John 12:31). Answerably to this, God has made Christ the Head of the Church and of angels.

"You are come unto . . . an innumerable company of angels" (Heb. 12:22). We are come to them as our fellow-citizens, in consequence of our faith in Christ. Our access to them is spiritual. We come to them now, while we are on earth and they in heaven. But we come to them not with our prayers, which is the doting superstition of Rome, and utterly destructive of the communion here asserted. For although there is a difference and distinction between their persons and ours as to dignity and power, yet as to this fellowship we are equal in it with them; as one of them expressly declared to the apostle John "I am your fellow-servant and of your brethren that have the testimony of Jesus" (Rev. 19:10). Upon which John Owen Said "nothing could be more groundless than that fellow-servants should worship one another"—nor absurd. We have access to all of them, not simply to this or that tutelar [guardian] angel, but to the whole company of them. We are come to them by virtue of the recapitulation of them and us in Christ, they and we being members of the same heavenly family and associated together in a common worship.

"What was the reason that the tabernacle was so full of 'cherubim?' Read Exodus 25:19 and observe there were two of them over the mercy-seat in the holy of holies. Read. Exodus 26:1 and mark how all the curtains of the tabernacle had cherubim wrought on them. Cherubim are angels (1 Pet. 1:12). Go from there to the temple of Solomon. There you have the cherubim again—on the mercy-seat, all the walls of the house, and its very doors (1 Kings 6:23, 29, 32). All this indicated that angels still fill the temple as well as men. Little do we think it, but the angels, as well as human beings, fill our churches and are present in our assemblies. Therefore are the women bidden to be modest and have their heads covered—the sign of their subordination—not only because of men, but because of the angels (1 Cor. 11:10), for surely that is the meaning of it. Because we are to be with them hereafter and to worship God together, therefore they come down and are present at the worship of God here with us" (T. Goodwin—slightly changed).

In Revelation 5, under the representative emblem of the "twenty-four elders," we behold the Church worshipping, singing a new song: "You are worthy to take the book and to open the seals of it, for You were slain and have redeemed us to God by Your blood, out of every kindred and tongue and people and nation, and have made us unto our God kings and priests, and we shall reign on the earth." Immediately after which the apostle tells us "And I behold, and I heard the voice of many angels, round the throne and the living creatures and the elders . . . saying with a loud voice, Worthy is the Lamb that was slain to receive power and riches and wisdom and strength and honor and glory and blessing" (vv. 9-12). The ascription of praise from the angels is mingled with the praise of the Church so as to comprise one entire worship. Thus the "gather together in one" of Ephesians 1:10 also included one great Choir or company of worshippers.

The holy angels are the adversaries of the wicked, for since such are the enemies of God they are their enemies too. Thus we read of the angel of the Lord standing in the way of perverse Balaam as "an adversary against him" (Num. 22:22). They were sent to destroy wicked Sodom (Gen. 19:1,13). One of them smote the camp of the Assyrians and slew nearly two hundred thousand of them in a night (2 Kings 19:35). Another slew the blasphemous Herod (Acts 12:23) in N.T. times. Observe how prominently they figure in the Apocalypse as the agents of God's judgments and the executioners of His vengeance. See Revelation 8:7-13; 15:1; 16:1-12. So also at the day of judgment "The Son of man shall send forth His angels and they shall gather out of His kingdom all things that offend and them which do iniquity, and shall cast them into a furnace of fire" (Matthew 13:41, 42).

How blessed the contrast to behold the ministrations of the angels unto the saints! "He shall give His angels charge over you, to keep you in all your ways" (Ps. 91:11)—a promise not only to Christ personally, but also to all the members of His mystical body. When the beggar died, his soul was "carried by angels into Abraham's bosom" (Luke 16:22). An angel delivered Peter from prison (Acts 12:7-10). In the Day to come Christ "shall send His angels with a great sound of a trumpet, and they shall gather together His elect from the four winds" (Matthew 24:31). In an earlier paragraph we called attention to the cherubim with the flaming sword barring our first parents from the tree of life (Gen. 3:24). But, in consequence of Colossians 1:20 and Ephesians 1:10, they now stand at the entrance of Paradise to admit the redeemed into it! The holy Jerusalem has "twelve gates, and at the gates twelve angels" (Rev. 21:12) and in that city is "the tree of life." (22:2).

"Behold, a ladder set up on earth and the top of it reached to heaven. And, behold, the angels of God ascending and descending on it" (Gen. 28:12). "Hereafter shall you see (with the eyes of faith—enlightened from the Scriptures) the heaven open, and the angels of God ascending and descending upon the Son of man" (John 1:51). Here we are shown plainly the grand Medium for uniting heaven and earth, the Foundation on which rests the intercourse between the angels and the redeemed. "The Son of man" views Christ as the last Adam, and is the Mediator's title of humiliation, while bearing sin. It is brought in here to emphasize the fact that it is His atonement, "the blood of His cross" (Col. 1:20) which is the meritorious ground of the restoration of the long-forfeited fellowship between the two branches of the one family in Christ. "If the partition wall between Jews and Gentiles is removed by the cross, and the enmity slain by it, the same thing holds true in reference to angels and men" (Geo. Smeaton).

Chapter 21
Its Scope-Concluded

It is not sufficiently realized that sin is the one great divisive, disrupting and destructive agency at work in every part and stratum of our world. It was sin that separated man from God, which produced a breach between him and the holy angels, and which operates to the alienating of one man from another. Among the many and dreadful effects of the Fall (which was itself an expression of enmity against God) is the enmity between man and man which has issued from it. That abominable thing which caused Adam to be driven out of Eden swiftly exhibited itself in the murderous hatred of Cain for Abel. Sin has not bred a quarrel with God, but between man and man, between brother and brother, between nation and nation. Not only do the unregenerate hate the regenerate, but they "live in malice and envy, hateful and hating one another" (Titus 3:3). The whole of human history is little more than a sad record of man's enmity against man—modified (though not eradicated) only where the Gospel has taken root.

As one has truly said, "There is in every man, if his nature were let out to the full, that in him which is 'against every man' as was said of Ishmael." Self-love is the greatest monopolist and dictator in this world, "for men shall be lovers of their own selves." What immediately follows? "Covetous . . . disobedient to parents . . . without natural affection, truce breakers, false accusers, incontinent, fierce, despisers of them that are good" (2 Tim. 3:2,3). Self-love is the regulating principle in every natural man. Self-love breaks all bonds and overrides all other considerations. And self-love is but another name for sin, for so far from seeking God's glory or the good of my fellows, it selfishly considers only my own interests. Since each nation is but an aggregate of individual sinners, self-interests regulate it, and therefore the nations are kept in a state of continual suspicion, jealousy and enmity one against another.

Now since Christ is the Savior, and the only Savior from sin, to Him was appointed the honor of healing the breaches made by sin. We have already seen how He reconciled God unto the Church and the Church unto Him, as we also dwelt at some length on His reconciliation of the Church to the celestial hosts, forming them into one holy and harmonious company. We are now to consider how He brought into the Church, welding them into one Body, two diverse peoples who had for many centuries been widely separated, and bitterly hostile to each other. That was indeed a miracle of grace, constituting as it does one of the greatest and grandest triumphs of the Atonement. We refer of course to the making of the Gentiles "fellow-heirs and of same Body and partakers of God's promise in Christ by the Gospel" (Eph. 3:6) with Jews. To appreciate that marvel let us carefully behold the awful and age-long alienation that existed between them.

We begin by contemplating that of the Jews against the Gentiles, for the quarrel originated with them. This is clearly intimated by "Gentiles in the flesh, who are called Uncircumcision by that which is called the Circumcision" (Eph. 2:12), for the word "called" there signified "dubbed." It was the Jews who first began using nick-names! Out of their carnal pride, they misused the privilege bestowed upon them by God as His peculiar people, to scorn the poor Gentiles, and this almost from the beginning. The sons of Jacob said, "To give our sister to one that is uncircumcised, that were a reproach to us" (Gen. 34:14), and afterwards the whole race of Jews, good and bad, used the term "uncircumcised" as a stigma. As by Samson (Judges 15:18), by Jonathan (1 Sam. 14:6), David (17:26, 36), Saul (31:4). Yea, they regarded it as worse than death itself to "die by the hands of the uncircumcised" or have "the daughters of the uncircumcised triumph" (2 Sam. 1:20). When they would accurse to the most degraded death, it was, Let him die the death of the uncircumcised.

This enmity of the Jews was expressed in their attitude toward and dealings with the Gentiles. Not only was there no communion between them in sacred things, but they deemed it an abomination to have any social intercourse with the Gentiles. In the latter they erred grievously, through perverting a particular precept, given upon a special ground, and making it of general application. Concerning the Ammonites and Moabites the Lord had said "You shall not seek their peace nor prosperity all your days forever" (Deut. 23:6), but as though foreseeing that the evil spirit in them would develop into a hatred of all nations and to prevent a wrong use of that precept, in the very next verse God bade them, "You shall not abhor an Edmonite, for he is your brother; you shall not abhor an Egyptian, because you were a stranger in his land" (v. 7). Yet the Jews ever carried themselves toward the Gentiles as though they were the scum of the earth.

It was for this reason that when our Savior asked water from the woman at the well, she was astonished and said, "How is it that you, being a Jew, ask drink of me, which am a woman of Samaria, for the Jews have no dealings with the Samaritans" (John 4:9). Yea, so intense was their animosity against the Gentiles, that the Jews would have' killed Paul for no other crime than this that he "brought Greeks also into the temple and has defiled this holy place" (Acts 21:28,31). Malice could not rise higher in any people against another than it did in the Jews for the Gentiles. They carried it so far that the apostle tells us "they please not God and are contrary to all men, forbidding us to preach to the Gentiles that they might be saved" (1 Thess. 2:15, 16). What hope was there of such enmity being removed, and of peace, love and concord displacing it?

How strong the Jewish prejudice was, how powerful the working of his enmity against the Gentiles, appears in him even after his conversion. This is forcibly illustrated in Acts 10, where we find God giving Peter a special vision in order to overcome his disinclination to carry the Gospel to those outside the pale of Judaism. When he arrived at the house of Cornelius he frankly admitted, "You know how that it is unlawful for a man that is a Jew to keep company, or come into one of another nation, but God has shown me that I should not call any man common or unclean" (v. 28). When this good news reached Jerusalem that "the Gentiles had also received the Word of God" and Peter returned to the brethren there, we are told that, so far from rejoicing over these new trophies of Divine grace, "they that were of the circumcision contended with him, saying, you went into men uncircumcised and did eat with them" (11:1-3).

Naturally the Gentiles resented their being held in such contempt by the Jews and were not slow to retaliate, though it must be confessed they were the more moderate of the two. And this was a righteous judgment upon them from God: "I will deliver them to be removed into all the kingdoms of the earth for their hurt: to be a reproach, and a proverb, and a taunt, and a curse in all places where I shall drive them" (Jer. 24:9). In the days of Ahasuerus, who ruled over one hundred and twenty-seven provinces, amongst which the Jews were scattered and in which they had enemies in all, it was only by special letters of appeal from the king that the Gentiles were restraining from falling on them (Esther 8:9). They were accused of being "hurtful unto kings and provinces, and that they have moved sedition within the same of old time" (Ezra 4:15). When the apostles were arrested in Philippi the charge preferred against them was "these men, being Jews, do exceedingly trouble our city" (Acts. 16:20).

But more. God Himself has made a distinction and difference between them, having dealt with and favored Israel as no other nation upon earth (Amos 3:2). He had assigned them their own special land, giving them a particular code of laws—moral, civil and religion—and set up His own exclusive worship in their midst. He had made of them a peculiar polity, having great privileges exclusive to itself, such as no other people ever enjoyed. From all of that the Gentiles were Divinely barred. As the apostle declares, they were "without Christ, being aliens from the commonwealth of Israel and strangers from the covenants of promise having no hope, and without God in the world" (Eph. 2:12). Those consequences followed from their being "without Christ," for He is both the substance and end of the covenants of Israel and the Revealer of God, and so of spiritual life. But in Christ all fleshly distinctions disappear, and through His mediation the Gentiles have been made partakers of Israel's "spiritual things" (Rom. 15:27). This is shown at length in Ephesians 2:14-22, unto which we now turn.

In approaching that passage it needs to be borne in mind that, the Spirit's principal design in it, as in all His ministrations, is to exalt Christ in our esteem. The incarnate Son glorified the Father on earth as He was never glorified here before or since, and therefore He was entitled to ask "Father, glorify Your Son" (John 17:1). That request received answer not only in His exaltation on High, not only in a redeemed people being quickened and united to Him to show forth His praises, but also in the further revelation made of Him in the N. T. An illustration of that is now to be before us. The Spirit's object in it is to give us an eminent instance of the efficacy of Christ's mediation by bringing to pass that which the united efforts of all men could never have accomplished, namely, the slaying of an age-long and inveterate enmity which existed between the two great branches of the human family, from each of which God takes a remnant to exemplify His sovereign grace. Ephesians 2 shows us how Christ abolished that which was the means or occasion of alienation between them.

"For He is our peace" (v. 14) objectively, what He is in Himself: as He is "our righteousness" (Jer. 23:6), "our life" (Col. 3:3), "our hope" (1 Tim. 1:1)—though there is that which is correspondent to each wrought in us. He is "our peace" because He is Himself "the Prince of peace" and because He is the great and glorious Peacemaker. Christ is at once the Author, the Substance, and Center of peace. In what follows the apostle supplies proofs or exemplifications. Christ is our peace between ourselves mutually, and He is our peace between God and us. The key to a right understanding of what follows lies in bearing in mind that duality. As verses 11-13 exhibit a dual alienation—of Gentiles from Jews, of both from God, so verses 14-17 treat of a double reconciliation opposite to it. And accordingly in verses 18-22 we are shown the grand twofold privilege which results from it: access into the favor of God (v. 18), the introduction of a new and united worship of Himself (vv. 19-22).

"For He is our peace: who has made both one and has broken down the middle wall of partition" (v. 14). He who is not only the Giver of Peace, but the Peace itself, has united together believing Jews and Gentiles. Those who previously were alienated, are reconciled by Him, because He has broken down that which divided and separated them. Of old God had "fenced" His vineyard (Isa. 5:1,2; Ps. 80:8; Matthew 21:33-43), or as the margin reads it "made a wall about it" which had barred the Gentiles from an entrance into Israel's spiritual things. The "middle wall of partition" is an expression which connotes the separating cause which existed between Jew and Gentile, but which was demolished by Christ when He had—as the Representative and Surety of each alike—"made both one" in Himself. As Christ's death rent the veil of the temple — the innermost barrier to God — so it destroyed the middle wall of partition.

"Having abolished in His flesh the enmity—the law of commandments contained in ordinances" (v. 15). This tells us how Christ broke down that which divided. The middle wall of partition is now designated "the enmity," and that in turn, is described as "the law of commandments, etc." Here, too, there is a double reference: first to the ceremonial law of Moses which excluded Gentiles from the Jews. Second to the Covenant of works which excluded both from God. "In His flesh" is the same as "by His blood" (v. 13) and "by the cross" (v. 16). By His sacrificial and atoning death the Law—both as a ceremonial system and as a rule of justification—was annulled. In the parallel passage (Col. 2:14) the word ordinances is connected with "the handwriting that was against us," that is, to a legal bond of indictment, which Christ took out of the way "nailing it to His cross."

"For to make in Himself of twain one new man, so making peace" (v. 15). In 2:10 the believer is declared to be "the workmanship of God," but there the glory of the creation is directly attributed to Christ, who is its Head and Life. The "twain" or "two" were the Jews and Gentiles, who were separate and hostile bodies, alike the children of wrath and dead in trespasses and sins. They are created anew so as to become "one new man" (collectively) and this by virtue of their federal union with Christ—therefore the "in Himself" "So making peace." the present participle is used because the operation is a continuous one the work is done, but the fruit of it is progressive. The long feud in the human family is healed. In Christ "there is neither Jew nor Greek" (Gal. 3:28)—both disappearing when the "enmity" that sundered them was abolished. There is now one fold, one Shepherd.

"And that He might reconcile both unto God in one body by the cross, having slain the enmity in this way" (v. 16). Here the "enmity" which Christ slew is the barrier which existed between God and men—created by sin; and not the enmity in our hearts against God, for it was slain by Christ's death and not by the working of His Spirit. To "reconcile" is to effect peace and unity between parties at variance. Christ reconciled both Jews and Gentiles unto God by propitiating Him, by satisfying the demands of His Law, in this way making it possible for Him to be just and yet the Justifier of the ungodly. There is no room for any uncertainty here. It was "by the cross" that Christ effected the reconciliation. The proximate design of a sacrifice is to appease God, and not to convert those for whom the offering is made. "Having slain the enmity" both amplifies and explains "by the cross." Christ's death removed God's wrath or judicial enmity from sinners.

And came and preached to you that were afar off (the Gentiles) and to them that were (in outward privileges) near (v. 17). As the "enmity" of verse 16 is the legal enmity of God, so the "peace" here is that "peace with God" (Rom. 5:1) into which Christ has brought all His redeemed. His "preaching" of it is after the cross, and therefore through His apostles (see 2 Cor. 5:20). It is the proclamation to those who savingly believe the Gospel that since the Law has been satisfied God is no longer hostile to us. Proof of that is "For through Him we both have access by one Spirit unto the Father" (v. 18)—which had been impossible unless His wrath had been removed or His enmity slain. Christ has done something very much more than simply "open a way to God" He has actually brought us to God (1 Pet. 3:18), inducted us into His grace or favor (Rom. 5:2). As God determined to magnify the exceeding riches of His grace by permitting the most heinous sins in the lives of some of those whom He chose unto salvation for the glory of His Son He suffered the strongest and bitterest animosity to possess the hearts of Jews and Gentiles, that the efficacy of His mediation might be displayed in constituting them one new man in Himself—blessedly exemplified when those, who formerly would not eat with one another, sit down together to partake of the Lord's Supper!

Chapter 22
Its Reception

This brings us to the manward side of the subject, and that will present more or less a difficulty unto some of our readers; not because of its abstruseness, but in seeking to ascertain its consistency and harmony with some other aspects presented previously. It concerns the ever-recurring problem of adjusting in our minds the conjunction of the Divine and human elements. Because that conjunction cannot always be stated with mathematical exactitude or in language fully intelligible to the average mind, the great majority are inclined to cut the knot and reject either the one or the other of those elements or factors. But if both be clearly set forth in the Word, whether or not we can perceive the precise relation between them or the definite point at which they meet, it is our bounden duty to believe and hold fast to both. If on the one hand Scripture teaches that Christ has effected reconciliation with God, Scripture just as plainly calls upon us to "be reconciled to Him." And it speaks of our "receiving the reconciliation." It is this latter aspect we must now be occupied with: what God requires from the sinner if he is to enter into the good of what Christ did for sinners.

There ought to be no need to labor this point at any length, and there had been none had not certain men—true servants of God we doubt not, who were thoroughly sound on almost every other part of that Faith once delivered to the saints, and whose ministry has deservedly been held in high esteem by the generations who succeeded them—departed from the Truth thereon and influenced many since their day to perpetuate a serious error. As we have previously pointed out, mutual alienation requires mutual reconciliation. The reconciliation of God to us and of us to God must answer the one to the other, for unless each party lay aside his enmity no real amity is possible. If peace were on one side only and hostility on the other, there would still be a breach. God must be propitiated; we must be converted: the one is as requisite as the other. As we have already shown at length how Christ reconciled God unto us, we must now enter into some detail of how we may be reconciled to God. That we are not about to depart from "the old paths" (Jer. 6:16) will appear from the following quotations.

"Although God the Father has transacted all these things from eternity and Jesus Christ has long since performed all that which might pacify and reconcile His Father and procure our atonement with His Father, yet it was withal agreed mutually then by Them that not a man, no, not any elect man, should have benefit by either, until they came to be reconciled . . . He that will be reconciled to God must part with and forsake all other friends and lovers, renounce and break off all interests and correspondence with them, and choose God for his sole Friend and Portion — he must choose God forever, to cleave to Him with full purpose of heart" (T. Goodwin vol. 6, pp. 122, 129). "We are actually justified, pardoned, and reconciled when we repent and believe. Whatever thoughts and purposes of grace God in Christ may have towards us from all eternity, yet we are under the fruits of sin till we become penitent believers ... That these are conditions which alone make us capable of pardon is evident" (T. Manton, vol. 12, 266).

"This reconciliation, purchased by the blood of Christ, is offered unto men by the Gospel upon certain articles and conditions, upon the performance whereof it actually becomes theirs, and without which, notwithstanding all that Christ has done and suffered, the breach still continues between them and God. And let no man think this a derogation from the freeness and riches of grace, for those things serve singularly to illustrate and commend the grace of God to sinners. As He consulted His own glory in the terms on which He offers us our peace, so it is His grace which brings our souls to these terms of reconciliation. And surely He has not suspended the mercy of our reconciliation upon unreasonable or impossible conditions. He has not said, If you will do as much for Me as you have done against Me I will be at peace with you; but the two grand articles of peace with God are repentance and faith" (J. Flavel vol. 1, p. 476).

"To make perfect reconciliation (which Christ is said in many places to do) it is required, first, that the wrath of God be turned away, His anger removed and all the effects of enmity on His part toward us. Secondly, that we be turned away from our opposition to Him and brought into voluntary obedience. Until both these be effected reconciliation is not perfected" (J. Owen, "The Death of Death." bk. 3, chap. 6, para. 1 on "Reconciliation") "A mediator must be accepted by both parties that are at variance, and they must stand to what the mediator does. As where two princes are at difference and a third interposes to make an agreement between them, they must both consent to accept of that prince for mediator and both put their concerns in his hand: he can be no mediator for him that does not accept of him in that relation . . . God has declared Himself fully contented and has complied with all the conditions of the first agreement (the everlasting covenant); it only remains now that man will accept of Him for those purposes for which God did constitute Him and comply with those conditions which God has settled. This is necessary: God saves no man against his will" (S. Charnock, vol. 3, p. 164).

Those excerpts supply a clear if brief idea of what was the almost uniform teaching of the Puritans on this subject. Probably they will come as a real surprise unto a considerable number of our readers who are wont to regard those men as the champions of orthodoxy and as the best-instructed scribes of the Gospel since the days of the apostles. If so, it is because they have imbibed subversive teaching which came from other men that followed the Puritans in the eighteenth century, men who though they upheld the banner of Truth, previously erected, yet in other things departed from the foundations laid down by their better-balanced predecessors. Though we highly respect these men too and freely acknowledge our indebtedness to many good things in their writings, yet we dare not and cannot follow them in those things wherein they relied more on logical reasoning than on the teaching of Holy Writ. And for the sake of those who have been misled by the errors of men who otherwise taught the Truth, it devolves upon us to at least make an attempt to lead them back into "the good way" (Jer. 6:16).

"Now then we are ambassadors for Christ, as though God did beseech by us: we pray in Christ's stead, be reconciled to God" (2 Cor. 5:20). That is the ringing call of the Gospel as it is addressed unto the unsaved. "Be reconciled to God:" cease your hostility against Him, throw down the weapons of your rebellion, turn from your wicked ways, abandon your idols, repent of your sins, sue for mercy in the name of Christ, receive forgiveness through His blood. But in certain more or less influential circles that is flatly rejected. It is blankly denied that the Gospel called upon the unsaved to be reconciled to God, or that He requires anything from sinners in order to the forgiveness of their sins. Nay it is argued that such an assertion as ours repudiates the free grace of God and denies the finished work of Christ, by inculcating salvation by works and making man in part his own Savior. If that were so, then it would necessarily follow that the most eminent and godly of the Puritans (quoted above) were guilty of those very crimes! But we deny that any such conclusion follows.

"Be reconciled to God" is both the demand of Divine holiness and the enforcement of human responsibility. But because that Gospel call clashed with the views of certain men, they attempted to explain away its real force, insisting that those words are addressed to saints and not to the unconverted. A certain air of plausibility is given to that view by an appeal to the fact that this verse is found in a church epistle, but if due attention be paid to its setting, and the scope of the apostle in the whole passage be rightly ascertained, then the seeming "plausibility" disappears and the untenability of such an interpretation is at once exposed. But in order to discover and exhibit the scope or design of the apostle here, careful attention has to be paid to the context and considerable ground must be covered by the expositor to make the same clear. We fear this may prove rather tedious to some of our friends, yet beg them to bear with us for the sake of others who need and for those who earnestly long for the opening-up of this passage.

Let us give first, in few and simple words, what we are convinced is the force of 2 Corinthians 5:20 and then state why we so understand it, setting forth the grounds on which our conviction rests. When the apostle wrote those words "Be reconciled to God" he was not exhorting saved or unsaved: rather was he giving a brief account of the evangelical message which he had been called to deliver to the latter. In the light of the immediate context we can come to no other conclusion. In the second half of v. 18 the apostle expressly declares that there had been given to him and his fellow-evangelists "the ministry of reconciliation," and then in verses 19-21 (and 6:1, 2) he tells us—as the opening "to wit" unequivocally shows—what that "ministry of reconciliation" consisted of, what were its principal elements and contents. Before proceeding further, let the reader carefully ponder verses 18-21 for himself, and see if he does not concur. If the meaning of verse 20 is still not clear to him, let him read again from verse 18 and omit the repeated "you" in verse 20, and all should be plain. But we will attempt a more thorough analysis of the passage.

As we pointed out in the opening paragraphs of the chapters on "the Prayers of the Apostles," certain false teachers were very active against Paul at Corinth, seeking to undermine his apostolic authority and destroy his influence and usefulness. It is that which accounts for what he says in 1 Corinthians 4:1; 9:1-5; 15:9-11, and 2 Corinthians 5:1,2; 10:2; 11:5, 12-16. It is that which explains why he was forced (by his adversaries) to vindicate his apostleship and point out that in authority, knowledge and effective grace, none excelled him: see 11:22-23 for his credentials. It seems quite evident from a close reading of those two epistles that his enemies had succeeded so far as to shake confidence in himself of some of his own converts there, and thus his appeals in 1 Corinthians 5:14-16; 2 Corinthians 3:14, 13:3 etc. From those passages it will be seen that Paul was on the defensive and obliged to justify himself and do what his modesty and humility detested—say much about himself and appear to resort unto boasting and self-laudation (2 Cor. 11:16-18). In the light of those references the apostle's scope in the epistle should be more easily perceived.

Throughout the third chapter he gives an account of how he had discharged the commission which he had received from his Master, acknowledging, tacitly, that he was no Judaiser (as were his opponents), but rather an able minister of the new testament or covenant (v. 6). In the fourth he continues the same subject, and makes mention of some of the trials which a faithful discharge of his commission had entailed (vv. 1, 8-14). Then, as was so often the case, his heart and mind (so to speak) ran away with him and he digressed to describe the rich compensation which God had provided for His servants and people in general—their afflictions being abundantly counterbalanced and recompensed by the glory awaiting them, which he continues to 5:10. But in 5:11 he returns to the subject of his own ministerial labors, making known the springs from which they issued. Having alluded to "the judgment-seat of Christ," he declared "knowing therefore the terror of the Lord, we persuade men." Nothing is more calculated to stir the soul of Christ's minister and make him earnest and faithful in dealing with his fellows than the solemn realization that naught but the "everlasting burnings" await all who die out of Christ. It is that which makes him cry to his hearers "flee from the wrath to come."

(1) "Knowing therefore the terror of the Lord (2) we persuade men:" the one was the cause, the other the effect. The "terror of the Lord" was not something of which the apostle stood in any doubt of, but a thing he knew—of which he was fully assured. And therefore he "persuaded men" at large, reasoning with, pleading with, urging them to flee for refuge and personally lay hold of the hope which he set before them in the Gospel. An illustration that this was the course which he followed, is supplied us in Acts 24:25, where we are told that, even when before one of his judges, "he reasoned of righteousness, temperance and judgment to come," so that "Felix trembled." Alas, how little of such zeal and fidelity is there today on the part of those who profess to be the servants of God; how little is there in their preaching which makes the hearer "tremble!" How little does the twentieth-century evangelist resemble those of the first. If the reader of this paragraph is a preacher, let him honestly measure himself by this verse and ask, Is the awful truth of the eternal punishment of the wicked in the Lake of Fire impelling me to so preach that in the day to come I shall be "pure from the blood of all," or am I deliberately withholding what I know would be unpalatable unto my congregation?

"But we are made manifest unto God" (v. 11). That was a solemn appeal by the apostle unto the Searcher of hearts of his sincerity and fidelity. And then he added, "and I trust also are made manifest in your consciences" (5:11): I cherish the hope that such zeal and honest dealing with souls will make it evident, to your conscience at least, that I am indeed and in truth an accredited servant of God. Can the reader, if he be a preacher, make the same appeal both to the Omniscient One and the conscience of his auditors? "For we commend not ourselves unto you, but give you occasion to glory on our behalf that you may have somewhat to answer them which glory in appearance and not in heart" (v. 12). It was not that the apostle would seek to ingratiate himself in the esteem of these unstable Corinthians, but that he reminded them of what they had already witnessed and experienced when he labored among them, and that, in order that they could effectually close the mouths of his detractors, who sought to take advantage of his absence by destroying the confidence of those who were his own children in the Faith.

"For whether we be beside ourselves, it is to God: or whether we be sober, it is for your cause" (v. 13). Here he replies to one of the charges which his adversaries had brought against him— that he was a wild fanatic. Says the apostle, even if I am mad, it is for God's glory that I have been so zealous; and if I had restrained myself within the bounds of sobriety, it was for your sakes. Whether he succeeded the limits of discretion as his enemies asserted, or whether he conducted himself decorously as men judged, it was not for himself: he had in mind only the glory of God and the good of His Church. "For the love of Christ constrains me" (v. 14): that was the second dynamic or motive-power of his ministry. That was what caused him to set aside all considerations of ease or self-aggrandizement and made him willing to be counted "the filth of the world, the offscouring of all things" (1 Cor. 4:13). Here again we see a blessed balance: the "terror of the Lord" and "the love of Christ" inspiring him in all his ministerial labors. The love of Christ for sinners for himself: the love of Christ filling his heart and engendering a love for sinners, made him willing to "spend and be spent" in labors "more abundant," and to get little more than misunderstanding and misrepresentation, jealousy, and bitter persecution for his pains.

Cannot the impartial reader see for himself the drift, the scope, the line of things of Paul in this passage? Having mentioned "the love of Christ" as constraining him to diligence in the ministry of the Gospel, he went on to enlarge upon the nature of that love: it was the One dying for the all (v. 14), and then to the end of verse 17 he describes some of the consequences and fruits of that love, upon which we must not now enlarge, as originally intended. The final fruits of Christ's love here enumerated are, that God "has reconciled us unto Himself by Jesus Christ, and has given to us the ministry of reconciliation" (v. 18). What that "ministry" consisted of he tells us in verses 19-21. It "consists of two parts. 1. A reconciliation wrought on God's part toward us, in the effecting of which Christ was concurrent with Him (v. 19). 2. A reconciliation on our parts, enforced from what God and Christ had done (v. 21), and this is equally necessary unto man's salvation as that reconciliation on God's part and Christ's part" (T. Goodwin vol. 6, p. 117). "The end of the ministry is to reconcile us to God, to prevail with us to lay down our enmity against Him and opposition to Him" (Owen on 2 Cor. 5:20).

"Now then we are ambassadors for Christ, as though God did beseech by us, we pray in Christ's stead, be reconciled to God" (v. 20). We trust it is now clear that in those words the apostle was "evidently giving an account of his commission and general ministry" (T. Scott). That he should here do so is quite in accord with what he had done in the previous epistle: see 1 Corinthians 2:2 and 15:1-3. Thus in this instance we believe that that most able expositor J. Gill erred in his interpretation of this verse—following as he did James Hussey rather than the earlier Puritans. So far from exhorting the saints unto "submission to providence and obedience to the discipline and ordinances of God," the apostle was stating how he exhorted the unsaved when preaching the Gospel to them. Had Gill's interpretation been valid, the twice stated "you" had been in the text! If any supplement be needed, it should be "men." "Be reconciled to. God" is the imperative demand of the Gospel to all who hear it being parallel with "Let the wicked forsake his way, and the unrighteous man his thoughts, and let him return unto the Lord, and He will have mercy upon him" (Isa. 55:7).

The apostle continues the same subject in chapter 6. "In this chapter (verses 1-10) the apostle gives an account of his general errand to all whom he preached to, with several arguments and methods he used" (M. Henry). It should be carefully noted that- not until 6:11 did the apostle directly address himself to the Corinthians! Now if Paul had been addressing the saints in 5:20, then in the opening verses of chapter 6 he must have been addressing their ministers, which is how Mr. Gill understood him. But in such case he would not have said "approving ourselves as the ministers of God" (v. 4) but "yourselves!" Thus it is manifest he was still vindicating himself and his fellow-apostles against the Judaisers. Not only were all who heard him preach the Gospel exhorted "be reconciled to God," but to "receive not the grace of God in vain," urging them not to procrastinate with the overtures of Divine mercy, but to recognize and realize that "now is the accepted time" (vv. 1, 2). Having been favored with the Gospel, let them not spurn it.

On 2 Corinthians 6:1 Owen said, "The grace of God may be considered two ways. 1. Objectively for the revelation or doctrine of grace, as in Titus 2:11, 12. So we are said to 'receive' when we believe and profess it, in opposition unto those by whom it is rejected. And this is the same with receiving the Word preached, so often mentioned in the Scriptures: Acts 2:41, James 1:21, which is by faith to give it entertainment in our hearts, which is the meaning of the word in this place." The "we" of 6:1 is the "we are ambassadors" of 5:20, and the "you receive not the grace of God in vain" (His gracious overture in the Gospel) are the same "you" as "be you reconciled to God." The meaning of "giving no offence in anything that the ministry be not blamed, but in all things approving ourselves as the ministers of God" (6:2, 4) is, that the apostles comported themselves in such a manner that there was nothing in their conduct which would hinder their Gospel preaching.

Chapter 23
Its Reception-Continued

In our last we sought to show that the words "be reconciled to God" (2 Cor. 5:20) are not an exhortation unto saints to acquiesce in the Divine providences or to render submission to His discipline and ordinances, but instead, that they form part of an account which the apostle was giving of his evangelical commission, of what his message was to men at large, and therefore those words express the call which the Gospel makes to the unsaved. Before turning from that verse let us point out that there is an expression in it which supplies an incidental yet very real and strong confirmation of what has been frequently insisted upon in this series. Again and again we have pointed out that in connection with reconciliation God is viewed specifically in His official and governmental (rather than in His essential or paternal) character, as Rector or Judge. In full accord with this His servants are here referred to as "ambassadors for Christ, as though God did beseech"—in no other connection are ministers of the Gospel so designated!

After all that was pointed out under our fourth main division (its Arrangement), when we dwelt at length on the glorious provision of the Everlasting Covenant, and all that was brought forward under our fifth division (its Effectuation), when we showed how Christ carried out all He had engaged Himself to do under that Covenant and the reward He earned—a "seed" for the travail of His soul; it might be thought that the elect were absolved and reconciled to God the moment the Savior triumphantly cried "It is finished." But not so. As Charnock pointed out, "We must distinguish between reconciliation designed by God, obtained by Christ, offered by the Gospel, and received by the soul." It is through failing to recognize and bear in mind those very real and necessary distinctions that we confuse ourselves, confounding what should be kept separate. It was their failure to distinguish between totally different aspects of the Truth which led some Arminians into teaching the gross error that the entire human race was reconciled to God by Jesus Christ, though most of them know it not.

For the purpose of simplification the fourfold distinction drawn by Charnock may be reduced unto a twofold one. A reconciliation which, in the language of lawyers, is de jure and one which is de facto, or in theological terms, the impetration or purchase of reconciliation by Christ and the application of it to us or our actual receiving of the same. This will be more intelligible to the average reader if we remind him of the difference between having a legal right to a thing and a right in it. Such is the case with a minor with reference to an inheritance. If but ten years old when his father died and willed an estate to him, as soon as the will was proved, he had a legal right to the estate—none else could claim it; but not until he was twenty-one could he enter into possession and enjoyment of it. The Holy Spirit uses that very figure in Gal. 4:1-7 when treating of dispensational differences of privilege under the old and new covenants.

It is by observing this fundamental distinction that we obviate a difficulty which a first reading of 2 Corinthians 5 might occasion. There we read "God has reconciled us to Himself by Jesus Christ" (v. 18), and then the call is made "be reconciled" (v. 20). But there is nothing whatever inconsistent between those two statements, or anything in them which should puzzle us. Paul was not there essaying a systematic exposition of the doctrine of reconciliation, but instead, was giving an account of his evangelical ministry or message in connection with it. As was shown in our last—by the quotation from T. Goodwin—that "ministry" consists of two parts: a reconciliation wrought on God's part and a reconciliation on our part toward God. The latter being equally necessary as the former. It is necessary because since the alienation exists on each side, both parties must set aside their enmity before amity is possible. It is necessary in order to the enforcement of human responsibility. It is necessary for us to be reconciled to God because that is what He requires of us, as the way He has appointed. But let us amplify that a little.

While a great deal has been written to show that in the transactions between the Father and the Mediator God determined to take full satisfaction unto His justice, and therefore ordained that His Son should be offered a sacrifice, much less has been written to demonstrate that the holiness of God required we must cease our revolt against Him before He can be reconciled to us or receive us into His favor. Yet the one is as true, as important, as necessary, as essential as the other. God is as jealous in the vindication and glorifying of one of His attributes as He is of another, and therefore if on the one hand we read that Christ is set forth "a propitiation through faith in His blood, to declare His righteousness" and "that He might be just and the Justifier of him that believes in Jesus" (Rom. 3:25, 26); on the other hand, we are told that He "has saved us and called us with a holy calling, not according to our works, but according to His own purpose and grace which was given us in Christ Jesus before the world began" (2 Tim. 1:9), addressing us thus: "as He which has called you is holy, so be holy in all manner of behavior."

In the wondrous and perfect salvation which God planned and provided for His people, infinite wisdom saw to it that each of His perfections should be owned and magnified, and if our presentation of the Gospel fails to exhibit that grand fact it is defective and partial. It is "to the praise of the glory of His grace in which He has made us accepted in the Beloved" (Eph. 1:6). It is "according to His mercy He saved us" (Titus 3:5). In order that the claims of His righteousness might be met He "spared not His own Son," abating not the least whit that justice demanded. Likewise He is resolved that "without holiness no man shall see the Lord" (Heb. 12:14). If He would not that the cup of death pass from Christ at His so earnest entreaty, most certain it is that He will not recede one iota from the requirements of His holiness in receiving us into His friendship, and therefore His inexorable demand is, "Let the wicked forsake his way, and the unrighteous man his thoughts, and let him return unto the Lord, and He will have mercy upon him, and to our God for He will abundantly pardon" (Isa. 55:7). For God to pardon those who persisted in their wicked ways would be to condone sin.

If there be a revolt in a kingdom, two things are required before peace can be restored and amity again prevail. The king must be willing to exercise clemency on a righteous basis and his subjects must cease their rebellion and become obedient to his scepter. Orderly government would be reduced to a farce if a pardon was offered unto those who continued to oppose the throne. Now the King of kings has announced His willingness and readiness to pardon any rebel among men, but only on the condition that he first throw down the weapons of his warfare against Him. The carnal mind is enmity against God, and obviously that enmity must cease before we can be reconciled to Him.

By nature and practice we are "alienated and enemies in our minds by wicked works" (Col. 1:21), and clearly those works must be confessed and repented of, hated and abandoned, before there can be peace between us and the thrice Holy One. God does not save us in our sins, but "from our sins" (Matthew 1:21). "But if while we seek to be justified by Christ, we ourselves also are found sinners, is therefore Christ the Minister of sin? God forbid" (Gal. 2:17).

In his chapter on what God requires from us in order to our reconciliation with God, T. Goodwin pointed out that "1. For the preparing us to be reconciled it is necessary that we be convinced that we are enemies to God, and that He accounts us such; and that so long as we remain in that estate, He is also an enemy to us, and can be no other. This what God in Christ has done gives demonstration of. He would not save us upon Christ's bare entreaty, but He would have satisfaction, and have Christ feel what it was to stand in the room of sinners. Yea, one end why God saved us by way of satisfaction to His justice, was that sinners pardoned might, in what Christ suffered, see and thoroughly apprehend what sin had deserved. And is it not then requisite that they should at least lay to heart and be sensible of their own treason and rebellions, and that God and they are at odds? Traitors must be convicted and condemned before they are capable of a legal pardon, as sentence must be pronounced before a legal appeal can be made. It is so in man's courts, and it is so in God's proceedings also. Neither indeed will men be brought so to sue out for His favor and prize His love till then, for it was never heard any man did heartily sue to one for pardon and peace with whom he did not first apprehend himself at variance.

2. It is necessary also that men apprehend the danger of going on in this estate; for though one should know another and himself to be enemies, if he thought his enemy were either careless or weak, he would slight reconciliation with him, and though sought unto would not seek it. He who is mentioned in Luke 14:31,32 was to sit down and consider if he were able to go out and meet his enemy, else he would never have sought conditions of peace. So the soul, until it apprehends and considers (finding God and itself enemies) what a sore enemy He is and what a fearful thing it is to fall into His hands, will not till then care to seek out to Him.

3. If one apprehended God implacable, not inclined to peace, or hard to be entreated, he would never come at Him either. Thus David, when Saul and he were at odds, suborned Jonathan secretly to observe what mind Saul bare towards him, and when he found him bent to kill him (1 Sam. 20:33), David came not at him.

4. The soul comes to be persuaded better things of God and things that accompany reconciliation, and conceives hope that reconciliation is to be had, and had for it. And therefore in all whom God means to reconcile to Himself, after He has humbled them He fixes a secret persuasion on their hearts that He is ready to be reconciled to them, if they will be reconciled to Him. God gives them a secret hint of His intended good will to them. He reveals what a gracious God He is, and how freely He pardons. . .the same God who from everlasting spoke unto His Son and wooed Him for us, does speak likewise secretly (inwardly) to a man's heart to allure and woo him to come into him" (T. Goodwin). In this way overcoming his reluctance, quieting his fears, and making him willing in the day of His power. As He employs the Law to impart a knowledge of sin, to convict is of our high-handed rebellion against the Most High, so He uses the Gospel to make known the wondrous provision He has made both to satisfy the claims of His Law and to meet deep need.

If it be asked, Since Christ has satisfied every requirement of God why are repentance and faith necessary from us? What has been said above should furnish a sufficient and satisfactory answer. It is because God is pleased to exercise pardoning mercy in such a way as is suited to all His perfections. It would be contrary to His wisdom to dispense the precious benefits of Christ's atonement to impenitent rebels. It would be contrary unto His governmental honor for Him to cast pearls before swine, to be trampled beneath their feet. It would be contrary unto His holiness for Him to bestow pardon upon one whom He knows would abuse such a favor—as though He granted a dispensatory power for him to sin with impunity. As it is no reflection upon the sufficiency of Christ's satisfaction that believers are called to suffer afflictions and death—for they are not penal inflictions for the satisfying of His justice, but are sent for the exercising of their graces (1 Pet. 1:7); so it in no way derogates from the perfections of Christ's satisfaction that sinners be required to repent and believe, for there is nothing meritorious about such exercises.

Goodwin then went on to point out, the sinner "must be set a-work to seek, as a condemned man, God and His favor in Christ, and peace and reconciliation through Him. He should pray to Him and He will be gracious ... God is the party superior, and it is fit the inferior should seek to the superior. He also is the person wronged, and though He be willing and desirous to be reconciled, yet He will have His favor prized. David longed to be reconciled to Absalom, yet he would be sought unto, for he would have his favor prized to the utmost and not cast away. Yea, and because the favor of God is better than life. He will be sought to with more earnestness and constancy that a man seeks for his life, 'you shall seek Me and find when you shall search for me with all your heart' (Jer. 29:13). 'If God has bidden us seek peace with men, yea, and to ensue it' (Ps. 34:14; 1 Pet. 3:11), that is, though it fly away and though He seems to reject us, yet to press upon Him—as David says my soul follows hard after you (Ps. 63:8). He will be sought unto with confession of and mourning for offending Him, for being in bitterness and mourning is joined with supplication for grace (Zech. 12:10). This is necessary to reconciliation because an acknowledgement is to be made (Jer. 3:13). God would be sought humbly unto by us, as those that are traitors and rebels. God will have men know when He pardons, that he knows what He pardons, and therefore will have them acknowledge what they deserve: 'that every mouth may be stopped and become guilty' (Rom. 3:19). If a man will become wise he must become a fool (1 Cor. 3:18); so a man that will become a friend to God must turn enemy against himself and judge himself worthy of destruction (Ezek. 36:31). . . .Where mourning for offending God is wanting, there is no sign of any good will yet wrought in the heart to God nor love to Him, without which God will never accept of a man...God will not pardon till He sees hope of amendment. Now until a man confesses his sin, and that with bitterness, it is an evidence he loves it (Job 20:12-14). While he hides it, spares it, and forsakes it not, it is sweet in his mouth. A man will never leave sin till he finds bitterness in it.

He must renounce all other friendships. The nature of reconciliation requires this, for friendship with anything else is enmity with God. 'Yea adulterers and, adulteresses, know ye not that the friendship of the world is enmity with God?' (James 4:4). As God will not have us serve other masters. so neither other friends. 'Whosoever does not forsake father and mother, etc., is unworthy of Me' says Christ (Luke 14:26). A friendship not only with proclaimed enemies—pen sins—but with all the things which the world has, is enmity with God. A believer may have a lordship over them, but not friendship with them. He may use them as strangers and servants, but not as friends, so as they have his heart. Friendship is entered into by choice—kindred is not so. So Jonathan chose David to be his friend (1 Sam. 20:30). As God did choose you, so also must you choose Him. As God chose you 'freely' (Hos. 14:4), out of good will, so must you choose Him freely. As He chose you forever, never to cast you off, so you are to choose Him forever. As nothing can separate from His love, so let nothing separate Him from yours.

Let your heart resign up itself and all that it has and devote it all unto God forever, to be commanded and used by Him. Thus did God for us — if He spared not His own Son, but with Him also freely gives us all things, let all you have be God's, giving up yourselves first unto the Lord (2 Cor. 8:5). Let God have all your understanding, will, affections, and whatever else. And let all be His, to command in anything as He pleases, and study how to set all a work for Him. Likeness of disposition is the only sure and lasting foundation of friendship, being the soul of it, for it is impossible two should long be friends unless they be one in their minds and affections, liking and loving the same things. 'Can two walk together except they be agreed' (Amos 3:3). Accordingly, a man that is thus reconciled must endeavor to walk and behave himself as a friend. The nature of reconciliation requires it. 'A man that has friends must show himself friendly' (Prov. 18:24). Therefore Christ said, 'You are My friends, if you do whatsoever I command you' (John

15:14). Watch over yourselves in all your ways and be fearful to displease Him and His goodness (Hos. 3:5).

God designed to set forth His love so as to attain the ends of loving. It is not to give forth peace only, but to manifest good will and kindness, as Luke 2:14 shows. Yea, the ground of His showing mercy is His love (Eph. 2:4). And although on our part our love and friendship to God is not the ground of His, yet it is the end or aim of His. Though He did not love us because we loved Him first, yet He loved us that we might love Him in return. Therefore in those He saves, if there were not wrought an inward principle of love and friendship, and good will mutual again to Him, that might answer His love to us, His love would not have its end, and would be finally cast away. For so we reckon love to be given away in loss when it is not answered in its kind, that is, with a true love in response. God would have His love valued and esteemed by those He saves, for love is the dearest thing that anyone has to bestow, because whoever has a man's love has all he has—for it commands all. If God's love be esteemed by us it will work holiness in us" (T. Goodwin, condensed and a few words altered).

We have quoted at such length from that excellent Puritan because while T. Goodwin was a high Calvinist (a supralapsarian) and magnified the free and sovereign grace of God as few have done, yet he was also an able evangelist, a faithful shepherd of souls. And though he was a strict particular-redemptionist, yet he also enforced human responsibility. And while he taught clearly the total depravity and utter ruin of fallen man, yet he also shunned not to state plainly and emphatically what God required from the unsaved. We could easily reproduce the same, in substance, from Owen, Manton, Bunyan, and others of the seventeenth century. How far some in the eighteenth and nineteenth centuries departed from their teaching we leave the reader to determine, as he may also decide how solemn and serious—or how unimportant—such departure was. Whether the unsaved in many a so-called "place of truth" have been lulled to sleep by a fatalistic presentation of the doctrine of election and by harping so much on the creature's inability to meet God's requirements, or whether they have been faithfully exhorted to repent and believe the Gospel.

Should the reader say, I mentally assent to most of what Goodwin wrote, but I find myself totally unable to comply with his directions, we ask, cannot you see that such a statement greatly aggravates your wickedness? Suppose I have grievously wronged and offended a dear friend of yours, and you came to me saying you deplored the breach between us, that your friend was willing to be friends again if I would put matters right and beg forgiveness. Suppose you pleaded with me to do the proper thing, and the only reply I made you was, I am unable to. What would you think? Would you not justly conclude that all I lacked was a willing heart? That the reason I would not seek unto the one I had injured was either because I hated him or because I was too proud to humble myself before him? You would judge rightly! So it is with the sinner and God. If we analyze his "cannot" it is because he is so wedded to his idols, so in love with sin, he will not forsake them. And anything in our preaching which comforts him in his "will not" is contrary to Truth.

Chapter 24
Its Reception-Continued

On this occasion we propose to treat of the present aspect of our subject in connection with the Covenant. There is a pressing need for this today, for while on the one hand most professing Christians are woefully ignorant about the Covenant, some others have been very faultily instructed in them. As on almost every other doctrinal and practical subject, the Puritans were much sounder than many of the outstanding Calvinists of the nineteenth century, for the sermons of the latter were sadly lacking in perspective. Those of men like Joseph Irons, and James Wells, were thoroughly lop-sided. While they rightly emphasized Divine sovereignty, they remissibly ignored human responsibility; while they had much to say about God's grace, they had little to say about the demands of His holiness: while magnifying the finished work of Christ, they were silent upon what God required from sinners before the benefits of it were applied to them. They were very fond of quoting "He has made with me an everlasting covenant, ordering in all things and sure" (2 Sam. 23:5), but they scarcely ever cited, and never expounded, "Incline your ear and come unto Ale: hear and your soul shall live: and I will make an everlasting covenant with you" (Isa. 55:3).

A covenant is a compact between two parties in which there is mutual stipulation and restipulation, the one promising certain benefits in return for the fulfilling of certain conditions by the other. Thus it was in the covenant or agreement entered into between Isaac and Abimelech (Gen. 26:28, 29) and between Jonathan and David (1 Sam. 20:16,1 7). God entered into covenant with Christ as the Head of the elect, and to that covenant He attached the demand of repentance, faith, and obedience from them.

Let us first consider the passage we quoted above from Isaiah 55 and which is so much ignored by many Calvinists. That chapter opens with a most blessed Gospel invitation, though there are one or two things in it which have been both misunderstood and disregarded. "Ho everyone that thirsts, come you to the waters" has been restricted unto a spiritual thirst, as though the invitation is made only unto souls Divinely quickened. That is an unwarrantable limitation. The Gospel call goes forth freely to all classes and conditions of men, addressing them simply as sinners—guilty, lost, needy sinners. Since they are sinners, they have no satisfying portion, yet they have a thirst for something more contenting, and therefore their quest for happiness. But since they are blinded by sin they know not what that satisfying portion consists of or where true happiness is found. They seek it, but seek it wrongly and in vain. Therefore the question is asked them, "wherefore do you spend your money for that which is not bread? And your labor for that which satisfies not." In this way is the Gospel called enforced.

"Come to the waters" which can quench your thirst and satisfy your heart. "And he that has no money, come you, buy and eat." The Inviter is a generous Benefactor who makes no charge for His benefits and bars not the poorest from a welcome to them. Nevertheless, those who would partake of them must "buy." That does not mean they must give something for those benefits and purchase them. But it does signify they must part with something, or otherwise the word "buy" would have no force. There are two things which the sinner must part with if he would be a participant of the Gospel feast: he must abandon his idols, and he must renounce his own goodness or righteousness. That which his idols, and he must renounce his own goodness or righteousness. That which Christ requires from the sinner is that he come to Him empty handed. If on the one hand that means he must bring no price with him, nothing seeking to merit his acceptance; on the other hand, it also means he must drop the world, and no longer cherish and cling to those objects or pleasures in which until this time he has sought to delight himself.

"Come you, buy and eat, yea, come, buy wine and milk, without money and without price." Three times over in that first verse is the word "come" used. It is the response which is required to the invitation made. It is a word calling for action, for voluntary action. It is a word too of clear yet necessary implication. One cannot come to a place without leaving another! The prodigal son had to quit the "far country" in order to turn unto the Father's house. The sinner must (in his affections and resolutions) turn his back upon the world if he would embrace Christ. Twice is the word "buy" found in it, to emphasize the fact that it is a definite and personal transaction which is here in view, and as we have already pointed out, to denote that something must be relinquished or parted with—whatever stand in opposition to Christ as seeking to hold the sinner's heart. While the "no money," "without money and with out price" stresses the truth that eternal life is not to be obtained by the works of the Law, but is a free gift, that we bring nothing with us to commend ourselves to God's favorable regard, but come simply as poverty-stricken beggars.

"Hearken diligently unto Ale, and eat that which is good, and let your soul delight itself in fatness" (v. 2). Listen to the voice of Wisdom which pleads with you to waste no more of your money on that which ministers not to your spiritual and eternal needs and your efforts after what has no power to afford you real and lasting satisfaction. Appropriate unto yourselves the riches of Divine grace as they are spread before you in the Gospel, and let your soul delight itself in that which will bring no disappointment with it or regrets afterward. "Incline your ear, and come unto Me." Too long have you hearkened to the sirens of your lusts and to the false promises of this world. Too long have you been deaf to My counsels and precepts, to My expostulations and warnings. Incline your ear "as you do to that which you find yourselves concerned in, and pleased with. Bow the ear, and let the proud heart stoop to the humbling methods of the Gospel; bend the ear this way you may hear with attention" (Matt. Henry). "Hear," that is, heed, respond, obey, comply with My demands. "Hear, and your soul shall live, and I will make an everlasting covenant with you." (v. 3).

Here, then, we learn plainly and definitely who are the characters with whom God proposes to make an everlasting covenant, and the terms with which they must comply if He is to do so. They are those who have freely sampled the lying vanities of this world and, like the poor prodigal, have found them to be naught but "husks." They are those who hitherto had closed their ears against Him, refusing to meet His requirements and steeling themselves against His admonitions. "Incline your ear" signifies. cease your rebellious attitude, submit yourselves to My righteous demand. They are those who are separated and alienated from the Holy One, at a guilty distance from Him—away in "the far country." "Come unto Me" means, throw down the weapons of your warfare and cast yourselves upon My mercy. They are those who are unquickened, destitute of spiritual life, as the "hear, and your souls shall live" clearly shows. Comply with those terms, says God, and I will make an everlasting covenant with you. It is human responsibility which is there being enforced. It is but another way of saying to sinners "Be reconciled to God."

As we pointed out in a former chapter, this enforcing of man's responsibility is most meet for the honor of God, and as the honor of the Father lies nearer to the heart of Christ than anything else, He will not dispense the benefits of His atonement except in that way which is most becoming to God's perfections. There is a complete accord between Christ's impetration of God's favor and the application of it. That is, between Christ's purchase of it and our actual entrance into the same. As the justice of God deemed it meet that His wrath should be appeased and His law vindicated by the satisfaction made by His Son, so His wisdom determined and His holiness ordered it that the sinner must be converted before pardon be bestowed upon him (Acts 3:19). We must be on our guard here, as everywhere, against extolling one of God's attributes above another. True, the Covenant is entirely of grace—pure, free, sovereign grace—nevertheless, here too grace reigns "through righteousness" (Rom. 5:21) and not at the expense of it. Christ died not to render any sinner secure in his carnality.

God will not disgrace his grace by entering into covenant with those who are impenitent and openly defying Him. To do so would make Him the Condoner of sin, instead of the implacable Hater of it. It is not that the sinner must do something in order to earn the grand blessings of the covenant, or that he must add his quota to the redemptive work of Christ. No, no he contributes not a mite to the procuring of them. That price, and infinitely costly it was, was fully paid by the Lord Jesus Himself. But though God requires naught from us by way of purchasing or meriting those blessings, He does in the matter of receiving them. "The honor of God would fall to the ground if we should be pardoned without our submission, without confession of past sin, or resolution of future obedience. For till then we neither know our true misery, nor are we willing to come out of it; for they that securely continue in their sins, despise both the curse of the Law and the grace of the Gospel" (Manton).

"And I will make an everlasting covenant with you, the sure mercies of David" (v. 3). It is of course the Messiah, the spiritual or antitypical David of whom God there speaks—(as He is also called "David" in Psalm 89:3, Jeremiah 30:9, Ezekiel 34:23, 24; 37:24, Hosea 3:5). If proof is needed that it is the Lord Jesus who is in view, Acts 13:34-37 supplies it. "The sure mercies of David" are the special and distinguishing favors which are reserved for and in due time bestowed upon God's elect. They are the grand privileges and benefits of the Covenant which God pledged Himself to impart unto Christ and His seed upon the completion of His engagement. They are "sure" because the promises of One who cannot lie, and because they are now dispensed by the victorious and risen Redeemer. They are revealed in the Gospel and presented for the acceptance of faith. "Behold I have given Him (the spiritual David) a Witness to the people, a Leader and Commander to the people" (Isa. 55:4). That tells us those "sure mercies" are dispensed in a way of righteousness and holiness. The Gospel presents Christ to us not only as a Redeemer, but a Teacher and Ruler. We are required to surrender to Him as our absolute Lord and voluntarily take His yoke upon us before He becomes our Savior and imparts rest unto our souls.

"For thus says the Lord, unto the eunuchs that keep my sabbaths and choose the things that please Me, and take hold of My covenant; even unto them will I give in My house and within My walls a place and a name better than of sons and daughters. I will give them an everlasting name that shall not be cut off Also the sons of the stranger that join themselves to the Lord, to serve Him, and to love the name of the Lord, to be His servants, every, one that keeps the sabbath from polluting it and takes hold of My covenant" (Isa. 56:4-6). Here we have spiritual and eternal blessings presented under the imagery of the Mosaic economy. It was an O. T. prophecy announcing the distinctive favors of the N. T. dispensation. Under the Mosaic law "eunuchs" were barred from entering the congregation of the Lord, and the "stranger" or Gentile was barred by the middle wall of partition; but under the Gospel era these restrictions would no longer abstain, for the grace of God should flow forth unto all without distinction. That which we would specially observe is the clause placed in italics, which sets forth the human side of things.

Let us notice carefully what is here predicated of those who "take hold of" God's covenant. They "keep the Sabbath from polluting it," that is, they have a concern for God's honor and a respect for His Law, and therefore keep holy that day which He has set apart unto Himself, requiring us to act as per the instructions of Isaiah 58:13. They "choose the things that please" the Holy One. They are not self-pleasers, or gratifiers of the flesh, but earnestly endeavor to abstain from whatever God has prohibited and to perform whatever He has enjoined; and this not by constraint or fear, but freely and cheerfully. They "join themselves to the Lord." They seek unto and cleave to Him. they do so in order "to serve Him and to love His name, to be servants." "Serve" Him means to be subject unto Him, to take their orders from Him, to promote His interests. They are resolved to "love His name." Their service is that of friends and not slaves, their faith is one which works by love and their obedience prompted by gratitude. Unless our service proceeds from love it is valueless. They had given Him their hearts, and therefore their faculties, talents, time and strength are dedicated and devoted unto Him. Such are the ones who "take hold of His covenant."

"In every covenant there is something given and something required. To take hold of God's covenant is to lay claim to the privileges and benefits promised and offered in it. Now this cannot be done unless we choose the things that please Him. That is, voluntarily and deliberately, not by chance but by choice, enter into a course of obedience wherein we must be pleasing or acceptable to Him: this is the fixed determination of our hearts" (Manton). And we never enter upon that course of obedience and do the things which are pleasing unto God until we have first chosen Him as our absolute Lord, our Supreme End, our highest Good and our everlasting Portion. Negatively, they can be "no taking hold of the covenant" until we cease all opposition to God. Positively, it is to embrace the Gospel offer and to comply with its terms. The covenant of grace is proffered to us in the Gospel and to take hold of the former is to heartily consent unto the latter and meet its requirements, giving ourselves to the Lord (2 Cor. 8:5)—freely, unreservedly, for time and eternity. Consent there must be, for none can enjoy the privileges of a charter which they never accepted and agreed to.

What has just been before us in Isaiah 56 is virtually parallel with 27:4 and 5. "Fury is not in Me (unless I am provoked by the rebellion of My creatures. In such case): Who would set the briers and thorns against me in battle? I would go through them, and I would burn them together." Such opposition against the Almighty is utterly futile. If they stir up His wrath, naught but the Lake of fire can be their portion, unless they avail themselves of His amnesty, throw down the weapons of their warfare against Him and be reconciled to Him, which is what is signified by "Or (as the only alternative to burning) let him take hold of My strength." Let him grasp My arm which is uplifted to smite and crush him. And how shall that be done? Thus, "that he may make peace with Me." That he may cease this sinful fighting against Me; "and He shall make peace with Me." God is ready and willing—on the ground of Christ's satisfaction—to lay aside His vengeance and be reconciled, if the sinner is willing to lay aside his awful enmity and become friends.

"This (Isa. 27:4, 5) may very well be construed as a summary of the doctrine of the Gospel, with which the church is to be watered every moment. Here is a quarrel supposed between God and man: for here is a battle fought and peace to be made. It is an old quarrel, ever since sin first entered. It is on God's part a righteous quarrel but on man's part most unrighteous. Here is a gracious invitation given us to make up this quarrel. Let him that is desirous to be at peace with god take hold on God's strength, on His strong arm, which is lifted up against the sinner to strike him dead; let him by supplication keep back the stroke. Pardoning mercy is called the power of the Lord; let him take hold of that. Christ crucified is the power of God, let him by a lively faith take hold on Him, as a sinking man catches hold of a plank that is within his reach, or as the malefactor took hold on the horns of the altar...it is vain to think of contesting with Him. It is like setting briers and thorns before a consuming fire. We are not an equal match for Omnipotence. This is the only way, and it is a sure way to reconciliation. Let him take this way to make peace with Me, and he shall make peace" (From. M. Henry).

"In those days and in that time, says the Lord, the children of Israel shall come, they and the children of Judah together, going and weeping. They shall go, and seek the Lord their God. They shall ask the way to Zion with their faces toward it, saying, Come, and let us join ourselves to the Lord in a perpetual covenant that shall not be forgotten" (Jer. 50:4, 5). The historical reference is to the liberty which Cyrus gave to the Hebrews to return unto their own land, consequent upon his overthrow of Belshazzar. Unacquainted with the road, the exiled Jews on leaving Babylon for Palestine, made inquiry about it. Their case supplied a type or adumbration of the spiritual experiences of God's people. "In those days" is an O. T. expression which pointed forward to this Christian era. It was therefore one of many evangelical prophecies couched in the language of an historical event. Whatever fulfillment that prophecy may or may not yet have for the Jewish people (and on that matter we refrain from any dogmatic statement) its present application is to sinners who have been awakened and convicted by the Spirit so that they are concerned about their spiritual and eternal interests.

Like those in the historical type, these seekers are issuing forth from a lifelong bondage—in sin. Convicted of their guilt and resolved to reform their ways, they are represented as "going and weeping" and determining to "seek the Lord their God," which in N. T. language would be "repenting" and being "converted." As Matthew Henry says "This represents the return of poor sinners to God. Heaven is the Zion they aim at as their end. On this they have set their hearts, toward this they have set their faces, and therefore they ask the way to it. They do not ask the way to heaven and set their faces to the world, nor set their faces toward heaven and go on at a venture without asking the way. In all true converts there are both a sincere desire to attain the end and a constant care to keep in the way." Their desire and design was to "join themselves to the Lord in a perpetual covenant." That was something they must do, and it is to that particular expression we would ask careful attention, for it has been totally ignored by hyper-Calvinists, who say nothing at all upon the human-responsibility side of the subject—what we must do before the benefits of the Covenant are actually made over to us.

Chapter 25
Its Reception-Concluded

There is a zeal which is not according to knowledge (Rom. 10:2), and the ecclesiastical history of the last three centuries supplies many sad examples of same. In opposing the Papist fiction of human merits, some went too far in the opposite direction and failed to enforce the necessity of good works. In protesting against a general or indefinite atonement and in contending for particular redemption, not a few hyper-Calvinists repudiated the free offer of the Gospel. Many handled the total depravity and spiritual inability of the natural man in such a manner that his responsibility was completely undermined. In their ardor to magnify the sovereign grace of God, men often lost sight of the moral requirements of His righteousness. There has been a lamentable lack of balance in presenting the inseparable truths of justification and sanctification, and the privileges and duties of believers. The perseverance of the saints in faith and holiness has not received nearly so much emphasis among Calvinists as has the Divine preservation of them, nor have they said one-tenth as much on repentance as on faith. The same grievous defect appears in many of the sermons preached on the Covenant. The Puritans were thoroughly sound and symmetrical on it, but some who followed them, though posing as the champions of Truth, were very lopsided.

"Gather My saints together unto Me: Those who have made a covenant with Me by sacrifice" (Ps. 50:5). This is still another verse which has been greatly if not totally neglected by those against whose partiality we complain. It also deals with the human side of things. There is a human side in connection with the Covenant. It is just as true that men must enter into covenant with God, as it is that He deigns to enter into covenant with them. In this verse we learn that one of the distinguishing marks of God's saints is that they have made a covenant with Him: That speaks of human action and not of Divine operations. The saints make a covenant with God "by sacrifice," for no valid paction [agreement, compact, bargain] can be entered into with Him apart from the intervention of a sacrifice. At the beginning of their national history Israel entered into a solemn covenant with Jehovah, and they did so by sacrifice. A graphic account of the same is furnished in Exodus 24. There is much there of outstanding interest and importance which we cannot now dwell upon; only a bare notice of the salient features will here be in order.

After Moses had received the Ten Commandments from the Lord, he returned and "told the people all the words of the Lord" (v. 3)—that obedience which He required from them. Their response was prompt and proper: "all the people answered with one voice and said, All the words which the Lord has said will we do." Moses then gave orders for oxen to be sacrificed unto the Lord: half of the blood he sprinkled on the altar, half he put into basins. Having written the words of the Lord in what is specifically called "the book of the covenant" he then read it unto the whole of the congregation, and they again vowed to be obedient (v. 7). Next Moses "took the blood and sprinkled it on the people and said, Behold the blood of the covenant." Thus was the covenant formally ratified: God binding Himself to the fulfilling of His promises and they binding themselves to His precepts, that they might avoid the penalty threatened and obtain the blessings promised. To that transaction the apostle refers in Hebrews 9:19, 20—"testament" should be "covenant." those slain oxen prefigured the sacrifice of Christ and the benefits accruing from there. The congregation represented "the Israel of God" (Gal. 6:16), and their compact with the Lord adumbrated the full surrender which believers make of themselves unto God when they respond to the call of the Gospel.

Christians also make a covenant with God, and they do so "by sacrifice." Christ's death was a real and true sacrifice: see Eph. 5:2. In all the sacrifices there was a shedding of blood without which there was no remission of sins, and as their antitype Christ's blood was poured out. Christ's death was a mediatory sacrifice, a propitiatory sacrifice, an accepted sacrifice,, and therefore an effectual one. It has all the virtues of a sacrifice. As the Rector and Judge of the universe God was pacified, as the party offended, by Christ's oblation. Christ made His soul an offering for sin and God accepted the same as a full satisfaction to His justice. So too His blood expiates the offences of His people: "when He had by Himself purged our sins, sat down on the right hand of the Majesty on high." When rightly appropriated His blood removes both the guilt and pollution of sin. So too it is adequate for the sinner himself, the offending party. When he avails himself of the preferred remedy and trusts in Christ's atonement, he is reconciled to God. No other sacrifice is needed by God nor is it by the sinner.

By His sacrifice Christ made and confirmed the new covenant. By virtue of His oblation Christ is authorized to offer the terms and dispense the benefits of it. "Now tile God of peace, that brought again from the dead the Lord Jesus, that great Shepherd of the sheep, through the blood of the everlasting covenant" (Heb. 13:20). Observe carefully the "blood of the everlasting covenant" has a double reference there. First, to God, as "The God of peace," that is, to God as pacified—His wrath appeased and His justice satisfied by a full recompense being made for our offences. Second, to Christ Himself: having satisfied to the uttermost farthing, God brought Him back from the dead and invested Him with His office of "the great Shepherd of the sheep." That is, as the One who had the right to rescue His strayed sheep out of the power of the roaring lion, and bring them into the fold to enjoy the privileges of the flock. And by Christ's sacrifice the benefits of the covenant are ratified and conveyed to us. That is evident from His own words at the institution of the Lord's supper: "this is My blood of the new covenant, which is shed for many, for the remission of sins" (Matthew 26:28)—the principal blessing. It is by the blood of the covenant we are pardoned, sanctified and perfected forever.

As Manton showed, our manner of entering into covenant with God is by the same moral acts as which Israel of old were conversant about the sacrifices and what they imported. Those sacrifices represented the defilement they had contracted by sin: by the killing of the beast, they owned that they deserved to die themselves. The oblations they brought to the tabernacle or temple were public testimonies of their guilt and pollution, an acknowledgement that their life was forfeit to God. As the apostle informs us "in those sacrifices there is a remembrance again made of sins" (Heb. 10:3); they kept before their offerers what they were as violators of the Law. Now the same obligation lies upon us if we would make a covenant with God by virtue of the great sacrifice of Christ. There must be the recognition that the curse of the law binds us over to eternal wrath and a subscription to that solemn fact by our conscience. There must be an acknowledgement of our guilt and pollution, and that, with broken heartedness. Unless we be deeply affected by our sinfulness and ruin Christ will be little valued by us.

The sacrifices appointed by God in the OT. era told forth His abundant mercy: that God had no pleasure in the death of the wicked, but rather that he turn from his wickedness and live. And in order that His mercy might be on a righteous basis, His love provided that which His justice demanded. That has been lost sight of by the dispensationalists, who erroneously represent the Mosaic economy as a stern regime of unrelieved justice. But it should ever be remembered that side by side with the moral law was the ceremonial, with its oblations and ablutions, where for-giveness and cleansing were obtainable for those who availed themselves of it. All through the O.T. era "mercy rejoiced against judgment" (Ex. 34:6, 7; Ps. 103:8; Isa. 1:18). That "The Lord is gracious and full of compassion, slow to anger, and of great mercy" was shown and believed in David's time (Ps. 145:8), for those blessed attributes were clearly revealed in the sacrifices—types as they were of Christ. So today the sinner who would enter into covenant with God should re-alize that He is merciful and in Christ has made full provision for his deep need. This is to be acknowledged by us with thankfulness and joy.

Those O.T. sacrifices were also so many obligations unto duty, for they instructed the offerer of that worship and obedience which he owed unto God. Since God required propitiation for sin, they were shown the need for conforming to His law, and whereas His mercy made provision for their past failure, gratitude should prompt them unto future subjection. Moreover, by offering a ram or an ox unto the Lord the one who brought it did in effect devote himself, with all his strength, unto Him. In this way the offerer was taught to yield himself unto His service. And so unto those who would make or renew a covenant with God, the N.T. word is "I beseech you, therefore, brethren, by the mercies of God, that you present your bodies a living sacrifice, holy, acceptable unto God, which is your reasonable service" (Rom. 12:1). That, as we showed at some length in a recent article, supplies an interpretation of the rites of the Law and of the "reason-able" part of the O. T. order of things. Thus, he who would make a covenant with God is required to give up himself wholly unto God with a sincere and firm resolution unto a new life of obedience to Him. If there is any reservation the covenant is marred in the making of it: "Their heart was not right with Him, neither were they steadfast in His covenant" (Ps. 78:37).

As the Puritan Win. Gurnall so faithfully remarked upon Psalm 50:5, "We are not Christians till we have subscribed this covenant, and that without any reservation. When we take upon us the profession of Christ's name, we enlist ourselves in His muster-roll and by it do promise that we will live and die with Him in opposition to all His enemies. He will not entertain us till we resign up ourselves freely to His disposal, that there may be no disputing with His commands afterwards, but as one under authority, go and come at His word." So too Manton: "You have no benefit by the covenant till you personally enter into the bond of it. It is true, God being pacified by Christ, offers pardon and acceptance on the condition of the covenant, but we do not actually partake of the benefits till we perform those conditions. Though the price is paid by Christ, ac-cepted by the Father, yet we have not an actual interest, through our own default, for not accept-ing God's covenant. What shall we do? Bless God for His grace. Own Christ as the Son of God, the Redeemer of the world, and the Fountain of our life and peace. Devote yourselves to God, to serve and please Him."

Not only are we required to take hold of God's covenant (Isa. 56:4,6), to make a covenant with God by sacrifice (Ps. 50:5), and to "join ourselves to the Lord in a perpetual covenant" (Jer. 50:5), but we are enjoined "Take heed unto yourselves lest you forget the covenant of the Lord your God" (Deut. 4:23) and "Be mindful always of His covenant" (1 Chron. 16:15). We are required to abide faithfully by the promises we made and the agreement we entered into when we chose Him to be our God and gave up ourselves unreservedly unto Him, for the promises of the covenant are made only unto such: "All tile paths of the Lord are mercy and truth unto such as keep His covenant and His testimonies" (Ps. 25:10). Of old the Lord complained, "His people have trans-gressed My covenant" (Judges 2:20). "Israel and Judah have broken My covenant" (Jer. 11:10). They themselves acknowledged "the children of Israel have forsaken Your covenant" (1 Kings 19:10). "They kept not tile covenant of God" (Ps. 78:10). So it is with the Christian when he de-parts from the Lord and enters upon a course of self-pleasing. Therefore, in order for a backslider to be restored, he must needs renew his covenant with God, for the recovery of such an one is a new "conversion" (Luke 22:32). And so he is required to "do the first works" (Rev. 2:5).

Now cannot certain of our readers see for themselves how unfair and unfaithful it is for preachers and writers to make so much of and quote so frequently such verses as 2 Samuel 23:5, Jeremiah 31:33,34; 32:40,41, and utterly ignore Isaiah 56:4-6, Jeremiah 50:5, Psalm 50:5 and those cited in the preceding paragraph. Cannot they perceive it is handling God's word deceitfully, and utterly misleading unto souls to be constantly comforting them with the "I wills" of God, yet remaining silent upon the "Be you," "you shall" and failing to press such exhortations? Cannot they see how dishonest it is to treat only of that covenant which God enters into with the elect before time began in the person of their Head, and say nothing of the covenant which we must make with God during this time-state? We ourselves should be guilty of the very partiality against which we inveigh were we to publish in booklet form the last four of our articles on Reconciliation in the 1944 volume and the first four in 1945 entitling them "The Covenant of Grace." if we failed to add to them what has been adduced in this chapter and the three preceding it, in which we have set before the reader the human side of things—what God requires from us.

God has appointed a "due order" or connection—a moral and righteous one—between the blessings purchased by Christ and the actual conveyance of them unto us, in which our responsibility is enforced. To quote from yet another of the able and godly Puritans: "Holiness is God's signature upon all heavenly doctrines, which distinguishes them from all carnal inventions. They have a direct tendency to promote His glory and the real benefit of the rational creature. Thus the way of salvation by Christ is most fit to reconcile God to man by securing His honor, and to reconcile man to God by encouraging his hope. . .The grace of the Gospel is so far from indulging sin that it gives the most deadly wound to it, especially since the tenor of the new covenant is that the condemned creature, in order to receive pardon and the benefits that are purchased, must receive the Benefactor with the most entire consent for his Prince and Savior. Thus the Divine wisdom has so ordered the way of salvation that, as mercy and justice in God, so holiness and comfort may be perfectly united in the reasonable creature" (Win. Bates, "The Harmony of the Divine Attributes" 1660). The death of Christ is not only the surest ground of comfort, but the strongest incentive to obedience.

We are advocating no new or strange doctrine when we insist that the Everlasting Covenant and the Gospel requires from us repentance and faith, full surrender unto God and the steadfast performance of obedience unto the end of our lives. "The obligation on us unto holiness is equal as unto what it was under the Law, though a relief is provided where unavoidably we come short of it. There is, therefore, nothing more certain than that there is no relaxation given us as unto any duty of holiness by the Gospel, nor any indulgence unto the least sin. But yet upon the supposition of the acceptance of sincerity, and a perfection of parts instead of degrees, with mercy provided for our failings and sins, there is an argument to be taken from the command unto indispensable necessity of holiness, including in it the highest encouragement to endeavor after it. For together with the command there is also grace administered, enabling us unto the obedience which God will accept. Nothing therefore can avoid or evacuate the power of this command and argument from it but a stubborn contempt of God arising from the love of sin" (J. Owen).

Probably there is another class of our readers who have never heard anything on the subject, as well as those who are acquainted only with the Divine side of it, who are ready to exclaim, If it is an imperative condition of salvation that man enters into a definite covenant with God, then that cuts me off entirely, for I have never made one with Him! Alas, it is sadly true that, through the laziness or unfaithfulness of the preachers they have sat under, many of the Lord's people know nothing, or next to nothing, about the Covenant of Grace. On the other hand, it is blessedly true that, in the mercy of God, though all unconscious to themselves, they had been led to comply with the terms of the Covenant. Though they knew not that they were truly (though not formally) entering into Covenant with God when they repented, believed the Gospel and received Christ Jesus as their Lord and Savior, yet such was the case. Each one who has really responded to the call in Isaiah 55:3 with him God has "made an everlasting covenant"— Nevertheless his ignorance of that fact does not excuse the Christian's failure to have learned from the Scriptures what they teach on it.

Let us now seek to remove one or two difficulties which may have been raised in the minds of our friends. When we affirm that God's ministers are to make a free offer of the Gospel to every creature and that they are to call upon all who hear it "be reconciled to God," that does not imply that the results of Christ's death are rendered uncertain, that the success of His redemptive work is suspended on the caprice of man's will. Not at all. It has been far too little recognized that God has more than one design in sending forth the Gospel. First, it is for the glory of Christ—a worldwide proclamation of His excellence. God intends that a universal testimony shall be borne to the person and work of the One who so superlatively honored Him. Second, the preaching of the Gospel is made a further test of corrupt nature, demonstrating that men love darkness rather than light. Third, God uses the Gospel as a remedial agency in curbing the wickedness of the world, for many are reformed by it who are never savingly transformed in this way, making this scene a safer place for His people to pass through. It is also the means by which He calls out His elect: the sieve in which the wheat is separated from the chaff.

But if Christ be the Head and Representative of His people, and as their Surety fulfilled every requirement of the Law, in their stead and earned its reward, must not every one of them be made partakers of that reward? Most assuredly, yet still in the order or way God has appointed. We must have the requisite qualification to make us meet for that reward. "This qualification is faith. As grace in God qualified God (if I may use the expression) for effecting reconciliation, so faith in us qualifies us for applying and enjoying it. Though Christ be the Purchaser, yet faith is the means of instating us in it. 'Being justified by faith, we have peace with God through our Lord Jesus Christ.' Not a man has peace with God till justified by faith. This inestimable favor is not conferred but upon men of good will, that value and consent to it. We must lay our hands upon the head of the sacrifice and own Him for ours. This is the bond which unites us to Christ the Purchaser, and by Him to God as the Author of reconciliation. It gives us a right to this peace, and at the last the comfort of it" (S. Charnock).

But does not God's requirement of faith from us leave the outcome of Christ's redemption uncertain? In no wise. Why not? Because Christ by His merits procured the Holy Spirit to work in His people what God requires from them to meet the terms of His covenant and to fulfill the conditions of the Gospel. "The purchase was made by Christ alone upon the cross, without any qualification in us; the application is not wrought without something in us concurring with it, though that also is wrought by the grace of God. God has ordained peace for us. There is a work to be wrought within us for the enjoyment of that peace: 'Lord, You will ordain peace for us, for You also have wrought all our works in us' (Isa. 26:12). The one is the act of God in Christ, the other is the act of God by the Spirit. Though the fire burn, if I would be warmed I must not run from it, but approach it" (Charnock). It is that work of Christ's Spirit within the elect which capacitates and causes them to abandon their idols, put forth faith, and makes them willing to be wholly devoted to God.

That was admirably set forth in the Westminster Confession of Faith—the joint and studied production of many of the ablest of the Puritans. "Man by his fall having made himself incapable of life by the first covenant, the Lord was pleased to make a second, commonly called the

Covenant of Grace: by which He freely offered unto sinners life and salvation by Jesus Christ, requiring of them faith in Him that they might be saved, and promising to give unto all those who are ordained unto life His Holy Spirit, to make them willing and able to believe." The grand change in our legal relation to God, secured by Christ's satisfaction, is infallibly followed by the great change in our experimental relation to God, as that is wrought in us by the Spirit's work of regeneration and sanctification, the one being the fruit of the other—the reward assured the Surety on behalf of those He represented. Our reconciliation to God (through the renewing of the Spirit) is the sure consequence of His reconciliation to us, and a faith which works by love, which goes out in acts of holy obedience, is the evidence of our new birth and of our having entered into covenant with God.

"We joy in God through our Lord Jesus Christ, by whom we have now received the reconciliation" (Rom. 5:11). It is through Him, by the working of His Spirit, that we have, by faith, been enabled to "receive the reconciliation" which the Mediator wrought out for us. From the Divine side of things the evangelist goes forth on no uncertain errand, for the invincible operations of the Spirit God makes the Gospel effectual unto each hearer chosen unto salvation. Yet from the human side of things the evangelist is required to enforce the responsibility of his hearers, calling on them to "be reconciled to God," to repent and believe the Gospel, to make a covenant with God, and so far from assuring them that God will work in their hearts what He requires of them (which would encourage them to remain in a state of inertia), he is to enforce God's righteous demands, press upon them the claims of Christ, and bid them flee for refuge to the hope set before them.

Chapter 26
Its Need Revisited

In the previous chapters we have shown at some length the need for and the nature of reconciliation being effected between God and those who have broken His Law. We have dwelt upon the amazing fact that, though He was the One wronged, yet God took the initiative and is the Author of recovering the rebellious unto Himself. We have seen how that project engaged His eternal counsels in the Everlasting Covenant, and that therein His wisdom found a way by which His love might flow forth unto the guilty without any sullying of His holiness of flouting of His justice, and how that the Son fully concurred in the Father's counsels and voluntarily performed the stupendous work in order to their accomplishment. We have already considered that which God requires from sinners if they are to become actual participants of the good of Christ's mediation and personally "receive the reconciliation" (Rom. 5:11). We are therefore now ready to contemplate the "results" of fruits of that reconciliation—the consequences which follow from the new relation to God and His Law which the sinner enters into upon his repentance and saving acceptance of the Gospel.

Causes and their effects need ever to be distinguished if we are to obtain something more than a vague and general idea of the things with which they are concerned. It is by confounding principles and their products that so many are confused. As we have shown in previous chapters, reconciliation is one of the principal results which issue from the sacrifice of Christ. Strictly speaking it has a fourfold cause. The will of the Father, or His eternal counsels, was its originating cause. The mediation of the incarnate Son is its meritorious and procuring cause. The work of the Spirit in the souls of the elect is the efficient cause, for it is by His gracious and invincible operations they are capacitated to do that which God requires of them before they become actual partakers of the benefits of Christ's mediation. The repentance and faith of the awakened and convicted sinner is the instrumental cause by which he is reconciled to God. We say that reconciliation is one of the principal results from Christ's sacrifice—redemption, remission, sanctification are others, and they are so intimately related that it is not easy to prevent an overlapping of them in our thoughts. But in what follows we shall treat, mainly, not of the effect of Christ's redemptive work, but rather the results of reconciliation itself.

Perhaps the most comprehensive of any single statement in Holy Writ concerning the outcome of reconciliation is found in that brief but pregnant word "Christ has also once suffered, the Just for the unjust, that He might bring us to God" (1 Pet. 3:18). "Bring us to God" is a general expression for the whole benefit which ensues from reconciliation, including the removal of all obstacles and impediments and the bestowment of all requisites and blessings. Formerly there was a legal hostility and moral dissimilarity between God and us, with the want of intercourse and fellowship, but now those who were once "far off" are "made nigh" (Eph. 2:13). In consequence of what Christ did and suffered, His people have been enstated into life, brought into the favor of God, become par-takers of the nature of God, have restored to them the image of God, are given access to God, are favored to have communion with Him and will yet enjoy the eternal and ineffable vision of Him. Let that serve as our outline.

1. The initial consequence of our reconciliation to God by Christ is that we have life: a life in Law. That is an aspect of our subject which, fundamental though it be, has received scarcely any attention from theologians and Bible teachers. It is one which is familiar to few of God's people, and therefore calls for both explanation and elaboration. By our sin and fall in Adam we died legally, our life-in-law was lost, for we came under its curse. The Divine Judge had threatened our federal head "In the day you eat of it, you shall surely die," and "in Adam all die" (1 Cor. 15:22). The case of each descendant of his upon entering this world is like that of a murderer in the condemned cell—awaiting the hour of execution unless he be reprieved. We are by nature "the children of wrath" (Eph. 2:3) and until we savingly believe in the Son "the wrath of God abides on us" (John 3:36). We have no life in Law, no title to its award, but are transgressors, and as such under its death sentence—"condemned already" (John 3:18).

The consequence of Adam's dying legally was that he also died spiritually: that is, his soul became vitiated and depraved. He lost the moral image of God and the capacity to enjoy Him or please Him. Legal death and spiritual death are quite distinct (John 5:24), the latter being entailed by the former. "By one man sin entered into the world, and death by sin, and so death passed upon all men" (Rom. 5:12)—not simply "entered into" all men, but "passed upon" them as a judicial sentence. "By the offence of one judgment came upon all men to condemnation" (Rom. 5:18). The guilt of the federal head was imputed unto all he represented—evidenced by so many dying in infancy, for since even physical death is part of the wages of sin and infants having not personally committed any, they must be suffering the consequences of the sin of another. But Adam died spiritually as well as legally, and his depravity is imparted to all his descendants, so that they enter this world both legally and spiritually "alienated from the life of God, through the ignorance that is in them, because of the blindness of their heart" (Eph. 4:18).

Now it is only by Christ, "the last Adam," that We can regain life either legally or spiritually. That they obtain spiritual life from Christ, is well understood by the saints, but His having secured for them a life in Law, most of them are quite ignorant about. Yet Rom. 5 is very emphatic on the point: "For if by one man offence death reigned by one (i.e. a single transgression), much more they which receive abundance of grace (to meet not only the original but their own innumerable transgressions) and of the gift of righteousness (i.e. the imputed obedience of Christ) shall reign in life by One, Jesus Christ. Therefore as by the one offence judgment came on all men to condemnation, even so by the righteousness of One the free gift came upon all men to justification of life" (Rom. 5:17, 18)—note well that last clause: not "the free gift entered into all men tin to regeneration of life." Justification is entirely a legal matter and concerns our status before the Lawgiver. As God's elect lost their life in law through the disobedience of their first federal head, so the obedience of their last Federal Head has secured for them a life in law.

Christ is the fountain of life unto all His spiritual seed, and that, not as the second Person in the Trinity, but as the God-man Mediator. "For it pleased the Father that in Him should all fullness dwell" (Col. 1:19), which has reference to Christ officially and not essentially. Failure to grasp that truth has resulted in some verses of Scripture being grievously misunderstood and misinterpreted, to the dishonoring of our blessed Lord. For instance, when He declared "For as the Father has life in Himself, so has He given to the Son to have life in Himself" (John 5:26) He was there speaking of Himself as incarnate. As God the Son, co-essential and co-glorious with the Father, He always had "life in Himself"—"in Him was life" (John 1:4) which refers to His essential person before He became incarnate. But as God-man Mediator the Father gave Him "to have life in Himself:" He gave Him a mediatorial life and fullness for His people. "As You have given Him power over all flesh, that He should give eternal life to as many as You have given Him" (John 17:2) presents the same aspect of Truth—Christ was there speaking as the Mediator, as is evident from His high priestly prayer which immediately follows.

"As the living Father has sent Me and I live by the Father, so he that eats Me even he shall live by Me." (John 6:57). That title "the living Father" respects Him in connection with the economy of redemption and expresses His supremacy over the office of His Son, as the One who covenanted and sent Him forth on His grand mission. In His Godhead the Son has life — has it essentially, originally, independently in Himself, as a Person co-eternal with the Father. But as Mediator, the life which Christ lived and lives to God, and which in the discharge of His mediatorial office He bestows on His people, is derived from and is dependent upon the will of the Father, for in office the Son is lower than and inferior to the Father—in that respect, and in that only, "My Father is greater than I" (John 14:28), He declared. In affirming that "I live by the Father" (John 6:57), Christ signified that His mediatorial life was sustained by the Father. Let it be clearly understood that in John 6:57 the Lord Jesus was speaking of Himself officially, mediatorially, and not essentially as God the Son.

"I live by the Father. "The Father prepared a body for Him (Heb. 10:5) and all the days of His flesh was upholding Him by the right hand of His righteousness. Christ definitely acknowledged this again and again, by the Spirit of prophecy and by His ministerial utterances: "Thou maintainest My lot . . . I have set the Lord always before Me. Because He is at My right hand, I shall not be moved" (Ps. 16:5,8). "I gave My back to the smiters and My cheeks to them that plucked off the hair. I hid not My face from shame and spitting. For the Lord God will help Me; therefore I shall not be confounded" (Isa. 50:5,6). "I came down from Heaven not to do My own will, but the will of Him that sent Me" (John 6.'38). "Believest thou not that I am in the Father and the Father in Me? The words that I speak to you I speak not of Myself, but the Father that dwells in Me, He does the works" . . . "as the Father gave Me commandment, even so I do" (John 14: 10,31). In all these passages He spoke as the dependent One, the Mediator.

By purchase Christ ratified His title to the mediatorial life—"Now the God of peace (the propitiated and reconciled One) that brought again from the dead (not "the," but "our") Lord Jesus, that great Shepherd of the sheep," nor as the God-man considered as a private person, that God raised Him—but as the God-man Mediator and Surety of His people—by His own essential power Christ emerged from the tomb (John 2:19; 10:17). By the right of conquest Christ secured the mediatorial life, being made a royal priest "after the power of an endless life"—"He asked life of You (cf. Ps. 2:8)! Thou gayest it Him, even length of days forever and ever" (Heb. 7:16; Ps. 21:5). He has an official right and title to life because He had "magnified the Law and made it honorable"(Isa. 42:21)—magnified it by rendering to it a personal, perfect and perpetual obedience in thought, word and deed, and that as the God-man Mediator, "For Moses described the righteousness which is of the Law, that the man who does these things shall live by them."

It has not been sufficiently recognized that the converse of "the wages of sin is death" is "the award of obedience is life!" The first man violated the Law and therefore suffered its penalty; but the last man fulfilled the Law and therefore obtained a right to its reward. Christ found the Commandment "unto life" (Rom. 7:10), and it was for that life (the reward of the Law) He "asked" (Ps. 21:5) and which He received (Heb. 6:16) after He had vanquished death. Christ "reigns in life" (Rom. 5:17, in "justification of life" (Rom. 5:18 and cf. Isa. 50:8, 1 Tim. 3:16). Christ now "lives unto God" (Rom. 6:10) and He does so as the last Adam, as our Representative. Christ's life in law is also that of His people: "Christ our life" (Col. 3:4). Christ is the sole fountain of life, the source from which our life—both legal and spiritual—flows. It is for this reason that the scroll on which are the names of God's elect is inscribed is called "the Lamb's book of life" (Rev. 21:27), it is the Mediator's book for "the Lamb" is always expressive of Christ as the Priest and sacrifice of His people, and it is His mediatorial life which He shares with us.

The antithesis of sin is righteousness, for as sin is the transgression of the Law (1 John 3:4) so righteousness is rightness or measuring up to the standard of right, and therefore consists of fulfilling the Law. And since the God-man Mediator perfectly obeyed it, we are told that "He is the end of the Law for righteousness to everyone that believes" (Rom. 10:4). Now just as sin and death cannot be separated, so righteousness and life are indivisible. A further appeal to Romans 5 establishes that: "they which receive abundance of grace and of the gift of righteousness shall reign in life by One, Jesus Christ. . . by the righteousness of One the free gift came upon all men into justification of lift as sin has reigned unto death, even so might grace reign through righteousness unto eternal life by ("in") Jesus Christ our Lord" (vv. 17, 18, 21)—in each case it is a premial life or one of reward from the Law. "Christ our life" (Col. 3:4): apart from Him we have no standing before the Law, no title to its award; but being federally and judicially one with Him, then that which was due Him in return for His perfect fulfillment of the Law's requirements is due those He represented.

Far too little attention has been paid to the first member in the antithesis presented in Deut. 28, namely, "that these blessings shall come on you and overtake you if you shall listen diligently to the voice of the Lord your God. Blessed shall you be... blessed shall be... blessed shall be... blessed shall you be when you come in and blessed shall you be when you go out" (verses 2-6); which is set over against "But. . . if you will not hearken unto the voice of the Lord your God to observe to do all His commandments. . . that all these curses shall come upon you and overtake you" etc. (v. 5 etc.). Just as surely as the Law pronounces a curse on those who break it, so the Law pronounces a blessing on those who keep it. The curse is death, and the blessing life, and that blessing the God-man Mediator obtained as the Surety of His people. As Christ is, objectively and by imputation, "our righteousness," so He is objectively and by imputation "our life." By Christ those who are reconciled to God have life in law, and that is the foundation of all the other results or consequences of their restoration to His judicial favor.

2. Pardon from God. "God was in Christ reconciling the world unto Himself, not imputing their trespasses unto them" (2 Cor. 5:19). The trespasses of God's penitent and believing people are not charged against them, because His wisdom discovered a way by which He might be fully recompensed for the wrong which our sins did unto His majesty — by imputing them to our Substitute and exacting vengeance upon Him for the same. Our iniquities were laid upon Him and because of them He suffered "the Just for the unjust." That which was the ground of reconciliation was likewise the ground of the pardon of our iniquities: "In whom we have redemption through His blood the forgiveness of sins, according to the riches of His grace" (Eph. 1:7). Remission was the ransom-price which Christ paid' unto God's justice, and therefore a principal part of our reconciliation is the remission of our sins. Remission of sins means that the guilt damnation of them is cancelled, and therefore that we are released from the penalty and punishment of them, and that, because the punishment was borne by Christ and God's wrath appeased.

Now observe how inseparably connected is the pardon of the believer's sins with his possessing a life in law before God. As we have shown above, obedience to the Law (in the person of our Surety) is righteousness, and where there is righteousness the Law bestows blessing, as surely as it pronounces a curse on all unrighteousness. Now what does the blessing of the Law consist of? Negatively, that it has naught against us, and where that is the case none can truly "lay anything to our charge." Positively, that it pronounces us righteous, and as such, entitled to its award and blessing. Therefore we are told "Blessed is he whose transgression is forgiven, whose sin is covered. Blessed is the man unto whom the Lord imputes not iniquity" (Ps. 32:1,2). Yet we need to be on our guard against drawing a false inference from this. As Christians we still transgress and therefore need to beg for daily forgiveness — as well as for daily bread, as Matt. 6:12

plainly shows. As Christ is required to ask and sue out the fruits of His mediation (Ps. 2:7), so we are enjoined to humbly sue out our right of forgiveness—Jeremiah 3:12; 1 John 1:9.

3. Peace with God. "Therefore being justified by faith, we have peace with God, through our Lord Jesus Christ" (Rom. 5:1). This verse has been commonly misunderstood, through supposing the "peace" there mentioned to be that which is subjective rather than objective. The verse is not speaking about that peace of conscience when assured of Divine forgiveness, when the burden of our sin is removed and left at the foot of the cross, nor to that "peace of God which passes all understanding," that keeps the hearts and minds of God's children when they are anxious for nothing, but in everything by prayer and supplication make known their requests unto God (Phil. 4:6,7); but to "peace with God." It is not a state of mind, but a relation to the Lawgiver which is in view. It is not tranquility of heart, but that relation which arises from the expiation of sin and consequent justification. "Peace with God" means that He no longer regards us as His enemies in the objective sense of the term, but are now the objects of His favor. It is that state of things which ensues from the cessation of hostilities. It means that the sword of Divine justice, which smote our Shepherd (Zech. 13:7), is now forever sheathed.

"Peace with God" means that we are no longer the objects of His displeasure, and therefore that we no more have any cause to dread the Divine vengeance. If due attention is paid to the first clause of Rom. 5:1 there should be no difficulty in understanding the second: the illative "therefore" pointing the connection. In the previous chapters the apostle had proved that all have sinned and come short of the glory of God, that they are guilty and under the condemnation of the Law. They are therefore viewed by Him as "enemies" and as such they are "without strength" or ability to help themselves. In blessed contrast therefrom in 5:1-11 the apostle described at length the glorious status and state of those who are justified by faith. Justification imports the forgiveness of sins (Rom. 4:5-7) and that imports "peace with God," that He is reconciled to us, that He no longer frowns but smiles upon us. To "peace with God" is added "through our Lord Jesus Christ" not "by the operation of the Holy Spirit" as had been the case if peace of conscience had been in view. As Christ is "our life" (Col. 3:4) objectively and legally, so He is "our peace" (Eph. 2:14) objectively and legally.

Just as spiritual life wrought in our souls through regeneration is the consequence of the legal life which we have in Christ, so inward peace or the purging of our consciences from dead works follows from the peace which Christ made (Col. 1:20) by the blood of His cross, though the measure of our inward peace is largely determined by the daily exercise of our faith (Rom. 15:13). Here again we may perceive how, intimately one result is linked with another. The antitypical Melchizedek is first "King of righteousness" "and then "King of peace" (Heb. 7:2). "The work of righteousness shall be peace." That is, the mediatorial work of Christ shall produce "peace with God," "and the effect of righteousness (as it is apprehended by faith), quietness and assurance forever" (Isa. 32:17). "We have peace with God" because "the chastisement of our peace" (Heb. peaces) "was upon Him" (Isa. 53:5). Peace here and hereafter, objectively and subjectively, with God and in the conscience the whole corrective or punishment which produced them was laid upon Christ. "By submitting to those chastisements Christ slew the enmity and settled the amity between God and man...and God not only saves us from ruin, but takes us into friendship. Christ was in pain, that we might be at ease" (Matt. Henry).

4. Brought into cod's favor. By nature, and by practice Christians were "the children of wrath, even as others" (Eph. 2:3), being under the curse of the Law—all the threatenings of God in full force against them. But condemnation, awful as it is, is not damnation—the sentence is not yet executed, and until it is, it is not irrevocable. But once the sinner savingly believes in Christ he stands in a new relation to God as Lawgiver and Judge. He is no longer under the condemning

power of the Law, but is "under grace." As the manslayer on having entered the city of refuge was, by a special constitution of mercy, secure from the avenger of blood (Num. 35:12), so the sinner who has "fled for refuge to lay hold on the hope set before us" in the Gospel (Heb. 6:18), is, by the gracious constitution of God, forever secured from the curse. All the threatenings which until this time belonged to him, no longer stand against him, but are reckoned by the Judge of all as having been executed on his Substitute, who was made a curse for His people. But more: the favor of God, Divine blessing, is now his status and portion.

When Christ reconciled the Church unto God He did more than put away her sins and avert the judicial wrath of God. He reinstated her in God's favor and opened the way for the full manifestation of His love unto her. The two things are clearly distinguished in Colossians 1:20. "Having made peace through the blood of His cross, by Him to reconcile all things unto Himself." As we have so often pointed out in these articles, "reconciliation" consists of two things: the removal of enmity, and the restoring of amity—the two parts of Christ's mediatorial work, respectively, effecting them. His bloodshedding or enduring the curse of the Law removed the enmity or "making peace," His obedience to the Law or bringing in "an everlasting righteousness" procuring the reward and entitling unto the Divine blessing. The shedding of Christ's atoning blood obtained for His people the remission or pardon of their sins. His meritorious obedience secured for them the justification of their persons in the high court of Heaven, or their admittance into God's judicial favor.

"Therefore being justified by faith, we have peace with God through our Lord Jesus Christ; by whom also we have access by faith into this grace wherein we stand" (Rom. 5:1, 2). As we pointed out in the last, "peace with God" refers not to a subjective experience but to an objective fact, that it signifies not tranquility of soul but a relation to the Lawgiver. Hostilities between the Divine Judge and His believing people have ceased. His sword of justice is sheathed, and therefore they no longer have cause to dread His vengeance. But that is more or less a negative thing: there is something else, something positive, something more blessed. That additional benefit is introduced in Romans 5:2 by the word "also." Suppose that one of the nobles of the land who stood high at court and enjoyed special privileges from his sovereign, should commit some grave offence against the throne, in fact turn traitor. We can imagine that, in his clemency the king might pardon the offender upon the acknowledgement of his crime and his suing for mercy, but we can scarcely conceive of the monarch restoring his subject to the intimacy and privileges he formerly enjoyed. Yet that is what Christ has done—restored apostate traitors to the full favor of God.

"By whom also we have access by faith into this grace wherein we stand." Christ has not only brought us into a legal state in which we are secure from God's wrath, but into one of intimate friendship with Him. It is indeed a great mercy that God has ceased to be offended with us, that He will never inflict any penal punishment upon us; but it is a far greater and grander blessing that He should regard us with pleasure and pour blessings upon us. "By whom also we have access" implies that by nature we did not, and that by our efforts we could not. Previous to conversion our standing was in disgrace, but now we are "accepted in the Beloved," (Eph. 1:6), or as it might more literally be rendered "graced in the Beloved." Christ has reinstated His people in the good will and perfect acceptance of God: "this is the true grace of God wherein you stand" (1 Pet. 5:12). We stand in the full favor of God, with not a single cloud between us. By the mediatorial work of Christ the believer has full right of approach to the Divine mercyseat, to gaze upon the face of a reconciled God, to dwell in His glorious presence for evermore. For this is no transient blessing which the obedience and bloodshedding of Christ has procured for His people, but a permanent and unalienable one. It is not only that they are admitted into God's favor, but it is "this grace wherein we stand"— in which you are eternally settled and established. It is not only that God will never again be at judicial enmity against them, but that He is forever their Friend. The blessings which Christ has obtained for His redeemed are not contingent or evanescent ones, for they are dependent upon nothing whatever in or from them, but are the unforfeitable procurements of His infinitely-meritorious righteousness. And therefore has the Father made a covenant-promise to His Son concerning those He transacted for, "I will not turn away from them to do them good" (Jer. 32:40). We have been received into the most cordial good will and everlasting favor of the Father.

5. Given access to God. The very first message from Heaven after the advent of the Prince of peace revealed the purpose for which the Son had become incarnate and made known what He would accomplish from His mission. "There was with the angel a multitude of the heavenly host praising God, and saying, Glory to God in the highest, and on earth peace, good will toward men" (Luke 2:13,14). That brief word contained a broad outline of the whole subject of reconciliation. First, it declared that the glory of God was its grand design, for that ever takes precedence of all other considerations. Second, it proclaimed that the issue of it would be peace on earth—not "in the earth," but a revolted province restored to fealty. Third, it announced, as the "and" connecting the first and second clauses shows, that God's glory and the good of His people go and in hand. Though He would show Himself a Friend to them, yet He would conserve His own interests and maintain His own honor. Fourth, it published the grand outcome: "good will toward men"—they brought into God's favor. The final clause may also be rendered "good will among men"—Jew and Gentile made one!

Now no sooner had the Peacemaker exemplified God's holiness, magnified His law, and pacified His wrath, in this way glorifying Him to the superlative degree, than we are told "Behold, the veil of the temple was rent in twain from the top to the bottom" (Matthew 27:5 1). That was a parable in action, and one possessed of profound spiritual significance. There were several other remarkable phenomena which immediately followed the death of Christ, but the Holy Spirit has placed first the rending of the temple veil. He calls our attention to that miraculous happening with the word "Behold"—bidding us pause and consider this marvel, be awed by it, amazed over it. That "veil" was a magnificent curtain hung between the holy place and the holy of holies, separating the one from the other, barring an entrance into the innermost chamber and shutting out from view its holy furniture from the sight of those in the second compartment. It was rent asunder at the moment Christ expired. Immediately the soul and spirit were separated from Christ's body, an invisible hand separated the veil.

Amazing synchronization was that! Christ was the true Tabernacle or Temple (John 1:14), and therefore when His flesh was rent (Heb. 10:20), there was an answering rending of the structure which typed forth His flesh. Well may we reverently inquire, What was signified by that? First, though subordinately, it signified a revelation of the O.T. mysteries. The veil of the temple was for concealment. 'Out of all the congregation of Israel only one man was ever permitted to enter the holy of holies, and he but once a year, and then in a cloud of incense—symbolizing the darkness of that dispensation. But now, by the death of Christ, all is laid open: the shadows give place to the substance, the mysteries are unveiled. Second, and dispensationally, the uniting of Jew and Gentile by the removal of the partition wall—the ceremonial law (Eph. 2:14, 15)—which had separated them. But third, and chiefly, that a new and living way had been opened unto God: the rending of the veil opened the door into the holiest, where He abode between the cherubim. The rending of the veil signified and announced free access unto God.

First, for Christ Himself. During the three hours of darkness the Redeemer was cut off from God. But when the veil was rent there was an anticipation of what is recorded in Hebrews 9:11,12. Though Christ did not officially enter Heaven till forty days after his resurrection, yet He acquired the right to enter immediately (as our Surety) when He cried "It is finished," and had a virtual admission. Therein we may perceive the conformity between the Head and the members of His Body: the moment a sinner savingly believes in Christ he has a title to enter heaven, yet he has to wait his appointed time ere he does so in the fullest sense. Second, for the redeemed. Christ has procured an entrance for them in spirit and by faith even now: "Having therefore, brethren boldness to enter into the Holiest by the blood of Christ, by a new and living way, which He has consecrated for us, through the veil, that is say His flesh" (Heb. 10:19, 20). We have a free access to the throne of grace. "Through Christ we both (believing Jews and Gentiles) have access by one Spirit unto the Father" (Eph. 2:18).

It was sin which estranged us from the Holy One. Upon his first transgression Adam was driven out of paradise. The whole congregation of Israel at Sinai were commanded to keep their distance. The unclean in Israel were debarred from the camp and tabernacle. By so many different emblems did the Lord signify that sin had obstructed our access to Him. "But now in Christ Jesus, you who sometime were far off are made nigh by the blood of Christ" (Eph. 2:13), because His blood put away our sins. The efficacy of His sacrifice and the virtue of His meritorious obedience conferred upon His believing people the right to draw near unto God. All legal distance is removed: reconciliation has been effected: access to God is their consequent privilege and right. What a wonder of wonders is this! that one who is by nature a depraved creature may by grace, and through the Mediator, not only approach unto God without servile fear, but may have blessed fellowship with Him. To come into His very presence as a consciously accepted worshipper is the distinguishing blessing of Christianity in contrast from Judaism, Romanism and all false religions..

6. Endowed with the sanctifying gifts of the Spirit. "For through Him we both have access by one Spirit unto the Father." The mighty work of the Spirit in us is as indispensable as the meritorious work of Christ for us in order to appear before God as acceptable worshippers. As it is by the obedience and sufferings of Christ we have the title of access to God, so it is by the regenerating and sanctifying operations of the Spirit we have personal meetness for the same. That was typed out of old under the Mosaic economy. Those who drew near unto Jehovah in the services of His house were required to have not only the consecrating blood applied to their persons, but to be sprinkled with the anointing oil (Lev. 8:24, 30). Three things are required if we are to worship God right. There must be knowledge in the understanding that we may be informed of what God approves and accepts, grace in the heart so that our communion with Him may be a real and spiritual one and not merely a bodily and formal one, strength in the soul for the exercise of faith, love, reverence and delight. By the Spirit alone are those three essentials imparted.

Now it is from a reconciled God, in virtue of Christ's meritorious work, that we receive the sanctifying Spirit. This is evident from the particular character in which the apostle addressed Deity in the following prayers: "And the very God of peace sanctify you wholly" (1 Thess. 5:23); "Now the God of peace, that brought again from the dead our Lord Jesus, that great Shepherd of the sheep, through the blood of the everlasting covenant, make you perfect in every good work to do His will, working in you that which is wellpleasing in His sight" (Heb. 13:20,21). The "God of peace" is the pacified and reconciled God, and the blessings which the apostle requested are bestowed or wrought in us by the Spirit. Christ prayed that His redeemed might be loved as He was loved of the Father (John 17)—not in degree, but in kind; and the sanctifying graces of the Spirit are the tokens and evidences of His love, the manifestations of His heart toward His people. Or, as Manton so beautifully expressed it, they are "the jewels of the covenant, with which the Spouse of Christ is decked."

Even the regenerate, harassed as they are by indwelling sin and hindered by their infirmities, can no more spiritually approach unto the Father without the gracious operations of the Spirit than they could without the mediation of Christ. The One supplies the experimental enablement, as the Other has the legal right. The Spirit's operations within us are imperative if our leaden hearts are to be raised above the things of time and sense, if our affections are to flow forth unto their rightful Object, if faith is to be duly acted upon Him, if a sense of His presence is to be felt in our souls. He alone can empower us experimentally to have real fellowship with God, so that He is glorified and we edified. How shall we ask for those things which are according to the Divine will unless the Spirit prompts us (Rom. 8:26)? How shall we "sing with grace in our hearts to the Lord" (Col. 3:16) without the Spirit's quickenings? How shall we bring forth fruit to the glory of God without the Spirit energizing us? And our enduement with the Spirit is one of the bestowments—the chief of them—of a reconciled God.

7. God's acceptance of our services. Those "services" may be broadly and briefly summed up as our obedience and worship. But says the self-emptied Christian, What can a poor, sinful creature like me possibly offer unto God which would be acceptable unto Him? The proud religionist may boast of his performances and plume his fine feathers, but not so one whose eyes have been anointed by the Spirit so that he sees himself in God's light. The one who is really "poor in spirit," realizes not only that his very righteousnesses as a natural man are as "filthy rags," but that his most spiritual works as a regenerate man are defective and defiled. How then shall such services be received by the Holy One? Some may experience a difficulty at this point and ask, Since the spiritual works of a Christian are wrought by the Holy Spirit, how can they be defiled? Answer: they are wrought by His agency and yet are performed by us. The purest water is fouled when it passes through a soiled pipe. The most brilliant lamp is blurred if it shines through a smoky chimney. Thus it is with what the Spirit produces through us.

But since our obedience and worship are to faulty and polluted, how can God accept them? Turn back to the first worshipper on this sin-cursed earth: "Abel brought of the firstlings of his flock and of the fat of them. And the Lord had respect unto Abel and to his offering" (Gen. 4:4). It was by faith Abel offered that "excellent sacrifice" (Heb. 11:4) which so blessedly foreshadowed the Lamb of God, and "the Lord had respect unto Abel and to his offering." The worshipper himself was first accepted and then his worship! Thus it has been. ever since. The person is first taken into God's favor, and then his services are acknowledged as well-pleasing unto Him. Yet that does not furnish a complete answer to the question. Other types have to be taken note of if we are to obtain a complete picture. On the forehead of Israel's high priest was a plate of pure gold bearing the inscription "Holiness to the Lord." He wore it that he might "bear the iniquity of the holy things which the children of Israel shall hallow in all their holy gifts, and it shall be always upon his forehead, that they may be accepted before the Lord" (Ex. 28:36-38). Christ bore the defects of our "holy things "and because of His holiness God accepts from us whatever is sincere.

"The sinful failings of our best actions are hid and covered: they are not examined by a severe Judge, but accepted by a loving Father" (Manton). That is true, but it fails to show how the Father is righteously able to act so graciously. It is not because there has been any relating of His holiness or lowering of His standard, but because our Surety made full satisfaction to God's holiness for the sinful failings of their best actions. But even that is not all, for it is largely negative: our sincere obedience and reverent worship is accepted by the Father because the same ascends to God perfumed with the merits of Christ. In Revelation 8:3 He is seen as the Angel of the Covenant, "And there was given unto Him much incense that He should add it to the prayers of all saints!" Thus it is "by Him" that we offer the sacrifice of praise to God (Heb. 13:15). As those made "priests unto God" (Rev. 1:6) we are to "offer up spiritual sacrifices," and they are "acceptable to God by Jesus Christ" (1 Pet. 2:5), and they are acceptable because He has effected a perfect reconciliation between God and the Church.

8. Our eternal security. In view of all that has been brought out under the previous heads, there is little need for us to enlarge upon this one. So perfect was the sacrifice which Christ offered to God on behalf of His Church that there is a perpetuity annexed to it: "by one offering He has perfected forever them that are sanctified" (Heb. 10:14). Its efficacy is of everlasting force and its merits are imputed to the believer without cessation. Christ made an end of sins, effected reconciliation for iniquity and brought in an everlasting righteousness (Dan. 9:24). That righteousness is imputed to His people and placed upon them as a robe (Isa. 61:10), and such is its virtue and vitality that it never wears out. But more: the risen Christ now serves continually as the Advocate of His people, pleading His sacrifice on their behalf, and suing out the benefits of it. "If when we were enemies we were reconciled to God by the death of His Son, much more being reconciled we shall be saved by His life" (Rom. 5:10). If while we were the objects of the Divine displeasure Christ restored us to God's favor, much more now that we are God's friends will He obtain pardon for our daily transgressions and secure our final salvation. The life of our risen Savior is the security of His people: "because I live, you shall live also" (John 14:19).

"Christ is not only the Mediator of reconciliation to make our peace, but the Mediator of intercession to preserve it. He only took away our sins by His death; He only can preserve our reconciliation by His life. As He suffered effectively by the strength of His Deity to make our peace, so He intercedes in the strength of His merit to preserve peace. He did not only take away, but 'abolished and slew the enmity' (Eph. 2:15,16). He slew it to make it incapable of living again, and if any sin stands up to provoke justice, He sits as an Advocate to answer the process (1 John 2:2). As God was in Christ reconciling the world, so He is in Christ giving out the fruits of that reconciliation, not imputing our trespasses unto us. Our constant access to God is by Christ. He sits in Heaven to lead us by the hand unto the Father, as a prince in favor brings a man into the presence of a gracious king" (Charnock). The sum of this, and the grand and infallible conclusion to which it all leads is, that nothing "shall be able to separate us from the love of God which is in Christ Jesus" (Rom. 8:39).

9. God for us—loving, providing for, protecting, blessing us. If we have been brought into His favor, and if He is the Ruler of the universe, then what will necessarily follow? This: that He will make "all things work together for our good" (Rom. 8:28). Nay more: "All things are yours: whether Paul, or Apollos, or Cephas or the world, or life, or death, or things present, or things to come; all are yours; and you are Christ's and Christ is God's"(1 Cor. 3:21-23). "Christ is God's" is a relation based upon the Mediatorial office. To Him, as the rightful Heir, God has given "all things" (Heb. 1:2), and by virtue of our relation to Christ, all things are ours—relatively, and subject to God's government for our good.

10. The beatific vision. On the resurrection morning, the body of the believer will be "fashioned like unto Christ's glorious body" (Phil. 3:21), then in spirit, soul and body, we shall be "like Him" (1 John 3:2), fully and eternally "conformed to the image of God's Son" (Rom. 8:29). Then will His prayer receive answer, "Father, I will that they also whom You have given Me, be with Me where I am, that they may behold My glory" (John 17:24).

Chapter 27
Its Need Revisited-Continued

Up to this point we have dealt, almost entirely, with the expository side of our subject. Now we turn to what is more the experimental aspect of it. Some of our readers will consider this the most important and vital part, while to others it will make no appeal, being in their judgment better omitted. Those who read principally for intellectual information must appreciate that which supplies new light on things, explains to them what is obscure, or opens to them a difficult passage of Scripture, and often look with disfavor on that which calls upon them to diligently inquire what use they are making of the light they have received, to what practical ends are they turning their new knowledge. Yet this should be the principal concern of each of us. The interpretation of a passage of Scripture is but a means to an end. The personal appropriation and application of it to my own heart and life is the great desideratum. The value of a book, or of an article, lies chiefly in this: does it help to deliver its reader from the evil powers of this world and serve to assist him in his journey Heavenwards?

Though the other aspects of this grand truth which have been before us may both interest and instruct the mind, yet they will afford little real comfort and lasting peace to the heart until I am personally satisfied that I am reconciled to God, and He is reconciled to me. It deeply concerns each one of us to ascertain whether the wrath of God or the smile of God is upon him, whether the Law curses him or pronounces him righteous. It is a matter of utmost moment for us to determine whether we are the serfs of Satan or the friends of Christ, whether we are in a state of nature or of grace. We are plainly warned in Scripture that "There is a generation that are pure in their own eyes, and yet is not washed from their filthiness" (Prov. 30:12), and if I really value my eternal interests then I shall seriously and solemnly inquire, am I one of that deluded company? Am I numbered among those who sincerely believe that they have been cleansed from their sins by the blood of Christ, but are sincerely mistaken? More than a mere inquiry needs to be made: there should be an earnest and definite investigation. "Examine yourselves whether you are in the faith, prove your own selves" (2 Cor. 13:5), yet that is the very task which the great majority of professing Christians refuse to undertake, and if it is pressed upon them, they see no need for engaging in it, firmly assured that all is well with them spiritually. It is natural for us to think well of ourselves, yet just to the extent that we are influenced by self-esteem will our judgment be prevented from forming a true estimate of ourselves. And while self-love and self-flattery rule our hearts, we shall decline this essential duty of self-examination. Pride produces presumption, so that its infatuated victims are secure in their conceit that they are heirs of Heaven, when in fact they have neither title nor meetness to it. Those thus bewitched cannot be induced to prosecute a course of self-examination, nor will they tolerate a searching and probing ministry, be it oral or written.

What madness has seized those who treat lightly what should become of their souls in eternity! And those who are unwilling for their profession to be thoroughly tested, are as truly numbered in that class as those who make no religious profession. Do you say, There is no need for my profession to be tested for it is a valid one, seeing that for years past I have been resting on the finished work of Christ. But my reader, God Himself bids those claiming to be His people "give diligence to make your calling and election sure" (2 Pet. 1:10), and He has given no needless exhortations. O pit not your vain confidence against infinite wisdom. Bare your heart to the Sword of the Spirit: shrink not from a faithful and discriminating ministry. Know you not that Satan employs a variety of tactics seeking to keep a firm hold upon his captives? And one of them is to prevent his deluded victims engaging in this very investigation—lest they should discover that, after all, their hope has rested on a foundation of sand.

"For every one that does evil hates the Light, neither comes to the Light, lest his deeds should be discovered" (John 3:20). Does not that place those who refuse to examine themselves whether they are in the faith and decline to be "weighed in the balances of the Sanctuary?" It certainly does. It ranks them among evil-doers. Despite all their religious pretensions, the solemn fact is that they "hate the Light" which exposes an empty profession, and therefore they "come not to the Light" to be tested by it. And why is this? Because they lack an honest heart, which desires to know the truth about themselves, no matter how unpalatable it is. Therefore it is that they find most distasteful and discomforting those sermons or articles which point out the differences between hypocrites and the sincere, and which show how closely the former may, in many ways, resemble the latter. Even if they began the work of self-examination it would prove so obnoxious as soon to be abandoned, and being under the power of a "heart that is deceitful above all things" would give themselves the benefit of the doubt.

But different far is it with those in whom a work of grace has been wrought. They have been made to realize something of the deceitfulness of sin and the awful solemnity of eternity, and therefore refuse to give themselves the benefit of any doubt, being determined at all costs to find out where they stand before God. Of each of them Christ declares "But he that does truth (is genuine and sincere) comes to the Light, that his (profession and) deeds may be made manifest, that they are wrought in (by) God" (John 3:21). He longs to know whether he is in a state of nature or of grace, and if his assurance of the latter is based on a conjectural persuasion or well-authenticated evidence, whether his faith in Christ is a natural one or "the faith of God's elect" (Titus 1:1), whether his repentance is "the sorrow of the world" which "works death," or that "godly sorrow" which "works repentance to salvation not to be repented of" (2 Cor. 7:10). There is hope for a man who is deeply exercised over such matters; but there is none for those who are complacently satisfied with a false peace.

Readiness to be searched and probed by the Word of God, willingness to go to much pains to learn whether I am treading the Narrow Way which leads unto Life, or whether I am on the clean side of that broad road which terminates in destruction, is a good sign. As there is nothing that a hypocrite dreads more than to have his rottenness exposed, so there is nothing which an honest heart more longs to know than the real truth about his state before God. The earnest prayer of such an one is, "Examine me, O Lord, and prove me, try my reins and my heart" (Ps. 26:2). But alas, those who are filled with a carnal confidence feel no need of begging the Lord to "prove" them, for they are quite sure that all is well with them. Many, so completely deceived are they by Satan, they imagine it would be an act of unbelief to do so. Poor souls, they "call evil good, and good evil," and "put darkness for light, and light for darkness" (Isa. 5:20).

"Examine me, O Lord, and prove me." Is that the cry of your soul, my reader? If it is not, then there is strong reason to fear you are yet fatally enthralled by Satan. One of the surest marks of regeneration is that such a soul cries frequently, "Search me, O God, and know my heart: try me, and know my thought: and see if there is any wicked way in me, and lead me in the way everlasting" (Ps. 139:23,24). Yet it should be pointed out that this must not be made a shelving of our responsibility, a substitute for the performance of our own duty. God has bidden us, "Examine yourselves whether you are in the faith," and every possible effort must be made by us to do so, taking nothing for granted, but resolutely and impartially scrutinizing our hearts, measuring ourselves by the Word, ascertaining whether or not we have the marks and evidences of regeneration. Like the Spouse we should say, "Let us get up early. . . let us see if the vine flourish" (Song of Sol. 7:11).

"Examine yourselves whether you are in the faith" clearly implies that a knowledge of our spiritual state is possible. As the natural man perceives his own thoughts, knows what views and motives regulate him, and is acquainted with his own designs and aims, so may the spiritual man. "Reflection and knowledge of self is a prerogative of a rational creature. We know that we have souls by the operations of them. We may know that we have grace by the effects of it, if we are diligent. As we may know by the beams of the sun that the sun is visible, if we shut not our eyes" (Charnock). Grace discovers itself in its affections and actions, in its operations and influence on the heart and life. If we observe closely the springs of our actions and "commune with our own heart" (Ps. 4:4), we shall have little difficulty in becoming acquainted with the state of our souls. "For what man knows the things of a man save the spirit of man which is in him"(1 Cor. 2:11).

In His parable of the Sower and the Seed our Lord likened those who hear the Word unto different kinds of soil which received the Seed, and the various results or yields from them. His obvious design was to supply us with criteria by which we may measure ourselves. If, then, I would properly examine myself, I must ascertain if I am no better than the wayside hearer, who heard the Word and "understood it not;" or the shallow-soil hearer, who received the Word with an evanescent "joy" and yet had "no root in himself" and soon fell away; or the thorny-ground hearer, who suffered the "care of this world and the deceitfulness of riches" to choke the Word and render him unfruitful. Or, if by grace Iam a good-ground hearer, of whom it is said—not simply that he "believes the Gospel," but—"which in an honest and good heart, having heard the Word, keep it, and bring forth fruit with patience" (Luke 8:15). That is the test: not knowledge, orthodoxy, or happy feelings, but FRUIT.

Unless a man knows himself to be a child of God he cannot rationally or lawfully take comfort from the promises which are addressed unto the saints. It is madness and presumption for me to flatter myself that God has declared He will do this and that for me, unless I am reliably assured that I am one of those to whom such declarations are made. It is the height of folly for me to believe that all things are working together for my good, unless I really love God (Rom. 8:28). On the other hand, if I am regenerate and decline to take comfort from the promises, I forsake my own mercies and allow Satan to deprive me of my legitimate portion. That it is not God's will for His people to remain in uncertainty is unmistakably clear from 1 John 5:13. He moved one of His apostles to write a whole Epistle for the express purpose that they might know they had eternal life, and that they may believe on the name of the Son of God.

Realizing full well that this is the most momentous investigation that any mortal can ever undertake, that sincere souls—conscious of how much is involved—will proceed carefully and cautiously, and making full allowance that an honest heart will be fearful of being deceived in the matter, yet we have never been able to understand why a regenerate soul should find it so difficult to determine whether he is in a state of nature or of grace. We are very much afraid that not a few of God's dear people have been hindered by the teaching they sat under and the general custom which prevailed in the circle where they were. It is indeed deplorable that many Protestants have echoed the dogma of Popery that it is presumptuous for any Christian to aver he knows that he has been made a new creature in Christ Jesus. The N. T. contains not a word in support, but much to the contrary. For a saint to doubt his acceptance by God is not a mark of humility but the fruit of unbelief.

We have been dealing with the Christian's assurance of his state before God in a more or less general way, let us now be specific and ask, How is an exercised soul to ascertain whether he has really been restored to the favor and friendship of God? By what criteria or rules is he to test himself in order to discover whether God is at peace with him? By what evidence may he be rationally assured that he is reconciled to the moral Ruler and Judge of this world? Surely that should not be difficult to determine. Is it possible for a truly converted person, who has passed through a radical change in his heart and life, in his thoughts, affections, and actions, to yet know nothing about it? Surely a person cannot be awakened out of a state of security in sin, to realize what a vile, unclean rebel he is, and to mourn over the same, and yet perceive nothing about it. For one to radically change his selfish and worldly pursuits, to lose relish for his idols, and to live a life of communion with God, and yet be uncertain such is his case, is impossible. Grace is as evident in its own nature as corruption is, and its operations and fruits are as manifest and unmistakable as are those of sin. Not only so in ourselves, but in our fellow-saints too. In a time like the present it is particularly easy to recognize those who are truly reconciled to God. The few friends of Christ stand out conspicuously among the vast multitude of His enemies. In a day when lawlessness abounds and every man does "that which is right in his own eyes" (Judges 21:25), those whose lives are ordered by God's Word cannot be mistaken. They "shine as lights in the world, in the midst of a crooked and perverse nation" (Phil. 2:15). Noah "walked with God" (Gen. 6:9) though he lived in the midst of the reprobate antediluvians. Elijah was jealous for the glory of God and faithful in maintaining His cause, though his lot was to dwell amid a people who had forsaken God's covenant, thrown down His altars, and slain His prophets (1 Kings 19:14).

It may be easier—we are by no means sure it is so—for one to serve God faithfully in a season of revival than in one of declension, and to journey Heavenwards in the company of a goodly number than to stand alone; but it is more difficult to identify the saints. As the fire evidences the pure gold, so a day either of bitter persecution or of wide-spread apostasy, enables us to discern who are out and out for the Lord, and those who have nothing more than a thin veneer of religion. When many of Christ's nominal disciples went back and walked no more with Him, He turned to the apostles and asked, "Will you also go away?" Whereupon Simon Peter acting as their spokesman said, "To whom shall we go? You have the words of eternal life" (John 6:68). "They have made void Your Law, therefore I love Your commandments above gold" (119:127). Such is the effect upon a true child of God of the defection of his fellows.

But returning to the individual who would ascertain whether or not he is reconciled to God. That problem may be reduced to a simple issue. You are either an enemy of God or the friend of God, plainly manifesting the one or the other in your conduct. It should not be difficult for you to determine in which class you are. "And you that were sometime alienated and enemies in your mind by wicked works, yet now has He reconciled" (Col. 1:21). The implication is inescapable. If you have been reconciled to God then you are no longer fighting against Him, and though as yet you are very far from being perfect, or all that you should be, nevertheless, no longer is your mind enmity against Him—ever engaged in wicked works. Nay, if reconciled, the very opposite is the case: you yearn for closer fellowship with Him, you love His Word, honestly endeavor to be regulated by it in all things, and in your measure, are bringing forth good works.

Yes, the issue is a very simple one: to be reconciled to God is for there to be mutual peace between Him and you, and peace is the opposite of war, as love is of hatred. It therefore follows that no soul who is at peace with sin can possibly be at peace with God, for sin is the open enemy of the Holy One. The question to be decided then is, Have I thrown down the weapons of my warfare against the Most High? Have I enlisted under the banner of a new Captain? If I am honestly and resolutely fighting against sin, then I must be reconciled to God: said Christ to His disciples, "he that is not against us is on our part" (Mark 9:30). There is no third condition: you are either for or against God, His friend or His foe. God's enemies are opposed to Him, leagued with all that is hostile to Him, doing what He forbids and flouting what He enjoins. If then I desire to please Him, am on the side of His friends, hating what He hates and loving what He loves, must I not be one with Him!

Chapter 28
Its Need Revisited-Continued

We commence this portion at the point where we left off in our last. Those who are at peace with sin are at enmity with God; but those who are reconciled to God are antagonistic to sin. It cannot be otherwise. Satan and God, sin and holiness, are diametrically and irreconcilably opposed. As the "scepter of righteousness" (Heb. 1:8) holds sway over the kingdom of God and of Christ, iniquity is the dominant power in the empire of Satan, "he that commits sin is of the Devil" (1 John 3:8). It therefore follows that all real Christians are opposed to Satan as the common enemy, and evince the same by fighting against sin. Satan's principal work lies in drawing men to sin, and therefore are the saints bidden "resist the Devil and he will flee from you" (Jas. 4:7); and again, "Be sober, be vigilant; because your adversary the Devil, as a roaring lion, walks about seeking whom he may devour" (1 Pet. 5:8). To resist the Devil is to refuse his temptations to fight against sin; contrariwise, to trifle with temptation and commit sin is to render service unto him.

The forwarding of sin is the Devil's main instrument to lead his subjects into more and more of a revolt against their Maker, and the more any yield to his solicitations, the more do they perform his work. To sin is "to give place to the Devil" (Eph 4:27), and to depart from Christ is to "turn aside after Satan" (1 Tim. 5:15). Whenever we knowingly sin we join with Satan in his battle against God. We take sides with him and strengthen his cause. How that awful consideration should restrain us and make us tread warily! How it should humble us before God when we have yielded to temptation and thus aided His arch-enemy! Again; the love of God and the love of the world cannot possibly stand together: "Know you not that the friendship of the world is enmity with God? Whosoever therefore will be a friend of the world is the enemy of God" (Jas. 4:4). Thus the lines are plainly drawn: if I am a friend of the world, the abettor of Satan, the servant of sin, I cannot possibly be at peace with God. But if I am reconciled to God, then I am in avowed and open antagonism to that evil trinity.

While any soul is at peace with sin, he is certainly not at peace with God, for He is ineffably holy and hates all sin. It was sin which caused the breach between Him and us: "they rebelled and vexed His Holy Spirit, therefore He was turned to be their Enemy and He fought against them" (Isa. 63:10). Since sin is the inveterate enemy of God and man it must be fought, or it will destroy us. Therefore His call is "be reconciled to God." When a soul really responds to that call he ceases his opposition to God and enlists under the banner of Christ. Christ becomes his "Captain" (Heb. 2:10) and he engages to fight against all His enemies. He severs his old allegiance with the world, the flesh and the devil, and binds himself by a solemn bond to live unto God and be the Lord's forevermore. From this time forward can be no truce between corruptions and grace, carnal reasonings and the teaching of Holy Writ. "Neither yield your members as weapons of unrighteousness unto sin, but yield yourselves unto God" (Rom. 6:13).

"You have not yet resisted unto blood, striving against sin" (Heb. 12:4). The leading thought of the context is, the need for faithful perseverance in a time of persecution and suffering. In the urging of this the apostle set before them (and us) the grand example of Jesus Christ, and how we should improve the same. Then he points out that, severe as had been the trials experienced, yet not so fearful as might yet be encountered. They had indeed suffered considerably (10:32, 33), but so far God had restrained their enemies from going to extreme lengths. The afflictions already undergone did not discharge them from their warfare. Rather must they continue in this to the point of being prepared to lay down their lives. That warfare consisted of "striving against sin"—sin in themselves, which inclined them to take the line of least resistance; sin in their persecutors, who sought to drive them to apostatize.

In Hebrews 12:4 the apostle continues to use the figure of the Public Games which he had employed in v. 1, only there he refers to the "race," while here he alludes to the mortal conflict or combat between gladiators, in which one contended for his life against another who had entered the lists against him. In like manner, the Christian has to contend with a mortal adversary, namely, sin, both external and internal. He is called upon to wrestle not with flesh and blood, but against the powers of darkness (Eph. 6:12), and therefore is he exhorted to take unto him "the whole armor of God." So too he is to strive against his own indwelling corruptions: "abstain from fleshly lusts which war against the soul" (1 Pet. 2:11). Those lusts are violent and powerful, ever seeking to dominate and regulate the soul, antagonizing the principle of grace, endeavoring to overcome our faith and prevent our obedience to God. Sin is a deadly enemy which will slay us unless we daily strive against it with determination of mind and resolute effort. Here then is one of the principal features which distinguishes the children of God from the children of the Devil. Here is an essential part of the evidence which clearly makes manifest those in whom a miracle of grace has been wrought. Here is the proof that I am reconciled to God. By nature sin is my element and I take to it as ducks do to the water and swine to the mire. By nature I delight in sin: do I not love myself? And in loving myself I am delighting in sin, for sin is part and parcel of my being. I was shapen in iniquity and conceived in sin (Ps. 51:5). If then I now hate my natural self, loathe sin, vigorously resist it, I must be a new creature in Christ Jesus, at peace with God. If I compare myself with what I was in my unregenerate days, is it not obvious that a radical change has taken place! Did I then abhor myself? No indeed, far from it. I was pleased with myself. Did I then look upon iniquity as that "abominable thing" which the Holy One hates and takes sides with Him against it? Alas, I did not: I thirsted after it, drank greedily of it, and took pleasure in it.

The natural man may indeed seek to overcome some grosser lust, the yielding to which humiliates his pride. He may seriously endeavor to conquer an unruly temper, that he may not be put to shame before his fellows. But that is a very different matter. One who is truly reconciled to God has voluntarily entered into a covenant to fight against sin as sin, and not merely this or that particular form and outbreaking of it. He is daily engaged in contending with his indwelling corruptions, resisting the Devil, refusing the allurements of the world, mortifying his members which are upon the earth. Here then is the matter reduced to its simplest possible terms, here is the plain but sufficient rule by which you may test the validity of your profession. You know whether or not you really are fighting against sin. We do not say fighting against it as faithfully, diligently, zealously as you ought to be. Nor do we say meeting with that success which you could wish. It is the fact itself we would have you consider: if you are really warring against indwelling sin you must be one with God.

Probably the reader says, Tell us more explicitly what you mean by fighting against sin. Very well. Fighting against sin implies that you hate it, for you do not war against anything you love. Likewise it signifies you earnestly desire to avoid it, keep away from it, have no commerce with it. To countenance sin is rebellion against God; to condemn and oppose sin is conformity to Him. If I hate sin and am engaged in a warfare against it, I shall not trifle with temptation but watch jealously for and seek to suppress the first motions of sin in my heart. When my corruptions clamor for satisfaction I shall earnestly endeavor to deny them. When the apostle averred, "I keep under my body and bring it into subjection" (1 Cor. 9:27), he was describing one aspect of his fight against sin. When another of the apostles enjoined, "Little children, keep yourselves from idols" (1 John 5:21), he was calling them unto a further part of the same conflict. It was an affectionate appeal for them to avoid, resist, and renounce will worship and whatever could captivate our affections.

This fighting against sin is from evangelical motives. Here too the line is clearly drawn between the regenerate and the unregenerate. Whatever resistance the latter make against sin it is from carnal or legal considerations. That which deters the natural man from the outward commission of evil is either pride or self-respect, because he would retain the good opinion of his fellows, or the fear of consequences. But different far is it with the spiritual man: he would hate and resist sin even if assured there is no Hell awaiting evil-doers hereafter! It is love of God, a desire to please Him, a concern for His glory, a horror of doing that which would sully his profession, bring shame upon the cause of Christ, or stumble any of His little ones. Therefore it is that when Satan gets the better of him and he is overtaken in a fault, he mourns before God. If we are reconciled to God we love Him, and repentance is the first expression of that love—the sorrowing part of it. Those fighting against sin do not "allow" or excuse their failures, but grieve over, confess them, and seek to prevent a repetition of the same. Let us repeat, it is not the measure of our success in this warfare, but the genuineness of our sincerity in it, which is the criterion by which we are to measure ourselves. As one of the old worthies said, "This is the seal which assures us the patent is the authentic grant of the Prince of peace." Or as John Owen put it, "Mortification of sin is the soul's opposition to self, wherein sincerity is most evident." To which we may add, none of our exercises and efforts have any sincerity in them—neither reading, hearing, praying nor worship—unless we are genuinely endeavoring to earnestly and vigorously resist sin. Sin is ever assailing the soul, contending for rule and sovereignty over it. But if a principle of grace is in my heart, then it will constantly challenge sin's right to usurp authority and oppose its assaults. "The subduing of our souls to God, the forming of us to a resemblance unto Him, is a more certain sign that we belong to Him, than if we had with Isaiah seen in vision His glory with all His train of angels about Him" (S. Charnock).

Granted, says the exercised soul, but there is so much in me that is not yet subdued to God, yea which is contrary to Him, and this it is which makes me seriously doubt my reconciliation. I fear that I should be uttering an idle boast and thinking of myself more highly than I ought to, if I declared myself to be engaged in seriously fighting against sin. Dear reader, hypocrites are never troubled over the deceitfulness of their hearts, nor are they concerned at all of being presumptuous, and if you really are exercised over such things, then must you not belong to a totally different class! Vain and empty professors are not exercised about their sincerity, but instead are filled with a self-confidence and sense of security which no expostulations or warnings of man can shake. They are total strangers to the jealous fears and holy exercises of soul which engage those with humble hearts. "They had rather go to hell on a feather bed than to Heaven in a fiery chariot" as one quaintly but solemnly expressed it.

Am I reconciled to God, at peace with Him? Yes, if I am daily and sincerely engaged in fighting against sin. But, says the reader, if I am engaged in such a fight, mine is a losing one, for the more I endeavor to resist my corruptions, the more fiercely do they oppose me and thwart my efforts. Yea, so often do my lusts master me, I can only conclude that I am still at war against God. Not so, if you take sides against your lusts and grieve over their prevalence. As it is not the fighting of a number of individuals belonging to two different countries which causes one of those states to declare war against another, but rather its consenting to and maintaining them in their hostility; so it is not the rising up of our lusts against our graces which constitutes an act of war against God, but only when we approve of them, consent to and defend their presumptuous enmity. While we take up and maintain a constant fight against God's enemies—no matter how often we may be worsted in the conflict—hating and disavowing their outrageous uprisings, the peace between God and us holds.

In the chapters on our reception of that peace which Christ effected Godwards on behalf of His people, we showed at some length what God requires from the sinner if he is to become a personal partaker of that peace, and every exercised reader should go carefully over those articles again with one particular design before him—to discover whether he or she has met those requirements. From the lengthy quotation from Goodwin (Feb. issue), it was shown that in preparing us to be reconciled to God it is necessary that we be convinced we are His enemies, and that He accounts us such. Thus, if the reader has never been painfully convicted of his revolt against the Most High, he is in no condition to seek reconciliation unto Him. If I have been made aware that I am a lifelong rebel against Heaven, that all my days have been spent in fighting against God, then I shall be sensible and deeply affected by such a realization. I shall mourn over my wickedness. I shall "remember my ways and be ashamed." I shall be "confounded" and have not one word to say in my self-defense (Ezek. 16:61-63).

If the Holy Spirit has awakened me from the sleep of self-security, opened my eyes to see my true character in the sight of God, filled me with horror and contrition over my dreadful enmity against Him, then I shall readily respond to that peremptory call, "Let the wicked forsake his way, and the unrighteous man his thoughts," and cease my hostility against the Lord. At first it will appear to me that I have sinned beyond the hope of forgiveness, that it is impossible God should ever be reconciled to such a rebel as I now know myself to be, that nought but the everlasting burnings can be the portion of such a wretch. But later, the same gracious Spirit who revealed to me my horrible plight, acquaints me that God has "thoughts of peace" (Jer. 29:11) toward those who throw down the weapons of their warfare against Him. But that seems too good to be true, and for a season the stricken soul finds itself unable to credit the same. To him it appears that a holy God can do nothing but abhor him, that a righteous God must surely exact vengeance upon him, that his doom is irrevocably sealed. Do you know anything of such an experience as that?

When God begins a work of grace in a soul He does not cease when it is but half finished. If He wounds it is that He may heal; if at first He drives to despair, later He awakens hope. When the Law has performed its office—of stripping us of our self-righteousness—then we are prepared to listen to the message of the Gospel, which tells of the garments of salvation provided for bankrupts. The glorious evangel of Divine grace announces that God is not implacable but inclinable unto peace, that His wisdom had found a way whereby the requirements of His holiness and the demands of His justice are fully met so that He can without sullying His honor, yea to the everlasting glory of His matchless name, show mercy to the very chief of sinners. As the soul begins to give credence to that good news, he is persuaded better things of God than his fears allowed, hope is born within him that even his case is not beyond remedy, and the sweet music is borne to his ears, "Let the wicked forsake his way, and the unrighteous man his thoughts, and let him return to the Lord, and He will have mercy upon him, and to our God, for He will abundantly pardon" (Isa. 55:7).

But it is in Christ, and Christ alone, that the thrice Holy God meets the sinner in pardoning mercy. Christ is the One who met His claims and endured His wrath on the behalf of all who put their trust in Him. Christ is the alone Mediator whereby transgressors can approach unto a reconciled God. It is the Lord Jesus who is "set forth a propitiation through faith in His blood" (Rom. 3:25). And therefore "He is able to save them to the uttermost which come unto God by

Him" (Heb. 7:25). It is in and through Christ that sinners may enter into covenant with God and by whom He enters into covenant with them, for Christ is "the Surety" (Heb. 7:22) and "the Mediator" (Heb. 8:6) of the covenant. Christ is the One who came "to seek and to save that which was lost" (Luke 19:10), and who declares "him that comes to Me I will in nowise cast out" (John 6:37). Have you gone unto Him as a desperately-ill person seeks a physician, or as a drowning man clutches to a life-buoy? You either have, or you have not; and it should not be difficult for you to determine. But am I come to Christ in the right way? Answer, the only right way is to come as a lost sinner, trusting in His merits.

Have you, then, complied with the terms expressed in Isaiah 55:1-3, for it is with those doing so that God makes an everlasting covenant. That is but another way of asking, Have you really embraced the Gospel offer, which is made freely to all who hear it? Have you seriously, thoughtfully, broken-heartedly received Christ as your own personal Lord and Savior? Have you exercised faith in His mediatorial sacrifice? Your faith may indeed have been so weak that you touched but the hem of His garment, yet if it was His garment, that was sufficient. The saving virtue lies not in our faith but in Christ, faith being simply the empty and leprous hand which lays hold of the great Physician. Every penitent believer may be infallibly assured on the Word of Him that cannot lie that his sins were all transferred to his blessed Surety and forever put away by Him; and that he is now made the righteousness of God in Christ (2 Cor. 5:21).

But the honest soul who would "make assurance doubly sure" should go further, and test himself by Psalm 50:5, Isaiah 56:4-6; Jeremiah 50:4,5. There we have described the character of those making a covenant with God and who "take hold of His covenant," and it is our wisdom and duty to seriously compare ourselves with those characters and ascertain whether we possess their marks. Have I surrendered to God as my absolute Lord and chosen Him to be my all-sufficient Portion? Have I renounced and relinquished the things which He hates and "chosen the things that please" Him? Have I given myself up to Him wholly to love and serve Him, and that not for a brief season only, but forever? Am I now manifesting the sincerity of my surrender by being concerned for His honor and having respect to His Law? Have the resolutions I formed at my conversion been translated into actual practice?—not perfectly so, but by genuine effort nevertheless. If so, then I have good reason to believe that I have savingly complied with His call "be reconciled to God."

Chapter 29
Its Need Revisited-Continued

Another criterion by which each of us should carefully measure himself is, Am I now a friend of God? That is a most pertinent and necessary inquiry, for, as was shown under a considerable variety of expressions when defining the meaning of reconciliation, that term signifies the bringing together of two persons who have previously been alienated, the changing of a state of enmity and hostility unto one of amity and friendship. By nature and by practice I was the enemy of God, hating and opposing Him; but if a work of grace has been wrought in my soul then I am now the friend of God, loving and serving Him. As this is a matter of deepest importance, both practically and experimentally, we propose to canvass it in some detail, endeavoring to do so along lines so clear and simple that no exercised soul should have any uncertainty in determining to which class he belongs.

"Abraham believed God and it was imputed unto him for righteousness, and he was called the friend of God" (Jas. 2:23). It seems passing strange that scarcely any of the commentators perceived the force of that last clause, interpreting it quite out of harmony with its setting. Most of them see in God's styling Abraham His "friend" an amazing instance of His sovereign grace and condescension, while a few regard the expression in the light of the extraordinary and intimate communion which the patriarch was permitted to enjoy with Jehovah. But what is there in the context which paves the way for any such climax? It was in no-wise the design of the Holy Spirit in this epistle to portray the wondrous riches of Divine grace, nor to describe the inestimable privileges they confer upon their recipients; rather was it to expose a worthless profession and supply marks of a valid one. James was not moved to refute the legality of Judaism, which insisted that we must do certain things in order to our acceptance by God, but was repelling Antinomianism, showing the worthlessness of a faith which bore no fruit.

In the days of the apostles, as in all succeeding generations, there were those bearing the name of Christians who supposed that a mere intellectual belief of the Gospel was sufficient to secure a passport for Heaven. There is not a little in the N.T. which was expressly written to refute that error, by an insistence upon holiness of heart and strictness of life being necessary in order to evince a saving faith in Christ. The principal design of James was to show that when God justifies or reconciles a sinner to Himself, He also works in that person a disposition which is friendly toward Him, a spirit and attitude which reciprocates His own benignity. In a genuine conversion an enemy is transformed into a friend to God, so that he loves Him, delights in Him, and serves Him. No one has any right to regard himself as a friend of God unless he has the character of one and conducts himself accordingly. If I am the friend of God then I shall be jealous of His honor, respect His will, value His interests, and devote myself to promoting the same; in a word, I shall "show myself friendly."

The apostle's scope is clear enough both from what immediately precedes and follows. In verse 20 he says, "But will you know, O vain man, that faith without works is dead," and in verse 24, "You see then how that by works a man is justified, and not by faith only." A bare mental assent to the Gospel is worthless, for it effects no change in the heart and walk of the one exercising it.

Fair words on the lips are downright hypocrisy unless they are borne out in our daily conduct. A faith in Christ which conforms not to His image is not the faith of God's elect. Saving faith produces good works. In verses 8 to 14 the apostle had insisted that the Gospel requires a sincere respect unto all the Divine commandments, while in verses 15-25 he shows what a real faith in them brings forth. This he illustrates first by the illustrious case of Abraham. It is to be duly noted that reference is not here made to the initial act of his faith when the Lord first appeared unto the patriarch in Ur of Chaldea, but rather to that memorable incident on mount Moriah recorded in Genesis 22.

Faith is not a passive thing but an active principle, operating powerfully within its possessor. "Faith works by love" (Gal. 5:6). Let those words be carefully pondered. "Faith works:" it is the very nature of it to do so, for it is a new, living and powerful energy, imparted to the soul at regeneration. "Faith works by love:" not by fear or compulsion, but freely and gladly. Such was the faith of Abraham: his faith "wrought with his works" (Jas. 2:22), and it wrought by love, for it was love to God which moved the patriarch, in obedience to His behest, to lay his dear Isaac upon the altar; and in this way he attested his friendship to God. "Friendship is the strength of love, and the highest improvement of it. 'Your friend' says Moses, 'who is as your own soul' (Deut. 13:6). Friendship is common to and included in all relations of love. A brother is (or ought to be) a friend; it is but friendship natural. Husband and wife are friends: that knot is friendship conjugal. In Song of Solomon 5 we have an instance of both: Christ called His church Sister, and then Spouse; and not contented with both, though put together, He added another compellation as the top of all, 'O My friends' (v. 11)."

In its first working faith comes to God as an empty-handed beggar to receive from Him, yet if it is a sincere and spiritual faith it will necessarily form the soul of its possessor unto a correspondent and answerable frame of heart unto God; thus if I come to Him for pardon and peace, and receive the same, the reflex or consequence will be the exercise of a filial and friendly spirit in me toward God. Faith is made the grateful recipient of all from God, yet on that very account it becomes the worker of love in the soul. In James 2:21-23 the apostle shows what a powerful working thing faith is: it molded Abraham's heart into friendship with God. A friend is best known or most clearly manifested in a time of trial. Thus it was in Genesis 22: the Lord there put Abraham to the proof, bidding him, "Take now your son, your only Isaac, whom you love . . . and offer him there for a burnt offering." And God so approved of his ready response as to own him as His "friend" from this time forward: see 2 Chronicles 20:7, Isaiah 41:8. And since He only calls things as they actually are, Abraham had truly conducted himself as such.

Let it next be pointed out that Abraham's case is not to be regarded as an exceptional or extraordinary one, but rather as a representative and typical one. As Romans 4:11 and 16 plainly teaches, Abraham is a pattern and father unto all believers. Those who are his spiritual children (Rom. 9:7,8) and seed (Gal. 3:7,29), "walk in the steps of that faith of our father Abraham" (Rom. 4:12) and "do the works of Abraham" (John 8:39), and they too are owned by the Lord as His "friends" (John 15:14). Observe that in both 2 Chronicles 20:7 and Isaiah 41:8 it is "the seed of Abraham Your friend," while in James 2:21 Abraham is expressly presented in that passage as "our father." Thus, this blessed appellation pertains to all his spiritual seed. For one to be owned by God as His "friend" imports that person has a friendly disposition of heart and deportment of life toward Him, as one friend bears unto another. Wherever a saving faith exists it frames the heart of its possessor into a friend-like temper and brings forth a friend-like carriage in our life.

"He was called the friend of God." While that indeed is a title of unspeakable dignity and honor, yet—though scarcely any appear to have perceived it—it is also (and chiefly) expressive of the inward disposition of a saint toward God, describing his love for Him and his bearing toward

Him. By our carriage and conduct we exemplify and ratify that character. The faith which justifies a sinner before God is one that works by love and is expressed in an obedient walk, earnestly endeavoring to please God in all things, and therefore the character and carriage of a Christian is appropriately expressed under the notion of friendship. In a truly marvelous way had God befriended Abraham, and the patriarch manifested his appreciation by conducting himself suitably to it. It is the law of friendship to answer it again with friendship: "A man that has friends must show himself friendly, and there is a Friend that sticks closer than a brother" (Prov. 18:24), and to Him we must show ourselves supremely friendly, doing nothing to displease or dishonor Him, but exercising subjection to Him, delighting in Him, and promoting His interests.

We will pass now from the general to the particular and consider some of the more obvious characteristics and marks of friendship, together with the duties and offices to be performed as are proper and suited to such a relationship—friendship too combines both privilege and duty, and we should be dishonest if we confined our remarks to one of them only, First of all then, between two friends there necessarily exists a close bond of union, a oneness of nature or at least similarity of disposition, so that they share in common the same likes and dislikes—not perhaps in every detail, but generally and essentially so. There can be no congeniality where there is no singleness and harmony of nature. It is the gift and dwelling of the Holy Spirit within the Christian which is the bond of union, and which capacitates him to hate what God hates and love what He loves. It is that oneness of nature and disposition which causes two persons to have a mutual regard and affection, and to look favorably on one another, in which the very essence of friendship consists. From all eternity God set His heart upon him, and now the reconciled one has given his heart to Him.

One has a very high regard for an intimate and proved friend. That God greatly values and esteems those whom He reconciles to Himself is clear both from His declarations concerning them and what He has done for them. He prizes them above the world and orders all things in its governance for the furthering of their good. "For lam the Lord your God, the Holy One in Israel, your Savior. I gave Egypt for your ransom, Ethiopia and Seba for you. Since you were precious in My sight, you have been honorable, and I have loved you" (Isa. 43:3,4). What a wondrous and blessed testimony is that! "He delivered me because He delighted in me" (2 Sam. 22:20). "How fair and how pleasant you are, O love for delights" (Song of Sol. 7:6) is His language respecting His Spouse, and She in return declares, "I sat down under His shadow with great delight, and His fruit was sweet to my taste" (2:3). So highly does the saint prize God in Christ that he avers, "Whom have I in heaven but You, and there is none upon earth that I desire besides You" (Ps. 73:25).

Since real and warm friends highly value and delight in one another it is their chief pleasure to share each other's company, being happiest when together. Thus it is between the reconciled soul and his heavenly Friend: "truly our fellowship is with the Father and with His Son Jesus Christ" (1 John 1:3). In nothing can the Christian more fitly evince his friendship with God than by a diligent endeavor to maintain a constant and intimate communion with Him. In addition to the regular tribute of his daily worship, if the soul of the believer is in a healthy condition, he will take occasion to frequently come into God's presence on purpose to. have communion with Him. Friendship is best maintained by visits, and the more free and less occasioned by urgent business, the more are they appreciated. David, owned as "a man after God's own heart"—the equivalent of Abraham's being called His "friend"—said, "O God, You are my God, early will I seek You . . . To see Your power and Your glory, so as I have seen You in the sanctuary. Because Your lovingkindness is better than life, my lips shall praise You. . . My soul shall be satisfied as with marrow and fatness, and my mouth shall praise You with joyful lips" (Ps. 63:1-5). That was the language of pure friendship.

Intimate converse and close communications characterize the dealings of one warm friend to another. Things which I would not discuss with a stranger, personal matters I would be silent upon to a mere acquaintance, I freely open to one I delight in. It is thus between God and the reconciled soul. It is so on His part: "The secret of the Lord is with them that fear Him, and He will show them His covenant" (Ps. 25:14). "The Lord spoke to Moses face to face (without restraint or reserve) as a man speaks unto his friend" (Ex. 33:11). Thus Scripture makes this freedom of communication one of the marks of spiritual friendship. So too we find the Lord Jesus saying to His beloved apostles, "Henceforth I call you not servants, for the servant knows not what his lord does: but I have called you friends; for all things that I have heard of My Father, I have made known unto you" (John 15:15). Do you, my reader, know anything of this experience? Are you in such close touch with Him as to make this (morally) possible? It is through His Word God now speaks to us: do you know what it is for your heart to "burn" while He talks with you by the way and "opens" to you the Scriptures (Luke 24:32)?

Yet this intimate conversation is not one-sided, but is reciprocal: the reconciled one finds liberty in opening his heart unto his heavenly Friend, as he does to none other. This is his holy privilege: "trust in Him at all times, you people, pour out your heart before Him" (Ps. 62:8). How do you treat your best earthly friend? When you have not seen him for a season, how warmly you welcome him, how freely you express your pleasure at meeting him again, what utterances of good will and delight do you make! Equally free should the saint be with his Lord. He should pour out his heart with joy and gladness. He should unrestrainedly avow his delight in the Lord. He should bring with him a sacrifice of praise, that is, the fruit of his lips, giving thanks (Heb. 13:15). Such will not only be acceptable unto Him, but it will give Him pleasure: it is on these occasions that He says, "Your lips, O My Spouse, drop as the honeycomb: honey and milk are under your tongue" (Song of Sol. 4:11)—such communications are sweet unto Me.

But there are times when one is so sorely troubled and weighed down that his expressions of delight and joy toward a loving friend will be restrained. True, yet that only affords occasion for another attribute of friendship to be exercised, namely, to freely unburden his heart unto him. Thus it is with the reconciled soul and God: he will speak to Him more freely and make mention of things which he would not to his nearest and dearest earthly friend. This is the Christian's privilege: to ease his heart before God. Said the Psalmist, "I poured out my complaint before Him, I showed before Him my trouble" (Ps. 142:2), and He deems Himself honored by such confidences. The more communion there is between God and us over our distresses, the more will He discover our secret faults, and the more will we disclose again to Him. The one is a sure consequence of the other. After speaking of our fellowship with God in 1 John 1:3, it is added, "If we confess our sins He is faithful and just to forgive us our sins." One great part of our friendship with God is the taking of Him fully into our confidence, as on His part it is to pardon us.

Having confidence in a friend we freely seek his help and advice. When describing a close friend David said, "we took sweet counsel together" (Ps. 55:14). And that is how we ought to treat our heavenly Friend, making use of Him, counting upon His favor and help in all our concerns. That is both our privilege and duty: "in all your ways acknowledge Him, and He shall direct your paths" (Prov. 3:6)—seek His counsel, give yourself up to His guidance. That little (and large) word "all" includes small things as well as great! In this the friendship of God excels that of others. We are loath to trouble an earthly friend about trifles, but we may spread the smallest matter before Him who has numbered the very hairs of our head. In this we honor Him, for it is an acknowledgement on our part that He rules all things, even the very least.

One is very careful in seeking to avoid giving any offence unto a dear friend and doing all in our power to please him. Apply that Godwards and it has reference to our obedience. Therefore do we find Christ saying, "You are My friends if you do whatsoever I command you" (John 15:14). That "if" is addressed to responsibility and is the testing of our profession. It is by obedience we evidence and approve ourselves to be His friends. Obedience goes much further than resisting sin and abstaining from wicked works: "cease to do evil, learn to do well" (Isa. 1:17). It is not sufficient to forbear the commission of sin if we perform not our duty. The fig tree was cursed not because it bore evil fruit, but because it was barren. There are many who, like the Pharisees, pride themselves on negations: I am not profane, immoral, irreligious. But that gives them no title to regard themselves as friends of Christ. Are they actually doing the things He has enjoined—this is the crucial test and characteristic mark of the reconciled.

Observe it is not "you shall be" but "you are My friends if you do." It is the doers of His Word whom the Lord owns as His friends: they who are as diligent in practicing His precepts as in shunning what He hates. And their obedience is not that of mercenary legalists nor the forced work of slaves, but is the voluntary and joyful response of loving and grateful hearts. An action may have the appearance of friendship when there is nothing of good will behind it. But none can impose upon the Lord—He knows when there is inward conformity to His will as well as outward compliance, when a person's "good works" are those of the formalist or of a loving heart. If they are the latter, we shall not pick and choose between His precepts, but "do whatsoever He commands?" "whatever your soul desires, I will even do it for you" (1 Sam. 20:4) said Jonathan to his friend. That is indeed the longing and aim of every reconciled soul but his infirmities and distempers often cause him to go halting.

Another characteristic or mark of friendship is confidence: "My own familiar friend in whom I trusted" (Ps. 41:3) said David. Nothing more readily undermines friendship than the harboring of suspicions. It is because we have proved the staunchness and affection of another that we count him our friend, and rely upon him. Thus it is with a reconciled soul and God. He has 'shown Himself to be graciously disposed unto me, giving me innumerable proofs of His lovingkindness and faithfulness, and that draws out my heart in confidence toward Him. The more I trust in Him and look to Him for help, the more is He pleased and honored by me, and the more do I show myself to be His friend. "Cast your burden upon the Lord" is His blessed invitation, for He desires not His child should be weighted down by it. "Casting all your care upon Him, for He cares for you" (1 Pet. 5:7). God would have His people act toward Him with holy familiarity, confiding in Him at all time, counting upon His goodness, reposing themselves in His love, making known their requests with thanksgiving, expecting Him to supply all their need. That is both our privilege and duty if we sustain to God the relationship of friends.

Where there is full confidence in a tried and trusted friend we place a favorable construction upon even those actions of his which may puzzle and perplex us. We refuse to impute evil to or harbor suspicions against him. Any fancied slight he has given, any apparent unconcern or unkindness he has shown, anything in his letters which we do not understand, we leave until we again see him face to face, quietly assured that a satisfactory explanation will be forthcoming from him. Thus it is with the saint and his heavenly friend. Some of His dealings sorely try and exercise him, yet he doubts not that He is too wise to err and too loving to be unkind. Some of His dispensations are exceedingly trying to flesh and blood, but a believing soul will "Judge not the Lord by feeble sense, but trust Him for His grace," realizing that "behind a frowning providence, He hides a smiling face." Thus it was with Job, "Though He slay me, yet will I trust Him." Love "thinks no evil" but favorably interprets the most mysterious of God's ways, knowing that He is making all things work together for our good.

There is no real reason why any one of ordinary intelligence should remain in doubt as to his spiritual state. If you faithfully examine yourself and honestly measure yourself by the different criteria we have mentioned in these articles, you should have no difficulty in determining whether you be still alienated from God or reconciled to Him. If you are at peace with Him then you are making common cause with Him, warring against His foes—the Devil, sin, the world. If you are reconciled to God, then you are His friend, evidencing the same by a friend-like disposition and deportment, conducting yourself toward Him, treating Him, as one friend with another. The Lord so add His gracious blessing that in His light each of us may see light.

Chapter 30
Its Need Revisited-Continued

This is an aspect of our subject which will by no means appeal to the empty professor, nor, we may add, to the backslider. The Antinomian is all for hearing about the free grace of God and His unforfeitable gifts, and if the preacher should point out that favors and privileges entail obligations, he is condemned by them for his legality; but if he is to receive his Master's "well done," he will not have the united approbation of a large congregation. It betrays a most unhealthy state of soul when we wish to hear only of what Christ did and procured for sinners, and little or nothing of what He requires from the beneficiaries of the same. God has inseparably joined together privilege and duty, relationship and obligation, and we are lacking an honest heart if we eagerly seize His promises and despise His precepts. It betrays a sad condition of soul if we are not anxious to ascertain "What does the Lord require of you" (Micah 6:8).

It is our firm conviction that one of the main causes for such a vast number of empty professors and backslidden believers in Christendom today was the disproportionate and unfaithful preaching of most of the prominent orthodox pulpits during the past century. Instead of giving a conspicuous place to what which tested profession, both doctrinally and practically, nominal saints were lulled into a false sense of security. Instead of insisting that conversion is but the beginning of the Christian life, an enlisting under the banner of Christ to "fight the good fight of faith," in which the Devil is to be steadfastly resisted and a ceaseless warfare waged against indwelling sin, the siren song of "Once saved, always saved" was dinned into the ears of those whose walk was thoroughly carnal and worldly. Instead of a searching and probing ministry the pulpit cried "Peace, peace" unto those still at enmity with God.

Those who were flattered as being "the stalwarts of the Faith" were often most partial in which aspects of the Faith they concentrated upon. Those whose proud boast it was that they "shunned not to declare all the counsel of God," were for the most part men who repudiated human responsibility and detested the word "duty." It is handling the Word of God deceitfully to emphasize the expression "ordained to eternal life" and to ignore "good works which God has before ordained that we should walk in them" (Eph. 2:10). It is withholding that which is profitable unto souls (Acts 20:20) to leave them in ignorance that Christ is "the Author of eternal salvation unto all them that obey Him" (Heb. 5:9). It is highly dishonoring to God when we pretend to magnify "the riches of His grace" if we fail to insist that His grace effectually teaches its recipients to be "denying ungodliness and worldly lusts, (that) we should live soberly, righteously, and godly in this present world" (Titus 2:11,12).

Having dwelt upon the privilege-side of our theme in previous articles of this series, we should be woefully lacking in proportion and completeness if we now failed to consider the duty-side of it. It behooves us to point out God's full rights and just claims upon us, as well as His rich favors and unmerited mercies unto us. It becomes the reader to whole-heartedly welcome our efforts to execute this part of our task. The language of a reconciled soul is, and must be, "What shall I render unto the Lord for all His benefits?" How shall I express my gratitude unto that blessed One who has shown me such unspeakable mercy? If the wrath of God is removed from me and

I am now taken into His unclouded and everlasting favor, how shall I now most fitly comport myself? Since such measureless love has been so freely lavished upon me, how can I best show forth my gratitude? That is the question we shall now endeavor to answer.

1. By fervent praise unto God. O what thanksgiving is due unto Him for His matchless grace! As it was the supreme demonstration of His love in sending forth His Son to make peace, that should be the principal spring of our thanksgiving. When God bids His people," Behold My Servant whom I uphold, My Elect in whom My soul delights," whom He gave "for a covenant of the people, for a light of the Gentiles. to open the blind eyes, to bring out the prisoners from the prison and them that sit in darkness out of the prison-house;" the use which He enjoins them to make of the same is, "Sing unto the Lord a new song" (Isa. 42:1-10). The initial response of one who realizes that his trespasses are no longer imputed to him, but instead that the perfect righteousness of Christ is reckoned to his account, must be "Bless the Lord, O my soul, and all that is within me bless His holy name" (Ps. 103:1). So too it should be his daily—as it will be his eternal—response.

"God might have destroyed us with less cost than He has reconciled us; for our destruction there was no need of His counsel, nor fitting out and sending His Son, nor opening His treasures; a word would have done it, whereas our reconciliation stood Him at much charge. It was performed at the expense of His grace and Spirit to furnish His Son to be a sacrifice for our atonement. An inexpressible wonder that the Father should prepare His Son a mortal body that our souls might be prepared for immortal glory" (S. Charnock). The apostle could not consider the will of our Father in this work without interrupting his discourse with a doxology: "to whom the glory be forever and ever. Amen" (Gal. 1:4,5); and such should be our response. As the angels rejoiced in the manifestation of the wisdom and power of God in the incarnation of His dear Son, much more should we rejoice at the triumphant outcome of His mission and of our personal interest in the same, joining with them in their "Glory to God in the highest."

Who is it, my reader, who makes you to differ from others? Is it not God? Then ascribe glory to Him. If He has made you to differ from others in the exercise of His sovereign mercy, do you differ from them in the sounding forth of His praises. When David considered the works of God's hand in the stellar heavens, he exclaimed "What is man that You are mindful of him," and if we consider what sovereign favor has wrought for and in the regenerate, well may we be overwhelmed with wonder. Pardon of but one sin would make us forever debtors to God, for every sin is a hatred of Him and renders us obnoxious to eternal torments. What then is due unto Him from those whom He has pardoned sins more in number than the hairs of their heads! O the marvel of it, that the one who is by nature a child of wrath should be made an heir of Heaven; that one so vile should be taken into the bosom of the Father! Thanks be unto God for His unspeakable gift.

2. By care to please God. Since He went to so much trouble and cost in restoring us, how our thoughts and affections should unitedly engage in earnestly endeavoring to please Him. The Decalogue is prefaced with "I am the Lord your God, which brought you out of the land of Egypt, out of the house of bondage," as an incentive and inducement for Israel to render cheerful obedience unto Him. "I am the Lord your God who in Christ has delivered you from eternal death and brought you into My everlasting favor" is the tenor of the Gospel—a far weightier motive for the Christian to place himself unreservedly at God's disposal. This it is which will demonstrate the worth and genuineness of our praise: whether it is merely an emotional spasm or the overflowing gratitude of a heart which has been won by Him. If our expressions of thanksgiving and worship are sincere, then the homage of our lips will be borne out by the honoring of God in our daily lives. Whenever I am tempted to gratify the flesh, my reply should be "How then can I do this great wickedness and sin against God" (Gen. 39:9); or "Is this your kindness to your Friend!" (1

Sam. 16:17). Shall I so evilly requite the One who has been gracious unto me?

The service which God requires from us is that of love, and not of compulsion. We must indeed keep our eyes on the Rule so that our actions may be conformed to its requirements, otherwise God will ask, "Who has required this at your hand?" (Isa. 1:12). But there must be something more: the Lord looks on the heart as well as the outward performances. Duties are not distinguished by their external garb, but by the spirit prompting them. A box of ointment with an affectionate regard for the Lord, nay a cup of cold water, is valued and registered. The smallest act of service unto God which issues from gratitude is prized by Him more highly than all the imposing works of men without it. It is at this very point that the saints differ radically from all others. Whatever are the religious performances of the legalist, the formalists, or the hypocrite, they proceed from some form of self-esteem. But that of the believer is wrought by gratitude. It is the love of Christ which constrains him, which moves him to take His yoke upon him, which so motivates him that his chief concern is to keep His commandments and show forth His praises.

If there is good will in the heart toward God it will be evidenced by choosing and doing the things which are pleasing unto Him. There will be a readiness of heart unto obedience, for love prepares and predisposes the heart unto what He requires from us. Good will in the heart toward God expresses itself in the actual performing of what He has enjoined, for the language of gratitude is "His commandments are not grievous" (1 John 5:3). When love to Rachel set Jacob a work it was not unpleasant to him, and though it took him seven years, he deemed it not long. So far from a reconciled soul feeling that God is a hard Master imposing a severe task upon him, he is thankful to have the opportunity to manifest his appreciation. When David made such costly preparations for the house of God, he asked "But who am I?" (1 Chron. 29:14), considering it a marvel of condescension that the great God should accept anything at his hands. So far from begrudging any self-sacrifice love will mourn that what has been done is so little and so imperfect, realizing that nothing can be too much or too good for the Lord—and not only too small to answer God's love, but to adequately express his own.

3. By trusting in God. Since He is reconciled to me and I to Him then it is both my privilege and duty to look to Him for the supply of every need and confidently expect the same. The Christian should habitually view Him as "the God of peace" and under that title and relationship implore Him for daily supplies of grace, for it is as such that He works in us "that which is well pleasing in His sight" (Heb. 13:20,21). God has promised to be "as the dew" unto His people under the Gospel (Hos. 14:5), and as the dew descends from a clear sky so does grace from the One who has blotted out our iniquities. We should look then continually for spiritual strength from God in Christ. All our approaches to Him should be begun and attended with a sense that we have been taken into His favor. In all His communications to His people God acts as reconciled to them, and so should we eye Him whenever we come to the throne of grace. As there is not one mercy God shows us but springs from this relationship, so every duty we offer to Him and petition we make of Him should rise from a sense of the same. This should cause us to believe with a holy boldness.

Here is a cordial for us in our sorest problems and trials. What can the greatest difficulty or acutest strait signify when God remains reconciled to the soul in Christ! Providence is ordered by our best Friend. This is the grand stay which Christ has furnished His disciples: "that in Me you might have peace; in the world you shall have tribulation" (John 16:33). Is not that a sufficient defence against all the roaring of men and the rage of Satan? Though the world frowns, God in Christ smiles upon you. It was a sense of their reconciliation to God which turned prisons into palaces and dungeons into chambers of praise for those who were persecuted by the ungodly. Here is a shield against fear, security against danger, a treasure against poverty. Under the sharpest affliction the believer may distinguish between God as a loving Father and avenging Judge. Carnal reason and sense will indeed dispute against faith, and while they are listened unto, faith will stagger; but if the heart turns to and is engaged with a reconciled God it will discern under the severest chastisement the rod of mercy, wielded by a love maintaining our best interests.

There should be an expecting of temporal mercies. If God was in Christ reconciling us to Himself, then most assuredly He will be in Christ giving forth all suited benefits. It is entirely inconsistent with His amity to withhold anything really needed by us, for in that case) as one pointed out, it would not then be a "much more" as Christ argued, but a much less: "If you then, being evil, know how to give good gifts unto your children, how much more shall your Father which is in heaven give good things to them that ask Him!" (Matthew 7:11). Yet it is to be borne in mind that it is only "good things" which He has promised to give, and that He alone is the proper judge as to what is "good." If God feeds the ravens, certainly He will not permit His friends to starve. If He spared not His only Son, He will not begrudge mere food and clothing. Our covenant God will deny His children nothing which is for their welfare. If we lived in the realization of that, how contented we would be in every situation!

4. By cherishing God's peace. "The remission of sins past gives not a permission for sins to come, but should be a bridle and a restraint" (Manton). "There is forgiveness with You that You may be feared" (130:4). The end of Christ's death cannot be separated: He is no Atoner for those He is not a Refiner, for He gave Himself to "purify unto Himself a peculiar people, zealous of good works" (Titus 2:4). As there was a double enmity in us—one rooted in our nature and another declared by wicked works, so there must be a change both in our state and an alteration of our actions. God and sin are irreconcilable enemies, so that where there is peace with one, there must be war with another. Fire and water would sooner agree than a peace with God and a peace with sin. "There is no peace, says my God to the wicked." We should be very tender of God's peace, that no breach fall out between us: "If I have done iniquity, I will do no more" (Job 34:32) must be our sincere desire and resolution, otherwise we are but hypocrites.

Peace was broken by the sin of the first Adam, and though it was restored by the last Adam, yet our obedience is necessary if we are to enjoy the fruits of it: "Great peace have they which love Your Law" (119:165). Then let us beware of relaxing in our watchfulness or of becoming self-confident in our ability to face temptations. "He will speak peace unto His people and to His saints, but let them not turn again to folly" (Ps. 85:8). "When we sought for pardon, sin was the great burden which lay upon our consciences, the wound which pained us at heart, the disease our souls were sick of; and shall that which we complained of as a burden become our delight? shall we tear open our wounds which are in a fair way of being healed, and run into bonds and chains again after we are freed from them?" (Manton). That were indeed crass folly, madness. Backsliders forsake their peace: as it is said of them, "they have forgotten their resting place" (Jer. 50:6). Peace can only be recovered as we repent of our sins and renew our covenant with God.

5. By using our access to God. The most blessed result or consequence of reconciliation is that believers have the right to approach unto God, and therefore it is their privilege to freely avail themselves of the same. "Having therefore, brethren, liberty to enter into the Holiest by the blood of Jesus.. .let us draw near with a true heart in full assurance of faith"(Heb. 10:19,22), that is, with a firm belief in the efficacy of Christ's sacrifice and a firm reliance upon the same. As God was in Christ reconciling, so He is in Him receiving our praises and petitions. As Christ made satisfaction for us by His death, so He provides the acceptance of our sacrifices and services by His merits. Though justification is a transcendent mercy, yet it would not complete our happiness unless we could commune with God. Peace was not the thing God ultimately aimed at—it

was but the medium. He would be our Friend, that there might be sweet intercourse between Him and His people. This is an inestimable privilege of which we should make constant use.

But those who would enjoy communion with the Lord must needs be careful to avoid everything which would separate from Him. He is a jealous God and will brook no rivals. If our fellowship with the Holy One is to be intimate and constant, then we must keep a close guard against grieving the Spirit. We must beware of cooling affections, slackening in the use of means and fighting against sin, slipping back into our old ways. If we neglect those duties there can be no real, acceptable or satisfying drawing nigh unto God. Christ has indeed opened a new and living way for His people into God's presence, and has provided them with both the right and title so to do; nevertheless there are certain moral qualifications required of them if they are to really draw nigh unto the Holy One—certainly those who simply offer cold and formal prayers do not do so.

There are many of God's own children who are cut off from conscious access to Him, for their sins have caused a breach (Isa. 59:1,2): "with the pure You will show Yourself pure; and with the forward You will show Yourself forward" (Ps. 18:26). Loose walking severs our communion with God, and then He acts distantly toward us: "How long will You hide Your face from me?" (Ps. 13:1) has been the sorrowful lament of many a wayward saint. Our folly must be repented of and humbly confessed before there can be restoration unto fellowship with God. If we would draw near unto Him it must be with "our hearts sprinkled from an evil conscience and our bodies washed with pure water" (Heb. 10:22) that is, our internal and external man cleansed from defilement, our members kept from evil and used for God. "Universal sanctification upon our whole persons and the mortification in an especial manner of outward sins are required of us in our drawing near to God" (J. Owen).

6. By rejoicing in God. How great should and may be the joy of believing souls! To be instated in the favor of God, to have the Almighty for our Friend, to have the light of His countenance shining upon us. The knowledge of that in the understanding is tidings of great joy, the sense of it in our hearts is "joy unspeakable and full of glory." Reconciliation and the realization of it are two distinct things. The one may be a fact, yet through unbelief or carelessness I may lack the assurance of it. But what comfort and happiness is his who has the assurance that he is at peace with God and the testimony that his conscience is sprinkled with the blood of the Lamb! Then, even though the fig tree blossom not, the fields yield no meat, and there are no herds in the stalls, "yet I will rejoice in the Lord, I will joy in the God of my salvation" (Hab. 3:18). "As sorrowful" over our sins, yet "always rejoicing" in the Lord (2 Cor. 6:10) is our bounden duty.

7. By devotedness to God. "You are not your own, for you are bought with a price. Therefore glorify God in your body and in your spirit" (1 Cor 6:19,20). That summaries the responsibilities of the reconciled. To conduct ourselves as those who are not only the creatures, the children, but the purchased property of God, in whom He has the sole right. Since He spared not His own Son for us, we should withhold nothing from Him, but present ourselves unreservedly to Him as "a living sacrifice," which is indeed "our reasonable service." We must spare no lust, nor indulge anything which is hateful to Christ, but denying self, take up our cross, and follow Him. Let us earnestly seek grace for the discharge of these duties.

Chapter 31
Its Need Revisited-Concluded

It might be thought that we had pretty well covered this aspect in the preceding section. Not so; there is another important phase of it which needs to be considered. Sin has not only alienated man from God, but man from man as well. Where there is no love to God there is no genuine love to our fellow-men. By nature we are totally depraved, and as such possessed of a radically selfish, evil, malicious disposition. "The poison of asps is under their lips, whose mouth is full of cursing and bitterness; their feet are swift to shed blood, destruction and misery are in their ways" (Rom. 3:13-17). The record of human history consists largely of a solemn demonstration of that fact. Envies and enmities have marked the relationships of one nation to another, one party against another, one individual against another. Frictions and feuds have been the inevitable outcome of a covetous and ferocious spirit among men, were they black or white, red or yellow.

It is only the restraining hand of God which holds men within bounds and prevents the social sphere from becoming worse than the jungle. Every once in a while that restraining Hand is largely withdrawn and then, despite all our vaunted progress, human nature is seen in its naked savagery. The truth is that men today are neither better nor worse than they were at the beginning of this Christian era. Speaking of God's own people during their unregeneracy, the apostle described them as "serving divers lusts and pleasures, living in malice and envy, hateful and hating one another" (Titus 3:3). Such are men the world over, though they will not own up to it, nor can they be expected to. Since the natural man is ignorant of his inherent and inveterate enmity against God, it not to be supposed that he is aware of harboring such a spirit against his neighbors. But if all the police were removed from this so-called civilized country, how long would it be before "hateful and hating one another" was plainly and generally manifested!

Fallen man not only requires to be reconciled to God but to his fellows, and where the one takes place the other necessarily follows. Reconciliation, as was shown, is one of the fruits of regeneration; for at the new birth a new principle is imparted to its subject, so that his enmity is displaced by amity. "Everyone that loves Him that begat, loves him also that is begotten of Him" (1 John 5:1). The reconciliation of a soul to God entails his reconciliation to all saints. Since God has been reconciled to the entire Church (considered as fallen) and its two main constituents (believing Jews and Gentiles) are made one, it follows that each Christian is, fundamentally, harmoniously united to all others. We say "fundamentally," for the work of Christ has federally and legally united them. But that is not all. He procured the Spirit for His Church and He—by the work of regeneration—makes them vitally one in a new creation. "For by one Spirit are we all baptized into one body, whether Jews or Gentiles, bond or free, and have all been made to drink into one spirit" (I Cor. 12:13).

As the Christian's reconciliation to God entails certain clearly marked responsibilities, so also does his reconciliation to all fellow-believers, and these are what we shall now be occupied with. Let us begin with that basic and comprehensive duty, "Endeavoring to keep the unity of the Spirit in the bond of peace" (Eph. 4:3). Concerning that simple precept there has been much confusion, both as to its meaning and requirement, with almost endless controversy about church union and divisions. Man, with his usual perversity, has changed that exhortation to "Zealously attempt to make and enforce a human unity," anathematizing all who will not subscribe and conform unto the same. Romanists have made the greatest outcry about church unity, vehemently contending that it is indispensably necessary that all Christians should submit to the papal authority, and that there is no salvation for anyone dying outside their communion. Thus, a visible and carnal union with an Italian pontiff is preferred to an invisible, spiritual and saving union with the Christ of God.

We do not propose to cover now the various efforts and devices of men since the Reformation to bring into existence organizations for unity and uniformity among professing Christians, both in creed and form of worship, such as State Churches "by law established," denominations which have laid claim to being the "true Church" or "churches of Christ," nor the high pretensions of those who rather more than a century ago denounced all sects and systems and alleged that they alone met on "the ground of Christ's Body" and "expressed" the unity of the Spirit, only to split up in a very short time into numerous factions and conflicting "fellowships." No, our object here is not to be controversial but constructive, to give a brief exposition of Ephesians 4:1-6, and then point out the practical application and bearing of the same. We cannot intelligently "keep the unity of the Spirit" until we rightly understand what that "unity" is; may He graciously be our Guide.

"I therefore the .prisoner of the Lord beseech you that you walk worthy of the vocation with which you are called. . . endeavoring to keep" etc. (Eph. 4:1-3). That exhortation holds the same place in this epistle as 12:1 does in that of the Romans, being placed at the forefront of the hortatory section, and we at once observe the verbal resemblances between them in the "therefore" by which it is supported, and the "I beseech you" the earnestness with which the call is made. Standing as it does at the beginning of the practical division of the epistle, taking precedence of all its other precepts, we have emphasized its deep importance. It was written by the apostle during his incarceration at Rome, but it is blessed to mark that He looked above Caesar, regarding himself as "the prisoner of the Lord." Therefore we find his heart was occupied not with his own danger or discomfort, but with the glory of Christ and the interests of His redeemed. He asked not the saints to "get up a petition" for his release, nor even to pray for it, but was concerned that they should conduct themselves in a way which would bring glory to his Master.

The "I therefore beseech you that you walk worthy. . . endeavoring to keep the unity of the Spirit in the bond of peace" requires that we carefully consult what precedes, for it is the contents of Ephesians 1-3 which explains the force of 4:1-3. First, it should be pointed out that the Greek word rendered "bond" is not the simple "desmos" but rather the compound "sun-desmos"—joining—bond. This at once links up with and is based upon the "fellow-citizens" of 2:19, the "being fitly framed together" and "built together" (2:21,22), and the "fellow-heirs, and a joint-body, and joint partakers of His promise" (3:6 —Greek), where in each case, the reference is to the union of believing Jews and Gentiles in the mystical Body of Christ. It is therefore an affectionate plea that those who in their unregenerate days had been bitterly hostile against each other, should now walk together in love and harmony. The same Greek word occurs in the parallel passage in Col. 3: "above all things put on charity, which is the joint bond of perfectness" (v. 14), which throws clear light on the verse we are now considering.

"I therefore. . . beseech you that you walk worthy of the vocation wherewith you are called," which is unto sonship—holiness and glory, conformity to the image of Christ. The inestimable privileges conferred upon those who are effectually called by God out of darkness into His marvelous light, obligates its favored recipients to order their lives accordingly. It requires from them a distinctive spirit, a particular disposition and temper, which is to be exercised and manifested in their dealings with fellow-saints. They are to conduct themselves with humility and gentleness, not with self-assertiveness and self-exaltation. They are required to seek the good and promote the interests of their brethren and sisters in Christ, and continually endeavor to preserve amity and concord among them, "to bear with one another in love as to those light occasions of offence or displeasure which could not be wholly avoided even among believers in this present imperfect state" (T. Scott).

For the Christian to walk worthily of his vocation is for him to live and act congruously, suitably for it. Here it has particular reference to the spirit and manner in which he is to practically conduct himself toward his fellow-saints, namely, by endeavoring to keep the unity of the Spirit in the bond of peace. That word "endeavoring" means far more than a half-hearted effort which ceases as soon as opposition is encountered. It signifies "give diligence," laboring earnestly, doing our utmost in performing this task. The nature of this duty is intimated with considerable definiteness by the particular graces which are here specified as needing to be exercised. Had that "unity" consisted of uniformity of belief—as many have supposed, then the saints had been exhorted unto the acquirement of "knowledge" and the exercise of "faith." Or had that unity been an ecclesiastical one which is to be framed or "expressed" on earth, then the call would be to the exercise of "faithfulness" and "firmness," in uncompromisingly resisting all innovations. But instead, it is "with all lowliness and meekness, forbearing one another in love."

Thus whatever is our angle of approach in seeking to define this controversial expression, whether it is from the contents of the previous chapters, the parallel passage in Colossians 3:14, or the congruity of the preceding verse, it should be clear that the "unity of the Spirit" which we are to diligently assay to keep "in the bond of peace" has no reference to the formation of an external and visible unification of all professing Christians, in which all differences in judgment and belief are to be dropped and where all worship is to conform to a common standard. The union of Christendom which so many enthusiasts have advocated would, in reality, consist of a unity in which principle gave way to policy, contending earnestly for the Faith once delivered to the saints would be displaced by the uttering of mere generalities and moral platitudes, and the masculine virtues degenerating into an effeminate affection of universal charity. Sheep and goats will never make amicable companions, still less so sheep and wolves. Variety and not uniformity marks all the works of God, whether it is in creation, providence or grace.

The unity of the Spirit is not an ecclesiastical one here on earth, nor is it one which God will make in Heaven by and by. Nor is it the unity of the mystical Body, for that can no more be broken than could a bone in the literal body of Christ (John 18:36). The very fact that it is "the unity of the Spirit" precludes any visible ecclesiastical unity. It is a fact subsisting to faith, without any evidence of it to sight. It is therefore a Divine, spiritual and present unity which is quite imperceptible to the senses. It is that unity of which the Spirit is the Author. It is the new creation of which He makes God's elect members by regeneration. Every soul indwelt by the Spirit is a part of that unity, and none others are. By being made members of the new creation we are brought into "the joint-bond of peace." Each soul indwelt by the Spirit is inducted into a company where enmity has been slain, in which the members are united as the fruit of Christ's sacrifice, and they are here enjoined to act in full harmony with this new relationship.

By virtue of his having the Spirit each Christian is in spirit united with all other regenerated souls, and he is to give diligence in practically observing that fact in all his converse and dealings with them. He is to earnestly avoid falling out with a brother or sister in Christ, being most careful to eschew everything having a tendency to cause a breach between them. He is to love all in whom he can discern any of the features of Christ, whether or not they belong to his own "church" or "assembly." He is to exercise good will unto all who are members the Household of Faith. He should be slow to take offence, and having himself received mercy, should ever be merciful unto others. God's reconciliation should be our rule in dealing with our brethren: "If God so loved us, we ought also to love one another" (1 John 4:11), and since His heart embraces the whole of His family, ours should do no less. If He is longsuffering to usward, we should be long-suffering to themward. "Be you therefore imitators of God as dear children" (Eph. 5:1).

Now the only possible way in which the reconciled soul can discharge this essential and blessed part of his responsibility is by exercising those graces enjoined in verse 2. After beseeching the saints to walk worthy of their vocation, Paul described the necessary qualifications for so doing, namely, "with all lowliness and meekness, forbearing one another in love." Lowliness of mind or humility is to have a mean estimate of myself, based upon the consciousness of my sinfulness and weakness. Let it be most attentively noted that the exercise of this grace comes first, and that it is not only "with lowliness," but "with all lowliness." Nothing so hinders our keeping the unity of the Spirit in the bond of peace as personal pride. Next comes "meekness," which signifies tractability, gentleness, mildness; an unresisting and uncomplaining temper. It is that lamb-like disposition which enables one to bear injury from others without bitterness and retaliating in a spirit of revenge. "Forbearing one another in love:" suppressing anger and ill feelings, patiently enduring the failings, foibles, and faults of my brethren, as they do (or should) mine.

Those grace of humility, meekness and longsuffering are to be manifested in keeping—recognizing and cherishing—that spiritual and invisible unity which there is between the children of God, loving all in whom they perceive His image doing everything in their power to further one another's interests and to promote harmony and concord. For the glory of God, the honor of Christ, and the good of His people, each believer is under bonds to exercise and manifest a spirit of good will unto his brethren; that is to override all natural peculiarities, all selfish interests, all party concerns. That does not mean a peace at any price, wherein we connive at error or condone the sins of an erring saint, making no effort to recover him. No indeed, the wisdom which is from above is "first pure, and then peaceable" (Jas. 3:17). If we perceive a professing Christian walking contrary to the Truth, we are to have no intimate fellowship with him, "yet count him not as an enemy, but admonish him as a brother" (2 Thess. 3:15); if he is suddenly overtaken in a fault we should, in the spirit of meekness, seek to restore him (Gal. 6:1).

Rightly did Matt. Henry point out that "The seat of Christian unity is in the heart or spirit; it does not lie in one set of thoughts and form or mode of worship, but in one heart or soul." In other words it lies in the exercise of a gracious and peaceable disposition. As that writer so aptly pointed out, "Love is the law of Christ's kingdom, the lesson of His school, and the livery of His family." If Christ is the Prince of Peace, then surely His disciples ought to be the children of peace, ever striving to maintain amity and harmony. The root cause of strife and dissension lies not in anything external, but within ourselves: "From where come wars and fightings among you? Come they not here even of your lusts that war in your members?" (Jas. 4:1). We should not rudely obtrude our ideas upon others, but rather wait until we are asked to state our views, and then do so with meekness and reverence (1 Pet. 3:15). The cultivation of an amiable disposition and peaceable temper is the best cement for binding saints together. In verses 4-6 the apostle mentions several motives to prompt unto a compliance with the duty expressed in Ephesians 4:1,3. "There is one Body, and one Sprit, even as you are called in one hope of your calling." What better grounds could believers have to love and act peaceably toward each other! They are fellow-members of the mystical body of Christ, they are indwelt by the same blessed Spirit, they are begotten unto the same glorious and eternal inheritance. Do they look forward to the time when they shall join "the spirits of just men made perfect"? Then let them anticipate that time and act now agreeably toward those they hope to dwell together with forever. "One Lord, one faith, one baptism." There may be different apprehensions of that Faith, different degrees of conformity to that Lord, different understandings of "baptism," but that must not alienate the heart of one

Christian from another. "One God, and Father of all," whose family all the reconciled belong to; and should not the members of that family cherish one another! Let that sevenfold consideration animate each of us to live in peace and brotherly affection with our fellow-saints.

The unity of the Spirit differs from the oneness of the Body, in that while we may either keep or break the former, we can do neither the one nor the other with the latter. The responsibility of those reconciled to each other is, negatively, to avoid anything which would mar that unity; and positively, to engage in everything that would further it. Pride, self-will, envy, bigotry, fleshly zeal about comparative trifles, are the causes of most of the frictions and fractions among believers. "Only by pride comes contention." (Prov. 13:19). That is the most fertile root of all—offence is taken because I do not receive that notice to which I deem myself entitled, or I am hurt because I cannot have my own way in everything. "A whisperer separates chief friends" (Nov. 16:28): but he can only do so by one giving ear to his malicious tales! An acquaintance of ours used to say unto those who come to her with evil reports of others, "Please take your garbage elsewhere: I decline to receive it."

"Therefore if you bring your gift to the altar, and there remember that your brother has anything against you; leave there your gift before the altar and go your way; first be reconciled to your brother, and then come and offer your gift" (Matthew 5:23,24). How emphatically that makes manifest the importance which God attaches to our keeping the unity of the Spirit in the bond of peace! When that unity has been broken, He desires not our gifts. If you have done a brother an injury and he has just cause of complaint, peace has been disrupted, and the Holy One requires you to right that wrong before He will receive your worship. "If I regard iniquity in my heart the Lord will not hear me" (Ps. 66:18). God is as much the Father of the offended one as He is of you, and He will receive nothing at your hand until you remove that stumblingstone from before your brother. No worship or service can possibly be acceptable to God while I cherish a malicious spirit toward any of His children.

When a minister of the Church of England gives notice of an approaching "Holy Communion" he is required to read unto those expecting to participate from an exhortation containing these words: "And if you shall perceive your offences to be such as are not only against God, but also against your neighbor, then you shall reconciled yourself unto them; being ready to make restitution and satisfaction, according to the uttermost of your power, for all injuries and wrongs done by you to any other; and being likewise ready to forgive others that have offended you, as you would have forgiveness of your offence at God's hand. For otherwise the receiving of the Holy Communion does nothing else than increase your damnation." Alas that there is so little of such plain and faithful warning in most sections of Christendom today, and that Christ is so often insulted by His "Supper" being celebrated in places where bitter feelings are cherished and breaches exist between the celebrants.

The following precepts are so many illustrations of Ephesians 4:3 and so many branches of the responsibility saintwards of each reconciled soul. "Have peace one with another" (Mark 9:50). "You ought also to wash one another's feet. . . love one another" (John 13:14,34). "Be kindly affectioned one to another with brotherly love, in honor preferring one another" (Rom. 12:10). "Admonish one another" (Rom. 15:14). "By love serve one another...bear one another's burdens" (Gal. 5:13; 6:2). "Be kind one to another, tender hearted, forgiving one another as God for Christ's sake has forgiven you" (Eph. 4:32). "In lowliness of mind let each one esteem other better than themselves" (Phil. 2:3). "Comfort yourselves together and edify one another"(1 Thess. 5:11). "Exhort one another. . . consider one another to provoke unto love and good works" (Heb. 3:13; 10:24). "Speak not evil one of another" (Jas. 4:11). "Use hospitality one to another. . . all of you be subject one to another" (1 Pet. 4:8; 5:5).

Conclusion

In the course of our explanation of this doctrine we have sought to make a comprehensive view of it as a whole and then to examine in detail its essential components. Truth is a unit, one harmonious whole, but with our very limited powers of comprehension we are incapable of receiving it as such: rather do we take it in "here a little, there a little." That is according as God has constituted us. When endeavoring to master a subject or problem which is presented to the mind, we are obliged to consider singly its several elements and branches. When partaking of material food we do not attempt to swallow it whole, but first break it into fragments and then masticate them. It is thus with the spiritual ailment which God has provided for the soul. Unless we carefully collate all that the Spirit has revealed on the subject, duly ponder each aspect and view it in its true perspective, we shall obtain nothing more than a vague and faulty conception of it.

Though Truth is a unit, it has two sides to it. It had in the communicating of it: it is a Divine revelation, yet it passed through the minds of holy men and is couched in their language. It is thus with its contents, as a whole and all its parts. There is both a Divine and a human side to it, issuing from God, addressed to men: revealing His heart and will, enforcing our responsibility. That necessarily presents a problem to the finite mind, the more so since our mind is impaired by the ravages of sin. As man is constructed, he is unable to take in both sides of the Truth at a single glance, being obliged to view each separately. Unless he does so, a distorted vision will inevitably ensue, for while contemplating but one half he will imagine that he is actually viewing the whole. Now those two sides of the Truth are not contradictory, but complementary. Since God is God, He must maintain His sovereign rights and enforce His authority; and since He has constituted man a moral agent, He deals with him accordingly—having absolute control over him, yet leaving him to act freely.

This twofoldness of truth is exhibited in every doctrine contained in Holy Writ, in every aspect of the Faith, in every branch of the Evangelical system, and it is in the maintaining of a due proportion and balance between them that the competency and helpfulness of any expositor chiefly appears, as it is also the hardest part of his task. Most conspicuously is this the case with the doctrine we have been treated of, for not only is reconciliation itself a mutual affair, but Scripture presents reconciliation as being both an accomplished thing and also as something now being effected—according as it is viewed from the standpoint of what Christ wrought at the cross, or from what is required of the sinner in order for him to personally enter into the good of what the Redeemer there procured. It is specially for the benefit of the young preacher—scores of which will read them—that these closing paragraphs are penned, for unless he is quite clear upon this distinction, his trumpet will give forth an uncertain sound.

When was God really reconciled to the Christian? At the cross or when he savingly believed the Gospel? That question has been discussed earlier, yet we believe that some will welcome a further elucidation. On this subject, as so many, the Puritans are much to be preferred to the best writers of the nineteenth century. "God is never actually reconciled to us, nor we to Him, till He gives us the regenerated Spirit" (T. Manton). "For the preparing us to be reconciled it is necessary that we are convinced that we are enemies to God, and that He accounts us such, and that so long as we remain in that state He is also an enemy to us" (T. Goodwin). "There is a double reconciliation here (2 Cor. 5:18,19). First, fundamental, at the death of Christ, whereby it was obtained, This is the ground of God's laying aside His anger. Second, actual or particular, when it is complied with by faith. This regards the application of it, when God does actually lay aside His enmity, and imputes sin no more to the person" (S. Charnock).

Elsewhere Charnock says, "He acts toward the world as a reconciling God towards believers as reconciled. He is reconcilable as long as He is inviting and keeps men alive in a state of probation." The Puritans drew a plain and broad line of demarcation between the impetration [to obtain by request] or purchase of salvation, and the actual application or bestowing of the same. "By impetration we mean the purchase of all good things made by Christ for us with and of the Father; and by application, the actual enjoyment of those good things upon our believing; as if a man paid a price for the redeeming of captives, the paying a price supplies the room of the impetration of which we speak, and the freeing of the captives is the application of it" (J. Owen). Christ merited and obtained the reconciliation of both sides, yet God is not reconciled to us nor are we to Him until we repent and believe. So it is in justification: Christ wrought out a perfect and everlasting righteousness for all His people, yet God does not impute that righteousness to any of them until they savingly believe the Gospel.

While most of the best theologians of the last century recognized the necessary distinction between the impetration and the application of reconciliation, yet often they failed to frame their postulates consistently therewith. For instance, one of the most eminent of them, and for whose works we have a high regard, stated, "On the ground of God's reconciliation to us, we are exhorted to be reconciled to Him, and the great motive or encouragement is His previous reconciliation." That such language was not simply a slip of the pen (to which all are liable) is clear from what follows in his next paragraph. "'The chastisement of our peace,' by which peace was procured, 'was upon Him, and with His stripes we are healed.' God was reconciled when that was done, and made justice cease to demand our punishment." It is because such teaching has been so widely received and has led to serious mischief in the evangelical ministry, that its erroneous character needs to be exposed.

To affirm that God is reconciled to sinners, or if you prefer it, to His elect, before they are reconciled to Him, is an unintentional but tacit repudiation of John 3:36: "He that believes not the Son shall not see life, but the wrath of God abides on him." Note it is not "the wrath of God shall come upon him," but it is on him now and remains so as long as he is an unbeliever. In these respects there is no difference whatever between the elect and the non-elect. All are "by nature the children of wrath," under the Covenant of Works, and therefore under the curse and condemnation of the Law. The work of Christ has not changed the attitude of a holy God toward a single soul who continues in love with sin and a rebel against Him. "He is angry with the wicked every day" (Ps. 7:11), and "the wrath of God is revealed from heaven against all ungodliness and unrighteousness of men" (Rom. 1:18). It is not until the sinner repents and savingly believes the Gospel that he passes from one state to another and the frown of God is displaced by His smile (John 3:18; 5:24). Of the elect (1 Pet. 2:10) it is that "which had not obtained mercy, but now have obtained mercy" (2:10).

This is another declaration from a nineteenth century theologian of high repute, and to whose works we are personally indebted not a little: "God is reconciled: He is no longer angry with the sinner, for he is no longer a sinner in the eye of God and His justice." Had he said, "the penitent and believing sinner," that would be blessedly true: instead he was discussing what Christ's work had accomplished Godwards. In the same paragraph he averred, "All the chosen people are redeemed," which is another statement badly in need of qualification and explanation. Christ indeed "gave Himself a ransom for all"—His people (1 Tim. 2:6), and He did so "that He might redeem us from all iniquity" (Titus 2:14), but none then unborn were actually "redeemed." The correct way to state it is this: redemption was purchased for all the chosen people by Christ, and "in due time" (1 Tim. 2:6) they are made partakers of that redemption by the effectual operation of the Holy Spirit. Believers alone are actually redeemed or emancipated, and it is of them such passages as Galatians 3:13; Ephesians 1:7; 1 Peter 1:18,19 speak.

It is only by attending closely to the exact wording of Scripture and refusing to go one iota beyond its statements, that we are preserved from confusion and error. Christ was made sin for us "that we might be made the righteousness of God in Him" (2 Cor. 5:21). It is not said that "Christ is the end of the Law for righteousness to all His people," but "to everyone that believes" (Rom. 10:4). "Though He was rich, yet for our sakes He became poor, that you through His poverty might be rich" (2 Cor. 8:9). He was "made a curse for us...that the blessing of Abraham might come to the Gentiles" (Gal. 3:13,14). Christ "suffered for sins, the Just for the unjust, that He might bring us to God" (1 Pet. 3:18). But we are not actually made rich or partakers of the blessing of Abraham, nor brought to God, until we repent and believe. As we must distinguish between the impetration and the application of the atonement, so also must we between the grace of God decreeing and the execution of the decree of His grace. The "all spiritual blessings" of Eph. 1:3 include regeneration, yet none are regenerate until effectually called by God.

"We were reconciled to God by the death of His Son" (Rom. 5:10) impetratively, for God has accepted Christ's ransom, yet He does not apply it till faith is exercised by us. Reconciliation, redemption and justification are alike the results of Christ's satisfaction, the blessings which He purchased for His people, but they are only bestowed upon them when they are personally reconciled to God. "God the Father justifies, through the Son, by the Spirit, who works faith to receive the same. But until those things meet together our persons are not properly justified, notwithstanding Christ has wrought out a complete righteousness" (W. Bridge, 1670), nor is God reconciled to us till the Spirit has wrought faith in our hearts. In the light of Romans 3:25 and 26 are we not fully warranted in saying that, Christ is set forth a propitiation through faith in His blood that God might be holy, and yet the Reconciler of him who ceases to defy His authority and sues for mercy through the Lord Jesus.

Though the governmental requirements of God demand that the sinner end his revolt before He will be reconciled to him, that by no means implies any doubt of Christ's satisfaction securing its designed effects. The atonement has done very much more than remove legal obstacles which previously stood in the way of friendship between God and men or opened the door for Him to bestow peace and pardon upon all who would accept them, as the Arminian speaks; it has absolutely guaranteed the salvation of all for whom it was made. So far from the word "might" in the passages quoted, above denoting uncertainty, it is expressive of design and intimates the sure consequence that follows from Christ's sacrifice. As the Westminster Confession of Faith so well puts it, "To all those for whom Christ purchased redemption, He does certainly and effectually apply and communicate the same," where the word "redemption" is used—as it often is in Scripture—as including all the blessings which it was the immediate object of Christ's death to procure.

That there is a human side to the Evangelical system by no means introduces an element of uncertainty into it or jeopardizes its success. "God is in one mind and who can turn Him? And what His soul desires, even that He does" (Job 13:13). The Arminian comes short of the full truth when he says, "All was done on Christ's part which was necessary to make possible the reconciliation and pardon of sinners, and it is now left with them whether they will receive or reject the Gospel offer," and that "since God has constituted man a moral agent, He requires his voluntary cooperation." Christ's sacrifice has made certain the reconciliation and redemption of all for whom it was offered, for it ensured that He would "see the travail of His soul and be satisfied."

Christ's impetration secured an infallible provision for the effectual application, namely, the gift of the Holy Spirit, who by His invincible operations should regenerate each of Christ's "seed" and work saving repentance and faith in them. Though eternal life, repentance and faith are the "gifts" of God, they are also the fruits of Christ's atonement, and are conferred upon all in whose room He suffered and died.

Instead of merely opening a door of salvation for the whole of Adam's posterity to enter if they feel disposed to, the atoning work of Christ has effectually secured the actual salvation, of all the people of God, for by the wisdom of the Divine counsels and the power of the Spirit they are brought to gladly concur with God's will, and put their trust in the blood of the Lamb. Nevertheless, God still enforces the righteous requirements of His government and treats with men according to their responsibility, sending forth His ambassadors to charge them with their wickedness, bidding them to be reconciled to God, and assuring them of His gracious acceptance upon their ceasing to fight against Him. Before the sinner can enjoy the benefits of Christ's death he must consent to return to the duty of the Law and live in obedience to God, for He will not pardon him while he continues to live in rebellion against Him. The Gospel calls upon men to repent of their sins, forsake their idols, and enter into solemn covenant with God, yielding themselves up unreservedly to Him, to henceforth live unto His glory.

The work of the evangelist is clearly defined: the O. T. precedes the New, the ministry of John the Baptist went before that of Christ, the substance of Romans 1-3 is to be preached before the truth of Romans 4 and 5 is proclaimed. His first duty is to preach the Moral Law, for "by the Law is the knowledge of sin" (Rom. 3:20): its requirements, its strictness, its spirituality, its curse, that his hearers may be brought to realize their guilty and lost condition. Coupled with this preaching of the Law must be a presentation of the character of the Lawgiver and His claims upon the creatures of His hand: that He is sovereign Lord, demanding unqualified submission to His will; that He is ineffably holy, hating all sin and iniquity; that He is inflexibly just and "will by no means clear the guilty," and will yet judge every man according to his works. Conviction of sin, by the application of the Law to the conscience, is the first step in the progress by which men are led to take hold of God's covenant. Peace with God, which the covenant established, will be sought and prized by none except those who are conscious of their guilt and dread the displeasure and vengeance of the Judge of all the earth.

The second duty of the evangelist is to preach the Gospel, and that, in such a manner, that he neither contradicts nor weakens what is pointed out in the preceding paragraph—though complementing it. He is to show that the principal design of God in sending His Son here was to magnify the' Law, to manifest His detestation of sin, to exhibit His justice; all of which was solemnly seen at the cross. He is then to open the wondrous grace of God in giving His Son to execute His mission and perform His work, not only for the glory of God but the good of sinners. He is to show the amazing thing is that God takes the initiative, that in Christ He makes the advances, that by Christ provision is made for the healing of the breach, and that He sends forth His servants to make overtures of peace, bidding sinners "be reconciled to Him"—to be converted, to repent of their sins, abandon their wicked ways, believe in the Lord Jesus Christ, and walk according to His precepts.

It is the duty of the evangelist to show that though Christ is read to be the Friend of sinners, yet He will not be the Minister of sin, but rather maintains the honor and interests of the Father at every point. His call is, "Come unto Me, all you that labor and are heavy laden, and I will give you rest." That is, Come unto Me, all you that have in vain sought satisfaction in gratifying self and partaking of the pleasures of sin, and are now weighed down with burdened consciences and a sense of the deserved wrath of God. "Take My yoke upon you. . . and you shall find rest unto your souls." That is, Own My scepter, surrender to My lordship, walk in obedience to My commandments, and rest of soul shall be your portion. The One who made satisfaction to God tells us the benefits of it are received only through our believing (John 3:16), and that is an act which principally respects the will. The belief is to "receive" Christ (John 1:12) as He is offered in the Gospel: to receive a whole Christ, to be our Prophet, Priest and King.

The work of the pastor or teacher is to further instruct those who have responded to the message of the evangelist. He is to show that as God out of Christ was an offended and threatening God, God in Christ is an appeased and promising God. He is to make it clear that the reason why those who responded to the call and appeal of the evangelist was not because they were in themselves wiser or better than those who reject it, but that it was God who made them to differ (1 Cor. 4:7). That God did so first, by choosing them in Christ before the foundation of the world; second, by giving them as sheep to the good Shepherd for Him to save; third, by causing the Holy Spirit to bring them from death unto life, illumine their understandings, convict them of their lost estate, and make them willing to receive Christ. Thus they have no cause for boasting, but every reason to ascribe all the glory unto the Triune God.

Should the young preacher say, I am not yet quite clear in my mind, especially does the doctrine of election puzzle me as to exactly how I should address the unsaved. Neither election nor particular redemption should in anywise cramp your style. Your commission is to preach the Gospel to "every creature" you can reach, and the Gospel is that "Christ Jesus came into the world to save sinners" (1 Tim. 1:15), and therefore you are warranted in telling your hearers that there is a Savior for every sinner out of Hell who feels his need of Him and is willing to comply with His terms. Your first business is to show him his need of Christ and count upon the Spirit's making your efforts effectual, assured that God's Word shall not return unto Him void, whether or not you are permitted to see its fruits. But if you are granted the privilege of seeing some comply with Christ's terms, then you may know that they are members of that Church which Christ loved and gave Himself for, and that the Spirit has now vitally united them to Him.

The evangelist's message is that there is salvation in Christ for all who receive Him as He is offered in the Gospel and put their trust in Him. Though Christ purchased reconciliation and justification for all His people, yet they do not receive the same until they repent and believe. God is willing to be on terms of amity with the sinner, yet He will not be so until the sinner submit to those terms. Christ has perfectly made peace with God, so that no other ransom or sacrifice is required, yet none are admitted into it until they make their peace with God. God has appointed a connection— a moral and holy one—between the blessings purchased by Christ and the actual conveyance of them to His people. Though Christ died in order to procure Heaven for them by His merits, He also died to procure for them the regenerating operations of His Spirit to prepare them for Heaven. The test or evidence of our compliance with God's terms is a life of voluntary obedience: "as many as walk according to this rule, peace be on them and mercy" (Gal. 6:16)—"mercy" toward their defects.

THE DOCTRINE
OF REVELATION

Contents

INTRODUCTION

During the past 15 years we have devoted nearly a quarter of each issue of Studies in the Scriptures to an expository unfolding of some portion of doctrinal truth, and were it possible to relive those years we should not alter that plan. Two Timothy 3:16, 17, mentions some of the principal uses and values which the sacred Scriptures possess for us, and the first mentioned is that they are "profitable for doctrine." There is an inseparable connection between doctrine and deportment: our convictions mold our characters—what we believe largely determines how we act—"as he thinketh in his heart, so is he" (Prov. 23:7). To be soundly indoctrinated and to be well-grounded in the Truth is one and the same thing, and nothing but the Truth operating in the soul will preserve us from error, either theoretical or practical. Of the primitive Christians it is said, "They continued steadfastly [1] in the Apostles' doctrine, and [2] fellowship, and [3] in breaking of bread, and [4] in prayers" (Acts 2:42), which at once indicates that they esteemed soundness in the Faith as of first importance, and were of a radically different spirit from those who are so indifferent to the fundamentals of Christianity, insinuating, if not openly saying, "It matters little what a man believes if his life is good."

The relation between sound doctrine and godly deportment is like unto that between the bones and flesh of the body, or between the tree and the fruit which it bears: the latter cannot exist without the former. The first Epistle of the New Testament exemplifies our remark: three-fourths of it is occupied with a laying down of the essentials of Christianity, ere the Apostle shows what is requisite for the adornment of the Christian character. The history of Christendom during the last four centuries strikingly illustrates our contention. Examine the writings of the Reformers, and what do you find? Why, that exposition of doctrine held the foremost place in their ministry: that was the light which God used to deliver so great a part of Europe from the popish ignorance and superstition which characterized "the dark ages"! The moral tendency upon the masses and the spiritual blessings communicated to God's people by doctrinal preaching appears in the time of the Puritans. Since that day, in proportion as the churches have departed from their doctrinal fidelity and zeal, has close walking with God, purity and uprightness before men, and morality in the masses declined.

Each of our previous doctrinal discussions has taken one thing for granted, namely, that the Scriptures (to which we constantly appealed) are the inspired Word of God. Until recently the majority of our readers were residents of the U.S.A., and since there was available a book which we had had published there on that basic and vital subject, there was the less need for us to write thereon in these pages. Moreover, we were fully justified in taking a belief of that truth for granted, for the inerrancy and Divine authority of Holy Writ is a settled axiom with all true Christians, seeing that it constitutes the foundation of all their faith and the ground of all their hope. But since our book on the Divine Inspiration of the Scriptures is not at present obtainable by our British and Australian readers (for we decline to handle it while the disparity between the pound and the dollar persists), and since the tides of skepticism and infidelity continue to advance and constitute such a solemn menace unto the young, we feel moved to make an effort to show how strong and how sure are the foundations on which the faith of the Christian rests.

What we propose doing in this book, namely, to make a serious attempt to assist some of those who have inhaled the poisonous fumes of infidelity and been left in a state of mental indecision concerning sacred things, is something quite different from the course we usually follow in our magazine, Studies in the Scriptures. In view of the bewilderment and uncertainty of many, and the shaken faith of others, it appears our duty to do so, and we trust our friends will make a point of reading this unto those of their children likely to need it, and that preachers will feel free to use portions in preparing special sermons or addresses for the young. Our principal object will be to set forth some of the numerous indications that the Bible is something far superior to any human production, but before doing that we must seek to establish the existence of its Divine Author. The later chapters will be designed chiefly for preachers or older students of the Word, presenting as they will, some of the rules which require to be heeded if the Scriptures are to be properly interpreted; and though their scope will go beyond the general title of "Divine revelation," yet they will complement and complete the earlier ones.

Under our present title, then, we purpose to treat (DV.) of that revelation which God has given or that discovery which He makes of Himself unto the sons of men. If we were writing a comprehensive and systematic treatise on the whole subject, we should devote a proportionate space unto the manifestations which God has made of Himself First, in creation, or the external world; second, in the moral nature—particularly the conscience—of man; third, in the controlling and shaping of human history by Providence. Fourth, in His incarnate Son; fifth, in the sacred Scriptures; sixth, in the saving revelation which He makes of Himself unto the souls of His regenerate people, and finally, in the beatific vision, when we shall "know as we are known." But, instead, we shall deal more briefly with the first four, and concentrate chiefly upon the Scriptures, presenting some of the evidences of their Divine Authorship, then pointing out some of the principles which govern their right interpretation, and then the application which is to be made of their contents. This is a considerable task to essay, rendered the more difficult because we desire to hold the interest of, and (under God) make this book profitable unto a considerable variety of readers—young and old, believers and unbelievers.

The present generation has, for the most part, been reared not only in an atmosphere of negative unbelief but of hostile unbelief. They live in a world where materialism and skepticism are rampant and dominant. In the great majority of homes the Sunday newspaper is the only thing read on the Lord's Day. Doubt as to moral and spiritual truth is distilled through a score of channels. Our seats of learning are hotbeds of agnosticism. Our literature, with rare exceptions, makes light of God, and jokes about sacred things. The newspapers, the radio broadcasts, public utterances and private conversations, are steadily but surely removing the foundations of righteousness and destroying what little faith in spiritual things still remain. The vast majority in the English-speaking world are totally ignorant of the contents of the Bible, know not that it is a Divine revelation, yea, question whether there be any God at all. Yet modern skepticism is rarely candid, but is rather a refuge in which multitudes are sheltering from an accusing conscience. With such we are not here concerned, for where a prejudiced mind and a caviling spirit obtain, argument is useless; and we can but leave them unto the sovereign mercy of the Lord.

Even those brought up in Christian homes are being corrupted by the paganism of modern education, are bewildered by the conflicting teachings they receive from parents and the school, and are harassed by doubts. Some of them are honestly seeking a resolving of their doubts, and it has become a pressing duty devolving upon the servant of God to recognize the mental conflict taking place in the minds of his youthful hearers, and to seek to meet their more immediate need by presenting some of the "Christian evidences." It is therefore our desire and will be our endeavor in the earlier chapters to be of some help unto those who may have become entangled in Satan's snares, who have been seriously disturbed by the infidelity of this age, but are willing to carefully examine some of the "strong reasons" by which it is rational to believe in the existence of a living and personal God and to receive the Scriptures as an authoritative and inerrent revelation from Him—and that it is not only the most horrible impiety but the height of irrationality to doubt the one or call into question the other.

There are some likely to deem our present procedure as being needless if not actually wrong, considering that the existence of God and the authority of His Word are matters to be reverently believed and not argued. Though we respect their conviction, we do not share the same. We fully agree that a rational discussion cannot produce anything but a rational faith, but even that should not be despised. Something has been accomplished if we can take away a stumbling block from the path of inquirers: the removal of weeds is necessary to prepare the garden for the seed. Though no external evidence, however weighty, can savingly convert the soul, it can carry conviction to the reason and conscience. Such arguments as we propose to submit are sufficient in themselves to beget in the mind a sober, intelligent, and firm judgment that there is a God and that the Bible is His inspired Word. It is much to be thankful for if we can bring the serious minded to respect and read the Scriptures, waiting for a spiritual confirmation. Intellectual persuasion and motives of credibility are not the ground on which a spiritual faith rests, yet they often prove (under the Divine blessing) a paving of the way thereunto.

Nor is an appeal unto external evidences of the Truth, which address themselves to and are apprehended by the reasoning faculty of our minds, without value to the child of God. They are confirmatory of his faith, support it against the oppositions and objections of others, and relieve the mind under temptations to doubt. In such a day as this, the young Christian especially needs all the help he can obtain in order to withstand the assaults of the Enemy. Even older ones are prone to give way to doubting, and cannot be too strongly established in the fundamentals of the Faith. Moreover, such a course serves to exhibit the excellence of our profession and the impregnable rock on which it is founded. It enables us to perceive what good grounds and satisfactory confirmation we have for the Faith which we avow. Wisdom is justified of her children (Matt. 11:19), and it behooves them to be equipped to justify their profession, if for no other reason than to close the mouths of gainsayers. A Christian should be capable of knowing and giving expression to the distinct and special reasons why he believes in God and reveres His Word—that he has something more substantial and valuable than human "tradition" to appeal unto.

Before entering upon our immediate task it should be acknowledged that it is not possible to prove the existence of God by mathematical demonstration, for if such proof were procurable there would be no room left for the exercise of faith. Yet, on the other hand, it must be pointed out that it is equally impossible to demonstrate the non-existence of the Creator. But though we cannot prove to a demonstration that God is, yet we can adduce evidence so clear and weighty as must impel, if not compel us to accept His existence as a fact. Those evidences, when carefully pondered, separately and together, afford the strongest possible ground for believing in the Divine Maker of Heaven and earth: the probability actually amounting to the height of moral certainty. There are certain great facts of Nature which call for an explanation, such as the existence of matter, the existence of motion, and the existence of life. The heathen had sufficient perspicuity to realize "Ex nihilo nihil"—from nothing, nothing comes; and if we reject the truth that "the worlds were framed by the Word of God" (Heb. 11:3), then we are left in complete darkness, without any hope of obtaining any satisfactory explanation of either the noumenon or phenomenon of existence.

Most careful consideration ought to be given unto the alternative offered by unbelief. The great enigma which has confronted the human race throughout the centuries, and challenged its sages to supply a solution, is the problem of the universe: how it came to be; and within that macrocosm, the microcosm man—his origin, his intelligence, his destiny. Every explanation that has been advanced, save only the one provided by the Bible, fails to carry conviction to the mind, much less meets the longings of the heart. But the Bible supplies a solution for those problems which has satisfied the reason and conscience of millions of people, yea, which has brought peace and joy to a countless number of souls. Skeptics have indeed rejected its explanation, but what have they offered in its place? Nothing but agnostic doubts and metaphysical vagaries so abstruse that none can understand them, or speculations so incredible and absurd that only those who prefer darkness to light will pay any heed unto them. Ponder well the immeasurable difference there is between Christianity and Infidelity, and despise not the former until you are quite sure the latter has something more solid and valuable to give you in its stead.

There is ample evidence both in the material and moral realm on which to base a rational and intelligent belief in the existence of God. Anyone who seriously examines that evidence and then turns and carefully considers what Infidelity has to offer as an alternative should have no difficulty at all in perceiving which is the more convincing, adequate, and satisfying. As the author of The Gordian Knot rightly pointed out, "Skepticism is a restless sea on which anyone who sails is tossed up and down and driven to and fro in endless uncertainty. There is no solid ground on which to stand until something true is found and believed." That is the alternative, the only one, for those who credit not the Scriptures. The Infidel would take from you the Bible, but what does he offer in its place but sneers and doubts! He scouts the idea of a personal Creator, but what explanation can he supply you of creation? He despises the Lord Jesus Christ, but to what other redeemer does he point as being able to save you from your sins, and induct you into an inheritance that is incorruptible and undefiled, that fades not away, but will endure for all eternity in Heaven?

Part One-The Existence of God

Chapter 1
THE EXISTENCE OF GOD
AS MANIFEST IN CREATION

The Bible opens with the words, "In the beginning God." He was in the beginning because Himself without beginning: the uncaused, self-existent and self-sufficient One—"from everlasting to everlasting, Thou art God" (Ps. 90:2). But the youthful, yet intelligent inquirer, will ask, And do you comprehend that? We candidly answer, Certainly not, for how could one who is finite comprehend the Infinite, a creature of time fully understand the Eternal One? Nevertheless, we believe it, being logically and rationally obliged to do so. There must of necessity be a First Cause, and if a first Cause, that Cause is obviously uncaused and self-existent. If that First Cause be the Originator of all other causes and effects, then it follows that Cause is not only self-existent but self-sufficient, or, in other words, all-mighty. Since we may ascertain something—often much—of the nature of a cause from the effects it produces, then from the effects perceptible to us in the visible universe, it is clearly evident that the First Cause must be endowed with life, with intelligence, with will, in a word, with Personality, and one infinitely superior to ours—which First Cause we recognize and own as God.

Though the opening words of the Bible take the existence of God for granted, yet what immediately follows supplies more than a hint where we may find irrefutable evidence that He is: "In the beginning God created the Heaven and the earth." It has been truly said, "We need no other argument to prove that God made the world than the world itself—it carrieth in it and upon it the infallible tokens of its original" (John Owen). That is true if we consider it simply in the mass: how came it to be? Three theories have been put forward to account for the existence of matter by those who believe not in its creation. First, that matter is eternal. But that solves no difficulty, in fact it involves one much more perplexing than any which Genesis 1:1 can give rise to. In itself matter is both inert and unintelligent: whence then its motion and marks of design? Second, by spontaneous generation. But not only is there no proof to support such a view, it is too self-evidently inadequate to merit discussion. Third, by evolution: concerning which we will now only point out—push that hypothesis backward, stage by stage, till you come to the first molecule or protoplasm, and to the question, How did it originate? No answer is forthcoming. Something could not evolve from nothing!

Though the universe could not evolve from nothing, it could be created by an eternal and all-mighty Creator! Assuming the existence of God, our difficulty is at once resolved. But with the universe spread before our eyes we do not have to assume God's existence. "Because the things which may be known of God is manifest in them; for God hath showed it unto them. For the invisible things of Him from the creation of the world are clearly seen, being understood by the things that are made, even His eternal power and Godhead, so that they are without excuse" (Rom. 1:19, 20). God may be rationally inferred by reasoning back from effect to cause. Intelligent arrangement, wise contrivance, marks of design argue an intelligent Designer. There are such palpable and innumerable impressions of Divine wisdom, power and goodness in the works of God that unprejudiced reason must necessarily conclude a Creator of whose perfections those impressions are the faint adumbrations. So true is this that atheists and all idolaters are left without any excuse. Thus it is apparent that the doubts of Infidels are either affected or arise from the determination to rid themselves of the idea of accountableness. "The fool hath said in his heart there is no God." (Ps. 14:1): it is moral depravity and not mental weakness which prompts such a desire.

"The heavens declare the glory of God and the firmament showeth His handiwork" (Ps. 19:1). The universe proclaims God both by its very existence and its wondrous composition. From whence proceeded this vast system, with its exquisite order, its perfect balance, and its enduring strength? Every effect must have an adequate cause. If the heavens do not declare the existence of God and scintillate with the reflections of His glory, let the Infidel tell us what they do bespeak. If the celestial bodies be nothing more than a fortuitous mass of atoms, flung together by unreasoning law or blind chance, then what has preserved them throughout the ages? What regulates their movements with more than clock-like precision? What invested the sun with light and actinic power? To put it on the lowest level—can skepticism furnish any answer to those questions which satisfies reason or appears adequate to common sense? If the thoughtful beholder of the stellar heavens perceives no evidence of a Divine Creator, then are we not obliged to sorrowfully exclaim, "None so blind as those who will not see"! It is true that a recognition of the Creator in His creation is no evidence of regeneration, for many who never open the Bible are convinced of the reality of His existence, yet such mental perception is much to be preferred to the stupidity of atheism or the darkness of agnosticism.

We pointed out that the origin of three essential things in Nature call for explanation from the attentive observer: matter, motion and life. Having considered the alternative solutions for the first, let us now contemplate the others. Concerning them we cannot do better than present to the reader a summary of what we deem a singularly able and convincing discussion by John Armour in his unique work (out of print), Atonement and Law.

As we contemplate the wondrous movement of bodies in the solar system, measuring time for us with absolute exactness, and as we rise to the conception of the harmonious motion of all bodies in space, measuring duration for all created beings, we cannot but be actuated with an intense desire to know the cause of this wondrous motion. But the question, what is the cause of the motion of the heavenly bodies in space? naturally resolves itself into the more general question: what is the cause of all motion? The ready, the only answer is force. But this raises the real question: what is the origin of force? Every investigation of that subject leads to the profound conviction that all force is traceable to life.

In the entire vegetable kingdom we have perpetual demonstration of the intimate and necessary relations of motion, force and life. Even the least instructed, who have no conception of the real activity or of the observable motion in all growing plants, cannot but know that the mighty forests are built up by vital force operating tirelessly century after century. Even they cannot but know that the whole world is covered over with the countless, varied and marvelous products and proofs of the mysterious, universally recognized, but invisible vital power. Only those who have patiently and perseveringly gazed into that limitless world into which the microscope is the only door, and have witnessed the amazing activity of vital force in plant life, can have any idea of the manner in which the entire vegetable kingdom testifies of the intimate relations of motion, force and life.

Let anyone spend but a few hours in watching the rapid and incessant motion in a small leaf (such as that of the Anacharis Alsinastrum) under one of the best microscopes art has been able to furnish, the field being less than ten thousandths part of an inch—in that small field can be distinctly seen twelve rows of cells with an average of five cells in each row. The current can be seen flowing rapidly along appropriate channels, like rivers with broken ice on the surface, while in each of the sixty oblong cells the fluids are seen circulating like eddies or whirlpools in a rushing stream. But for the perfection which microscopic art has attained, this amazing activity would never have been suspected or credited. Witnessing this activity in the ten-thousandth part of an inch on the surface of a small leaf, what would be the impression upon the mind could we look upon a single tree, discerning the activity of vital force in every part of it with the same degree of clearness? While we cannot do this, imagination can transfer what we have seen in the leaf under the microscope to all the leaves of the forest, to all vegetation on the globe, for in every cell of every living plant there is substantially the same vital activity.

Whether we look upon forest or field, the eye of the mind should discern not merely motionless forms of life, but everywhere intensely active vital power Were we capable of seeing the real activity of the vital force in the living tree, it would be to us scarcely less wonderful than the "great sight" which Moses turned aside to see; nor could it fail to produce in us a sense of the Divine presence not unlike that which he experienced. This vital action, which man and all created intelligences must ever strive to behold, and may ever more and more clearly discover, God Himself alone sees as it is.

The same line of remark might be followed out at length in regard to force and motion in every department of the animal kingdom. Here also the life is the force, and force that never ceases to produce activity. In the ova vitalized, and from that instant, on and on through all vicissitudes, motion is demonstrably uninterrupted till death, or rather the cessation of motion is death. The only absolute test of life is vital action. When this has ceased it is proof that vital force has ceased— that vitality is extinct. Nor is there the slightest ground to believe that this vital action, having ceased for an instant, can start again of itself. Vital activity can no more begin in plant or animal organism in which it has once ceased than in matter in which it never existed. The animal kingdom, then, is a witness, and in all its extent, with myriad voices in perfect unison, it declares, "All motion is from vital force." The testimony of these two kingdoms is both positive and negative. Their witness agrees: "In us all motion is from vital force." "With us all motion ceases when vital force ceases."

When we come, however, to man, and consider the motion traceable to him, we have to deal with a very different problem, and unless we give special attention we shall probably leave out of the estimate the vastly greater part of the evidence in this case. For man, unlike all other living beings on earth, or at least infinitely beyond other beings on earth, has the power to produce motion, not merely by force of muscle without skill, but he has the power to originate and sustain motion on a grand scale by means of the vital force of brain as well. The savage who should cast a stone a little way into the sea by strength of arm, or from a sling, or shoot an arrow from his bow, or propel his little boat a few miles from the shore in a calm sea, would give proof of the extent of his power. Clearly, in each case, from that of the stone which could be hurled but a few yards to that of the vessel which might be propelled perhaps as many miles, the motion would be wholly attributable to vital force of muscle and brain, or to skill and strength.

The civilized man who constructs and launches the ocean steamer that plows its furrow through the sea, in calm and storm, for thousands of miles gives proof of his power to produce motion by skill and strength. The ocean steamer that circumnavigates the globe, displacing the water and defying the storm, is, as one might truthfully say, hurled around the world; and its motion, in that entire revolution, is as clearly traceable to vital force of hand and brain in the civilized man, as is that of the stone from the hand, or the arrow from the bow, of the savage. Let an honest inquirer light upon the ocean steamer at any stage of its long journey. Let him search the vessel from keel to top-mast. Finding no life in hull or rigging, no life in coal or fire, no life in water or steam, no life in engine or propeller, shall he say, "This vessel does not owe its force and motion to life at all." If he so determine, he is not a philosopher but a fool. For every part of the vessel, from keel to top-mast, is eloquent in its testimony to the vital force of combined skill and strength of man in its construction. And this we may recognize with all the confidence with which, on approaching an eight-day clock in the middle of the week, we recognize its onward movement as the vital force of the constructor of the clock, combined with the vital force of the person who wound it up—for not only is the vital force of the hand that wound the clock as truly the cause of its continued motion as though that hand had never for an instant been withdrawn, but the vital force of the contriver and the actual constructor, though he may have passed away centuries ago, is as clearly prolonged as would be the vital force of the hand that wound the clock, though the very next hour it were cold and motionless in death.

I have ventured to dwell longer on this illustration because of the argument it furnishes in favor of the recognition of vital force as the cause of other and infinitely grander movements.

We come now to a stage in our investigations in which, unless we exercise the utmost vigilance, we shall utterly fail to interpret the transcendent scene where there is an aggregate of motion in comparison with which all we have hitherto considered is but as the small dust of the balance. As to rapidity, the swiftest we have as yet contemplated is as that of the snail; as to vastness of orbit, even that of the ocean steamer around the globe is but as the "finger ring of a little girl"—as we contemplate motion on a scale so grand, motion of bodies so vast and so numerous, motion in orbits a scarcely perceptible arc of which has been traversed since man appeared on earth, motion which highest created intelligences must regard with never-ending wonder and admiration—shall we begin to detach, in our conception, motion from force, or force from that which lives? If we do, how can we any longer pretend that we are consistent, scientific or philosophical? All motion hitherto considered has been traceable to that which lives. Why at this stage begin to question whether that which moves is moved by force or whether force proceeds from life? Motion on a small scale we have found is from vital force. All the motion that man has ever been able to trace to its source he has found to proceed from life. There is not a shred of trustworthy evidence that any visible thing on earth has the power to originate motion. And the invisible power that causes all the motion we can at all trace to its source is always vital power.

We have traced force and motion from that in the smallest seed in plant life and that of the ova in animal life, and have found force and motion ever proceed from that which lives. Why, then, when we stand in the presence of the most wondrous motion—motion that speaks of force beyond all conception—do we, all at once, lapse from the conviction that motion must proceed from force and that force must proceed from life? Doubt comes in where evidence is most abundant. A stone seen moving through the air we believe was hurled by some lad, though we see him not. A cannon ball crossing the bay we do not doubt was sent by persons having skill and power. An ocean steamer driven around the world we know owes its force and motion to skill and power of living beings. When we see mighty orbs moving in space, why do we raise any question regarding the origin of motion and force? The only shadow of reason that can be imagined is that we cannot readily conceive of a Being infinite, ever-present, and all-mighty, the Source of all motion, all force producing all motion in the universe. In a vastly higher sense than that in which the motion of the steamship in mid-ocean is to be attributed to man, all motion in the universe, including that produced in and by vital organisms in this world and in all worlds, is to be attributed to the Infinite, the Ever-living, the Almighty. In the presence of the moving universe may we not exclaim: "Power belongs unto God"?

Why should we hesitate to accept the conclusions thus reached? The data furnished to all men leave them without excuse. The soundness of the reasoning by which I have undertaken to prove that motion, mere motion, as recognized everywhere in the universe, since it assures us of the universality of law, is to us direct proof of the existence of the Ever-living, Ever-present Lawgiver is confidently submitted to the judgment of candid and competent reasoners.

The great timepiece of the universe in its surpassing grandeur and glory may continue to move with absolute exactness and utmost harmony from age to age and century to century. The multitudes of mankind may continue to look upon it mainly to see what time of day it is, as indicated upon the broad dial-plate that meets their gaze, and never reflect that this grand time-measurer, like every poor imitation of it man has ever constructed, measures time by means of motion, and motion sustained by force, this force in its turn necessarily from the living, traceable to the living. Yet there may be those who shall find time, even in this busy age, to look with prolonged and steadfast gaze, with awakened and quickened powers, and with intense interest upon the ever-present and never-exhausted wonders of that aggregate of motion before which all effort towards estimate is perfectly powerless. And when favorably situated therefor, the truly evidential nature of God's glorious work may flash out even as the noonday itself, so that, before this one surpassing demonstration of the power and presence of God, all doubts shall be driven away. Even as night itself is chased around our globe by the glorious king of day; so that thenceforward, even to life's close, they shall live in the noonday splendor of unquestioning faith—faith, not vision, for God gives everywhere and in all things not merely proof that He is, but that He is and must be forever more the Invisible.

But though invisible, God is neither the Incredible nor the Unknowable, for He has set before all men "the invisible things of Him" and these "are clearly seen, being understood by the things that are made, even His eternal power and Godhead, so that they are without excuse." Among the visible things of Him which are clearly seen, that is, clearly and fully recognized by all men—motion, force and life—have place; for by these are made known the universality of law, the presence, power and glory of the Ever-living, Ever-present Lawgiver.

Not only does the existence of matter, of motion, and of life, testify that God is, but the magnitude and magnificence of creation announce the same grand truth: the work reveals the Workman. "The massive dome of St. Peter's, rising 400 feet, and ablaze with the masterpieces of Italian art, declares an architect and artist—someone who planned, built, decorated it. This is a thought in stone and tells of a thinker. It did not grow of itself, or come to be by some mysterious "evolution" or "development." Atoms never could arrange themselves in such harmonious relations, or fall accidentally into such marvelous combination. Blind chance never built that cathedral in Rome. There must have been a controlling intelligence—an intelligent control. Yet some would have us believe that the vaster Dome of Heaven with its millions of starry lamps, surmounting a grander Temple of Creation, had neither Architect to plan nor Builder to construct! The author of the Epistle to the Hebrews indulged in no mere poetic rhapsody when he wrote, "Every house is built by someone: but He who built all things is God."

"The thoughtful observer must feel that in the heavens there is not only a testimony to a Creator, but a partial revelation of His character and attributes. Such a work and workmanship not only reveal a Workman, but hint what sort of workman He is. For example, as no bounds have ever been found in the universe, it is natural to infer an infinite Creator. The vast periods discovered by astronomy suggest His eternity. The forces of the universe, displaying stupendous power, bespeak His omnipotence. Waste, everywhere going on and needing perpetual resupply, demands omnipresence. The exact proportion and wise adaptation of every part to each other, and of all to the great whole, tell of omniscience, which includes both infinite knowledge and wisdom. The Being who survives and guides all the changes of this universe must Himself be immutable; and He who lavishes upon His work such wealth of splendor and variety of beauty must be both infinitely rich in resources and versatile in invention. So also the universal harmony by which the whole mechanism is regulated, indicates a character of infinite perfection in harmony with itself. Thus, seen from no higher point of view than the scientific and philosophical, the dome of the sky bears, wrought on its expanse, in starry mosaics, 'There is a God'" (The Gordian Knot).

Descending from the heavens to the planet on which we reside, here, too, we are confronted with phenomena, both in the general and the particular, both in nature and number, for which no explanation is adequate save that of an all-mighty, benevolent, and infinitely wise Creator. Upon the surface of this earth are incalculable hosts of creatures, varying in size from gnats to elephants, each requiring its regular food, the total amount of which for a single day defies human computation if not the imagination. Those creatures are not set down in a dwelling-place where the table is bare, but where there is abundance for them all; nor are they furnished merely with a few necessities, but, instead, with a great variety of luxuries and dainties. From whence proceed such ample and unfailing supplies? From Nature, says the materialist. And what or whom endowed Nature to bear so prolifically and ceaselessly? To which no intelligent reply is forthcoming. Only one answer satisfactorily meets the case: from the living God! "He causeth the grass to grow for the cattle and herb for the service of men: the earth is full of Thy riches. These all wait upon Thee, that Thou mayest give them meat in season. Thou openest Thy hand, they are filled with good" (Ps. 104:14).

The continuous fertility of the earth after 6,000 years of incessant productiveness can only be satisfactorily explained by attributing the same unto the riches and bounty of its Maker. That one generation of creatures is succeeded by another, in endless procession, on its surface, to find such an illimitable store of food available for them, is nothing but a stupendous miracle, the marvel of which is lost upon us either through our thoughtlessness or because of its unfailing and regular repetition. The constant supplies which God causes the earth to yield for such myriads of beings is just as remarkable as the original production of the place in which they were to live, for the annual re-fertilization of the earth is actually a continuous creation. To quote again from Psalm 104: as the reverent beholder contemplates the revived countenance of Nature in the springtime, he cannot but turn his eyes unto the living God and exclaim, "Thou renewest the face of the earth" (v. 30). Beholding as he does the barren fields, the leafless trees, the frozen ground, and often the sunless skies, during the dreary months of winter, and seeing everything covered in white, it appears that the earth has grown old and died, that a pall of snow has fallen to hide its forbidding features. And what could man do, what could all the scientists in the world do, if winter should be prolonged month after month, and year after year? Nothing, but slowly yet surely die of starvation.

But the Creator has declared, "While the earth remaineth, seed-time and harvest shall not cease" (Gen. 8:22), and therefore He makes good that promise each year, by causing winter to give place to spring and "renewing the face of the earth." The world is as full of creatures today as though none had ever died, for as soon as one generation passes from it, it is at once replaced by another, coming to a larder already well filled for it. And again we insist, that was made possible and actual only by God's having "renewed the face of the earth." And what a marvelous thing that is, yea, a series of marvels. That such a variety of food, so perfectly adapted to the greatly varying digestive organs of insects, animals and men, so replete with nourishment, so attractive in appearance, should be produced by soil, than which nothing is more insipid, sordid, and despicable. What a pleasing variety of fruits the trees bear: how beautifully colored, elegantly shaped and admirably flavored! Shall we be struck most with agreeable astonishment at the Cause of such effects or at the manner of bringing them into existence?

"The heavens declare the glory of God; and the firmament showeth His handiwork" (Ps. 19:1). The stellar heavens proclaim the attributes of their Maker, bespeaking not only His existence but His excellence—while the atmospheric heavens exhibit His unique skill, revealing to us both their Author and His wondrous wisdom. Upon the former many have discussed, but the latter has received very much less notice. The "firmament" signifies "the expanse" and, as distinct from the sphere of the more distant planets, refers to the atmosphere surrounding the earth—the air in which the clouds are seen. The Hebrew verb rendered "showeth" means to "place before" for our thoughtful inspection, as challenging our most serious and reverent contemplation. Though the atmosphere be not an object of our sight, and for that reason is little regarded, it is a most remarkable contrivance or apparatus, a source of many advantages to us, and one which richly repays those who carefully consider it and take pleasure in "seeking out" the works of the Lord (Ps. 111:2).

The atmospheric pressure upon a person of ordinary stature is equal to the weight of 14 tons, and it scarcely needs to be pointed out that the falling upon him of a very much lighter object would break every bone in his body and drive all breath out of his lungs. Why then is it that we suffer no inconvenience from it, nay, thrive therein and enjoy it? Here is a phenomenon which, if thus viewed, is not unlike that which so awed Moses of old when he beheld the miracle of the burning bush—the combustible substance all aflame and yet not consumed. And by what means are we preserved from that which, considered abstractly, is such a deadly menace? The Creator's having so devised that the air permeates the whole of our body, and by its peculiar nature pressing equally in all directions, all harm and discomfort is prevented—"the heads of the thigh and arm bones are kept in their sockets by atmospheric pressure" (International Encyclopedia).

The air, commissioned by its benign Author, performs many offices for the good of mankind. While it covers us without any conscious weight, the air reflects, and thereby increases the life-giving heat of the sun. The air does this for us much as our garments supply additional heat to our bodies. If the reader has, like the writer, climbed a mountain and reached a point 13,000 feet above sea level, then he has proved for himself how considerably the solar warmth is diminished as the quality of the air becomes more attenuated. At its base the climb was comfortably warm, but had we remained a night on its summit, death by freezing would have been the outcome. What reason have we, then, to bless the Disposer of all things for placing us at a level where we suffer no ill or inconvenience from the atmosphere, for the combined wisdom of men could no more moderate it than regulate the actions of the ocean!

The air co-operates with our lungs, thereby ventilating the blood and refining the fluids of the body, stimulating the animal secretions, and regulating our natural warmth. We could live for months without the light of the sun or the glimmering of a star, but if deprived of air for a very few minutes we quickly faint and die. Not to us alone does this "universal nurse" (as Hervey eloquently styled her) minister: it is this gaseous element enveloping the earth which both sustains and feeds all vegetable life. Again—the air conveys to our nostrils those minute particles (effluvia) which are emitted by odiferous bodies, so that we are both refreshed by the sweet fragrance of flowers and warned by offensive smells to withdraw from a dangerous situation or beware of injurious food. So, by the undulating motions of the air, all the diversities of sound are conducted to the ear, for if you were placed in a room from which all air had been withdrawn and a full orchestra (wearing artificial respirators) played at fortissimo, not a sound would you hear.

Not only does the air waft to our senses all the charming modulations of music and the elevating influences of refined and edifying conversation, but it also acts as a seasonable and faithful monitor. For example, should I be walking along the road, my eyes looking off unto some object, or my mind so absorbed that I am completely off my guard, and a vehicle be bearing down upon me from behind, though my eyes perceive not my danger, yet my ear takes alarm and informs me of my peril, even while it be some distance away, and with kindly if clamorous importunity bids me act for my safety. Let us then inquire, what is it that has endowed the atmosphere with such varied and beneficent adaptations, so that it diffuses vitality and health, retains and modifies solar heat, transmits odors and conveys sound? Must we not rather ask "Whom?" and answer, "This also cometh from the LORD of hosts, which is wonderful in counsel and excellent in working" (Isa. 28:29).

"Hearken unto this, O Job: stand still and consider the wondrous works of God. Dost thou know when God disposed them [i.e., the winds and clouds, the thunder and lightning, the frost and rain], and caused the light of His cloud to shine? Dost thou know the balancing of the clouds, the wondrous works of Him who is perfect in knowledge" (Job 37:14-16). The same queries are addressed unto each of us, and call for calm and quiet reflection. "Stand still and consider the wondrous works of God" which appear in the firmament. That is, cease for an hour from your feverish activities and devote yourself, as a rational creature, unto serious reflection, and compose yourself for thoughtful contemplation. "Consider" what is brought forth in, by, and from the atmosphere, and then be filled with reverent wonder and awe. Ponder well the fact that water is much denser and far heavier than air, and yet it rises into it, makes a way through it, and takes up a position in its uppermost regions! One would just as soon expect the rivers to run backward to their source; yet Divine wisdom has contrived a way to render it not only practicable but a matter of continual occurrence.

There in the firmament we behold an endless succession of clouds fed by evaporation from the ocean, drawn thither by the action of the sun. The clouds are themselves a miniature ocean, suspended in the air with a skill which as far transcends that of the wisest man as his knowledge does that of an infant in arms. It is because so very few "stand still and consider" the amazing fact of millions of tons of water being suspended over their heads and sustained there in the thinnest parts of the atmosphere, that such a prodigy is lost upon them. The writer recalls the impressions made upon him over 30 years ago as he was driven around the Roosevelt Dam in Arizona and inspected that great engineering feat: probably some of our readers have experienced similar ones as they have beheld some huge reservoir of human contrivance. But what are they in comparison with the immeasurably vaster quantities of water which, without any conduits of stone or barriers of cement, are suspended in the clouds, and kept there in a buoyant state!

The clouds, as another pointed out, "travel in detached parties, and in the quality of itinerant cisterns round all the terrestrial globe. They fructify by proper communications of moisture the spacious pastures of the wealthy and gladden with no less liberal showers the cottager's little garden. Nay, so condescending is the benignity of the great Proprietor that they satisfy the desolate and waste ground, and cause, even in the most uncultivated wilds, the bud of the tender herb to spring forth, so that the natives of the lonely desert, those savage herds which know no master's stall, may nevertheless experience the care and rejoice in the bounty of an all-supporting Parent" (James Hervey). But what most fills us with wonderment is that these celestial reservoirs, so incalculably greater than any of human construction, should be suspended in the air. This it was which so evoked the admiration of both Job and Eliphaz: "He [said the former] bindeth up the waters in His thick clouds, and the cloud is not rent under them" (Job 26:8) notwithstanding their prodigious weight.

One of the things attributed to God in Holy Writ is that He has fixed "the bound of the sea by a perpetual decree, that it cannot pass it; and though the waves thereof toss themselves, yet they cannot prevail; though they roar, yet can they not pass over it" (Jer. 5:22). If it be not its Maker whose mandate had determined the bounds of the sea, who has fixed its limits? Certainly not man, for he who cannot control himself is scarcely competent to issue effective orders to the ocean. That was made fully evident in the days of Noah, when for the first and last time God gave the waters their full freedom, and dire was the consequence, for the whole human race was helpless before them. Without that Divine decree the impetuous sea would again overflow the earth, for such is its natural propensity. But by the mere fiat of His lips God immutably controls this turbulent element. On some coasts high cliffs of rock serve as impregnable ramparts against the raging main, but in others—to evince God is confined to no expedients, but orders all things according to the counsel of His own will—He bids a frail bank of earth curb the fury of its angry waves.

But wonderful as it is that, by the Divine ordinance, a narrow belt of contemptible sand should confine the sea to its appointed limits, yet to us it seems even more remarkable that such immense volumes of water are held in the air within the compass of the clouds. Writing thereon, one of the ablest of the Puritans pointed out: "There are three things very wonderful in that detention of the waters. First, that the waters, which are a fluid body and love to be continually flowing and diffusing themselves, should yet be stopped and stayed together by a cloud, which is a thinner and so a more fluid body than the water. It is no great matter to see water kept in conduits of stone or in vessels of brass, because these are firm and solid bodies, such as the water cannot penetrate nor force its way through; but in the judgment of Nature, how improbable is it that a thin cloud should bear such a weight and power of waters, and yet not rend nor break under them! This is one of the miracles in Nature, which is therefore not wondered at because it is so common, and which because it is constant is not inquired into.

"Second, as it is a wonder that the cloud is not rent under the weight of water, so that the cloud is rent at the special order and command of God. At His word it is that the clouds are locked up, and by His word they are opened. As in spiritual things so in natural: 'He openeth, and no man shutteth; He shutteth, and no man openeth.' Third, this also is wonderful that when at the word of God the cloud rents, yet the waters do not gush out like a violent flood all at once, which would quickly drown the earth, but descend in moderate showers, as water through a colander, drop by drop. God carrieth the clouds up and down the world, as the gardener does his watering-can, and bids them distil upon this or that place as Himself directeth. The clouds are compared to 'bottles' in Job 38:37, and those God stops or unstops, usually as our need requires, and sometimes as our sin deserves. 'I have withholden the rain from you' (Amos 4:7), and He can withhold it till the heavens above us shall be as brass and the earth under us as iron. 'I will also command the clouds that they rain no rain upon it' (Isa. 5:6)" (Joseph Caryl, 1643).

There were still other features of the handiwork of God in the firmament which Job was enjoined to stand still and consider, namely, that God "caused the light of His cloud to shine," and "the balancing of the clouds," which are denominated "the wondrous works of Him which is perfect in knowledge" (37:15, 16). Upon the expanse of ether overhead we behold scenes infinitely more exquisite than any which a Turner or a Raphael could produce: sights so delicately colored, so subtle in texture, so vast in extent, they could do no justice unto in their attempts to reproduce. What artist's brush can begin to portray the splendors of the eastern sky as the monarch of the day emerges from his rest, or the entrancing magnificence of the western horizon as he retires to slumber? The Hebrew verb for "shine" in Job 37:15, means to shine in an illustrious manner, as in Deuteronomy 33:2 (and cf. Ps. 50:1), and "the light of the cloud" refers to the light of the sun's reflection from or upon a watery cloud, producing that wonderful phenomenon the rainbow, which is so conspicuous and beautiful, so desirable and attractive, so mysterious and marvelous.

"Dost thou know the balancings of the clouds?" (Job 37:16). Can you explain how such prodigious volumes of water are suspended over your head and held there in the thinnest parts of the atmosphere? Can you tell what it is which causes those ponderous lakes to hang so evenly and hover like the lightest down? What poises those thick and heavy vapors in coverings so much lighter and thinner than themselves, and prevents their rushing down more impetuously than a mountain torrent? Must we not again employ the personal pronoun, and answer, "HE bindeth up the waters in His thick clouds, and the cloud is not rent under them" (26:8). Who puts the clouds, as it were, into scales, and so orders their weight that one does not overpower another, but rather hang evenly? This is another of the wondrous works of God, who makes the clouds smaller or larger, higher or lower, according to the service He has appointed and the use He makes of them: nothing but the Divine wisdom and power can satisfactorily account for such a prodigy.

Yes, "He bindeth up the waters in His thick cloud." Those masses of water do not remain stationary in the firmament by themselves, nor could they, for, being so much heavier than the air, they would naturally fall of their own weight and power at once in disorder and ruin to the land beneath. It is God who makes them behave and perform His bidding. By some secret power of His own, God fetters them so that they cannot move until He permits. And though these waters be of such mighty bulk and weight, they do not rend the fleecy filament which contain them. "The thick cloud is not rent under them": the same Hebrew word is rendered "divided" in Psalm 78:13 where the reference is to the Almighty cleaving a way for His people through the Red Sea. There is a natural tendency and power in those waters to rend the clouds, but until God bids them, they are held in place, delicately poised, mysteriously but perfectly balanced.

"Which doeth great things and unsearchable, marvelous things without number. Who giveth rain upon the earth, and sendeth waters upon the fields" (Job 5:9, 10). Observe the tense of the verb in the first sentence: it is not only that God "has done" or that He "will do" great things, though both be true, but that He now "doeth" as a present and continued act, for us to take notice of today. Among those stupendous and inscrutable wonders is His sending of the rain, which, though an almost daily provision, is something which men can neither manufacture nor regulate. We do not have far to go in order to inquire or actually see these "marvelous things": they are near to hand, of frequent occurrence, and, if closely looked into, every shower of rain discovers the wisdom, power and goodness of God. Nature works not without the God of nature, and its common blessings are not dispensed without a special providence. The course of nature only moves as it is turned by the hand of its Maker and directed by His counsels. The heaviest clouds distil no water until they receive commission from God to dissolve.

"For He maketh small the drops of water: they pour down rain according to the vapor thereof, which the clouds do drop and distil upon man abundantly" (Job 36:27, 28). "Rain is the moisture of the earth drawn up by the heat of the sun into the middle region of the air, which being there condensed into clouds, is afterward, at the will of God, dissolved and dropped down again in showers" (Joseph Caryl). Though an ordinary and common work of God, yet it is a very admirable one. The Psalmist tells us God "prepareth rain for the earth" (147:8). He does so by the method just described, and then by "making small" its drops, for unless He did the latter, it would pour down in a flood. That, too, is a work of His power and mercy, for the earth could not absorb solid volumes of water at once.

"Also can any understand the spreadings of the clouds?" (Job 36:29). Fully so? No, as the diverse and inadequate theorizings of men go to show. It is almost amusing to examine the various answers returned by philosophers and scientists to the question. What holds the clouds in position? The heat of the sun, say some. But if that were the case rain would fall during the night only, whereas the fact is that as many clouds break and empty themselves in the daytime as during the hours of darkness. By the winds, which keep them in perpetual motion, say others. But how can that be, for sometimes the clouds unburden themselves when a hurricane is blowing, and at others in a dead calm. By their sponginess, which permits their being permeated by the air, thus holding them in place, say others. Then why do light and heavy clouds alike move and evaporate? We are logically forced to rise higher, to the will and power of God It is also of His mercy that the clouds serve as a cool canopy over our heads and break the fierce heat and glare of the sun.

Let us pause here and make practical application of what has been before us. These wonders of nature, so little considered by the majority of our fellows, should speak loudly to our hearts. They should awe us, humble us, bow us in wonderment before the Author of such works. But it is more especially the children of God we now have in mind, and particularly those who are in straits and trouble, whose way is hedged up, whose outlook appears dark and foreboding. As we have contemplated such marvels of Divine wisdom and power, should not our faith be strengthened, so that we look upward with renewed confidence unto our heavenly Father? Must we not, in view of such prodigies, join with the Prophet in exclaiming, "There is nothing too hard for Thee" (Jer. 32:17)? Cannot He who has commissioned the very atmosphere to perform so many useful and benevolent offices for our good, relieve our temporal distress? Cannot He who sustains such mighty volumes of water over our head, also support and succor us? Cannot He who paints the glorious sunrise shine into our soul and dissipate its gloom? Consider the rainbow, not only as a mystery and marvel of nature, but also as a sacramental sign, as a token of God's covenant faithfulness.

That is the use we should make of "the wondrous works of Him who is perfect in knowledge." That is how we should "consider" them, and the conclusion we should draw from them. There is no limit to the power of that One who, in the beginning, made Heaven and earth, and who throughout the centuries has preserved them. When we are confronted with difficulties which seem insurmountable, we should look above, around, below—and beholding the marvelous handiwork of God commit ourselves and our case into His hands with full assurance. When Hezekiah was confronted with the formidable hosts of Sennacherib he sought refuge in the Divine omnipotence, spreading that king's haughty letter before the Lord and appealing to Him as, "Thou hast made Heaven and earth" (2 Kings 19:15), and therefore can vanquish for us our enemies. So, too, the Apostles, when forbidden by the authorities to preach the Gospel, appealed to God as the One who "made Heaven and earth, and the sea, and all that in them is" (Acts 4:24). Rest, then, in this blessed and stimulating truth, that "nothing is too hard" for Him who has loved you with an everlasting love!

"The sea is His and He made it" (Ps. 95:5). The ocean and its inhabitants present to our consideration as many, as varied, and as unmistakable, evidences of the handiwork of God as do the stellar and atmospheric heavens. If we give serious thought to the subject, it must fill us with astonishment that it is possible for any creatures to live in such a suffocating element as the sea, and that in waters so salty they should be preserved in their freshness; and still more so that they should find themselves provided with abundant food and be able to propagate their species from one generation to another. If we were immersed in that element for a few minutes only, we should inevitably perish. Were it not for our actual observation and experience, and had we but read or heard that the briny deep was peopled with innumerable denizens, we should have deemed it an invention of the imagination, as something utterly impracticable and impossible. Yet by the wisdom and power of God not only are myriads of fishes sustained there, but the greatest of all living creatures—the whale—is found there. In number countless, in bulk matchless, yet having their being and health in an element in which we could not breathe!

As it is with us in the surrounding air, so it is with the fish in their liquid element: the principle of the equal transmission of pressure enables their frail structures to bear a much greater pressure and weight than their own without being crushed—the air and the fluids within them pressing outward with a force as great as the surrounding water presses inward! Moreover, "They are clothed and accoutered in exact conformity to their clime. Not in swelling wool or buoyant feathers, nor in flowing robe or full-trimmed suit, but with as much compactness and with as little superfluity as possible. They are clad, or rather sheathed, in scales, which adhere closely to their bodies, and are always laid in a kind of natural oil—which apparel nothing can be more light, and at the same time so solid, and nothing so smooth. It hinders the fluid from penetrating their flesh, it prevents the cold from coagulating their blood, and enables them to make their way through the waters with the greatest possible facility. If in their rapid progress they strike against any hard substance, this their scaly doublet breaks the force of it and secures them from harm" (James Hervey).

Being slender and tapering, the shape of fishes fits them to cleave the waters and to move with the utmost ease through so resisting a medium. Their tails, as is well known, are extremely flexible, consisting largely of powerful muscles, and act with uncommon agility. By its alternate impulsion, the tail produces a progressive motion, and by repeated strokes propels the whole body forward. Still more remarkable is that wonderful apparatus or contrivance, the air-bladder, with which they are furnished, for it enables them to increase or diminish their specific gravity, to sink like lead or float like a cork, to rise to whatever height or sink to whatever depths they please. As these creatures probably have no occasion for the sense of hearing, for the impressions of sound have very little if any existence in their sphere of life, to have provided them with ears would have been an encumbrance rather than a benefit. Is that noticeable and benignant distinction to be ascribed to blind chance? Is it merely an accident that fishes, that need them not, are devoid of ears which are found in all the animals and birds? The cold logic of reason forbids such a conclusion.

A spiritually minded naturalist has pointed out that almost all flat fish, such as soles and flounders, are white on their underside but tinctured with darkish brown on the upper, so that to their enemies they resemble the color of mud and are therefore more easily concealed. What is still more remarkable, Providence, which has given to other fishes an eye on either side of the head, has placed both eyes on the same side in their species, which is exactly suited unto the peculiarity of their condition. Swimming as they do but little, and always with their white side downward, an eye on the lower part of their bodies would be of little benefit, whereas on the higher they have need of the quickest sight for their preservation. Admirable arrangement is that! Where nothing is to be feared, the usual guard is withdrawn; where danger threatens their guard is not only placed, but doubled! Now we confidently submit that such remarkable adaptations as all of these argue design, and that, in turn, a designer, and a Designer, too, who is endowed with more than human wisdom, power and benignity.

"One circumstance relating to the natives of the deep is very peculiar, and no less astonishing. As they neither sow nor reap, have neither the produce of the hedges nor the gleanings of the field, they are obliged to plunder and devour one another for necessary subsistence. They are a kind of licensed bandit that make violence and murder their professed trade. By this means prodigious devastation ensues, and without proper, without very extraordinary recruits, the whole race would continually dwindle and at length become totally extinct. Were they to bring forth, like the most prolific of our terrestrial animals, a dozen only or a score, at each birth, the increase would be unspeakably too small for consumption. The weaker species would be destroyed by the stronger, and in time the stronger must perish, even by their successful endeavors to maintain themselves. Therefore to supply millions of assassins with their prey and millions of tables with their food, yet not to depopulate the watery realms, the issue produced by every breeder is almost incredible. They spawn not by scores or hundreds, but by thousands and tens of thousands. A single mother is pregnant with a nation. By which amazing but most needful expedient, a periodical reparation is made proportional to the immense havoc" (James Hervey).

"Speak to the earth, and it shall teach thee; and the fishes of the sea shall declare unto thee" (Job 12:8). Mute though the fishes be, yet they are full of instruction for the thoughtful inquirer. Study them intelligently and your mind shall be improved and your knowledge increased. And what is it that the dumb fishes declare unto us? Surely this: that there is a living God, who is "wonderful in counsel and excellent in working" (Isa. 28:29); that the creature is entirely dependent on the Creator, who fails not to supply all its needs; that ready obedience to the Divine will becomes the creature, and is rendered by all save rebellious man. In exemplification of that last fact, let us call attention to that amazing phenomenon of countless multitudes of finny visitors crowding upon our shores at the appointed season of the year, and in an orderly succession of one species after another. What is equally remarkable, though less known, is the fact that as they approach, the larger and fiercer ones—who would endanger the lives of the fishermen and drive away the ones which provide us with food-are restrained by an invisible Hand and impelled to retire into the depths of the ocean. As the wild beasts of the earth are directed by the same overruling Power to hide themselves in their dens, so the monsters of the deep are laid under a providential interdiction!

If we survey with any degree of attention the innumerable objects which the inhabitants of this earth present to our view, we cannot but perceive unmistakable marks of design, clear evidences of means suited to accomplish specific ends, and these also necessarily presuppose a Being who had those ends in view and devised the fitness of those means. Order and harmony in the combined operation of many separate forces and elements point to a superintending Mind. Wise contrivances and logical arrangements involve forethought and planning. Suitable accommodations and the appropriate and accurate fitting of one joint to another unquestionably evinces intelligence. The mutual adjustment of one member to another, especially when their functions and properties are correlated, can no more be fortuitous than particles of matter could arrange themselves into the wheels of a watch. The particular suitability of each organ of the body for its appointed office comes not by accident. Benevolent provision and the unfailing operation of law, logically imply a provider and a lawgiver. The fitting together of parts and the adoption of means to the accomplishment of a definite purpose can only be accounted for by reference to a designing Will. Thus, the argument from design may be fairly extended so as to include the whole range of creation and the testimony it bears in all its parts to the existence of the Creator.

Forcibly did Professor John Dick argue, "If we lighted upon a book containing a well-digested narrative of facts, or a train of accurate reasoning, we should never think of calling it a work of chance, but would immediately pronounce it to be the production of a cultivated mind. If we saw in a wilderness a building well-proportioned and commodiously arranged and furnished with taste, we should conclude without hesitation and without the slightest suspicion of mistake that human will and human labor had been employed in planning and erecting it. In cases of this kind, an atheist would reason precisely as other men do. Why then does he not draw the same inference from the proofs of design which are discovered in the works of creation? While the premises are the same, why is the conclusion different? Upon what pretext of reason does he deny that a work, in all the parts of which wisdom appears, is the production of an intelligent author? And attribute the universe to chance, to nature, to necessity, to anything, although it should be a word without meaning, rather than to God?"

"He that planted the ear, shall He not hear? and He that formed the eye, shall He not see?" (Ps. 94:9). The manifest ability of the ear to receive and register sounds, and of the eye for vision, argues an intelligent Designer of them. The Infidel will not allow that conclusion, but what alternative explanation does he offer? This—there may be adaptation without design, as there may be sequence without causation. Certain things, he tells us, are adapted to certain uses, but not made for certain uses: the eye is capable of vision, but had no designing author. When he is asked, How is this striking adaptation to be accounted for apart from design, he answers, Either by the operation of law, or by chance. But the former explanation is really the acknowledgment of a designer, or it is mere tautology, for that law itself must be accounted for, as much as the phenomena which come under it. The explanation of "chance" is refuted by the mathematical doctrine of probability. The chance of matter acting in a certain way is not one in a million, and in a combination of ways, not one in a trillion. According to that theory, natural adaptation would be more infrequent than a miracle, whereas the fact is that adaptation to an end is one of the most common features of nature, occurring in innumerable instances.

When the Psalmist said, "I am fearfully and wonderfully made" (Ps. 139:14), he gave expression to a sentiment which every thoughtful person must readily endorse. Whether that statement be taken in its widest latitude as contemplating man as a composite creature—considering him as a material, rational and moral being— or whether it be restricted to his physical frame, yet it will be heartily confirmed by all who are qualified to express an opinion thereon. Regarding it in its narrower scope, the composition and construction of the human body is a thing of amazing workmanship. To what extent David was acquainted with the science of anatomy we know not, but in view of the pyramids and the Egyptians' skill in embalming the body (and "Moses was learned in all the wisdom of the Egyptians"— Acts 7:22—and doubtless passed on much of the same unto his descendants) and the repeated statement of Holy Writ that "there is nothing new under the sun," we certainly do not believe the ancients were nearly so ignorant as many of our inflated moderns wish to think. But be that as it may, the outward structure of the body, the ordering of its joints and muscles for the service of its tenant, the proportion of all its parts, the symmetry and beauty of the whole cannot but strike with wonderment the attentive student of the human frame.

This living temple has aptly been termed "the masterpiece of creation." Its sinews and muscles, veins and blood, glands and bones, all so perfectly fitted for their several functions, are a production which for wisdom and design, the adaptation of means to ends, not only far surpasses the most skillful and complicated piece of machinery ever produced by human art, but altogether excels whatever the human imagination could conceive. That the nutritive power of the body should be working perpetually and without intermission replacing waste tissue; that there should be a constant flowing of the blood and beating of the pulses, that the lungs and arteries (comprised of such frail and delicate substances) should move without cessation for 70 or 90 years—for 900 years before the Flood!—presents a combined marvel which should fill us with astonishment and awe, for they are so many miracles of omniscience and omnipotence. But turning to the more obvious and commonplace, the human hand and eye, let us conclude this chapter with a rather longer quotation than usual from The Gordian Knot, for it calls attention to features which, though equally remarkable, the most untrained are able to appreciate.

"The human hand was obviously meant to be the servant of the entire body. It is put at the extremity of the arm, and the arm is about half the length of the body, and, as the body can bend almost double, the hand can reach any part of it. The hand is at the end of an arm having three joints, one at the shoulder, one at the elbow, one at the wrist, and each joint made on a different pattern so as to secure together every conceivable motion—up and down, sidewise, backward and forward, and rotary. The hand is made with four fingers and an opposing thumb, which secures a double leverage, without which no implement or instrument could be securely grasped, held, or wielded, and so strangely are the fingers molded of unequal lengths that they exactly touch tips over a spherical surface, such as a ball or the round handle of a tool.

"There are two hands—opposite and apposite to each other in position and construction, so that they exactly fit each other and work together without interference, making possible by joint action what neither could accomplish alone. Montaigne, referring to one only of the hand's many capacities—a gesture—says: 'With the hand we demand, promise, call, dismiss, entreat, deny, encourage, accuse, acquit, defy, flatter, and indicate silence; and with a variety and multiplication that almost keeps pace with the tongue.' The hand is so strikingly capable of being used to express conceptions and execute designs that it has been called 'the intellectual member.'

"The human eye is perfect in structure and equally perfect in adaptation. It is placed in the head like a window just under the dome, to enable us to see farthest; placed in front, because we habitually move forward; shielded in a socket of bone for protection to its delicate structure, yet protected from that socket by a soft cushion; provided with six sets of muscles to turn it in every direction; with lids and lashes to moisten, shut it in, protect it and soothe it; with tear ducts to conduct away excess of moisture; and having that exact shape—the only one of all that might have been given—to secure distinct vision by refracting all rays of light to a single surface, which is known in science as the ellipsoid of revolution.

"By a wonderful arrangement of iris and pupil it at once adapts itself to near and far objects of vision and to mild or intense rays of light, and, most wonderful of all, the human eye is provided in some inscrutable manner with the means of expressing the mind itself, so that one may look into its crystal depths and see intellectuality, scorn, and wrath, and love, and almost every spiritual state and action' (Dr. E. F. Burr).

"The eye of man has taught us the whole science of optics. It is a camera obscura, with a convex lens in front, an adjustable circular blind behind it; a lining of black to prevent double and confusing reflections; fluids, aqueous and vitreous, to distend it; a retina or expansion of the optic nerve to receive the images of external objects; with minute provision for motion in every direction; and, most wonderful of all, perhaps, perfect provision against the spherical and chromatic aberration which would produce images and impressions ill-defined and false colored. Yet the microscope shows these lenses themselves to be made up of separate folds, in number countless, the folds themselves composed of fibers equally countless, and toothed so as to interlock. And with all this, perfect transparency is preserved!

"It is in the minutiae of creation, perhaps, that the most surprising marvels, mysteries and miracles of creative workmanship are often found. It is here also that the works of God so singularly differ from the works of man. However elaborate man's work it does not bear minute microscopic investigation. For instance, the finest cambric needle becomes coarse, rough and blunt under the magnifying lens, whereas it is only when looked at with the highest power of the microscopic eye that Nature's handiwork really begins to reveal its exquisite and indescribable perfection. Where the perfection of man's work ends, the perfection of God's work only begins.

"The proofs of this perfection in minutiae are lavishly abundant. When a piece of chalk is drawn over a blackboard, in the white mark on the board, or the powder that falls on the floor, are millions of tiny white shells, once the home of life. The dust from the moth's wing is made up of scales or feathers, each as perfect as the ostrich plume. The pores of the human skin are so closely crowded together that 75,000 of them might be covered by a grain of sand. The insect's organ of vision is a little world of wonders in itself. In the eye of a butterfly 34,000 lenses have been found, each perfect as a means of vision. The minute cells in which all life, vegetable and animal, reside present as true an evidence of the mysterious perfection of individual workmanship and mutual adaptation as the constellations that adorn the sky, and equally with them declare the glory of God! How it speaks of a Creator who can lavish beauty even on the stones, and who carries the perfection of His work into the realm of the least as well as the greatest!"

Chapter 2
THE EXISTENCE OF GOD
AS REVEALED IN MAN

Creation makes manifest the Creator, and having considered some of the mighty products of Omnipotence therein, we turn now to that which comes closer home unto each of us. We are not obliged to go far afield and turn our attention to objects in the heavens or the depths of the ocean in order to find evidences of God's existence—we may discover them in ourselves. Man himself exhibits a Divine Maker, yea, he is the chief of His mundane works. Accordingly we find that Genesis I, after giving a brief but vivid account of how the heavens and earth were called into existence by a Divine fiat and both of them furnished for the benefit of the human race, God made man last—as though to indicate he is the climax of His works. In each other instance we are told "God said," "God called," "God created," etc., but in our case there is a marked difference: "And God said, Let Us make man in Our image, after Our likeness" (1:26), as if to signify (speaking after the manner of men) there was a special conference of the Divine Trinity in connection with the formation of that creature who should be made in the Divine image. All the works of God bear the impress of His wisdom, but man alone has stamped upon him the Divine likeness.

The fact that man was made by the Triune God and "in Their image" plainly indicates that he was constituted a tripartite being, consisting of spirit and soul and body—the first being capable of God-consciousness, the second of self-consciousness, and the third of sense-consciousness. The dual expression, "in Our image, after Our likeness," imports a twofold resemblance between God and man in his original condition: the former referring to the holiness of his nature, the latter to the character of his soul—which competent theologians have rightly distinguished as "the moral image" and the "natural image" of God in man. That is a real and necessary distinction, and unless it be observed we inevitably fall into error when contemplating the effects of man's defection from God. To the question, Did man lose the image of God by the Fall? the orthodox rightly answer in the affirmative; yet many of them are quite at a loss to understand such verses as Genesis 9:6 and James 3:9, which teach that fallen man retains the image of God. It was the moral image which was destroyed when he apostatized, and which is restored to him again at regeneration (Eph. 4:24; Col. 3:10). Fallen man is made in the image of his fallen parent, as Genesis 5:3, and Psalm 51:5 solemnly attest. But fallen man still has plainly stamped upon him the natural image of God, evidencing his Divine origin. What that "natural image" consists in we will now consider.

We have called attention to some of the wonders observable in the human body, and if God bestowed such exquisite workmanship upon the casket, what must be the nature of the gem within it! That "gem" is the spirit and soul of man, which was made in the natural image of God— we shall not here distinguish between them, but treat of them together under the generic term "soul." If the human body bears upon it the impress of the Divine hand, much more so does the soul with its truly remarkable faculties and capabilities. The soul is endowed with understanding, will, moral perception, memory, imagination, affections. Man is comprised and possessed of something more than matter, being essentially a spiritual and rational being, capable of communion with his Maker. There was given unto man a nature nobler than of any other creature on earth. Man is an intelligent being, capable of thinking and reasoning, which as much excels the instinct of animals as the finished product of the artist's brush does the involuntary raising of his hand to protect his face, or the shutting of his eye without thought when wind blows dust into it. From whence, then, has man derived his intelligence?

The soul is certainly something distinct from the body. Our very consciousness informs us that we possess an understanding, yea, an intelligent entity which, though we cannot see, yet is known by its operations of thinking, reasoning, remembering. But matter possesses no such properties as those, no, not in any combination of its elements. If matter could think, then it would still be able to do so after the soul was absent from the body. Again—if matter had the power of thought, then it would be able to think only of those things which are tangible and material, for no cause can ever produce effects superior to itself. Intelligence can no more issue from non-intelligence than the animate from the non-animate. A stone cannot think, nor a log of wood understand a syllogism. But the human soul is not only capable of thinking, it can also commune with itself, rejoice in itself. Nor is its ability to rationalize restricted to itself: it is so constituted that it can apprehend and discourse of things superior to itself. So far from being tied down to the material realm, it can soar into the heavens, cognize the angels, and commune with the Father of spirits.

Consider the vastness of the soul's capacity! What cannot it encompass? It can form a concept of the whole world, and visualize scenes thousands of miles away. As one has pointed out, "it is suited to all objects, as the eye to all colors or the ear to all sounds." How capacious is the memory to retain so much, and such variety! Consider the quickness of the soul's motions: nothing is so swift in the whole course of nature. Thought is far more rapid in its action than the light-waves of ether: in a single moment fancy may visit the Antipodes. With equal facility and agility it can transport itself into the far away past or the distant future. As the desires of the soul are not bounded by material objects, so neither are its motions restrained by them. Consider also its power of volition. The will is the servant of the soul, carrying out its behests, yet it knows not how its commissions are received. Now matter has no power of choice, and what it is devoid of it certainly cannot convey. As man's intelligence must have its source in the supreme Mind, so his power of volition must proceed from the supreme Will.

The nature of man also bears witness to the existence of God in the operations and reflections of his conscience. If the external marvels of creation exhibit the wisdom and power of the Creator, this mysterious faculty of the soul as clearly exemplifies His holiness and justice. Whatever be its nature or howsoever we define it, its forceful presence within presents us with a unique phenomenon. This moral sense in man challenges investigation and demands an explanation—an investigation which the Infidel is most reluctant to seriously make, and for which he is quite unable to furnish satisfactory explanation. "Conscience is a court always in session and imperative in its summons. No man can evade it or silence its accusations. It is a complete assize. It has a judge on its bench, and that judge will not be bribed into a lax decision. It has its witness stand, and can bring witnesses from the whole territory of the past life. It has its jury, ready to give a verdict, "guilty" or "not guilty," in strict accordance with the evidence, and it has its sheriff, Remorse, with his whip of scorpions, ready to lash the convicted soul. The nearest thing in the world to the bar of God is the court of conscience. And though it be for a time drugged into a partial apathy or intoxicated with worldly pleasure, the time comes when in all the majesty of its imperial authority this court calls to its bar every transgressor and holds him to a strict account" (A. T. Pierson).

Conscience is that which conveys to the soul a realization of right and wrong. It is that inward faculty which passes judgment upon the lawfulness or unlawfulness of our desires and deeds. It is an ethical instinct, a faculty of moral sensibility, which both informs and impresses its possessor, being that which, basically, constitutes us responsible creatures. It is an inward faculty which is not only of a vastly superior order, but is far keener in perception than any of the bodily senses: it both sees, hears and feels. Its office is twofold: to warn us against sin and to prompt us unto the performance of duty— and this it does according to the light shining into it—from natural reason and Divine revelation. Though the heathen be without the Bible, yet their conscience passes judgment on natural duties and unnatural sins. Hence, the more spiritual light a person has, the greater his responsibility, and it is according to that principle and on that basis he will be dealt with at the grand Assize. "That servant which knew his lord's will and prepared not, neither did according to his will, shall be beaten with many stripes. But he that knew not, and did commit things worthy of stripes, shall be beaten with few. For unto whomsoever much is given, of him shall be much required" (Luke 12:47-48). Punishment will be proportioned to light received and privileges enjoyed.

To this moral sensibility of man as the basis of his accountability, the Apostle refers in Romans 2: "For when the Gentiles [heathen] which have not the Law, do by nature the things contained in the Law, these, having not the Law, are a law unto themselves" (v. 14). The "nature" of anything is the peculiarity of its being, that in virtue of which it is what it is: it is that which belongs to its original constitution, in contradistinction from all that is taught or acquired. This ethical sense is an original part of his being, and is not the product of education—a power of discrimination by which he distinguishes between right and wrong is created in man. The natural light of reason enables the uncivilized to distinguish between virtue and vice. All, save infants and idiots, recognize the eternal difference between good and evil: they instinctively, or rather intuitively, feel this or that course is commendable or censurable. They have a sense of duty: the natural light of reason conveys the same. Even the most benighted and degraded give evidence that they are not without a sense of obligation: however primitive and savage be their mode of life, yet the very fact that they frame some form of law and order for the community, proves beyond any doubt they have a definite notion of justice and rectitude.

The very nature of the heathen, their sense of right and wrong, leads to the performing of moral actions. In confirmation thereof, the Apostle went on to say, "which show the work of the Law written in their heart, their conscience also bearing witness [to the existence of God and their accountability to Him], and their thoughts the meanwhile [or "between themselves," margin] accusing or excusing [the conduct of themselves and of] one another" (Rom. 2:15). The "work of the Law" is not to be understood as a power of righteousness operating within them, still less as their actual doing of what the Law requires; but rather the function or design of the Law, which is to direct action. The natural light of reason informs them of the distinction between right and wrong. "Their conscience also bearing witness," that is, in addition to the dictates of reason, for they are by no means the same thing. Knowledge of duty and the actions of conscience are quite distinct: the one reveals what is right, the other approves of it, and condemns the contrary. They have sufficient light to judge between what is honest and dishonest, and their moral sense makes this distinction before commission of sin, in the commission, and afterward—as clearly appears in their acquitting or condemning one another.

Those who have given Romans 2:14 any serious thought must have been puzzled if not stumbled by the statement that those in Heathendom, "do by nature the things contained in the Law," since they neither love the Lord God with all their hearts nor their neighbors as themselves—the sum of what it requires. The American Revised Version is much to be preferred: "Do by nature the things of the Law," which describes not the yielding of obedience to the Law, but the performing of its functions. The proper business of the Law is to say, This is right, that is wrong; you will be rewarded for the one, and punished for the other. To command, to forbid, to promise, to threaten—these are "the things of the Law," the "work" of it (v. 15). The Apostle's assertion is this—an assertion exactly accordant with truth, and directly bearing on his argument: "The Gentiles who have no written Divine Law, perform by nature from their very constitution, to themselves and each other, the functions of such a law. They make a distinction between right and wrong, just as they do between truth and falsehood. They cannot help doing so. They often go wrong by mistaking what is right and what is wrong, as they often go wrong by mistaking what is true and what is false. But they approve themselves and one another when doing what they think right; they disapprove themselves and one another when they do what they think to be wrong; so that, though they have no written law, they act the part of a law to themselves. This capacity, this necessity of their nature, distinguishes them from brutes, and makes them the subjects of Divine moral government. In this way they show 'that the work of the law'—the work which the Law does—is 'written in their hearts,' woven in their constitution, by the actings of the power we call conscience. It is just, then, that they should be punished for doing what they know to be wrong, or might have known to be wrong" (Professor Brown).

Man is the only earthly creature endowed with conscience. The beasts have consciousness and a limited power to acquire knowledge, but that is something very different. Certain animals can be made to obey their masters. With the aid of a stick, even a cow may be taught to refrain from plucking the green leaves over the garden fence, which her mouth craves—the memory of the beatings she has received for disobedience incline her to forgo her inclinations. Much more intelligent is a domesticated dog: he can be trained to understand that certain actions will meet with reward, while others will receive punishment. But memory is a very different thing from that ethical monitor within the human breast, which weighs whatever is presented to the mind and passes judgment either for or against all our actions, secretly acquainting the soul with the right and wrong of things. Wherever we go, this sentinel accompanies us: whatever we think or do, it records a verdict. Much of our peace of mind is the fruit of a non-accusing conscience, while not a little of our disquietude is occasioned by the charges of wrong-doing which conscience brings against us.

Conscience is an integral part of that light which "lightens every man which comes into the world." Forceful testimony is borne to its potency by the rites of the heathen and their self-imposed penances, which are so many attempts to appease the ones they feel they have offended. There is in every man that which reproves him for his sins, yea, for those to which none other is privy, and therefore the wicked flee when no man pursues (Prov. 28:1). At times the stoutest are made to quail. The most hardened have their seasons of alarm. The specter of past sins haunts them in the night watches. Boast loudly as they may that they fear nothing, yet "there were they in great fear where no fear was" (Ps. 53:5)—an inward horror where there was no outward occasion for uneasiness. When there is no reason for fright, the wicked are suddenly seized with panic and made to tremble like an aspen leaf, so that they are afraid of their own shadows.

The fearful reality of conscience is plainly manifested by the fact that men who are naturally inclined to evil nevertheless disapprove of that which is evil, and approve of the very good which they practice not. Even though they do not so audibly, the vicious secretly admire the pure, and while some be sunk so low they will scarcely acknowledge it to themselves, nevertheless they wish they could be like the morally upright. The most blameworthy will condemn certain forms of evil in others, thus evincing they distinguish between good and evil. Whence does that arise? By what rule do they measure moral actions, but by an innate principle? But how comes man to possess that principle? It is not an attribute of reason, for at times reason will inform its possessor that a certain course of conduct would result in gain to him, but conscience moves him to act in a way which he knows will issue in temporal loss. Nor is it a product of the will, for conscience often acts in opposition to the will, and no effort of the will can still it. It is a separate faculty which, in various degrees of enlightenment and sensitiveness, is found in civilized and uncivilized.

Now even common sense tells us that someone other than ourselves originated this faculty. No law can be without a lawgiver. From whence, then, this law? Not from man, for he would annihilate it if he could. It must have been imparted by some higher Hand, which Hand alone can maintain it against all the violence of its owner, who, were it not for this restraining monitor, would quickly reduce the world to a charnel house. If, then, we reason rationally, we are forced to argue thus: I find myself naturally obliged to do this and shun that, therefore there must be a Superior who obliges me. If there were no Superior, I should myself be the sole judge of good and evil, yea, I should be regulated only by expediency and recognize no moral distinctions. Were I the lord of that principle or law which commands me, I should find no conflict within myself between reason and appetite. The indubitable fact is that conscience has an authority for man that cannot be accounted for except by its being the voice of God within him. If conscience were entirely isolated from God, and were independent of Him, it could not make the solemn, and sometimes the terrible impressions it does. No man would be afraid of himself if self were not connected with a higher Being than himself.

As God has not left Himself without witness among the lower creatures (Acts 14:17), neither has He left Himself without witness within man's own breast. There is not a rational member of the human race who has not at some time more or less smarted under the lashings of conscience. The hearts of princes, in the midst of their pleasures, have been stricken with anguish while their favorites were flattering them. Those inward torments are not ignorant frights experienced only by children, which reason throws off later on, for the stronger reason grows, the sharper the stings of conscience, and not the least so in maturity and old age. It often operates when wickedness is most secret. Numerous cases are on record of an overwhelming terror overtaking wrongdoers when their crimes were known to none, and they have condemned themselves and given themselves up to justice. Could that self-accuser originate from man's own self? He who loves himself would, were it possible, destroy that which disturbs him. Certainly conscience has received no authority from its possessor to lash himself, to spoil the pleasures of sin, to make him "like the troubled sea, which cannot rest."

The very fact there is that in man which condemns him for sins committed in secret, argues there is a God, and that he is accountable unto Him. He has an instinctive dread of a Divine Judge who will yet arraign him. "They know the judgment of God" (Rom. 1:32) by an inward witness. It is a just provision of the Lord that those who will not reverently fear Him, have a tormenting fear of the future. Why is it that, despite all their efforts to escape from the conclusion that God is, they dread a retribution beyond death?—often demonstrated by the most callous wretches in their last hours by asking for a chaplain or "priest." If there be no God, why do men strive to silence conscience and dispel its terrors? And why are their efforts so unavailing? Since they cannot still its accusations, some Higher Power must maintain it within the soul. That the most enlightened nations recognize men have no right to force the conscience, is a tacit acknowledgment it is above human jurisdiction, answerable only to its Author. Conscience is the vicegerent of God in the soul, and will torment the damned for all eternity.

Chapter 3
THE EXISTENCE OF GOD
AS SEEN IN HUMAN HISTORY

Since God is the Creator of all things, He is their perpetual Preserver and Regulator. And since man is the chief of His earthly creatures, it is unthinkable that God has left him entirely to himself. The same all-mighty Being who created every part of it, directs the vast machinery of the universe and controls equally all the hearts and actions of men. But the same unbelief which seeks to banish God from the realm of creation, denies that He has any real place or part in the moral government of the world. The one, it is said, is regulated by the (impersonal) "laws of Nature," while man, endowed with "free will," must not be interfered with, but left to work out his own destiny, both individually and collectively considered. We have shown how utterly irrational is such a view as it pertains to the material sphere, and it is no more difficult to demonstrate how thoroughly untenable it is as applied to the moral realm. The palpable facts of observation refute it. The affairs of every individual, the history of each nation, the general course of human events—all bear evidence of a higher Power super-intending the same.

In reading history most people are contented with a bare knowledge of its salient facts, without attempting to trace their causes or ascertain the connection of events. For the most part they look no farther than the motives, designs and tendencies of human nature. They perceive not that there is a philosophy of history. They rise not to the realization that the living God has absolute sway over this scene, that amid all the confusion of human wills and interests, all the malice and wickedness of Satan and his agents, the Lord God omnipotent reigns—not only in Heaven but over this earth—shaping all its affairs, directing all things to the outworking of His eternal purpose. Because the reading of human history is done so superficially, and few have more than a general acquaintance with its character, our present line of argument may not be so patent or so potent to some. Nevertheless, it should be more or less obvious unto any person of ordinary intelligence that in the course of the centuries there are clear marks of an over-ruling and presiding Power above the human.

Since there can be no effect without a previous cause, no law without a law-giver, neither do events come to pass fortuitously. Any thoughtful student of history is obliged to conclude that its records are something more than a series of disconnected and purposeless incidents: rather do they evince the working out of a plan. True, its wheels often appear to move slowly, and not infrequently at cross-purposes, nevertheless, the sequel shows they work surely. It is in the combination of events leading up to some grand end that the workings of Divine Providence most clearly appear. As we perceive the wisdom of the Creator in so admirably fitting each member of the human body to perform its designed functions, so we may discern the hand of the moral Ruler of this world in the adapting of appropriate means to the accomplishment of His ends, in the suitability of the instruments He has selected thereunto, in making each separate human actor play his part, each individual contribute his quota in producing the desired effect. As in the mechanism of a watch, each pivot is in place, each wheel in motion, so that the main-spring guides its index, so in the complicated machinery of history every single circumstance pays its mite toward the furthering of some grand object.

Proofs of a presiding Providence are to be found in the life of each individual. Where is the man who has not passed through experiences which made him feel in his heart there must be a God who watches over him? In the unexpected and remarkable turns in the course of his affairs, in the sudden thoughts and unaccountable decisions which lead to most important results, in his narrow escapes from grave danger, he has evidence of a higher power at work. Even the most giddy and thoughtless are, at times, forced to take notice of this. That we are under a Moral Government which dispenses rewards and punishments in a natural way is also plain to our sense and proved by personal experience. Vicious actions speedily meet with retribution, by involving their perpetrator in disgrace, by often reducing him to poverty, subjecting him to bodily disease and mental suffering, and brining about an untimely death. On the other hand, we find that virtuous actions not only result in inward peace and satisfaction, but lead to respect, health and happiness.

If there be no living God presiding over this scene, how can we possibly account for the almost exact ratio between the two sexes? Each year there are born into this world millions of males and of females, and yet the balance between them is perfectly preserved. Their parents had no say in the matter, nor did medical science regulate it! The only rational explanation is that the sex of each child is determined by the Creator. Again—if there be no personal Creator fashioning human countenances, how are we to explain their unvarying variation? The features of the human countenance are but few in number, yet so much does their appearance differ, both singly and in their combination, that out of countless millions no two people look exactly alike! Suppose the opposite. If a likeness were common, what incalculable inconvenience and confusion would ensue. If only 100 men in a single large city had the same build and countenance, impersonation would be practiced without fear of detection, and criminals could not be identified. Such endless dissimilarities among those descended from common parents must have the Almighty for their Author.

That the One from above regulates all human affairs is demonstrated on every side of us, look where we may. In the instances alluded to above, the individual is entirely passive, for it is by no decision of his that he is born male or female, black or white, a giant or a dwarf. But consider something yet more striking, namely, that even our voluntary actions are secretly directed from on high. Each year hundreds of thousands of both young men and women choose their ordinary vocations or careers: what is it which moves them to make a proportionate selection from such a variety of alternatives? Is it nothing but blind chance that each generation is supplied with sufficient physicians and dentists, lawyers and school teachers, mechanics and manual laborers? Many of our youth emigrate: what hinders all from doing so? Some prefer a life on the land, others on the sea— why? Take something still more commonplace: today I have written and mailed seven letters—suppose every adult in Great Britain did the same! The complicated machinery of modern life would speedily break down and utter chaos would obtain were not an omniscient and omnipresent Being regulating it.

It may be objected that the machinery of our complex social life does not always run smoothly—that there are strikes and lock-outs which result in much inconvenience, that at times the railroads are blocked with traffic, that hotels are overcrowded, and so on. Granted, yet such occurrences are the exception rather than the rule. But we may draw an argument of Divine Providence from the very commotions and confusions which do obtain in the world. Seeing it does occasionally pass through disturbances, is it not evident that there must be a mighty Power balancing these commotions, yea curbing them, so that they do not speedily issue in the total ruin of the world? The same One who has put the fear of man into wild beasts and a natural instinct for them to avoid human habitations, preferring to resort unto the jungles and deserts, to prowl for their prey in the night, and in the morning return to their caves and dens, sufficiently places His restraining hand upon the baser passions of men as to ensure that degree of law and order which makes life possible amid fallen and depraved creatures. Were that restraining Hand altogether removed, any guarantee of safety and security would be non est.

God is no idle Spectator of the affairs of this earth, but is the immediate Regulator of all its events, and that, not only in a general way, but in all particulars, from the least to the greatest. If, on the one hand, not a sparrow falls to the ground without the Divine will (Matt. 10:29), certain it is that on the other no throne can be overturned without His ordering. "For of Him, and through Him, and to Him, are all things: to whom be glory forever. Amen" (Rom. 11:36). God is not only "King of saints," but He is "King of nations" (Jer. 10:7) as well. God reigns as truly over His foes as He does over His friends, and works through Satan and his demons as truly as by His holy angels. "The king's heart is in the hand of the Lord, and He turneth it whithersoever He will" (Prov. 21:1). God presides over the deliberations of parliaments and influences the decisions of cabinets. Human governments act only as they are moved by a secret power from Heaven. Jehovah rules in the councils of the ungodly equally as in the prayerful counsels of a church assembly. The designs, decisions and actions of all men are directed by Him unto those ends which He has appointed, yet that in nowise annuls their moral agency or lessens their own guilt in sinning.

The government of this world is as much a work of God as was the creation of it, and while there be some things as inscrutable about the one as the other, yet each alike bears unmistakably upon it the Divine impress. There are riddles in each which the wisest cannot solve, but there are also wonders in each before which all should be awed. Broadly speaking, the moral government of God consists of two things: in directing the creatures' actions, in apportioning rewards and punishments according to the actions of rational creatures. No evil comes to pass without His permission, no good without His concurrence; no good or evil without His over-ruling—ordering it to His own ends. "The eyes of the LORD are in every place, beholding the evil and the good" (Prov. 15:3), and in His balances everything is weighed. The distributions of Divine mercy and of vengeance are, to some extent, apportioned in this life, but more particularly and fully will they be made manifest in the Day to come. God rules in such a way that His hand should be neither too evident nor too secret, and by adopting this middle course, room is left for the exercise of faith, while the unbelief of Infidels rendered without excuse.

Nothing happens simply because it must, that is, of inexorable necessity. Fate is blind, but Providence has eyes—all is directed by wisdom and according to design. The history of each nation is the outworking of the Divine plan and purpose concerning it. Yet it is equally true that the history of each nation is determined by its own attitude toward God and His Law. In the experience of each one it is made to appear that "Righteousness exalteth a nation, but sin is a reproach to any people" (Prov. 34:3). Thus the Word of God and the Providence of God are complementary: the former sheds light on the latter, while the latter illustrates and exemplifies the former. Therefore in His government of this world, God displays His manifold perfections: His wisdom and goodness, His mercy and justice, His faithfulness and patience. The rise, progress and triumphs of each nation, as also its decline, fall and ignominy, are according to both the sovereign will and the perfect righteousness of the Lord. He rules "in the midst of His enemies" (Ps. 110:2), yet His rule is neither capricious nor arbitrary, but a wise and just one. The prosperity of nations generally tends to the increase of vice through affording fuller opportunity to indulge its lusts; and in such cases sore calamities are necessary for the checking of their wickedness, or, when it has come to the full, to destroy them as the Egyptian and Babylonian empires were.

The history of Israel affords the most striking example of what has been pointed out above. So long as they honored God and walked in obedience to His Law, so long they prospered and flourished—witness their history in the days of Joshua and David. But when they worshipped the idols of the heathen and became unrighteous in their conduct man with man, sore chastisements and heavy judgments were their portion, as in the times of the judges and of the Babylonian captivity. Observe, too, the futile attempts made by the most powerful of their enemies to secure their extirpation: the efforts of Pharaoh, of Haman, of Sennacherib to overthrow the purpose of Jehovah concerning His people resulted only in their own destruction. Note how an exact retribution—"poetic justice," worldlings would call it—overtook Jezebel: "In the place where dogs licked the blood of Naboth" (1 Kings 21:19), who was murdered at the orders of that wicked queen, there was her corpse consumed by dogs (2 Kings 9:36). On the other hand, behold how God blessed those who showed kindness to His people: as Rahab and the whole of her family being delivered when Jericho was destroyed because she had sheltered the two Israeli spies; and the Shunnamite woman supernaturally provided for throughout the sore famine for her befriending of the Prophet Elijah. What incredulity regards as "coincidences" right reason views as wondrous providences.

The book of Esther furnishes a most vivid illustration and demonstration of the invisible yet palpable working of God in human affairs. In it we are shown the Jews brought to the very brink of ruin, and then delivered without any miracle being wrought on their behalf. The very means employed by their enemies for their destruction were, by the secret operations of God, made the means of their deliverance and glory. Writing thereon, Carson rightly said: "The hand of God in His ordinary Providence linked together a course of events as simple and as natural as the mind can conceive, yet as surprising as the boldest fictions of romance." The series of events opened with the king of Persia giving a banquet. Heated with wine, that monarch gave orders for his royal consort to appear before the assembled revelers. Though such a request was indecorous and distasteful to the queen, yet it is remarkable she dared to disobey her despotic husband. Whether a sense of decency or personal pride actuated her, we know not—but in voluntarily acting according to her own feelings, she ignorantly fulfilled the will of Him whom she knew not. That the king should subject her to a temporary disgrace for her refusal to heed his behest might be expected, but that he should give up forever one whom he so much admired is surprising.

How extraordinary it was that the deposing of Vashti made way for the elevating of a poor Jewess to the rank of queen of the Persian empire! Was it nothing but a "happy coincidence" that she should be more beautiful than all the virgins of over a 100 provinces? Was it only a piece of "good luck" that the king's chamberlain was pleased with her from the first moment of her arrival, and that he did all in his power to advance her interests? Was it simply "fortunate" for her that she instantly met with favor when the king set eyes upon her? Was it only by blind chance that the conspiracy of two of the king's servants was thwarted and that Mordecai and all his people were saved from disaster? Haman was sure of victory, having obtained the king's decree to execute his bloody designs. Why was it, then, that the king was sleepless one night, and why should he arise and, to pass the time away, scan the court records? Why did his eye happen to alight on the reported discovery of the plot on his own life? Why had Mordecai been the one to uncover the scheme and his name entered into the report? Why was the king now—at this critical juncture in Israel's affairs—so anxious to ascertain whether Mordecai had been suitably rewarded? Cold logic is not sufficiently credulous to regard these things, and the grand sequel to them all, as so many fortuitous events.

The book of Esther plainly evinces that the most trifling affairs are ordered by the Lord to subserve His own glory and effect the good of His own people. Though He works behind the scenes,

He works none the less. He does indeed govern the inanimate world by general laws of His own appointing, yet He directs their operations-or suspends them when He pleases—so as to accomplish what He has decreed. He has also established general moral laws in the government of mankind, yet He is not tied by them: sometimes He uses means, at others He uses none. As the sun and rain minister to the nourishment and comfort of the righteous and wicked alike, not from the necessity of general laws but from the immediate Providence of Him who has ordained all things, so the free determinations of men are so controlled from on high that they effect the eternal designs of God. So, too, the Book of Esther reveals that it is in the combination of incidents the working of Providence most plainly appears. There is a wonderful series of linking events which lead to the accomplishment of God's glorious purpose: the actions of each person are links in the chain to bring about some appointed result—if one link were removed the whole chain would be broken. All lines converge on and meet in one center: all things concur to bring about the decreed event.

If the record of any Gentile nation were fully chronicled, and had we sufficient discernment and perspicuity, we should perceive as definite a connection between one event—which now appears to us isolated—and another, and the hand of God controlling them as in the history of Israel. But even a fragmentary knowledge of general history should be sufficient to reveal to any man the directing hand of God in it and the testimony it bears to the truth of the Bible. It abounds in illustrations that, "The race is not to the swift, nor the battle to the strong" (Eccl. 9:11). The most numerous and powerful armies are no guaranty of success, as has frequently been demonstrated. Providence disposes the event: without any miraculous interference the best trained and equipped forces have been defeated by much weaker ones. The discovery of America by Columbus, in time for that land to afford an asylum for persecuted Protestants, the invention of printing just before the Reformation, the destruction of the "Invincible Armada" of Spain, are more than "coincidences." Why has England always had a man of outstanding proportions—genius, valor, dynamism, dogged determination—at each critical juncture of her history? Cromwell, Drake, Nelson, Wellington, Churchill—all were the special gifts of God to a people under His peculiar favor.

A real, if mysterious, Providence is obviously at work, controlling the gradual growth of each empire and of the combination of nations: as in the federation of the ten kings of Revelation 17:16, 17—the Divine plan is brought to fruition by those whose intention it is to accomplish their own purpose. "For God hath put it in their hearts to fulfill His will," though that in nowise lessens their sin: none but the hand of the Almighty can bring good out of evil and make the wrath of His enemies to praise Him. The more their chronicles be studied, the stronger should be our conviction that only the action and interposition of God can account for many of the outstanding events in human history. The rise and careers of individual tyrants also illustrates the same principle. How often have the workings of Providence verified the Word that "the triumphing of the wicked is short" (Job 20:5). At longest it is but brief because limited by the span of this life, whereas their sufferings will be eternal. But often God blows upon the plans of ambitious oppressors, crosses their imperious wills, and brings them to a speedy ruin in this world: He did so with Napoleon, the Kaiser, Mussolini and Hitler! He raised them on high that He might cast them down by a more terrible fall.

We have called attention to the revelation which God has made of Himself in human history, that is, to the cumulative evidence which the affairs of individuals and of nations furnish that a Divine Person has full control over those affairs, and orders and directs them all unto the accomplishment of His own eternal purpose. The Ruler of this world makes use of the opinions and motives, the resolves and actions of men, yea, overruling their very crimes to further His design and promote His own glory. Every occurrence upon the stage of human events is not only to be traced back to the Divine counsels, but should be viewed as the outworking of a part of His vast plan. We should behold God in all the intrigues of courts and governments, in all the caprices of monarchs, in all the changes of kingdoms and empires; yea, in all the persecutions of the righteous, as really and as truly as in the progress of the Gospel: though in the former it is more the secret workings of His justice, as it is the more open manifestations of His grace in the latter. "The lot is cast into the lap, but the whole disposing thereof is of the LORD" (Prov. 16:33) whether or not we perceive it.

The One who rules the planets is equally master of every human despot. We supplied proof of that in connection with Ahasuerus. Consider now another example. As a judgment upon their long-continued sinfulness, God delivered the Jews into the hands of an invading power, and suffered the flower of their nation to be carried captive into Babylon. Yet His judgment was tempered with mercy, for He assured His covenant, though wayward people, that after 70 years they should return to Palestine. That promise was definite and sure: but how was it to receive its fulfillment? They were utterly incapable of delivering themselves from the midst of the mightiest empire on earth, and there was no friendly and powerful nation demanding their emancipation. How, then, was the Lord's Word to be made good? God had indeed delivered their forefathers from Egypt by a series of great marvels, but from Babylon He freed them without a single miracle. The manner in which He did so supplies a striking example of His providential workings and an illustrious illustration of how He shapes the history of nations.

"Now in the first year of Cyrus king of Persia, that the word of the LORD by the mouth of Jeremiah might be fulfilled, the LORD stirred up the spirit of Cyrus king of Persia, that he made a proclamation throughout all his kingdom, and put it also in writing, saying, Thus saith Cyrus king of Persia, The LORD God of Heaven hath given me all the kingdoms of the earth; and He hath charged me to build Him a house at Jerusalem, which is in Judah. Who is there among you of all His people? his God be with him, and let him go up to Jerusalem which is in Judah, and build the house of the LORD God of Israel (He is the God), which is in Jerusalem. And whosoever remaineth in any place where he sojourneth let the men of his place help him with silver, and with gold, and with goods, and with beasts, beside the freewill offering for the house of God that is in Jerusalem" (Ezra 1:1-4).

This is the famous Cyrus whose name occupies a prominent place upon the scroll of secular history. He was the ordained conqueror of Babylon, and when the empire of Nebuchadnezzar and Darius fell before his sword, instead of keeping the Jews in bondage, he decreed their liberation. But why should he do so? Was he a worshipper of Jehovah and a lover of His people? Far from it: he was a heathen idolater! The prophecy of Jeremiah had evidently been read by him, though it effected not his conversion, for he continued a devotee of his own gods. But God so impressed his mind by that prophecy, and secretly wrought in him a desire and determination to free the Jews that he made an authoritative proclamation to that effect. God gave His people favor in the eyes of the Persian king, and wrought in him both to will and to do of His good pleasure; yet in the forming and carrying out of his decision, Cyrus acted quite freely. Thus with the greatest of ease God can affect His own purpose, and without the use of force remove any obstacle standing in the way.

If (as so many students of prophecy believe) God has predestined that the Jews shall, after centuries of weary wandering among the Gentiles, once more occupy the land of Palestine, and if His time be now ripe for the fulfillment of that decree, then neither the Arabs nor anyone else can prevent their doing so. Whatever method or means God uses will in no wise alter the fact that there will be spread before the eyes of the world a demonstration that One immeasurably superior to man is ordering its affairs. Time will show: but up to now it looks as though God is repeating what He did in and through Cyrus. First, He moved the British Government to take over the mandatory control of Palestine, which has been administered for a quarter of a century at great inconvenience and at heavy cost of life and money, without a "thank you" from anyone. Now He has "stirred up the spirit" of the U.S. Government to insist on the entry of more and more Jews into that land. God has "His way in the whirlwind" (Nahum 1:3).

Let us now carefully consider the objection of the skeptic. If an infinitely wise and benevolent Being be in full control of all the affairs of earth, then why is there so much evil, so much suffering and sorrow? Justice is a rare commodity between individuals or nations— the ruthless and powerful seize the prey, while the conscientious and honest are despoiled. Mercy appears to be mainly a consideration of prudence, for who acts generously or leniently when another is thwarting his own interests?—witness, for example, the toll of the road. If a God of love presides over the scene, then why has He permitted the horrible holocaust of the past few years, with such widespread havoc and misery? The first answer is, Because the earth is inhabited by a rebellious race, which has revolted from its Maker, and is now being made to feel that "the way of transgressors is hard" (Prov. 13:15). Since man himself was the one who deliberately dashed into pieces the cup of felicity which was originally placed in his hands, he has no legitimate ground for complaint if he now finds that the potion which he has brewed for himself is as bitter as gall and wormwood.

The Infidel may reject with scorn the contents of the first three chapters of Genesis, but in so doing he casts away the only key which unlocks to us the meaning of human history, the only explanation which rationally accounts for the course of human affairs. If it be true that man was made by a holy and gracious God and was under moral obligations to serve and glorify Him, and if instead of so doing he cast off allegiance to Him and apostatized, what would we expect the consequences to be? Why, that man should be made to feel His displeasure and reap what he had sown. If this world lies under the righteous curse of its Creator because of man's sin and its Ruler be displaying His justice in punishing offenders and vindicating His broken Law, in what other ink than that of blood and tears may we expect human history to be written?! Does the alternative hypothesis of evolution offer a more satisfactory solution? Very far from it. If man started at the bottom of the ladder and during the course of the ages has gradually ascended, if the human race be slowly but surely improving, how comes is it that this twentieth century has witnessed such an unprecedented display of savagery and degradation?!

If an omniscient and beneficent God be governing this world, why is there so much wickedness and wretchedness in it? We answer, in the second place, to demonstrate the truth of His own Word The accounts which that Word gives of the corruptions of human nature have been widely refused, as being too gloomy a diagnosis of the same. The descriptions furnished by Scripture of man's depravity have been haughtily despised by the wise of this world. Nevertheless, the annals of human history furnish abundant verification of the same. It may not be palatable to read, "Behold, I was shapen in iniquity, and in sin did my mother conceive me" (Ps. 51:5), that "man is born like a wild ass's colt" (Job 11:12), that "The wicked are estranged from the womb, they go astray as soon as they be born, speaking lies" (Ps. 58:3)—yet universal observation discovers clear proof of the verity of the same. Children do not have to be taught to be intractable, to lie and steal. Remove restraints, leave them to themselves, and it quickly appears what is born and bred in them. The widespread juvenile delinquency of our own day is very far from exemplifying any progress of the human race!

It certainly is not flattering to proud human nature to be told in the unerring Word of Truth, that, as the result of the Fall, man's heart is "deceitful above all things and desperately wicked"

(Jer. 17:9), yet every newspaper we open contains illustrations of the teaching of Christ that, "out of the heart proceed evil thoughts, adulteries, fornications, murders, thefts, covetousness, wickedness, deceit, lasciviousness, an evil eye, blasphemy, pride, foolishness: all these evil things come from within, and defile the man" (Mark 7:21-23). Thousands of years ago God described mankind thus: "Their throat is an open sepulcher: with their tongues they have used deceit, the poison of asps is under their lips, whose mouth is full of cursing and bitterness. Their feet are swift to shed blood. Destruction and misery are in their ways, and the way of peace have they not known" (Rom. 3:13-17). And why is this? The closing words of the same passage tell us: "There is no fear of God before their eyes" (v. 18). Who that has any acquaintance with the chronicles of history can deny that indictment? Who with the present state of society before his eyes can deny it? The very Word of God which men will not receive by faith is being verified in their very sight!

Why does God permit so much human misery? We answer, in the third place, to manifest the glory of His own perfections. The frightful calamity of war causes many to deny or seriously doubt the reality of Divine Providence, for when that fearful scourge falls upon the nations, it appears to them that Satan, rather than the Lord, has charge of things and is the author of their troubles. At such a time God's own people may find it difficult to stay their minds on Him and rest implicitly in His wisdom and goodness. Yet the Word reveals that God is no mere distant Spectator of the bloody conflicts of men, but that His righteous and retributive agency is immediately involved therein, though that neither mitigates the guilt of the human instigators nor destroys their free agency. Their consuming egotism, insatiable greed, horrible barbarities—proceed entirely from themselves and are of their own volition; nevertheless, the Most High directs their lusts to the execution of His own designs and renders them subservient to His own honor.

The affairs of nations are ordered by a Divine hand. Their rise, development and progress are "of the Lord," so also are their decline, adversities and destruction. God's dealing with Israel of old was not exceptional, but illustrative of His ways with the Gentiles throughout the last 19 centuries. While Israel's ways pleased the Lord, He made their enemies to be at peace with them; but when they gave themselves up to idolatry and lasciviousness, war was one of His sore scourges upon them. Whenever Divine judgment falls upon either an individual or a nation, it is because sin has called loudly for Him to vindicate His honor and enforce the penalty of His Law. Yet warning is always given before He strikes: "space to repent" is provided, the call to forsake that which displeases Him, opportunity to avert His wrath—and if this warning be disregarded and the opportunity to escape His vengeance be not improved—then is His judgment doubly righteous. Ordinarily God makes use of men—a Nebuchadnezzar, a Caesar, a Hitler—as the instruments by which His judgment is inflicted, thereby demonstrating His sovereignty over all, who can do nothing without Him, yet who must play the part which He has ordained.

In various ways does the Ruler of this world manifest the glory of His attributes. By the display of His infinite patience in bearing with so much longsuffering those who defy Him to His face and continue in their obduracy. By exhibiting the exceeding riches of His mercy in sometimes calling the most outrageous rebels out of darkness into His marvelous light, bringing them to repentance and granting them pardon: thus it was with King Manasseh and Saul of Tarsus. By manifesting the strictness of His untempered justice in hardening others in sin to their own destruction. "Behold therefore the goodness and the severity of God: on them which fell, severity; but toward thee goodness, if thou continue in His goodness: otherwise thou shalt also be cut off" (Rom. 11:22). By showing forth His wondrous power, both in directing and curbing human passions. "Surely the wrath of man shall praise Thee [as that of Pharaoh's was made to do]: the remainder of wrath shalt Thou restrain" (Ps. 76:10), for He holds in check the fiercest as much as He sets bounds to the turbulent seas.

The depravity of human nature, the potency and prevalence of evil, and the power and malice of the Wicked One in whom the whole world lies, only makes more evident and wonderful the Providence of God. Since holiness be so universally hated and the saints of the Lord so detested and persecuted by the great majority of their fellow men, had not God so signally interposed for their preservation, the last of His people had long since perished amid the enmity and fury of their implacable enemies. Were there no other evidence that the living God governs this world, this one should suffice: that though His servants and sons have been so strenuously opposed in this scene, yet they have never been totally rooted out of it; that though the most powerful governments have sought their complete destruction, and though they were weak and possessed of no material weapons, yet a remnant always survived!—as real a marvel that is as the preservation of the three Hebrew youths in the fiery furnace of Babylon.

What has just been pointed out has not received the attention which it justly claims, for it is a conspicuous feature of history and one that has been frequently repeated. The saints of God in Old Testament times, in the early centuries of this Christian era, and throughout the Dark Ages, when both pagan and papal Rome made the most determined efforts to completely annihilate them, had good reason to confess, "If it had not been the LORD who was on our side, when men rose up against us, then they had swallowed us up quick, when their wrath was kindled against us. Then the waters had overwhelmed us, the stream had gone over our soul; then the proud waters had gone over our soul. Blessed be the LORD who hath not given us as a prey to their teeth" (Ps. 124:2-6). It is quite possible, perhaps likely, that before this present century has run its course, the restraining hand of God will again be wholly removed from their foes and His people subjected to martyrdom. Should such prove the case, He will, unto the end, maintain to Himself a witness in the earth.

Why is there so much suffering and sorrow in this world? Fourth, for the good and gain of God's own people. As there is not a little in the realm of creation which sorely puzzles both the naturalist and the scientist—as there is much in God's written Word that is opposed to proud reason—so many of His governmental works often appear profoundly mysterious. That the wicked should prosper so much and flourish as the green bay tree, while the righteous are often in sore straits and at their wit's end to make ends meet; that the most unscrupulous attain unto positions of prestige and power, while the most virtuous and pious have been counted as "the offscouring of all things," and ended their days in a dungeon or by suffering a cruel martyrdom; that when God's judgments fall upon a nation they are no respecter of persons, the relatively innocent suffering from them as severely as the most guilty—these and similar cases which might be instanced present real problems to those who reflect upon the same.

True, but the more thoughtfully they be examined, especially in view of the hereafter, the less difficulty they present. The thoughts of the materialist and skeptic extend no farther than the narrow bounds of this life, and consequently he sees these things in a false perspective. Because of their misuse of them, the temporal mercies enjoyed by the wicked become a curse, hardening them in their sins and fattening them for the slaughter. On the other hand, afflictions often prove a blessing in disguise unto believers, weaning their affections from the things of earth and causing them to seek their joy in things above. God often thwarts their carnal plans because He would have their hearts occupied with better objects. The more they are dissatisfied in the creature and discover that everything under the sun yields only vanity and vexation of spirit, the more inducement have they to cultivate a closer communion with the One who can fully satisfy their souls.

It is not meet that the righteous should always be in a prosperous and happy case in their temporal estate, for then they would be most apt to seek their rest therein. On the other hand, if their portion were that of unrelieved affliction and misery, while the lot of the wicked was uniformly one of plenty and ease, that would be too severe a trial of faith. Therefore God wisely mixes His dispensations with each class respectively. God so orders His Providences that His people shall live by faith and not by sight or sense. That is not only for their happiness, but for God's honor. He frequently regulates things so that it may appear that the saints trust Him in the dark as well as in the light. An outstanding example of that is seen in the case of Job, who was afflicted as few have ever been. Yet in his blackest hour he averred, "though He slay me, yet will I trust in Him" (13:15). How greatly is He glorified by such conduct! Tribulations are needful for the testing of profession, that the difference between the wheat and the chaff may appear. Heresies are necessary that lovers of Truth may be made manifest (1 Cor. 11:19). Trials are indispensable, that patience may have her perfect work.

If in every instance the righteous were rewarded and the wicked punished in this life, the Day of judgment would be fully anticipated: but by furnishing some present instances of both the one and the other, the great Assize is presaged and the government of God vindicated. If temporal mercies and spiritual blessings were now evenly distributed, no demonstration would be made of the absolute sovereignty of Him who dispenses His favors as He pleases, and bestows upon or withholds from each individual that which seems good unto Himself. There are not more inequalities in the dispensations of Providence than in the realm of creation. In its widest aspect there is a noticeable and striking balance observable in the apportionment of mercies. As in Old Testament times Divine favors were largely confined to the seed of Abraham, so in the New Testament era unto the Gentiles. Something analogous thereto is seen in God's conduct toward the eastern and western parts of the earth. For 2,000 years after the Flood, learning, government and piety were largely confined to the east, while our forefathers in the west were a horde of savages. For the last 2,000 years the Gospel, with all its beneficent by-products, has traveled westward. Perhaps in the next 2,000 years it will again move eastward.

The living God controls all circumstances, commands all events, rules every creature, makes all their energies and actions fulfill His will, provides a sure and comfortable resting place for the heart. The present outlook may be dismal, but God reigns and is making all things work together for the glory of His name and the good of His people. If the human race is to occupy this earth for several more generations, or perhaps many centuries, then certain it is that out of the throes through which it is now passing shall issue the furtherance of the Gospel and the promotion of Christ's kingdom. The annals of human affairs can only be read intelligently and interpreted aright as we perceive that history is His-story. In the final Day of Manifestation it will be plain to all that, "He hath done all things well"; meanwhile, faith now knows that it is so.

Chapter 4
THE EXISTENCE OF GOD AS UNVEILED IN THE LORD JESUS CHRIST

In the dispensations of His Providence, the revelation which God has made of Himself unto mankind has been a progressive one. First, He is manifested in the realm of creation, and that with sufficient clearness as to leave all without excuse if they perceive not that He is. Second, God is revealed in man himself, so that his very constitution evinces his Divine origin and his conscience bears witness of his accountability to his Maker. Third, God is plainly to be seen in human history: most patently in His dealings with the Jews during the past 35 centuries; yet with sufficient clearness everywhere as to attest that He is the moral Governor of this world, the Regulator of human affairs. But over and above these—O wonder of wonders—God has become incarnate. In the Person of His blessed and co-equal Son, God deigned to clothe Himself in our flesh and blood and manifest Himself unto the sons of men. For the space of 33 years He appeared among men and displayed His glory before their eyes; yea, gave proof of His matchless mercy by performing a work, at infinite cost to Himself, which has made it possible for Him to righteously save the very chief of sinners.

"In the beginning was the Word, and the Word was with God, and the Word was God. . . and the Word became flesh and dwelt among us" (John 1:1, 14). It is by means of words that we make known our wills, reveal the caliber of our minds and the character of our hearts, and communicate information unto others. Appropriately, then, is Christ designated, "The Word of God," for He has made the Transcendent immanent, the incomprehensible God intelligible to us. Thus, too, is He denominated "the image of the invisible God" (Col. 1:15) and the "Alpha and the Omega" (Rev. 1:8)—the One who spells out the Deity unto us. "The only begotten Son, which is in the bosom of the Father, He hath declared" or "told Him forth" (John 1:18). In Christ's life of impeccable purity, we behold God's holiness; in His utter selflessness, God's benevolence; in His peerless teaching, God's wisdom; in His unrivalled miracles, God's power; in His gentleness and longsuffering, God's patience; in His love and grace, the outshining of God's glory.

The record of Christ's unprecedented life is found in the four Gospels. Those Gospels were written by men who were constantly in Christ's company during the days of His ministry, being an ungarnished record of what they personally saw with their own eyes and heard with their own ears. Numerous copies of those Gospels have been in known existence since the first century of this Christian era. Only three explanations of them are feasible. First, that they were written by deluded fanatics. But the character of their contents, the calmness of their tenor, the absence of anything savoring of enthusiasm, cause anyone capable of weighing evidence to promptly reject such an hypothesis. The dreams of visionaries had never received such widespread credence. Second, that they were the inventions of deceitful men. But that could not be, otherwise their contemporaries had exposed them as impostors. Wicked men could not have devised the Sermon on the Mount. Third, that they were written by honest men, who chronicled actual facts.

The Person of the Lord Jesus presents a baffling problem, yea, an insoluble enigma unto infidelity. Skepticism is quite unable to supply any rational explanation of the phenomenon which He presents. Yet, "what think ye of Christ?" is a question which cannot be avoided or evaded by anyone who professes to use his reasoning powers or lays any claim to being an educated person. The obvious fact confronts believer and unbeliever alike that the appearing of Jesus Christ on the stage of this world has exerted a more powerful, lasting, and extensive influence than has any other person, factor, or event that can be named. To say that Christ has revolutionized human history is only to affirm what His bitterest foes are compelled to acknowledge. He dwelt in no palace, led no army, overthrew no mundane empire, yet His fame has spread to the ends of the earth. He wrote no book, framed no philosophy, erected no temple—yet He occupies a place in literature and religion which none else has ever achieved. How is this to be explained? Unbelief can furnish no answer! Nor can it refute, for the historicity of Christ is established far more conclusively than that of Socrates and Plato.

Viewed simply from the human plane the Lord Jesus presents a phenomenon which admits of no human explanation. The law of heredity cannot account for Him, for He transcends all merely racial characteristics. Though according to the flesh He was the Son of Abraham, yet He is bounded by no Jewish limitations. Instead, He is the Man of men, the Pattern Man. The Englishman and the Dutchman, with their vastly different racial temperaments, the stolid German and the warm Italian behold their Ideal in Christ: He rises above all national restrictions. The law of environment cannot explain Him, for He was born in poverty, lived in a small town, received no collegiate training, toiled at the carpenter's bench. Such an environment was not conducive to the development of thought and teaching which was to enlighten the whole world. Christ transcends all laws. There is nothing provincial about Him. "The Son of man" is His fitting title, for He is the Representative Man.

Christ was not tinctured or affected by the age in which He lived. And that can be said of no one else. Study the characters and teaching of any of the outstanding figures of history, and we are at once aware that they were colored by their own generation. By common consent we make certain allowances for those who lived in former times, and agree that it would not be just to measure them by present-day ideals. Men of the most sterling worth were, in measure, marred by the crudities, coarseness, or superstitions of their contemporaries. But the Lord Jesus is the grand Exception. You may test Him by the light of this twentieth century—if light it be—or you may judge Him by any century, and no lack or blemish is to be found in Him. His teaching was pure Truth without any mixture of error, and therefore it stands the test of all time. His teaching was neither affected by the prevailing traditions of Judaism, by that of Grecian philosophy, nor by any other influence then abroad. The timeless value of Christ's teaching is without parallel. That of Socrates and Plato has long since become obsolete, but Christ's is as pertinent and potent now as the day He uttered it.

There is no part of Christ's teaching which the subsequent growth of human knowledge has had to discredit. Therein it is in marked contrast with that of all other men, whose dicta have to be constantly revised and brought up to date. There is a universal quality to His teaching which is found in none other's—an originality, a loftiness, an adaptability. There is nothing petty, local, or transient about it. It is of general application, suited to all generations and to all peoples. It possesses a vital and vitalizing freshness without a parallel. It is profound enough for the mightiest intellect, practical enough for the artisan, simple enough for the little child. It is profitable for youth, for maturity, and old age alike. It furnishes that which is needed by those in prosperity, brings comfort to those in adversity, and has imparted a peace which passes all understanding to thousands who lay upon beds of suffering, and while they passed through the valley of the shadow of death. Those are facts attested by a multitude of witnesses whose testimony cannot be fairly impeached.

Unto Christ the master minds of the ages have paid homage. Such mighty intellects as Lord Bacon and Isaac Newton, Michael Faraday and Lord Kelvin, Milton and Handel; Calvin and John Locke, and a host of others who towered above their fellows in mental acumen and genius, bowed before Him in adoring worship. Not that Christianity is in any need of human patronage to authenticate it, but that it may be evinced to the thoughtful ones of this rising generation that Christians are far from being a company of credulous simpletons. Christianity is not something suited only to little children or old ladies in their dotage. When the young men of this age behold such hard-headed men as General Dobbie, the valiant defender of Malta, and Field Marshal Montgomery, the Commander-in-chief of the British Army, unashamedly acknowledging Christ as their personal Lord and Savior, they have before them that which clearly challenges them to seriously consider the claims of Christ and carefully examine His teachings— instead of contemptuously ignoring the same as something unworthy of their best attention.

Napoleon Bonaparte, the military genius of a century ago, declared, "Alexander, Caesar, Charlemagne and myself have founded empires, but upon what did those creations of our genius depend? Upon force. Jesus Christ alone established His empire upon love, and to this very day millions would die for Him. I think I understand something of human nature, and I tell you, those were men and I am a man; Jesus Christ is more than a man. I have inspired multitudes with such an enthusiastic devotion that they would have died for me . . .but to do this it was necessary that I should be visibly present, with the electric influence of my looks, of my words, of my voice. When I saw men and spoke to them, I lighted up the flame of self-devotion in their hearts. Christ alone has succeeded in raising the mind of men toward the Unseen, that it becomes insensible to the barriers of time and space. Across a chasm of 1,800 years Jesus Christ makes a demand which is, beyond all others, difficult to satisfy.

"He asks for the human heart. He will have it entirely for and to Himself. He demands it unconditionally, and forthwith His demand is granted. Wonderful! In defiance of time and space, the soul of man, with all its powers and faculties, is annexed to the empire of Christ. All who simply believe in Him experience that remarkable, supernatural love towards Him. This phenomenon is unaccountable: it is altogether beyond the scope of man's creative powers. Time, the great destroyer, is powerless to extinguish this sacred flame; time cannot exhaust its strength, nor put a limit to its reign. This it is which strikes me most. I have often thought of it. This it is which proves to me quite convincingly the Divinity of Jesus Christ." Paul Richter said of Christ: "The holiest among the mighty, the mightiest among the holy, who with His pierced hands has lifted empires off their hinges, turned the stream of centuries out of its channel, and still governs the ages."

Alexander, Napoleon, Lincoln, are dead, and we refer to them in the past tense. But not so with Christ. We do not think or speak of Him as One who was, but as One who is. The Lord Jesus is far more than a memory. He is the great "I am": the same yesterday and today and forever. He is more real to mankind, His influence still more prevalent, His followers more numerous in this twentieth century than they were in the first. On what principle, scientifically, can we rationally account for the dynamical influence of the Lord Jesus today? That One now at a distance of almost two millenniums is still molding human thought, attracting human hearts, transforming human lives, with such mighty sway that He stands forth from all other teachers as the sun makes the stars recede into dimness and pale before the luster of His refulgence. As a strictly scientific question, the mystery of Christ's influence demands an adequate solution. It requires neither science nor philosophy to deny, but it does to explain. The only satisfactory explanation is that Christ is God, omnipotent and omnipresent.

We call attention now to what has well been termed "The Logic of the Changed Calendar": what follows is an enlargement of some notes we made nearly forty years ago from a book entitled The Unrealized Logic of Religion. Few people stop to inquire for an explanation of one of the most amazing facts which is presented to the notice of everybody, namely, the fact that all civilized time is dated from the birth of Jesus Christ. This is the twentieth century, and from what event are those centuries dated? From the birth of a Jew, who, according to the view of Infidels, if He ever existed, was a peasant in an obscure province, who was the author of no wonderful invention, who occupied no throne, who died when, as men count years, He had scarcely reached his prime, and who died the death of a criminal. Now if the Lord Jesus Christ were nothing more than what skeptics will allow, then is it not utterly unthinkable that the chronology of the civilized world should be reckoned from His birth? The effect must correspond to the cause, and there is no agreement between such a phenomenon and such an inadequate producer.

To have some common measure of time is, of course, a necessity of organized society, but where shall we find an adequate starting point for the calendar?—i.e., one which will be acceptable to all civilized nations! A world-shattering victory, the founding of some many-centuried city, the birth of a dynasty, the beginning of a revolution: some such event, it might reasonably be expected, would give time a new starting point. But no conqueror's sword has ever cut deep enough on Time to leave an enduring mark. The Julian era, the Alexandria era, the era of the Sileucidae—all had their brief day and have vanished. There is for civilized men but one suitable, enduring and universally recognized starting point for civilized time, and that is the manger at Bethlehem! And how is that strange yet startling fact to be explained? It was imposed neither by the authority of a conqueror, the device of priests, the enactment of a despot, nor even by Constantine; but by slow and gradual consent.

The name of Jesus Christ did not emerge in the calendar till five centuries after His death—a space of time long enough for Him to be forgotten had He been an impostor. It took another 500 years to become universally accepted; and the process is linked to no human name. Here, then, is a phenomenon that skepticism cannot explain: that without any conspiracy of Christian fanatics Jesus Christ has altered the almanacs of the world. The one event which towers above the horizon of history serves as a landmark to measure time for all civilized races. The Lord of time has indelibly written His signature across time itself; the years of the modern world being labeled by common consent the years of our Lord! Every letter you receive (though penned by an atheist), every newspaper carrying the date of its issue (though published by Communists), bears testimony to the historicity of Christ! The One who entered this world to shape its history to a new pattern changed its calendar from A.M. to A.D.

All that had transpired previously in human history counted for nothing. The name of the most famous of the world's generals or of its most powerful monarchs was not deemed worthy to be imprinted upon all succeeding centuries. By a deep, unanimous, inarticulate and yet irresistible instinct, each nation has recognized and recorded on its almanacs the true starting point of its life. Several attempts have been made to establish another point of departure for recorded time. Islam has made a faint but broken mark upon the centuries, relating time to the sword; but the Moslem almanac is confined to but a cluster of half-civilized races. La Place, the astronomer, proposed to give stability and dignity to human chronology by linking it to the stars, but the world approved not. France sought to popularize its Revolution, and count 1793 as year one, but her calendar lasted but 13 years. The centuries belong to Christ and pay homage to Him by bearing

His name!

Men and women of all ages, who are at present being tossed to and fro upon a sea of doubt, there is no reason why you should remain there. It will be your own fault if you fail to secure firm ground to stand upon. You may imagine Christians make an idle boast when they affirm "we know," and declare, "That is exactly what you do not: you suppose, you hope, you believe. The dream may be alluring, the hope pleasing, but you cannot be sure." If so, you err. The children of God have infallible proof, and if you follow the right course, assurance will be yours too. The value and Divinity of Christ's teaching may be personally verified by yourself. How? "If any man will do His will," said Christ, "he shall know of the doctrine" (John 7:17). If you will read the record of it in the Gospels, submit to Christ's authority, conform to His requirements, regulate your life by His precepts, then you shall obtain a settled conviction that He "spoke as never man spoke," that His are the words of Truth.

Nay, further. If you be an honest inquirer, prepared to follow the Truth wherever it leads—and it will be out of the mists of skepticism and away from the fogs of uncertainty—you may obtain definite and conclusive proof that Christ is and that He is the Rewarder of those who diligently seek Him. His invitation is, "If any man thirst, let him come unto Me and drink" (John 7:37), and upon compliance, He promises to satisfy that thirst. Test Him for yourself If the empty cisterns of this world—their poor pleasures or their intellectual speculations—have failed to satisfy your soul, Christ can. He declares, "Come unto Me all ye that labor and are heavy laden, and I will give you rest" (Matt. 11:28). If you have toiled in vain for peace and your conscience be burdened with a sense of guilt, then cast yourself on the mercy of Christ right now, and you shall find "rest unto your soul"—such as this world can neither give nor take away. Then you, too, will know the reality and certainty of His so great salvation. Put Him to the test!

Part Two-The Holy Bible
Chapter 5
THE HOLY BIBLE GOD'S WRITTEN COMMUNICATION

In our preceding chapters we have called attention to some of the evidences which demonstrate the existence of God as seen in the revelation which He has made of Himself in creation, in man himself, in His shaping of human history, and in the Person of His incarnate Son. We turn now to that written communication which He has vouchsafed us, namely, the Scriptures, commonly designated "the Bible," which means "The Book," or more reverently "The Holy Bible"—the Book which is separated from and exalted above all others, the Sacred Book. Concerning it the Psalmist averred, "Thou hast magnified Thy Word above all Thy name" (Ps. 138:2): that is, beyond all previous manifestations of the Divine Being. In the Holy Scriptures God has made a full discovery of Himself and a complete disclosure of His will. There His glories are set forth in their meridian clarity and splendor. The Word is a glass in which the character and perfections of God may be seen, and in order to become better acquainted with Him we need to more diligently peruse the same. Alas that so very few of this generation do so. Alas that so many preachers discourage such a duty.

Nearly 40 years ago, in one of our earliest publications, we wrote: "To all who are acquainted with the spiritual conditions of our day it is apparent that there is being made at this time a determined attempt to set aside the authority of the Bible. In the press, the pulpit and the pew, its Divine Authorship is being questioned and denied. The Serpent's words to Eve 'Yea, hath God said?' are being heard in every quarter of Christendom. The ancient 'landmarks' of our fathers are being abandoned, the foundation of our religion undermined, and for the most part the Bible is no longer regarded as the Word of God.

"In every age the Bible has been the object of attack and assault: every available weapon in the Devil's arsenal has been used in the effort to destroy the Temple of God's Truth. In the first days of the Christian era the attack of the enemy was made openly—the bonfire being the chief instrument of destruction. But in these 'last days' the assault is made in a more subtle manner, and comes from a more unexpected quarter. The Divine origin of the Scriptures is now disputed in the name of 'Scholarship' and 'Science,' and that, too, by those who profess to be the friends and champions of the Bible. Much of the learning and theological activities of the hour are concentrated in the attempt to discredit and destroy the accuracy and authority of God's Word. The result is that thousands of nominal Christians are plunged into a sea of doubt and tossed about by every wind of the destructive 'Higher Criticism.' Many of those who are paid to stand in our pulpits and defend the Truth of God are now the very ones engaged in sowing the seed of unbelief and destroying the faith of those to whom they minister."

Today we behold some of the fearful crops which have resulted from that evil sowing: "some of," we say, for it is greatly to be feared that the full harvest does not yet appear. Shocking and appalling is the situation which is already spread before us. It has become increasingly evident, even to man who make no pretensions unto spirituality, that the restraining hand of God has been more and more removed from the world, till a spirit of utter lawlessness and recklessness now possesses a large proportion of mankind. But only those with an anointed eye can perceive why this is so, namely because the influence formerly exerted by God's Word was suppressed. The majority of church-goers of the preceding generations had instilled into them doubts upon the authenticity of Holy Writ: theological professors and "up-to-date" preachers openly denied its supernatural character. Once the awe-inspiring authority of God's Word was removed, the most potent bridle upon the lusts and passions of the masses was gone. Where there is no longer any fear of Divine judgment after death, what is left to curb the activities of sin?

The present state of society is due to the infidelity of "the churches" during the past century, and the apostasy of Christendom began by losing its grip upon the basic truth of the Divine inspiration of the Scriptures. And there is no hope whatever of Christendom being recovered from its present corrupt condition and woeful plight until it regains that grip, until it recognizes and avows that the Bible is a messenger from Heaven, a direct communication from God, imperiously demanding complete subjection of conscience to its authority and total subjugation of the mind and will to its requirements. It has, therefore, become the imperative duty of God's servants to put first things first: to affirm with clarion voice the Divine inspiration and authority of the Holy Bible, to present to their hearers some of the many "infallible proofs" by which it is authenticated, that they may "know the certainty of those things" (Luke 1:4) wherein they are instructed. Thereby God Himself will be honored, a sure foundation laid for faith to rest upon, the only specific provided for the disease of materialism and infidelity, and the lone barrier against the inroads of Romanism.

There is not a shadow of doubt in our mind that Rome was behind the "Higher Criticism" movement of the last century, just as she was of the introduction and spread of Arminianism in England (through Laud) shortly after the Reformation. The Papacy was shrewd enough to recognize that the authority of God's Word must be undermined and its influence upon the nation weakened, before she had any hope of bringing it within her deadly toils. There is nothing she hates and dreads so much as the Bible, especially when it is circulated among the common people in their own tongue, as was clearly shown in the days of Queen Mary, of infamous memory. The organization of the Bible Societies, with their enormous output, was a rude shock to Rome, but she promptly countered it through "Modernism," by discrediting the inerrancy of the Scriptures. The promulgation of the so-called "Higher Criticism" has done far more for the spread of infidelity among the masses than did the coarse blasphemies of Tom Paine; and it is among those who have no settled convictions that Rome wins most of her converts!

Now, the most effective way to oppose error is to preach the Truth, as the way to dispel darkness from a room is to let in or turn on the light. Satan is well pleased if he can induce those whom God has called to expound His Law and proclaim His Gospel to turn aside and seek to expose the fallacies of the various cults and isms. When the disciples of Christ informed Him that the Pharisees were offended at His teaching, He bade them, "Let them alone: they be blind leaders of the blind" (Matthew 15:14)—waste no time upon them. When the servants of the Householder asked permission to remove the tares which His enemy had sown in His field, He forbade them (Matthew 13:29). The business of Christ's ministers is to sow, and continue sowing the good Seed, and not to root up tares! Their work is to be a positive and constructive one, and not merely a negative and destructive thing. Their task is to "preach the Word" (2 Tim. 4:2), faithfully and diligently, in dependency upon the Spirit, looking to God for His blessing upon the same. And what is so urgently needed today is that they proclaim with earnest conviction, "All Scripture is given by inspiration of God" (2 Tim. 3:16).

That claim is no empty one, but rather one that is attested by unimpeachable witnesses and verified by incontrovertible evidence. It bears in it and upon it the infallible tokens of its Divine origin, and it is the bounden duty and holy privilege of God's servants to present, simply and convincingly, some of the various and conclusive evidence which demonstrates the uniqueness of the Bible. They cannot possibly engage in a more important and needed task than in seeking to establish their hearers in the Divine inspiration of the Scriptures, for it is of the greatest possible moment they should be thoroughly settled in that truth. The human mind cannot engage itself with any inquiry more momentous than this: "Has the Bible come from God? Is it a Divine revelation and communication addressed unto us personally from our Maker?" If it is, then it has claims upon us such as are possessed by no other writings. If it is not, then it is a wicked imposter, utterly unworthy of our serious consideration. Those are the sole alternatives. Hence, this is "the doctrine of doctrines: the doctrine that teaches us all others, and in virtue of which alone they are doctrines" (Gaussen).

Before we call attention to some of the abundant and varied evidence which makes manifest the Divine inspiration of the Scriptures, perhaps we should meet an objection which a few may be inclined to raise: Is it not largely a waste of time for you to furnish demonstration of a truth which no genuine Christian doubts? We do not think so. All of God's people are not equally well established, and in any case faith cannot have too firm a foothold, especially in a day when the tide of infidelity is seeking to sweep everything away into the sea of skepticism. It is good for Christians themselves to be more fully assured that they have not followed "cunningly devised fables," but have an unmistakable, "Thus saith the Lord" as the foundation of all their hopes. Moreover, as another has pointed out, "Faith needs food as well as foothold, and it is upon these Divine verities, so plainly revealed and so clearly established in the Word of Truth, that faith finds its choicest provision."

Further, these evidences are of value to the Christian in that they enable him to give an intelligent and rational answer to those who inquire after knowledge. God requires His people to "be ready always to give an answer to every man that asketh you a reason of the hope that is in you, with meekness and reverence" (1 Pet. 3:15). Thus we must be able to reply to any who seriously ask us, Wherefore do you believe the Bible to be the Word of God? But our chief desire and design will be to furnish young preachers with material to use in sermons, aimed at resolving the perplexities and removing the doubts which perturb not a few of their hearers, and so counter and nullify the infidelities of modern "education." Yet here again we must anticipate an objection: Since the regenerate alone are capable of discerning spiritual things, why attempt to convince the unregenerate that the Bible is a Divine book? If faith be the sole ear competent to hear the voice of God, why try to reason with unbelievers?

While it is true that no arguments, however convincing in themselves, can remove the veil of prejudice from the understanding of the unregenerate or convert the heart unto God, yet that is far from allowing that such means possess no value. It has often been said by good men that the Scriptures are addressed to faith. That is true, yet only a part of the truth, for if it were taken absolutely it must follow they are not addressed to any devoid of faith, which is a palpable error. Our Lord bade the skeptical Jews, "search the Scriptures," and declared, "He that rejecteth Me and receiveth not My words hath one that judgeth him: the Word that I have spoken the same shall judge him in the last day" (John 12:48), thereby showing plainly the natural man is under binding obligations to heed and be subject unto the Word! The fact is that the Word is addressed to man as a rational creature, as a moral agent, as a responsible being, and it carries its own evidence—evidence which is addressed both to the reason and conscience.

"These arguments are such as are able of themselves to beget in the minds of men—sober, humble, intelligent and unprejudiced—a firm opinion, judgment and persuasion that the Scripture doth proceed from God" (J. Owen). They are evidences which show the irrationality of infidelity, and render those faced with them without excuse for rejecting the same. They are such as nothing but perverse prejudice can restrain men from assenting thereto. It is a fact that of those who have written against the Bible not one has soberly and seriously undertaken to refute the evidence which they knew had been adduced for the veracity of its history, the fulfillment of its miracles, and the purity and consistency of its doctrine. They close the mouths of gainsayers. Such arguments afford relief to the mind from the objections of skeptics, for if weighed impartially they must produce a moral assurance of the truth of Scripture. Thus they dispose the mind to approach the Bible with confidence and pave the way for receiving it as God's Word.

Such arguments go to show that Christians are not a company of credulous simpletons, but have good reason for their faith. They are a means of strengthening and establishing those who have accepted the Bible on less satisfactory grounds. Few look farther than human authority and public countenance. The majority believe the Scriptures in the same way as Mohammedans do the Koran: because it is the tradition of their fathers. But wisdom is to be justified of her children, so that they walk in her ways by a rational choice. When the Spouse is asked, "What, is thy Beloved more than another beloved?" (Song. 5:9), she is not backward in making reply; and when the worldling asks, "What, is your Bible above what the heathen appeal to in support of their superstitions," we should be able to give an intelligent answer.

Nevertheless some are still apt to conclude it is useless to enter into such a discussion, insisting that the Bible is to be believed and not argued about, that arguments at best will only produce a human faith. But it is not a thing to be despised if we can prepare the young to respect God's Word, and then seek the Spirit's confirmation. Sometimes a human faith makes way for a Divine. The testimony borne by the woman from the well issued in that very sequel: "Now we believe, not because of thy saying, but we have heard Him ourselves and know that this is indeed the Christ, the Savior of the world" (John 4:39, 42). It is much to be thankful for when we can persuade people upon good grounds that the Bible is the Word of God, so that they are induced to make trial of it for themselves, for often that leads to their obtaining an experimental verification from the Holy Spirit. The revelation which God has made of Himself unto mankind through His wondrous works, both in creation and in providence, are addressed unto their reasoning faculty, and render them without excuse for their unbelief of His existence. Equally so is the more complete discovery of Himself which God has given to the world in His written Word addressed to the intelligence and conscience of those favored with it, and therefore will it in the Day to come condemn all who refused to conform unto the Divine will as it is there made known to them. Hence it behooves preachers to press the inerrancy and Divine authority of the Holy Bible.

Chapter 6
THE HOLY BIBLE ADDRESSED
TO REASON AND CONSCIENCE

That the Living Oracles of Truth are addressed to the reason of men as well as their conscience is definitely established by the fact that God Himself appeals to prophecy in proof of the unrivalled character of the communications He made through His servants. Their messages were retrospective as well as prospective, treating of things of the remotest antiquity as well as of those which lay centuries ahead, and thus commanded the entire horizon of history past and future. Their Divine Author places such peculiar value and attaches such importance to those supernatural disclosures as an evidence of inspiration that not less than seven times in the prophecy of Isaiah alone He challenges any false faith or idolatrous cult the world over to produce any revelations like unto His. "Produce your cause, saith the LORD; bring forth your strong reasons, saith the King of Jacob. Let them bring forth and show us what shall happen: let them show the former things, what they be, that we may consider them and know the latter end of them, or declare us things for to come" (41:21, 22).

"Behold, the former things are come to pass, and new things do I declare: before they spring forth I tell you of them" (42:9). "Let all the nations be gathered together and let the people be assembled: who among them can declare this, and show us former things? [such as the creation of the earth, and everything else recorded in the book of Genesis]: let them bring forth their witnesses, that they may be justified [in their claims]; or let them hear, and say, it is truth" (43:9). "I have declared the former things from the beginning; and they went forth out of My mouth, and I showed them; I did them suddenly, and they came to pass" (48:3). None of the seers of false religion can show either "the former things" or the "latter things": their outlook is restricted to the present. Only the Omniscient One can endow His messengers with a vision which reaches back before history began and which looks forward to ages not yet historic.

Again—that the Word of God is addressed to the reason of men is proven from the fact that appeal is made to the miracles recorded therein. "And many other signs [i.e. miracles—Acts 2:22] truly did Jesus in the presence of His disciples (who have recorded many of them] which are not written in this book. But these are written that ye might believe that Jesus is the Christ, the Son of God: and that believing, ye might have life through His name" (John 20:30, 31). The record of the various wonders wrought by God are given in Scripture not merely to furnish information, but to convince us that He is the Author of the Book which chronicles the same, and to bring our hearts and lives in full submission to His authority—and that we receive as our personal Lord and Savior the One who is Himself God manifest in flesh, and therefore the final Spokesman from Heaven. Those whom God employed as His penmen gave to the world a Divine revelation, and He accredited the same with due evidences, so that any receiving them are left without excuse if they despise and reject them.

Now it should be quite evident that if God is to give a personal communication unto fallen man, who is full of unbelief and skepticism, it will be supported with something more than the ordinary evidence of human testimony—that it will be supplemented by extraordinary evidence. A Divine revelation will be confirmed by Divine insignia. If God is to speak audibly to those who forsook Him, it can only be in a way out of the common course. If He commissions messengers to declare His will, they must possess such credentials as demonstrate that they come from Him. Each Prophet sent from Him must be authenticated by Him. Those bearing supernatural messages will reasonably be expected to possess supernatural seals and be accompanied with supernatural phenomena. If God directly intervenes to instruct and legislate for the children of men, then clearly revelations and miracles must cooperate and combine. But here the Infidel will at once demur, and deny that miracles are either possible or credible.

Nothing is easier than for an atheist to affirm that since the universe exists by eternal necessity and is subject to no change, that miracles cannot take place; but it is impossible for him to make anything approaching a satisfactory demonstration of that assertion. We do not propose to enter upon a lengthy discussion of the subject, deeming it sufficient to appeal to what has been presented in the previous chapters as proof that God is, that He created the universe, and is now presiding over it. And then to point out, first, that what men term "the course of nature" is nothing but the agency of God. To declare that either a suspension or an alteration of the laws of nature is impossible, is to endow those laws with the attributes of Deity, and to be guilty of the absurdity of saying that the Lawgiver is subordinate to His own laws. The workman is ever superior to his works, and if God be the Creator and Governor of Heaven and earth then He must be free to interfere in His own works whenever He pleases, and to make such interference manifest, by suspending or altering those laws by which He is pleased normally to regulate them.

"What is called the usual course of nature, then, is nothing else than the will of God, producing certain effects in a continual, regular, constant and uniform manner; which course or manner of acting being in every moment arbitrary, is as easy to be altered at any time as to be preserved. . . . To assert the impossibility of a miracle is absurd, for no man can prove, nor is there any reason to believe, that to work a miracle is a greater exercise of power than those usual operations which we daily witness. To restore life to a dead body and to bring it forth from the grave is not attended with any more difficulty than to communicate life to a fetus and to bring it forth from the womb. Both are equally beyond the power of man; both are equally possible with God. In respect of the power of God, all things are alike easy to be done by Him. The power of God extends equally to great things as to small, and to many as to few; and the one makes no more difficulty or resistance to His will than the other" (Robert Haldane).

To proceed one step farther. In a world which is upheld and governed by the living God, miracles are not only possible but credible, because probable. If the arrangement of nature be designed for the glory of its Maker and the good of His creatures, then it becomes in the highest degree likely that when any end of extraordinary importance is to be attained, that the laws of nature in their uniform course should be altered and made subservient to that event, that it should be heralded and evinced by extraordinary manifestations. Not only will the laws of the natural world become subservient to any great moral end, but they will be made to promote it. Since the laws of nature be under the direct management of their own Legislator, then not only may He moderate those laws at His own pleasure, but it is reasonable to conclude that He will make those modifications palpable and visible to His creatures when He purposes to effect some unusual influence upon them. Miracles could only be incredible if they were contrary to God's known perfections or contradicted some prior revelation of His will.

"Everything we see is, in one sense, a miracle: it is beyond our comprehension. We put a twig into the ground, and find in a few years' time that it becomes a tree; but how it draws its nourishment from the earth, and how it increases, we know not. We look around us, and see the forests sometimes shaken by storms, at other times yielding to the breeze; in one part of the year in full leaf, in another naked and desolate. We all know that the seasons have an effect on these things, and philosophers will conjecture at a few immediate causes; but in what manner these causes act, and how they put nature in motion, the wisest of them know not. When the storm is up, why does it not continue to rage? When the air is calm, what rouses the storm? We know not, but must, after our deepest researches into first causes, rest satisfied with resolving all into the power of God. Yet, notwithstanding we cannot comprehend the most common of these appearances, they make no impression on us, because they are common, because they happen according to a stated course, and are seen every day. If they were out of the common course of nature, though in themselves not more difficult to comprehend, they would still appear more wonderful to us, and more immediately the work of God.

"Thus, when we see a child grow into a man, and, when the breath has left the body, turn to corruption, we are not in the least surprised, because we see it every day; but were we to see a man restored from sickness to health by a word, or raised to life from the dead by a mere command, though these things are not really more unaccountable, yet we call the uncommon even a miracle, because it is uncommon. We acknowledge, however, that both are produced by God, because it is evident that no other power can produce them. Such, then, is the nature of the evidence which arises from miracles; and we have no more reason to disbelieve them, when well attested and not repugnant to the goodness or justice of God, only because they were performed several ages ago, than we have to disbelieve the more ordinary occurrences of Providence which passed before our own time, because the same occurrences may never happen again during our lives. The ordinary course of nature proves the Being and Providence of God; these extraordinary acts of power prove the Divine commission of that person who performs them" (T. H. Horne).

Finally, miracles are not only possible and credible, but, as indicated in an earlier paragraph, in certain circumstances they are necessary. If there was to be a restoration of that intercourse with God which men had severed and forfeited by their defection, it must obviously be by supernatural means. Divine revelation, being of an extraordinary nature, requires extraordinary proofs to certify it. Since it was not to be a revelation made separately to every individual, conveyed to his mind in such a way as should remove all doubting, but rather a revelation communicated to a few and then published to the world, it follows that miracles were called for to confirm the testimony of the messengers of God, to convince others that they spoke by higher authority than their own, and therefore the necessity of miracles was in proportion to the necessity of a revelation being made. By the miracle performed through His servants God gave proof to those who heard them that they were not being imposed upon by fraud when they claimed to utter a, "Thus saith the Lord."

A miracle is a supernatural work. It is something which could not be produced by the laws of nature, and it is therefore a deviation from their normal operations. A miracle is an extraordinary Divine work, where an effect is produced contrary to the common course of nature. God was pleased to perform such prodigies to testify His approbation of those who acted as His mouthpieces, to avouch their messages— the miracles they performed were their letters patent. Whatever God has confirmed by miracles is solemnly and authoritatively ratified. The miracles wrought by Moses and Elijah, and by the Apostles of the New Testament were such as were manifestly beyond the powers of any creature to produce and therefore they attested the Divine origin of their messages. Obviously, God would not work such wonders through imposters or in order to confirm lies, but only to witness unto the truth of a Divine revelation—see Mark 16:20; Hebrews 2:4; though miracles were both probable and necessary to authenticate unto men a revelation from God, yet it could not reasonably be expected that such sensible tokens or marks of Divine interposition should be renewed in every age or to each individual in the world, for that would completely subvert the regular order of things which the Creator has established. Nor was there any need for such a continual repetition of miracles. Once Christianity was established in the world, those extraordinary interventions of God ceased. It was fitting that they should, for God does nothing unnecessarily. The Jews, every time they heard the Law read to them, did not expect a recurrence of the supernatural happenings of Sinai: those were one solemn confirmation of the Ten Commandments, which were to serve for all generations. Likewise, the Christian doctrine is the same now as it was in the first century, and will remain unchanged to the end of the world: we have a sure and authentic record of it in the Bible. Miracles, like any other facts, may be certified by reliable testimony.

It is by means of testimony that we obtain by far the greater part of our knowledge, and the trustworthiness of such testimony may be as conclusive as sense or mathematical demonstration. Evidence is necessary to establish the fact of revelation, though revelation existed before a line of Scripture came to be written. Those to whom the revelation was not personally made are required to believe it on the testimony of those who received it from the mouth of God. And it is just as unreasonable and illogical not to credit those witnesses as it would be to decline the trustworthiness of the atlas. I might as well refuse to believe there is any such country as New Zealand because I have never seen it for myself or personally spoken to those who have lived there, as reject the Bible as a Divine revelation because I did not personally witness the miracles God wrought to attest its original penmen, nor have had personal converse with them. It is only by the evidence of testimony of their contemporaries and then through historians that we know such men as Alexander and Napoleon ever existed.

"On the same grounds of historical testimony, but furnished to us in a measure far more extensive, and connected moreover with a variety of other kinds of evidence, we are assured of the fact that Jesus Christ appeared in the world and that He was born, and lived, and died, in the country of Judea. This is attested by contemporary historians, and no man acquainted with history can be so absurd as to admit the reality of the existence of Julius Caesar and at the same time deny that of Jesus Christ. This is admitted by the greatest enemies of Christianity; and it is also acknowledged on all hands that the Christian religion which is professed at this day took its rise from Jesus Christ, and in the age in which He lived. Till then it is never mentioned; but from that period it begins to be noticed by historians, and shortly after becomes the subject of public edicts, and later produces revolutions in government, both more important and more permanent than that which Julius Caesar effected" (Robert Haldane).

We have pointed out that our knowledge of and belief in all those events of the past which we did not personally behold are based upon the testimony of witnesses, and that we who live in this twentieth century have far better and surer evidence—judged from an historical standpoint—to be assured that Jesus Christ was an historical reality, than we have for believing that Julius Caesar existed. The only objection made against that fact which has even the appearance of substance is, that whereas the history of Julius Caesar followed the ordinary course of events, that of Jesus Christ was radically different, so much so that the latter makes a far greater demand upon our credence than does the former. Those who preceded us have shown that this objection, so far from presenting any real difficulty, only serves to render our belief easier, for it calls attention to just what should be expected in such a case, thereby rendering it more credible. Had the career of Jesus Christ flowed in normal channels—were there no extraordinary features to mark it, then we should indeed have good reason to suspect the records of it.

If Jesus Christ were the Son of God incarnate then we should naturally expect Him to be born in a way none other ever was. If He came here on a unique mission, of supreme importance to the whole human race—a Divine Mission, having for its purpose a climacteric display of God's perfections, and the saving of His people with an everlasting salvation—then His life would obviously be without any parallel, yea, characterized by the supernatural. The very nature of His mission required that miracles should attest His teaching. Those very miracles being matter of fact, evident to the senses of those who witnessed them, of such a nature they could not be misunderstood, were, equally with common occurrences, the subject of credible testimony. They were not of a momentary nature, but permanent in their effects. They were not performed in secret, but in broad daylight in the midst of multitudes. They were not few only, but numerous. They were not performed only in the presence of friends but before enemies, and under a government and priesthood which bitterly hated their Performer and the doctrine He supported.

The miracles wrought by the Lord Jesus were, both in their beneficent character and in their wondrous nature, worthy of Him who did them and of the mission which engaged Him. They were not performed as spectacular displays of power, but directed to such gracious and practical ends as feeding the hungry and healing the sick. Moreover, it is to be carefully borne in mind that those wonders were specifically predicted centuries before He was born at Bethlehem. Wrought as they were in the open, before friends and foes alike, had there been any deception practiced, it must have been detected But the fiercest of His detractors were compelled to acknowledge their reality (John 11:47; 12:18, 19), though ascribing them to a diabolical influence. It is an historic fact that Christ's miracles were not denied in the age in which they were performed, nor for many centuries afterwards. They are related to us by eye-witnesses and are inseparably connected with the rest of the history of which they form apart. They are in perfect accord with what the rest of the Bible reveals of the power and goodness of God.

When Moses beheld the bush burning and not consumed, and heard the voice of the Lord speaking to him therefrom, not only were his senses convinced, but the awe-inspiring effect upon his heart was self-attesting evidence that the living God was there revealed to him. But those to whom he related that startling experience, especially when he declared he had then received a Divine commission to act as their leader, would require some convincing proof that God had indeed spoken to him. When the Lord bade him return into Egypt and inform the elders of Israel that the God of their fathers had appeared unto him in Horeb, Moses was fearful that his report would be received with skepticism, saying, "They will not believe me, nor hearken to my voice." Whereupon the Lord, in His condescending grace, told him to cast his rod on the ground, and it became a serpent; and take it by the tail and it became a rod in his hand; so that repeating these miracles, "they may believe that the LORD God . . .hath appeared unto thee" (Ex. 4:1-5). Thereby the mission which God had entrusted unto Moses would be confirmed beyond all dispute.

Upon this particular point we know of none who has written more lucidly and convincingly than Mr. J. C. Philpot, from whom we shall now quote and paraphrase. "In such a matter as Divine revelation, which, being supernatural, is to fallen men naturally incredible, there is a necessity that the ordinary evidence of human testimony should be as it were backed and supplemented by extraordinary evidence, that is, the evidence of miracle and prophecy . . . Let us see the combined effect of testimony and miracle when Moses goes to execute his mission." "Moses and Aaron went and gathered together all the elders of the children of Israel. And Aaron spake all the words which the LORD had spoken unto Moses, and did the signs in the sight of the people. And the people believed: and when they heard that the LORD had visited the children of Israel, and that He had looked upon their affliction, then they bowed their heads and worshipped" (Ex. 4:29-31).

"First, there is testimony: 'And Aaron spoke all the words which the LORD had spoken unto Moses.' Next there is miracle: 'And did the signs in the sight of the people.' Thirdly, there is belief

'And the people believed.' Fourthly, there is worship: 'they bowed their heads and worshipped.' Thus we see that the weakness of testimony ["weak" under such circumstances as those—a single weakness unto an unexpected and unprecedented occurrence: A.W.P.] is made up for and supplemented by the strength of a miracle. Without testimony, the miracle would be purposeless; without a miracle, the testimony would be inefficacious. Testimony is to miracle what Aaron was to Moses—'instead of a mouth'; and miracle is to testimony what Moses was to Aaron—'instead of God' (Ex. 4:16). But why should a miracle possess this peculiar strength? For this simple reason: that it shows the special interposition of the Almighty. Thus the magicians, when baffled and confounded, confessed to Pharaoh, 'This is the finger of God' (Ex. 8:19)."

Another instance of the place and value of miracles in connection with testimony is found in 1 Kings 18. Half a century before, 10 of Israel's tribes had revolted from the throne of David. Jeroboam their king had set up the worship of the golden calves in Dan and Bethel, which marked the extremities of his kingdom. Two generations had grown up in idolatry and, "for a long season Israel [in contradistinction from Judah] had been without the true God, and without a teaching priest, and without law" (2 Chron. 15:3). But in the days of the wicked Ahab, God raised up the Prophet Elijah, and His messenger announced that, "there shall not be dew nor rain these years, but according to my word" (1 Kings 17:1), and for three years there was an unbroken drought (James 5:17), which resulted in famine and great distress. Yet when the Lord's hand was lifted up in such manifest judgment "they would not see" (Isa. 26:11), but Jezebel slew the Prophets of the Lord (1 Kings 18:13), while Ahab vowed vengeance upon Elijah himself. Nor did the common people evince any sign of repentance.

Elijah gave orders that all Israel should be gathered together unto mount Cannel, with the 450 prophets of Baal and the 400 prophets of the grove. He then came unto the people and said, "How long halt ye between two opinions: if the LORD be God, follow Him; but if Baal, follow him. And the people answered him not a word" (1 Kings 18:21)—apparently because they were nonplussed, perceiving not how the controversy might be determined. Whereupon the servant of God proposed, "Let them therefore give us two bullocks: and let them choose one bullock for themselves, and cut it in pieces, and lay on wood, and put no fire under; and I will dress the other bullock, and lay it on wood, and put no fire under. And call ye on the name of your god, and I will call on the name of the LORD: and the God that answereth by fire, let Him be God. And all the people answered and said, It is well spoken" (vv. 23, 24). The controversy should be decided by a miracle! Nothing could be fairer than what Elijah proposed; no test more convincing than the one here put to the proof. The people unanimously assented, and forthwith the trial was made.

For hours the prophets of Baal called upon their god to answer by fire, but there was no response; they leaped up and down at the altar, cutting themselves with knives till the blood gushed out upon them, but there was not "any that regarded"—the desired fire fell not. After their vain pretensions had been fully exposed, Elijah, to make more evident the miracle that followed, called for four barrels of water and poured it on the bullock which he had cut up and upon the wood until, "the water ran round about the altar, and he filled the trench also with the water." Then Elijah prayed unto the Lord God of Abraham, Isaac and Jacob saying, "Let it be known this day that Thou art God in Israel, and I Thy servant, and that I have done all these things at Thy Word. Hear me, O LORD, hear me, that this people may know that Thou art the LORD God, and that Thou hast turned their hearts back again" (vv. 36, 37). Nor did the Prophet supplicate in vain. "Then the fire of the LORD fell and consumed the burnt sacrifice, and the wood, and the stones, and the dust, and licked up the water that was in the trench. And when the people saw they fell on their faces, and they said, The LORD He is the God; the LORD, He is the God" (vv. 38, 39).

Now what we would particularly note in that memorable scene on Carmel is the light which it casts upon the evidential value of miracles. That was made unmistakably plain in Elijah's prayer. The supernatural fire which came down from Heaven in the sight of that vast assembly, consuming not only the bullock but the very stones on which it was laid, and the water in the trench round about the altar, was designed to make manifest, first, that Jehovah was God in Israel. Second, that Elijah was His authorized servant. Third, that his mission and work was according to the Word of the Lord. Fourth, that God still had designs of mercy in turning the hearts of Israel back again unto Himself. Here, then, is another case in point where the evidence of testimony was ratified by the evidence of a miracle. The mission of Elijah was authorized by the miracles performed in answer to his prayers: the special interposition of God attested the Divine origin of his message, for obviously the Lord would not work such wonders in answer to the petitions of an impostor. God was pleased to perform those prodigies to testify His approbation of those who served as His mouthpieces, thereby leaving "without excuse" all who turned a deaf ear unto them.

Herein we may at once perceive how futile and senseless is the method followed by the "Modernists" and "Higher Critics." They are obliged to acknowledge the canonicity of the books of the Bible, for the whole of the Old Testament was translated into the Greek more than 200 years before Christ. While there is independent evidence for the existence of the books of the New Testament from a very early date in the Christian era: yet they refuse to believe the miracles recorded in them. But that is utterly irrational. One has but to read attentively either the Pentateuch, the four Gospels, or the Acts, to discover that their historical portions and their miraculous portions are so intimately related we cannot logically accredit the former without accrediting the latter. They necessarily stand or fall together: if the history is true, so also are the miracles; if the miracles be spurious, so is the history. We could not delete the miraculous plagues upon Egypt and the supernatural destruction of Pharaoh and his hosts at the Red Sea without rendering completely meaningless the historical portions of the book of Exodus. The same holds good of the book of Acts: remove the miracles recorded therein, and much of the narrative become unintelligible.

The same feature obtains in connection with the wonders wrought by the Savior. "Take, for instance, the raising of Lazarus from the dead. How can we separate the narrative from the miracle, or the miracle from the narrative? To see this more clearly, let us look at the narrative as distinct from the miracle. How simply, and so to speak naturally, is it related, and with what a minuteness and particularity of circumstances, which could not from their very nature have been invented. The name of the sick and dying man; the place where he lived, not far from Jerusalem, and therefore open to the closest investigation and examination; the names of his two sisters; the absence of Jesus at the time; the deep grief of Martha and Mary, and yet the way in which it was shown, so thoroughly in harmony with their characters elsewhere given (Luke 10:38-42). The arrival of Jesus: His conversation with them; His weeping at the tomb, and the remarks of the bystanders—what an air of truthfulness pervades the whole! There is nothing exaggerated, nothing out of place, nothing but what is in perfect harmony with the character of Jesus as reflected in the mirror of the other Gospels.

"But this narrative portion of the sickness and death of Lazarus cannot he separated from the miraculous portion—the raising of him from the dead. The first precedes, explains, introduces, and harmonizes with the second. Without the narrative the miracle would be unintelligible. It would float on the Gospel as a fragment of a shipwrecked vessel on the waves of the sea, furnishing no indication of its name or destination. So without the miracle the narrative would be useless and out of place, and of no more spiritual value than the sickness and death of a good man who died yesterday. But narrative and miracle combined, interlaced and mutually strengthening each other form a massy web which no Infidel fingers can pull to pieces. What we have said with respect to the miracle wrought at the grave of Lazarus is equally applicable to the other miraculous works of our blessed Lord. Narrative introduces the miracle, and miracle sustains the narrative—their combined effect being to prove that Jesus was the Son of God, the promised Messiah of whom all the Prophets testified" (J. C. Philpot).

To the miracles which He wrought, the Lord Jesus again and again appealed as evidence of His Divine mission. Thus, His forerunner, while languishing in prison and dismayed by his non-deliverance therefrom, sent two of his disciples unto Him with the inquiry, "art Thou He that should come, or do we look for another?" To which our Lord made reply, "Go and show John again those things which ye do hear and see; the blind receive their sight, the lame walk, the lepers are cleaned, and the deaf hear, the dead are raised up, and the poor have the Gospel preached unto them" (Matthew 11:4, 5). The Lord there authenticated the Gospel which He preached by the supernatural works He performed: those displays of Divine goodness and power being the plain and irrefutable evidence that He was the Messiah "who should come," according to the unanimous declarations of the Old Testament Prophets. On another occasion, after mentioning the testimony which John had borne unto Him, the Redeemer said, "But I have greater witness than of John: for the works which the Father hath given Me to finish, the same works that I do bear witness of Me, that the Father hath sent Me" (John 5:33, 36).

When the unbelieving Jews came and said unto Him, "How long dost Thou make us to doubt? If Thou be the Christ, tell us plainly." Jesus answered them, "I told you, and ye believed not; the works that I do in My Father's name, they bear witness of Me" (John 10:24, 25). If it be asked, How could any eye-witnesses of those mighty works refuse to believe if they were indeed proofs of His Divine mission? Because, since they rejected His teaching, God blinded their eyes and hardened their hearts (John 12:37-40). But others were convinced. Many believed in His name, when they saw the miracles which He did (John 2:23); and on the feeding of the great multitude with five loaves and two small fishes, we are told, "Then those men, when they had seen the miracle that Jesus did, said, This is of a truth that Prophet that should come into the world" (John 6:14). Said Nicodemus, "We know that Thou art a Teacher come from God: for no man can do these miracles that Thou doest, except God be with Him" (John 3:2): such displays of Divine power demonstrated that His mission and message were Divine.

Another striking illustration and exemplification of the value of miracles authenticating one employed upon a Divine mission is found in Acts 2. Less than two months after the death and resurrection of the Lord Jesus, and His subsequent departure from this world, we find the Apostle Peter declaring openly, "Ye men of Israel, hear these words: Jesus of Nazareth, a man approved of God among you by miracles and wonders and signs, which God did by Him in the midst of you as ye yourselves also know" (v. 22). This was not said to a company of Christians in private, but to a vast "multitude" in Jerusalem (vv. 5, 6). It formed part of an appeal made to the whole mass of the Jewish populace, and it was not contradicted by them, as it most certainly had been if Peter were making an empty boast. The Apostle was reminding them that Christ had dispossessed demons, raised the dead, not in a corner, but in the most public manner. Those miracles were incontestable, and the significance of them could not be gainsaid: they were so many testimonies from God of His approbation of the One who wrought them. They declared and demonstrated that Jesus Christ was the promised Messiah and Savior. They certified His mission and doctrine. Much failure attaches to us at every point. Our paramount desire to enjoy intimate and unbroken fellowship with the Lord, though sincere, is neither as intense nor as constant as it should be. Our efforts after the realization of that desire, our use of those means which promote communion with Him, are not as diligent and wholehearted as is incumbent upon us. Our pressing forward unto the mark set before us is often most feeble and faulty. But there is no failure with our God: His purpose will be accomplished, He will perfect that which concerns us (Ps. 138:8).

Chapter 7
THE HOLY BIBLE FILLS MAN'S NEED FOR DIVINE REVELATION

If the Bible is the Word of God, if it immeasurably transcends all the productions of human genius, then we should naturally expect it to be attested by marks which evince its Divine origin. That such an expectation is fully realized we shall, at some length, seek to show. Those marks are not vague and uncertain, but definite and unmistakable, and are of such a character as man could not be the author of them. The indications that the Bible is a Divine revelation are numerous, various, and conclusive. They are such as appeal severally to those of different tastes and temperaments, while taken together they present a case which none can invalidate. The Bible is furnished with such credentials as only those blinded by prejudice can fail to recognize it is a messenger from Heaven. They are of two kinds—extraordinary [miracles and prophecies] and ordinary, and the latter may be distinguished again between those which are objective and subjective—the one addressed to reason, the other capable of verification in experience. Each has the nature of a distinct witness, yet there is perfect agreement between them—united, yet independent.

1. Man's Need. We may well draw our first argument for an intelligible and authoritative revelation of God from our imperative requirement of the same. We have presented evidence to show God exists, that He created man a rational and moral being, endowed with the power to distinguish between good and evil, and, therefore, that he was [originally] capable of knowing God, obeying Him, and worshipping Him. But man could neither intelligently obey nor acceptably worship God unless he first had a direct revelation from Him of how He was to be served. In order for there to be intercourse between man and his Maker, he must first receive from Him a communication of His mind prescribing the details of his duty. Accordingly we find that immediately after the creation of Adam and Eve God gave them a particular statute. He first informed them what they might do (Gen. 2:16), and then specified what they must not do. Thus, from the outset, was man made dependent upon his Creator for a knowledge of His will, and thus, too, was his fidelity unto Him put to the proof.

If such were the case with man in his pristine glory, as he was made in the moral image of God, how much greater is his need of a Divine revelation since he has left his first estate, lost the image of God, and become a fallen and depraved creature! Sin has defiled his soul: darkening his understanding, alienating his affections, vitiating all his faculties. Should a critical objector here say, But you are now assuming what has not yet been proved, for you are taking for granted the authenticity of Genesis 3 [wherein the defection of man from his Maker is recorded]. It should be sufficient reply at this stage to ask, What other alternative remains? Only this: that God created man in his present woeful plight, that he has never been in any better condition. But is not such a concept abhorrent even to reason? Surely a perfect God would not create so faulty a creature. Could One who is infinitely pure and holy make man in the awful state of iniquity in which we now behold him? How, then, has man become such a depraved being?

Why is it that the world over, mankind are so intractable and wayward, that so many are regulated by their lusts rather than reason, that if the restraints of human law and government were removed and everyone given free rein, the earth would speedily become a charnel-house? During the first half of this twentieth century, despite our vaunted education and civilization, enlightenment and progress, we have witnessed the most appalling proofs of human depravity, and that on a scale of enormous magnitude. So far from beholding any indication that man is slowly but surely ascending from the ape to the Divine, there is abundant evidence to show that the larger part of our race has descended to the level of the beasts. But how comes this to be, if man at the beginning was a sinless and holy creature? Apart from the Bible, no satisfactory answer is forthcoming: neither philosophy nor science can furnish any satisfactory explanation. Here again we see the urgent need of a revelation from God: that Divine light may be cast upon this dark mystery, that we may learn how man forfeited his felicity and plunged himself into misery.

What has just been pointed out makes manifest yet another aspect of man's deep need of a plain revelation from God. Man is now a fallen and polluted creature—no one who reads the newspapers or attends the police courts can question that. How, then, do the ineffable eyes of God regard him? How is it possible for fallen creatures to regain their former glory? Reason itself tells us that one who has rebelled against God's authority and broken His laws cannot at death be taken into His presence, there to spend a blissful eternity, without his sins being first pardoned and his character radically changed. The convictions of conscience reject any such anomaly. But apart from Divine revelation, how are we to ascertain what will satisfy the thrice holy God? In what way shall a guilty soul be pardoned, a sinful soul be purified, a polluted creature made fit for the celestial courts? All the schemes and contrivances of human devising fail utterly at this vital point—at best they are but a dream, a guess. Dare you, my reader, risk your eternal welfare upon a mere peradventure?

Turning back from the future to the present: how is God to be worshipped by man? Such a question is necessarily raised by the being and character of God and of man's relationship to Him as His creature. That the Deity should be acknowledged, that homage ought to be rendered unto Him, has been owned by the majority of our fellows in all climes and ages. True, their conceptions of Deity have varied considerably, and so, too, their ideas of how to honor Him; yet the conscience of all nations has convicted them that some form of worship is due unto God. It has been generally felt and avowed that there should be an acknowledgment of our dependency upon God, that supplications for His favor should be offered, that confessions of sin should be made, that thanksgivings for His mercies should be returned. Low as man has fallen, yet until he be steeped in vice, the dictates of reason and the promptings of his moral nature have informed him that God ought to be worshipped. Yet without a special revelation from God, how is it possible for any man to know that he worships aright, that his efforts to honor God are acceptable to Him? The crude and debasing idol worship of those who are ignorant of or have spurned God's Word will clearly evince the need for such a revelation.

From the works of creation, the voice of conscience, and the course of Providence, we may learn enough of God and of our relation to Him as to make us the accountable creatures of His government. But of that knowledge which is necessary to our salvation, we can discover nothing whatever. Unwritten revelation is inadequate to meet the needs of a sinner. We need a further revelation in order to learn our real character and ascertain how we may be acceptable unto God. Creation as such exhibits no Savior, announces no redemption, and supplies not the least indication that the forgiveness of sins is possible, much less likely. If we break the laws of nature we must suffer the penalty. Ignorance will not exempt us nor will penitence remit the suffering. Nature's laws are inexorable and are no respecter of persons. A child falling into the fire will be burned as surely as the vilest criminal. If we had nothing more than the visible world from which to draw our conclusions, we could never infer a hope of mercy for the transgressor of law. Nor would our moral instincts hold out any prospect of future relief—for conscience condemns us and informs us that punishment is just.

Religion [from re-ligo "to bind back"] must have something to tie to. It must have a foundation, a basis, an ultimate appeal. What is that appeal? Many say tradition: to the teaching of "the Fathers," to the decree of Councils, to an authority lodged in the Church as a Divine corporation, indwelt and made infallible by the presence of the Holy Spirit. That is the doctrine of Rome—a doctrine which binds to a system assumed to be supernatural, but which is "as shifting as the decrees of councils have shifted, contradictory as the statements of church fathers have been conflicting, blind and confusing; a congeries of truths and errors, of affirmations, and denials, of half lights and evasions from Origen to Bellarmine" (G. S. Bishop). The Papacy's claim to be the seat of Divine authority is refuted by historic fact and personal experience. Her career has been far too dark and checkered, her influence on human life, liberty and progress, much too unsatisfactory for any impartial investigator to be deceived by such an arrogant pretension.

Others make their own instincts the supreme arbiter. That which commends itself to their "intuitions" or appeals to their sentiments is accepted, and whatever accords not therewith is spurned. But since temperaments and tastes differ so widely, there could be no common standard to which appeal may be made, and by which each one might test the rightness or wrongness of his preferences. Each separate individual would become a law unto himself: nay, if nothing be right or good save what I approve of, then I am my own god. This may be termed the religion of nature, and it accounts for every vagary from the myths of Paganism to the self-delusion of miscalled "Christian Science," for everything put forth from Homer to Huxley. Such self-limitation exposes its utter poverty. Self cannot advance beyond the bounds of an experience which is limited by the present. How can I know anything about the origin of things unless I be taught by One who existed before them? Apart from a special revelation from God, what can I possibly know of what awaits me after death?

Human reason is the ultimate court of appeal for the majority of this generation. But reason is not uniform: what appears to be logical and credible to one man, seems the very opposite to another. Most of what was pointed out in the last paragraph obtains equally here—reason can know nothing of what it has no experience. The great subject of controversy between Infidels and Christians is whether reason [the intellect and moral faculties] be sufficient to enable us to attain all that knowledge which is necessary for bringing us to virtue and happiness. That question is not to be answered by theorizing but by experiment; not by conjectures, but facts. It must be submitted to the test of history. At what conclusions did the reason of the ancient Egyptians, Greeks and Romans arrive? So far from formulating any adequate conception of Deity, they worshipped birds and beasts, and invented gods of the most revolting character. There was no agreement among their most renowned thinkers. Their systems of moral philosophy were woefully defective and their framers notoriously profligate. Even today where the Bible is rejected reason rises no higher than agnosticism: I know not—whether there be a God, a soul which survives the death of the body, or what the hereafter may hold.

If it be asked, What purpose does reason serve in connection with spiritual things? We answer, first, its province is to form a judgment of the evidence of Christianity: to investigate and to estimate the grounds on which it claims to be a Divine revelation. Its duty is to weigh impartially and determine the force of such arguments as we have advanced in the preceding discussion and those we will present. Second, its office is to examine carefully the contents of Scripture, to acquaint ourselves with its teachings, to attentively consider the demands they make upon us—which we could not do if we had no more understanding than the irrational beasts. Third, its function is to subordinate itself unto the authority of Divine revelation—the absurdity of the opposite is self-evident. Reason is certainly not to constitute the judge of what God says, but is rather to consider and test the evidence which demonstrates that He has spoken. The wisdom of God is not placed on trial before the bar of human foolishness. Man is the scholar, and not the Teacher—his reason is to act as a servant and not a lord. We act most reasonably when we thankfully avail ourselves of the light which God has vouchsafed us in His Word.

Having shown the limitations and inadequacy of man's own faculties—manifested everywhere in the records of history, both ancient and modern—we return to our opening postulate: man's need of a special and infallible revelation from God. He needs such in order to deliver from a state of spiritual ignorance—a state which is fraught with the utmost peril to his soul. Consider how prone is the mind of man to embrace error, how ready and fertile to invent new religions. Even when unfallen, man required that his path of duty be made known to him by his Maker. Much more so does man, considered as a fallen creature, require an unerring Mentor to instruct him in spiritual things, one outside himself, infinitely above him. In a world of conflicting opinions and ever-changing theories, we must have a sure Touchstone, an unvarying Standard, an ultimate Authority to which appeal can be made. Amid all the sins and sorrows, the problems and trials of life, man is in urgent need of a Divine Guide to show him the way to present holiness and happiness and to eternal glory.

2. A Presumption in its favor. This follows logically from all we have presented. Since man sorely needs such a revelation from God, and He is able to furnish it, then there is a strong probability that He will do so. He who endowed man with his intellectual faculties, is certainly capable of granting him a further degree of light by some other medium. "Revelation is to the mind what a glass is to the eye, whether it be intended to correct some accidental defect in its structure, or to enlarge its power of vision beyond its natural limits" (Professor Dick). To argue that we should be uncertain whether such a revelation be genuine or not would be tantamount to saying that because there are so many impostors in the world, therefore there is no truth—that because so many are deceived, none can be sure that he is right. It is both presumptuous and unreasonable to affirm that God is unable to supply a communication unto mankind which is lacking in those marks that would authenticate it as coming from Himself. Cannot Deity legibly inscribe His signature on the work of His own hand?

We might indeed draw the conclusion that since man is so vilely apostatized from his Maker, that God will justly abandon him to misery. Yet we perceive that, notwithstanding the criminal conduct of His creatures, God still makes His sun to shine and the rain to fall upon them, providing them with innumerable blessings. Thoroughly unexpected as it might well be, we behold God exercising mercy unto the sinful sons of men, ameliorating those evils which they have brought upon themselves, and providing means by the use of which their sufferings are much alleviated. Though we could not from those things warrantably draw the conclusion that God would proceed any further in our behalf, yet if He should be pleased to extend His care unto our souls as well as our bodies, it would only be an enlargement of the scope of that benevolence already displayed in His provisions for us. It would be in perfect accord with the method He has employed with His creatures, if He further interposed to rescue fallen men from ignorance, guilt and perdition.

"From man at the head of creation, down to the lowest organized structure, there is not a necessity for which provision has not been made, and that in exact proportion to its wants. You yourself came into this world a poor, helpless, naked infant, full of necessities, and would have perished from the womb unless provision had been made for you. Who filled for you your mother's breast with milk and your mother's heart with love? But you have a soul as well as a body—no less naked, no less necessitous. Shall then the body have its necessities, and those be provided for—and shall the soul have its necessities too, and for it no provision made? Is there no milk for the soul as well as the body? no 'sincere milk of the Word' that it may grow thereby?" (J. C. Philpot). The goodness of God, the benevolence of the Creator, the mercy of our Governor, all point to the likelihood of His ministering to this supreme need of ours, without which everyone of us must assuredly perish.

Brother Philpot draws a further argument in support of this conclusion from the relations which God sustains to us as our sovereign Master and our judge, pointing out that a master's will must be known before it can be obeyed, that a judge's law must be declared before it can be transgressed. Why are theft and murder punished? Because the law of the land expressly forbids those crimes under a prescribed penalty; but since no human statute prohibits ingratitude, none are penalized in human courts for the same. It is a recognized principle that "where there is no law there is no transgression" (Rom. 4:15). Then does it not clearly follow from this that God will give unto us His laws—direct, positive, authoritative laws, binding upon us by Divine sanctions? How could He justly punish what He has not forbidden? And if He has forbidden sin, how and when has He done so? Where is the statute book, written by His dictation, which makes known His will to us? If it be not the Bible, we are left without any!

If it would be a far greater tax upon our credulity to believe that the universe had no Maker, than that, "In the beginning God created the heavens and the earth." If it involves immeasurably greater difficulty to regard Christianity as being destitute of a Divine Founder, than to recognize that it rests upon the Person and work of the Lord Jesus Christ. Then is it not far more unreasonable to suppose that God has left the human race without a written revelation from Him, than to believe the Bible is such? There are times when the most thoughtful are uncertain as to which is the right course to pursue, when the most experienced need a guide their own wisdom cannot supply—will the One who furnishes us with fruitful seasons deny us such counsel? There are sorrows which rend the hearts of the stoutest—will He who has given us the beautiful flowers and singing birds to regale our senses, withhold that comfort we so much need in the hour of bereavement? Which is the more reasonable—that the Maker of sun and moon should provide a Lamp for our feet, or leave us to grope our way amid the darkness of a ruined world?!

Chapter 8
THE HOLY BIBLE DECLARES IT COMES FROM GOD HIMSELF

We have presented a portion of that abundant evidence which makes it unmistakably manifest that God has given us a clear revelation of Himself in creation, in the constitution of man (physical, mental, and moral), in His government of this world (as evinced in the annals of history), in the advent to this earth of His incarnate Son, and in the Holy Scriptures. We based our first argument that the Bible is an inspired communication from God on the fact that man is in urgent need of a written revelation, because his own faculties—especially as he is now a fallen and sinful creature—are insufficient as a guide to virtue and eternal happiness. Second, that there is therefore a presumption in favor of the Bible's being a revelation from God, since man urgently needs such and God is well able to supply it. Since all nature evinces that a merciful Creator has made suitable provision for every need of all His creatures, it is unthinkable that this supreme need of the highest of His earthly creatures should be neglected.

We now come to point 3: Its own claims. These are unambiguous, positive, decisive, leaving us in no doubt as to what the Scriptures profess to be. The Bible declares that, as a Book, it comes to us from God Himself. It urges that claim in various ways. Its very names proclaim its Source. It is repeatedly denominated "The Word of God." It is so denominated because as we express our thoughts and make known our intentions by means of words, so in His Book God has disclosed His mind and declared His will unto us. It is called "The Book of the LORD" (Isa. 34:16) because He is its Author and because of the Divine authority with which it is invested, demanding our unqualified subjection to its imperial edicts. It is termed "The Scripture of Truth" (Dan. 10:21) because it is without confusion, without contradiction, without the slightest mixture of error—infallible in every verse, every word, every letter inspired—Divine. It is designated "The Word of Life" (Phil. 2:16) because it is invested with the very breath of the Almighty, indelible and indestructible, in contradistinction from all the perishing productions of man. It is entitled "The Oracles of God" (Rom. 3:2) because in it God Himself is the Speaker.

The Bible proclaims itself to be a Divine revelation, a direct and inerrent communication from the living God, that He "spoke by the mouth of His holy Prophets, which have been since the world began" (Luke 1:70). They announce that "the Law of the LORD is perfect" (Ps. 19:7)—without flaw or blemish; that "the Word of God is quick and powerful" (Heb. 4:12)—living, pungent, dynamic. They claim that "the Word of the Lord endureth forever" (1 Pet. 1:25)—surviving all the passages of time, withstanding all the efforts of enemies to destroy it. They affirm themselves to be "the Holy Scriptures, which are able to make thee wise unto salvation" (2 Tim. 3:15). The article there is emphatic, being used to distinguish the Sacred Writings from all others, to aver their excellence and eminence over all the writings of men. The Holy One is their Author, they treat of the holy things of God, and call for holy hearts and lives from their readers. And just so far as our characters are formed and our conduct regulated by their precepts, will the fruits of holiness appear in our lives.

The instruments which God employed to bring to us the Word were themselves conscious of and frankly owned to the fact that they were but His mouthpieces or penmen. Again and again we find them avowing that truth. "Joshua said unto all the people, Thus saith the LORD" (24:2). "The LORD spoke thus to me" (Isa. 8:11). "Hear ye for the LORD hath spoken" (Jer. 13:15). "Hear this word that the LORD hath spoken" (Amos 3:1). "The mouth of the LORD of hosts hath spoken it" (Micah 4:4). Said the royal Psalmist, "The Spirit of the LORD spake by me, and His Word was in my tongue" (2 Sam. 23:2). So, too, when the Apostles quoted a passage from the Old Testament they gave their testimony to the same truth. When Peter addressed the disciples, he said, "this Scripture must needs have been fulfilled which the Holy Spirit spoke by the mouth of David" (Acts 1:16). "Who by the mouth of thy servant David hast said" (Acts 4:25). "Well spoke the Holy Spirit by Isaiah the Prophet" (Acts 28:25). Whoever were the human spokesmen or writers, the language of the Scriptures is the very Word of God.

Not once or twice, but scores of times, there are passages which, without any preamble or apology, declare, "Thus saith the Lord." In the Bible, God is the Speaker. Chapter after chapter in Leviticus opens with, "And the Lord spoke, saying." And so it runs to the end of the chapter. Moses was but a scribe, God the Author of what is recorded. The question of Inspiration is, in its ultimate analysis, the question of Revelation itself. If the Book be Divine, then what it says of itself is Divine. The question is one of Divine testimony, and our business is simply to receive that testimony—without doubting or quibbling, with thankful and unreserved submission to its authority. When God speaks He must be heeded. "If at this moment yonder heavens were opened—the curtained canopy of star-sown clouds rolled back; if amid the brightness of light ineffable, the Dread Eternal were Himself seen rising from His throne, and heard to speak in voice audible, it could not be more potent, more imperative, than what lies now before us upon Inspiration's pages" (G. S. Bishop).

God requires us to receive and accredit His Word, and to do so on His own ipse dixit. All faith rests on testimony, and the testimony on which faith in the Scriptures reposes is amply sufficient to support it, for it is Divine. "If we receive the witness of men, the witness of God is greater. ... he that believeth not God hath made Him a liar, because he believeth not the record that God gave" (1 John 5:9, 10). If the witness of men of respectability and integrity be received in the judicatories of all nations, then most assuredly the witness of God is infinitely more worthy of our acceptance. The best of men are fallible and fickle, yet in matters of the greatest importance their testimony is credited—the affairs of the world would soon come to a standstill if it were not so. Then with how much more confidence may we receive the testimony of Him who is infallible and immutable, who can neither deceive nor be deceived?! How unspeakably dreadful the alternative: if we believe not God's record, that is virtually calling Him a liar—regarding Him as a false witness! May the reader be delivered from such wickedness.

Now we proceed to point 4: No other explanation is even feasible. Whence comes the Bible is a question deserving of the very best attention of every serious mind. The subjects of which it treats are of such tremendous importance both to our present welfare and our future felicity, that the question of its derivation calls for the most diligent examination. The Bible is here, and it must be accounted for. It holds a unique place in the literature of mankind and it has exerted an unrivalled influence in molding the history of the world; and therefore it calls loudly for an adequate rationale to be given of its origin. Only three explanations are possible: the Bible is either a deliberate imposter, manufactured by wicked men; or it is the product of deluded visionaries, who vainly imagined they were giving forth inspired messages from Heaven; or else it is what it claims to be: an infallible and authoritative revelation from God Himself unto the sons of men. Between those three alternatives every thoughtful investigator of the matter must choose. If he ponders carefully the first two and tests them by the evidence adduced in favor of the Bible's being a Divine communication, he should have no difficulty in perceiving they are not only inadequate, but utterly absurd.

It is proverbial that "water will not rise above its own level," as it is self-evident that no cause can produce any effect superior to itself. Equally incredible is it that wicked men should bring forth a Book which has done far more than all other books combined (except those drawn from the Bible) in promoting morality and producing holiness. Grapes do not grow upon thistles! To assert that the Bible was produced by evil men is refuted by the very character of its teachings, which uniformly condemn dishonesty and declare that "all liars shall have their part in the Lake which burneth with fire and brimstone" (Rev. 21:8). It is thoroughly irrational to suppose that the authors of the most impious and gigantic literary fraud ever imposed upon mankind (if such it be) should invent for themselves such a fearful doom as that! It must also be remembered that some of the penmen of the Bible laid down their lives for a testimony to its verity; but the annals of history contain no record of men willingly suffering martyrdom for a known lie—from which neither they nor their families received any advantage.

Another class of skeptics dismiss the Bible as the fanciful flights of poets, the ravings of mystics, the extravagances of enthusiasts. Much in it is no doubt very beautiful, yet it is as unsubstantial as a dream, with no reality corresponding thereto, and those who credit the same are living only in a fool's paradise. They say, If there be a God, He is so absolute and transcendent, so remote from this scene, as to take no personal notice of our affairs; that it is both unphilosophical and a slur on His greatness to affirm (as the ancient Psalm does), "Like as a father pitieth his children, so the Lord pitieth them that fear Him." Thus we are asked to believe that mystics and fanatics have invented a god with more tender and nobler attributes than the real God has. But to say that fancy has devised a superior god than actually exists is the acme of irrationality. Were it possible for us to choose what kind of excellence deity should possess, would we not include among them pity linked with infinite power, using that power as its servant to tenderly minister unto the suffering?

Surely this is the most amazing chimera that has ever been invented: that men have endowed God with grander qualities than He really possesses, that they have predicated of Him a perfection which He is incapable of exercising. Rather must we affirm that that wondrous statement, "God so loved the world that He gave His only begotten Son, that whosoever believeth in Him should not perish, but have everlasting life" (John 3:16), is a revelation which opens to us a new moral kingdom, a kingdom of unimaginable benignity and grace. The message of redemption is a Divine light breaking in upon us from Above, a revelation that proves itself. That God should send here His own Son, clothed with our humanity, to seek and to save rebels against His government, to suffer in their stead, and by His death make full atonement for their sins, to provide His Spirit to conform them to His image, to make them His joint heirs and sharers of His eternal glory, is a concept which had never entered human heart or mind to conceive. Yet it is worthy and becoming of our Maker. The Gospel is the noblest force which has ever touched human character.

As another has pertinently asked, "Is it a dishonor to God that, being great, He stoops to us? Does it make Him less? Is it a reproach to Him that He gives Himself to us? Would it be more for His glory if He mocked us? It is this very wedlock of the wisdom that planned the heavens— the measureless Power that guides the stars—with the tenderness that stoops to the whispered prayer of a child, that counts the tears of a widow, that hears the sighs of the prodigal—which makes the unconceivable greatness of God. It completes the mighty curve of His attributes. And is it credible that we can conceive this amazing greatness and yet God not be capable of it? . .

. The Bible represents God as saying, 'My thoughts are not your thoughts, nor My ways your ways, for as the heavens are higher than the earth so are My thoughts above your thoughts and My ways above your ways.' And this ought to be true! The realities of God ought to be nobler than the dreams of men. It would be the perplexity and despair of man if this were not so" (The Unrealized Logic of Religion).

Equally false is it to assert, as some ignorant Infidels have done, that we owe the Bible to the Church. It is an indubitable historical fact that the larger part of the Bible was in known existence more than 200 years before the dawn of the Christian era, and every doctrine, every precept and promise contained in the New Testament is based upon that earlier revelation. Such was the sufficiency of the Old Testament Scriptures that Paul could say they were "able to make wise unto salvation." While it is true that Christian churches existed before the New Testament was written, yet it must be borne in mind that there was the spoken Word by Christ and His Apostles ere the first of those churches was formed. On the day of Pentecost the Old Testament was quoted and expounded, the revelation of God in Christ was proclaimed, and it was upon the acceptance of that Word that the New Testament came into being. Thus, the fact is that the Word created the Church and not vice versa. It was only after some of the Apostles had died and others were engaged in extensive travel that the need arose for the permanent embodiment of the final portions of God's revelation, and this was given gradually in the New Testament. From that time until now, the written Word has taken the place of the original spoken Word.

For centuries before the inauguration of Christianity, the Jews beheld the books which comprised the Old Testament as being the genuine productions of those Penmen whose names they bear, and they were unanimously considered by them, without any exception or addition, to have been written under the immediate direction of the Spirit of God. Those books of the Old Testament had been preserved with the utmost veneration and care, and at the same time had been jealously guarded from any spurious or apocryphal writings. It is a fact well authenticated that while the Jews of Christ's day were divided into numerous sects, which stood in the most direct opposition to one another, yet there was never any difference among them respecting the divinity and authority of the sacred writings. Josephus appealed to the public records of different nations and to many historical documents existing in his day, as indisputable evidence, in the opinion of the Gentile world, of the verity and fidelity of those portions of Israel's history to which he referred. Even to this day the bulk of the religious Jews retain an unshakable conviction of the Divine origin of their religious laws and institutions. Yet their own Scriptures record their unparalleled hardness of heart, resistance to the light God gave them, and their rejection and murder of their own Messiah—things which would have been accorded no place in a spurious production.

That the Jews did not manufacture the Old Testament—on which the New is largely based—is apparent from other considerations. The immense disparity between the Old Testament as a book, and the Hebrew people as a nation, shows that the knowledge of God and of Divine things contained in the former, but wanting in the latter, came ab extra, that it was communicated from on high. One has but to read the writings of Josephus, the Jewish Targum and Talmud, or the Kabbala, to recognize at once the vast difference there is between them and the Holy Scriptures. That might be illustrated at great length, from many different angles, but we will confine ourselves to a single feature, and treat of it in a way that the ordinary reader will have no difficulty in following: the extreme exclusiveness of the Jews, and then call attention to a number of passages in the Old Testament which cannot possibly be accounted for in the light of that dominant national characteristic.

There has never been another people so outstandingly clannish in sentiment and so provincial in outlook as the Jews: nor had any other equal reason for so being. God dealt with them as with no other nation: "You only have I known of all the families of the earth" (Amos 3:2). "He hath not dealt so with any nation" (Ps. 147:20). He forbade Israel to have anything to do with the religion of other nations, prohibited all marriages with them, and the learning of their ways. Yet they carried the spirit of bigotry and exclusiveness to an unwarrantable extent—far beyond the requirements of Scripture. Their violent prejudice appears in that statement, "the Jews have no dealings with the Samaritans" (John 4:9), in Peter's reluctance to go unto Cornelius, and the unwillingness of the Christian Church at Jerusalem to believe the grace of God extended to the uttermost part of the earth. Nevertheless, the fact remains that the teaching of the Old Testament was very far from inculcating that the Israelites must confine their benevolent affections within the narrow bounds of their own twelve tribes. No spirit of bigotry breathes in the sacred songs sung in their temple.

"God be merciful unto us and bless us, and cause His face to shine upon us. Selah. That Thy way may be known upon the earth, Thy saving health among all nations. Let the people praise Thee, O God, let all the people praise Thee. O let the nations be glad and sing for joy: for Thou shalt judge the people righteously and lead the nations upon earth" (Ps. 67:1-4). "All nations whom Thou hast made shalt come and worship Thee, O Lord, and shall glorify Thy name" (Ps. 86:9). "O sing unto the LORD a new song. Sing unto the LORD all the earth. Sing unto the LORD, bless His name: show forth His salvation from day to day. Declare His glory among the heathen, His wonders among the people . . . Give unto the LORD the glory due unto His name, bring an offering and come into His courts" (Ps. 96:1-3, 8). Who, we ask, put such words as those into the Psalmist's mouth? Who caused them to be given a permanent record on the Sacred Scroll? Who preserved them intact for the thousand years which followed till the advent of Christ, during which interval the Jews were possessed of most fanatical egotism and the bitterest hatred of the Gentiles!?

The same striking feature appears even in the Pentateuch. "Thou shalt speak and say before the LORD your God, A Syrian ready to perish was my father: and he went down into Egypt and sojourned there with a few, and became a nation, great, mighty and populous. And the Egyptians evil entreated us and afflicted us, and laid upon us hard bondage" (Deut. 26:5, 6). The whole of that remarkable passage (vv. 4-10)—which Israel was required to recite before God at one of her most solemn acts of worship—should be carefully weighed. What could more effectually repress their national pride than that confession? But who instructed them to make such a humble acknowledgment of their lowly origin? Who bade them utter this perpetual avowal of their base beginnings? And more—it was on the very basis of their lowly origin and the sore oppression their fathers had suffered in a foreign land that a number of most un-"Jewish" laws were framed—laws which bade them pity and relieve the stranger. If that fact be critically pondered it should be evident that such precepts could not have originated from such a bigoted and hard-hearted people.

Those precepts were quite contrary to flesh and blood. It is natural for sinful men to strongly resent harsh treatment, for the memory of it to cherish rancor and malevolence, to feed the spirit of revenge, so that if the positions should be reversed they would "get even." Instead, we find the Mosaic Law enjoining the very opposite—inculcating the warmest and purest benevolence toward the wretched and defenseless of other nations. "Thou shalt not vex a stranger nor oppress him; for ye were strangers in the land of Egypt" (Ex. 22:21). Yea, more—"The stranger that dwelleth with you shall be unto you as one born among you, and thou shalt love him as thyself" (Lev. 19:34). Now, my reader, what explanation can possibly account for such benign statutes?—statutes which were repeatedly flouted by Israel! Who was it that originated and inculcated such unselfish tenderness? Who taught the haughty Jews to return good for evil? Who but the One who is both "no respecter of persons," and, who is "very pitiful and of tender mercy" (James 5:11).

It also requires to be pointed out that the Pentateuch contains a narration of many events which took place in the actual lifetime, yea, before the eyes, of the very people who were called upon to receive those books as authentic. Thus there was no opportunity for Moses, or anyone else, to palm off upon the Hebrews a lot of fictions, for each one of them would know at once whether the records of their cruel bondage in Egypt, the judgments which Jehovah is said to have executed there, and the miraculous deliverance of His people at the Red Sea, were true or not. Had those events been of a commonplace character, few perhaps had been sufficiently interested to scrutinize the narratives of them, still less have taken the trouble to refute them, were they untrue. But in view of their extraordinary nature, and especially since those miracles were designed to authenticate a new religion upon which their future hopes were to be based and by which their present deportment was to be regulated, it is unthinkable that a whole nation gave a mechanical assent, and still more so that they unitedly endorsed evidence which they knew to be false, especially when those same narratives inculcated a code of conduct which they certainly had never designed of their own accord.

But more—not only were many of the Mosaic institutions radically different from those practiced by all other nations, and from what the Hebrews had themselves observed in Egypt, they also involved numerous rites which required constant attention and which must have been most irksome and unpleasant. Moreover, those ceremonies subjected the Israelites to considerable expense by the costly sacrifices they were frequently required to offer and the tithes they were commanded to pay the priests. Furthermore, some of the laws bound upon them were of such a character that it is altogether unaccountable, on the principles of political wisdom, that any legislator should have proposed or that a whole nation should meekly have submitted to them. Such was the law of the Sabbath year, which forbade them tilling or sowing the ground for a whole twelve months (Ex. 23:10, 11). Such was the law ordering all the males to journey from every part of the land to the tabernacle (Deut. 16) —leaving their homes unprotected. Such was the law which prohibited their king multiplying horses (Deut. 17:16); and more especially the law of jubilee, when all mortgaged property had to be restored to the original owners and all slaves freed (Lev. 25:10).

Now we submit that it is utterly incredible to suppose that any sane legislator would, on his own authority, have imposed enactments which interfered so seriously with both private and public liberty, and which involved such hazards as the people dying of starvation while their fields lay fallow, and their wives and children being murdered by invaders when all their menfolk were far removed from them. Still more inconceivable is it that, instead of bitterly resenting and openly revolting against such unpopular statutes, the whole nation should quietly acquiesce therein. It is quite pointless to say that Israel was imposed upon by Moses, that he deceived them into believing those laws were of Divine authority. No such deception was possible, for the simple reason that the entire nation was assembled at Sinai and had witnessed the supernatural and awe-inspiring phenomena when the Lord had descended and given those Laws audibly—they had with their own ears heard a portion of it published. Israel's reception of such a Law can only be accounted for on the basis that they were fully assured it proceeded from God Himself.

Having demonstrated that the Scriptures could not have been manufactured by either wicked impostors or deluded fanatics, that they were not invented by the Christian Church or the ancient Jews, we are shut up to the only remaining alternative, namely, that they are a revelation from God—His own inspired and infallible Word. No other choice is left; no other explanation is credible. Every other attempt to explain their origin is found, upon critical examination, to be not only altogether inadequate, but utterly absurd. If a thinking man finds it difficult, nay, impossible, to explain a created universe apart from a Divine Creator, it is no less so for him to account for the Book of books without a Divine Author. This is a matter which admits of no compromise: if the Bible has come to us from God, then it has claims upon us which infinitely transcend those of all other writings. If it is not from God, then it is an impious fraud, unworthy of our attention. There is no middle ground! Moreover, if the Bible is not what it claims to be, then we are left without any revelation which, with any reliability or authority, can impart to us the knowledge of God or warrant its reception by mankind!

We now come to the 5th point—It bears the hallmark of genuineness: the contents of the Bible are just what might be looked for. What are the essential characteristics we should expect to find in a written communication from God unto fallen mankind? Would they not be, first, the imparting to us of a knowledge of the true God; and second, of that instruction which is best suited to our varied needs? Such is precisely what we have in the Bible. The grand truth taught throughout the Sacred Scriptures is that God does all things for His own glory and for the manifestation of His own perfections. And is not that exactly in accord with right reason? Once men are led to entertain any true conceptions of the Supreme Being, they are brought to the irresistible conclusion that One who is self-existent and self-sufficient, the Creator and Proprietor of the universe, could not be swayed by any creature or moved to action from a regard to anything outside of Himself, or irrespective of Himself—that in all His works—both of creation and providence, He will have a supreme regard unto His own honor and the maintaining of His own perfections.

If, then, the Bible is the Word of God, proceeding from Himself, stamped with the autograph of His own authority, we naturally expect to find it possessed of that characteristic and directed to that end. Thus in fact it is. The cardinal design of the Sacred Scriptures is to make God known, to exhibit the peerless excellence of His character, to teach us the homage and adoration which are His due. Their supreme end is to display to us the glorious attributes of God, that we may learn to form the most elevated conceptions of His Being, our own entire dependence upon Him, our deep obligations to show forth His praise. The scope of the entire Bible is to teach us our relations to God, and that the business of our lives is to give Him His true place in our hearts, to act always so as to please Him. Yet the very reverse of that is what obtains in human practice: in view of which we are forced to conclude that had men originated the Bible its teaching thereon had been very different, and that it had contained no such statements as, "The LORD hath made all things for Himself" (Prov. 16:4), "Whatsoever ye do, do all to the glory of God" (1 Cor. 10:31).

Again—would we not naturally expect to find a revelation from God couched in a strain very different from that in which one man speaks to another? Since the Creator is so high above the creature, does it not befit Him to address us in terms which become His august majesty? Such is just what we find in the Bible. Its instructions are delivered to us not in an argumentative form, but in an authoritative manner, for while arguments are suited to equals, they would be quite out of place for the Allwise when directing the ignorant. Its precepts are not proffered to us as so much good advice which we are free to heed or not at our pleasure, but rather as imperial edicts which we disregard to our eternal undoing. The commandments of Scripture admit of no questioning: "Thou shalt," and "Thou shalt not," are its peremptory terms. In the most uncompromising way, and without the least semblance of apology, the Bible claims the absolute right to dictate unto all men what they should do, condemns them for their failure, and pronounces sentence of judgment upon every offender. From Genesis to Revelation the contents of Holy Writ are set forth in dictatorial language beyond which there is no appeal. It speaks throughout as from an infinitely elevated plane.

Moreover, the Bible does not single out for address merely the ignorant and the base, but issues its orders unto all classes alike. The cultured as well as the illiterate, the high as well as the low, the rich equally with the poor are imperatively told what they must do and from what they must abstain. And that one feature alone places the Bible, my reader, in a class by itself. If it possessed not the same, then we should have grave reason to suspect its authenticity. It would be most incongruous for the Ancient of Days to use a conciliatory tone and employ the language of obsequiousness when vouchsafing a communication to creatures who are but of yesterday. So far from the language of dogmatism being unsuited, it is exactly what might be looked for in a revelation from the Most High. Nevertheless, the dictatorial ring of the Bible accords it a unique place in the realm of literature. There is no other book in the world which demands, on pain of eternal perdition, the total submission of all mankind unto its authority; as there is none other which pronounces a fearful curse on anyone who has the audacity to take away from its contents. The ring of imperial authority which sounds through all its chapters indicates that it is the voice of the living God who is the Speaker.

Yet it will also follow that if the Bible be a Divine revelation, then it must be suited to the needs of man, and not simply this or that man, but of all without distinction. One of the clearest marks of the handiwork of God in the material creation is that of design and adaptation—that all His productions are perfectly fitted to answer the ends for which they are made—as the human hand to perform so many different tasks. We should therefore expect to find this same characteristic stamped upon the Bible; nor is that expectation disappointed! It imparts to us the knowledge of God's glorious character and our relations to Him, and reveals the means by which we may regain His favor and secure our own eternal happiness. The Holy Scriptures furnish us with an accurate diagnosis of the human heart and all its manifold workings. They describe to us our enemies and make known the stratagems which they employ, and how they are to be resisted and overcome. They discover to us the character of that malady which has smitten our moral nature, and the great Physician who is able to recover us therefrom. They specify the most serious of the dangers which menace us, and faithfully warn us against the same. They supply instruction which if heeded promotes our welfare in every way.

The Bible makes known to us how wisdom, strength, and true joy are to be obtained here, and how Heaven may be our portion hereafter. It supplies salutary counsels which are admirably suited to all our varied circumstances. It is adapted equally to the young as to the aged, to those in prosperity or those in adversity. Its language is simple enough for those of little education, yet it has depths in it which the most learned cannot fathom. In the Scriptures there is as great a variety as there is in Nature, something to meet the most diverse temperaments and tastes: history, poetry, biography, prophecy, legislation—the essentials of hygiene, profound mysteries, and a message of glad tidings to those in despair. Moreover, the Bible is self-explanatory. No reference library is required to be consulted in order to arrive at the meaning of anything in it: one part interprets another. The New Testament supplements the Old, and by patiently comparing Scripture with Scripture the diligent reader may ascertain the significance of any figure, symbol, or term used therein; though its spiritual secrets are disclosed only unto the prayerful and the obedient.

As the light is accommodated to the eye and the eye formed and fitted to receive the light, so though the Scriptures have come from Heaven, yet are they perfectly suited to those who live on earth. They contain all the information that is required by man as a moral and accountable being. There is no important problem relating to either our temporal or eternal welfare upon which the Bible does not supply excellent counsel. Though its contents be ineffably sublime, they are at the same time intensely practical, meeting every moral and spiritual need, adapted alike to Jew and Gentile, ancient or modern, rich or poor. The Bible not only makes known how the State should be governed and the Church ordered, but it furnishes full instruction to direct the individual and to regulate the home. In a word, the Bible is qualified to be a lamp unto our feet and a light unto our path. When, then, we examine this Book which claims to come from God, and find it possesses all those marks and evidences which could reasonably be expected or desired, that it is exactly suited to answer all the ends of a Divine revelation, we are obliged to conclude that our Creator has graciously met our deep need, and therefore that revelation should be received by us with the utmost reverence and welcomed with the deepest thanksgiving.

Let us move on to the 6th point—Christ and the Scriptures. What was His attitude toward them? What was His estimate of them? What use did He make of them? The answers to those questions are of supreme importance and must settle the matter once and for all, for what is the opinion of any man worth when placed over against the verdict of the Son of God! Give, then, your best attention while we seek to furnish a reply to those inquiries. Negatively, Christ never cast the slightest doubt upon their validity or called into question their authenticity. When His detractors reminded Him, "Moses wrote unto us" such and such a thing, He did not say that Moses was wrong, but told them they "erred, not knowing the Scriptures" (Mark 12:19-24). When a lawyer sought to ensnare Him, so far from brushing aside the authority of the Scriptures, He enforced the same, saying, "What is written in the Law?" (Luke 10:26). When engaged in any controversy, His invariable appeal was unto the Old Testament, and declared that what David said was "by the Spirit," (Mark 12:36). Not once did He intimate that it was unreliable and untrustworthy.

But let us turn to the positive side. Behold the Lord Jesus when He was assaulted by the Devil, and note well that the only weapon He made use of was the Sword of the Spirit. Each time He repulsed the Tempter with a sentence from the Old Testament (Matthew 4)! And observe that as soon as that mysterious conflict was over, God—to evince His approbation of Christ's conduct—sent angels to "minister unto Him" (Mark 1:13). Mark how He commenced His public ministry, by entering the synagogue, reading from the Prophet Isaiah, and saying, "This day is this Scripture fulfilled in your ears" (Luke 4:16-21). Hear Him as He declared, "Think not that I am come to destroy the Law or the Prophets: I am not come to destroy, but to fulfil. For verily I say unto you, Till Heaven and earth pass, one jot or tittle shall in no wise pass from the Law till all be fulfilled" (Matthew 5:17, 18). He had come to enforce the teachings of the Old Testament in their minutest detail, to honor and magnify the same, by rendering a personal and perfect obedience to them. He owned the Scriptures as "the Word of God" (Mark 7:13) just as they stood—without any reservation or qualification—thereby authenticating all the books of the Old Testament.

So far from regarding the Old Testament as being full of myths and fables, He taught that Abraham, Lot, Moses, Daniel, were real entities. He expressly ratified the very incidents at which the skeptics scoff: the Flood, the destruction of Sodom and Gomorrah by fire from Heaven (Luke 17:28-29), Jonah being three days and nights in the whale's belly (Matthew 12:40), thereby denying they were but "folk lore," and establishing their historicity. Christ placed the words of Moses on a par with His own—(John 5:46, 47). Jesus said, "If they hear not Moses and the Prophets, neither will they be persuaded though one rose from the dead" (Luke 16:31), which again evinces our Lord's estimate of the Old Testament. It was of supreme authority to Him. When vindicating Himself for affirming His Deity, after quoting from the Psalms He added, "and the Scripture cannot be broken" (John 10:35)—it is infallible, inviolable. When engaged in prayer to the Father He solemnly declared, "Thy Word is Truth" (John 17:17): not simply contains the Truth, or even is true, but "is Truth"—without the least tincture of error, the word of Him "that cannot lie" (Titus 1:2).

When His enemies came to arrest Him in the Garden and Peter drew his sword, the Savior rebuked him, saving, "Thinkest thou that I cannot pray to My Father, and that He shall at once give Me more than twelve legions of angels," yet note well how He at once added, "But how then shall the Scripture be fulfilled, that thus it must be?" (Matthew 26:53, 54). Very blessed is that: showing that the written Word was what regulated His every action, and that it was His strong consolation in His darkest hour. Reverently behold Him on the Cross, and observe Him placing homage upon the sacred Psalter by using its words when undergoing the extreme anguish of Divine desertion (Ps. 22:1; Matthew 27:46). But more—"Jesus . . . that the Scripture might be fulfilled, saith, I thirst" (John 19:28). There was yet one detail predicted of His dying sufferings which had not been accomplished, namely, that, "in My thirst they gave Me vinegar to drink" (Ps. 69:21), and therefore in subjection to the Divine authority of the Old Testament, He cried "I thirst"! After rising in triumph from the grave, we find our blessed Lord again magnifying the Scriptures: "Beginning at Moses and the Prophets, He expounded unto them in all the Scriptures the things concerning Himself" (Luke 24:27).

Thus we are left in no doubt whatever of Christ's attitude toward, estimate of, and the use which He made of the Scriptures. He ever treated them with the utmost reverence, affirmed their Divine authority, and considered that one word of theirs put an end to all controversy. He averred the Old testament was "the Word of God," entirely inerrant, verbally inspired, as a whole and in all its parts. He affirmed that the Scriptures are the final court of appeal, and asserted their perpetuity. For the Christian, the testimony of Christ is final: he requires no further evidence or argument. Nor should the non-Christian. It is the height of absurdity to suppose that One who was endowed with infinitely superior wisdom to Solomon should have been imposed upon by a fraud; as it would be horrible blasphemy to say that He knowingly set His imprimatur upon what He knew to be false. Whose judgment, my friend, do you prefer: that of the so-called "advanced thinkers" or the verdict of the Son of God? Which deem you the more trustworthy?

Chapter 9
THE HOLY BIBLE IS UNIQUE

We come now to our 7th point—Its uniqueness. Viewed simply as a book, the Bible stands far apart from all others. Amid the writings of the ancients or the productions of our moderns there is nothing which, for a moment, bears comparison with it. The Bible not only occupies a prominent place in literature, but an unrivalled one. Consider its amazing circulation. The number of its editions is to be counted not by the dozen or even the hundreds, but literally by the thousands. And not merely tens or hundreds of thousands of copies have been printed, but hundreds of millions! That at once separates it by an immeasurable distance from everything penned by man. Consider its unequalled translation. It has been rendered into almost all the multitudinous dialects of the earth. Those of nearly every nation now have the Bible in their own tongue. It has been printed in more than 600 languages! That too, is without any parallel. The most famous and popular compositions of men have not been translated into one tenth as many tongues. Consider its by-products: countless works have been devoted to its exposition, millions of sermons preached and published on portions of it. That also is without any precedent.

Consider further the laborious indexes which have been made upon its contents. There are voluminous concordances which not only list every word used in the Scriptures, but all the occurrences of them—in many cases scores, and in not a few, hundreds of references. Now we do not possess complete concordances of any of the writings of the most renowned human author, wherein is collated every occurrence of each word he used. And why? Because no such nicety, no such significance, pertains to his language as makes the sense of a passage or the force of an argument turn upon a single word. Much less has the ablest of human authors employed all his terms with exact consistency and correspondence throughout the whole of his writings. Yet such is the case with the Bible—wherein no less than forty different men were used as its scribes! The Concordance loudly proclaims the uniqueness of the Bible. It tacitly declares that not simply this or that term, but every word from Genesis to Revelation is God-breathed, and that every occurrence of each word was directed by His unerring wisdom.

The perpetuity of their text is unique. The Sacred Scriptures were written originally in Hebrew and Greek, which are the only languages that, dating back of all tradition, are still recognized as living vehicles of thought. The language spoken in the streets of modern Athens is identically the same, to its very accents, as that used by Plato and Socrates, yea, of Homer's Iliad, which was composed almost 3,000 years ago. In like manner, the Hebrew of the Talmud is the Hebrew of the book of Genesis. What a remarkable survival, or rather a miracle, of Divine power! That becomes more apparent when we contrast how other ancient tongues have long since passed away. The Egyptian language used by the builders of the pyramids has perished. The Syrian used by Rabshakeh is no more. The dialect spoken by the original Britons is now unknown. Yet the Hebrew employed by Moses is spoken by the Jewish rabbi today, and the Greek used by the Apostle Paul is heard in Salonica at this hour. Here, then, is a striking and unparalleled fact: that the languages in which God wrote His Word have outlived all their contemporaries and have remained unchanged throughout the centuries!

Even on its surface the Bible differs from all other books. That appears in the style of its writings. Two languages were used which are quite diverse in their manner of inscription. The Hebrew is written and read from right to left, whereas the Greek (and all modern languages) is written and read from left to right. The Scriptures make no comment upon that arresting and striking contrast, but leaves the reader to interpret the fact in the light of their contents. Once attention be focused upon the same, its significance is at once apparent: in the singular reversal of its text the Bible teaches us the two most fundamental and radical facts in human history: man's apostasy from God, and his restoration. The "right hand" is that of dignity and privilege (Ps. 110:1), the "left hand" is that of disgrace and condemnation (Matthew 25:41). The Old Testament, written in Hebrew, is an amplification of that statement, "man being in honor abideth not" (Ps. 49:12), being a record of his departure from God, with all its evil consequences. The New Testament, written in Greek, has for its leading theme how the wanderer is restored to God, how the prodigal returns to the Father's house.

As another has pointed out, the uniqueness of the Bible appears (again) in that its conjugation of the Hebrew verb puts man in his proper place. "In all Occidental languages the verb is conjugated from the first person to the third—'I,' 'Thou,' 'He.' The Hebrew, in reversal of the human thought, is conjugated from the third down and backward to the first: beginning with God, then my neighbor, then myself last—'He,' 'Thou,' 'I.' This is the Divine order: self-obliterating and beautiful." That peculiarity is very much more than an interesting detail in philology: it embodies and expresses a profound spiritual truth. It accords God His due pre-eminence, and thereby teaches us that all right thinking must start with Him and work downward to man. For that very reason the Scriptures open with the words, "In the beginning GOD." No theology can be sound unless it makes that Truth its foundation and starting point. The initiative is ever with God: "we love Him because He first loved us" (1 John 4:19). Once God is accorded His rightful place in our affections, man is automatically put where he belongs—but which, apart from Divine revelation and Divine grace, he never takes!

Our 8th point—Its delineation of God. The portrayal of Deity supplied by the Bible is so very different from and so vastly superior to that furnished by all other sources—we are forced to conclude it cannot be of human invention. Beginning with the Old Testament, let us single out two statements which were penned by Moses. "Hear, 0 Israel, the LORD our God is one Lord" (Deut. 6:4). That is a startling, yea, a unique declaration, at complete variance with the conceptions of all His contemporaries. Polytheism, or a belief in and worship of a plurality of gods, prevailed universally among the heathen. Whence then did Moses obtain his knowledge of the true God, who is one in His essence? Certainly not from the Egyptians, for their king confessed, "I know not the LORD" (Ex. 5:2). "The LORD God, merciful and gracious, longsuffering and abundant in goodness and truth, keeping mercy for thousands, forgiving iniquity and transgression and sin, and that will by no means clear the guilty"—who continue impenitent and despise an atoning sacrifice (Ex. 34:6, 7). Such a conception of the Divine perfections is as far beyond the reach of man's mind as Heaven is above the earth. Search the philosophers, the mystics, and religious teachers of the ancients, and nothing can be found which in the least resembles such a blessed conception of God as that.

"For thus saith the high and lofty One that inhabiteth eternity, whose name is Holy: I dwell in the high and holy place, with him also that is of a contrite and humble spirit." "Thus saith the Lord, The heaven is My throne and the earth is My footstool: where is the house that ye build unto Me? And where is the place of My rest? For all those things hath Mine hand made, and all those things have been, saith the Lord: but to this man will I look, even to him that is poor and of a contrite spirit" (Isa. 57:15; 66:1, 2). The majesty of such language at once distinguishes it from all human compositions and evinces it was not fabricated by the brain of man. But suppose for the sake of argument that the mind of man had soared to such an elevated conception of Deity as is portrayed in the first part of those passages, it had certainly not conceived of what follows in the second part. Therein God is presented not only in the greatness of His infinite excellence above all creatures, but also in His amazing condescension unto the meanest of men. Those verses not only exhibit the transcendence of the Creator, but make known the marvels of His grace, "which He accounts His own glory" (Eph. 1:6).

Turning to the New Testament, we will confine ourselves to three brief statements: "God is spirit" (John 4:24), "God is light" (1 John 1:5), "God is love" (1 John 4:8). Those three descriptions of Deity furnish us with a truer and more elevated view of Him than could the most elaborate definitions of human eloquence and genius. They announce the spirituality, the purity, and the benevolence of God. The first purports to be a record of words spoken by Christ during His earthly ministry; the second and third to be inspired declarations given by the Holy Spirit through a human instrument. If their Divine origin be denied, then the skeptic is faced with this problem: all three were penned by an unlettered fisherman! Whence did he derive such conceptions?—conceptions before which philosophy is abashed. The sublimity and the comprehensiveness of those brief expressions are without any peer, or even parallel. If they originated from one unlearned, it would be a much greater marvel and miracle than that he wrote them under Divine dictation. Much more might be added by entering into a detailed enumeration of all the wondrous attributes of God, but sufficient has been pointed out to establish how immeasurably grander is the Bible's delineation of God than anything found in the writings of men.

Our 9th point—Its representation of man. The account which the Bible gives of man is radically different from that supplied by all human compositions. That sin and misery exist, yea, abound in the world, is a patent fact, however unpleasant it may be. The daily newspapers report it, the police courts illustrate it, the prisons witness thereto. Nor is this fearful moral disease confined to any one nation, or even limited to any particular strata of society, but is common to all. It is no new epidemic, for it has prevailed in all periods of history. Every human attempt to banish or even curb it has failed. Legislation, education, increased wages and improved environments have produced no change for the better. Sin is too deeply rooted and widely spread in human nature for the remedial efforts of social reformers to extirpate it. The wisest men who reject the Divine explanation of this tragic mystery are completely in the dark as to the real nature and origin of the malady. The Bible is the only book in existence which truly describes the sinful condition of man, accurately diagnoses his case, and ascribes it to an adequate cause. It teaches that as a result of his defection from God at the beginning of human history, he is a fallen, ruined, guilty, lost creature.

The picture which the Scripture gives of man is a deeply humiliating one, radically different from all drawn by human pencils. It is so because human writers describe how man views himself and how he appears in the eyes of his fellows—the Bible alone informs us what man is in the sight of God! His unerring Word affirms, "There is none righteous: no, not one" (Rom. 3:10)—not a single member of our race who is conformed to the Divine Rule. That Word solemnly asserts, "There is none that doeth good" (Rom. 3:12) according to the Divine Standard of conduct: not one in his natural condition whose actions proceed from a holy principle, acts out of love to God, or with an eye only to His glory. Such statements as those are much too unpalatable to proud human nature to have been made by any who sought to palm off an alleged communication from Heaven designed for universal acceptance. The Bible also shows why we cannot meet the just requirements of our Maker: each of us is "shapen in iniquity" and conceived in sin (Ps. 51:5). Depravity is transmitted from parent to child: each one enters this world with a defiled nature, with a bent toward evil.

Since the fountain is polluted, all the streams issuing therefrom are foul. Fallen Adam "begat a son in his own [moral] likeness, after his [sinful] image" (Gen. 5:3), and thus it has been with each succeeding generation. "Man is born like a wild ass's colt" (Job 11:12)— thoroughly intractable, hating restraint, wanting to have his own way. Think you, my reader, such a description of human nature as that was invented by man? "The wicked are estranged from the womb: they go astray as soon as they are born, speaking lies" (Ps. 58:3). Entering this world "alienated from the life of God" (Eph. 4:18), that which is bred in the bone quickly comes out in the flesh. No child requires to be taught to tell lies—it is natural for him to do so, and the more he is left free to "develop his own personality" without "inhibitions," the more will his delinquency appear. "Man at his best estate is altogether vanity" (Ps. 39:5)—an empty bubble, yea, as vain as a peacock. He is as unsubstantial as the wind. "Men of high degree are a lie: to be laid in the balance they are altogether lighter than vanity" (Ps. 62:9). Man, who so glories in himself, would never originate such an estimate of himself.

Instead of making Satan the author of all our iniquities, the Holy Bible teaches, "For from within, out of the heart of men, proceed evil thoughts, adulteries, fornication, murders, thefts, covetousness, wickedness, deceit, lasciviousness, an evil eye, blasphemy, pride, foolishness; all these evil things come from within and defile the man" (Mark 7:21-23). External temptations would have no power unless there was something within us to which they could appeal: a lighted match is a menace to a barrel of gunpowder, but not so to one filled with water! That explains why all the efforts of statesmen, educators, and social reformers are unavailing to effect any improvement of man—they are incapable of reaching the seat of his moral disease; at most, they can but place outward restraints on him. It is vain to move the hands of a watch or polish its case if the mainspring be broken. "The heart is deceitful above all things and desperately wicked" (Jer. 17:9), is another concept which would never originate in the human mind, for it is quite contrary to our ideas and too abasing for our acceptance. Such a pride-withering delineation of human nature as the Bible furnishes could have been supplied by none other than God Himself.

The Bible not only paints human nature in the colors of truth and reality, but it also reveals how it has come to be what it now is. The existence of moral evil has been acknowledged in every age, for it was far too palpable and potent to be denied, but whence it came and how it originated proved to be a problem which the wisest, without Divine revelation, were unable to solve. To ascribe it to the malignity of matter (as some of the ancients did) is a manifest absurdity, for matter possesses no moral qualities, and could not corrupt the heart and mind, however closely it were placed in connection with them. The Scriptures inform us that, "Man being in honor abideth not" (Ps. 49:12). The Hebrew word for man, there, is Adam, and that verse informs us that the father of our race continued not in the state of purity in which God created him. He disobeyed his Maker, lost his innocence by his own fault, and having corrupted himself, has communicated his depravity unto all his descendants. "By one man sin entered the world, and death by sin; and so death passed upon all men, for that all have sinned" (Rom. 5:12). The root was vitiated, and therefore every part of the tree springing from it is tainted.

We now come to point 10—Its teaching on sin. As might well be expected, the teaching of Holy Writ thereon is as different from that of fallen man's as is light from darkness. So long as it breaks not forth in open crime, to the injury of their own interests, those of this world regard sin lightly and minimize its seriousness. In many quarters sin is regarded as being merely a species of ignorance, and the sinner is looked upon as more to be pitied than blamed. The various terms which are commonly used as substitutes for sin indicate how inadequate and low is the popular conception: infirmities, mistakes, shortcomings, youthful follies they speak of—rather than iniquities, transgressions, disobedience, wickedness. In the Bible sin is never palliated or extenuated, but from first to last its heinousness and enormity are insisted upon. The Word of Truth declares that "sin is very grievous" (Gen. 18:20), that "abominable thing" which the Lord "hates" (Jer. 44:4). It regards sin as being "red like crimson" (Isa. 1:18), and declares it to be "exceeding sinful" (Rom. 7:13). It likens sin to "the poison of asps," to the "scum" of a seething pot, to the loathsome disease of leprosy.

The Bible declares "the thought of foolishness is sin" (Prov. 24:9)—what human mind devised such a standard as that?! It teaches that "whatsoever is not of faith is sin" (Rom. 14:23), so that unbelief and doubting are reprobate. It insists that, "to him that knoweth to do good, and doeth it not, to him it is sin" (James 4:17), so that sins of omission, equally with those of commission, are condemned. Yea, sins of ignorance are culpable (Lev. 5:17), for with God's Word in our hands ignorance is inexcusable. Holy Writ teaches that sin is more than an act, namely, an attitude which precedes and produces the action. "Sin is lawlessness" (1 John 3:4 R.V.), spiritual anarchy, a state of rebellion against the Lawgiver Himself. It insists that we are sinners by nature before we are sinners by practice. It does not restrict its indictments to any particular class, but declares that "all have sinned and come short of the glory of God." Now a book which uniformly depicts sin as a vile and hideous thing, which strips man of every excuse, which declares that "every imagination of the heart of man is only evil continually" (Gen. 6:5), and which brings in "all the world guilty before God" (Rom. 3:19) could not have been created by fallen creatures, but must have come from the thrice Holy One.

The same applies with equal force to the teaching of the Scriptures concerning the punishment of sin. A defective view of sin necessarily leads to an inadequate conception of what is due unto it. Man looks at sin and its deserts solely from the human viewpoint, but the Bible exhibits its malignity in the light of God's broken Law, and shows it to be one of infinite enormity and guilt, which—where the atoning sacrifice of Christ be rejected—demands and receives eternal punishment. The Word of Truth reveals that all who die in their sins will be consciously tormented forever and ever in "Hell fire," and there will not be a drop of water to relieve the sufferer. The sphere of their anguish is described as "the blackness of darkness forever," for not a ray of hope ever enters there, and where there is "wailing and gnashing of teeth." None but the Holy One, who alone is capable of determining what is due to rebels against Himself, could have lifted the veil and given us a glimpse of the terrible character of sin's wages. The fact that this solemn truth is so distasteful to all and so widely rejected, and yet occupies a place of so much prominence in the Bible, is one of the many proofs that it is not of human origin.

Let us proceed to the 11th point—Its historical parts. Much of the Bible consists of historical narratives, yet both their contents and the style in which they are written at once distinguish them from all others. They cover a period of no less than 4,000 years! The Old Testament contains the oldest records of the world, dating far back of the chronicles of men, yea, of the dimmest traditions of all nations, save the Jewish, and therefore the Scriptures of the Old Testament are many centuries older than any other historical records. Herodotus, who has been styled "the Father of History," was born a thousand years after Moses!—the penman employed by God in writing the Pentateuch. They not only impart information which none of the writings of antiquity contain, but are in striking contrast with the legendary fables of early Greece and Rome. The Bible alone supplies us with any knowledge of the affairs of this world during its first 15 centuries. Antedating all human historians, God Himself has made known to us how the earth came into existence, how the nations originated, and has given a brief but succinct account of the antediluvian era which terminated in the Flood—all of which matters are entirely beyond our imagination.

The opening verses of Genesis stand in a class entirely by themselves. Their teaching upon the creation of the universe out of nothing is quite peculiar to Holy Writ. Such an idea is not to be found in the most rational and refined systems of secular writers. Even where an intelligent Architect was conceived of, as in the speculations of Plato and Aristotle, yet he was portrayed as working upon existing material, on eternal matter. While the hypothesis favored by the earlier Egyptians and Babylonians was that everything, including the stars and this earth, has developed from the inherent power of the sun. For reconditeness of theme and yet simplicity of language, for comprehensiveness of scope and yet brevity of description, for scientific exactitude and yet the absence of technical terms, nothing can be found in all literature which for a moment compares with the opening chapter of the Bible. Its Divine revelation stands out in marked separation, not only from the meaningless cosmogonies of the ancients and the senseless mythologies of the heathen, but equally from the laborious jargon of our moderns who essay to write upon the origin of things, and which are out of date almost as soon as published.

Again—the historical portions of the Bible, alone, supply us with a satisfactory explanation of the present state of the world. As was pointed out earlier, the earth exhibits numerous marks of intelligence and benignity, yet they are neither of unvaried orderliness nor of unmixed benevolence. If on the one hand we behold the fertile fields and beauties of nature, on the other there are icy wastes, vast deserts, death-dealing volcanoes. It is apparent that this earth has experienced some fearful convulsion, by which its original structure has been deranged. It is still subject to earthquakes, devastating tornadoes and tidal waves. Man and this earth are manifestly adapted to each other; nevertheless there are many examples of such discrepancy. Why is this? Certainly not because of any imperfection in the Creator. Then why? The Bible alone accounts for these abnormalities, and it does so in a way without the wisdom and power of the Creator being impeached. It reveals that, as the result of sin, God is now dealing in justice and holiness with His refractory subjects, as well as in goodness and mercy with the creatures of His hand.

The uniqueness of Scripture history appears not only in the disclosures which are made, but also in its style and omissions. Its method of chronicling events is radically different from all other histories. It only just touches upon, and often entirely ignores, matters which had been of most interest to men of the world, whereas it frequently treats at length of things which they had deemed of no importance. How amazingly brief is the account given the creating and furnishing of this earth! Man had never restricted that to a single chapter, and then have devoted more than 10 others to the tabernacle and its erection. No indeed: the wisdom of this world would had regarded the grand edifice of the universe as worthy of a much fuller description than that of a religious tent! Nothing is told us of the "seven wonders" of the ancient world. Men of renown are passed by in silence, while the pastoral lives of insignificant individuals are narrated. The great empires of antiquity are scarcely alluded to, and then only as they touch the interests of Israel. A principle of selection obtains such as no secular historians adopt, and the events singled out are set down as a plain record of facts, without any attempt of the writers to mingle their own reflections with them.

The design of sacred history is entirely different from that of all others. Its aim is not simply to preserve the memory of certain occurrences, but to teach us the knowledge of God and His salvation, and to show us our deep need of the same. Its purpose is not merely to narrate bare facts, but rather impart important moral instruction. It does very much more than convey us a knowledge of events, an account of which is nowhere else obtainable—the agency of God in connection with those events is constantly brought out. That which uninspired historians either overlook or deliberately ignore is made prominent, namely, the Divine displeasure against sin. The historical portions of Scripture display to us throughout, the excellence of the Divine character, and set before us His governing of this world. Sacred history is very much more than an authentic record of human affairs: it exhibits the perversity and folly, the instability and unbelief of human nature, and reveals the springs from which our actions proceed. In its narratives the thoughts and secret motives of men are discovered, and that in a manner and to an extent which none but the great Searcher of hearts was capable of doing. The real character of man is unveiled as in no other writings.

"The Bible describes, in action and exhibition, the perfections of Jehovah as fully as the proclamation in which He declares Himself to be longsuffering and of great mercy, forgiving iniquity, transgression and sin. It delineates the deceitfulness and desperate wickedness of the heart, as forcibly and distinctly as the annunciation's of the Prophets, when they aloud and spare not" (Robert Haldane). It emphasizes the providential interposition of God in human affairs and His ways with men. Therein we are shown what a mad and bitter thing it is for either an individual or a nation to forsake the living God—and, contrariwise, what blessings attend those who walk in subjection and fellowship with Him. Consequently its narratives are of great practical value: not only in a general way by showing how God punishes sin and rewards righteousness, but by specific and personal illustrations of the same. Vital ethical and spiritual lessons are thereby inculcated, and from the lives of different individuals we are taught what examples are worthy of our emulation and what evils and dangers it will be our wisdom and profit to avoid. Thus those sacred narratives afford us scope for constant meditation. Into the inspired history is most wondrously interwoven all the doctrines and duties promulgated by Christ and His Apostles.

But the grand design of the Old Testament was to make manifest the need for, the nature of, and the various preparations made unto the redemptive work of Christ. Everything else was subordinated unto an anticipation of the all-important advent of God's Son to this earth and the inauguration of the Christian era. As there is one central object in the heavens which far surpasses in glory all other planets, so the Person and mission of the Lord Jesus Christ is accorded the place of pre-eminence in the Sacred Volume. That was what regulated the principle of selection as to what should or should not be recorded in the Bible. Hence it is that the history of Adam and his posterity during the first 2,000 years is condensed into but eleven chapters, and why very little indeed is said about them—special attention being directed only unto those individuals from which the promised Messiah was to spring. For the same reason, from Genesis 12 onwards we are occupied almost entirely with the history of Abraham and his descendants. The lives of the Patriarchs are described in much more detail, that we may perceive the sovereignty and grace of God in His choice of and dealings with them; and that we may obtain a better view of the stock from which Christ, according to His humanity, was to issue.

Most of the Old Testament is a history of the nation of Israel, and it, too, is written in a manner quite different from all others, for as one has well said, "It is recorded by the unerring hand of Truth." No effort is made to magnify the virtues of Israel, nor is there the least attempt to hide their vices. Had those records been composed by uninspired Jews, then obviously they would have labored to present the most attractive picture possible of their own people, and therefore no reference would had been made unto their base ingratitude and hard-heartedness. Particularly would a forgery have sought to impress other nations with the might, valor, and military genius of the Jews. But so far from that, their faint-heartedness and defeats are frequently recorded. The capture of Jericho and the conquest of Canaan are not attributed to the brilliance of Joshua and the bravery of his men, but to the Lord's showing Himself strong in their behalf. Nor did the victories granted them proceed from partiality or caprice, for only while they walked in obedience to God's Law did He crown their efforts with success. It is noteworthy that the sacred history of the Old Testament ends at the point where credible secular history begins, for the occupation of Palestine by the Persians, Greeks and Romans is recorded by Xenophon and his successors.

And finally, point 12—Its typical teachings. Since the incarnation of His Son, with the attendant blessings of redemption, was the grand object contemplated by God from the dawn of human history, He ordered everything in the early ages of the world to pave the way for the same, particularly in the educating of His people concerning it. It pleased God to first preach the Gospel to them by means of parables, by symbolical instruction and typical occurrences which foreshadowed the Person and work of the future Redeemer. Therein lies the key which opens many a chapter of the Old Testament, which to those lacking, it appears not only of little interest but unworthy of a place in a Divine revelation. But once their scope and significance be recognized, we perceive in those ancient institutions and religious rites such a wondrous anticipation of and perfect correspondence with what is set forth more openly in the New Testament as no human wisdom could have devised. There is a pre-arranged harmony between type and antitype as no mortal could invent; a prophetic meaning in them which only God could have given. The fitness of the types and the agreement of the antitypes lie not so much in their external resemblance as in the essential oneness of the ideas they embody and express and their relations to each other.

The types are so many outward emblems and visible signs appointed by God to portray spiritual objects. They were so constructed and arranged as to express in symbolical form the great truths and principles which are common alike to all dispensations, such as the holiness of God and its requirements, the sinfulness of sin and its polluting effects, the necessity for a Mediator. Under the Levitical ceremonies there was set forth a palpable exhibition of sin and salvation, the purification of the heart, and the dedication of the person and life unto God. His method of revelation was first to portray heavenly things by means of earthly, to make known eternal realities through temporal events, to exhibit to the physical senses what was later presented more directly to the mind. Thereby was indicated on a lower plane what was to be accomplished on a far higher one. Visible things were made to image and prepare the way for the disclosure of the more spiritual mysteries of Christ's kingdom. In that way the earlier dispensations were made the servants for getting ready the stage of things to come. God so modeled the institutions of Israel's worship as to set before their eyes the cardinal doctrines of Christianity, the one being a stepping-stone to the other. During the immaturity of God's family celestial things were more easily grasped when set forth in a corporate form than by abstract statements about them.

The events recorded in the Old Testament were actual occurrences, yet they also presaged the more excellent things which were promised. Divine Providence so molded human history that in many instances there was made a typical representation of the work of redemption. That was set forth, in its broad outlines, in the days of Noah. The fearful flood which God sent upon the world of the ungodly made known His intense hatred of sin and the punishment which it entails. Yet before that judgment fell, merciful warning was made and time given for repentance; but the wicked repented not. In the ark we behold the gracious provision which God made for those who feared Him. Noah and his family sought refuge therein, and accordingly they were preserved from the overflowing scourge. That ark was the only place of deliverance. It was therefore a prophetic sign of Christ as the sole Savior of sinners, and the security of those who sheltered therein shadowed forth the deliverance from the wrath to come of those who flee to Christ. There was room in the ark for all who availed themselves of it, and the Redeemer has promised to receive and cast out none who come to Him. The dove sent forth by Noah was an emblem of the Holy Spirit, and her return to the ark with an olive leaf in her mouth spoke of that assurance which believers have that God is now at peace with them.

The whole history of Israel was a typical one and was made to adumbrate the experience of God's people in the days of their unregeneracy, the provisions made by God for their deliverance, and the complete salvation which He effects for them. The cruel bondage suffered by the Hebrews in Egypt under the merciless oppression of Pharaoh supplies a vivid picture of our natural servitude unto sin and Satan. Their crying in the brick kilns and their groaning under the whips of their taskmasters spoke of those smiting of conscience and sorrows of heart when God convicts us of our rebellion against Him and when He makes sin to become exceedingly burdensome and bitter to our souls. The utter inability of those Israelite slaves to free themselves from the galling yoke of their masters portrayed the helplessness of the natural man, his complete impotence to deliver himself from the dominion of sin. The sovereign grace of God in raising up a deliverer in the person of Moses pointed forward to the Redeemer emancipating His people. The appointment of the lamb and the efficacy of its sprinkled blood to shelter from the angel of death on the Passover night revealed yet more clearly what is now proclaimed by the Gospel. While the destruction of Pharaoh and his hosts at the Red Sea, and Israel's sight of the "Egyptians dead upon the sea shore" (Ex. 14:30), told of the completeness of the Christian's salvation—the putting away of his sins from before the face of God.

The subsequent history of Israel after their miraculous exodus from Egypt while on their way to Canaan foreshadowed, in a remarkable and unmistakable manner, the experiences of Christians from the tune they are born again until their entrance into Heaven. Israel's long journey across the wilderness supplies a graphic picture of the believer's passage through this world. Once the heart has been really captivated and won by the loveliness of Christ, the things of time and sense lose their charm and this world becomes a dreary desert to him. As the wilderness, with its sterile sands and waterless wastes, was a place of trials unto the Hebrews, so this world is made the place of testing unto the graces of the saints. But as God ministered unto Israel of old, so He has made full provision to meet our every need. They had the pillar of cloud by day and of fire by night to direct their course, and we have the Word of God as a lamp unto our feet and the Holy Spirit to interpret it for us. As God furnished them with manna from on high, so He has given us "exceeding great and precious promises" to feed upon. As He caused water to flow from the smitten rock for Israel, so He now revives the souls of the contrite. As He enabled them to overcome Amalek, so His grace is sufficient for us.

That remarkable feature of the Old Testament Scriptures which we are now dealing with is a very comprehensive one, and a large volume might readily be written thereon. The whole of the Mosaic ritual possessed a typical and spiritual significance. The tabernacle in which they worshipped was an emblematic representation of Christ and His Church, and by ordaining that more than a dozen chapters should be devoted to an account of its structure, its furniture, and its setting up, while but a single chapter describes the creating and peopling of this earth! This tells us that in the Divine estimation, the latter is of infinitely more importance than the former. The world was made for Christ (Col. 1:16) and His people (2 Cor. 4:15), as a platform upon which the celestial hierarchies "might be known by [or rather "through"—dia] the Church, the manifold wisdom of God" (Eph. 3:10). The tabernacle was God's dwelling-place in the midst of Israel. Its holy courts, its sacred vessels, the priesthood which ministered there: the sacrifices they offered, were, to their minutest detail, all, so many object lessons brought down to our finite capacity, setting forth the grand truths of Divine revelation, without which we could not so fully understand what is set forth in the New Testament.

Many of the outstanding characters of the Old Testament adumbrated Christ in the varied relations He sustained. Adam presaged His federal headship (Rom. 5:14), Moses His prophetical office (Deut. 18:18), Melchizedek His priestly (Ps. 110:4), David His kingly (Rev. 5:5). The checkered experiences through which Joseph passed foreshadowed Christ both in His humiliation and His exaltation. Joshua typified Him as the Securer of the inheritance. The miraculous birth of Isaac prefigured the supernatural incarnation; the murder of Abel, His death; the budding of Aaron's rod, His resurrection. Every perfection of Christ's character, each office that He sustained, all the aspects of His redemptive work—Godwards, manwards, and sin-ward—were indicated by or through one and another of the historical persons of the Patriarchal and Mosaic eras. That so very much in the Jewish Scriptures should be adapted to image the Person and history of the Savior cannot be accounted for on any other hypothesis than that God Himself is the Author of them. The spiritual instruction conveyed by the Old Testament narratives, their deeper and hidden meanings, the great number and variety of the types, their anticipations of and perfect accord with what is taught in the New Testament, clearly demonstrate that Judaism and Christianity—so dissimilar in their externals, so opposite in their incidentals, yet uniting in their essentials—both belong to the same Lord.

Chapter 10
THE HOLY BIBLE TEACHES
THE WAY OF SALVATION

The uniqueness of the Bible appears most conspicuously here, as anyone may ascertain for himself by comparing the teaching of the so-called "sacred books" of all human religions. The difference between what is revealed in the Scripture of Truth and the systems of men upon the attainment of holiness and eternal felicity is like unto that between light and darkness. At no other point does the celestial nature of the Bible shine forth more unmistakably than in the plan of redemption which is made known therein. The good news which it heralds to ruined and lost sinners is such as was undiscoverable by the light of nature, yet is authenticated by its own intrinsic excellence. The Gospel which is published in the Bible attests itself by virtue of its matchless merits. It discovers its Divine origin by a proclamation of truth which is self-evident. There is no need for an appeal to be made unto any external testimonies, for a true perception of the Gospel demonstrates its Divine nature. That which is affirmed in the Gospel is manifest by its own assertion as something far surpassing all the inventions of the human mind.

The Gospel itself is light, for its central Object is "the Light of the world" (John 8:12). The advent of Jesus Christ to this earth was predicted as the rising of "the Sun of righteousness" (Mal. 4:2), and the universal spread of His Gospel is represented under the figure of that grand fountain of natural light diffusing His beams over every part of the earth (Ps. 19:1-5, and cf. Rom. 10:17, 18). Now light necessarily proves itself for it is self-evident, needing nothing to manifest it. It serves to discover other objects, but requires nothing to discover itself. "Whatsoever doth make manifest is light" (Eph. 5:13), and the Gospel makes manifest the perfections of God, setting forth an open discovery of them before our minds, beyond any other of His wondrous works. Therefore is this Divine revelation, this message of glad tidings unto condemned criminals, designated "the glorious Gospel of the blessed God" (1 Tim. 1:11) because His ineffable glories are there so brightly displayed. The consummate wisdom of God is evidenced far more eminently in the work of redemption than in any of His marvels in creation or in Providence, so that none but the blind can be unconvinced thereby.

The Gospel evinces its Divinity by the solution which it offers to a problem for which the combined wisdom of all mankind can furnish no adequate solution. That problem is succinctly stated thus: "How, then, can man be justified with God? or how can he be clean that is born of a woman?" (Job 25:4). The problem is twofold: legal, and moral, respecting man's relation to the Divine Law, and his fitness for the celestial Temple. Man is a transgressor of the Divine Law. Every member of the human race is such. Anything short of perfect and perpetual obedience to the Divine commandments in thought and word and deed constitutes one a transgressor. Measured by such a standard, each of us must plead guilty, for we come far short of it. The Law condemns us: how, then, can we be acquitted? On what possible ground can the righteous Judge declare us to be entitled to the award of the Law? But more—we are fallen and sinful creatures, and as such unfit to dwell in the immediate presence of the ineffably holy God. How shall we get rid of our defilement? How do we obtain that unsullied purity to make us meet for Heaven?

Let us briefly amplify the several elements which enter into that problem.

1. The requirements of God's Law. They are founded upon the perfections of its Framer, and therefore nothing less than spotless holiness is demanded of us. Negatively, it proscribes not only wrong deeds and corrupt counsels of the heart, but—as no human legislation ever did—it also prohibits evil desires and propensities, so that all unchaste imaginations are forbidden, as also the spirit discontent, envy, revenge—anything which is contrary to the perfections of God Himself is interdicted. Positively, the Divine Law demands from us an entire, unreserved, and uninterrupted yielding of soul and body, with all their faculties and powers, unto God and His service. It requires not only that we love Him with all our heart and strength, constantly, but that love to Him must actuate and regulate all our actions unvaryingly. Nor is that unreasonable, for we are all God's creatures, made for His glory, and originally created without sin, in His own image and likeness.

2. The charge preferred against us: "there is none righteous, no, not one" (Rom. 3:10). Not a single member of our fallen race measures up to the holy standard which our Maker and Governor has set before us—not one who meets the just requirements of His Law. Nor is there one who has made a genuine, wholehearted, and sustained effort to do so. So far from subordinating all his interests to the will of God, the natural man follows the desires and devices of his own heart, giving place to God only so far as that is pleasing to himself. Though he owes his very life to His daily care, yet he has no concern for His glory. He is ungrateful, unruly, ungodly, abusing God's mercies, despising His reproofs, trampling under foot His commandments. And therefore "all the world stands guilty before God" (Rom. 3:19).

3. The sentence of the Law. This is clearly stated in the Divine Word. "Cursed is everyone that continueth not in all things which are written in the Book of the Law to do them" (Gal. 3:10). Whoever violates a single precept of that Law exposes himself to the displeasure of God, and to His just punishment as the expression of that displeasure. No allowance is made for ignorance, no distinction is made between persons, no relaxation of its strictness is possible. "The soul that sinneth it shall die," is its inexorable pronouncement. No exception is made whether the transgressor be young or old, rich or poor, Jew or Gentile: the wages of sin is death, for "the wrath of God is revealed from Heaven against all ungodliness and unrighteousness of men" (Rom. 1:18).

4. The judge Himself is inflexibly just, "that will by no means clear the guilty" (Ex. 34:7). In the high court of Divine justice, the Lord interprets the Law in its sternest aspect and judges rigidly according to the strictness of its letter. "He is a holy God, He is a jealous God: He will not forgive your transgressions and your sins" (Josh. 24:19). God is inexorably righteous, and will not show any partiality either to the Law or to its violator. "But we are sure that the judgment of God is according to truth against them which commit such things.., who will render to every man according to his deeds" (Rom. 2:2, 6). He has determined that His Law shall be faithfully upheld and its sanctions strictly enforced.

5. The sinner is unquestionably guilty. It is not merely that he has infirmities, or that he has done his very best, yet failed to attain unto absolute perfection. He has set at naught God's authority, and has proved a proud rebel rather than a loyal subject. He has gone his own way and gratified himself, without any concern for the Divine honor. Morally respectable he may be in the sight of his fellows, but a criminal before the Divine tribunal. It is impossible for any man to clear himself of the solemn charge: he can neither disprove the accusations which the Law prefers against him, nor vindicate himself for the perpetration of them.

Here, then, is how the case stands. The Law demands flawless and continuous obedience to its precepts in heart and in act, in motive and performance. God charges us with having failed to meet those just requirements, and declares us guilty. The Law then pronounces sentence of condemnation, and demands the infliction of the death penalty. The One before whose tribunal we stand is omniscient, and cannot be imposed upon; He is inflexibly just and swayed by no sentimental considerations. We are unable to refute the charges of the Law, unable to vindicate our sinful conduct, unable to offer any reparation or atonement for our crimes. Truly our case is desperate to the highest degree.

Here, then, is the problem. How can God justify the willful transgressor of His Law without justifying his sins? How can He receive him into His favor without being the Patron of a rebel? How can God deliver him from the penalty of His broken Law without going back upon His word that He, "will by no means clear the guilty"? How can life be granted to the culprit without repealing the sentence, "the soul that sinneth it shall die"? How can mercy be shown to the sinner without justice being flouted? That is a problem which none of the jurists of this earth could solve, one which must forever have baffled every finite intelligence. Yet, blessed be His name, God has, in His consummate wisdom, devised a way whereby the chief of sinners can be dealt with by Him as though he were entirely innocent. Nay, more—He pronounces him righteous, up to the required standard of the Law, and entitled to its reward of eternal life. The Gospel provides a plain, satisfactory, and glorious solution to that problem, and therein evidences its Divinity. To that solution we now direct the reader's attention.

That solution may be summed up in one word, namely, substitution, though a million words could not express all the stupendous wonders attending the same. God decreed that salvation should be provided for transgressors and, in order that His righteousness might not be compromised, determined that Another should take their place, and in their stead make a full satisfaction to the Divine Law, by rendering a flawless obedience to it. But where was to be found one suitable for this task, for, first, he must be a sinless being? There was not a single candidate among the sons of men, for the whole human race was guilty. From whence, then, could a substitute be found? Suitable, we say, for not only must he be without sin, but his obedience to the Law must possess such super-abounding worth as to pay the debts not of one sinner, but of all sinners for whom it was vicariously performed. His obedience must needs possess more merit than their total demerits. That necessarily excluded all the angels, for as creatures of God they themselves were obligated to render perfect obedience to Him, and in so doing merely performed their duty; consequently no merit attached to the same, and so there was no excess for others.

Further, none would be suitable save one who could act in his own absolute right, one who in himself was neither a subject nor a servant, otherwise he could merit nothing for others: he that has nothing that is absolutely his own cannot pay any price to redeem others. He must be a person possessed of infinite dignity and worthiness, so that he might be capable of meriting infinite blessing. He must be endowed with infinite power and wisdom to qualify him for such a stupendous undertaking. He must be one of unchanging integrity and immutable faithfulness, or he could not be depended upon for such a momentous task. He must be one of matchless mercy and love to willingly serve as the Substitute and die in the room of fallen and depraved men. It was also requisite that he should be a person infinitely dear unto God the Father, in order to give an infinite value to his transaction in God's esteem. Now where, my reader, was such a one to be found? Had that question been propounded to the ablest of men, yea, to a conclave of angels, it had remained unanswered forever.

But "The things which are impossible with men are possible with God" (Luke 18:27). That problem which was far above the compass of all creatures was solved by Omniscience. The surpassing goodness and infinite wisdom of God selected His own Son for the undertaking, for He was in every way fit, possessing in Himself all the requisite qualifications. But here another problem, no less than the former, presented itself. The Son was absolute Sovereign in Himself: how then could He serve? He was infinitely above all law: how then could He perform obedience to law? He was the Lord of Glory, worshipped by all the heavenly hosts: how then could He be substituted in the place of worms of the dust? Moreover, as their Substitute, He must not only fulfill all the preceptive requirements of the Law, but He must also take upon Him their sins and expiate their guilt; He must suffer the Law's condemnation, endure its penalty, receive the awful wages of sin. But how could One of such infinite dignity enter such depths of humiliation? How could the ineffably Holy One be judicially "made sin" for them? How could the Blessed One be made a curse? How could the Lord of Life die?

As another has said, "If God had declared who the person is that should do this work and had gone no further, no creature could have thought which way this person could have performed the work. If God had told them that His own Son must be the Redeemer, and that He alone was a fit person for the work, and that He was a person every way sufficient for it, but had proposed to them to contrive a way how this fit and sufficient Person should succeed, we must conclude that all created understandings would have been utterly at a loss." Yet the Gospel makes known the wondrous and glorious solution to that problem, a solution which had never entered the mind of man to conceive, and in the revelation made of that salvation the Gospel bears unmistakably the impression of Divine wisdom and carries its own evidence of its Divinity.

The manifold wisdom of God determined that His Son should become the Representative and Surety of sinners and so be substituted in their place. But who else would have thought of such a thing: that the Son should occupy the place of rebels and become the Object of Divine wrath! And in order for the Son to be the sinner's Surety, He must render satisfaction to the Law in man's own nature! What created intelligence had deemed such a thing possible: that a Divine Person should become incarnate and be both God and man in one Person! Had God made known such a marvel, what finite intelligence could have devised a way whereby the Son should become flesh without partaking of the pollution of fallen human nature! Not only that the finite should become finite, the Ancient of Days an infant, but that He should be born of a woman without being tainted by the virus of sin! No angel had ever dreamed of the miracle of the virgin birth, whereby an immaculate human nature was produced in Mary's womb by the operation of the Holy Spirit, so that "a holy thing" (Luke 1:35), spotless and impeccable, was born by her! But that was no mystery to Divine wisdom. The Son of God became the Son of man.

And so we might continue, paragraph after paragraph, pointing out that the circumstances of Christ's birth, the details of His life, the reception which He met with from the world, the character of His mission, the nature of His death, His triumphant resurrection from the tomb, His ascension into Heaven, His there being crowned with honor and glory, seated at the right hand of the Majesty on high, now reigning as King of kings and Lord of lords—each and all of which transcend the powers of human imagination. But a word requires to be added upon the application of Christ's work to His people. How shall they partake of the benefits of His redemption without robbing Him of His glory? By what means shall their enmity be subdued and their wills be brought into subjection to Him? That was a further problem which no man could have solved. It is by the Spirit's communicating to them a new nature, making them sensible of their wretchedness and need, and causing them to stretch forth the beggar's hand and receive eternal life as a free gift. Though indwelling sin be not removed in this life, Christ's love has so won their hearts that it is now their fervent desire and sincere endeavor to live daily so as to please and glorify Him.

Now we submit to the critical reader that the Gospel is stamped with the Divine glory, that the wisdom of God appears conspicuously in the way of salvation that it exhibits. In its unique contrivances, its accomplished designs, its glorious ends, its blessed fruits, its stupendous wonder in transforming lawless rebels into loving and loyal subjects, we have that which is worthy of Omniscience. Never had it entered into the heart of man to conceive not only of Hell-deserving sinners being saved in a way suited to all the Divine perfections, but which also provides for their being personally conformed unto the image of God's Son, made "like Him" in holiness and happiness, made "joint heirs" with Him and eternal sharers of His glory. When impartially examined, it is self-evident that the Gospel is not of human origin. Certainly the Jews did not invent it, for they were its bitterest enemies. Nor the Gentiles, for they knew nothing about it until the Apostles preached it to them. Nor did the Apostles themselves, for at first they were offended at it (Matthew 16:21, 22). The Gospel is of God: thanks be unto Him for His unspeakable gift!

In what way shall depraved and guilty creatures be delivered from wickedness and punishment and restored to holiness and happiness, is the most difficult as well as important question which can engage the mind. Such an inquiry is of no interest to a pleasure-loving trifler, but is of vast moment to the sin-convicted soul. He knows that God is justly displeased with him, but how He shall become reconciled and receive him into His favor, passes his comprehension. A sense of guilt makes him afraid of God: how shall the cause of that fear be removed? Those are difficulties which human religions do not resolve and before which reason is silent. No amount of present repentance and reformation can cleanse the blotted pages of the past. When brought face to face with the dread realities of death, judgment, and eternity, the soul is appalled. A vague hope in the general mercy of God suffices not, for that leaves His justice unsatisfied. The Gospel alone provides a satisfactory solution to these problems and peace for the burdened conscience.

Neither sorrowing nor amendment of conduct can right the wrongs of which the sinner is guilty before God, nor can he by any self-effort change himself for the better, still less fit himself for Heaven. A sinner may be filled with bitter remorse for his vicious excesses, but tears will not heal his diseased body or deliver him from an early grave. The gambler will condemn himself for his folly, but no self-recriminations will recover his lost estate or save him from spending his remaining years in poverty. Thus it is evident that when it comes to the blotting out of his iniquities before God and the obtaining of a new nature which renders him fit for the Divine presence, man must look outside himself. But where is he to look for deliverance from himself for sin has made fallen man averse to fellowship with the Holy One? How then shall he desire, seek after, delight in that which is repellent to him? He is bidden to look unto One who is "mighty to save" (Isa. 63:1). The Gospel presents a Divine Physician who can heal the moral leper, yea, give eternal life to one who is spiritually dead. The Lord Jesus is "able to save unto the uttermost them that come unto God by Him" (Heb. 7:25). His salvation is an all-sufficient and everlasting one, freely offered, "without money and without price." Such a Savior, such a salvation, is of no human invention; therefore the Book which makes them known must be Divine.

It may be asked, If the Gospel be self-evident, why do not all men believe it? The answer is, "This is the condemnation, that light is come into the world, and men loved darkness rather than light, because their deeds were evil" (John 3:19). The great majority deliberately close their eyes and steel their hearts against its appeal, because that appeal clashes with their corruptions and worldly interests. Not until men solemnly contemplate the character of God, their relation to Him as the subjects of His government, and their utter unpreparedness for His awful tribunal, will they seriously consider the claims of His Gospel. As food is relished most by the famished, as health is valued highest by those who have suffered a painful and protracted illness, so the Gospel is only welcomed by those who realize they are under the curse of a sin-hating God, stricken with a moral malady which no human remedy can relieve, hastening to hopeless eternity. Nevertheless, he who believes not shall be damned.

Chapter 11
THE HOLY BIBLE
ITS FULFILLED PROPHECIES

If the Bible is a human invention it ought not to require very much perspicuity to discover and demonstrate its imposture. The Scriptures claim to be of Divine inspiration, but if that claim is an empty and unfounded one, then it should be no hard matter to prove it is so. The Bible not only treats considerably of history and moral instruction, but it contains not a little prophecy, and that not in dark and dubious language, like that of the pretended Sibylline Oracle, such as that ambiguous answer made to the inquiry of Croesus when he was about to engage the Persians in war: "Croesus, having passed the river Hilys, shall overturn a great empire"—which would be verified whether his own kingdom or that of the Persians was subverted. Radically different are the predictions of Holy Writ. They are clear and definite, enter into specific and minute details, and in many instances are too plain to be misunderstood. Thus, the dispute between the Christian and the Infidel may be reduced to a short and simple issue: if Scripture prophecy be Divinely inspired then it will be accomplished; if it be spurious, it will not be.

Since the words "prophecy" and "prediction" are frequently used in a loose and general sense in present-day parlance, it is requisite that we should carefully define our term. By a "prophecy" we mean the annunciation of some future event which could not have been foreknown by natural means or arrived at by logical deduction from present data. Such are scores of predictions recorded in the Bible hundreds of years ago, and which have been accurately verified by history. They are entirely different from weather forecasts, which are more often wrong than right, and merely announce climatic conditions a few days ahead. To bear any resemblance to the prophecies of Scripture, they would have to prognosticate the specific temperature, the direction of the wind, the precise rainfall upon a certain city or country on a given day, 500 years hence! The reader will readily perceive that all of the scientists and astronomers in the world possess no such prevision as that. Yet the Bible abounds with forecasts far more wonderful.

It requires no prophetic spirit to declare that, life permitting, a certain male infant will develop into a child, and then into a man; but it would to announce from his cradle whether he will be a fool or a wise man, a failure or success; and still more so to predict the exact span of his life, and where and how he will die. A well-informed politician may foretell how soon there will be a general election, and which party will win the same; but he is quite incapable of foreseeing the political, social, economic and religious condition of his country 100 years from now. And, likewise, it would be completely beyond his powers to give the name and describe the character of its ruler in that day. An experienced statesman may indeed discern the speedy breakup of his state, and from the temper of its subjects deduce that it is likely to collapse under a fearful revolution, but he could not predict and describe the successive changes of empires centuries in advance—changes which depend upon countless unknown incidents. Yet the Bible does that very thing!

Sagacious conjecture is very different from Scripture prediction. Prophecy is, as one has well defined it, "the eyes of the omniscient God reading the predestinated future, and revealing the secret to His servants, the Prophets." It is demonstrated to be such by the actual accomplishment of the same as testified to by the records of history. And it is highly significant that sacred history ends where profane history—that part of it, at least, which is commonly regarded as reliable—begins, so that the great changes in world affairs which the Divine seers foretold are confirmed by secular recorders of events, thereby effectually closing the mouths of skeptics. Thus the remarkable predictions of Daniel concerning the rise, the career, and the character of the great Gentile powers which occupied the stage during the last six centuries before the advent of Christ may be fully checked from the chronicles of heathen historians, who, entirely unacquainted with the Old Testament (which then existed only in the Hebrew language), were quite unaware that they were narrating the fulfillment of the same.

The book of Daniel contains prophetic visions which describe one momentous event after another that has come before the observance of the whole world: events so unlikely, so startling, and so far-reaching, that no wisdom could possibly have foreseen the same—least of all, so far in advance. It was therein revealed that four successive world kingdoms should arise, to be followed by a spiritual and everlasting kingdom set up by God Himself. Those four empires are viewed under the figure of wild beasts, to denote their strength, ferocity, and agility. It was therein foretold that they should come forth from "the great sea" (Dan. 7:2, 3), which in Scripture always has reference to the Mediterranean, thereby defining the center of their territorial origin. By that limitation of four, God made it known that after the Babylonian, Medo-Persian, Grecian, and Roman empires there should never again be another kingdom commensurate with those. Charlemagne, Napoleon, the Kaiser, Hitler, in their insatiable greed, coveted and strove to form one, but in vain. Equally so will prove the ambitions of Moscow. [Written in 1948].

It is an incontrovertible fact that no Infidel has ever dared to meet the great body of Scripture prophecy, nor seriously attempted a reply to the many books written thereon, calling attention to their accomplishment. Either they are silently ignored, or dismissed with some such scurrilous remark that the Scripture prophecies are "a book of falsehoods," as Tom Paine's accusation in his blasphemous Age of Reason (Part 2, pages 44, 47). Let the reader judge for himself from the following. Almost 100 years before the event, the Lord announced through Isaiah that Babylon should be destroyed by the Medes and Persians. "Behold, I will stir up the Medes against them. . .And Babylon, the glory of kingdoms, the beauty of the Chaldees' excellency, shall be as when God overthrew Sodom and Gomorrah. . .Go up, O Elam [the ancient name of Persia]; besiege, O Media. . .Babylon is fallen" (Isa. 13:17, 19; 21:2, 9). Utterly unlikely as such a catastrophe then appeared, nevertheless, Herodotus and Xenophon record its literal fulfillment!

Again, Daniel, more than 200 years before the event, foretold the overthrow of the Medo-Persian empire by the arms of Greece, under the direction of Alexander the Great, depicting the government of the latter under the symbol of a the-goat with a notable horn between his eyes. That prophecy, in figurative language, is found in Daniel 8:3-7, and then (vv. 20-21) its meaning is explained in plain terms: "the ram which thou sawest having two horns, are the kings of Media and Persia. And the rough goat is the king of Grecia, and the great horn that is between his eyes is the first king." Ask the historians of those times, Diodorus and Plutarch, if that were a falsehood! In his Antiquities (Jud. 11:8) Josephus tells of Alexander's journey to Jerusalem for the purpose of dealing severely with the Jews, and how that when he was shown by the high priest a copy of the prophecy of Daniel announcing that a Grecian monarch should overthrow Persia, was so deeply impressed that, contrary to his invariable course, he showed remarkable favor to the Jews.

The same Daniel went on to announce that upon the death of Alexander his vast empire should be divided between four of his principal generals, each of whom should have an extensive dominion (8:8, 22), which, as profane historians record, is precisely what took place. But more—he also predicted that out of one of those four branches of the Grecian empire would arise one who, at first weak and obscure, should become "exceeding great," blatant and impious, and that he would meet with no ordinary end (8:9, 12, 23-25). Therein was accurately described the infamous career of Antiochus Epiphanies, king of Syria. In that remarkable prophecy it was plainly intimated that that monster should, by means of flattery and treachery, accomplish his evil designs; and because of the degeneracy of the Jews would be permitted for a time to ravish their country, profane their temple, and put many of them to death; yet, that in the heyday of his career he should be cut off by a sudden visitation from Heaven. All of which was fulfilled to the letter!

Daniel also went on to herald the rise of yet a fourth kingdom. As he foretold that the Babylonian should be succeeded by the Medo-Persian and it by the Grecian, so in turn would this be vanquished by another yet more powerful. It is described as being "strong as iron: for as much as iron breaketh in pieces and subdueth all" (2:40); and as "diverse from all the others, exceeding dreadful" and which "shall devour the whole earth, and shall tread it down and break it in pieces" (7:19, 23). Therein was given, more than 500 years beforehand, a delineation of the Roman empire, as differing from the others in its democratic form of government, in the irresistible might of its military power, and in its world-wide dominion (compare Luke 2:1). Finally, Daniel announced that "in the days of these kings" (2:44) should "the God of Heaven set up a kingdom which shall never be destroyed" (2:44; 7:13, 14). And it was in the days of the Caesars that the Son of God became incarnate and established His spiritual kingdom, which, despite all the efforts of Satan and his emissaries to overthrow it, continues to this very hour. What proofs of Divine inspiration are these!

But let us now come to a phenomenon which falls more immediately before our own observation, namely, the Jews. To the man of affairs the Jews present an interesting, yet perplexing problem, for they are the greatest paradox of the ages. No other nation was so highly favored by God, yet none has ever been so severely chastised by Him. They are the only people to whom God ever gave a land, yet the only one which for so many centuries have been without one. They are the only nation to whom God ever immediately gave a king, yet for 2,000 years they have been without a ruler or head. They are the outstanding miracle of history. Scattered throughout the earth, they are yet a unit; dispersed among the Gentiles, yet unassimilated by them. They are not wanted anywhere, yet because of their financial strength, needed everywhere. Taxed and plundered as no others have ever been, yet the wealthiest of all people. Persecuted and slaughtered as no other nation, yet miraculously preserved from annihilation.

The Bible alone supplies the key to their history. Not only so—the Bible described, in numerous particulars, their history long in advance. We will now single out but a few from the many scores. Two thousand years before the event, their conquest by the Romans and the terrors of the siege of Jerusalem were graphically depicted: see Deuteronomy 28:49-57—the passage is too lengthy to quote here, but let the reader be sure to consult it. The worldwide dispersion of the Jews was foretold centuries in advance: "And the LORD shall scatter thee among all people, and from the one end of the earth even unto the other" (Deut. 28:64). The restless migrating of the Jews was made known ages before their actual dispersion: "And among those nations shalt thou find no ease, neither shall the sole of thy foot have rest: but the LORD shall give thee a trembling heart, and failing of eyes, and sorrow of mind" (Deut. 28:65). So literally has that been fulfilled that "the wandering Jew" has become a proverbial expression adopted by all modem nations!

The taunts universally passed upon them were prophetically declared: "thou shalt become an astonishment, a proverb, and a byword among all nations whither the LORD shall lead thee"

(Deut. 28:37). Who has not heard the expression, "as greedy as a Jew"! When one man gets the better of another by means of tricky dealings, it has become the custom throughout the English-speaking world to say "he Jew'd me." Literally has he become a "Proverb and a byword." Their survival, despite all the efforts of men to exterminate them, was made known: "when they be in the land of their enemies, I will not... destroy them utterly" (Lev. 26:44). The preservation of their national distinctness was expressly predicted: "lo, the people shall dwell alone, and shall not be reckoned among the nations" (Num. 23:9). Though scattered throughout the whole earth, they still subsist—unassimilated by the Gentiles—as a distinct people! And so we might go on. Let the reader carefully bear in mind that all of those fore-announcements were made upwards of 3,000 years ago! Such forecasts manifestly render imposture out of the question: they must have been God-breathed.

We now call attention to that which is central in prophecy, namely, the amazing description supplied of the Messiah many centuries before He came to this earth. A full portrait of Him was drawn in advance: one inspired artist after another adding fresh details, until the picture was complete. The Prophets, with one consent, gave witness to the Lord Jesus Christ, so that nothing remarkable befell Him and nothing great was done by Him which they did not foretell. Those prophecies were in the hands of the Jews, and translated into the Greek, generations before His birth, and were so well known that the Apostle Paul could say to king Agrippa that he taught no things, "than those which the Prophets and Moses did say should come: that Christ should suffer and that He should be the first that should rise from the dead" (Acts 26:22, 23). Thus did the fulfillment exactly correspond to the predictions made long before, for it pleased God to supply such an exact description of the Messiah that His identity should be indubitably established when He appeared among men: and thus the Jews were condemned by their Prophets for rejecting Him.

The supernatural character of our Lord's humanity was declared when it was said that He should be the woman's "Seed" (Gen. 3:15), unbegotten by a man: conceived and born of a "virgin" (Isa. 7:14). In Genesis 9:25-28, it was made known through which of the three sons of Noah the Messiah should issue, namely, Shem: for God would "dwell" in his "tents." Later, it was revealed that Christ, according to the flesh, should be of the Abrahamic stock (Gen. 22:18, and cf. Matthew 1:1). Still further was the compass narrowed, for of the twelve sons of Abraham's grandson, Judah was chosen (Gen. 49:10). Out of all the families of Judah, He would spring from the house of Jesse (Isa. 11:1). The place of His birth was specified (Micah 5:2). The very time of His advent was mentioned (Dan. 9:24-26). So definite were the Old Testament prophecies concerning Christ that the hope of Israel became the Messianic hope: all their expectations centered in His appearing. It is therefore the more remarkable that their sacred Scriptures contained another set of prophecies, telling of His being despised by His own nation and put to a shameful death.

Though Christ would preach good tidings to the meek, bind up the brokenhearted, and proclaim liberty to the captives of sin and Satan (Isa. 61:1), and though He should open the eyes of the blind, unstop the ears of the deaf, and make the lame leap as a hart (Isa. 35:5, 6), yet utterly incredible as it appeared, He would be "despised and rejected of men" (Isa. 53:3). His back would be smitten, the hair plucked out of His cheeks, and His face covered with the vile spittle of those who hated Him (Isa. 1:6). He would be sold for "thirty pieces of silver" (Zech. 11:13), brought as a lamb to the slaughter, taken from prison and judgment, "cut off out of the land of the living" (Isa. 53:8). His death by crucifixion was revealed a thousand years beforehand (Psa. 22:1). So, too, His being crucified with malefactors (Isa. 53:12), His being derided upon the Cross (Ps. 22:7, 8), His being offered vinegar to drink (Psa. 69:2 1), as well as the soldiers gambling for His garments (Ps. 22:1 8)—were all described. It was also foretold that He should rise from the dead (Ps. 16:1, 2), and ascend into Heaven (Ps. 68:18).

But perhaps the most remarkable feature about the prophecies concerning Christ is their paradoxical character. He was to be the seed of David, which should proceed out of his bowels (2 Sam. 7:12), and at the same time be David's "Lord" (Ps. 110:1). He was to be both "the Son of man" (Dan. 7:13) and "the mighty God" (Isa. 9:6); "a Man of sorrows and acquainted with grief" (Isa. 53:3), yet "anointed with the oil of gladness above His fellows" (Ps. 45:7). He was to be One in whom Jehovah's "soul delighted" (Isa. 42:), yet "smitten of God and afflicted" (Isa. 53:4). In one passage it was fore-announced, "Thou art fairer than the children of men" (Ps. 45:2), in another, "His visage was so marred more than any man" (Isa. 52:14). It was said that, "Messiah shall be cut off, and shall have nothing" (Dan. 9:26, margin), yet "of the increase of His government and peace there shall be no end" (Isa. 9:7). He would "make His grave with the wicked" (Isa. 53:9), yet would be made "higher than the kings of the earth" (Psa. 89:27). The fulfillment in New Testament times of those apparently glaring contradictions evinced there was perfect harmony between them; yet is it not evident that such seeming inconsistencies as those had ever been inserted in an imposture!

Now we submit to the skeptical reader that the fulfillment of all those prophecies demonstrated the Divine origin of the Book which contains them. They were given not in the form of a vague generalization, but with a precision and minuteness which no human sagacity could possibly have supplied. Again and again have men attempted to foretell the future, but only to meet with failure; the anticipations of the most far-seeing are repeatedly mocked by the irony of events. Man stands before such an impenetrable veil that he knows not what a day may bring forth. How then shall we explain the hundreds of detailed prophecies recorded in the Scriptures which were fulfilled to the letter centuries after they were given? Only one explanation is rational, adequate, and satisfactory: they were revealed by God Himself. It is the prerogative of God alone to declare the end from the beginning, and the numerous, varied, and detailed predictions recorded in the Bible, demonstrate beyond a doubt that that Book is His own inspired and infallible Word. The prophecies of Scripture are supernatural: nothing in the remotest degree resembling or even aiming to do so, is to be found in any of the religions of the world. Prophecy is as truly the product of Omniscience as miracles are of Omnipotence.

Chapter 12
THE HOLY BIBLE
MORE UNIQUE CHARACTERISTICS—1

1. Its doctrine. Probably that heading would be more intelligible unto most of our readers had we employed the plural number. As a matter of fact, it is at this very point that its uniqueness first appears. Error is diverse and multiform, but Truth is harmonious and one. Scripture speaks of "the doctrines of demons" (1 Tim. 4:1) and "the doctrines of men" (Col. 2:22), which are "divers and strange doctrines" (Heb. 13:9), but whenever it refers to that which is Divine, the singular number is always used. Thus "the doctrine" (John 7:17; 1 Tim. 4:16), "the Apostles' doctrine" (Acts 2:42), "sound doctrine" (1 Tim. 4:1), "good doctrine" (1 Tim. 4:6), "the name of God and His doctrine" (1 Tim. 6:3). Yet, like a single diamond with its many facets or the rainbow combining all the colors, the doctrine of God has numerous and distinct aspects, which to our finite minds are best apprehended singly. Nevertheless, they are not like so many separate pearls on a string, but rather resemble branches growing out of a single tree. What we term "the doctrines of grace" are only so many parts or phases of the revealed favor of God unto His people.

The more time one devotes to a prayerful and diligent perusal of "the doctrine of Christ" (2 John 9), the more will he perceive not only the spiritual excellence of each of its parts, but also their perfect harmony, their intimate relation to one another, and the mutual furtherance of all unto the same end. It is ignorance of the whole which lies behind the supposition that any one part conflicts with another. It is designated "the doctrine which is according to godliness" (1 Tim. 6:3), for when truly believed it produces and promotes piety. It is a mold into which the mind is cast and from which it receives its impress (Rom. 6:17, margin). An observing eye will easily perceive that a distinct spirit attends different religions and different systems of the same religion which, over and above natural temperament, stamps their respective adherents. Thus it was at the beginning: those who received "another Gospel" received with it "another spirit" (2 Cor. 11:4), and hence we read of "the spirit of truth and the spirit of error" (1 John 4:6). Scripture doctrine produces holiness of character and conduct because it proceeds from the Holy One.

It would require a whole volume to do justice to this argument and illustrate it at length. The doctrine of the Godhead is unique. That God must be one is an axiom of sound reason, for there could not be a plurality of supreme beings. But that God should be one in His essence or nature, yet three in His Persons, is something which mere reason could never have discovered. That God is Triune, a trinity in unity, transcends infinite intelligence, and therefore never originated therefrom. That it is clearly set forth in the Bible evinces its verity. The doctrine of federal headship is peculiar to Divine revelation. That one should legally represent the many, that the many should be dealt with judicially according to the conduct of the one, is a truth which has no place at all in any human religion. Yet the Bible teaches explicitly that the guilt of Adam's transgression is reckoned to the account of all his natural descendants, so that because of it they stand condemned before God—a thing far too unpalatable for human invention. The merits of the obedience of the last Adam is reckoned to the account of all His spiritual seed, so that they are all accounted righteous before God—something far too wonderful to be of human contrivance.

The doctrine of Divine grace is equally unique. It is a truth peculiar to Divine revelation, a concept to which the unaided powers of man's mind could never have risen. Proof of this is seen in the fact that where the Bible has not gone, grace is quite unknown. Not the slightest trace of it is to be found in any of the religions of heathendom, and when missionaries undertake to translate the Scriptures into the natives' tongues, they can find no word which in any wise corresponds to the Bible word "grace." Grace is something to which none has any rightful claim, something which is due unto none; being mere charity, a sovereign favor, a free gift. Divine grace is the favor of God bestowing inconceivable blessings upon those who have no merits and from whom no compensation is demanded. Nay, more— grace is exercised unto those who are full of positive demerits. How completely grace sets aside all thought of worth in its subject appears from that declaration, "being, justified freely by His grace" (Rom. 3:24); that word, "freely," signifies "without a cause," and is so rendered in John 15:25—justified gratuitously, for nothing!

Grace is a Divine provision for those who are so corrupt that they cannot better their evil natures; so averse to God they will not turn unto Him; so blind they perceive not His excellence; so deaf they hear Him not speaking unto them; so dead spiritually that He must open their graves and bring them forth on to resurrection ground if ever they are to be saved. Grace implies that its object's condition is desperate to the last degree: that God might justly leave him to perish—yea, that it is a wonder of wonders He has not already cast him into Hell. That grace is told out in the Gospel, which is not a message of good advice, but of good news. It is a proclamation of mercy, sent not to the good, but to the bad. It offers a free, perfect, and everlasting salvation "without money and without price," and that to the chief of sinners. To the convicted conscience, salvation by grace alone seems too good to be true. Grace is God acting irrespective of the sinner's character, not as a Demander but as a Giver—to the ill-deserving and Hell-deserving—who have done nothing to procure His favor, but everything to provoke His wrath.

There are other portions of doctrine taught in the Scriptures which by virtue of their very transcendence indicate their Divine source, as, for example, that of the sovereignty of God and the responsibility of man. It is a dictate of sound reason that if God be God—God in fact as well as in name—then He must have full control of all His creatures and regulate their every action in subservience to His own glory. It is equally self-evident that if man be created a moral agent, he must be endowed with the power of choice, and as such, be answerable unto God for all his volitions. So teaches the Bible: on the one hand that God is working all things after the counsel of His own will, not only in Heaven but also "among the inhabitants of the earth, and none can stay His hand" (Dan. 4:35); and on the other that "every one of us shall give account of himself to God" (Rom. 14:12). Yet no human intellect is able to explain how that responsibility of man consists with the fact that God has eternally predestinated his every action and infallibly directs the same without the least violence to his will.

The same seeming paradox appears in the doctrine of man's spiritual impotence and accountability: that the fallen creature is in such complete bondage to sin that he is incapable of performing a spiritual act, yea, of originating a spiritual desire or thought, and yet is justly held blameworthy for all his moral perversity and impiety—that none can come to Christ except they be drawn (John 6:44), yet are condemned for not coming to Him (John 3:18). So, too, the doctrine of particular redemption: that Christ acted as the Surety of and made atonement for the sins of God's elect only; yet that the Gospel makes a free and bona fide offer of salvation unto all who hear it. In like manner, the complementary doctrines of the saints' preservation by God and the imperative necessity of their own perseverance in faith and holiness—that no child of God can perish eternally, yet that he is in real danger of so doing as long as he is left in this world. Such things appear to be utterly inconsistent to human reason, which is sure evidence that no impostors, would have placed so much in the Bible as is foolishness to the natural man.

Another unmistakable hallmark of the genuineness of the several branches of the doctrine of Holy Writ is the manner in which they are set forth therein. They are not presented as so many expressly defined articles of faith or items of a creed. There is no formal statement of the doctrine of regeneration or of sanctification: rather are there many brief references to each scattered throughout the whole of the sacred writings. They are introduced more incidentally than systematically. Instead of being drawn up as so many propositions, they are illustrated and exemplified in the practical history of individuals. So different from man's method, yet characteristic of the ways of God! Man reduces botany to a system, but the Creator has not set out the flowers and trees in separate beds and fields according to their species, but has distributed them over the earth in beautiful variety. In like manner, He has not gathered into one chapter the whole of any one truth, but requires us to search and collate the numerous references to it, which are mingled with exhortations, warnings and promises. God's Word is addressed not only to our understanding but to our conscience, and no doctrinal statement is made without some practical end being answered.

Another striking feature of Biblical doctrine is its orderly presentation. As in the processes of nature, so there is a gradual unfolding of each particular doctrine. The diligent student will find that every vital truth made known in Scripture is seen first in the blade, then in the ear, and then in the full com in the ear. Thus, for example, with the Messianic prophecies: the germinal announcement in Genesis 3:15, the fuller revelation in Isaiah 53, the complete fulfillment in the New Testament. So with God's justifying of a sinner: briefly hinted at in Genesis 15:6, more plainly disclosed in Psalm 32:1, 2, fully expounded in Romans 4. The Bible is more than a book: it is a living organism, growth marking all its parts.

All through Scripture there is seen a systematic advance in the communication of Truth. In Genesis, the basic doctrine repeatedly exemplified is that of election; in Exodus, redemption by blood and power; in Leviticus, the chosen and redeemed are brought nigh to God as worshippers. Then the complementary side of things is set before us: in Numbers, our passage through this wilderness-world; in Deuteronomy, the enforcing of responsibility. While in Joshua we behold the people of God entering into and enjoying their heritage. What unmistakable progress is there! The same feature marks the New Testament. In the Gospels, Christ accomplishing the work of salvation; in Acts, the proclamation thereof; in the Epistles, salvation experienced by the members of His mystical Body; in Revelation, the saved in Glory around the Lamb. Such progress demonstrates both the unity of Scripture and continuity of its inspiration. Behind all the varied penmen is one Author working according to a definite plan.

2. Its precepts. This is another aspect of our many-sided subject which deserves as many separate chapters as space requires us to condense into paragraphs. At no other point does the heavenly origin of the Bible appear more plainly than the exalted standard it sets forth and the conduct it requires from us. Therein it is in marked contrast with the writings of all who oppose the Bible. Infidels and atheists have no ethical standard, yea, their code is utterly subversive of all morality. So too it differs radically from the teaching of the best of the ancient moralists and philosophers. They far surpass the most celebrated maxims of the sages and religionists, and immeasurably transcend the best statutes of all human legislation. The Divine precepts embrace every relation and duty, and not only prohibit all evil but promote all virtue. They reprehend practices which all other systems approve or tolerate, and inculcate duties they omit. The laws of man reach no farther than human action, but those of God the fountain from which all actions proceed. If the laws of God were universally obeyed this earth would be a scene of universal peace

and good will.

The world approves of ambition, the eager pursuit of wealth, fondness of pleasure, and in many instances applauds pride, ostentation, contempt of others, and even the spirit of revenge— whereas the precepts of Scripture condemn all of those in every form and degree. They require us to renounce the world as a source of happiness and to set our affection upon things above (Col. 3:2). They repress the spirit of greed: "having food and raiment, let us be therewith content" (1 Tim. 6:8). "Labor not to be rich" (Prov. 23:4); "lay not up for yourselves treasures upon earth" (Matt. 6:19); and warn that "the love of money is the root of all evil." They bid us "lean not unto thine own understanding. . . be not wise in thine own eyes" (Prov. 3:5, 7), and prohibit all self-confidence: "he that trusteth in his own heart is a fool" (Prov. 28:26). Not only do they reprehend the spirit of revenge (Rom. 12:19; 1 Pet. 3:9), but they enjoin upon us, "Love your enemies, bless them that curse you, do good to them that hate you, and pray for them that despitefully use and persecute you" (Matthew 5:44). Such precepts as those never originated in any human mind, my reader.

In these precepts morality and duty are advanced to their highest pitch. "All things whatsoever ye would that men should do to you, do ye even so to them" (Matthew 7:12). Many of them are entirely against the bent of nature: as "rejoice not when thine enemy falleth, and let not thine heart be glad when he stumbleth" (Prov. 24:17); "If thine enemy be hungry, give him bread to eat" (Prov. 25:21); "In honor preferring one another" (Rom. 12:10); "let each esteem each other better than themselves" (Phil. 2:3). None others so "holy, just and good" (Rom. 7:12). Such statements as the following were never devised by man: "When thou doest thine alms, let not thy left hand know what thy right hand doeth: that thine alms may be in secret" (Matthew 6:3, 4). "Whether therefore ye eat or drink, or whatsoever ye do, do all to the glory of God" (1 Cor. 10:31); "Let all bitterness, and wrath, and anger, and clamor, and evil speaking, be put away from you, with all malice: and be ye kind one to another, tender hearted, forgiving one another" (Eph. 4:31, 32). "Giving thanks always for all things unto God" (Eph. 5:20); "Rejoice evermore" (1 Thess. 5:16).

"Be ye therefore perfect, even as your Father which is in Heaven is perfect" (Matthew 5:48). The only objection which an Infidel could bring against the precepts of Scripture is that such an exalted standard of conduct as they inculcate is manifestly unattainable by imperfect creatures. That is readily admitted, yet so far from making against them, it only serves to exhibit the more clearly the design and wisdom of their Divine Author. In requiring from fallen creatures that which they cannot perform in their own strength, God does but maintain His own rights, for our having lost our original power does not release us from rendering to God that fealty and honor which is His due. Moreover, they are admirably designed to humble us, for our unsuccessful attempts to meet their demands make us the more conscious of our infirmities, and thereby pride is abased. They are intended to awaken within us a personal sense of dependence upon Divine aid. Where there is a genuine desire and endeavor to obey those statutes, they will be turned into earnest prayer for help—nor will assistance be denied the seeking soul. Thus, the seeming foolishness of God is seen to surpass the feigned wisdom of man.

One other remarkable feature about the precepts of the Bible calls for a brief notice, namely, the motives by which they are enforced. No appeal is made to vanity, selfishness, or any of the corrupt propensities of our nature. Obedience to them is urged by no consideration of what our fellows will think or say of us, nor how we shalt further our own temporal interests. Rather are the animating motives drawn from respect to God's will, hope of His approbation, concern for His glory, gratitude for His mercies, the example that Christ has left us, and the claims which His sacrifice has upon us. Christians are bidden to forgive one another because God has for Christ's sake forgiven them (Eph. 4:32). Wives are called on to submit themselves unto their own husbands as the Church is subject unto Christ, and husbands to love their wives "even as Christ also loved the church" (Eph. 5). Servants are required to be obedient unto their masters in singleness of heart "as unto Christ" (Eph. 6:5), while their employers are to act toward their servants in the knowledge, that they also "have a Master in Heaven" (Col. 4:1). Christ's commandments are to be kept out of love to Him (John 14:15). How radically different are such inducements as those from urging that which will win the esteem of our fellows! Not that which will promote our own temporal interests, but what "is right" (Eph. 6:1) is that which the Holy Spirit presses upon us.

A final word to the preacher: The solemn fact is that every unsaved hearer is "dead in trespasses and sins" (Eph. 2:1), devoid of any spiritual perception or sensibility, incapable of any spiritual action—such as evangelical repentance and saving belief of the Gospel. Nothing short of a miracle of grace can bring a lost soul from death unto life, and nothing but the almighty and invincible power of God can accomplish the same (Eph. 1:19). It therefore follows that neither your faithfulness nor your earnestness can, of itself, save a single sinner: you will simply be "beating the air" unless the Holy Spirit is pleased to graciously accompany the Word with power and apply it to the heart of your hearer. None but the blessed Spirit can effectually convince of sin, and bring an unsaved person to realize his desperate condition and dire need. Even the Word itself only becomes "the Sword of the Spirit" as He wields it, and we cannot warrantably look unto Him to do so if we grieve Him by using fleshly means and worldly methods. It is unbelief in the imperative necessity of the Spirit's operations which has caused so many churches to descend to the level of the circus, and evangelists to conduct themselves like showmen. Humbly seek His presence and blessing, and trustfully count upon the same.

3. Its promises, which hold out the highest felicity of which man is capable. There is a natural instinct in the human heart after happiness, yea, after eternal happiness; yet instead of looking unto God for the same, the unregenerate try to find it in the creature. They fondly imagine that satisfaction is to be obtained in things visible, that it is to be found through the medium of the senses. But in vain do they gratify their bodily lusts: material things cannot satisfy the longings of an immaterial spirit. The springs of the earth are unable to quench the thirst of the soul. Wealth does not, for the millionaire is still a stranger to contentment. The honors of the world are but empty baubles, as their securers quickly enough discover. The eager devotees of pleasure find there is no real happiness in any form of amusement. Serious souls are at a loss to know where to look for that which will reward their quest. "There are many that say, Who will show us any good?" (Ps. 4:6): they neither know what it consists of, nor where it to be found.

Hence it is that the Lord says unto them, "Wherefore do ye spend money for that which is not bread? and your labor for that which satisfieth not? Hearken diligently unto Me, and eat ye that which is good, and let your soul delight itself in fatness. Incline your ear and come unto Me: hear and your soul shall live" (Isa. 55:2, 3). God has "shown" what substantial and lasting "good" consists of, and where it is to be obtained. He has made known the same unto us in the wondrous and blessed promises of His Word: "Eye hath not seen, nor ear heard, neither have entered into the heart of man, the things which God hath prepared for them that love Him. But God hath revealed them unto us by His Spirit" (1 Cor. 2:9, 10). This is yet another of the many excellence's of the Bible: that its promises set forth the greatest happiness of which we are capable of enjoying. The One who gave us being is alone capable of putting real gladness into the human heart. That gladness comes to us not through the delights of sense, but consists in communion with the One who is the sum of excellence.

The promises of Scripture are the assurances which God has given us that He will bestow the best of blessings, for this life and also for the life to come, on those who seek them in the right spirit and comply with their terms. From the many hundreds which are scattered throughout the Bible we can but single out a few specimens. The sum of them is that the soul of man shall delight itself in God Himself as its everlasting portion. But that is impossible until the guilty conscience has been pacified, and that can only be through the knowledge of His forgiveness of sin. Therefore we begin with the evangelical promises which are addressed unto sinners. "Let the wicked forsake his way, and the unrighteous man his thoughts; and let him return unto the LORD, and He will have mercy upon him, and to our God, for He will abundantly pardon" (Isa. 55:7). "Come unto Me [Christ] all ye that labor and are heavy laden, and I will give you rest" (Matthew 11 :28)—peace of conscience, rest of soul, joy of heart. What precious promises are those! They are the promises of Him that cannot lie.

God has solemnly pledged Himself to bestow a free, full and eternal salvation upon every penitent sinner who comes to Him as a beggar and relies upon His Word. Not only to blot out all his iniquities, but to clothe him with the robe of Christ's righteousness, to receive him as a son, and to henceforth supply his every need. He has promised to be "a sun and shield" unto all such, to "give grace and glory," and that "no good thing will He withhold from them that walk uprightly" (Ps. 84:11). The promises of Satan are every one of them lies, those of man unreliable, but every one of God's is infallibly sure. The writer can testify that after forty years of Christian experience, in his travels around this earth, he has never met with a single person who trusted God and found that His promises mocked him. At the close of his long life Joshua said unto Israel, "ye know in all your hearts and in all your souls that not one thing hath failed of all the good things which the LORD your God spoke concerning you: all are come to pass unto you" (23:14). So, too, acknowledged Solomon: "Blessed be the Lord that hath given rest unto His people Israel according to all that He promised: there hath not failed one word" (1 Kings 8:56).

"Call upon Me in the day of trouble: I will deliver thee" (Ps. 50:15). That is a promise which every person may test for himself. We can personally bear emphatic witness that many times have we put that word to the proof and never found it wanting; and many, many others, too, can bear witness that the living God is a prayer-hearing and prayer-answering God. That is an argument—a well-attested one—which no Infidel can answer. There is no gainsaying the fact that thousands of men and women have called upon God in the day of their trouble and were miraculously and gloriously delivered by Him. What a monument to God's faithfulness in honoring His promises was raised by George Muller of Bristol, whose 2,000 orphans were daily fed and clothed in answer to believing prayer! In like manner shall everyone who puts his trust in the Divine promises yet receive fulfillment of that most amazing word; "when He [Christ] shall appear, we shall be like Him" (1 John 3:2)—perfectly conformed to His holy image! The Divine promises unmistakably bespeak their Author to be none other than "the God of all grace" (1 Pet. 5:10).

4. Its profundity. There are books in the writer's library which thirty years ago he read with no little pleasure and profit. Some of them he has recently re-read—with mingled disappointment and thankfulness. In the past they were helpful to him: but today they are too elementary to be of service to him. As he outgrew the clothes of childhood, so every minister of the Gospel who continues to pursue his studies assiduously will advance beyond the primers of his theological youth. Yet no matter how intensely nor for how many years he may study God's Word, he will never advance beyond it, either spiritually or intellectually. What a laborious and thankless task would it be to read through the ablest human production twenty times! Yet many who have read through the Bible scores of times have testified that it was more attractive and edifying to them than ever. The deeper any regenerate soul digs into the wondrous contents of the Bible, the more will he discover that it contain a boundless and fathomless ocean of Truth, and an inexhaustible mine of precious treasure.

The Bible treats of the most exalted subjects which can engage the mind of man. It rises above the merely human and temporal, and occupies it readers with God, the unseen world, eternity. Everything is shown to be related to Him whose throne is eternal in the heavens. Human conduct is viewed not so much as it appears unto their performers and fellows, but rather as it appears in the eyes of the Holy One and in the light of the final Day of reckoning. There are many things in Scripture which are above the capacity of man to have devised. Such as a Trinity of Persons in the Godhead, the Divine incarnation and virgin birth of Christ, the union of the human nature to a Divine Person, the manner in which the Holy Spirit operates upon souls. A delineation of fallen nature is given such as neither philosophy nor medical science could furnish; the secret workings of the heart are exposed in a manner in which no analysis of the self-styled "psychiatrists" could supply. Parts of human history are chronicled not for the purpose of magnifying man but to show how far the human race has departed from God, and what obstacles stand in the way of recovery to holiness and happiness. Heaven and the everlasting bliss of the redeemed are portrayed not in a manner to gratify curiosity, still less to appeal unto the corruptions of the natural man, but to that place into which nothing that defiles can enter.

The profundity of its teaching appears throughout the pages of the Sacred Volume. The origin of sin, the fall of man, the federal relation of Adam to his posterity, the transmission of his own nature to all his descendants, the consistency of man's freedom with God's sovereignty, his total depravity with his accountability, the justification of a believing sinner by the imputed righteousness of Christ, his union to Him as a member of His mystical body admit of no philosophical explanation. They defy intellectual dissection and cannot be mapped out so as to show their precise points of contact or mode of union with each other. They are not reducible to a system of "common sense," but rather are presented as awful and insoluble mysteries. They possess depths which no man can sound and heights which none can scale. Yet so far from stumbling the reverent student of the Bible, those very mysteries are just what he expects to find in a book written by the Most High. They are designed to humble the arrogance of man, by a demonstration of his intellectual limitations, and should cause him to exclaim, "O the depth of the riches of the wisdom and knowledge of God! how unsearchable are His judgments and His ways past finding out!" (Rom. 11:33).

5. Its simplicity. Here is a remarkable phenomenon: that combined with real profundity there is the utmost simplicity. Here again we find the same thing characterizing the Word of God as appears in His works of creation: while there is much that is occult, yet there is much more that is plain and obvious. Though there be hidden prophecies and difficult doctrines, yet on all practical matters and points of duty the Scriptures are so clear that they may be understood by the dullest minds. What is more explicit than the precepts? "The testimony of the Lord is sure, making wise the simple" (Ps. 19:7). Though there be things in the Bible which are sufficient to confound the proudest efforts of human reason, yet it does not, as to its general tenor, require either genius or crudition to grasp its terms, but is adapted to the level of the unsophisticated. Since its contents are of universal concern, they are presented in language suited to the capacity of all. That which concerns man's temporal well-being and everlasting felicity is written so distinctly that the wayfaring man, though a fool, need not err therein. Though there be depths which no leviathan can swim, yet the babe in Christ may safely wade in its refreshing streams.

Though the Bible is full of majesty, yet the naked Truth itself is presented in a manner suited to the meanest capacity. God graciously accommodates Himself to our limitations, setting forth His mighty power under such a figure as the baring of His arm, and represents Heaven unto His people as "the Father's house" in which are many mansions. Its very unaffectedness is perfectly suited to the gravity of its Author. Its penmen employed not the "enticing words of man's wisdom," but wrote "in demonstration of the Spirit and of power." The Bible is not written in the style of the "classics": there is an entire absence of any appearance of art. Take the four Gospels. Their obvious design is to magnify the Redeemer, yet they never resort to the usual method of elaborate praise. There is a plain statement of His virtuous life, yet no eulogizing of His perfections. His most gracious works are plainly recorded, and no attempt is made to heighten their effect. His wondrous miracles are chronicled as matters of fact, to speak for themselves, no comment being passed upon them, no note of admiration affixed to them. They are sufficient to suitably impress our minds, without any remarks from the narrators. In all of this the candid mind will perceive the signature of Truth, an ungarnished account of events which actually took place.

6. Its impartiality. To fully appreciate this striking feature of the Bible, the reader needs to cast his mind back to the conditions prevailing in society during the centuries when it was written. Women were then the mere chattel of men, slavery was extensively practiced, and with the utmost rigor, while kings reigned with the most despotic sway. Yet the teachings of Holy Writ are without the least bias, requiring obedience to their imperial edicts from all classes alike. So far from being written to keep the oppressed in awe and subjection, rulers and ruled are the subjects of its authoritative commands. Kings and subjects are bound by the same laws, liable to the same punishments, encouraged by the same promises. God's Word declares, "there is no difference, for all have sinned and come short of the glory of God" (Rom. 3:22, 23); while it also announces, "Whosoever shall call upon the name of the Lord shall be saved" (Rom. 10:13). Such declarations as those were entirely foreign to the spirit and sentiments which universally prevailed in the day of God's Prophets and Apostles.

The Gospel of Christ is designed for no privileged class, but is to be preached to "every creature" (Mark 16:15). It does not prescribe one way of salvation for the rich and another for the poor: rather does it affirm on the one hand, "How hardly shall they that have riches enter into the kingdom of God!" (Mark 10:23), and on the other, "God hath chosen the poor of the world" (James 2:5). There is no toadying to the scholar or sage: "Thou has hid these things from the wise and prudent, and hast revealed them unto babes" (Matthew 11:25). Husbands are bidden to "love their wives as their own bodies" (Eph. 5:28), and masters are enjoined to treat their servants in manner which comports with the fact that they, too, have a Master in Heaven with whom "there is no respect of persons" (Eph. 6:9). No such declaration as the following was ever coined by an impostor: "There is neither Jew nor Greek, there is neither bond nor free, there is neither male nor female: for ye are all one in Christ Jesus" (Gal. 3:28).

7. Its comprehensiveness. God's Word is a compendious and complete Rule of Life, so that we may be "thoroughly furnished unto all good works" (2 Tim. 3:17). Every truth in it is designed to influence our character and conduct. It contains full and explicit instructions for all our relative duties. No case has ever occurred, or ever will, for which adequate provision has not been made in its invaluable treasury. Here are directions suited to any situation in which we may find ourselves. Whether its reader be young or old, male or female, rich or poor, illiterate or learned, he may find that which will supply all his need. That any should read it without receiving any benefit therefrom is due alone to his own vanity or perversity. His duty and his danger are plainly marked out as though it had been written for him alone! Its very fullness proclaims its Author: it is a revelation and communication from the Infinite One. Its contents have supplied material for thousands of books and matter for millions of sermons.

The Bible is more than a book: it is a library. Its history covers a period of 4,000 years. Its prophecies extend to literally dozens of nations. Its teachings respect good and evil, God and man, time and eternity. It makes known how He is to be worshipped acceptably. It informs us how His blessing may be secured upon the home. It reveals its secrets of health and longevity. Here is milk for babes, meat for the strong, medicine for the sick, relief for the weary, consolation for the dying. The particular experience of every believer is so vividly delineated therein that whoever reads it aright may discover, by His grace, his precise state and degree of progress. In the Bible is stored up more true wisdom, which has endured the trials of the centuries, than the sum total of thinking done by men since the day of human history down to the present hour. Of all the books in the world the Bible alone can rightly be said to be comprehensive and complete. It needs no addendum. It has been truly affirmed, "If every book but the Bible were destroyed, not a single spiritual truth would be lost" (Torrey). The comprehensiveness and fullness of the Scriptures is yet another of their innumerable evidences which demonstrate their Divine inspiration.

Chapter 13
THE HOLY BIBLE
MORE UNIQUE CHARACTERISTICS—2

8. Its conciseness. Here is yet another remarkable feature which distinguishes the Bible from other books: though it be the most comprehensive of all, yet the most compact. Though it contains a complete library, having no less than sixty-six books within its covers, yet a small-print copy may be carried in one's pocket. Though there is here an amazing fullness, yet no excessive length. There is an abundance of matter wrapped up in a few words. An epitome of the heavens and earth, an account of the forming of this world into an habitable globe, the creation of its denizens, the making of man, the formation of woman, their state in Paradise, a description of the garden of Eden—are all condensed into two chapters which require but two pages! If "brevity" be "the soul of with," then here is the quintessence of wisdom. A vivid description of the fall of our first parents, how it was brought about, with the effects thereof; to which is subjoined the appearing of the Lord, their arraignment by Him, with their trial, sentence, and expulsion from the garden, are all given within the space of only twenty-four verses! So briefly narrated, yet all-sufficient to answer every purpose for which the revelation of the same is made to us.

Within the space of seven chapters we have the creation and furnishing of the world, the apostasy of our first parents, the birth of Abel and Cain, an account of their worship of God, the murder of the former, and an enumeration of seven generations of the latter—with a description of 10 of the progenitors of Christ. In addition, we find in them an account of the wickedness of men, the announcement of God that He purposed to destroy the earth and the human race; His detailed instructions to Noah for the building of an ark, in which were to be preserved himself, his family, and representatives of all living creatures. Then we have described the coming of the flood, the destruction of the old world, and the salvation of all within the ark! All the wisdom of men could not have expressed and compressed subjects of such vast importance and interests within so brief a compass. Moses himself could not, unless he had been inspired by the Holy Spirit. No book besides the Bible contains so much in so short a space. The brevity of Scripture is beyond imitation. The wisdom of God is most gloriously displayed in revealing so much in language so simple and so succinct. There is nothing within the wide range of human literature which in the least resembles this striking yet little noticed feature.

The unique brevity of Holy Writ only becomes really apparent when we compare the biographies which men have written and the systems of religion which they have drawn up. The Jews have joined to the Scriptures their Talmud, to which they affix equal authority— the one followed by most of their rabbis consists of 12 folio volumes; while the Romanists receive with the same veneration the writings of "the fathers," the decisions of the "councils," the vast accumulations of synod edicts and papal decrees and bulls, and a mass of "traditions" respecting both faith and morals. Who among uninspired historians and narrators would or could have recorded the birth, life, ministry, miracles, sufferings, death, resurrection and ascension of Christ in less than 1,200 lines? Who among them could have related the history of Christianity during the first thirty of its most memorable years within the space of thirty pages? For fullness and brevity, dramatic description yet terseness of language, for outlines of sermons, details of miraculous conversions, intervention of angels, all pictured with a few brief touches, there is nothing comparable to the Acts of the Apostles. What but the Divine Mind could have comprehended in so small a book as the Bible such an immense store of information and instruction?

9. Its Numerics. As the Creator has been pleased to provide an endless variety in Nature, which appeals to widely different tastes and temperaments both as it respects objects for the eye, sounds for the ear, scents for the nose and flavors for the palate, so He has deigned to supply many different kinds of evidence for the inspiration of His Word, which are suited to all kinds of minds. As one man prefers this dish or flower to that, so one investigator will be more impressed and convinced by a particular line of demonstration than another. It is with that fact in mind we have prepared this material and multiplied their divisions. All of them will not appeal with equal potency and pertinence to the same reader: what strikes one most forcibly may seem not at all interesting to another, while what one finds unimpressive may settle the matter for another. Thus with the argument we are about to expound. Some may deem it fanciful and unsatisfactory, while others will not only find it interesting and instructive, but weighty and conclusive.

Our present argument may be briefly stated thus: as there are innumerable evidences of mathematical design in God's works of creation, we should naturally look for the same in His Word. If the One who "telleth the number of the stars" (Ps. 147:4), who "bringeth out their host by number" (Isa 40:26), who "weigheth the waters by measure" (Job 28:25), should vouchsafe to grant the sons of men a written revelation, it is to be expected that it will bear similar evidences of numerical significance and exactitude. If the heavenly bodies move with such unfailing regularity that an eclipse can be calculated centuries in advance of its occurrence, and if all of our chronometers are set by the motion of the sun, which never varies a fraction of a second, then it is to be anticipated that similar phenomena will appear in the Holy Scriptures. Nor is such an expectation disappointed: rather does it receive abundant confirmation and illustration. Everywhere in the Bible there are to be found the same evidences of a supreme Mathematical Mind as appear to the careful observer in the material realm.

Those marks of mathematical design are seen both in the general and in the particular For example, 12 is the number of rule or government. Thus, the only theocracy or nation immediately governed by God, and in whose midst He set up His throne, comprised 12 tribes; and when Christ established His spiritual kingdom upon earth, He ordained 12 Apostles to be His ambassadors. Now both Scripture and common observation tell us that God has set in the heavens, "two great lights: the greater light to rule the day and the lesser light to rule the night" (Gen. 1:16). In perfect accord with that fact, day and night alike have 12 hours, each hour consisting of 60 minutes (12 x 5), with 12 months for the year. From the remotest ages of antiquity astronomers have divided the stellar heavens into the "12 signs of the Zodiac"; so, too, the vast circle of the heavens has been divided into 360 degrees or 12 x 30. But why should 12 thus pervade the heavens? Why not 10 or fourteen? Man can give no reason. But Scripture supplies the explanation: "the heavens do rule" (Dan. 4:26), and 12 is the number which stands for that!

The very structure of the Bible evinces numerical design and arrangement. First we have the five books of the Pentateuch, like basal blocks. They are surmounted by the 12 historical books— Joshua to Esther. Next follow the five "poetical"—Job, Psalms, Proverbs, Ecclesiastes, Song of Solomon. Then come the five major Prophets, succeeded by the 12 minor ones. Above these are the five historical books of the New Testament, then the 21 Epistles (by five writers!), and over all, like a crowning dome, the Apocalypse. It will be seen that five is the number which occurs most frequently, appearing conspicuously at four points: at the beginning of the Old Testament and at the beginning of the New Testament; the other two in the center of the Bible! Nor will the student of Scripture be surprised at this when he discovers that the numerical significance of that number is Divine grace. Hence five is the dominant number in the Tabernacle; and hence too, the five great offerings of Leviticus 1-6. "This mathematical law, pervading the Book, is at least a hint of the mathematical mind of the Author, who reveals the same regard to the symmetry of number and form in the material universe ("The Bible and Spiritual Life," A. T. Pierson).

Before passing from the more general to the particular, let us point out that Bible numerics assure us of the integrity of the Canon of Scripture. How so? The very number of its books intimates the Canon is complete. The Old Testament has in it 39, or 3 x 13, and three is the number of manifestation and 13 of apostasy: its dominant theme being the apostasy of man and of Israel. The New Testament has just 27 books, or the cube of three: 3 x 3 x 3, and three is the number of God and of manifestation—God fully and finally manifested in the incarnate and risen Christ. Now take out a single book, or add one (like "Asher"), and that significance will disappear! But as it is in Nature, so with the Bible: its wonders and perfections, especially in minutiae, are only perceptible to the studious investigator. When examined under the microscope the flakes of snow and even the scales of the herring (as the writer recently saw for himself) are formed and arranged after perfect geometrical patterns. In like manner, the number of times a word or an object is found in the Bible is always in strict harmony with the meaning possessed by that numeral.

As others before us have pointed out, four is the number of the world or earth. The fourth day of Genesis 1 saw the material creation completed—the fifth and sixth being devoted to furnishing and peopling the earth. It is divided into four quarters: north, east, south, west. It has four seasons: spring, summer, autumn and winter. The fourth clause in the Family Prayer is, "Thy will be done on earth." Four Gospels present our Lord's earthly ministry. Five, which is 4 + 1 (God coming to the aid of the creature), is the number of grace. The fifth day's work in Genesis 1 illustrates: "life" and "God blessed them" occurring, for the first time. When Joseph signified his peculiar favor unto the beloved Benjamin, "his mess was five times so much" as that of any of his brethren (Gen. 43:34), and while he provided change of raiment for them, he gave "five changes of raiment to Benjamin" (Gen. 45:22). The fifth clause in the Family Prayer is "Give us this day," etc. The 50th year was that of "jubilee." Six is the number of man, for he was made on the sixth day, and see Revelation 13:18. There were six cities of refuge for the manslayer (Num. 35:13). In the Bible there are six words for "man"—four in the Old Testament and two in the New. Our Lord was crucified by men and for men at "the sixth hour"!

Seven, as is well known, is the number of perfection: how exceedingly striking, then, that in Matthew 1:17, the Holy Spirit informs us there were "14 generations" from Abraham to David, 14 from David to the Babylonian captivity, and 14 from the captivity till Christ: or 42 in all. And 42 is 7 x 6: the 42nd generation from Abraham being the perfect Man! Stand in holy awe, my reader, before such Divine handiwork: Eight signifies a new beginning. It was Noah, "the eighth person" (2 Pet. 2:5), who stepped out of the ark onto the earth to begin a new order of things. Circumcision was to be administered on the eighth day (Gen. 17:12). On the eighth day Israel's priests entered upon their service (Lev. 8:33, and 9:1). On that day the leper was cleansed (Lev. 14:10, 11), and the Nazarite was restored (Num. 6:10). Just eight penmen were employed by God on the New Testament. Thirteen is the number of revolt or apostasy: "Twelve years they served Chedorlaomer, and in the 13th year they rebelled" (Gen. 14:4). Note Esther 3:13! In Mark 7:21, 22, our Lord enumerated 13 features of man's apostate heart. The "dragon," the arch-apostate, is mentioned just 13 times in the New Testament. Much of the above has been culled from Numbers in Scripture, by E. W. Bullinger—unobtainable.

The same meaning appears in their multiples. Thus, one of the significations of two is that of witness (John 8:17; Rev. 11:3), and 14 speaks of perfect or complete witness, as in Nehemiah 8:4, the 14 Epistles of Paul. Fifteen (5 x 3) is a manifestation of grace: 2 Kings 20:6; Leviticus 23:6, 34, 39. Ten is the number of responsibility (Gen. 18:22; 24:55; Ex. 34:28), and therefore when Christ graciously fed the multitude and they were required to partake in an orderly manner—"make them sit down by fifties [5 x 10] in a company" (Luke 9:14). Jude is the 26th book (13 x 2) in the New Testament and its obvious theme is apostasy, witnessing unto and against it: verses 4-8, 11-13, 24—a fitting prelude to the Revelation. When the Jews treated Paul as an apostate, they laid upon him "forty stripes save one"—39 or 13 x 3 (2 Cor. 11:24)! Thus, all through the Scripture numbers are not used haphazardly but with design. Not only so, but though they are employed by no less than 40 penmen, yet always with uniform precision; which can only be accounted for on the ground that all were inspired by one and the same Spirit.

10. Its reserve. Had the Bible been of human origin—a fraud passed on upon the world—exactly the opposite had been the case. When human writers take up matters of extraordinary interest they deal with them dramatically rather than prosaically, and in a manner which will appeal to lovers of the sensational. But there is nothing like that in the Scriptures: instead, a holy constraint rests upon its scribes. When secular writers arouse curiosity they endeavor to satisfy it, whereas the sacred penmen lift not a finger to remove the veil from off the mysteries of which they treat. They never draw upon the imagination, nor indulge in that speculation which is so prominent in the authors and disciples of all heathen religions. That can only be accounted for on the ground that the Holy Spirit suppressed their natural proclivities. The Divine inspiration of the Bible appears not only in what is said, but equally in what is not said. Its silences are as eloquent as its speech. No explanation is given of the modus of the three Persons in the Godhead—in marked contrast to the presumptuous reasonings of not a few theologians, who sought to be wise above what is written.

How scanty the information furnished on many things upon which the human heart craves light! In the historical portions men and nations appear abruptly, raising the curtain of oblivion, stepping to the front of the stage for a brief moment, and then disappearing into the unknown. It is full of gaps which human authors would have filled in. How often we wish the Evangelists had been more communicative. Had they been left to their own wisdom, the Gospels had been much fuller and lengthier! No description is given of the bodily appearance of Christ: they say not a word about His stature, complexion, or features. What is yet more remarkable, except for one brief statement concerning Him as a boy of twelve, the first 30 years of our Lord's life are passed over in complete silence, which is very different from the fabled accounts of the Apocryphal writers! There is not the least gratifying of idle curiosity in the Bible, but a noticeable repressing of the same. Nothing is told us of the experiences of the soul—either redeemed or reprobate—immediatcly after death, and little about the Eternal State. The Scriptures are not for entertainment, but are given for practical and spiritual ends.

While Holy Writ makes known many facts unto us, it does so no further than they contribute to the design of the Holy Spirit and are for our moral instruction. Very little information is furnished, and sometimes none at all, concerning the amanuenses of God—we do not even know who wrote the books of Ruth and Esther. No account is given of the closing hours of Peter, Paul and John. It is not thus with uninspired historians and biographers! How natural for the Apostle John to have spoken of our Lord's mother in terms of adulation, yet not a word does he utter which affords the least support to the sickly sentimentality and blasphemous idolatry of the Popish Mariolatry. Only once is she mentioned after Christ's ascension, and then at a prayer meeting: not as the object of supplication, but taking her place among brethren and sisters as a supplicant (Acts 1:14)! Frequent mention is made in the Gospels of "the devils" or "demons," yet nowhere are we told anything about who or what they are. There are many matters of which we should welcome information, but the Bible is silent thereon, because such knowledge respected not our duty nor would it have promoted personal piety. But nothing concerning our well-being is omitted. An account is given of how the human race became infected with the virus of sin, but not a word on the origin of evil.

11. Its ingenuousness. Had the historical portions of the Old Testament been a spurious production, how vastly different had been their contents! Each of the books was written by a son of Abraham, yet nowhere do we find his posterity flattered. So far from extolling the virtues of the Jewish nation, it is uniformly portrayed as an ungrateful, rebellious, and sinful people. There is scarcely a book in the Old Testament which does not relate that which is most unfavorable and highly disgraceful to them. Nowhere do we find their bravery eulogized, and never are their victories ascribed either to their valor or military genius. Success is always attributed unto Jehovah, their God. In like manner, their defeats are referred unto Him, as withholding His power because their evil conduct had justly displeased Him. Their defeats are accounted for neither by misfortune nor bad generalship, but to their own wickedness restraining a holy God from showing Himself strong in their behalf. Now such a God is not the creation of the human mind, nor are such historians actuated by the common principles of human nature. Time after time Israel's subjugation by heathen nations is faithfully chronicled.

The Jewish historians have also impartially recorded the numerous backslidings and spiritual declensions of their own people. One of the outstanding truths of the Old Testament is the unity of God, that beside Him there is none else, that all others are false gods, and that the paying of any homage to them is the sin of all sins. Yet the idolatry of Israel is frankly and repeatedly recorded. The guilt of some of their leading men is mentioned, as that of Aaron and Solomon. Nor is there the slightest attempt made to excuse such appalling wickedness: instead, it is openly censured and roundly condemned. Nor do the writers spare themselves or omit that which is to their discredit. Moses concealed not the reflection cast upon his own tribe (Gen. 34:30; 49:5), nor the incest of his parents (Ex. 6:20), or the rebellion of his sister (Num. 12:1). He failed not to set down his own faults and failings, but frankly tells us of his disinclination to respond to Jehovah's call (Ex. 4:10-14), his murmuring against God (Num. 11:11-14), his lack of faith after so many Divine interpositions on his behalf (Num. 10:12), and the Lord's displeasure against him because of his disobedience (Num. 27:12-14). Such unsparing fidelity is found not in those who are left free to follow the bent of their own hearts.

The same unusual feature is found in the New Testament. John the Baptist is presented as a most eminent personage: miraculously born, the Lord's forerunner, accorded the high honor of baptizing Him. Where had human wisdom and sentiment placed him among the Savior' s followers? Surely, as the most distinguished and favored of His attendants, set at His right hand. Whereas he was granted no familiar discourse with Him, but was treated with apparent neglect, suffered to be cast into prison through no fault of his own, left there unvisited. See him harassed with unbelief, doubting whether or not He was the true Messiah. Had his character been the invention of fraud, nothing had been said of his lapse of faith. The same shocking unbelief is recorded of the Apostles, who not only basely deserted Christ in the hour of His crisis, but had no expectation of His rising from the dead—nay, when informed that He had done so, were full of skepticism. A spurious history had omitted such glaring blemishes. But the Bible characters are painted in the colors of truth and nature, and in the unrivalled honesty of its penmen we have yet another evidence that they wrote by Divine inspiration and not by natural impulse.

12. Its majestic tone. If God is the Author of the Bible we should naturally expect to find in it

a loftiness of tone and majesty of diction which surpasses all human productions. And such is indeed the case, especially in those portions of it which more especially treat of the Divine perfections. Amidst great plainness of speech and homeliness of expression, adapted to that meanest capacity, there is often an elevation of spirit and grandeur of language which not only command attention but fill with reverent awe. Thus, "Hear O heavens, and give ear O earth, for the LORD hath spoken" (Isa. 1:2). "The LORD reigneth, let the people tremble" (Ps. 99:1). It would be the height of presumption for any creature to speak thus, yet perfectly fitting for the Almighty to do so. When the Son of God became incarnate, the people who heard Him declared that, "He taught with authority, and not as the scribes" (Matthew 7:29), and the very officers sent to arrest Him testified, "never man spoke like this Man" (John 7:46). The same qualities mark God's written Word. It possesses a sovereign majesty which is unrivalled and inimitable.

Though the contents of the Bible are not presented pompously or bombastically, but calmly and with becoming dignity, there is yet an unmistakable elevation of style and an august solemnity of diction which is without parallel. God speaks therein and reveals the glory of His excellence. His supremacy, His omniscience, His holiness, His immutability, His faithfulness, His goodness and grace, are set forth in a manner worthy of Himself, yet at the same time admirably suited to our weakness. The most laborious efforts of scholars and rhetoricians are insipid in comparison with those passages which are particularly designed to convey to us due apprehensions of the One with whom we have to do. "He sitteth upon the circle of the earth, and the inhabitants thereof are as grasshoppers; that stretcheth out the heavens as a curtain, and spreadeth them out as a tent to dwell in" (Isa. 40:22). Yet, "He shall feed His flock like a shepherd: He shall gather the lambs with his arm, and carry them in His bosom, and shall gently lead those that are with young" (Isa. 40:11).

We adduce but one other specimen. "O LORD my God, Thou art very great; Thou art clothed with honor and majesty. Who coverest Thyself with light as with a garment: who stretchest out the heavens like a curtain: Who layeth the beams of His chambers in the waters: who maketh the clouds His chariot: who walketh upon the wings of the wind: Who maketh His angels spirits; His ministers a flaming fire: Who laid the foundations of the earth, that it should not be removed forever. Thou coveredst it with the deep as with a garment: the waters stood above the mountains. At Thy rebuke they fled; at the voice of Thy thunder they hasted away" (Ps. 104:1-7). Where shall we fine in human compositions anything as chaste, so elevated, so sublime!

13. Its undesigned coincidences. Infidel challengers of the Scriptures and deniers of their Divine inspiration have shown some industry and ingenuity in gathering together apparent contradictions between different statements in the Bible. But such alleged contradictions are only apparent, and betray the ignorance and misapprehension of those who urge them. The men who present them are merely retailing old trivial objections, which have been refuted again and again. On the other hand, those who undertake the defense of the Bible may appeal to innumerable proofs not only of its general harmony but also of its detailed consistency and verbal precision. The veracity of Holy Writ is demonstrated by hundreds of undesigned coincidences in them, or the uncollaborated agreement of one part with another. Though the Bible has in it 66 books, written by 40 penmen, covering so many generations of the world, relating to widely different states of society, containing such a variety of matter upon so many different subjects, and abounding in supernatural incidents, yet it exhibits concord in all its parts, which becomes increasingly evident the more closely it is examined. Their consonance without collusion is too uniform to be accidental, and too incidental to have been mutually planned.

That which gives greater force to this argument is its self-evident feature that the perfect agreement of all its writers is undesigned on their part. The closer their productions be scanned, the more is it manifest that their perfect unity was not studied but casual. This line of argument was developed at considerable length by Paley and later by J. I. Blunt, who fully evinced the minute agreement and yet unpremeditated concurrence of one writer with another. The value of such evidence cannot be overestimated. As Professor Blunt pointed out, "It does not require many circumstantial coincidences to determine the mind of a Jury as to the credibility of a witness in our courts even when the life of a fellow creature is at stake." When independent narrators describe an incident in detail and there is no discrepancy but perfect accord between their several accounts, we logically conclude that they have related actual occurrences—the more so when there is no indication of conference or contrivance. We shall now condense a number of examples from those authors.

After Joseph's brethren had cast him into the pit, we are told that, "they lifted up their eyes and looked, and behold a company of Ishmeelites came from Gilead, with their camels bearing spicery and balm and myrrh, going to carry it down to Egypt" (Gen. 37:25). Now this, by no means an obvious incident to have suggested itself, does appear to be a very natural one to have occurred. But what is more to our point, it tallies exactly with what we read of elsewhere, yet in a passage which has no reference whatever to the one just cited, namely, "Joseph commanded the physicians to embalm his father... and the Egyptians mourned three score and ten days" (Gen. 50:2, 3). It was the practice of the Egyptians to embalm their dead, and hence the Ishmeelites would find a ready market in Egypt for their spices! Again—when during the famine, Joseph possessed himself on the king's account of all the land of Egypt, "he did not buy the land of the priests" (Gen. 47:22)—as a specially favored class, they were exempted. In perfect accord is the fact that the final mark of the king's regard for Joseph was his giving him to wife, "the daughter of Potipherah the priest" (Gen. 41 :45)—showing that the priests were held in peculiar esteem by their monarch.

"Moses gave. . . two wagons and four oxen unto the sons of Gershon, according to their service; and four wagons and eight oxen to the sons of Merari" (Num. 7:7, 8). Why twice as many to the one as to the other? No reason is expressly stated, yet if we turn to an earlier chapter—separated by sundry details on other matters—we discover for ourselves a satisfactory explanation: the sons of Gershon carried the lighter part of the tabernacle furniture (Num. 4:25), those of Merari the heavier (Num. 4:32, 33). Does cunning contrivance or truth lie behind that? "But he [Israel's king] shall not multiply horses to himself" (Deut. 7:16). The governors of Israel rode on "white asses (Judges 5:10, and cf. Joshua 15:18; 1 Sam. 25:23), and it was the asses and not the horses of Kish which were lost (1 Sam. 9:3). News of Absalom's death was brought to David by runners on foot (2 Sam. 18:21-23). Thus it appears quite incidentally in the history of Israel that for several centuries they had no horses—a coincidence of reality which had never occurred in a fiction.

When praising the Lord for deliverance from their enemies, Deborah mentioned there was not "a shield or spear" among the Israelites (Judg. 5:8). Strange though that be, it fully accords with several other details found in that book. Ehud "made him a dagger" (3:16), Shamgar slew the Philistines "with an ox goad" (3:31), Jael had to improvise and use a tent pen, (4:21), Samson searched in vain for a weapon till he "found a new jawbone of an ass" (15:15). Yet more remarkable was Gideon's victory over the Midianites with trumpets and broken pitchers, with their satirical cry of faith "the sword of the Lord and of Gideon" (7:15-22). No explanation is furnished by the writer of Judges, nor does he link together those incidents. But when we turn to 1 Samuel 13:19-22, they are fully accounted for, for there we are told that when the Philistines subdued Israel they suffered "no smith throughout the land"! Those who are qualified to weigh evidence will perceive in such "undesigned coincidences the marks of truth—the more convincing since our attention is not directly called to them.

"Goliath of Gath" (1 Sam. 17: 4). Let us mark the value of that casual mention of the giant's town—a detail of such little importance that its insertion or omission apparently mattered nothing. In Numbers 13:32, 33, we are informed that, "the sons of Anak were men of great stature." Later, that Joshua "cut off the Anakim from the mountains and utterly destroyed their cities," but a few remained "in Gaza, in Gath, and in Ashdod" (Josh. 11:22). Thus 1 Samuel 17:4 is found to square with those independent statements in Numbers and Joshua—in the mouth of those three witnesses the veracity of history being established! In 1 Samuel 22:3, 4, David trusted his father and mother to the protection of the Moabites. Why he made such a strange and dangerous choice we are not told. Had not the book of Ruth come down to us, the mystery had been left unexplained, but there we learn that the grandmother of David's father was "a Moabitess" (Ruth 4:17), and thus the propriety of his selection of their place of refuge appears—yet only by comparing the two books together is the circumstance accounted for.

The undesignedness of many passages in the Gospels is overlooked in our familiar acquaintance with them. For instance, why were the sick brought to Jesus "when the even was come" (Matthew 8:16)? From the parallel passages, (Mark 1:21; Luke 4:31) we learn that the transaction took place on the Sabbath—which ended at sunset (Lev. 23:32). Then from Matthew 12:10—an entirely independent passage—we discover there was a superstition among the Jews that, "it was not lawful to heal on the Sabbath day." No explanation is given in Matthew 8:16, and had it not been for the accounts of Mark and Luke we had not known it was "the Sabbath"! How came it to pass that Peter, a stranger, who had entered the house in the night, and under circumstances of some disorder, was identified by the maid in the porch (Matthew 26:71)? John 18:16, tells us: he had stood there with John until "her that kept the door" admitted them—one Gospel minutely confirming the other.

The Bible, my reader, consists of no cunningly devised fables, but authentic records of momentous events. They court examination and will sustain the most diligent scrutiny, evidencing themselves to be eminently trustworthy and faithful accounts of actual happenings. While they relay much that is extraordinary, miracles many and mighty, yet confidence in the historicity is established by the numerous marks of reality, consistency, and accuracy which the ordinary matters of fact combined with them constantly exhibit. The exact agreement between incidental statements in widely separated parts of the Bible argues the truthfulness of each of them. The closer we check one narrative with another the more does the veracity of the writers appear. Thus, when I find Paul affirming that from "a child" Timothy had "known the Scripture" (2 Tim. 3:1 5)—which necessarily implies at least one Jewish parent—and then discover his mother was "a Jewess" (Acts 16:1), I am compelled by the very obliquity of such a statement to accept it as inerrant.

14. Its dispassionate poise. In all the historical narratives of Old and New Testaments alike there is a most noticeable absence of any expression of feeling on the part of those who penned them. One and all maintain candor and calmness when chronicling the most pathetic or the most atrocious incidents. There is no trace anywhere of their own delight or anger—not a single outburst of that personal bitterness and rancor which so often mar the writings of uninspired men. Instead, we behold a mild equanimity and quiet dignity breathing throughout the sacred pages. Thus, when the fall of our first parents, with all its disastrous consequences, is recorded, it is without any reflections of the scribe annexed thereto. The murder of Abel is related, but no recriminations are cast upon Cain. Even when informing us there was "no room in the inn" for Joseph and Mary, and that the newly born Savior was perforce laid in a manger, the evangelist indulges in no cutting invectives upon those who so grievously insulted the Son of God.

When another evangelist records the ferocious and wicked attempt of Herod upon the life of the infant Savior by ordering all the children in Bethlehem under the age of two to be slain, he voices no horrified denunciation at such brutality; and when he relates how the legal parents of Christ had to flee into Egypt in order to escape from the murderous designs of that king, he pronounces no railing accusation upon him, such as an ordinary writer had deemed fit. Another of them tells us of the tetrarch of Galilee vilely yielding to the demand of a dancing girl that the head of John the Baptist be brought to her on a platter, but refrains from all aspersion upon the woman's baseness and the weakness and wickedness of his consenting to the murder of our Lord's fore-runner—and with unparalleled honesty states that, "the king was exceeding sorry" (Mark 6:26). It was not that the evangelists were devoid of feeling, but that they were so completely under the control of the One who moved them to write that their natural passions were wholly subdued.

Still more remarkable is the entire absence of any reproaches from the evangelists upon the glaring injustice of the judges of the Redeemer, the horrid indignities to which He was subjected during His last hours, and the blasphemous taunts hurled at Him as He hung upon the tree. Their temperate and unvarnished description of Christ's trial and crucifixion is without paral-lel. Instead of indignantly upbraiding Caiaphas and Pilate, instead of hot strictures upon the hypocritical priests and Pharisees, instead of strong declamations of the brutal soldiers—there is nothing but the calm discharge of their task as sacred historians. How entirely different from the temper and tone of the ordinary biographer when recounting the injuries of those he loves or highly esteems! So, too, in the accounts of our Lord's resurrection—what an opportunity did that unique event afford the evangelists to break forth in accents of admiration! What an occasion was it for extolling the powers of their triumphant Redeemer! Instead, there is only a brief ac-count of the bare facts of the case. Surely it is patent that such moderation and sobriety can only be accounted for on the ground that the Holy Spirit fully controlled them, that as the amanuen-ses of God they wrote not by natural impulse, but by Divine inspiration!

15. Its amazing anticipations. A few words need to be said upon the scientific reliability of the Bible. First, there is not a word which clashes with any known fact discovered since it was written. Therein it differs radically from the Shafter of the Hindus (which affirms the moon to be 50,000 leagues higher than the sun!), the Koran of Mahomet (which teaches the mountains were created "to prevent the earth from moving"!), the statement of Pope Zanchary (which denied the antipodes), or the blunders which the latest generation of scientists find in the writings of their immediate predecessors. Second, the Bible makes known "secrets of Nature" of which all con-temporary writings were totally ignorant. Space permits of but few illustrations to show that the Bible has always been far in advance of "science."

There is not a little recorded in Holy Writ of which the ancients knew nothing, but which was verified long afterwards. For example: "Which maketh Arcturus, Orion, Pleiades, and the cham-bers of the south" (Job 9:9): centuries after that was said the southern hemisphere was un-known! "He stretcheth out the north over the empty place, and hangeth the earth upon nothing" (Job 26:7): sustaining it in space without any material support, kept in position by the center of gravity. As Dr. Leathers (King's College London) pointed out, "Job, more than 3,000 years ago, described in the language of scientific accuracy the condition of our globe." "Or ever the silver cord [the spinal column] be loosed, or the golden bowl [the skull] be broken, or the pitcher be broken at the fountain, or the wheel be broken in the cistern" (Eccl. 12:6). The lungs take in and pour out air as a pitcher does water. The heart is "the wheel" on which the pitcher is brought up from the cistern: one of its lobes receives blood from the veins, the other lobe casts it out again, pulsing it through the arteries. Therein the circulation of the blood was figuratively described long before Hervey discovered it!

Any good encyclopedia will inform its readers that in the 17th century AD., Sir Isaac Newton discovered the "law" of the circular motion of the wind; yet long before, Solomon had declared, "The wind goeth toward the south, and turneth about the north; it whirleth about continually, and the wind returneth again to his circuits" (Eccl. 1:6). It will likewise attribute to Newton the discovery of "the law of evaporation," yet the Bible had previously made known, "He causeth vapors to ascend from the ends of the earth" (Ps. 135:7). One would think from man's writings that the scientists had invented these things! But many centuries before coal was first mined, Job declared, "As for the earth out of it cometh bread, and under it is turned up as it were fire" (28:5): combustible material which provides the most suitable fuel for the furnace. Millenniums before Henry Ford was born, Nahum. (2:4) foretold, "The chariots shall rage in the streets, they shall justle one against another in the broad ways: they shall seem like torches, they shall run like the lightnings"!

In Genesis 15:5, God said to Abraham, "Look now toward Heaven, and tell the stars, if thou be able to number them," while in Jeremiah 33:22, we read, "the host of Heaven cannot be numbered." When those verses were penned, none on earth had the least idea there was a countless number of stars. Ptolemy made a catalogue of the whole sphere of the heavens and made them to be but three thousand and fifty! But when Galileo turned his telescope on the heavens, he discovered there were many more than had been seen by the naked eye; when Lord Roosse used his great reflector, he found they were to be numbered by the millions; and when Hershel examined the "milky way," he learned it was composed of countless myriads! How came it that Moses and Jeremiah used expressions so far in advance of the knowledge of their day, unless guided by Omniscience? "Thus shall it be in the day when the Son of Man shall be revealed: in that day. . . . he that is in the field . . . in that night there shall be two in bed, the one shall be taken and the other left" (Luke 17:30-35). How strikingly accurate: day on one side of the earth, night on the other!—a fact quite unknown in Luke's time!

16. Its ineffable purity. This appears relatively, by comparing the Bible with other writings, for it far excels all human codes of law in its injunctions, prohibitions, and motives as the light of a sunny day does that of a foggy one. It is equally evident when considered absolutely in itself as no other book, the turpitude and horrid nature of sin as "that abominable thing" which God hates (Jer. 44:4), and which we are to detest and shun. It never gives the least indulgence or dispensation to sin, nor do any of its teachings lead to licentiousness. It sternly condemns sin in all its forms, and makes known the awful curse and wrath of God which are its due. It not only reproves sin in the outward lives of men, but discovers the secret faults of the heart, which is its chief seat. It warns against its first motions, and legislates for the regulating of our spirits, requiring us to keep clean the fountain from which are the issues of life (Prov. 4:23). Its promises are made unto holiness, and its blessings bestowed upon the pure in heart. The ineffable and exalted holiness of the Bible is its chief and peculiar excellence, as it is also the principal reason why it is disliked by the majority of the unregenerate.

The Bible forbids all impure desires and unjust thoughts, as well as deeds. It prohibits envy (Prov. 23:17), and all forms of selfishness (Rom. 15:1). It requires us to "cleanse ourselves from all filthiness of the flesh and spirit, to perfect holiness in the fear of God" (2 Cor. 7:1), and bids us "abstain from all appearance of evil" (1 Thess. 5:22)—injunctions which are quite foreign to the "moralists" of the ancients! Heavenly doctrine is to be matched with heavenly character and conduct. Its requirements penetrate into the innermost recesses of the soul, exposing and censuring all the corruptions found there. The law of man goes no farther than "thou shalt not steal," but that of God, "thou shalt not covet." The law of man prohibits the act of adultery, that of God reprehends the looking upon a woman to lust after her (Matt. 5:28). The law of man says, "thou shalt not murder," that of God forbids all ill-will, malice or hatred (1 John 3:15). It strikes directly at that which fallen nature most cherishes and craves:

"Woe unto you when all men shall speak well of you" (Luke 6:26)— a denunciation of no human invention! It prohibits the spirit of revenge, enjoins the forgiveness of injuries, and, contrary to the self-righteousness of our hearts, inculcates humility.

Though we have now set forth no fewer than thirty separate lines of evidence for the Divine Authorship of the Scriptures, we are far from having exhausted the subject. We might have shown that the Divine inspiration of the Bible is attested by its miraculous preservation through the centuries, its unrivalled influence upon humanity, its perennial freshness, its inexhaustible fullness, its marvelous unity, its verification in Christian experience—but we have previously written thereon. Separate sections could have been devoted to the setting forth of its minute accuracy, its pride-abasing contents, its inculcation of altruism, its power to search the conscience, its intense realism— dealing not with theorizing and idealizing, but the actualities of life, its utter unworldliness, its sanctifying tendency, its teaching on Providence—but we hesitate lest the reader be wearied, and because young preachers should now be able to work them out for themselves.

Part Three-God's Subjective Revelation

Chapter 14
GOD'S SUBJECTIVE REVELATION IN THE SOUL

We would be woefully unfaithful to our calling and fail lamentably in the exercise of our present task did we not here issue a plain and solemn warning—one which we beg each reader, and especially the young preacher to seriously take to heart, namely that something more than an intellectual belief in the existence of God and the inspiration of His Word is necessary to the soul's recovery. There are multitudes now in Hell who lived and died in the firm belief that God is and that the Bible is a communication from Himself unto the children of men. It is one thing for the mind to be assured that creation must have a Divine Creator, and quite another for the heart to be yielded up to Him. There is a radical difference between mental assent to the evidences of God's existence, and a wholehearted consent to take Him as my God—my only Lord, my chief Good, my supreme End—subject to Him, delighting in Him, seeking His glory. So too with His Word. It is one thing to be thoroughly persuaded of the uniqueness and excellence of its contents, yet it is quite another to submit to its authority and be regulated by its precepts. One may greatly admire the plan of redemption revealed therein, and yet have no acquaintance with its saving power!

The evidence we have presented for the existence of God and the arguments produced in demonstration of the Divine Authorship of the Bible, are amply sufficient for that purpose, yet they are incapable of regenerating a single person or of producing saving faith in anyone. Though they be such as no Infidel can refute, though they thoroughly expose the utter irrationality of skepticism—they will not be effectual in bringing one soul from spiritual death unto spiritual life. They are indeed sufficient to intellectually convince anyone who will impartially weigh the same, but they are unable to accomplish a spiritual transformation in the soul. Though they are strong enough to produce an historical faith, they are not strong enough to work saving faith. Something more is necessary for that. However desirable and valuable be a mental assent to the Bible's being the Word of God, we must not rest satisfied therewith. There is a vital difference between perceiving the transcendence of its teaching, its immeasurable superiority to all the writings of men, and having a personal experience in our own soul of its sanctifying virtue. That can be acquired by no study or pains on our part, nor can it be imparted by the ablest reasoner or most searching preacher.

In the introductory chapter we stated that after treating of the manifestations which God has made of Himself in creation, in the moral nature of man, in His shaping of human history, in His incarnate Son and in the sacred Scriptures, we would consider that saving revelation which He makes of Himself in the souls of His people. In each of the others, it was an objective revelation of God which engaged our attention; but we now concern ourselves with a subjective or inward revelation of Himself. This is a much more difficult branch of our subject, and one which requires to be handled with great care and reverence; yet it is the most vital of all so far as the eternal interests of the soul are concerned, and therefore one which it behooves each of us to give our best attention unto. There are few duties to which professing Christians are so reluctant to apply themselves—they would not think of crossing a river in a boat with an insecure and leaky bottom, and yet will venture into the ocean of eternity on an untested (and, most probably, unsound) faith. All around us are those who mistake a theoretical knowledge of the Gospel for a saving acquaintance therewith.

There is a vast difference between being firmly persuaded that God is, and knowing God for myself, so as to have access to Him, communion with Him, delight in Him. Such a knowledge of Him cannot be obtained by any efforts on our part. It is impossible for a man by any exercise of his rational and reasoning powers—by acquired knowledge in the arts and sciences, by philosophy or astronomy—to attain to the least spiritual knowledge of God. The existence of God may be known, His works seen and admired, His Word read and stored up in the mind, and yet without any true and saving knowledge of the Triune Jehovah. No human study or learning can impart to us one spiritual idea of God and His Christ, or convey the slightest acquaintance with Him. The reader of these lines may acknowledge God, confess Him to be sovereign, holy, just and good, and yet be entirely ignorant of Him to any good purpose. An infinite Being cannot be cognized by finite reason. "Canst thou by searching find out God?" (Job 11:7). We may indeed say of His wondrous works, "Lo these are parts of His ways," yet after the most exhaustive investigation and examination of them we are obliged to add, "but how little a portion is heard of Him" (Job 26:14).

God can only be known as He is supernaturally revealed to the heart by the Spirit through the Word. None can be brought to a spiritual and saving knowledge of God apart from Divine illumination and communication. Hear what Christ Himself declared on the subject: "neither knoweth any man the Father, save the Son, and he to whomever the Son will reveal Him" (Matthew 11:27). They may entertain correct opinions of Him, have Scriptural ideas of Him in their brains, but know Him they do not and cannot, unless Christ, by His Spirit, make Him manifest to the soul. To the Jews He averred, "It is My Father that honoreth Me: of whom ye say that He is your God Yet ye have not known Him" (John 8:54, 55). So it is today, with the vast majority of preachers and professing Christians: they mistake a notional knowledge of God for an experiential acquaintance with Him. The Lord Jesus said, "I thank Thee, O Father, Lord of Heaven and earth, because Thou hast hid these things from the wise and prudent, and hast revealed them unto babes" (Matthew 11:25). "Unto babes,"—unto those whom Divine grace has made simple and teachable, little in their own eyes, conscious of their ignorance, and who cling to Him in their dependence.

When Peter owned the Savior as, "The Christ, the Son of the living God," Jesus answered, "Blessed art thou Simon Bar-jona, for flesh and blood hath not revealed it unto thee, but My Father which is in Heaven" (Mart. 16:17). Peter had long been in possession of the Old Testament, yet despite its prophecies so manifestly fulfilled in and by the Lord Jesus, it was not sufficient of itself to produce in Peter a saving conviction that Jesus was the Messiah. Nor were His wondrous miracles enough to bring spiritual assurance to Peter's heart—they did not even to the multitudes who witnessed them!

Nor is the Word of God, even in its unadulterated purity, adequate of itself to save souls. This too was unmistakably and solemnly demonstrated by the preaching of Christ: the great majority of those who listened to Him remained unaffected, or else had their native enmity against Him fanned into a flame. Nothing external to man can impart to him a saving knowledge of God or His Christ. There must be a supernatural application of the Truth made unto the heart by the special power of God before it can be spiritually apprehended.

Not without good reason did the most favored of the Old Testament Prophets exclaim, "Who bath believed our report? And to whom is the arm of the LORD revealed?" (Isa. 53:l)—the second question answering the former. That evangelical Prophet, like most of God's servants in all ages, had many Gospel hearers, but few in whose hearts a supernatural work of Divine grace was wrought. The "arm of the LORD" is a figurative expression for His invincible power (Ps. 136:12). The Lord, in His conquering might, is revealed subjectively by inward manifestation, with life and efficacy in the soul. In 1 Corinthians 2:4, the same expression is termed, "in demonstration of the Spirit and of power." Where there is not that powerful work of the Spirit in the heart, there is no genuine conversion. In order to do that, something more than faithful preaching is necessary: there must be a distinct, personal, peculiar, immediate, miraculous and effectual work of the Spirit: "a certain woman named Lydia...whose heart the Lord opened, that she attended unto [took unto her] the things which were spoken of Paul" (Acts 16:14).

"You may listen to the preacher,
God's own Truth be clearly shown:
But you need a greater Teacher
From the everlasting Throne.
Application is the work of God alone."

The most fearful and fatal delusion now so prevalent in most sections of so-called "evangelical" Christendom is that a saving belief in Christ lies within the power of the natural man, that by performing what is naively termed "a simple act of faith," he becomes a new creature. That is to make the sinner the beginner of his own salvation! He takes "the first step," and God does the rest; he believes, and then God renews him—which is a blatant denial of the imperative necessity of the work of the Holy Spirit. The fact is, if there is one time more than another when a man is absolutely dependent upon the Spirit's power, it is at the beginning, for the most formidable difficulty lies there. To savingly believe in Christ is a supernatural act and is the direct product of a supernatural work of grace in the soul. Fallen and depraved man has no more power to come to Christ evangelically than he has merit of his own to entitle him to God's favor. He is as completely dependent on the Spirit's gracious operation within him as he is upon Christ's worthiness without him. Fallen man is spiritually dead (Eph. 2:1), and a dead soul cannot "co-operate," any more than a physical corpse can with an undertaker.

"The natural man receiveth not the things of the Spirit of God, for they are foolishness unto him; neither can he know them, because they are spiritually discerned" (1 Cor. 2:14). The "things Of the Spirit" signify contents of the Word of Truth, for they were penned under His immediate inspiration. The "natural man" is man in his fallen and unrenewed state while the sinner remains unregenerate, he "receiveth not" either the Divine Law or the Gospel. That requires a word of explication: the natural man can, and often does, receive the things of the Spirit in the letter of them as so many propositions or statements, but he cannot apprehend them as does one who has been made the subject of a miracle of grace. They are "foolishness"—absurd, unattractive, distasteful to him. Yea, he "cannot know them"— he is disqualified to perceive their verity and value; "because they are spiritually discerned," and spiritual discernment he has none. The sinner has to be transformed from a natural into a spiritual man before he has any spiritual perception. "Except a man be born again he cannot see the kingdom of God" (John 3:3). Only in God's light can we see light (Ps. 3 6:9), and in order to do that, we must be brought out of that darkness in which sin has enveloped the soul.

The natural man, by reading and hearing, is competent to receive the things of God in their grammatical sense and to acquire an accurate mental notion of them, but is quite incapable of receiving a spiritual image of them in his understanding, of taking them into his affections, of cordially accepting them with his will. They are neither discerned by him in their Divine majesty and glory, delighted in by him, nor obeyed. The things of the Spirit are not only addressed to the intellect as true, but to the conscience as obligatory, to the affections as good and lovely, to the will to be yielded unto. The unregenerate are entirely unable to recognize by an inward experience their surpassing weight and worth. They may indeed receive the Truth of God into their brains, but they never receive "the love of the Truth" (2 Thess. 2:10) in their affections. The natural man is insensible alike to the authority and the excellence of the things of the Spirit of God, because his whole inward state is antagonistic to them. There must be congeniality between the perceiver and the thing perceived: only the pure in heart can see God. We not only need the Spirit objectively to reveal unto us the things of God, but He must make us subjectively spiritual men before we can receive them into our hearts.

As the eye is fashioned to take in sights, and the ear, sounds—as the faculties of the mind are fitted to think, reason, and retain concepts, so God must make the heart of fallen man suitable unto spiritual things ere he can receive them. There must be a correspondence between the object apprehended and the subject apprehending, as there is between the qualities of matter and the senses of the body which cognize them. As I cannot truly appreciate in oratorio—no matter how acute my hearing—unless I have a musical ear and refined taste, neither can I delight in spiritual things until I be made spiritual. Between God and fallen man there is no living relation, no agreement. The "beauty of holiness" cannot be perceived by one who is in love with and blinded by sin. There is no harmony between the sinner's spirit and the Holy Spirit. No matter how simply and clearly the things of God be set before the natural man, nor how logically and accurately he may reason about them, he cannot receive them in their actuality and spirituality, for he has no spiritual sight to discern their wisdom and goodness, no taste to relish their loveliness and sweetness, no capacity to take in their desirability and glory.

"The light shineth in darkness, and the darkness comprehended it not" (John 1:5). Though "the Light of the world" stood before them, they saw in Him no beauty that they should desire Him. Something more than an external revelation of Him is necessary, even such as that described in: "For God who [in the beginning] commanded the light to shine out of darkness, hath shined in our hearts, to give the light of the knowledge of the glory of God in the face of Jesus Christ" (2 Cor. 4:6). The unregenerate have their "understanding darkened, being alienated from the life of God, through the ignorance that is in them, because of the blindness of their heart" (Eph. 4:18), and they have no more ability or power of their own to dispel the same than had the deep to dissipate the darkness which abode upon it (Gen. 1:2). In the darkness of a heart which, in its native condition, is a chamber of spiritual death, God shines with a light that is none other than Himself. The One who is light irradiates the benighted soul, and in His light it now sees the fullness of truth and grace shining in the face of Jesus Christ. By sovereign fiat and miraculous power the soul is now enabled to discern the glory of the Divine perfections manifested in and through the Redeemer.

For several generations past there has been a woeful ignoring of what has been pointed out above. There has been little recognition of the fact, and still less acknowledgment of it, that all which the Father has purposed and contrived, all that the Son has done and suffered for the redemption of His people, is unavailable and ineffective to their souls until the Holy Spirit applies the same. The inestimable blessings of the Father's love, through the Son's mediation, are only brought home to the souls of the elect by the testimony, power and operations of the Spirit. But during the last century, the majority of "evangelists" displayed a zeal which was not according to knowledge. In their efforts to show the simplicity of "the way of salvation," they ignored the difficulties of salvation (Luke 18:24; 1 Pet. 4:18); and in their pressing the responsibility of men to believe, repudiated the fact that none can do so savingly until the Spirit imparts faith. One of His titles is "the Spirit of faith" (2 Cor. 4:13), because He is the Author and Communicator of it. Faith is "the gift of God" (Eph. 2:8): not offered for man 's acceptance, but actually bestowed: "the faith of the operation [not of man's will, but] of God" (Col. 2: 12)—"who by Him do believe in God" (1 Pet. 1:21).

The work of the Spirit in the heart is as indispensable as was the work of Christ on the Cross. The necessity for the Spirit's inward and effective operations are from the darkness, depravity and spiritual emptiness of fallen human nature. He alone can discover to us our dire need of Christ, convict us of our lost and ruined condition, create within us a hatred and horror of sin, bring us to consent to Christ's scepter, and make us willing in the day of His power to take Christ's yoke upon us. By nature we are totally averse to holiness, and from birth have been accustomed to doing evil only. It is impossible for us to take into the arms of our affection a holy Christ until the Spirit of life in Christ Jesus first takes hold of us. Moreover, there is a transcendency in spiritual things which far exceeds the highest flight of natural reason. Nature stands in need of grace in order for the heart to be rightly disposed to receive the things of God, and no human culture or education can effect that. A Gospel which comes to us from Heaven can only be savingly known by an inward revelation from Heaven. The Gospel is a revelation of Divine grace, such as had never entered the heart of man to conceive, still less is it capable of comprehending it—their Author must apply it to the heart.

The Gospel consists of supernatural truth and it can only be perceived in a supernatural light. True, an unregenerate person may acquire a theoretical concept and notional knowledge of the Gospel, but that is a radically different thing from a spiritual and experimental knowledge thereof: the latter is possible only by the effectual application of the Spirit. The natural man lacks both will and power to turn unto Christ. Do some of our readers regard that as "dangerous teaching"? Then we would remind them of the words of the Lord Jesus, "No man can come to Me, except the Father who hath sent Me draw him" (John 6:44). We who are "darkness" by nature must be made "light in the Lord" (Eph. 5:8) ere we can enjoy the light of the Lord. As we cannot see the sun in the heavens but in its own light, neither can we see the Sun of righteousness but by the beams of His sacred illumination. "When it pleased God, who separated me from my mother's womb, and called me by His grace, to reveal His Son in me" (Gal. 1:15, 16). There Paul gives us an account of his conversion, ascribing it wholly unto God: unto His foreordination, His effectual call, His miraculous and inward illumination by the Spirit.

The Holy Scriptures, which are inspired of God, contain a clear and full revelation of His will concerning our faith and practice. They are able to make us wise unto salvation through faith which is in Christ Jesus, and having done so, by them the man of God is "thoroughly furnished unto all good works" (2 Tim. 3:15-17). Great things are ascribed to those Scriptures and the most blessed effects are declared to be produced by them. "The Law of the LORD is perfect, converting the soul; the testimony of the LORD is sure, making wise the simple; the statutes of the LORD are right, rejoicing the heart; the commandment of the LORD is pure, enlightening the eyes" (Ps. 19:7, 8). In all ages the child of God has acknowledged, "Thy Word is a lamp unto my feet, and a light unto my path" (Ps. 119:105). All of the Christian's peace and joy, assurance and expectation, proceeds from the knowledge which he has of the love and grace of God as declared in His Word. Nevertheless, it remains that the operations of the Holy Spirit within our souls are imperative and indispensable: the Gospel needs to come to us—not only at first, but throughout our Christian lives—"not in word only, but in power, and in the Holy Spirit" (1 Thess. 1:5). Our reception of the Truth is due alone to the interposition and secret workings of an Almighty power in our hearts, making it effectual to our conviction, conversion and consolation.

Chapter 15
GOD'S SUBJECTIVE REVELATION
IS ESSENTIAL

Our urgent need for something more than an external revelation from God, even though it be a written communication from Him, inspired and inerrant, was intimated in our last chapter in a general way. Now to be more specific. Our need of an immediate and inward discovery of God in the soul, or for a supernatural work of grace to be wrought in the heart in order to fit us for a saving knowledge of Him and the receiving of His Truth, arises from the power which sin has upon man. Sin has such a hold upon the affections of the unregenerate that no human arguments or persuasions can divorce their heart from it. Sin is born and bred in man (Ps. 51:5), so that it is as natural for fallen man to sin as it is for him to breathe. Its power over him is constantly increased by long-continued custom, so that he can no more do that which is good than the Ethiopian can change his skin (Jer. 13:23). It is his delight: "It is sport to a fool to do mischief (Prov. 10:23). Sinners have no other pleasure in this world than to gratify their lusts, and therefore they have no desire to mortify them. It has such a maddening effect upon them that, "their hearts are fully set in them to do evil" (Eccl. 8:11). Nothing but the might of God can change the bent of man's nature and the inclination of his will.

The impossibility of a sinner's coming to Christ without an effectual call from God, or His quickening application of the Word to his heart, appear again from the strong opposition of fallen man. "Three things must be wrought upon a man before he can come to Christ. His blind understanding must be enlightened, his hard and rocky heart must be broken and melted, his stiff, fixed, and obstinate will must be conquered and subdued—but all these are effects of supernatural power. The illumination of the mind is the peculiar work of God (2 Cor. 4:6). The breaking and melting of the heart is the Lord's own work: it is He that gives repentance (Acts 5:31). It is the Lord that takes away the heart of stone, and gives an heart of flesh (Ezek. 36:26); it is He that pours out the spirit of contrition upon man (Zech. 12:10). The change of the natural bent and inclination of the will is the Lord's sole prerogative (Phil. 2:13)" (John Flavell). None but the Almighty can free sin's slaves or deliver Satan's captives. It is a work of infinite power to impart grace to graceless souls, to make those who are carnal and worldly to become spiritual and heavenly. The call of God is to holiness (1 Thess. 4:7), and nothing but omnipotence can make the unholy respond thereto.

The same must be said of the nature of that faith by which the soul comes to Christ. Everything in faith is supernatural. Its implantation is so (John 1:12, 13). "It is a flower that grows not in the field of nature. As the tree cannot grow without a root, neither can a man believe (savingly) without the new nature, whereof the principle of believing is a part" (Thomas Boston). No vital act of faith can be exercised by any man until a vital principle has been communicated to him. The objects of faith are supernatural—Divine, heavenly, spiritual, eternal, invisible—and such cannot be apprehended by fallen man: his line is far too short to reach to them. The tasks allotted faith lie not within the compass of mere nature—to deny self, to prefer Christ before the dearest relations of flesh and blood, to adopt His Cross as the principle of our lives, to cut off the right hand and pluck out right-eye sins—are contrary to all the dictates of natural sense and reason. The victories of faith bespeak it to be supernatural: it overcomes the strongest oppositions from without (Heb. 11:33, 34), purges the most deep-seated corruptions within (Acts 15:9), and resists the most charming allurements of a bewitching world (1 John 5:4). Nothing short of that mighty power which raised Christ from the dead and exalted Him to the right hand of God can enable a depraved creature to savingly believe (Eph. 1:19, 20).

Divine teaching is absolutely essential for the reception and learning of Divine things, and without it all the teaching of men—even of God's most faithful and eminent servants—is inefficacious. God Himself cannot be apprehended merely by the intellectual faculty, for He is spirit (John 4:24), and therefore can only be known spiritually. But fallen man is carnal and not spiritual, and unless he be supernaturally brought out of darkness into God's marvelous light, he cannot see Him. This Divine teaching is promised: "Good and upright is the LORD: therefore will He teach sinners in the way" (Ps. 25:8). Sinners are subjects on whom He works, elect sinners, on whom He works savingly: "all Thy children shall be taught of the LORD" (Isa. 54:13). In them God makes good His assurance, "I will give them a heart to know me" (Jer. 24:7), and until He does so there is no saving acquaintance with Him. No book learning can acquire it: "According as His Divine power hath given unto us all things that pertain unto life and godliness, through the knowledge of Him that hath called us to glory and virtue" (2 Pet. 1:3). That Divine power communicates life to the soul, light to the understanding, sensitivity to the conscience, strength to the affections, a death-wound to our loving knowledge of Him" (2 Pet. 1:3) consists of such a personal discovery of God to the heart as conveys a true, spiritual, affecting perception and recognition of His surpassing excellence. God is revealed to it as holy and gracious, clothed with majesty and authority, yet full of mercy and tender pity. Such a view of Him is obtained as causes its favored subject, in filial and adoring language, to exclaim, "I have heard of Thee by the hearing of the ear, but now mine eye seeth Thee" (Job 42:5). God Himself has become an awe-inspiring but blessed reality to the renewed soul. He is beheld by the eye of faith, and faith conveys both a demonstration and an inward subsistence of the objects beheld. The Father is now revealed to the heart (Matthew 11:27). The word "reveal" means to remove a veil or covering, and so exhibit to view what before was hidden. The blessed Spirit, at regeneration, removes that film of enmity which sin has produced, that blinding veil which is upon the depraved mind (2 Cor. 3:14), that "covering" which is "cast over all people" (Isa. 25:7).

The saving revelation which is made to an elect sinner is not a creating of something which previously had no existence, nor is it ab extra to the Word: nothing is ever revealed to the soul by the Holy Spirit which is not in the Scriptures. It is most important that we should be quite clear on this point, or we shall be in danger of mysticism on the one hand or fanaticism on the other. "To expect that the Spirit will teach you without the Word is rank enthusiasm, as great as to hope to see without eyes: and to expect the Word will teach you without the Spirit is as great an absurdity as to pretend to see without light—and if any man says the Spirit teaches him to believe or do what is contrary to the written Word, he is a mad blasphemer. God has joined the Word and the Spirit, and what God has joined together let no man put asunder" (W. Romaine). "The Spirit of God teaches and enlightens by His Word as the instrument. There is no revelation from Him but what is (as to our perception of it) derived from the Scriptures. There may be supernatural illuminations and strong impressions upon the mind in which the Word of God has no place or concern, but this alone is sufficient to discountenance them, and to prove they are not from the Holy Spirit" (John Newton).

There is real need to labor this point, for not a few highly strung people and those with vivid imaginations have been deceived thereon, supposing that strange dreams, extraordinary visions, abnormal sights and sounds, are the means or manner in which the Holy Spirit is made manifest to the soul. Those who look for any such experience are far more liable to be deluded by Satan than enlightened by the Holy Spirit. The Spirit supplies no new and different revelation today from that which He has already made in the written Word. God indeed spoke to His servants of old by dreams and extraordinary means and made known to them hidden mysteries and things to come—but a "vision and prophecy" is forever "sealed up" (Dan. 9:24). Through Paul it was announced that prophecies should "fail" (be given no more) and tongues should "cease" (1 Cor. 13:8), and they did so when the Canon of Scripture was completed. All of the Divine will, so far as it can be of any use to us in the present life, is already clearly made known to us in the Old and New Testaments. The testimony of the Spirit in the Scriptures is a "more sure Word" than any voice from Heaven (2 Pet. 1:19)!

The most fearful curse is pronounced upon those who presume to add to or diminish from the testimony of God in the Scriptures (Rev. 22:18, 19). It is plain to the Christian that Mohammed, John Smith and Mrs. Eddy who pretended to be the recipients of special revelations from God, were lying impostors. Others who claim to have received any Divine communications of their own souls, over and above what is contained in or may be rightly deduced from God's infallible Word, are themselves deceived, and on highly dangerous ground. "God does not give the Spirit to His people to abolish His Word, but rather to render the Word effectual and profitable to them" (Calvin on Luke 24:45). The Holy Scriptures "are able to make wise unto salvation" (2 Tim. 3:15), yet not apart from the Spirit; the Spirit illuminates, yet never apart from the Word. The Spirit has first to open our sin-blinded understandings, before the light of the Word (2 Pet. 1:19) can enter our souls. He alone can seal the Truth upon the heart. The things revealed in the Bible are real and true, but the natural man cannot perceive their spiritual nature, nor is he vitally affected by them, for he has no inward experience of the realities of which they treat.

By means of religious education and personal application to the study of the same, the natural man can obtain a good understanding of the letter of Scripture, and discourse fluently and orthodoxly thereon; yet the light in which he discerns them is but a merely natural or mental light; and while that be the case his experience is the same as that of those described in 2 Timothy 3:7—ever learning and never able to come to the [spiritual, Divine experiential] knowledge of the truth." The religion of the vast majority in Christendom today is one of tradition, form, or sentiment—destitute of one particle of vital and transforming power. Unless the Spirit of God has regenerated and indwells the soul, not only the most pleasing ritual but the most orthodox creed is worthless! Reader, you may be an ardent "Calvinist," subscribe heartily to the soundest "Articles of Faith," assent sincerely to every sentence in the Westminster Confession and Catechism, and yet be dead in trespasses and sins. Yea, such is your sad condition at this very moment, unless you have really been "born of the Spirit" and God has revealed His Son in you (Gal. 1:16).

"A man can receive nothing, except it be given him from Heaven" (John 3:27). How little is that statement understood by the majority of professing Christians! How unpalatable it is to the self-sufficient Laodiceans of this age, ignorant as they are of their wretchedness, poverty and blindness (Rev. 3:17). Though the wisdom and power of the Creator manifestly appear in every part of His creation, yet when the first Gospel preacher was sent to the Gentiles he had to declare, "the world by wisdom knew not God" (1 Cor. 1:21). Though the Jews had the Holy Scriptures in their hands and were thoroughly familiar with the letter of them, yet they knew neither the Father nor His Son when He appeared in their midst. Nor are things any better today. One may accept the Bible as God's Word and assent to all that it teaches, and still be in his sins. He may believe that sin is a transgressing of God's Law, that the Lord Jesus is alone the Savior of sinners, and even be intellectually convinced that without holiness no man shall see the Lord, and yet be entirely ignorant of God to any good purpose. Until a miracle of grace is wrought within them, the state and experience of all men—spiritually speaking—is, "Hearing, ye shall hear, and not understand; seeing, ye shall see, and not perceive" (Acts 28:26). They cannot do so until the veil of pride and prejudice, carnality and self-interest be removed from their hearts, by God's grace.

The soul must be Divinely renovated before it is capable of apprehending spiritual things. The careful reader will have noticed that the marginal rendering of John 3:27, is: "A man can take unto himself nothing, except it be given him from Heaven." He must first be given a disposition in order to do so. What a word was that of Moses to the Israelites: "Ye have seen all that the LORD did before your eyes in the land of Egypt . . . Yet the LORD hath not given you a heart to perceive, and eyes to see, and ears to hear, unto this day" (Deut. 29:2-4)—they took not to them the implications of what God had done so as to profit therefrom. Many have "the form of knowledge and of the truth in the Law" (Rom. 2:20) in their heads, but are total strangers to the power of it in their hearts. Why is this the case? Because the Spirit has not made an effectual application of it to them:

they have received no inward revelation of it in their souls. Let us furnish a specific illustration: "For I was alive [in my own esteem] without the Law once: but when the commandment came, sin revived, and I died" (Rom. 7:9). From earliest childhood Saul of Tarsus had been thoroughly acquainted with the words of the Tenth Commandment, but until the hour of his spiritual quickening they had never searched within and "pricked him in the heart" (Acts 2:37).

Hitherto, that "Hebrew of the Hebrews" was proud of his orthodoxy, for had he not been brought up at the feet of Gamaliel, taught according to the perfect manner of the Law of the fathers, and was zealous toward God (Acts 22:3)? Conscientious in the performing of duty, living an irreproachable life, "touching the righteousness which is in the law, blameless" (Phil. 3:6) in his outward walk, he was thoroughly pleased with himself. But when the Spirit of God applied to his conscience those words, "thou shalt not covet," his complacency was rudely shattered. When God gave him grace to perceive and feel the spirituality and strictness of the Divine Law, that it prohibited inward lustings, all unholy and irregular desires, he was convicted of his lost condition. He now saw and felt a sea of corruption within. He realized he stood condemned before the bar of a holy God, under the awful curse of His righteous Law, and he died to all self-esteem and self-righteousness. When the Law was Divinely brought home to his conscience in shattering power, it was like a bolt from the blue, smiting him with compunction: he became a dead man in his own convictions, a justly sentenced criminal.

Have you, my reader, experienced God's Word to be "quick and powerful, and sharper than any two edged sword, piercing even to the dividing asunder of soul and spirit"? Have you found it to be "a discerner of the thoughts and intents of the heart" (Heb. 4: 12)—of your heart? You have not merely by the reading of it, nor by the hearing of it. That Word must be applied by an Almighty hand before it cuts a soul to the quick: only then is it "the sword of the Spirit"—when He directs it. It is only by the blessing and concurrence of the Spirit that the Word is made to produce its quickening, searching, illuminating, convicting, transforming and comforting effects upon the soul of any man. Only by the Spirit is the supremacy of the Word established in the soul. It is by His teaching that there is conveyed a real apprehension of the Truth, so that the heart is truly awed and solemnized, by being made to feel the authority and majesty of the Word. Only then does any man realize the vast importance and infinite value of its contents. By the inward work and witness of the Spirit the regenerate have a personal and infallible source of evidence for the Divine inspiration and integrity of the Scriptures to which the unregenerate have no access.

Spiritual life is followed by Divine light shining into the heart, so that its favored subject perceives things to be with him exactly as they are represented in the Word. The Spirit makes use of His own Word as a vehicle for communicating instruction. The Word is the instrument, but He is the Agent. The holiness of God, the spirituality of His Law, the sinfulness of sin, his own imminent peril, are now discovered to the soul with a plainness and certainly which as far exceed that mental knowledge which he previously had of them as an ocular demonstration exceeds a mere report of things. By the Spirit's teaching he obtains radically different thoughts of God, of self, of the world, of eternity, than he ever had before. Things are no longer general and impersonal to him: "thou art the man" has become the conviction of his conscience. He no longer challenges that awful indictment, "the carnal mind is enmity against God, and is not subject to the Law of God, neither indeed can be" (Romans 8:7), for he is painfully aware of the awful fact that he has been a lifelong rebel against Heaven. He no longer denies his total depravity, for the Spirit has given him to see there is "no soundness" in him—that there is nothing in him by nature but deadness, darkness, corruption, unbelief and self-will.

Those who are inwardly taught of God discover there is abundantly more of evil in their defiled natures and sinful actions than ever they realized before. There is as great and real a difference between that general notion which the natural man has of sin and that experiential and intuitional knowledge of it which is possessed by the Divinely quickened soul as there is between the mere picture of a lion and being confronted by a living lion as it meets us roaring in the way. In the light of the Spirit, sin is seen and felt to be something radically different from how the natural man conceives it. None knows what is in the heart of fallen man but God. He has delineated the same in His Word, and when the Spirit opens the eyes of the sinner's understanding, he sees himself in its mirror to be exactly as God has there portrayed him—with a heart which is "deceitful above all things and desperately wicked" (Jer. 17:9). His secret imaginations are now discovered to him; his pride, his presumption, his awful hypocrisy are beheld in all their hideousness. The sight and sense which the illumination of the Spirit gives him of his wickedness and wretchedness is overwhelming: he realizes he is a leprous wretch before a holy God—he sees himself as irreparably ruined—lost.

Chapter 16
GOD'S SUBJECTIVE REVELATION
THE HOLY SPIRIT MUST QUICKEN

We have dwelt upon the revelation which God has made of Himself in the material universe, in the moral nature of man, in the shaping of human history, in His incarnate Son, and in the Holy Scriptures. We have pointed out that while the evidence which the first three supply for the existence of God is ample to expose the irrationality of skepticism, and to show that the Infidel is without excuse, and that while the testimony of the last two transmit to us a clear and full communication of the Divine will and make plain our path of duty, yet none of them nor all combined are sufficient of themselves to bring any man—fallen and sinful as he now is—to a saving knowledge of and relation to the thrice Holy One. While the natural man may be intellectually assured of God's existence, that Christ is His Son, that the Bible is His inspired Word, and that while he may acquire an accurate theoretical understanding of the Scriptures, he cannot either discern, receive, or relish them spiritually and experimentally—and in order thereto, he must first be made spiritual, "born of the Spirit" (John 3:6), become "a new creature in Christ" (2 Cor. 5:17).

The absolute necessity for a supernatural work of grace upon the human heart to fit it for the taking in of a spiritual knowledge of spiritual things was shown from its indisposedness unto them because of its native depravity, from the might and enthralling power which sin has over it, as well as from the transcendency of Divine things over the scope of human reason, and of the nature of that faith by which alone they can be apprehended. In a word, that an answerableness or correspondency between the object apprehended and the subject apprehending is indispensable. But what accord or concord is there between an infinitely holy God and a totally depraved and defiled sinner? And thus the work of the Spirit within the sinner is as imperative as is the work of Christ for him. The Word itself does not produce its quickening, searching, convicting and converting effects except by the blessing and concurrence of Him who of old moved holy men to write it. In short, before anyone can obtain a saving and sanctifying knowledge of God, he must make a personal, supernatural, inward discovery of Himself to the soul. As none but God can change night into day, so He alone can bring a sinner out of darkness into His own marvelous light.

"All thy children shall be taught of the LORD" (Isa. 54:13). There is a teaching of God without which all the teaching of man—even that of His most gifted and faithful servants—is ineffectual and inefficacious. The One by whom the elect are taught is the Holy Spirit, and therefore is He rightly called, "The Spirit of wisdom and revelation" (Eph. 1:17). Not because He reveals to the soul anything which is not found in the Word itself. But first, because it was by His own wisdom and revelation that the penmen of Scripture were enabled to write what they did; and second because it is by His operations that what they wrote is now made effectual unto their souls. He begins by regenerating them—imparting to them a principle of spiritual life, without which they are incapacitated to see the things of God—(John 3:3). Then He makes to their renewed mind a real and spiritual application of the same, so that they are realized in the heart, and are found to be Divine realities. By the work of the Spirit, the soul obtains an actual experience of the things contained in the Scriptures, thereby receiving fulfillment of that promise, "I will put My Law in their inward parts, and write it in their hearts" (Jer. 31:33).

All of God's children are taught by Him, yet not in the same degree, nor in the same order of instruction. God exercises His sovereignty here, as everywhere, being tied by no rules or regulations. That there is variety in the influences of the Spirit is intimated in that figurative expression, "Come from the four winds, O Breath, and breathe upon these slain, that they may live" (Ezek. 37:9), and is more definitely stated in, "There are diversities of operation, but it is the same God which worketh all in all" (1 Cor. 12:6). Though God ever acts as He pleases, and always with unerring wisdom, and where His people are concerned, in infinite grace; usually His operations upon their souls follow more or less a general pattern. But in every instance such a revelation of God is made to the soul, as none can understand or appreciate except those who have been made the favored subjects of the same. It is accompanied by a life and light, power and pungency, such as no preacher can possibly impart. An effectual application of the Truth is then made so that its recipient is enabled to know and feel his own personal case before God—to see himself in His light, to have an actual experience of things which hitherto were only hearsay to him.

Here we should, perhaps, anticipate an objection. Some may be inclined to think that in the two chapters preceding this one and in what follows here, we have wandered somewhat from our present subject. That we are supposed to be treating of that immediate and inward, that personal and saving revelation which God makes of Himself to the soul: whereas we appear to be bringing in that which is extraneous and irrelevant, by describing the varied experiences through which a soul passes just prior to and in his conversion. But in reality, the objection is pointless. As "the fear of the Lord is the beginning of wisdom," so an inward knowledge of God Himself is the beginning of spiritual life and the first entrance into vital godliness. "This is life eternal that they might know Thee, the only true God, and Jesus Christ whom Thou hast sent" (John 17:3). There cannot be any evangelical conviction and contrition, still less a coming to Christ and resting upon Him, until God Himself is known. We never move toward God in Christ until He directly shines in our hearts (2 Cor. 4:6), and thus the efficacious cause of faith is neither the clearness of our minds nor the pliability of our wills, but our effectual call by God from death unto life.

As no artist would undertake to draw a picture which would exactly resemble every face in each feature and particular, yet may produce an outline which will readily distinguish a man from any other creature, so we shall not essay to give such a delineation of regeneration and conversion as will precisely answer to every Christian's experience in its circumstances, but rather one which should be sufficient to distinguish between a supernatural work of grace and that which pertains to empty professors. All births are not accompanied by equal travail, either in duration or intensity, yet it is often the case that those who have the easiest entrance into this world are the greatest sufferers in infancy and childhood. So some of God's children experience their acutest pangs of conviction before conversion and others afterward, but sooner or later each is made to feel and mourn the plague of his own heart. "The first actings of faith are, in most Christians, accompanied with much darkness and confusion of understanding; but yet we must say in the general that wherever faith is, there is so much light as to discover to the soul its own sins, dangers, and wants, and the all-sufficiency, suitableness, and necessity of Christ for the supply and remedy of all; and without this, Christ cannot be received" (John Flavell).

The selfsame light which discovers the holiness of God to a soul necessarily reveals its own vileness. Though the Spirit does not enlighten in the same measure or bring different ones to perceive things in the same order, yet sure it is that He teaches everyone certain fundamental lessons, and that, in a manner and to an extent which they never understood before. "They that are whole need not a physician, but they that are sick," and before one will savingly betake himself to the Great Physician he is made conscious of his need of His ministrations. When a soul is quickened and illuminated by the Holy Spirit, his heart is opened to a sight and sense of sin. A work of Divine grace is made perceptible first on the conscience, so that its subject is given to realize the exceeding sinfulness of sin. He now perceives how offensive it is unto God and how destructive unto his own soul. The malignity of sin in its very nature is seen as a thing contrary to the Divine Law. He who had previously felt himself secure, now realizes he is in terrible danger. If he is one who was already a professing Christian, he now knows that he was mistaken, deluded—that what he thought to be peace, was nothing but the torpor of an unawakened conscience.

Conviction of sin is followed by a wounding of the heart, for life is accompanied not only with light but feeling also, otherwise its subject would be a moral paralytic. The sinner is filled with shame, compunction, horror and fear. He apprehends his own wickedness and pollution to be such as none other was ever guilty of. He sees himself to be utterly undone, and cries "Woe is me." He no longer laughs at what is recorded in Genesis 3, or any longer has any doubt about Adam's fall, for he perceives his sinful image in himself—conveyed to him at his very conception, a defiled nature from birth. He has been given an experiential insight into the mystery of iniquity. He now realizes that so far from having lived to the glory of God, self-gratification has been his sole occupation. "Against. Thee, Thee only have I sinned, and done evil in Thy sight" (Ps. 51:4) is now his anguished lament. He thinks there was never a case so desperate as his, and fears there is no hope of forgiveness. Now his heart "knoweth its own bitterness."

This anguish of heart is something radically different from that sorrow for sin which is sometimes found in graceless souls, which usually consists of being ashamed because of their fellows or a chagrin at their own folly. Even Judas repented of betraying his Master, but not with a "godly sorrow" (2 Cor. 7:10). It is not the degree but the nature of our sorrow for sin which evidences whether or not it be produced by the grace of God. That grief for sin which issues from a gracious principle is concerned for having flouted God's authority, abused His mercies, and been indifferent whether his conduct pleased or displeased Him. Whereas the sorrow of the natural man proceeds only from self-love: his grief is that he wrecked his own interests and brought misery upon himself. The quickened soul is now thoroughly ashamed and abased. He no longer makes excuses, but takes sides with God and unsparingly condemns himself. The guilt of sin lies heavily upon him, as an intolerable burden. The sentence of the Law is pronounced in his conscience. He perceives that there is no soundness in him, that his case is desperate to the last degree. How can I escape my merited doom? is now his great concern.

Those who have not sat under a preaching of the Gospel of the grace of God wherein Christ is freely offered to all who hear it, and have reached the stage described above, are now at their wit's end. The condition and case of such a one is no worse than it was formerly, but the scales have been removed from his eyes and he sees himself in God's light. The soul is now brought to a state of utter unrest and disquietude: not only unable to find any satisfaction in the creature, but even to obtain the slightest relief from the things of time and sense. He seeks help and peace here and there, only to find they are "cisterns which hold no water." He is at a total loss about deliverance, and sees no way of escape from that eternal doom to which he now realizes he is fast hastening. He once thought that a little repentance would save him, or a cry to God for mercy would suffice for pardon, but he now finds "the bed is shorter than a man can stretch himself on, and the covering narrower than he can wrap himself in" (Isa. 28:20). Neither meet his dire need.

What shall become of me? is now the question which wholly absorbs his thoughts. If, like a drowning man seeking some object that he may grasp to support him, he turns unto professing Christians and inquires in what way the Lord dealt with their souls and how they obtained relief—sometimes he will receive a little encouragement, but more often that which dampens his faint hope that God will yet be gracious unto him that he perish not. As he listens to what one and another relates, he realizes that it is not the path which he is treading, that he has not experienced the things which they did, and he is brought to the place of self-despair. He wishes that he had never been born, for he fears that in spite of all his convictions and anguish he may be lost forever. He feels his utter helplessness and has an experiential realization that he is "without strength" (Rom. 5:6). Yet so far from this sense of his impotency producing apathy and inertia, he is increasingly diligent in making use of the means of grace: he now searches the Scriptures as he never did before, and cries from the depths of his soul, "Lord save me" (Matthew 14:30).

"Understandest thou what thou readest?" said Philip to the Ethiopian eunuch. "How can I?" he replied, "except some man should guide me" (Acts 8:27-33). Nevertheless, he read the Scriptures, and God graciously and savingly met with him therein, using Philip as His instrument to preach Jesus unto him. None but Christ can save a sinner: He alone can remove the burden of guilt, cleanse the conscience, speak peace to the heart. As sin is loathed and hated, and self-righteousness is renounced, room is made in the soul for Christ. There is no true desire for Him until the utter vanity of this world has been felt—that its most alluring pursuits and pleasures are nothing better than the husks which the swine feed on. Sin must be made bitter as wormwood to us, before Christ can be sweet to the heart. God must wound the conscience by the lashing of His Law, ere the healing balm of Christ's blood is longed for. Like the prodigal in the far country, the soul must be brought to the place where it cries, "I perish with hunger," before the rich provisions of the Father's house are really sought.

It is in this way the blessed Spirit prepares the heart for the receiving of Christ. By giving him to understand his condition and case: his sins, his guilt, his pollution, his emptiness, his personal demerit, his misery. By giving him such a sense of the same as causes him to die unto himself, to renounce himself, to abhor himself to acknowledge that the worst that God says of him in His Word is true. Thereby the Holy Spirit shows him that he is exactly suited to Christ, who is "mighty to save," and who does save "to the uttermost them that come unto God by Him" (Heb. 7:25). He makes him to realize that he is a fit subject for the Great Physician to exercise his loving kindness upon, to heal him of his loathsome leprosy, to pardon his innumerable sins, to supply all his need out of the exceeding riches of His glorious grace. The Holy Spirit is pleased to show the self-condemned soul that Christ has nothing in His heart against him, that He is full of compassion, of infinite power, in every way meet for him; that He came into the world with the express purpose to "seek and to save that which was lost" (Luke 19:10). Thus is Christ made desirable unto him.

But it is one thing to perceive our need for and the perfect suitability of Christ and to have longings after Him, and quite another for Him to be made accessible and present to us. There has to be an inward discovery of Him to the soul before He is made a reality unto it and laid hold of by him. Said the Savior, "This is the will of Him that sent Me, that everyone that seeth the Son and believeth on Him, may have everlasting life" (John 6:40). Note well the order of those two verbs: there must be a "seeing" of the Son with the eye of the soul before there can be any saving believing on Him. In other words, the same One who has removed the scales of pride and prejudice from the sinner's eyes to behold his own abject state, must show him the glorious Object on which his trust is to be reposed. The light of the Gospel now shines into his heart, and he is enabled to behold "the King in His beauty." When He is beheld thus it must be said, "flesh and blood hath not revealed this unto thee," but it has been supernaturally communicated by the Spirit.

Christ is now made known as "Fairer than the children of men," as wholly suited to and all-sufficient for the stricken sinner. The soul is now assured that, "the Son of God is come, and has given him an understanding that he may know Him that is true" (1 John 5:20). The heart is taken with Him, attracted by Him, drawn to Him, and cries, "Lord I believe, help Thou mine unbelief." A convincing and fully-persuading realization of the truth of the Gospel concerning Christ is his. The Spirit has vouchsafed no new and different revelation of Christ than what was in the written Word, but He has given a supernatural efficacy unto the Gospel to his soul, as truly as the blowing of the rams' horns was made by God to cause the walls of Jericho to fall down. The hour has come when the hitherto dead soul hears the voice of the Son of God, and hearing, lives (John 5:25). His voice has come to him with quickening energy. The saving knowledge of Christ which is thus obtained is a vastly different thing from having a good opinion or orthodox conception of Him: He is now realized to be everything which the justice of an angry God required for satisfaction and everything which is required by the most indigent soul.

Christ now dwells in his heart by faith, and the testimony of such a one is, "One thing I know, that, whereas I was blind, now I see" (John 9:25), and neither man nor Satan can make him deny it. Before the Holy Spirit, in His sovereign and invincible power, dealt with my soul, I was "blind": blind to the just claims of Christ's holy scepter, blind so that I saw in Him no beauty that I should desire Him, blind to my own folly in spending money for that which was not bread and by seeking contentment and satisfaction away from Him. But now I see": see His surpassing loveliness and superlative worth, see that He loved even me and gave Himself for me. I see that His precious blood cleanses me from all sin. I see that He is the only One worth living on and living for. Hear him singing from the heart, "Thou O Christ are all I want, more than all, in Thee I find." Hear him as he avers with the Apostle, "I count all but loss for the excellency of the knowledge of Christ Jesus my Lord" (Phil. 3:8). Behold him, as lost in wonder, love, and praise, he bows in adoration and exclaims, "Thanks be unto God for His unspeakable gift."

How different is such a coming to Christ, closing with Him, and knowledge of Him, from that of the deluded and empty professors! Rightly did the Puritan Flavell declare, "Coming to Christ notes a supernatural and almighty power, acting the soul quite above its own natural abilities in this motion. It is as possible for the ponderous mountains to start from their bases and centers, mount aloft into the air, and there fly like a wandering atom hither and thither, as for any man of himself, i.e., by a pure natural power of his own, to come to Christ. It was not a stranger thing for Peter to come to Christ walking upon the waves of the sea, than for his or any man's soul to come to Christ in the way of faith." It is only as the Spirit quickens the dead soul, makes him sensible of his desperate condition and deep need, reveals Christ as an all-sufficient Savior, and by a powerful inclining of his will, that he is brought to cast himself on Him, and that he obtains for himself a saving experience of the Gospel, in contradistinction from a mere hearsay knowledge of it.

This personal and secret revelation of God in the soul is a miracle, as truly and as much so as when darkness enveloped the chaos of Genesis 1:3, and God by a mere fiat said, "Let there be light, and there was light." This is clear from, "For God, who commanded the light to shine out of darkness, hath shined in our hearts unto the light of the knowledge of the glory of God in the face [or "Person"] of Jesus Christ" (2 Cor. 4:6). In His own ordained hour, by a sovereign and almighty act on His part, a supernatural, saving and sanctifying knowledge of God is communicated to the souls of each of His elect. This knowledge of God is spiritual and altogether from above, being wholly Divine and heavenly. Being miraculous, this unique experience is profoundly mysterious. Its favored subject contributes nothing whatever to it, not so much as desiring or soliciting the same. "There is none that seeketh after God. . . the way of peace have they not known: there is no fear of God before their eyes" (Rom. 3:11, 17, 18). It could not be otherwise, for by nature all are, spiritually speaking, "dead in trespasses and sins" (Eph. 2:1). There can be no spiritual sight of spiritual objects, no spiritual hearing, still less any spiritual actions, until spiritual life is imparted to the soul.

No one can possibly have any spiritual hatred of sin, any pantings after holiness, any saving faith in Christ, until he has actually "passed from death unto life." In every instance where God graciously gives this inward and vivifying revelation of Himself. He declares, "I am found of them that sought Me not" (Isa. 65:1)—the subsequent seeking of the soul is the reflex, the consequence, the effect, of His initial seeking it. As we love Him because He first loved us (1 John 4:19), so we call upon Him (Rom. 10:13), because His effectual call (1 Pet. 2:9), preceded and capacitated ours. The "Spirit of life" (Rom. 8:2) must first join Himself to the spiritually-dead soul in quickening power, before he has any spiritual life or light. In that initial operation of the Spirit, the soul is wholly passive and unconscious. Regeneration is not something which we actually "receive," but is wrought in its subject once and for all. Was not natural life communicated to me without any act of mine? What act did I perform when a living soul was imparted to me? Nothing: it was utterly impossible that I should. Being and life were Divinely given to me without any volition whatever on my part.

The soul must be Divinely renovated before it is able to discern or relish spiritual things. The natural man, totally depraved as he is, can neither perceive the reality of spiritual things, be impressed with their excellence, or have his affections drawn after them. How can the natural man savingly believe in Christ when he has no grace, no power of will upwards, no sufficiency in himself? Coming to Christ is a spiritual motion, for it is the soul going out to Him. But motion presupposes life, and as there can be no natural motion or movement without natural life, so it is spiritually. Deny that, and you deny the indispensability of the Spirit's work of grace to bestow life, light and sight. Something in addition to life and light is required: the Spirit must remove from our eyes the scales of pride and enmity before we can perceive our ruined condition. Coming to Christ imports both a sense of need and a hope of relief: it is an actual closing with Him as He is freely offered to sinners in the Gospel, by a practical assent of the understanding and hearty consent of the will.

By the Spirit alone are we awakened from the sleep of carnal sloth and unconcern for our eternal welfare. By Him alone are we given to perceive the spirituality and strictness of the Divine Law, and feel its condemning power in our conscience. The Spirit alone shows us ourselves and brings us to realize that our very nature is a sewer of filth. He reveals to us our desperate need of Christ, who overcomes our hostility to Him, and makes us willing to receive Him as our Prophet to teach and instruct us, our Priest to atone and make intercession for us, our King to rule over and fight for us. It is wholly by His powerful operation that Christ is formed in us "the hope of glory." By Him alone do we obtain an experimental and intuitional knowledge of Christ. Said the Savior, "He shall glorify Me, for He shall receive of Mine, and shall show it unto you. All things that the Father hath are Mine: therefore said I that He shall take of mine and shall show it unto you" (John 16:14, 15). "Show it," not in the mere letter of it (there is no need for Him to do that, for by a little diligence we can grasp the literal or grammatical meaning for ourselves), but in the spirituality, blessedness and power thereof.

The preciousness and potency of the things of Christ are set home on the renewed mind by the grace and energy of the Spirit in such a manner that the believer is inwardly assimilated thereto. He shows them not to his reasoning faculty but to his heart, and in such a way as to impress a real image thereof, fixing the same indelibly in his affections. The Spirit is He who gives unto him soul-satisfying, heart-warming apprehensions of the Savior's love, so that at times he is quite lifted out of himself, his thoughts being raised above the things of time and sense, to be entirely absorbed with the "altogether lovely" One, and thus vouchsafes him an earnest and foretaste of his eternal joy. It is the Spirit's special office to magnify Christ: to make Him real unto His redeemed, to endear Him to their souls, until He becomes their "All in all." Every true thought entertained of Christ, every exercise of the believer's affections upon Him, is through the effectual influence of the Spirit. All true fellowship and communion which the Christian has with the Redeemer, all practical conformity unto His holy image, is by the Spirit's gracious operations. We are completely dependent upon Him for every spiritual breath we draw and spiritual motion we make.

But we have been somewhat carried away—it is not easy for love to heed the requirements of logic! The last three paragraphs should have been preceded by the statement that, though an inward revelation of God to the soul be both truly miraculous and profoundly mysterious, yet it may be identified and known to its participant. To the participant we say, for it is no less impossible to explain the same by mere words to one who has had no actual experience of the same, than it would be to convey any intelligible concept of color to one born blind or of sound to one born totally deaf. It may be known by its attendants and by its fruits. When life and being were given me naturally, all that followed was but the effects and consequences of the same. In due time I was brought forth into the world—a feeble and needy, but living and active creature, yet entirely dependent upon others. So at regeneration the soul has spiritual life imparted to it, is born again, and all that follows in the experiences of that soul is but the effects and fruits thereof, making manifest the reality of it, so that by comparison of its present history with its past, and by an examination of both in the light of Holy Writ, the great change may be clearly and indubitably informed.

God has endowed the soul with the power of reflection, so that it may be conscious of its own condition and operations. Therefore does He bid professing Christians, "Examine yourselves whether ye be in the faith, prove your own selves. Know ye not your own selves, how that Jesus Christ is in you, except ye be reprobates?" (2 Cor. 13:5). The Psalmist tells us, "I commune with mine own heart, and my spirit made diligent search" (77:6). God has so wondrously constituted man that he is able to look within and form a judgment of himself and of his actions, and at regeneration he is given "the spirit of a sound mind" (2 Tim. 1:7) so that he may form an impartial and true judgment of himself While some are too introspective, others are not sufficiently so for their own good. The regenerate soul has power not only to put forth a direct act of faith upon Christ, but also to discern that act: "I know whom I have believed" (2 Tim. 1:12). In this way Christians may attain unto a certainty of their saving knowledge of and union with Christ. The more so since they have received the gift of the blessed Spirit, by which "they might know the things that are freely given to them of God" (I Cor. 2:12). "Hereby know we that we dwell in Him, and He in us, because He hath given us of His Spirit" (1 John 4:13), which is apparent from His operations within us.

It most highly concerns each reader to examine and try his knowledge of God, and make sure it be something more than a merely natural and notional one, namely that he has been favored with a spiritual and experiential discovery of God to his soul. "Being alienated from the life of God, through the ignorance that is in them . . . have given themselves over unto lasciviousness. But ye have not so learned Christ: if so be ye have heard Him, and have been taught by Him, as the truth is in Jesus: that ye put off concerning the former conversation the old man" (Eph. 4:18-22). There a contrast is drawn between the unregenerate Gentiles and the Ephesian saints. The latter had learned both from the precepts and example of Christ. The question for them to make sure about was, Had they really been taught inwardly and effectually by Him, so that a vital change was evident in their character and conduct? That "if so be" intimated that nothing was to be taken for granted. They must put themselves to the proof and ascertain whether the truth dwelt in and regulated them as it did the Savior: whether in short, the teaching they had received was inoperative or whether it had produced a radical change in their daily lives. By its fruit is the tree known.

The inward and immediate revelation of God to a soul is made manifest by its accompaniments. It is accompanied by a principle of life, of grace, of holiness. It is attended with light and warmth and power, producing a great and glorious change within, renovating each faculty of the soul. Therein it differs radically from the "conversions" of modem evangelism which effects no such change. It is attended with the opening of the eyes of the understanding, enabling its subject to see God, Christ, self, sin, the world, eternity—in a light he did not previously. Such sights, under the gracious influences of the Spirit, lead to the experiences of conviction, contrition, and conversion, described in the preceding chapters. The quickened soul not only now discovers the true nature of sin, but feels the guilt and burden of it, and unfeignedly sorrows for and hates it. He is brought to realize the worthlessness of all self-help and creature performances. He is enabled to take in, little by little, a knowledge of Christ from the Word, by which means he is led to an acquaintance with Him and his will is brought to a full surrender to Him. Thus there is an efficacy accompanying the Spirit's teaching which is not found in any man's teaching: illuminating the understanding, searching the conscience, engaging the affections, drawing the heart unto it, sanctifying the will.

As there is both an outward and an inward "hearing" of the things of God (Acts 26:26), an ineffectual "learning of the Truth" (2 Tim. 3:7), and an effectual one (Eph. 4:20-22), so there is a knowledge of God which is inefficacious (Rom. 1:21), and a knowledge of Him which is saving (John 17:3). How am I to ascertain that mine is the latter? Answer: from its effects. It is not the quantity but the quality, not the degree or extent of the knowledge but the kind of it that matters and that is evidenced by its products. A real Christian may have a far inferior intellectual grasp of the Truth than has an unregenerate theologian, and yet possess a spiritual and sanctifying knowledge thereof to which the theologian, after all his studying, is a stranger. Concerning all the renewed God says, "But the Anointing which ye have received of Him abideth in you, and ye need not that any man teach you: but as the same Anointing teacheth you of all things, and is truth, and is no lie, and even as it hath taught you, ye shall abide in it" (1 John 2:27). That "Anointing" is the Person and operations of the Holy Spirit, and where He indwells a soul no man is needed to teach him there is a God, that the Bible is His Word, that Christ is an all-sufficient Savior, etc.

Let us now describe some of the effects of this Divine anointing. First, it is a realizing knowledge. Its grand Object is no longer known theoretically and inferentially, but actually and immediately, not by a process of reasoning but intuitively. God, who is spirit and invisible, is made visible and palpable to the soul. Does that strike some of our readers as being too strong a statement? It would not, had they experienced the same, and it should not, if they be at all familiar with Holy Writ, for of Moses it is said, "he endured as seeing Him who is invisible" (Heb. 11:27). God was real to his faith, though imperceptible to his senses. At the new birth such a discovery of God is made to the heart that its subject avers with Job, "I have heard of Thee by the hearing of the ear, but now mine eye seeth Thee" (42:5). The recipient of that manifestation is awed by a sense of His majesty, His authority, His power, His holiness, His glory. Such a revelation of the Most High is overwhelming: he dare not trifle any longer with Him, for he now knows something of the being and character of the One with whom he has to do. In like manner, the Gospel becomes to him something very different from merely an external proclamation by God's servants—it now is "the ministration of the Spirit" (2 Cor. 3:8) inwardly.

In the light of God the soul sees things as they actually are. Hitherto, if he had not a false concept of them, it was but a notional acquaintance at best. But now he views himself the present life, the hereafter, as God does, perceiving that all under the sun is but vanity and vexation of spirit. When truth is applied by the Holy Spirit its authority and spirituality are discerned, its power and pungency are felt, its savor and sweetness are tasted, its excellence and uniqueness are realized. When God is inwardly revealed to a person he becomes better acquainted with Him in five minutes this way, than in a lifetime of reading books and hearing sermons about Him. It is not an acquired knowledge, but an infused one, obtained by no mental efforts, but is Divinely imparted. As a very different image is begotten in the mind by actually seeing a person face to face than by looking upon his portrait, so by the secret operations of the Spirit a spiritual subsistence of God is wrought in the soul. Let the ablest artist paint a picture of the sun, let him use the brightest pigments and most brilliant colors, yet what a wan and insipid representation does he make in comparison to the shining and splendor of the sun itself! Glorious apprehensions of God and His Christ are conveyed and begotten in the renewed soul by the Spirit. He has now "seen" the Son (John 6:40) for himself, has "heard" His voice (John 5:25), "handled" Him by faith (1 John 1:1), "tasted that the Lord is gracious" (1 Pet. 2:3).

Second, it is a convincing and certifying knowledge. By this inward and gracious teaching of God there is given to the heart such personal evidence of the wonders of wisdom and the riches of His grace as set forth in the Gospel, that he is fully persuaded of the same. A firm and unshakeable assurance of the verity of what is revealed in the written Word is conveyed to the soul, for the Spirit works an inward experience of the same in him, so that their reality and actuality is known and acknowledged. There is an ocular demonstration made to him by the light of the Word and the power of the Spirit revealing and applying them to the one born again, so that the teachings of the Scripture and the experiences of the believer, by these means, answer to one another as do the figures in the wax and the engravings in the seal. As a Spirit-taught person reads the Bible, especially much in the Psalms or a chapter like Romans 7, he finds the workings of his heart are accurately portrayed there, and says, "That is exactly my case." Such an experience supplies far stronger proof than can either reason or sense, and though faith be occupied with things not seen by the eyes of the body and which are far above the reach of reason, yet it produces a conviction and certainty which is more conclusive and invincible than any logical demonstration.

The internal witness of the Spirit is much more potent and satisfying than all arguments grounded upon human reasoning. The natural man may be intellectually convinced that the Bible is the Word of God, and yet never have had an experiential sense of the spirituality of His Law and a heart-conviction that he is a guilty transgressor of it. He may entertain no doubt whatever that the Lord Jesus is the only refuge from the wrath to come, and still be a complete stranger in his soul to His so-great salvation. A spiritual assurance that the Scriptures are Divine can no more be obtained without the inward witness of the Spirit than can a spiritual understanding of their contents. It is an essential part of His distinctive work to produce a spiritual and supernatural faith in the hearts of God's elect, so that they receive the Word on the alone testimony of its Author. When that faith has been communicated, he can no more doubt the integrity of the Scriptures for he now "knows the certainty of those things wherein he has been instructed" (Luke 1:4). Such an assurance will cause him to cling to the Truth and confess it though there were not another person on earth who did so. He now values the Bible as his dearest earthly possession, and no matter how he might be tempted to do so, will steadfastly refuse to "sell" or part with the Truth.

Third, it is an affecting knowledge. The notions possessed by the natural man, Scriptural though they be, exert no spiritual influence upon him and produce no godliness of character or conduct. They are inoperative, ineffectual, inefficacious. He may perceive clearly that sin is hateful to God and harmful to himself, that if cherished and continued in, it will certainly damn him, yet his lusts dominate him. He may be well informed upon the excellence of holiness, and the necessity of possessing it if ever he is to enter Heaven, yet self-love and self-interests turn the scales and prevent his seeking it wholeheartedly. A natural knowledge of spiritual things penetrates no deeper than the brain, neither influencing the heart nor moving the will. The empty professor may subscribe sincerely to the doctrine of man's total depravity, but it never moves him to cry from the depths of an anguished soul, "O wretched man that I am." The doctrinal light which the unregenerate have is like that of the moon's: it quickens not, possesses no warmth, produces no fruit. A merely theoretical knowledge of the Scriptures, however accurate or extensive it may be, leaves the heart dead, cold, barren.

Radically different is that spiritual knowledge which God imparts to the renewed mind. It has a vitalizing, convincing, moving and powerful effect upon the whole of the inner man. It conveys a real subsistence of Divine things to the soul, so that the understanding discerns and knows them, the affections delight in and cleave to them, the will is influenced and moved by them. "Thus saith the LORD, the Redeemer, the Holy One of Israel: I am the LORD thy God which teacheth thee to profit" (Isa. 48:17). He teaches so much of the evil of sin as makes it the most bitter and burdensome thing in the world to us. He teaches us so much of our need for and the worth of Christ as moves us to freely take His yoke upon us—which none do unless they have been Divinely tamed. Spiritual light is like that of the sun's, which not only illuminates, but warms and fructifies, and therefore is Christ designated, "The Sun of righteousness" (Mal. 4:2). All the real teaching of the Spirit has a powerful tendency to draw away from self unto Christ, to a fixation in and living upon Him to find all our springs in Him, to prove Him to be our everlasting strength.

Fourth, it is a humbling knowledge. This is another unmistakable effect of an immediate and supernatural revelation of God to a person. That spiritual illumination and inward teaching lays the soul low before God. Therein it differs radically from self-acquired learning and the intellectual teaching we absorb from men, for that only serves to feed our conceit: such knowledge "puffeth up" (1 Cor. 8:1). Truth itself when unapplied by the Spirit is only unsanctified knowledge, adding to our store of information but producing no lowliness of heart. But when the Lord teaches a soul, the bladder of self-sufficiency is punctured, and there is a "casting down imaginations, reasonings, and every high thing that exalteth itself against the knowledge of God" (2 Cor. 10:5). He now renounces his own wisdom and becomes as a "little child." The soul is brought to realize not that he is lacking in instruction, but that he is incapable of making a good use of what he already knows. He is now sensible that he needs to be Divinely taught how to effectually translate his knowledge into practice. The letter of God's precepts may be fixed in his mind, but how to perform them he knows not, and therefore does he cry, "Teach me, O LORD, the way of Thy statutes" (Ps. 119:33), "Teach me to do Thy will" (Ps. 143:10).

Of too many Laodicean "Christians" must it be said, "thy wisdom and thy knowledge it hath perverted thee [caused you to turn away]" (Isa. 47:10) from the only One who can effectually anoint blind eyes. But the wisdom which is from above is a self-emptying one, making its possessor cry, "Lord, teach me to pray" (Luke 11:1), and when he does, it is in a very different manner from the polished periods and eloquent language of what are termed pulpit "invocations." The natural man will ask for relief when in temporal distress, though he has no sense of need for spiritual mercies. But one taught of God is painfully conscious of the fact that, "he knows not what he should pray for as he ought," and has "groanings which cannot be uttered," and that makes him implore the help of the Holy Spirit. Such a one prays, "Give me understanding that I may learn Thy statutes." "Incline my heart unto Thy testimonies." "Quicken Thou me in Thy way." "Teach me good judgment." "Order my steps in Thy Word and let not any iniquity have dominion over me" (Ps. 119:73, 40, 66, 133). Thus the soul is taught how perfectly suited is God's Word to his deep need.

Fifth, it is a transforming knowledge. When God savingly reveals Himself to a person, a real and radical change is effected in him, so that the one alienated from Him is now reconciled to Him. The light of Divine grace is a prevailing and overcoming one, producing an altered disposition toward God, so that the one who shrank from Him pants after Him. Not only is Christ now feared, but adored. Divine teaching not only slays enmity against God, but conveys to the soul an answerableness to His holiness. It is affirmed of all such, "but ye have obeyed from the heart that form of doctrine whereto ye were delivered" (Rom. 6:17), i.e., the mold of teaching into which you have been cast. At regeneration the heart is made tender and the will tractable. The characters of the renewed are formed by the Truth—for a corresponding impression is made thereon. Their hearts and lives are modeled according to the tenor of the Gospel. Truth is received not only in the light of it, but in the love of it as well. The inward inclinations are changed and framed according to what the Word enjoins, the faculties being fitted to respond thereto. He delights in the Law of God after the inward man, and chooses the things that please God (Isa. 56:4).

The sanctifying discovery of God to the soul not only slays its enmity unto Him, subdues the lusts of the flesh, removes carnal prejudices against His holy requirements, but stirs up the affections after them. No longer is there a murmuring against the exalted standard which God sets before us, but rather a reaching forth and striving to measure up to it. The Spirit's effectual application of the Word is always accompanied by a drawing out of the heart unto God, so that its subject is sensibly affected by His majesty and authority, His love and grace, His forbearance and goodness. So great was the change wrought in those who had been converted under his ministry, the Apostle could say of one company, "Ye are manifestly declared to be the Epistle of Christ ministered [instrumentally] by us, written not with ink, but with the Spirit of the living God" (2 Cor. 3:3). And why? Because, beholding as in a mirror the glory of the Lord, they were changed "into the same image from glory to glory, as by the Spirit of the Lord" (v. 18): changed from pride to humility, from self-love to self-loathing, from self-seeking to Christ-pleasing.

Sixth, it is an operative knowledge. There are multitudes in Christendom today who "profess they know God, but in works [not "words"] deny Him" (Titus 1:16). Much Truth has entered their ears and eyes, but it results only in idle notions, useless speculations, and frothy talk. Whereas those who by grace are made partakers of the Divine nature have a disposition and impulse unto the performance of duty, and therefore they not only long after communion with God, but diligently endeavor to please and glorify Him in their daily lives. At the new birth God puts His Law into their souls and writes it upon their hearts (Jer. 31:33), and that moves its favored recipient to exclaim "How love I Thy Law!" (Ps. 119:97), and to manifest that love by diligently seeking to comply with the Divine precepts. The Spirit is given to the elect that He may "cause them to walk in God's statutes" (Ezek. 34:27). A saving knowledge of God constrains the soul unto obedience to Him: not perfectly so in this life, yet a real responding to His requirements. No sooner did the light of God shine supernaturally into the heart of Saul of Tarsus than he cried, "Lord, what wilt Thou have me to do?" "Being made free from [the guilt and dominion of] sin, and became servants to God, ye have your fruit unto holiness" (Rom. 6:22).

When the Holy Spirit effectually applies the Truth unto a person, he responds thereto: the soul is quickened and solemnized, God is revered, the affections are elevated, the will is given an inclination to deny self, renounce the world, resist the Devil. Thus it was with the Thessalonian saints: "For this cause thank we God without ceasing, because when ye received the Word of God which ye heard of us, ye received it not as the word of men; but as it is in truth, the Word of God which effectually worketh in you that believe" (1 Thess. 2:13). It effectually prevails over sloth, the fear of man, worldly interests, everything which stands in opposition to it. "Who teacheth like Him?" (Job 36:22). Divine teaching is both efficacious and intensely practical. As God's creative words were mighty and effectual (Gen. 1), 50 are His teaching words (John 6:63; 15:3). "Hereby we do know that we know Him, if we keep His commandments" (1 John 2:3). Keeping His commandments is the evidence and proof of a saving knowledge of God. Though the obedience of a Christian be far from flawless, yet is it real, spontaneous, sincere, impartial. Where no such obedience exists, then "he that saith I know Him and keepeth not His commandments [by prayerful and genuine endeavor] is a Liar" (1 John 2:4).

Seventh, it is a satisfying knowledge. The language of every truly regenerated and converted soul is, I ask for no better Savior than Christ, I desire no other peace than God's—which passes all understanding; I need no superior Director through the mazes of this world than the infallible Scriptures. Though his station in life be the humblest and meanest, the one who has been Divinely quickened would not change places with those in highest office. The one in whose heart the supernatural light of God has shone, making him wise unto salvation, counts all other knowledge as comparatively worthless. Though he be a financial pauper, yet the one who has had the scales of prejudice and unbelief removed from his eyes, and Christ "revealed in him," knows himself to be infinitely richer than the godless millionaire. The one who has had the Divine Law effectually applied to his conscience, his sins set before him in the light of God's holiness, and has found cleansing and healing in the atoning blood of the Lamb, had rather be a doorkeeper in the house of the Lord than dwell in the mansions of the wicked. Joint heirs with Christ envy not the great of this world; those who are clothed with His righteousness look not with grudging eye upon those clothed in silks and flashing with diamonds.

Yes, this knowledge is a heart-satisfying one. It cannot be otherwise, for it is engaged with an all-sufficient Object. Nothing outside of Christ can suit the soul. Satisfaction is not to be found in ourselves, for we are mutable and dependent creatures. Nor in any of the things of time and sense, for they all perish with the using. Christ alone is the Fountain of Life and Happiness. He is all-sufficient for us, "for it hath pleased the Father that in Him should all fullness dwell" (Col. 1:19), and therefore can He amply supply our every want. He is "altogether lovely," the perfection of beauty. He excels all on earth, out-shines all in Heaven. The infinite mind of God Himself finds contentment in the Lord Jesus, declaring Him to be "Mine Elect, in whom My soul delighteth" (Isa. 42:1). Every genuinely saved person readily sets to his seal that Christ is true when He avers, "Whosoever drinketh of this Water [the failing wells of earth] shall thirst again [as Solomon found, though he drank deeply from them all]. But whosoever drinketh of the water that I shall give him, shall never thirst; but the water that I shall give him shall be in him a well of water springing up into everlasting life" (John 4:13, 14). A Divine discovery of the fullness, suitability, and excellence of Christ meets every need and satisfies every longing of the soul.

Let every reader, as he values his soul and its eternal interests, carefully and honestly test himself by what has been set before him. As the sin of Adam could not hurt us unless he had been our head by way of generation, so the righteousness of Christ cannot enrich us unless He be our Head by regeneration. There must be union with Him before we partake of His benefits. The bands of union are life and the Spirit on His part, faith and love on ours. There is no coming and cleaving to Christ in a saving way until the soul has "learned of the Father" (John 6:45). We have described some of the characteristics and effects of that "learning." Speculative knowledge produces no spiritual fruit: no humility, no poverty of spirit, no broken-heartedness, no godly sorrow. Divine knowledge manifests a heart-searching, sin-discovering, conscience-convicting, soul-humbling, Christ- magnifying attitude. When Isaiah beheld the Holy One he exclaimed "Woe is me! for I am undone" (Isa. 6:5). Have you ever been brought to the place where you have made such a confession? When Daniel had a vision of the Lord with "His face as the appearance of lightning and His eyes as lamps of fire," he tells us, "my comeliness was turned in me into corruption, and I retained no strength" (10:6, 8). Has anything resembling that been duplicated in your experience?

Try yourself, we beseech you, by what has been pointed out. Assume not that all is well with you. Examine yourself, and your knowledge of Divine things. You may not know the very day of your regeneration, nor how it was brought about, but the evidences of it are apparent. Which do you really love the more: the pleasures of sin or the beauty of holiness? Which do you genuinely value most: God or the creature? Which are you actually serving: self or Christ? A sanctifying knowledge of God results in the heart being divorced from the things formerly cherished and idolized, and now cleaving to objects disliked and shunned. When the Spirit shines into the heart and reflects His own light from the Word into it, the soul is forevermore out of conceit with itself. When the Lord fully discovered Himself unto Job, he cried, "Behold, I am vile" (40:4). Have you ever been made conscious of the same thing before Him? Do you now perceive that, in yourself, you are a corrupt and polluted creature? Has the blessed Spirit made Christ real and precious to you? If so, there has been a radical change in your heart and life. When Christ was revealed to Paul, he had a contempt for all things else, ardent desires after Him, supreme delight in Him, and was willing to suffer the loss of all things for His sake (Phil. 3:8, 9). A saving knowledge of Christ gives us to prove the sufficiency of His grace, sustaining the soul amid trials (2 Cor. 12:9).

"Being confident of this very thing, that He which hath begun a good work in you will perform it until the day of Jesus Christ" (Phil. 1:6). That which we have sought to describe is only commenced at regeneration and conversion: henceforth we are to "grow in grace and in the knowledge of our Lord and Savior Jesus Christ" (2 Peter 3:18). Our native spiritual blindness is only partly cured in this life, so that we "see through a glass darkly." Believers are still completely dependent upon the Lord that He should "open their understanding, that they might understand the Scriptures" (Luke 24:45). They need to beg Him to make good unto them that promise, "The path of the just is as the shining light, that shineth more and more unto the perfect day" (Prov. 4:18). As the work of God is carried on in the soul, the Spirit shows him more and more what a Hell-deserving wretch he is in himself, causes him to groan frequently over his corruptions and failures, makes him more deeply sensible of his need and suitableness unto Christ, brings him more and more in love with the Savior, and stirs him unto an increased diligence in endeavoring to serve and honor Him. However far a saint may advance in an experiential acquaintance with Him, it is his privilege and duty to pray that he may be, "increasing in the knowledge of God" (Col. 1:10).

It is very necessary that the young Christian should clearly recognize that God's work of grace in the soul is not completed in this life. There are some of His people who look within themselves for a faith that is not hampered with unbelief, for a love that is ever warm and constant, for pantings after holiness that vary not in fervor and regularity. They look for an obedience which is well-nigh perfect, and because they are unable to find that this is their case, conclude themselves to be unregenerate. They fail to realize that the evil principle of "the flesh" is left in them, and remains unchanged unto the end. It is indeed their bounden duty to mortify its lustings and to make no provision for the same (Rom. 13:14), nevertheless, they will frequently have occasion to complain, "iniquities prevail against me" (Ps. 65:3), and daily will they need to avail themselves of that fountain opened to the Lord's people for sin and for uncleanness (Zech. 13:1). If they do not, if they trifle with temptations, consort with the ungodly, allow unconfessed sins to accumulate on the conscience, they will soon relapse into a sickly state of soul, lose their relish for the things of God, have their graces languish, and then they will be unable to discern in their hearts and lives the seven marks named above. A backslider will not find the fruits of righteousness in his soul.

It is also necessary to point out here that there is a radical difference between the manner of the Spirit's working in regeneration and His subsequent operations. In the former, He wrought upon us as we were "dead in sin," and consequently entirely passive therein. But after He has quickened us into newness of life, we concur with Him. That is to say, we are required to use the means of grace, especially the reading of God's Word, meditating on its contents, praying for grace to conform thereto. The blessed Spirit will set no premium on slothfulness. We are to Work, but He graciously assists: "Likewise the Spirit also helpeth our infirmities." As we are "led by the Spirit" to walk in the paths of righteousness, conscience testifies in our favor, and "the Spirit Himself beareth witness with our spirit that we are the sons of God" (Rom. 8:14, 16). But if we become careless and excuse ourselves therein, then the Spirit is grieved and obstructed, His comforts are withheld, and we taste the bitterness of our folly. The chastening rod falls on us till we repent of our waywardness and turn again unto the Lord. When matters are righted with God, the Spirit stirs us afresh to the use of means and again takes of the soul-satisfying things of Christ and shows them unto us.

Finally, let it again be emphasized that all the inward teachings of God are perfectly agreeable to the written Word. The revelations made by the Spirit to the souls of God's elect and which constitute their own actual "experience," and the revelation which He has made in the sacred Scriptures never conflict (Isa. 59:21). When God speaks to the heart of man, whether it be in a way of conviction, consolation, or instruction in duty, He always honors the Bible by making express use of its words. Thus the written Word is the sole standard by which we must try all the teaching we have received: all must be weighed in the balances of the Sanctuary. "To the Law and to the Testimony: if they speak not according to this Word, it is because there is no light in them" (Isa. 8:20). Without that Divine safeguard we lay ourselves open to gross fanaticism and fatal deception. Whatever spiritual knowledge you think you have received, if it accords not wholly with God's Word, it is not of Divine revelation, but is either of human imagination or Satanic insinuation. "The Word contains the revelation of Christ; the Holy Spirit from the Word reveals Christ. In a spiritual apprehension of Him eternal life is begotten in the soul, which while it is full of Christ, yet we do not see and believe on Him to life eternal until the Lord the Spirit be our Teacher and Instructor" (S. E. Pierce).

In conclusion, let us draw a few inferences from all that has been before us. (1) Herein we behold the sovereignty of God, who divides the light from the darkness as He pleases. Divine grace is discriminating (Rom. 9:18). That particularity in which Christ dealt with souls still exists: "It is given unto you to know the mysteries of the kingdom of Heaven, but to them it is not given" (Matthew 13:11). (2) Hence we see the deep importance of distinguishing between that knowledge of the things of God which is naturally acquired and that which is Divinely taught the soul, and the need for ascertaining whether my knowledge is producing spiritual fruit in my life. It is a safe criterion to apply that whatever originates with self always aims at and terminates on self; whereas that which is from the Spirit draws out the heart and will unto Christ. (3) That those upon whom the Sun of righteousness has arisen cannot be sufficiently thankful or praise Him enough. How grateful we should be if we "know the joyful sound" (Ps. 89:15) and have found peace and joy in Christ! Well may we with wonderment exclaim, "Lord, how is it that Thou wilt manifest Thyself unto us, and not unto the world?" (John 14:22). (4) Why so few who hear the Gospel are truly saved under it. How different were the effects produced by the same Seed on the several soils (Luke 8:5-8): the heart must be plowed and harrowed before it is made an "honest and good" one (v. 15). (5) Why so many keen-brained and well-educated people are left in spiritual ignorance, while simple and illiterate souls are made wise unto salvation. (6) How that the preacher is wholly dependent upon the Holy Spirit. The ablest minister of the Word can no more of himself win souls to Christ than experienced fishermen could catch a single fish until He gave success (Luke 5:5). Neither the gifted Paul nor the eloquent Apollos was "anything": it is God "that giveth the increase" (1 Cor. 3:7). Often the most carefully prepared and earnestly delivered sermons produce no fruit, while a plain and ordinary one is blest of God. (7) How highly should the Christian prize the illumination of the Spirit and be looking continually to Him for instruction. He needs not a plainer Bible, but a clearer vision. I know no more of God to any good purpose than as I have been and am being taught of Him!

Part Four-Revelation in Glory

Chapter 17
REVELATION IN GLORY
THIS LIFE AND LIFE HEREAFTER

We have now arrived at the grand climax of our subject, and well may we beg the Lord to enlarge our hearts that we may take in a soul-rapturing view thereof. Having traced out—most imperfectly—the revelation which God has made of Himself in the created universe, in the moral nature of man, in His shaping of human history, in His incarnate Son, in the sacred Scriptures, and in the saving discovery which He makes of Himself in the souls of His elect at their regeneration and conversion, we shall now endeavor to contemplate something of that manifestation which the Triune God will make in and through Christ unto His saints in Heaven. That experiential knowledge of and communion with God which the believer has here on earth is indeed a real, affectionate and blessed one, so that at times he is lifted out of himself and made to rejoice with joy unspeakable— yet it is but an earnest and a foretaste of what he shall enjoy hereafter! At death he enters into a life which amply compensates for all the trials and tribulations he experiences in this world. Said one who had endured persecution in every form: "For I reckon that the sufferings of this present time are not worthy to be compared with the glory which shall be revealed in us" (Rom. 8:18).

The profession of the Gospel subjects the believer to peculiar hardships, for it requires him to deny self, take up his cross daily, and serve under the banner of One who is despised and rejected of men generally. To follow the example which Christ has left us involves having fellowship with His sufferings and enduring His reproach, and the more fully we be conformed to His holy image the more shall we be hated, ridiculed and opposed by the world—especially by its graceless professors. In certain periods of history, and in some countries today, particularly fierce and sore persecution was experienced by the saints; but everywhere and in all generations they have found, in different ways and degrees that, all who are determined to live godly in Christ Jesus "shall suffer persecution" (2 Tim. 3:12). Yet that is only one side of the present experience of Christians: they also enjoy a peace which passeth all understanding, and have blessed fellowship with Christ as He walks and talks with them along the way. Moreover, "the hope which is laid up for them in Heaven," whereof they have heard in the Word of the truth of the Gospel (Col. 1:5), causes them, like Moses of old, to "esteem the reproach of Christ greater riches than the treasures of Egypt, for he had respect unto the recompense of the reward" and by faith "endured, as seeing Him who is invisible" (Heb. 11:26. 27).

Such is the experience of God's people, and ought to be so increasingly by all of them: looking off from the things seen and temporal unto those which are unseen and eternal. With the eye of faith fixed steadfastly upon the Captain of their salvation, they should run with patience the race set before them. Though a very small part of this world be their portion, they are to "look for a City which hath foundations, whose Maker and Builder is God." Though called upon to suffer temporal losses for Christ's sake, they are to remember that in Heaven, "they have a better and enduring substance." If they be the objects of scorn and infamy, they can rejoice that their names are written in Heaven, and will yet be honored by Christ, not only before the Father and the holy angels, but before an assembled universe He will not be ashamed to call brethren. If their affections be really set upon things above, then having food and raiment they will therewith be content. If they have the assurance they are heirs of God and joint-heirs with Christ, it will be a small matter when worms of the earth cast out their names as evil and shun their company. If believing anticipations of the glorious future be theirs, then the joy of the Lord will be their strength.

If the would-be disciple of Christ is enjoined to sit down first and count the cost (Luke 14:28), let him also make an inventory of the compensations. How rich those compensations are, how great "the recompense of the reward" is, may be estimated by many considerations:

1. From the contrast presented by our present sufferings. "For our light affliction, which is but for a moment, worketh for us a far more exceeding eternal weight of glory" (2 Cor. 4:17). The sufferings of God's people in this world are, considered in themselves, often very heavy and grievous, and in many cases long protracted. If, therefore, they be "light" when set over against their future bliss, how great that bliss must be! The paucity of human language to express it is seen in the piling up of one term upon another: it is a "weight," it is an "exceeding weight," even a "far more exceeding weight," yea, it is an "eternal weight of glory."

2. From the Divine promises. "Blessed are ye when men shall revile you . . . for great is your reward in Heaven" (Matthew 5:11-12): who can gauge what He terms "great"! "Then shall the righteous shine forth as the sun in the kingdom of their Father" (Matthew 13:43). "Enter thou into the joy of thy Lord" (Matthew 25:21).

3. From our relationship to God. The saints are designated His children and heirs, and it is not possible for Almighty God to invest created beings with higher honor than that. This sonship is not that which pertains to them as creatures, and which in a lower sense other creatures share—but rather is it a peculiar privilege and dignity which belongs to them as new creatures in Christ Jesus. As such they are nearer and dearer unto God than the unfallen angels. Therefore the riches of the saints are to be estimated by the riches of God Himself!

4. From the declared purpose of God. "And hath raised us up together, and made us sit together in the heavenlies in Christ Jesus: that in the ages to come He might show the exceeding riches of His grace, in His kindness toward us through Christ Jesus" (Eph. 2:6, 7). If, then, God has designed to make a lavish display of the fullness of His favor unto His people, how surpassingly glorious will such a demonstration of it be! As another has said, "When the Monarch of the universe declares His purpose of showing how much He loves His people, the utmost stretch of imagination will struggle in vain to form even a slight conception of their glory."

5. From the saints being God's inheritance. All creatures are God's property, but the saints are His in a peculiar sense. They are expressly denominated "God's heritage" (1 Pet. 5:3), which imports that all other things compared with them are trifling in His view. On them He sets His heart, loving them with an everlasting love, valuing them above the angels. That affords another standard by which we may measure their future felicity. Well might the Apostle pray that the eyes of our understanding should be enlightened, that we might know, "what is the hope of His calling, and what the riches of the glory of His inheritance in the saints" (Eph. 1:18). According as God has glory in the saints, they themselves will be glorious.

6. From the love which Christ bears them. Of that love they have the fullest proof in His infinite condescension to become incarnate for their sakes, in the unparalleled humiliation into which

He entered in His producing for them a perfect robe of righteousness, and in His making a full atonement for all their sins. That involved not only a life of poverty and shame, of enduring the contradiction of sinners against Himself, but of suffering the wrath of God in their stead. Such love defies description and is beyond human comprehension. If He so loved us when we were enemies, what will He not bestow on us as His friends and brethren!

7. From the reward God has bestowed upon Christ. This also affords us a criterion by which we may gauge what awaits the saints. The stupendous achievements of Christ have been duly recognized by the Father and richly recompensed. That reward is one which is proportioned to the dignity of His person, one which is answerable to the revenue of honor and praise which His infinitely meritorious work brought to God, and which is commensurate with the unparalleled sufferings He endured and the sacrifice He made. When God gives He does so—as in all His other actions—in accord with whom and what He is. He has highly exalted the Redeemer, and given Him the name which is above every name. In John 17:22 we find the Lord Jesus making mention to the Father of "the glory which Thou hast given Me." Oh, what a transcendent and supernal glory that will be! And that glory He shares with His beloved people: "the glory which Thou gayest Me, I have given them"! That which pertains to the heavenly Bridegroom is also the portion of His Bride. "To him that overcometh will I grant to sit with Me in My throne, even as I also overcame and am set down with My Father in His throne" (Rev. 3:21). The Head and His members form one body, and therefore, "when He who is our life shall appear, then shall we also appear with Him in glory" (Col. 3:4).

While the Scriptures make no attempt to gratify a carnal curiosity concerning the nature and occupations of that life into which the regenerate enter when they pass out of this world, yet sufficient is told them to feed hope and gladden their hearts. While it is stated that "eye hath not seen, nor ear heard, neither have entered into the heart of man the things which God hath prepared for them that love Him" (1 Cor. 2:9), let it not be overlooked that the same passage goes on to say, "But God hath revealed them unto us by His Spirit: for the Spirit searcheth all things, yea the deep things of God" (v. 10). Yes, He has, to no inconsiderable extent, graciously revealed the same in the Word of Truth, and while we are to beware of lusting to be, "wise above what is written," we should spare no pains to be made wise to what is written. If the unregenerate go to such trouble and expense in manufacturing telescopes and erecting observatories in order to examine the stellar planets, and take such delight in each fresh discovery they make, yet never expect to personally possess those distant stars, how intense should be our interest in those glories of Heaven which will soon be ours forever!

Not only has God been pleased to reveal to His people something of the blissful future awaiting them, but even while still, in this vale of tears, He favors them at times with real foretastes of the same. Though at present we are able to form only the most imperfect and indistinct ideas of the saints' felicity in Heaven, nevertheless, in those moments of high elevation of soul, when the believer is abstracted from external things and absorbed with contemplating the perfections of God, he joins heartily with the Psalmist in exclaiming, "Whom have I in Heaven but Thee? and there is none upon earth that I desire besides Thee" (Ps. 73:25). Not only at conversion, when the soul rejoices in the knowledge of sins forgiven and of his being accepted in the Beloved, but afterwards, in seasons of intimate fellowship with the Lord, the conscious motions of sin are suppressed, and he is sensible only of the exercise of holy desires, love and joy. Such an experience is a real "earnest" of that which he will enjoy to a far greater degree when he is delivered from the body of this death (indwelling corruptions) and is "present with the Lord," no longer viewing Him through a mirror, but beholding Him "face to face."

It is at the second coming of Christ or at death that the believer in Him enters into the glorified state, and therefore, before examining what Holy Writ has to say upon the latter, we propose to enter into some detail on what it teaches concerning his dissolution. Since the vast majority of the redeemed enter Heaven through the portals of death—for they have been doing so for almost 6,000 years, and the New Testament seems to intimate there will be very few indeed of them upon earth at the Redeemer's return—it is appropriate that we should do so. Moreover, there is a real need for us to, for in certain quarters scarcely anything has been given out, either orally or in writing, for the instruction and comfort of God's people upon the dying of the saint. Not only does nature shrink from the experience, and unbelief paint it in black, but the Devil is not inactive in seeking to strike terror into their hearts. Not a few have been deprived of the blessed teaching of the Word thereon, because they have been erroneously led to believe that for a Christian to think much about death, or seek to prepare himself for it, is dishonoring to Christ and utterly inconsistent with "looking for that blessed hope" and living in the daily expectation of His glorious appearing.

That there is no real inconsistency between the two things is clear from many considerations. Whether the Savior will return before "the millennium" or not until the close of earth's history—whether His coming be "imminent," or whether certain events must first take place—this is sure—that the Apostle Paul was among the number of those who "waited for God's Son from Heaven" (1 Thess. 1:10). Nevertheless, that did not deter him from communicating a most comforting and assuring description of what takes place at the death of a Christian (2 Cor. 5:1-8). Let us also point out that when exhorting the New Testament saints to run with patience the race which is set before them, the first motive which the Holy Spirit supplies for the same is to remind them that they are "compassed about with so great a cloud of witnesses" (Heb. 12: 1)— the reference being to those whose testimony is described in the previous chapter, of whom it is said, "these all died in faith" (Heb. 11:13), and where the triumphant deaths of Isaac, Jacob and Joseph are most blessedly depicted (vv. 20-22). We propose, then, to dwell upon the death of a child of God, the accompaniments or attendants of the same, and the glorious sequel thereto.

One of the distinguishing features of the Holy Scriptures and one of the many proofs of their Divine inspiration is their blessed illumination of the grave and the revelation they vouchsafe concerning the hereafter. The light of nature and the best of pagan philosophy could provide no certainty about the next life. The famous Aristotle, when contemplating death, is said to have expressed himself thus: "Anxius vixi, dubius morioa, nesci quo vado," which signifies, "I have lived in anxiety, I am dying in doubtfulness, and know not where I am going." How delightful the contrast of a Christian who can affirm, "having a desire to depart, and to be with Christ, which is far better" (Phil. 1:23). How profoundly thankful should we be unto God for His Holy Word! It not only reveals to us the way of salvation, makes clear the believer's path of duty, but it irradiates the valley of shadows and lifts a comer of the veil, affording to us a view of Immanuel's land. If God's people made a more prayerful and believing study of and meditated upon what the Word teaches about their departure from this world and their Homegoing, death would not only be divested of its terrors, but would be welcomed by them.

That there is a radical difference between the death of a believer and of an unbeliever is clear from many passages. "The wicked is driven away in his wickedness, but the righteous hath hope in his death" (Prov. 14:32), upon which Thomas Boston well said: "This text looks like the cloud between the Israelites and the Egyptians: having a dark side towards the latter and a bright side towards the former. It represents death like Pharaoh's jailer, bringing the chief butler and the chief baker out of prison: the one restored to his office, and the other to be led to his execution. It shows the difference between the godly and ungodly in their death: who, as they act a very different part in life, so in death have a very different exit. . . The righteous are not driven away as chaff before the wind, but led away as a bride to the marriage chamber, carried by the angels into Abraham's bosom. The righteous man dies not in a sinful state, but in a holy state. He goes not away in sin, but out of it. In his life he was putting off the old man, changing his prison garments; and now the remaining rags of them are removed, and he is adorned with robes of glory. He has hope in his death: the well-founded expectation of better things than he ever had in this world."

Proverbs 14:32 is but one of many passages in the earlier Scriptures which evince that the Old Testament saints were far from being in the dark regarding death or what lay beyond it. They knew that in God's presence is "fullness of joy, at Thy right hand there are pleasures forevermore" (Ps. 16:11). Said David, "I will behold Thy face in righteousness: I shall be satisfied, when I awake, with Thy likeness" (Ps. 17:15). And again, "Surely, goodness and mercy shall follow me all the days of my life; and I will dwell in the house of the LORD forever" (Ps. 23:6). It is true that life and immortality have been brought more fully to light through the Gospel (2 Tim. 1:10), nevertheless, it is clear that from the dawn of human history, the light of Divine revelation had, for the saints, illuminated the tomb. "Thou shalt guide me with Thy counsel and afterward receive me to glory" (Ps. 73:24), which, as a summary, goes as far as anything taught in the New Testament. "Many of them that sleep in the dust of the earth shall awake: some to everlasting life, some to shame and everlasting contempt" (Dan. 12:2). And therefore, it is said of all those who died in faith that, having seen the promises of God afar off, they "were persuaded of them and embraced them, and confessed that they were strangers and pilgrims on the earth" (Heb. 11:13).

Before proceeding further, let us face the question, Why does a child of God die? Since physical death be one of the consequences of sin, and since the Lord Jesus has paid the whole of its wages, and therefore put it away for His people, why should any of them have to enter the grave? A number of reputable writers whom we have consulted deem that a great and insoluble mystery, while others evade it by saying that such presents no greater problem than sin's remaining in us after regeneration. But neither of those things should present any difficulty: both are designed for God's glory and their good. As Proverbs 14:32 shows, there is a vast difference between the death of the righteous and that of the wicked. Death is not sent to the former as a penal infliction, but comes to him as a friend—to free him from all further sorrow and suffering—to induct the heir of glory into his inheritance. Why should a Christian die? sufficient for the disciple to be as his Master, and "made conformable unto His death." What a fearful hardship had the saints from Pentecost onwards been obliged to remain on earth till the end of time! Surely it is an act of Divine love to remove them from the vale of tears! But could not God have translated them to Heaven without seeing death, like He did Enoch and Elijah? Yes, but they were exceptions; and in such case Christ would not have the glory of raising their bodies from the dust and fashioning them like unto the body of His glory!

Chapter 18
REVELATION IN GLORY
THE JOY OF DEATH AND HEAVEN

We are now to consider some of the details revealed in Scripture about the death of a child of God. It is a most important and practical subject, and, though a solemn one, a very blessed one too; for it is then that the saint enters into glory. Let it be pointed out that if we are prepared for God's summons to pass from this life, then, whether His messenger be death or the appearing of the Lord of life, we shall be equally ready. On the other hand, those who are unprepared for death, yet profess to be daily looking for that Blessed Hope, are woefully deceiving themselves that they will be among the number who shall be caught up to meet the Lord in the air. What we have here said requires no proof: it is self-evident that since a saint's departure from this scene is in order for him to enter the presence of God, that if he be prepared for that, it can make no difference to his soul whether death or Christ personally be the one to conduct him thither. Let the Christian make his calling and election sure (2 Pet. 1:10) by ascertaining that he has a valid title to Heaven through Christ (Rom. 5:11) and a personal meetness by the miracle of the new birth (John 3:5; Col. 1:12), and he has no good reason to dread either death or the Redeemer's return.

Death may be defined as the dissolution of that union which exists between the constituent elements of human nature: it is a separating of the immaterial part of man from the material, an emerging of the soul from the body. But that severance in the Christian for a while produces no separation of either his soul or his body from the Lord Jesus. The union there is between the redeemed and regenerate members of Christ's mystical body and their glorious Head is indissoluble and endless, and is both the basis and security of every blessing they enjoy in time and eternity. His people are as truly His in death as in life. Their union with Christ is the same, nor is their interest in Him lessened. As the beloved Hawker said, "The covenant rots not in the grave, however their bodies molder into dust." Moreover, that separation which the believer sustains of soul and body at death is but for a season; and among other blessings with which it is accompanied, will be amply compensated on the resurrection morning, when an everlasting union shall be effected between them, nevermore to be broken.

Let us now consider four expressions used in the New Testament in connection with the death of a believer, none of which, be it noted, contains the least suggestion of an experience to be dreaded. (1) The Apostle Paul spoke of his decease as a departing from this world: "having a desire to depart, and be with Christ, which is far better" (Phil. 1:23). Young's concordance defines the word as signifying "to loose up (an anchor)." It is a nautical term, which describes a vessel leaving her temporary moorings. The figure is a suggestive and picturesque one. The hour for sailing has arrived. The anchor is weighed, the gangway raised, the ropes are released, and fond farewells are said and waved to beloved friends who have come to see us off The ship now moves gently away from the quay, down the river, into the vast reaches of the ocean beyond. That is what death is to a Christian: a loosening of those moorings which bound him to the earth, a gliding out into a life of freedom, a going forth unto another Country. This same figure is used again in "the time of my departure is at hand" (2 Tim. 4:6)—the exact hour of sailing has been Divinely appointed!

(2) The Apostle Peter likened his impending dissolution unto the taking down of a tent: "knowing that shortly I must put off this my tabernacle, as our Lord Jesus Christ hath showed me" (2 Pet. 1:14, and, cf. John 21:18, 19). In the previous verse he had similarly spoken of his body, declaring that he would continue urging upon the saints their obligations and duties "as long as I am in this tabernacle," or better "tent." The body, for whose wants the majority of our fellows are as anxious as though it were the whole man, is but a tent. The figure is a very suggestive one. A "tent" is a frail structure, designed only for temporary occupation, is suited for use in the wilderness, and is exchanged for a "house eternal in the heavens." In the verse Peter employed a mixed metaphor, as Paul did in 2 Corinthians 5:1-4, where the breaking up of the earthly house of our tabernacle is spoken of as our being "unclothed." Here, then, is the Christian concept of death: it is no more terrible or distressing than the removing of a tent (which is easily taken down), or the putting off of our garments when retiring to rest—to be resumed at the dawn of a new day!

(3) Death is likened unto an exodus. The term is used first in connection with our Savior: when He was transfigured before His disciples on the holy mount, there talked with Him Moses and Elijah, "who spoke of His decease, which He should accomplish at Jerusalem" (Luke 9:3 1). The Greek word is exodos and is found again in Hebrews 11:22, where it is recorded that, "By faith Joseph when he was a dying [in Egypt] made mention of the departing [exodos] of the children of Israel." It is hardly to be thought that Moses and Elijah would confine their speech unto Christ's death, but would rather converse upon "the sufferings of Christ and the glory that should follow" (1 Peter 1:1 1). Dr. Lightfoot was of the opinion that Christ's exodus included His ascension, pointing out that Israel's exodus from Egypt was a "triumphant and victorious one." The term literally means "exit," and Manton regards its scope in Luke 9:31, as including Christ's death, resurrection (Acts 2: 24) and ascension (Luke 24:51). Peter also made use of the same term when he referred to his own "decease" or exodus (2 Pet. 1:15), thereby giving it a general application unto all of God's people.

Here, then, is another simple but suggestive figure to express the blessedness of a believer's departure from this life. Like the previous one, this also imports the going forth on a journey; but, in addition, the leaving behind of the house of bondage and the making for the promised inheritance—the antitypical Canaan. There is a striking analogy between the death of a Christian and Israel's emancipation from the cruel slavery of Pharaoh. One of the distinct features of the Christian's life in this world is his groaning under the burden of indwelling sin (Rom. 8:23; 2 Cor. 5:2), a crying "who shall deliver me from the body of this death?" But death is, for him, a snapping of his fetters, an escaping from the bonds that hold him, a going forth from sin and sorrow into freedom and immortality. Israel's exodus from Egypt was a leaving behind of all their enemies, and such is death for the saint: the world, the flesh, the Devil—all that opposes God and hinders him forever done with. Israel's exodus included their safe passage through the Red Sea, a crossing over unto the farther shore, their faces turned unto the land of milk and honey. How eagerly should the Christian welcome death!

(4) The death of God's people is likened unto a sleep. This is the most familiar figure of all, and since it is used much more frequently in the Scriptures, and because certain errorists have perverted its meaning, we will dwell longer upon it. To the saints in his day the Apostle said, "But I would not have you to be ignorant, brethren, concerning them which are asleep" (1 Thess. 4:13). We regard it as a mistake to restrict that to their bodies: obviously it is their persons ("them") which are "asleep"; yet that by no means warrants the conclusion which some have drawn—that at death the soul passes into a state of total inactivity and unconsciousness. Such a verse proves

too much for the case of "soul sleeping," for it would make it teach that the soul died with the body, since "sleep" is here an image of death; which would be in direct variance with our Lord's words, "Fear not them which are able to kill the body, and are not able to kill the soul" (Matthew 10:28). Even in this life, when the body is soundly asleep, the soul or mind is not inactive, as our dreams manifestly evidence.

Whether or not Luke 16:19-31, is a "parable," certain it is that our Lord was there setting forth the condition of both the righteous and the unrighteous immediately after death, and if their souls then pass into a state of oblivion His language would be utterly misleading where He declared the one to be "comforted" and the other "tormented" (v. 25). So, too, His promise to the dying thief had been meaningless unless he was to enjoy the company of Christ in Paradise that day and enter upon all the delights of that place. Further, it would not be true that "death" is one of the things which is unable to separate believers from receiving manifestations of God's love and their enjoyment of the same (Rom. 8:3 8, 39) if they pass from this world into a state of insensibility. Again, Paul, who was favored with such intimate and precious fellowship with Christ in this world, had never been in any "strait" between his desire to remain in the flesh for the sake of his converts and his longing to "depart," had the latter alternative meant the complete suspension of all his faculties, without any communion with God. Nor had he spoken of "the spirits of just men made perfect" (Heb. 12:23) if they are without life and light, peace and joy, immediately after death.

While rejecting the false glosses put upon this figurative expression, let us be careful the enemy does not rob us of its true import, and thereby deprive us of the comfort it contains. Was it not for the consolation of His disciples (and all His people) that the Savior said: "I go to awake our friend Lazarus out of his sleep" (John 11:11)? Again, we are told that after the first Christian martyr had knelt down and prayed for his enemies, he "fell asleep" (Acts 7:60)! How much more was conveyed by that statement of the inspired historian than had he merely said that Stephen expired! Amid the curses of his foes, and while their stones were crushing the life from his body, he "fell asleep." Inexpressibly blessed is that! As the sleep of the body brings welcome relief when it is racked with pain, so death delivers from spiritual warfare and puts an end to all the wounding of the believer's soul by indwelling sin. As sleep gives rest from the toils and burdens of the day, so that we are oblivious to the perplexities and trials which harass our waking hours, so death for the saint puts an end to all the things which occasioned him anxiety and distress down here: he is released, henceforth, from all cares and troubles.

No doubt the principal idea which this figure should convey to us is the entire harmlessness of death. What is there in sleep to dread? Instead of being an object of horror, it is a merciful provision of God's for which we should be most grateful. It comes to us not as a rough and terrifying foe, but approaches gently as a kind friend. Christ has removed the "sting" from death (1 Cor. 15:56, 57), and therefore it can no more harm one of His redeemed than could a hornet whose power to injure has been destroyed. In employing this comforting metaphor, God would have His people assured that they have nothing more to fear from the article of death than in lying down on their beds to slumber. Again—sleep is of but brief duration: a few hours of repose, and then we arise refreshed and reinvigorated for the duties of another day. In like manner, death is but a sleep, an entering into rest, and resurrection will be the restoration and glorification of our bodies. Finally, death is likened to a sleep to intimate how easily the Lord will quicken our mortal bodies. The skeptic may ridicule as an impossibility the truth of resurrection, but to Christ it will be simpler than waking a sleeper. A slumbering person is aroused most easily by one speaking to him, and "the hour is coming, in the which all that are in the graves shall hear His voice" (John 5:28)!

In addition to those figurative expressions, which so manifestly depict the harmlessness of death,

God has made many plain statements in His Word for the comfort and assurance of His saints. It is evident from Genesis 15 that He preached the Gospel to Abraham in clear terms: not only the basic doctrine of justification by faith and the righteousness which is imputed to the believer, but also that state of blessedness into which all His people enter immediately upon their death. First, He made known to the "father" or prototype of all the faithful of what Heaven is and wherein the happiness of the saints consists: "I am thy Shield" in this life, "and thy exceeding great Reward" in the life to come (v. 1). For as Goodwin pointed out, "Reward is after the finishing of work, and what is this reward but the blessedness of Heaven? Christ Himself says no other, nor no more, of it, 'The Lord is the portion of Mine inheritance.' For the joy that was set before Him, He endured the Cross knowing that 'in Thy presence is fullness of joy.'" Second, God informed him what the condition of his soul should be: "thou shalt go to thy fathers in peace" (v. 15). No wonder Balaam said, "Let me die the death of the righteous, and let my last end be like his" (Num. 23:10).

What a blessed declaration is this: "Precious in the sight of the LORD is the death of His saints" (Ps. 116:15)—then certainly it ought not to be dreadful in theirs! That verse presents an aspect of our subject which is all too little considered by Christians. They look at it, as at most other things, too much from the human angle—but here we have what may be termed the Godward side of a believer's death—it is precious in His sight! The Hebrew word yaqar is rendered "costly" in 1 Kings 5:17, "honorable" in Psalm 45:9, "excellent" in Psalm 36:7. It occurs again in "precious stones" (1 Kings 10:10), yea, is used of Christ Himself—"a precious Cornerstone." Whatever form it takes, and no matter what be the attendant circumstances, such is the death of His people unto the Lord: an honorable, costly, excellent, precious thing. Note well the words, "in the sight of the LORD": His eyes are fixed upon them in a peculiar and special manner. Their death is precious unto Him because it releases them from sin and sorrow, because it is sanctified by His own death for them, because it is a taking unto His immediate presence those upon whom He set His heart from all eternity, because they are the trophies of His own victory, and because they then "enter into the joy of their Lord."

In the closing verses of 1 Corinthians 3 a number of things are mentioned as pertaining to God's children: "all things are yours: whether Paul or Apollos, or Cephas, or the world, or life, or death, or things present, or things to come; all are yours." Those words were first addressed to shame some who sought pre-eminence in the house of God and whose affections were too much set upon things on the earth; yet they are full of instruction and comfort for us today. The ministry of God's servants, the things God has provided for us in the world, life or death, are equally ours. Death is ours not by way of punishment and curse, but as a privilege and blessing. It is ours not as an enemy, but as a friend. It is our conquered foe, and is not to be feared, for it has neither strength nor sting to harm us: Christ, our victorious Captain, has disarmed it of both—"He hath abolished [rendered null and void] death" (2 Tim. 1:10). Life and death are administered by God so as to fulfill His gracious designs unto His people. Death is theirs because they share in Christ's triumphs over it, because it furthers their interests and ministers to their wellbeing, because it is a means of their inexpressible advantage, removing them from a world of ills, conducting them into a world of glory and bliss.

What a word is this: "And I heard a voice from Heaven, saying unto me, Write, Blessed are the dead which die in the Lord from henceforth: Yea, saith the Spirit, that they may rest from their labors; and their works do follow them" (Rev. 14:13). Here was a special and immediate revelation from Heaven. It was to be placed upon imperishable record for the comfort of believers to the end of time. "Blessed are the dead": pronounced so by God, happy in themselves. Not "blessed shall they be," at the resurrection morning, though that will be their case; but "blessed are" they at the moment. Why? Because they "die in the Lord": whether conscious of the fact or not, they die in union and communion with Him, His smile of approbation resting upon them. To die in the Lord is "to die in the favor of God, in a state of peace with Him as members of His mystical body" (Thomas Manton). But more: they are blessed "from henceforth," without delay or cessation, which at once gives the lie to their lapsing into a state of entire unconsciousness. "Yea, saith the Spirit." Here is solemn confirmation: the Holy Spirit maketh affidavit" (Manton). They "rest from their labors": not only the toils of their temporal callings, but their conflicts with sin. "And their works do follow them": we carry nothing out of the world with us but the conscience and comfort of what we have done for God" (Manton).

We continue by borrowing a few thoughts (though clothing them mostly in our own language) from Boston's counsels on why a Christian should be reconciled to death, and then how to prepare for it. Some dread the prospect of leaving behind their wives and children in this cold world: yet they have a reliable Guardian to commit them unto. Says He, "Leave thy fatherless children: I will preserve them alive, and let thy widows trust in Me" (Jer. 49:11). But death will remove me from my dearest friends! True, yet it will conduct you unto your best Friend; and if those you leave are God's children, you will meet them again in Heaven. But the approach and pains of death are sometimes very dreadful! Not nearly so terrible as pangs of conscience caused by apprehensions of Divine wrath—remember that each pang of bodily disease brings you a step nearer unto a soul made every whit whole. But I am naturally timorous, and the very thoughts of death alarm me! Then familiarize yourself with it by frequent meditations thereon, and especially view the bright side of the cloud, and by faith look beyond it.

That there may be a readier disposition of heart and preparedness of mind, make it your care to "have always a conscience void of offense toward God and men" (Acts 24:16). Walk closely with God, maintain a diligent and strict course in the way of His precepts; and because of the infirmities which cleave to us in this present state, renew your repentance daily and be ever washing in that Fountain which has been opened for sin and for uncleanness. Be constantly engaged in weaning your heart from this world. Let the mantle of earthly enjoyments hang loosely upon you, that it may be easily dropped when the summons comes to depart for Heaven. Set your affections, more and more, upon things above, and pass through this wilderness scene as a stranger and pilgrim. We are ready for Heaven when our heart is there before us (Mathew 6:21). Be diligent in laying up evidences of your title to Heaven, for the neglect of so doing renders uncomfortable the dying pillar of many a Christian. Grieve not the Holy Spirit, so that He will bear witness with your spirit that you are a child of God (Rom. 8:16).

Though our specific subject is that revelation with which God favors His people in Heaven, yet because the great majority of them pass thereto through the door of death, and since quite a number of our readers have been denied the comforting teaching of Scripture thereon, we have taken the opportunity to write upon the same. We come now to consider some of the accompaniments of a Christian's death.

Among these, first place must be given unto the presence of the Lord with him at that time. While it is blessedly true that He never leaves nor forsakes them, being with them "always" (Matthew 28:20), yet He is with them in a special manner at certain crucial times. This idea seems to be clearly borne out by the statement that God is "a very present help in trouble" (Ps. 46:1), as though He draws nearest of all to us in the seasons of acutest need. Do we not have an illustration and example of that fact when the three Hebrews were cast alive into Babylon's furnace, and the king beheld Another walking with them in the midst of the fire? "And the form of the fourth is like the Son of God" said he (Dan. 3:25).

Again—has not the Lord declared, "Fear not, for I have redeemed thee, I have called thee by thy name: thou art Mine. When thou passest through the waters, I will be with thee; and through the rivers, they shall not overflow thee" (Isa. 43:1, 2). How blessedly that was demonstrated at the Red Sea, where God so gloriously showed Himself strong on behalf of His people; and again at the Jordan, which was more definitely a figure of the safe passage of believers through death. Was not the passing of Israel dry shod through Jordan into Canaan a blessed adumbration of the saints' harmless exit from this world and entrance into their everlasting inheritance? As Jehovah manifested Himself most conspicuously on those occasions, so— whether perceived by them or not—He is, in a most particular sense, present with His beloved ones as they walk through the valley of the shadow of death. Said the Psalmist, "I will fear no evil, for Thou art with me: Thy rod and Thy staff they comfort me" (Ps. 23:4). Thy rod and Thy staff: "by which Thou governs and rules Thy flock—the emblems of Thy sovereignty and of Thy gracious care" (Spurgeon).

The meaning of those figures is plain: it is by His Word and Spirit that the good Shepherd governs and cares for His sheep, and is their "comfort" in the hour of their supreme crisis. That the believer is granted a special supply of the Divine Comforter at that hour can scarcely be doubted. "The Spirit was given us for that purpose, as a brother is said to be 'born for adversity' (Prov. 17:17). Certainly He who was given for a comfort to you all through your life long, and has delivered you out of all your distresses and fears, will carry you through this; and though your heart should for a while fail you, together with your flesh, yet God and His Spirit will not fail you (Ps. 73:26). The interest of the Spirit's own glory moves Him. No captain rejoices more to bring his vessel home into harbor, after he has sailed it safely through so many storms, than the Holy Spirit rejoices to bring a soul He has wrought upon and who was committed to His trust, safe to Heaven" (Thomas Goodwin). Let it be noted that "the supply of the Spirit of Jesus Christ" is given not only in life but also in death (Phil. 1:19, 20)!

2. The soul is rid of sin. There shall in no wise enter into the new Jerusalem "anything that defileth, neither whatsoever worketh abomination" (Rev. 21:27). No serpent shall find admittance into the celestial paradise, nor will any who are still polluted by him. Not only the holiness of God, but the happiness of the saints also require that they be freed from all evil ere they enter Heaven, or otherwise their bliss would be marred. Their communion with and delighting themselves in the Lord is hindered down here by the sin which still cleaves to them. From the moment of the new birth until the moment a regenerated person leaves this world, "the flesh lusteth against the spirit and the spirit against the flesh," and since those two principles of action are "contrary the one to the other" it follows that he "cannot do the things that he would" (Gal. 5:17), and daily has he occasion to lament, "O wretched man that I am." Even when the power of God subdues the ragings of sin within His children, they are not delivered from its inbeing. But when the Divine summons to the soul comes to depart hence, it is entirely delivered from inbred corruption. The conflict is then ended; the victory over sin is complete. No propensity to evil remains, no guilt of conscience or defilement shall ever again be contracted.

"Although the whole troop of evils, like the army of Egypt, will pursue me (as it did Israel) to the borders of the sea, death ends the warfare—'The Egyptians whom ye have seen today, ye shall see them again no more forever' (Ex. 14:13). O the inconceivable blessedness which immediately opens at death to every redeemed and regenerated child of God!" (Robert Hawker). Yet it is not death itself which effects this blessed purification of the soul. That is evident not only from the cases of Enoch and Elijah, who were caught up to Heaven without dying, but of those saints, too, who will be alive on earth at the personal return of Christ (1 Cor. 15:51; 1 Thess. 4:17). No, it is produced by the supernatural operation of God. It is the Lord Himself fitting His "temple" (2 Cor. 6:16) for His fuller and final possession. It is to be noted that Christ cleansed the temple at Jerusalem twice: at the beginning of His ministry (John 2:15-17) and again near the close thereof (Luke 19:45), which adumbrated His twofold cleansing of the hearts of His redeemed. At conversion they are purged from the love, the guilt, and the dominion of sin; at death they are delivered from its very inbeing and presence.

3. Enlarging of their faculties. We regard that expression, "the spirits of just men made perfect" (Heb. 12:23), as denoting not only their being purged of all evil and misery, but also of their being capacitated to take in immeasurably more good and happiness than ever they did previously. Sin has not only greatly impaired the vitality and functions of the body, but it has considerably injured the health and defiled and limited the faculties of the soul; and therefore the latter will experience a grand elevation when rid of the incubus of sin. As the resurrected body will be possessed of powers far transcending its present ones, so when the soul is glorified its faculties will be much greater—the understanding no longer beclouded, the affections purified, the will emancipated. In its present state the soul, even when engaged in spiritual acts, is sadly cramped and hampered, but upon its dismissing from the body, the Holy Spirit will strengthen, enlarge, and elevate the faculties of the soul, raising them up to a suitability and harmony with their new life in Heaven. Then will the believer know even as he is known (1 Cor. 13:12).

It was, we believe, to this gracious operation of the Spirit that David referred in Psalm 23:5, where, after describing his passage through the valley of the shadow of death and before mentioning his dwelling in the house of the Lord forever, he declared: "Thou anointest my head with oil: my cup runneth over." In Old Testament typology "oil" was the outstanding type of the Holy Spirit (cf. 1 John 2:27), and as the Lord Jesus was anointed by the Spirit at the beginning of His ministry (Acts 10:3 8) and again at the completion of it (Ps. 45:7; Acts 2:33), so the believer is anointed by Him first at conversion (2 Cor. 1:21, 22) and then receives a fuller infusion of Him at death. Then it is that mortality is "swallowed up of life" (2 Cor. 5:4)-words which are "as applicable unto the condition of the soul then, as at the resurrection they are applicable to the condition of the body" (Thomas Goodwin). As that eminent expositor pointed out: "In 1 Corinthians 15, where the change of the body is insisted on, Paul says, 'this mortal shall put on immortality; this corruptible, incorruption,' but here he says 'swallowed up of life,' which is the proper happiness of the soul." We will condense below the rest of his remarks thereon.

"Though the soul in the substance of it be immortal, yet take the condition of life which it now leads and it may be most truly said to have a 'mortality' adhering to it, yea, inhering in it as the adjunct of it. There is a mortal state the person is in. There is an animal life, as one calls it; there is a dying life, a life of death, in which as to a great part the soul now lives; and it is this present state, or this dying life of the soul, which causes believers to 'groan, being burdened,' and which the Apostle here terms 'mortality,' but which he assures us will, at its dismissal from the body, be 'swallowed up of life'—that which is life only, and only deserves the name of life: the true and eternal life, life indeed. For what is life? 'This is life eternal, that they might know Thee the only true God and Jesus Christ whom Thou hast sent' (John 17:3). It is a peculiar life of living in God, as knowing Him and seeing Him face to face." The soul which hitherto had been so trammeled by sin shall then be taken into a life so rich, so full, so overflowing with abundance, as to rid it in a moment of all misery and imperfection, freeing and perfecting all its faculties.

4. Perfuming of their persons. This too is intimated in Psalm 23, a part of which we have somewhat anticipated. It seems to us that each experience described in verses 4-6 receives a general fulfillment throughout the life of a saint, and a particular one at his death. Thus, "though I walk through the valley of the shadow of death" well expresses his journey through the wilderness, for though men term this world, "the land of the living," it would be far more accurate to designate it "the land of the dying." The shadow of the grave is cast heavily across it; nevertheless, such language also suitably describes the believer's passage through the article of death. "I will fear no evil": why should he? A "valley," in contrast with a "mountain," suggests easy travel, and a

"shadow" cannot harm him! Moreover, the "shadow" necessarily presupposes the presence of light. Unbelief may talk of "the dark valley of death"—not so David. It was far otherwise with him: the Light of life (John 8:12) was there, as his words acknowledge: "for Thou art with me"—to support, to guard, to comfort, to rejoice. "With me" now in a peculiarly intimate and special way.

The One present was Jehovah, whom David knew and owned as "my Shepherd" in the opening verse. But observe a striking alteration in his language in the latter part of the Psalm. In the first three verses all the pronouns referring to the Lord are in the third person: "He maketh me to lie down in green pastures. He leadeth me. He restoreth my soul." But in the last three verses David changes to the second person: "Thou art with me. Thy rod [not "His" rod] and Thy staff. Thou preparest a table before me, Thou anointest my head." Why the variation? Ah, there is something inexpressibly blessed in that change. During life the believer speaks of the Lord—"He leadeth me"; but as he enters the valley of the shadow he speaks to the Lord, for He is there by his side! How much we miss through our careless and hurried reading of God's Word! How we need to weigh and ponder every jot and tittle in it. Sometimes the tense of the verb, at others the number of the noun marks that which is most important for us to observe; here the change of pronouns brings out a precious line of truth.

Having acknowledged the presence of the good Shepherd in the valley and the comfort derived from His gracious care, the Psalmist next went on to say: "Thou preparest a table before me in the presence of mine enemies." In Scripture, the "table" always speaks of fellowship, and that of the most intimate kind (Luke 22:21), and here it tells of the Lord's communion with the dying saint, and the loving and full provision He has made to supply his every need. His "enemies" may refer to the forces of evil, who would make their final assault upon him if they could. But they are prevented from doing so, for God has promised "the end of that man is peace" (Ps. 37:37). His enemies are not only thwarted, but mocked by the Lord in this "table." Then as he emerges from the valley, the believer exclaims, "Thou anointest my head with oil"—as Moses did the heads of the priests as they were on the point of entering upon their tabernacle privileges and duties (Ex. 28:41; 29:7), thereby preparing them for the presence of God. Thus the Redeemer puts upon the soul His own blessed fragrance as it enters into the courts above. Then David exultantly declared, "and I shall dwell in the house of the LORD forever." Thus this remarkable Psalm portrays the saint's happy life (vv. 1-3), comfortable death (vv. 4, 5), and blissful eternity (v. 6).

5. An angelic convoy. This is clear from our Lord's statement in Luke 16:22: "And it came to pass that the beggar died, and was carried by the angels into Abraham's bosom." Abraham is the father of all them that believe (Rom. 4:11), and is here shown to be in Paradise. His "bosom" speaks of the place of peculiar privilege (John 1:18; 13:23): the once-despised beggar, counted unworthy of a seat at the rich man's table on earth, is accorded a position of honor on high— placed next to the eminent Patriarch. The same gracious provision has God made for the safe conduct of each of His people in their journey from earth to Heaven: "He shalt give His angels charge over thee, to keep thee in all thy ways" (Ps. 91:11). Angelic ministry occupies, most probably, a far more extensive place in the lives of believers than any of them realize. "These encamp about them in the time of their life, and surely will not depart in the day of their death. These happy ministering spirits are attendants on the Lord's bride, and will doubtless carry her safely home to His house. The Captain of the saints' salvation is the Captain of this holy guard: He was their Guide even unto death, and He will be their Guide through it, too" (Thomas Boston).

What we are now considering presents another most blessed though little-known contrast between the death of the righteous and the death of the unrighteous. The souls of the former are carried to Heaven by the holy angels, the souls of the latter are seized by demons and taken to Hell. In Luke 12:20, Christ declared that God would say to the rich boaster, "Thou fool, this night do they require thy soul" (margin, and see Greek). Upon which, after affirming, "the devils take others' souls away," Thomas Goodwin, the Puritan, asked: "Who are they?" And his answer, "Hell is a prison (1 Pet. 3:19) and the judge delivers to the officer, and the officer casts into prison (Luke 12:58). This 'officer' is the Devil that hales souls to that prison." In this convoy or guard of angels for the redeemed, saints are conformed to their Head, when He was "carried up to Heaven" (Luke 24:5 1). "The chariots of God are twenty thousand, even thousands of angels: The Lord is among them . . . Thou hast ascended on high" (Ps. 68:17, 18). "Angels were the chariots in which Christ rode, and these the guard that attends believers" (Gill). Thus, the soul of the saint is conducted in state from his earthly house to his heavenly abode.

Immediately after death, without any interval of waiting either long or short, the ransomed soul is inducted into Paradise. The heir of glory enters at once upon his eternal inheritance: "absent from the body, present with the Lord" (2 Cor. 5:8). This needs emphasizing in certain quarters, where the idea seems to obtain that the glorification of the saint's soul awaits the time of the glorification of his body. We do not like to see Protestants employing the term "intermediate state" (in contrast with "the eternal state"), for it savors too much of the imaginary "Limbo" of the Romanists; greatly preferring the "disembodied" and the "resurrection state." Immediately at death spirits of just men are "made perfect" in knowledge, in holiness, in blessedness. Mortality is then "swallowed up of life": as Goodwin expressed it, the soul "is now all life and joy in God the Fountain of life." As we shall seek to show, the request of Christ in John 17:24, receives its fulfillment in the experience of His redeemed as soon as they leave this earth—the beatific vision is then theirs.

In the very moment of his dismissal from the body, the Savior receives His redeemed into the actual possession of that eternal heritage which He has purchased for them. It was this reception for which the expiring Stephen made request when he said, "Lord Jesus receive my spirit" (Acts 7:59), and as Thomas Goodwin pointed out: "He not only receives it into His own bosom, but He brings it to God and presents it to Him with a joy infinitely more abounding than can be in us. Then it is that Christ is glorified and rejoices in us, and so we may be said rather to die to the Lord and His interest than to ours." Then it is that He "sees of the travail of His soul and is satisfied." While at a later date Christ will present the entire company of His people to Himself a glorious Church, "not having spot or wrinkle, or any such thing" (Eph. 5:27), yet He does so to each individual member of it at death, as His words to the dying thief clearly implied. Oh, what praise is due unto Him for having extracted the sting from death and robbed it of all its terrors! What cause have we to exclaim, "Thanks be unto God which giveth us the victory through our Lord Jesus Christ!"

What has been before us should surely make it easier to bear the trials through which a Christian may now be passing: at longest they are but for a moment in comparison with the eternity of bliss awaiting him. How faith should feed upon and hope anticipate the same! With what contentment should such a prospect fill us! What little reason have we to envy the deluded worshippers of Mammon, even though such now be clothed in purple and fine linen and fare sumptuously every day. How the contemplation of what God has prepared for them that love Him should wean their hearts from the perishing baubles of this world. How the certainty of being "with Christ" forever should make them desire to depart from this scene. How the knowledge that at death they will be forever done with sin and sorrow should make them willing to die. Why should any believer be reluctant to long to go unto the eternal Lover of his soul, especially when he learns from Scripture what full provision God has made for his passage to Him and that it is an easy and pleasant one? Oh, that all our ambitions and longings may be swallowed up in that of the Psalmist's: "One thing have I desired of the Lord, that will I seek after: that I may dwell in the house of the LORD all the days of my life, to behold the beauty of the LORD" (27:4).

Chapter 19
REVELATION IN GLORY
THE STATE OF SAINTS IN GLORY

We have shown that there is a real and radical difference between the death of a believer and that of an unbeliever, and having contemplated some of the accompaniments of a Christian's departure from this world we are now ready to consider how he exists in the disembodied state. It is not to be wondered at that the unregenerate should be thoroughly befogged at this point, for they are so materialistic that they find it very difficult to form a definite concept of anything that is incorporeal and intangible. But those who, by God's grace, enjoy a real communion with Him who is "Spirit" (John 4:24), ought not to flounder on this matter, for they have proved by experience how much more important is the soul than the body, and how infinitely more real and satisfying are spiritual objects than the perishing things of time and sense. So far from regarding his soul as a mysterious, nebulous and indefinable thing, the believer looks upon it as a living, intelligent, sentient being—his real self We should view a disembodied soul as one which has cast off its earthly clothing and is now appareled in a garment of light, or, to use the language of Scripture, "clothed in white raiment" (Rev. 3:5; 4:4).

At death the soul of the saint is freed from all the limitations which sin had imposed upon it, and its faculties are then not only purified, but elevated and enlarged. It will be like a chrysalis emerging from its cramped condition, or a bird liberated from a cage, now free to spread its wings and soar aloft. It is true the body is a component part of man's complex being, yet we must endeavor to view it in a due proportion. Which is the more important: the tenant or his tenement, the individual or the tent in which he resides? It must be borne in mind that the soul derives not its powers from the body. That is clear from the Divine account of man's creation: after his body had been formed, and as a separate act, God "breathed into his nostrils the breath of life, and the man became a living soul" (Genesis 2:7). The mind is the noblest part of our being, and therefore it must find exercise and satisfaction in the disembodied state, otherwise we should not be "blessed" or happy (Rev. 14:13) immediately after death. "It is the mind maketh the man; it is our preferment above the beasts that God hath given us a mind to know Him" (Thomas Manton).

"The soul can and does operate without the use of bodily organs in its present state, and in many things stands in no need of them. The rational soul thinks, reasons and discourses without the use of them. Its powers and faculties need them not: the will is directed and guided by the understanding; and the understanding has to do with objects in the consideration of which bodily organs are in no way assisting. As in the consideration of God, His nature and perfections; of angels and their nature; and of a man's own spirit, and the things of it—it penetrates into without the help of any of the instruments of the body. It can consider of things past long ago, and of things very remote and at a great distance; and such objects as are presented to it by the senses, it reasons about them without making use of any of the organs of the body. And if it can operate without the body, it can exist without it; for since it is independent of it in its operations, it is independent of it in its being. Since it can exist without it, it can act in that separate state of existence without it. Wherefore since it dies not with the body, it is not affected as to its operations, by the absence of it, nor at death becomes insensible as that is" (John Gill).

Yet, obvious as is what has been pointed out above, the majority of Christians seem to suppose that it is impossible for us to form any definite ideas of what it is to be disembodied, or of that state into which the saint enters at death, or of what the medium is by which he will know, enjoy, and have fellowship with the Lord in that state. While they remain content with such slothful ignorance, it is not to be expected that any further light will be vouchsafed them—"According to your faith be it unto you" (Matthew 9:29) holds good at this point as much as it does anywhere else. Not a curious and unbridled imagination, but a Scripturally informed and regulated faith ever has to do with God and His written Word. If His Word be searched prayerfully, diligently and expectantly for Divine instruction on these things it will not be confused. From some of the accounts given in the sacred volume we may gather some real apprehensions on these subjects, yea, much more than is generally attended to. To these accounts we shall now turn.

The case of those servants of God who were favored with ecstatic raptures and supernatural visions while their bodies were inactive and senseless shows most clearly that the soul can function without any assistance from the body. Micaiah said unto the king of Israel, "I saw the LORD sitting on His throne, and all the host of Heaven standing by Him, on His right hand and on His left" (1 Kings 22:19). Though the Prophet was in the body, it was not with his natural eyes that he gazed upon such a scene as that. Again, a similar sight was granted Isaiah, and in addition he listened to the very words of the seraphim as they cried unto one another, "Holy, holy, holy is the LORD of hosts: the whole earth is full of His glory" (Isa. 6:1-5), and yet the eyes and ears of his body could no more have "seen the King, the LORD of hosts," nor heard those acclamations of Divine homage than could those of our bodies lying cold in death. God is Spirit, incorporeal: and His ineffable glory cannot be seen by the corporeal senses of any creature: it was therefore a visionary representation which was made to the spirit of His messenger.

Ezekiel tells us while among the captives by the river of Chebar, "the heavens were opened and I saw visions of God" (1:1). At the close of the first chapter of his prophecy, he describes one of those celestial revelations. He says, "And above the firmament that was over their heads [i.e. the cherubim] was the likeness of a throne as the appearance of a sapphire stone, and upon the likeness of the throne was the likeness as the appearance of a Man above it. And I saw as the color of amber, as the appearance of fire round about within it, from the appearance of His loins even upward, and from the appearance of His loins even downward, and I saw as it were the appearance of fire, and it had brightness round about. As the appearance of the bow that is in the cloud in the day of rain, so was the appearance of the brightness round about. This was the appearance of the likeness of the glory of the Lord" (vv. 26-28). From the words we have placed in italics it is obvious that the Prophet was under the supernatural influx of the Holy Spirit, and that his spiritual faculties were granted a visionary sight of the Savior before He became incarnate.

The experiences of Daniel also supply some illumination on the matter we are now considering: the capabilities of the soul abstracted from the body. First, he informs us: "I saw in the night visions. . . the Ancient of days did sit, whose garment was white as snow, and the hair of His head like the pure wool. His throne was like the fiery flame and his wheels as burning fire. A fiery stream issued and came forth from before Him: thousand thousands ministered unto Him, and ten thousand times ten thousand stood before Him" (7:7-10). "Then I lifted up mine eyes and looked, and behold a certain Man clothed in linen, whose loins were girded with fine gold of Uphaz. His body also was like the beryl and His face as the appearance of lightning, and His eyes as lamps of fire, and His arms and His feet like in color to polished brass, and the voice of His words like the voice of a multitude. And I Daniel alone saw the vision" (10:5-7). A sight of

Christ was there presented to the eyes of the Prophet's mind. They were opened and raised to an extraordinary degree; and they were closed again after the vision passed. His faculties were supernaturally elevated, or he could not have seen Christ thus. He tells us, "there remained no strength in me" (v. 8), so that he was in the body. As his body did not prevent his seeing this vision, neither will the absence of ours prevent us seeing Christ by sight and vision of soul.

A very similar, though perhaps not identical, case is that of Peter, of whom we read that, "he fell into a trance, and saw Heaven opened, and a certain vessel descending unto him, as it had been a great sheet knit at the four comers, and let down to the earth; wherein were all manner of four-footed beasts of the earth, and wild beasts, and creeping things, and fowls of the air. And there came a voice to him, Rise. Peter; kill, and eat. But Peter said, Not so, Lord, for I have never eaten anything that is common or unclean. And the voice spoke unto him again the second time, What God hath cleansed call not thou common. This was done thrice: and the vessel was received up again into Heaven" (Acts 10:10-16). The dictionary defines a trance as "a state in which the soul appears to be absent from the body, as to be wrapped in vision," because at such a time, all the normal activities (save that of the heart) and sensibilities of the body are suspended. The most remarkable feature of this incident is that Peter was not only able to see and hear, but also to reason and speak, to express his religious prejudice—and his, "Not so, Lord," demonstrates that sin has defiled our inner being, and that the soul needs to be purified before it can be admitted into the immediate presence of God on high.

Still more pertinent is the case of the Apostle Paul. In 2 Corinthians 12 he relates an extraordinary experience with which God had favored him. He declares, "I knew a man in Christ above fourteen years, ago, (whether in the body, I cannot tell; or whether out of the body, I cannot tell: God knoweth;) such an one caught up to the third heaven. And I knew such a man, (whether in the body, or out of the body, I cannot tell: God knoweth;) How that he was caught up into paradise and heard unspeakable words which it is not lawful [or "possible"—margin] for a man to utter," and this he recites as an illustration of "visions and revelations of the Lord" (vv. 1-4). It is remarkable that twice over in those verses, the Apostle should register his inability to determine whether or not he was in the body at the time he was translated to Heaven and heard and saw such wondrous things. If the soul were incapable of recognizing objects when it is detached from the body, then most assuredly Paul had never been at any such loss as he here mentions. From the language employed it is clear that the soul is capable of attending to the most important and blessed things of all when it is out of the body, and thus that death will not deprive it of its capabilities and sensibilities.

Finally, the experience which the beloved John had in the Isle of Patmos supplies us with further help on this point. He, too, was favored with a vision of Christ, an account of which he gives in the first chapter of the Revelation, and the effect which it had upon him. The glorious form of the Savior shone forth before him beyond what it did on the mount of transfiguration. The splendor of it was more than the Apostle could bear in his embodied state—"when I saw Him, I fell at His feet as dead" (v. 17). He described how the Lord Jesus acted toward him and what He said to him: "And He laid His right hand upon me, saying unto me, Fear not" (v. 17). He tells us that immediately prior to this supernatural experience, "I was in the spirit" (v. 10), or, more literally, "I became in spirit": that is, he passed out of the condition of normal human consciousness into the supernormal. The same expression occurs again in Revelation 4:2, "I became in spirit and, behold, a throne was set in Heaven": he was elevated to a new mode of consciousness and sphere of existence—in which mortal imperfections had no place—in which all bodily activities and sensations were completely suspended, and in which the soul was wholly under a Divine influence, entirely abstracted from all corporeal things, being fully controlled by the spirit.

It appears to the writer that from the accounts cited above, from both the Old and New Testaments, we may form some real, definite, and spiritual conceptions concerning the saints in their disembodied state. The soul will be detached from all occupation with natural things and entirely fixed upon Divine objects. The mind or spirit will be lifted above the natural or mortal state and be illumined and engaged with supernatural things. As those saints were favored with visions of Christ while in their bodies, yet their bodies were of no use to them at the time, so all of the redeemed when dismissed from their bodies are granted a view of Christ for which their physical senses are not needed—such a complete and immediate view of Him as fills them with admiration and adoration. If it be asked what will be the medium by which disembodied believers will know, enjoy and have fellowship with the Lord, the answer is furnished by, "Now we see in a mirror [American R.V.] obscurely, but then face to face" (1 Cor. 13:12). The "mirror" is the Word (Jam. 1:23-25) and the medium of perception is faith; but in Heaven the soul will have an unobscured sight of Christ and the whole invisible world will be opened, so that we shall see as we are seen or "know as we are known," by means of intuitional light and knowledge, crystal-clear intellectual and spiritual views of Christ and the Father in Him, by the indwelling Holy Spirit.

At the separation of the soul from the body it, or better he or she, enters into a state of which he has had no previous experience, yet the anticipation of the same should not occasion the slightest uneasiness—for Christ Himself passed out of the world and entered that state the same way. It is no untrodden path, for thousands of God's people have already gone over it. Immediately upon its dismissal from the body, such a change passes upon the soul that regeneration is then completed by being instantaneously and forever delivered from the whole being of sin and death. As we cannot enter Christ's spiritual kingdom of grace except by the new birth and a translation out of darkness into His marvelous light, neither can any of His redeemed (prior to His second coming) enter the kingdom of Christ's glory save by death. At that moment mortality is swallowed up of life. While death will bring a great difference in me, it will make none in my Savior to me. "For whether we live, we live unto the Lord; and whether we die, we die unto the Lord: whether we live therefore, or die, we are the Lord's. For to this end Christ both died, and rose, and revived, that He might be Lord both of the dead and living" (Rom. 14:8, 9). While I am in the body Christ ministers to me and supplies my every need, and when He summons me to leave the body, that will afford Him opportunity to express His love to me in a new way, introducing me into Heaven, there to behold His glory.

Luke 16:9 represents another aspect of the experience of saints upon their leaving of this scene. "And I say unto you, Make to yourselves friends of the mammon of unrighteousness, that, when ye fail, they may receive you into everlasting." As Goodwin remarked, "Those everlasting habitations there mentioned are in Heaven, where there are many mansions." This verse is part of the parable of "the unjust steward," and here the Lord made a practical application of the same. He bids His disciples emulate the wisdom (though not the wickedness) of him who has an eye to the future. The "mammon of unrighteousness" is the coinage of this world, in contrast with the "true riches" of the Spirit. The saints are to expend their earthly means, however small, in works of piety and charity, and thereby "make to themselves friends." "Our Lord here exhorts us to provide for ourselves a comfortable reception to the happiness of another world, by making good use of our possessions and enjoyments in this world" (Manton). The soul's passage out of this life is termed a "failing"—of the body—and its entrance on high as a being welcomed home by those to whom he had ministered upon earth. "The poor saints that are gone before to glory receive them that in this world distributed to their necessities" (Matthew Henry).

The above verse is one of several which makes it clear that there will be the personal recognition of the saints in the next life. The question was asked Luther a little while before his death whether we should know one another in the other world, to which he answered by observing the case of Adam, who knew Eve to be flesh of his flesh and bone of his bone whom he had never seen before. "How did he know this," asked Luther, "but by the Spirit of God, by revelation?" And then he said, "so shall we know parents, wives and children in the other world, and that more perfectly." To which we may add, How otherwise can those of whose conversion and edification Gospel-ministers have been the instruments be their "joy and crown of rejoicing" in the day to come (1 Thess. 2:19) unless the one is able to identify the other? A further hint on the subject is supplied by the Apostles knowing Moses and Elijah on the mount, for they had never beheld them previously nor seen any statue or picture of them, for such was not allowed among the Jews.

It has long been our conviction that the glorious scene which the three Apostles witnessed on the holy mount was designed (among other ends) to furnish us with a glimpse of the blessed condition and delight of the glorified So ravished was Peter by the sight that he exclaimed: "Lord, it is good for us to be here" (Matthew 17:4), and would fain have remained there. As Manton said: "So was he affected with joy in the presence and company of Christ, and Moses and Elijah appearing with Him, that all his natural comforts and relations were forgotten." They were granted a foretaste of the life to come, for those who enter that blessed state will never desire to come out of it. The account of the transfiguration is prefaced by the statement: "And after six days" (Mathew 17:1) and, "It came to pass about an eight days after" (Luke 9:28): thus it was a seventh day (the perfect number!) event—a foreshadowing of the eternal Sabbath. The central figure was Christ Himself in resplendent glory. Talking with Him were Moses and Elijah: the one who had survived death, the other who had never expired—types of those saints alive on earth at Christ's second coming.

Not only does the above incident teach us that the departed saints preserve their individual identities and are recognizable, but the fact that the Apostles were permitted to see them, and to hear their discourse with Christ intimates that the society of saints is a part of Heaven's blessedness, and that the Old Testament saints (represented by Moses and Elijah) and those of the New (the Apostles) are all together with Christ. Is not the same fact indicated by our Lord's words, "I say unto you, That many shall come from the east and west, and shall sit down with Abraham, and Isaac, and Jacob, in the kingdom of Heaven" (Matthew 8:11)? Still another passage which witnesses to the truth that the company of the redeemed and our fellowship with them is an adjunct of Heaven's blessedness is Hebrews 12:22, 23, where among other privileges we are said to have come to "the spirits of just men made perfect." That same passage also makes mention of "an innumerable company of angels." If the Bethlehem shepherds were filled with joy as they heard the heavenly hosts praising God, what delight will it give us to mingle our voices with the angelic choirs! Yet these things are but secondary, for as Rutherford well said: "The Lamb is all the glory in Immanuel's land," or, as Matthew 17 shows us, Moses and Elijah soon faded from the Apostles' view, and they "saw no man save Jesus only" (v. 8)!

Though God has not given us the Scriptures in order to gratify an idle carnal curiosity, it has pleased Him graciously to reveal sufficient in them to satisfy the spiritual aspirations and expectations of His people concerning the life to come. Nevertheless, it is neither the prayerless nor the indolent who apprehend and enjoy much therein. We have shown from the Word of Truth that the saint dies in union and communion with the Lord, that an angelic guard of protection and honor conducts him to the Father's House on high, that he is there greeted by those believers whom he had befriended upon earth and who have entered before him into their inheritance, and that Christ Himself receives him and presents him faultless before the throne of His glory with exceeding joy. We have seen that the company of the redeemed and our fellowship with them, yes, and with the holy angels also, constitutes a part of Heaven's blessedness, yet that such privileges are entirely subordinate to the blissful communion we shall have with Christ Himself. The supreme and climacteric joy will be found in that One who occupies both the central and supreme throne in Heaven. Nor would any saint have it otherwise. Christ is the One who loved him and gave Himself for him, and therefore He is not only his Savior, his Beloved, but his "All" (Col. 3:11).

Well might the Psalmist, under the Spirit of inspiration, exclaim: "O how great is Thy goodness which Thou hast laid up for them that fear Thee, which Thou hast wrought for them that trust in Thee" (Ps. 31:19). A part of that which God, in His eternal purpose, designed for His people is entered into and enjoyed by them during their earthly pilgrimage; but far more is "laid up for them" for their eternal felicity. The good or best wine is reserved for the end—for the marriage feast (John 2:10)—and its inexpressible excellence is indicated by the, "O how great!" Then it is that we shall participate in the consummation of God's "so great salvation": we shall be as happy and as blessed as it is possible for creatures to be. "They shall be abundantly satisfied with the fatness of Thy house, and Thou shalt make them drink of the river of Thy pleasures. For with Thee is the fountain of life: in Thy light shall we see light" (Ps. 36:8, 9). It is blessed to note that in the Hebrew word for "pleasures," there is the plural of "Eden." As Home said: "In Heaven alone the thirst of an immortal soul after happiness can be satisfied. There the streams of Eden will flow again." To drink of that "river" (cf. Rev. 22:1) we understand to signify to be favored with an unclouded knowledge of God and a pure affection to Him.

There are two of the Divine titles which ought to appeal particularly unto believers: "the God of all grace" (1 Pet. 5:10) and "the God of glory" (Ps. 29:3). The former is much the better known one, yet it is the latter which receives the most prominence in Scripture. There we read of "the Father of glory" (Eph. 1:17), while the Son is styled "the King of glory" (Ps. 24:7), and "the Lord of glory" (1 Cor. 2:8), and the Comforter is termed "the Spirit of glory" (1 Pet. 4:14). Those appellations speak not only of what God is in Himself essentially, but also of what He is in His relations and acts unto His dear people. As S. E. Pierce pointed out, "the God of glory expresses what He hath prepared for us, what He will bestow upon us, and what He will be to us in the house eternal in the heavens." "Glory" imports an excellency (Matthew 4:8), yea, a height of excellency (2 Pet. 1:17), and therefore that place and state of blessedness into which believers enter immediately after death, and into which their Forerunner was "received," is designated "Glory" (1 Tim. 3:16). It is striking to note that the Hebrew word (tabod) means both "weight" and "glory," as though to tell us that what seems so nebulous unto men is that which alone possesses substance and solidity—explaining the Apostle's expression, "an exceeding weight of glory," in 2 Corinthians 4:17.

"Glory" is connected with that which is exceedingly lovely to look upon, for when we read of "the glory of his countenance" (2 Cor. 3:7), we know it was no ordinary beauty and radiance which illumined the face of Moses when he came down from the mount, but one that was too dazzling for the beholders to gaze upon, so that he had to cover it with a veil (Ex. 34:35). So, too, Paul tells us that when the Savior appeared to him on the way to Damascus, "there shone from Heaven a great light upon me." No ordinary light was it, for he added: "I could not see for the glory of that light" (Acts 22:6, 11). Thus it is in Heaven itself: the celestial city "had no need of the sun, neither of the moon to shine in it, for the glory of God did lighten it, and the Lamb is the light thereof" (Rev. 21:23). What then must be "the riches of His glory" (Eph. 3:16)! During their sojourn here believers are made partakers of "the riches of His grace" (Eph. 1:7), but in the life to come God will "make known the riches of His glory on the vessels of mercy, which He had afore prepared unto glory" (Rom. 9:23) and they are "His riches in glory by Christ Jesus" (Phil. 4:19).

That a revelation of God in Christ unto His saints in glory will satisfy every longing of the renewed heart is implied in the request of Philip, "show us the Father, and it sufficeth" (John 14:8), for that is an indirect acknowledgment that there is such a sufficiency in viewing Him as will be enough to completely content all the insatiable desires of the soul. Three tenses are used in connection with the saint's absorption with Christ's excellence. First, "we beheld His glory, the glory as of the only begotten of the Father, full of grace and truth" (John 1:14), which is realized at our conversion, when a supernatural revelation of Christ is made to the heart. Second, "But we all, with open face, beholding as in a mirror the glory of the Lord, are changed into the same image from glory to glory as by the Spirit of the Lord" (2 Cor. 3:18), which is a progressive experience in the Christian's life, as by the exercise of faith upon the personal and official perfections of Christ, as they are set forth in the written Word and under the gracious agency of the Spirit, we are transformed being assimilated to His holy image. Third, "Father, I will that they also whom Thou hast given Me, be with Me where I am: that they may behold My glory" (John 17:24), which is realized when they are removed from earth to Heaven.

We are, from our regeneration to our glorification, taking in Christ into our renewed understanding. It is but little that we now apprehend of Him, yet the least degree of spiritual apprehension of Him received into our hearts from the Word of Truth renders Him more precious to us than the gold of Ophir. Imperfect though it be, yet even in this life the genuine Christian has a real and solid, convincing and affecting knowledge of Christ. By the gracious operations of the Spirit, his faith is called into exercise in such a manner that it obtains both evidence and subsistence of the things of God in the soul (Heb. 11:1). As the eye of the body conveys to the mind an image of the object beheld, so faith (which is the eye of the soul) takes in a true knowledge of Christ, so that He is "formed within" him (Gal. 4:19). Thereby he procures as accurate a knowledge of His Person as he ever will in Heaven. When the believer shall see Christ "face to face," it will be identically the same Person he formerly beheld by faith, through a mirror obscurely. It will be no stranger to whom he needs an introduction that the believer will meet with on high, but One whom he savingly knew here below, and with whom he enjoyed an all-too-brief, yet real and precious, fellowship.

Let there be no mistake upon this point: in this life every born again Christian experiences the truth of those words: "Whosoever drinketh of the water that I shall give him shall never thirst, but the water that I shall give him shall be in him a well of water springing up into everlasting life" (John 4:14). That does not mean he will not desire a more complete knowledge of Christ, deeper draughts of His love, sensible enjoyments of Him—but that a satisfying portion is now his. He "thirsts" indeed, yet not for any other portion, but for larger measures of it. He will never more be without that which will abundantly meet his every longing. The saints in Heaven know more of Christ, but they do not know Him more truly than they did on earth. By the Spirit the mind is enlightened to receive the true and saving knowledge of Christ, and we are brought to believe on Him with all our hearts. By Him we are "given an understanding that we may know Him that is true" (1 John 5:20). The Spirit is graciously pleased to reveal Christ to us as He is set forth in the Word—nevertheless, each of us yearns with Paul "that I may know Him"—more perfectly (Phil. 3:10).

Further and grander manifestations of God will be enjoyed by saints in Heaven than on earth, yet this will be different only in degree, and not in kind, from that which is vouchsafed His people in this life. It will indeed immeasurably exceed in fullness and clarity anything which they are now capable of enjoying, but for substance it will be the same. Grace is glory in the bud; glory is grace in full fruition. The good wine of the kingdom is sampled by them now, but their cup of bliss will then be full to overflowing. Even here the Spirit shows us "things to come" (John 16:13), but there we shall enter into the full possession of them. That communion with Christ in glory which the redeemed enjoy at present, those refreshings in which they participate from the fountain of His love—are termed "the firstfruits of the Spirit" (Rom. 8:23)—samples of the harvest of blessedness awaiting them as a cluster of the luscious grapes of Canaan was brought to Israel before they entered the Land (Num. 13:23). Such experiences are also termed "the earnest of the Spirit in our hearts" (2 Cor. 1:22). An "earnest" is a small token of the whole yet to come, a partial payment of the thing itself; what we now enjoy is a foretaste of the coming feast.

"The fullness of the felicity of Heaven may appear if we compare with it the present joys and comforts of the Holy Spirit. Such they are as that the Scripture styles them strong consolation (Heb. 6:18), full joy (John 15:11), joy unspeakable and full of glory (1 Pet. 1:8), abounding consolation (2 Cor. 1:5). And yet all the joy and peace that believers are partakers of in this life is but as a drop in the ocean, as a single cluster to the whole vintage, as the thyme or honey upon the thigh of a bee to the whole hive fully fraught with it, or as the break and peep of day to the bright noontide. And yet these tastes of the water, wine, and honey of this celestial Canaan, with which the Holy Spirit makes glad the hearts of believers, are far more desirable and satisfactory than the overflowing streams of all earthly felicities. And there are none who have once tasted of them, but say as the Samaritan woman did: 'Lord, give me that water, that I thirst not, neither come hither to draw' (John 4:15). So also the first and early dawnings of the heavenly light fill the soul with more serenity, and ravish it with more pure joy, than the brightest sunshine of all worldly splendor can ever do" (W. Spurstow, 1656).

To see God in His Word and works is the happiness of saints on earth; but to see Him in Christ face to face will be the fullness of their blessedness in Heaven. None can doubt that the Apostle Paul was favored with the most intimate, exalted and frequent communion with Christ down here; yet he declared that to depart and be with Him is "far better" (Phil. 1:23). He did not say, "to depart and be in Paradise," but "to be with Christ"! So again—"absent from the body, present with the Lord"—not, "safe at home in Heaven." From earliest times it was announced, "unto Him shall the gathering of the people be" (Gen. 49:10). That receives a threefold fulfillment at least: at conversion, when they are drawn to Him by the power of the Father (John 6:44); in the assembly to worship Him by the power of the Spirit (Matthew 18:20); at death or His return, when He brings them to Himself on high. "My Beloved is gone down into His garden to gather lilies" (Song. 6:2). Christ comes into His "garden" (the local church) sometimes to plant new lilies, and at others to crop and gather old ones, to remove them into His paradise ("garden") above. "Gather My saints together unto Me, those that have made a covenant with Me by sacrifice" (Ps. 50:5).

"Father, I will that they also, whom Thou hast given Me, be with Me where I am; that they may behold My glory, which Thou hast given Me" (John 17:24). Too many of our moderns would postpone the realization of that request until the "Eternal State," but there is nothing in Scripture which intimates that the saints will have to await the resurrection morning ere they shall gaze upon their glorified Lord. It should be quite clear to the reader from all that we have set before him that the obscure, partial and transient enjoyment of Christ which is his in this life is turned into a clear, full, perfect and permanent enjoyment of Him immediately after death. The beatific vision will then be his—designated such because, having been freed from all the darkness and limitation which indwelling sin places upon the soul, he will then be able to take in his full measure of bliss. At first his vision of Christ will be wholly spiritual and intellectual: after the resurrection it will be corporeal also. In Heaven the Son will be seen in all the surpassing dignity and splendor of His Person, His perfections shining forth in cloudless luster. "Then how should believers long to be with Him! Most men need patience to die; a believer should need patience to live!" (John Flavel).

On high the Christian will have an immediate, uninterrupted and satisfying view of the Lord of glory. In Him the Incomprehensible Three will be manifested in the uttermost display of Their excellences, before all the holy angels and saints. It is that which will be the supreme blessedness of Heaven, and which each believer shall forever behold, filling him with such concepts of the Divine glory as he can never express. He will be eternally admiring the same, rejoicing in it, having communion with God over it, praising Him for it. The heart will then be everlastingly fixed upon Christ as its Center. The glory of Christ is very dear unto the saints. They have a spiritual perception of it now, but a far greater apprehension of it will be theirs when they are removed from this vale of tears and are "present with the Lord." Then shall they behold the King in His beauty, and that supernatural sight shall be theirs forever. Paul could go no higher than, "so shall we ever be with the Lord." Not merely beholding His glory as spectators, but taken into intimate fellowship with the same.

How overwhelming must be the first open sight of Christ! What will our feelings be when, without any intervening medium, we shall behold the Son of God? Who can fitly visualize our first meeting with the eternal Lover of our souls? What stretch of imagination can comprehend the experience of soul as we behold Him who is "altogether lovely"? No doubt the Christian reader has, like this scribe, attempted to anticipate those moments when he will first gaze upon that Blessed One whose visage was (through pain and suffering) more marred than any others, but which now shines with a splendor exceeding that of the mid-day sun, and which will beam with love as He welcomes to Himself another of His redeemed. Doubtless, when we behold His glorified humanity, which is personally united to the Divine nature, and is exalted far above all principalities and powers, we shall be lost in wonder, love and praise. If the wise men fell down and worshipped Him when they saw Him as "a young child with Mary, His mother, in the house," what will be our feelings when we see Him seated upon the Father's throne? Such views shall we then have of His excellence as will satiate our souls with holy admiration and joy inexpressible.

Our efforts to anticipate that blissful experience will be aided somewhat if we bear in mind that we shall then be completely rid of sin and that selfishness of character which mars even the regenerate in this life. "Everything we now enjoy, though even of a spiritual nature, is tinged with self If we contemplate the glories of God in His trinity of Persons, as revealed us in Christ: if we feel our souls going forth under the Divine leading of the Holy Spirit in sweet communion with the Father, and with His Son Jesus Christ—if the soul be led to bless God, when at any time receiving love-tokens of pardon, consolation, strength, or any of the 10,000, times 10,000 marks of grace, like the dew from Heaven, coming to us from the Lord—in all these, self and self-interest is mingled. But there is an infinitely higher source of pure unmixed felicity, which the disembodied spirit will immediately enter upon when all selfishness is lost in the love of God" (Robert Hawker). There the soul will be lifted up above itself, absorbed entirely with God in Christ, independent of what He is to us and all that He has done for us.

Christ, the God-man Mediator, is the grand Center of Heaven's blessedness and the all-engrossing Object of its inhabitants. "In the midst of the throne, and of the four living creatures, and in the midst of the elders, stood a Lamb, as it had been slain" (Rev. 5:6). And the hosts surrounding Him sing: "Thou art worthy to receive honor, and glory, and blessing" (vv. 11, 12). It is the contemplation of this most glorious Christ which will constitute the holiness and happiness of the saints for all eternity. To behold His beauty will be infinitely more than all the benefits we derive from Him. Our refined and enlarged intellectual and spiritual faculties will be so engaged with and exercised upon Him that it will be impossible for us to fall again into sin. In Him dwells all the fullness of the Godhead personally. In and through Him the Triune God is displayed before elect angels and saints, reflecting on them the full blaze of the Divine perfections. It is a Christ who is "The brightness [effulgence] of God's glory" (Heb. 1:3) that we shall forever enjoy.

Christ is the Medium and Mirror in which the redeemed shall see God. "In Him we shall behold the manifestation of the Father, Son and Holy Spirit, as far as the invisibility of the Divine essence can admit of revelation" (Robert Hawker), and so far as finite creatures will be capable of apprehending it.

As all the glory of the sun is inherent in itself and is only apparent in the object it shines upon, so all the glory of Heaven centers in Christ and is treasured up in Him for them—as all grace is (2 Tim. 2: 1)—and He imparts it unto them. Our blessedness in Heaven will not be independent of the Lord, but conveyed to us out of His fullness. "Christ's glory, as the God-man, is that of the Godhead dwelling personally in Him. That glory is founded upon the union of the human nature with the nature of God. This glory breaks forth and shines through His human nature, as if the sun were encompassed with a case of clear crystal—how glorious would that crystal be!" (Goodwin). Christ's glory is so inherently and essentially in Himself that He is designated "the Lord of glory," and His ineffable beauty will be so beheld by us as to be reflected upon us, as the countenance of Moses shone with a more-than-natural light after his communion with Jehovah. Christ has indeed an incommunicable glory, yet according to our capacity we shall be partakers of the glory which the Father has "given" Him (John 17:22).

Chapter 20
REVELATION IN GLORY
CONCLUSION

The glorification of the saint commences upon his departure from this world, but it is not consummated until the morning of the resurrection, when his body shall be "raised in glory" (1 Cor. 15:43). Then will he be fully "conformed to the image of His Son" (Rom. 8:29). It is observable that in the process of conforming, the members of Christ's mystical body partake of the experiences of their Head. As He suffered on this earth before He entered into His glory, so do they, for the rule holds good here that the servant is not above his Master, who purchased all that the servant is to enjoy. As His glorification was in distinct stages, so is theirs. His glorification began in His victory over sin and death, when He came forth triumphant from the grave. It was greatly advanced when he ascended and sat down at the right hand of the Majesty on high. Yet that did not complete it, for He is awaiting a more thorough conquest of His enemies (Heb. 10:13) and the completion of the Church which is His "fullness" or "complement" (Eph. 1:23): "When He shall come to be glorified in His saints and to be admired in all them that believe" (2 Thess. 1:10). Ours begins at regeneration, when we receive "the Spirit of glory" as an earnest of our inheritance. It will be greatly augmented at death, for the soul is then purged of all defilement, and enters the Father's House. But our complete glorification will not be until our bodies are raised, reunited to our souls, and "fashioned like unto His glorious body."

As Christ Himself is not in every way complete (Eph. 1:23) until the entire company of His redeemed are about Him and fully conformed to Him—for not till then will He "fully see of the travail of His soul and be satisfied"—neither is the glorification of Christians complete until their souls and bodies are united together again, for Christ redeemed the body as well as the soul (Rom. 8:23), and if the Old Testament saints were not perfect without New Testament believers (Heb. 11:40), then by the same reason the soul will be imperfect without the body. The charge God gave to Christ was not only to lose none of "them" given to Him by the Father (John 18:9), but also that He should lose "nothing" of them, but "should raise it up again at the last day" (John 6:39). As Goodwin pointed out, "God hath the soul of Abraham with Him above, yet still He reckons to have not Abraham, that is the whole of him, until the resurrection; from thence Christ argued that Abraham must rise because God is called Abraham's God (Matthew 22:32)." The hope of Christ Himself, while His body lay in the grave (although His soul was in Paradise) was fixed upon the resurrection of His body. "Therefore My heart is glad, and My glory rejoiceth: My flesh also shall rest in hope. For Thou wilt not leave My soul in Sheol [the unseen world], neither wilt Thou suffer Thine Holy One to see corruption. Thou wilt show Me the path of life" (Ps. 16:9-1 1).

That expectation of the Savior's was also shared by the Old Testament saints. This is evident from the language of Job: "And though after my skin worms destroy this body, yet in my flesh shall I see God: whom I shall see for myself, and mine eyes shall behold, and not another" (19:26, 27). And again from the words of David: "As for me, I will behold Thy face in righteousness: I shall be satisfied, when I awake with Thy likeness" (Ps. 17:15). As the death of the body is likened unto "sleep," so the figure of "awaking" is used of its resurrection. Not until then will entire satisfaction (of spirit and soul and body) be the saint's—for only then will the eternal purpose of God concerning him be fully realized. Note how comprehensive and sublime was this expectation, to "behold Thy face," which proves that Old Testament believers possessed as much light on the subject as we are now favored with, for the New Testament contains nothing higher than "they shall see His face" (Rev. 22:4). Not only so, but they turned it into practical use, and lived in the blessed power and enjoyment of the same. In Psalm 17:14 David makes mention of the "men of this world" who flourished like a green bay tree and had all their carnal hearts could desire of natural things. But far was he from envying them or being discontented with his lot because he realized they had "their portion in this life," and said, "As for me, I will behold Thy face in righteousness"—he anticipated the joy of the life to come

To behold God's face by faith is both our duty and comfort in this life, yet that can only be as we are clothed with the righteousness of Christ and as we maintain practical righteousness by obedience to God's revealed will. To behold the Lord by open vision will be our occupation and enjoyment in the next life. But what is meant by, "I shall be satisfied, when I awake, with Thy likeness"? Not a few have experienced difficulty in supplying an answer. Their spiritual instincts tell them those words cannot mean that the soul will find its contentment in God's image then being perfectly stamped upon itself; yet at first glance that is what they seem to signify. Manton appears to have given the true interpretation when he said: "In Heaven we look for such a vision as makes way for assimilation, and such assimilation to God as maketh for complete satisfaction and blessedness." There will be no self-satisfaction there, but rather entire absorption with and satisfaction in Christ. "That blessedness consists of three things. 1. The open vision of God and His glory: the knowledge of God will then be perfect, and the enlarged intellect filled with it. 2. The participation of His likeness: our holiness will there be perfect: this results from the former—'we shall be like Him, for we shall see Him as He is' (l John 3:2). 3. A complete and full satisfaction resulting from all this. There is no satisfaction for a soul but in God: in His face and likeness, His good will toward us, and His good work in us" (Matthew Henry).

It is solemnly true that the wicked will also yet behold the face of God in Christ, for it is written, "Behold, He cometh with clouds; and every eye shall see Him, and they also which pierced Him": yet how vastly different will be their case! They will look upon Him but briefly and not perpetually, with shame and sorrow and not with confidence and joy—upon their Judge and not their Savior. So far from such a sight filling them with satisfaction, "all kindreds of the earth shall wail because of Him" (Rev. 1:7), yea, they shall say to the mountains and rocks, "Fall on us, and hide us from the face of Him that sitteth on the throne and from the wrath of the Lamb; for the great day of His wrath is come, and who shall be able to stand?" (Rev. 6:17). None will be able to stand, be he king or subject, rich or poor, save those who "have washed their robes and made them white in the blood of the Lamb." These latter are "before the throne of God, and serve Him day and night in His temple, and He that sitteth upon the throne shall dwell among them. They hunger no more, neither thirst any more. . . For the Lamb which is in the midst of the throne shall feed them, and shall lead them unto living fountains of water" (Rev. 7:15-17), finding His joy in ministering to them, as theirs will be in such ministry.

"At the resurrection there will be a glory upon the body as well as upon the soul: a glory equal to that of the sun, moon and stars. The body which is sown in the earth in corruption, a vile body, corrupted by sin, and now by death, shall be raised in incorruption, no more to be corrupted by sin, disease or death. What is sown in dishonor, and has lost all its beauty and glory, and become nauseous and fit only to be the companion of worms, shall be raised in glory—in the utmost perfection and comeliness, fashioned like to the glorious body of Christ—and shine like the sun in the firmament of Heaven. What is sown in weakness, having lost all its strength, and carried by others to the grave, shall be raised in power—strong and hale, able to move itself from place to place—and will attend the service of God and the Lamb without weakness and weariness—there will be no more complaint of this kind: 'the spirit is willing, but the flesh is weak.' What is sown a natural body, or an animal one, which while it lived was supported with animal food, shall be raised a spiritual body: not turned into a spirit, for then it would not have flesh and bones, as it will have; but it will subsist as spirits do, without food, and no more die; then it will be no encumbrance to the soul, as now, in spiritual services, but assisting to it, and befitted for spiritual employments and to converse with spiritual objects." (J. Gill). When the glorified soul and the glorified body are united, there will then be a full accession of glory to the whole man, and his enjoyments will then be entered into in a larger and more sensible manner.

Let us now consider the various features of a saint's glorification, or those things which constitute his eternal bliss. First, a perfection of knowledge. This is clear from "now I know in part, but then shall I know even as also I am known." This does not mean we shall become omniscient, or possessed of infinite knowledge, but that our knowledge will be free from all doubt and error, and as full as our finite faculties will permit. We shall not only enjoy a greater means of knowledge, but our capacity to take in will be immeasurably increased. That sight of God in Christ which will be ours will not only irradiate our minds but enlarge our understandings. We shall perceive the glory of God with the eyes of our mind fully enlightened. The rays of that glory will shine into our souls so that they will be filled with the knowledge of God, and with the whole good pleasure of His will, in all His vast designs of grace unto us. That which is revealed in Scripture, and upon which we now exercise faith and hope, shall then be fully experienced by us.

Second, a perfection of union and communion, both with Christ and fellow believers. Henceforth, there will be no more differences of opinion, cooling of affections, or breaches between Christians. Then will be fully realized that prayer, "that they may be one, even as We are one: I in them, and Thou in Me, that they may be made perfect in one" (John 17:22, 23). The very reading of those words should fill our hearts with holy amazement, and the actualization of them will fill us with adoration. The oneness between the Father and the Son is such that they partake of the same ineffable blessedness, each enjoying it equally with the other. And that is the likeness, by way of similitude, of the final union between the Redeemer and the redeemed—ours will be like Theirs! As the union between the Father and the Son is a real, spiritual, holy, indestructible, and inexpressibly glorious one, such will be that between Christ and His Church in Heaven. There is a grace union between them here, but it is the glory union which is referred to in the above verses. "He will be theirs, and will bless them forever. He will be all around them and within them, the light of their understandings, the joy of their hearts, the object of their perpetual praise" (John Dick). Christ will remain the everlasting bond of union between God and the saints.

Third, a perfection of love. Even now Christ has the first place in their hearts (otherwise they would not be real Christians), yet how often their affection toward Him wanes. Real need has each of us to pray, "O may no earth-born cloud arise, to hide You from Your servant's eyes." But, blessed be God, such a thing will be unknown there. It will be impossible to constantly contemplate the excellence of God without continually loving Him. "In this world the saints prefer Him to their chief joy, and there are seasons when their hearts go out to Him with an ardor which no created object can excite, with desire for the closest union and the most intimate fellowship. But this flame will glow more ardently in the pure atmosphere of Heaven.

The fervour of his affection will never abate, nor will anything occur to suspend it or turn it into a different channel. God will always maintain the pre-eminence and appear infinitely greater and better than all other beings" (John Dick). There will be a perpetual cleaving of heart to Him without change or weariness, a love that never ceases working communion with God.

Fourth, a perfection of holiness. "Now they are in part made 'partakers of the Divine nature,' but then they shall perfectly partake of it. That is to say, God will communicate to them His own image, making all His goodness not only pass before them, but pass into them, and stamp the image of all His own perfections upon them, so far as the creature is capable of receiving the same; from whence shall result a perfect likeness to Him, in all things in and about them" (Thomas Boston). "If our view of the glory of Christ by faith is assimilating now, and 'changes into the same image from glory to glory' (2 Cor. 3:18), what will a full view, a clear sight, of Him do? Then will the great end of predestination—to be conformed to the image of the Son of God—be completely answered. The soul, with all its powers and faculties, will bear a resemblance to Christ. Its understanding will have a clear discernment of Him, the bias of the mind will be wholly toward Him, the will will be entirely subject to Him, the affections will be in the strongest manner set upon Him, and the memory will be fully stored with spiritual and heavenly things" (John Gill).

Fifth, a perfection of glory. Of old it was promised, "The Lord will give grace and glory" (Ps. 84:11): as surely as He has given us the one, will He the other. "But we are bound to give thanks always to God for you, brethren beloved of the Lord, because God hath from the beginning chosen you to salvation through sanctification of the Spirit and belief of the truth: whereunto He called you by our Gospel, to the obtaining of the glory of our Lord Jesus Christ" (2 Thess. 2:13, 14). That was what God had in mind for His people in eternity past:

nothing less would satisfy His heart. Observe well that it is "the glory of our Lord Jesus Christ." Our glory cannot be independent of Him, but the glory which the Father has given Him, He gives us (John 17:22), so that we share His very throne (Rev. 3:21)! As He is the Head of grace, ministering to our every need, so He is the Head of glory and will communicate the same to us in Heaven. He will shine forth in all His glory so that His bride will reflect the splendor of it. Angels will be spectators of it, but not the sharers. It will be a glory revealed in the saints which is beyond all comparison (Rom. 8:18; 2 Thess. 1:10), and a glory put upon them which is inconceivable (Ps. 45:13; Rev. 21:11), so that, "when Christ, who is our life, shall appear, then shall we also appear with Him in glory" (Col. 3:4), in shining robes of ineffable purity and beauty.

Sixth, a perfection of joy. "Joy sometimes enters into us now, but it has much to do to get access while we are encompassed with sorrows; but then, joy shall not only enter into us, but we shall enter into it, and swim forever in an ocean of joy; where we shall see nothing but joy wherever we turn our eyes" (Boston). Our joy will be pure and unmixed, without any dregs of sorrow. "In Thy presence is fullness of joy, at Thy right hand there are pleasures forevermore" (Ps. 16:11). The object of our happiness will not be a creature, but God Himself. The presence and communion of the Lamb will afford us everlasting delight. All that the spouse is represented in the Song as longing for, she will then have, and a thousand times more. Christ will then say, "Enter thou into the joy of thy Lord" (Matthew 25:21), sharing with us His own joy. Perfect serenity of mind, complete satisfaction of heart, will be ours, without interruption forever. As we are told that in that day the Lord God, "will rest in His love, He will joy over thee with singing" (Zeph. 3:17), so will it be with His people.

Seventh, a perfection of praise. In Revelation 15:2, the heavenly saints are seen "having the harps of God"—the emblem of praise. At present our best worship is faulty, for both our knowledge of God and our love to Him are sadly defective—but when we come into His presence and are filled with all His fullness (Eph. 3:19), we shall render to Him that which is His due. Then shall we fully realize our infinite indebtedness to His grace, and our hearts will overflow with gratitude. A glorified soul will be far better capacitated to estimate and appreciate the wondrous riches of

His grace than it can be in its present state, and therefore our adoring homage will be immeasurably more fervent and raised to a higher pitch. The infinite perfections of the Triune Jehovah, His love unto the Church collectively and to each of its members individually—the revelation and manifestation of His glory in Christ, the salvation which He provided for them at such fearful cost to Himself, contain an all-sufficiency for perpetual praise and thanksgiving throughout the endless ages. His praises can never be exhausted: for all eternity we shall find fresh matter in Him for thanksgiving.

"And there shall be no more curse; but the throne of God and of the Lamb shall be in it; and His servants shall serve Him. And they shalt see His face, and His name shalt be in their foreheads" (Rev. 22:3, 4). That is not only the final but the ultimate word on this glorious subject. In the beatific vision it is not upon His "back parts" we shalt look, as did Moses upon the mount (Ex. 33:23), but we shall "see His face"! We shall not be limited to touching the hem of His garment, nor to embracing His feet, but shall actually and personally feast our eyes upon His peerless countenance. That sacred head which once was crowned with thorns is now adorned with diadem resplendent; and that blessed face which was covered with the vile spittle of men will forever beam with love upon His own. Oh, what an ineffable sight! No longer will our eyes be clouded by sin or dimmed by old age. Nor will such bliss be ours for a brief season only, but forevermore. There will be a perfect and perpetual influx of delight as we view Him in the inconceivable radiance of His manifested glory.

"They shall see His face." There will be many other objects to behold, but nothing in comparison with Him! Those mansions which Christ has gone to prepare for His beloved must be indescribably lovely. The holy angels, the cherubim and seraphim, will be present to our sight. The Patriarchs and Prophets, the Apostles and martyrs, some of our own dear kindred who were washed in the blood of the Lamb. But chief and foremost, claiming our notice and absorbing our attention, will be our best Beloved. Then it is we shall receive the fullest and grandest answer to our oft-repeated prayer, "God be merciful unto us, and bless us, and cause His face to shine upon us" (Ps. 67:1). To see the King's face is to enjoy His favor (2 Sam. 14:24, 32). But it also signifies to have the most intimate and immediate communion with Him, that we shall then be the recipients of the fullest and most lavish discoveries of His love—beholding Him with both the eyes of our understandings and of our glorified bodies. All distance will then be removed. Every veil will then be done away with. All we longed for perfectly realized.

Nothing will then be lacking to the absolute completeness of our happiness; and, what is far better, nothing will be lacking to complete the happiness of Christ. That "joy" which He "set before Him" or held in view, as He "endured the Cross" (Heb. 11:2), will then be fully His, for we shall not only be with Him, but like Him, conformed to His image. "His name shall be in their foreheads." Then will it openly appear to all beholders that they belong to Him and bear His holy image, since they shall perfectly reflect Him. As the "name" represents the person, so we shall bear His likeness, giving expression to those who see us who and what He is. We shall be publicly acknowledged as His (cf. Rev. 14:1).

Christ will everlastingly delight in the Church, and the Church will everlastingly delight in Him. There will be mutual intercourse, an unrestrained opening of the heart one to another. In communion communications are made by both parties. One party bestows favor upon another, and the recipient reciprocates by giving back to the donor, according to the benefit received, grateful acknowledgment— those communications, from both sides, flowing from love and union. Thus we read, "Now ye Philippians know that. . . no church communicated with me as concerning giving and receiving, but ye only" (4:15). Paul and the Philippian saints were united in heart and had spiritual fellowship together in the Gospel (1:5). Out of love to him, they communicated in a temporal way, they being, the active givers, he the passive receiver. Then, in return for their kindness, the Apostle communicated by acknowledging their beneficence, thanking them for it. This may help us a little to form some idea of what our communion with Christ in Heaven will be like. As the vine conveys sap to the branch, so the branch responds by bearing leaves and fruit. Christ will continue to be the Giver, and we the receivers. This will issue in the overflowing of our love, and in return, we shall pour out praise and thanksgiving, adoration and worship.

> "He and I in one bright glory
> Endless bliss shall share;
> Mine, to be forever with Him;
> His, that I am there."

THE DOCTRINE
OF SANCTIFICATION

Contents

Chapter 1
INTRODUCTION

In the articles upon "The Doctrine of Justification" we contemplated the transcendent grace of God which provided for His people a Surety, who kept for them perfectly His holy law, and who also endured the curse which was due to their manifold transgressions against it. In consequence thereof, though in ourselves we are criminals who deserve to be brought to the bar of God's justice and there be sentenced to death, we are, nevertheless, by virtue of the accepted service of our Substitute, not only not condemned, but "justified," that is, pronounced righteous in the high courts of Heaven. Mercy has rejoiced against judgment: yet not without the governmental righteousness of God, as expressed in His Holy law, having been fully glorified. The Son of God incarnate, as the federal head and representative of His people, obeyed it, and also suffered and died under its condemning sentence. The claims of God have been fully met, justice has been magnified, the law has been made more honorable than if every descendant of Adam had personally fulfilled its requirements.

"As respects justifying righteousness, therefore, believers have nothing to do with the law. They are justified 'apart from it' (Rom. 3:21), that is, apart from any personal fulfillment thereof. We could neither fulfill its righteousness, nor bear its course. The claims of the law were met and ended, once and forever, by the satisfaction of our great Substitute, and as a result we have attained to righteousness without works, i.e., without personal obedience of our own. 'By the obedience of one shall many be constituted righteous' (Rom. 5:19). There may indeed, and there are, other relations in which we stand to the law. It is the principle of our new nature to rejoice in its holiness: 'we delight in the law of God after the inner man.' We know the comprehensiveness and the blessedness of those first two commandments on which all the Law and the Prophets hang: we know that 'love is the fulfilling of the law.' We do not despise the guiding light of the holy and immutable commandments of God, livingly embodied, as they have been, in the ways and character of Jesus; but we do not seek to obey them with any thought of obtaining justification thereby.

That which has been attained, cannot remain to be attained. Nor do we place so great an indignity on 'the righteousness of our God and Savior,' as to put the partial and imperfect obedience which we render after we are justified, on a level with that heavenly and perfect righteousness by which we have been justified. After we have been justified, grace may and does for Christ's sake, accept as well-pleasing our imperfect obedience; but this being a consequence of our perfected justification cannot be made a ground thereof. Nor can anything that is in the least degree imperfect, be presented to God with the view of attaining justification. In respect of this, the courts of God admit of nothing that falls short of His own absolute perfectness" (B. W. Newton).

Having, then, dwelt at some length on the basic and blessed truth of Justification, it is fitting that we should now consider the closely connected and complementary doctrine of Sanctification. But what is "sanctification": is it a quality or position? Is sanctification a legal thing or an experimental? that is to say, Is it something the believer has in Christ or in himself? Is it absolute or relative? by which we mean, Does it admit of degree or no? is it unchanging or progressive?

Are we sanctified at the time we are justified, or is sanctification a later blessing? How is this blessing obtained? by something which is done for us, or by us, or both? How may one be assured he has been sanctified: what are the characteristics, the evidences, the fruits? How are we to distinguish between sanctification by the Father, sanctification by the Son, sanctification by the Spirit, sanctification by faith, sanctification by the Word?

Is there any difference between sanctification and holiness? if so, what? Are sanctification and purification the same thing? Does sanctification relate to the soul, or the body, or both? What position does sanctification occupy in the order of Divine blessings? What is the connection between regeneration and sanctification? What is the relation between justification and sanctification? Wherein does sanctification differ from glorification? Exactly what is the place of sanctification in regard to salvation: does it precede or follow, or is it an integral part of it? Why is there so much diversity of opinion upon these points, scarcely any two writers treating of this subject in the same manner. Our purpose here is not simply to multiply questions but to indicate the many sidedness of our present theme, and to intimate the various avenues of approach to the study of it.

Diversive indeed have been the answers returned to the above questions. Many who were ill-qualified for such a task have undertaken to write upon this weighty and difficult theme, rushing in where wiser men feared to tread. Others have superficially examined this subject through the colored glasses of creedal attachment. Others, without any painstaking efforts of their own, have merely echoed predecessors who they supposed gave out, the truth thereon. Though the present writer has been studying this subject off and on for upwards of twenty-five years, he has felt himself to be too immature and too unspiritual to write at length thereon; and even now, it is (he trusts) with fear and trembling he essays to do so: may it please the Holy Spirit to so guide this thoughts that he may be preserved from everything which would pervert the Truth, dishonor God, or mislead His people.

We have in our library discourses on this subject and treatises on this theme by over fifty different men, ancient and modern, ranging from hyper-Calvinists to ultra-Arminians, and a number who would not care to be listed under either. Some speak with pontifical dogmatism, others with reverent caution, a few with humble diffidence. All of them have been carefully digested by us and diligently compared on the leading points. The present writer detests sectarianism (most of all in those who are the worst affected by it, while pretending to be opposed to it), and earnestly desires to be delivered from partisanship. He seeks to be profited from the labors of all, and freely acknowledges his indebtedness to men of various creeds and schools of thought. On some aspects of this subject he has found the Plymouth Brethren much more helpful than the Reformers and the Puritans.

The great importance of our present theme is evidenced by the prominence which is given to it in Scripture: the words "holy, sanctified" etc., occurring therein hundreds of times. Its importance also appears from the high value ascribed to it: it is the supreme glory of God, of the unfallen angels, of the Church. In Ex. 15:11 we read that the Lord God is "glorious in holiness"—that is His crowning excellency. In Matt. 25:31 mention is made of the "holy angels," for no higher honor can be ascribed them. In Eph. 5:26, 27 we learn that the Church's glory lieth not in pomp and outward adornment, but in holiness. Its importance further appears in that this is the aim in all God's dispensations. He elected His people that they should be "holy" (Eph. 1:4); Christ died that He might "sanctify" His people (Heb. 13:12); chastisements are sent that we might be "partakers of God's holiness" (Heb. 12:10).

Whatever sanctification be, it is the great promise of the covenant made to Christ for His people. As Thos. Boston well said, "Among the rest of that kind, it shines like the moon among the lesser stars—as the very chief subordinate end of the Covenant of Grace, standing therein next to the glory of God, which is the chief and ultimate end thereof. The promise of preservation, of the Spirit, of quickening the dead soul, of faith, of justification, of reconciliation, of adoption, and of the enjoyment of God as our God, do tend unto it as their common center, and stand related to it as means to their end. They are all accomplished to sinners on design to make them holy." This is abundantly clear from, "The oath which He swore to our father Abraham: that He would grant unto us, that we, being delivered out of the hand of our enemies, might serve Him without fear, in holiness and righteousness before Him all the days of our life" (Luke 1:73-75). In that "oath" or covenant, sworn to Abraham as a type of Christ (our spiritual Father: Heb. 2:13), His seed's serving the Lord in holiness is held forth as the chief thing sworn unto the Mediator—deliverance from their spiritual enemies being a means to that end.

The supreme excellency of sanctification is affirmed in Prov. 8:11, "For wisdom is better than rubies; and all things that may be desired are not to be compared to it." "Everyone who has read the book of Proverbs with any attention must have observed that Solomon means by 'wisdom' holiness, and by 'folly' sin; by a wise man a saint, and by a fool a sinner. 'The wise shall inherit glory: but shame shall be the promotion of fools' (Prov. 13:35): who can doubt whether by 'the wise' he means saints, and by 'fools' sinners! 'The fear of the Lord is the beginning of wisdom' (Prov. 9:10), by which he means to assert that true 'wisdom' is true piety or real holiness. Holiness, then, is 'better than rubies,' and all things that are to be desired are not to be compared with it. It is hard to conceive how the inestimable worth and excellency of holiness could be painted in brighter colors than by comparing it to rubies—the richest and most beautiful objects in nature" (N. Emmons).

Not only is true sanctification an important, essential, and unspeakably precious thing, it is wholly supernatural. "It is our duty to enquire into the nature of evangelical holiness, as it is a fruit or effect in us of the Spirit of sanctification, because it is abstruse and mysterious, and undiscernible unto the eye of carnal reason. We say of it in some sense as Job of wisdom, 'whence cometh wisdom, and where is the place of understanding, seeing it is hid from the eyes of all living, and kept close from the fowls of heaven; destruction and death say, We have heard the fame thereof with our ears: God understandeth the way thereof, and He knoweth the place thereof. And unto man He said, Behold, the fear of the Lord that is wisdom, and to depart from evil is understanding' (28:20-23, 28). This is that wisdom whose ways, residence, and paths, are so hidden from the natural reason and understandings of men.

"No man, I say, by mere sight and conduct can know and understand aright the true nature of evangelical holiness; and it is, therefore, no wonder if the doctrine of it be despised by many as an enthusiastic fancy. It is of the things of the Spirit of God, yea, it is the principal effect of all His operation in us and towards us. And 'these things of God knoweth no man but the Spirit of God' (I Cor. 2:11). It is by Him alone that we are enabled to 'know the things that are freely given unto us of God' (v. 12) as this is, if ever we receive anything of Him in this world, or shall do so to eternity. 'Eye hath not seen, nor ear heard, neither have entered into the heart of man, the things that God hath prepared for them that love Him': the comprehension of these things is not the work of any of our natural faculties, but 'God reveals them unto us by His Spirit' (vv. 9, 10).

"Believers themselves are oft-times much unacquainted with it, either as to their apprehension of its true nature, causes, and effects, or, at least, as to their own interests and concernment therein. As we know not of ourselves, the things that are wrought in us of the Spirit of God, so we seldom attend as we ought unto His instruction of us in them. It may seem strange indeed, that, whereas all believers are sanctified and made holy, they should not understand nor apprehend what is wrought in them and for them, and what abideth with them: but, alas, how little do we know of ourselves, of what we are, and whence are our powers and faculties even in things natural. Do we know how the members of the body are fashioned in the womb?" (John Owen)

Clear proof that true sanctification is wholly supernatural and altogether beyond the ken of the unregenerate, is found in the fact that so many are thoroughly deceived and fatally deluded by fleshly imitations and Satanic substitutes of real holiness. It would be outside our present scope to describe in detail the various pretentions which pose as Gospel holiness, but the poor Papists, taught to look up to the "saints" canonized by their "church," are by no means the only ones who are misled in this vital matter. Were it not that God's Word reveals so clearly the power of that darkness which rests on the understanding of all who are not taught by the Spirit, it would be surprising beyond words to see so many intelligent people supposing that holiness consists in abstinence from human comforts, garbing themselves in mean attire, and practicing various austerities which God has never commanded.

Spiritual sanctification can only be rightly apprehended from what God has been pleased to reveal thereon in His holy Word, and can only be experimentally known by the gracious operations of the Holy Spirit. We can arrive at no accurate conceptions of this blessed subject except as our thoughts are formed by the teaching of Scripture, and we can only experience the power of the same as the Inspirer of those Scriptures is pleased to write them upon our hearts. Nor can we obtain so much as a correct idea of the meaning of the term "sanctification" by limiting our attention to a few verses in which the word is found, or even to a whole class of passages of a similar nature: there must be a painstaking examination of every occurrence of the term and also of its cognates; only thus shall we be preserved from the entertaining of a one-sided, inadequate, and misleading view of its fullness and many-sidedness.

Even a superficial examination of the Scriptures will reveal that holiness is the opposite of sin, yet the realization of this at once conducts us into the realm of mystery, for how can persons be sinful and holy at one and the same time? It is this difficulty which so deeply exercises the true saints: they perceive in themselves so much carnality, filth, and vileness, that they find it almost impossible to believe that they are holy. Nor is the difficulty solved here, as it was in justification, by saying, Though we are completely unholy in ourselves, we are holy in Christ. We must not here anticipate the ground which we hope to cover, except to say, the Word of God clearly teaches that those who have been sanctified by God are holy in themselves. The Lord graciously prepare our hearts for what is to follow.

Chapter 2
ITS MEANING

Having dwelt at some length upon the relative or legal change which takes place in the status of God's people at justification, it is fitting that we should now proceed to consider the real and experimental change that takes place in their state, which change is begun at their sanctification and made perfect in glory. Though the justification and the sanctification of the believing sinner may be, and should be, contemplated singly and distinctively, yet they are inseparably connected, God never bestowing the one without the other; in fact we have no way or means whatsoever of knowing the former apart from the latter. In seeking to arrive at the meaning of the second, it will therefore be of help to examine its relation to the first. "These individual companions, sanctification and justification, must not be disjoined: under the law the ablutions and oblations went together, the washings and the sacrifices" (T. Manton).

There are two principal effects that sin produces, which cannot be separated: the filthy defilement it causes, the awful guilt it entails. Thus, salvation from sin necessarily requires both a cleansing and a clearing of the one who is to be saved. Again; there are two things absolutely indispensable in order for any creature to dwell with God in heaven: a valid title to that inheritance, a personal fitness to enjoy such blessedness—the one is given in justification, the other is commenced in sanctification. The inseparability of the two things is brought out in, "In the Lord have I righteousness and strength" (Isa. 45 :24); "but of Him are ye in Christ Jesus, who of God is made unto us wisdom, and righteousness, and sanctification, and redemption" (1 Cor. 1:30); "but ye are washed, but ye are sanctified, but ye are justified" (1 Cor. 6:11); "If we confess our sins, He is faithful and just to forgive us our sins, and to cleanse us from all unrighteousness" (1 John 1:9).

"These blessings walk hand in hand; and never were, never will be, never can be parted. No more than the delicious scent can be separated from the beautiful bloom of the rose or carnation: let the flower be expanded, and the fragrance transpires. Try if you can separate gravity from the stone or heat from the fire. If these bodies and their essential properties, if these causes and their necessary effects, are indissolubly connected, so are our justification and our sanctification" (James Hervey, 1770).

"Like as Adam alone did personally break the first covenant by the all-ruining offence, yet they to whom his guilt is imputed, do thereupon become inherently sinful, through the corruption of nature conveyed to them from him; so Christ alone did perform the condition of the second covenant, and those to whom His righteousness is imputed, do thereupon become inherently righteous, through inherent grace communicated to them from Him by the Spirit. 'For as by one man's offence death reigned by one, much more they which receive the abundance of grace and the gift of righteousness, shall reign in life by one, Jesus Christ' (Rom. 5:17). How did death reign by Adam's offence? Not only in point of guilt, whereby his posterity were bound over to destruction, but also in point of their being dead to all good, dead in trespasses and sins. Therefore the receivers of the gift of righteousness must thereby be brought to reign in life, not only legally in justification, but also morally in sanctification" (T. Boston, 1690).

Though absolutely inseparable, yet these two great blessings of Divine grace are quite distinct. In sanctification something is actually imparted to us, in justification it is only imputed. Justification is based entirely upon the work Christ wrought for us, sanctification is principally a work wrought in us. Justification respects its object in a legal sense and terminates in a relative change—a deliverance from punishment, a right to the reward; sanctification regards its object in a moral sense, and terminates in an experimental change both in character and conduct— imparting a love for God, a capacity to worship Him acceptably, and a meetness for heaven. Justification is by a righteousness without us, sanctification is by a holiness wrought in us. Justification is by Christ as Priest, and has regard to the penalty of sin; sanctification is by Christ as King, and has regard to the dominion of sin: the former cancels its damning power, the latter delivers from its reigning power.

They differ, then, in their order (not of time, but in their nature), justification preceding, sanctification following: the sinner is pardoned and restored to God's favor before the Spirit is given to renew him after His image. They differ in their design: justification removes the obligation unto punishment; sanctification cleanses from pollution. They differ in their form: justification is a judicial act, by which the sinner as pronounced righteous; sanctification is a moral work, by which the sinner is made holy: the one has to do solely with our standing before God, the other chiefly concerns our state. They differ in their cause: the one issuing from the merits of Christ's satisfaction, the other proceeding from the efficacy of the same. They differ in their end: the one bestowing a title to everlasting glory, the other being the highway which conducts us thither. "And an highway shall be there,...and it shall be called The way of holiness" (Isa. 35:8).

The words "holiness" and "sanctification" are used in our English Bible to represent one and the same word in the Hebrew and Greek originals, but they are by no means used with a uniform signification, being employed with quite a varied latitude and scope. Hence it is hardly to be wondered at that theologians have framed so many different definitions of its meaning. Among them we may cite the following, each of which, save the last, having an element of truth in them. "Sanctification is God-likeness, or being renewed after His image." "Holiness is conformity to the law of God, in heart and life. Sanctification is a freedom from the tyranny of sin, into the liberty of righteousness." "Sanctification is that work of the Spirit whereby we are fitted to be worshippers of God." "Holiness is a process of cleansing from the pollution of sin." "It is a moral renovation of our natures whereby they are made more and more like Christ." "Sanctification is the total eradication of the carnal nature, so that sinless perfection is attained in this life."

Another class of writers, held in high repute in certain circles, and whose works now have a wide circulation, have formed a faulty, or at least very inadequate, definition of the word "sanctify," through limiting themselves to a certain class of passages where the term occurs and making deductions from only one set of facts. For example: not a few have cited verse after verse in the O. T. where the world "holy" is applied to inanimate objects, like the vessels of the tabernacle, and then have argued that the term itself cannot possess a moral value. But that is false reasoning: it would be like saying that because we read of the "everlasting hills" (Gen. 49:26) and the "everlasting mountains" (Hab. 3:6) that therefore God cannot be everlasting"—which is the line of logic (?) employed by many of the Universalists so as to set aside the truth of the everlasting punishment of the wicked.

Words must first be used of material objects before we are ready to employ them in a higher and abstract sense. All our ideas are admitted through the medium of the physical senses, and consequently refer in the first place to external objects; but as the intellect develops we apply those names, given to material things, unto those which are immaterial. In the earliest stages of human history, God dealt with His people according to this principle. It is true that God's sanctifying of the sabbath day teaches us that the first meaning of the word is 'to set apart," but to argue from this that the term never has a moral force when it is applied to moral agents is not worthy of being called "reasoning"—it is a mere begging of the question: as well argue that since in a majority of passages "baptism" has reference to the immersion of a person in water, it can never have a mystical or spiritual force and value—which is contradicted by Luke 12:50; 1 Corinthians 12:13.

The outward ceremonies prescribed by God to the Hebrews with regard to their external form of religious service were all designed to teach corresponding inward duties, and to show the obligation unto moral virtues. But so determined are many of our moderns to empty the word "sanctify" of all moral value, they quote such verses as "for their sakes I sanctify Myself" (John 17:19); and inasmuch as there was no sin in the Lord Jesus from which He needed cleansing, have triumphantly concluded that the thought of moral purification cannot enter into the meaning of the word when it is applied to His people. This also is a serious error—what the lawyers would call "special pleading": with just as much reason might we insist that the word "tempt" can never signify to solicit and incline to evil, because it cannot mean that when used of Christ in Matthew 4:1; Hebrews 4:15!

The only satisfactory way of ascertaining the meaning or meanings of the word "sanctify" is to carefully examine every passage in which it is found in Holy Writ, studying its setting, weighing any term with which it is contrasted, observing the objects or persons to which it is applied. This calls for much patience and care, yet only thus do we obey that exhortation "prove all things" (I Thess. 5:21). That this term denotes more than simply "to separate" or "set apart," is clear from Num. 6:8 where it is said of the Nazarite, "all the days of his separation he is holy unto the Lord," for according to some that would merely signify "all the days of his separation he is separated unto the Lord," which would be meaningless tautology. So again, of the Lord Jesus we are told, that He was "holy, harmless, undefiled, separate from sinners" (Heb. 7:26), which shows that "holy" means something more than "separation."

That the word "sanctify" (or "holy"—the same Hebrew or Greek term) is far from being used in a uniform sense is dear from the following passages. In Isaiah 66:17 it is said of certain wicked men, "They that sanctify themselves, and purify themselves in the gardens behind one tree in the midst, eating swine's flesh." In Isaiah 13:3 God said of the Medes, whom He had appointed to overthrow the Babylonian empire, "I have commanded My sanctified ones, I have also called My mighty ones, for Mine anger." When applied to God Himself, the term denotes His ineffable majesty, "Thus saith the high and lofty One that inhabiteth eternity, whose name is Holy" (Isa. 57:15 and cf. Psa. 99:3; Hab. 3:3). It also includes the thought of adorning and equipping: "thou shalt anoint it to sanctify it" (Ex. 29:36 and cf. 40:11); "anoint him to sanctify him" (Lev. 8:12 and cf. v. 30), "If a man purge himself from these, he shall be a vessel unto honor, sanctified and meet for the Master's use" (2 Tim. 2:21).

That the word "holy" or "sanctify" has in many passages a reference to a moral quality is clear from such verses as the following: "Wherefore the law is holy, and the commandment holy and just and good" (Rom. 7:12)—each of those predicates are moral qualities. Among the identifying marks of a scriptural bishop are that he must be "a lover of hospitality, a lover of good men, sober, just, holy, temperate" (Titus 1:8) each of those are moral qualities, and the very connection in which the term "holy" is there found proves conclusively it means much more than an external setting apart. "As ye have yielded your members servants to uncleanness and to iniquity, even so now yield your members servants to righteousness unto holiness" (Rom. 6:19): here the word "holiness" is used antithetically to "uncleanness." So again in 1 Corinthians 7:14, "else were your children unclean, but now are they holy" i.e. martially pure.

That sanctification includes cleansing is clear from many considerations. It may be seen in the types, "Go unto the people, and sanctify them today, and tomorrow, and let them wash their clothes" (Ex. 19:10)—the latter being an emblem of the former. As we have seen in Romans 6:19 and I Corinthians 7:14, it is the opposite of "uncleanness." So also in 2 Timothy 2:2! the servant of God is to purge himself from "the vessels of dishonor" (worldly, fleshly, and apostate preachers and churches) if he is to be "sanctified" and "meet for the Master's use." In Ephesians 5:26 we are told that Christ gave Himself for the Church, "that he might sanctify and cleanse it," and that, in order that He "might present it to Himself a glorious Church, not having spot or wrinkle or any such thing, but (in contrast from such blemishes) that it should be holy" (v. 27). "If the blood of bulls and goats, and the ashes of a heifer sprinkling the unclean, sanctifieth to the purifying of the flesh" (Heb. 9:13): what could be plainer!—ceremonial sanctification under the law was secured by a process of purification or cleansing.

"Purification is the first proper notion of internal real sanctification. To be unclean absolutely, and to be holy, are universally opposed. Not to be purged from sin, is an expression of an unholy person, as to be cleansed is of him that is holy. This purification is ascribed unto all the causes and means of sanctification. Not that sanctification consists wholly herein, but firstly and necessarily it is required thereunto: 'I will sprinkle clean water upon you, and ye shall be clean; from all your filthiness and from all your idols will I cleanse you!' (Ezek. 36:25). That this sprinkling of clean water upon us, is the communication of the Spirit unto us for the end designed, I have before evinced. It hath also been declared wherefore He is called 'water' or compared thereunto. The next verse shows expressly that it is the Spirit of God which is intended: 'I will put My Spirit within you, and cause you to walk in My Statutes.' And that which He is thus in the first place promised for, is the cleansing of us from the pollution of sin, which in order of nature, is proposed unto His enabling us to walk in God's statutes (John Owen).

To sanctify, then, means in the great majority of instances, to appoint, dedicate or set apart unto God, for a holy and special use. Yet that act of separation is not a bare change of situation, so to speak, but is preceded or accompanied by a work which (ceremonially or experimentally) fits the person for God. Thus the priests in their sanctification (Lev. 8) were sanctified by washing in water (type of regeneration: Titus 3:5), having the blood applied to their persons (type of justification: Rom. 5:9), and being anointed with oil (type of receiving the Holy Spirit: 1 John 2:20, 27). As the term is applied to Christians it is used to designate three things, or three parts of one whole: first, the process of setting them apart unto God or constituting them holy: Hebrews 13:12; 2 Thessalonians 2:13. Second, the state or condition of holy separation into which they are brought: I Corinthians 1:2; Ephesians 4:24. Third, the personal sanctity or holy living which proceeds from the state: Luke 1:75; 1 Peter 1:15.

To revert again to the 0. T. types—which are generally the best interpreters of the doctrinal statements of the N. T., providing we carefully bear in mind that the antitype is always of a higher order and superior nature to what prefigured it, as the substance must excel the shadow, the inward and spiritual surpassing the merely outward and ceremonial. "Sanctify unto Me all the firstborn . . . it is Mine" (Ex. 13:2). This comes immediately after the deliverance of the firstborn by the blood of the paschal lamb in the preceding chapter: first justification, and then sanctification as the complementary parts of one whole. "Ye shall therefore put difference between clean beasts and unclean, and between unclean fowls and clean: and ye shall not make your souls abominable by beast, or by fowl, or by any manner of living thing that creepeth on the ground, which I have separated from you as unclean. And ye shall be holy unto Me: for I the Lord am holy, and have severed you from other people, that ye should be Mine" (Lev. 20:25, 26). Here we see there was a separation from all that is unclean, with an unreserved and exclusive devotement to the Lord.

Chapter 3
ITS NECESSITY

It is our earnest desire to write this article not in a theological or merely abstract way, but in a practical manner: in such a strain that it may please the Lord to speak through it to our needy hearts and search our torpid consciences. It is a most important branch of our subject, yet one from which we are prone to shrink, being very unpalatable to the flesh. Having been shapen in iniquity and conceived in sin (Ps. 51:5), our hearts naturally hate holiness, being opposed to any experimental acquaintance with the same. As the Lord Jesus told the religious leaders of His day, "This is the condemnation, that light is come into the world, and men loved darkness rather than light" (John 3:19), which may justly be paraphrased "men loved sin rather than holiness," for in Scripture "darkness" is the emblem of sin the Evil one being denominated "the power of darkness"— as "light" is the emblem of the ineffably Holy One (1 John 1:5).

But though by nature man is opposed to the Light, it is written, "Follow peace with all, and holiness, without which no man shall see the Lord" (Heb. 12:14). To the same effect the Lord Jesus declared "Blessed are the pure in heart, for they shall see God" (Matt. 5:8). God will not call unto nearness with Himself those who are carnal and corrupt. "Can two walk together except they be agreed?" (Amos 3:3): what concord can there be between an unholy soul and the thrice holy God? Our God is "glorious in holiness" (Ex. 15:11), and therefore those whom He separates unto Himself must be suited to Himself, and be made "partakers of His holiness" (Heb. 12:10). The whole of His ways with man exhibit this principle, and His Word continually proclaims that He is "not a God that hath pleasure in wickedness, neither shall evil dwell with Him" (Ps. 5:4).

By our fall in Adam we lost not only the favor of God, but also the purity of our natures, and therefore we need to be both reconciled to God and sanctified in our inner man. There is now a spiritual leprosy spread over all our nature which makes us loathsome to God and puts us into a state of separation from Him. No matter what pains the sinner takes to be rid of his horrible disease, he does but hide and not cleanse it. Adam concealed neither his nakedness nor the shame of it by his fig-leaf contrivance; so those who have no other covering for their natural filthiness than the externals of religion rather proclaim than hide it. Make no mistake on this score: neither the outward profession of Christianity nor the doing of a few good works will give us access to the thrice Holy One. Unless we are washed by the Holy Spirit, and in the blood of Christ, from our native pollutions, we cannot enter the kingdom of glory.

Alas, with what forms of godliness, outward appearances, external embellishments are most people satisfied. How they mistake the shadows for the substance, the means for the end itself. How many devout Laodiceans are there who know not that they are "wretched and miserable, and poor and blind, and naked" (Rev. 3 :17). No preaching affects them, nothing will bring them to exclaim with the prophet, "0 my God, I am ashamed, and blush to lift up my face to Thee my God" (Ezra 9:6). No, if they do but preserve themselves from the known guilt of such sins as are punishable among men, to all other things their conscience seems dead: they have no inward shame for anything between their souls and God, especially not for the depravity and defilement of their natures: of that they know, feel, bewail nothing.

"There is a generation that are pure in their own eyes, and yet is not washed from their filthiness" (Prov. 30:12). Although they had never been cleansed by the Holy Spirit, nor their hearts purified by faith, (Acts 15:9), yet they esteemed themselves to be pure, and had not the least sense of their foul defilement. Such a generation were the self-righteous Pharisees of Christ's day: they were constantly cleansing their hands and cups, engaged in an interminable round of ceremonial washings, yet were they thoroughly ignorant of the fact that within they were filled with all manner of defilement (Matt. 23:25-28). So is a generation of churchgoers today; they are orthodox in their views, reverent in their demeanor, regular in their contributions, but they make no conscience of the state of their hearts.

That sanctification or personal holiness which we here desire to show the absolute necessity of, lies in or consists of three things. First, that internal change or renovation of our souls, whereby our minds, affections and wills are brought into harmony with God. Second, that impartial compliance with the revealed will of God in all duties of obedience and abstinence from evil, issuing from a principle of faith and love. Third, that directing of all our actions unto the glory of God, by Jesus Christ, according to the Gospel. This, and nothing short of this, is evangelical and saving sanctification. The heart must be changed so as to be brought into conformity with God's nature and will: its motives, desires, thoughts and actions require to be purified. There must be a spirit of holiness working within so as to sanctify our outward performances if they are to be acceptable unto Him in whom "there is no darkness at all."

Evangelical holiness consists not only in external works of piety and charity, but in pure thoughts, impulses and affections of the soul, chiefly in that disinterested love from which all good works must flow if they are to receive the approbation of Heaven. Not only must there be an abstinence from the execution of sinful lusts, but there must be a loving and delighting to do the will of God in a cheerful manner, obeying Him without repining or grudging against any duty, as if it were a grievous; yoke to be borne. Evangelical sanctification is that holiness of heart which causes us to love God supremely, so as to yield ourselves wholly up to His constant service in all things, and to His disposal of us as our absolute Lord, whether it be for prosperity or adversity, for life or death; and to love our neighbors as ourselves.

This entire sanctification of our whole inner and outer man is absolutely indispensable. As there must be a change of state before there can be of life—"make the tree good, and his fruit (will be) good" (Matt. 12:33)—so there must be sanctification before there can be glorification. Unless we are purged from the pollution of sin, we can never be fit for communion with God. "And there shall in no wise enter into it (the eternal dwelling place of God and His people) anything that defileth, neither whatsoever worketh abomination" (Rev. 21:27). "To suppose that an unpurged sinner can be brought into the blessed enjoyment of God, is to overthrow both the law and the Gospel, and to say that Christ died in vain" (J. Owen, Vol. 2: p. 511). Personal holiness is equally imperative as is the forgiveness of sins in order to eternal bliss.

Plain and convincing as should be the above statements, there is a class of professing Christians who wish to regard the justification of the believer as constituting almost the whole of his salvation, instead of its being only one aspect thereof. Such people delight to dwell upon the imputed righteousness of Christ, but they evince little or no concern about personal holiness. On the other hand, there are not a few who in their reaction from a one sided emphasis upon justification by grace through faith alone, have gone to the opposite extreme, making sanctification the sum and substance of all their thinking and preaching. Let it be solemnly realized that while a man may learn thoroughly the scriptural doctrine of justification and yet not be himself justified before God, so he may be able to detect the crudities and errors of "the Holiness people," and yet be completely unsanctified himself. But it is chiefly the first of these two errors we now desire to expose, and we cannot do better than quote at length from one who has most helpfully dealt with it.

"We are to look upon holiness as a very necessary part of that salvation that is received by faith in Christ. Some are so drenched in a covenant of works, that they accuse us for making good works needless to salvation, if we will not acknowledge them to be necessary, either as conditions to procure an interest in Christ, or as preparatives to fit us for receiving Him by faith. And others, when they are taught by the Scriptures that we are saved by faith, even by faith without works, do begin to disregard all obedience to the law as not at all necessary to salvation, and do account themselves obliged to it only in point of gratitude; if it be wholly neglected, they doubt not but free grace will save them nevertheless. Yea, some are given up to such strong Antinomian delusions, that they account it a part of the liberty from bondage of the law purchased by the blood of Christ, to make no conscience of breaking the law in their conduct.

"One cause of these errors that are so contrary one to the other is that many are prone to imagine nothing else to be meant by 'salvation' but to be delivered from Hell, and to enjoy heavenly happiness and glory; hence they conclude that, if good works be a means of glorification, and precedent to it, they must also be a precedent means of our whole salvation, and if they be not a necessary means of our whole salvation, they are not at all necessary to glorification. But though 'salvation' be often taken in Scripture by way of eminency for its perfection in the state of heavenly glory, yet, according to its full and proper signification, we are to understand by it all that freedom from the evil of our natural corrupt state, and all those holy and happy enjoyments that we receive from Christ our Savior, either in this world by faith, or in the world to come by glorification. Thus, justification, the gift of the Spirit to dwell in us, the privilege of adoption (deliverance from the reigning power of indwelling sin. A. W. P.) are parts of our 'salvation' which we partake of in this life. Thus also, the conformity of our hearts to the law of God, and the fruits of righteousness with which we are filled by Jesus Christ in this life, are a necessary part of our 'salvation.'

"God saveth us from our sinful uncleanness here, by the washing of regeneration and renewing of the Holy Spirit (Ezek. 36:29; Titus 3:5), as well as from Hell hereafter. Christ was called Jesus, i.e., a Savior: because He saves His people from their sins (Matt 1:21). Therefore, deliverance from our sins is part of our 'salvation,' which is begun in this life by justification and sanctification, and perfected by glorification in the life to come. Can we rationally doubt whether it be any proper pert of our salvation by Christ to be quickened, so as to be enabled to live to God, when we were by nature dead in trespasses and sins, and to have the image of God in holiness and righteousness restored to us, which we lost by the fall; and to be freed from a vile dishonorable slavery to Satan and our own lusts, and made the servants of God; and to be honored so highly as to walk by the Spirit, and bring forth the fruits of the Spirit? and what is all this but holiness in heart and life?

"Conclude we, then, that holiness in this life is absolutely necessary to salvation, not only as a means to the end, but by a nobler kind of necessity—as part of the end itself. Though we are not saved by good works as Procuring causes, yet we are saved to good works, as fruits and effects of saving grace, 'which God hath prepared that we should walk in them' (Eph. 2:10). It is, indeed, one part of our salvation to be delivered from the bondage of the covenant of works; but the end of this is, not that we may have liberty to sin (which is the worst of slavery) but that we may fulfill the royal law of liberty, and that 'we may serve in newness of spirit, and not in the oldness of the letter' (Gal. 5:13; Rom. 7:6). Yea, holiness in this life is such a part of our 'salvation' that it is a necessary means to make us meet to be partakers of the inheritance of the saints in heavenly light and glory: for without holiness we can never see God (Heb. 12:14), and are as unfit for His glorious presence as swine for the presence-chamber of an earthly king.

"The last thing to be noted in this direction is that holiness of heart and life is to be sought for earnestly by faith as a very necessary part of our 'salvation.' Great multitudes of ignorant people that live under the Gospel, harden their hearts in sin and ruin their souls forever, by trusting on Christ for such an imaginary 'salvation' as consisteth not at all in holiness, but only in forgiveness of sin and deliverance from everlasting torments. They would be free from the Punishments due to sin, but they love their lusts so well that they hate holiness and desire not to be saved from the service of sin. The way to oppose this pernicious delusion is not to deny, as some do, that trusting on Christ for salvation is a saving act of faith, but rather to show that none do or can trust on Christ for true 'salvation' except they trust on Him for holiness, neither do they heartily desire true salvation, if they do not desire to be made holy and righteous in their hearts and lives. If ever God and Christ gave you 'salvation', holiness will be one part of it; if Christ wash you not from the filth of your sins, you have no part with Him (John 13:8).

"What a strange kind of salvation do they desire that care not for holiness! They would be saved and yet be altogether dead in sin, aliens from the life of God, bereft of the image of God, deformed by the image of Satan, his slaves and vassals to their own filthy lusts, utterly unmeet for the enjoyment of God in glory. Such a salvation as that was never purchased by the blood of Christ; and those that seek it abuse the grace of God in Christ, and turn it into lasciviousness. They would be saved by Christ, and yet be out of Christ in a fleshly state; whereas God doth free none from condemnation but those that are in Christ, that walk not after the flesh, but after the Spirit; or else they would divide Christ, and take a part of His salvation and leave out the rest; but Christ is not divided (1 Cor. 1:13). They would have their sins forgiven, not that they may walk with God in love, in time to come, but that they may practice their enmity against Him without any fear of punishment. But let them not be deceived, God is not mocked. They understand not what true salvation is, neither were they ever yet thoroughly sensible of their lost estate, and of the great evil of sin; and that which they trust on Christ for is but an imagination of their own brains; and therefore their trusting is gross presumption.

"The Gospel-faith maketh us to come to Christ with a thirsty appetite that we may drink of living water, even of His sanctifying Spirit (John 7:37, 38), and cry out earnestly to Him to save us, not only from Hell, but from sin, saying, 'Teach us to do Thy will; Thy Spirit is good' (Ps. 143:10); 'Turn Thou me, and I shall be turned' (Jer. 31:18); 'Create in me a clean heart, O God, and renew a right spirit within me' (Ps. 51:10). This is the way whereby the doctrine of salvation by grace doth necessitate us to holiness of life, by constraining us to seek for it by faith in Christ, as a substantial part of that 'salvation' which is freely given to us through Christ" (Walter Marshall, 1692).

The above is a much longer quotation than we usually make from others, but we could not abbreviate without losing much of its force. We have given it, not only because it is one of the clearest and strongest statements we have met with, but because it will indicate that the doctrine we are advancing is no novel One of our own, but one which was much insisted upon by the Puritans. Alas, that so few today have any real scriptural apprehension of what Salvation really is; alas that many preachers are substituting an imaginary 'salvation' which is fatally deceiving the great majority of their hearers. Make no mistake upon this point, dear reader, we beg you: if your heart is yet unsanctified, you are still unsaved; and if you pant not after personal holiness, then you are without any real desire for God's salvation.

The Salvation which Christ purchased for His people includes both justification and sanctification. The Lord Jesus saves not only from the guilt and penalty of sin, but from the power and pollution of it. Where there is a genuine longing to be freed from the love of sin, there is a true desire for His salvation; but where there is no practical deliverance from the service of sin, then we are strangers to His saving grace. Christ came here to "Perform the mercy promised to our fathers, and to remember His holy covenant: the oath which He swore to our father Abraham; that He would grant unto us, that we being delivered out of the hand of our enemies might serve Him without fear, in holiness and righteousness before Him all the days of our life" (Luke 1:72-75). It is by this we are to test or measure ourselves: are we serving Him "in holiness and righteousness?" If we are not, we have not been sanctified; and if we are unsanctified, we are none of His.

Chapter 4
ITS NECESSITY
(COMPLETED)

In the first part of our treatment of the necessity of sanctification it was shown that, the making of a sinner holy is indispensable unto his salvation, yea, that sanctification is an integral part of salvation itself. One of the most serious defects in modern ministry is the ignoring of this basic fact. Of only too many present-day "converts" does it have to be said, "Ephraim is a cake not turned" (Hos. 7:8)—browned underneath, unbaked on the top. Christ is set forth as a fire-escape from Hell, but not as the great Physician to deal with the malady of indwelling sin, and to fit for Heaven. Much is said upon how to obtain forgiveness of sins, but little is preached on how to be cleansed from its pollutions. The necessity for His atoning blood is set forth, but not the indispensability of experimental holiness. Consequently, thousands who mentally assent to the sufficiency of Christ's sacrifice, know nothing about heart purity.

Again; there is a woeful disproportion between the place which is given to faith and the emphasis which the Scriptures give to that obedience which flows from sanctification. It is not only true that "without faith it is impossible to please God" (Heb. 11:6), but it is equally true that without holiness "no man shall see the Lord" (Heb. 12:14). Not only are we told "in Christ Jesus neither circumcision availeth anything, nor uncircumcision, but a new creation" (Gal. 6:15), but it is also written, "Circumcision is nothing, and uncircumcision is nothing, but the keeping of the commandments of God" (1 Cor. 7:19). It is not for nothing that God has told us, "Godliness is profitable unto all things, having promise of the life that now it, and of that which is to come" (1 Tim. 4:8). Not only is there in all the promises a particular respect unto personal, vital, and practical "godliness," but it is that very godliness which, pre-eminently, gives the saint an especial interest in those promises.

Alas, how many there are today who imagine that if they have "faith ,"it is sure to be well with them at the end, even though they are not holy. Under the pretense of honoring faith, Satan, as an angel of light, has deceived, and is still deceiving, multitudes of souls. But when their "faith" be examined and tested, what is it worth? Nothing at all so far as insuring an entrance into Heaven is concerned: it is a power-less, lifeless, and fruitless thing; it is nothing better than that faith which the demons have (James 2:19). The faith of God's elect is unto "the acknowledgement of the truth which is after godliness" (Titus i :i). Saving faith is a "most holy faith" (Jude 20): it is a faith which "purifieth the heart" (Acts 15:9), it is a faith which "worketh by love" (Gal. 5:6), it is a faith which "overcometh the world" (1 John 5:4), it is a faith which bringeth forth all manner of good works (Heb. 11). Let us now enter into detail, and show more specifically wherein lies the necessity for personal holiness.

Our Personal holiness is required by the very nature of God. Holiness is the excellence and honor of the Divine character. God is called "rich in mercy" (Eph. 2:4), but "glorious in holiness" (Ex. 15':II) : His mercy is His treasure, but holiness is His glory. He swears by this perfection: "Once have I sworn by My holiness" (Psa. 89:35). Over thirty times is He called "The Holy One of

Israel." This is the superlative perfection for which the angels in Heaven and the spirits of just men made perfect do so much admire God, crying "Holy, holy, holy" (1 Sa. 6:3; Rev. 4:8). As gold, because it is the most excellent of the metals, is laid over inferior ones, so this Divine excellency is laid upon all connected with Him: His sabbath is "holy" (Ex. 16:33), His sanctuary is "holy" (Ex. 15:13), His name is "holy" (Psa. 99:3), all His works are "holy" (Ps. 145:17). Holiness is the perfection of all His glorious attributes: His power is holy power, His mercy is holy mercy, His wisdom is holy wisdom. \

Now the ineffable purity of the Divine nature is everywhere in the Scriptures made the fundamental reason for the necessity of holiness in us. God makes the holiness of His own nature the ground of His demand for holiness in His people: "For I am the Lord your God: ye shall therefore sanctify yourselves, and ye shall be holy, for I am holy" (Lev. 11:4). The same fundamental principle is transferred to the Gospel, "But as He which hath called you is holy, so be ye holy in all manner of behavior; because it is written, Be ye holy, for I am holy" (1 Pet. 1 :15, 16). Thus God plainly lets us know that His nature is such as, unless we be sanctified, there can be no intercourse between Him and us. "For I am the Lord that bringeth you up out of the land of Egypt, to be your God: ye shall therefore be holy, for I am holy" (Lev. 11:45). Without personal holiness the relationship cannot be maintained that He should be our God and we should be His people.

God is "of purer eyes than to behold evil, and canst not look on iniquity" (Hab. 1:13). Such is the infinite purity of His nature, that God cannot take any pleasure in lawless rebels, filthy sinners, the workers of iniquity. Joshua told the people plainly that if they continued in their sins, they could not serve the Lord, "for He is a holy God" (Joshua 24:19). All the service of unholy people toward such a God is utterly lost and thrown away, because it is 'entirely inconsistent with His nature to accept of it. The apostle Paul reasons in the same manner when he says, "Let us have grace whereby we may serve God acceptably with reverence and godly fear: for our God is a consuming fire" (Heb. 12:28,29). He lays his argument for the necessity of grace and holiness in the worship of God from the consideration of the holiness of His nature, which, as a consuming fire will devour that which is unsuited unto and inconsistent with it.

He who resolveth not to be holy must seek another god to worship and serve, for with the God of Scripture he will never find acceptance. The heathen of old realized this, and liking Dot to retain the knowledge of the true God in their hearts and minds (Rom. 1:28), and resolving to give up themselves unto all filthiness with greediness, they stifled their notions of the Divine Being and invented such "gods" to themselves, as were unclean and wicked, that they might freely conform unto and serve them with satisfaction. God Himself declares that men of corrupt lives have some secret hopes that He is not holy: "Thou thoughtest that I was altogether such an one as thyself: but I will reprove thee" (Psa. 50:21). Others, today, while professing to believe in God's holiness, have such false ideas of His grace and mercy that they suppose He will accept them though they are unholy.

"Be ye holy, for I am holy." Why? Because herein consists our conformity to God. We were originally created in the image and likeness of God, and that, for the substance of it, was holiness—therein consisted the privilege, blessedness, preeminence of man over all the lower creatures. Wherefore, without this conformity unto God, with the impress of His image and likeness upon the soul, we cannot stand in that relation unto God which was designed us in our creation. This we lost by the entrance of sin, and if there be not a way for us to acquire it again, we shall forever come short of the glory of God and the end of our creation. Now this is done by our be-coming holy, for therein consists the renovation of God's image in us (Eph. 4:22-24 and cf. Col. 3:10). It is utterly vain for any man to expect an interest in God, while he does not earnestly endeavor after conformity to Him.

To be sanctified is just as requisite as to be justified. He that thinks to come to enjoyment of God without holiness, makes Him an unholy God, and puts the highest indignity imaginable upon Him. There is no other alternative: we must either leave our sins, or our God. We may as easily reconcile Heaven and Hell, as easily take away all difference between light and darkness, good and evil, as procure acceptance for unholy persons with God. While it be true that our interest in God is not built upon our holiness, it is equally true that we have none without it. Many have greatly erred in concluding that, because piety and obedience are not meritorious, they can get to Heaven without them. The free grace of God towards sinners by Jesus Christ by no means renders holiness needless and useless. Christ is not the minister of sin, but the Main-tamer of God's glory. He has not purchased for His people security in sin, but salvation from sin.

According to our growth in likeness unto God are our approaches unto glory. Each day both writer and reader is drawing nearer the end of his earthly course, [A. W. Pink finished his earthy course on July 15, 1952] and we do greatly deceive ourselves if we imagine that we are drawing nearer to Heaven, while following those courses which lead only to Hell. We are woefully deluded if we suppose that we are journeying towards glory, and yet are not growing in grace. The believer's glory, subjectively considered, will be his likeness to Christ (1 John 3:2), and it is the very height of folly for any to think that they shall love hereafter what now they hate. There is no other way of growing in the likeness of God but in holiness: thereby alone are we "changed into the same image from glory to glory" (2 Cor. 3:18)—that is, from one degree of glorious grace to another, until by one last great change shall issue all grace and holiness in eternal glory.

But is not God ready to pardon and receive the greatest and vilest sinner who comes unto Him by Christ? Is not His mercy so great and His grace so free that He will do so apart from any consideration of worth or righteousness of their own? If so, why insist so much on the indispensability of holiness? This objection, though thousands of years old, is still made. If men must be holy, then carnal reasoners can see no need of grace: and they cannot see how God is gracious if men perish because they are unholy. Nothing seems more reasonable to carnal minds than that we may live in sin because grace has abounded. This is met by the apostle in Rom. 6:1, where he subjoins the reasons why, notwithstanding the superaboundings of grace in Christ, there is an indispensable necessity why all believers should be holy. Without the necessity of holiness in us, grace would be disgraced. Note how when He proclaimed His name "gracious and merciful," the Lord at once added, "and will by no means clear the guilty" i.e. those who go on in their sins without regard unto obedience.

2. Our personal holiness is required by the commands of God. Not only is this so under the covenant of works, but the same is inseparably annexed under the covenant of grace. No relaxation unto the duty of holiness is granted by the Gospel, nor any indulgence unto the least sin. The Gospel is no less holy than the Law, for both proceeded from the Holy One; and though provision be made for the pardon of a multitude of sins and for the acceptance of the Christian's imperfect obedience, yet the standard of righteousness is not lowered, for there is no abatement given by the Gospel unto any duty of holiness nor any license unto the least sin. The difference between those covenants is twofold: under that of works, all the duties of holiness were required as our righteousness before God, that we might be justified thereby (Rom 10:5)—not so under grace; no allowance was made for the least degree of failure (James 2:10)—but, now, through the mediation of Christ, justice and mercy are joined together.

Under the Gospel commands for universal holiness, respect is required unto three things. First, unto the authority of Him who gives them. Authority is that which obligates unto obedience: see Mal. 1:6. Now He who commands us to be holy is our sovereign Lawgiver, with absolute right to prescribe that which He pleases, and therefore a non-compliance is a despising of the

Divine Legislator. To be under God's command to be holy, and then not to sincerely and earnestly endeavor always and in all things so to be, is to reject His sovereign authority over us, and to live in defiance of Him. No better than that is the state of every one who does not make the pursuit of holiness his daily and chief concern. Forgetfulness of this, or failure to heed it as we ought, is the chief reason of our careless walking. Our great safeguard is to keep our hearts and minds under a sense of the sovereign authority of God in his commands.

Second, we must keep before our minds the power of Him who commands us to be holy. "There is one Lawgiver who is able to save and to destroy" (James 4:12). God's commanding authority is accompanied with such power that He will eternally reward the obedient and eternally punish the disobedient. The commands of God are accompanied with promises of eternal bliss on the one hand, and of eternal misery on the other; and this will most certainly befall us according as we shall be found holy or unholy. Herein is to be seen a further reason for the indispensable necessity of our being holy: if we are not, then a holy and all-powerful God will damn us. A due respect unto God's promises and threatenings is a principal liart of spiritual liberty: "I am the almighty God: walk before Me, and be thou perfect" (Gen. 17:1): the way to walk up-rightly is to ever bear in mind that He who requires it of us is Almighty God, under whose eyes we are continually. If, then, we value our souls, let us seek grace to act accordingly.

Third, respect is to be had unto the infinite wisdom and goodness of God. In His commands God not only maintains His sovereign authority over us, but also exhibits His righteousness and love. His commands are not the arbitrary edicts of a capricious despot, but the wise decrees of One who has our good at heart. His commands "are not grievous" (1 John 5:3): they are not tyrannical restraints- of our liberty, but are just, wholesome, and highly beneficial. It is to our great ad-vantage to comply with them; it is for our happiness, both now and hereafter, that we obey them. They are a heavy bur-den only unto those who desire to be the slaves of sin and Satan: they are easy and pleasant unto all who walk with God. Love for God carries with it a desire to please Him, and from Christ may be obtained that grace which will assist us thereto— but of this, more later, D. V.

Our personal holiness is required by the Mediation of Christ. One principal end of the design of God in sending His Son into the world was to recover us unto that state of holiness which we had lost: "For this purpose the Son of God was manifested, that He might destroy the works of the Devil" (1 John 3:8). Among the principal of the works of the Devil was the infecting of our natures and persons with a principle of sin and enmity against God, and that evil work is not destroyed but by the introduction of a principle of holiness and obedience. The image of God in us was defaced by sin; the restoration of that image was one of the main purposes of Christ's mediation. Christ's great and ultimate design was to living His people unto the enjoyment of God to His eternal glory, and this can only be by grace and holiness, by which we Ire made "meet for the inheritance of the saints in light."

Now the exercise of Christ's mediation is discharged under His threefold office. As to His priestly, the immediate effects Were the making of satisfaction and reconciliation, but the mediate effects are our justification and sanctification: "Who gave Himself for us, that He might redeem us from all iniquity, and purify unto Himself a peculiar people, zealous of good works" (Titus 2:14)— no unholy people, then, have any sure evidence of an interest in Christ's sacrifice. As to His prophetic office, this consists in His revelation to us of God's love and will: to make God known and to bring us into subjection unto Him. At the very beginning of His prophetic ministry we find Christ restoring the Law to its original purity—purging it from the corruptions of the Jews: Matt. 5. As to His kingly office, He subdues our lusts and supplies power for obedience. It is by these things we are to test ourselves. To live in known and allowed sin, and yet expect to be saved by

Christ is the master deception of Satan.

From which of Christ's offices do I expect advantage? Is it from His priestly? Then has His blood cleansed me? Have I been made holy thereby? Have I been redeemed out of the world by it? Am I by it dedicated to God and His service? Is it from His prophetic office? Then have I effectually learned of Him to "deny ungodliness and worldly lusts, and to live soberly, righteously, and godly in this present world?" (Titus 2:12). Has He instructed me unto sincerity in all my ways, in all my dealings with God and men? Is it from His Kingly office? Then does He actually rule in me and over me? Has He delivered me from the power of Satan and caused me to take His yoke upon me? Has His scepter broken the dominion of sin in me? Am I a loyal subject of His kingdom? If not, I have no rightful claim to a personal interest in His sacrifice. Christ died to procure holiness, not to secure an indulgence for unholiness.

Our personal holiness is required in order to the glory of Christ. If we are indeed His disciples, He has bought us with a price, and we are "not our own," but His, and that to glorify Him in soul and body because they are His: 1 Cor. 6:19, 20. He died for us that we should not henceforth live unto ourselves, but unto Him who redeemed us at such fearful cost. How, then, are we to do this? In our holiness consists the principal part of that revenue of honor which the Lord Jesus requires and expects from His disciples in this world. Nothing glorifies Him so much as our obedience; nothing is a greater grief and reproach to Him than our disobedience. We are to witness before the world unto the holiness of His life, the heavenliness of His doctrine, the preciousness of His death, by a daily walk which "shows forth HIS praises" (1 Peter 2:9). This is absolutely necessary if we are to glorify Him in this scene of His rejection.

Nothing short of the life of Christ is our example: this is what the Christian is called to "follow." It is the life of Christ which it is his duty to express in his own, and he who takes up Christianity on any other terms woefully deceives his soul. No more effectual reproach can be cast upon the blessed name of the Lord Jesus than for His professing people to follow the lusts of the flesh, be conformed to this world, and heed the behests of Satan. We can only bear witness for the Savior as we make His doctrine our rule, His glory our concern, His example our practice. Christ is honored not by wordy expressions, but by a holy conversation. Nothing has done more to bring the Gospel of Christ into reproach than the wicked lives of those who bear His name. If I am not living a holy and obedient life this shows that I am not "for" Christ, but against Him. (N. B. Much in this article is a condensation of John Owen on the same subject, Vol. 3, of his works.)

Chapter 5
ITS PROBLEMS

It should hardly be necessary for us to explain that when speaking of the problem of sanctification we refer not to such as unto God, but rather as it appears unto our feeble perceptions. But in these days it is not wise to take anything for granted, for not only are there some ready to make a man an offender for a word, if he fails to express himself to their satisfaction, but there are others who need to have the simplest terms defined unto them. No, it would be blasphemy to affirm that sanctification, or anything else, ever presented any problem to the great Jehovah: Omniscience can never be confronted with any difficulty, still less an emergency. But to the Christian's finite under-standing, deranged as it has been by sin, the problem of Holiness is a very real and actual one; far more perplexing, we may add, than that presented by the subject of justification.

There are various subsidiary difficulties in sanctification, as we intimated in the fourth and fifth paragraphs of the Introductory article, such as whether sanctification itself be a quality or a position, whether it be legal or experimental, whether it be absolute or progressive; all of which need to be cleared up in any satisfactory treatment of this theme. But far more intricate is the problem itself of how one who is a moral leper can be fit to worship in the Sanctuary of God. Strange to say this problem is the acutest unto those who are the most spiritual. Self-righteous Pharisees and self-satisfied Laodiceans are in no wise troubled over the matter. Antinomians cut the knot (instead of untying it) and deny all difficulty, by asserting that the holiness of Christ is imputed to us. But those who realize God requires personal holiness, yet are conscious of their own filthiness, are deeply concerned thereupon.

Things are now, generally, at such a low ebb, that some of our readers may be surprised to find us making any reference at all to the problem of sanctification. In most places, today, either the doctrine taught is so inadequate and powerless, or the practice maintained is so defective, that few are likely to be exercised in conscience over the nature of that holiness without which none shall see the Lord. The claims of God are now so whittled down, the exalted standard which Scripture sets forth is so disregarded, heart purity (in which vital godliness so largely consists) is so little emphasized, that it is rare to find any concerned about their personal state. If there be some preachers zealously warning against the worthlessness of good works to save where there be no faith in Christ, there are far more who earnestly cry up an empty faith, which is unaccompanied by personal holiness and obedience.

Such a low standard of spiritual living now prevails, that comparatively few of the Lord's own people have any clear or disturbing conceptions of how far, far short they come of measuring up to the holy model which God has set before us in His Word. Such feeble and faulty ideals of Christian living now prevail that those who are preserved from the grosser evils which even the world condemns, are "at ease in Zion." So little is the fear of God upon souls, so faintly are the majority of professing Christians conscious of the plague of their own hearts, that in most quarters to speak about the problem of sanctification, would be talking in an unknown tongue. A fearful miasma has settled down upon nine-tenths of Christendom, deadening the senses, blunting spiritual perceptions, paralyzing endeavor after deeper personal piety, till almost anything is regarded as being acceptable unto God.

On the other hand, there is no doubt that some of us have intensified the problem, by creating for ourselves additional and needless difficulties, through erroneous ideas of what sanctification is or what it involves in this life. The writer has been personally acquainted with more than one who was in abject despair through failing—after the most earnest and resolute efforts—to attain unto a state which false teachers had told them was attainable in this life, and who terminated their mortal wretchedness by committing suicide; and it has long been a wonder to him that thousands more who heed such teachers do not act likewise. There is no need to multiply difficulties: scriptural sanctification is neither the eradication of sin, the purification of the carnal nature, nor even the partial putting to sleep of the "flesh"; still less does it secure an exemption from the attacks and harassments of Satan.

Yet, on the other side, we must not minimize the problem, and reduce it to such simple proportions that we suppose a complete solution thereto is provided by merely affirming that Christ is our sanctification, and in himself the believing sinner remains unchanged to the end of his earthly course. If we die unholy in ourselves, then we are most assuredly lost for eternity, for only the "pure in heart" shall ever see God (Matt. 5:8). What that purity of heart is, and how it is to be obtained, is the very real problem which sanctification raises. It is at the heart God looks (1 Sam. 16:7), and it is with the heart we need to be most concerned, for "out of it are the issues of life" (Prov. 4:23). The severest woes were pronounced by Christ upon men not because their external conduct was foul, but because within they were "full of dead bones, and all uncleanness" (Matt. 23:27).

That personal holiness is absolutely essential for an entrance into Heaven was shown at length in our last chapter, and that what men regard as the lesser pollutions of sin just as effectually exclude from the kingdom of God as do the most heinous crimes, is clear from 1 Cor. 6:9, 10. The question which forces itself upon us is, How shall men be sanctified so as to suit an infinitely pure God? That we must be justified before we can stand before a righteous God is no more obvious than that it is necessary that we must be sanctified so as to live in the presence of a holy God. But man is utterly without holiness; yea, he is impure, foul, filthy. The testimony of Scripture on this point is plain and full. "They are corrupt, they have done abominable works, there is none that doeth good. The Lord looked down from haven upon the children of men, to see if there were any that did understand, and seek God. They are all gone aside, they are all together become filthy" (Ps. 14:1-3).

The testimony of Scripture is that all men are vile and polluted; that they are, root and branch, source and stream, heart and life, not only disobedient, but unholy, and therefore unfit for God's presence. The Lord Jesus who knew what was in man, makes this clear enough when, revealing with His own light that loathsome den, the human heart, He says, "Out of the heart of men proceed evil thoughts, adulteries, fornications, murders, thefts, covetousness, wickedness, deceit, lasciviousness, an evil eye, blasphemy, pride, foolishness: all these evil thing come from within" (Mark 7:21-23). Nor must we forget that the confession of saints concerning themselves has always corresponded to God's testimony. David says, "Behold, I was shapen in iniquity, and in sin did my mother conceive me" (Ps. 51). Job declared, "Behold I am vile; I abhor myself." Isaiah cried out, "Woe is me, for I am undone; because I am a man of unclean lips.., for mine eyes have seen the King, the Lord of hosts."

But the most remarkable confession of this absolute vileness is contained in an acknowledgment by the Old Testament church—a sentence which has been taken up by all believers as exactly expressing what they all have to say of their condition by nature: "But we are all as an unclean thing, and all our righteousnesses are as filthy rags" (Isa. 64:6). Strong language indeed is that, yet not one whit too strong to depict the mud and mire into which the Fall has brought us. If, then, when considering the doctrine of justification we found it appropriate—in view of man's self-will, lawlessness, and disobedience—to ask, "How shall a man be just with God? " it is no less so now we are contemplating the doctrine of sanctification to inquire—in view of man's uncleanness and filthiness—"Who shall bring a clean thing out of an unclean?" (Job 14:4).

We have no more power to make ourselves holy than we have to unmake or unbeing ourselves; we are no more able to cleanse our hearts, than we are to command or direct the winds. Sin in dominion is the "plague" of the heart (1 Kings 8:38), and as no disease is so deadly as the plague, so there is no plague so deadly as that of the heart. "Can the Ethiopian change his skin, or the leopard his spots? Then may ye also do good that are accustomed to do evil" (Jer. 13:23). The proud cannot make himself humble; the carnal cannot force himself to become spiritual; the earthly man can no more transform himself into a heavenly man than he can make the sun go backward or the earth fly upward. Sanctification is a work altogether above the powers of human nature: alas that this is so little realized today.

Even among those preachers who desire to be regarded as orthodox, who do not deny the Fall as a historical fact, few among them perceive the dire effects and extent thereof. "Bruised by the fall," as one popular hymn puts it, states the truth far too mildly; yea, entirely misstates it. Through the breach of the first covenant all men have lost the image of God, and now bear the image of the Devil (John 8:44). The whole of their faculties are so depraved that they can neither think (2 Cor. 3:5), speak, nor do anything truly good and acceptable unto God. They are by birth, altogether unholy, unclean, loathsome and abominable in nature, heart, and life; and it is altogether beyond their power to change themselves.

Not only so, but the curse of the law lying upon them has severed all spiritual relation between God and them, cutting off all communion and communication with Heaven. The driving from the Garden of Eden of our first parents and the establishment of the cherubim with the flaming sword at its entrance, denoted that in point of justice they were barred from all sanctifying influences reaching them—that being the greatest benefit man is capable of, as assimilating him to God Himself or rendering him like Him. The curse has fixed a gulf between God and fallen creatures, so that sanctifying influences cannot pass from Him unto them, any more than their unholy desires and prayers can pass unto Him. It is written, "The sacrifice of the wicked is an abomination unto the Lord" (Prov. 15:8). And again, "The thoughts of the wicked are an abomination to the Lord" (v.26).

It has, then, been rightly said that our sanctification "is no less a mystery than our justification" (T. Boston). As the depravity of human nature has always been so manifest that it could not escape notice even in the world, so in all ages men have, been seeking to discover a remedy for the same, and have supposed a cure could be achieved by a right use of their rational, faculties. But the outcome has always been, at best, but an outward show and semblance of sanctification, going under the tame of "moral virtue." But so far is that from meeting the requirements of Him who is Light, that men themselves, once their eyes are (in any measure) anointed with heavenly eye salve, perceive their moral virtue to be as "filthy rags," a menstrous cloth. Until men are regenerate and act from a principle of grace in the heart, all their actions are but imitations of real obedience and piety, as an ape would mimic a man.

It is a common error of those that are unregenerate to seek to reform their conduct without any realization that their state must be changed before their lives can possibly be changed from sin to righteousness. The tree itself must be made good, before its fruit can possibly be good. As well attempt to make a watch go, whose mainspring is broken, by washing its face and polishing its back, as for one under the curse of God to produce any works acceptable to Him. That was the great mistake Nicodemus labored under: he supposed that teaching was all he needed, so that he might adjust his walk to the acceptance of Heaven. But to him the Lord Jesus declared, "Marvel not that I said unto thee, Ye must be born again" (John 3:7): that was only another way of saying, Nicodemus, you cannot perform spiritual works before you possess a spiritual nature and a spiritual nature cannot be had until you are born again.

Multitudes have labored with great earnestness to subdue their evil propensities, and have struggled long and hard to bring their inward thoughts and affections into conformity with the law of God. They have sought to abstain from all sins, and to perform every known duty. They have been so devout and intent that they have undermined their health, and were so fervent in their zeal that they were ready to kill their bodies with fastings and macerations, if only they might kill their sinful lusts. They were strongly convinced that holiness was absolutely necessary unto salvation, and were so deeply affected with the terrors of damnation, as to forsake the world and shut themselves up in convents and monasteries; yet all the while ignorant of the mystery of sanctification—that a new state must precede a new life.

It is positively asserted by Divine inspiration that, "They that are in the flesh cannot please God" (Rom. 8:8). Alas, how few understand the meaning of those words "in the flesh;" how many suppose they only signify, to be inordinately addicted to the baser passions. Whereas, to be "in the flesh" is to be in a state of nature—fallen, depraved, alienated from the life of God. To be "in the flesh" is not simply being a personal transgressor of God's holy law, but is the cause of all sinfulness and sinning. The "flesh" is the very nature of man as corrupted by the fall of Adam, and propagated from him to us in that corrupt state by natural generation. To be "in the flesh" is also being in complete subjection to the power of the Devil, who is the certain conqueror of all who attempt to fight him in their own strength or with his own weapons. The flesh can no more he brought to holiness by man's most vehement endeavors, than he can bring a dead carcass to life by chafing and rubbing it.

The varied elements which entered into the problem of Justification were: God's law requires from us perfect obedience to its statutes; this we have utterly failed to render; we are therefore under the condemnation and curse of the law; the Judge Himself is inflexibly just, and will by no means clear the guilty: how, then, can men be shown mercy without justice being flouted? The elements which enter into the problem of Sanctification are: the law requires inward as well as outward conformity to it: but we are born into this world with a nature that is totally depraved, and can by no means be brought into subjection to the law (Rom. 8:7). God Himself is ineffably pure, how then can a moral leper be admitted into His presence? We are utterly without holiness, and can no more make ourselves holy than the Ethiopian can change his skin. Even though a holy nature be imparted by regeneration, how can one with the flesh, unchanged, within him, draw near as a worshipper unto the Heavenly Sanctuary? How can I as a person possibly profess myself as holy, while conscious that I am full of sin? How can I honestly profess to have a "pure heart," while realizing a sea of corruption still rages within me? If my state must be changed before anything in my life is acceptable to God, what I possibly do?—I cannot unmake myself. If I know that polluted and vile, and utterly unsuited unto the thrice holy how much less can He regard me as fit for His presence?

Chapter 6
ITS SOLUTION

In connection with the grand truth of sanctification there is both a mystery and a problem: the former relates to the unregenerate; the latter is what exercises so deeply the regenerate. That which is hidden from the understanding of the natural man is, why his best performances are unacceptable unto God, no matter how earnestly and devoutly they be done. Even though he be informed that the tree must be made good if its fruit is to be wholesome, in other words, that his very state and nature must first be made acceptable unto God before any of his works can be so, he has not the remotest idea of how this is to be accomplished. But that which perplexes the spiritual man is, how one who is still full of sin may justly regard his state and nature as being acceptable unto God, and how one who is a mass of corruption within can honestly claim to be holy. As the Lord is pleased to enable we will consider each in turn.

The natural man is quite ignorant of the mystery of sanctification.

Though he may—under the spur of conscience, the fear of Hell, or from desire to go to Heaven—be very diligent in seeking to conquer the activities of indwelling sin and exceedingly zealous in performing every known duty, yet he is quite in the dark as to why his state must be changed before his actions ran be acceptable unto God. That upon which he is unenlightened is, that it is not the matter which makes a work good and pleasing to God, but the principles from which that work proceeds. It is true that the conscience of the natural man distinguishes between good and evil, and religious instruction may educate him to do much which is right and avoid much that is wrong; nevertheless, his actions are not done out of gratitude and in a spirit of loving obedience, but out of fear and from a servile spirit; and therefore are they like fruit ripened by art and forced in the hothouse, rather than normally by the genial rays of the sun.

"Now the end (design) of the commandment (or law) is love out of a pure heart, and a good conscience, and faith unfeigned" (I Tim. 1:5). Nothing less than this will meet the Divine requirements. Only those actions are pleasing to God which have respect unto His commandment, which proceed from gratitude unto Him for His goodness, and where faith has respect unto His promised acceptance and blessing. No works are approved of Heaven except they possess these qualities. A sense of duty must sway the conscience, disinterested affection must move the heart, and faith in exercise must direct the actions. Hence, should I be asked why I do thus and so? the answer should be, Because God has commanded it. And if it be further enquired, And why such earnestness and affection? the answer ought to be, Because God requires my best, and I desire to honor Him with the same. Obedience respects God's authority; love, His kindness; faith, His bounty or reward.

"Whether therefore ye eat, or drink, or whatsoever ye do, do all to the glory of God" (1 Cor. 10:31). This must be our design—the glory of God—if our actions are to meet with His approval. Whether it be the discharge of our temporal duties, the performing of deeds of charity and kindness, or acts of piety and devotion, they must be executed with this aim: that God may be honored by our conformity to His revealed will. The natural man, when in sore straits, will cry fervently unto God, but it is only that his wants be supplied. Many will contribute liberally of their means to the relief of sufferers, but it is to be seen of men" (Matt. 6:2). People are religious on the Sabbath and attend public worship, but it is either to satisfy an uneasy conscience or in the hope of earning Heaven thereby.

From what has been said above it should be clear that the best deeds of the unregenerate fall far short of the Divine requirements. The actions of the natural man cannot receive the approbation of Heaven, because God is neither the beginning nor the end of them: love for Him is not their spring, glorifying Him is not their aim. Instead, they issue from the workings of corrupt self, and they have in view only the advancement of self. Nor can it be otherwise. Water will not rise above its own level, or flow uphill. A pure stream cannot issue from an impure fountain. "That which is born of the flesh is flesh" (John 3:6), and will never be anything but flesh: educate, refine, religionize the flesh all we may, it can never become spirit. The man himself must be sanctified, before his actions are purified.

But how shall men be sanctified so as to be suited unto the presence of an infinitely pure God? By nature they are utterly without holiness: they are "corrupt, filthy, an unclean thing." They have no more power to make themselves holy than they have to create a world. We could tame a tiger from the jungle far more easily than we could our lusts. We might empty the ocean more quickly than we could banish pride from our souls. We might melt marble more readily than our hard hearts. We might purge the sea of salt more easily than we could our beings of sin. "For though thou wash thee with niter, and take thee much soap, yet thine iniquity is marked before Me, saith the Lord God" (Jer. 2:22).

Why "when we were in our best condition by nature, when we were in the state of original holiness, when we were in Adam vested with the image of God, we preserved it not. How much less likely then, is it, that now, in the state of lapsed and depraved nature, it is in our power to restore ourselves, to reintroduce the image of God into our souls, and that in a far more eminent manner than it was at first created by God? What needed all that contrivance of infinite wisdom and grace for the reparation of our nature by Jesus Christ, if holiness, wherein it doth consist, be in our power, and educed out of the natural faculties of our souls? There can be no more fond imagination befall the minds of men, than that defiled nature is able to cleanse itself, or depraved nature to rectify itself, or we, who have lost that image of God which He created in us, and with us, should create it again in ourselves by our own endeavors" (John Owen).

Yet, let it be pointed out that this impotency to measure up to the requirements of God is no mere innocent infirmity, but a highly culpable thing, which greatly aggravates our vileness and adds to our guilt. Our inability to measure up to the standard of personal piety which God has appointed, lies not in a lack of executive power or the needful faculties, but in the want of a willing mind and a ready heart to practice true holiness. If men in a natural state had a hearty love and liking to true holiness, and a fervent and sincere endeavor to practice it, and yet failed in the event, then they might under some pretense plead for this excuse (as many do), that they are compelled to sin by an inevitable necessity. But the fact is that man's impotency lies in his own obstinacy—"Ye will not come to Me" (John 5:40) said the Lord Jesus.

Inability to pay a debt does not excuse a debtor who has recklessly squandered his estate; nor does drunkenness excuse the mad or violent actions of a drunkard, but rather aggravates his crime. God has not lost His right to command, even though man through his wickedness has lost his power to obey. Because the flesh "lusteth against the Spirit" (Gal. 5:17), that is far from an extenuation for not being in subjection to Him. Because "every one that doeth evil hateth the light," that is far from justifying them because they "loved darkness" (John 3:19, 20); yea, as the Savior there so plainly and solemnly states, it only serves to heighten their criminality—"This is the condemnation." Then "How much more abominable and filthy is man, which drinketh iniquity like water?" (Job 15:16) that cannot practice holiness because he will not.

It is because men do not make a right use of their faculties that they are justly condemned. The soul in an unsanctified person is not dead, but is a living and acting principle; and therefore it is able to understand, desire, will, reason, and improve its opportunities, or redeem the time. Though the natural man is unable to work grace in his own heart, yet he is able to attend and wait upon the means of grace. An unsanctified person may as well go to hear a sermon as attend a theatre: he has the same eyes for reading the Scriptures as the newspaper or a novel: he may as well associate himself with those who fear an oath, as with those who delight to blaspheme that Name at which all should tremble. In the day of judgment unsanctified persons will be damned not for cannots, but for will not:.

Men complain that they cannot purify themselves, that they cannot cease from sin, that they cannot repent, that they cannot believe in Christ, that they cannot live a holy life. But if only they were honest, if they were duly humbled, if they sincerely grieved over the awful hold which sin has obtained upon them, they would fly to the throne of grace, they would cry unto God day and night for Him to break the chains which bind them, deliver them from the power of Satan and translate them into the kingdom of His dear Son. If they were but sincere in their complaint of inability, they would go to God and beg Him to sprinkle clean water upon them, put His Spirit within them, and give them a new heart, so that they might walk in His statutes and keep His judgments (Ezek. 36:25-28). And it is just because they will not, that their blood justly lies upon their own heads.

"Cleanse your hands, ye sinners; and purify your hearts, ye double-minded' (James 4:8). Outward separation from that which is evil and polluting is not sufficient: purity of heart is also indispensable. "Behold, Thou desirest truth in the inward parts" (Psa. 51:6). The Divine law not only prohibits stealing, but also insists "Thou shall not covet," which is a lusting of our souls rather than an external act. Holiness of nature is required by the law, for how else shall a man love the Lord his God with all his heart, soul, mind, and strength, and his neighbor as himself? God is essentially holy by nature, and nothing can be so contrary to Him as an unholy nature. Nothing can be so contrary as opposite natures. How can a wolf and a lamb, or vulture and a dove, dwell together? "What fellowship hath righteousness with unrighteousness? and what communion hath light with darkness? and what concord hath Christ with Belial?" (2 Cor. 6:14, 15).

How, then, is this mystery cleared up? By what method, or in what way, have the sanctified become blest with a nature which makes them meet for the ineffable presence of God? By what process does the evil tree become good, so that its fruit is wholesome and acceptable? Obviously, we cannot here supply the full answer to these questions, or we should be anticipating too much that we desire to bring out in later chapters. But we will endeavor to now indicate, at least, the direction in which and the lines along which this great mystery is cleared—lines which most assuredly would never have entered our hearts and minds to so much as conceive; but which once they are viewed by anointed eyes, are seen to be Divine and satisfying. The Lord graciously assist us to steer clear of the rocks of error and guide us into the clear and refreshing waters of the truth.

As we have shown, it was quite impossible—though it was their bounden duty—for those whom God sanctifies to personally answer the requirements of His holy law: "Who can say, I have made my heart clean, I am pure from sin?" (Prov. 20:9). Wherefore, for the satisfaction of the law, which requires absolute purity of nature, it was settled as one of the articles in the Everlasting Covenant, that Christ, the Representative of all who would be sanctified, should be a Man of an untainted and perfectly pure nature, which fully met the requirements of the law: "For such an

High Priest became us—holy, harmless, undefiled, separate from sinners" (Heb. 7:26). The meeting of that requirement necessitated two things: first, that the Head of His people should be born with a holy human nature; second, that He should retain that holiness of nature inviolate unto the end. Let us consider, briefly, each of these separately.

There was a holy nature given to Adam as the Root of mankind, to be kept by him and transmitted to his posterity by natural generation. Upon that ground the law requires all men to be born holy, and pronounces them unclean and "children of wrath" (Eph. 2:3) in the contrary. But how can this demand be met by those who are born in sin? They cannot enter again into their mother's womb, and be born a second time without sin. Even so, the law will not abate its demand. Wherefore it was provided that Christ, the last Adam, should, as the Representative and Root of His spiritual seed, be born perfectly holy; that whereas they brought a sinful nature into the world with them, He should be born "that holy thing" (Luke I :35). Consequently, in the reckoning of the law all believers are born holy in the last Adam. They are said to be "circumcised" by the circumcision of Christ (Col. 2:11), and circumcision necessarily presupposes birth!

But more was required. It was necessary that the Second Man should preserve His holy nature free from all spot or defilement, as He passed through this world of sin. The law not only demands holiness of nature, but also that the purity and integrity of that nature be preserved. Wherefore to satisfy this "demand," it was provided that the believers' federal Head should preserve His ineffable purity unstained. "He shall not fail" (Isa. 42:4). The first man did fail: the fine gold soon became dim: the holiness of his nature was quickly extinguished by sin. But the Second Man failed not: neither man nor devil could corrupt Him. He preserved the holiness of His nature unstained, even to the end of His life. And so of His sanctified, viewing them in Himself, He declares, "Thou art all fair, My love; there is no spot in thee" (Song of 5. 4:7).

But while that completely meets the judicial side, satisfying the demands of the law, something more was yet required to satisfy the heart of God and meet the experimental needs of His people. In view of their being actually defiled in Adam when he sinned, they are defiled in their own persons so that not only is his guilt imputed to them, but his corruption is imparted to them in the nature they have received him by generation. Therefore, not only were the elect legally born holy in Christ their Head, but from Him they also receive a holy nature: it is written, "The first man Adam was made a living soul; the last Adam was made a quickening Spirit" (1 Cor. 15:45). This is accomplished by that gracious and supernatural working of the third person in the Godhead, whereby the elect are vitally united to their head so that "he that is joined unto the Lord is one spirit" (1 Cor. 6:17).

"Therefore if any man be in Christ, he is a new creature: old things are passed away; behold, all things are become new" (2 Cor. 5:17). Our being united to Christ, through the Spirit, by faith, makes us partakers of the same spiritual and holy nature with Him, as really and as actually as Eve (type of the Church) was made of one nature with Adam, being bone of his bone and flesh of his flesh. Because believers are united to Christ the Holy One, they are "sanctified in Christ Jesus" (1 Cor. 1:2). The believer being one with Christ is made "a new creature," because He is such a Stock as changes the graft into its own nature: "If the Root be holy, so are the branches" (Rom. 11:16). The same Spirit which Christ received "without measure" (John 3:34) is communicated to the members of His body, so that it can be said, "Of His fullness have all we received, and grace for grace" (John 1:16). Being united to Christ by faith, and through the communication of the quickening Spirit from Christ unto him, the believer is thereupon not only justified and reconciled to God, but sanctified, made meet for the inheritance of the saints in light, and made an heir of God.

Chapter 7
ITS SOLUTION
(COMPLETED)

At the beginning of the former chapter it was pointed out that in connection with the grand truth of sanctification there is both a mystery and a problem: the former relating to the unregenerate, the latter causing concern to the regenerate. That which is hidden from the knowledge of the natural man is, why his best works are unacceptable to God. Tell him that all his actions—no matter how carefully and conscientiously, diligently and devoutly, executed—are rejected by God, and that is something entirely above the reach of his understanding. He knows not that his breaking of the law in Adam has brought in a breach between himself and God, so that while that breach remains, the favor of God cannot flow out of him, nor his prayers or offerings pass in to God. The Lord will no more receive anything at the hands of the natural man than He would have respect unto the offering of Cain (Gen. 4). And had He left all men in their natural estate, this would have held true of the whole race until the end of time.

Inasmuch as all men were given a holy nature—created in the image and likeness of God—in their representative and root, to be transmitted to them by him, before the law was given to Adam, it follows that the law requires a holy nature from each of us, and pronounces a curse wherever it finds the opposite. Though we are actually born into this world in a state of corruption and filth (Ezek. 16:3-6, etc.), yet the law will not abate its just demands upon us. In consequence of the sin which indwells us—which is so much a part and parcel of ourselves that everything we do is defiled thereby—we are thoroughly unable to render unto the law that obedience which it requires; for while we are alienated from the life of God, it is impossible that any outward acts of compliance with the law's statutes can proceed from those principles which it alone can approve of, namely, disinterested love and faith unfeigned. Consequently, the state of the natural man, considered in himself, is entirely beyond hope.

The provision made by the manifold wisdom and sovereign grace of God to meet the desperate needs of His people was stipulated for in terms of the Everlasting Covenant. There it was agreed upon by the Eternal Three that the Mediator should be the Son of man, yet, that His humanity should be not only entirely free from every taint of original sin, but should be purer than that of Adam's even when his Creator pronounced him "very good." This was accomplished by the supernatural operation of the Holy Spirit in the virgin birth, and by the Son of God taking into personal union with Himself "that holy thing" which was to be born of Mary. Inasmuch as Christ, the God-man Mediator, entered this world not as a private Person, but as a public, as the Representative and Head of God's elect, in the reckoning of the law they were born holy in their Surety and Sponsor, and so fully measure up to its requirements. Christ and His mystical body have never been viewed apart by the law.

But this, unspeakably blessed though it be, was not all. A perfect legal standing only met half of the need of God's elect: in addition, their state must be made to accord with their standing. This also has been provided for by the measureless love of the God of all grace. He so ordered that, just as the guilt of Adam was imputed to all for whom He acted, so the righteousness of Christ should be imputed to all for whom He transacted: and, that just as spiritual death—with all its corrupting effects—should be transmitted by Adam to all his posterity, so the spiritual life of Christ—with all its gracious influences— should be communicated to all His seed. As they received a sinful and impure nature from their natural head, so the sanctified receive a sinless and pure nature from their spiritual Head. Consequently, as they have borne the image of the earthy, so they shall bear the image of the heavenly.

Some of our readers may, perhaps, conclude that all difficulty in connection with this aspect of our subject has now been of, but a little reflection on the part of the believer soon remind him that the most perplexing point of all has yet to be cleared up. Though it be true that every essential requirement of the law has been met for the sanctified by their glorious Head, so that the law righteously views them as holy in Him; and though it be true that at regeneration they receive from Christ, by the Spirit, a new and holy nature, like unto His; yet the old nature remains, and remains unchanged, unimproved. Yea, to them it seems that the carnal nature in them is steadily growing worse and worse, and more active and defiling every day they live. They are painfully conscious of the jest that sin not only remains in them, but that it pollutes their desires, thoughts, imaginations, and acts; and to prevent its uprisings they are quite powerless.

This presents to an honest heart and a sensitive conscience a problem which is most acute, for how can those who abhor themselves be pleasing unto the thrice holy One? How can those conscious of their filthiness and vileness possibly be fit to draw nigh unto Him who is ineffably and infinitely pure? The answer which some have returned to this agonized enquiry based upon an erroneous deduction from the words of Paul "it is no more I that do it, but sin that dwelleth in me": Rom. 7:20—will by no means satisfy them. To say it is not the regenerate person, but only the flesh in him, which sins, is to invent a distinction which repudiates the Christian's responsibility and which affords no relief to a quickened conscience. Scripture is far too plain on this point to justify a mistake: Old and New Testament alike insist it is the person who sins—"against Thee. . . have I sinned" (Ps. 51). Paul himself concludes Romans 7 by saying, "O wretched man that I am!"

Where other matters are concerned, men have more sense than to fall back upon such a distinction as some modern theologians are so fond of insisting upon: it never occurs to them to argue thus in connection with temporal things. Imagine one before a judge, who was charged with theft, acknowledging his offence, but disowning all responsibility and culpability on the ground that it was his "evil nature" and not himself which did the stealing! Surely the judge would be in a quandary to decide whether prison or the madhouse was the right place to send him. This reminds us of an incident wherein a "Bishop" was guilty of blasphemy in the House of Lords (where all "Bishops" have seats). Being rebuked by his manservant, he replied, "It was the 'lord' and not the 'bishop' who cursed." His servant responded, "When the Devil gets the 'lord' where will the 'bishop' be!" Beware, my reader, of seeking to clear yourself by throwing the blame upon your "nature."

Somewhere else, then, than in any supposed distinction between the sanctified person and his old nature, must the solution to our problem be sought. When one who has been walking with God is tripped up by some temptation and falls, into sin, or when indwelling corruption surges up and (for the time being) obtains the mastery over him, he is painfully aware of the fact; and that which exercises him the most is not only that he has sinned against the One who is nearer and dearer to him than all else, but that his communion with Him is broken, and that he is no longer morally fit to come into His sacred presence. Whilst his knowledge of the Gospel may be sufficient to allay any haunting fears of the penal consequences of his sins, yet this does not remove the defilement from his conscience. This is one important respect in which the unregenerate and regenerate differ radically: when the former sins it is the guilt (and punishment) which most occupies his thoughts; but when the latter, it is the defiling effects which most exercises his heart.

There are two things in sin, inseparably connected and yet clearly distinguishable, namely, its criminality and its pollution. The pollution of sin is that property of it whereby it is directly opposed unto the holiness of God, and which God expresseth His holiness to be contrary unto. Therefore it is said, He is "of purer eyes than to behold iniquity, and canst not look on evil" (Hab. 1:13)—it is a vile and loathsome sight to Him who is the Light. Hence doth He use that pathetic entreaty, "Oh, do not this abominable thing that I hate" (Jer. 44:4.). It is with respect unto His own holiness that God sets forth sin by the names of everything which is offensive, objectionable, repulsive, abominable. Consequently, when the Holy Spirit convicts of sin, He imparts such a sight and sense of the filth of sin, that sinners blush, are ashamed, are filled with confusion of face, are abased in their own esteem, and abashed before God.

As we are taught the guilt of sin by our own fear, which is the inseparable adjunct of it, so we are taught the filth of sin by our own shame, which unavoidably attends it. Under the typical economy God not only appointed sacrifices to make atonement for the guilt of sin, but also gave various ordinances for purification or ceremonial cleansing from the pollution thereof. In various ways, during Old Testament times, God instructed His people concerning the spiritual defilement of sin: the distinction between clean and unclean animals, the different natural distempers which befoul the body, the isolating of the leper, the accidental touching of the dead which rendered people religiously unclean by the law, are cases in point. All of them prefigured internal and spiritual pollution, and hence the whole work of sanctification is expressed by "a fountain opened...for sin and for uncleanness" (Zech. 13:1)—that is, for the purging away of them.

So inseparable is moral pollution from sin, and a sense of shame from a consciousness of the pollution, that whenever a soul is truly convicted of sin, there is always a painful sense of this filthiness, accompanied by personal shame. Only as this is clearly apprehended, are we able to understand the true nature of sanctification. The spiritual comeliness of the soul consists in its conformity to God. Grace gives beauty: hence it is said of Christ that He is "Fairer (or "more beautiful") than the children of men," and that beauty consisted in his being made in the image of God, which constituted the whole harmony and symmetry of his nature, all his faculties and actions having respect unto God. Therefore, that which is contrary to the image of God—depravity, contrary to grace—sin, hath in it a deformity which mars the soul, destroys its comeliness, disrupts its order, and brings deformity, ugliness, vileness.

Whatever is contrary to holiness or the image of God on the soul, is base, unworthy, filthy. Sin dishonors and degrades the soul, filling it with shame. The closer we are permitted to walk with God and the more we see ourselves in His light, the more conscious are we of the deformity of sin and of our baseness. When our eyes were first opened to see our spiritual nakedness, how hideous did we appear unto ourselves, and what a sense of our pollution we had! That was but the reflex of God's view, for He abhors, loathes, and esteems as an abominable thing whatever is contrary to His holiness. Those who are made "partakers of the Divine nature" (2 Pet. 1:4), do, according to their measure, but see themselves with God's eyes, as wretched, naked, shameful, loathsome, hideous and abominable creatures; and therefore do they, with Job, "abhor" themselves.

The last four paragraphs are, in part, a condensation from John Owen; and from them we may clearly perceive that it is they who are truly sanctified and holy, who are the most deeply sensible of the root of corruption which still remains within them, and which is ever springing up and producing that which defiles them; and therefore do they greatly bewail their pollutions, as that which is most dishonoring to God and most disturbing to their own peace; and earnestly do they endeavor after the mortification of it. A remarkable corroboration is found in the fact that the most godly and holy have been the very ones who most strongly affirmed their sinfulness and most loudly bewailed the same. It was one whom God Himself declared to be a "perfect (sincere) and an upright man, one that feareth God, and escheweth evil" (Job 1:8) who declared "Behold, I am vile" (40:4). It was one "greatly beloved" of God (Dan. 10:19), who acknowledged "my comeliness was turned in me into corruption" (10:8). It was he who was caught up to the third heaven and then returned again to earth who moaned, "O wretched man that I am! who shall deliver me from the body of this death?" (Rom. 7:24).

From the quotations just made from the personal confessions of some of the most eminent of God's saints, it is perfectly plain to any simple soul that a "pure heart" cannot signify one from which all sin has been removed, nor can their language possibly be made to square with the utopian theory that the carnal nature is eradicated from any believer in this life. Indeed it cannot; and none but they who are completely blinded by Satan would ever affirm such a gross absurdity and palpable lie. But this requires us now to define and describe what a "pure heart" consists of, according to the scriptural meaning thereof. And in our efforts to supply this, we shall have to try and guard against two evils: providing a pillow for empty professors to comfortably rest upon; and stating things in such a way that hope would be killed in the regenerate.

First, a "pure heart" is one which has experienced "the washing of regeneration and renewing of the Holy Spirit" (Titus 3:5). That takes place at the new birth, and is maintained by the Spirit throughout the Christian's life. All that this involves we cannot now state at any length. But, negatively, it includes the purifying of the believer's understanding, so that it is no longer fatally blinded by Satan, but is supernaturally illumined by the Spirit: in consequence, the vanity of worldly things is now perceived. The mind is, in great measure, freed from the pollution of error, and this, by the shining in of the light of God's truth. It includes, negatively, the cleansing of the affections, so that sin is no longer loved but loathed, and God is no longer shrunk from and avoided, but sought after and desired.

From the positive side, there is communicated to the soul at regeneration a nature or principle which contains within itself pure desires, pure intentions, and pure roots of actions. The fear of God is implanted, and the love of God is shed abroad in the heart. In consequence thereof, the soul is made to pant after God, yearn for conformity to His will, and seeks to please Him in all things. And hence it is that the greatest grief of the Christian arises from the hindering of his spiritual longings and the thwarting of his spiritual aspirations. A pure heart is one that loathes impurity, and whose heaviest burden is the realization that such an ocean of foul waters still indwells him, constantly casting up their mire and dirt, polluting all he does. A "pure heart," therefore, is one which makes conscience of foolish, vile imaginations, and evil desires. It is one which grieves over pride and discontent, mourns over unbelief, and enmity, weeps in secret over unholiness.

Second, a "pure heart" is one which has been "sprinkled from an evil conscience" (Heb. 10:22). An "evil conscience" is one which accuses of guilt and oppresses because of unpardoned sin. Its possessor dreads the prospect of the day of judgment, and seeks to banish all thoughts of it from his mind. But a conscience to which the Spirit has graciously applied the atoning blood of Christ obtains peace of mind, and has confidence to draw nigh unto God: in consequence, superstition, terror and torment is removed, and an aversion to God is displaced by a joy in God. Hence, also, third, we read "purifying their hearts by faith" (Acts 15:9). As unbelief is a principle which defiles, so faith is a principle which purges, and that, because of the object which it lays hold of.

Faith looks away from self to Christ, and is enabled to realize that His blood "cleanseth us from all sin" (1 John 1:7).

Every Christian, then, has a "pure" heart in the particulars given above. But every Christian does not have a "clean" heart (Ps. 51 :10). That which pollutes the heart of a Christian is un-judged sin. Whenever sin is allowed by us, communion with God is broken, and pollution can only be removed, and communion restored, by genuine repentance—a condemning of ourselves, a mourning over the sin, and unsparing confession of the same, accompanied by a fervent desire and sincere resolution not to be overtaken by it again. The willing allowance and indulgence of any known sin cannot exist with a clean heart. Rightly, then, did John Owen say of repentance: "It is as necessary unto the continuance of spiritual life, as faith itself." After the repentance and confession, there must be a fresh (and constant) recourse unto that Fountain which has been "opened for sin and for uncleanness," a fresh application by faith of the cleansing blood of Christ: pleading its merits and efficacy before God.

In this chapter (in two sections) we have sought to answer the questions at the close of the fifth chapter. We have met every demand of the law in the person of our Surety. We are made meet for the inheritance of the saints in light, because all the value of Christ's cleansing blood is reckoned to our account. We are capacitated to draw nigh unto God now, because the Holy Spirit has com-municated to us the very nature of Christ Himself. By faith we may regard ourselves as holy in Christ. By regeneration we have received a "pure heart:" proof of which is, we hate all impurity, although there is still that in us which delights in nothing else. We are to maintain communion with God by cleansing our own hearts (Ps. 73:13), and that, through constant mortification, and the daily and unsparing judgment of all known sin in and from us.

importance. Third, by discovering the true nature of sin, for holiness is its opposite. Fourth, by remembering that sanctification is an integral and essential part of salvation itself, and not an extra. Fifth, by following up the clue given us in the threefold meaning of the term itself.

What is connoted by the holiness of God? In seeking an answer to this question very little help is to be obtained from the works of theologians, most of whom contented themselves with a set of words which expressed no distinct thing, but left matters wholly in the dark. Most of them say that God's holiness is His purity. If it be enquired, in what does this purity consist? the usual reply is, In that which is opposite to all sin, the greatest impurity. But who is the wiser by this? That, of itself, does not help us to form any positive idea of what God's purity consists of, until we are told what sin really is. But the nature of sin cannot be experimentally known until we apprehend what holiness is, for we do not fully learn what holiness is by obtaining a right idea of sin; rather must we first know what holiness is in order for a right knowledge of sin.

A number of eminent theologians have attempted to tell us what Divine holiness is by saying, It is not properly a distinct attribute of God, but the beauty and glory of all His moral perfections. But we can get no concrete idea from those words, until we are told what is this "beauty and glory." To say it is "holiness" is to say nothing at all to the point. All that John Gill gives us for a definition of God's holiness is, "holiness is the purity and rectitude of His nature." Nath Emmons, the perfector of the "New England" scheme of theology, tells us, "Holiness is a general term to express that goodness or benevolence which comprises everything that is morally amiable and excellent." Though sound in their substance, such statements are too brief to be of much service to us in seeking to form a definite conception of the Divine Holiness.

The most helpful description of God's holiness which we have met with is that framed by the Puritan, Stephen Charnock, "It is the rectitude or integrity of the Divine nature, or that conformity of it in affection and action to the Divine will, as to His eternal law, whereby He works with a becomingness to His own excellency, and whereby He hath a delight and complacency in everything agreeable to His will, and an abhorrence of everything contrary thereto." Here is something definite and tangible, satisfying to the mind; though perhaps it requires another feature to be added to it. Since the law is "a transcript" of the Divine mind and nature, then God's holiness must be His own harmony therewith; to which we may add, God's holiness is His ordering all things for His own glory, for He can have no higher end than that—this being His own unique excellency and prerogative.

We fully concur with Charnock in making the will of God and the law of God one and the same thing, and that His holiness lies in the conformity of His affections and actions with the same; adding, that the furtherance of His own glory being His design in the whole. Now this concept of the Divine holiness—the sum of God's moral excellency—helps us to conceive what holiness is in the Christian. It is far more than a "position" or "standing." It is also and chiefly a moral quality, which produces conformity to the Divine will or law, and which moves its possessor to aim at the glory of God in all things. This, and nothing short of this, could meet the Divine requirements; and this is the great gift which God bestows upon His people.

What was it that Adam had and lost? What was it which distinguished him from all the lower creatures? Not simply the possession of a soul, but that his soul had stamped upon it the moral image and likeness of his Maker. This it was which constituted his blessedness, which capacitated him for communion with the Lord, and which qualified him to live a happy life to His glory. And this it was which he lost at the fall. And this it is which the last Adam restores unto His people. That is clear from a comparison of Colossians 3:10 and Ephesians 4:23: the "new man," the product of regeneration, is "renewed in knowledge (in the vital and experimental knowledge of God Himself: John 17:3) after the image of Him that created him," that is, after the original likeness which was bestowed upon Adam; and that "new man" is distinctly said to be "created in righteousness and true holiness" (Eph. 4:24).

Thus, what the first Adam lost and what the last Adam secured for His people, was the "image and likeness" of God stamped upon the heart, which "image" consists of "righteousness and holiness." Hence to understand that personal and experimental holiness which the Christian is made partaker of at the new birth, we have to go back to the beginning and ascertain what was the nature or character of that moral "uprightness" (Eccl. 7:29) with which God created man at the beginning. Holiness and righteousness was the "nature" with which the first man was endowed; it was the very law of his being, causing him to delight in the Lord, do those things which are pleasing in His sight, and reproduce in his creature measure God's own righteousness and holiness. Here again we discover that holiness is a moral quality, which conforms its possessor to the Divine law or will, and moves him to aim only at the glory of God.

What is sin? Ah, what man is capable of supplying an adequate answer: "Who can understand his errors?" (Ps. 19:12). A volume might be written thereon, and still much be left unsaid. Only the One against whom it is committed can fully understand its nature or measure its enormity. And yet, from the light which God has furnished us, a partial answer at least can be gathered. For example, in 1 John 3:4 we read, "Sin is the transgression of the law," and that such transgression is not confined to the outward act is clear from "the thought of foolishness is sin" (Prov. 24:9). But what is meant by "sin is the transgression of the law?" It means that sin is a trampling upon God's holy commandment. It is an act of defiance against the Lawgiver. The law, being "holy and just and good" it follows that any breach of it is an evil and enormity which God alone is capable of estimating.

All sin is a breach of the eternal standard of equity. But is more than that: it reveals an inward enmity which gives to the outward transgression. It is the bursting forth of that pride and the self-will which resents restraint, which repudiates control, which refuses to be under authority, which resists rule. Against the righteous restraint of law, Satan opposed a false idea of "liberty" to our first parents—"Ye shall be as gods." And he is still plying the same argument and employing the same bait. The Christian must meet it by asking, Is the disciple to be above his Master, the servant superior to his Lord? Christ was "made under the law" (Gal. 44), and lived in perfect submission thereto, and has left us an example that we should "follow His steps" (1 Pet. 2:21). Only by loving, fearing, and obeying the law, shall we be kept from sinning.

Sin, then, is an inward state which precedes the evil deeds. It is a state of heart which refuses to be in subjection to God. It is a casting off the Divine law, and setting up self-will and self pleasing in its stead. Now, since holiness is the opposite of sin this helps us to determine something more of the nature of sanctification. Sanctification is that work of Divine grace in the believer which brings him back into allegiance to God, regulating his affections and actions in harmony with His will, writing His law on the heart (Heb. 10-16), moving him to make God's glory his chief aim and end. That Divine work is commenced at regeneration, and completed only at glorification. It may be thought that, in this section, we have contradicted what was said in and earlier paragraph. Not so; in God's light we see light. Only after the principle of holiness has been imparted to us, can we discern the real character of sin; but after it has been received, an analysis of sin helps us to determine the nature of sanctification.

Sanctification is an integral part of "salvation." As this point was dwelt upon at length in the third chapter, there is less need for us to say much upon it here. Once it be clearly perceived that God's salvation is not only a rescue from the penalty of sin, but is as well, and chiefly, deliverance from the pollution and power of sin—ultimating in complete freedom from its very presence there will be no difficulty in seeing that sanctification occupies a central place in the process. Alas that while there are many who think of Christ dying to secure their pardon, so few today consider Christ dying in order to renew their hearts, heal their souls, bring them unto obedience to God. One is often obliged to wonder if one out of each ten professing Christians is really experimentally acquainted with the "so great salvation" (Heb. 2:3) of God!

Inasmuch as sanctification is an important branch of salvation, we have another help towards understanding its nature. Salvation is deliverance from sin, an emancipation from the bondage of Satan, a being brought into right relations with God; and sanctification is that which makes this actual in the believer's experience—not perfectly so in this life, but truly so, nevertheless. Hence sanctification is not only the principal part of salvation, but it is also the chief means thereto. Salvation from the power of sin consists in deliverance from the love of sin; and that is affected by the principle of holiness, which loves purity and piety. Again, there can be no fellowship with God, no walking with Him, no delighting ourselves in Him, except as we tread the path of obedience (see 1 John 1:5-7); and that is only possible as the principle of holiness is operative within us.

Let us now combine these four points. What is scriptural sanctification? First, it is a moral quality in the regenerate—the same in its nature as that which belongs to the Divine character—which produces harmony with God's will and causes its possessor to aim at His glory in all things. Second, it is the moral image of God—lost by the first Adam, restored by the last Adam—stamped upon the heart, which "image" consists of righteousness and holiness. Third, it is the opposite of sin. Inasmuch as all sin is a transgression of the Divine law, true sanctification brings its possessor into a conformity thereto. Fourth, it is an integral and essential part of "salvation," being a deliverance from the power and pollution of sin, causing its possessor to love what he once hated, and to now hate what he formerly loved. Thus, it is that which experimentally fits us for fellowship with and the enjoyment of the Holy One Himself.

Chapter 9
ITS NATURE
(CONTINUED)

The threefold signification of the term "to sanctify." Perhaps the simplest and surest method to pursue in seeking to arrive at a correct understanding of the nature of sanctification is to follow up the meaning of the word itself, for in Scripture the names of things are always in accurate accord with their character. God does not tantalize us with ambiguous or meaningless expressions, but the name He gives to a thing is a properly descriptive one. So here. The word "to sanctify" means to consecrate or set apart for a sacred use, to cleanse or purify, to adorn or beautify. Diverse as these meanings may appear, yet as we shall see they beautifully coalesce into one whole. Using this, then, as our principal key, let us see whether the threefold meaning of the term will open for us the main avenues of our subject.

Sanctification is, first of all, an act of the triune God, whereby His people are set apart for Himself—for His delight, His glory, His use. To aid our understanding on this point, let it be noted that Jude 1 speaks of those who are "sanctified by God the Father," and that this precedes their being "preserved in Jesus Christ and called." The reference there is to the Father choosing His people for Himself out of the race which He purposed to create, separating the objects of His favor from those whom He passed by. Then in Hebrews 10:10 we read, "we are sanctified through the offering of the body of Jesus Christ once for all": His sacrifice has purged His people from every stain of sin, separated them from the world, consecrated them unto God, setting them before Him in all the excellency of His offering. In 2 Thessalonians 2:13 we are told, "God hath from the beginning chosen you to salvation, through sanctification of the Spirit, and belief of the truth": this refers to the Spirit's quickening work by which He separates the elect from those who are dead in sin.

Sanctification is, in the second place, a cleansing of those who are to be devoted to God's use. This "cleansing" is both a legal and an experimental one. As we prosecute our subject, it needs to be constantly borne in mind that sanctification or holiness is the opposite of sin. Now as sin involves both guilt and pollution, its remedy must meet both of those needs and counteract both of those effects. A loathsome leper would no more be a fit subject for Heaven than would one who was still under the curse. The double provision made by Divine grace to meet the need of God's guilty and defiled people is seen in the "blood and water" which proceeded from the pierced side of the Savior (John 19:34). Typically, this twofold need was adumbrated of old in the tabernacle furniture: the laver to wash at was as indispensable as the altar for sacrifice. Cleansing is as urgent as forgiveness.

That one of the great ends of the death of Christ was the moral purification of His people is clear from many scriptures. "He died for all, that they which live should not henceforth live unto themselves, but unto Him which died for them, and rose again" (2 Cor. 5:15); "Who gave Himself for us, that He might redeem us from all iniquity, and purify unto Himself a peculiar people, zealous of good works" (Titus 2:14); "How much more shall the blood of Christ, who through the eternal Spirit offered Himself without spot to God, purge your conscience from dead works to serve the living God" (Heb. 9:14); "Who His own self bear our sins in His own body on the tree, that we, being dead to sins, should live unto righteousness" (1 Pet. 2:24). From these passages it is abundantly plain that the purpose of the Savior in all that He did and suffered, was not only to deliver His people from the penal consequences of their sins, but also to cleanse them from the pollution of sin, to free them from its enslaving power, to rectify their moral nature.

It is greatly to be regretted that so many when thinking or speaking of the "salvation" which Christ has purchased for His people, attach to it no further idea than deliverance from condemnation. They seem to forget that deliverance from sin—the cause of condemnation—is an equally important blessing comprehended in it. "Assuredly it is just as necessary for fallen creatures to be freed from the pollution and moral impotency which they have contracted, as it is to be exempted from the penalties which they have incurred; so that when reinstated in the favor of God, they may at the same time be more capable of loving, serving, and enjoying Him forever. And in this respect the remedy which the Gospel reveals is fully suited to the exigencies of our sinful state, providing for our complete redemption from sin itself, as well as from the penal liabilities it has brought upon us" (T. Crawford on "The Atonement"). Christ has procured sanctification for His people as well as justification.

That cleansing forms an integral element in sanctification is abundantly clear from the types. "For if the blood of bulls and of goats, and the ashes of an heifer sprinkling the unclean, sanctifieth to the purifying of the flesh" (Heb. 9:13). The blood, the ashes, the sprinkling, were all God's merciful provision for the "unclean" and they sanctified "to the purifying of the flesh"—the references being to Leviticus 16:14; Numbers 19:2, 17, 18. The antitype of this is seen in the next verse, "How much more shall the blood of Christ, who through the eternal Spirit offered Himself without spot to God, purge your conscience from dead works to serve the living God." The type availed only for a temporary and ceremonial sanctification, the Antitype for a real and eternal cleansing. Other examples of the same thing are found in, "Go unto the people, and sanctify them today and tomorrow, and let them wash their clothes" (Ex. 19:10); "I will sanctify also both Aaron and his sons, to minister to Me in the priest's office" (Ex. 29:44)—for the accomplishment of this see Exodus 40:12-15, where we find they were "washed with water," "anointed" with oil, and "clothed" or adorned with their official vestments.

Now the substitutionary and sacrificial work of Christ has produced for His people a threefold "cleansing." The first is judicial, the sins of His people being all blotted out as though they had never existed. Both the guilt and the defilement of their iniquities are completely removed, so that the Church appears before God "as the morning, fair as the moon, clear as the sun" (Song of S. 6:10). The second is personal, at "the washing of regeneration and renewing of the Holy Spirit." The third is experimental, when faith appropriates the cleansing blood and the conscience is purged: "purifying their hearts by faith" (Acts 15:9), "having our hearts sprinkled from an evil conscience, and our bodies washed with pure water" (Heb. 10:22). Unlike the first two, this last, is a repeated and continuous thing: "If we confess our sins, He is faithful and just to forgive us our sins, and to cleanse us from all unrighteousness" (1 John 1:9). We hope to amplify these different points considerably when we take up more definitely our sanctification by Christ.

Sanctification is, in the third place an adorning or beautifying of those whom God cleanses and sets apart unto Himself. This is accomplished by the Holy Spirit in His work of morally renovating the soul, whereby the believer is made inwardly holy. That which the Spirit communicates is the life of the risen Christ, which is a principle of purity, producing love to God; and love to God implies, of course, subjection to Him. Thus, holiness is an inward conformity to the things which God has commanded, as the "pattern" (or sample) corresponds to the piece from which it is taken. "For ye know what commandments we gave you by the Lord Jesus. For this is the will of God, your sanctification" (1 Thess. 4:2, 3), i.e., your sanctification consists in a conformity to His will. Sanctification causes the heart to make God its chief good, and His glory its chief end.

As His glory is the end God has in view in all His actions—ordering, disposing, directing everything with this design—so conformity to Him, being holy as He is holy, must consist in setting His glory before us as our ultimate aim. Subjective sanctification is that change wrought in the heart which produces a steady desire and purpose to please and honor God. This is not in any of us by nature, for self-love rules the unregenerate. Calamities may drive the unsanctified toward God, yet it is only for the relief of self. The fear of Hell may stir up a man to cry unto God for mercy, but it is only that he may be delivered. Such actions are only the workings of mere nature—the instinct of self-preservation; there is nothing spiritual or supernatural about them. But at regeneration a man is lifted off his own bottom and put on a new foundation.

Subjective sanctification is a change or renovating of the heart so that it is conformed unto God—unto His will, unto His glory. "The work of sanctification is a work framing and casting the heart itself into the word of God (as metals are cast into a die or mould), so that the heart is made of the same stamp and disposition with the Word" (Thos. Goodwin). "Ye have obeyed from the heart that form (or "pattern") of doctrine whereto ye were delivered" (Rom. 6:17). The arts and sciences deliver unto us rules which we must conform unto, but God's miracle of grace within His people conforms them unto the rulings of His will, so as to be formed by them; softening their hearts so as to make them capable of receiving the impressions of His precepts. Below we quote again from the excellent remarks of Thos. Goodwin.

"The substance of his comparison comes to this, that their hearts having been first, in the inward inclinations and dispositions of it, framed and changed into what the Word requires, they then obeyed the same Word from the heart naturally, willingly; and the commandments were not grievous, because the heart was framed and moulded thereunto. The heart must be made good ere men can obey from the heart; and to this end he elegantly first compares the doctrine of Law and Gospel delivered them, unto a pattern or sampler, which having in their eye, they framed and squared their actings and doings unto it. And he secondly compares the same doctrine unto a mould or matrix, in to which metal is being delivered, have the same figure or form left on them which the mould itself had; and this is spoken in respect of their hearts."

This mighty and marvelous change is not in the substance or faculties of the soul, but in its disposition; for a lump of metal being melted and moulded remains the same metal it was before, yet its frame and fashion is greatly altered. When the heart has been made humble and meek, it is enabled to perceive what is that good, and perfect, and acceptable will of God, and approves of it as good for him; and thus we are "transformed by the renewing of our mind" (Rom. 12:2). As the mould and the thing moulded correspond, as the wax has on it the image by which it was impressed, so the heart which before was enmity to every commandment, now delights in the law of God after the inward man, finding an agreeableness between it and his own disposition. Only as the heart is supernaturally changed and conformed to God is it found that "His commandments are not grievous" (1 John 5:3).

What has just been said above brings us back to the point reached in the preceding chapter (or more correctly, the first sections of this chapter, namely, that holiness is a moral quality, an inclination, a "new nature," a disposition which delights itself in all that is pure, excellent, benevolent. It is the shedding abroad of God's love in the heart, for only by love can His holy law be "fulfilled." Nothing but disinterested love (the opposite of self-love) can produce cheerful obedience. And, as Romans 5:5 tells us, the love of God is shed abroad in our hearts by the Holy Spirit. We are sanctified by the Spirit indwelling us, He producing in and through us the fruits of holiness. And thus it is that we read, "But know that the Lord hath set apart him that is godly for Himself" (Ps. 4:3).

In the preceding (portion of this) chapter we asked, "How can it be discovered whether or not we have been sanctified, unless we really know what sanctification is?" Now let it be pointed out that our sanctification by the Father and our sanctification by Christ can only be known to us by the sanctification of the Spirit, and that, in turn, can only be discovered by its effects. And this brings us to the ultimate aspect of the nature of our sanctification, namely, that holy walk, or course of outward conduct, which makes manifest and is the effect of our inward sanctification by the Spirit. This branch of our subject is what theologians have designated our "practical sanctification." Thus, we distinguish between the act and process by which the Christian is set apart unto God, the moral and spiritual state into which that setting apart brings him, and the holy living which proceeds from that state; it is the last we have now reached. As the "setting apart" is both privative and positive—from the service of Satan, to the service of God— so holy living is separation from evil, following that which is good.

Thos. Manton, than whom none of the Puritans are more simple, succinct, and satisfying, says, "Sanctification is threefold. First, meritorious sanctification is Christ's meriting and purchasing for His Church the inward inhabitation of the Spirit, and that grace whereby they may be sanctified: Hebrews 10:10. Second, applicatory sanctification is the inward renovation, of the heart of those whom Christ hath sanctified by the Spirit of regeneration, whereby a man is translated from death to life, from the state of nature to the state of grace. This is spoken of in Titus 3:5: this is the daily sanctification, which, with respect to the merit of Christ, is wrought by the Spirit and the ministry of the Word and sacraments. Third, practical sanctification is that by which those for whom Christ did sanctify Himself, and who are renewed by the Holy Spirit, and planted into Christ by faith, do more and more sanctify and cleanse themselves from sin in thought, word, and deed: (1 Pet. 1:15; 1 John 3:3).

"As to sanctify signifieth to consecrate or dedicate to God, so it signifieth both the fixed inclination or the disposition of the soul towards God as our highest lord and chief good, and accordingly a resignation of our souls to God, to live in the love of His blessed majesty and a thankful obedience to Him. More distinctly (1) it implieth a bent, a tendency, or fixed inclination towards God, which is habitual sanctification. (2) A resignation, or giving up ourselves to God, by which actual holiness is begun; a constant using ourselves to Him, by which it is continued; and the continual exercise of a fervent love, by which it is increased in us more and more, till all be perfected in glory.

As to sanctify signifieth to purify and cleanse, so it signifies the purifying of the soul from the love of the world. A man is impure because, when he was made for God, he doth prefer base trifles of this world before his Maker and everlasting glory: and so he is not sanctified that doth despise and disobey his Maker, he despiseth Him because he preferreth the most contemptible vanity before Him, and doth choose the transitory pleasure of sinning before the endless fruition of God. Now he is sanctified when his worldly love is cured, and he is brought back again to the love and obedience of God. Those that are healed of the over-love of the world are sanctified, as the inclinations of the flesh to worldly things are broken."

"And the very God of peace sanctify you wholly; and I pray God your whole spirit and soul and body be preserved blameless unto the coming of our Lord Jesus Christ" (1 Thess. 5:23). There was probably a threefold reference in the apostle's request. First, he prayed that all the members of the Thessalonian church, the entire assembly, might be sanctified. Second, he prayed that each individual member might be sanctified entirely in his whole man, spirit and soul and body. Third, he prayed that each and all of them might be sanctified more perfectly, moved to press forward unto complete holiness. 1 Thessalonians 5:23 is almost parallel with Hebrews 13:20, 21. The apostle prayed that all the parts and faculties of the Christian might be kept under the influence of efficacious grace, in true and real conformity to God; so influenced by the Truth as to be fitted and furnished, in all cases and circumstances, for the performance of every good work. Though this be our bounden duty, yet it lies not absolutely in our own power, but is the work of God in and through us; and thus is to form the subject of earnest and constant prayer.

Two things are clearly implied in the above passage. First, that the whole nature of the Christian is the subject of the work of sanctification, and not merely part of it: every disposition and power of the spirit, every faculty of the soul, the body with all its members. The body too is "sanctified." It has been made a member of Christ (1 Cor. 6:15), it is the temple of the Holy Spirit (1 Cor. 6:19). As it is an integral part of the believer's person, and as its inclinations and appetites affect the soul and influence conduct, it must be brought under the control of the spirit and soul, so that "every one of us should know how to possess his vessel in sanctification and honor" (1 Thess. 4:4), and "as ye have yielded your members servants to uncleanness and to iniquity, even so now yield your members servants to righteousness unto holiness" (Rom. 6:19).

Second, that this work of Divine grace will be carried on to completion and perfection, for the apostle immediately adds, "Faithful is He that calleth you, who also will do it" (1 Thess. 5:24). Thus the two verses are parallel with "Being confident of this very thing, that He which hath begun a good work in you will finish it until the day of Jesus Christ" (Phil. 1:6). Nothing short of every faculty and member of the Christian being devoted to God is what he is to ever aim at. But the attainment of this is only completely realized at his glorification: "We know that when He shall appear, we shall be like Him" (1 John 3:2)—not only inwardly but outwardly: "Who shall change our vile body, that it may be fashioned like unto His glorious body" (Phil. 3:21).

Chapter 10
ITS NATURE
(COMPLETED)

That which we have labored to show in the previous chapters of this book is the fact that the sanctification of the Christian is very much more than a bare setting apart of him unto God: it is also, and chiefly, a work of grace wrought in his soul. God not only accounts His people holy, but actually makes them so. The various materials and articles used in the tabernacle of old, when dedicated to God, were changed only in their use, but when man is dedicated to God he is changed in his nature, so that not only is there a vital difference between him and others, but a radical difference between him and himself (1 Cor. 6:11)—between what he was, and now is. That change of nature is a real necessity, for the man himself must be made holy before his actions can be so. Grace is planted in the heart, from whence its influence is diffused throughout all departments of his life. Internal holiness is a hatred of sin and a love of that which is good, and external holiness is the avoiding of the one and the pursuing of the other. Wherever there a change of heart fruits will appear in the conduct.

Like "salvation" itself—according to the use of the term is Scripture (see 2 Tim. 1:9, salvation in the past; Phil. 2:12, salvation in the present; Rom. 13:11, salvation in the future) and in the actual history of the redeemed—so sanctification must be considered under its three tenses. There is a very real sense in which all of God's elect have already been sanctified: Jude 1; Hebrews 10:10; 2 Thessalonians 2:13. There is also a very real sense in which those of God's people on earth are daily being sanctified: 2 Corinthians. 4:16; 7:1; 1 Thessalonians 5:23. And there is also a real sense in which the Christian's (complete) sanctification is yet future: Romans 8:30; Hebrews 12:23; 1 John 3:2. Unless this threefold distinction be carefully borne in mind our thoughts are bound to be confused. Objectively, our sanctification is already an accomplished fact (1 Cor. 1:2), in which one saint shares equally with another. Subjectively, our sanctification is not complete in this life (Phil. 3:12) and varies considerably in different Christians, though the promise of Philippians 1:6 belongs alike to all of them.

Though our sanctification be complete in all its parts, yet it is not now perfect in its degrees. As the newborn babe possesses a soul and body, endowed with all their members, yet they are undeveloped and far from a state of maturity. So it is with the Christian, who (in comparison with the life to come) remains throughout this life but a "babe in Christ" (1 Pet. 2:2). We know but "in part" (1 Cor. 13:12), and we are sanctified but in part, for "there remaineth yet very much land to be possessed" (Josh. 13 :1). In the most gracious there remains a double principle: the flesh and the spirit, the old man and the new man. We are a mixture and a medley during our present state. There is a conflict between operating principles (sin and grace), so that every act is mixed: there is tin mixed with our silver and dross with our gold. Our best deeds are defiled, and therefore we continue to feed upon the Lamb with "bitter herbs" (Ex. 12:8).

Holiness in the heart discovers itself by godly sorrowings and godly aspirations. "Blessed are they that mourn: for they shall be comforted" (Matt. 5:4): "mourn" because of the swellings of pride, the workings of unbelief, the surging of discontent; "mourn" because of the feebleness of their faith, the coldness of their love, their lack of conformity to Christ. There is nothing which more plainly evidences a person to be sanctified than a broken and contrite heart—grieving over that which is contrary to holiness. Rightly did the Puritan John Owen say, "Evangelical repentance is that which carrieth the believing soul through all his failures, infirmities, and sins. He is not able to live one day without the constant exercise of it. It is as necessary unto the continuance of spiritual life as faith is. It is that continual, habitual, self-abasement which arises from a sense of the majesty and holiness of God, and the consciousness of our miserable failures." It is this which makes the real Christian so thankful for Romans 7, for he finds it corresponds exactly with his own inward experience.

The sanctified soul, then, is very far from being satisfied with the measure of experimental holiness which is yet his portion. He is painfully conscious of the feebleness of his graces, the leanness of his soul, and the defilements from his inward corruption. But, "Blessed are they which do hunger and thirst after righteousness" (Matt. 5:6), or "they that are hungering and thirsting" as the Greek reads, being the participle of the present tense; intimating a present disposition of the soul. Christ pronounces "blessed" (in contrast from those under "the curse") they who are hungering and thirsting after His righteousness imparted as well as imputed, who thirst after the righteousness of sanctification as well as the righteousness of justification—i.e., the Spirit infusing into the soul holy principles, supernatural graces, spiritual qualities, and then strengthening and developing the same. Such has been the experiences of the saints in all ages, "As the hart panteth after the waterbrooks, so panteth my soul after Thee, O God. My soul thirsteth for God, for the living God; when shall I come and appear before God?" (Ps. 42:1, 2).

One of the things which prevents so many from obtaining a right view of the nature of sanctification is that scarcely any of the bestowments of the Gospel are clearly defined in their minds all being jumbled up together. While every spiritual privilege the believer enjoys is the fruit of God's electing love and the purchase of Christ's mediation, and so are all parts of one grand whole, yet it is our loss if we fail to definitely distinguish them one from the other. Reconciliation and justification, adoption and forgiveness, regeneration and sanctification, all combine to form the present portion of those whom the Father draws to the Son; nevertheless, each of these terms stands for a specific branch of that "great salvation" to which they were appointed. It makes much for our peace of mind and joy of heart when we are able to apprehend these thinks severally. We shall therefore devote the remainder of this chapter unto a comparison of sanctification with other blessings of the Christian.

Regeneration and sanctification. It may appear to some who read critically our articles on "Regeneration" and who have closely followed what has been said in our discussion of the nature of sanctification, that we have almost, if not quite, obliterated all real difference between what is wrought in us at the new birth and what God works in us at our sanctification. It is not easy to preserve a definite line of distinction between them, because they have a number of things in common; yet the leading points of contrast between them need to be considered if we are to differentiate them in our minds. We shall therefore occupy the next two or three paragraphs with an examination of this point, wherein we shall endeavor to set forth the relation of the one to the other. Perhaps it will help us the most to consider this by saying that, in one sense, the relation between regeneration and sanctification is that of the infant to the adult.

In likening the connection between regeneration and sanctification to the relation between an infant and an adult, it should be pointed out that we have in mind our practical and progressive sanctification, and not our objective and absolute sanctification. Our absolute sanctification, so far as our state before God is concerned, is simultaneous with our regeneration. The essential thing in our regeneration is the Spirit's quickening of us into newness of life; the essential thing in our sanctification is that thenceforth we are an habitation of God, through the indwelling of the Spirit, and from that standpoint all the subsequent progressive advances in the spiritual life are but the effects, fruits, and manifestations of that initial consecration or anointing. The consecration of the tabernacle, and later of the temple, was a single act, done once and for all; after, there were many evidences of its continuance or perpetuity. But it is with the experimental aspect we would here treat.

At regeneration a principle of holiness is communicated to us; practical sanctification is the exercise of that principle in living unto God. In regeneration the Spirit imparts saving grace; in His work of sanctification, He strengthens and develops the same. As "original sin" or that indwelling corruption which is in us at our natural birth, contains within it the seeds of all sin, so that grace which is imparted to us at the new birth contains within it the seeds of all spiritual graces; and as the one develops and manifests itself as we grow, so it is with the other. "Sanctification is a constant, progressive renewing of the whole man, whereby the new creature doth daily more and more die unto sin and live unto God. Regeneration is the birth, sanctification is the growth of this babe of grace. In regeneration, the sun of holiness rises; in sanctification it keepeth its course, and shineth brighter and brighter unto the perfect day (Prov. 4:18). The former is a specific change from nature to grace (Eph. 5:8) the latter is a gradual change from one degree of grace to another (Ps. 84:7), whereby the Christian goeth from strength to strength till he appear before God in Zion" (Geo. Swinnock, 1660).

Thus, the foundation of sanctification is laid in regeneration, in that a holy principle is then first formed in us. That holy principle evidences itself in conversion, which is a turning away from sin to holiness, from Satan to Christ, from the world to God. It continues to evidence itself under the constant work of mortification and vivification, or the practical putting off of the old man and the putting on of the new; and is completed at glorification. The great difference then between regeneration and experimental and practical sanctification is that the former is a Divine act, done once and for all; while the latter is a Divine work of God's grace, wherein He sustains and develops, continues and perfects the work He then began. The one is a birth, the other the growth. The making of us practically holy is the design which God has in view when He quickens us: it is the necessary means to this end, for sanctification is the crown of the whole process of salvation.

One of the chief defects of modern teaching on this subject has been in regarding the new birth as the summum bonum of the spiritual life of the believer. Instead of its being the goal, it is but the starting point. Instead of being the end, it is only a means to the end. Regeneration must be supplemented by sanctification, or otherwise the soul would remain at a standstill if such a thing were possible: for it seems to be an unchanging law in every realm that where there is no progression, there must be retrogression. That spiritual growth which is so essential lies in progressive sanctification, wherein all the faculties of the soul are more and more brought under the purifying and regulating influence of the principle of holiness which is implanted at the new birth, for thus alone do we grow up into Him in all things, which is the Head, even Christ" (Eph. 4:15).

Justification and sanctification. The relation between justification and sanctification is clearly revealed in Romans 3 to 8: that Epistle being the great doctrinal treatise of the N. T. In the 5th chapter we see the believing sinner declared righteous before God and at peace with Him, given an immutable standing in His favor, reconciled to Him, assured of his preservation, and so rejoicing in hope of the glory of God. Yet, great as are these blessings, something more is required by the quickened conscience, namely, deliverance from the power and pollution of inherited sin. Accordingly, this is dealt with at length in Romans 6, 7, 8, where various fundamental aspects of sanctification are treated. First, it is demonstrated that the believer has been judicially cleansed from sin and the curse of the law, and that, in order that he may be practically delivered from the dominion of sin, so that he may delight in and serve the law. Union with Christ not only involves identification with His death, but participation in His resurrection.

Yet though sanctification is discussed by the apostle after his exposition of justification, it is a serious error to conclude that there may be, and often is, a considerable interval of time between the two things, or that sanctification is a consequent of justification; still worse is the teaching of some that, having been justified we must now seek sanctification, without which we must certainly perish—thus making the security of justification to depend upon a holy walk. No, though the two truths are dealt with singly by the apostle, they are inseparable: though they are to be contemplated alone, they must not be divided. Christ cannot be halved: in Him the believing sinner has both righteousness and holiness. Each department of the Gospel needs to be considered distinctly, but not pitted against each other. Let us not draw a false conclusion, then, because justification is treated of in Romans 3 to 5 and sanctification in 6 to 8: the one passage supplements the other: they are two halves of one whole.

The Christian's regeneration is not the cause of his justification, nor is justification the cause of his sanctification—for Christ is the cause of all three; yet there is an order preserved between them: not an order of time, but of nature. First we are recovered to God's image, then to His favor, and then to His fellowship. So inseparable are justification and sanctification that sometimes the one is presented first and sometimes the other: see Romans 8:1 and 13: 1 John 1:9; then Micah 7:19 and 1 Corinthians 6:11. First, God quickens the dead soul: being made alive spiritually, he is now capacitated to act faith in Christ, by which he is (instrumentally) justified. In sanctification the Spirit carries on and perfects the work in regeneration, and that progressive work is accomplished under the new relation into which the believer is introduced by justification. Having been judicially reconciled to God, the way is now open for an experimental fellowship with Him, and that is maintained as the Spirit carries forward His work of sanctification.

"Though justification and sanctification are both of them blessings of grace, and though they are absolutely inseparable, yet they are so manifestly distinct, that there is in various respects a wide difference between them. Justification respects the person in a legal sense, is a single act of grace, and terminates in a relative change; that is, a freedom from punishment and a right to life. Sanctification regards him in an experimental sense, is a continued work of grace, and terminates in a real change, as to the quality both of habits and actions. The former is by a righteousness without us; the latter is by holiness wrought in us. Justification is by Christ as a priest, and has regard to the guilt of sin; sanctification is by Him as a king, and refers to its dominion. Justification is instantaneous and complete in all its real subjects; but sanctification is progressive" (A. Booth, 1813).

Purification and sanctification. These two things are not absolutely identical: though inseparable, they are yet distinguishable. We cannot do better than quote from G. Smeaton, "The two words frequently occurring in the ritual of Israel, 'sanctify' and 'purify,' are so closely allied in sense, that some regard them as synonymous. But a slight shade of distinction between the two may be discerned as follows. It is assumed that ever-recurring defilements, of a ceremonial kind, called for sacrifices which removed, and the word 'purify' referred to these rites and sacrifices which removed the stains which excluded the worshipper from the privilege of approach to the sanctuary of God, and from fellowship with His people. The defilement which he contracted excluded him from access. But when this same Israelite was purged by sacrifice, he was readmitted to the full participation of the privilege. He was then sanctified, or holy. Thus the latter is the consequence of the former. We may affirm, then, that the two words in this reference to the old worship, are very closely allied; so much so, that the one involves the other. This will throw light upon the use of these two expressions in the N. T.: Ephesians 5:25, 26; Hebrews 2;11; Titus 2:14. All these passages represent a man defiled by sin and excluded from God, but readmitted to access and fellowship, and so pronounced holy, as soon as the blood of sacrifice is applied to him." Often the term "purge" or "purify" (especially in Hebrews) includes justification as well.

Objective holiness is the result of a relationship with God, He having set apart some thing or person for His own pleasure. But the setting apart of one unto God necessarily involves the separating of it from all that is opposed to Him: all believers were set apart or consecrated to God by the sacrifice of Christ. Subjective holiness is the result of a work of God wrought in the soul, setting that person apart for His use. Thus "holiness" has two fundamental aspects. Growing out of the second, is the soul's apprehension of God's claims upon him, and his presentation of himself unto God for His exclusive use (Rom. 12:1; etc.), which is practical sanctification. The supreme example of all three is found in Jesus Christ, the Holy one of God. Objectively, He was the One "whom the Father hath sanctified and sent into the world" (John 10:36); subjectively, He "received the Spirit without measure" (John 3 :34); and practically, He lived for the glory of God, being absolutely devoted to His will—only with this tremendous difference: He needed no inward purification as we do.

To sum up. Holiness, then, is both a relationship and a moral quality. It has both a negative and a positive side: cleansing from impurity, adorning with the grace of the Spirit. Sanctification is, first, a position of honor to which God has appointed His people. Second, it is a state of purity which Christ has purchased for them. Third, it is an inducement given to them by the Holy Spirit. Fourth, it is a course of devoted conduct in keeping therewith. Fifth, it is a standard of moral perfection, at which they are ever to aim: 1 Peter 1:15. A "saint" is one who was chosen in Christ before the foundation of the world (Eph. 1:4), who has been cleansed from the guilt and pollution of sin by the blood of Christ (Heb. 13:12), who has been consecrated to God by the indwelling Spirit (2 Cor. 1:21, 22), who has been made inwardly holy by the impartation of the principle of grace (Phil. :6), and whose duty, privilege, and aim is to walk suitable thereto (Eph. 4:1).

Chapter 11
Its Author

God Himself is the alone source and spring of all holiness. There is nothing of it in any creature but what is immediately from the Holy One. When God first created man, He made him in His own image, that is, "in righteousness and true holiness (Eph. 4:24 and cf. Col. 3:10). The creature can no more produce holiness of himself than he can create life: for the one he is just as much dependent upon God as he is for the other How much less, then, can a fallen creature, polluted and enslaved by sin, sanctify himself? More easily could the Ethiopian change his skin or the leopard his spots, than a moral leper make himself pure. Where any measure of real holiness is found in a human heart its possessor must say with Paul, "By the grace of God I am what I am" (1 Cor. 15:10). Sanctification, then, is the immediate work and gift of God Himself.

No greater delusion can seize the minds of men than that defiled nature is able to cleanse itself, that fallen and ruined man may rectify himself, or that those who have lost the image of God which He created in them, should create it again in £ themselves by their own endeavors. Self-evident as is this truth yet pride ever seeks to set it aside. Self-complacency assumes that obligation and ability are co-extensive. Not so. It is true that God requires and commands us to be holy for He will not relinquish His rights or lower His standard. Yet His command no more denotes that we have the power to comply, than His setting before us a perfect standard implies we are able to measure up to the same. Rather does the one inform us that we are without what God requires, the other should humble us into the dust because we come so far short of the glory of God.

But so self-sufficient and self-righteous are we by nature it also needs to be pointed out that, the very fact God promises to work in His people by His grace both indicates and demonstrates that of themselves they are quite unable to meet His demands. Ponder for a moment the following: "I will put My law in their inward parts, and write it in their hearts; and will be their God, and they shall be My people" (Jer. 31:31), "I will give them one heart, and one way, that they may fear Me forever, for the good of them, and of their children after them: and I will make an everlasting covenant with them, that I will not turn away from them to do them good; but I will put My fear in their hearts, that they shall not depart from Me" (Jer. 32:39,40), "A new heart also will I give you, and a new spirit will I put within you: and I will take away the stony heart out of your flesh, and I will give you a heart of flesh; and I will put My Spirit within you, and cause you to walk in My statutes" (Ezek. 36:26, 27). In those blessed assurances, and nowhere else, is contained the guarantee of our sanctification: all turns upon God's power, grace, and operations. He is the alone accomplisher of His own promises.

The Author of our sanctification is the Triune God. We say "the Triune God," because in Scripture the title "God," when it stands unqualified, is not used with a uniform signification. Sometimes "God" refers to the first Person in the Trinity, sometimes to the second Person, and sometimes to the Third. In other passages, like 1 Corinthians 5:28, for instance, it includes all the three Persons. Each of the Eternal Three has His own distinctive place or part in connection with the sanctification of the Church, and it is necessary for us to clearly perceive this if we are to have definite views thereof. We have now reached that stage in our prosecution of this subject where it behooves us to carefully trace out the particular operations of each Divine Person in connection with our sanctification, for only as these are discerned by us will we be prepared to intelligently offer unto each One the praise which is His distinctive due.

In saying that the Author of sanctification is the Triune God, we do not mean that the Father is the Sanctifier of the Church in precisely the same way or manner as the Son or as the Holy Spirit is. No, rather is it our desire to emphasize the fact that the Christian is equally indebted unto each of the three Divine Persons, that his sanctification proceeds as truly from the Father as it does from the Holy Spirit, and as actually from the Son as it does from either the Spirit or the Father. Many writers have failed to make this clear. Yet it needs to be pointed out that, in the economy of salvation, there is an official order observed and preserved by the Holy Three, wherein we are given to see that all is from the Father, all is through the Son, all is by the Holy Spirit. Not that this official order denotes any essential subordination or inferiority of one Person to another, but that each manifests Himself distinctively, each displays His own glory, and each is due the separate adoration of His people.

It is most blessed to observe there is a beautiful order adopted and carried on by the Eternal Three through all the departments of Divine love to the Church, so that each glorious Person of the Godhead has taken part in every act of grace manifested toward the mystical Body of Christ. Though all Three work conjointly, yet there are distinct Personal operations, by which they make way for the honor of each other: the love of the Father for the glory of the Son, and the glory of the Son for the power of the Holy Spirit. Thus it is in connection with the subject now before us. In the Scriptures we read that the Church is "sanctified by God the Father" (Jude 1), and again, "Wherefore Jesus also, that He might sanctify the people with His own blood, suffered without the gate" (Heb. 13:12), and yet again, "God hath from the beginning chosen you to salvation through sanctification of the Spirit" (2 Thess. 2:13). Each Person of the Godhead, then, is our Sanctifier, though not in the same manner.

This same cooperation by the Holy Three is observable in many other things. It was so in the creation of the world: "God that made the world and all things therein, seeing that He is Lord of heaven and earth" (Acts 17:24), where the reference is plainly to the Father; of the Son it is affirmed "All things were made by Him, and without Him was not anything made that was made" (John 1:3); while in Job 26:13 we are told, "By His Spirit He bath garnished the heavens." So with the production of the sacred humanity of our Redeemer: the super-natural impregnation of the Virgin was the immediate effect of the Spirit's agency (Luke 1:35), yet the human nature was voluntarily and actively assumed by Christ Himself: "He took upon Him the form of a servant" (Phil. 2:7 and cf. "took part" in Heb. 2:14); while in Hebrews 10:5 we hear the Son saying to the Father, "a body hast Thou prepared Me."

Our present existence is derived from the joint operation of the Divine agency of the blessed Three: "Have we not all one Father? hath not one God created us?" (Mal. 2:10); of the Son it is said, "For by Him were all things created, that are in heaven and that are in earth" (Col. 1:16); while in Job 33:4 we read, "The Spirit of God hath made me, and the Breath of the Almighty hath given me life." In like manner, the "eternal life" of believers is indiscriminately ascribed to each of the Divine persons: in Romans 6:23 it is attributed to the bounty of the Father, 1 John 5 :11 expressly assures us that it "is in the Son," while in Galatians 6:8 we read, "he that soweth to the Spirit shall of the Spirit reap life everlasting." By the Father we are justified (Rom. 8:33), by Christ we are justified (Isa. 53:11), by the Spirit we are justified (1 Cor. 6:11). By the Father we are preserved (1 Pet. 1 :5), by the Son we are preserved (John 10:28), by the Spirit we are preserved (Eph. 4:30). By the Father we shall be raised (2 Cor. I :9), by the Son (John 5:28), by the

Spirit (Rom. 8:11).

The actions of the Persons in the Godhead are not unlike to the beautiful colors of the rainbow: those colors are perfectly blended together in one, yet each is quite distinct. So it is in connection with the several operations of the Holy Three concerning our sanctification. While it be blessedly true that the Triune God is the Author of this wondrous work, yet, if we are to observe the distinctions which the Holy Scriptures make in the unfolding of this theme, they require us to recognize that, in the economy of salvation, God the Father is, in a special manner, the Originator of this unspeakable blessing. In connection with the whole scheme of redemption God the Father is to be viewed as the Fountain of grace: all spiritual blessings originating in His goodness, and are bestowed according to the good pleasure of His sovereign will. This is clear from Ephesians 1:3: "Blessed be the God and Father of our Lord Jesus Christ, who hath blessed us with all spiritual blessings in the heavenlies in Christ."

That the Father is the Sanctifier of the Church is obvious from 1 Thessalonians 5:23, "And the very God of peace sanctify you wholly: and I pray God your whole spirit and soul and body be preserved blameless unto the coming of our Lord Jesus Christ Here He is acknowledged as such, by prayer being made to Him for the perfecting of this gift and grace. So again in Hebrews 13:20, 21, we find the apostle addressing Him as follows, "Now the God of peace, that brought again from the dead our Lord Jesus, that great Shepherd of the sheep, through the blood of the everlasting covenant, make you perfect m every good work to do His will, working in you that which is well pleasing in His sight, through Jesus Christ." It is the furthering of this work within His people for which the apostle supplicates God. In both passages it is the Father who is sought unto. "By the which will we are sanctified, through the offering of the body of Jesus Christ once for all" (Heb. 10): here the sanctification of the Church is traced back to the sovereign will of God as the supreme originating cause thereof, the reference again being to the eternal gracious purpose of the Father, which Christ came here to accomplish.

Further proof that the first Person in the Divine Trinity is the immediate Author of our sanctification is found in Jude 1: "To them that are sanctified by God the Father, and preserved in Jesus Christ, called." Note it is not simply "them that are sanctified by God," but more specifically "By God the Father." Before attempting to give the meaning of this remarkable text, it needs to be pointed out that it is closely connected with those words of Christ in John 10:36, "Say ye of Him, whom the Father hath sanctified, and sent into the world, Thou blasphemest because I said, I am the Son of God?" Our Lord was there referring to Himself not as the second Person of the Godhead absolutely considered, but as the Godman Mediator, for only as such was He "sent" by the Father. His being "sanctified" before He was "sent," has reference to a transaction in Heaven ere He became incarnate. Before the foundation of the world, the Father set apart Christ and ordained that He should be both the Head and Savior of His Church, and that He should be plenteously endowed by the Spirit for His vast undertaking.

Reverting to Jude 1, we would note particularly the order of its statements: the "sanctified by God the Father" comes before "preserved in Jesus Christ, called." This initial aspect of our sanctification antedates our regeneration or effectual call from darkness to light, and therefore takes us back to the eternal counsels of God. There are three things in our verse: taking them in their inverse order, there is first, our "calling," when we were brought from death unto life; that was preceded by our being "preserved in Jesus Christ," i.e., preserved from physical death in the womb, in the days of our infancy, during the recklessness of youth; and that also preceded by our being "sanctified" by the Father, that is, our names being enrolled in the Lamb's book of life, we are given to Christ to be loved by Him with an everlasting love and made joint-heirs with Him forever and ever.

Our sanctification by the Father was His eternal election of us, with all that that term connotes and involves. Election was far more than a bare choice of persons. It included our being predestined unto the adoption of children by Jesus Christ to Himself (Eph. 1:15). It included our being made "vessels unto honor" and being "afore prepared to glory" (Rom. 9:21, 22). It included being "appointed to obtain salvation by our Lord Jesus Christ" (1 Thess. 5 :9). It included our being separated for God's pleasure, God's use, and "that we should be to the praise of His glory" (Eph. 1:12). It included our being made "holy and without blame before him" (Eph. 1:4). This eternal sanctification by God the Father is also mentioned in 2 Timothy 1:9, "Who hath saved us, and called us with a holy calling, not according to our works but according to His own purpose and grace, which was given us in Christ Jesus before the world began."

As we pointed out in the last paragraph of the preceding chapter, "Sanctification is, first, a position of honor to which God hath appointed His people." That position of honor was their being "chosen in Christ before the foundation of the world" (Eph. 1:4), when they were constituted members of His mystical Body by the eternal purpose of God. 0 what an amazing honor was that! a place in glory higher than that of the angels being granted them. Our poor minds are staggered before such wondrous grace. Here, then, is the link of connection between John 10:36 and Jude 1: Christ was not alone in the mind of the Father when He "sanctified" Him: by the Divine decree, Christ was separated and consecrated as the Head of a sanctified people. In the sanctification of Christ, all who are "called saints" were, in Him, eternally set apart, to be partakers of His own holy standing before the Father! This was an act of pure sovereignty on the Father's part.

As it is not possible that anything can add to God's essential blessedness (Job 22:2, 3; 35:7), so nothing whatever outside of God can possibly be a motive unto Him for any of His actions. If He be pleased to bring creatures into existence, His own supreme and sovereign will must be the sole cause, as His own manifestative glory is His ultimate end and design. This is plainly asserted in the Scriptures: "The Lord hath made all things for Himself: yea, even the wicked for the day of evil" (Prov. 16 :4), "Thou hast created all things, and for Thy pleasure they are and were created" (Rev. 4:11), "Who hath first given to Him, and it shall be recompensed unto him again? For of Him, and through Him, and to Him, are all things: to whom be glory forever, Amen" (Rom. 11:35, 36). So it is in the ordaining of some of His creatures unto honor and glory, and appointing them to salvation in bringing them to that glory: nought but God's sovereign will was the cause, nought but His own manifestative glory is the end.

As we have shown in previous chapters, to "sanctify" signifies to consecrate or set apart for a sacred use, to cleanse or purify, to adorn or beautify. Which of these meanings has the term in Jude 1? We believe the words "sanctified by God the Father" include all three of those definitions. First, in that eternal purpose of His, the elect were separated from all other creatures, and predestinated unto the adoption of sons. Second, in God's foreviews of His elect falling in Adam, the corrupting of their natures, and the defilement which their personal acts of sin would entail, He ordained that the Mediator should make a full atonement for them, and by His blood cleanse them from all sin. Third, by choosing them in Christ, the elect were united to Him and so made one with Him that all His worthiness and perfection becomes theirs too; and thus they were adorned. God never views them apart for Christ.

"To the praise of the glory of His grace, wherein He hath made us accepted in the Beloved" (Eph. 1:6). The Greek word for "accepted" is "charitoo," and Young's Concordance gives as its meaning "to make gracious." It occurs (as a passive participle, rather than in its active form, as in Eph. 1:6) again only in Luke i :~8, where the angel said to the Virgin, "Hail, highly favored one," which Young defines as "to give grace, to treat graciously," and in his Index "graciously accepted or much graced." This, we believe, is the exact force of it in Eph. I :6: "according as He hath much graced us in the Beloved." A careful reading of the immediate context will show that this was before the foundation of the world, which is confirmed by the fact that the elect's being "much graced in the Beloved" comes before "redemption" and "forgiveness of sins" in verse 7!—note too the "hath" in verses 3, 4, 6 and the change to "have" in verse 7!

Here, then, is the ultimate reference in "sanctified by God the Father" (Jude 1). As we have so often pointed out in the previous chapters "sanctification" is not a bare act of simply setting apart, but involves or includes the adorning and beautifying of the object or person thus set apart, so fitting it for God's use. Thus it was in God's eternal purpose. He not only made an election from the mass of creatures to be created; He not only separated those elect ones from the others, but He chose them "in Christ," and "much graced them in the Beloved !" The elect were made the mystical Body and Bride of Christ, so united to Him that whatever grace Christ hath, by virtue of their union with Him, His people have: and therefore did He declare, "Thou hast loved them AS Thou loved Me" (John 17:23). 0 that it may please the Holy Spirit to so shine upon our feeble understandings that we may be enabled to lay hold of this wondrous, glorious, and transcendent fact. "Sanctified by God the Father :" set apart by Him to be Body and Bride of Christ, "much graced" in Him, possessing His own holy standing before the Throne of Heaven.

Chapter 12
Its Procurer

We have now reached what is to our mind the most important and certainly the most blessed aspect of our many-sided subject, yet that which is the least understood in not a few circles of Christendom. It is the objective side of sanctification that we now turn to, that perfect and unforfeitable holiness which every believer has in Christ. We are not now going to write upon sanctification as a moral quality or attribute, nor of that which is a matter of experience or attainment by us; rather shall we contemplate something entirely outside ourselves, namely, that which is a fundamental part of our standing and state in Christ. That which we are about to consider is one of those "spiritual blessings" which God has blest us with "in the heavenlies in Christ" (Eph. 1:3). It is an immediate consequence of His blood-shedding, and results from our actual union with Him as "the Holy One of God." It is that which His perfect offering has sanctified us unto, as well as what it has sanctified us from.

Among all the terrible effects and fruits which sin produces, the two chief are alienation from God and condemnation by God: sin necessarily excludes from His sanctuary, and brings the sinner before the judgment seat of His law. Contrariwise, among all the blessed fruits and effects which Christ's sacrifice procures, the two chief ones are justification and sanctification: it cannot be otherwise. Inasmuch as Christ's sacrifice has "put away" (Heb. 9:26), "made an end" (Dan. 9:24) of the sins of His people, they are not only freed from all condemnation, but they are also given the right and the meetness to draw nigh unto God as purged worshippers. Sin not only entails guilt, it defiles; and the blood of Christ has not only secured pardon, it cleanses. Yet simple, clear, and conclusive as is this dual fact, Christians find it much harder to apprehend the second part of it than they do the first.

When we first believed in Christ, and "the burden of our sins rolled away," we supposed that (as one hymn expresses it) we would be "happy all the day." Assured of God's forgiveness, that we had entered His family by the new birth, and that an eternity with Christ in unclouded bliss was our certain inheritance, what could possibly dampen our joy? Ah, but it was not long before we discovered that we were still sinners, living in a world of sin: yea, as time went on, we were made more and more conscious of the sink of iniquity that indwells us, ever sending forth its foul streams, polluting our thoughts, words and actions. This forced from us the agonized inquiry, How can such vile creatures as we see, feel, and know ourselves to be, either pray to, serve, or worship the thrice holy God? Only in His own blessed Word can be found a sufficient and a satisfying answer to this burning question.

"The epistle to the Romans, is, as is well known, that part of Scripture in which the question of justification is most fully treated. There, especially, we are taught to think of God as a Judge presiding in the Courts of His holy judgment. Accordingly, the expressions employed throughout that epistle are 'forensic,' or 'judicial.' They refer to our relation to God, or His relation to us, in His judicial Courts—the great question there being, how criminals can be brought into such a relation to Him, as to have, not criminality, but righteousness, imputed to them.

"But if, in the epistle to the Romans, we see God in the Courts of His judgment, equally in the epistle to the Hebrews we see Him in the Temple of His worship. 'Sanctified' is a word that has the same prominence in the epistle to the Hebrews that 'justified' has in the epistle to the Romans. It is a Temple-word, descriptive of our relation to God in the Courts of His worship, just as 'justified' is a forensic word, descriptive of our relation to God in the Courts of His judgment. Before there can be any question about serving or worshipping God acceptably, the necessity of His holiness requires that the claims both of the Courts of His judgment, and also of the Courts of His worship, should be fully met. He who is regarded in the, judicial Courts of God as an unpardoned criminal, or who, in relation to the Temple of God, is regarded as having the stains of his guilt upon him, cannot be allowed to take his stand among God's servants. No leper that was not thoroughly cleansed could serve in the Tabernacle. The existence of one stain not adequately covered by compensatory atonement, shuts out from the presence of God.

"We must stand 'uncharged' in relation to the judicial Courts of God and imputatively 'spotless' in relation to the Courts of His worship: in other words, we must be perfectly 'justified' and perfectly 'sanctified' before we can attempt to worship or serve Him. 'Sanctification,' therefore, when used in this sense, is not to be contrasted with justification, as if the latter were complete, but the former incomplete and progressive. Both are complete to the believer. The same moment that brings the complete 'justification' of the fifth of Romans, brings the equally complete 'sanctification' of the tenth of Hebrews—both being equally needed in order that God, as respects the claims of His holiness, might be 'appeased' or 'placated' toward us; and therefore equally needed as prerequisites to our entrance on the worship and service of God in His heavenly Temple: for until wrath is effectually appeased there can be no entrance into heaven.

"The complete and finished sanctification of believers by the blood of Jesus, is the great subject of the ninth and tenth of the Hebrews. 'The blood of bulls and goats' gave to them who were sprinkled therewith a title to enter into the courts of the typical tabernacle, but that title was not an abiding title. It was no sooner gained than it was lost by the first recurring taint. Repetition therefore of offering and repetition of sprinkling was needed again and again. The same circle was endlessly trodden and retrodden; and yet never was perpetuity of acceptance obtained. The tabernacle and its services were but shadows; but they teach us that, as 'the blood of bulls and goats' gave to them who were sprinkled therewith a temporary title to enter into that typical tabernacle; so, the blood of Christ, once offered, gives to all those who are once sprinkled therewith (and all believers are sprinkled) a title, not temporary, but abiding, to enter into God's presence as those who are sanctified for Heaven" (B. W. Newton).

"We are sanctified through the offering of the body of Jesus Christ once for all... For by one offering He hath perfected forever them that are sanctified" (Heb. 10:10, 14). These blessed declarations have no reference whatsoever to anything which the Spirit does in the Christian, but relate exclusively to what Christ has secured for them. They speak of that which results from our identification with Christ. They affirm that by virtue of the Sacrifice of Calvary every believer is not only counted righteous in the Courts of God's judgment, but is perfectly hallowed for the Courts of His worship. The precious blood of the Lamb not only delivers from Hell, but it also fits us for Heaven.

By the redemptive work of Christ the entire Church has been set apart, consecrated unto and accepted by God. The grand truth is that the feeblest and most uninstructed believer was as completely sanctified before God the first moment that he trusted in Christ, as he will be when he dwells in Heaven in his glorified state. True, both his sphere and his circumstances will then be quite different from what they now are: nevertheless, his title to Heaven, his meetness for the immediate presence of the thrice Holy One, will be no better than it is to-day. It is his relation to Christ (and that alone) which qualifies him to enter the Father's House; and it is his relation to Christ (and that alone) which gives him the right to now draw nigh within the veil. True, the believer still carries around with him "this body of death" (a depraved nature), but that affects not his perfect standing, his completeness in Christ, his acceptance, his justification and sanctification before God. But, as we said in an earlier paragraph, the Christian finds it much easier to believe in or grasp the truth of justification, than he does of his present perfect sanctification in Christ. For this reason we deem it advisable to proceed slowly and enter rather fully into this aspect of our subject. Let us begin with our Lord's own words in John 17:19, "For their sakes I sanctify Myself, that they also might be sanctified through the truth." Unto what did Christ allude when He there spoke of sanctifying Himself? Certainly He could not possibly be referring to anything subjective or experimental, for in His own person He was "the Holy One of God," and as such, He could not increase in holiness, or become more holy. His language then must have respect unto what was objective, relating to the exercise of His mediatorial office.

When Christ said, "For their sakes I sanctify Myself," He denoted that He was then on the very point of dedicating Himself to the full and final execution of the work of making Himself a sacrifice for sin, to satisfy all the demands of God's law and Justice. Christ, then, was therein expressing His readiness to present Himself before the Father as the Surety of His People to place Himself on the altar as a vicarious propitiation for His Church. It was "for the sake" of others that He sanctified Himself: for the sake of His eleven apostles, who are there to be regarded as the representatives of the entire Election of Grace. It is on their behalf, for their express benefit, that He set Himself apart unto the full discharge of His mediatorial office, that the fruit thereof might redound unto them. Christ unreservedly devoted Himself unto God, that His people might reap the full advantages thereof.

The particular end here mentioned of Christ's sanctifying Himself was "that they also might be sanctified through the truth," which is a very faulty rendering of the original, the Greek preposition being "in" and not "through," and there is no article before "truth." The marginal rendering, therefore, is much to be preferred: "that they might be truly sanctified"—Bagster's interlinear and the R. V. give "sanctified in truth." The meaning is "that they might be" actually, really, verily "sanctified"—in contrast from the typical and ceremonial sanctification which obtained under the Mosaic dispensation: compare John 4:24; Col. 1:6; 1 John 3:18 for "in truth." As the of Christ's sanctifying Himself—devoting Himself as whole burnt offering to God, His people are perfectly sanctified their sins are put away, their persons are cleansed from all defilement; and not only so, but the excellency of His infinitely meritorious work is imputed to them, so that they are perfectly acceptable to God, meet for His presence, fitted for His worship.

"For by one offering He hath perfected forever them that sanctified" (Heb. 10:14)—not by anything which the Spirit works in them, but solely by what Christ's sanctifying of Him-self has wrought for them. It is this sanctification in and through Christ which gives Christians their priestly character, the title to draw near unto God within the veil as purged worshippers. Access to God, or the worship of a people made nigh by blood, was central in the Divinely appointed system of Judaism (Heb. 9 :13). The antitype, the substance, the blessed reality of this, is what Christ has secured for His Church. Believers are already perfectly sanctified objectively, as the immediate fruit of the Savior's sacrifice. Priestly nearness is now their blessed portion in consequence of Christ's priestly offering of Himself. This it is, and nought else, which gives us "boldness to enter into the Holiest" (Heb. 10:19).

Many Christians who are quite clear that they must look alone to Christ for their justification before God, often fail to view Him as their complete sanctification before God. But this ought not to be, for Scripture is just as clear on the one point as on the other; yea, the two are therein inseparably joined together. "But of Him are ye in Christ Jesus, who of God is made unto us wisdom, and righteousness, and sanctification, and redemption" (I Cor. 1 :30). And here we must dissent from the exposition of this verse given by Chas. Hodge (in his commentary) and others of his school, who interpret "sanctification" here as Christ's Spirit indwelling His people as the Spirit of holiness, transforming them unto His likeness. But this verse is speaking of that sanctification which Christ is made unto us, and not that which we are made by Christ—the distinction is real and vital, and to ignore or confound it is inexcusable in a theologian.

Christ crucified (see the context of 1 Cor. 1:30—verses 17, 18, 23), "of God is made unto us" four things, and this is precisely the same way that God "made Him (Christ) to be sin for us" (2 Cor. 5:21), namely, objectively and imputatively. First, Christ is "made unto us Wisdom," objectively, for He is the One in whom all the treasures of wisdom and knowledge are hid, it is true that by the Spirit we are made wise unto salvation, nevertheless, we are far from being as wise as we ought to be—see 1 Corinthians 8:2. But all the wisdom God requires of us is found in Christ, and as the "Wisdom" of the book of Proverbs, He is ours. Second, Christ is "made unto us Righteous-ness," objectively, as He is Himself "The Lord our righteous-ness" (Jer. 23 :6), and therefore does the believer exclaim, "In the Lord have I righteousness and strength" (Isa. 45 :24). As the law raises its accusing voice against me, I point to Christ as the One who has, by His active and passive obedience, met its every demand on my behalf.

Third, Christ is "made unto us Sanctification," objectively: in Him we have an absolute purity, and by the imputation to us of the efficacy and merits of His cross-work we who were excluded from God on account of sin, are now given access to Him. If Israel became a holy people when sprinkled with the blood of bulls and goats, so that they were readmitted to Jehovah's worship, how much more has the infinitely valuable blood of Christ sanctified us, so that we may approach God as acceptable worshippers. This sanctification is not something which we have in our own persons, but was ours in Christ as soon as we laid hold of Him by faith. Fourth, Christ is "made unto us Redemption," objectively: He is in His own person both our Redeemer and Redemption—"in whom we have redemption" (Eph. 1:7). Christ is "made unto us Redemption" not by enabling us to redeem ourselves, but by Himself paying the price.

1 Corinthians 1:30, then, affirms that we are complete in Christ: that whatever the law demands of us, it has received on our account in the Surety. If we are considered as what we are in ourselves, not as we stand in Christ (as one with Him), then a thousand things may be "laid to our charge." It may be laid to our charge that we are woefully ignorant of many parts of the Divine will: but the sufficient answer is, Christ is our Wisdom. It may be laid to our charge that all our righteousnesses are as filthy rags: but the sufficient answer is, that Christ is our Righteousness. It may be laid to our charge that we do many things and fail to do many others which unfit us for the presence of a holy God: but the sufficient answer is, that Christ is our Sanctification. It may be laid to our charge that we are largely in bondage to the flesh: but the sufficient answer is, Christ is our Redemption.

1 Corinthians 1:30, then, is a unit: we cannot define the "wisdom" and the "sanctification" as what the Spirit works in us, and the "righteousness" and the "redemption" as what Christ has wrought for us: all four are either objective or subjective. Christ is here said to be "sanctification" unto us, just as He is our righteousness and redemption. To suppose that the sanctification here spoken of is that which is wrought in us, would oblige me to explain the righteousness and redemption here spoken of, as that which we had in ourselves; but such a thought Mr. Hodge would rightly have rejected with abhorrence. The righteousness which Christ is "made unto us" is most certainly not the righteousness which He works in us (the Romanist heresy), but the righteousness which He wrought out for us. So it is with the sanctification which Christ is "made unto us it is not in ourselves, but in Him; it is not an incomplete and progressive thing, but a

perfect and eternal one.

God has made Christ to be sanctification unto us by imputing to us the infinite purity and excellency of His sacrifice. We are made nigh to God by Christ's blood (Eph. 2:13) before we are brought nigh to Him by the effectual call of the Spirit (1 Pet. 2:9): the former being the necessary foundation of the latter—in the types the oil could only be placed upon the blood. And it is on this account we "are sanctified in Christ Jesus, called saints" (1 Cor. ':2). How vastly different is this—how immeasurably superior to—what the advocates of "the higher life" or the "victorious life" set before their hearers and readers! It is not merely that Christ is able to do this or willing to do that for us, but every Christian is already "sanctified in Christ Jesus." My ignorance of this does not alter the blessed fact, and neither does my failure to clearly understand nor the weakness of my faith to firmly grasp it, in anywise impair it. Nor have my feelings or experience anything whatever to do with it: God says it, God has done it, and nothing can alter it.

Chapter 13
Its Procurer
(CONTINUED)

It has been pointed out in the earlier chapters of this book that the Scriptures present the believer's sanctification from several distinct points of view, the chief of which are, first, our sanctification in the eternal purpose of God, when in His decree He chose us in Christ "that we should be holy and without blame before Him" (Eph. 1:4). That is what is referred to at the beginning of Hebrews 10:10, "by the which will we are sanctified." This is our sanctification by God the Father (Jude 1), which was considered by us in the 11th chapter under "The Author of our Sanctification." Second, there is the fulfilling of that "will" of God, the accomplishing of His eternal purpose by our actual sanctification through the sacrifice of Christ. That is what is referred to in "Wherefore Jesus also, that He might sanctify the people with His own blood, suffered without the gate" (Heb. 13:12). This is our sanctification by God the Son, and is what we are now considering. Third, there is the application of this sanctification to the individual by the Holy Spirit, when He separates him from those who are dead in sins by quickening him, and by the new birth imparting to him a new nature. This is our sanctification by God the Spirit.

Fourth, there is the fruit of these in the Christian's character and conduct whereby he is separated in his life and walk from the world which lieth in the Wicked one, and this is by the Holy Spirit's working in him and applying the Word to him, so that he is (in measure—for now we see "through a glass darkly") enabled to apprehend by faith his separation to God by the precious blood of Christ. Yet both his inward and outward life is far from being perfect, for though possessing anew and spiritual nature, the flesh remains in him, unchanged, to the end of his earthly pilgrimage. Those around him know little or nothing of the inward conflict of which he is the subject: they see his outward failures, but hear not his secret groanings before God. It is not yet made manifest what he shall be, but though very imperfect at present through indwelling sin, yet the promise is sure "when He shall appear we shall be like Him; for we shall see Him as He is."

Now though in this fourth sense our practical sanctification is incomplete, this in nowise alters the fact, nor to the slightest degree invalidates it, that our sanctification in the first three senses mentioned above is entire and eternal, that "by one offering Christ hath perfected forever them that are sanctified" (Heb. 10:14). Though these three phases of the believer's sanctification are quite distinct as to their development or manifestation, yet they are blessedly combined together, and form our one complete acceptance before God. That which we are here considering has to do with the objective side of our subject: by which we mean that it is something entirely outside of ourselves, resulting from what Christ has done for us. It is that which we have in Christ and by Christ, and therefore it can be received and enjoyed by faith alone. 0 what a difference it makes to the peace and joy of the soul once the child of God firmly grasps the blessed truth that a perfect sanctification is his present and inalienable portion, that God has made Christ to be unto him sanctification as well as righteousness.

Every real Christian has already been sanctified or set apart as holy unto God by the precious blood of the Lamb. But though many believers are consciously and confessedly "justified by His blood" (Rom. 5:9), yet not a few of them are unwittingly dishonoring that blood by striving (in their desires after holiness of life) to offer God "entire consecration" or "full surrender" (as they call it) in order to get sanctified—so much "living sacrifice" they present to God for so much sanctification. They have been beguiled into the attempt to lay self on some imaginary "altar" so that their sinful nature might be "consumed by the fire of the Spirit." Alas, they neither enter into God's estimate of Christ's blood, nor will they accept the fact that "the heart is deceitful above all things and incurably wicked" (Jer. 17:9). They neither realize that God has "made Christ to be sanctification unto them" nor that "the carnal mind is enmity against God" (Rom. 8:7).

It is greatly to be regretted that many theologians have confined their views far too exclusively to the legal aspect of the atonement, whereas both the Old Testament types and the New Testament testimony, with equal clearness, exhibit its efficacy in all our relations to God. Because we are in Christ, all that He is for us must be ours. "The blood of Christ cleanses us from all sin, and the believer does not more truly take his place in Christ before the justice of God as one against whom there is no charge, than he takes his place in Christ before the holiness of God as one upon whom there is no stain" (Jas. Inglis in "Way-marks in the wilderness," to whom we are indebted for much in this and the preceding chapter). Not only is the believer "justified by His blood" (Rom 5:9), but we are "sanctified (set apart, consecrated unto God, fitted and adorned for His presence) through the offering of the body of Jesus Christ once for all" (Heb. 10:10). It is this blessed aspect of sanctification which the denominational creeds and the writings of the Puritans almost totally ignored.

In the Larger Catechism of the Westminster Assembly the question is asked, "What is sanctification?" To which the following answer is returned: "Sanctification is a work of God's grace, whereby, they whom God hath before the foundation of the world chosen to be holy, are in time through the powerful operation of His Spirit, applying the death and resurrection of Christ unto them, renewed in their whole man after the image of God; having the seeds of repentance unto life and all other saving graces, put into their hearts, and those graces so stirred up, increased, and strengthened, as that they more and more die unto sin and rise unto newness of life."

Now far be it from us to sit in judgment upon such an excellent and helpful production as this Catechism, which God has richly blest to thousands of His people, or that we should make any harsh criticisms against men whose shoes we are certainly not worthy to unloose. Nevertheless, we are assured that were its compilers on earth today, they would be the last of all to lay claim to any infallibility, nor do we believe they would offer any objection against their statements being brought to the bar of Holy Scripture. The best of men are but men at the best, and therefore we must call no man "Father." A deep veneration for servants of God and a high regard for their spiritual learning must not deter us from complying with "Prove all things: hold fast that which is good" (1 Thess. 5:21). The Bereans were commended for testing the teachings even of the apostle Paul, "And searched the Scriptures daily whether those things were so" (Acts 17:11). It is in this spirit that we beg to offer two observations on the above quotation.

First, the definition or description of sanctification of the Westminster divines is altogether inadequate, for it entirely omits the most important aspect and fundamental element in the believer's sanctification: it says nothing about our sanctification by Christ (Heb. 10:10; 13:12), but confines itself to the work of the Spirit, which is founded upon that of the Son. This is truly a serious loss, and affords another illustration that God has not granted light on all His Word to any one man or body of men. A fuller and better answer to the question of, "What is sanctification?" would be, "Sanctification is, first, that act of God whereby He set the elect apart in Christ before the foundation of the world that they should be holy. Second, it is that perfect holiness which the Church has in Christ and that excellent purity which she has before God by virtue of

Christ's cleansing blood. Third, it is that work of God's Spirit which, by His quickening operation, sets them apart from those who are dead in sins, conveying to them a holy life or nature, etc."

Thus we cannot but regard this particular definition of the Larger Catechism as being defective, for it commences at the middle, instead of starting at the beginning. Instead of placing before the believer that complete and perfect sanctification which God has made Christ to be unto him, it occupies him with the incomplete and progressive work of the Spirit. Instead of moving the Christian to look away from himself with all his sinful failures, unto Christ in whom he is "complete" (Col. 2:10), it encouraged him to look within, where he will often search in vain for the fine gold of the new creation amid all the dross and mire of the old creation. This is to leave him without the joyous assurance of knowing that he has been "perfected forever" by the one offering of Christ (Heb. 10:14); and if he be destitute of that, then doubts and fears must constantly assail him, and the full assurance of faith elude every striving after it.

Our second observation upon this definition is, that its wording is faulty and misleading. Let the young believer be credibly assured that he will "more and more die unto sin and rise unto newness of life," and what will be the inevitable outcome? As he proceeds on his way, the Devil assaulting him more and more fiercely, the inward conflict between the flesh and the Spirit becoming more and more distressing, increasing light from God's Word more and more exposing his sinful failures, until the cry is forced from him, "I am vile; 0 wretched man that I am," what conclusion must he draw? Why this: if the Catechism-definition be correct then I was sadly mistaken, I have never been sanctified at all. So far from the "more and more die unto sin" agreeing with his experience, he discovers that sin is more active within and that he is more alive to sin now, than he was ten years ago!

Will any venture to gainsay what we have just pointed out above, then we would ask the most mature and godly reader, Dare you solemnly affirm, as in the presence of God, that you have "more and more died unto sin?" If you answer, Yes, the writer for one would not believe you. But we do not believe for a moment that you would utter such an untruth. Rather do we think we can hear you saying, "Such has been my deep desire, such has been my sincere design in using the means of grace, such is still my daily prayer; but alas, alas! I find as truly and as frequently today as I ever did in the past that, "When I would do good, evil is present with me; for what I would, that do I not; but what I hate, that do I" (Rom. 7). Ah, there is a vast difference between what ought to be, and that which actually obtains in our experience.

That we may not be charged with partiality, we quote from the "Confession of Faith" adopted by the Baptist Association, which met in Philadelphia 1742, giving the first two sections of their brief chapter on sanctification: 1. "They who are united to Christ, effectually called, and regenerated, having a new heart and a new spirit in them through the virtue of Christ's death and resurrection, are also (a) farther sanctified, really and personally, through the same virtue, (b) by His Word and Spirit dwelling in them; (c) the dominion of the whole body of sin is destroyed, (d) and the several lusts thereof more and more weakened and mortified, and they more and more quickened and strengthened in all saving graces, to the practice of all true holiness, without which no man shall see the Lord. 2. This sanctification is throughout in the whole man, yet imperfect in this life; there abideth still some remnants of corruption in every part, whence ariseth a continual and irreconcilable war."—Italics ours.

Like the previous one, this description of sanctification by the Baptists leaves something to be desired, for it makes no clear and direct statement upon the all-important and flawless holiness which every believer has in Christ, and that spotless and impeccable purity which is upon him by God's imputation of the cleansing efficacy of His Son's sacrifice. Such a serious omission is too vital for us to ignore. In the second place, the words which we have placed in italics not only perpetuate the faulty wording of the Westminster Catechism but also convey a misleading conception of the present condition of the Christian. To speak of "some remnants of corruption" still remaining in the believer, necessarily implies that by far the greater part of his original corruption has been removed, and that only a trifling portion of the same now remains. But something vastly different from that is what every true Christian discovers to his daily grief and humiliation.

Contrast, dear reader, with the "some remnants of corruption" remaining in the Christian (an expression frequently found in the writings of the Puritans) the honest confession of the heavenly-minded Jonathan Edwards: "When I look into my heart and take a view of its wickedness, it looks like an abyss infinitely deeper than Hell. And it appears to me that, were it not for free grace, exalted and raised up to the infinite height of all the fullness of the great Jehovah, and the arm of His grace stretched forth in all the majesty of His power and in all the glory of His sovereignty, I should appear sunk down in my sins below Hell itself. It is affecting to think how ignorant I was when a young Christian, of the bottomless depths of wickedness, pride, hypocrisy, and filth left in my heart." The closer we walk with God, the more conscious will we be of our utter depravity.

Among the Thirty-nine Articles of the Church of England (Episcopalian) there is none treating of the important doctrine of sanctification! We believe that all the Reformation "standards" (creeds, confessions, and catechisms) will be searched in vain for any clear statement upon the perfect holiness which the Church has in Christ or of God's making Him to be, imputatively, sanctification unto His people. In consequence of this, most theological systems have taught that while justification is accomplished the moment the sinner truly believes in Christ, yet is his sanctification only then begun, and is a protracted process to be carried on throughout the remainder of this life by means of the Word and ordinances, seconded by the discipline of trial and affliction. But if this be the case, then there must be a time in the history of every believer when he is "justified from all things" and yet unfit to appear in the presence of God; and before he can appear there, the process must be completed—he must attain what is called "entire sanctification" and be able to say "I have no sin," which, according to 1 John 1:8, would be the proof of self-deception.

Here, then, is a real dilemma. If we say we have no sin, we deceive ourselves; and yet, according to the doctrine of "progressive sanctification," until we can say it (though it be inarticulately in the moment of death) we are not meet for the inheritance of the saints in light. What an awful thought it is, that Christ may come any hour to those who realize that the process of sanctification within them is incomplete. But more: not only are those who have no complete sanctification unfit for eternal glory, but it would be daring presumption for them to boldly enter the Holiest now—the "new and living way" is not yet available for them, they cannot draw near "with a true heart in full assurance of faith." What wonder, then, that those who believe this doctrine are plunged into perplexity, that such a cloud rests over their acceptance with God. But thank God, many triumph over their creed: their hearts are better than their heads, otherwise their communion with God and their approach to the throne of His grace would be impossible.

Now in blessed contrast from this inadequate doctrine of theology, the glorious Gospel of God reveals to us a perfect Savior. It exhibits One who has not only made complete satisfaction to the righteous Ruler and Judge, providing for His people a perfect righteousness before Him, but whose sacrifice has also fitted us to worship and serve a holy God acceptably, and to approach the Father with full confidence and filial love. A knowledge of the truth of justification is not sufficient to thus assure the heart: there must be something more than a realization that the curse of the law is removed—if the conscience be still defiled, if the eye of God rests upon us as unpurged and unclean, then confidence before Him is impossible, for we feel utterly unfit for His ineffable presence. But forever blessed be His name, the precious Gospel of God announces that the blood of Christ meets this exigency also.

"Now where remission of these (sins) is, there is no more offering for sin. Having therefore, brethren, boldness to enter into the Holiest by the blood of Jesus" (Heb. 10:18, 19). The same sacrifice which has procured the remission of our sins, provides the right for us to draw nigh unto God as acceptable worshippers. "By His own blood He entered in once into the Holy Place, having obtained eternal redemption for us" (Heb. 9:13). Now that which gives the One who took our place the right to enter Heaven itself, also gives us the right to take the same place. That which entitled Christ to enter Heaven was "His own blood," and that which entitles the feeblest believer to approach the very throne of God "with boldness," is "the blood of Jesus." Our title to enter Heaven now, in spirit, is precisely the same as Christ's was!

The same precious blood which appeased the wrath of God, covers every stain of sin's guilt and defilement; and not only so, but in the very place of that which it covers and cleanses, it leaves its own excellency; so that because of its finite purity and merit, the Christian is regarded not only as guiltless and unreprovable, but also as spotless and holy. Oh to realize by faith that we are assured of the same welcome by God now as His beloved Son received when He sat down at the right hand of the Majesty on high. God views us in Christ His "Holy One," as possessing a holiness as perfect as is the righteousness in which we are accepted, both of them being as perfect as Christ Himself. "In us, as we present ourselves before Him through Christ, God sees no sin! He looks on us in the face of His Anointed, and there He sees us purer than the heavens" (Alex. Carson).

Chapter 14
Its Procurer
(COMPLETED)

There is a perfect sanctification in Christ which became ours the moment we first believed in Him—little though we realized it at the time. There will also be a perfect conformity to this in us, an actual making good thereof, when we shall be glorified and enter that blessed realm where sin is unknown. In between these two things is the believer's present life on earth, which consists of a painful and bewildering commingling of lights and shadows, joys and sorrows, victories and defeats—the latter seeming to greatly preponderate in the cases of many, especially so the longer they live. There is an unceasing warfare between the flesh and the spirit, each bringing forth "after its own kind," so that groans ever mingle with the Christian's songs. The believer finds himself alternating between thanking God for deliverance from temptation and contritely confessing his deplorable yielding to temptation. Often is he made to cry, "O wretched man that I am!" (Rom. 7:24). Such has been for upwards of twenty-five years the experience of the writer, and it is still so.

Now just as in the commercial world there are a multitude of medical charlatans announcing sure remedies for the most incurable diseases, and filling their pockets at the expense of those who are foolish enough to believe their fairy-tales; so there are numerous "quacks" in the religious world, claiming to have a cure for indwelling sin. Such a paragraph as we have just written above, would be eagerly seized by these mountebanks, who, casting up hands and eyes of holy horror, would loudly express their pity for such "a needless tragedy." They would at once affirm that such an experience, so largely filled with defeat, was because the poor man has never been "sanctified," and would insist that what he needed to do was "to lay his all on the altar" and "receive the second blessing," the "baptism of the Spirit," or as some call it, "enter into the victorious life" by fully trusting Christ for victory.

There are some perverters of the Gospel who, in effect, represent Christ as only aiding sinners to work out a righteousness of their own: they bring in Christ as a mere make-weight to supply their deficiency, or they throw the mantle of His mercy over their failures. Some of the religious quacks we have referred to above would be loud in their outcry against such a travesty of the grace of God in Christ, insisting that we can be justified by nought but His blood. And yet they have nothing better to set before their dupes when it comes to "perfect sanctification" or "full salvation through fully trusting Jesus." Christ they say will aid us in accomplishing what we have vainly attempted in our own strength, and by fully trusting Him we now shall find easy what before we found so arduous. But God's Word supplies no warrant to expect sinless perfection in this life, and such teaching can only tend to fatal deception or bitter disappointment.

Those we have referred to above generally separate justification and sanctification both in fact and in time. Yea, they hold that a man may pass through the former and yet be devoid of the latter, and represent them as being attained by two distinct acts of the soul, divided it may be by an interval of years. They exhort Christians to seek sanctification very much as they exhort sinners to seek justification. Those who attain to this "sanctification," they speak of as being inducted into a superior grade of Christians, having now entered upon "the higher life." Some refer to this experience as "the second blessing:" by the first, forgiveness of sins is received through faith in the Atonement; by the second, we receive deliverance from the power (some add "the presence") of sin by trusting in the efficacy of Christ's Name—a dying Savior rescues from Hell, an everliving Savior now delivers from Satan.

The question may be asked, But ought not the Christian to "present his body a living sacrifice unto God?" Most assuredly, yet not for the purpose of obtaining sanctification, nor yet for the improving or purifying of "the flesh," the sinful nature, the "old man." The exhortation of Romans 12:1 (as its "therefore" plainly shows—the "mercies of God" pointing back to 5:1,2; 6:5, 6; 8:30, etc.) is a call for us to live in the power of what is ours in Christ. The presenting of our bodies "a living sacrifice to God" is the practical recognition that we have been sanctified or consecrated to Him, and we are to do so not in order to get our bodies sanctified, but in the gracious assurance that they are already "holy."

The Christian cannot obtain a right view of the truth of sanctification so long as he separates that blessing from justification, or while he confines his thoughts to a progressive work of grace being wrought within him by the Holy Spirit. "But ye are washed, but ye are sanctified, but ye are justified in the name of the Lord Jesus, and by the Spirit of our God" (1 Cor. 6:11): observe that we are "sanctified" just as we are "justified—in the Name of Another! "That they may receive forgiveness of sins, and inheritance among them which are sanctified by faith" (Acts 26:18): when we receive the "forgiveness" of our sins, we also receive "an inheritance among them that are sanctified by faith." The prayer of Christ, "Sanctify them through Thy truth: Thy Word is truth" (John 17:17), is fulfilled as we obtain a spiritual knowledge of the Truth by the power of the Holy Spirit. It is not by self-efforts, by any "consecration" of our own, by attempts to "lay our all on the altar" that we enter into what Christ has procured for His people, but by faith's appropriation of what God's Word sets before us.

In Christ, and in Him alone, does the believer possess a perfect purity. Christ has consecrated us to God by the offering of Himself unto Him for us. His sacrifice has delivered us from defilement and the ensuing estrangement, and restored us to the favor and fellowship of God. The Father Himself views the Christian as identified with and united to His "Holy One." There are no degrees and can be no "progress" in this sanctification: an unconverted person is absolutely unholy, and a converted person is absolutely holy. God's standard of holiness is not what the Christian becomes by virtue of the Spirit's work in us here, but what Christ is as seated at His own right hand. Every passage in the New Testament which addresses believers as "saints"—holy ones—refutes the idea that the believer is not yet sanctified and will not be so until the moment of death.

Nor does the idea of a progressive sanctification, by which the Christian "more and more dies unto sin," agree with the recorded experience of the most mature saints. The godly John Newton (author of "How sweet the name of Jesus sounds," etc.) when speaking of the expectations which he cherished at the outset of his Christian life, wrote, "But alas! these my golden expectations have been like South Sea dreams. I have lived hitherto a poor sinner, and I believe I shall die one. Have I, then, gained nothing? Yes, I have gained that which I once would rather have been without—such accumulated proof of the deceitfulness and desperate wickedness of my heart as I hope by the Lord's blessing has, in some measure, taught me to know what I mean when I say, 'Behold I am vile!' I was ashamed of myself when I began to serve Him, I am more ashamed of myself now, and I expect to be most ashamed of myself when He comes to receive me to Himself. But oh! I rejoice in Him, that He is not ashamed of me!" Ah, as the Christian grows in grace, he grows more and more out of love with himself.

"And thou shalt make a plate of pure gold, and grave upon it, like the engravings of a signet, Holiness to the Lord. And thou shalt put it on a blue lace, that it may be upon the miter; upon the forefront of the mitre it shall be. And it shall be upon Aaron's forehead, that Aaron may bear the iniquity of the holy things, which the children of Israel shall hallow in all their holy gifts; and it shall be always upon his forehead, that they may be accepted of "before the Lord" (Ex. 28:36-38). These verses set before us one of the most precious typical pictures to be found in the Old Testament. Aaron, the high priest, was dedicated and devoted exclusively to the Lord. He served in that office on the behalf of others, as their mediator. He stood before God as the representative of Israel, bearing their names on his shoulders and on his heart (Ex. 28:12, 29). Israel, the people of God, were both represented by and accepted in Aaron.

That which was set forth in Exodus 28:36-38 was not a type of "the way of salvation" but had to do entirely with the approach unto the thrice holy God of His own sinning and failing people. Though the sacrifices offered on the annual day of atonement delivered them from the curse of the law, godly individuals in the nation must have been painfully conscious that sin marred their very obedience and defiled their prayers and praises. But through the high priest their service and worship was acceptable to God. The inscription worn on his forehead "Holiness to the Lord," was a solemn appointment by which Israel was impressively taught that holiness became the House of God, and that none who are unholy can possibly draw near unto Him. In Leviticus 8:9 the golden plate bearing the inscription is designated "the holy crown," for it was set over and above all the vestments of Aaron.

Now Aaron foreshadowed Christ as the great High Priest who is "over the House of God" (Heb. 10:21). Believers are both represented by and accepted in Him. The "Holiness to the Lord" which was "always" upon Aaron's head, pointed to the essential holiness of Christ, who "ever liveth to make intercession for us." Because of our legal and vital union with Christ, His holiness is ours: the perfections of the great High Priest is the measure of our acceptance with God. Christ has also "borne the iniquity of our holy things"—made satisfaction for the defects of our worship—so that they are not laid to our charge; the sweet incense of His merits (Rev. 8:3) rendering our worship acceptable to God. By Him not only were our sins put away and our persons made acceptable, but our service and worship is rendered pleasing too: "To offer up spiritual sacrifices, acceptable to God by Jesus Christ" (1 Pet. 2:5).

Here, then, is the answer to the pressing question, How can a moral leper be fitted for the presence of God? We need a perfect holiness as well as a perfect righteousness, in order to have access to Him. The Holy One cannot look upon sin, and were we to approach Him in a way wherein He could not look upon us as being perfectly holy, we could not draw nigh unto Him at all. Christ is the all-sufficient answer to our every problem, the One who meets our every need. The precious blood of Jesus has separated the believer from all evil, removed all defilement, and made him nigh unto God in all the acceptableness of His Son. How vastly different is this from that conception which limits sanctification to our experiences and attainments! How definitely better is God's way to man's way, and how far are His thoughts on this above ours!

Now it is in the New Testament Epistles that we are shown most fully the reality and substance of what was typed out under Judaism. First, we read, "For both He that sanctifieth and they who are sanctified are all of one" (Heb. 2:11). Christ is both our sanctification and our Sanctifier. He is our Sanctifier, first, by His blood putting away our sins and cleansing us from all defilement. Second, by the operations of the Holy Spirit, for whatever He doth, He does as "the Spirit of Christ" who procured Him (Psa. 68:18 and Acts 2:33) for His people. Third, by communicating a holy life unto us (John 10:10): the whole stock of grace and holiness is in His hands, He communicating the same unto His people (John 1:16). Fourth, by appearing in Heaven as our representative: He being "Holiness to the Lord" for us. Fifth, by applying and blessing His Word to His people, so that they are washed thereby (Eph. 5:26). He is our sanctification because the holiness of His nature, as well as His obedience, is imputed to us (1 Cor. 1:30).

"We are sanctified through the offering of the body of Jesus Christ once for all" (Heb. 10:10). The Christian will never have right thoughts on this subject until he perceives that his sanctification before God was accomplished at Calvary. As we read, "And you, that were sometime alienated and enemies in your mind by wicked works, yet now hath He reconciled in the body of his flesh through death, to present you holy and unblameable and unreprovable in His, sight" (Col. 1:21, 22): By His work at the cross, Christ presents the Church unto God in all the excellency of His perfect sacrifice. In these passages it is not at all a question of any work which is wrought in us, but of what Christ's oblation has secured for us. By virtue of His sacrifice, believers have been set apart unto God in all Christ's purity and merits, a sure title being accorded them for Heaven. God accounts us holy according to the holiness of Christ's sacrifice, the full value of which rests upon the least instructed, the feeblest, and most tried Christian on earth.

So infinitely sufficient is Christ's oblation for us that "by one offering He hath perfected forever them that are sanctified" (Heb. 10:14). As we read again, "Ye are complete in Him" (Col. 2:10), and this, because His work was complete. All true believers are in the everlasting purpose of God, and in the actual accomplishment of that purpose by the Lord Jesus, perfectly justified and perfectly sanctified. But all believers are not aware of that blessed fact; far from it. Many are confused and bewildered on this subject. One reason for that is, that so many are looking almost entirely to human teachers for instructions, instead of relying upon the Holy Spirit to guide them into the truth, and searching the Scriptures for a knowledge of the same. The religious world today is a veritable "Babel of tongues," and all certainty is at an end if we turn away from the Word (failing to make it our chief study) and lean upon preachers. Alas, how many in professing Protestantism are little better off than the poor Papists, who receive unquestioningly what the "priest" tells them.

It is only as we read God's Word, mixing faith therewith (Heb. 4:2) and appropriating the same unto ourselves, that the Christian can enter into God's thoughts concerning him. In the sacred Scriptures, and nowhere else, can the believer discover what God has made Christ to be unto him and what He has made him to be in Christ. So too it is in the Scriptures, and nowhere else, that we can learn the truth about ourselves, that "in the flesh (what we are by nature as the depraved descendants of fallen Adam) there dwelleth no good thing" (Rom. 7:18). Until we learn to distinguish (as God does) between the "I" and the "sin which dwelleth in me" (Rom. 7:20) there can be no settled peace. Scripture knows nothing of the sanctification of "the old man," and as long as we are hoping for any improvement in him, we are certain to meet with disappointment. If we are to "worship God in the Spirit" and "rejoice in Christ Jesus" we must learn to have "no confidence in the flesh" (Phil. 3 :3).

"Wherefore Jesus, also, that He might sanctify the people with His own blood, suffered without the gate" (Heb. 13:12). The precious blood of Christ has done more than simply make expiation for their sins: it has also set them apart to God as His people. It is that which has brought them into fellowship with the Father Himself. By the shedding of His blood for us, Christ made it consistent with the honor and holiness of God to take us as His peculiar people; it also procured the Holy Spirit who has (by regeneration) fitted us for the privileges and duties of our high calling. Thus, Christ has sanctified His people both objectively and subjectively. We are "sanctified with His own blood," first, as it was an oblation to God; second, as its merits are imputed to us; third, as its efficacy is applied to us.

Christ's blood "cleanseth us from all sin" (1 John 7) in a threefold way. First, Godwards, by blotting out our sins and removing our defilement from His view (as Judge). Second, by procuring the Holy Spirit, by whom we receive "the washing of regeneration" (Titus 3:5). Third, by our consciences being "purged" (Heb. 9:14) as faith lays hold of these blessed facts, and thus we are fitted to "serve the living God!" Herein we may perceive how God puts the fullest honor on His beloved Son, by making Him not only the Repairer of our ruin and the triumphant Undoer of the Serpent's work (1 John 3:8), but also giving us His own perfect standing before God and communicating His own holy nature unto His people—for a branch cannot be in the true vine without partaking of its life.

In the person of Christ God beholds a holiness which abides His closest scrutiny, yea, which rejoices and satisfies His heart; and whatever Christ is before God, He is for His people—"whither the Forerunner is for us entered" (Heb. 6:20), "now to appear in the presence of God for us" (Heb. 9:24)! In Christ's holiness we are meet for that place unto which Divine grace has exalted us, so that we are "made to sit together in the heavenlies in Christ Jesus" (Eph. 2:6) This is not accomplished by any experience, separated by a long process from our justification, but is a blessed fact since the moment we first believed on Christ. We are in Christ, and how can anyone be in Him, and yet not be perfectly sanctified? From the first moment we were "joined to the Lord" (1 Cor. 6:17), we are holy brethren, partakers of the heavenly calling" (Heb. 3:1). This is what the Christian's faith needs to lay hold of and rest on, upon the authority of Him that cannot lie. Nevertheless, the best taught, the most spiritual and mature Christian, apprehends the truth but feebly and inadequately, for now "we see through a glass darkly."

True, there is such a thing as a growth in the knowledge of sanctification, that is, providing our thoughts are formed by the Word of God. There is an experimental entering into the practical enjoyment of what God has made Christ to be unto us, so that by faith therein our thoughts and habits, affections and associations are affected thereby. There is such a thing as our apprehending the glorious standing and state which Divine grace has given us in the Beloved, and exhibiting the influence of the same upon our character and conduct. But that is not what we are here treating of. That which we are now considering is the wondrous and glorious fact that the Christian was as completely sanctified in God's view the first moment he laid hold of Christ by faith, as he will be when every vestige of sin has disappeared from his person, and he stands before Him glorified in spirit and soul and body.

But the question may be asked, What provision has God made to meet the needs of His people sinning after they are sanctified? This falls not within the compass of the present aspect of our subject. Yet briefly, the answer is, The ministry of Christ on high as our great High Priest (Heb. 7:25) and Advocate (1 John 2:1); and their penitently confessing their sins, which secures their forgiveness and cleansing (1 John 1:9). The sins of the Christian mar his communion with God and hinder his enjoyment of His salvation, but they affect not his standing and state in Christ. If I judge not myself for my sinful failures and falls, the chastening rod will descend upon me, yet wielded not by an angry God, but by my loving Father (Heb. 12:5-11).

We are not unmindful of the fact that there is not a little in this chapter which worldly-minded professors may easily pervert to their own ruin—what truth of Scripture is not capable of being "wrested"? But that is no reason why God's people should he deprived of one of the choicest and most nourishing portions of the Bread of Life! Other chapters in this book are thoroughly calculated to "preserve the balance of truth."

Chapter 15
Its Securer

The Christian has been sanctified by the triune Jehovah: infinite wisdom and fathomless grace so ordered it that he is indebted to each of the Eternal Three. The Lord God designed that all the Persons in the blessed Trinity should be honored in the making holy of His people, so that each of Them might be distinctively praised by us. First, the Father sanctified His people by an eternal decree, choosing them in Christ before the foundation of the world and predestinating them unto the adoption of children. Second, the Son sanctified His people by procuring for them a perfect and inalienable standing before the Judge of all, the infinite merits of His finished work being reckoned to their account. Third, God the Spirit makes good the Father's decree and imparts to them what the work of Christ procured for them: the Spirit is the actual Securer of sanctification, applying it to their persons. Thus the believer has abundant cause to adore and glorify the Father, the Son, and the Holy Spirit.

It is very remarkable to observe the perfect harmony there is between the different operations of the Eternal Three in connection with the making holy of the elect, and the threefold signification of the term "sanctification." In an earlier chapter we furnished proof that the word "to sanctify" has a threefold meaning, namely, to separate, to cleanse, to adorn. First, in Scripture a person or thing is said to be sanctified when it is consecrated or set apart from a common to a sacred use. So in the eternal decree of the Father, the elect were separated in the Divine mind from countless millions of our race which were to be created, and set apart for His own delight and glory. Second, where those persons and things are unclean, they must be purified, so as to fit them for God's pleasure and use. That was the specific work assigned to the Son: His precious blood has provided the means for our purification. Third, the persons or things sanctified need to be beautified and adorned for God's service: this is accomplished by the Holy Spirit.

It is also striking and blessed to note the relation and order of the several acts of the Holy Three in connection with our sanctification. The source of it is "the eternal purpose" or decree of God: "by the which will we are sanctified" (Heb. 10:10). The substance of it was brought forth by Christ when He fully accomplished God's will on our behalf: "that He might sanctify the people with His own blood" (Heb. 13:12). The securer of it is the Holy Spirit, who by His work of grace within applies to the individual the sanctification which the Church has in its Head: "being sanctified by the Holy Spirit" (Rom. 15:16). It is not until the Comforter takes up His abode in the heart that the Father's will begins to be actualized and the Son's "work" evidences its efficacy toward us. This glorious gift, then, is let down to us from the Father, through the Son, by the Spirit.

If we consider the nature of Christ's work for His people and the perfection of their standing in Him before God, it could not for a moment be supposed that this having been accomplished by the grace, wisdom, and power of God, that their state should be left unaffected—that their position should be so gloriously changed, yet their condition remain as sinful as ever; that they should be left in their sins to take comfort from their immunity to Divine wrath. The degradation, pollution, and utter ruin of our nature; our estrangement from God, spiritual death, and our whole heritage of woe are the immediate consequences of sin. And what would forgiveness, justification, and redemption in Christ mean, if deliverance from all those consequences did not directly and necessarily follow? Our being made the righteousness of God in Christ (2 Cor. 5:21) would be but an empty name, if it does not imply and entail recovery from all that sin had forfeited and deliverance from all that sin had incurred. Thank God that, in the end (when we are glorified), will be perfectly effected.

It is true that when Christ first seeks out His people He finds them entirely destitute of holiness, yea, of even desire after it; but He does not leave them in that awful state. No, such would neither honor Him nor fulfill the Father's will. Glorious as is the triumph of Divine grace in the justification of a sinner, through the work of Christ as Surety, yet even that must be regarded as a means to an end. See how this is brought out in every scriptural statement of the purpose of grace concerning the redeemed, or the design of the mission and sufferings of the Redeemer: "I am come that they might have life, and that they might have it more abundantly" (John 10:10); "Who gave Himself for us, that He might redeem us from all iniquity, and purify unto Himself a peculiar people, zealous of good works" (Titus 2:14); "Whereby are given unto us exceeding great and precious promises, that by these ye might be partakers of the Divine nature, having escaped the corruption that is in the world through lust" (2 Pet. 1:4); "Behold what manner of love the Father hath bestowed upon us, that we should be called the sons of God" (1 John 3:1).

Since we are made the righteousness of God in Christ the result of this in the Christian, must, ultimately, correspond with that perfection. In other words, nothing short of perfect fellowship with the Father and with His Son can answer to His having died on account of our sins and risen again on account of our justification; and having risen, become the Head f and Source of an entirely new life to all who believe on Him. The aim of the Father's love and of the Son's grace, was not only that we might have restored to us the life which we lost in Adam, but that we should have "life more abundantly;" that we should be brought back not merely to the position of servants—which was the status of unfallen Adam—but be given, the wondrous place of sons; that we should be fitted not simply for an earthly paradise, but for an eternity of joy in the immediate presence of God in Heaven.

Now it is on the ground of what Christ did and earned for His people, and with a view to the realization of the Father's purpose of their glorification, that the Holy Spirit is given to the elect. And it makes much for His praise and for their peace that they obtain a clear and comprehensive view of His work within them; nor can that be secured by a hurried or superficial study of the subject. His operations are varied and manifold; yet all proceeding from one foundation and all advancing toward one grand end. That which we are now to consider is the "sanctification of the Spirit," an expression which is found both in 2 Thessalonians 2:13 and 1 Peter 1:2. The connection in which the expression occurs in the two passages Just mentioned, clearly intimates that the sanctification of the Spirit is an integral part of our salvation, that it is closely associated with our "belief of the truth," and that it precedes our practical obedience.

John Owen's definition of the Spirit's sanctification, based on 1 Thessalonians 5:23 is as follows, "Sanctification is an immediate work of the Spirit of God on the souls of believers, purifying and cleansing of their natures from the pollution and uncleanness of sin, renewing in them the image of God, and thereby enabling them from a spiritual and habitual principle of grace, to yield obedience unto God, according unto the tenor and terms of the new covenant, by virtue of the life and death of Jesus Christ. Or more briefly: it is the universal renovation of our natures by the Holy Spirit, into the image of God, through Jesus Christ." Full and clear though this definition be, we humbly conceive it is both inadequate and inaccurate: inadequate, because it leaves out several essential elements; inaccurate, because it confounds the effects with the cause. Later, he says, "In the sanctification of believers the Holy Spirit doth work in them, in their whole souls—

their minds, wills, and affections—a gracious, supernatural habit, principle, and disposition of living unto God, wherein the substance or essence, the life and being, of holiness doth consist."

In an article thereon S. E. Pierce said, "Sanctification, or Gospel-holiness, without which no man shall see the Lord, comprehends the whole work of the Spirit of God within and upon us, from our regeneration to our eternal glorification. It is the fruit and blessed consequence of His indwelling us, and the continued effect of spiritual regeneration, i.e., in begetting within us a nature suited to take in spiritual things, and be properly affected by them. Regeneration is the root and sanctification is the bud, blossom and fruit which it produces. In our regeneration by the Holy Spirit we are made alive to God, and this is manifested by our faith in Christ Jesus. Our lusts are mortified because we are quickened together with Christ. And what we style the sanctification of the Spirit, which follows after regeneration hath taken place within us, consists in drawing forth that spiritual life which is conveyed to our souls in our new birth, into acts and exercise on Christ and spiritual things, in quickening our graces, and in leading us to walk in the paths of holiness, by which proof is given that we are alive to God through Jesus Christ our Lord." This, we believe is preferable to Owens, yet still leaving something to be desired.

Exactly what is the sanctification of the Spirit? Personally, we very much doubt whether that question can be satisfactorily answered in a single sentence, for in framing one, account needs to be taken of the change which is produced in the believing sinner's relationship to God, his relationship to Christ as the Head of the Church, his relationship to the unregenerate, and his relationship to the Divine law. Positionally, our sanctification by the Spirit results from our being vitally united to Christ, for the moment we are livingly joined to Him, His holiness becomes ours, and our standing before God is the same as His. Relatively, our sanctification of the Spirit issues from our being renewed by Him, for the moment He quickens us we are set apart from those who are dead in sins. Personally, we are consecrated unto God by the Spirit's indwelling us, making our bodies His temples. Experimentally, our sanctification of the Spirit consists in the impartation to us of a principle ("Nature") of holiness, hereby we become conformed to the Divine law. Let us consider each of these viewpoints separately.

Our union to Christ is the grand hinge on which everything turns. Divorced from Him, we have nothing spiritually. Describing our unregenerate condition, the apostle says, "at that time ye were without Christ," and being without Him, it necessarily follows "being aliens from the commonwealth of Israel, and strangers from the covenants of promise, having no hope, and without God in the world" (Eph. 2:12). But the moment the Holy Spirit makes us livingly one with Christ, all that He has becomes ours, we are then "joint-heirs with Him." Just as a woman obtains the right to share all that a man has once she is wedded to him, so a poor sinner becomes holy before God the moment he is vitally united to the Holy One. Everything which God requires from us, everything which is needed by us, is treasured up for us in Christ.

By our union with Christ we receive a new and holy nature, whereby we are capacitated for holy living, which holy living is determined and regulated by our practical and experimental fellowship with Him. By virtue of our federal union with the first Adam we not only had imputed to us the guilt of his disobedience but we also received from him the sinful nature which has vitiated our souls, powerfully influencing all our faculties. In like manner, by virtue of our federal union with the last Adam, the elect not only have imputed to them the righteousness of His obedience, but they also receive from Him (by the Spirit) a holy nature, which renews all the faculties of their souls and powerfully affects their actions. Once we become united to the Vine, the life and holy virtue which is in Him flows into us, and brings forth spiritual fruit. Thus, the moment the Spirit unites us to Christ, we are "sanctified in Christ Jesus" (1 Cor. 1:2).

It is axiomatic that those whom God separates unto Himself must be suited to Himself, that is, they must be holy. Equally clear is it from the Scriptures that, whatsoever God does He is determined that the crown of honor for it should rest upon the head of Christ, for He is the grand Center of all the Divine counsels. Now both of these fundamental considerations are secured by God's making us partakers of His own holiness, through creating us anew in Christ Jesus. God will neither receive nor own anyone who has the least taint of sin's defilement upon him, and it is only as we are made new creatures in Christ that we can fully measure up to the unalterable requirements of God. Our state must be holy as well as our standing; and as we showed in the last three chapters Christ Himself is our sanctification, so now we seek to point out that we are actually sanctified in Christ—personally and vitally.

"But of Him are ye in Christ Jesus" (1 Cor. 1:30)—"of Him" by the power and quickening operation of the Spirit. Christians are supernaturally and livingly incorporated with Christ. "For we are His workmanship, created in Christ Jesus" (Eph. 2:10): that new creation is accomplished in our union with His person. This is our spiritual state: a "new man" has been "created in righteousness and true holiness" (Eph. 4:24), and this we are exhorted to "put on" or make manifest. This is not at all a matter of progress or attainment, but is true of every Christian the moment he is born again. The terms "created in righteousness (our justification) and true holiness" (our sanctification) describe what the "new man" is in Christ. It is not simply something which we are to pursue though that is true, and is intimated in the "put ye on;" but it is what all Christians actually are: their sanctification in Christ is an accomplished fact: it is just because Christians are "saints" they are to lead saintly lives.

The believer begins his Christian life by having been perfectly sanctified in Christ. Just as both our standing and state were radically affected by virtue of our union with the first Adam, so both our standing and state are completely changed by virtue of our union with the last Adam. As the believer has a perfect standing in holiness before God because of his federal union with Christ, so his state is perfect before God, because he is now vitally united to Christ: he is in Christ, and Christ is in him. By the regenerating operation of the Spirit we are "joined unto the Lord" (1 Cor. 6:17). The moment they were born again, all Christians were sanctified in Christ with a sanctification to which no growth in grace, no attainments in holy living, can add one iota. Their sanctification, like their justification, is "complete in Him" (Col. 2:10). Christ Himself is their life, and He becomes such by a personal union to Himself which nothing can dissolve. From the moment of his new birth every child of God is a "saint in Christ Jesus" (Rom. 1:7), one of the "holy brethren" (Heb. 3:1); and it is just because they are such, they are called upon to live holy lives. 0 what cause we have to adore the grace, the wisdom, and the power of God!

When one of God's elect is quickened into newness of life a great change is made relatively, that is, in connection with his relation to his fellowmen. Previously, he too was both in the world and of it, being numbered with the ungodly, and enjoying their fellowship. But at regeneration he is born unto a new family, even the living family of God, and henceforth his standing is no longer among those who are "without Christ:" "Who hath delivered us from the Power of darkness, and hath translated us into the kingdom of His dear Son" (Col. 1:13). Thus, when one is made alive in Christ by the Holy Spirit, he at once becomes separated from those who are dead in trespasses and sins and therefore this is another aspect of the "sanctification of the Spirit." This was typed out of old. When the Lord was revealed unto Abraham, the word to him was "Get thee out of thy country, and from thy kindred" (Gen. 21:1). So again it was with Israel: no sooner were they delivered from the Angel of Death by the blood of the lamb, than they were required to leave Egypt behind them.

Personally we are sanctified or consecrated unto God by the Spirit's indwelling us and making our bodies His temples. As He came upon Christ Himself ("without measure") so, in due time, He is given to each of His members: "ye have an Unction (the Spirit) from the Holy One"—Christ; "the Anointing (the Spirit) which ye have received of Him (Christ) abideth in you" (1 John 2:20, 27)—it is from this very fact we receive our name, for "Christian" means "an anointed one," the term being taken from the type in Psalm 133:2. It is the indwelling presence of the Holy Spirit which constitutes a believer a holy person. That which made Canaan the "holy" land, Jerusalem the "holy" city, the temple the "holy" place, was the presence and appearing of the Holy One there! And that which makes any man "holy" is the perpetual abiding of the Spirit within him. Needless to say, His indwelling of us necessarily produces fruits of holiness in heart and life—this will come before us in the sequel.

Amazing, blessed, and glorious fact, the Holy Spirit indwells the regenerate so that their bodies become the temples of the living God. "The Holy Spirit descends on them and enters within them, in consequence of their union with Christ. He comes from Heaven to make known this union between Christ and them. He is the Divine Manifester of it. He dwells in us as a well of water springing up into everlasting life. He abides with us as our Divine Comforter, and will be our Guide even unto death, and continue His life-giving influences in us and dwell in us, filling us with all the fullness of God in Heaven forever" (S. E. Pierce).

This indwelling of the Spirit is, in the order of God, subsequent to and in consequence of our being sanctified by the blood of Jesus; for it is obvious that God could not "dwell" in those who were standing under the imputation of their guilt. The Holy Spirit, therefore, from the very fact of making our bodies His temples, attests and evidences the completeness and perpetuity of the sanctification which is ours by the sacrifice of Christ. He comes to us not to procure blessings which Christ hath already purchased for us, but to make them known to us: "Now we have received, not the spirit of the world, but the Spirit which is of God; that we might know the things that are freely given to us of God" (1 Cor. 2:12). He comes to sustain those in whom the life of Christ now is.

Chapter 16
Its Securer
(COMPLETED)

"Sanctification of the Spirit" (2 Thess. 2:13) is a comprehensive expression which has a fourfold significance at least. First, it points to that supernatural operation of the Spirit whereby a sinner is "created in Christ Jesus" (Eph. 2:10), made vitally one with Him, and thereby a partaker of His holiness. Second, it tells of the vital change which this produces in his relation to the ungodly: having been quickened into newness of life, he is at once separated from those who are dead in sins, so that both as to his standing and state he is no longer with them common to Satan, sin and the world. Third, it speaks of the Spirit Himself taking up His abode in the quickened soul, thereby rendering him personally holy. Fourth, it refers to His bringing the heart into conformity with the Divine law, with all that that connotes. Before taking up this last point, we will offer a few more remarks upon the third.

The coming of this Divine and glorious Person to indwell one who is depraved and sinful is both a marvel and a mystery: a marvel that He should, a mystery that He would. How is it possible for Him who is ineffably holy to dwell within those who are so unholy? Not a few have said it is impossible, and were it not for the plain declarations of Scripture thereon, probably all of us would come to the same conclusion. But God's ways are very different from ours, and His love and grace have achieved that which our poor hearts had never conceived of. This has been clearly recognized in connection with the amazing birth, and the still more amazing death of Christ; but it has not been so definitely perceived in connection with the descent of the Spirit to indwell believers.

There is a striking analogy between the advent to this earth of the second person of the Trinity and the advent of the third person, and the marvel and mystery of the one should prepare us for the other. Had the same not become an historical fact, who among us had ever supposed that the Father had suffered His beloved Son to enter such depths of degradation as He did? Who among us had ever imagined that the Lord of glory would lie in a manger? But He did! In view of that, why should we be so staggered at the concept of the Holy Spirit's entering our poor hearts? As the Father was pleased to allow the glory of the Son to be eclipsed for a season by the degradation into which He descended, so in a very real sense He suffers the glory of the Spirit to be hid for a season by the humiliation of His tabernacling in our bodies.

It is on the ground of Christ's work that the Spirit comes to us. "Whatever we receive here is but the result of the fullness given to us in Christ. If the Spirit comes to dwell in us as the Spirit of peace, it is because Jesus by His blood, once offered, hath secured for us that peace. If the Spirit comes as the Spirit of glory, it is because Jesus has entered into and secured glory for us. If the Spirit comes as the Spirit of sonship, it is because Jesus has returned for us to the bosom of the Father and brought us into the nearness of the same love. If the Spirit comes to us as the Spirit of life, it is because of the life hidden for us in Christ with God. The indwelling of the Spirit therefore being a result of the abiding relation to God into which the resurrection and ascension of our Lord has brought us, must of necessity be an abiding presence. Consequently, the sanctification which results from the fact of His presence in us and from the fact of the new man being created in us, must be a complete and abiding sanctification—as complete and as abiding as the relation which Christ holds to us in redemption as the Representative and Head of His mystical body" (B. W. Newton).

Yet let it be pointed out that, the blessed Spirit does not allow our hearts to remain in the awful condition in which He first finds them; and this brings us to our fourth point. In Titus 3:5 we read "according to His mercy He saved us, by the washing of regeneration, and renewing of the Holy Spirit." All that is comprehended in this "washing" we may not be able to say, but it certainly includes the casting of all idols out of our hearts, to such an extent that God now occupies the throne of it. By this "washing of regeneration" the soul is so cleansed from its native pollution that sin is no longer loved, but loathed; the Divine law is no longer hated, but delighted in; and the affections are raised from things below unto things above. We are well aware of the fact that this is the particular point which most exercises honest consciences; yet, God does not intend that our difficulties should be so cleared up in this life that all exercise of heart should be at an end.

Though it be true that the flesh remains unaltered in the Christian, and that at times its activities are such that our evidences of regeneration are clouded over, yet it remains that a great change was wrought in us at the new birth, the effects of which abide. Though it be true that a sea of corruption still dwells within, and that at times sin rages violently, and so prevails that it seems a mockery to conclude that we have been delivered from its domination; yet this does not alter the fact that a miracle of grace has been wrought within us. Though the Christian is conscious of so much filth within, he has experienced the "washing of regeneration." Before the new birth he saw no beauty in Christ that he should desire Him; but now he views Him as "the Fairest among ten thousand." Before, he loved those like himself; but now he "loves the brethren" (1 John 3:14). Moreover, his understanding has been cleansed from many polluting errors and heresies. Finally, it is a fact that the main stream of his desires runs out after God.

But "the washing of regeneration" is only the negative side: positively there is "the renewing of the Holy Spirit." Though this "renewing" falls far short of what will take place in the saint at his glorification, yet it is a very real and radical experience. A great change and renovation is made in the soul, which has a beneficial effect upon all of its faculties. This "renewing of the Holy Spirit" has in it a transforming power, so that the heart and mind are brought into an obedient frame toward God. The soul is now able to discern that God's will is the most "good and acceptable and perfect" (Rom. 12:2) of all, and there is a deep desire and a sincere effort made to become conformed thereto. But let it be carefully noted that the present and not the past tense is employed in Titus 3:5—not ye were washed and renewed, but a "washing" and "renewing:" it is a continual work of the Spirit.

Ere proceeding to show further the nature of the Spirit's work in the soul in His sanctifying operations, let it be pointed out that what our hearts most need to lay hold of and rest on is that which has been before us in the last few chapters. The believer has already been perfectly sanctified in the decree and purpose of the Father. Christ has wrought out for him that which, when reckoned to his account, perfectly fits him for the courts of God's temple above. The moment he is quickened by the Spirit he is created in Christ," and therefore "sanctified in Christ:" thus both his standing and state are holy in God's sight. Furthermore, the Spirit's indwelling him, making his body His temple, constitutes him personally holy—just as the presence of God in the temple made Canaan the "holy land" and Jerusalem the "holy city."

It is of the very first importance that the Christian should be thoroughly clear upon this point. We do not become saints by holy actions—that is the fundamental error of all false religions. No, we must first be saints before there can be any holy actions, as the fountain must be pure before its stream can be, the tree good if its fruit is to be wholesome. The order of Scripture is "Let it not be once named among you, as becometh Saints" (Eph. 5:3), and "but now are ye light in the Lord: walk as children of light" (Eph. 5 8); "in behavior as becometh holiness" (Titus 2:3). God first sets our hearts at rest, before He bids our hands engage in His service. He gives life, that we may be capacitated to render love. He creates in us a sanctified nature, that there may be sanctified conduct. God presents us spotless in the Holiest of all according to the blood of sprinkling, that, coming forth with a conscience purged from dead works, we may seek to please and glorify Him.

It is the creating of this holy nature within us that we must next consider. "It is something that is holy, both in its principle, and in its actions; and is superior to anything that can come from man, or be performed by himself. It does not lie in a conformity to the light of nature, and the dictates of it; nor is it what may go by the name of moral virtue, which was exercised by some of the heathen philosophers, to a very great degree, and yet they had not a grain of holiness in them; but were full of the lusts of envy, pride, revenge, etc., nor does it lie in a bare, external conformity to the law of God, or in an outward reformation of life and manners: this appeared in the Pharisees to a great degree, who were pure in their own eyes, and thought themselves holier than others, and disdained them, and yet their hearts were full of all manner of impurity.

"Nor is it what is called restraining grace: persons may be restrained by the injunction of parents and masters, by the laws of magistrates, and by the ministry of the Word, from the grosser sins of life; and be preserved, by the providence of God, from the pollutions of the world, and yet not be sanctified. Nor are gifts, ordinary or extraordinary, sanctifying grace: Judas Iscariot no doubt had both, the ordinary gifts of a preacher, and the extraordinary gifts of an apostle; yet he was not a holy man. Gifts are not graces: a man may have all gifts and all knowledge, and speak with the tongue of men, and angels, and not have grace; there may be a silver tongue where there is an unsanctified heart. Nor is sanctification a restoration of the lost image of Adam, or an amendment of that image marred by the sin of man; or a new vamping up of the old principles of nature" (John Gill).

Having seen what this holy nature, imparted by the Spirit, is not; let us endeavor to define what it is. It is something entirely new: a new creation, a new heart, a new spirit, a new man, the conforming of us to another image, even to that of the last Adam, the Son of God. It is the impartation of a holy principle, implanted in the midst of corruption, like a lovely rosebush growing out of a dung-heap. It is the carrying forward of that "good work" begun in us at regeneration (Phil. 1:6). It is called by many names, such as "the inward man" (2 Cor. 4:16) and "the hidden man of the heart" (1 Pet. 3:4), not only because it has its residence in the soul, but because our fellows can see it not. It is designated "seed" (1 John 3 :9) and "spirit" (John 3:6) because it is wrought in us by the Spirit of God. It is likened to a "root" (Job 19:28), to "good treasure of the heart" (Matt. 12:35), to "oil in the vessel" (Matt. 25:4)—by "oil" there is meant grace, so called for its illuminating nature in giving discernment to the understanding, and for its supplying and softening nature, taking off the hardness from the heart and the stubbornness from the will.

It is in this aspect of our sanctification that we arrive at the third meaning of the term: the blessed Spirit not only separates from the common herd of the unregenerate, cleanses our hearts from the pollution of sin, but He suitably adorns the temple in which He now dwells. This He does by making us partakers of "the Divine nature" (2 Pet. 1:4), which is a positive thing, the communication of a holy principle, whereby we are "renewed after the image of God." When the Levites were to minister in the holy place, not only were they required to wash themselves, but to put on their priestly attire and ornaments, which were comely and beautiful. In like manner, believers are a holy and royal priesthood (1 Pet. 2:5), for they have not only been washed from the filth of sin, but are "all glorious within" (Ps. 45:13). They have not only had the robe of imputed righteousness put upon them (Isa. 61:10), but the beautifying grace of the Spirit has been implanted in them.

It is by the reception of this holy principle or nature that the believer is freed from the domination of sin and brought into the liberty of righteousness, though not until death is he delivered from the plague and presence of sin. At their justification believers obtain a relative or judicial sanctification, which provides for them a perfect standing before God, by which they receive proof of their covenant relationship with Him, that they are His peculiar people, His "treasure," His "portion." But more, they are also inherently sanctified in their persons by a gracious work of the Spirit within their souls. They are "renewed" throughout the whole of their beings; for as the poison of sin was diffused throughout the entire man, so is grace. It helps not a little to perceive that, as Thos. Boston pointed out long ago in his "Man's Fourfold State," "Holiness is not one grace only, but all the graces of the Spirit: it is a constellation of graces; it is all the graces in their seed and root."

Yet let it be pointed out that, though the whole of the Christian's person is renewed by the Spirit, and all the faculties of his soul are renovated, nevertheless, there is no operation of grace upon his old nature, so that its evil is expelled: the "flesh" or principle of indwelling sin is neither eradicated nor purified nor made good. Our "old man" (which must be distinguished from the soul and its faculties) is "corrupt according to the deceitful lusts," and remains so till the end of our earthly pilgrimage, ever striving against the "spirit" or principle of holiness or "new man." As the soul at the very first moment of its union with the body (in the womb) became sinful, so it is not until the moment of its dissolution from the body that the soul becomes inherently sinless. As an old divine quaintly said, "Sin brought death into the world, and God, in a way of holy resentment, makes use of death to put an end to the very being of sin in His saints."

Many readers will realize that we are here engaged in grappling with a difficult and intricate point. No man is competent to give such a clear and comprehensive description of our inward sanctification that all difficulty is cleared up: the most he can do is to point out what it is not, and then seek to indicate the direction in which its real nature is to be sought. As a further effort toward this it may be said that, this principle of holiness which the Spirit imparts to the believer consists of spiritual light, whereby the heart is (partly) delivered from the darkness in which the Fall enveloped it. It is such an opening of the eyes of our understandings that we are enabled to see spiritual things and discern their excellency; for before we are sanctified by the Spirit we are totally blind to their reality and beauty: such passages as John 1:5; Acts 26:18; 2 Corinthians 4:6; Ephesians 5:8; Colossians 1:13; 1 Peter 2:9 (read them!) makes this clear.

Further, that principle of holiness which the Spirit imparts to the believer consists of spiritual life. Previous to its reception the soul is in a state of spiritual death, that is, it is alienated from and incapacitated toward God. At our renewing by the Spirit, we receive a vital principle of spiritual life: compare John 5:24; 10:11, 28; Romans 8:2; Ephesians 2:1. It is by this new life we are capacitated for communion with and obedience to God. Once more; that principle of holiness consists of spiritual love. The natural man is in a state of enmity with God; but at regeneration there is implanted that which delights in and cleaves to God: compare Deuteronomy 30:6; Romans 5:5; Galatians 5:24. As "light" this principle of holiness affects the understanding, as "life" it influences and moves the will, as "love" it directs and moulds the affections. Thus also it partakes of the very nature of Him who is Light, Life, and Love. "Let the beauty of the Lord be upon us" (Ps. 90:17) signifies "let this principle of holiness (as light, life, and love) be healthy within and made manifest through and by us.

But we must now turn to the most important aspect of all, of the nature of this principle of holiness, whereby the Spirit sanctified us inherently. Our experimental sanctification consists in our hearts being conformed to the Divine law. This should be so obvious that no labored argument should be required to establish the fact. As all sin is a transgression of the law (I John 3 :4), so all holiness must be a fulfilling of the law. The natural man is not subject to the law, neither indeed can he be (Rom. 8:7). Why? Because he is devoid of that principle from which acceptable obedience to the law can proceed. The great requirement of the law is love: love to God, and love to our neighbor; but regarding the unregenerate it is written, "ye have not the love of God in you" (John 5 42). Hence it is that God's promise to His elect is "The Lord thy God will circumcise thine heart, and the heart of thy seed, to love the Lord thy God with all thine heart" (Deut. 30:6)—for "love is the fulfilling of the law."

This is the grand promise of the Covenant: "I will put My laws into their mind, and write them in their hearts" (Heb. 8:10); and again, "I will put My Spirit within you, and cause you to walk in My statutes" (Ezek. 36:27). As we said in the preceding article: when Christ comes to His people He finds them entirely destitute of holiness, and of every desire after it; but He does not leave them in that awful condition. No, He sends forth the Holy Spirit, communicates to them a sincere love for God, and imparts to them a principle or "nature" which delights in His ways. "They that are in the flesh cannot please God" (Rom. 8:8). Why? Because any work to be pleasing to Him must proceed from a right principle (love to Him), be performed by a right rule (His Law, or revealed will), and have a right end in view (His glory); and this is only made possible by the sanctification of the Spirit.

Experimental holiness is conformity of heart and life to the Divine law. The law of God is "holy, just and good" (Rom. 7:12), and therefore does it require inward righteousness or conformity as well as outward; and this requirement is fully met by the wondrous and gracious provision which God has made for His people. Here again we may behold the striking and blessed cooperation between the Eternal Three. The Father, as the King and Judge of all, gave the Law. The Son, as our Surety, fulfilled the Law. The Spirit is given to work in us conformity to the Law: first, by imparting a nature which loves it; second, by instructing and giving us a knowledge of its extensive requirements; third, by producing in us strivings after obedience to its precepts. Not only is the perfect obedience of Christ imputed to His people, but a nature which delights in the law is imparted to them. But because of the opposition from indwelling sin, perfect obedience to the law is not possible in this life; yet, for Christ's sake, God accepts their sincere but imperfect obedience.

We must distinguish between the Holy Spirit and the principle of holiness which He imparts at regeneration: the Creator and the nature He creates must not be confounded. It is by His indwelling the Christian that He sustains and develops, continues and perfects, this good work which he has begun in us. He takes possession of the soul to strengthen and direct its faculties. It is from the principle of holiness which He has communicated to us that there proceeds the fruits of holiness—sanctified desires, actions and works. Yet that new principle or nature has no strength of its own: only as it is daily renewed, empowered, controlled, and directed by its Giver, do we act "as becometh holiness." His continued work of sanctification within us proceeds in the twofold process of the mortification (subduing) of the old man and the vivification (quickening) of the new man.

The fruit of the Spirit's sanctification of us experimentally, appears in our separation from evil and the world. But because of the flesh within, our walk is not perfect. Oftentimes there is little for the eye of sense to distinguish in those in whom the Spirit dwells from the moral and respectable wordlings; yea, often they put us to shame. "It doth not yet appear what we shall be." "The world knoweth us not." But the heart is washed from the prevailing love of sin by the tears of repentance which the Christian is moved to frequently shed. Every new act of faith upon the cleansing blood of Christ carries forward the work of experimental sanctification to a further degree. As Naaman was required to dip in the Jordan again and again, yea, seven times, till he was wholly purged of his bodily leprosy; so the soul of the Christian—conscious of so much of the filth of sin still defiling him—continues to dip in that "fountain opened for sin and for uncleanness." Thank God, one day Christ will "present to Himself a glorious Church, not having spot or wrinkle, or any such thing" (Eph. 5:27).

Chapter 17
Its Rule

Having considered the distinct acts of the Father, the Son, and the Holy Spirit in the sanctification of the Church, we must now carefully inquire as to the Rule by which all true holiness is determined, the Standard by which it is weighed and to which it must be conformed. This also is of deep importance, for if we mistake the line and plummet of holiness, then all our efforts after it will be wide of the mark. On this aspect of our subject there also prevails widespread ignorance and confusion today, so that we are obliged to proceed slowly and enter rather lengthily into it. If one class of our readers sorely needed—for the strengthening of their faith and the comfort of their hearts—a somewhat full setting forth of the perfect sanctification which believers have in Christ, another class of our readers certainly require—for the illumination of their minds and the searching of their conscience—a setting forth in detail of the Divinely-provided "Rule."

In previous chapters we have shown that holiness is the antithesis of sin, and therefore as "sin is the transgression (a deviation from or violation of) the Law" (1 John 3:4), holiness must be a conformity to the Law. As "sin" is a general term to connote all that is evil, foul, and morally loathsome, so holiness" is a general term to signify all that is good, pure, and morally virtuous or vicious, praiseworthy or blameworthy, as they express the desires, designs, and choices of the heart. As all sin is a species of self-love—self-will, self-pleasing, self-gratification—so all holiness consists of disinterested or unselfish love—to God and our neighbor: 1 Corinthians 13 supplies a full and beautiful delineation of the nature of holiness: substitute the term "holiness" for "love" all through that chapter. As sin is the transgressing of the Law, so love is the fulfilling of the Law (Rom. 13:10).

The spirituality and religion of man in his original state consisted in a perfect conformity to the Divine Law, which was the law of his nature (for he was created in the image and likeness of God), with the addition of positive precepts. But when man lost his innocence and became guilty and depraved, he fell not only under the wrath of God, but also under the dominion of sin. Consequently, he now needs both a Redeemer, and a Sanctifier; and in the Gospel both are provided. Alas that so often today only a half Gospel, a mutilated Gospel, is being preached—whereby sinners are made "twofold more the children of Hell" than they were before they heard it! In the Gospel a way is revealed for our obtaining both pardoning mercy and sanctifying grace. The Gospel presents Christ not only as a Deliverer from the wrath to come (1 Thess. 1:10), but also as the Sanctifier of His Church (Eph. 5:26).

In His work of sanctifying the Church Christ restores His people unto a conformity to the Law. Before supplying proof of this statement, let us carefully observe what it is which the Law requires of us. "Jesus said unto him, thou shalt love the Lord thy God with all thy heart, and with all thy soul, and with all thy mind. This is the first and great commandment. And the second is like unto it, Thou shalt love thy neighbor as thyself. On these two commandments hang all the Law and the Prophets" (Matt. 22:37-40). Christ here summed up the ten commandments in these two, and every duty enjoined by the Law and inculcated by the Prophets is but a deduction or amplification of these two, in which all are radically contained. Here is, first, the duty required—love to God and our neighbor. Second, the ground or reason of this duty—because He is the Lord our God. Third, the measure of this duty—with all the heart.

The grand reason why God, the alone Governor of the world, ever made the Law, requiring us to love Him with all our hearts, was because it is, in its own nature, infinitely just and fitting. That Law is an eternal and unalterable Rule of Righteousness, which cannot be abrogated or altered in the least iota, for it is an unchanging expression of God's immutable moral character. To suppose that He would ever repeal or even abate the Law—when the grounds and reasons of God's first making it remain as forcible as ever, when that which it requires is as just and meet as ever, and which it becomes Him as the moral Ruler of the universe to require as much as ever—casts the highest reproach upon all His glorious perfections. Such a horrible insinuation could have originated nowhere else than in the foul mind of the Fiend, the arch-enemy of God, and is to be rejected by us with the utmost abhorrence.

To imagine God repealing the moral Law, which is the rule of all holiness and the condemner of all sin, would be supposing Him to release His creatures from giving unto Him the full glory which is His due, and allowing them to hold back a part of it at least. It supposes Him releasing His creatures from that which is right and allowing them to do that which is wrong. Yea, such a vile supposition reflects upon God's very goodness, for so far from it being a boon and benefit to His creatures, the repealing or altering this Law, which is so perfectly suited to their highest happiness, would be one of the sorest calamities that could happen. If God had rather that heaven and earth should pass away than that the least jot or tittle of the Law, should fail (Matt. 5:18), how steadfastly should we resist every effort of Satan's to rob us of this Divine rule, weaken its authority over our hearts, or prejudice us against it.

In the light of what has been pointed out, how unspeakably horrible, that vile blasphemy, to imagine that the Son Himself should come from Heaven, become incarnate, and die the death of the cross, with the purpose of securing for His people a rescinding or abating of the Law, and obtain for them a lawless liberty. What! had He so little regard for His Father's interests and glory, for the honor of His Law, that He shed His precious blood so as to persuade the great Governor of the world to slacken the reins of His government and obtain for His people an impious license? Perish the thought. Let all who love the Lord rise up in righteous indignation against such an atrocious slur upon His holy character, and loathe it as a Satanic slander—no matter by whom propagated. Any Spirit-taught reader must surely see that such a wicked idea as the affirming that Christ is the one who has made an end of the Law, is to make Him the friend of sin and the enemy of God!

Pause for a moment and weigh carefully the implications. How could God possibly vindicate the honor of His great name were He to either repeal or abate that law which requires love to Him with all our hearts? Would not this be clearly tantamount to saying that He had previously required more than was His due? Or, to put it in another form, that He does not now desire so much from His creatures as He formerly did? Or, to state the issue yet more baldly: should God now (since the cross) relinquish His rights and freely allow His creatures to despise Him and sin with impunity? Look at it another way: to what purpose should Christ die in order to secure an abatement from that Law? What need was there for it? or what good could it do? If the Law really demanded too much, then justice required God to make the abatement; in such case the death of Christ was needless. Or if the Law required what was right, then God could not in justice make any abatement, and so Christ died in vain!

But so far from Christ coming into this world with any such evil design, He expressly declared, "Think not that I am come to destroy the Law, or the Prophets; I am not come to destroy, but to fulfill. For verily I say unto you, Till heaven and earth pass, one jot or one tittle shall in no wise pass from the Law, till all be fulfilled, Whosoever therefore shall break one of these least commandments, and shall teach men so, he shall be called the least in the kingdom of heaven: but whosoever shall do and teach them, the same shall be called great in the kingdom of heaven" (Matt. 5:17-19). This is the very thing He condemned the Pharisees for all through this chapter. They, in effect, taught this very doctrine, that the Law was abated, that its exacting demands were relaxed. They affirmed that though the Law did forbid some external and gross acts of sin, yet it did not reprehend the first stirrings of corruption in the heart or lesser iniquities.

For instance, the Pharisees taught that, murder must not be committed, but there was no harm in being angry, speaking reproachfully, or harboring a secret grudge in the heart (Matt. 5:21-26). That adultery must not be committed, yet there was no evil in having lascivious thoughts (vv. 27-30). That we must not be guilty of perjury, yet there was no harm in petty oaths in common conversation (vv. 33-37). That friends must not be hated, yet it was quite permissible to hate enemies (vv. 43-47). These, and such like allowances, they taught were made in the Law, and therefore were not sinful. But such doctrine our Savior condemned as erroneous and damning, insisting that the Law requires us to be as perfect as our heavenly Father is perfect (v. 48), and declaring that if our righteousness exceed not that of the scribes and Pharisees we could not enter the kingdom of heaven (Matt. 5:20). How far, then, was our holy Lord from abating God's Law, or lessening our obligations to perfect conformity to it!

The fact of the matter is (and here we will proceed to adduce some of the proofs for our statement at the beginning of the fourth paragraph), that Christ came into the world for the express purpose of giving a practical demonstration, in the most public manner, that God is worthy of all that love, honor, and obedience which the Law requires, and that sin is as great an evil as the punishment of the Law implies, and thereby declared God's righteousness and hatred of sin, to the end that God might be just and yet the Justifier of every sincere believer. This Christ did by obeying the precepts and suffering the death-penalty of the Law in the stead of His people. The great design of the incarnation, life and death of our blessed Lord was to maintain and magnify the Divine government, and secure the salvation of His people in a way that placed supreme honor upon the Law.

The chief object before the beloved Son in taking upon Him the form of a servant was to meet the demands of the Law. His work here had a prime respect to the Law of God, so that sinners should be justified and sanctified without setting aside its requirements or without showing the least disregard to it. First. He was "made under the Law" (Gal. 4:4)—amazing place for the Lord of glory to take! Second, He declared, "Lo, I come: in the volume of the book it is written of Me, I delight to do Thy will, O my God; yea, Thy Law is within My heart" (Ps. 40:7, 8)—enshrined in His affections. Third, He flawlessly obeyed the commands of the Law in thought, and word, and deed: as a Child He was subject to His parents (Luke 2:51); as Man He honored the sabbath (Luke 4:16), and refused to worship or serve any but the Lord His God (Luke 4:8). Fourth, when John demurred at baptizing Him, He answered "Thus it becometh us to fulfill all righteousness" (Matt. 3:15)—what a proof of His love for the Lawgiver in submitting to His ordinance! what proof of His love for His people in taking His place alongside of them in that which spake of death!

The truth is, that it was God's own infinite aversion to the repeal of the Law, as a thing utterly unfit and wrong, which was the very thing which made the death of Christ needful. If the Law might have been repealed, then sinners could have been saved without any more ado; but if it must not be repealed, then the demands of it must be answered by some other means, or every sinner would be eternally damned. It was because of this that Christ willingly interposed, and "magnified the Law and made it honorable" (Isa. 42:21), so securing the honor of God's holiness and justice, so establishing His law and government, that a way has been opened for Him to pardon the very chief of sinners without compromising Himself to the slightest degree. "As many as are of the works of the Law are under the curse. . . Christ hath redeemed us from the curse of the Law, being made a curse for us" (Gal. 3:10, 13).

Christ loved His Father's honor far too much to revoke His Law, or bring His people into a state of insubordination to His authority; and He loved them too well to turn them adrift from "the perfect Law of liberty." Read carefully the inspired record of His life upon earth, and you will not discover a single word falling from His lips which expresses the slightest disrespect for the Law. Instead we find that He bade His disciples do unto men whatsoever we would that they should do unto us because "this is the Law and the Prophets" (Matt. 7:12). In like manner Christ's apostles urged the performance of moral duties by the authority of the Law: "Owe no man anything, but to love one another: for he that loveth another hath fulfilled the Law" (Rom. 13:8); "Children, obey your parents in the Lord, for this is right: honor thy father and mother, which is the first commandment with promise" (Eph. 6:1, 2). The apostle John exhorted believers to love one another as "an old commandment which ye had from the beginning" (1 John 2:7). And, as we shall yet show at length, the Law is the great means which the Spirit uses in sanctifying us.

Here, then, is a "threefold cord" which cannot be broken, a threefold consideration which "settles the matter" for all who submit to the authority of Holy Scripture. First, God the Father honored the Law by refusing to rescind it in order that His people might be saved at less cost, declining to abate its demands even when His own blessed Son cried, "If it be possible, let this cup pass from Me." God the Son honored the Law by being made under it, by perfectly obeying its precepts, and by personally enduring its awful penalty. God the Spirit honors the Law by making quickened sinners see, feel, and own that it is "holy, and just, and good" (Rom. 7:12) even though it condemns them, and that, before ever He reveals the mercy of God through Jesus Christ unto them; so that the Law is magnified, sin is embittered, the sinner is humbled, and grace is glorified all at once!

There are some who will go with us this far, agreeing that Christ came here to meet the demands of the Law, yet who insist that the Law being satisfied, believers are now entirely freed from its claims. But this is the most inconsistent, illogical, absurd position of all. Shall Christ go to so much pains to magnify the Law in order that it might now be dishonored by us! Did He pour out His love to God on the Cross that we might be relieved from loving Him! It is true that "Christ is the end of the Law for righteousness to everyone that believeth" (Rom. 10:4)—for "righteousness" (for our justification), yes; but not for our sanctification. Is it not written that "he that saith he abideth in Him ought himself also to walk even as He walked" (1 John 2:6), and did not Christ walk according to the rule of the Law? The great object in Christ's coming here was to conform His people to the Law, and not to make them independent of it. Christ sends the Spirit to write the Law in their hearts (Heb. 8:10) and not to set at nought its holy and high demands.

The truth is that God's sending His Son into the world to die for the redemption of His people, instead of freeing them from their obligations to keep the Law, binds them the more strongly to do so. This is so obvious that it ought not to require arguing. Reflect for a moment, Christian reader, upon God's dealings with us. We had rebelled against the Lord, lost all esteem for Him, cast off His authority, and practically bid defiance to both His justice and His power. What wonder, then, had He immediately doomed our apostate world to the blackness of darkness forever? Instead, He sent forth His own dear Son, His only Begotten, as an Ambassador of peace, with a message of good news, even that of a free and full forgiveness of sins to all who threw down the weapons of their warfare against Him, and who took His easy yoke upon them.

But more: when God's Son was despised and rejected of men, He did not recall Him to Heaven, but allowed Him to complete His mission of mercy, by laying down His life as a ransom for all who should believe on Him. And now He sends forth His messengers to proclaim the Gospel to the ends of the earth, inviting His enemies to cease their rebellion, acknowledge the Law by which they stand condemned to be holy, just and good, and to look to Him through Jesus Christ for pardon as a free gift, and to yield themselves to Him entirely, to love Him and delight themselves in Him forever. Is not this fathomless love, infinite mercy, amazing grace, which should melt our hearts and cause us to "present our bodies a living sacrifice, holy, acceptable unto God" which is indeed our "reasonable service" (Rom. 12:1)?

O my Christian reader, that God out of His own mere good pleasure, according to His eternal purpose, should have stopped thee in thy mad career to Hell, made thee see and feel thy awful sin and guilt, own the sentence just by which thou wast condemned, and bring thee on thy knees to look for free grace through Jesus Christ for pardon, and through Him give up thyself to God forever. And that now He should receive thee to His favor, put thee among His children, become your Father and your God, by an everlasting covenant; undertake to teach and guide, nourish and strengthen, correct and comfort, protect and preserve; and while in this world supply all thy need and make all things work together for thy good; and finally bring thee into everlasting glory and blessedness. Does not this lay thee under infinitely deeper obligations to Love the Lord thy God with all thine heart? Does not this have the greatest tendency to animate thee unto obedience to His righteous Law? Does not this engage thee, does not His love constrain thee, to seek to please, honor and glorify Him?

Chapter 18
Its Rule
(CONTINUED)

We trust it has now been clearly proved to the satisfaction of every Truth-loving reader that the great object in Christ's coming here was to magnify the Law and satisfy its righteous demands. In His fulfilling of the Law and by His enduring its penalty, the Lord Jesus laid the foundation for the conforming of His people to it. This is plainly taught us in, "For what the Law could not do (namely, justify and sanctify fallen sinners—neither remit the penalty, nor deliver from the power of sin) in that it was weak through the flesh (unable to produce holiness in a fallen creature, as a master musician cannot produce harmony and melody from an instrument that is all out of tune) God sending His own Son in the likeness of sin's flesh and for sin, condemned sin in the flesh, that (in order that) the righteousness of the Law (its just requirements) might be fulfilled in us" (Rom. 8:3, 4).

This was the design of God in sending His Son here. "That He would grant unto us, that we, being delivered out of the hand of our enemies, might serve Him (be in subjection to Him) without fear, in holiness and righteousness before Him all the days of our life" (Luke 1:74, 75). "Who gave Himself for us, that He might redeem us from all iniquity, and purify unto Himself a peculiar people, zealous of good works" (Titus 2:14). "Who His own self bare our sins in His own body on the tree, that we, being dead to sins, should live unto righteousness" (1 Pet. 2:24). These and similar passages, are so many different ways of saying that Christ "became obedient unto death" in order that His people might be recovered to obedience unto God, that they might be made personally holy, that they might be conformed to God's Law, both in heart and life. Nothing less than this would or could meet the requirements of the Divine government, satisfy God's own nature, or glorify the Redeemer by a triumphant issue of His costly work.

Nor should it surprise any to hear that nothing short of heart-conformity to the Law could satisfy the thrice Holy One. "The Lord seeth not as man seeth: for man looketh on the outward appearance, but the Lord looketh on the heart" (1 Sam. 16:7). We have read the Old Testament Scriptures in vain if we have failed to note what a prominent place this basic and searching truth occupies: anyone who has access to a complete Hebrew-English concordance can see at a glance how many hundreds of times the term "heart" is used there. The great God could never be imposed upon or satisfied with mere external performances from His creatures. Alas, alas, that heart religion is rapidly disappearing from the earth, to the eternal undoing of all who are strangers to it. God has never required less than the hearts of His creatures: "My son, give Me thine heart" (Prov. 23:26).

"Only take heed to thyself, and keep thy soul diligently, lest thou forget the things which thine eyes have seen, and lest they depart from thy heart all the days of thy life" (Deut. 4:9). "Circumcise therefore the foreskin of your heart, and be no more stiffnecked" (Deut. 10:16, and cf. Jer. 10:25, 26). "Keep thy heart with all diligence, for out of it are the issues of life" (Prov. 4:23). "Therefore also now, saith the Lord, turn ye even to Me with all your heart, and with fasting, and with weeping, and with mourning: and rend your hearts and not your garments; and turn unto the Lord your God, for He is gracious and merciful" (Joel 2:12, 13). The regenerate in Israel clearly recognized the high and holy demands which the Law of God made upon them: "Behold, Thou desirest truth in the inward parts" (Ps. 51:6); and therefore did they pray, "Search me, O God, and know my heart: try me, and know my thoughts; and see if there be any wicked way in me, and lead me in the way everlasting" (Ps. 139:23, 24).

Now as we pointed out in our last, the Lord Jesus affirmed that the full requirements of the Law from us are summed up in, "Thou shalt love the Lord thy God with all thy heart, and with all thy soul, and with all thy mind; thou shalt love thy neighbor as thyself" (Matt. 22:37, 39). It was to restore His people to this that Christ lived and died: to recover them to God, to bring them back into subjection to Him (from which they fell in Adam), to recover them to the Lawgiver. Christ is the Mediator between God and men, and by Christ is the believing sinner brought to God. When He sends His ministers to preach the Gospel it is "to open their eyes, to turn them from darkness to light, and from the power of Satan to God" (Acts 26:18). "All things are of God, who hath reconciled us to Himself by Jesus Christ" (2 Cor. 5:18). To the saints Paul wrote "Ye turned to God from idols, to serve the living and true God" (1 Thess. 1:9). Of Christ it is written "He is able also to save them to the uttermost that come unto God by Him" (Heb. 7:25); and again, "Christ also hath once suffered for sins, the Just for the unjust, that He might bring us to God" (1 Pet. 3:18)—to the God of the Old Testament, the Lawgiver!

Let us now consider how Christ recovers His people unto a conformity of the Law, how He restores them unto the Lawgiver. Since that which the Law requires is that we love the Lord our God with all our hearts, it is evident, in the first place, that we must have a true knowledge of God Himself: this is both requisite unto and implied in the having our affections set upon Him. If our apprehensions of God be wrong, if they agree not with the Scriptures, then it is obvious that we have but a false image of Him framed by our own fancy. By a true knowledge of God (John 17:3) we mean far more than a correct theoretical notion of His perfections: the demons have that, yet they have no love for Him. Before God can be loved there must be a spiritual knowledge of Him, a heartfelt realization of His personal loveliness, moral excellency, ineffable glory.

By nature none of us possess one particle of genuine love for God: so far from it, we hated Him, though we may not have realized the awful fact, and had we done so, would not have acknowledged it. "The carnal mind is enmity against God, for it is not subject to the Law of God, neither indeed can be" (Rom. 8:7): those are equivalents, convertible terms. Where there is enmity toward God, there is insubjection to His Law; contrariwise, where there is love for God, there is submission to His Law. The reason why there is no love for God in the unregenerate is because they have no real knowledge of Him: this is just as true of those in Christendom as it is of those in heathendom—to the highly privileged and well-instructed Jews Christ said, "Ye neither know Me, nor My Father" (John 8:19, 54). A miracle of grace has to take place in order to this: "For God, who commanded the light to shine out of darkness, hath shined in our hearts, to give the light of the knowledge of the glory of God in the face of Jesus Christ" (2 Cor. 4:6); "We know that the Son of God is come, and hath given us an understanding, that we may know Him that is true" (1 John 5:20).

This true knowledge of God consists in our spiritually perceiving Him (in our measure) to be just such an One as He actually is. We see Him to be not only Love itself, the God of all grace and the Father of mercies, but also Supreme, infinitely exalted above all creatures; Sovereign, doing as He pleases, asking no one's permission and giving no account of His actions; Immutable, with whom there is no variableness or shadow of turning; ineffably Holy, being of purer eyes than to behold evil and canst not look on iniquity; inflexibly Just, so that He will by no means clear the guilty; Omniscient, so that no secret can be concealed from Him; Omnipotent, so that no creature can successfully resist Him; the Judge of all, who will banish from His presence into everlasting woe and torment every impenitent rebel. This is the character of the true God: do you love Him, my reader?

Second, a high esteem for God is both requisite unto and is implied in loving Him. This high esteem consists of exalted thoughts and a lofty valuation of Him from the sight and sense we have of His own intrinsic worthiness and excellency. To the unregenerate He says, "Thou thoughtest that I was altogether such a one as thyself" (Ps. 50:21), for their concepts of God are mean, low, derogatory. But when the Spirit quickens us and shines upon our understandings we discern the beauty of the Lord, and admire and adore Him. We join with the celestial hosts in exclaiming, "Holy, holy, holy, is the Lord of hosts." As we behold, as in a glass, His glory, we see how infinitely exalted He is above all creatures, and cry, "Who is like unto Thee, O Lord, among the gods? who is like Thee, glorious in holiness, fearful in praises, doing wonders?" yea, we confess "Whom have I in heaven but Thee? and there is none upon earth that I desire besides Thee" (Ps. 73:25).

Now this high estimate of God not only disposes or inclines the heart to acquiesce, but to exult in His high prerogatives. From a consciousness of His own infinite excellency, His entire right thereto, and His absolute authority over all, occupying the throne of the universe, He presents Himself as the Most High God, supreme Lord, sovereign Governor of all worlds, and demands that all creatures shall be in a perfect subjection to Him; deeming those who refuse Him this as worthy of eternal damnation. He declares, "I am the Lord, and beside Me there is no God: My glory will I not give to another: thus and thus shall ye do, because I am the Lord." As it would be the utmost wickedness for the highest angel in heaven to assume any of this honor to himself, yet it perfectly becomes the Almighty so to do: yea, so far above all is He, that God is worthy of and entitled to infinitely more honor and homage than all creatures together can possibly pay to Him.

When the eyes of our hearts are open to see something of God's sovereign majesty, infinite dignity, supernal glory, and we begin to rightly esteem Him, then we perceive how thoroughly right and just it is that such an One should be held in the utmost reverence, and esteemed far above all others and exulted in: "Sing unto the Lord all the earth" (Ps. 96:1). A spiritual sight and sense of the supreme excellency and infinite glory of the Triune Jehovah will not only rejoice our hearts to know that He is King of kings, the Governor of all worlds, but we are also thankful and glad that we live under His government, and are His subjects and servants. We shall then perceive the grounds and reasons of His Law: how infinitely right and fit it is that we should love Him with all our hearts and obey Him in everything; how infinitely unfit and wrong the least sin is, and how just the threatened punishment. We shall then also perceive that all the nations of the earth are but as a drop in the bucket before Him, and that we ourselves are less than nothing in His sight.

Third, a deep and lasting desire for God's glory is both requisite unto and is implied in our loving Him. When we are acquainted with a person who appears very excellent in our eyes and we highly esteem him, then we heartily wish him well and are ready at all times to do whatever we can to promote his welfare. It is thus that love to God will make us feel and act toward His honor and interests in this world. When God is spiritually beheld in His infinite excellency, as the sovereign Governor of the whole world, and a sense of His infinite worthiness is alive in our hearts, a holy benevolence is enkindled, the spontaneous language of which is, "Give unto the Lord, O ye kindreds of the people, give unto the Lord glory and strength: give unto the Lord the glory due unto His name" (Ps. 96:6, 7). "Be thou exalted O God, above the heavens; let Thy glory be above all the earth" (Ps. 57:5). As self-love naturally causes us to seek the promotion of our own interests and self-aggrandizement, so a true love to God moves us to put Him first and seek His glory.

This holy disposition expresses itself in earnest longings that God would glorify Himself and honor His great name by bringing more of our fellow-creatures into an entire subjection to Himself. The natural longing and language of true spiritual love is, "Our Father which art in heaven, Hallowed be Thy name; Thy kingdom come; Thy will be done on earth as it is in heaven." When God is about to bring to pass great and glorious things to the magnifying of Himself, it causes great rejoicing: "Let the heavens rejoice and let the earth be glad . . . He shall judge the world with righteousness, and the people with His truth" (Ps. 96:11, 13). So too when God permits anything which, as it seems to us, tends to bring reproach and dishonor upon His cause, it occasions acute anguish and distress: as when the Lord threatened to destroy Israel for their stiffneckedness, Moses exclaimed "What will become of Thy great name? what will the Egyptians say!"

From this disinterested affection arises a free and genuine disposition to give ourselves entirely to the Lord forever, to walk in His ways and keep all His commandments. For if we really desire that God may be glorified, we shall be disposed to seek His glory. A spiritual sight and sense of the infinite greatness, majesty, and excellency of the Lord of lords, makes it appear to us supremely fit that we should be wholly devoted to Him, and that it is utterly wrong for us to live to ourselves and make our own interests our last end. The same desire which makes the godly earnestly long to have God glorify Himself, strongly prompts them to live unto Him. If we love God with all our hearts, we shall serve Him with all our strength. If God be the highest in our esteem, then His honor and glory will be our chief concern. To love God so as to serve Him is what the Law requires; to love self so as to serve it, is rebellion against the Majesty of heaven.

Fourth, delighting ourselves in God is both requisite unto and is implied in our loving Him. If there be a heartfelt realization of God's personal loveliness and ineffable glory, then the whole soul must and will be attracted to Him. A spiritual sight and sense of the perfections of the Divine character draw out the heart in fervent adoration. When we "delight in" a fellow-creature, we find pleasure and satisfaction in his company and conversation; we long to see him when absent, rejoice in his presence, and the enjoyment of him makes us happy. So it is when a holy soul beholds God in the grandeur of His being, loves Him above all else, and is devoted to Him entirely—now he delights in Him supremely. His delight and complacency is as great as his esteem, arising from the same sense of God's moral excellency.

From this delight in God spring longings after a fuller acquaintance and closer communion with Him: "0 God, Thou art my God; early will I seek Thee: my soul thirsteth for Thee, my flesh longeth for Thee in a dry and thirsty land, where no water is: to see Thy power and Thy glory . . because Thy lovingkindness is better than life . . . my soul followeth hard after Thee" (Ps. 63:1-8). There is at times a holy rejoicing in God which nothing can dim: "Although the fig tree shall not blossom, neither shall fruit be in the vines; the labor of the olive shall fail, and the fields shall yield no meat; the flock shall be cut off from the fold, and there shall be no herd in the stalls; Yet I will rejoice in the Lord, I will joy in the God of my salvation" (Hab. 3:17, 18). From this delight in God arises a holy disposition to renounce all others and to live wholly upon Him, finding our satisfaction in Him alone: "0 Lord our God, other lords besides Thee have had dominion over us but by Thee only will we make mention of Thy name" (Isa. 26:13); "I count all things but loss for the excellency of the knowledge of Christ Jesus my Lord: for whom I have suffered the loss of all things, and do count them but dung, that I may win Christ" (Phil. 3 :8). As the proud man seeks contentment in creature honors, the worldling in riches, the Pharisee in his round of duties, so the true lover of God finds his contentment in God Himself.

That these four things are a true representation of the nature of that love which is required in the first and great commandment of the Law, upon which chiefly hang all the Law and the Prophets, is manifest, not only from the reason of things, but from this: that such a love lays a sure and firm foundation for all holy obedience. Only that love to God is of the right kind which effectually influences us to keep His commandments: "Hereby we do know that we know Him, if we keep His commandments. He that saith I know Him, and keepeth not His commandments is a liar, and the truth is not in him. But whoso keepeth His Word, in him verily is the love of God perfected" (1 John 2:3-5). But it is evident from the very nature of things that such a love as this will effectually influence us so to do. As self-love naturally moves us to set up self and its interests, so this love will move us to set up God and His interests. The only difference between the love of saints in heaven and of saints on earth is one of degree.

Having shown that the great object in Christ's coming to earth was to magnify the Law (by obeying its precepts and suffering its penalty), and that by so doing He laid a foundation for the recovering of His people to the Lawgiver, it now remains for us to consider more specifically how He conforms them to the Law. This, as we have just seen, must consist in His bringing them to lay down the weapons of their warfare against God, and by causing them to love God with all their heart. This He accomplishes by the sending forth of His blessed Spirit to renew them, for "the love of God is shed abroad in our hearts by the Holy Spirit which is given to us" (Rom. 5:5). It is the special and supernatural work of the Spirit in the soul which distinguishes the regenerate from the unregenerate.

Previously we have shown at length that the regenerating and sanctifying work of the Spirit is an orderly and progressive one, conducting the soul step by step in the due method of the Gospel: quickening, illuminating, convicting, drawing to Christ, and cleansing. That order can be best perceived by us inversely, according as it is realized in our conscious experience, tracing it backward from effect to cause. (5) Without the Spirit bringing us to Christ there can be no cleansing from His blood. (4) Without the Spirit working in us evangelical repentance there can be no saving faith or coming to Christ. (3) Without Divine conviction of sin there can be no godly sorrow for it. (2) Without the Spirit's special illumination there can be no sight or sense of the exceeding sinfulness of sin, wherein it consists—opposition to God, expressed in self-pleasing. (1) Without His quickening us we can neither see nor feel our dreadful state before God: spiritual life must be imparted before we are capable of discerning or being affected by Divine things.

It is by the Spirit we are brought from death unto life, given spiritual perception to realize our utter lack of conformity to the Divine Law, enabled to discern its spirituality and just requirements, brought to mourn over our fearful transgressions against it and to acknowledge the justice of its condemning sentence upon us. It is by the Spirit we receive a new nature which loves God and delights in His Law, which brings our hearts into conformity to it. The extent of this conformity in the present life, and the harassing difficulty presented to the Christian by the realization that there is still so much in him which is opposed to the Law, must be left for consideration in our next chapter.

Chapter 19
Its Rule
(CONTINUED)

It has been pointed out in earlier chapters that our practical sanctification by the Spirit is but His continuing and completing of the work which He began in us at regeneration and conversion. Now saving conversion consists in our being delivered from our depravity and sinfulness to the moral image of God, or, which is the same thing, to a real conformity unto the moral Law. And a conformity to the moral Law (as we showed in our last chapter), consists in a disposition to love God supremely, live to Him ultimately, and delight in Him superlatively; and to love our neighbors as ourselves, with a practice agreeing thereto. Therefore a saving conversion consists in our being recovered from what we are by nature to such a disposition and practice.

In order to this blessed recovery of us to God, Christ, by His Spirit applies the law in power to the sinners understanding and heart, for "the Law of the Lord is perfect, converting the soul" (Ps. 19:7). That effectual application of the Law causes the sinner to see clearly and to feel acutely how he had lived—in utter defiance of it; what he is—a foul leper; what he deserves—eternal punishment; and how he is in the hands of a sovereign God, entirely at His disposal (see Rom. 9:18). This experience is unerringly described in, "For without (the Spirit's application of) the Law, sin was dead (we had no perception or feeling of its heinousness). For I was alive without the Law once (deeming myself as good as anyone else, and able to win God's approval by my religious performances); but when the commandment came (in power to my conscience), sin revived (became a fearful reality as I discovered the plague of my heart), and I died" (to my self-righteousness)—Romans 7:8, 9.

It is then, for the first time, that the soul perceives "the Law is spiritual" (Rom. 7:14), that it requires not only outward works of piety, but holy thoughts and godly affections, from whence all good works must proceed, or else they are unacceptable to God. The Law is "exceeding broad" (Ps. 119:96), taking notice not only of our outward conduct but also of our inward state; "love" is its demand, and that is essentially a thing of the heart. As the Law requires love, and nothing but love (to God and our neighbor), so all sin consists in that which is contrary to what the Law requires, and therefore every exercise of the heart which is not agreeable to the Law, which is not prompted by holy love, is opposed to it and is sinful. Therefore did Christ plainly declare, "Whosoever looketh on a woman to lust after her hath committed adultery with her already in his heart" (Matt. 5:28).

God requires far more than a correct outward deportment: "Behold, Thou desirest truth in the inward parts" (Ps. 51:6). The Law takes cognizance of the thoughts and intents of the heart, saying, "thou shalt not covet, which is an act of the soul rather than of the body. When a sinner is brought to realize what the high and holy demands of the Law really are, and how utterly he has failed to meet them, he begins to perceive something of the awfulness of his condition, for "by the Law is the knowledge of sin" (Rom. 3:20). Now it is that the awakened sinner realizes how justly the Law condemns and curses him as an inveterate and excuseless transgressor of it. Now it is that he has a lively sense in his own soul of the dreadfulness of eternal damnation. Now it is he discovers that he is lost, utterly and hopelessly lost so far as any self-help is concerned.

This it is which prepares him to see his dire need of Christ, for they that are whole (in their self-complacency and self-righteousness), betake not themselves to the great Physician. Thus the Law (in the hands of the Spirit) is the handmaid of the Gospel. Was not this the Divine order even at Sinai? The moral law was given first, and then the ceremonial law, with its priesthood and sacrifices: the one to convict of Israel's need of a Savior, the other setting forth the Savior under various types and figures! It is not until sin "abounds" in the stricken conscience of the Spirit-convicted transgressor, that grace will "much more abound" in the estimation and appreciation of his Spirit-opened heart. In exact proportion as we really perceive the justice, dignity, and excellency of the Law, will be our realization of the infinite evil of sin; and in exact proportion to our sense of the exceeding sinfulness of sin will be our wonderment at the riches of Divine grace.

Then it is that "God, who commanded the light to shine out darkness, shines in our hearts, unto the light of the knowledge of the glory of God in the face of Jesus Christ" (2 Cor. 4:6). As an experimental sense of the glory of God's righteousness in the Law and of His grace in the Gospel is imparted to the soul by the Spirit, the sinner is moved to return home to God, through the Mediator, to venture his soul and its eternal concerns upon His free grace, and to give up himself to be His forever—to love Him supremely, live to Him entirely, and delight in Him superlatively. Hereby his heart begins to be habitually framed to love his neighbor as himself, with a disinterested impartiality; and thus an effectual foundation is laid in his heart for universal external obedience, for nothing but a spontaneous and cheerful obedience can be acceptable to God, an obedience which flows from love and gratitude, an obedience which is rendered without repining or grudging, as though it were a grievous burden to us.

It is thus that Christ, by His Spirit, conforms us to God's Law. First, by enlightening our understandings, so that we perceive the spirituality of the Law, in its high and meet demands upon our hearts. Second, by bringing us to perceive the holiness and justice of its requirements. Third, by convicting us of our lifelong trampling of the Law beneath our feet. Fourth, by causing us to mourn over our wicked defiance of its authority. And fifth, by imparting to us a new nature or principle of holiness. Now it is that the Lord puts His laws into our minds and writes them in our hearts (Heb. 8:10). Thus, so far from the grace of the Gospel "making void the Law," it "establishes" it (Rom. 3:31) in our consciences and affections. A spiritual and universal obedience is what the Law demands.

The principal duties of love to God above all, and to our neighbors for His sake, are not only required by the sovereign will of God, but are in their own nature "holy, just and good" (Rom. 7:12), and therefore meet for us to perform. These are the two main roots from which issue all other spiritual fruits, and apart from them there can be no holiness of heart and life. And the powerful and effectual means by which this end is attained is the grand work of the Spirit in sanctifying us, for by that our hearts and lives are conformed to the Law. He must bestow upon us an inclination and disposition of heart to the duties of the Law, so as to fit and enable us unto the practice of them. For these duties are of such a nature as cannot possibly be performed while we have a disinclination from them.

As the Divine life is thus begun, so it is carried on in the soul much after the same order. The Spirit of God shows the believer, more and more, what a sinful, worthless, Hell-deserving wretch he is in himself, and so makes him increasingly sensible of his imperative need of free grace through Jesus Christ, to pardon and sanctify him. He has an ever-deepening sense of those two things all his days, and thereby his heart is kept humble, and Christ and free grace made increasingly precious. The Spirit of God shows the believer more and more the infinite glory and excellency of God, whereby he is influenced to love Him, live to Him, and delight in Him with all his heart; and thereby his heart is framed more and more to love his neighbor as himself. Thus "the path of the just is as the shining light, that shineth more and more unto the perfect day" (Prov. 4:18).

The last paragraph needs the following qualifications: the Spirit's operations after conversion are attended with two differences, arising from two causes. First, the different state the subject is in. The believer, being no longer under the Law as a covenant, is not, by the Spirit, filled with those legal terrors arising from the fears of Hell, as he formerly was (Rom. 8:15); rather is he now made increasingly sensible of his corruptions, of the sinfulness of sin, of his base ingratitude against such a gracious God; and hereby his heart is broken. Second, from the different nature of the subject wrought upon. The believer, no longer being under the full power of sin nor completely at enmity against God, does not resist the Spirit's operation as he once did, but has a genuine disposition to join with Him against sin in himself; saying, Lord, correct, chasten me, do with me as Thou wilt, only subdue my iniquities and conform me more and more unto Thy image.

A few words now upon the relation of the Gospel. First, the grace of the Gospel is not granted to counterbalance the rigor of the Law, or to render God's plan of government justifiable so as to sweeten the minds of His embittered enemies. The Law is "holy, just, and good" in itself, and was so before Christ became incarnate. God is not a tyrant, nor did His Son die a sacrifice to tyranny, to recover His injured people from the severity of a cruel Law. It is utterly impossible that the Son of God should die to answer the demands of an unrighteous Law. Second, the Law, as it is applied by the Spirit, prepares the heart for the Gospel: the one giving me a real knowledge of sin, the other revealing how I may obtain deliverance from its guilt and power. Third, the Law, and not the Gospel, is the rule of our sanctification: the one makes known what it is that God requires from me, the other supplies means and motives for complying therewith.

Fourth, the Law and the Gospel are not in opposition, but in apposition, the one being the handmaid of the other: they exist and work simultaneously and harmoniously in the experience of the believer. Fifth, the high and holy demands of the Law are not modified to the slightest degree by the Gospel: "Be ye therefore perfect, even as your Father which is in heaven is perfect" (Matt. 5 48); "But as He which hath called you is holy, so be ye holy in all manner of conversation" (1 Pet. 1:15) is the standard set before us. Sixth, thus the Christian's rule of righteousness is the Law, but in the hands of the Mediator: "Being not without law to God, but under the law to Christ" (1 Cor. 9:21)—beautifully typed out in the Law being given to Israel at Sinai after their redemption from Egypt, through Moses the typical Mediator (Gal. 3:19). Seventh, herein we may see the seriousness of the God-dishonoring error of all those who repudiate the moral law as the Christian's rule of life.

"The holy Law of God and the Gospel of His grace reflect the Divine glory, the one upon the other reciprocally, and both will shine forth with joint glory eternally in Heaven. The Law setting forth, in the brightest light, the beauty of holiness, and the vileness and fearful demerit of sin, will show the abounding grace that hath brought the children of wrath thither, with infinite luster and glory; and Grace will do honor to the Law, by showing in sinners, formerly very vile and polluted, the purity and holiness of the Law fully exemplified in their perfect sanctification; and Christ, the Lamb that was slain, by whom the interests of the Law and of Grace have been happily reconciled and inseparably united, will be glorified in His saints and admired by them who believe" (James Fraser, "The Scriptural doctrine of Sanctification," 1760).

It is, then, by the regenerating and sanctifying work of His Spirit that Christ brings His people to a conformity unto the Law and to a compliance with the Gospel. "But we all, with open face, beholding as in a glass the glory of the Lord, are changed into the same image from glory to glory, by the Spirit of the Lord" (2 Cor. 3:18). The "glory of the Lord" is beheld by us, first, as it shines in the glass of the Law—the glory of His justice and holiness, the glory of His governmental majesty and authority, the glory of His goodness in framing such a Law, which requires that we love Him with all our hearts, and, for His sake, as His creatures, our neighbors as ourselves. The "glory of the Lord" is beheld by us, second, as it shines forth in the glass of the Gospel—the glory of His redeeming love, the glory of His amazing grace, the glory of His abounding mercy. And, as renewed creatures, beholding this, we are "changed (the Greek word is the same as Christ being "transfigured") into the same image, from glory to glory (progressively, from one degree of it to another) by the Spirit of the Lord:" that is, into a real conformity to the Law, and a real compliance with the Gospel.

The Gospel calls upon us to repent, but there can be no genuine repentance until we see and feel ourselves to be guilty transgressors of the Law, and until we are brought by the Spirit to realize that we are wholly to blame for not having lived in perfect conformity to it. Then it is we clearly realize that we thoroughly deserve to be damned, and that, notwithstanding all our doings and religious performances. Yea, then it is that we perceive that all our previous religious performances were done not from any love for God, or with any real concern for His glory, but formally and hypocritically, out of self-love, from fear of Hell, and with a mercenary hope of gaining Heaven thereby. Then it is that our mouth is stopped, all excuses and extenuations silenced, and the curse of the Law upon us is acknowledged as just. Then it is that seeing God to be so lovely and glorious a Being, we are stricken to the heart for our vile enmity against Him, and condemn ourselves as incorrigible wretches. Such are some of the elements of genuine repentance.

The Gospel calls upon us to believe, to receive upon Divine authority its amazing good news: that a grievously insulted God has designs of mercy upon His enemies; that the Governor of the world, whose Law has been so flagrantly, persistently, and awfully trampled upon by us, has, in His infinite wisdom, devised a way whereby we can be pardoned, without His holy Law being dishonored or its righteous claims set aside; that such is His wondrous love for us that He gave His only begotten Son to be made under the Law, to personally and perfectly keep its precepts, and then endure its awful penalty and die beneath its fearful curse. But when a sinner has been awakened and quickened by the Holy Spirit, such a revelation of pure grace seems "too good to be true." To him it appears that his case is utterly hopeless, that he has transgressed beyond the reach of mercy, that he has committed the unpardonable sin. One in this state (and we sincerely pity the reader if he or she has never passed through it) can no more receive the Gospel into his heart than he can create a world. Only the Holy Spirit can bestow saving faith.

The Gospel calls upon us to obey, to surrender ourselves fully to the Lordship of Christ, to take His yoke upon us, to walk even as He walked. Now the yoke which Christ wore was unreserved submission to the will of God, and the rule by which He walked was being regulated in all things by the Divine Law. Therefore does Christ declare, "If any man will come after Me, let him deny himself, and take up his cross, and follow Me" (Matt. 16:24), for He has left us an example that we should follow His steps. It is their refusal to comply with this demand of the Gospel which seals the doom of all who disregard its claims. As it is written, "The Lord Jesus shall be revealed from Heaven, with His mighty angels, in flaming fire, taking vengeance on them that know not God, and that obey not the Gospel" (2 Thess. 1:7, 8); and again, "For the time is come that judgment must begin at the house of God: and if it first begin at us, what shall the end be of them that obey not the Gospel of God!" (1 Pet. 4:17). But such obedience as the Gospel requires can only be rendered by the sanctifying operations of the gracious Holy Spirit.

Marvelous indeed is the change which the poor sinner passes through under the regenerating and converting operations of the Spirit in his soul: he is made a new creature in Christ, and is brought into quite new circumstances. Perhaps the closest analogy to it may be found in the experience of orphan children, left without any guardian or guide, running wild and indulging themselves in all folly and riot; then being taken into the family of a wise and good man and adopted as his children. These lawless waifs are brought into new surroundings and influences: love's care for them wins their hearts, new principles are instilled into their minds, a new temper is theirs, and a new discipline regulates them; old things have passed away, all things have become new to them. So it is with the Christian: from being without God and hope in the world, from running to eternal ruin, they are delivered from the power of darkness and brought into the kingdom of Christ. A new nature has been communicated to them, the Spirit Himself indwells them, and a reconciled God now bestows upon them a Father's care, feeding, guiding, protecting them, and ultimately conducting them into everlasting glory.

Chapter 20
Its Rule
(COMPLETED)

The Unchanging moral Law of God, which requires us to love Him with all our hearts and our neighbors as ourselves, is the believer's rule of life, the standard of holiness to which his character and conduct must be conformed, the line and plummet by which his internal desires and thoughts as well as outward deeds are measured. And, as has been shown, we are conformed to that Law by the sanctifying operations of the Holy Spirit. This He does by making us see and feel the heinousness of all sin, by delivering us from its reigning power, and by communicating to us an inclination and disposition of heart unto the requirements of the Law, so that we are thereby fitted and enabled to the practice of obedience. While enmity against God reigns within—as it does in every unregenerate soul—it is impossible for love to give that obedience which the Law demands.

We concluded our last chapter by showing something of the marvelous and radical change which a sinner passes through when he is truly converted to God. One who has really surrendered to the claims of God approves of His Law: "I love Thy commandments above gold; yea, above fine gold. Therefore I esteem all Thy precepts concerning all things to be right; and I hate every false way" (Ps. 119:127, 128). And why do not the unregenerate do likewise? Because they have no love for a holy God. But believers, loving a holy God in Christ, must love the Law also, since in it the image of His holiness is displayed. The converted have a real inclination of heart unto the whole Law: "The Law of Thy mouth is better unto me than thousands of gold and silver . . . all Thy commandments are faithful" (Ps. 119:72, 86). There is in the regenerate a fixed principle which lies the same way as the holy Law, bending away from what the Law forbids and toward what it enjoins.

The converted habitually endeavor to conform their outward conduct to the whole Law: "0 that my ways were directed to keep Thy statutes! Then shall I not be ashamed, when I have respect unto all Thy commandments" (Ps. 19:5, 6). They desire a fuller knowledge of and obedience to the Law: "Teach me, ? Lord, the way of Thy statutes; and I shall keep it unto the end. Give me understanding, and I shall keep Thy Law; yea, I shall observe it with my whole heart. Make me to go in the path of Thy commandments, for therein do I delight" (Ps. 119:33-35). Should any object that these quotations are all made from the Old Testament (waiving now the fact that such an objection is quite pointless, for regeneration and its effects, conversion and its fruits, are the same in all ages), we would point out that the apostle Paul described his own experience in identically the same terms: "I delight in the Law of God after the inward man . . . with the mind I myself serve the Law of God" (Rom. 7:22, 26). Thus Christ conforms His people to the Law by causing His Spirit to work in them an inclination toward it, a love for it, and an obedience to it.

But at this point a very real and serious difficulty is presented to the believer, for a genuine Christian has an honest heart, and detests lies and hypocrisy. That difficulty may be stated thus: If conversion consists in a real conformity to the holiness of God's Law, with submission and obedience to its authority, accompanied by a sincere and constant purpose of heart, with habitual endeavor in actual practice, then I dare not regard myself as one who is genuinely converted, for I cannot honestly say that such is my experience; nay, I have to sorrowfully and shamefacedly lament that very much in my case is the exact reverse. So far from the reigning power of sin being broken in me, I find my corruptions and lusts raging more fiercely than ever, while my heart is a cage of all unclean things.

The above language will accurately express the feelings of many a trembling heart. As the preceding chapters upon the Rule of our sanctification have been thoughtfully pondered, not a few, we doubt not, are seriously disturbed in their minds. On the one hand, they cannot gainsay what has been written, for they both see and feel that it is according to the Truth; but on the other hand, it condemns them, it makes them realize how far, far short they come of measuring up to such a standard; yea, it plainly appears to them that they do not in any sense or to any degree measure up to it at all. Conscious of so much in them that is opposed to the Law, conscious of their lack of conformity to it, both inwards and outwards, they bitterly bewail themselves, and cry, "O wretched man that I am" (Rom. 7:24).

Our first reply is, Thank God for such an honest confession, for it supplies clear evidence that you are truly converted. No hypocrite—except it be in the hour of death—ever cries "0 wretched man that I am." No unregenerate soul ever mourns over his lack of conformity to God's Law! Such godly sorrow, dear Christian reader, will enable you to appropriate at least one verse of Scripture to your own case: "My tears have been my meat day and night" (Ps. 42:3), and those words proceeded not from the bitter remorse of a Judas, but were the utterance of one who had exclaimed "As the hart panteth after the water brooks, so panteth my soul after Thee, ? God" (Ps. 42:1). Alas that so many today are ignorant of what constitutes the actual experience of a Christian: defeat as well as victory, grief as well as joy.

Whilst it be a fact that at regeneration a new nature is imparted to us by the Holy Spirit, a nature which is inclined toward and loves the Law, it is also a fact that the old nature is not removed, nor its opposition to and hatred of the Law changed. Whilst it be a fact that a supernatural principle of holiness is communicated to us by the Spirit, it is also a fact that the principle and root of indwelling sin remains, being neither eradicated nor sublimated. The Christian has in him two opposing principles, which produce in him a state of constant warfare: "For the flesh lusteth against the spirit, and the spirit against the flesh: and these are contrary the one to the other; so that ye cannot do the things that ye would" (Gal. 5:17). That "cannot" looks both ways: because of the restraining presence of the "spirit," the "flesh" is prevented from fully gratifying its evil desires; and because of the hindering presence of the "flesh," the "spirit" is unable to fully realize its aspirations.

It is the presence of and the warfare between these two natures, the "flesh" and the "spirit," the principles of sin and holiness, which explain the bewildering state and conflicting experience of the real Christian; and it is only as he traces more fully the teaching of Holy Scripture and carefully compares himself therewith, that light is cast upon what is so puzzling and staggering in his experience. Particularly it is in the seventh of Romans that we have the clearest and most complete description of the dual history of a converted soul. Therein we find the apostle Paul, as moved by the Spirit, portraying most vividly and intimately his own spiritual biography. There are few chapters in the New Testament which the Devil hates more than Romans 7, and strenuously and subtly does he strive to rob the Christian of its comforting and establishing message.

As we have shown above, the Christian approves of the Law, and owns it to be "holy and just and good" (Rom. 7:12). He does so, even though the Law condemns many things in him, yea condemns all in him which is unholy or ungodly. But more: the Christian condemns himself—

"For that which I do, I allow not: for what I would, that do I not, but what I hate, that do I" (Rom. 7:15). So far from sin affording him satisfaction, it is the Christian's greatest grief. The more he perceives the excellency of God and what He is entitled to from His creatures, and the more he realizes what a debtor he is to Divine grace and the loving obedience he ought to render out of gratitude, the more acute is the Christian's sorrow for his sad and continual failures to be what he ought to be and to live as he should.

Our second answer to one who is deeply distressed over the raging of his lusts and fears that he has never been soundly converted, is this: the fact is, that the more holy a person is, and the more his heart is truly sanctified, the more clearly does he perceive his corruptions and the more painfully does he feel the plague of his heart; while he utters his complaints in strong expressions and with bitterness of soul. In God's light we see light! It is not that sin has greater control of us than formerly, but that we now have eyes to see its fearful workings, and our consciences are more sensitive to feel its guilt. An unregenerate person is like a sow wallowing in the mire: his impurities and iniquities afford him satisfaction, and give him little or no concern, no, not even the unholiness of his outward practice, much less the unholiness of his heart.

There is a notable difference between the sensibilities and expressions of the unconverted and the converted. An unregenerate person, who indulges freely in a course of evil practice, will nevertheless give a favorable account of himself: he will boast of his good-heartedness, his kindness, his generosity, his praiseworthy qualities and good deeds. On the other hand, persons truly holy, even when kept pure in their outward behavior, yet conscious of their indwelling corruptions, will condemn themselves in unsparing language. The unholy fix their attention on anything good they can find in themselves, and this renders them easy in an evil course. But a truly sanctified person is ready to overlook his spiritual attainments and fruits, and fixes his attention, with painful consciousness, on those respects in which he kicks conformity to Christ.

A Christian will say, I thought I had tasted that the Lord is gracious and that my heart had undergone a happy change, with a powerful determination toward God and holiness. I concluded I had some sound evidence of true conversion and of a heart that was really regenerated. Yet I knew the effect should be to grow in grace, to advance in holiness, and to be more delivered from sin. But alas, I find it quite otherwise. If there is grace in me, it is becoming weaker, and even though my outward conduct be regulated by the precepts of the Law, yet in my heart sin is becoming stronger and stronger—evil lusts, carnal affections, worldly desires, and disorderly passions, are daily stirring, often with great vehemence, defiling my spirit. Alas, after all, I fear my past experience was only a delusion, and the dread of the final outcome often strikes terror throughout my whole soul.

Dear friend, it is true that there is much in every Christian which affords great cause for self-judgment and deep humbling of ourselves before God; yet this is a very different matter from sin obtaining fuller dominion over us. Where sin gains power, there is always a corresponding hardening of heart and spiritual insensibility. Sin is served willingly by the wicked, and is sweet and pleasant to them. But if you sorrow over sin, sincerely and vigorously oppose it, condemn yourself for it, then old things have passed away and all is become new. "Christians may be assured that, a growing sensibility of conscience and heart sorrow for sin, is among the chief evidences of growth in grace and of good advances in holiness, that they are likely to have on this side of Heaven. For the more pure and holy the heart is, it will naturally have the more quick feeling of whatever sin remaineth in it" (Jas. Fraser, 1760).

The dual experience of the Christian is plainly intimated in Paul's statement: "So then with the mind I myself serve the Law of God, but with the flesh, the law of sin" (Rom. 7:25). But some one may reply, the opening verse of the next chapter says, "There is therefore now no condemnation to them which are in Christ Jesus, who walk not after the flesh, but after the spirit." Ah, note the minute accuracy of Scripture: had it said, "who act not according to the flesh" we might well despair, and conclude for a certainty we were not Christians at all. But "walking" is a deliberate course, in which a man proceeds freely, without force or struggle; it is the reverse of his being dragged or driven. But when the believer follows the dictates of the flesh, it is against the holy desires of his heart, and with reluctance to the new nature! But does not Romans 8:4 affirm, that Christ died in order that "the righteousness of the Law might be fulfilled in us?" Again we answer, admire the marvelous accuracy of Scripture; it does not say, "the righteousness of the Law is now fulfilled in us." It is not so, perfectly, in this life, but it will be so at our glorification.

Perhaps the reader is inclined to ask, But why does God suffer the sinful nature to remain in the Christian: He could easily remove it. Beware, my friend, of calling into question God's infinite wisdom: He knows what is best, and His thoughts and ways are often the opposite of ours (Isa. 55:8). But let me ask, Which magnifies God's power the more: to preserve in this wicked world one who still has within him a corrupt nature, or one that has been made as sinless as the holy angels? Can there be any doubt as to the answer! But why does not God subdue my lusts: Would it not be more for His glory if He did? Again, we say, Beware of measuring God with your mind. He knows which is most for His glory. But answer this question: If your lusts were greatly subdued and you sinned far less than you do, would you appreciate and adore His grace as you now do?

Our third answer to the deeply exercised soul who calls into question the genuineness of his conversion, is this: Honestly apply to yourself the following tests. First, in seasons of retirement from the noise and business of the world, or during the sacred hours of the Sabbath, or in your secret devotions, what are your thoughts, what is the real temper of your mind? Do you know God, commune with and delight in Him? Is His Word precious, is prayer a welcome exercise? Do you delight in God's perfections and esteem Him for His absolute supremacy and sovereignty? Do you feel and lament your remaining blindness and ignorance; do you mourn over your lack of conformity to God's Law and your natural contrariety to it, and hate yourself for it? Do you watch and pray and fight against the corruptions of your heart? Not indeed as you should, but do you really and sincerely do so at all?

Second, what are the grounds of your love to God? from what motives are you influenced to love Him? Because you believe He loves you? or because He appears infinitely great and glorious in Himself? Are you glad that He is infinitely holy, that He knows and sees all things, that He possesses all power? Does it suit your heart that God governs the world, and requires that all creatures should bow in the dust before Him, that He alone may be exalted? Does it appear perfectly reasonable that you should love God with all your heart, and do you loathe and resist everything contrary to Him? Do you feel yourself to be wholly to blame for not being altogether such as the Law requires? Third, is there being formed within you a disposition to love your neighbor as yourself, so that you wish and seek only his good? and do you hate and mourn over any contrary spirit within you? Honest answers to these questions should enable you to ascertain your real spiritual state.

"The holiness which the Gospel requireth will not be maintained either in the hearts or lives of men without a continual conflict, warring, contending; and that with all diligence, watchfulness, and perseverance therein. It is our warfare, and the Scripture abounds in the discovery of the adversaries we have to conflict withal, their power and subtlety, as also in directions and encouragements unto their resistance. To suppose that Gospel obedience will be kept up in our hearts and lives without a continual management of a vigorous warfare against its enemies, is to deny the Scripture and the experience of all that believe and obey God in sincerity. Satan, sin, and the world, are continually assaulting of it, and seeking to ruin its interest in us. The Devil will not be resisted, which it is our duty to do (1 Pet. 5:8, 9) without a sharp contest; in the management whereof we are commanded to 'take unto ourselves the whole armor of God' (Eph. 6:12). Fleshly lusts do continually war against our souls (1 Pet. 2 :11), and if we maintain not a warfare unto the end against them, they will be our ruin. Nor will the power of the world be any otherwise avoided than by a victory over it (1 John 5 :4), which will not be carried without contending.

"But I suppose it needs no great confirmation unto any who know what it is to serve and obey God in temptations, that the life of faith and race of holiness will not be persevered in without a severe striving, laboring, contending, with diligence and persistence; so that I shall take it as a principle (notionally at least) agreed upon by the generality of Christians. If we like not to be holy on these terms, we must let it alone, for on any other we shall never be so. If we faint in this course, if we give it over, if we think what we aim at herein, not to be worth the obtaining or persevering by such a severe contention all our days, we must be content to be without it. Nothing doth so promote the interest of Hell and destruction in the world, as a presumption that a lazy slothful performance of some duties and an abstinence from some sins, is that which God will accept of as our obedience. Crucifying of sin, mortifying our inordinate affections, contesting against the whole interest of the flesh, Satan, and the world, and that in inward actings of grace, and all instances of outward duties, and that always while we live in this world, are required of us hereunto" (John Owen, 1660).

From all that has been said it should be evident that the Christian needs to exercise the greatest possible care, daily, over the inward purity of his heart, earnestly opposing the first motions of every fleshly lust, inordinate affection, evil imagination, and unholy passion. The heart is the real seat of holiness. Heart-holiness is the chief part of our conformity to the spiritual Law of God, nor is any outward work considered as holy by Him if the heart be not right with Him—desiring and seeking after obedience to Him—for He sees and tries the heart. Holiness of heart is absolutely necessary to peace of mind and joy of soul, for only a cleansed heart can commune with the thrice Holy God: then keep thy heart with all diligence, for out of it are the issues of life" (Prov. 4:23).

In the last paragraph we have said nothing which in anywise clashes with our remarks in the body of this article; rather have we emphasized once more another aspect of our subject, namely, the pressing duty which lies upon the Christian to bring his heart and life into fuller conformity with the Law. It would be a grievous sin on the part of the writer were he to lower the standard which God has set before us to the level of our present attainments. Vast indeed is the difference between what we ought to be and what we actually are in our character and conduct, and deep should be our sorrow over this. Nevertheless, if the root of the matter be in us, there will be a longing after, a praying for and a pressing forward unto increased personal and practical holiness.

N. B. This aspect of our theme has been purposely developed by us somewhat disproportionately. The supreme importance of it required fullness of detail. The prevailing ignorance called for a lengthy treatment of the subject. Unless we know what the Rule of Sanctification is, and seek to conform thereto, all our efforts after holiness will and must be wide of the mark. Nothing is more honoring to God, and nothing makes more for our own true happiness, than for His LAW to be revered, loved, and obeyed by us.

Chapter 21
Its Instrument

Paul was sent unto the Gentiles "to open their eyes, to turn them from darkness to light and the power of Satan unto God, that they might receive forgiveness of sins and inheritance among them which are sanctified by faith that is in me" (Acts 26:18). Two extremes are to be guarded against in connection with the precise relation that faith sustains to the various aspects of salvation: disparaging it, and making too much of it. There are those who expressly deny that faith has any actual part or place in the securing of the same. On the other hand, there are some who virtually make a savior out of faith, ascribing to it what belongs alone to Christ. But if we adhere closely to Scripture and observe all that is said thereon (instead of restricting our attention to a few passages), there is no excuse for falling into either error. We shall therefore make a few remarks with the object of refuting each of them.

"But without faith it is impossible to please God" (Heb. 11:6). We are saved by faith (Luke 7:50). We are justified by faith (Rom. 5:1). We live by faith (Gal. 2:20). We stand by faith (2 Cor. 1:24). We walk by faith (2 Cor. 5:7). We obey by faith (Rom. 1:5). Christ dwells in our hearts by faith (Eph. 3:17). We overcame the world by faith (1 John 5:4). The heart is purified by faith (Acts 15:9). All duties, for their right motive and end, depend upon it. No trials and afflictions can be patiently or profitably borne unless faith be in exercise. Our whole warfare can only be carried on and finished victoriously by faith (1 Tim. 6:12). All the gifts and graces of God are presented in the promises, and they can only be received and enjoyed by us in a way of believing. It is high worship to be strong in faith giving glory to God. In view of all this, we need not be surprised to read that we are "sanctified by faith."

But in what way does faith sanctify us? To answer this question properly we must carefully bear in mind the principal aspects of our subject, which have already been considered by us in the previous chapters of this book. First, faith has nothing to do with the Father's setting us apart and blessing us with all spiritual blessings in Christ before the foundation of the world: it is one of the God-dishonoring and creature-exalting errors of Arminianism to affirm that Christians were elected on the ground that God foresaw they would believe. Second, our faith was in no sense a moving cause to Christ's becoming the Surety of His people and working out for them a perfect holiness before God. Third, faith has no influence in causing the Holy Spirit to separate the elect from the reprobate, for at the moment He does this they are dead in trespasses and sins, and therefore totally incapable of performing any spiritual acts. Fourth, faith will not contribute anything unto the Christian's glorification, for that is solely the work of God; the subject of it being entirely passive therein. "Whom he justified, them he also glorified."

Thus faith, important though it be, plays only a secondary and subordinate part in sanctification. It is neither the originating, the meritorious, nor the efficient cause of it, but only the instrumental. Yet faith is necessary in order to a saving union with Christ, and until that be effected none of the blessings and benefits which are in Him can be received by us. It seems strange that any who are well versed in the Scriptures and who profess to be subject to their teachings, should question what has just been affirmed. Take such a declaration as "them that believe to the saving of the soul" (Heb. 10:39). True, we are not saved for our believing, yet equally true is it that there is no salvation for any sinner without his believing. Every blessing we receive from Christ is in consequence of our being united to Him, and therefore we cannot receive the holiness there is in Him until we are "sanctified by faith." Furthermore, faith is necessary in order to the reception of the purifying Truth, in order to practical deliverance from the power of sin, and in order to progress or growth in personal holiness.

Before proceeding further let it be pointed out that the faith which the Gospel requires, the faith which savingly unites a sinner to Christ, the faith which issues in sanctification, is very much more than the bare assent of the mind to what is recorded in the Scriptures concerning the Lord Jesus; it is something far different from the mere adoption of certain evangelical opinions regarding the way of salvation. The Day to come will reveal the solemn fact that thousands went down to Hell with their heads filled with orthodox beliefs—which many of them contended for earnestly and propagated zealously, just as the Mohammedan does with the tenets and principles of his religion. Saving faith, my reader, is the soul's surrender to and reliance upon the Lord Jesus Christ as a living, loving, all-sufficient Savior, and that, upon the alone but sure testimony of God Himself. When we say "an all-sufficient Savior" we mean One in whom there is a spotless holiness as well as perfect righteousness for those who come to Him.

Faith lays hold of Christ as He is offered to sinners in the Gospel, and He is there presented not only for justification but also for the sanctification of all who truly believe on Him. The glorious Gospel of grace not only heralds One who delivers from the wrath to come but as giving title to approach now unto the thrice holy God. Moreover, faith accepts a whole Christ: not only as Priest to atone for us, but as a King to reign over us. Faith, then, is the instrument of our sanctification. Faith is the eye which perceives the gracious provisions which God has made for His people. Faith is the hand which appropriates those provisions. Faith is the mouth which receives all the good that God has stored up for us in Christ. Without faith it is impossible to please God, and without the exercise of faith it is impossible to make any real progress in the spiritual life.

Many of the Lord's people rob themselves of much of their peace and joy by confounding faith with its fruits; they fail to distinguish between the Word of God believed and what follows from believing it aright. Fruit grows on the tree, and the tree must exist before there can be fruit. True obedience, acceptable worship, growth in grace, assurance of salvation, are what faith produces, and not what faith itself is: they are the effects of faith working, and not definitions of the nature of faith. Faith derives its being from the Word of God, and all its fruits are the result of believing. What God has spoken in His Word demands belief from all to whom the Word comes. Faith and the Word of God, then, are related as the effect and the cause, because "faith cometh by hearing, and hearing by the Word of God" (Rom. 10:17). When faith comes by the inward "hearing," then we assent to what God has said, and we rely upon His faithfulness to make good what He has promised; until that has been effected there can be no fruits of faith.

It is, then, of much importance to correctly define what faith is, for a mistake at this point is not only dishonoring to God, but injurious to the soul and inimical to its peace. Faith is a childlike taking God at His Word and resting on what He has said. It is a depending on Christ to bestow those blessings and graces which He has promised to those who believe. How is a sin-defiled soul to become a partaker of the cleansing efficacy of the blood of the Lamb? Only by faith. The purifying virtue of Christ's blood, and the administration of the Spirit, for the application to make it effectual unto our souls and consciences, is exhibited in the promises of the Gospel; and the only way to be made a partaker of the good things presented in the promises is by faith. God Himself ordained this instrumental efficacy unto faith in the Everlasting Covenant, and nothing is more honoring to Him than the exercise of real faith.

Returning to our earlier question, In what way does faith sanctify us? We answer, first, by uniting us to Christ, the Holy One. Oneness with Christ is the foundation of all the blessings of the Christian, but it is not until he is actually united to Christ by faith that those blessings are really made over to him. Then it is that Christ is "made unto us wisdom, and righteousness, and sanctification, and redemption" (1 Cor. 1:30). It is faith which receives Christ's atonement, for God hath set forth Christ "a propitiation through faith in His blood" (Rom. 3:25), and His infinitely meritorious blood not only justifies but sanctifies too. Thus there is no intrinsic virtue in faith itself, instead, its value lies wholly in its being the hand which lays hold of Him who possesses infinite virtue. For this very reason faith excludes all boasting (Rom. 3:27), and therefore any "believing" which produces self-gratulation or results in self-satisfaction is most certainly not the faith of the Gospel.

Second, faith sanctifies the believer by enabling him to enjoy now what is his in Christ and what will be his in himself in Heaven. Faith sets to its seal that the testimony of God is true when He declares that "we are sanctified through the offering of the body of Jesus Christ once for all" (Heb. 10:10). Faith assures its possessor that though he is still a fallen creature in himself, and as such a sinner to the end of his earthly course, yet in Christ he is perfectly holy, having the same immaculate standing before God as does his Head and Surety; for "as He is, so are we in this world" (1 John 4:17). Thus faith is "the evidence of things not seen" (Heb. 11:1) by the natural eye, nor felt by the natural senses. Faith projects us out of this scene entirely and carries the heart into Heaven itself—not a natural faith, not a preacher-produced faith, but Gospel faith, imparted by the Holy Spirit.

But let us not be mistaken at this point. The faith of which we are here treating is not a blind fanaticism. It does not ignore the presence of indwelling sin. It does not lose its eyes to the constant activities of the flesh. It refuses to tone down the vile fruits which the flesh produces, by terming them peccadillos, ignorance, mistakes, etc. No, faith has clear vision and perceives the infinite enormity of all that is opposed to God. Faith is honest and scorns the hypocrisy of calling darkness light. But faith not only sees the total depravity of natural self and the horrible filth which fouls every part of it, but it also views the precious blood which has satisfied every claim of God upon those for whom it was shed, and which cleanses from all sin those who put their trust in it. It is neither fanaticism nor presumption for faith to receive at its face value what God as declared concerning the sufficiency of Christ's sacrifice.

Third, faith sanctifies as it derives grace from the fullness in which there is in Christ. God has constituted the Mediator the Source of all spiritual influences and faith is the instrument by which they are derived from Him. Christ is not only a Head of authority to His Church, but also a Head of influence. "But speaking the truth in love, may grow up into Him in all things, which is the Head, even Christ: from whom the whole body fitly joined together and compacted by that which every joint supplieth, according to the effectual working in the measure of every part, maketh increase of the body unto the edifying of itself in love" (Eph. 4:15, 16). That "effectual working in the measure of every part" is by supplies of grace being received from Christ, and that grace flows through the appointed channel of faith. As the Lord Jesus declared unto the father of the demon-tormented son, "If thou canst believe, all things are possible to him that believeth" (Mark 9:28); and to the two blind beggars who cried unto Him for mercy, "According to your faith be it unto you" (Matt. 9:29). How earnest and importunate should we be, in begging the Lord to graciously strengthen and increase our faith.

It is by faith laying hold upon a full Christ that the empty soul is replenished. All that we need for time as well as eternity is to be found in Him; but the hand of faith must be extended, even though it grasp but the hem of His garment, if virtue is to flow forth from Him into us. As Samson's strength was in his locks, so the Christian's strength is in his Head. This the Devil knows full well, and therefore does he labor so hard to keep us from Christ, causing the clouds of unbelief to hide from our view the radiant face of the Sun of righteousness, and getting us so occupied with our miserable selves that we forget the great Physician. As it is by the sap derived from the root which makes the branches fruitful, so it is by the virtue which faith draws from Christ that the believer is made to abound in holiness. Hence the exhortation, "Thou therefore, my son, be strong in the grace that is in Christ Jesus" (2 Tim. 2:1).

Fourth, faith sanctifies because it cleanses the soul. "And God, which knoweth the heart, bare them witness, giving them the Holy Spirit, even as He did unto us; and put no difference between us and them, purifying their hearts by faith" (Acts 15:8, 9). It is by faith the heart is "sprinkled from an evil conscience" by the blood of Christ. It is by faith the affections are lifted unto things above, and thereby disentangled from the defiling objects of the world. It is by the exercise of faith a that the "inward parts" (Ps. 51:6) are conformed in some measure unto the Rule of righteousness and holiness, for "faith worketh by love" (Gal. 5:6), and "love is the fulfilling of the Law" (Rom. 13:10). It is to be duly noted that in Acts 15:9 the apostle did not say" their hearts were purified by faith;" instead, he used the present tense "purifying," for it is a continuous process which lasts as long as the believer is hereupon earth. This aspect of our sanctification is not complete till we are released from this world.

Fifth, faith sanctifies because it is by this we hold communion with Christ, and communion with Him cannot but nourish the principle of holiness within the regenerate. Thus faith is sanctifying in its own nature, for it is exercised upon spiritual objects. "But we all with open face beholding (by faith) as in a glass the glory of the Lord, are changed into the same image from glory to glory, by the Spirit of the Lord" (2 Cor. 3:18). Faith is a transforming grace because it causes the soul to cleave unto the Divine Transformer. As it was faith which made us to first lay hold of Christ, so it impels us to continue coming unto Him; and if the woman who touched the hem of His garment by faith secured the healing of her body, shall not those who cleave to Christ continue obtaining from Him the healing of their spiritual maladies!

Sixth, faith sanctifies because it appropriates the commandmetsts of God and produces obedience. We are sanctified "by the Truth" (John 17:17), yet the Word works not without an act on our part as well as of God's. It is naught but blind enthusiasm which supposes that the Scriptures work in us like some magical charm. How solemn is that passage "but the Word preached did not profit them, not being mixed with faith in them that heard it" (Heb. 4:2). The Word avails us nothing if it be not received into a trustful heart and faith be acted upon it. Therefore do we read, "seeing ye have purified your souls in obeying the truth through the Spirit" (1 Pet. 2:22): it is only as the Truth is received upon the authority of God, given a place in our affections, and yielded to by the will, that our souls are "purified" by it. The more faith causes us to run in the way of God's commandments, the more is the soul delivered from the defiling effects of self-pleasing.

Seventh, faith sanctifies because it responds to the various motives which God has proposed to His people, motives to stir them up unto their utmost endeavors and diligence in using those ways and means which He has appointed for preventing the defilements of sin, and for cleansing the conscience when defilement has been contracted. As faith receives the Word as God's, its Divine authority awes the soul, subdues enmity, and produces submission. The effects of faith are that the soul trembles at the Divine threatenings, yields obedience to the Divine precepts, and gladly embraces the Divine promises. Herein, and in no other way, do we obtain unfailing evidence of the reality and genuineness of our faith. As the specie of a tree is identified by the nature of the fruit which it bears, so the kind of faith we have may be ascertained by the character of the effects which it produces. Some of those effects we have sought to describe in the last few paragraphs.

Chapter 22
Its Instrument
(COMPLETED)

Having presented an outline in our last chapter of the part which faith plays in sanctification, we shall now endeavor, under God, to offer consolation unto some of our sin-burdened, doubt-harassed, Satan-tormented brethren and sisters in Christ. "Comfort ye, comfort ye, My people, saith your God." (Isa. 40:1). And why? Because God's children are the most deeply distressed people on the face of the earth! Though at times they experience a peace which passeth all understanding, revel in that love which passeth knowledge, and rejoice with joy unspeakable, yet for the most part their souls are much cast down, and fears, bondage, groans, constitute a large part of their experience. They may for a brief season be regaled by the wells and palm trees of Elim, but most of their lives are lived in the "great howling wilderness" (Deut. 32:10), so that they are often constrained to say, "Oh that I had wings like a dove! for then would I fly away, and be at rest."

Such a distressful experience causes many of the regenerate to very seriously doubt whether they are real Christians. They cannot harmonize their gloom with the light-heartedness they behold in religious professors all around them. No, and they need not wish to. The superficial and apostate religion of our day is producing nothing but a generation of flighty and frothy characters, who scorn anything sober, serious, and solemn, and who sneer at that which searches, strips, and abases into the dust. God's Isaacs must not expect to be understood and still less appreciated by the "mocking" Ishmaels (Gen. 21:9), for though these dwell for a while in Abraham's household, yet a different mother has borne them. Unless the sin distressed and fear-tormented believer is "as a sparrow alone upon the housetop" (Ps. 102:7), then he will have to say "mine heritage is unto me as a speckled bird, the birds round about are against me" (Jer. 12:9)—there is no oneness, no fellowship.

Many of God's dear children are like Asaph. "But as for me, my feet were almost gone; my steps had well-nigh slipped. For I was envious at the foolish, when I saw the prosperity of the wicked. For there are no bands in their death: but their strength is firm. They are not troubled as other men, neither are they plagued like other men. Therefore pride compasseth them about as a chain: violence covereth them as a garment. Their eyes stand out with fatness they have more than heart could wish. They are corrupt, and speak wickedly: concerning oppression, they speak loftily" (Ps. 73:2-8). As Asaph beheld the prosperity of these people he was staggered, supposing that God was with them and had deserted him.

The spiritual counterpart of this is found in modern Laodicea. There is a generation of professing Christians who appear to enjoy great religious "prosperity." They have considerable knowledge of the letter of Scripture; they are experts in "rightly dividing the Word;" they have great light upon the mysteries of prophecy; and are most successful as "soul winners." They have no ups and downs in their experience, no painful twistings and turnings, but go on in a straight course with light hearts and beaming countenances. Providence smiles upon them, and they never have a doubt as to their acceptance in Christ. Satan does not trouble them, nor is indwelling sin a daily plague to them. And the poor Christian, conscious of his weakness, his ignorance, his poverty, his vileness, is sorely tempted to be "envious" of them, for they seem to have "more than heart could wish," while the longings of his heart are denied him, and that which he pursues so eagerly continues to elude his grasp.

Ah, but note well some of the other characteristics of this prosperous company. Pride compasseth them about as a chain" (Ps. 73 :6). Yes, they are utter strangers to humility and lowliness. They are pleased with their peacock feathers, knowing not that God views the same as "filthy rags." "Concerning oppression, they speak loftily" (Ps. 73:8). God's children are oppressed, sorely oppressed, by their corruptions, by their innumerable failures, by the hidings of the Lord's face, by the accusations of Satan. They are oppressed over the workings of unbelief, over the coldness of their hearts, over the insincerity of their prayers, over their vain imaginations. But these Laodiceans, "speak loftily," ridiculing such things, and prate of their peace, joy, and victory. "Therefore His people, return hither: and waters of a full cup are wrung out to them" (Ps. 73:10), for as real Christians listen to the "testimonies" of the "higher life" people, they conclude that it would be the height of presumption to regard themselves as Christians at all.

Behold these are the ungodly," continues Asaph, "who prosper in the (religious) world; they increase in riches" (Ps. 73:12). And as he was occupied with them, contrasting his own sad lot, a spirit of discontent and petulance took possession of him. "Verily I have cleansed my heart in vain" (Ps. 73:13)—what is all my past diligence and efforts worth? I am not "prosperous" like these professors: I do not have their graces or attainments, I do not enjoy the peace, assurance, and victory, they have. Far from it: "For all the day long I have been plagued, and chastened every morning" (Ps. 73:14). Ah, that was holy Asaph's experience, my reader; is it yours? If so, you are in goodly company, much as the present-day pharisees may despise you.

Then the Psalmist was checked, and realized his wrong in giving way to such wicked sentiments. "If I say, I will speak thus, behold, I shall offend against the generation of Thy children" (Ps. 73:15). Yes, the generation of God's children will be offended when they hear one of their brethren saying it is "vain" to use the appointed means of grace because those have not issued in deliverance from indwelling sin. "When I thought to know this, it was too painful for me; until I went into the sanctuary of God, then understood I their end. Surely Thou didst set them in slippery places; Thou castedst them down into destruction" (Ps. 73 :16-18). How unspeakably solemn! Instead of these prosperous Laodiceans having a spiritual experience high above those whose hearts plague them "all the day long," they were total strangers to real spirituality. Instead of being among the chief favorites of God, they had been set by Him in the "slippery places" of error and false religion, to be eventually "cast down into destruction."

What a warning is this, my sin-harassed brother, not to envy those who are strangers to the plague of their own hearts, who groan not "being burdened" (2 Cor. 5:4), and who cry not "O wretched man that I am" (Rom. 7:24). Envy not the proud Laodiceans, who are "rich and increased with goods and have need of nothing;" and know not that they are "wretched, and miserable, and poor, and blind, and naked" (Rev. 3:17). Instead, be thankful if God has made you "poor in spirit"—feeling that you are destitute of every spiritual grace and fruit; and to "mourn" over your barrenness and waywardness; for none other than Christ pronounces such characters "blessed." And why should you think it strange if you are among that little company who are the most distressed people on earth? Have you not been called into fellowship with Christ, and was He not "The Man of sorrows" while He tabernacled in this world? If He sorrowed and suffered so much in enduring the penalty of sin, will you complain because God is now making you groan daily under the felt workings of the power of sin?

The fact of the matter is that very much of that which now passes for sanctification is nothing but a species of pharisaism, which causes its deluded votaries to thank God that they are not like other men; and sad it is to find many of the Lord's people adding to their miseries by grieving over how far they come behind the lofty attainments which they imagine these boasters have reached unto. A true and God-honoring "Christian testimony," my reader, does not consist in magnifying self, by telling of attainments and excellences which, with apparent humility, are ascribed to Divine enabling. No indeed, very far from it. That "witness" which is most honoring to the Lord is one which acknowledges His amazing grace and which magnifies His infinite patience in continuing to bear with such an ungrateful, heard-hearted, and unresponsive wretch.

The great mistake made by most of the Lord's people is in hoping to discover in themselves that which is to be found in Christ alone. It is this, really, which causes them to become so envious and discontented when they behold the spurious holiness of some and the carnal attractiveness of others. There is such a thing as "the goodliness" of the flesh, which is "as the flower of the field" (Isa. 40:6), yet as the very next verse tells us "the Spirit of the Lord bloweth upon it." But so easily are the simple deceived today they often mistake such "goodliness" for godliness. Why, my reader, a man (or woman) in his personal makeup may be as meek and tractable as a lamb, he may be constitutionally as kind and grateful as a spaniel, and he may be temperamentally as cheerful as a lark; yet there is not a grain of grace in these natural qualities. On the other hand, the Christian, in his natural temperament, is likely to be as gloomy as an owl or as wild as a tiger; yet that does not disprove grace within him.

"For ye see your calling, brethren, how that not many wise men after the flesh, not many mighty, not many noble, are called: But God hath chosen the foolish things of the world to confound the wise; and God hath chosen the weak things of the world to confound the things which are mighty; and base things of the world, and things which are despised hath God chosen, and things which are not (non-entities, ciphers) to bring to nought things that are: that no flesh should glory in His presence" (1 Cor. 1:26-29). If this passage were really received at its face value, many of God's sin-afflicted and doubting children would find the key that unlocks much which is bewildering and grievous in their experience.

In His determination to magnify His sovereign grace God has selected many of the very worst of Adam's fallen race to be the everlasting monuments of His fathomless mercy—those whom Luther was wont to designate "The Devil's riff-raffs." This is very evident too from "Go out quickly into the streets and lanes of the city, and bring in hither the poor, and the maimed, and the halt, and the blind" (Luke 14:21)—the most unlikely ones as guests for a royal feast, the waifs and strays of society! There are thousands of moral, upright, amiable people who are never effectually called by the Spirit; whereas moral perverts, thieves, and awful-tempered ones are regenerated. When such are born again they still have vile inclinations, horrible dispositions, fiery tempers, which are very hard to control, and are subject to temptations that many of the unregenerate have no first-hand acquaintance with.

Hundreds more of God's children, whose animal spirits are much quieter by nature and whose temperament is more even and placid, yet are plagued by a spirit of pride and self-righteousness, which is just as hateful in the sight of God as moral degeneracy is to respectable worldlings. Now unless the thoughts of such are formed from the Scriptures, they are sure to entertain erroneous conceptions which will destroy their peace and fill them with doubts and fears, for upon a fuller discovery and clearer sight of the sea of corruption within, they will conclude they have never passed from death unto life. But to call into question our regeneration because we fail to obtain deliverance from the power of indwelling sin, is a great mistake; the new birth neither removes nor refines the flesh, but is the reception of a nature that feels sin to be an intolerable burden, and that yearns after holiness above everything else.

If I have really come to Christ as a leprous and bankrupt sinner, utterly despairing of self-help, and have put my trust in the sufficiency of His sacrifice, the Scripture affirms that God has made Christ to be sanctification to me (1 Cor. 1:30) and that I have received a spirit of holiness from Him. Now faith accepts this blessed fact notwithstanding an ocean of corruption and the continued raging of sin within. My peace of mind will, then, very largely depend upon faith's continued apprehension of the perfect salvation which God has provided for His people in Christ, and which in Heaven they shall enjoy in their own persons. After the sinner has come to Christ savingly, the Holy Spirit gives him a much fuller discovery of his vileness, and makes him a hundredfold more conscious of how much there is in his heart that is opposed to God than ever he realized previously; and unless faith be daily in exercise, the activities of the flesh will slay his assurance—instead, they ought to drive him closer and closer to Christ.

O my Christian reader, what a difference it would make were you to steadily realize the truth that, every temptation you encounter, every defeat you suffer, every distressing experience you pass through, is a call and a challenge for the exercise of faith. You complain that you are still the subject of sin, that it cleaves to you as the flesh does to your bones, that it mixes with your duties and defiles every act you perform. You often feel that you are nothing but sin. When you attempt to walk with God, inward evil rises up and stops you. When you read His Word or endeavor to pray, unbelieving thoughts, carnal imaginations, worldly lusts, seek to possess your soul. You strive against them; but in vain. Instead of improvement, things grow worse. You beg of God for humility, and pride rises higher; you cry to Him for more patience, but apparently His ear is closed. Ah, you are now learning the painful truth that in your flesh there dwelleth "no good thing."

Yes, but what is a poor soul to do in such a harrowing case? How is it possible for him to preserve any peace in his conscience? When the believer is so sorely attacked by sin and Satan, how is he to defend himself? Nothing but faith in the sure Word of God can keep him from sinking into abject despair. This is the very time for him to maintain his trust in the sufficiency of Christ's blood and the excellency of His imputed righteousness. His faith is now being tried by the fire that it may come forth as gold. It is by such experiences the genuineness of his faith is put to the proof. The believer is cast into the furnace that faith may conflict with unbelief, and though he will be hard put to it, yet victory is sure. The proof of his victory is faith's perseverance (amid a thousand waverings) unto the end. Remember, my reader, that the test of perseverance is not how we act in the face of success, but how we conduct ourselves under a long series of defeats. "For a just man falleth seven times, and riseth up again" (Prov. 24:16).

Let it not be overlooked that we can no more take our place before God now as accepted worshippers without a perfect holiness, than we can enter Heaven without it; but that perfect holiness is to be found in Christ alone—the practical holiness of the Christian is, at present, but a very, very faint reflection of it. The more I feel my utter unworthiness and total unfitness to approach unto God and call upon Him in my own name, the more thankful I should be for the Mediator, and the unspeakable privilege of calling upon God in Christ's name. And it is faith which counts upon the glorious fact that the thrice holy God can exercise His grace and goodness toward one so vile as I, and that, consistently with His majesty and justice—Christ has honored the Law infinitely more than my sins dishonor it. One who feels that, as a Christian, he is "an utter failure," and who is conscious of his continued abuse of God's mercies, can only draw nigh to God with confidence as he exercises faith in the infinite merits of Christ.

As we stated at the beginning, our principal object in writing this chapter is, under God, to comfort His sin-distressed, doubt-harassed, Satan-tormented people. We are not unmindful that among the ranks of nominal Christians there are, on the one hand, many "having a form of godliness, but denying the power thereof; ever learning and never able to come to the knowledge of the Truth" (2 Tim. 3:5, 7), who will regard as highly "dangerous" much of what we have said; while on the other hand, there are "ungodly men, turning the grace of God into lasciviousness" (Jude 4), who are likely to abuse the same by adopting it as an intellectual opinion, from which they may derive peace in their defiance of God. Yet notwithstanding these likely eventualities, we shall not withhold a needful portion of the children's bread.

Those who claim to have received the "second blessing" and be "entirely sanctified" in themselves, have never seen their hearts in the light of God. Those who boast of their sinless perfection are deceived by Satan, and "the truth is not in them" (1 John 1:8). Two things ever go together in the experience of a genuine believer: a growing discovery of the vileness of self, and a deepening appreciation of the preciousness of Christ. There is no solid ground for a believer to rest upon till he sees that Christ has fully answered to God for him. In exact proportion to his faith will be his peace and joy. "Ye are complete in Him" (Col. 2:10): believers now possess a perfect holiness in the Covenant-Head, but at present they are far from being perfect in the grace which flows to them from Him. God honors and rewards that faith which is exercised upon our holiness in Christ: not necessarily by subduing sin or granting victory over it, but by enabling its possessor to continue cleaving to Christ as his only hope.

O my Christian reader, be content to be nothing in yourself, that Christ may be your all. O to truly say "He must increase, but I decrease (John 3 :30). Growth in grace is a being brought more and more off from self-complacency and self-dependency, to an entire reliance upon Christ and the free grace of God through Him. This temper is begun in the believer at regeneration, and like the tiny mustard seed it at last develops into a large tree. As the Christian grows in grace he finds himself to be increasingly full of wants, and further off than ever from being worthy to receive the supply of them. More and more the spirit of a beggar possesses him. As the Spirit grants more light, he has a growing realization of the beauty of holiness, of what Christ is entitled to from him; and there is a corresponding self-loathing and grief because he is so unholy in himself and fails so miserably to render unto Christ His due.

Fellowship with God and walking in the light as He is in the light, so far from filling the Christian with self-satisfaction, causes him to groan because of his darkness and filthiness—the clearer light now making manifest what before was unperceived. Nothing is more perilous to the soul than that we should be occupied with our achievements, victories, enjoyments. If Paul was in danger of being exalted by the abundance of the revelations vouchsafed him, can the danger be less of our being puffed up with thoughts of spiritual progress, spiritual conquests, spiritual excellences. And yet the cherishing of such thoughts is the very thing which is now being increasingly encouraged by the religious quacks of the day. No matter what fellowship with Christ be enjoyed, what growth in grace be made, it will ever remain true that "we that are in this tabernacle do groan, being burdened" (2 Cor. 5:4).

So far from what we have said in this chapter encouraging a real Christian to entertain low views of sin, it is only in the vital and experimental knowledge of the same that a life of holiness begins. Nothing will cause a renewed soul to hate sin so much as a realization of God's grace; nothing will move him to mourn so genuinely over his sins as a sense of Christ's dying love. It is that which breaks his heart: the realization that there is so much in him that is opposed to Christ. But a life of holiness is a life of faith (the heart turning daily to Christ), and the fruits of faith are genuine repentance, true humility, praising God for His infinite patience and mercy, pantings after conformity to Christ, praying to be made more obedient, and continually confessing our disobedience. Daydreaming about complete deliverance from indwelling sin, seeking to persuade ourselves that the flesh is becoming less active, cannot counter-balance the humbling reality of our present state; but our corruptions should not quench a true Gospel hope.

Those who have read the previous chapters of this book cannot suppose that we have any design to lower the standard of the Christian life, or to speak peace to deluded souls who "profess that they know God, but in works deny Him" (Titus 1:16). Some indeed may charge us with encouraging light views of the sinfulness of sin, yet it must be remembered that the grand truth of Divine grace has ever appeared "dangerous" to mere human wisdom. A worldly moralist must think it subservient of the very foundations of virtue to proclaim to men, without regard to what they have done, and without stipulation as to what they are to do, "Believe on the Lord Jesus Christ and thou shalt be saved." If I believed that says the unrenewed man, I would take my fill of sin, without fear or remorse. Ah, but a saving faith from God is always accomplished by a principle which hates sin and loves holiness; and the greatest grief of its possessor is, that its aspirations are so often thwarted. But those very thwartings are the testings of faith, and should daily drive us back to Christ for fresh cleansings. Lord, increase our faith.